55,60:61

THE POLITICAL BASIS
OF
ECONOMIC DEVELOPMENT

An Exploration in Comparative Political Analysis

*A Study from The Center for Comparative Political Analysis
Department of Political Science, University of Minnesota*

by
ROBERT T. HOLT
University of Minnesota

and

JOHN E. TURNER
University of Minnesota

NEW PERSPECTIVES
IN
POLITICAL SCIENCE

D. VAN NOSTRAND COMPANY, INC.
PRINCETON, NEW JERSEY
TORONTO   NEW YORK   LONDON

To

Debra and Susan, Ann, and Sharon

D. VAN NOSTRAND COMPANY, INC.
120 Alexander St., Princeton, New Jersey
(*Principal Office*)
24 West 40 Street, New York 18, New York

D. VAN NOSTRAND COMPANY, LTD.
358, Kensington High Street, London, W.14, England

D. VAN NOSTRAND COMPANY (Canada), LTD.
25 Hollinger Road, Toronto 16, Canada

Contents

ACKNOWLEDGMENTS v

PROLOGUE 1

1 THE MODERN POLITICAL SYSTEM AND THE PROCESS OF POLITICAL DEVELOPMENT 7

2 A FRAMEWORK FOR THE STUDY OF THE POLITICAL BASIS OF ECONOMIC GROWTH 39

3 GOVERNMENTAL STRUCTURES AND PROCEDURES OF GOVERNING: AN OVERVIEW 66

4 FUNCTIONS OF GOVERNMENT AND PROCEDURES OF GOVERNING—I: ADAPTATION AND GOAL ATTAINMENT 100

5 FUNCTIONS OF GOVERNMENT AND PROCEDURES OF GOVERNING—II: PATTERN MAINTENANCE AND INTEGRATION 171

6 THE TAKE-OFF STAGE: JAPAN AND ENGLAND 233

7 THE MAJOR HYPOTHESES 292

EPILOGUE 336

APPENDIX: THE CHANGING SOVIET POLITY, 1930-1964 343

BIBLIOGRAPHY 383

INDEX 407

Acknowledgments

THE MANY DEBTS ACCUMULATED BY THE AUTHORS IN THE PREPARA-
tion of this study are matched only by their gratitude to those individuals who were extremely generous with their time in aiding the
work of the project. Brief mention in a preface is small repayment
indeed for the advice and counsel which proved to be so helpful
during the various stages of the study.

The authors must first acknowledge the assistance given to them
by their colleagues at the University of Minnesota. In the Department
of Political Science, Professors William H. Flanigan, Edwin Fogel-
man, and Thomas M. Scott read an early draft of the manuscript and
made thoughtful comments. Professors Paul W. Bamford, Romeyn
Taylor, and John B. Wolf of the Department of History also provided
valuable advice on bibliography and content. A special debt of gratitude is owed to Professors Leonid Hurwicz and Jacob Schmookler,
scholars in the field of economics, who spent a great many hours in
discussing the theoretical problems and in critically examining the
manuscript. In receiving the expert counsel so generously provided
by these local scholars, the authors came to appreciate more fully the
vast intellectual resources which are available at the University of
Minnesota.

The writers of this work are grateful, too, to a number of scholars
from other universities who constructively criticized the manuscript.
These scholars included Professors Oliver E. Benson, University of
Oklahoma; George I. Blanksten, Northwestern University; and
Fred W. Riggs, University of Indiana. Professor Ramon H. Myers
of the University of Hawaii made available an interesting article
from his own research.

A portion of the theoretical framework was developed while one
of the authors was a Fellow at the Center for Advanced Study in
the Behavioral Sciences. This work owes much to colleagues at the
Center, especially Professors McKim Merriott, Rodney Needham,
and Robin Williams, with whom some of the theoretical issues were
discussed. At that time Professor Joseph LaPalombara read and
criticized an early version of Chapter 1. During the same period, the
other author was a Fulbright Research Fellow at the London School

of Economics, where he benefited from long discussions with Professors Leonard Schapiro and Alec Nove.

To all of these scholars the authors are most grateful, but, in congruence with the tribal customs of academe, we assume full responsibility for errors of fact and interpretation.

The authors are especially grateful to the Graduate School of the University of Minnesota whose leading personnel offered kind encouragement and awarded several grants which helped to get the project started. In addition, financial assistance from the Winton Fund was of considerable help to both authors—both at the outset of the study and during the final stages.

For short periods of time, the authors also benefited from the research assistance of several willing helpers, including Mr. T. J. Su and William Frame of the University of Hawaii; Mr. Paul H. B. Godwin, Mr. John V. Gillespie, Miss Susan Lampland, Mr. Richard Erikson, and Dr. Jacques Henry of the University of Minnesota. Miss Jean Belden, Miss Sally Smith, Miss Barbara Hosking, Miss Ruth Wilson, and Mrs. Patricia Hayman-Chaffey assisted in typing portions of the manuscript.

The greatest cost of this study was underwritten by the wives and children of the authors. Unfortunately, the authors were unable to obtain financial support which would have provided adequate research assistance and some relief from their regular academic responsibilities. This meant that the research and writing had to be done during spare time, and that the authors were in major part their own research assistants—a time-devouring responsibility in a project of this sort. This difficulty, however, was more than offset by the willingness of the authors' families (though not always without comment) to be evening and weekend widows and orphans. The dedication of this work is the authors' tribute to four lovely children who seemed somehow to understand far beyond their years. For the time being, the wives will have to be content with other statements.

Prologue

THE ACADEMIC STUDY OF POLITICS IS TYPICALLY RESPONSIVE TO THE pressing problems of the day. The large-scale involvement of the United States in international affairs during and after World War II, for example, has provoked new interest in the analysis of international relations. The protracted conflict between the East and the West has stimulated the growth of research in communism and the countries that embrace this philosophy. Similarly, since the decade of the 1950's, as new nations emerged from colonial status in greater numbers and as older but underdeveloped countries embarked upon programs of economic development, political scientists have turned their attention to an analysis of the process of political modernization.

When a discipline is confronted with new phenomena which must be described and explained, its traditional tools of analysis often prove to be inadequate for the task and need to be sharpened or even replaced by better instruments. New concepts may have to be developed and old ones redefined in order to provide a solid conceptual underpinning for empirical research and theoretical development. The adequacy of the new conceptual frameworks, of course, will ultimately be determined by the type and quality of the research they engender and by the explanatory power of the theories in which they are used. Within the last decade, a rapidly expanding army of social scientists has begun to tackle the problems inherent in the analysis of economic development. Prominent in this army is a number of imaginative political scientists who are studying carefully the political aspects of modernization. As their research on new phenomena begins to build up, it is important for their work to be subjected to preliminary examination, not only for the research findings but also for the methodological contribution. Such analyses will permit scholars to assess tentatively the usefulness of the concepts that have been

1

employed and to determine whether the conceptual schemes meet the requirements of concept formation in a scientific discipline.

The research on development underlines the importance of conceptual frameworks which, being multidisciplinary in nature, draw from economics, sociology, anthropology, psychology, history, and political science. Each of these disciplines has much to contribute in the formulation of meaningful generalizations about man and his environment. If the political scientist is to make his contribution, he must be aware of the work that is being done in related disciplines. Thus, in cases where it is desirable, conceptual frameworks may be drawn from these disciplines and properly employed in ordering the data of political science. The political scientist, however, must be more than a mere borrower; when he adopts an analytical framework from a sister discipline, it is used to systematize data that are different from the data for which the framework was originally designed. Since this provides an additional test for the usefulness of the framework, the political scientist should be in a position to suggest modifications which could increase the utility of the conceptualization.

In many instances, of course, the political scientist will find it necessary to construct his own conceptual frameworks. In developing these designs, he should be concerned explicitly with the manner in which these new frameworks may be integrated with the methodological work being done in other fields.

For more than fifteen years, the world of scholarship has witnessed considerable lament over the absence of "truly comparative" studies in the field of political science. Although the criticism and self-examination have generated much intellectual ferment, it is interesting to observe that the reader of political science literature is still likely to encounter more lamentations than actual comparative studies. This situation, which can be largely explained in terms of the inherent difficulties involved in comparative research, may also stem in part from the failure to recognize the purpose of such research.

A number of social scientists have drawn attention to the comparative method as a device for controlling variation when the variables under examination cannot be manipulated directly. In carefully designed comparative research, the scholar who seeks to test hypotheses dealing with macro-social phenomena is able to find something approximating the controlled laboratory experiment.[1] This research, for anyone who agrees with George P. Murdock, must be cross-cultural comparative research: "There can never be any generally valid science of man which is not specifically adapted to, and tested with reference to, the diverse manifestations of human . . . societies differing from our own. . . ." [2] In many respects political science as a discipline has not been mainly oriented toward the development of a "generally valid [political] science of man." Its commitment to a comparative field appears to be based more upon its deep empirical tradition than upon a predisposition to test systematically hypotheses that are theoretically significant.

The comparative method, however, may be used for another purpose, which may be even more appropriate for political science in its present stage of development; it is toward this use that the present study is directed. We have subtitled the monograph *An Exploration in Comparative Political Analysis.* We use the term *exploration* for the explicit purpose of labeling our work an *exploratory study.* By an exploratory study we mean research appropriately designed to *generate* hypotheses—not to *test* them—and to provide the rationale which will justify future research aimed at testing these propositions.

An exploratory study is made up of several necessary components. In the first place, there must be an analysis of the relevant literature to determine what the leading scholars have to say on the subject and to examine critically the conceptual bases of their work. Such a critique not only lays before the reader the essential elements of and conflicting views about the problem but also draws his attention to the methodological contributions and limitations of other approaches. In light of these, it provides some justification for the methodological decisions which will have to be made in any given study. If advances are to be made in the pursuit of knowledge in any area, the microscope of criticism should be focused upon the very best scholarship that has been done in the field. In any scientific discipline, the best approach which is being taken today may prove to be somewhat limited or even inadequate for the research tasks of tomorrow. What is to be useful in tomorrow's research effort, however, will have to be built upon the best that exists today.

A second necessary component of an exploratory study is the development of the conceptual framework which is to be employed. This framework contains the concepts in terms of which the phenomena under examination are to be described and the emerging hypotheses will be stated.

The third element is the collection of empirical data. These data should be collected from research sites chosen in such a way that the variables can be manipulated in a prescribed manner. In the presentation of these data, there should be an explicit statement concerning what variables are being manipulated and how the selection of the research sites accomplishes the desired manipulation.)

(The fourth aspect is the analysis of the data and the formulation of hypotheses from the patterns of similarity and difference which appear. In any exploratory research, of course, the number of cases which can be treated is likely to be somewhat restricted, and for this reason the hypotheses may be of limited generality, or may even conceal spurious components. These dangers, however, may be mitigated to some extent by taking a fifth step. It is possible for the researcher to take the empirically generated hypotheses and to identify the existing theory (or set of theories) from which these hypotheses might also have been drawn, and then to restate them in the form that they would assume if they had initially been deduced from a theory (or theories). In this restated form, they are likely to be at the highest level of generalization, given the present state of knowledge, and least likely to embrace spurious components. Furthermore, the testing of the hypotheses in this form will contribute to the testing of the theory (or theories) with which the hypotheses have been linked.

Every exploration is something of an adventure—an attempt to probe in a tentative way some unknown, neglected but nevertheless promising areas. Some explorations, of course, turn out to have great payoff, but many of them end up with little return. It is probably for this reason that only the hardy—or the foolhardy—ever embark upon such undertakings. Whether an exploration has been fruitful or fruitless, however, cannot be determined until the journey, however uncertain, has been completed. By the same token, the outcome of an exploratory study similar to that we have just outlined cannot be ascertained until the hypotheses which have been generated are tested in field research.

/ Since the main objective of our exploratory study is to develop hypotheses which can be tested in future studies, it is important to provide potential critics with an explicit statement of the intellectual justification of our work./For this reason we have included in this volume all of the components of an exploratory study (as outlined above), and we have attempted to present them in logical and developmental order. In Chapter 1, there is a critique of the most significant methodological works which are related to our own research. This critique is focused upon the writings of scholars who have made the most significant contributions to the solution of crucial methodological problems. While at times we draw attention to certain limitations in their respective approaches or findings, we do not question but wholeheartedly applaud their pioneering efforts and the significance of their research. Those readers who are not especially interested in methodological issues may find it advisable to begin their reading in Chapter 2, where we present the conceptual framework which we are employing in this study. The empirical data are to be found in Chapters 3, 4, 5, and 6. The over-all analysis and the statement of the hypotheses are reserved for Chapter 7.

In more specific terms, the purpose of this work is to present a conceptual framework for the analysis of political factors in economic growth, and to develop hypotheses on the role of these factors at a certain stage of economic development. Before we move to the analytical discussions in Chapters 1 and 2, it may be wise to alert the reader to the empirical focus of the study. In order to manipulate in a desired manner the variables that concern us, we have concentrated attention upon France, 1600-1789; China, 1644-1911; Japan, 1603-1868; and England, 1558-1780. Shortly after the final dates listed, Japan and England entered upon a period of rapid industrialization, whereas France and China lagged behind in varying degrees. If there are significant political requirements for economic growth, and if there was no obvious technological factor at work, we should expect to find certain political similarities between France and China, on the one hand, that distinguish them from Japan and England on the other. The patterns of similarity and difference will be used as a basis for developing hypotheses concerning the political requirements for economic growth at the stage of early industrialization.

These hypotheses are developed for the purpose of testing them in field research in contemporary modernizing countries. But because the technological and historical contexts of the industrialization experiences we are studying are so different from those of contemporary developing nations, it is necessary for us to refine the hypotheses by examining them in relationship with existing theories in social science, primarily for the purpose of establishing the level of generality at which they are operating. Further discussion concerning the problems involved in testing the hypotheses in field studies will be found in the closing pages of the work, where they can be examined in the light of the empirical data that have been presented.

We have also included a treatment covering the take-off stage in

Japan and England (Chapter 6), not so much for the purpose of generating hypotheses, but rather to demonstrate how the conceptual framework might be applied at other stages of economic development. For the same reason we have added a short treatment of the Soviet Union from 1930 to 1965 in the appendix.

Before we turn to the body of the study itself, it is important to caution the reader about what we are *not* attempting to do. We are not attempting to provide a complete account of why England and Japan managed to industrialize while France and China tended to lag behind. Indeed, our interest is not so much with these four cases themselves as with the use of the cases as a basis for developing generally applicable hypotheses. In this study we are concerned *only with domestic political factors* that had an influence upon economic growth. Obviously, there were other factors that were important— such as foreign wars and international involvements—but these lie outside the boundary of our present interests. This monograph, in other words, focuses specifically and entirely upon the political basis for economic development, and we have purposely excluded other factors, however important they may be, from our consideration. Those who are interested in these other factors should be encouraged to undertake exploratory studies aimed at generating additional hypotheses.

NOTES

1. Emile Durkheim, *The Rules of the Sociological Method,* pp. 125-140; S. F. Nadel, *The Foundations of Social Anthropology,* pp. 222-227; Talcott Parsons, *The Structure of Social Action,* pp. 742-743.

2. George P. Murdock, "Anthropology as Comparative Science," *Behavioral Science,* Vol. 2, No. 4, October 1957, p. 249.

CHAPTER 1

The Modern Political System
and the Process of Political Development

A THEORY OF POLITICAL MODERNIZATION IS A SPECIAL THEORY OF social change. Although this is recognized, at least implicitly, by most political scientists, few writers on political development attempt to discuss the kind of social change theory with which they are working. References to theorists of social change are almost negligible. Such an oversight does not mean that the theories used by political scientists are original with them and bear little relationship to the theories of social change employed by other social scientists. A more likely explanation is that a single approach tends to dominate the field; when nearly everyone agrees, there is little to discuss.

In the most common approach to the study of political modernization, change is conceived as a transmutation of one type of political system to another. Writers in the field define these two basic types as polar opposites, an approach that is hardly unique. Tönnies, Maine, Redfield, and others employed similar concepts of social development. While these theorists may have focused their attention upon different aspects of social structure, they tended fundamentally to view social change as nonreversible movement between two poles on a continuum (_Gemeinschaft-Gesellschaft,_ status-contract, folk-secular).[1] Contemporary students of political modernization have developed more complex formulations, which differ in three respects: they do not focus on a single dimension; they typically identify a midpoint in the developmental process which they label as "transitional"; and they often introduce qualifications which are intended to modify the essentially dichotomous nature of their schema.[2] These modifications do not conceal the basic similarity with the approach of Tönnies, Maine, and Redfield.

7

THE "MODERN POLITICAL SYSTEM"

In the contemporary approach to the study of political development, a crucial concept is that of a *modern political system*.[3] The process of political modernization is usually conceived as development from a traditional stage through a transitional stage to a modern stage. The main features which distinguish these three stages are identified primarily in comparison with the modern political system as the basic model. Thus students of political development describe the essential characteristics of the modern system; they then identify the traditional system as possessing opposite characteristics; and they distinguish the transitional system as one that is in the process of development between the modern and traditional and has important features of both.

Although the concept *modern political system* is widely used and is the core of analysis in many studies, few scholars have defined it explicitly. After attempting to draw common elements out of the definitions of a number of writers, we abandoned the task when we discovered that the definitions were either too implicit or were drawn in large part from the works of one of the leading scholars of political development, Gabriel A. Almond. We found that by analyzing Almond's relatively explicit formulation, we were able to cover most of what is significant in the field.[4] The writings of this theorist have served as a catalyst for fresh thinking about comparative politics, and it must be emphasized that, in examining his approach, we do not deprecate it but praise his considerable contribution. Indeed, it is a tribute to the clarity of his presentation and to his great influence that so much of the conceptual work done in this field can be embraced by an analysis of his views.

Almond's Formulation

In Almond's formulation, the modern political system is distinguished from the traditional on two major dimensions: (1) structural differentiation-structural nondifferention and (2) secular-theocratic. In addition, there are several secondary dimensions which point up certain aspects of *style*.[5]

STRUCTURAL DIFFERENTIATION. Some notion of differentiation—the existence of highly specialized and functionally specific roles and structures—enters into most definitions of the modern political system, but without refinement this concept has little utility. It is not very useful, for example, when it is applied solely to the increase in the agencies or units of government that have specialized activities. A state that owns and manages the means of production would, *ceteris paribus,* have more specialized agencies of government than one which does not, and hence would be regarded as more modern. Measured by this standard, a federal system would be more modern than a unitary system.[6] Obviously, such a formulation does not carry the analysis very far.

Almond's concept of structural differentiation is more distinct and much more refined. He is not concerned with the sheer multiplication of specialized government agencies. According to his formulation, structural differentiation exists when there are structures in the political system that have a "functional distinctiveness, and which tend to perform . . . a regulatory role in relation to that function within the political system as a whole."[7] Thus, in order to talk meaningfully about structural differentiation, it first becomes necessary to identify the functions that all political systems have in common. Almond classifies these functions into two main categories—input functions and output functions. The input functions are (1) political socialization and recruitment, (2) interest articulation, (3) interest aggregation, and (4) political communication. The output functions are (1) rule making, (2) rule application, and (3) rule adjudication.[8] A differentiated political system has in each of these functional areas specialized and distinct structures which tend to regulate that function for the system as a whole. In every political system, for example, there are structures that have an interest articulation function. A system in which the interests of kinship groups, religious bodies, professional organizations, labor unions, and the like must *pass through* and be *processed by* associational interest groups is more differentiated in its interest articulation than a system in which the various nonassociational groups *feed* their interests directly into the political system. A political system in which the dominant interest aggregating structures are political parties, which feed relatively well-aggregated interests into the rule-making and rule-application structures, is more differentiated than a political system in which interest aggregation occurs primarily within the interest groups, legislatures, and government bureaucracies, with little regulation by any single specialized structure. A government that has specialized structures dominating, respectively, the rule-making, rule-application, and rule-adjudication functions is more differentiated than one in which *all* of these functions are controlled and directed by some other structure, such as the elite of the political party.[9]

THE SECULAR AND THE THEOCRATIC. Although Almond's notion of structural differentiation is explicitly and clearly stated, the other major dimension—the secular-theocratic—receives only brief mention. Almond does not offer a precise and detailed definition, and his references to it do not clearly indicate the formulation he might favor.[10] Since he makes little use of this dimension, however, the lack of definition is understandable and does not affect his subsequent analysis.

THE MODERN STYLE. One of the significant concepts in Almond's monograph is that of *style*—the mode or manner in which a function is performed. Modern systems may be distinguished from traditional ones on the basis of the style with which each of the functions is performed. It will be useful to indicate briefly the style which Almond considers to be modern and that which he regards as traditional for each of the input functions.

The modern style of political socialization is predominantly specific and universalistic. Because of these characteristics, it "creates a distinct loyalty and membership on the part of the individual in the general political system, and a tendency to penetrate and affect the socialization processes of other social systems, such as the family and church, so that they introduce general citizenship content into their socialization processes." [11] The traditional style of political socialization is predominantly diffuse and particularistic, and tends to engender loyalty to a specific local group (kinship or territorial) and only indirectly to the larger political system.

The style of political recruitment is measured on an ascriptive-achievement dimension, as well as on a particularistic-universalistic dimension.[12] In no society, of course, are the criteria of political recruitment entirely ascriptive and particularistic or entirely achievement-oriented and universalistic. Even in what would generally be considered the most modern societies, individuals may be appointed to political positions because of family, status, or other factors that are not germane to the tasks to be performed. But the more modern the system, the more important are achievement and universalistic criteria; the more traditional the system, the more consequential are ascriptive and particularistic criteria.[13]

In treating the style of interest articulation that is associated with the modern political system, the Almond formulation identifies four types of interest groups: (1) institutional, (2) nonassociational, (3) anomic, and (4) associational.[14] Only when the interest-group system is dominated by associational interest groups do interest-group structures regulate the performance of the articulation function. Thus differentiated structures of interest articulation can occur only when there is a predominance of associational interest groups. Hence the modern political system is a system in which there is a primacy of associational interest groups.

The style of interest articulation is measured on four dimensions: (1) manifest-latent, (2) specific-diffuse, (3) general-particular, and (4) instrumental-affective. The style of associational interest groups tends to be toward the manifest, specific, general, and instrumental poles of these continua. The other types of interest groups tend to be associated with the latent, diffuse, particular, and affective style of interest articulation. Thus we can conclude that interest articulation in the modern political system tends to be manifest, specific, general, and instrumental.[15]

Interest aggregation can be a function of many different structures —legislatures, executives, government bureaucracies, interest groups, or political parties. Only a party system of certain types, however, is able to regulate this function for the political system as a whole, and thus the distinctively modern style of political aggregation is associated with these types of party systems. But the style of interest aggregation is defined by the way in which types of parties (not party systems) perform their aggregating function. There are three types: (1) secular, "pragmatic," bargaining parties; (2) absolute value-oriented, *Weltanschauung* or ideological parties; (3) particularistic, or traditional parties.[16] Only when the party system is dominated by secular, "pragmatic" bargaining parties will the interest aggregation function be regulated by a specialized structure. Thus the modern style of interest aggregation is associated with secularism, pragmatism, and bargaining.[17]

The modern political communication system is characterized as being autonomous, neutral, and penetrative. While the descriptive terms "autonomous" and "neutral" have common-sense meanings, the "penetrative" feature requires further explanation. Almond accepts the position of Katz that a technically modern communication system involves a "two-step flow." [18] Messages are carried by mass media, but their impact upon individuals can be understood only if the mediating role of certain primary groups is taken into account. It is the opinion leaders in these informal groups who interpret the messages and make them relevant to the recipients. A "penetrative" communication system is one that pierces deeply into these primary groups and reduces, although certainly does not obliterate, the independent role of the opinion leaders in the communication process.[19]

The style of political communication is measured on four dimensions: (1) manifest-latent, (2) specific-diffuse, (3) *generalistic*-particularistic, and (4) affectively neutral-affective. Although the modern political system has many latent, diffuse, particularistic, and affective messages, the specialized, autonomous, and neutral media of communication (aided by associational interest groups and aggregative political parties) translate these into manifest, specific, generalistic, and neutral messages and dispatch them to the *proper addresses* in the political system.[20] The modern is distinguished from the traditional style of political communication by its predominantly manifest, specific, generalistic, and neutral characteristics.

Almond does not treat the modern style of the three output functions with the same detail as he does the style of input functions. He does, however, illustrate the differences between the output system of modern Western governments and the output functions of traditional political systems in the non-Western world. His distinction between the modern and the traditional output functions is primarily that of structural differentiation. The modern output system has specific, autonomous structures that regulate each of the three output functions —rule making, rule application, and rule adjudication. In the traditional system, specialized structures for these functions do not exist.

In summary, then, Almond conceives of the modern political system as being structurally differentiated and secular, and as a system in which the input functions are performed in a specified style.

Critique of Almond's Formulation

Almond's conceptual analysis of the modern political system brings a stimulating approach to the study of comparative politics, providing a useful framework for the analysis of some highly significant problems in cross-cultural research. Indeed, a part of the scheme employed in this monograph reflects the influence of Almond's contribution. His framework, however, appears to have several limitations which prevent it from being completely effective as a basis for developing more general theories of political modernization. It is difficult to apply on a broad basis to include both historical and contemporary cases. The formulation also tends in effect to equate the modern political system with the modern Anglo-American democratic system. We have two further criticisms which probably represent a minority point of view: its definitions employ too many dimensions, and it neglects the problem of variation in the *societal functions* of government. These points are important enough to merit some elaboration.

IDENTITY OF THE MODERN WITH THE MODERN DEMOCRATIC. Difficulties with Almond's formulation begin to emerge when one attempts to apply it in a broad comparative analysis of political modernization. It is hard, for example, to adjust the framework for a study of modernization in societies that have adopted a totalitarian form of government. According to Almond's definition, the Soviet Union does not have a modern political system. It is highly undifferentiated—indeed, by his prescription a totalitarian system is the most undifferentiated that one would find in societies having central political structures at all. The Soviet system contains no "autonomous" structures that regulate, respectively, the rule-making, rule-application, and rule-adjudicating functions; these are regulated by the Communist Party. The Party also regulates the various input functions either by itself or by dominating any non-Party structures that may be involved in these functions.

While a totalitarian system must be labeled traditional according to the criterion of differentiation, curious anomalies emerge when one examines the style in which input functions are performed. A totalitarian system is characterized by the fact that interests, although they exist in abundance, tend to be suppressed, and the regime expends great effort in preventing their articulation in the political system unless they are approved by the Party. In the Soviet Union after Stalin's death, more interests were apparently articulated than had previously been the case, and the style in which they were articulated reveals a curious combination of modern and nonmodern features. The interests of writers (and a few other professional groups) were articulated in a style that was latent (nonmodern), highly specific and particular (modern), and noninstrumental (nonmodern).

The articulation of writers' interests in post-Stalin Russia was latent in the sense that they were usually not explicitly expressed, appearing in the disguised form of novels and poetry, or in the oblique remarks and nonverbal actions and reactions of people who attended the occasional writers' conferences. Their articulated interests, however, were specific and particular. For the most part, the writers were concerned to free themselves from Party supervision; they voiced few demands for changes in the society or in the basic power structure of the political system. While the desires of the writers, if satisfied, might have long-term ramifications for the society as a whole, their immediate demands called for a measure of freedom for themselves as professional people, so that they could adhere to the norms of their art.

Another case of interest articulation in Russia's post-Stalin period was that of the legal profession over the revision of the criminal code. In addition to being specific, this articulation appears to have been extremely manifest and somewhat more general. Shortly after Stalin's death, the Supreme Soviet authorized the Minister of Justice to survey the outdated criminal code with a view toward major reforms in the definition of crime and in trial procedures. Seizing upon this opportunity, many legal specialists engaged in a prolonged discussion in the press on the changes that were needed, some going so far as to advocate reforms in line with Western standards of justice. Eventually these specialists drew up a set of draft proposals, which they submitted to the political authorities. What could be more manifest and specific than open statements in the press from the lawyers, or the preparation of draft codes by the legal specialists themselves? The demand for substantive and procedural changes affecting the rights of lawyers and defendents, however, is hardly a particular demand. If all the wishes of the legalists were to have been granted, they would have had an impact upon the entire political system, for they would probably have brought changes in the basic process of social control at all levels of the society. Crucial institutions of justice would have been dramatically changed. As it turned out, of course, the regime refused to accept some of the proposals of the specialists and eventually modified a number of those they accepted.[21]

These illustrations of the style of interest articulation in post-Stalin Russia suggest that, while the Almond categories of analysis call attention to significant aspects of interest articulation in a totalitarian society, they appear to be more relevant to the process of democratization than to the process of modernization as such.[22]

A totalitarian system also presents a strange mixture of modern and nonmodern elements in the socialization and political communication functions. Neither the structures of political socialization nor the structures of political communication are autonomous; they do not tend to regulate the functions in their respective areas. The socialization process, however, certainly aims to create a "distinct loyalty and membership on the part of the individual in the general political system, and a tendency to penetrate and affect the socialization processes of other social systems, such as the family and church, so that they introduce general citizenship content into their socialization processes." By this measure the process of political socialization in the modern totalitarian state is the most modern known.[23] The political-communication structures are neither autonomous nor neutral (and hence are nonmodern), but the process of political communication is exceedingly "penetrative." Indeed, the army of trained agitators and the system of manipulated mass participation which are employed in the Soviet Union make its political communication system the most penetrative in history.[24]

In using Almond's definition of a modern political system, the student is forced either to classify the totalitarian system as transitional (which creates some problems to be analyzed below) or to treat modernization in the totalitarian context as an aberration from normal democratic development. But to regard it as a deviation from an expected or desired pattern does little to facilitate the analysis of the totalitarian case within a comparative framework.[25]

In addition to the problem of fitting totalitarian systems into the Almond scheme, one may encounter difficulty in placing some primitive political systems within the framework. Two important dimensions in the Almond formulation are those of achievement-ascription and universalism-particularism. Achievement-oriented and universalistic criteria of political recruitment are characteristic of modern political systems, while traditional and primitive systems are more ascriptively and particularistically oriented.

Research on primitive systems, however, has raised a few tentative doubts about such a classification. Smith's remarkable study of government and politics among the Hausa (a tribe in northern Nigeria) reveals, for example, a primitive political system in the nineteenth century which had institutionalized a remarkable degree of achievement-oriented and universalistic criteria for recruitment and promotion. Indeed, the institutional devices for suppressing nepotism and personal favoritism in appointments to public office before the Fulani domination in the early nineteenth century may have been more achievement-oriented and universalistic than those in Tsarist Russia prior to World War I or those in England before 1830.[26]

Smith's description also indicates that, despite the lack of a legislature in the modern sense of the term, there existed a single differentiated group in the government that dominated the rule-making function (policy-making, in Smith's terms), another that dominated rule application (administration, in Smith's terms), and a third that specialized in rule adjudication. Thus the government of the Hausa was more structurally differentiated than government in a modern totalitarian system. A rigorous application of Almond's criteria leaves one with little choice but to rate the political system of the Hausa in the nineteenth century at least as modern as the Soviet political system in 1965.[27]

The small number of studies of primitive political systems as detailed and precise as Smith's makes it difficult to provide direct evidence that the government of the Hausa was not atypical to the point of being unique. There is, however, some indirect evidence concerning the use of achievement-oriented criteria in primitive societies. Udy's study of 150 work organizations drawn from a relatively large sample of preindustrial societies indicates that in almost 20 per cent of the societies for which information is available (20 out of 111), achievement was emphasized.[28] While recruitment on an achievement basis in work organizations is no guarantee that political recruitment was based on the same criteria, one must not overlook the possibility that recruitment patterns in work organizations might be carried over into the political system. These data suggest that achievement criteria are far more common in traditional and primitive societies than is usually supposed, and more research is needed to determine the usefulness of an achievement-ascription dimension to distinguish between modern and nonmodern political systems.[29]

THE PROBLEM OF MANY DIMENSIONAL DEFINITIONS. Almond differentiates the modern political system from the traditional on the basis of 17 to 20 separate dimensions, two of which are major and the rest secondary. It is clear from his definition that the United States today has a modern political system, while France at the time of Louis XIV had a traditional system. It is equally clear that both the Soviet Union and contemporary India must be classed as transitional, but they are classed as transitional for very different reasons. In the Soviet Union, the characteristics that are modern are exceedingly modern—aspects of the political-communication and political-socialization functions are probably more modern than those in the United States—while those that are nonmodern are exceedingly nonmodern (there exists, for example, virtually no structural differentiation as Almond defines it). India is classified as transitional because the characteristics of that political system fall somewhere between modern and traditional on many of the dimensions. The usefulness of any measuring device—and Almond's concepts may be viewed as a "device" for measuring the degree of modernization—is limited when some of the different components vary independently of one another, or when in some samples they may be negatively correlated to a high degree. Its limitations may be compared to those of a device which is designed to measure *blackness* but which does not enable the user to distinguish between a gray slab and a black-and-white checkerboard, each of which is equally "black."

This sort of a problem is a probable consequence of any definition that employs so many dimensions. It is desirable to limit the definitional criteria as much as possible, perhaps to only one or two dimensions, and to examine the others as empirical correlates of the dimensions, in terms of which a system type is defined.

The response to this argument is obvious: the student should compare political systems on each of the dimensions without making any attempt to compound the measures into some general concept of the modern and the traditional. Thus India and the Soviet Union would not both be classified as transitional, but attention would be drawn to the dimensions on which they are similar and to the dimensions on which they are different. But, conceptually speaking, this is not forward movement, for it is a step away from developing a basis for the construction of general theory. The Almond formulation does not fall into this trap, for it is concerned with the analysis of political systems as complete entities.

NEGLECT OF SOCIETAL FUNCTIONS. Although Almond has developed what is essentially a structural-functional framework, he focuses his attention exclusively upon the political system as the unit of analysis and does not consider the functions of political structure from the point of view of the society.[30] Indeed, he regards it as a step backwards for the student to concern himself with the general societal functions of a political system, contending that such an approach will eventually lead to a consideration of the general "integrating" and "adapting" functions of all political systems. Such a focus, he argues, rules out the sharp definitions necessary if one is to compare highly differentiated systems with relatively undifferentiated systems.

The definitions of politics which identify it with such general societal functions as "integration" and "adaptation" fail us from this point of view. It is of course true that political systems typically perform the functions of maintaining the integration of a society, adapting and changing elements of the kinship, religious, and economic systems, protecting the integrity of political systems from outside threats, or expanding into and attacking other societies. But to identify politics with social integration and adaptation is a regressive step, scientifically speaking. It represents a return to a dull tool, rather than an advance to a sharper one, for if in pursuit of the political system we follow the phantoms of integration and adaptation, we will find ourselves including in the political system churches, economies, schools, kinship and lineage groups, age-sets, and the like.[31]

The usefulness of a structural-functional framework may be jeopardized if structures (or systems) are defined in terms of their "functions" or "purposes," because statements relating structures and functions would then have a heavy tautological component. In other words, structures and functions would be logically linked, and one could not investigate empirically many of the relationships between the two because they would be related by definition. But if political structures are defined independently of their functions, the determination of their functions vis-à-vis the societies becomes a legitimate and significant line of investigation. Because of his unwillingness to pursue the "phantoms of integration and adaptation" in his definition of the political system, Almond excludes an examination of the societal functions of the political system.[32]

The consequences of this exclusion do not become clear if attention is focused entirely upon modern political systems, all of which have similar societal functions. In primitive and traditional systems, however, there is a considerable range of variation in the functions of government. Schapera has documented this very well in his studies of primitive tribes. His discussion of the differences in the functions of chiefs among the Bantu, Hottentot, Bergdama, and Bushmen is summed up by his statement that in "South Africa the constitutional functions of chiefs and their assistants vary greatly from one people to another." He is, of course, referring to the societal functions of government.[33]

Brief reference to some comparisons will illustrate the consequences that a neglect of the societal functions of government may have for an understanding of political modernization. Take, for example, four political systems: (1) the contemporary United States, (2) the contemporary Soviet Union, (3) the United States around 1840, and (4) imperial Russia around 1840. How would a student, employing Almond's criteria, rank them on a modern-nonmodern continuum? Contemporary United States would be the most modern, the United States around 1840 would be second, and contemporary Soviet Union and imperial Russia around 1840 would probably rank close together in positions three and four. If one takes into consideration the societal functions of government, however, there emerge some important similarities between contemporary United States and contemporary Soviet Union which differentiate them from their nineteenth-century predecessors. The political systems in both societies have significant economic control and regulatory activities (adaptive and integrative functions), and they have important social welfare functions (tension-management functions).[34] The differences between the two are not functional, that is, *what* is done; the differences are largely procedural, that is, *how* what is done is done.[35] If one is concerned with contrasting democratic and nondemocratic systems, procedural considerations are of major importance. But if one is studying modernization, the societal functions of government may be of greater significance.[36]

In summary, Almond's definition of the modern political system is a valuable and insightful formulation for the study of the development of democratic systems. It draws attention to factors that have been neglected, as, for example, the identification of certain structures and styles of interest articulation which may be as important for the existence of democratic government as certain kinds of political parties. The need, however, for an expanded definition of a modern political system that will embrace totalitarian forms and include the societal functions of government prompts students of political modernization to experiment with modified definitions, as well as to explore the possibility of alternative approaches.

THE "PROCESS" OF POLITICAL MODERNIZATION

Our methodological discussion thus far has been concentrated upon the definition and application of the concept *modern political system*. Because there is a growing body of literature on the *process* of political modernization, it will be instructive, before turning to the analytical framework of the present study, to glance briefly at selected studies of this process with a view toward examining a major methodological issue.

Political scientists of a behavioral persuasion rely heavily upon the research and theory in other behavioral sciences—psychology, sociology, economics, and anthropology. It often seems as though each political scientist has his own small group of theorists from whom he receives intellectual stimulation, frameworks of analysis, and sometimes even data. In some instances, the ideas and approaches which political scientists borrow from sister disciplines are the subjects of controversy within those disciplines, but are introduced into political science with very little discussion of the points of contention which engage other social scientists.

At this point in our discussion, we should like to examine two different conceptualizations used by students of political modernization, and to relate them to an important controversy which has been raging among certain anthropologists and sociologists. The issue is whether psychological or sociological factors should be used to explain social structural (or social system) phenomena.[37]

Before presenting an illustration of each conceptual approach, it will be necessary to define our terminology. By a *conceptualization of the causal sequence* we mean a specification of the independent, intervening, and dependent variables that are conceived to be operating.[38] In studies of political modernization, the dependent variable is a type of political system, for example, a modern political system. For some political scientists, the independent and intervening variables are largely psychological; for others, they are sociological. To illustrate these two approaches, we shall draw upon the works of David E. Apter and Lucian W. Pye.

A Sociological Conceptualization

Apter's studies of political change in Africa are an excellent illustration of a sociological conceptualization of the developmental process.[39] This can be seen by reviewing just one of the questions with which he is concerned. In part, Apter's objective is to explain what kind of a modernizing regime evolves in countries that are in a transitional stage of development. To facilitate his analysis, Apter has developed three models of the forms that the transitional political system may take: a *mobilization* model, a *consociational* model, and a model of the *modernizing autocracy*.

A mobilization system is one in which a single party dominates the regime and "engages in drastic and thorough reorganization of the society." [40] The mobilization system has the following characteristics: (1) Authority is structured hierarchically. (2) The party demands *total allegiance* from the individual. (3) The party enjoys great *tactical flexibility*. "It is tactical- rather than policy-oriented, and has a remarkable freedom of action with a minimum of accountability." (4) The party is dominated by the principle of *unitarism*. It establishes its own subordinate units and opposes the formation of other solidarity groupings which might be able to challenge the party's supremacy. (5) There is considerable *ideological specialization*. Ideology, instead of being a motivating factor, is used to support action that appears to be necessary on the grounds of expediency.[41]

 The consociational system represents a "joining together of constituent units which do not lose their identity when merging in some form of union."[42] It has the following characteristics: (1) Authority is *pyramidal*. Rather than being concentrated at the center, power is dispersed among constitutent units and the central organization. (2) There is a tolerance of *multiple loyalties*. Individuals may belong to political parties without making a total commitment either to a leader or to the goals of the party organization. (3) There is a *necessity for compromise*. (4) Since there are diverse and competing social and political subgroups, the social order is *pluralistic*. (5) There is *ideological diffuseness*. This does not mean, however, that ideology is unimportant. On the contrary, it is the cement that holds together the alliances among the constituent units, binding them into a unity which rests on more than a transient, coincidental common interest.[43]

The modernizing autocracy is a system in which change can be adopted and absorbed by the traditional system of authority. It has the following characteristics: (1) *Authority is hierarchical,* but, unlike the mobilization system, authority at any given moment is vested in the leadership role, not in the individual leader himself. (2) There is a principle of *exclusivism*. "To belong means not to belong to another social grouping of a similar nature and not to divide one's fundamental allegiance. Within this allegiance, however, persons can belong to a range of voluntary associations and political groups." (3) There is *strategic flexibility* (freedom to develop long-term plans) but little tactical flexibility, particularly of a sort that might "jeopardize the authority principle." (4) The organizational structure tends to be *unitary*. (5) The ideology tends to be *neotraditional*.[44]

One of the significant contributions of Apter's work is a theory that explains why one rather than another of these systems develops (or will develop) during the transitional stage of political development. In the terms used in this monograph, Apter's conceptualization of the variables involved in his study of African cases may be expressed as follows: the independent variable is the structure and practices of British colonialism; the intervening variable is the type of traditional system on which these structures and practices impinged; and the dependent variable is the type of system that emerged in the transitional stage. For example, in Ghana a mobilization system emerged, Nigeria developed a consociational system, and in Uganda (or more particularly in Buganda) a modernizing autocracy evolved.

Although Apter recognizes some differences in the colonial experiences in West and East Africa, he feels that for his purposes he can treat them as basically similar.[45] Thus the differences in the type of transitional system that develops are due largely to the type of traditional system which existed prior to the impact of the West. The crucial differences in the traditional political system are to be found in (1) the type of authority structure, and (2) the type of values which are dominant in the system. Apter conceives of two types of authority systems, *pyramidal,* and *hierarchical,* and two types of values, *consummatory* and *instrumental.* Since any combination of authority structure and dominant value patterns is possible, on the basis of these two components four types of traditional systems are within the realm of possibility: (1) hierarchical and instrumental, (2) pyramidal and instrumental, (3) hierarchical and consummatory, and (4) pyramidal and consummatory.[46] Apter presents this typology in the following table.[47]

| | Authority Type | |
Value Type	A. Hierarchical	B. Pyramidal
I. Instrumental	(IA)	(IB)
II. Consummatory	(IIA)	(IIB)

The Ashanti, the most significant precontact traditional system in Ghana, was of type IIB (pyramidal authority and consummatory values). The Baganda, the dominant tribal people in Uganda, were of type IA (hierarchical authority and instrumental values).

What happened after the colonial impact pushed these two societies along the path toward modernization? Instrumental values are an essential part of a modern system. Thus the value requirement of a modern system clashed directly with the dominant value type in Ashanti. As the consummatory values were inextricably related to the pattern of traditional authority, the substitution of instrumental values undermined the entire traditional political system, As Apter points out:

What had hitherto been reinforcing social institutions of the consummatory system of Ashanti rapidly broke down into competing power groups and sources of internal antagonism and weakness. Thus conflicts of youth and age, royals against nonroyals, and slaves against non-slaves all represented conflict over the continuing strength of particularistic criteria which could be reconciled only so long as older religious and institutional checks were distributed.[48]

Apter goes on to say:

Where the consummatory system prevailed, there developed fierce competition between traditional and secular leaders to monopolize allegiance. This was expressed by the latter in efforts to build overarching and autocratic institutions which by autocratic means fostered egalitarianism in political recruitment and the exercise of authority. The problem was to prevent social atomism while mobilizing those resources of the society which could capitalize on change itself. This put exceedingly heavy burdens on political nationalists whose need for organizational control and support becomes all important. *This led to the development of the mobilization system in Ghana.*[49]

In Buganda, by contrast, instrumental values were dominant in the traditional system. Modernization could be introduced without challenging the basis of legitimacy and thus without stimulating pressures to modify the traditional authority structure, accommodated as it was to instrumental values. "In Buganda the autocratic principle prevailed and the two oligarchies, British and Baganda, worked alongside one another. They were in constant competition but they did not challenge each other's legitimacy. Both were oriented to efficiency and performance." [50] By selecting certain aspects of the modern system and incorporating them into the traditional, the traditional autocracy in Buganda became a modernizing autocracy.

It is possible to schematize the conceptualization which underlies Apter's theory as follows:

Independent Variable	*Intervening Variable*	*Dependent Variable*
	(Traditional system)	(Transitional type)
	Pyramidal, consummatory →	Mobilizational system
	↗ traditional system	
Colonial impact		
	↘ Hierarchical, instrumental →	Modernizing autocracy
	traditional system.	

In Apter's theory, it should be observed, all the variables are social system variables, as Apter defines such variables.[51]

In this analysis we must also take note of what Apter is not doing. He does not argue that Nkrumah's personality was a significant factor in explaining the development of a mobilization regime in Ghana either because such a system suited his personality or because a vast number of people in Ghana were attracted to his personality and style of rule. Apter recognizes that a charismatic personality is probably essential to a successful mobilization regime, but, as we interpret his position, he would argue that if Nkrumah had attempted to come to power in Buganda, he would either have had to give up his attempt to develop a mobilization regime or be unsuccessful in his efforts. While Apter recognizes the importance of psychological variables in an explanation of why an individual is attracted to a mobilization party, he does not attempt to explain the existence of the party in terms of the personality factors that may be involved in an individual's decision to affiliate.[52]

A Psychological Conceptualization

Pye has developed what is one of the most intriguing psychological explanations of social system phenomena. His book on Burma, *Politics, Personality, and Nation Building,* is a model for the clear presentation of field-research findings in a theoretical framework which is worthy of careful consideration. He is explicitly concerned with the role of personality factors in that phase of political development which he refers to as nation building. His major concern is indicated in the following passage:

> In order to avoid the excessively static bias of, say, classical anthropology while not going to the other extreme of, say, traditional economics in which change is seen as no more complex than rational choice, it will be helpful to elucidate the details of the relationships between personality and social change. This can usefully be done by first analyzing the various phases of the political socialization process and then noting the significance for social change of the different types of cultural values and attitudes produced by the socialization process. The theme running throughout such an analysis must be the quest of individuals to achieve appropriate political and social indentities in their changing worlds.[53]

It is a tribute to the clarity of Pye's work that his central thesis may be summarized in propositional form:[54]

1. Large, complex, effective and thus flexible organizational forms are a crucial feature of a modern society.

2. Large, complex organizations cannot be flexible and effective unless, in addition to their formal structures, there exist significant informal structures, especially informal channels of communication.
3. Only individuals who have developed *associational sentiments* can form and effectively participate in these informal structures.
4. Individuals who are insecure and distrustful cannot manifest associational sentiments.

Therefore:

5. Organizations in which a significant proportion of the members are insecure and distrustful cannot have effective informal structures.

Therefore:

6. A modern society (which by definition has large, complex, effective, and hence flexible organizations) cannot develop when the crucial large-scale organizations have a disproportionate number of insecure and distrustful individuals in them.

Pye finds that the Burmese administrator, because of his socialization experiences in the native culture and because of the impact of acculturation, is insecure and distrustful and has not developed associational sentiments. The following passage presents the essential elements of the author's interpretation:

The urge to withhold confidence in subordinates permeates almost all hierarchical relationships within the present-day Burmese bureaucracy. Thus barriers are established to casual, relaxed, and informal relationships, creating a situation especially disturbing to men who initially learned that government service could and should offer warm, close, and exciting personal associations. Now all relationships seem to be cold and indifferent. There is an increased need to emphasize status considerations in order to insure one's security in the hierarchy. The result is an enveloping sense of isolation and loneliness. In addition to feeling that they have been under constant attack from politicians on the outside, the senior administrators feel themselves about to be waylaid and criticized by people within their establishments.

The feelings of isolation and insecurity of course breed further distrust and the belief that discipline should be more strongly enforced, which, when combined with the basic Burmese desire for status but fear of decision and choice, tend to choke off the flow of communication within the administrative service. Superiors cannot share their problems with subordinates, and subordinates feel it necessary to adhere rigidly to correct form and procedure in all their dealings with their superiors. There is thus a profound psychological reason why it is impossible to hold staff meetings within the Burmese bureaucracy, and why superiors and subordinates cannot explore operational problems together. Trial and error and free discussion might only prove that superiors are fallible. *And here we find the basic psychological reason why the Burmese administrative class clings so tenaciously to formal procedure. Confronted with a pervasive sense of insecurity, everyone must fall back on the safest course of action; everyone must adhere strictly to form, to procedure, to ritual.*[55]

Pye's conceptualization is very clear. A personality characteristic of the Burmese administrators (a "sense of insecurity") is the independent variable; a characteristic of the bureaucratic structure (the strict adherence to procedure, form, and ritual) is the intervening variable; nation building (in this case, slow progress of) is the dependent variable.[56]

Another example of Pye's psychological conceptualization is found in his explanation of the high incidence of acts of violence in Burmese society. In attempting to explain this phenomenon, he recognizes that some of it stems from the disruptive impact of the West upon traditional Burmese life. He argues, however, that other traditional societies have been disrupted without giving rise to a comparable degree of violence. In other words, he feels that the greater amount of violence in Burmese society, as contrasted with other transitional societies, cannot be accounted for by the Western impact. He explains the difference by postulating a causal role for certain personality factors. The early socialization experience of the Burmese (particularly the relationship between mother and child) produces a personality that seeks warm and close personal relationships, but it also develops a personality which fears that such behavior may elicit hostile responses. Thus the source of the violence (and of the gentleness) in Burmese society is a "deep-seated fear of provoking others." [57] Pye goes on to state that "the acculturation process tends to reinforce a sense of distrust towards precisely those who would appear to be anxious to help, for helping is the same as controlling; when people are being changed from traditionals into moderns, they are likely to be hypersensitive to the deeply felt sensation of being changed and manipulated by others who always protest that they are only being helpful." [58]

In Pye's analysis of Burmese society, a personality factor (a deep-seated fear of provoking others) is the independent variable, the impact of the West (or of "world culture") is the intervening variable, and the high incidence of violence is the dependent variable.[59]

Psychological Versus Sociological Conceptualizations

In the language of the philosophy of science, what we have referred to as a psychological explanation is a *reductive* explanation. It attempts to explain the phenomena in a given field in terms of another field that is microscopic to it. For example, Pye tries to explain nation building (or failures in nation building), which involves the use of group or collective concepts, in terms of the personality characteristics and behavior of individuals who make up the collectivities. In this sense his explanation is reductive. By contrast, Apter's explanation of the type of regime that emerges during the transitional stage of development tries to account for variation among social system phenomena in terms of social system phenomena. Psychological factors are either absent from or nonessential to his analysis; there is no attempt at reduction. An explanation of this sort may be designated as an *emergent* explanation.[60]

The language of the philosophy of science has been introduced in order to help establish some methodological guidelines. In some respects, reductive and emergent explanations compete with each other. For any given macro-social phenomenon, the scholar may attempt to provide either a reductive or an emergent explanation. But if he attempts to present a reductive explanation, the data he must use are entirely different from the data he would use for an emergent explanation. Apter, for example, would have had to uncover a different sort of empirical data if he had undertaken a reductive explanation. Because the kind of data called for by one type of explanation is of little relevance to the other type of explanation, it is important for the scholar to make the best possible decision concerning the kind of explanation he is seeking before he begins to collect the empirical data. Some of the work in the philosophy of science is very useful in helping to make this decision.

In principle, there is no doubt that the reductive explanation is preferable. Closure, autonomy, and perfect knowledge are *ideal goals* in the development of any scientific theory, and reductive explanations come closest to reaching these goals. However, enormous difficulties stand in the way of researchers and theorists who try to provide reductive explanations for the kinds of complex macro-social phenomena that are encountered in the study of political modernization. The major obstacle is the absence of a set of *composition laws* which would enable the scholar to generalize from the characteristics of the interaction between two individuals to the pattern of interaction among many individuals.

Pye's analysis of Burma contains no composition laws of this type. This gap is, of course, readily understandable and excusable. Few composition laws have been developed thus far in the behavioral sciences, and the kind that are necessary to make Pye's theory "complete" would be discouragingly complex. It is conceivable that such laws do not even exist and, if this is the case, a reductive explanation would not be possible. But if a reductive explanation is undertaken, composition laws are required, and their absence in Pye's work is one reason for the weakness of his explanation, which will be discussed below.

Although in principle less desirable than a reductive explanation, the emergent explanation is acceptable on grounds of logic. This point is made in order to counter the argument that the explanation of group phenomena in terms of group phenomena requires the scholar to attribute supra-individual characteristics to these phenomena; in other words, that it requires him to defend the existence of *emergent properties,* which is a logically untenable position. But it is not necessary for the scholar who seeks an emergent explanation to hold this view, as Brodbeck clearly indicates:

> The belief that there are no emergent *properties* rests on our criterion of the meaningful. It is thus, broadly speaking, a matter of logic. The assumption that the *laws* of group behavior are or are not, as the case may be, emergent with respect to laws about individuals is a matter of fact, a matter for empirical determination.[61]
>
> Explanatory emergence . . . refers to laws of group behavior, which, *even though their terms are defined as they should be,* are still not derivable from the laws, including whatever composition laws there are, about individual behavior. This is *in fact* the case at present [in the behavioral sciences].[62]

It is doubtful that there will be at least for a very long time any composition laws which will make possible reductive explanations of macro-political phenomena. But, regardless of what the future may bring forth, at the present time composition laws are far beyond our grasp. Given this situation, we have no alternative but to seek emergent explanations. However, we do not expect the reader to underwrite this methodological decision merely on the basis of an abstract argument. For this reason we shall return briefly to an analysis of

Pye's theory in order to illustrate more clearly the problem of the reductive explanation. In considering Pye's analysis further, we shall be concerned with two aspects of the problem: (1) the deductive power of the Pye formulation; and (2) the limitations of personality theory as an explanation of macro-social phenomena. Following this discussion, we shall indicate that certain sociological conceptualizations may be uncovered in the literature of the social sciences, and that these may be substitutable alternatives for Pye's psychological explanation.

THE DEDUCTIVE POWER OF PYE'S THESIS. One of the implications of Pye's work is that successful nation building is dependent upon bureaucracies that are staffed by psychologically secure individuals who are able to form associational sentiments; in the absence of such people in the major bureaucracies, nation building cannot proceed. Unfortunately, the studies of nation building in a variety of societies necessary to test this proposition directly have not yet been made. It is, however, interesting to examine Pye's thesis in light of the work of the psychological theorist upon whom he draws heavily, Eric H. Erikson, and his important concepts of *ego identity* and *identity crisis*.

We can hypothesize that the struggles of large numbers of people in any society to realize their own basic sense of identity will inevitably be reflected in the spirit of the society's political life, and thus, more specifically, that those conscious and subconscious elements most crucial in determining the individual's identity crises must have their counterparts in the shared sentiments of the polity. We must assume that in transitional societies in which the socialization process fails to give people a clear sense of identity there will be related uncertainty in the political culture of the people.

Although many citizens in transitional societies may be disturbed by the consequences of cultural diffusion and the need to adjust to the changing times, it is those intimately associated with power and politics who are the most disturbed over their own sense of identity. In part this is because their access to power leaves them peculiarly sensitive to the possibilities of advantage and disadvantage, being superior or inferior, honored or shamed, effective or ineffective. In part it is because they are the most deeply touched by the acculturation process, and they may have experienced moments of insight into the real meaning of being a modern man in a modern country, and forever after been left disturbed by the knowledge that on the matters that really count they have been rationalizing rather than describing the realities of their society. Their ambivalences have undermined their sense of judgment, of property, of tastes; their self-confidence has been sapped to the point where these men are consciously anxious about their own worth and unsure of their own identities.[63]

In an earlier section of the book, the argument is clearly stated:

> . . . the search for individual identity hinges on the existence of a national identity, and the latter calls for a coherent and consensus-bound political process; but people cannot fundamentally respect their political spokesmen when they are not sure that they can respect themselves, and so back to the issue of personal integrity and identity. A dilemma is framed: the need for self-identity produces the need for a nation-state, and the need for reassurance of individual worth produces the need for a politics of status—and yet such a politics is inconsistent with the requirements of nation building.[64]

The use of Erikson's concepts may provide some interesting insights into the problems of nation building. They are useful, however, primarily to gain a deeper understanding of some of the personality tensions and strains suffered by individuals in a transitional society; they do not seem to provide much basis for explaining the process of nation building. More specifically, they do not go very far in answering the question of why some nations modernize quickly and with relative ease, while others struggle for generations without making much progress.

One is struck, for example, by the similarities between Pye's discussion of the identity crisis and its consequences in Burma and Erikson's discussion of Germany. While Pye calls attention to the conflict between the traditional culture and the "world culture" in Burma, Erikson says of Germany:

> Germany has been impressed by *foreign values*. Her attitude toward these values, and their relation to her own cultural diversity, constitute a clinical problem hard to define. But one may say that no other young nation of similar size, density, and historical diversity of population, with a similar lack of natural frontiers, is exposed to cultural influences as divergent in their nature and as disturbing in their succession as the influences emanating from Germany's neighbors. As is true for the elements which make for individual anxiety, it is the consistent mutual aggravation of all these items which has never allowed German identity to crystallize. . . . [65]

The conflict between the traditional culture and the world culture which Pye finds in Burma is thus akin to the conflict between the *cosmopolitan* German and the *provincial* German as reported by Erikson.[66]

Germany has had a prolonged identity crisis, and the German bureaucrat is often characterized as being excessively formal and ritualistic. Yet these do not seem to have inhibited the development of "large, complex, effective, and flexible" organizations.[67] Few nations in Western Europe were as close to their feudal past as was Germany in the nineteenth century; few nations had as far to go to reach a modern status; yet few covered the ground so quickly.

On the basis of the variable that Pye postulates as significant in nation building, one cannot account for both the lack of progress in Burma and the speed of German development during the last half of the nineteenth century. It is doubtful, too, that this analysis sheds much light on the differences between the nation building of China and Japan during the nineteenth and twentieth centuries.

THE GENERAL PROBLEM OF PSYCHOLOGICAL CONCEPTUALIZA-TIONS. The difficulties involved in the use of psychological concepts as major variables in a theory of political change may point to intrinsic weaknesses in any essentially psychological interpretation. Two major considerations tempt one to suggest this possibility. In the first place, roles in well-defined social settings tend to be tightly defined, and the norms governing behavior tend to be unambiguous. Thus there is little leeway for individual personality factors to affect behavior significantly.[68] A second factor may be operating even when the social setting is not well defined. It is possible that concepts used to differentiate personalities cannot be used to make significant discriminations in behavior. For example, political scientists who use psychological conceptualizations tend to employ terms like *insecurity, distrust,* and *aggression.* However, an individual who has, for example, pervasive feelings of insecurity may rely on one or more defense mechanisms to enable him to cope with his insecurity. He may *regress, rationalize,* and/or *repress.* An individual who has feelings of aggression may rely on *projection* or *reaction formation.* Not only are the behavioral manifestations of different defense mechanisms different, but the behavioral manifestations of the same defense mechanism may be different in different people. For example, the person who relies heavily on projection to help deal with his aggressive feelings may be a retiring, indecisive type, or he may be decisive and aggressive, displaying such intolerance of ambiguity that he cannot accept indecision in himself or in others.[69] In light of these considerations, one might suggest that Pye could hypothetically have found in Burma the opposite of his actual findings—great decisiveness and resoluteness—and explain such characteristics on the same psychological grounds as he explains the ineffectualness, indecision, and impotency.[70]

It should be noted that, in making these comments, we are in no way criticizing the field of personality psychology. Indeed, one of the problems of psychological explanations of macro-social phenomena may derive from the fact that theories of individual behavior are so much more advanced than the theories dealing with macro-social phenomena that it is extremely difficult to bring the former to bear upon the latter.

SOCIOLOGICAL ALTERNATIVES. In a number of studies, bureaucratic structures have been compared on dimensions of rigidity, formalism, and ritualistic behavior, and observed differences have been accounted for by social-structural variables.

In her study of two wards in a hospital, for example, Coser found that in the medical ward the relationships among individuals occupying different roles were formal and ritualistic, while in the surgical ward there was great informality.[71] Although in the surgical ward there was little delegation of authority from the chief resident to the doctors and nurses on the floor, the medical ward was characterized by a scalar delegation of authority from the chief resident to the assistant resident on to the interns and from the interns to the head nurse. Coser suggests that "where the rank hierarchy below the top decision-makers is not very strict and the delegation of authority not well-defined, informal relations are built across status lines." [72] Where authority is specifically delegated at various levels and when there are advantages to be gained by a consensual style of decision making, such informal relationships tend not to develop and the organization displays signs of ritualism. According to Coser, there is evidence to suggest that the development of informal relations in some organizations and the development of formal relations and ritualistic behavior in others are largely functions of the formal structure and the nature of the task of the organization rather than of a "professional" or personality trait.[73]

In *The Dynamics of Bureaucracy*, Blau presents data which bear upon this discussion. Like Pye, he employs psychological terms like *insecurity*, but his use of these concepts in explanatory propositions is entirely different. In a governmental agency, a unit which Blau calls *Section A* showed "ritualistic adherence to the existing order," while in *Section B* (engaged in the same task as Section A) there was informal cooperation among the employees, which at times led to a disregard of official regulations but which resulted in increased effectiveness.[74] Blau found that the members of *Section A* were more anxious and insecure than were the members of *Section B*. But he does not refer to them as insecure or anxious personalities. Members of *Section A* were on probation for their civil service appointments, while members of *Section B* held permanent appointments. Thus the crucial difference between *Section A* and *Section B* is a structural one; the roles are defined differently with regard to the occupants' rights to permanent employment.[75] In the explanatory proposition, this structural characteristic is the independent variable, and the presence or absence of informal, cooperative groups is the dependent variable. A personality variable—feelings of insecurity and anxiety—is an intervening factor. But it should be noted that none of the variation in the dependent variable is accounted for by changes in this factor. There is no need to explore an individual's socialization experiences and culture conflicts to find a reason for the insecurity, because little, if any, of the variation in the dependent variable is accounted for by the characteristics of the individual's personality before he entered the organization. Feelings of security or insecurity are related directly to the role the individual occupies, and they simply form a link between the independent variable and the dependent variable. The variation between *Section A* and *Section B* is accounted for by a different definition of roles and a different structuring of these roles, not by personality differences.

This is not to suggest, however, that the explanation of excessive formalism and ritualism presented by either Coser or Blau can account for these phenomena in the Burmese bureaucracy. The data necessary to support such a conclusion are not available. But these studies indicate that there are good sociological conceptualizations within which the characteristics of formalism and ritualism may be explained.

It is also possible to explain the higher incidence of violence and other forms of disruptive behavior in one transitional society than in another in sociological terms. It may be that in two traditional societies the structures and mechanisms of social control are different, and that the beginning of the modernization process undercuts the traditional structures more in one than in the other. If this is the case, it is likely that the incidence of violence will be higher in the society where the traditional structures have been undercut most completely, until new structures can be developed to bring disruptive behavior under control.[76] We are not asserting that the traditional social-control structures in Burma were undermined more than those of a transitional country with a lower incidence of violence. We do not have the data necessary to support such an explanation. We make this point merely to illustrate a sociological conceptualization that may be used as an alternative to Pye's psychological explanation.

METHODOLOGICAL GUIDELINES

This brief critique of significant approaches to the study of political modernization influenced in large measure some of the methodological decisions which have been made in this exploratory study and which are reflected in the following chapters. The major guidelines that have been drawn from the critique may be listed in summary form as follows:

1. A useful approach to the study of political modernization must be able to accommodate both the democratic and autocratic/ totalitarian cases.
2. Different types of systems should be *defined* by a very limited number of characteristics.
3. Particular attention must be devoted to the societal functions of government.
4. Given the present state of development in the behavioral sciences, significant psychological (reductive) explanations of macro-social phenomena are not yet possible, and efforts should be focused upon sociological (emergent) explanations, with an explicit attempt to achieve maximum closure and autonomy.

NOTES

1. The dichotomous schema of various scholars interested in social development have been examined and a high degree of interrelationship shown. See Linton C. Freeman and Robert F. Winch, "Societal Complexity: An Empirical Test of a Typology of Societies," *American Journal of Sociology*, Vol. 62, No. 5, March 1957, pp. 461-466. On social change theories, see Everett E. Hagen, *On the Theory of Social Change*; H. Ian Hogbin, *Social Change*; Don Martindale, *Social Life and Cultural Change*; Wilbert E. Moore, *Social Change*; Marshall D. Sahlins and Elman R. Service, *Evolution and Culture*; Pitirim Sorokin, *Social and Cultural Dynamics*; Julian H. Steward, *Theory of Culture Change*.
2. These qualifications, however, seem to be little more than attempts to avoid being accused of adapting a dichotomous scheme (reflecting a milieu in which such an analysis is considered an oversimplification), rather than significantly affecting the underlying dichotomy in its essentials.
3. There are several important exceptions to this generalization. For example, David E. Apter in *The Gold Coast in Transition* is concerned with the development of a democratic political system rather than with the more general problem of a modern political system. Karl W. Deutsch focuses attention upon

the modern society rather than on the modern political system. (See "Social Mobilization and Political Development," *American Political Science Review,* Vol. 55, No. 3, September 1961, pp. 493-514.) His approach has something in common with what we propose in Chapter 2.

4. The works of Apter are again the most notable exception. Some of his significant ideas are presented below, pp. 20-24.

5. Gabriel A. Almond, "A Functional Approach to Comparative Politics," the introduction to G. A. Almond and J. S. Coleman (eds.), *The Politics of Developing Areas,* p. 5. For additional examples of Almond's position, see Gabriel A. Almond and Sidney Verba, *The Civic Culture;* Gabriel A. Almond, "Political Systems and Political Change," *American Behavioral Scientist,* Vol. 6, No. 10, June 1963, pp. 3-10; and "A Developmental Approach to Political Systems," *World Politics,* Vol. 17, No. 2, January 1965, pp. 183-214.

6. This kind of problem, of course, does not arise if one uses a criterion of differentiation to define a modern society rather than to define a modern political system.

7. Almond, "A Functional Approach to Comparative Politics," p. 18.

8. *Ibid.,* p. 17. These terms have been so widely used in the literature in recent years that it is not necessary to present definitions here.

9. *Ibid.,* p. 18.

10. In an earlier article, Almond does define what he means by a *secular political culture*: "By a secular political culture I mean a multi-valued political culture, a rational-calculating, bargaining, and experimental political culture. . . . A secularized political system involves an individuation of and a measure of autonomy among the various rôles. Each one of the rôles sets itself up autonomously in political business, so to speak. There tends to be an arms-length bargaining relationship among the rôles." ("Comparative Political System," *Journal of Politics,* Vol. 18, No. 3, August 1956, pp. 391-409). In "A Functional Approach to Comparative Politics," Almond treats this same point when discussing the style in which input functions are performed. See below, p. 11.

11. Almond, "A Functional Approach to Comparative Politics," p. 30.

12. *Ibid.,* pp. 31-33.

13. *Ibid.,* p. 32. This is, of course, a *ceteris paribus* proposition.

14. *Ibid.,* p. 33.

15. *Ibid.,* pp. 34-35. The meaning of the first three dimensions should be clear, since ordinary definitions apply. However, the fourth dimension—instrumental-affective—may need some amplification. It is the difference between a rational, calculated means for achieving a specified end, and an affected, emotionally loaded orientation to means-ends relationships.

16. *Ibid.,* p. 43.

17. *Ibid.,* pp. 43-44. Almond makes a distinction between "interest aggregation" and "interest integration." A totalitarian party "integrates" rather than "aggregates" interests.

18. Elihu Katz, "The Two-Step Flow of Communication: An Up-to-Date Report on a Hypothesis," *Public Opinion Quarterly,* Vol. 24, No. 1, Spring 1957, pp. 61-78. See also E. Katz and P. F. Lazarsfeld, *Personal Influence,* Chapters 1-3.

19. Almond, "A Functional Approach to Comparative Politics," pp. 48-49.

20. *Ibid.,* p. 49. The generalistic-particularistic continuum which Almond applies to political communication is different from the generalistic-particularistic continuum which he uses to characterize the style of political recruitment. In the former case, he is emphasizing the nature of the political message that

is being communicated—whether it is a particular or general message; in the latter case, he is referring to the basis on which individuals are recruited into political roles.

21. John E. Turner, "Soviet Politics: Old and New," in Robert T. Holt and John E. Turner (eds.), *Soviet Union: Paradox and Change*, pp. 23-27.

22. In the appendix of this book, there is a discussion of changes in the post-Stalin period that appears to be relevant to an analysis of modernization.

23. On the socialization functions of schools and youth groups which are dominated by the Party, see Merle Fainsod, *How Russia Is Ruled*, Chapter 9.

24. See Alex Inkeles, *Public Opinion in Soviet Russia: A Study in Mass Persuasion*.

25. This is the position taken by Edward Shils, who has called the modernity of the Soviet Union a "tyrannically deformed manifestation of potentialities which are inherent in the process of modernisation," since its pressures for "mobilisation of the masses" lead to a "coerced conformity" rather than to personal liberties and freely given consent. See his "Further Observations on Mrs. Huxley," *Encounter*, Vol. 17, No. 4, October 1961, p. 45.

26. M. G. Smith, *Government in Zazzau, 1800-1950*, pp. 42-67.

27. In making these estimates, we are not weighting the various dimensions on which modernization is measured. Almond gives no indication that they should be weighted.

28. Stanley H. Udy, Jr., *Organization of Work*, pp. 39-43, 109. For further treatment, see also S. N. Eisenstadt, *From Generation to Generation*.

29. Almond is careful to point out that no system is completely modern, as he defines the term. There will always be traditional elements present. However, he certainly holds that, as a system moves toward the modern pole of his various dimensions, it becomes more modern. (See his "A Functional Approach to Comparative Politics," pp. 24-25.)

30. The failure to study comparatively the societal functions of government is, of course, typical of the whole field of political science. See below, pp. 50-57.

31. Almond, "A Functional Approach to Comparative Politics," p. 5.

32. *Ibid.*, p. 5.

33. I. Schapera, *Government and Politics in Tribal Societies*, pp. 87-88.

34. The terminology in parentheses is further discussed below, pp. 51-54.

35. For further treatment, see below, pp. 50-55.

36. For further treatment, see below, pp. 293-328.

37. Among the most active contestants, one finds Rodney Needham, *Structure and Sentiment* versus George C. Homans and D. M. Schneider, *Marriage, Authority and Final Causes*. The Homans and Schneider volume is a critique of Claude Levi-Strauss, *Les structures élémentaires de la parenté*, while Needham's work is a lively defense of Levi-Straus. For an account of the controversy, including the role of other combatants, see F. G. Lounsbury's review of Needham, *American Anthropologist*, Vol. 64, No. 6, December 1962, pp. 1302-1310.

Others who subscribe generally to what we would call a sociological conceptualization are Max Gluckman (see *Order and Rebellion in Tribal Africa*, especially the introduction) and E. R. Leach (see *Rethinking Anthropology*).

An excellent example of a psychological conceptualization is found in Hagen, *On the Theory of Social Change*.

38. See T. R. Vallance, "Methodology in Propaganda Research," *Psychological Bulletin*, January 1951, pp. 32-61, and Robert T. Holt and Robert W. van de Velde, *Strategic Psychological Operations and American Foreign Policy*, pp. 52-65.

39. Apter, *The Gold Coast in Transition*, and *The Political Kingdom in Uganda.*

40. Apter, *The Political Kingdom in Uganda*, p. 22.

41. *Ibid.*, p. 23.

42. *Ibid.*, p. 24. (Italics in original.)

43. *Ibid.*, p. 24-25.

44. *Ibid.*, pp. 25-27.

45. *Ibid.*, p. 448.

46. *Ibid.*, pp. 85-91.

47. *Ibid.*, p. 90.

48. *Ibid.*, p. 444.

49. *Ibid.*, p. 446. (Emphasis added.)

50. *Ibid.*, p. 445.

51. In Chapter 2 we shall define social system variables in a more restricted manner than does Apter.

52. Apter, *The Political Kingdom in Uganda*, p. 443.

53. Lucian W. Pye, *Politics, Personality, and Nation Building: Burma's Search for Identity*, p. 44.

54. *Ibid.*, p. 44. These propositions have been abstracted from the text on pp. 51-54. See also pp. 264-265.

55. *Ibid.*, p. 228. (Emphasis added.)

56. Since Pye makes no attempt to apply his scheme to several countries, it is a little more difficult to identify the causal sequence that he is dealing with. It is perfectly clear, however, that, *ceteris paribus*, he would account for differences in the progress toward nation building by psychological factors.

57. Pye, *Politics, Personality, and Nation Building*, p. 139.

58. *Ibid.*, p. 139.

59. Note that Pye emphasizes the impact of the West on *individuals*, in marked contrast with Apter's emphasis on the impact of the West on traditional social systems.

60. See May Brodbeck, "Methodological Individualisms: Definitions and Reduction," *Philosophy of Science*, Vol. 25, No. 1, January 1958, pp. 1-22.

61. *Ibid.*, p. 6.

62. *Ibid.*, pp. 19-20.

63. Pye, *Politics, Personality, and Nation Building*, pp. 52-53.

64. *Ibid.*, pp. 4-5.

65. Erik H. Erikson, *Childhood and Society*, p. 305.

66. *Ibid.*, p. 306.

67. It is interesting to observe—more in support of Pye's position than our own—that in the Wehrmacht, the most Prussian of German organizations, individuals exhibited great capacity for what Pye would call associational sentiments. See Edward A. Shils and Morris Janowitz, "Cohesion and Disintegration in the Wehrmacht in World War II," *Public Opinion Quarterly*, Vol. 12, No. 2, Summer 1948, pp. 280-315.

68. Robert E. Lane, *Political Life*, pp. 99-100.

69. For further discussion, see any relevant psychology textbook, for example, Norman Cameron and Ann Magaret, *Behavior Pathology*, pp. 217-245, 337-371. It is also interesting to compare the way in which a psychological concept like aggression is developed and used by a psychologist, with the way it is employed in political science writings. Compare Pye, for example, with Leonard Berkowitz, *Aggression: A Social Psychological Analysis*, especially Chapters 6-7, 10.

70. A more fundamental criticism of psychological explanations of social-

structural and social system phenomena may be developed from a critique of the theories of socialization that are involved. Political scientists tend to draw their socialization theories from works published before 1955, the intellectual foundations of which were developed in the late 1930's. Many recent works in anthropology have been extremely critical of these classical formulations. See, for example, Anthony F. Wallace, *Personality and Culture.*

71. Rose L. Coser, "Authority and Decision-making in a Hospital: A Comparative Analysis," in James D. Thompson *et al., Comparative Studies in Administration,* pp. 119-130.

72. *Ibid.,* p. 127.

73. *Ibid.,* p. 129. A process of self-recruitment in which individuals with certain personality types join groups with social structures that are most compatible with their personality characteristics would, of course, give rise to a correlation between personality type and social-structural type.

74. Peter Blau, *The Dynamics of Bureaucracy,* p. 208.

75. *Ibid.,* p. 208.

76. In many respects, the analysis made by Marion J. Levy, Jr., in "Contrasting Factors in the Modernization of China and Japan," in Simon Kuznets, Wilbert E. Moore, and Joseph J. Spengler, *Economic Growth: Brazil, India, Japan,* pp. 496-536, is similar to the one we are suggesting as an alternative to Pye. For further discussion, see below, pp. 172-193, 313-314.

CHAPTER 2

A Framework for the Study of the Political Basis of Economic Growth

THE FACT THAT STUDIES OF POLITICAL MODERNIZATION BETRAY some conceptual limitations is neither surprising nor requiring of apology. After all, political scientists have been actively concerned with the analysis of political development for only about a decade, and much of their work has been pioneering and experimental. The shortcomings are overshadowed by the remarkable progress that has been made. However, as scholars continue their search for more useful concepts, more valid theories, and more revealing research, the pace of scholarly progress will be measured to a significant degree by the frequency with which the concepts and theories become outdated. This process may be accelerated through continuous examination and criticism of the existing corpus of theories and concepts, and by experimenting with new ones when the old ones have outlived their usefulness.

The approach to the study of political modernization which we are presenting was developed in part as a response to the criticism of previous work in the field—criticism advanced by other writers, as well as that which we have projected.[1] In an attempt to develop a more adequate concept of the modern political system, we first examined some of the research that has been done in economic development. It did not seem difficult to identify the features of a modern economy that would persist in any form of economic organization, whether capitalist, mixed, socialist, or Communist. But the analysis of economic development theory unfortunately provided little assistance in the formulation of a new definition of a modern political system. It did, however, suggest that some features of a modern political system might develop as a consequence of political problems that are created by a rapidly growing economy, and that some of the aspects of a modern economy may require certain political forms if they are to evolve. For this reason we concluded that it might be fruitful to study political modernization specifically in relationship to economic development.

There is, of course, a rich literature on what might generally be called the economic basis of politics. But our attention is attracted to the opposite problem—the political basis of economic development. At the outset, we address ourselves to one fundamental question: What are the *functions of government* and the *procedures of governing* that are with a high probability required for economic growth at the various *stages of economic development?* This question opens the door to a number of meaningful research projects and suggests tentative solutions to some of the conceptual problems which were encountered in the last chapter. Before discussing these, however, it is necessary to define the three major concepts we are to use: *functions of government, procedures of governing,* and *stages of economic growth.*

STAGES OF ECONOMIC GROWTH

Despite protestations to the contrary, any social scientist who even utters the words *stages of economic growth* will very likely find himself associated with the ideas set forth in W. W. Rostow's best-selling book of the same title.[2] To be associated with the book is to be associated with the penetrating (and not altogether dispassionate) criticism that has been made of it.[3] At the beginning of this discussion, however, it is imperative that we make our position clear vis-à-vis Rostow and his critics. While we do use the concept of stages of economic growth (but with different meaning) and we borrow some of Rostow's terminology, we do *not* employ a Rostowian scheme in this study, because we differ fundamentally with him on crucial definitions. In order to acknowledge properly our intellectual debt to Rostow, while at the same time disassociating ourselves from many of his ideas, we shall present our concept of the stages of economic growth along with an analysis of Rostow's and of the criticism he has drawn.[4]

Rostow defines five stages of economic growth: (a) traditional, (b) preconditions for take-off, (c) take-off, (d) drive to maturity, and (e) high mass consumption.[5] The central concept involved in his whole scheme is that of *take-off.* The other categories have little meaning unless the usefulness of this concept has been demonstrated. We shall therefore begin the discussion of our adaptation of Rostow with a treatment of *take-off*.

Take-off

In somewhat graphic terms, Rostow identifies the take-off as that stage of economic growth where compound interest first "gets built into the society's structure." [6] More specifically, he seems to identify take-off by the presence in a society of three factors:

(1) A rise in the rate of productive investment from, say, 5 per cent or less to over 10 per cent of national income (or net national product, (NNP));

(2) The development of one or more substantial manufacturing sectors, with a high rate of growth;

(3) The existence or quick emergence of a political, social and institutional framework which exploits the impulses to expansion in the modern sector and the potential external economy effects of the take-off and gives to growth an on-going character. [7]

In another section of his work, he says of take-off:

This view of the take-off is, then, a return to a rather old-fashioned way of looking at economic development. The take-off is defined as an industrial revolution, tied directly to radical changes in methods of production, having their decisive consequence over a relatively short period of time. [8]

A major criticism of Rostow's concept of the take-off centers around the view of economic development: that there occurs at a certain point a sudden increase in growth rates which clearly differentiates the take-off from what went before. Cairncross asks:

Is there a genuine discontinuity rather than a simple acceleration of growth? If so, in what form does the discontinuity show itself? In what sense does the discontinuity herald a decisive break with the past? And is it conceivable that this discontinuity is of such character that it can be identified with a precise span of time, normally twenty years?

It may well be that Rostow could make a case for a kink in the rising curve of industrial output early in the process of industrialization. But the evidence which he provides in this book is not very convincing. . . . [9]

Part of the problem seems to be that the direct evidence on his historical cases necessary to demonstrate a case of "kink in the rising curve" is not available. This lack, however, is not a fatal weakness if good inferential support exists.

Far more significant are certain conceptual weaknesses in Rostow's definition which make it unacceptable. The striking feature of take-off from our point of view is that it represents the beginning of a period of economic development in which growth rates are markedly higher than before. An increase in investment rates "from, say, 5 per cent or less to over 10 per cent of national income (or net national product)" is not an adequate definition for our study, because we wish to hold open the empirical possibility of investment rates of over 10 per cent of NNP which do *not* result in rapid economic growth. Furthermore, we do not want to include by definition such characteristics as the "existence or quick emergence of a political, social and institutional framework which exploits the impulses to expansion. . . ." To include these elements by definition rules out the fascinating empirical question of *what kind* of "political, social and institutional framework" is necessary if such startling growth rates are to be achieved.

The present study calls for a definition of take-off that is exclusively and directly formulated in economic forms. Any other factors associated with take-off—institutional changes, technical developments, etc.—would be empirically related but not included by definition. For this kind of definition we rely heavily on the work of Simon Kuznets. He sees *modern* economic growth—as distinguished from previous historical cases of economic growth—as having certain distinctive characteristics: a "sustained and substantial rise in product per capita" and in almost all cases a "sustained and substantial rise in population." [10]

Following Kuznets, we date the beginning of modern economic growth—take-off—as that decade in which there developed a "sustained and substantial rise in product per capita." [11] "Substantial" is, of course, a slippery term. To have meaning for empirical research, some figure will have to be arbitrarily assigned to indicate what we mean by "substantial" growth. While an exact number is not important in this study, we might suggest a figure of not less than a 15 per cent increase in per capita product (in constant prices) per decade. [12]

Although Kuznets is one of Rostow's more penetrating critics, he presents data that suggest the usefulness of a definition of take-off similar to the one we are advancing. He has computed the increase in product per capita for nineteen countries from the earliest period for which reliable data are available up to the early 1950's. (The earliest figures he works with are for France in 1840.) He then uses the known rate of growth for each country to extrapolate back into the period for which no precise data exist. This extrapolation indicates that if those countries with known growth rates of more than 15 per cent per decade in product per capita had grown at similar rates in the earlier period, they would have had almost no income per capita in very recent history. For example, the French growth rate from 1841 to 1953 was 13.8 per cent per decade. Had France grown at that rate in the period 1745 to 1840, the French income per capita in 1745 would have been about $50.00 (in purchasing power of 1952-1954). All evidence points to the fact that it was much higher than that. Thus the growth rate from 1745 to 1840 must have been much lower than it was in succeeding decades.[13]

This is a convincing argument that there was a marked increase in growth per capita at a certain time—that there was a *kink* in the curve. Direct evidence taken from the English experience reveals a marked increase in per capita product beginning about 1785, when growth per decade rose to about three times the average for the rest of the century.[14]

It is also reasonable to assume that take-off marks a *watershed* in the structural configuration in a society. We doubt that rates of growth of 15 per cent per decade or more over several decades were possible before the advent of a modern industrial technology. Decreasing returns on capital investment may set in too quickly on the investment in preindustrial plant to make such growth rates possible. We further assume that the social-structural and cultural context necessary to maintain even a limited industralized economy is strikingly different from that which is most probable in a society with an economy at the traditional stage.

Besides objecting to Rostow's definition of take-off, some critics feel that there is an unwarranted determinism in his argument—he implies that once take-off has been achieved, an economy will continue along the road to maturity.[15] Whether this is a reasonable interpretation of Rostow or not, we explicitly exclude it from our scheme. When an economy has begun to grow at something like 15 per cent per decade in product per capita, we shall regard it as having entered the take-off stage. But this is no guarantee that economic growth on an advancing scale will continue. Indeed, such growth will not continue unless the "requisites" and "prerequisites" for the take-off stage are fulfilled. Hopefully, our proposed study will set forth hypotheses concerning the political prerequisites and requisites that must be fulfilled if the various stages of economic growth are to be completed. These hypotheses, if verified, would be a partial basis for predicting, for example, whether or not an economy in which capital is invested at a rate of 15 per cent of net national product will take off and continue to grow.

Traditional Society and the Preconditions for Take-off

The delineation of a specific stage of economic development which is labeled *preconditions for take-off* appears to be a doubtful procedure. If a particular stage has preconditions, is it not reasonable to conceive that the other stages also have preconditions? That is, in addition to preconditions for take-off, are there not preconditions for the *drive to maturity* and for the *maturity* stages?

We prefer to use the concept of *prerequisite* (instead of precondition), not to refer to any specific stage of development, but as a concept that is analytically related to all stages. We also accept the possibility that some prerequisites for a given stage of development may not be satisfied until *after* that stage has begun. The recognition of this possibility suggests a further conceptual refinement: A measure of precision will be added to the analysis if a distinction is made between *requisites* and *prerequisites*.[16] Prerequisites must be satisfied before an economy *can move into a given stage;* requisites must be satisfied before a given stage *can be completed.*

It must be understood that we do not look upon either the requisites or the prerequisites as a set of specific conditions that must be satisfied before any given stage can be begun or completed. On the contrary, we recognize that there may be various alternatives or substitutes. In other words, there is a range of factors, several combinations of which may satisfy the requisites or prerequisites. We do not, however, postulate unlimited substitutability. Two factors may be substitutes for each other, while neither is necessarily a substitute for a third factor. We would also suppose that the presence of one factor rather than its alternative may limit the substitution of other factors. Let us, for example, assume that $a, b, c,$ and d are prerequisites for a given stage of development, and that x is an alternative for $a,$ and that y is an alternative for $d.$ It is possible that if x is present rather than a, y cannot be substituted for d and still satisfy the set of prerequisites. The acceptable combinations would be: $a, b, c,$ and d or $x, b, c,$ and d or $a, b, c,$ and $y.$[17]

Although we recognize the possibility that alternative factors may satisfy requisites or prerequisites, we anticipate that the presence of a given factor rather than its alternative may be explained in terms of another set of conditions in the societies under consideration.

Since we are not using the concepts of requisites and prerequisites to apply to a specific pretake-off stage (as Rostow uses his comparable concept of precondition), we must develop a different concept of the traditional economy.[18] Rostow defines a traditional society directly: "limited production functions, based on pre-Newtonian science and technology, and on pre-Newtonian attitudes towards the physical world." [19] In our work, however, we define it residually: Any economy that has not yet reached take-off is a traditional economy. Using this definition, we conceive of different types of societies that have traditional economies. For our purposes, the most significant distinction is between those societies that have in a traditional stage met the prerequisites for take-off and those that have not.

The Modern Economy and the Drive to Modernity

Economies generally considered to be modern have several characteristics: The basic economic structure has been set and remains relatively stable, the economies of scale are relatively well exploited, few new industries (in terms of percentage of total) develop, a great demand is manifest for a wide variety of high quality products, and a high degree of interdependence exists among various industries and among various geographical areas. For our definition of a modern economy, however, attention has been concentrated solely upon the last characteristic—interindustry and interregional dependence.

This definition may be operationalized by constructing an input-output matrix on an industry-by-industry basis. The ideal modern economy would be one in which there are no empty cells. Table 2.1 schematizes the modern economy, while Table 2.2 represents the nonmodern economy.[20] (In these schematic presentations, letters have been substituted for figures.) The final statement of a definition of a modern economy (which is of no concern at this time) would be as a ratio of empty cells to the total number of cells. (Some decision would have to be made concerning the point at which a numerical entry in a cell is so insignificant that it should be treated as empty.) When this ratio is below some arbitrarily set low figure, the economy would be regarded as modern.

Although an enormous amount of empirical data has to be col-

TABLE 2.1. IDEAL MODERN ECONOMY   TABLE 2.2. NONMODERN ECONOMY

TABLE 2.1. IDEAL MODERN ECONOMY

0/0	1	2	3	4	5	6	7	8	9	10	11	12	13	14	15	D	T
1	x	x	x	x	x	x	x	x	x	x	x	x	x	x	x	d	t
2	x	x	x	x	x	x	x	x	x	x	x	x	x	x	x	d	t
3	x	x	x	x	x	x	x	x	x	x	x	x	x	x	x	d	t
4	x	x	x	x	x	x	x	x	x	x	x	x	x	x	x	d	t
5	x	x	x	x	x	x	x	x	x	x	x	x	x	x	x	d	t
6	x	x	x	x	x	x	x	x	x	x	x	x	x	x	x	d	t
7	x	x	x	x	x	x	x	x	x	x	x	x	x	x	x	d	t
8	x	x	x	x	x	x	x	x	x	x	x	x	x	x	x	d	t
9	x	x	x	x	x	x	x	x	x	x	x	x	x	x	x	d	t
10	x	x	x	x	x	x	x	x	x	x	x	x	x	x	x	d	t
11	x	x	x	x	x	x	x	x	x	x	x	x	x	x	x	d	t
12	x	x	x	x	x	x	x	x	x	x	x	x	x	x	x	d	t
13	x	x	x	x	x	x	x	x	x	x	x	x	x	x	x	d	t
14	x	x	x	x	x	x	x	x	x	x	x	x	x	x	x	d	t
15	x	x	x	x	x	x	x	x	x	x	x	x	x	x	x	d	t
H	h	h	h	h	h	h	h	h	h	h	h	h	h	h	h	h	t

TABLE 2.2. NONMODERN ECONOMY

0/0	1	2	3	4	5	6	7	8	9	10	11	12	13	14	15	D
1	x		x	x	x				x	x	x		x			d
2	x	x	x	x	x		x		x	x	x	x	x	x		d
3		x	x						x							d
4		x							x							d
5		x	x	x					x	x			x			d
6	x	x	x	x	x	x	x		x	x	x	x	x	x		d
7	x		x	x	x		x		x	x	x	x	x			d
8	x	x	x	x	x	x	x	x	x	x	x	x	x	x	x	d
9									x							d
10		x	x						x	x						d
11		x	x	x					x	x	x		x			d
12	x		x	x	x				x	x	x	x				d
13		x	x						x	x			x			d
14	x		x	x	x		x		x	x	x	x	x	x		d
15	x	x	x	x	x	x	x		x	x	x	x	x	x	x	d
H	h	h	h	h	h	h	h	h	h	h	h	h	h	h	h	h

TABLE 2.4.

TABLE 2.3. NONMODERN ECONOMY SHOWING HIERARCHICAL STRUCTURE

0/0	9	4	3	10	13	5	11	1	12	7	14	2	6	15	8	D	T
9	x															d	t
4	x	x														d	t
3	x	x	x													d	t
10	x	x	x	x												d	t
13	x	x	x	x	x											d	t
5	x	x	x	x	x	x										d	t
11	x	x	x	x	x	x	x									d	t
1	x	x	x	x	x	x	x	x								d	t
12	x	x	x	x	x	x	x	x	x							d	t
7	x	x	x	x	x	x	x	x	x	x						d	t
14	x	x	x	x	x	x	x	x	x	x	x					d	t
2	x	x	x	x	x	x	x	x	x	x	x	x				d	t
6	x	x	x	x	x	x	x	x	x	x	x	x	x			d	t
15	x	x	x	x	x	x	x	x	x	x	x	x	x	x		d	t
8	x	x	x	x	x	x	x	x	x	x	x	x	x	x	x	d	t
H	h	h	h	h	h	h	h	h	h	h	h	h	h	h	h	d	t

NONMODERN ECONOMY SHOWING BLOCK TRIANGULAR STRUCTURE

0/0	1	2	3	4	5	6	7	8	9	10	11	12	13	14	15	D
1	x	x	x	x												d
2	x	x	x	x												d
3	x	x	x	x												d
4	x	x	x	x	x	x	x	x								d
5	x	x	x	x	x	x	x	x								d
6	x	x	x	x	x	x	x	x								d
7	x	x	x	x	x	x	x	x								d
8		x	x	x	x	x	x	x	x	x						d
9		x	x	x	x	x	x	x	x	x						d
10			x	x	x	x	x	x	x	x	x					d
11			x	x	x	x	x	x	x	x	x					d
12			x	x	x	x	x	x	x	x	x					d
13								x	x	x	x	x	x	x	x	d
14								x	x	x	x	x	x	x	x	d
15								x	x	x	x	x	x	x	x	d
H	h	h	h	h	h	h	h	h	h	h	h	h	h	h	h	h

(See note on facing page.*)

lected and analyzed before this definition can be applied, the definition itself is clear and precise. It has an additional advantage. The input-output matrix reveals not only the structure that is a useful indicator of a modern economy, but it may also indicate certain other specific structures associated with nonmodern economies. In other words, although the pattern of empty and full cells may appear to be random, a reordering of the industries may reveal an important pattern. For example, Table 2.3 contains precisely the same data that are found in Table 2.2. The industries, however, have been reordered, and there is revealed a specific structure in which certain industries have a hierarchical relationship one to another. An industry in any given row receives inputs only from all those "below" it and feeds its output only into all those above it. For example, industry 9 in the far left column requires inputs from all other industries but delivers its output only to final demand. In contrast, industry 8 in the far right-hand column delivers its outputs to all other industries as well as to final demand, but receives its inputs only from households.[21]

Table 2.4 shows another kind of nonmodern structure, a "block triangular" structure. In this type of economy, the various "blocks" of industries are highly interdependent, but one "block" is in a specific hierarchical relationship to another.[22]

How, then, do we differ from Rostow in our concept of a modern economy? Rostow uses the term *mature* rather than *modern* and defines maturity as the "period when a society has effectively applied

---

*TABLES 2.1-2.4

The internal structures of various model economies are revealed by schemetized input-output tables. x's signify inputs from an industry in a given horizontal row to industries in vertical columns intersected by the row; d's signify the input from each industry to *final demand* (D); t's signify the total output (T) of each industry; h's signify the inputs of prime factors from *household services* (H). Table 2.1 shows a completely *interdependent* economy and thus is completely *modern* by our definition. Table 2.2 shows a random pattern of partial interdependence and would not be modern by our definition. Table 2.3 contains identically the same data as Table 2.2 but they have been rearranged (note the sequence of numbers denoting industries in both rows and columns). This *triangulation* of the table reveals a hierarchical relationship between the various industries (see text above). Table 2.4 shows a *block triangular* model in which there is a high degree of interdependence among certain groups of industries, and these blocks have a hierarchical relationship. (These tables have been adapted from Wassily Leontief, "The Structure of Development," *Scientific American*, Vol. 209, No. 3, September 1963, p. 149.)

the range of (then) modern technology to the bulk of its resources." [23] We do not wish to define a type of social system in terms
of its nonhuman environment, preferring, for reasons extraneous
here, to leave the environment in which a certain type of social system may operate open to empirical investigation. Rostow also tends
to use the concept of maturity to refer more to a "point" marking the
end of the drive to maturity stage rather than to a stage itself. In his
framework the stage that follows drive to maturity seems to be the
age of high mass consumption. We conceive of a modern stage in
which high mass consumption may, but not necessarily will, develop.[24]

Some attention must also be paid to what lies beyond modernity,
as well as to what lies between take-off and modernity. Rostow suggests but does not discuss in detail a stage beyond that of high mass
consumption. We also conceive of a postmodern stage, but since it
has not as yet become relevant to our research interests, we have not
attempted to define it with rigor.

The definition of the stage between take-off and modernity is more
crucial to our present interests. On this point there is much of Rostow that we should like to adopt in principle. According to his analysis, the beginning of take-off is associated with the application of the
existing modern technology to one or more of the leading sectors of industry. When take-off is regarded as a stage (in some places Rostow
seems to treat it as a point), the conclusion of the stage is taken to be
the time when the existing modern technology has been fully applied
in the leading sector(s). The drive to maturity begins when that modern technology is spread from the leading sectors to other industries,
and it is concluded when the modern technology is applied to all
significant industries.

Although we should like to adopt this conceptualization, two objections immediately come to mind. First, the question of whether or
not economic modernization occurs by an initial application of modern technology to a leading sector, and, following the modernization
of that sector(s), by spreading technology to other sectors, is an
empirical matter. Rostow's evidence that this is the course of modernization is not conclusive. If modernization does not occur in this
pattern with a high frequency, one cannot use Rostow's definition to
distinguish between take-off and drive to maturity.[25] The second objection to Rostow's conceptualization stems in part from our reluc-

tance to define a type of social system in terms of its nonhuman environment.

Although preliminary investigation indicates that there are different functional and procedural requisites and prerequisites for a take-off stage and a drive to the modernity stage (as the latter is intuitively identified), we have not yet developed an acceptable alternative to Rostow's definition. This remains a conceptual problem to which we must devote attention sometime in the future, when we expand our research to include post-take-off stages of development.

Summary of Definitions of Stages of Economic Growth

For heuristic reasons, we postulate five stages of economic development: (1) traditional economy, (2) take-off, (3) drive to modernity, (4) modernity, and (5) postmodernity. The traditional economy is defined residually as any economy that has not reached the beginning of take-off. Take-off is defined as beginning in the decade in which product per capita begins to increase at a *substantial* rate (15 per cent per decade is the figure suggested). The end of the take-off stage and the drive to modernity stage have not yet been defined. The mature economy is defined as one in which there is a high degree of interindustry integration, as measured by an input-output matrix.

These definitions differ from those of Rostow primarily in two ways. First, our definitions apply strictly to the economy, not to an entire society. Any noneconomic characteristics of the society will be associated with the various stages as empirical research demonstrates a relationship; they will not be included as characteristic of a given stage by definition. Second, we do not conceive of a specific "preconditions for take-off" stage. Rather, we use the concepts of prerequisite and requisite to apply to all stages of economic growth. The modernity stage, for example, has preconditions that are as significant as those of take-off.

It should be emphasized again that we do not view these stages as steps in an inevitable developmental sequence. The conceptual scheme keeps open the possibility of a "reverse movement." For example, an economy in a modern stage might be greatly disrupted by war and much of the physical plant destroyed. The postwar rebuilding period may well have the characteristics of drive to modernity rather than modernity, and we would not hesitate to classify it as such.

Some scholars—although few political scientists are among them—

object to any kind of "stage approach" to the study of development. Typically, the major objection is the common-sense observation that history unfolds continuously, not in discrete stages. We, of course, do not challenge this perceptive observation. When there is little adequate theory for the explanation and prediction of developmental phenomena, however, it may be useful to conceive of development in terms of stages. The *stage* framework is a heuristic device. When the various stages have been defined, their characteristics are investigated empirically. If this research indicates that characteristics commonly associated with one stage are not associated with others, a useful step has been taken in the direction of theory development. We agree with Kuznets: "Stages . . . are a classificatory device, governed by the working assumption that the generality of observation and invariance of analytical relations secured thereby are maximized."[26]

Having examined one important element in our conceptual framework—the stages of economic growth—we must now turn to the two other major concepts within the scheme, and we shall handle in turn the *functions of government* and the *procedures of governing*.

THE FUNCTIONS OF GOVERNMENT

The concept *function* has been used in the social sciences in many different ways. Political scientists often use the term to refer to the classical powers of government. In this sense, the "functions" of government are to legislate, to execute, and to adjudicate. As we have already seen, Almond's use of the term includes not only these "functions" but also certain extragovernmental "functions" of the political system. Almond, however, employs the term to refer to what more appropriately might be called *processes* or *procedures* of governing. "How are interests articulated?" "How are interests aggregated?"— these are the questions that Almond typically asks. *How* what is done is done is a question that involves procedure. *What* is done is a question that is related to function.

The concept *function,* as used in this study, draws more heavily upon sociology than upon political science.[27] Function is defined as the *system relevant* effects of a structure passing through time. Structure is defined as a patterned interrelationship of roles.[28] A few illustrations will indicate why it is necessary to include the phrase "system relevant" in the definition. One effect of the heart is the sound of the heart-beat. The heart sound, however, is not a function of the heart, for it is not relevant to the physiological system of which the heart is a part. Another example is more directly pertinent to this study. One effect of a government[29] may be the execution of a man accused and found guilty of homicide. The imposition of capital punishment, however, is not a function of government but an *activity* of government. An activity is what a structure *does*. A function is what a structure *does* that is relevant to the system of which it is a part.[30] An activity is not distinguishable from a function on the basis of the concrete behavior involved, but only in relationship to a conceptual framework and the chain of referents which that framework provides. If it is postulated, for example, that the maintenance of the basic values of a society (pattern maintenance) is a functional requisite of the social system at the societal level, and if the postulated theory of social control recognizes capital punishment for the violation of basic norms as one technique that can help to maintain conformity to values, the the activity of government in executing a man for committing homicide may be regarded as a contribution of government to the satisfaction of the pattern-maintenance function. The activity is the execution of a man; the function is pattern maintenance.

Activities of government may be looked upon as raw data. Hence, one of the major tasks of analysis is to link activities with specific functions. In order to do this, it is necessary, first, to specify the system under consideration, and, second, to postulate a set of functional requisites for that system. It is essential to specify the system under consideration because an activity that may contribute to the satisfaction of a functional requisite at one system level may be not functional at another system level.[31] It is necessary to postulate a set of functional requisites because, in our formulation, system relevance can be established most efficaciously in terms of system *requiredness*.[32]

The system we are concerned with is the social system at the societal level.[33] For our functional requisites we have adapted the conceptualization developed by Parsons. He and his associates have postulated that any social system has four basic functional requisites: (1) adaptation, (2) goal attainment, (3) pattern maintenance and tension management, and (4) integration.[34]

ADAPTATION. Any social system at the societal level exists in an environment that has a nonhuman, or material, component. The character of this material environment is determined by the land surface of the area being occupied, the flora and fauna, and the tools and other means of production. If it is to survive, any social system at the societal level must be able to adapt itself to this nonhuman aspect of the environment; adaptation thus becomes an important functional requisite of the system. Interaction with the material component of environment must lead to the accumulation of disposable resources which can be used to realize the goals of the system as a whole, as well as the goals of individuals and subsystems.[35]

The processes that are relevant to the satisfaction of the adaptive functional requisite are those typically associated with economics—the processes of production, of resource allocation, and of resource management.[36]

GOAL ATTAINMENT. In every society there are certain goals that are considered to be goals of the society as a whole, as distinguished from those of individuals within the society. These goals are not terminal states of existence which can in any sense be finally achieved. They consist, rather, of sets of desired relationships with the environment, and, since the environment is continually changing (at least, potentially), goal attainment involves a cluster of on-going activities. The environment within which goal attainment takes place is exceedingly complex. It includes an aspect of both the nonhuman and cultural environments, as well as an environment of relationships with other societies with which there is contact.

One of the most important goals of the society is the preservation of the society itself. Hence, activities relating to the defense of the realm are involved in goal attainment. In this case, the relevant component of environment consists of other societies. The achievement of societal goals also involves the preservation of certain relationships with important deities. In this respect, many activities that can be classified as religious—such as national religious rituals—contribute to the satisfaction of the goal-attainment requisite. The relevant aspect of environment in this field is the cultural system.

Of the various processes which are involved in the satisfaction of the goal-attainment requisite, the most significant for this study is that of mobilizing societal resources for a societal effort. This process involves the raising of public revenue and the creation of credit, which includes the development of an adequate monetary system.

PATTERN MAINTENANCE. One of the unique features of the conceptualization which we present is the rigid distinction drawn between the social system and the cultural (belief-value) system.[37] There are no values in the social system; values are considered to be environmental to it. In other words, the cultural system is on one of the boundaries of the social system. This cultural system (belief-value system) specifies the goals for the social system as a whole and for the roles within it, as well as the acceptable means for attaining these goals. One of the functional requisites of the social system is to maintain conformity with the belief-value system. Hence, three major processes are involved in the pattern-maintenanace functional requisite.[38] First, provision must be made for passing the primary values on from one generation to the next, or an *enculturation* process.[39] Second, the *social-control* process is concerned with the application of punishment for the violation of the prescriptions of the value system. Third, there is a process to prevent the development of situations—or to control situations that have already developed—that are likely to encourage large number of actors to violate basic norms. Prolonged unemployment and galloping inflation in a modern industrial society are examples of these kinds of situations. Their control involves what we call a *tension-management* process.[40]

INTEGRATION. In any social system at the societal level, there is differentiation of roles.[41] If interdependent roles are differentiated, they must be integrated. Hence, one of the functional requisites of the social system is to provide for the integration of the interdependent units (roles and structures) in the social system.

The activities of the basic units that are necessary for the achievement of an acceptable degree of integration are partially specified by the norms of the society. Hence, the integration problem is partially *solved* by maintaining conformity to these norms. Thus the integration functional requisite involves aspects of the social-control process.[42] But all of the behavior that is required if basic units are to be sufficiently integrated cannot be achieved simply by manipulating the mechanisms of social control successfully. In every social system there is some behavior that is not prohibited by norms but is nevertheless malintegrative. Furthermore, there is some behavior that is integrative even though it is in violation of norms.

If the activities of the occupants of various interdependent roles are to be properly integrated, information concerning such matters as reciprocal role expectations and demands must be communicated to the individuals who occupy the roles. Thus a communication process is involved in the satisfaction of the integration requisite. Since the interests of the various role occupants, however, are likely to be divergent to some degree, a coercive process (but one that, by definition, does not involve the use of legitimate violence) is also involved.

The manner in which these various processes operate to meet the integration functional requisite may be illustrated by the operation of the market (a powerful integrating mechanism) in a free economy. Role relationships within the market are governed in part by a set of norms which specify such matters as enforceable and nonenforceable contracts and define acceptable and fraudulent business practices. These norms, which place limits on the alternative choices available to participants, are not generated by the market, but are part of the setting in which it operates. The behavior that conforms to the norms is typically more integrative than that which is not. One cannot, however, account for the integrating effects of the market simply in terms of the normative system which governs it. The market also generates vast amounts of information which enable the participants to fit their plans into the plans of others, and which therefore contribute to the integration of the system.[43]

There is, moreover, an element of coercion involved in market relationships. The interests of the various participants are to some extent disparate, and not all of those who engage in the market have equal power. Under these circumstances, some participants are able to coerce others into acting in ways that may be integrative for the system as a whole.

Methodological Choices

Because some of the methodological choices we have made differ greatly from what is typical in political science and because they differ considerably from the Parsonian scheme from which so much has been borrowed, several aspects of our functional framework should be highlighted.

1. We draw a rigid analytical distinction between a social system and a cultural system, and we differentiate both from a collectivity. Briefly, a collectivity is a plurality of interacting actors. A society is a particular kind of collectivity. From any collectivity may be abstracted a system consisting of a patterned relationship of interdependent roles—a social system—and another consisting of a patterned interrelationship of beliefs and values—a cultural system. In order to keep these two systems logically independent so that they may be interrelated by a set of empirically testable laws, we define a role

solely in terms of behavior. Role expectations (beliefs and/or values) are not included in this definition of a role.[44]

2. Since we define cultural system and social system in a way that makes them logically independent, we view the environment of the

Figure 2.1. *Schematic View of the Social System in Its Environment.* Some of the major aspects of our view of the social system are presented in this paradigm. Note (1) the position of the integrative function requisite in the center indicating that it is heavily concerned with activities that relate the other requisites to each other; (2) the complex environment. Compare with Parson's paradigm in Parsons and Semelser, *Economy and Society,* p. 19.

social system in a unique fashion. The paradigm in Fig. 2.1 indicates this position.

As can be seen, three different aspects of the environment of the social system bear different relationships to the four functional requisites. The cultural system is part of the environment that bears heavily upon the pattern-maintenance and goal-attainment areas, and sec-

ondarily upon the integration area. The material (or nonhuman) component of environment relates to adaptive and goal-attainment requisites. Other collectivities—in the case of the social system at the societal level, these would be other societies—form part of the environment for the goal-attainment functional requisite.

3. This analysis is deliberately and explicitly a macro-analysis. We
are concerned with the social system at the societal level. We are not
concerned with the small group interactions that might be important
to economic growth. It is not that we consider the small group interactions to be unimportant. Rather, we *assume* that, when dealing with
change over long periods of time, one may treat the activities of
small groups in different societies as constants. These groups may
well mediate the impact of some of the macro-forces we are dealing
with, but we are assuming for the moment that any variation in the
effect that small groups have on macro-structures and functions among
societies can be accounted for by the macro-structure of the social
system, or by the environment, or by both.[45]

4. We are employing the functional requisite framework in a manner different from that intended by Parsons. Our general concern is
with the range of concrete structures that can contribute to the satisfaction of the four functional requisites under specific conditions, and
with the effect of different structuring upon social change. More particularly, of course, we shall focus our attention upon the differing
contributions that are made by a specific concrete structure, namely,
government. We hypothesize, generally, that government must make
a contribution to the satisfaction of certain functional requisites and
must not make a contribution to others if the economy is to develop.
Furthermore, we hypothesize that the contribution which government
must and must not make differs from one stage of economic growth
to another.[46]

5. When we use the term *functions of government,* this is a short-
hand way of referring to an activity (or set of activities) of government that contributes to the satisfaction of a given functional requisite of the social system at the societal level.

PROCEDURES OF GOVERNING

Having defined a function of government as a set of governmental
activities contributing to the satisfaction of a functional requisite of
the social system at the societal level, we use the concept *procedures
of governing* to refer generally to the manner in which these functions

are performed. "What is done" is the functional question. "How what is done is done" is the procedural problem. A wide range of problems, however, must be treated under the general rubric of procedures of governing. The first to be considered—a familiar one in the literature of political science—deals with the characteristics of the various processes involved in governing.[47]

Characteristics of the Processes of Government

It is useful in this study to distinguish analytically between a number of different processes of government. A distinction will be made between a *policy-making* process and a *policy-enforcing* process. A second distinction will be drawn between *governmental* processes and *extragovernmental* processes.[48] Characteristics of the government aspect of policy making and policy enforcing will be analyzed in terms of the authority structure of decision making and in terms of the communication networks and their operation.

AUTHORITY STRUCTURES. In this study, the crucial aspect of authority structures accounting for differences in characteristics of the policy-making process is the degree of *resolution* in the structure. A highly resolved authority structure is one in which there is a clear rank-order of policy-making roles and structures. This greatly reduces the probability that any conflicting policies will be developed simultaneously. A highly resolved authority structure is also characterized by the fact that few roles or substructures are able to veto or otherwise nullify a policy that has been decided by others.

In the empirical analysis presented in the following chapters, the resolution of the authority structure is the only aspect of the authority structure of policy making considered, since it was the only one that appeared to be related to any of the variations between the two sets of cases which are analyzed. In treating the procedures of governing with regard to other problems, however, one would probably want to analyze the basis of legitimacy. The procedures would very likely be different, for example, depending upon whether the basis of legitimacy is traditional, rational-legal, or charismatic.[49]

Other aspects of the authority structure in relationship to policy enforcement, however, are significant for this study. First of all, we are interested in the *reliability* of the structure. If authority is defined as the "ability to issue orders, instructions, and commands with the probability that they will be obeyed," [50] the reliability of the authority structure is the magnitude of that probability. The higher the probability that an order will be obeyed, the greater the reliability of the structure.

Secondly, we are concerned with the *clarification* of the authority structure. When there is a single hierarchy of enforcement operating through a single chain of command, the authority structure is highly clarified. When a number of hierarchies are involved in the enforcement of a given policy, with no clear order of precedence and dominance being established, the effectiveness of each hierarchy is reduced and the structure is *unclarified*.

Whereas the reliability and clarification aspects of the authority structure of the enforcement process deal solely with relationships within the official agencies themselves, the third aspect we are concerned with—*techniques of securing compliance*—involves relationships between the official enforcers of policy and those to whom the policy is directly applied. We are interested in the variety of techniques that may be employed, and in the degree to which raw coercion and terror can be employed, as contrasted with more subtle means of persuasion.[51]

INFORMATION NETWORKS. In the assessment of differences in decision-making procedures in both policy making and policy enforcing, the second important factor is that of information networks. As Karl Deutsch has so cogently demonstrated, government may fruitfully be regarded as a self-steering mechanism.[52] The concepts and analytical tools of cybernetics can then provide considerable insight into the procedures of governing.[53] In many ways, the most useful of these concepts is that of a *feedback* system—"a communications network that produces action in response to an input of information, and *includes the results of its own action in the new information by which it modifies its subsequent behavior.*"[54] The characteristics of a feedback system that are of procedural concern are *lag* and *gain*. Lag is the amount of time that elapses between the beginning of movement toward an objective (or from the beginning of any deliberate change in the course toward an objective), and the moment when corrective action is taken in response to information that has been received concerning the appropriateness of the course being pursued.[55] Gain is the magnitude of the corrective measures that are taken in the interval between any two feedback messages.[56] There are, for example, great procedural differences between an enforcement process in which considerable time passes between a given attempt to enforce a policy and the receipt of information about the effectiveness of such action (long lag), and an enforcement process in which such information is available immediately after each attempt (short lag).[57] Almost as significant are differences between a process in which there is an enormous increase in coercive measures as a response to the action of a few people who do not react properly to a policy (large gain), as contrasted with a process in which response to a large number of people not complying to a policy is very mild (small gain).[58]

A second feature of information networks which is of interest is the *memory*.[59] With regard to memory, a number of procedural questions may be asked. How is information coded and classified for storage (storage both of the initial information and of the classification code)? How is information retrieved? What is the time interval between a request for stored information and its receipt? Unfortunately, almost no direct information is available on these aspects of decision-making procedures in any of the four societies with which we are concerned. The case has had to be built from circumstantial evidence, and will be discussed in some detail in Chapter 7, where additional conceptual clarification will be presented.

A third aspect of importance in the information networks is *efficiency*. The more efficient the system, the smaller the information loss. We shall be interested in comparing procedures of governing on the basis of the efficiency of the information transfer.[60]

Finally, we are concerned with the *reliability* of communication channels—the probability that a message will arrive at its proper destination. In detailed empirical studies of the seventeenth and eighteenth centuries, concern with reliability may involve studies of highwaymen and warlords who were able to cut off the flow of messages from a province to the central government. If we assume, however, that these kinds of factors are operating with about equal significance in all cases, and, in any event, are irrelevant to communications whose origin and destination are limited to the central government itself, attention can be concentrated upon the *redundancy* of the system—the number of different channels a message may take in order to reach its destination. As the redundancy increases, the reliability increases.[61]

EXTRAGOVERNMENTAL PROCESSES. The procedures of governing can hardly be understood unless attention is paid to a number of extragovernmental processes, that is, those processes that influence decision making but do not involve governmental structures. Almond's treatment of input functions[62] appears to be a useful way of approaching the study of these extragovernmental processes. In our study of procedures, for example, we are interested in the types of structures that may be involved in interest articulation (institutional, nonassociational, anomic, and associational), and the style in which interests are articulated (manifest-latent, specific-diffuse, general-particular, instrumental-affective). Likewise, characteristics of parties and party systems and the style of interest aggregation are procedural matters of consequence. No attempt will be made to discuss these extragovernmental procedures in this monograph, because no discrimination can be made between the two sets of cases on the basis of these considerations. In these cases, they appear to have no predictive significance.[63]

Other Procedural Considerations

There is a general category of factors which we label as *procedural* because they deal with the *way* in which something is done rather than referring to what is done. This category, however, is very different from the decision-making procedures treated earlier. Although we have found it difficult to define these other procedural considerations sharply, they are easy to illustrate. For example, all of the governments treated in this study engaged in taxation, but the way in which taxes were applied was different. The governments levied different kinds of taxes, and the assessments fell differentially upon different segments of the population. These governments also had regulations controlling social mobility (and thus were involved in the integration function), but the type of mobility that was allowed or forbidden differed in the two sets of cases. We are tentatively treating these differences as procedural, but unfortunately we are able to offer very little conceptual analysis at this time.

SUMMARY

The conceptual framework presented in this chapter embraces three categories, in terms of which the analysis is undertaken—*stages of economic growth, functions of government,* and *procedures of governing.*

The framework establishes five stages of economic growth: traditional, take-off, drive to modernity, modern, and postmodern. Three of these stages—the traditional, the take-off, and the modern—will be used in the exploratory case studies which follow. It must be emphasized that these stages have been defined solely by economic criteria. Each stage is conceived as having prerequisites and requisites—

prerequisites must be satisfied before a stage can be begun, while requisites must be satisfied before a stage can be completed.

In this conceptual framework, we define a function of government as the contribution that government makes to the satisfaction of a functional requisite of the social system at the societal level. A social system has been defined entirely in terms of roles and structures, without a belief-value (cultural) component. Four functional requisites of the social system at the societal level have been postulated: (1) adaptation, which is concerned with the relationship of the social system to the nonhuman part of environment; (2) goal attainment, which is concerned with the achievement of system goals in relationship to the material environment, the cultural environment, and other societies; (3) pattern maintenance, which is concerned with maintaining conformity to the belief-value (cultural) system; and (4) integration, which is concerned with achieving necessary coordination among differentiated but interdependent roles.

The third major category of analysis—the procedures of governing—deals with the manner in which functions are performed. It focuses attention upon the procedural characteristics of government activities, the procedural characteristics of politically relevant, extragovernmental activities, and the different substantive policies which governments may pursue in making a contribution to the satisfaction of a functional requisite.

It is the main purpose of this monograph to apply this framework of analysis to certain societies which have had different economic growth experiences. In analyzing these societies, we shall attempt to discover whether they manifest differences in functions of government and in procedures of governing, and whether the differences suggest hypotheses of explanatory and predictive consequence.

NOTES

1. See, for example, Leonard Binder, *Iran: Political Development in a Changing Society,* pp. 1-58; Frederick W. Frey, "Political Development, Power, and Communications in Turkey," in Lucian W. Pye (ed.), *Communications and Political Development,* pp. 298-326; and Joseph LaPalombara, "Bureaucracy and Political Development: Notes, Queries, and Dilemmas," in Joseph LaPalombara (ed.), *Bureaucracy and Political Development,* pp. 34-61; and Fred W. Riggs, "The Theory of Developing Polities," *World Politics,* Vol. 16, No. 1, October 1963, pp. 147-171.

2. Walt W. Rostow, *The Stages of Economic Growth.*

3. See, for example, reviews by A. K. Cairncross in *The Economic History Review,* Vol. 13, No. 3, April 1961, pp. 450-458; H. J. Habakkuk in *The Economic Journal,* Vol. 71, No. 283, September 1961, pp. 601-604; Simon

Kuznets, "Notes on the Take-off," in Theodore Morgan, George W. Betz, and N. K. Choudhry, *Readings in Economic Development*, pp. 201-213.

4. There will be some who object to any *stage* approach. This general problem is treated below, pp. 49-50.

5. Rostow, *The Stages of Economic Growth*, pp. 4-16.

6. *Ibid.*, p. 36.

7. *Ibid.*, p. 39. It should be noted that Rostow introduces these three points with the phrase "take-off is defined as requiring. . . ."

8. *Ibid.*, p. 57.

9. Cairncross, *The Economic History Review*, Vol. 13, No. 3, April 1961, p. 454.

10. Simon Kuznets, *Six Lectures on Economic Growth*, p. 14.

11. For statistical tables indicating per capita growth in about twenty countries, see *ibid.*, pp. 20-22, 27.

12. Actually, our definition is far more complex than this, but in this exploratory study we do not wish to spend several pages discussing and defending it. The important refinement includes the introduction of a population growth factor which allows per capita growth rates at less than 15 per cent per capita per decade if population increases are very great. We also take the 15 per cent figure to be a three-decades average, in which case take-off may begin before the 15 per cent rate has actually been achieved.

13. Kuznets, *Six Lectures on Economic Growth*, pp. 25-29.

14. Phyllis Deane and W. A. Cole, *British Economic Growth, 1688-1959*, pp. 80-81.

15. See, for example, Cairncross's review in *The Economic History Review*, Vol. 13, No. 3, April 1961.

16. For an interesting treatment of the concepts of prerequisites for economic growth, see Alexander Gerschenkron, *Economic Backwardness in Historical Perspective: A Book of Essays*, pp. 31-51. Our distinction between requisite and prerequisite draws heavily upon Marion J. Levy, Jr., *The Structure of Society*, pp. 43-45, 71-76.

17. Gerschenkron also explicitly discusses the idea of the substitutability of requisites in *Economic Backwardness in Historical Perspective*, pp. 31-51.

18. Note that here, as elsewhere, we refer to stages in the growth of the economy, not the society.

19. Rostow, *The Stages of Economic Growth*, p. 4.

20. Wassily Leontief, "The Structure of Development," *Scientific American*, Vol. 209, No. 3, September 1963, p. 149.

21. *Ibid.*, pp. 150-151.

22. It is likely that certain kinds of structuring of the economy will be associated with each stage of economic growth. We shall not, however, attempt to define any stage other than the modern in structural terms. The relationship between other stages and the structuring of the economy will be left open for empirical investigation and theorizing.

23. Rostow, *The Stages of Economic Growth*, p. 59.

24. *Ibid.*, pp. 73-92. Rostow is somewhat unclear about how he conceives of maturity and high mass consumption. We have used the term *modern* rather than *mature* in order to escape some of the stagnationist connotations of the latter. However, we probably take some parts of Alvin Hansen's theories more seriously than do many economists. In brief, we hypothesize that the modern economy, more than the immediately preceding stage, places tighter constraints upon the tolerable range of variation in the contribution by government to the satisfaction of the adaptive, goal-attainment, and integrative functional requi-

sites. When the functions of government are outside these constraints, *stagnation* is a possible consequence. See below, pp. 372-375.

25. It is interesting to compare Rostow's ideas on this point with Hirschman's notions of unbalanced growth. See Albert O. Hirschman, *The Strategy of Economic Development*, pp. 62-69, 205-208.

26. Kuznets, "Notes on the Take-off," in Morgan *et al., Readings in Economic Development*, p. 202. See also Bert F. Hoselitz, "Theories of Stages of Economic Growth," in Bert F. Hoselitz *et al., Theories of Economic Growth*, pp. 193-238. Even in most precise sciences, it is often difficult to deal with continuous change, and it is assumed for purposes of analysis that change takes place in discrete steps. (See W. Ross Ashby, *An Introduction to Cybernetics*, p. 9.)

27. We draw most heavily upon Levy, *The Structure of Society*; Robert K. Merton, *Social Theory and Social Structure*, pp. 19-84; and Talcott Parsons, *The Social System*. For a penetrating criticism of functionalism, see Carl G. Hempel, "The Logic of Functional Analysis," in Llewellyn Gross (ed.), *Symposium on Sociological Theory*, pp. 271-307.

28. This definition is adapted from Levy, *The Structure of Society*, pp. 57-58.

29. We define government as a concrete structure which has access to legitimate violence for enforcing its decisions upon the occupants of roles that lie outside of the structure itself.

30. Hempel objects to using function synonymously with effect. (See "The Logic of Functional Analysis," p. 279.) Note that we are not using the terms synonymously but treat function as a subclass of effects.

31. See Merton, *Social Theory and Social Structure*, p. 51, on nonfunctional consequences.

32. Much of this conceptual framework dealing with the functions of government is adapted from a forthcoming work by Robert T. Holt which treats the functions of government in primitive societies. The reasons for many of the conceptual decisions we are making are discussed at length in that work.

33. We define a social system as a patterned relationship of interdependent roles; a society is a plurality of interacting individuals with other special characteristics. Thus, unlike most writers, we do not consider a society to be a social system. A social system is one of several systems that may be abstracted from a society (of from any other collectivity). We must, therefore, use the somewhat awkward phrase "social system at the societal level."

34. Talcott Parsons and Neil J. Smelser, *Economy and Society*. It must be emphasized that we are adapting Parsons' and Smelser's scheme. The major modifications which have been made will be discussed in some detail below. One obvious difference is that we use the term *requisite* rather than *imperative*. For a good discussion of the four functional requisites, see Chandler Morse, "The Functional Imperatives," in Max Black (ed.), *The Social Theories of Talcott Parsons*, pp. 100-153. It should be pointed out that Hoselitz has employed this Parsonian framework in the analysis of development problems. (See "Levels of Economic Performance and Bureaucratic Structures," in Joseph LaPalombara [ed.], *Bureaucracy and Political Development*, pp. 168-198.)

35. Karl Polanyi, Conrad Arensberg, and Harry W. Pearson (eds.), *Trade and Market in the Early Empires*, pp. 239-321.

36. Parsons and Smelser label the adaptive requisite, viewed as a system in its own right, as the *economy*, and this term suggests many of the processes that are involved. However, not every process that is normally regarded as economic is involved in the adaptive function. See below, pp. 100-126, 293-312.

37. This is one of our major modifications of Parsons and Smelser. For further discussion, see below, pp. 54-56.

38. The idea of processes that are related to the various functions is another departure from Parsons and Smelser. Logically, we conceive of processes as the intervening variables in a causal sequence in which structure is the independent variable and function the dependent variable. For further discussion, see Holt's forthcoming work on primitive societies, Chapter 3.

39. Note that enculturation is not used synonymously with socialization.

40. The treatment of tension management as a process is, of course, another basic departure from Parsons and Smelser.

41. In more formal terminology, we are postulating that role differentiation is an *analytical structural requisite* of any social system. See Levy, *The Structure of Society*, pp. 299-348.

42. The distinction we draw between the social-control process that relates to pattern maintenance and the social-control process that relates to integration is taken from Durkheim, who differentiates between *repressive* sanctions and *restitutive* sanctions. Within our framework, the former relate to pattern maintenance and the latter to integration. See Émile Durkheim, *The Division of Labor in Society*, pp. 68-69, and below, pp. 171-172, 194.

43. See F. A. Hayek, "The Use of Knowledge in Society," *The American Economic Review*, Vol. 35, No. 4, September 1945, pp. 519-530.

44. This type of formulation is more different from a Parsonian framework than is apparent on the surface. Parsons also attempts to analyze social action partially in terms of the analysis of a social system and a cultural system. He also conceives of the role as the basic unit in the social system. "For most purposes *the conceptual unit of the social system is the role*" (Talcott Parsons and Edward A. Shils [eds.], *Toward a General Theory of Action*, p. 190). Beliefs and values are the basic units in the cultural system. (See A. L. Kroeber and Talcott Parsons, "The Concepts of Culture and of Social System," *American Sociological Review*, Vol. 23, No. 5, October 1958, p. 583.) The big difference comes in the definition of role. To Parsons the primary ingredient of a role is the *role expectation*. (See *Toward a General Theory of Action*, p. 190.) Role expectations are patterns of beliefs and values. Thus the *primary ingredient* of the "conceptual unit of the social system" is defined in terms of the basic unit of the cultural system. Many of the propositions that link the social system and the cultural system will be tautologies, true by definition rather than as empirically testable laws or hypotheses.

Parsons also tends to treat culture as an aspect of the social system rather than as an analytically distinguishable subsystem on the same level of generality. For example, sentences like "There is crucially important interdependence between cultural patterns and the other elements of the social system . . ." (Talcott Parsons, *The Social System*, p. 15), and "There can be no possible doubt of the importance of 'empirical lore' as part of the cultural tradition of every social system" (*ibid.*, p. 332), indicate that culture is a subsystem of the social system. As astute an observer as Karl Deutsch interprets Parsons as maintaining that "the integrative function is carried on to the largest extent by the subsystems of *culture*. . . ." (*The Nerves of Government*, p. 117).

In our formulation, a society is not a type of social system, nor is culture a *part of* the social system.

45. In recent years political science and sociology may have suffered from an absence of concern with a macro-analysis of social systems. See Edward A. Shils, "The Macrosociological Problem," in Donald P. Ray (ed.), *Trends in Social Science*, pp. 60-83.

46. In the terms of Marion Levy, upon whom we draw so heavily, we are concerned with the concrete structural requisites of a particular type of society. (See *The Structure of Society*, pp. 198-207.) We might also point out that what we shall attempt to do is what Hempel argues cannot be done. (See "The Logic of Functional Analysis," pp. 286.)

47. The emphasis of political science upon the procedures of governing, as distinguished from the functions of government, can be illustrated by a very simple exercise. The considerations that are of fundamental concern to any systematic discipline are revealed by factors that underlie the classification schemes which have been developed. In classifications of political systems according to party systems—one-party, two-party, multiparty—the significant emphasis is clearly being placed upon the procedures of governing. (See Maurice Duverger, *Political Parties*, pp. 392-393.) Easton's proposals for criteria of classification are explicitly based on an attempt to differentiate between political systems on the basis of *how* they operate. (See David Easton, "Classification of Political Systems," *PROD*, Vol. 1, No. 1, September 1957, p. 4). The taxonomies developed in the 1950's, principally for use in the study of developing countries, indicate a primary emphasis on the structure of authority and the procedures of governing. (See, for example, David E. Apter, *The Political Kingdom in Uganda*, pp. 3-9.)

48. All of these would be included under the general rubric of *decision making*, as this concept is used by Richard C. Snyder. (See Richard C. Snyder, H. W. Bruck, and Burton Sapin, *Foreign Policy Decision-making*, pp. 14-185.)

49. Max Weber, *The Theory of Social and Economic Organization*, pp. 324-391; Snyder *et al.*, *Foreign Policy Decision-making*, p. 110.

50. Snyder *et al.*, *Foreign Policy Decision-making*, p. 116.

51. Samuel Krislov, *The Perimeters of Force*, unpublished paper read at the annual meeting of the American Political Science Association, New York, 1963.

52. Deutsch, *The Nerves of Government*, p. ix.

53. For an introduction to the theory of communication and control, see Norbert Wiener, *Cybernetics*, and Ashby, *An Introduction to Cybernetics*.

54. Deutsch, *The Nerves of Government*, p. 88. See also p. 187.

55. *Ibid.*, pp. 88-89, 187-188.

56. *Ibid.*, pp. 88-89, 187-188.

57. In comparative cross-cultural studies, it might be more useful to compare the lag and gain in two different systems as ratios to *load*—the amount of information needed to reach an objective—rather than to make absolute comparisons. Our data do not permit such refinement at this stage.

58. See Wiener, *Cybernetics*, pp. 95-115.

59. Deutsch, *The Nerves of Government*, pp. 85-86.

60. *Ibid.*, pp. 187-188.

61. William H. Pierce, "Redundancy in Computers," *Scientific American*, Vol. 210, No. 2, February 1964, pp. 103-112.

62. For a review, see Chapter 1 above, pp. 9-12.

63. This may be due to the inadequacy of the source material we have to deal with. Interest articulation, in Almond's terms, is not a subject about which one can find much comparative analysis in political histories.

CHAPTER 3

Governmental Structures and Procedures of Governing: An Overview

CONCEPTS AND CONCEPTUAL FRAMEWORKS—LIKE THE ONES PRE-
sented in the previous chapter—are of consequence only if they provide a useful framework for the development and statement of
significant hypotheses. These hypotheses, of course, do not emerge
directly from the conceptual framework itself, but may be developed
in two different ways. First, one may attempt to state existing, relevant theories in the social sciences in terms of these concepts, and
then seek to derive hypotheses from the theories. Second, one may
undertake an exploratory study in which he analyzes empirical cases
in terms of the concepts presented and develops hypotheses from the
patterns of similarities and differences which are revealed. We shall
begin the development of hypotheses by the latter method. In this and
the following two chapters, we shall briefly analyze a number of empirical cases in an exploratory way, and in Chapter 7 we shall attempt to formulate hypotheses that appear to be justified by the analysis.

The first cases to be treated are France in the last two centuries of
l'ancien régime (1600-1789), Manchu China (1644-1911), Tokugawa Japan (1603-1868), and England from the late Tudor period
until the third quarter of the eighteenth century (1558-1780). These
four societies have in common a number of features which may be
summarized by two major points: (1) their economies were all pre-
take-off; and (2) they all had polities that would be classified by
most political scientists as "traditional."

Despite important elements of similarity, however, England and
Japan were able to achieve take-off within a relatively short time
after the techniques and processes of early industrialization had be-

66

come known to them, while France and China did not. England, the first state to enter the take-off stage, was able to do so in the closing decades of the eighteenth century—an event closely associated in time with important technical developments in the textile and ferrous-metal industries. Japan was largely isolated from the main currents of Western development until the middle of the nineteenth century, but once Western technology became available, it spread very rapidly. Shortly after the Meiji Restoration, the Japanese economy reached the take-off stage.

China and France, on the other hand, lagged considerably in their industrial development; knowledge about production techniques and processes was available in these two countries long before their economic growth rates began to accelerate rapidly. Although China was opened to Western influence on a large scale in the 1840's, she made little industrial headway. Chinese leaders made half-hearted attempts to modernize in the closing decades of the nineteenth century and took more energetic steps after the turn of the twentieth century. But economic take-off was certainly not achieved by the time of the revolution in 1911, and there is some doubt that the Chinese Communists have even yet reached that stage.

According to recent analyses of economic growth in France, the French economy made little advance from the revolution in 1789 until 1815, and it developed at only a slightly faster pace from 1815 to 1850.[1] Economic growth at rates that are associated with take-off did not occur until the latter half of the nineteenth century. The question naturally arises as to whether the knowledge of production techniques and processes which was available in England in the latter part of the eighteenth century was also available in France. If France did not have access to this knowledge, her delay in achieving economic take-off may be attributed to purely technical factors.

There is evidence to indicate, however, that the French economy had technological knowledge and experience upon which to draw. In the textile industry the inventions associated with Arkwright and Cartwright were introduced into France between 1775 and 1780.[2] Large coke-burning steel furnaces existed in the 1780's, and bellows, hammers, and drills were being operated by steam power. Large-scale production units could be found in a number of industries. By 1787, for example, there was in operation a metallurgical plant capable of producing 10,000,000 *livres* of cast iron each year; by 1789 there was a coal mine which employed 4,000 workers and utilized the energy of 600 horses and 12 steam engines; in 1790 there were in existence textile plants with 6,000 spools driven by steam.[3] Thus it would appear that an advanced level of technological knowledge was available in France. The examples cited, however, are isolated cases which simply indicate that France did not lag much behind England in technical knowledge; this industrial technology did not become diffused throughout the economy for many decades.

Since England reached the take-off stage by the 1790's, it may be assumed that she met the prerequisites sometime during the period 1560-1790. Japan, which reached the take-off stage in the 1890's, satisfied the prerequisites during the Tokugawa era. In contrast, France, we postulate, had not met the prerequisites by 1790, and China had not met them by 1911. From this point of view, one would expect to find patterns of similarity between France and China which distinguish them from England and Japan. The patterns of similarity and difference emerging from an analysis of these four case studies will hopefully provide the basis for the development of our hypotheses.

Our attention, of course, is concentrated upon similarities and differences in the functions of government and in the procedures of governing as political prerequisites for economic take-off. It is conceivable that, in the periods under consideration, all four countries met the *political* prerequisites for take-off, but that France and China did not satisfy some of the nonpolitical prerequisites. If this is the case, the patterns of political similarities and differences will not be relevant to the problem of achieving take-off. As will be seen in Chapter 7, however, the hypotheses that emerge from this exploratory study are compatible with a body of social theory, and hence probably of relevance to the basic problem.

Before proceeding to the case studies, it is necessary to utter a final word of caution. The monograph would undoubtedly be better balanced if we had included a case of an economy that achieved take-off during the contemporary period, so that we might compare it with the historical cases. It appears, however, to be much more difficult to glean detailed material from secondary sources for a contemporary modernizing economy than for the four cases we have selected. But, since we are primarily interested in developing hypotheses concerning the political basis of economic growth that are general enough to be applied to states whose comparable periods of economic development are in different centuries, it makes little difference what cases we select for the exploratory study so long as they manifest patterns of similarity and difference which enable us to examine the effect of variation in the significant factors. It is our intention eventually to test the hypotheses on a sample which includes contemporary cases.

The analysis of differences in the functions of government and the procedures of governing, upon which the development of our hypotheses depends, will be facilitated by a brief review of the major features of government in the four countries during the periods under consideration.

FRANCE (1600-1789)

As one reviews the structure of French government and the procedures of governing during the seventeenth and eighteenth centuries, so many changes in detail emerge that generalization may seem hazardous. Some of the changes that occur, however, are not important to the main themes of this study. It makes little difference to our problem, for example, whether the monarch was "his own first minister" (for example, Louis XIV) and made many key decisions himself, or whether one of the monarch's appointees (for example, Richelieu) wielded dominant power in government. But other changes and differences over time are important. We need, for example, to take note of the increasing ineffectiveness of the central government after the middle of the eighteenth century. For purposes of this study, we shall concentrate upon the period of Louis XIV's personal reign (1643-1715), because this period can be used to illustrate the characteristics of governance during both the seventeenth and eighteenth centuries.[4]

The government of prerevolutionary France represents one of the best historical examples of an absolute monarchy sanctioned by *divine right.* Even the political theorists and lawyers attributed to the monarch virtually unlimited authority and power, and the writings of Louis XIV leave little doubt that, in his view, God had granted to him both the right to rule as he saw fit and the ability to provide France with the best possible government. This does not mean that he failed to consult with advisers. Indeed, during the opening years of his reign his consultation with advisers became formalized through the emergence of a number of councils and advisory positions. Since these institutions had existed in previous periods, sometimes under different names, much of what will be described is also applicable to the French government under Richelieu during an earlier part of the seventeenth century.[5]

Under Louis XIV there were four councils of primary significance: the *conseil d'état et privé* (commonly known as the *conseil des parties*); the *conseil d'en haut* (or *conseil d'état*); the *conseil des dépêches*; and the *conseil des finances* (frequently referred to as the *conseil royale.*).

The *conseil des parties,* the oldest of these bodies, had had in the sixteenth and early seventeenth centuries a broad and ill-defined sphere of competence. It dealt with matters of justice and finance, as well as with general administration. Under Louis XIV its authority was more precisely defined as the "supreme regulator and interpreter of all laws, private or public, within the kingdom. It was capable of judging even in the first instance and of directing all courts or parlements as to their procedure and duties." [6]

The *conseil d'état,* which was usually presided over by the king, handled important affairs of state, both domestic and external, and was at times the final authority in judicial cases of a civil or administrative nature.

The *conseil des dépêches* and the *conseil des finances* dealt with the administrative and regulative problems of the realm. The former had jurisdiction over a wide range of state affairs: the relation of the provinces to the central government; the administration of communities and municipal corporations; temporal matters of the churches; public works; supervision of the nobility; and brevets for governors, commandants, and other offices of the monarch. The *conseil des finances,* more than the others, was the creation of Louis XIV and of his *contrôleur-général,* Jean-Baptiste Colbert, although it was the direct descendant of the "Grand Directory" of Louis XIII. This council set the tax levies and the proportion of direct taxes to be paid by each *généralité;* it drew up contracts with tax farmers for the collection of indirect taxes, and it supervised their execution; it kept the treasury accounts; it created (or abolished) offices and supervised their sale; and it provided for grants of privilege to various industries.

Although the range of authority of these four councils[7] overlapped to some degree, no single council acted as a check upon the others in a way that limited the capability of the government to act decisively. In no sense were they competing veto groups. In the terms presented in Chapter 2, the authority structure of policy making was highly resolved.

The various councils did not operate in such a manner as to block effective action by the central authority for three major reasons: (1) At any given time there were only a few positions of any potential or actual policy-making significance. During the reign of Louis XIV, for example, there were only ten of these posts—four ministers of state, four secretaries of state, a chancellor, and a *contrôleur-général*. A few important men held more than one of these positions, and most of them occupied seats on the important councils, thus minimizing the danger that sharp differences of opinion might develop among the four agencies.[8] (2) The men who held strategic posts usually met informally with the king, and many of the major decisions were made in this way. (3) The men who held important offices had no significant independent basis of power, serving merely at the pleasure of the strong men in the government—Richelieu under Louis XIII, Louis XIV himself after the death of Mazarin, and Fleury during part of the reign of Louis XV.

Ranum has presented fascinating examples of how a chief minister like Richelieu could apply pressure to a strong-willed official whose office gave him a measure of independence. Claude de Bullion, Superintendent of Finance, was sometimes in a position to thwart certain of Richelieu's policies by delaying the financial resources that were needed to put them into effect. An officer with the power and prestige of a Superintendent of Finance, however, could not arrange marriages for his children without the permission of the king. When Bullion asked Louis to approve a marriage for his son, the response was not clear. He then asked Richelieu to intercede in his behalf. After a delay of six months, during which Bullion had raised the matter several times, Richelieu eventually agreed to secure the royal assent on condition that Bullion would agree to conduct himself in a more compliant fashion as Superintendent of Finance. As soon as an agreement was signed, the king saw fit to grant royal approval for the marriage.[9]

During the closing decades of Louis XIV's rule, the deliberative councils suffered a noticeable decline in influence as a result of what Pagès refers to as a change from an absolute monarchy to an administrative monarchy. More and more decisions were made by the king in consultation with only the secretaries responsible for their enforcement, and, under these circumstances, policy-making procedures took on an anonymous, bureaucratic coloration. At the end of Louis' reign, Pagès argues, it was no longer legitimate, as it had been in earlier years, to draw a distinction between the government and the administration.[10] While the absolute monarchy with deliberative councils of some significance was a typical feature of French government in the seventeenth century, the administrative monarchy with its more bureaucratic and secretive procedures was characteristic of the eighteenth century.

Regardless of which system we focus our attention upon, however, it is clear that the policy-making structure in France was, in comparison with England, highly resolved. Moreover, its sphere of competence was extremely broad. The central authority, which was wielded by a very few men, made decisions ranging from waging war and converting Protestants to establishing minimal levels of salt consumption and prescribing the number of threads in the warp of a piece of fabric.[11]

But a knowledge of the central decision structure leads to only a partial understanding of the political system of prerevolutionary France. Decisions made by powerful leaders are of little consequence unless they can be enforced. In France during this period, the enforcement of statutes, decrees, and regulations rested largely in the hands of the *intendants,* who were full-time professional agents of the central government.[12]

The origin of the office can be traced back to the middle of the sixteenth century, and it was used effectively early in the reign of Henri IV. The system of intendants was expanded by Richelieu, and these officials became such efficient agents of the royal power that one of the major objectives of the nobility at the time of the *Fronde* was to secure their abolition.[13] When, under Louis XIV, decisions of the central government were designed to penetrate more deeply into French society, the intendant became an indispensable official for their enforcement.

Their formal title *intendants de justice, de police et de finance, commissaires départis pour l'exécution des ordres du roi* suggests the wide range of their authority and responsibility. The intendant was, in the first place, an investigator—a collector of the information and intelligence needed to form the policies which governed the social, economic, and political life of France in such intricate detail. Second, he was the official with major responsibility for enforcing the decisions of the central government in the provinces. To carry out this important task, he had the coercive power of the state at his disposal. He could call upon the police—or even the standing army—to secure obedience from the reluctant and the perverse. Finally, the intendant had impressive judicial powers, including authority in special instances to supersede all regular courts by creating special tribunals, which he usually dominated and which rendered judgments that could rarely be appealed.[14] The powers of the intendant were specified in the commission which he received at the time of his appointment. It must be emphasized, however, that the intendant had wide discretionary authority to interpret and apply the policies of the central government. In order to enforce a given edict, both according to its letter and spirit, he might feel that the situation required action that lay outside the legal authority granted by his commission. In such a case, he might take action immediately and then write to Paris for authorization.[15]

To help him in his work, the intendant could appoint assistants (*subdélégués*) who were directly responsible to him. Although this practice was frowned upon by Colbert, it became regularized by the early eighteenth century. Indeed, even before the death of Louis XIV, there were some intendancies which had from 50 to 100 *subdélégués* operating as agents of the intendant, either in smaller geographical subdivisions or in special administrative assignments, like tax collection.[16] When the central government dispatched special agents (as, for example, the *inspecteurs des manufactures*) to the provinces to handle particular tasks, they typically reported to and worked under the supervision of the intendants.

In an age characterized by the purchase of office, when wealth and inheritance as much as any other criteria determined who would hold most (if not the most important) posts, the intendant was indeed an exceptional official.[17] His job never became a sinecure. Until the revolution, he was the reliable agent of the central government. Much of the success of the central authorities in dominating virtually any local interest or authority with which it was in conflict was owed to the intendant.[18]

Another important component of the enforcement machinery of the central government was the *lieutenants généraux de police*. First created for Paris in 1667, they became established officials in all the major and minor cities of France by the end of the century, serving with the intendants as representatives of the royal power.[19]

Two other political structures which existed in the local areas merit brief examination: the governorships of the provinces and the *parlements*. The governors held appointment from the king and were legally his highest representatives in the provinces. Typically selected from the ranks of the high nobility, some were essentially superfluous to the process of governing, while others served as active supporters and instruments of royal policies. Important for our purposes is the fact that these officials were dependent upon the king; they were able to develop few independent bases of strength which would allow them to be effective spokesmen for local or class interests hostile to the policies of the central authority. When the governors played an influential role, they were significant mainly as agents of the royal power.[20]

The parlements were a political structure of a somewhat different type. Altogether there were twelve of these bodies,[21] the most important of which was the Parlement of Paris. Although their members liked to trace the origin of the parlements back to the ancient assemblies described by Tacitus,[22] the Parlement of Paris did not in fact become a distinct body until early in the fourteenth century. Their own theory also held that the various parlements were originally one body, the provincial organizations having been split off from the one in Paris. This view, however, fitted the needs of the *parlementaires* of the seventeenth and eighteenth centuries more than it adhered to historical facts. Some of the provincial parlements had developed out of old seignorial courts.

The parlements were primarily judicial bodies. In all but extraordinary cases, they were the supreme courts of the realm. They attempted, however, to invade the legislative field through the devices of *registration* and *remontrance*. At one time, *registration* merely involved the formal process of recording the laws in the register, but eventually a sort of "judicial review" developed. The laws were not passively registered but were examined and discussed for the purpose of discovering whether the statutes had flaws in them, or whether they violated established precedents and traditions. If the laws were found to be defective, the king would be so informed through a *remontrance*. In the seventeenth century, the parlements claimed the right to refuse registration until the monarch had made the modification in the statute that was demanded. In support of their alleged right, they claimed—at least when the Estates General was not being summoned by the king—that they were representatives of the nation and therefore had a legitimate legislative role.

The magistrates of the parlements were in a stronger position than most opponents of royal power. They were members of the nobility, the *noblesse de la robe*. Their titles accompanied their offices, which in most cases had originally been purchased but which could be sold or passed on to heirs. By the beginning of the eighteenth century, the leading magistrates were able to trace their titles back several generations and were among the wealthiest men in France.

Some of the most significant political struggles in France during the seventeenth and eighteenth centuries were between the parlements and the crown. Until after 1750, the king was able to win all of these contests. He could force the registration of his laws by a *lit de justice* and other techniques. He could overrule unfavorable decisions by action of his high councils, and he could even deprive the parlements of their jurisdiction over certain cases by ordering, for example, an intendant to establish a special tribunal.

In short, the authority structure of policy making was highly *resolved*. A very few men had the authority to make decisions on a wide variety of matters, and they could count on a *reliable* bureaucracy equipped with a number of techniques designed to gain compliance and to faithfully put into effect every policy.

CHINA (1644-1911)

In examining the decision-making structure of imperial China, we shall focus our attention upon the Manchu period. This phase of Chinese history affords a clear view of imperial institutions in operation, since the Manchu conquerors followed to a large extent the patterns that had been characteristic of the earlier Ming dynasty (1368-1644). The Ming rulers had greatly increased the power and prestige of the imperial throne and had developed a central government apparatus which was markedly superior to that of previous regimes.[23] Thus the Manchu conquerors inherited and, *until the regime became weakened in the middle of the nineteenth century,* continued in operation a highly unified and centralized political structure.

Ruling as the "Son of Heaven," the Chinese emperor was theoretically the living source of all authority.[24] As supreme ruler, he held full authority in the legislative, executive, and judicial spheres, and was entitled to intervene by decree in virtually any area of Chinese life. Although the private ownership of land was sanctioned, the emperor regarded himself as the custodian of all property and reserved the right to interfere with it through seizure or taxation.[25] He claimed authority to levy assessments upon the population in the form of money, goods, or direct labor, and he issued decrees governing manner of dress and style of living. As the highest human authority on law and the dispenser of justice, he issued legislative edicts against which there was theoretically no recourse. The system provided no legal safeguards against the exactions of the throne or its official representatives.

Although at times certain officials around the throne might exert influence over the emperor, and occasionally one or two of them might wield delegated authority to conduct the affairs of state, the monarch was usually an autocrat who insisted upon being the final arbiter on all important questions and who tolerated no veto groups.[26] The high officials of state played a subordinate role in the decision-making structure, and served merely as advisers to the throne. The Ming rulers had dismantled the premiership, taking over the powers of this office for themselves, and their Manchu successors did not re-establish the post.[27] The emperor's advisers were required to submit important matters to him for his approval, while minor problems might be handled by a top administrator. Since "important matters" were not defined, however, the emperor could intervene in any governmental affair.[28] The monarch had the right to appoint, promote, remove, or punish his officials, and there is evidence to indicate that he exercised this authority freely, often intimidating or chastizing his subordinates and occasionally resorting to physical brutality. Government officials whose tenure was dependent upon the emperor's whim were hardly in a position to resist his policies effectively. "From the grand secretaries and ministers of the six departments down to an insignificant clerk in the remote corner of the empire, appointment or dismissal, reward or punishment, [were] all given directly by the emperor himself." [29]

Assisting the emperor at the palace and supervising the work of the state administration were two advisory councils and a set of administrative boards.[30] Since council members usually served on the administrative boards, the number of leading state officials was very small. The more traditional of the advisory councils—the Grand Secretariat—consisted of six high-ranking chancellors who counseled with the monarch on policy matters and conducted ceremonial affairs. The Grand Council, composed of four to six ministers, was formed in 1730 to advise the throne in military matters, but it gradually encroached upon the jurisdiction of the Grand Secretariat, taking over its significant advisory powers if not its prestige. This body issued decrees announcing imperial decisions, sent orders to provincial officials, tried important cases on order of the emperor, and handled other state business. Central administration was handled by six boards[31]—usually comprised of two ministers, four vice-ministers, and a host of subordinate directors, auditors, and secretaries—which dealt with civil service matters, ritual observances, finance, national defense, legal affairs, public works, and the regulation of weights and measures. As a rule, the highest posts in the central government were not awarded to individuals who had purchased their way into the civil service. In an attempt to control their bureaucracy, the Manchu rulers employed the traditional system of censorial supervision. The Censorate, which was made up of six Censors-General and a legion of regular censors for the administrative departments and the provinces, was responsible for checking on the activities of public officials at all levels of government (including the center), for auditing accounts, and for supervising public works projects. Thus, as was the case with France, the authority structure of policy making was highly resolved, and the emperor's sphere of legal competence was unrestricted.

There were, of course, practical limits upon the emperor's jurisdiction.[32] He was restricted by the customs and traditions of the country, by the precepts of Confucianist doctrine, and by the precedents established by earlier monarchs. He could, to be sure, issue decrees in violation of the mores of the society, but to do so would invite trouble. Under the "Mandate of Heaven" concept, the Chinese monarch was obligated to govern well. If conditions in the country deteriorated, there was the possibility that he would be faced with rebellion which could overthrow his regime and establish a new dynasty. It was unwise, in other words, for an emperor to rule without regard for the feelings of his people, especially the scholar-officials and the other gentry, who were influential in molding public opinion. Finally, the task of governing such a huge territory and the enormity of the state's business made it necessary for the ruler to delegate responsibility to subordinate officials at the capital and in the provinces.

To control and administer affairs in the provinces, the emperors of China developed a highly symmetrical system of administration, buttressed by an army of military bannermen stationed at strategic points throughout the empire.[33] The tiers of the administrative hierarchy descended from the province through the prefectures, subprefectures, and cantons down to the districts, which embraced the villages and the towns. In addition to these regular subdivisions, there was the circuit, a specially defined area for the administration of such government activities as the collection of customs, the administration of the salt industry, and the development and maintenance of transportation facilities. The lines of responsibility ran directly from the government officials in the districts to the emperor and his ministers in Peking. A viceroy was in charge of one to three provinces, while nearly every province was also under the direct supervision of a governor. Assisting the governor in the administration of provincial affairs were several commissioners—Finance, Judicial, Education—who were appointed directly by the emperor. Below the provincial commissioners were the circuit intendants who handled such problems as transportation, salt administration, postal service, and grain collection in several prefectures. The prefect who was in charge of a prefecture was the administrative link between the leading provincial authorities and the main official in the district, the magistrate. As the need arose, the emperor would dispatch special commissioners to the provinces to deal with any unique problems that might have developed, and, in similar fashion, high provincial officials could send out special agents vested with authority to act in their behalf.

All of these provincial and local officials were regarded as servants of the crown, and, while they enjoyed a certain amount of discretion in the administration of their territories, they had little influence on central policy making as such. Indeed, the emperor sought to hedge them about by all sorts of controls in an effort to keep them loyal to him. Rather than relying upon a hereditary system of civil servants, the emperor recruited his officials by competitive examination, the training for which included heavy doses of Confucianist indoctrination. Once appointed to office by the monarch or his ministers, these government officials were subjected to an intricate system of checks and balances. They were not permitted to select their own subordinates. Offices were usually held by more than one person so that they could watch each other, and in some instances an official might hold several positions part time and thus be blocked from developing an area of personal strength. These high-ranking servants were encouraged to report the shortcomings of their colleagues and were at all times subject to scrutiny by eunuchs who were loyal to their master and by members of the Censorate who were on the lookout for cases of corruption, disloyalty, and misuse of power.

The key official in this system of administration was the district magistrate—a functionary who was comparable in many respects to the French intendant. Since he was responsible for collecting taxes, maintaining order, dispensing relief, preserving roads and buildings, and settling disputes, he combined in his office the executive, legislative, and judicial roles. The magistrate was the main point of contact between the inhabitants of the villages and towns and the agents of the central government who were superior to him in the hierarchy. In carrying out his assignments he worked in close contact with the village elders, family councils, and other social groupings. As in the case of the higher-ranking officials, the emperor sought to keep his magistrates under firm control. The normal term of appointment was for three years, and a policy of periodic rotation was designed to prevent an individual from sinking deep roots in a local area. In an effort to insulate these officials from familial and interest-group pressures, they were not permitted to serve in their native localities, and they were forbidden to marry a resident of the area without special permission.

Since it was virtually impossible for the magistrate to handle all the details of district administration personally, he and his superiors were forced to lean heavily upon the residents and social organizations of the localities. Very often a clan would dominate the life of a village, and the government would use it as an instrument of control. The gentry of the area—retired officials and degree-holders hopefully waiting for office—were always active in organizing community projects that would ordinarily be the work of government itself. The gentry, for example, initiated and managed many irrigation schemes, local industries, the distribution of relief, the building and maintenance of transportation routes, and similar projects. Exercising great influence over ordinary citizens in their communities, the gentry were useful to the government in the collection of taxes and the maintenance of order. Government administration worked best when there was a harmonious relationship between the officials and these local magnates. Being dependent upon the gentry made it imperative for the emperor to control them as much as possible.[34] This the government attempted to accomplish in part through the examination system, setting quotas for admittance to the examinations (and hence to gentry status) and keeping the aspirants so busy preparing for the examinations that they had little time to become restive. The government also sought to thwart the influence of this group by establishing local organizations of control that were independent of them and under separate leadership. When, for example, the *pao-chia* (for police control) and *li-chia* (for tax collection) systems[35] were set up, the government saw to it that commoners rather than gentry were placed in charge, thus vesting ordinary citizens with state authority as a counterweight to gentry influence and power. The selection of village leaders and local managers was, of course, subject to approval by the magistrate, and community groups which served as auxiliary agencies of control operated directly under his authority. At times government officials would assign several local organizations to the same activity so that the overlap would encourage one to act as a check upon the other and thus prevent cliques from developing centers of power beyond the reach of the emperor's agents.[36] While the magistrate was forced to lean heavily upon the gentry who resided in his bailiwick, it is important to recognize that he could designate the people with whom he would work. In other words, it was possible for a local official to impair the political influence of a prominent gentry family which happened to be creating difficulty.

The government, of course, was not always successful in maintaining tight control, and it disintegrated rapidly after the middle of the nineteenth century. The effectiveness of the system depended to a large extent upon how reliable and efficient the magistracy was. While it is difficult to generalize about the effectiveness of government administration in so large a territory, most authorities agree that government in local areas was reasonably efficient during the opening decades of new dynastic rule. However, they also agree that inefficiency and corruption tended to become rampant as time advanced, weakening the control system, as happened under the Manchus in the middle of the nineteenth century. It must also be remembered that the government administrator was forced to operate within the framework of a political tradition that laid stress upon the inactive, unobtrusive role of government. While government was expected to engage in certain activities and perform certain necessary functions, its main goal was to keep the people happy, even if this meant leaving them relatively undisturbed. This responsibility, of course, fell largely upon the district magistrates, who were understandably reluctant to enforce policies that would violate the customs and sentiments of the local communities and thus precipitate unrest. In a sense, the magistrate was caught between two sets of pressures. On the one hand, he was subject to a flood of edicts and ordinances from Peking, and was threatened with *serious punishment* if he neglected his duty to the emperor. On the other hand, he was motivated to trim the orders of his superiors to fit the peculiar conditions of his district;

otherwise, the local citizens might become unhappy and set off disturbances which would be unfavorably recorded in a report to the central authorities. Faced with these cross-pressures, the magistrate was often inclined to assume as little responsibility as was congenial with his continuance in the job.

In general, however, the magistrate in China was responsible more to his administrative superiors than to the communities he supervised. Since he was a stranger to his district and was usually not there long enough before reassignment to become caught in the web of personal obligations, the leaders of the towns and villages could probably exert less influence over him than would otherwise have been the case.[37] Moreover, the government official was in several important respects oriented toward Peking, looking to the emperor for promotion and being subject to the elaborate control system which was centered in the capital. Even the gentry, upon whom the government had come to depend for assistance in local administration, ordinarily identified their interests with those of the regime, even though they might engage in rebellious activity during periods of adversity.[38] As Hsiao has pointed out, it would be erroneous to assume that the rural gentry as a group were antagonistic to the government:

> On the contrary, retired officials and titled or aspirant scholars usually had an interest in upholding the existing regime. As scholars they ordinarily prepared for or participated in the competitive examinations; their attitudes and views were therefore conditioned in varying degrees by the precepts of imperial Confucianism. They were in general loyal to the empire, even though they held no offices and had no political responsibility. Officials temporarily or permanently retired to their home villages had no desire to antagonize the government or to challenge the authorities. And while scholars did not have exactly the same status as officials, they were potential officials, or "expectants." Unless a scholar was bitterly disappointed in his aspirations, he generally preferred political stability to political upheaval.[39]

Thus, local government in China was for the most part geared to the administrative machine at the emperor's palace. Besides exercising considerable control over provincial finance, the central authorities were in a position to manipulate the bureaucratic apparatus through the enforcement of a uniform administrative code and through the appointment, removal, and even the corporal punishment of local officials.[40]

In comparing the political systems of China and France, it becomes apparent that both countries had a highly resolved authority structure of policy making which was dominated by a single ruler, until the decline of the central governments. Both the Chinese and French monarchs made use of advisory councils staffed by a handful of men who served at the pleasure of the monarchs themselves. These councils never developed autonomous strength, and as a rule they were able to put up little resistance to the policies of the ruler. Eventually France developed into an administrative monarchy similar to the system that China had had for a long time. The decision-making structures in the two countries had a wide sphere of competence. There were few legal limits on the finance power, and the ruler could theoretically intervene in virtually any realm of life. While the rulers in both countries did in fact issue edicts governing a broad range of activities, the central authority in China was usually expected to pay greater heed to tradition, custom, and precedent. In carrying out the policies of the central government, the rulers of both countries developed a system of administration which covered the entire country and extended in a direct line from the center through the provinces and prefectures as far down as the district.

This administration was staffed by a paid, professional bureaucracy which devoted full time to its responsibilities and which was subject to an elaborate system of controls. At the local level, the French ruler encountered difficulty with the parlements, but he was able to employ techniques that usually enabled him to make his will prevail. In China, the monarch was forced to rely upon the good will of the local gentry who were often a source of trouble, but as a rule the gentry class tended to identify its interests with the goals of the monarchy and, except for periods of crisis, enjoyed a vested interest in the status quo.

Japan (1603-1868)

The political system of Japan during the period under consideration has been characterized as a centralized stage of feudalism which developed following a long epoch of internal chaos and clan strife. Its inception dates from the end of the sixteenth century when the military efforts of several effective clan leaders led to the establishment of a central government which could at least maintain order, and when in 1603 Tokugawa Ieyasu, who had emerged as the strongest of the clan chieftains, received the appointment of *shōgun* (generalissimo). The establishment of his capital at Edo (the old name for Tokyo) ushered in a regime that was to endure for more than 250 years.

Since the Tokugawa clan had bested but had not destroyed a number of other power centers in the society, Ieyasu and his successors did not have a free hand in designing a political system that was completely to their liking. It will help us to understand the Tokugawa system if we examine briefly the political situation in Japan at the outset of the period, before we turn to a description of the decision-making structure and administrative system of the Tokugawa rulers.

By the time the Tokugawa seized control, the feudal pattern had already been well established, and the shogunate was forced to operate within the framework of that pattern. In theory, the shogun received his appointment from the imperial throne, an institution that commanded too much reverence to be overturned. Regarded as being of divine descent, the emperor had been forced into meditative seclusion very early in Japanese history, and although he continued to be recognized as *de jure* sovereign, the real powers of government had long been wielded by dominant clan leaders in the name of and under commission by the royal house.[41] Thus, in a legal sense, the shogun was merely the chief minister of the emperor. Moreover, the Tokugawa clan, although the most powerful by demonstrated military prowess, was only one among many strong families which occupied the territory of Japan. Under the shogun's direct control were the provincial domains of the Tokugawa family and its branches. Although these areas were scattered throughout forty-seven of the sixty-eight provinces and included the major cities, they constituted only about a quarter of the Japanese realm.[42] The rest of the country the Tokugawa rulers were forced to apportion among two types of feudal lords: (1) the *fudai daimyō* (inside lords)—176 in number—who in most instances had been hereditary vassals of the Tokugawa prior to 1600 and who had been allied with Ieyasu during his military struggles; and (2) the *tozama daimyō* (outside lords)—a total of eighty-six—most of whom had been strong enough to resist Ieyasu until the final conquest.

Thus, at the inception of the Tokugawa regime, the shogun was forced to conciliate a large number of feudal lords, including his own vassals, and he was not in a strong enough position to deny them the right to hold the lands that many of them had long occupied on a hereditary basis.[43] The threat of the tozama chieftains, especially during the opening decades of the Tokugawa era, made it imperative for the shogunate to interfere with their feudal domains (*han*) as little as possible. Since the Tokugawa rulers did not wish to stir up antagonism among potential competitors, their system of government was of necessity a pragmatic synthesis of central and local controls.

Unlike France and China, the central decision-making structure of Tokugawa Japan was as a rule not dominated by a single ruler but by a small group of councilors, who were usually high-ranking fudai daimyo.[44] The Council of State (*Gorōju*), consisting usually of four or five elders who often served for life and selected their own successors on a hereditary basis, theoretically advised the shogun on important policy matters. In reality, they exercised a high degree of power, especially after the middle of the seventeenth century. In addition to making policy, these elders dealt with the leading daimyo, selected officials to fill high executive posts in the capital, and supervised the national administrative machine. According to Wigmore, from the time of Iyemitsu, the third shogun (1623-1651), "there was probably not a single occupant of that commanding position [except Yoshimune, the eighth shogun (1716-1745)] who did not register without hesitation whatever decree the councilors agreed upon." [45] A step below the Council of State was the Junior Council (*Wakadoshiyori*), which was made up of two to six young fudai daimyo and which supervised the conduct of feudal vassals below the rank of daimyo. While the Council of State usually had a dominant voice in policy making, crucial decisions on some occasions were made by the shogun's personal favorites, strong heads of the Tokugawa branch families, or other "unseen powers" behind the shogunal throne.

This system was not conducive to the effective determination and execution of policy at the center. As Sansom points out:

[The functions of the] various officers were ill-defined. Moreover, [the system] had the serious defect of being so devised as to discourage initiative, for its high offices were duplicated or their functions were discharged not by individuals but by councils, because it was thought necessary to guard against the monopoly of power by one person. Further, its operations were hampered by a system of rotation, under which the elders and the highest commissioners took turns of duty for a month, and were therefore apt to muddle or procrastinate; and this fault tended to throw real power into the hands of persons behind the scenes, such as chamberlains, masters of ceremonies, or even officials in the women's apartments.[46]

It is not surprising, therefore, that the decrees issued from the shogun's palace were not only numerous but often inconsistent, suffering from a lack of coordination.[47] Moreover, since the families of tozama daimyo were usually excluded from high offices, the important policy-making and administrative positions tended to become hereditary in the families of the fudai daimyo, and "rigid class distinctions sadly limited the talent available for all posts." [48]

In the case of the Tokugawa central government, then, it is apparent that the authority structure of policy making was not resolved, nor did the central policy makers enjoy in practice a broad sphere of competence. To be sure, the Tokugawa rulers laid claim to a wide range of jurisdiction. They issued decrees preventing extensive contact with the outside world, excusing debtors from payment of their obligations, prohibiting the sale of land, denying the right of internal migration, and censuring luxurious living. But the important point is that the regime was frequently unsuccessful in making its policies prevail. This was partly due to the fact that a sizable portion of the country remained in the hands of the tozama daimyo, who were never completely defeated and who jealously guarded their autonomy with their own private armies. Hence, the shogun was never able to enforce many of his policies effectively within their domains. Moreover, the continual threat of the tozama lords forced the shogun to rely upon his fudai vassals (as well as his private retainers, the *hatamoto*) for protection.[49] Dependent upon the fudai daimyo as defenders against the tozama daimyo and as recruits for his administrative machine, the shogun was understandably reluctant to risk their good will by intervening more than was absolutely necessary in the affairs of their estates. Always present was the possibility that the stronger lords might grow less than enthusiastic in their support of the shogun, or might even conspire with the tozama daimyo against him.

The shogun, however, did develop techniques to keep the daimyo in line and prevent them from challenging his hegemony.[50] The feudal lords were required to sign an oath of loyalty to the shogun, promising not to give assistance to the regime's enemies. Theoretically, the shogun could dispossess the feudatories of their lands, and while there were many instances of such punitive action, most of the tozama daimyo, especially in remote regions, were in little danger of losing their domains. The shogun, however, assigned his dependable retainers to fiefs adjacent to the lands of his competitors and made sure that his friends occupied estates along the main highways and near strategic towns. Social and business contacts between the daimiates were discouraged, and travel beyond the confines of the han was rendered difficult by a passport system and by barriers erected along the major transportation routes. The shogun required his sanction to marriages between lordly families, and he forbade the daimyo to have any contact with the emperor's court in Kyoto except through prescribed channels. The daimyo were also required to secure shogunal permission to build or repair castles on their estates, and feudatories in the maritime regions were forbidden to build ships beyond designated size.

Especially burdensome to the daimyo was the *sankin-kōtai* system, under which the feudal lords and some of their *samurai* (warriors) were compelled to reside for several months each year at Edo, and when they returned to their domains for alternate residence, they were required to leave their wives and families at the capital as hostages. The cost of travel and the maintenance of two residences, however, were not the only financial burdens placed upon the daimyo. For the most part, the shogun's policy aimed to keep his lordly rivals in weakened condition. The shogun often made assessments upon the daimyo for public projects of various sorts, and he would order them to build shrines, roads, or public buildings in their local areas at their own expense. Some shoguns even encouraged the daimyo to live in luxury so that their financial resources would become depleted. The shogun, however, did not impose a system of regular, direct taxation upon the feudal lords.

Since the daimyo—especially the tozama—enjoyed considerable autonomy within their own fiefs, being left to conduct their own affairs so long as they performed their obligations to the shogun and did not threaten his position, the Tokugawa rulers had to develop indirect methods for gleaning intelligence about internal developments. To keep posted on the activities of the daimyo, lesser nobles, and the people, they employed a hierarchy of censors (*metsuke*) who functioned under the councils of state in Edo. Although the various ranks of censors had some judicial responibilities, their main task was to report violations of shogunal regulations and to uncover dissident elements among the feudal elite. The chief censors in Edo were known as the "eyes and ears of the shogun."

The shogun exercised more direct controls over his own domain (including the major cities) and at times in certain fudai territories. The areas under direct shogunal rule were governed by commissioners whom he appointed from among his retainers, taking into account the local customs of the region. Officials in the districts, who were designated as *gundai* and *daikan* according to their rank, exercised the ordinary functions of governmental administration, especially tax assessment and collection, the maintenance of order, and the settlement of disputes. The cities that lay within the shogun's direct jurisdiction were administered by magistrates, usually two or three in number, who rotated their duties and functioned both as administrators and judges. In the districts and cities, local headmen and elders had some administrative responsibility and acted as middlemen between the shogun's officials and ordinary citizens.

The rudimentary bureaucracy at the shogun's disposal was in large measure recruited from the fudai daimyo.[51] Successful work in government service on the part of the fudai vassals often resulted in an increase of their land holdings—rewards that tended to make them increasingly concerned about their private affairs. Thus the fudai administrators in the shogun's service not only had competing demands upon their time and energy but were also vulnerable to local pressures and conflicts of interest. They might, for example, be reluctant to enforce central government policies that appeared adverse to their own private concerns, unless their lack of zeal were likely to risk serious punitive action from Edo. The shogun, to be sure, was able to enforce certain unambiguous edicts that were basic to his control system—for example, those dealing with the forced residence of the daimyo and samurai in Edo. These edicts were probably enforceable because the shogun was willing to resort to military force in order to secure compliance to rules that were so fundamental to maintaining his regime in power. But on less consequential matters the flow of decrees issuing from Edo was so large and the ordinances themselves were often so confusing or even contradictory, that the provincial administrator who disliked a given line of policy could procrastinate in its enforcement in the hope that a succeeding edict would soon modify it. Not always sure what rules were in effect at a given time, the local official was inclined to follow the customs of his area, paying due respect to the promulgation of the shogun's instructions, but, as often happened, doing little to enforce them.[52] Despite his efforts, the shogun was usually not successful in making his administrators more diligent.

In the huge area that constituted the domains of the fudai and tozama lords and was beyond the direct reach of the shogun, there was fairly wide cope for the genius and enterprise of individual daimyo and their samurai, even when such activity was not officially sanctioned. Similarly, within an individual daimiate, the reins of government, while firmly in the hands of the feudal lord or his administrators, were not pulled too tightly.[53] Administration was centered in the castle town where the daimyo lived with most of his samurai. For the administration of his fief, he leaned heavily upon the samurai who became the real rulers of the domain. The samurai-magistrates who were stationed in strategic districts throughout the realm, however, were often content to let the headmen and peasants of the villages handle many of their own affairs. The magistrate's main tasks were to relay the edicts of the lord to the inhabitants of the villages and to give the elders whatever assistance they needed. Thus, within his own territory, the daimyo and his administrative retainers often tended to give slack rein to the local citizens so long as they met their tax quotas and did not disturb the tranquility of the fief.

Unlike the powerful men in the governments of France and China, the Japanese shogun did not usually make policy on his own, but was checked by the members of his high council, who in turn would limit the policy-making roles of each other. Although he had direct control over his own lands, which were extensive, he had only *indirect control over a large section of the country,* being content to leave well enough alone in the tozama estates and in many of the fudai domains. In a very real sense, the shogunate was unable to develop a single line of bureaucracy that was capable of reaching into all corners of Japan.[54] Lacking a bureaucracy that he could really call his own, the shogun was forced to rely for much of his administration upon the fudai daimyo, some of whom were concerned with protecting their own interests, even at the expense of the central government. The only policies that the central government could regularly enforce were those so important to its existence (like the sankin-kotai system) that military intervention might be justified.

ENGLAND (1558-1780)

The period we are concerned with in our study of England embraces some of the most crucial developments in English political and constitutional history. During the sixteenth and early seventeenth centuries, the monarchy was regenerated, and it became a strong executive instrument; but during the succeeding decades the kingship was stripped of much of its authority and its power transferred to legislative chambers. In this study, however, we are not concerned with the details of English constitutional development. In examining the decision-making and administrative structures of this long period, it will be necessary for us to look at the finished weave rather than to untangle the individual threads.

Traditionally, the English monarch formulated policy with the advice of a body of councilors. This group, which eventually became known as the Privy Council, exercised important powers of policy making during the latter part of the fourteenth century up to about 1450.[55] The Council was powerful enough to restrain the king and at times was able to usurp some of the royal prerogative. With the growth of royal power under the Tudors, however, the role of the Privy Council as a policy-making group rapidly declined, and it became more of an administrative machine. As consultants to the throne, the monarch came to rely upon *individual members* of the Privy Council and upon his secretaries, the latter becoming very influential in policy formulation, especially in their role as intermediaries between the crown and parliament.[56]

These individual advisers to the throne were appointed by the king and held office only at his pleasure. At times they might be able to restrain such powerful personalities as the Stuart monarchs, while at other times a headstrong king would insist upon a particular set of policies and the resistance would have to come from other political bodies rather than from the councilors. As opposition from these quarters grew increasingly fierce under the Stuarts, the occupant of the throne came to depend upon his ministerial advisers more and more. During the reign of Charles II, there emerged an offspring of the Privy Council—the cabinet—and the members of this body came eventually to act in concert rather than as individuals. William III soon discovered that his policies were likely to be formulated more effectively if he selected ministers whose views corresponded with the views of the parliamentary majority.

Thus, as far as the initiation of crown policy is concerned, the king in pre-Tudor times was greatly influenced by his Privy Council acting as a group; during the Tudor and early Stuart periods, the monarch was more autonomous, although he often solicited the advice of individual councilors and his secretaries; and beginning in the late Stuart era and continuing thereafter, the king became increasingly dependent upon his advisers, gradually relinquishing power to another council, namely, the cabinet.

The king and his councilors, however, were exercising a prerogative that was limited, even under the "absolutism" of the Tudors.

Early in English history, the medieval nobility had united against the king, forcing him to recognize the ancient rights of his subjects, and the uncertain boundaries of royal authority acted as a curb upon succeeding monarchs. In contrast with France and China, "divine right" and the "mandate of heaven" found little support among political theorists and constitutional lawyers in England. Indeed, no theory of absolute monarchy was advanced until the kingship had already entered the stage of decline.[57] It was understood that the king was bound by the law, both statutory and customary. When Henry VIII needed support in his struggle with the Papacy, he made expedient use of the parliament, and it came to be a recognized norm that the monarch possessed no legislative authority except in collaboration with the representative body of the nation. This meant that the king was not entitled to levy new taxes by a simple decree issued by himself and his councilors. With this financial hold over the monarch, the members of parliament were prompted to increase their own authority by bargaining with the crown, agreeing from time to time to supply the necessary funds on condition that certain royal policies be modified. A further restraint upon the king was exercised by the law courts, which, in upholding the law to which the king was bound, had authority to block important policies and actions of the crown.

Thus, in addition to the king and his councilors, the central policy-making structure included the parliament and the courts, both of which had authority to withhold approval of major crown policies. Since the struggle over the limits of the royal prerogative ensued during the entire period covered by this study, both parliament and the crown played crucial roles in the policy-making structure. The king was entitled to veto acts of the parliament, and either or both of the two chambers could veto policies of the crown. Parliament, however, was not a cohesive body. The nobility and high ecclesiastical officials sat in the House of Lords, while the House of Commons was made up of landowning and commercial interests. Thus, before major policy could be formulated, approval had to be secured from three independent groups (the Lords, the Commons, and the crown), each of which had somewhat differing interests. The objection of any single component in the policy-making structure would result in the veto of a given policy or in its modification into more acceptable form.

Another type of veto over the policies of the crown was that exercised by the common law courts. If a strong-willed king attempted to rule without parliamentary assent—or even when the parliament had agreed to an unpopular policy—the royal decrees could be discarded or the statutes limited in their operation by the common law courts, over which the monarch had little direct control. Because of the significant influence exerted by the judges over the ordinances issuing from Westminster, the common law courts must also be regarded as part of the policy-making structure.[58]

Unlike France and China, the authority structure of policy making in England was not resolved. In comparison with Japan, of course, the institutional framework in the English system was considerably different. But when one examines the procedural characteristics and veto potential of central policy making in the two societies—the features with which this study is concerned—the similarities between the two become more apparent.

As in the other cases, the central government of England concerned itself with detailed aspects of English life, and it promulgated a wide variety of decrees which were calculated to remedy pressing economic and social problems. It prohibited the enclosure of agricultural lands, forbade industry to be moved to the countryside, set standards for wages and apprenticeship, granted monopolistic privileges, and established regulations governing the consumption of commodities and the quality of manufactured articles. While some of these admonitions and programs were relatively successful at times, the central government as a rule experienced difficulty in making its policies prevail. Not only did the crown often encounter resistance from parliament and from the common law courts, but it also suffered from the lack of an effective enforcement mechanism.

Within the central government, primary responsibility for the enforcement of decrees and statutes fell upon the Privy Council,[59] which in its heyday was composed of about forty members, including both nobility and commoners. The Council operated through a system of committees, including several regional councils (such as the Council of the North and the Council of Wales and the Marches), which wielded the administrative powers of the parent body in the provinces. As the central core of English administration, the Privy Council handled a vast scope of state business which in a later day was taken over by the executive departments. At the king's request, it issued decrees regulating virtually every realm of English life—commerce, industry, finance, religion, justice, and the press. It supervised the work of regional, county, and local authorities, calling them to account when royal decrees went unheeded. On regular occasions most of the Privy Councilors sat as members of the Star Chamber, a special court which enforced royal proclamations that had not as yet received parliamentary sanction. The scope of the Chamber's judicial activities was as wide as the business of the state, and it had virtually a free hand to render any type of judgment except the death penalty. When wealthy, influential leaders in the localities oppressed the less fortunate and escaped censure in the local courts, they were summoned to Westminster to answer before the Star Chamber for their behavior. In this way ordinary citizens had some recourse against local magnates who had violated regulatory decrees but whose influence with local juries enabled them to avoid punishment.

While the Privy Council, especially under the Tudors, attracted noteworthy administrators and had a number of points to its credit, it was in general an unwieldy and inefficient instrument of royal rule. It and the Star Chamber were attempting to remedy from the center the laxity of administration that the crown was unable to prevent throughout the countryside. The task of administering England with barely an embryo civil service at its command was too great for agencies of this sort. Moreover, the Council was usually split by factional rivalries, and very often the Privy Councilors themselves had serious conflicts of interest. When the monarch, for example, decided to prohibit enclosures of agricultural land, the members of his Council were among the biggest offenders.[60] Similarly, during the reign of James I, Spain gained some influence in the Council by paying bribes and pensions to certain members.[61] By 1660 the Star Chamber had been abolished by parliament on the ground that it had become a tyrant's weapon, and the Privy Council itself had begun to decline in importance. This meant that until a new administrative structure was erected at the center (and placed under the control of parliament), the local agents of the crown were without even the central discipline that the Council had attempted to enforce upon them.[62]

In administering the realm, the king and the Privy Councilors did not have at their command a full-time, paid, professional bureaucracy which could be relied upon to carry out central policies in the localities. In early times the government of each county had been under the supervision of the sheriff, but in the fourteenth and fifteenth centuries the powers of this office were gradually transferred to other officials. The Lords Lieutenant, for example, who were appointed by the king usually from among the nobility, took over from the sheriffs the task of organizing and commanding the militia of the counties and served as the supervisory agents of the crown.[63] The main burden of local administration, however, fell upon the justices of the peace, who were nominated by the Lords Lieutenant and commissioned as official representatives of the crown. Assisting the justices of the peace were a number of parish officials—the surveyor, constable, clerk, relief administrator, and others—who functioned under their direction.

The administrative hierarchy extending from the Privy Council down to the local areas proved to be an unreliable instrument for the enforcement of the central government's orders in the countryside. The main spokes in the local administrative wheel were the justices of the peace, upon whom the king came to depend almost entirely for the enforcement of his ordinances. As early as the thirteenth century, these officials had served in a limited capacity as conservators of the peace. As social disorders became widespread, the crown gradually widened the scope of their authority.[64] By the end of the fifteenth century, the justices were engaged in more activities than had ever before been assigned to local officials, and they became increasingly important during the period with which we are concerned.

Usually there were from twenty to sixty justices of the peace commissioned for each county, the total reaching about 2,000 in the period under consideration.[65] Their mandate to enforce royal decrees gave them responsibility for maintaining order and for trying certain types of criminal cases, as well as for administering a broad range of policies at the local level. They supervised the maintenance of roads, the distribution of poor relief, the collection of some local taxes, the inspection of industrial products and commercial transactions, the licensing of taverns, and similar activities. At various times they were also given important assignments of a special character, such as the periodic examination and adjustment of wage scales. In carrying out their judicial and administrative duties, the justices of the peace were subject to the scrutiny of the circuit judges and, until its decline, the Privy Council.

Although the crown had originally expanded the authority of the justices in an attempt to strengthen its hold over the local areas, these officials, in contrast with the French intendants, never became the bureaucratic instrument of the central government. The people who were appointed to these posts were landed gentry of the localities, who were largely concerned with their own private interests and the interests of the communities they administered.[66] Since they were the unpaid servants of the crown, they were forced to live on the incomes from their own estates—a condition that gave them a large degree of independence from the authorities in Westminster. Moreover, they did not govern as "outsiders" in strange territory. As natives of the area, they were thoroughly familiar with the life and problems of their own bailiwicks and were inclined to let their local conerns take precedence over royal command. This meant that when crown edicts ran counter to the interests of their home territories or of their own social class, the king could never be certain that his proclamations would be enforced. The justices of the peace were drawn from the same social stratum as many members of the House of Commons— indeed, some justices also held seats in the House—and when parliament would lose a battle with the king over a particular issue, the justices were likely to be unsympathetic with the policy when they were ordered to administer it. Thus the local administrators of the counties, especially in the eighteenth century, exercised a large measure of autonomy, and, as Trevelyan points out, when the local squires felt strongly against certain of the crown's policies, the king was sometimes left without any bureaucratic instrument for governing the countryside.[67]

Since the central authorities experienced difficulty in having their decrees enforced throughout the country, the king and his ministers from time to time appointed special commissioners to carry out special supervisory assignments. These officials were sometimes dispatched to the counties to keep a watchful eye on the justices of the peace. Although this system of control occasionally operated smoothly—as, for example, during the early phases of Elizabethan poor law administration—it did not as a rule prove to be very effective. When the crown decided that it was necessary to check the quality and prices of textiles, it established a system of inspectors (*aulnagers*) to do the checking. This method of control failed miserably, however, for the inspectors tended to levy special charges upon the merchants and the customers without doing very much inspecting. Indeed, the merchants were able most of the time to evade the system.

SUMMARY

Although differing in certain detail, the governments of France and China had many structural and procedural characteristics in common. In both, the authority structure of policy making was well resolved;

policy was made in each instance by the monarch with the assistance of a small, well-coordinated group of advisers. No competing group held the power of veto; there was no institutionalized system of *checks and balances.* Moreover, the central government in each country possessed a reliable bureaucracy for the enforcement of its decisions throughout the countryside, and the agents of the central authorities had at their disposal a wide range of techniques to secure compliance to official directives. They could, for example, gently persuade the potential dissidents, or more severely tax the communities that did not comply, or even call into operation the instruments of violence held in reserve by the state.

Japan and England, on the other hand, display some marked contrasts with France and China. In neither government was there a resolved authority structure of policy making, for checks and balances were built into each system. Furthermore, neither government possessed a bureaucratic instrument to enforce throughout its territory the policies that were formulated at the center. And even if an agent of the central government wanted to enforce a given policy, he often did not have available the techniques needed to secure compliance from elements in the population which offered vigorous resistance to the edicts of the central policy makers.

NOTES

1. See Institute de Science Économique Appliquée, "La croissance économique française," in Milton Gilbert (ed.), *Income and Wealth,* pp. 45-100; Bert F. Hoselitz, "Entrepreneurship and Capital Formation in France and Britain since 1700," in National Bureau Committee for Economic Research, *Capital Formation and Economic Growth,* pp. 292-293.

2. Henri Sée, *Economic and Social Conditions in France during the Eighteenth Century,* p. 169; Charles Ballot, *L'introduction du machinisme dans l'industrie française,* pp. 44-83, 175-179; John Hammond and Barbara Hammond, *The Rise of Modern Industry,* p. 45; Rondo E. Cameron, *France and the Economic Development of Europe, 1800-1914,* pp. 7-8.

3. Sée, *Economic and Social Conditions in France during the Eighteenth Century,* pp. 170-171; Ballot, *L'introduction du machinisme dans l'industrie française,* pp. 385-405, 440. Coke was first used in France in 1769.

4. For a treatment of government during the entire period of our interest, see Ernest Lavisse, *Histoire de France,* Volumes VI-IX, especially Vol. IX by H. Carré, P. Sagnac, and E. Lavisse. Our discussion is based largely upon G. Pagès, "Le gouvernement et l'administration monarchique en France à la fin du règne de Louis XIV" (in four parts), in *Revue bimensuelle des cours et conférences,* Vol. 38, 1936, No. 1, pp. 1-9; No. 4, pp. 289-297; No. 7, pp. 610-619; and No. 8, pp. 703-712; Phillippe Sagnac, "Louis XIV et son administration," *Revue d'histoire politique et constitutionnelle,* Vol. 3, No. 1, January 1939, pp. 23-47; Orest A. Ranum, *Richelieu and the Councillors of Louis XIII;*

James E. King, *Science and Rationalism in the Government of Louis XIV, 1661-1683.*

5. For an earlier period, see Ranum, *Richelieu and the Councillors of Louis XIII*; Roland Mousnier, "Le Conseil du Roi de la mort de Henri IV au gouvernement personnel de Louis XIV," *Études d'histoire moderne et contemporaine*, Vol. 1, 1947, pp. 29-67.

6. King, *Science and Rationalism in the Government of Louis XIV, 1661-1683*, p. 119.

7. Pagès, "Le gouvernement et l'administration monarchique en France à la fin du règne de Louis XIV," pp. 3-9. There were other councils, but they were of less significance.

8. *Ibid.*, pp. 3-9.

9. Ranum, *Richelieu and the Councillors of Louis XIII*, pp. 152-153.

10. Pagès, "Le gouvernement et l'administration monarchique en France à la fin du règne de Louis XIV," pp. 295-297.

11. There were, of course, aspects of French life into which the government could not effectively penetrate. Many of the feudal relationships which existed in the countryside could not have been greatly modified by decisions of the central government in the seventeenth century. Nor could the clergy, who, in addition to their divine ministry, carried on most of the education, regulated marriages, and so on, have been effectively removed from these tasks. Some of the provinces that had been recently incorporated into the kingdom had formal agreements with the monarch (capitulations) which preserved some significant features of local autonomy. But during the eighteenth century, the administrative organs of the central government grew stronger and were in a position to penetrate more deeply into French society. (See Sagnac, "Louis XIV et son administration," pp. 25-36.)

As will become clear in the following chapters, our primary concern is with the centralization or decentralization of *economic* decision making in government. On the situation in France, Charles W. Cole's summary point is of interest: "From 1683 to the inauguration of the five-year plan by the Soviet government in Russia, no conscious and directed effort to develop a nation's industrial life was so prolonged, so thorough, so permeating, so far-reaching as that of Colbert" (*Colbert and a Century of French Mercantilism*, Vol. II, p. 362).

We have no desire to get into the argument about whether or not the *ancien régime* was centralized. Such a term has significance only in the comparative sense. In comparison with England and Japan, we shall argue, the authority structure of policy making in France was highly resolved, and the enforcement mechanism was clarified and highly reliable.

12. On the intendant, in addition to works cited in note 4 above, see Eli F. Heckscher, *Mercantilism*, Vol. I. pp. 152-153; Alexis de Tocqueville, *The Old Regime and the French Revolution;* Allen Johnson, *The Intendant as a Political Agent under Louis XIV*; Paul Ardashev, *Les intendants de province sous Louis XVI;* Henri Fréville, *L'intendance de Bretagne (1689-1790)*, Vols. I-III; Pierre Dubuc, *L'intendance de Soissons sous Louis XIV, 1643-1715.*

13. Paul R. Doolin, *The Fronde*, p. 59.

14. Pagès, "Le gouvernement et l'administration monarchique en France à la fin du règne de Louis XIV," pp. 706-709.

15. Sagnac, "Louis XIV et son administration," p. 29.

16. *Ibid.*, pp. 31-35.

17. It should be pointed out that the intendants were appointed largely from

among the ranks of the *maître des requêtes,* many of whom purchased their offices. However, the intendancies themselves were not venal.

18. We do not mean to imply that the central government, through the instrument of the intendant, destroyed all local autonomy. But up until the middle of the eighteenth century, any major dispute between local interests and central government interests was likely to be resolved in favor of the latter.

19. Sagnac, "Louis XIV et son administration," p. 36. He calls this structure modern.

20. For example, at the time of the Fronde, the Duke d'Épernon, governor of Guyenne, fought loyally for the government against an army raised by the Parlement of Bordeaux, but when it seemed advantageous for the government to remove him from his position, there was no difficulty. (See Doolin, *The Fronde,* pp. 30-31, 38-40.)

21. On the parlements, see Roger Bickart, *Les parlements et la notion de souveraineté nationale au XVIII° siècle;* Paul H. Beik, *A Judgment of the Old Regime;* Franklin L. Ford, *Robe and Sword.*

22. Beik, *A Judgment of the Old Regime,* pp. 36-48.

23. For a short treatment of Ming institutions, see Charles O. Hucker, *The Traditional Chinese State in Ming Times (1368-1644).*

24. On the Manchu system of government, see P. C. Hsieh, *The Government of China, 1644-1911,* pp. 39-98; S. Wells Williams, *The Middle Kingdom,* Vol. I, pp. 382-516.

25. Norman Jacobs, *The Origin of Modern Capitalism in Eastern Asia,* pp. 22-23.

26. See Edmund Backhouse and J. O. P. Bland, *Annals and Memoirs of the Court of Peking,* especially pp. 247-268, 343-373, 391, 429.

27. John K. Fairbank, *Chinese Thought and Institutions,* pp. 210-211.

28. Hsieh, *The Government of China, 1644-1911,* p. 35. See also Thomas R. Jernigan, *China's Business Methods and Policy,* p. 346.

29. Hsieh, *The Government of China, 1644-1911,* p. 31, quoting the *Huang Chao Wen Hsien Tung Kao.* In reality, of course, the clerks were a part of the magistrate's household.

30. See C. F. Wu, *Chinese Government and Politics,* pp. 11-20; S. K. Chen, *The System of Taxation in China in the Tsing Dynasty, 1644-1911,* pp. 11-22.

31. The administrative boards were as follows: The Board of Civil Service, Board of Rites, Board of Revenue, Board of War, Board of Punishments, and Board of Works. There were also several auxiliary agencies, including the Colonial Office and the Academy of Letters.

32. Hsieh, *The Government of China, 1644-1911,* pp. 38-40.

33. On provincial and local administration, see K. Hsiao, *Rural China: Imperial Control in the Nineteenth Century,* pp. 289-320; Edwin O. Reischauer and John K. Fairbank, *East Asia, the Great Tradition,* pp. 299-302; T. T. Ch'ü, *Local Government in China under the Ch'ing, passim.*

34. See Hsiao, *Rural China,* pp. 6-7, 45-74; Franz Michael, "State and Society in Nineteenth-century China," *World Politics,* Vol. 7, No. 3, April 1955, pp. 427-428; Ch'ü, *Local Government in China under the Ch'ing,* pp. 168-169, 175-177, 180-188.

35. Eventually the pao-chia took over both functions.

36. See Hsiao, *Rural China,* pp. 501-502.

37. See Chen, *The System of Taxation in China in the Tsing Dynasty, 1644-1911,* pp. 29-30.

38. See Hsiao, *Rural China,* p. 418.

39. *Ibid.,* p. 317.

40. See Ch'ü, *Local Government in China under the Ch'ing,* especially pp. 1, 6-7, 193-194.

41. In addition to the performance of ceremonial functions, the emperor had authority over foreign affairs, although the shogun retained the power of veto.

42. E. Herbert Norman, *Japan's Emergence as a Modern State: Political and Economic Problems of the Meiji Period,* pp. 13-14.

43. William E. Griffis, *The Mikado's Empire,* p. 272; George Sansom, *A History of Japan, 1334-1615,* pp. 404-406.

44. See James Murdoch, *A History of Japan,* Vol. III, pp. 4-8; Harold S. Quigley, *Japanese Government and Politics,* pp. 9-10; George Sansom, *A History of Japan, 1615-1867,* p. 141. For other general treatments of the Tokugawa system, see Edwin O. Reischauer, "Japanese Feudalism" in Rushton Coulborn (ed.), *Feudalism in History,* pp. 26-48; John W. Hall, "The Nature of Traditional Society: Japan," in Robert E. Ward and Dankwart A. Rustow, *Political Modernization in Japan and Turkey,* pp. 14-41; John W. Hall, *Tanuma Okitsugu, 1719-1788: Forerunner of Modern Japan,* pp. 21-27.

45. John H. Wigmore, "Materials for the Study of Private Law in Old Japan," *Transactions of the Asiatic Society of Japan,* Supplement to Vol. 20, 1892, Part I, p. 29. See also J. H. Gubbins, "Some Features of Tokugawa Administration," *Transactions of the Asiatic Society of Japan,* Vol. 50, December 1922, pp. 74-75.

46. George B. Sansom, *Japan, A Short Cultural History,* p. 457.

47. Matsuyo Takizawa, *The Penetration of Money Economy in Japan,* p. 136.

48. Sansom, *Japan, A Short Cultural History,* p. 457.

49. On the fudai daimyo as administrators, see Albert M. Craig, *Chōshū in the Meiji Restoration,* pp. 362-369.

50. See Norman, *Japan's Emergence as a Modern State,* pp. 14-15: Murdoch, *A History of Japan,* Vol. III, pp. 16-23; Griffis, *The Mikado's Empire,* pp. 276-277; Walter G. Dickson, *Japan,* pp. 192-222.

51. See Craig, *Chōshū in the Meiji Restoration,* pp. 362-369. The shogun also made use of the hatamoto and other private retainers.

52. Takizawa, *The Penetration of Money Economy in Japan,* pp. 135-136.

53. See Thomas C. Smith, *The Agrarian Origins of Modern Japan,* pp. 202-204.

54. See Marion J. Levy, Jr., "Contrasting Factors in the Modernization of China and Japan," in Simon Kuznets, Wilbert E. Moore, and Joseph J. Spengler, *Economic Growth: Brazil, India, Japan,* pp. 515-516; Yosoburo Takekoshi, *The Economic Aspects of the History of the Civilization of Japan,* Vol. II, p. 476.

55. Albert V. Dicey, *The Privy Council,* pp. 33-42.

56. See Richard H. Gretton, *The King's Government: A Study of the Growth of Central Administration.*

57. See Franklin Baumer, *The Early Tudor Theory of Kingship.*

58. See below, pp. 124-125.

59. On the Privy Council, see Dicey, *The Privy Council*; Almeric W. Fitzroy, *The History of the Privy Council*; Edward R. Turner, *The Privy Council of England in the Seventeenth and Eighteenth Centuries, 1603-1784,* Vols. I and II.

60. Milton Briggs and Percy Jordan, *Economic History of England,* pp. 108-109.

61. Turner, *The Privy Council, of England in the Seventeenth and Eighteenth Centuries, 1603-1784,* Vol. I, p. 85.

62. William H. B. Court, *A Concise Economic History of Britain: From 1750 to Recent Times*, p. 109.

63. Stanley B. Chrimes, *English Constitutional History*, pp. 136-138.

64. See W. E. Lunt, *History of England*, pp. 258-259; Heckscher, *Mercantilism*, Vol. I, pp. 246-263.

65. Conyers Read, *The Government of England under Elizabeth*, pp. 17-18; Gilbert Slater, *The Growth of Modern England*, pp. 29-35.

66. See Ephraim Lipson, *The Economic History of England*, Vol. I, pp. 155-156; Fritz Caspari, *Hamanism and the Social Order in Tudor England*, p. 4; Joseph R. Tanner, *English Constitutional Conflicts in the Seventeenth Century, 1603-1689*, p. 78; George M. Trevelyan, *English Social History: A Survey of Six Centuries, Chaucer to Queen Victoria*, p. 352.

67. Trevelyan, *English Social History*, pp. 170-171.

CHAPTER 4

Functions of Government and Procedures of Governing— I: Adaptation and Goal Attainment

A PATTERN OF SIMILARITY AND DIFFERENCE IS ALREADY BEGINNING to emerge. The central decision structures and procedures in France show some similarity to those in China, as do the bureaucratic structures employed in enforcing the centrally made decisions throughout the country. Even more significant, France and China resemble each other precisely with respect to those features that distinguish these two countries from Japan and England.

Of greater importance to this study than these general structural and procedural considerations, however, is the pattern of similarity and difference in the contribution of government to the four functional requisites. In this chapter, we shall examine the adaptive and goal-attainment requisites and lay out the empirical basis for some of our major hypotheses.[1]

THE ADAPTIVE FUNCTIONAL REQUISITE

According to our definition, the adaptive functional requisite involves those activities that are necessary if the social system is to adapt to its material environment. Processes of production, of resource allocation, and of resource management are of primary significance. Much of the contribution of government to the satisfaction of this requisite will thus include activities that involve the government's participation directly in the economic order.

France

In treating government and the adaptive functional requisite in France, we shall be largely interested in the period from about 1660 until the revolution. This date has not been chosen because it marks any significant break with the past, for most of the activities that concern us had precedents in the sixteenth century.[2] The patterns of activity which we shall examine, however, become much more distinct during the time Colbert was the chief architect of economic policy.

For our purposes the activities of the French government that contributed significantly to the satisfaction of the adaptive requisite during this era may be conveniently arranged in three categories: (1) government support of economic endeavor; (2) government regulation of economic enterprises; and (3) practices and procedures employed in the enforcement of regulations.

GOVERNMENT SUPPORT OF ECONOMIC ENDEAVOR. Economic policy in prerevolutionary France was characterized by generous government support to specific entrepreneurs in certain favored industries. Although a few firms were directly owned and managed by the state, the government as a rule channeled its assistance to the economy through the *grants of privilege,* which were awarded to individual manufacturers. Such a grant could carry with it a number of lucrative concessions and entitlements: direct subsidies from the royal treasury, loans without interest, and monopolistic rights to manufacture and distribute certain products over a designated geographic area. It might also exempt an entrepreneur and his employees from certain taxes, especially the *taille* and the *gabelle,*[3] and from the onerous obligation to quarter troops. Some grants even made it possible for a nobleman to invest in a manufacturing concern without impairing his noble status.[4]

Specialists in French economic history find it difficult to estimate the amount of state aid given to industry during the last 120 years of the *ancien régime.* There can be little doubt, however, that the amount was significant. Martin has compiled the allocations for direct state subsidies on an annual basis from 1664 through 1690, and the total for this period was 1,979,983 *livres tournois.*[5] While these direct grants were undoubtedly important, the indirect subsidies were of even greater consequence. Tax exemption for the owner of an establishment and his employees reduced the expense of operating the firm and enabled him to confer benefits upon his workers without increasing his labor costs. When the government granted monopoly rights to an entrepreneur or contracted for the purchase of his products at a fixed price, he reaped the advantage of a guaranteed market.

Similarly, loans supplied by the state without interest gave certain business men access to free capital. Some loans—because they were never repaid—were really outright gifts. Boissannade estimates that from 1664 to 1883 the amount of indirect subsidies reached a total of about 16,000,000 livres. His calculation, however, is probably conservative.[6] Although these statistics on direct and indirect subsidies are taken from the period when Colbert was *contrôleur-général,* they should not be regarded as atypically high. Economic privileges granted by the government, especially tax immunities and monopoly rights, were even more prevalent under Colbert's successors.[7]

It is apparent, then, that the government played an important role in deciding which entrepreneurs in a given industry had the lowest probability of failing, and in determining into which industry the marginal livre should go.

GOVERNMENT REGULATION OF ECONOMIC ENTERPRISES. The French government exercised a broad measure of control over the major segments of the economy. A grant of privilege not only conferred benefits upon the recipient but also imposed upon him a set of obligations. The terms of the grant often required an entrepreneur to produce specified amounts of a commodity at a standard level of quality, and the government sometimes ordered him to employ certain production techniques. Government regulation of economic activities, however, was not restricted to the royal manufacturers. The controlling arm of the political authorities extended to virtually all manufacturing industries, commerce, and mining.

When an economic enterprise fell within the orbit of government supervision, the regulations were applied to nearly every aspect of production and distribution. They provided detailed product specification, they prescribed the processing techniques which were to be utilized, and they defined the terms and conditions of employment. Cole has made available the regulations that were characteristic in the state's supervision of the textile industry, and these may be presented as an example of the detailed regulation of industry generally. These regulations specified, among other things, the acceptable way to dry wool,[8] the type of dyes to be used and the dyeing process to be employed, the number of threads in the warp, and the minimal size of a finished fabric. Many of the official rules applied to the labor force in a textile establishment. They detailed the length of service required for a worker to become a master and the number of apprentices a master might employ. They also enumerated the conditions under which a journeyman might be hired or fired—prohibiting a master, for example, from enticing a worker from another establishment. These types of government regulations, which were stringent and detailed in Colbert's time, grew even more detailed in the eighteenth century. Whereas the silk regulations of 1667, for example, had only fourteen articles dealing with technical matters, the regulations of 1737 contained fifty-one articles.[9]

In scope and depth, these government regulations were comparable to the regulations of the guilds which flourished throughout Western Europe during the Middle Ages. In point of fact, the ancient guild rules served as models for the economic regulations handed down by the French government, and one can detect similarity in language and detail. During the seventeenth and eighteenth centuries, the French guilds themselves were in effect supported by the government; special guild rules were given the sanction of state law, and the enforcement machinery of the guilds was closely geared to that of the state.[10] Thus, while the guild organization of industry had already declined in England, the guilds in France, under the tutelage of the state, were increasing in number almost until the revolution, as the power of the government was brought to the support of the old and the new regulations alike.[11]

ENFORCEMENT PRACTICES AND PROCEDURES. Since the intendants enjoyed, as we have seen, a wide sphere of competence in implementing the laws and decrees of the central government, it was to be expected that they would be assigned important responsibility for enforcing industrial regulations.[12] However, the number of regulations and the minuteness of their detail, as well as the propensity of some citizens to evade them, prompted the government to create a more elaborate enforcement mechanism. In 1669, Colbert established a special corps of administrators, the *inspecteurs des manufactures,* whose principal task was to enforce the regulations applicable to industry. The size of the corps kept pace with the need, increasing from eighteen *inspecteurs* in 1669 to twenty-four in 1683 and to thirty-four in 1715. The number continued to grow until the revolution.[13] Later, in the eighteenth century, the central government set up other offices to supervise even further the machinery of regulation. In 1727, for example, several *inspecteurs généraux* were appointed to direct the work of the *inspecteurs des manufactures.* At various times the *lieutenants généraux de police* were also involved in these regulatory activities.[14]

In the eighteenth century, the *inspecteurs des manufactures* at the district level were entitled to appoint assistants to represent them and to carry out their work in the various manufacturing centers of the area.[15] The *inspecteurs* also called upon certain municipal officials— like the *maires* (mayors) and the *échevins* (aldermen)—and the wardens of the guilds to help them enforce industrial regulations. In an attempt to clothe the town authorities with effective supervisory power, the central government issued to them special orders which provided that the *maires* and *échevins,* as well as other designated officials, were to have "original jurisdiction over cases involving the size, quality, marking, value or manufacture of goods, and also bleaching, dyeing and wages." In cases involving amounts less than 150 livres their decisions were to be final. The procedure was to be summary, without benefit of lawyers or prosecutors.[16] To the wardens of the guilds the government assigned certain routine tasks of enforcement, such as the inspection of shops, machines, materials, and finished products.[17]

Violations of the regulations were punishable by fines, confiscation of goods, or imprisonment of the offenders. The central government might also threaten to increase the taille for those municipalities whose officials were lax in enforcing the regulations.[18] The following case illustrates how the central government could make its will prevail over the parlements in the event of a clash between the two over the enforcement of economic regulations. A dyer who had been fined 40 livres by local officials appealed the case to the Parlement of Paris, which ruled in favor of the dyer. The central government then issued a decree reversing the decision of the Parlement. This decree also reconfirmed the authority of municipal officials to handle summarily cases involving fines of less than 150 livres, and it underlined the admonition against the appeal of adverse decisions by authorizing a fine of 100 livres against any offender who sought to take such cases to the Parlement.[19]

Thus the central government was able to fashion an effective administrative mechanism for the regulation of economic activities. Although the supervisory *inspecteurs* were an important part of this mechanism, the main responsibility for enforcement rested upon the intendants, who directed the work of the town and guild officials. As the staffs of the intendants' offices grew in the eighteenth century, the intendants could command greater facilities for the detailed regulation of industrial enterprises. When they dealt with violations, they could confidently rely upon the support of their superiors in Paris.

We do not mean to imply, however, that every regulation was always carried out to the letter. Indeed, the frequency with which some decrees were reissued, often with preambles bemoaning the absence of adequate enforcement, attests to the hiatus between the proclaiming of a regulation and enforcement practices. When we recall the difficulties encountered by the American authorities in enforcing prohibition, even with the sophisticated techniques of law enforcement unknown in the eighteenth century, we can appreciate the obstacles which must have existed. It is, of course, impossible to develop any absolute measure of the effectiveness of law enforcement in France during this period. Our purpose is served, however, by a comparative estimate. The reports of the intendants and the records of the courts indicate that the regulation of manufacturing and commercial industries by the French state were enforced much more stringently than they were in England.[20]

China

As in the case of prerevolutionary France, the government of Manchu China contributed significantly to the satisfaction of the adaptive functional requisite, playing a particularly important role in large-scale economic activity.

GOVERNMENT SUPPORT OF ECONOMIC ENDEAVOR. From ancient times the government of China had utilized the resources of the state to keep the land productive. The intensive cultivation of the fields required an adequate system of water control, and the central government had always taken the lead in taming the rivers to prevent floods and to channel the water to the farmlands. The imperial government not only initiated and directed extensive reclamation and irrigation projects of its own, usually employing *corvée* labor, but often subsidized local irrigation schemes that were undertaken by the gentry of the localities. In similar fashion, the central authorities sponsored programs of flood control and provided grants to local areas for this purpose.[21] The government also developed an intricate system of canal and river transport to facilitate the collection of taxes and grain tribute and the supplying of food to the cities.[22]

In addition to subsidizing agricultural production, the Chinese government was active in the distribution of farm produce. It developed

an "ever-normal granary" system under which the government purchased grain surpluses in times of plenty and either loaned grain to
the peasants or sold it to them below market price when harvests were
bad.[23] At various times, when officials felt it necessary to bring
down prices or to curb monopoly, the government would set up its
own warehouses and supply commodities to individual distributors
through a license system. Thus, by purchasing farm commodities and
by collecting taxes on agricultural produce, the government became
the main collector and distributor of such items as grain and silk,
commanding sufficient power to fix the prices of these commodities.[24] Handling directly such a large proportion of the farm products in an agrarian economy meant that the government inevitably
played a dominant role in the economic life of the country.

As Hucker points out, the central government as early as the Ming
dynasty usually produced the manufactured items that were consumed by the government itself.[25] "Peking," he indicates, "abounded
with armories, textile factories, metalwork shops, leatherwork shops,
saddlery shops, paint shops, apparel factories, wineries, and the like,
all operated by the Ministry of Works or by eunuchs, to provide the
court and the central government with their commodity needs." The
government also operated weaving and dyeing enterprises and pottery
works in other cities, and it produced most of the porcelain that was
used in the country. Thus the state was not only the sole producer of
many commodities but also the largest single consumer of its produce.

In addition to being the principal manufacturer of the goods that it
consumed, the Chinese government also "exercised monopolistic control over the production and distribution of commodities that were
essential to the population at large and susceptible to private monopolistic exploitation."[26] This meant that large-scale operations like
mining were under the strict control of the government,[27] and that
the production of and trade in such items as iron, salt, tea, matches,
silk, wine, and tobacco were the prerogative of the state and not an
unrestricted preserve for private investment and entrepreneurship.
Some staples, such as salt, could be produced only in particular regions and had to be distributed on a wide scale to consumers
throughout the country. In order to derive revenue from these commodities, as well as to insure adequate production and distribution,
the government established administrative agencies in the producing
areas, setting production quotas and taking over the finished products
through compulsory purchase. The agencies then sold the commod-

ities to private merchants under a government-imposed quota and license system.[28]

While these licenses entitled the holders to engage in lucrative business operations and represented grants of privilege to favored individuals, the allocation of special privileges to private individuals by the government became more widespread in the latter part of the nineteenth century, when political leaders began seriously to encourage the development of modern industry. At that time private entrepreneurs who wanted to build factories or develop transportation routes were able to secure government funds in the form of loans and subsidies, as well as liberal tax allowances.

As in the case of France, lack of data and the difficulty in breaking down hidden expenditures make it impossible to determine the amount of state aid given to industry under the Manchu regime, or to estimate accurately the proportion of capital formation attributable to the direct and indirect subsidies and concessions given to certain industries and individuals by the government. Scattered information, however, suggests that the amount was significant. Chen, for example, lists as permanent appropriations of the central government in the nineteenth century 307,833 taels for silk manufacturing and 1,618,-081 taels for the conservation of rivers and ponds.[29] According to the revenue budget for 1911, public industries (excluding railways and telegraph) produced approximately 46,600,900 taels, the second highest source of revenue, following closely behind the land tax. In that year the government spent approximately 5,600,400 taels on the public industries, 2,400,000 on the administration of agriculture and industry, and 4,515,270 on public works.

GOVERNMENT REGULATION OF ECONOMIC ENTERPRISES. Although Chinese tradition dictated that the central government minimize its activities in certain areas of life, the fact remains that virtually all phases of economic activity were potentially vulnerable to government intervention, and the span of government controls over the economy—or private controls reinforced by government—was in reality of considerable breadth. Whereas the French monarchy controlled the economy largely through the regulation of private firms, the Chinese government was able to impose its regulations directly upon the large-scale economic activities over which it held direct control. The mining industry was especially characterized by strict government regulation, and, even where the government permitted a measure of private enterprise, it levied a heavy assessment in kind (especially in the case of copper) and reserved the right to purchase a large proportion of the output at a low price.[30] At various times during the Manchu era, the central authorities either prohibited mining activities in certain areas, or placed serious restrictions upon those who sought to develop the industry.[31]

When the government exercised strict monopolistic control over a given branch of production, it often sought to regulate the supply and the price of the commodities by licensing private individuals to engage in the manufacture, transport, and sale of these commodities. The best illustration of this practice was to be found in the salt industry.[32] Since salt was in great demand throughout the empire, the business of producing and selling it became extremely large and profitable, and enterprising individuals eagerly sought government licenses to participate in the indistry. In Ming times the government permitted merchants to engage in the salt trade only after they had transported grain to military garrisons on the frontier. After having performed this task, the merchants were issued certificates authorizing them to purchase government salt and to sell it to distributors in the interior.

Under the Manchus, however, the salt certificates could be purchased for cash, and the salt trade fell into the hands of about thirty rich merchants who dominated the several hundred transport merchants and lesser salt retailers. In a sense those who were able to buy their way into the Chinese salt trade enjoyed a privileged position somewhat akin to the grants of privilege in France. Many of the gentry participated in the salt business, and the government eventually established in some provinces special examination quotas for the sons of salt merchants, thereby enabling them to try for coveted posts in the civil service.[33]

A similar situation obtained in the field of foreign trade, which the government also kept firmly under its control. For a very long time China had no foreign trade of any significance, and what little there was took the form of "tribute payments" to the emperor, who offered in exchange gifts to the visiting representatives of other nations. By the time that Western nations became interested in Chinese trade, however, the imperial court had decided to confine the contacts with foreigners to the single port of Canton. To carry out this trade with the foreign "barbarians," the central government awarded a monopoly of all foreign commerce to a guild of thirteen merchants (the

Cohong), most of whom became wealthy as a result of this concession.

Quite apart from the state monopolies, however, the Chinese government was meticulous in regulating a great many economic enterprises. According to Chinese tradition, the emperor was expected to safeguard the welfare of his people, and this obligation entitled him to intervene in economic transactions.[34] Financial institutions (such as pawnshops) and many businesses dealing with wholesale trade were operated under charter from the government.[35] Since the central authorities distrusted traveling merchants who were thought to spread alien ideas throughout the countryside, these merchants were required to secure appropriate permits from the government before they could engage in their business. Licenses issued by the military governors were required of merchants who wished to carry on trade with the nomads in Inner Mongolia. It was a strict rule that such trade be negotiated on a cash-and-carry basis, and it was illegal for merchants to enter Mongolian territory to seek payment for debts owed them. Violation of the strict edicts governing the trade in Inner Mongolia resulted in punishment which ranged from expulsion and loss of license to death.[36] Government regulations involving economic enterprises throughout the empire frequently applied not only to the prices of commodities but also to the quantity and quality of the merchandise, and official inspectors were employed to enforce the required standards. These edicts, for example, provided that household utensils not strong enough for use were to be confiscated, that pieces of cloth below a stipulated size were to be returned to the manufacturers, and that merchants who sold substandard goods were to be flogged.[37]

Even more than was the case with France, the Manchu rulers depended upon the guilds as agencies for enforcing the rules of trade.[38] Membership in a guild was virtually compulsory for those who wished to engage in major types of commercial activity, and the organization exercised strong disciplinary powers over all who joined. The guilds established and enforced regulations governing wages and prices, the number and types of apprentices, and the weight and quality of merchandise. In assuming responsibility for the detection of faulty business practices, the guilds enjoyed the full support of the government, however much they might clash with the political authorities on tax matters. The government, for example, would not support the victims of a boycott, which was a powerful weapon over those who violated guild regulations. According to the rules of most guilds, offenses and disputes involving the members were to be submitted to the trade organization *before* the cases could be taken into the state courts. In cases where the guilds had been bypassed, the magistrates were likely to refer them to the guilds for decision.[39] If a guild found one of its members guilty of a serious offense, the culprit would be turned over to the authorities. A member who was in trouble but who, after investigation, was supported by his trade organization would have a portion of his legal costs defrayed by the guild. When a case came before a magistrate, he usually endorsed the prior decision of the guild. Chinese courts were strongly inclined to support guild rules, often citing them as though they were statutory enactments. Government officials decided civil suits in accordance with the customs of the locality, and these customs were usually the norms that had been given sanction by the guilds.[40] As Vinacke points out, "the successful magistrate kept on good terms with the guild officers, aiding them, when necessary, in the enforcement of guild rules and penalties, and working with and through them in the performance of the duties of his office."[41]

ENFORCEMENT PRACTICES AND PROCEDURES. Although smuggling and corruption were conspicuous features of Chinese economic and political life, the government attempted to enforce its regulations through the elaborate network of state administrators. These enforcement efforts were usually much more successful when a new ruling house first seized power than in its declining stages when the administrative brooms had worn thin and no longer swept so clean. As indicated earlier, the Manchu system began noticeably to disintegrate after 1850.

At the local level, of course, the burden of enforcement fell upon the district magistrate, who was directly responsible to his administrative superiors in the echelons above him. All these officials, from the viceroy down to the magistrate, were in a position to employ special agents to assist them in enforcing the regulations which flowed from Peking. In addition, the officials in the Censorate were instructed to keep a close watch over the administration of government affairs, and they had particular responsibility in the supervision of public works. The Department of Public Works also had responsibility in this field, including the inspection of weights and measures. Besides these regular officials, the government depended upon special inspectors to check the weight and quality of merchandise. The circuit intendants supervised the salt industry, the collection and transportation of grain, the waterways, and similar economic activities. After the turn of the twentieth century, when the government was promoting industrial development, it established the post of intendant of industries to inspect the work in factories and workshops.

As already indicated, however, a great deal of the regulation of economic activities was enforced by the guilds, with the overt support of the government.[42] The guilds, for all practical purposes, fixed the rules of trade in the private sectors of the economy and enforced compliance. These organizations usually had their own inspectors—and some employed spies—to check upon violations of the manufacturing and trading codes. In some areas, teams of guild inspectors, accompanied by a government policeman, would inspect the market places for substandard merchandise, turning the defrauding merchants over to the guilds for appropriate punishment. Sometimes the inspectors would question suspected offenders, and, after determining the nature of the violations, hand them over to the police. Punishment meted out by the guilds to their erring members was usually severe. If a guild member were found guilty of a breach of the commercial code, he could be fined, he could have some of his property confiscated, he could be flogged, or he could be expelled from the fraternity. Expulsion would probably result in commercial disaster for the offender, since, under guild rules, no other guild member was permitted to have any dealings with him. A guild member found guilty of a serious offense would probably be arrested by the guild and turned over to the government authorities.

Japan

In turning to Japan, it must be noted that the extent of the contribution made by the shogun's government to the satisfaction of the adaptive functional requisite was significantly less than it was in France and China. This can be demonstrated by a brief examination of the government's support and regulation of the economy and the means by which the regulations were enforced.

GOVERNMENT SUPPORT OF ECONOMIC ENDEAVOR. The Japanese shogun did not employ grants of privilege comparable either in nature or in scale to those that were distributed by the French monarch, and the tax concessions which he made were markedly different from the French model. The direct ownership and management of large-scale enterprise, which was characteristic of China, was not nearly so prevalent in Japan. The central government, for example, did not develop a unified system of water supply, and each clan or village was often left to handle the irrigation problem on its own.[43]

The central government of Japan, however, did develop several kinds of direct support of economic endeavor. Although figures on actual expenditure are lacking, one of the most significant of the government's activities appears to have been its support of land reclamation.[44] The shogun often furnished subsidies to those who were willing to engage in reclamation projects. In many cases, the work would be financed by merchant capital, and the government subsidy would consist of the remission or reduction of taxes on the reclaimed land. That the reclamation policy was largely successful is suggested by the fact that the fields under cultivation more than doubled during the Tokugawa period.[45]

Another type of government support for economic endeavor was especially noticeable during the early decades of Tokugawa rule. The shogun tried to encourage merchants to settle in his cities by giving them free business sites and liberal tax exemptions.[46] The townsmen of Osaka, for example, were excused indefinitely from the payment of taxes on their houses and lots. It must be emphasized, however, that these kinds of subsidies and tax concessions were hardly similar to those included in the French grants of privilege, since the Japanese made no systematic attempt to discriminate among various entrepreneurs in the same industry or to favor a certain industry.

When it came to direct economic management, the shoguns for the most part confined their activities to mining.[47] In the sixteenth century, the most important mines, especially those producing copper and precious metals, fell under the direct control (but not necessarily the ownership) of the shogunate, and the Tokugawa shoguns did their best to exploit them and make them productive. Ieyasu, for example, sought to increase the skill of the miners, and he enlisted the aid of Portuguese experts to help develop the metallurgical arts.[48] The interest of the central government in mining was directly related to the shogunal monopoly of the coinage, which was usually supervised by a government servant of noble rank.

During the closing years of Tokugawa rule, especially after the visit of Commodore Perry, the shogun began to take a more direct and active interest in the support of economic development.[49] He solicited the aid of foreign technicians, sent Japanese managers and students abroad for technical study, encouraged the importation of foreign machinery, and undertook the construction of dockyards, ironworks, and other industrial establishments which were based upon Western models. But even this type of activity involved relatively small amounts of capital when compared with the governmental expenditures of France and China.[50]

GOVERNMENT REGULATION OF ECONOMIC ENTERPRISES. While the shogun's efforts to support economic endeavor, both directly and indirectly, were on a relatively small scale, his government made numerous and significant attempts to regulate economic activity. These regulatory policies included control over the location of industry, prices and wages, and licensing.

The central authorities in Edo sought to protect agriculture against the inroads of commerce and manufacturing by trying to regulate the location of industry. Their primary aim was to confine industrial enterprises to the established centers and to prevent the movement of industry to the countryside.[51] On at least six occasions during the eighteenth and nineteenth centuries, for example, the government banned silk-weaving in the countryside, and the Kyoto merchants were forbidden to go into the rural areas to purchase silk cloth. The frequency of the decrees suggests that they were not very effective, and the prevalence of industry in the countryside by the nineteenth century is further testimony to the regime's inability to enforce its directives. In some of the rural industries, for example, there were work places employing as many as 100 people. By 1846, in the province of Kiryu, some 267 weaving establishments housed a total of more than 5,000 looms.[52]

Related to the policy of keeping industry out of the countryside were the shogun's regulations designed to keep the peasants on the land. Many decrees were issued prohibiting rural folk from moving to the cities, and peasants who lived in Edo were ordered to return to their native villages. Large numbers of peasants, however, left their farms to pursue other occupations.[53] As part of the program to stabilize agriculture, the shogunate in 1643 prohibited the sale of land (except in one province). But despite severe penalties, even against the officials who registered the sales, the law was frequently violated either in fact or in spirit through such devices as long-term leases.[54]

Throughout most of the Tokugawa period, the regime tried to regulate the price of rice and to prevent brokers from making huge profits from fluctuations in the value of this commodity.[55] At times the government tried to control the price by purchasing supplies of rice itself, while at other times it sought to establish the price by edict. Sometimes the shogun even loaned money to rice dealers to enable them to corner the market and thus push up the price. None of these measures, however, could be effectively enforced.

Other attempts on the part of the central government to regulate prices met with as little success. When the shogun tried to prohibit greenhouse men from selling vegetables out of season at inflated prices, the magistrates were unable to cope effectively with the wave of evasions of the restriction.[56] Similarly, when money-changers were forbidden by the shogun to enter into an association for the purpose of increasing their fees, the regulations could not be enforced, and ultimately the matter had to be turned over to the guilds.[57] Attempts to reduce pawnbroking rates provoked the brokers into closing their shops, and the shogun suffered loss of prestige.[58] As early as 1657, the central authorities had trouble with the rising charges in the building trade, and they ordered the builders to adhere to the "customary rates." When these edicts were violated, the government, besides threatening punishment, began to set wage rates in the industry. It was still trying to resolve the problem in the middle of the nineteenth century.[59] Other experiences with price and wage regulation were equally disheartening.[60]

The Tokugawa rulers also attempted to control certain types of commercial and industrial activities through a system of licensing. Under this arrangement, a limited number of individuals would pay a fee for the privilege of producing or dealing in certain commodities or of conducting trade in specified geographic regions. In many areas, however, the licensing schemes broke down, primarily because the shogun's government was often unable to protect the monopolies it had granted.[61] In the cinnebar trade, for example, the legitimate license-holders encountered such competition from illegal operators that the government in 1696 was forced to handle the problem by issuing more licenses.[62] Two years later, the Edo government placed restrictions upon the use of gold and silver foil for ornamentation because it was needed in coinage. But by 1705, the government itself was forced to undertake the sale of foil in order to curb illicit transactions, and even this scheme had to be abandoned within four years.[63] From time to time the shogun also took steps to curb speculation, excess profit-making, and cornering of the market, but most of these regulations proved to be unworkable.[64]

Perhaps the most far-reaching of the commercial regulations were those controlling foreign trade. Early in the Tokugawa period, the shogun embarked upon a policy of "isolation," closing the country to foreign trade except for Dutch and Chinese merchants who were granted certain trading privileges at Nagasaki, a city under the shogun's direct control. This restricted commercial intercourse with two foreign nations was officially regarded as a monopoly of the shogun. The monopoly, however, was often violated, especially by the hostile tozama clans in the south, who secretly sent their young samurai abroad for technical study and whose contact with foreigners became more frequent and open as the Tokugawa regime neared its end.[65] The central authorities even experienced great difficulty in keeping their grip upon the trading activities at Nagasaki.[66] The town authorities at the port developed a high degree of local autonomy, for the shogun's representatives, who lacked knowledge about business methods and practices, were inclined to leave matters to the city elders. Eventually much of the commerce in the port fell under their control, and their personal wealth grew correspondingly. When the central authorities sought to impose restrictions, their efforts were frustrated by smugglers and by the city-wide trading association which kept a double set of books. At times the merchants shipped out of the country more than their legal allotments of copper, and the shogun was forced to bear the loss. They also defrauded the shogun in the ginseng trade, and, when the Edo government sent out an inspector, he reported that the members of the trading association had been falsifying their accounts. As it turned out, however, the government was unable to bring the problem under control. Evasions of this sort were highly profitable, and many of the merchant barons at Nagasaki amassed huge fortunes by deceiving the central authorities.[67]

ENFORCEMENT PRACTICES AND PROCEDURES. It is apparent, then, that the central government of Tokugawa Japan did not make much of a contribution to the satisfaction of the adaptive functional requisite through its regulation of the economy. The decrees that were sent out from the shogun's palace were not enforced widely enough or regularly enough to make the regulatory policies effective. This is not surprising when one recalls the nature of the central decision-making structure, as described in Chapter 3. The fact that the administrative agencies were headed by a commission rather than by a single individual, that key administrators were rotated frequently, and that the central government was not in full command of the entire country contributed to the seeming inability of the shogunate to develop consistent policies and to enforce them vigorously.

The problem of enforcing the decrees of the central government presented special difficulties. As we have seen, the shoguns were forced to rely upon a bureaucracy which was largely staffed by the fudai daimyo, and was inadequate to penetrate the domains of the tozama lords. Within their own territories, the fudai daimyo would hardly be inclined to enforce enthusiastically the policies of the central government if the policies conflicted with their own interests. This was likely to be the case with much of the economic regulation that was applied outside the cities. The growth of manufacturing and commerce in the countryside, for example, was often to the advantage of both the tozama and fudai daimyo. By the same token, the shogun was unable to prevent the alienation of farm lands within the daimyo estates or to curb the speculative business practices that flourished there, because these areas were beyond his direct control.[68]

Thus, in contrast with France and China, the shogun did not have at his disposal a hierarchy of dependable administrative officials whose personal interests did not interfere with the faithful execution of the economic regulations which were issued in Edo. The Tokugawa rulers, to be sure, developed an intricate network of investigative agents who kept their eyes upon the feudal lords. While this device was perhaps adequate for exposing a disloyal lord whose behavior might justify the use of military force, it was a poor substitute for a regular civil service that could be made responsible for enforcing economic regulations. Violations of these decrees, however, were hardly serious enough to risk military action, which might provoke the recalcitrant lords into joint action against the regime.

It is a bit more difficult to explain why the economic regulations were not enforced more effectively in the large cities, which were directly under the jurisdiction of the Edo government and where the shogun could employ administrative agents responsible to the central government. Unlike the French intendant, however, the Japanese administrative official in the cities did not wield clear-cut authority. Each urban center had two or three magistrates who were supposed to look out for the shogun's interests. But these officials were required to rotate their duties—a system that was hardly conducive to the consistent enforcement of policies that might encounter strong local resistance. Moreover, the shogun's agents in the cities were not equipped to cope with the deceptions of the experienced merchants who carried on their negotiations behind the scenes, out of the sight of inspectors. Confronted by resistance from powerful local groups, the Edo representative was often tempted to let well enough alone, since local outbursts would reflect upon his administration and might cost him his job.[69] The difficulty of regulating economic life in the cities was further compounded by the fact that many of the provinces that sent goods to the urban centers were beyond the effective jurisdiction of the shogun's government.[70]

In seeking to enforce their regulations in the economic sphere, the Tokugawa rulers were unable to make as effective use of the guilds as did the governments of France and China. One reason why this was the case is that the Japanese guilds were a different kind of organization.[71] Although powerful guilds (*za*) had developed during the thirteenth and fourteenth centuries, they had declined by the time the Tokugawa clansmen seized control, being superseded by merchant associations (*nakama*), which were much less restrictive than the earlier organizations. Since at the outset the new guilds multiplied rapidly and placed no limits upon the number of members, their inherently monopolistic character was weakened. During the first century of Tokugawa rule, the central authorities were as a rule hostile to the guilds, which experienced great difficulty in imposing controls upon their members without the ultimate backing of the government. Eventually, however, when the violations of their regulations became too burdensome, the guilds petitioned the government for official recognition of their customary trading practices. In 1721, the shogunal authorities granted sanction to the merchant associations, seizing the opportunity to use them for a tighter control of commerce and to exact tribute ("thank money") from them in return for their official licenses.

But by this time the guilds were unable to become an effective mechanism for enforcing restrictions in the economic realm. They could not, for example, control the new industries which were mushrooming in the countryside. Even when a guild grew powerful and monopolistic, the shogun, who had come to rely upon the charter fees, was reluctant to enforce upon it the official controls that were considered by the merchants to be objectionable. When a guild was weak and faced competition from many unlicensed operators, it could not be effective in regulating an entire industry. Moreover, the government tended to extend monopoly privileges to other individuals (often in other cities), or even to grant charters to competing guilds.

In this way it became difficult for a single group of entrepreneurs to secure a tight, guaranteed monopoly; with so many groups operating legally in a given trade, they could not be effective in regulating economic activities throughout the industry.

Finally, in 1842, the shogun dissolved the guilds, apparently in an attempt to reduce prices. This action gave an impetus to individual enterprise. The ban on merchant associations was lifted in 1851, but the guilds re-emerged with greatly reduced powers. They were not only weakened by government regulations—rules against restrictive membership, excessive entrance fees, and certain monopolistic practices—but also the entrepreneurs from the countryside were developing greater wealth and power and were now in a better position to compete with their commercial cousins in the cities.

England

As was true of Japan, the extent of the English government's contribution to the satisfaction of the adaptive functional requisite was significantly less than it was in France and China. If legislation were to be effective, it had to be approved by the crown, the Lords, and the Commons. Since different economic interests were represented in these three bodies, it was difficult to achieve consensus on economic matters. And even when the central government could hammer out agreement on a policy, more often than not it encountered great difficulty in enforcing it.

GOVERNMENT SUPPORT OF ECONOMIC ENDEAVOR. To a limited degree in the sixteenth and seventeenth centuries, the English monarch supported monopolies, provided subsidies, and issued exemptions from certain taxes and other obligations. In the case of monopolies designed to encourage new industries—a small proportion of the monopolies granted—the crown sometimes granted subsidies and usually provided immunity from certain government requirements. At times the central authorities paid bounties on shipbuilding and fishing, and made provision for the supply of building materials and for the repair of harbors.[72] The crown also encouraged the immigration of aliens who brought with them technical know-how and supplies of capital.[73] In many instances the government provided the new settlers from the Continent with special facilities and declared them exempt from guild regulations.

A case which illustrates what often happened when the English government undertook direct support of an industry is that of the alum industry. In the sixteenth century the monarch granted control of this industry to a group of private patentees.[74] In 1609, however, the king took over the alum mines and farmed them out to contractors. Four years later, after this contractual arrangement had failed, the crown appointed its own managers to operate the mines, but within a few years the government lost an investment of about £100,-000 as a result of unwise expenditure and corruption on the part of its agents. Subsequent attempts by the king to withdraw from direct management of the alum industry by farming out the mines proved to be unsuccessful, and the crown kept having to intervene in the operation of the enterprises with a conspicuous lack of success.

Thus, compared with France, the English efforts at direct and indirect support of the economy were of little consequence. Even during the period of the government's greatest activity in the economic field, the proportion of gross capital formation that could be attributed to direct allocation by the central government was very small indeed.

GOVERNMENT REGULATION OF ECONOMIC ENTERPRISES. The most common types of monopolies that were granted by the central government in England were not related, as they were in France, to programs designed to pour public money into economic development.[75] Instead they were more closely related to the crown's efforts to collect revenue and/or to regulate economic activities. The revenue-producing aspect of the monopolies will be treated below in our discussion of goal attainment; their role as devices of economic regulation will concern us in this section.

Monopolies and other forms of licensing represented significant attempts by the central government to control economic activity. If an individual were to pay the crown for monopolistic privileges, he naturally expected the government to keep other producers out of the industry. This sort of regulation of access into a trade or industry was applied at one time or another to such industries as salt, glass, iron, playing-cards, soap, aqua vitae, oil, cloth, alum, gunpowder, gold or silver thread, calamine-stone, and other products. The history of these state-granted monopolies, however, was roughly the same in every industry where the system was tried. The king and his government experienced difficulty in enforcing effectively for any length of time the privileges they had granted. The unreliability of the enforcement apparatus, the lack of effective techniques to secure compliance, and the action of the courts which voided many of the crown's edicts combined to make the state-sponsored program of regulation through monopolies largely unsuccessful.

Long before the beginning of the industrial revolution in England, the central government had largely abandoned its policy of granting monopolies. The patents of monopoly provoked fierce resistance among the people, especially the merchants and the gentry, who objected to the exorbitant price increases and the narrowing of business opportunities. In 1601, Queen Elizabeth revoked some of the monopolies, and she conceded to the jurisdiction of the common law courts the determination of whether a patent was injurious to trade and industry. In 1624, the Statute of Monopolies limited the authority of the crown to issue letters of patent except for inventors and companies. For a time, especially while Charles I was on the throne, the exceptions made to companies provided a loophole in the law, and the king attempted to reap profits by granting monopoly rights to groups of merchants, many of whom were already engaged in the business. For more than a decade after 1629, the crown entered into contracts with companies of merchants and manufacturers, demanding payment in return for the issuance of patents. These schemes, however, were not entirely successful, for the patentees were usually well enough established in the particular line of business. Since many merchants and entrepreneurs were already enjoying the privileges presumably granted by the crown, they had no qualms about violating parts of their contracts. By this time the king had both common law and statute law against him, and the members of the House of Commons were not enthusiastic about underwriting the crown's claims which would increase its financial independence. In 1640, the Long Parliament terminated nearly all of the industrial patents, and a system which had never really flourished was for the most part destroyed.

Although the patents of monopoly, in addition to limiting the number of participants of an industry, included regulations governing the production and sale of goods, the central government sought to impose restrictions upon nearly all segments of the economy, especially after the decline of the guilds. These ordinances aimed to control the quality of merchandise, to regulate the processes of production, to prevent a rise in prices, and to direct the general economy in a manner reminiscent of the French kings.[76] In the sixteenth and seventeenth centuries, the crown issued minute rules concerning the quality of hops and malt in brewing, the size of bricks, and the type of materials to be used in the manufacture of thread, leather, soap, glass, tobacco, and a host of other products. The regulations that were applied to the textile industry were particularly detailed, specifying the kind and weight of materials to be utilized and the dimensions of the finished product. Textile manufacturers were also ordered to refrain from using "gig mills" and "tenter-frames." Included in the government's regulatory programs were provisions designed to hold down the prices of staple commodities so that ordinary people could buy them.

While these regulations were detailed and numerous and while most of them were presumably in effect during the period under consideration,[77] there is little more to be gained at this point in further elaboration. More important than the number and detail of the regulations is the fact that the government lacked the ability to enforce them.

Another set of official decrees and statutes attempted to regulate certain aspects of "labor relations," especially wage rates and the terms of apprenticeship. By the middle of the sixteenth century, the guild system had broken down, and in 1563 the crown and parliament enacted the Statute of Artificers which sought to regulate the wages of craftsmen and their terms of employment. Under this law, the justices of the peace were entrusted with the task of assessing the wage rates of workmen once a year with a view toward establishing just scales of remuneration. It also made a seven-year period of apprenticeship compulsory for all industrial workers. The Statute of Artificers, which was supplemented by other laws from time to time, remained on the books for more than two centuries.

The record of enforcement of the Statute of Artificers was not a good one from the government's point of view. The courts, as we shall see, interpreted the law as narrowly as possible, excluding from its operation many of the large-scale industries. The wage provisions of the law apparently received their best enforcement during the first century of its operation.[78] The pattern of wage enforcement, however, appears to have been spotted. Many of the justices of the peace were reluctant to make annual assessments in their localities, and it was common practice in some areas for them to reissue the same wage scales year after year. Sometimes the magistrates even ignored their own assessments, and, when they set wage rates that provoked the wrath of local entrepreneurs, they were inclined not to attempt to enforce them. During the eighteenth century, the system of wage readjustment was no longer applied on a broad scale, and freedom of contract in wage matters grew more prevalent.[79]

The government also tried to prevent the movement of industry away from the established manufacturing towns to the countryside.[80] During the fifteenth and sixteenth centuries, the cloth merchants began to extend their business into the rural areas where they purchased wool, hired farm folk to spin and weave it, and then sold the finished product. Since these activities were carried on outside the corporate limits of the older towns, the merchants were not bound by the restrictions of the guilds on trading practices, night work, number of apprentices employed, and so forth. This meant that adventuresome entrepreneurs could experiment with new forms of industrial organization in areas where there was an abundant supply of unregulated labor. The growth of this new industry encouraged farm laborers to leave their fields and to take up alternative forms of employment. This development was not pleasing to the government, and through a series of enactments the central authorities attempted to prevent the peasants from leaving the land and to restrict industry to the older town settlements. The problem of enforcing these statutes, however, rendered most of them inoperative, and by the 1620's the crown had abandoned its efforts to stop the spread of industry to the rural areas.

Equally ineffective was the policy pursued by the Tudor kings and their successors of protecting the customary land rights of freeholders and tenants by resisting the enclosure movement.[81] A series of statutes beginning in the latter part of the fifteenth century was designed to halt the enclosures, and the government sought to provide relief for victims of the enclosures through appeals to the Privy Council and the Court of Requests. These laws, however, were easily evaded, partly because those responsible for their enforcement were among the worst violators.

ENFORCEMENT PRACTICES AND PROCEDURES. Regardless of which aspect of government regulation of the economy is examined, the record in nearly every case forces one to a conclusion which may be summed up in a single sentence: The policy was unsuccessful because it could not be enforced. As E. Misselden asserted in 1623, "It were better to have fewer laws with better execution." [82] Unlike the monarchs of France and China, the English rulers were unable to rely heavily upon the guilds as instruments of enforcement, for these organizations had lost much of their capacity to regulate industrial affairs when entrepreneurs moved their operations to the countryside, beyond the orbit of guild control.[83]

In the sixteenth and early seventeenth centuries, as we have seen, the Privy Council and its various committees were the central gears in the administrative machine. They issued orders to the justices of the peace, and they summoned violators to Westminster when the local officials failed to apprehend them. After the Privy Council was stripped of much of its authority in the middle of the seventeenth century, however, the central administrative machinery was dismantled, and the local officials were left largely to their own devices in enforcing the policies of the central government.

In carrying out its commands in the local areas, then, the crown throughout this entire period was almost entirely dependent upon the part-time, voluntary services of the justices of the peace. These magistrates were natives of the localities they administered and were extremely sensitive to the needs and interests of their bailiwicks. When an order of the Privy Council was inimical to the "general welfare" of their regions, their loyalty to their own localities was likely to take precedence over their obligations to the crown unless great pressure was exerted from the center. They were understandably reluctant to enforce the regulations on apprenticeship when such action might create unemployment in their areas for which they would be expected to provide relief. Moreover, many of the justices were themselves deeply involved in the development of new industries and were fundamentally out of sympathy with most of the regulations the crown ordered them to enforce.[84] Indeed, the magistrates were frequently guilty of violating the crown's industrial codes. This was recognized very early by Edward VI: "Those men should be put from being justices of the peace that be touched or blotted with those vices that be against these new laws to be established; for no man that is in fault himself, can punish another for the same offence." [85] That the justices would rather evade than enforce many of the regulations was also acknowledged by the Privy Council in 1596-1597: "When the justices of peace . . . , whose duty is to reform those abuses, are themselves authors and maintainers of the same, no marvel though the poor people find no remedy nor our orders take effect." [86] A clothier who served as a magistrate was hardly a disinterested party when he set the wage scales for his own industry, but when clothiers were ordered not to serve as justices, many of them nevertheless remained in their posts.[87]

Nef reports a case which illustrates very well how the private interests of the justices of the peace interfered with their obligations to the crown, thus creating difficult enforcement problems.[88] The town charter at Bridgwater provided that no individual was to be permitted to brew or sell ale unless the malt had been ground at certain water-driven mills which were owned jointly by the crown and the Earl of Hertford. Before very long, however, the mayor of the town, who was also a justice of the peace, built a horse mill for grinding malt, setting himself up as a business competitor to the monopoly he was supposed to enforce. But more than this, he used the power of his office to force the brewers to use his mill, and he diverted the water supply so that the competing mill was unable to run at full capacity. When he was haled into court for his action, the crown was unable to make its case prevail against him. In a similar incident involving the enforcement of the salt patent, the biggest smuggler of salt turned out to be the justice of the peace who had personally received orders from the Privy Council to enforce the patent.[89]

If a justice of the peace did decide to bring the violator of an economic regulation into a common law court, he discovered that the judge and the law were often more in sympathy with the offender than with the crown. The common law courts could render a law inoperative or whittle down its effects in three ways. First, they could interpret statutes or decrees so narrowly as to significantly diminish their scope. The courts, for example, held that the Statute of Artificers applied only to those industries in existence when the law was passed in 1563. This meant that all of the new large-scale industries which mushroomed during the course of the next century—the drapery industry, certain metal trades, brickmaking, milling, and many others—were exempt from the restrictions of the law, and entrepreneurs were free to make their own labor contracts and to employ nonapprenticed workers.[90]

Second, the common law judges frequently ruled that the methods used to enforce a regulation violated the rights of the king's subjects. At the end of the sixteenth century, for example, the government issued patents to a number of people authorizing them to enter private dwellings and other buildings in order to search for saltpeter, which was necessary in the manufacture of gunpowder.[91] By the beginning of the seventeenth century, opposition to most patents of monopoly had grown formidable, and the saltpetermen were especially vulnerable. In 1625 the foremost judges in England placed restrictions upon the king's claim to saltpeter earth, upholding the right of a citizen to keep the king's agents off his property.

Third, the common law judges, taking the view that the common law had precedence over statute law (and particularly over royal decrees that had not been sanctioned by parliament), might void a regulation from Westminster on the ground that it violated the ancient property rights of English citizens. The monarch's attempts to develop mining as a crown monopoly were thwarted in this manner.[92] The early English sovereigns had claimed a universal regale over all minerals and ores beneath the soil. In the middle of the sixteenth century, the crown commissioned a number of individuals to develop and work the mines royal. These patentees were given authority to purchase land at reasonable rates and to use crown timber, and they were exempted from payment of certain tax assessments. As early as the 1560's, however, the judges established the principle that the monarch could press no claim upon the mines unless they contained precious metals, and later decisions held that these metals had to be present in substantial quantity before the rights of the crown could be honored.

Faced with the lax administration by the justices of peace and the hostility of the common law courts, the king and the Privy Council were compelled to search for ways to reinforce the inadequate system of control.[93] One method of improving the administration was through the appointment of men to enforce very specific provisions of the law. As early as the thirteenth century, for example, aulnagers were appointed to inspect each piece of cloth and to give it a seal if it conformed to the official regulations. By the seventeenth century, however, the clothmakers were simply purchasing the seals, and their products went to market without being inspected. In the middle of the sixteenth century, municipal officials were ordered to appoint public searchers who were responsible for uncovering defective merchandise. Neither of these attempts to develop more effective enforcement procedures met with a high degree of success.

Another way in which the king sought to strengthen his enforcement machinery was by having the Privy Council, the Star Chamber, the Court of Requests, and similar bodies summon offenders to Westminister for trial when the local magistrates refused to charge them or when local juries refused to convict. Such procedures worked a financial hardship on the poor complainants, and the central courts could not possibly handle all the violations.

The fate of the governmentally-established soap monopoly is an illustration of how these attempts to rely more heavily on central administration broke down. For a number of years the government tried to ferret out independent soapmakers, to try them before the Star Chamber, and to punish them with fines or imprisonment.[94] The local authorities were so hostile to the patent that the king was forced to send out special commissioners charged with its enforcement and even to develop a special set of officials who were directly subject to the monarch's command. Eventually, however, both the patentee and the Privy Council were forced to enter into negotiations with the principal offenders who purchased immunity against punishment for their violations.

Summary

In summary, then, it should be noted that the French government made a significant contribution to the satisfaction of the adaptive requisite through its grants of privilege, and that the government of China made a similar contribution through its participation in irrigation projects, the distribution of agricultural produce, the production of items consumed by state agencies, and the granting of monopoly privileges to particular individuals to sell specified staples. In both France and China, the government sought to regulate economic activities in minute detail. To achieve this objective, the imperial authorities relied heavily upon a centrally controlled bureaucratic apparatus, which worked closely with viable guild organizations.

In Japan and England, on the other hand, the government did not contribute very significantly to the support of economic endeavor. In both countries, the government did not participate to any great extend in the direct ownership and management of large-scale enterprise, and its grants of privilege to favored individuals fell wide of the mark because very often they could not be enforced against interlopers. Although the central authorities in Japan and England sought to enforce detailed regulations upon economic enterprises, they suffered from the lack of an effective, pervasive bureaucracy and from the absence of a broad range of techniques for securing compliance. Moreover, in both countries, the guild organizations were not as powerful as they were in France and China, and for this reason they could not be relied upon as efficient enforcement agents.

THE GOAL-ATTAINMENT FUNCTIONAL REQUISITE

Although the government in any society is likely to make a major contribution to satisfying the functional requisite of goal attainment by becoming involved in several of the relevant processes, this study is primarily concerned with only one of these processes: the mobilization of the society's resources for a societal effort. Two types of activities are involved in mobilizing these resources—those relating to the assessment and collection of state revenues, and those relating to the creation of credit.[95] Since the governments in all four cases were engaged in these activities, at least to some extent, the similarities or differences to be found will be largely procedural. Our concern, in other words, is with the systematic uniformities and divergencies in the manner in which state revenue was accumulated and the way in which credit was created.

France

In France, the decisions on who should be taxed, the amount of the assessment, and the method of collection were made by the king in consultation with his chief advisers. In the central policy-making structure the divergent interests of different classes of taxpayers were not directly represented, and there was little opportunity to block systematically decisions to increase old taxes or to levy new ones. Other than the size of the economy itself, the only significant limit upon the government's power to tax was the chronic shortage of state funds which prompted the monarch and his ministers to opt for small, immediate income in exchange for larger revenues over the long run. Before the mechanics of this choice can be explained, however, it will be useful to discuss the sources of state revenue in France.

TYPES OF TAXES AND THEIR YIELD. The greatest revenue-producing tax during the *ancien régime* was the taille, an assessment that could be either real or personal. In the former case, the tax rate was applied to the value of tangible property, while in the case of the latter it was levied upon income from all sources, or, alternatively, upon presumed wealth of all sorts.

In deciding the amount of money to be collected by the taille, the central authorities, as a first step, ordered the intendants to report on the ability of their respective provinces to pay the assessment. Armed with this information, as well as some estimates on the need for revenue, the king and the appropriate council then determined the total amount of the tax to be levied and the proportion that was to be collected from each province. Each intendant was instructed to forward to the central government a certain sum of money after he had collected the taille. In discharging his responsibilities, the intendant was expected to distribute the tax burden among the regions and municipalities in his district. In similar fashion a lower official, the *élu,* would levy an assessment upon each parish, and, finally, the tax collector collected the taille that was due from the individual taxpayer.[96] The *receveurs des tailles* were responsible for receiving the tax payments and for sending the receipts each month to the *receveurs généraux* who resided in Paris and who kept a general account in which the revenues from direct taxes were deposited.

Another important source of revenue for the French government was the gabelle—a tax on salt which was especially hated by the ordinary citizen. Despite the fact that it was not collected in all the provinces,[97] the yield of the gabelle during the seventeenth century was surpassed only by that of the taille.

The gabelle was collected through a virtual royal monopoly on salt. Some of the salt works were owned by the state, and the private producers in the industry were forced to sell all of their salt to royal warehouses at prices fixed by government officials. The fact that this "taxed salt" sold at from four to ten times the price that would ordinarily have been charged on the open market provided great incentive for smuggling. The government, of course, took vigorous action to prevent such illegal activities, and offenders—smugglers and customers alike—could expect long terms of servitude in the galleys. The central authorities even sought to alleviate the problem of smuggling by forcing people to buy minimum amounts of legal salt. In this way the customers' needs were partially met, and the opportunities of the smugglers were somewhat diminished. The annual receipts of the gabelle rose from about 460,000 *livres tournois* in 1523 to almost 20,-000,000 in 1641, and by 1783 they can be estimated at over 50,000,-000 livres.[98]

Although the nobility and clergy could not claim blanket exemption from the gabelle, most of them did enjoy exemptions of one sort or another. Many of the people in these social groups were permitted to purchase their salt directly from the government warehouses at a greatly reduced price.[99]

In addition to the gabelle, the French government levied a number of other indirect taxes. Sales taxes, called *aides,* were collected in about half of the French territory, being levied upon wholesale transactions or upon retail trade. In 1661 these taxes yielded 5,000,000 livres, but by 1783 the amount of revenue from this source had increased to 51,500,000 livres. *Traites* were essentially internal customs duties levied upon the movement of goods from one province to another. Although Colbert sought to eliminate these duties, his efforts were unsuccessful, and they remained in effect until 1787. Besides the aides and the traites, the government also collected fees on private sales of property and on the recording of transactions and other acts by notaries.

These indirect taxes—gabelle, aides, traites, and similar levies—were collected by "tax farmers." In charge of this operation were the farmers-general, who were usually a group of wealthy capitalists organized into a financial society. (There were only forty of them after a reorganization in 1726.) Collectively the farmers-general had a contract with the government under which they were given authority to collect the indirect taxes in return for the payment of a fixed annual sum to the royal treasury. In the eighteenth century the members of this group had about 20,000 employees working for them in the business of tax collection. An individual tax farmer could earn about 50,000 livres annually.[100]

Toward the end of the seventeenth century, the government introduced a new kind of assessment, the *capitation.* This was a poll tax levied in 1695 as a war emergency measure, but it was collected continually from 1701 until the revolution. For purposes of this tax, the public was divided into twenty-two classes according to presumed wealth, and each category paid a different amount ranging from one livre to 2,000 livres annually. Generally the clergy, some of the nobility, and a number of provinces purchased exemption from the capitation assessment. A similar type of tax, the *dixième,* was first levied in 1710, and was a direct assessment of 10 per cent. The rate was lowered to 5 per cent in 1750 (and the name was changed to *vingtième*), but was increased to 15 per cent in 1783. Again, the clergy, some members of the nobility, and some regions were permitted to purchase immunity.

Although the royal treasury often needed replenishing during the seventeenth and eighteenth centuries—indeed, at times it was bankrupt—there is no evidence to indicate that the central government lacked adequate powers of taxation. The financial plight of the government was more an indication of its enormous propensity to spend. Nef estimates that between 1540 and 1640 the revenues from taxation in France at least doubled, while in England all the crown revenue—from other sources as well as from taxation—remained at about the same level. By the end of his rule, Louis XIII was collecting from three to four times as much revenue from each of his subjects as Charles I was collecting per capita from people in England.[101] The tax revenues of the French monarch increased even further during the eighteenth century, partly as a result of the new tax levies already discussed.

Perhaps more significant than a discussion of the kinds of taxes that were levied is the question of which groups in the society footed the tax bill. As suggested earlier, the clergy and many of the nobility managed to escape the most onerous forms of taxation, and to the degree that agricultural wealth was in the hands of these groups, it bore a relatively light share of the tax burden. The enterprising craftsman or business entrepreneur who invested his savings in physical plant and inventories was hit heavily by the taille, the capitation, and the *dixième-vingtième* unless he held a grant of privilege that provided exemption.

OTHER SOURCES OF REVENUE. The central treasury in France could not depend entirely upon taxation to finance its activities, but commanded other sources of revenue. For example, it continued to collect old feudal dues until the revolution.[102] At times the monarch exacted interest-free loans from some of his subjects, and he was known to be careless about paying these debts.

A major portion of the king's income was derived from the sale of offices and the accompanying titles. Mousnier has compiled data on the income from the sale of offices both in absolute terms and as a percentage of total government revenue for the period 1600-1643. The proportion of state revenue that came from the sale of offices ranged from 3.75 per cent to 52 per cent. In 14 of the 44 years the figure was 30 per cent or more, and in two of the years it was 5 per cent or less. The mean was 21.8 per cent.[103]

During the reign of Louis XIV, government income from the sale of offices and titles reached new heights. There are, of course, limits upon the number of offices that can be created and sold at a profitable price. When the practice of passing on the offices and titles through inheritance became widespread, the crown experienced greater difficulty in selling newly created offices. Other strategies had to be devised. The problem, however, was no particular strain upon the imagination of Louis XIV. Nine times during his reign he proceeded to revoke certain categories of titles that had already been issued. On one occasion, for example, all the letters of patent conferring noble rank of a certain class were revoked, and on another occasion all of the letters issued after a given date were recalled. These revocations, of course, usually contained a proviso that exemption from the edict could be purchased, and in most cases the appropriate response was forthcoming.[104] At times of great financial need, prospective buyers of office were even *forced* to purchase noble status, leading one writer to comment that the king transformed commoners into noblemen in the same way that he made Catholics out of Protestants—with *dragonnades*. In more normal times, however, the king had little difficulty in finding buyers.

CREATION OF CREDIT. As equally important to goal attainment as the direct mobilization of societal resources through taxation is the creation of credit. This is an aspect of goal attainment on which Parsons and Smelser place a great deal of emphasis.[105]

In modern societies, the government is actively engaged in the creation of credit through banking systems which are state-owned or state-controlled. In *ancien France,* however, there was no government bank of any consequence,[106] and for this reason the government's role in banking activities need not concern us.

But even if government does not sponsor an adequate banking system, it can still make a significant contribution toward credit creation by maintaining a relatively stable currency. The maintenance of a stable currency, however, was something that was not accomplished in France until about fifty years before the revolution. Indeed, until that time the government actually followed policies that helped to make the monetary system unstable.

In order to explain how and why this was the case, it is necessary to distinguish between the monetary units that were used to make payments and those that were simply units of account. On the one hand, there were the *louis d'or,* the *écus d'argent,* and the billon or vellon currency (consisting mostly of copper) which were the coins of the realm. On the other hand, there was the money of account—the *livre tournois,* the *sou,* and the *denier tournois,* which were simply accounting units used to facilitate the handling of the many types of coin in circulation. The coins themselves carried no exterior markings of value, and since the legal value of the coin was fixed by the crown, the equivalence of coin in terms of units of account was easily manipulated. As a matter of fact, nearly 300 changes were made between 1300 and 1700, and about forty of these took place in the closing years of the seventeenth century.

The crown made these changes in order to help mitigate the shortage of bullion—a constant complaint in France during the sixteenth and seventeenth centuries—and to attempt to prevent the flight or hoarding of undervalued coins. In the terminology of the day, these changes in the value of money were effected by *augmentations* or *diminutions*. Augmentations, which decreased the metallic equivalent of the livre, required that the coins be taken to the mint so that a new mark could be imprinted (occasionally, the coins were melted down and recast), and the coins that were not brought in were legally proscribed. Diminutions, which increased the metallic content of the livre, were nominal in their operation, consisting merely of a decree by the crown that certain coins would be revalued.

The royal treasury, of course, was able to profit from manipulations of the currency. The monarch could benefit from an augmentation—he was able to decrease, for example, the value of his debts by giving fewer *new* coins for the *old* ones he had borrowed. Very often, in order to profit maximally from a revaluation, the king would have an augmentation preceded by a series of preparatory diminutions in anticipation of the actual augmentation.[107]

A specific illustration will help to explain this type of currency manipulation by the regime. On January 1, 1690, the *écu* was worth 3 livres 6 sous, but on August 1, 1693, as a result of four successive diminutions, the *écu* was worth 3 livres 2 sous. The *écu* was then increased as the result of an augmentation to 3 livres 12 sous on October 1, 1693. During the years 1700-1701, changes were made at an interval of two or three months; in 1708, the interval became one month.[108]

The constant revaluation of the currency did not cease until 1726, when under Louis XV the livre was finally standardized and stabilized, and currency manipulation ceased to be a conspicuous part of royal monetary policy.[109]

China

As in the case of France, the important decisions on public finance were made by the monarch, in consultation with his advisers but without any check by a legislative body representing the interests of the taxpaying public. The only important restraint upon the political authorities who might be interested in raising the land tax rates was the possibility that such action might provoke rebellion. Recurring treasury deficits, as we shall see, led to land tax increases in disguised form, the imposition of new taxes, and the adoption of policies designed to produce immediate income at the expense of larger revenues over the long term.

The central authorities in China, like their counterparts in France, fixed the size of their budget and then apportioned it among the various provinces according to the wealth of their resources, and the provincial administrators in turn assigned revenue quotas to the administrative subdivisions within their territory. At the bottom of the scale, the responsibility for actual tax collection fell to the district magistrate. Frequently the central government would assess the more wealthy provinces in order to finance projects in the poorer areas, ordering them to transfer the funds directly to the expenditure sites without transmitting the revenue through the national treasury. In any event, when the tax quotas were determined, the government officials at each administrative level would usually collect more than the quotas they were expected to send forward to the higher authorities, using the surplus to finance government operations within their jurisdiction and to augment their official salaries. In other words, only a part of the tax revenue collected found its way to the imperial treasure chest in Peking.[110]

TYPES OF TAXES AND THEIR YIELD. Throughout most of the Manchu era, the principal source of revenue was the land tax, which supplied more than three-fourths of the total state revenue until the last quarter of the nineteenth century.[111] Originally the land tax was a separate assessment on property which was paid in money and in kind. In addition, the government imposed a levy in the form of official labor service (*corvée*). Under the Ming dynasty, however, the labor conscription was converted to a monetary levy and combined with the land tax into a single system. Similarly, under the Manchu rulers, labor service was eventually merged with the tax on land to facilitate ease of collection, as was the head tax which they introduced.

About a decade before the merger of these two taxes, the emperor had decreed that henceforth the assessment on land was to be "fixed and immutable."[112] As the government officials in the provinces felt the need for additional funds, however, they succeeded in increasing the land tax through various ruses. They would levy an additional charge, for example, for melting the local currency into standard silver taels, and they would impose a "compensation tax" for the loss of silver in the melting.[113] Although the official rate of exchange was only 1,000 copper coins for 1 silver tael, local officials were known to charge four or five times that amount. Under these circumstances, the surtaxes became very heavy, varying from 10 per cent to as much as 50 per cent of the original assessment.[114] Although the emperor objected to these practices from time to time, the central authorities eventually legalized them.

In addition to the ordinary land tax, the Peking government also levied upon certain areas of the country tributary assessments in kind.[115] Provinces rich in particular resources were ordered to supply the government with such items as silk, copper, wax, timber, and porcelain. The provinces adjacent to the Yangtze paid tribute in grain in order that the population of Peking could be fed. Even when assessments were collected in kind, the taxpayer was not free from the accretions of the surcharges. In the case of grain, for example, he could be assessed for losses incurred in storage and shipment, or for a money equivalent in grain that exceeded the market price.[116]

Another important source of revenue during the Manchu period was the profit derived from the salt industry, which was in effect a tax reflected in the price of the commodity. As we have seen, the production and distribution of salt was under strict control by the government, although private individuals were licensed to engage in the trade. Administrative officials levied taxes and storage charges at the site of manufacture, the wholesale establishments, the depots, and the retail outlets—all of which were passed on to the consumer in the form of a greatly inflated price.[117] During periods of financial crisis, the government would increase the price of salt as a means of augmenting its revenue.[118] Until the middle of the nineteenth century, the salt tax along with the tax on metals (also a government monopoly) was usually second to the land tax as a source of public funds, and even after 1850 it continued to be among the major producers of revenue.

In addition to the levy on salt, the government imposed taxes that affected business enterprise.[119] Assessments were levied upon the production of reeds for fuel and thatched roofs; the transportation of tea; the sale of fish, sauces, and oils; mineral products from private mining; and the cultivation of poppies. Government officials also made use of octroi and local production taxes, stamp duties, and charges on the sale of property and the transfer of titles. Heavy taxation was imposed upon both the merchant and the consumer, commodities being assessed both before and after sale and the same merchandise being taxed each time it was moved to a different locale.[120] In addition, the government collected fees for the issuance of licenses which were required for all sorts of mercantile operations. These miscellaneous taxes were probably a more lucrative source of revenue for local officials than for the central authorities, and they were levied with increased frequency after the Taiping rebellion.

At the time of this disorder, the Manchu rulers faced serious financial difficulties, since they could no longer count upon revenue from the land and salt taxes in the areas of rebellion.[121] The rapidly increasing costs of government would probably have necessitated additional sources of tax revenue even without the rebellion. In an attempt to devise new sources of income for the public treasury, the authorities turned their attention to commerce and industry, introducing a special tax known as the *likin*. It was applied on a limited scale in 1853, but before long it was being collected in all of the provinces that were not under the control of the Taiping rebels. Traditionally, the Chinese had made use of a domestic customs levy, imposing duties on the movement of goods past certain points of collection. The liken, however, was a vastly expanded transit tax levied upon the value or weight of commodities and collected at stations or barriers in all the trade centers and along the main trade arteries. By the time of the revolution in 1911, revenue from the likin was nearly as important as the land tax as a revenue producer.[122]

These taxes bore unequally upon the several segments of the population. The gentry, for example, tended to shoulder less of the tax burden than any other social group.[123] They were exempted from the payment of all personal taxes, such as the head tax, and they and the members of their families were freed from the obligation of *corvée* labor service. For a time they were also legally exempt from a portion of the land tax, although this exemption was eventually removed. When the head tax and conscription service were amalgamated with the land tax, however, the gentry often managed to delay payment in the hope of eventually evading them entirely. As Chang points out, the exemptions from labor service or the converted tax relieved the gentry from a "substantial part of the tax burden. In practice their advantage was even greater, since their privileged positions enabled them frequently to escape extra charges and to pay less or none of the land tax for which they were supposed to be held responsible." [124]

Thus in China, as was the case in France, to the degree that agricultural land was held by the gentry, it tended to escape the full burden of taxation. The merchant and private manufacturer tended to pay proportionately higher taxes than the landed gentry. As we have seen, they were forced to pay license fees for the privilege of conducting their business, and, when they wanted to transport merchandise, they were subject to exactions at every likin barrier. Always on the lookout for new sources of funds, the government naturally turned to the merchants who constituted a wealth-accumulating group and who suffered from an official distrust of mercantile activities. In any event, the tax burdens grew increasingly heavy during the Manchu period, as evidenced by the expansion of revenue from *all* sources from 28,381,039 taels at the beginning of the era to 263,610,-000 taels at the termination of Manchu rule.[125] By paying both the direct and indirect levies assessed upon them, the merchants (as well as the peasants) were forced to carry a disproportionate share of the load.

OTHER SOURCES OF REVENUE. With the growing demands upon the imperial treasury, the Manchu rulers and the local officials were continually on the watch for lucrative sources of revenue. Local administrators, whose official salaries were shockingly low, not only levied extra charges wherever possible but also sought to cut themselves in on profitable business activities, exacting the appropriate "squeeze" in return for "protection." To meet their problems, the Peking authorities often solicited "contributions" from opulent subjects in order to defray the expenses of particular government schemes.

Many of these "contributions" were really cash payments in return for social titles and offices, for the Manchu authorities, like their counterparts in France, frequently resorted to the sale of social rank and appointments to office as a means of fattening the public purse. Although this practice in China dates back several centuries, it reached new heights during the Manchu era, when money began to compete significantly with legitimate academic attainment as a means of achieving high social status, that is, entry into the gentry class.[126]

Even before the financial crisis generated by the Taiping rebellion, the sale of titles and offices, especially in the lower echelons, was widespread in China. In the period from 1821 to 1852, the purchase of more than 315,000 studentships in the Imperial Academy produced nearly 34,000,000 taels of revenue, while similar sales between 1799 and 1820 brought into the government coffers almost 41,000,000 taels.[127] These transactions involved the sales of titles (more numerous than the purchase of actual office) which awarded status to the recipient and which was a requirement for advancement to office itself. Accession to office usually required an additional purchase at a much higher price. According to Chang, the title of circuit intendant might be purchased for more than 5,000 taels, but the actual office could command twice that price.[128] He estimates that among the upper gentry—those who actually held office or official titles—80,000 of them in the pre-Taiping period had risen via the examination route, while 40,000 had achieved their position through purchase. Approximately one-third the entire gentry group (350,000 individuals) were in the "purchase" category.[129]

Although the data are somewhat more scattered after 1850, they indicate clearly that the sale of titles and offices grew increasingly frequent following the outbreak of the Taiping rebellion. So financially pressed was the regime that it began to reduce the purchase price, selling some posts that had earlier commanded 1,000 taels for about 200 taels, or even 100 in the provinces.[130] Indeed, provincial officials called for blank title registrations so that the transactions could be expedited more quickly. In one province alone during a six-month period in 1860, some 600 titles were purchased. Among the upper gentry in the post-Taiping era, 100,000 had risen through examination, but an equal number had purchased their position. In the entire gentry group, 36 per cent (approximately 530,000 individuals) had bought their way up the ladder.[131]

CREATION OF CREDIT. The Manchu government was never able to develop and sustain an effective, stable system of credit in the territory under its control, and, when Western nations became active in China in the nineteenth century, they were forced to establish modern banks of their own which usually supplied investment loans to Chinese entrepreneurs. The native banks, which were usually affiliated with the bankers' guild but which operated as private partnerships, were not required to maintain cash reserves, and for the most part they did not enjoy the confidence of the Chinese citizen.[132] These banks, as well as ordinary moneylending agencies, were often managed by members of the gentry class and were closely linked with government, since the decisions of government officials (or official "protection") were crucial to their operation.[133] Around 1800, a national chain of remittance banks was established by enterprising businessmen of Shansi province, but these banks were chiefly concerned with transmitting funds, especially state revenue, from one place to another rather than with providing long-term loans for the development of productive enterprise.[134] Many of the Shansi bankers held official rank and had close connections with government.[135] In the absence of adequate credit institutions, the pawnshops became flourishing businesses by the middle of the eighteenth century, especially in the rural areas, making short-term loans on such commodities as grain, silk, and cotton and enabling many businessmen to engage in speculation.[136] Whereas the number of pawnshops totaled 7,685 in 1685, it had jumped to 23,139 by 1812, declining in the latter half of the nineteenth century because of inflation and competition from more effective banking institutions. Most of the pawnbroking loans were short-term advances for purposes of consumption rather than for long-term commercial or industrial investment. The gentry were also active in this business, cashing in on the high interest rates which often exceeded 3 per cent per month.[137]

The lack of a reliable credit system forced businessmen to depend upon currency for the major portion of their transactions.[138] Unfortunately, however, the monetary system was clumsy and unstable, suffering from the absence of a uniform standard. Copper coined by the government was a common medium of exchange, but there were many types of copper coins, and their value differed from place to place.[139] Silver ingots were another form of currency, but silver was left largely in private hands, unregulated by law, and the actual weight of the silver tael varied from area to area. It was possible that in a given city as many as sixty different kinds of currency would be in use, each continually fluctuating in value with itself and in relationship with other types of coins.[140] Under these circumstances, the money exchanges were kept very busy, and, according to custom, they extracted a fee for each transaction. After 1890, the value of certain currencies varied from mint to mint; and in December 1920 the Shanghai Tramway Company lost 29 per cent of its revenue through the depreciation of the fares that had been collected.[141] The issuance of paper money was equally chaotic, for the government introduced no effective system of regulation. From time to time notes were issued by the central government, by individual provinces, and by banks, private money-changers, and ordinary business concerns.[142] The government's unwillingness or inability to foster an efficient system of credit and monetary exchange handicapped business operations and placed a heavy burden upon merchants and consumers.

Japan

Since the direct rule of the Tokugawa ranged over only a portion of the Japanese area, the shogun's financial system through which most of the government revenue was collected was not nation-wide in scope. The first Tokugawa shogun, Ieyasu, saw fit not to impose a regularized system of taxation upon the feudal daimyo or upon the peasants who inhabited their domains.[143] This meant that each of the local lords had his own tax system, controlling exclusively the tax resources within his dominion, and the only "revenue" which the shogun could collect from these territories were "gifts" from the daimyo and the special assessments he might levy for public projects.

Within his private domain, the shogun and his advisers decided who should be taxed and the method of collection, but they had to give heed to the prevailing customs and "rules." [144] If the rate of land taxation exceeded the customary assessment, for example, the Edo government would encounter difficulty in collecting the revenue. That this age-long practice placed certain limits upon the shogunate is suggested by the fact that from 1716 to 1841 (a difficult financial period, for the most part) the average tax rate varied only from 33.02 per cent to 37.65 per cent.[145] The peasants, who bore the lion's share of the tax burden, played no formal role in deciding financial matters and could make their grievances visible only by lodging complaints with the government agents or by engaging in rebellion. The merchants, on the other hand, became a much more powerful group whose interests the shogun could not always afford to ignore. The central authorities were very slow to recognize that merchant wealth could be a lucrative source of revenue, and, by the time they decided that it could be systematically taxed, the merchants had grown sufficiently strong to make their protests heard.[146] Indeed, some wealthy entrepreneurs became the financial advisers of the shogun, and occasionally he sought the advice of the leaders of the commercial world on the financial questions of the day.[147] Thus, while the merchant group did not have formal representation in government circles as a matter of right, their wealth and power sometimes vaulted them into positions of influence where they could block or modify adverse policies through formal or informal pressure.

Within a daimial estate, of course, the local lord would decide taxation policy, levying assessments upon the land and upon other property and resources peculiar to his domain.[148] Although custom weighed heavily in determining the tax rates, some daimyo made excessive demands upon the inhabitants of their areas. Here again the peasant had little say in financial affairs, but members of the merchant class were often in a position to exert some influence, especially since the daimyo sought to attract them to their domains and sometimes made them business agents or consultants.[149]

TYPES OF TAXES AND THEIR YIELDS. Although the daimyo were not directly taxed by the Edo government, they did contribute in a variety of ways to the relief of the central treasury.[150] They assumed responsibility for the administration and defense of their home territories, and they furnished contingents of soldiers for guard duty in the capital and other strategic areas. They also met assessments levied by the central government for the building of castles, dikes, roads, and other public works, and, as we shall see, they sent to the shogun at regular intervals specified types of "gifts" which were really a form of "tribute tax."

It was anticipated, however, that the shogun (like the English monarch) would pay the expenses of his government largely out of the revenue derived from his own estates. The income from his private lands was the biggest item on the credit side of his budget, constituting about half of his total revenue.[151] This income might occasionally be augmented if he increased his holdings by dispossessing some daimyo of their fiefs; often when he seized such lands, however, he distributed most of them among his own retainers without adding a great deal to his own patrimony.[152]

Most of the income from the shogun's private domains came from the land tax, which was levied upon the peasants with serious penalties for nonpayment.[153] Although the rates varied with the type of land, they seem to have ranged from 30 per cent to 50 per cent of the crop yields. The usual practice was for the peasant to pay his assessment in rice, which was then sold by the shogun's agents and the proceeds in coin turned over to his treasury. The land tax, it should be noted, tended to favor the most enterprising and productive peasants. The assessment was based upon the periodic land surveys, and the tax remained the same until the land was surveyed again. This meant that a farmer who had sufficient capital to introduce technical improvements and thereby increased the yield was able to enjoy his gain tax free. In this way the improved lands of the relatively well-to-do peasants bore proportionately less of the tax burden than the poorer farms whose production records showed no rise.

By the middle of the eighteenth century, the growing demands upon the government had outrun the shogun's resources, and his financial plight forced him increasingly to look for alternative sources of revenue.[154] In addition to levying surtaxes on land, the shogun at various times imposed assessments on special kinds of property, such as fisheries, rivers, ponds, forests, water wheels, and urban land frontage. With increasing frequency, he sought to tax the resources of commerce and industry, usually through a system of licenses or charters: shipping, foreign trade, stock farms, dyers, second-hand dealers, whalers, sake-brewing, building construction, and the dealers or retailers in staples. From time to time, the shogun also levied special taxes on the ordinary citizens of his realm to pay for rice storage, official travel, ceremonial functions, and so on. Many of these taxes were temporary, and were sometimes discontinued when business was depressed.

In the early stages of Tokugawa rule, the shoguns failed to realize the importance of the merchants as a potential source of tax revenue.[155] As we have already seen, they invited private entrepreneurs to the cities and favored them with liberal tax exemptions, and, even when the central authorities began later to tax this group, the assessments tended to be relatively light. The merchants at Nagasaki, for example, were privileged to engage in a lucrative commerce with foreign traders, and their tax payments to the public treasury included only license fees and assessments on their residential property. The taxation of commerce and industry by the Edo government and the local lords tended to be "piecemeal, and not very effective," enabling the merchants to carry a disproportionately light share of the total tax burden.[156] According to one estimate of the situation in 1842—an era of high merchant taxation, compared with the early decades of Tokugawa rule—the breakdown of the tax load was as follows: peasants, 84 per cent; samurai, 12 per cent; and merchants, 4 per cent (not including their forced loans).[157]

By the time commerce and industry had fallen within the orbit of the shogunate's tax system, the merchants had grown powerful enough to resist some of the proposed levies. One of the early shoguns, for example, sought to impose a tax on goods in order to obtain money for a pilgrimage, but the results were so disappointing that he had to resort to currency manipulation.[158] During the Tanuma era (1767-1786), when a tax was imposed upon the silk trade, the wholesalers resisted the levy by refusing to purchase any more silk from the manufacturers. The depressed market in cloth soon prompted them to petition the government to abolish the tax.[159] During the closing decades of Tokugawa rule, the merchants increasingly opposed government interference with their commercial activities, and toward the end of the shogunate a number of ministers were removed from their posts because they had been unsuccessful in dealing with the powerful merchants.[160]

OTHER SOURCES OF REVENUE. In addition to ordinary tax receipts, the shogunate derived some revenue from the forests that lay within the Tokugawa domains and from the mines that were under the control of the central authorities.[161] These sources of income, however, proved to be uncertain and irregular and could hardly be regarded as dependable forms of public finance. After 1625, for example, the production of gold and silver rapidly diminished, leaving only copper as the mainstay of the mining industry. But apparently the Edo government did not take full advantage of the copper market, and the official price was lower than what the demand of merchants and foreign traders would have justified.

A more lucrative source of shogunal revenue took the form of "gifts" from the feudal daimyo, presented both in kind and in money.[162] Some of these gifts were offered regularly during certain seasons of the year, while others were sent forward on special ceremonial or festive occasions. At the outset of the Tokugawa period these donations were "gifts" in the ordinary sense of the term, and the lords presented them to the shogun lest they be suspected of disloyalty. As the pattern of feudal relationships became more settled, however, the Edo government issued decrees prescribing the nature and presentation of the gifts, and the presents from the daimyo tended to become a form of "tribute tax." The prescriptions governing this type of revenue became important midway in the Tokugawa period when some daimyo were inclined to present their gifts to certain feudal lords who had grown in power and influence. In addition to their obligation to present the shogun with gifts of this type, the lords of the outlying domains were expected to help finance his special projects, such as the building of castles, the construction of roads, and the erection of fortifications.

Another source of revenue for the Edo government was the "thank money" or fees collected from the merchants and guilds in return for charters permitting them to engage in specialized lines of industry or trade. These assessments, which do not appear to have been excessive, were usually paid at the time the monopoly was granted, and thereafter on an annual basis. The Nagasaki merchants, who probably enjoyed the most lucrative monopoly, paid only small compensation for their privileges, the amount of their assessment fluctuating from time to time. As the financial position of the central government deteriorated, the shogun tended to rely more heavily upon the "thank money." This is one of the reasons why the Edo authorities granted more and more charters, some of them competitive with those of existing guilds. When merchants engaged in illegal trading practices, the shogun was sometimes inclined to look the other way lest he deprive himself of the revenue gathered from this source.

As merchant wealth grew more visible, however, the shogun searched for ways to tap it in order to enlarge the public purse. Occasionally he confiscated the property of rich merchants who lived in lavish style, but such extreme action tended to generate discontent in the business community and was not as fruitful as "thank money." [163] Somewhat more successful were the shogun's efforts to draw upon the profits of commerce by imposing forced loans (*goyōkin*) upon well-to-do merchants and entrepreneurs.[164] Exactions of this sort were resorted to in the 1760's on the assumption that the merchants were contributing relatively little to the public treasury but were deriving great benefits from the state. Technically these contributions were loans for which the shogun was to pay interest, but in fact many of them were never repaid. Revenue from the merchant "contributions" was used to balance the budget when the shogunate's expenditures for public works, relief, and adjustments in the price of rice had grown excessive. In meeting these demands, however, the merchants were sometimes able to exact concessions from the central authorities. The government, for example, often promised not to confiscate merchant wealth, and sometimes the merchants as a group would negotiate reductions in the size of the loans that were levied upon them.

When the shogun became particularly hard-pressed for money, he resorted to debasement of the currency—an important source of public revenue in the closing decades of Tokugawa rule when forced loans and other sources of income became harder to obtain.[165] Such a practice, of course, was facilitated by the central government's monopoly over the coinage of metal. According to a report of the period 1828-1837, the Edo authorities made a profit of more than 9,000,-000 *ryō* by reducing the metallic content of the currency.[166] During this phase of Tokugawa rule, the income derived from recoinage accounted for approximately one-third of the total revenue collected by the shogun.[167]

CREATION OF CREDIT. The course of economic development during the Tokugawa period demanded an exchange system that would operate with some degree of regularity and uniformity over wide areas of territory. Even before the advent of the Tokugawa, the rise of the castle towns had fostered the growth of trade, encouraging the use of money in commercial transactions. The Tokugawa control system further stimulated economic expansion and the growth of a monetary system, for the daimyo who were forced to make periodic journeys to the shogun's capital at Edo found it convenient to convert their rice into money in order to meet the expenses of travel and residence. Thus, during this stage of Japan's development, markets expanded beyond the confines of the daimyo estates, money came into more general circulation, and the merchants began to develop a system of credit to meet their commercial needs.

Although the Tokugawa monetary system varied in effectiveness from time to time and suffered, especially during the latter part of the era, from debasement, the central government played a more active role in promoting a national currency than did the government of China. The unification of currency in Japan was begun and carried forward by the Tokugawa predecessors—Nobunaga and Hideyoshi—and the first Tokugawa ruler, Ieyasu, improved upon their work.[168] Thus at the outset the government assumed monopoly control over the coinage, forbidding the daimyo to engage in such practices, and the monetary system, based upon gold, silver, and copper, became much more standardized than in the past. Despite the establishment of a single, country-wide system under the control of the central government, however, there was the continual problem of adjusting the ratio of value among the three types of currency, and in general the system deteriorated, especially when the Edo authorities sought to make a profit through recoinage.[169] After 1765, the government permitted certain lords to mint iron and copper coins of their own, but the situation was never as chaotic as it was in China. At times some of the stronger shoguns set about to improve the currency and to gain its wide acceptance at uniform value. Under Yoshimune, for example, the central government embarked upon a program of recoinage without attempting to make a profit, and it established by law a fixed premium for the old coins.[170]

On the issuance of paper money, the Tokugawa rulers tended to take a conservative position. It was not until 1867 that they promulgated a decree authorizing the issuance of such money by the central government, and the ordinance was withdrawn shortly thereafter.[171] The shogunate also attempted to restrict the use of paper money by the daimyo, but it was largely unsuccessful in enforcing the restrictions, since the daimyo, prohibited from minting coins, asserted their right to issue notes.[172] Unless the daimyo were rich enough to have banking reserves in Osaka to redeem their notes, their paper currency was accepted only within their private domains. This meant that at any given time a wide variety of paper notes, some more valuable than others, would be circulating within the country. Since the daimyo were forced to buy goods and services outside their dominions, however, they needed a supply of money coins to meet their obligations, and this need helped to sustain the development of a national currency. The demand for money on the part of the daimyo and other groups in the society meant that they had to convert their rice into a common medium of exchange, and the merchants began to play an important role as middlemen in commercial transactions.

For its day Tokugawa Japan developed a fairly widespread and efficient credit system.[173] At the outset, of course, credit arrangements developed among the members of a given guild. As the commercial world grew more complex, however, an intricate system of credit institutions arose to facilitate business transactions among the merchants, daimyo, and the government in various sections of the country. Merchants who had performed as money-changers and exchange brokers eventually became bankers, and in this capacity they bought and sold currency, accepted deposits, made loans, and issued checks. The banking system at Osaka, which was the hub of the commercial world, sprang into being as early as the 1630's, and ultimately most of the business of the city was conducted by bank notes which were widely negotiable.

By the closing decades of the seventeenth century, ten of the leading Osaka financiers were organized to control banking transactions and to act on behalf of the government when necessary. The privileged position of the "Big Ten" was symbolized by their right to wear two swords and by their exemption from ordinary civic duties. These financiers acted as a central bank, handling government transactions and operating as the ultimate lending agency. They also sanctioned the entry of other people into the banking business, enforcing common regulations upon them. Other bankers besides the Big Ten were organized into subordinate institutions which handled the business in particular geographic areas. This pattern of organization was designed to regulate the banking industry from the center, to establish a mechanism for the settlement of commercial disputes before they reached the courts, and to provide the government with a hierarchy of control over the money market and the issuance of credit.

By the same token, individual merchants and wholesalers in different cities entered into credit relationships with each other, employing such instruments as bills of exchange, promissory notes, and checks issued upon bank deposits. At the behest of certain merchants, the shogun consented to having his monetary revenue, which had been converted from rice, transmitted to Edo by credit bills. The merchants would issue the notes upon receipt of the money, use the money to purchase their supplies, and then sell the supplies in Edo in time to pay off the notes when they became due. In this way the shogun was saved the expense of transporting the heavy coins, and the merchants were given the use of government money free for about sixty days. The Mitsui family was instrumental in developing this exchange system which soon expanded to other firms in many parts of the country.

It is important to recognize that the Tokugawa government gave firm support to the development of an efficient credit system.[174] The instruments of credit, for example, were for the most part given protection under the law and, if attempts at conciliation failed, were enforceable in the courts. While the central authorities sought to keep unsecured money claims involving interest ("money suits") out of the regular courts, they were concerned to give protection to money claims that were backed by security but which did not draw interest ("main suits"). These two types of suits were handled separately on certain fixed days of the court calendar. The debtors in money suits were treated more gently than were the defendants in main suits; they were usually given time to make limited payments until their obligations were discharged, though in cases of default the courts would issue an order of execution. When it came to main suits, however, the court judgment generally required that the debtor pay his debts in full on a prescribed date, and if he failed to do so, enough of his property was delivered to the creditor to cover the obligation. A favorable court decision also gave the creditor high priority in the distribution of a debtor's estate.

England

The English king, like the Japanese shogun, was not the unchallenged master of his ship when it came to financing the voyage into the modern age. From early times it was expected that he would finance the administration of the realm from his traditional feudal revenues—income from the crown lands, profits from the dispensation of justice, customary duties on imports and exports, and dues from feudal obligations. A number of these ancient levies had become fixed by usage and could not be increased without raising howls of public protest. The king was entitled to summon parliament when he needed supplementary revenue, but it was generally understood that this would be done only in cases of emergency, like domestic unrest or foreign war.

During the sixteenth century, the English monarchs began to feel the financial pinch, as they tried to adjust their relatively fixed revenue yields to the steadily increasing demands upon the state—expenditures to conduct wars, to quell rebellions in Ireland, to regulate commerce and industry on a national scale, and to help carry out welfare activities. As their financial condition worsened, the rulers were often forced to farm out the collection of the customs in order to insure a guaranteed revenue, to borrow money against the future collection of taxes, and even to pawn their property, including the crown jewels. The situation grew especially critical during the reigns of James I and Charles I, when the public treasury was depleted and the occupants of the royal palace tottered on the knife-edge of bankruptcy. Clearly the ordinary sources of crown revenue were inadequate to meet government needs, and additional income would have to be found.

In seeking a way out of his financial plight, however, the king was handicapped by the limitations placed upon the royal prerogative, for both parliament and the courts were vigorously asserting their rights against the crown. The monarch was not entitled to levy certain assessments merely by issuing a royal edict, and when he summoned parliament to more frequent sessions, the members seized the opportunity to exact concessions from him and to whittle away the authority of the crown.[175] When the king sought to increase his extraparliamentary revenue, he impinged further upon the rights of his subjects, thus creating new grievances for which the members of parliament would demand redress. As parliament grew in stature and importance, it insisted upon its right to approve the imposition of major taxes as well as any increases in existing levies. And as the landowning and business interests increased their representation in the House of Commons, they strongly resisted taxation measures that would hurt them financially. The result was that the English people—and especially the entrepreneurial classes—carried a relatively light tax burden, and the king, who was often compelled to follow an unpopular course of action in order to relieve his treasury, became embroiled with powerful forces in the society and eventually lost his long, drawn-out struggle with the parliament.

TYPES OF TAXES AND THEIR YIELD. Direct taxes were never as important a source of revenue in England as they were in France and China. As one reign succeeded another, they became proportionately less significant to the public treasury than customs duties and excise duties, at least until parliament was able to bring the crown more tightly under its control.[176] The imposition of direct taxes upon the king's subjects tended to provoke popular resistance which made assessments difficult to collect. As a rule it was understood that the government would resort to direct taxation only in times of dire emergency.

The traditional form of direct taxation was the "fifteenth" and the "tenth." [177] Originally this tax was levied as a fraction of a citizen's "movables" or personal property—a fifteenth in the case of a county and a tenth for a town. When the assessment generated opposition in the 1330's, it was gradually converted into a fixed sum from each local district, and the local authorities apportioned the amount of their obligation among the residents within their jurisdiction. Until its abolition in 1623, this tax usually produced about £39,000 annually for the king's treasury, although at times certain areas (like the "decaying" towns) would be exempted from payment. When this fixed amount of revenue was insufficient, parliament would sanction an assessment upon the counties and towns equal to several fifteenths and tenths.

Since the levy of the fifteenth and tenth proved to be inadequate to meet the crown's financial needs, the Tudor monarchs supplemented it with the "subsidy." [178] This was usually a tax of four shillings for every pound of land value and two shillings and eight pence in the pound for personal property valuation. Further subsidies were granted to Queen Elizabeth by imposing a levy of six shillings in the pound upon the clergy. As in the case of the fifteenth and tenth, the assessment of property values soon became stable, and each subsidy grant tended to the same as the one preceding. The tax yield from these subsidies was far below expectations. Whereas at the outset of Elizabeth's reign the subsidy was producing about £100,000, the yield had dropped to £80,000 by the time of her death. Six subsidies granted in 1640-1641 brought in only £420,000, and four subsidies levied upon the clergy and laity in 1663 produced only £282,000.

The yield from this form of direct taxation hardly corresponded with the rapidly expanding wealth of the country during this period. In Gloucester, for example, where prosperous merchants had bought land, only 79 people paid £10 or more of subsidy, while among the wealthy of London, no one was assessed at more than £200 worth of personal property.[179] The inability of the crown to tap the fortunes of landowners and entrepreneurs was recognized by Sir Walter Raleigh. "Our estates that be £30 or £40 in the queen's books," he pointed out, "are not the hundredth part of our wealth." [180] The disappointing return from the subsidy resulted in its abandonment in 1663. After experimenting with a system of monthly assessments, parliament instituted in 1691 a tax of four shillings in the pound on both land and personal property values, but the revenue from this tax also tended to become fixed, and the tax itself eventually became an imposition on land.

At various times the monarch sought to augment his revenue by instituting a poll tax, which was usually graduated according to rank and income.[181] When this capitation levy was first introduced in the fourteenth century, it precipitated fierce resistance from the peasants. Revived in 1513, it produced only £50,000 out of an estimated revenue of £160,000. It was reinstituted on several occasions by Charles I and Charles II for military purposes, but it proved to be such an unpopular assessment that evasions were commonplace. The tax in 1692 produced only about half of the revenue that was expected, and this method of public finance was dropped after 1698.

Equally unpopular among the people was the hearth tax, which was introduced in 1662.[182] This measure levied a tax of two shillings upon every hearth in a house (except for poor domiciles), thus getting at people in the lower economic brackets who did not ordinarily pay direct assessments. Rigorous enforcement involved house-to-house inspection, which met with widespread resistance and rendered collection difficult. During the last year of its operation, the hearth tax produced revenue in the amount of £200,000, but the crown abandoned it in 1689. Seven years later parliament approved a somewhat less objectionable house tax which levied two shillings upon every home, the rate rising according to the number of windows in a dwelling.

When Charles I tried to finance his government without summoning parliament, he issued a series of writs for "ship money." [183] While it had always been understood that the port towns would supply their quotas of ships for the navy during times of emergency, Charles' policy was to order the ports to furnish in peacetime a number of ships of prescribed size, or to pay the crown an equivalent in money. Furthermore, he soon began to levy this assessment upon the inland towns as well as the ports. This was considered to be a form of direct taxation without parliamentary consent, and opposition to these measures increased with each new effort to collect the money. Popular feeling was so strong in some sections of the country that the constables refused to proceed with the assessments. During the period from 1634 to 1642, the attempts to collect the ship money yielded a total of about £742,000. This method of public finance was brought under parliamentary control by the Long Parliament, which assembled in 1640.

Although the government had experimented with a graduated income tax in the fifteenth century, the scheme was quickly dropped and was not revived until 1799 when William Pitt introduced an income tax to help finance the war with France. [184] This represented the government's first real attempt to tap the new wealth which had long been accumulating in the kingdom.

In an effort to enforce these direct taxes in the face of popular resistance, the government established an elaborate network of collection agents. [185] A high commissioner, who was directly responsible to the exchequer, was appointed for each shire, and commissioners were placed in charge of the various districts under his jurisdiction. These commissioners selected a large number of collectors to act as their agents, and they had authority to obtain payment by sale of the property of delinquent taxpayers. In the case of the hearth tax, special inspectors or "chimney men" were entitled to enter people's homes to make sure that the assessments were accurate. The collectors, however, usually encountered difficulty in trying to obtain the desired amount of revenue from the king's subjects. As early as the fifteenth century, for example, the people of the north resisted the subsidy, and, when the Earl of Northumberland tried to assist the commissioners, he was slain.[186] It was perhaps expecting too much for the commissioners to enforce realistic assessments upon their prosperous neighbors and associates when they themselves were making tax payments far below what their actual wealth justified. The English people did not take kindly to the imposition of direct taxes, and most attempts to introduce new forms of raising revenue in this way met with such stubborn opposition from the landlords, merchants, entrepreneurs, and ordinary citizens that the new levies proved to be unsuccessful.[187]

An important part of the crown revenue was derived from customs duties imposed upon the import or export of such commodities as wool, liquor, currants, silk cloth, tobacco, tea, and other merchandise. The collection of this revenue by the king was of long standing, and, when the direct taxes turned out to be fixed in their yield, he sought to increase his nonparliamentary income by issuing new rate scales from time to time and by levying supplementary imposts without legislative consent—a policy that incurred the anger of the merchants. In 1688, port duties were the most lucrative of all the tax levies, contributing £992,000, to the public treasury, an amount roughly equal to the revenue produced by the hearth tax and the excise taxes combined.[188] As time advanced, however, the customs revenue increased proportionately much less than did the other forms of indirect taxation, producing in 1739 only £1,400,000, or about one-fourth of the total tax resources. After 1567 the customs were for the most part farmed out to private individuals, often to prosperous merchants, who paid a fixed rent to the crown for the privilege of collecting the duties.[189]

The excise tax, which was introduced in 1643, was levied upon articles of consumption produced domestically.[190] At the Restoration a "hereditary excise" was granted to the king in return for the abolition of his ancient feudal dues, and "temporary" excises, which tended to become permanent, were levied from time to time, especially on spirits. Although the excise levies were unpopular, they came to be an increasingly significant source of crown revenue as the king and parliament grew pressed for funds. Whereas the excise tax produced only about one-third of the tax revenue in 1688, the proportion had increased to more than one-half by 1739. By the end of the eighteenth century, the excise was levied on approximately 27 different articles.[191] It must be recognized, too, that the issuance of licenses to individuals who desired to engage in a particular line of business was really a disguised excise tax, since in most instances the license fees were passed on to the consumer in the form of higher prices.

In examining the English tax system during this period, one is struck by the relatively light tax burden which was carried by the people until the beginning of the nineteenth century. As pointed out earlier, Louis XIII in France was probably able to collect about three or four times as much from each of his subjects than was Charles I, even though the middle and lower classes in France were probably less able to afford the assessments.[192] The situation was admirably summarized by Francis Bacon: "He that shall look into other countries, and consider the taxes, and tallages, and impositions, and assizes, and the like, that are everywhere in use, will find that the Englishman is *most master of his own valuation* and the least bitten purse of any nation in Europe." [193]

Among the English taxpayers themselves, the merchants and entrepreneurs were touched more lightly than other groups in the population. The poorer classes bore more than their share of the burden as a result of the increased prices caused in part by the customs and excise duties. The landowners, too, whose property was stationary and visible, were hit harder than the tradesmen and other business groups, for the personal property tax enacted in 1691 became in practice a tax on the land.[194] The taxes paid by the business and industrial classes bore little relationship to the wealth they were rapidly amassing. What property taxes they paid were at a fixed rate and based upon outmoded assessments; they paid no income taxes until 1799 and no inheritance taxes of any consequence until late in the nineteenth century.[195] As Dowell asserts, wealth during this period was expanding rapidly, but "the rich paid but a very small quota to the ordinary taxes." [196]

OTHER SOURCES OF REVENUE. In financing the rising costs of government, the king was continually on the lookout for nonparliamentary sources of revenue, since parliament and the courts kept restricting his power of taxation and his subjects kept resisting increased or new levies. As we have seen, he received some income from his personal lands, but the size of his patrimony rapidly diminished when he was forced to put his lands up for sale in order to balance the crown budget. This was especially true of James I and Charles I, who each derived about £650,000 during the course of their reigns from the sales of crown property.[197] For a long time the monarchs also secured revenue from the traditional feudal dues, but parliament abolished these at the time of the Restoration, guaranteeing the crown an annual grant of £100,000 to be financed by the hereditary excise.

The crown also derived some revenue from the issuance of charters, patents of monopoly, and licenses which authorized individuals or companies to engage in particular trades, businesses, or professions. In early times, the king had granted charters to the towns and market areas in return for fees and annual payments—a practice that eventually loosened the crown's control over the towns and market places. As the financial plight of the Tudor and Stuart monarchs grew more desperate, they resorted increasingly to the issuance of monopoly privileges to favored individuals or groups in return for the payment of an initial fee and an annual rent in fixed sum or an amount based upon units of production or sale. The patents of monopoly, however, proved to be an uncertain source of income for the crown. They provoked such storms of protest that many of them had to be canceled, they became difficult to enforce because enterprising people found ways to evade them, and the monarch could not command an efficient enough bureaucracy to insure that the proper amount of revenue would be sent to the treasury. Apparently Charles I was somewhat more successful in utilizing the monopolies as a source of public finance than were his predecessors.[198] The alum patent, which at the outset had required outlays of crown capital, produced £126,000 in the period from 1629 to 1640, and the soap monopoly brought a total of £122,000 from 1634 to 1640. The patent on playing cards and dice provided the crown with £750 annually. While other monopolies were producing modest amounts during Charles' reign, the coal, salt, and brickmaking patents were not enforced for very long and produced little revenue.

Ordinary licenses which authorized individuals to peddle merchandise, to sell tobacco and strong beverages, to do auctioneering, to operate hackney coaches, or to engage in other occupations turned out to be annual permits for which the crown collected yearly fees in addition to the larger initial payment. Occasionally these could be manipulated in order to produce a windfall for the exchequer. In 1570, for example, the licenses of all alehouses were canceled and their owners forced to procure new charters before they could do business.[199] By the end of the reign of Charles I, the wine licenses were producing an annual revenue of £30,000, while the tobacco licenses were bringing in an additional £13,000.[200]

Although impecunious English kings sought to copy the French system of collecting revenue from the sale of offices, the practice never became widespread, and the crown could not gain a regularized income of any large amount from this source.[201] The sale of offices apparently reached its peak in the period of 1612-1628, but even during this time the traffic was never on a scale even closely comparable to that of France and China. One reason for this was the limited number of offices at the disposal of the king. The central government, as we have noted, functioned with a small bureaucracy, turning most of the administrative responsibility over to the local authorities; apart from the customs, there were relatively few opportunities to purchase lucrative posts in tax farming; and both parliament and the courts tended to resist the efforts of the monarch to create new offices. Existing officeholders were inclined to look upon their posts as proprietory holdings which were beyond the reach of the king. They insisted upon the right to appoint their own subordinates (usually for a fee) and to sell their offices themselves. This meant that the crown treasury derived little benefit from such transactions. Even in the local areas, where the bulk of the government business was carried on, the number of purchasable posts was much smaller than in France and China. According to one study, for example, there were in London area "at least 163" offices at the beginning of the eighteenth century, and these represented a value of £107,-860. A number of large offices, to be sure, were at the disposal of the king, and he was able to use these as a source of revenue. In 1620, for example, Sir Henry Montague is reported to have paid the crown £20,000 for the Lord Treasurership. Sales of this magnitude were often disguised as royal loans. In any event, it is important to recognize that the traffic in the sale of offices was much more limited in England than in France and China, that a large proportion of the sales was among officials themselves and from these the crown derived little benefit, and that the monarch's share of offices available for sale grew even smaller after the Restoration.

The early Stuarts were deeply involved in the sale of honors, but here again the practice never grew as widespread as it did in France and China. Financially hard-pressed, these monarchs sought to increase the number of titles available and to secure varying fees for dispensing the honors.[202] But the number of titles they distributed was comparatively very small, and the revenue derived from the sale of honors was never a large part of the crown's budget. When the sale of titles was at its peak under the Stuart monarchs, approximately £200,000 were paid out in known transactions, a large portion of which went to the members of the king's entourage rather than to the monarch himself.

The crown sometimes attempted to increase its revenue through gifts and benevolences.[203] Queen Elizabeth, for example, received gifts from the nobility and the more prosperous gentry on special occasions, and certain towns were known to have offered collective gifts. When James I needed money to meet the crises in international relations, he attempted to secure gifts or benevolences from his subjects, exerting considerable pressure upon them. In 1614, he ordered the sheriffs and justices of the peace to collect gifts for him, but even under duress his people contributed only £66,000. Other attempts to solicit benevolences were even less successful. On one occasion he managed to get £28,000 from the Privy Council and the City of London, but the rest of his subjects kept their purses closed. Despite the king's threats to appoint people to public office without remuneration or to assess them quotas of supplies for the army, his people did not respond enthusiastically to his financial pleas.

When Charles I attempted to persuade his people to make a gift to the crown and they refused to comply, he resorted to the method of forcing loans.[204] The justices of the peace were ordered to collect from every person an amount equal to what he would have received had parliament granted him four subsidies. The judges of the courts, however, refused to certify that this method of public finance was legal, and the crown's efforts to collect the loan failed. Benevolences and loans without the consent of the parliament were prohibited in 1628 under the Petition of Right.

The crown also resorted to loans of a nonpublic nature in an effort to balance its budget. Frequently the king borrowed money from private individuals, using as security the anticipated revenues from licenses and monopolies. After the revolution in 1688, the king was forced to carry on his war with France with considerable amounts of borrowed money. As a result, the debts of the crown expanded rapidly, a sizable fraction of the notes being held by foreign investors. Since the authority of the king had by this time become severely limited, the parliament was compelled to assume more responsibility for financing the state administration, and ways had to be found to fund and to repay the public debt in a systematic fashion. It was partly in response to this need that parliament granted a charter to the Bank of England.[205]

CREATION OF CREDIT. Compared with France, the English were able to develop a relatively stable currency early in the period we are concerned with, partly because there was very much less debasement of the coinage.[206] Henry VIII and Edward VI had caused much hardship by cheapening the currency, but Queen Elizabeth ordered all of the debased coins to be brought to a special mint and exchanged for new coins of truer value—a policy that greatly strengthened the country's monetary basis. Since the English people relied upon silver to settle their domestic transactions and upon gold to pay their foreign accounts, the government experienced considerable difficulty in maintaining a proper ratio which would prevent the withdrawal of the overvalued coins from circulation and the outflow of one or the other metals to foreign countries. The authorities tried to resolve the problem by assigning arbitrary values to both the silver and gold coins. After some experimentation along this line, the government finally adopted the gold standard in the eighteenth century. Thus, when compared with most other countries, England after Elizabeth suffered relatively little from alterations in the currency, and by the middle of the eighteenth century the country enjoyed the benefits of a single standard of value. The comparatively stable system of currency helped to foster reliable methods of extending credit. The rapid increase in commercial activity in the sixteenth century stimulated an increase in the use of credit which the government was unable to restrict.[207] Inland bills of credit soon became transferable through the custom of merchants, and by the beginning of the eighteenth century these bills of credit had been given legal sanction, and promissory notes had been made assignable by endorsement. By the middle of the nineteenth century, the vast majority of business transactions in London were being serviced by checks, a practice that was growing more widespread in the countryside.

The strength of the credit system, of course, was exhanced by the growth of an effective banking system, as well as by the development of the law of contract and tort. A long struggle over the question of usury had eventually resulted in the official sanction of this practice—a development that set the stage for the growth of banking institutions.[208] For a long time, the merchants and financiers kept their uninvested funds either on their own premises or in the Tower of London. The confiscations by Charles I, however, made the Tower an unreliable place to deposit private cash, and people with money began to deposit their excess funds with the goldsmiths of London. By the end of Elizabeth's reign, this practice had already been made secure by certain rulings laid down by the common law judges.[209] Under the common law, the property which an individual handed over to a second person for safekeeping remained the property of the original depositor. The courts held that this principle applied to the money that was deposited with the goldsmiths, provided that the money was placed in a sealed box. Before very long, the goldsmiths began to pay interest for the funds that were entrusted to them, because they were making loans to individuals who needed credit.

The need for credit, however, far exceeded the goldsmiths' ability to provide it, and after the Restoration businessmen felt the need for a broader system of banking institutions. Fortunately for them, the government was also in need of great amounts of credit, and its financial plight eventually resulted in the establishment of the Bank of England.[210] The crown, whose revenues were inadequate to meet its obligations, had long been accustomed to borrowing money from abroad. However, when the sources of foreign credit began to dry up, it was forced to turn to domestic suppliers, especially when it had to meet the costs of war. Toward the end of the seventeenth century, the struggle with France created a financial crisis for the monarch, who had accumulated a large debt but who could not command sufficient confidence among the masses to borrow large enough loans from them. When additional credits were needed in 1694, the government granted a charter to a group of merchants for the establishment of a large, private bank with authority to receive deposits, grant loans, and issue notes of credit. The Bank provided a secure base for the issuance of paper money, and it enabled parliament to exert greater control over the loans negotiated by the crown—a situation that encouraged greater stability in the financial world.

The credit system was further expanded through the development of provincial banks, many of which were organized by wealthy merchants who had accounts with the Bank of England.[211] While only a few of these banks were in existence in 1750, they were operating in nearly every market town by the end of the century. The release of coins through these banks increased the purchasing capacity of the ordinary citizen, and the need for credit precipitated by the expanding market was met by these banking institutions which gathered in the surplus cash of small savers. That more money was being injected into the investment stream is indicated by the decline in the interest rate, which fell from 8 per cent in 1695 to only 3 per cent in 1760.[212]

Summary

In all of these four cases, the government made similar contributions to the satisfaction of the goal-attainment functional requisite; in each instance it mobilized societal resources. There were, however, important procedural differences. The amount of revenue which the central authorities derived from taxes and allied sources was much greater in France and China than it was in Japan and England. Furthermore, in both France and China, the most prestigious classes tended to escape the brunt of the tax system, while the members of the merchant and entrepreneurial class were hit heavily by the tax collector. In Japan and England, on the other hand, the aristocratic classes were not permitted to evade their responsibilities in the field of public finance, while the mercantile and industrial groups bore a relatively light tax burden. When it came to the matter of establishing a healthy system of credit, we find that the central authorities in France and China failed to establish a uniform system of currency and habitually manipulated the value of their coins, thereby impeding the creation of credit by private individuals. In Japan and England, however, the government had more success in stabilizing the currency, and a more effective system of credit was developed.

THE ADAPTIVE AND GOAL-ATTAINMENT REQUISITES: PATTERNS OF SIMILARITY AND DIFFERENCE

In considering the contribution of government to the satisfaction of the adaptive and goal-attainment functional requisites in these four cases, the following patterns appear to emerge:

1. In both France and China, the government made a significant contribution to the adaptive functional requisite. Through special grants and/or direct government ownership or support, large amounts of investment capital were poured into the economy. By controlling

this investment, the government made important decisions about which industries would be developed and which firms (or individuals) within a given industry would be supported. In addition, the government enunciated minute regulations concerning how much of what products would be produced by specified production techniques. In seeking to enforce these regulations, the government operated through a relatively effective bureaucratic apparatus and through a strong guild structure.

2. In Japan and England, by contrast, the direct contribution by government to the adaptive functional requisite was of much less consequence. In these two countries, there was little government ownership or government management of productive enterprise, and relatively less government capital was poured into investment. Again, in comparison with France and China, the regulation of trade and manufacturing was not nearly so effective. The central authorities in Japan and England, of course, attempted to regulate industry and commerce on a broad scale and in great detail. But they were hampered in their efforts not only by the lack of a resolved structure of policy making but also by the absence of a reliable enforcement mechanism. The governments in both countries were unable to command the services of a dependable bureaucracy that extended into all sections of their territory, and the weakness of the guild organizations made it difficult for the authorities to employ them effectively as regulatory agents.

3. Although, as we have just seen, the government in all four cases contributed to the satisfaction of the goal-attainment functional requisite, the mercantile and manufacturing groups in France and China were forced to carry a disproportionately larger share of the financial burden than the aristocracy, and, in addition, a viable system of credit was not developed.

4. In Japan and England, the aristocratic classes were unable to escape so much of the tax burden, while the resources of industry and commerce were not subjected to oppressive tax measures. In these two countries, moreover, a fairly effective credit system was fostered.

NOTES

1. One note of caution is necessary. No attempt has been made to examine in detail all of the activities of government that are conceivably related to these two requisites. In this study, presentation has been limited to those activities that enable us to distinguish between our two sets of cases.

2. For the period 1540 to 1640, see John U. Nef, *Industry and Government*

in France and England, 1540-1640. For other comments on an earlier period, see Germain Martin, *La grande industrie sous le règne de Louis XIV, 1660 à 1715,* pp. 22-23; Charles W. Cole, *Colbert and a Century of French Mercantilism,* Vol. I, pp. 365-369.

3. For a description of these taxes, see below, pp. 127-128.

4. For details on the grants of privilege, see P. Boissonnade, *Colbert,* pp. 38-50; Cole, *Colbert and a Century of French Mercantilism,* Vol. I, pp. 235-239; Vol. II, pp. 135-216. Certain cities also enjoyed monopoly privileges. (See Warren C. Scoville, "The French Economy in 1700-1701: An Appraisal of the Deputies of Trade," *The Journal of Economic History,* Vol. 22, No. 2, June 1962, pp. 242-243.)

5. Martin, *La grande industrie sous le règne de Louis XIV,* p. 414. The figures presented by Boissannade for 1669-1672 are in some cases significantly higher than Martin's. His estimate of total grants from 1664 to 1683 is 3,700,-000 livres. In one year (1669) grants totaled 535,705 livres. They were insignificant during the Dutch War (1672-1678), but were increased again at its conclusion. Boissannade also points out that Colbert forced municipalities to make direct subsidies, but no estimate of the amount involved is given. (See *Colbert,* p. 49.)

It is exceedingly difficult to provide much information which will make the sums given in livres very meaningful. On the basis of information given by Goubert, one can estimate that the livre was worth about two man-days of labor in the wool industry in the seventeenth century. (See Pierre Goubert, *Beauvais et le Beauvaisis de 1600 à 1730,* p. 327.) Nef reports that Queen Elizabeth's ministers considered the pound sterling to be the equivalent of ten livres tournois in 1581-1582. By about 1640, the livre tournois had depreciated in value relative to the pound so that one pound was worth about fourteen livres tournois. (See *Industry and Government in France and England, 1540-1640,* pp. 126, fn. 13; 128, fn. 20.) Nef also reports that between 1540 and 1640 the annual wages earned by an unskilled workman in England seldom rose above £5 to £6, and almost never reached £10. (*Ibid,* p. 11.)

6. Boissannade, *Colbert,* pp. 49-50. See also Cole, *Colbert and a Century of French Mercantilism,* Vol. II, p. 134; Martin, *La grande industrie sous le règne de Louis XIV,* pp. 10-16 (see pp. 315-324 for some examples); Germain Martin, *La grande industrie en France sous le règne de Louis XV,* pp. 197-232. For some fascinating illustrations of the problems that the government involvement in industry created for one entrepreneur, see Paul W. Bamford, "Entrepreneurship in Seventeenth and Eighteenth Century France: Some General Conditions and a Case Study," *Explorations in Entrepreneurial History,* Vol. 9, No. 4, April 1957, pp. 204-213.

7. Martin, *La grande industrie en France sous le règne de Louis XV,* pp. 210-232; Henri Sée, *Economic and Social Conditions in France during the Eighteenth Century,* pp. 151-161; Bamford, "Entrepreneurship in Seventeenth and Eighteenth Century France," pp. 205-206.

8. See Cole, *Colbert and a Century of French Mercantilism,* Vol. II, pp. 378-379, 408-409. Additional details are presented in the works of Boissannade and Martin, cited in note 6 above.

9. Cole, *Colbert and a Century of French Mercantilism,* pp. 398, 415. In 1700, all but two deputies of the Council of Trade subscribed to the view that "commerce is presently too constrained both internally and externally. More than anything else it needs to be free." (Scoville, "The French Economy in 1700-1701," p. 234.)

10. Cole, *Colbert and a Century of French Mercantilism,* Vol. II, p. 436. See also Eli F. Heckscher, *Mercantilism,* Vol. I, pp. 140-152.

11. D. C. Coleman, "Economic Problems and Policies," in F. L. Carsten (ed.), *The New Cambridge Modern History*, Vol. V, pp. 40-41.

12. For examples of the instructions to the intendant to enforce the regulations, see Cole, *Colbert and a Century of French Mercantilism*, Vol. II, p. 428.

13. *Ibid.*, p. 417. See also Martin, *La grande industrie sous le règne de Louis XIV*, pp. 116-124; *La grande industrie en France sous le règne de Louis XV*, pp. 88-99; Heckscher, *Mercantilism*, Vol. I, pp. 153-155.

14. Martin, *La grande industrie sous le règne de Louis XIV*, pp. 337-341. However, the intendant was the key enforcement official. The first of the sixty-five articles of instructions for the *inspecteurs* directed them to report to the intendant for orders. See Cole, *Colbert and a Century of French Mercantilism*, Vol. II, 418-426 for a translation of these instructions.

15. Martin, *La grande industrie sous le règne de Louis XIV*, pp. 121-122.

16. Cole, *Colbert and a Century of French Mercantilism*, Vol. II, p. 429.

17. *Ibid.*, p. 434.

18. *Ibid.*, pp. 439-440.

19. *Ibid.*, p. 440.

20. See Heckscher, *Mercantilism*, Vol. I, pp. 166-175, 295; Nef, *Industry and Government in France and England, 1540-1640*, pp. 13-57; Cole, *Colbert and a Century of French Mercantilism*, Vol. II, pp. 431-441.

21. K. C. Hsiao, *Rural China: Imperial Control in the Nineteenth Century*, pp. 284-286; T. T. Ch'ü, *Local Government in China under the Ch'ing*, pp. 155-156.

22. See, for example, C. T. Hu, "The Yellow River Administration in the Ch'ing Dynasty," *Far Eastern Quarterly* (now *Journal of Asian Studies*), Vol. 14, No. 4, August 1955, pp. 505-513.

23. See Hsiao, *Rural China*, pp. 144-146.

24. See L. S. Yang, *Money and Credit in China: A Short History*, p. 8.

25. Charles O. Hucker, *The Traditional Chinese State in Ming Times (1368-1644)*, p. 31.

26. *Ibid.*, p. 32.

27. See E. Balazs, "The Birth of Capitalism in China," *Journal of the Economic and Social History of the Orient*, Vol. 3, Part 2, August 1960, pp. 207-211.

28. Hucker, *The Traditional Chinese State in Ming Times*, p. 32; S. K. Chen, *The System of Taxation in the Tsing Dynasty, 1644-1911*, p. 77.

29. Chen, *The System of Taxation in the Tsing Dynasty*, pp. 33, 43-44.

30. Balazs, "The Birth of Capitalism in China," pp. 207-211.

31. Ellsworth C. Carlson, *The Kaiping Mines (1877-1912)*, pp. 12-21.

32. See Balazs, "The Birth of Capitalism in China," pp. 211-213; P. T. Ho, "The Salt Merchants of Yang-chou: A Study of Commercial Capitalism in Eighteenth-Century China," *Harvard Journal of Asiatic Studies*, Vol. 17, No. 1-2, June 1954, pp. 130-168; Hosea B. Morse, *The Trade and Administration of the Chinese Empire*, pp. 100-103.

33. C. L. Chang, *The Chinese Gentry: Studies on Their Role in Nineteenth-Century Society*, p. 184.

34. Norman Jacobs, *The Origin of Modern Capitalism in Eastern Asia*, pp. 30-32, 48-50.

35. Tadashi Negishi, *Chūgoku no Girudo* (Guilds of China), p. 27.

36. *Ta-Ch'ing hui-tien shih-li* (The Collected Institutes of the Ch'ing Dynasty, Cases and Precedents), Li Fan Yuan, Chuan 983, Kuang Hsu Edition, 1899, U. S. Library of Congress microfilm copy, pp. 1-4.

37. Negishi, *Chūgoku no Girudo*, p. 24.

38. For a discussion of Chinese guilds, see "Chinese Guilds and Their

Rules," *The China Review,* July-August 1883, pp. 5-9; D. J. Macgowan, "Chinese Gilds or Chambers of Commerce and Trade Unions," *Journal of the China Branch of the Royal Asiatic Society,* Vol. 21, (1886), pp. 133-192; Hosea B. Morse, *The Gilds of China;* Edward T. Williams, *China, Yesterday and Today,* pp. 189-204; John S. Burgess, *The Guilds of Peking;* Sidney D. Gamble, *Peking: A Social Survey,* pp. 161-202; Negishi, *Chūgoku no Girudo.*

39. Sybille Van der Sprenkel, *Legal Institutions in Manchu China: A Sociological Analysis,* p. 95.

40. See Macgowan, "Chinese Guilds or Chambers of Commerce and Trade Unions," p. 140; Thomas R. Jernigan, *China's Business Methods and Policy,* pp. 109-110; Williams, *China, Yesterday and Today,* pp. 203-204.

41. Harold M. Vinacke, *A History of the Far East in Modern Times,* p. 13.

42. On the disciplinary powers of the guilds, see Gamble, *Peking,* p. 192; Williams, *China, Yesterday and Today,* p. 195.

43. Takao Tsuchiya, *The Development of Economic Life in Japan,* p. 32.

44. Takao Tsuchiya, "An Economic History of Japan," *Transactions of the Asiatic Society of Japan,* (2nd Series), Vol. 15, December 1937, p. 156; John W. Hall, *Tanuma Okitsugu, 1719-1788: Forerunner of Modern Japan,* pp. 63-64. See also George Sansom, *A History of Japan, 1615-1867,* p. 181.

45. See Neil S. Smith (ed.), *Tokugawa Japan,* p. 19.

46. See Charles D. Sheldon, *The Rise of the Merchant Class in Tokugawa Japan, 1600-1868* pp. 8-11; Y. Takekoshi, *The Economic Aspects of the History of the Civilization of Japan,* Vol. I, p. 522.

47. There were some government monopolies, chiefly related to foreign trade, and these were operated through a license system, which was only partially effective. See below, pp. 142-143.

48. Takekoshi, *The Economic Aspects of the History of the Civilization of Japan,* Vol. I, p. 546. The central authorities also established an iron monopoly in 1780, but this encountered opposition and had to be abandoned seven years later. (See John W. Hall, *Tanuma Okitsugu, 1719-1788,* p. 77.)

49. George C. Allen, *A Short Economic History of Modern Japan, 1867-1937,* p. 22; Thomas C. Smith, "Introduction of Western Industry to Japan during the Last Years of the Tokugawa Period," *Harvard Journal of Asiatic Studies,* Vol. 11, June 1948, p. 141.

50. While considering the support of economic endeavor by the central government in Japan, some mention should be made of the types of economic enterprises that were being sponsored by the individual daimyo in their respective domains. Many of the feudal lords sought to develop the resources of their own territories. They produced and sold for commercial purposes such commodities as sugar, candles, paper, wax, textiles, glass, indigo, and silk. (See Albert M. Craig, *Chōshū, in the Meiji Restoration,* especially pp. 27-29, 45-50; Smith "Introduction of Western Industry to Japan during the Last Years of the Tokugawa Period," pp. 149-151; K. I. Choi, "Tokugawa Feudalism and the Emergence of the New Leaders of Early Modern Japan," *Explorations in Entrepreneurial History,* Vol. 9, No. 2, December 1956, pp. 79-80. For a report of economic activities in Yonezawa, see Robert N. Bellah, *Tokugawa Religion: The Values of Pre-Industrial Japan,* p. 112.) In the declining years of the Tokugawa, this manufacturing activity was extended into such things as shipbuilding, munitions works, and small-scale factories. These activities, however, did not necessarily involve agents of the local government in the economic enterprises. Although it seems impossible to differentiate between the two, a distinction should be drawn between a daimyo investing his private funds and a daimyo investing tax revenues which he had collected. In the case of a feudal lord investing his private funds, he was acting as a private entrepreneur, and

the investment did not involve *government* activity. Some daimyo granted concessions to private individuals as a means of encouraging economic activity within their fiefs. In some instances they established government agencies to direct commercial and industrial enterprises within their territories.

51. See Thomas C. Smith, *The Agrarian Origins of Modern Japan*, p. 76; Matsuyo Takizawa, *The Penetration of Money Economy in Japan*, p. 80.

52. Edwin O. Reischauer and John K. Fairbank, *East Asia, the Great Tradition*, pp. 640-641.

53. Smith, *The Agrarian Origins of Modern Japan*, pp. 111-112; Sheldon, *The Rise of the Merchant Class in Tokugawa Japan, 1600-1868*, pp. 11-12, 27; Eijiro Honjo, *The Social and Economic History of Japan*, pp. 173-177.

54. Takizawa, *The Penetration of Money Economy in Japan*, pp. 72-74; Tsuchiya, "An Economic History of Japan," pp. 153, 159; Honjo, *The Social and Economic History of Japan*, pp. 38-39, 238.

55. See Hall, *Tanuma Okitsugu, 1719-1788*, p. 62: Takizawa, *The Penetration of Money Economy in Japan*, pp. 65, 106; Takekoshi, *The Economic Aspects of the History of the Civilization of Japan*, Vol. II, pp. 248-250, 299-300, 491; Honjo, *The Social and Economic History of Japan*, 220-224.

56. Takizawa, *The Penetration of Money Economy in Japan*, p. 68.

57. *Ibid.*, pp. 44-45.

58. Smith, *Tokugawa Japan*, p. 103. Sheldon points out that usury restrictions in general were not obeyed. (See *The Rise of the Merchant Class in Tokugawa Japan, 1600-1868*, p. 79.)

59. Takizawa, *The Penetration of Money Economy in Japan*, pp. 63-64.

60. See Smith, *The Agrarian Origins of Modern Japan*, pp. 111-112.

61. This happened in the oil-making industry of Yamato province. (See Smith, *The Agrarian Origins of Modern Japan*, p. 79. See also Hall, *Tanuma Okitsugu, 1719-1788*, pp. 75-76.)

62. Takekoshi, *The Economic Aspects of the History of the Civilization of Japan*, Vol. II, pp. 480-481.

63. Takizawa, *The Penetration of Money Economy in Japan*, p. 37.

64. Takekoshi, *The Economic Aspects of the History of the Civilization of Japan*, Vol. II, p. 491.

65. See Allen, *A Short Economic History of Modern Japan, 1867-1937*, p. 16; George C. Allen and Audrey G. Donnithorne, *Western Enterprise in Far Eastern Economic Development: China and Japan*, pp. 188-189.

66. See Takekoshi, *The Economic Aspects of the History of the Civilization of Japan*, Vol. II, pp. 124-182.

67. *Ibid.*, especially p. 135.

68. Tsuchiya, "An Economic History of Japan," p. 159; Smith, *Tokugawa Japan*, p. 101.

69. See Takekoshi, *The Economic Aspects of the History of the Civilization of Japan*, Vol. II, pp. 134-135, 248; Takizawa, *The Penetration of Money Economy in Japan*, p. 89; Hall, *Tanuma Okitsugu, 1719-1788*, p. 119.

70. Takizawa, *The Penetration of Money Economy in Japan*, p. 137.

71. The materials on the merchant guilds in Tokugawa Japan have been drawn from John H. Wigmore, "Materials for the Study of Private Law in Old Japan," *Transactions of the Asiatic Society of Japan, Transactions of the Asiatic Society of Japan*, Vol. 20, Supplement, 1892. Part I, pp. 143-158; Takekoshi, *The Economic Aspects of the History of the Civilization of Japan*, Vol. I, pp. 233-243, Vol. II, pp. 136-140, 482; Takizawa, *The Penetration of Money Economy in Japan*, pp. 55-59, 66; Smith, *Tokugawa Japan*, pp. 13, 79-116; Allen, *A Short Economic History of Modern Japan, 1867-1937*, pp. 13-14, 23; Reischauer and Fairbank, *East Asia, The Great Tradition*, pp. 639-641; Yetaro Kinoshita, *The Past and Present of Japanese Commerce*, pp. 87-88;

John W. Hall, "The Tokugawa Bakufu and the Merchant Class," *Occasional Papers*, No. 1, 1951, pp. 26-33.

72. Milton Briggs and Percy Jordan, *Economic History of England*, pp. 98-99. Although a few of the subsidized industries were successful, the costs of production were often so high that their markets were restricted, and when the subsidy was exhausted, they went out of business. (Herbert Heaton, *Economic History of Europe*, p. 397.)

73. Briggs and Jordan, *Economic History of England*, pp. 100-102, 160-162. See also M. W. Flinn, *An Economic and Social History of Britain*, pp. 98-100; William S. Reid, *Economic History of Great Britain*, p. 163.

74. See William H. Price, *The English Patents of Monopoly*, pp. 82-101; Ephraim Lipson, *The Economic History of England*, Vol. III, pp. 372-373.

75. See Lipson, *The Economic History of England*, Vol. III, pp. 352-386; Price, *The English Patents of Monopoly*, pp. 3-46, 62-81, 102-132; Flinn, *An Economic and Social History of Britain*, pp. 98-100; Nef, *Industry and Government in France and England, 1540-1640*, pp. 89-120; Hermann Levy, *Monopolies, Cartels, and Trusts in British Industry;* M. A. Abrams, "The English Gold- and Silver-Thread Monopolies, 1611-1621," *Journal of Economic and Business History*, Vol. 3, No. 3, May 1931, pp. 382-406.

76. See Nef, *Industry and Government in France and England, 1540-1640*, pp. 28-30, 47-48, 50-52; Reid, *Economic History of Great Britain*, p. 178; Lipson, *The Economic History of England*, Vol III, pp. 319-330.

77. A report published in 1792 listed no less than 311 laws governing the operation of the woolen trade alone. (See Lipson, *The Economic History of England*, Vol. III, p. 319.)

78. On the wage assessments, see *ibid.*, pp. 256-263, 274-276; Hugh O. Meredith, *Outlines in the Economic History of England: A Study in Social Development*, p. 193; Frederick C. Dietz, *An Economic History of England*, p. 258; William Ashley, *The Economic Organization of England: An Outline History*, p. 105.

79. See Lipson, *The Economic History of England*, Vol. III, pp. 266-270.

80. See *ibid.*, Vol. II, p. 68; Flinn, *An Economic and Social History of Britain*, p. 101; Reid, *Economic History of Great Britain*, p. 144; Richard H. Gretton, *The English Middle Class*, pp. 100-101.

81. See Nef, *Industry and Government in France and England, 1540-1640*, pp. 132-134; Dietz, *An Economic History of England*, p. 258; Lipson, *The Economic History of England*, Vol. I, pp. 154-157.

82. Quoted in Lipson, *The Economic History of England*, Vol. III, p. 319.

83. See *ibid.*, pp. 330-351; Reid, *Economic History of Great Britain*, pp. 142-143, 178; Nef, *Industry and Government in France and England, 1540-1640*, p. 26; Stella Kramer, *The English Craft Gilds and the Government: An Examination of the Accepted Theory Regarding the Decay of the English Craft Gilds;* William Cunningham, *The Growth of English Industry and Commerce in Modern Times*, p. 26.

84. See Nef, *Industry and Government in France and England, 1540-1640*, pp. 46, 56-57; Heckscher, *Mercantilism*, Vol. I, pp. 251, 260-261.

85. Quoted in Lipson, *The Economic History of England*, Vol. I, p. 156.

86. Quoted in *ibid.*, Vol. II, p. 430.

87. Ashley, *The Economic Organization of England*, p. 104.

88. Nef, *Industry and Government in France and England*, 1540-1640, pp. 52-53.

89. Edward Hughes, *Studies in Administration and Finance, 1558-1825: With Special Reference to the History of Salt Taxation in England*, pp. 62-63.

90. See Lipson, *The Economic History of England*, Vol. III, pp. 263-264,

281-282; G. N. Clark, *The Wealth of England from 1496 to 1760*, pp. 86-87; Barry Supple, *Commercial Crisis and Change in England, 1600-1642: A Study in the Instability of a Mercantile Economy*, p. 155; T. K. Derby, "The Repeal of the Apprenticeship Clauses of the Statute of Apprentices," *The Economic History Review*, Vol. 3, No. 1, January 1931, pp. 67-87.

91. See Nef, *Industry and Government in France and England, 1540-1640*, pp. 89-98; Lipson, *The Economic History of England*, Vol. III, pp. 358-359.

92. On the participation of the English crown in mining ventures, see Nef, *Industry and Government in France and England, 1540-1640*, pp. 98-101; Price, *The English Patents of Monopoly*, pp. 49-61; Cunningham, *The Growth of English Industry and Commerce in Modern Times*, pp. 59-61.

93. See Lipson, *The Economic History of England*, Vol. III, p. 327.

94. See especially Price, *The English Patents of Monopoly*, pp. 119-122.

95. Talcott Parsons and Neil J. Smelser, *Economy and Society*, pp. 56-64.

96. For an interesting example of this process, see Pierre Dubuc, *L'intendance de Soissons sous Louis XIV, 1643-1715*, pp. 199-200. The intendant could petition the central government for a reduction in the tax quota for his district. See A. Babeau, *La Province sous l'ancien régime*, Vol. II, p. 151, for an example of a reduction received by Turgot when he was intendant in the Limousin. For a discussion of exemptions from the taille, see below, pp. 181-182. A good general discussion of taxes and their yields is found in Maurice Block, *Statistique de la France comparée avec les autres états de l'Europe*, Vol. I, pp. 332-342.

97. In the middle of the sixteenth century, a number of provinces purchased perpetual exemption from the gabelle for 1,743,500 livres. This is one example of how the need for immediate income reduced tax revenues in the long run. See Nef, *Industry and Government in France and England, 1540-1640*, pp. 76-83. A more detailed account for a later period is to be found in E. P. Beaulier, *Les Gabelles sous Louis XIV*.

98. Nef, *Industry and Government in France and England, 1540-1640*, p. 83. Nef further reports that this figure of 20,000,000 livres was twice the annual revenue of the English king a decade before the civil war. For the 1783 estimate, see Block, *Statistique de la France*, Vol. I, pp. 335-336.

99. Nef, *Industry and Government in France and England, 1540-1640*, p. 82; Roland Mousnier, *La vénalité des offices sous Henri IV et Louis XIII*, p. 413.

100. Phillippe Sagnac, *La formation de la société française moderne*, Vol. II, pp. 60-61. Sagnac argues that the bad reputation of the farmers-general was not gained from the profits earned directly from their tax collections but from the disreputable speculation in which some of them engaged and from which they profited greatly. For a slightly different view, see Mousnier, *La vénalité des offices sous Henry IV et Louis XIII*, pp. 415-416.

101. Nef, *Industry and Government in France and England, 1540-1640*, p. 128.

102. Block, *Statistique de la France*, Vol. I, p. 337.

103. Mousnier, *La vénalité des offices sous Henry IV et Louis XIII*, pp. 391-392.

104. Franklin L. Ford, *Robe and Sword*, p. 110.

105. Parsons and Smelser, *Economy and Society*, pp. 56-64.

106. For a treatment of some of the banking endeavors of the old regime, see Herbert Lüthy, *La banque protestante en France de la révocation de l'édit de Nantes à la révolution*, Vol. I and II.

107. On currency, see Marc Bloch, *Esquisse d'une histoire monétaire de l'Europe*; Lüthy, *La banque protestante en France*; Franc C. Spooner, *L'économie mondiale et les frappes monetaires en France, 1493-1680*.

108. Lüthy, *La banque protestante en France*, Vol. I, p. 99.

109. Even though the currency was stabilized in 1726, it took several decades before merchants had any faith in the resolve of the government to refrain from further manipulation.

110. See R. Montgomery Martin, *China: Political, Commercial, Social*, Vol. I, p. 180; Ch'ü, *Local Government in China under the Ch'ing*, pp. 26-28, 194-195.

111. See Edwin G. Beal, Jr., *The Origin of Likin (1853-1864)*, p. 3. Some writers estimate the proportion at two-thirds.

112. On the land tax and the disguised increases, see Morse, *The Trade and Administration of the Chinese Empire*, pp. 85-94; Ch'ü, *Local Government in China under the Ch'ing*, pp. 28-32, 131-140.

113. See C. W. Shou, *Democracy and Finance in China: A Study in the Development of Fiscal Systems and Ideals*, pp. 127-129; S. K. Chen, *The System of Taxation in China in the Tsing Dynasty, 1644-1911*, pp. 51-54.

114. P. C. Hsieh, *The Government of China, 1644-1911*, pp. 194-196.

115. See Morse, *The Trade and Administration of the Chinese Empire*, pp. 94-95; Ch'ü, *Local Government in China under the Ch'ing*, pp. 140-144.

116. Shou, *Democracy and Finance in China*, p. 129.

117. See Chen, *The System of Taxation in China in the Tsing Dynasty, 1644-1911*, pp. 79-80; Ch'ü, *Local Government in China under the Ch'ing*, pp. 145-147.

118. E. H. Parker, *China: Her History, Diplomacy, and Commerce from the Earliest Times to the Present Day*, p. 239.

119. See Shou, *Democracy and Finance in China*, pp. 126-130; Ch'ü, *Local Government in China under the Ch'ing*, pp. 144-145.

120. T. Pêng (ed.), *Chung-kuo chin tai shou kung yeh shih tzŭ liao 1840-1949* (Historical Materials on China's Modern Handicraft Industries), Vol. I, p. 452.

121. The most comprehensive treatment of the new source of revenue, the likin, is to be found in Beal, *The Origin of Likin*. See especially pp. 9-10.

122. Srinivas R. Wagel, *Finance in China*, pp. 340-341.

123. See Chang, *The Chinese Gentry*, pp. 37-50; Ch'ü, *Local Government in China under the Ch'ing*, pp. 185-188.

124. Chang, *The Chinese Gentry*, p. 41.

125. Hsieh, *The Government of China, 1644-1911*, p. 204.

126. P. T. Ho, *The Ladder of Success in Imperial China: Aspects of Social Mobility, 1368-1911*, p. 47.

127. *Ibid.*, p. 34. The first figure excludes one province, and the second figure excludes two.

128, Chang, *The Chinese Gentry*, p. 30 fn. 116.

129. *Ibid.*, pp. 132, 137.

130. *Ibid.*, pp. 107-109.

131. *Ibid.*, pp. 132, 137.

132. Wagel, *Finance in China*, pp. 225-229, 237; Frank J. Goodnow, *China: An Analysis*, p. 65.

133. C. L. Chang, *The Income of the Chinese Gentry*, pp. 149-152.

134. John K. Fairbank, Alexander Eckstein, and L. S. Yang, "Economic Change in Early Modern China: An Analytic Framework," *Economic Development and Cultural Change*, Vol. 9, No. 1, October 1960, pp. 9-10; L. S. Yang, *Money and Credit in China: A Short History*, pp. 81-84.

135. Chang, *The Income of the Chinese Gentry*, pp. 177-178.

136. See Yang, *Money and Credit in China*, pp. 5-7, 73-74.

137. *Ibid.*, pp. 98-103.

138. See Fairbank, Eckstein, and Yang, "Economic Change in Early Modern China," pp. 10-11.

139. See Allen and Donnithorne, *Western Enterprise in Far Eastern Economic Development*, pp. 102-105.

140. Morse, *The Trade and Administration of the Chinese Empire*, pp. 145-146.

141. Allen and Donnithorne, *Western Enterprise in Far Eastern Economic Development*, p. 105.

142. See Yang, *Money and Credit in China*, pp. 68-70.

143. Takekoshi, *The Economic Aspects of the History of the Civilization of Japan*, Vol. I, p. 548.

144. *Ibid.*, Vol. II, pp. 306-312. Takekoshi points out: "The farmers had established usages and customs as regards taxes, to which they held strongly, refusing to allow them to be destroyed. The samurai . . . were well aware that they could not ignore these old usages and customs, and force whatever impositions they liked upon the farmers, and were inclined to respect them. . . . The farmers remained obedient to their lords as long as the latter did not trespass over this line, while the lords realized what would be the result if they did go beyond the line and impose taxes which did not fall in with the established customs and usages among the farmers." (*Ibid.*, Vol. III, pp. 392-393.)

145. *Ibid.*, Vol. II, pp. 306-310. Excluding two decades when the average rate was 37 per cent, the range of tax levies becomes 33.02 per cent to 34.66 per cent.

146. See below, pp. 141-142.

147. See, for example, Takekoshi, *The Economic Aspects of the History of the Civilization of Japan*, Vol. II, pp. 104-105.

148. Tsuchiya, "An Economic History of Japan," p. 152; Wigmore, "Materials for the Study of Private Law in Old Japan," Part I, pp. 114-119.

149. See Reischauer and Fairbank, *East Asia, the Great Tradition*, p. 634; Takizawa, *The Penetration of Money Economy in Japan*, p. 102; Norman Jacobs, *The Origin of Modern Capitalism in Eastern Asia*, p. 121.

150. See Reischauer and Fairbank, *East Asia, the Great Tradition*, pp. 607-608.

151. Sho Sawada, "Financial Difficulties of the Edo Bakufu" (translated by Hugh Borton), *Harvard Journal of Asiatic Studies*, Vol. 1, No. 3-4, November 1936, p. 317. For an account of Tokugawa revenues in 1842, see Eijiro Honjo, "On the Finance of the Tokugawa Government," *Kyōto University Economic Review*, Vol. 6, No. 2, December 1931, pp. 16-33.

152. Takekoshi, *The Economic Aspects of the History of the Civilization of Japan*, Vol. II, p. 305.

153. On the land tax, see *ibid.*, Vol. I, pp. 554-555, Vol. II, pp. 305-312; Reischauer and Fairbank, *East Asia, the Great Tradition*, pp. 629-630; Wigmore, "Materials for the Study of Private Law in Old Japan," Part I, pp. 120-125; Tsuchiya, "An Economic History of Japan," p. 223; Thomas C. Smith, "Landlords and Rural Capitalists in the Modernization of Japan," *The Journal of Economic History*, Vol. 16, No. 2, June 1956, pp. 176-179; Sansom, *A History of Japan, 1615-1867*, pp. 99-100, 104-105, 109.

154. See Hall, *Tanuma Okitsugu, 1719-1788*, p. 80; Takekoshi, *The Economic Aspects of the History of the Civilization of Japan*, Vol. II, pp. 313-320.

155. Takizawa, *The Penetration of Money Economy in Japan*, pp. 100-101; Eijiro Honjo, *Economic Theory and History of Japan in the Tokugawa Period*, p. 198.

156. See Reischauer and Fairbank, *East Asia, the Great Tradition*, pp. 632, 636.

157. Honjo, *Economic Theory and History of Japan in the Tokugawa Period*, p. 198.

158. Sawada, "Financial Difficulties of the Edo Bakufu," pp. 314-315. See also Hall, *Tanuma Okitsugu, 1719-1788*, pp. 124-125.

159. See Sawada, "Financial Difficulties of the Edo Bakufu," p. 320; Hall, *Tanuma Okitsugu, 1719-1788*, pp. 80-81; Takizawa, *The Penetration of Money Economy in Japan*, pp. 140-141.

160. Takizawa, *The Penetration of Money Economy in Japan*, p. 141.

161. See Takekoshi, *The Economic Aspects of the History of the Civilization of Japan*, Vol. II, pp. 179, 304-305.

162. See *ibid.*, Vol. I, pp. 550-552, Vol. II, pp. 318-320.

163. Takizawa, *The Penetration of Money Economy in Japan*, pp. 103-104.

164. Honjo, *The Social and Economic History of Japan*, pp. 40-42, 114-115, 285-286, 324-327.

165. On the debasement of the currency, see Takekoshi, *The Economic Aspects of the History of the Civilization of Japan*, Vol. III, pp. 208-222.

166. See Sawada, "Financial Difficulties of the Edo Bakufu," p. 322. The average annual profit amounted to 7,558 ryō between 1832-1842. (Takekoshi, *The Economic Aspects of the History of the Civilization of Japan*, Vol. III, p. 219.)

167. Hall, *Tanuma Okitsugu, 1719-1788*, p. 73. For an account of the profit made by the government from the exchange between gold and silver in connection with the Dutch trade, see Takekoshi, *The Economic Aspects of the History of the Civilization of Japan*, Vol. II, p. 160.

168. See Takekoshi, *The Economic Aspects of the History of the Civilization of Japan*, Vol. II, pp. 30-35.

169. See Hall, *Tanuma Okitsugu, 1719-1788*, pp. 68-73.

170. Takekoshi, *The Economic Aspects of the History of the Civilization of Japan*, Vol. II, p. 302, Vol. III, p. 39.

171. Wigmore, "Materials for the Study of Private Law in Old Japan," Part I, p. 168.

172. *Ibid.*, p. 168; Tsuchiya, "An Economic History of Japan," p. 211; Choi, "Tokugawa Feudalism," p. 75.

173. See Sydney Crawcour, "The Development of a Credit System in Seventeenth-Century Japan," *The Journal of Economic History*, Vol. 21, No. 3, September 1961, pp. 342-360; Wigmore, "Materials for the Study of Private Law in Old Japan," Part I, pp. 172-181; Tsuchiya, "An Economic History of Japan," pp. 215-220; Takekoshi, *The Economic Aspects of the History of the Civilization of Japan*, Vol. II, p. 278, Vol. III, pp. 42-50.

174. Wigmore, "Materials for the Study of Private Law in Old Japan," Part I, p. 181; Takekoshi, *The Economic Aspects of the History of the Civilization of Japan*, Vol. III, p. 50; Dan F. Henderson, *Conciliation and Japanese Law: Tokugawa and Modern*, Vol. I, pp. 102-115.

175. Joseph R. Tanner, *English Constitutional Conflicts in the Seventeenth Century, 1603-1689*, p. 9.

176. See below, pp. 239-240.

177. See Lipson, *The Economic History of England*, Vol. I, pp. 520-521; Stephen Dowell, *A History of Taxation and Taxes in England: From the Earliest Times to the Year 1885*, Vol. I, pp. 85-91, 110-111.

178. Dowell, *A History of Taxation and Taxes in England*, Vol. I, pp. 144-158, 161, Vol. II, p. 29; A. M. Chambers, *A Constitutional History of England*, pp. 148-149.

179. Dowell, *A History of Taxation and Taxes in England*, Vol. I, pp. 149, 157.

180. Quoted in *ibid.*, p. 150.

181. *Ibid.*, Vol. I, pp. 91-103, 129-130, 161, Vol. II, pp. 29, 45-46.

182. *Ibid.*, Vol. II, pp. 26-27, 38-40, 52.

183. *Ibid.*, Vol. I, pp. 210-223; Dietz, *An Economic History of England*, p. 250.

184. Since it was not a popular measure and was looked upon as a temporary, wartime levy, the tax was repealed in 1816. It was reintroduced in 1841-1842, and thereafter became a permanent levy.

185. See Dowell, *A History of Taxation and Taxes in England*, Vol. I, pp. 153-154.

186. *Ibid.*, pp. 123, 129, 157.

187. The crown's conspicuous lack of success with direct taxation meant that it was forced to rely heavily upon indirect methods of obtaining revenue from its citizens. As late as the Napoleonic Wars, when the government had at last resorted to an income tax, customs and excise duties accounted for nearly half of the public revenue, while direct taxes never produced more than one-third. (See William H. B. Court, *A Concise Economic History of Britain: From 1750 to Recent Times*, p. 148.)

188. See Dowell, *A History of Taxation and Taxes in England*, Vol. I, p. 195, Vol. II, pp. 34, 109.

189. G. E. Aylmer, *The King's Servants: The Civil Service of Charles I*, p. 39; Dietz, *An Economic History of England*, p. 175.

190. See Dowell, *A History of Taxation and Taxes in England*, Vol. II, pp. 8-24, 34, 109.

191. Chambers, *A Constitutional History of England*, p. 156.

192. Nef, *Industry and Government in France and England, 1540-1640*, p. 128.

193. Quoted in Dowell, *A History of Taxation and Taxes in England*, Vol. I, p. 158.

194. See *ibid.*, Vol. II, pp. 50-52.

195. From 1695 to 1706, a tax on burials was levied according to rank and income. The assessment on the estates of persons who had earned £50 or more per year, or whose property exceeded £600, was £1-4-0. (Dowell, *A History of Taxation and Taxes in England*, Vol. II, p. 543.)

196. *Ibid.*, Vol. I, p. 198.

197. Dietz, *An Economic History of England*, p. 246.

198. See Price, *The English Patents of Monopoly*, p. 42; Nef, *Industry and Government in France and England, 1540-1640*, pp. 115-117.

199. Briggs and Jordan, *Economic History of England*, p. 113.

200. Price, *The English Patents of Monopoly*, p. 42.

201. K. W. Swart, *Sale of Offices in the Seventeenth Century*, pp. 45-67; Aylmer, *The King's Servants*, pp. 219-240, 449. See also John H. Barcroft, *Buckingham and the Central Administration, 1616-1628*.

202. Dietz, *An Economic History of England*, p. 250; Charles R. Mayes, "The Sale of Peerages in Early Stuart England," *The Journal of Modern History*, Vol. 29, No. 1, March 1957, pp. 21-37; Lawrence Stone, "The Inflation of Honours, 1558-1641," *Past and Present*, No. 14, November 1958, p. 64.

203. See Dowell, *A History of Taxation and Taxes in England*, Vol. I, pp. 202-203; W. E. Lunt, *History of England*, pp. 436-437.

204. Lunt, *History of England*, p. 450.

205. Richard Pares, *Limited Monarchy in Great Britain in the Eighteenth Century*, p. 11.

206. See Lipson, *The Economic History of England*, Vol. III, pp. 62-84;

Supple, *Commercial Crisis and Change in England, 1600-1642*, p. 167; Gretton, *The English Middle Class*, pp. 186-187.

207. Lipson, *The Economic History of England*, Vol. III, pp. 219-221; Meredith, *Outlines in the Economic History of England*, pp. 220-221; Leland Jenks, *The Migration of British Capital to 1875*, p. 245.

208. Lipson, *The Economic History of England*, Vol. III, pp. 227-229; Meredith, *Outlines in the Economic History of England*, pp. 220-221; R. D. Richards, "The Pioneers of Banking in England," *Economic History*, Series No. 4, January 1929, pp. 485-502.

209. Dietz, *An Economic History of England*, p. 239.

210. On the Bank of England, see Lipson, *The Economic History of England*, Vol. III, pp. 233-244.

211. Gretton, *The English Middle Class*, p. 215; Gilbert Slater, *The Growth of Modern England*, p. 141.

212. Reid, *Economic History of Great Britain*, p. 184.

CHAPTER 5

Functions of Government
and Procedures of Governing—
II: Pattern Maintenance and Integration

THE CONTROL OF DEVIANT BEHAVIOR AND THE COORDINATION OF interdependent roles are examples of the kinds of activities that are associated with pattern maintenance and integration. At first glance, these activities do not appear to be as crucially related to economic development as do resource allocation, resource management, and resource mobilization, which were treated in Chapter 4. It is interesting to observe, however, that most writers who mention the political conditions necessary for economic development deal with what we have defined as pattern maintenance and integration.[1]

Although there are some differences in the contribution made by the respective governments to the satisfaction of the pattern-maintenance and integration requisites in our two sets of cases, the more striking are differences in procedure—distinctions in the manner in which the various governments made essentially the same functional contribution.

In Chapter 2, the pattern-maintenance functional requisite was defined as being concerned with the maintenance of conformity to the basic values of the cultural system, and the integration requisite as being concerned with securing coordination among differentiated but interdependent roles. Of the several processes involved in each of these functions, one is common to both: the social-control process, which will be of prime concern in this chapter. It is that process by which coercion is used to compel behavior that is in conformity with norms, and/or to punish for behavior that violates norms.

In distinguishing between those aspects of the social-control process that are relevant to pattern maintenance and to integration respectively, we referred to Durkheim's distinction between *repressive sanctions* and *restitutive sanctions*. It will be useful at this point to discuss these two groups of sanctions more fully. Durkheim distinguishes between the two as follows:

> Every precept of law [norm] can be defined as a rule of sanctioned conduct. Moreover, it is evident that sanctions change with the gravity attributed to precepts, the place they hold in the public conscience, the role they play in society. It is right, then, to classify juridical rules [norms] according to the different sanctions which are attached to them.
>
> They are of two kinds. Some consist essentially in suffering, or at least a loss, inflicted on the agent. They make demands on his fortune, or on his honor, or on his life, or on his liberty, and deprive him of something he enjoys. We call them repressive. They constitute penal law. It is true that those which are attached to rules which are purely moral have the same character, only they are distributed in a diffuse manner, by everybody indiscriminately, whereas those in penal law are applied through the intermediary of a definite organ; they are organized. As for the other type, it does not necessarily imply suffering for the agent, but consists only of *the return of things as they were,* in the re-establishment of troubled relations to their normal state, whether the incriminated act is restored by force to the type whence it deviated, or is annulled, that is, deprived of all social value. We must then separate juridical rules [norms] into two great classes, accordingly as they have organized repressive sanctions or only restitutive sanctions. The first comprise all penal law; the second, civil law, commercial law, procedural law, administrative and constitutional law, after abstraction of the penal rules which may be found there.[2]

In the scheme employed in this study, repressive sanctions identify the social-control process related to pattern maintenance, while restitutive sanctions identify the social-control process related to integration.[3]

THE PATTERN-MAINTENANCE FUNCTIONAL REQUISITE

Our major concern with the contribution of government to the satisfaction of the pattern-maintenance functional requisite is with the degree to which repressive sanctions are *legal sanctions* (and thus, by definition, involve government), rather than *nonlegal sanctions*. The problem can be better understood if it is placed in a slightly broader context. Four types of sanctions can be employed at a macro-social level: (1) *retaliation-compensation,* (2) *withdrawal of reciprocity,* (3) *supernatural sanctions,* and (4) *legal sanctions.* Whereas legal sanctions are applied by government, the other sanctions in our formulation are not defined in terms of a particular social structure (except that government is excluded), and may be employed by a number of different concrete structures.[4]

In primitive and traditional societies, there is a fairly wide range of variation in the reliance that is placed upon these different types of sanctions. The problem is to determine the extent of the government's contribution to the satisfaction of the pattern-maintenance requisite by assessing the degree to which repressive sanctions are legal (involving the government) rather than retaliation-compensation, withdrawal of reciprocity, or supernatural (not involving government).[5]

In this chapter, we are concerned with two types of norms that are supported by repressive sanctions. The first are those that in a modern society are associated with criminal (as opposed to private) law, and in some societies with violations of religious prescriptions. These are norms that apply universally (or nearly so) to all members of a society. We shall be interested, but only briefly, in whether or not the government in the four societies under consideration was actively involved in applying repressive sanctions for violations of this type of norm, which we shall for convenience label as *norms defining criminal behavior*.

We must also focus attention upon the maintenance of conformity to another type of norm, the enforcement of which is modern societies rarely involves repressive sanctions, but which in traditional societies frequently does. These are norms that govern the manner or style of living associated with social rank in the stratification system, and hence are not applied universally, but only to specified segments of the population.

Government Enforcement of Norms that Define Criminal Behavior

Since the empirical data on this topic do not draw as distinctive patterns as they do for the other topics we are treating, the organizational treatment of this subject will be somewhat different. It will be helpful first to discuss briefly the theory relating to government enforcement of norms defining criminal behavior and economic development,[6] and then to sketch in some of the data relating to our two sets of cases.

One of the political conditions of economic growth which is frequently mentioned in the literature is that government must maintain law and order at a reasonably high level. Spengler's statement is typical: "Law, order, and security must be maintained, and their maintenance must be accompanied by a minimal degree of public probity, since otherwise improbity, together with its uneven incidence, will too markedly reduce the effectiveness of the arrangements designed for the maintenance of law, order, and security." [7]

A part of what Spengler is discussing is what we refer to as the government's contribution to pattern maintenance, especially in the enforcement of norms that apply universally.[8] This formulation, however, raises a number of questions. While it is clear that economic growth cannot occur if the social order is utterly chaotic, few scholars have addressed themselves to the problem of how much chaos can be tolerated. Soviet society was certainly not *peaceful* and *orderly* during the 1930's. A great deal of chaos resulted from the forced collectivization of agriculture and a series of extensive purges. The collectivization drive produced a loss of life estimated to be many thousands, while masses of Soviet citizens were arrested during the course of the purges. This may have been law; it was not order and security. However, the Soviet economy grew at a remarkable rate.

An even more crucial question, in the terms of this study, is whether or not the *government* must make a significant contribution to the maintenance of law and order. There are societies, of course, in which other structures have a more significant involvement in maintaining conformity to norms than does the government. The question is not only whether the maintenance of some minimal level of conformity to basic norms is a condition of economic growth, but also whether this minimal level can be maintained *only* if the government becomes significantly involved.

Unfortunately, the four cases treated in this monograph shed little light on the problem. In France, England, and Japan the government contributed significantly to pattern maintenance by enforcing many of the norms that defined criminal behavior, while in China the government relied quite heavily upon other structures for the enforcement of these norms.

In France, it will be remembered, the intendant was, among other things, *intendant de police,* and he performed the full range of duties implied in that title, including at times presiding over tribunals which handed down legal decisions. In addition to the ordinary intendants, there were also the *lieutenants généraux de police,* who were more specifically concerned with apprehending offenders against the fundamental norms of the society. An army of subordinate local officials assisted the intendants and the lieutenants in capturing and punishing criminals. The fact that the French fleet had a huge appetite for men who could be made to row in the galleys provided an incentive for government officials to diligently seek out those persons who might qualify for long terms of servitude.

In England, an elaborate system of courts and judicial officials was gradually developed over several centuries to handle criminal offenses. The extraordinary courts directly linked with the Privy Council (such as the Star Chamber and the Court of Requests) were initially established as an arm of the executive to maintain law and order, and they tried a wide range of criminal cases. From the thirteenth century there appeared the Court of the King's Bench, which was the main regular court of the central authorities responsible for the enforcement of criminal law. It supervised the work of the local courts, and was entitled to have a case transferred to its calendar if the local officials seemed unlikely to render proper justice. A special link between the central courts and the local courts was provided by a group of itinerant judges who traveled about their circuits hearing criminal cases at regular intervals. At the local level, the key officials responsible for maintaining the peace and punishing criminals were the justices of the peace. In early times, the justices were themselves expected to search out the offenders, arrest them, and try the cases. Eventually, however, they enlisted the services of special constables who, operating under the direction of the justices, were charged with the detection and pursuit of criminals. The justices were thus able to devote their attention to the hearing of criminal cases, and for this purpose they held Quarter Sessions, which had jurisdiction over all but the gravest of felonies. During the seventeenth century, crimes that carried sentences of death were handled by the itinerant judges. The procedures against criminals became more humane in the eighteenth century, but the system was severe throughout most of the period with which we are concerned.[9] Many crimes were excluded from the traditional "benefit of clergy," [10] and the number of capital offenses was very large. While comprehensive data on the enforcement of criminal law are not available for the entire country during these centuries, there are scattered reports from individual counties for limited periods. In Devonshire during 1598, for example, out of the 387 prisoners who were tried for felonies, 74 were hanged, more than half of whom had been condemned by the Quarter Sessions of the justices of the peace.

During the Tokugawa period, Japan was under the rule of military clans which governed through a system of martial law. Besides exhorting his subjects to follow the path of moral rectitude and be loyal to their political superiors, the shogun would often issue detailed commands, which were read to the people by local officials. At the village level, the headmen were responsible to the district administrators and magistrates for the maintenance of peace and order, and they were usually required to bring important criminal matters to the attention of their administrative chiefs. Indeed, the headman himself was often punished for the crimes of his fellow villagers, and sometimes an entire village would be fined for the criminal behavior of its members. Within their respective han, the daimyo were responsible for detecting and punishing deviant behavior, although they were not entitled to carry out the death penalty without approval from the Edo authorities. The central officials ordinarily had considerable authority to approve or set aside the penalties that had been imposed by lower courts. As noted earlier, the shogun established an elaborate system of censorial inspection and espionage, which operated effectively in uncovering the most serious violations of the official codes. The metsuke not only served as inspectors but also performed as circuit judges. Working closely with them was an army of police, many of whom carried out their surveillance activities in secret while acting as priests or innkeepers. The schedule of punishments for the violation of basic norms was very severe, including sentences of death, especially in the case of commoners, for such crimes as theft, arson, and treason. These harsh penalties were designed to deter others from following a similar course of criminal behavior.[11]

In considering these three cases, it is important to observe that in England and Japan, where many economic regulations could not be effectively enforced, the government was successful in apprehending and punishing criminals. The enforcement mechanism was apparently more reliable in this regard.

The case that deviates from the common pattern is China.[12] Although the government in Manchu China contributed to the enforcement of basic norms, other nongovernmental structures were also involved to a significant degree, and in a sense the government *operated through* these other structures. Under the concept of joint responsibility, for example, the family or clan, the village, and the guild were accountable for the unlawful behavior of any member of the group. Indeed, the clan leaders were authorized to punish those members who had violated the basic norms of the society, and if the offenders refused to accept the decision of their elders, the entire clan would indict him before the state authorities. By the same token, the leaders of nongovernmental organizations who failed in their responsibility to punish the criminals in the group were themselves vulnerable to punishment. A magistrate would also be liable to discipline if he failed to punish a lawbreaker, or even if he failed to anticipate the crime. Although punishment was often tailored to fit the circumstances of a case, the penalties were designed to make violations of the codes unappealing, and 3,900 crimes were listed as punishable by death.

In China, then, conformity to fundamental norms was enforced through the combined use of governmental and nongovernmental controls, more so than in the other cases, including Japan. If the family, clan, or guild leaders failed to punish an offender, the political authorities stepped in directly to insure that the appropriate penalty would be paid. Apparently this system worked fairly effectively so long as the dynasty itself maintained a reasonably efficient bureaucracy. Whether or not the norms of the society could continue to be enforced by the political structure alone when the nongovernmental structures were breaking down is difficult to determine; when these structures began to lose their effectiveness, especially in the twentieth century, the central government itself had largely ceased to exist. It is impossible to say whether the government ceased to be effective in pattern-maintenance functions because it was unable to operate unless kinship and other social groups played their traditional role, or whether the central bureaucracy itself had become so weakened that it could not exert the direct control that it might have been able to do a century earlier.

Government Enforcement of Norms that Apply to Specific Classes

In every society except the most simple, differentiation is made on the basis of prestige, and values are assigned to certain manners of living. Some styles of life are regarded as superior, while others are relegated to an inferior category. Certain kinds of behavior may be considered desirable for the occupant of a given rank (governed by precepts); other kinds of behavior may be compulsory or forbidden (governed by norms).[13] In this study, we shall seek to determine whether the different styles of living associated with various ranks in the society were governed by norms, and if so, whether these norms were enforced by legal sanctions or by nonlegal sanctions.[14] In order to examine this aspect of pattern maintenance, it will be necessary to discuss the rank-order of social classes in each of the four countries and to determine how the social hierarchy was reinforced.

FRANCE. In outlining social stratification in *ancien France,* the student's attention is immediately focused upon the legal division of the society into three estates: the nobility, the clergy, and the *third estate.*[15] Although the latter category technically included all Frenchmen who were not members of the clergy or the nobility, it is with the bourgeoisie that we are primarily concerned. The breakdown into the three estates represents a good starting-point for the analysis of social classes in France, but it needs elaboration.

Nobility. Although the size of the nobility in eighteenth-century France has been estimated at various numbers, scholars are agreed that this group comprised only a small part of the total population. Sée accepts the estimate of 80,000 noble families, embracing about 400,000 individuals.[16] After a careful analysis of original and secondary sources, Ford arrives at a figure of 58,000 families, or about 200,000 individuals.[17] Since the population in France in 1715 was about 20,000,000,[18] a conservative calculation would place the nobility at about one per cent of the total inhabitants. These figures, in both absolute and proportional terms, are strikingly larger than comparable statistics for England.[19] Two obvious reasons account for the difference. First, in France, no rule of primogeniture applied to titles; all of the sons of a nobleman could legally belong to the noble class.[20] Second, the probability that a member of the bourgeoisie would achieve noble status (through purchase, for example) was much greater in France.

It would be a mistake to view the nobility as a homogeneous class. Enormous differences in wealth existed between a poor, rural *hobereau* and the First President of the Parliament of Paris.[21] But more important for our purposes than differences in wealth was the distinction between the *noblesse de l'épée* and the *noblesse de la robe.* The former were the descendants of the old feudal military nobility; the latter were the magistrates of the sovereign courts, most of whom had either purchased their titles along with their offices or had inherited originally purchased titles from their ancestors. Many other offices were put up for sale, and these carried titles with them. Very often the holders of these titles were also referred to as members of the nobility of the robe.[22]

Before the revolution, the nobility shared with the clergy the positions of top prestige in French society. It should not be assumed, however, that the members of this group exercised great power. Ford draws attention to Louis XIV's policy of "seeking to minimize the extent to which any subject could combine in his own person high degrees of both external grandeur and actual power, or, stated in other terms, the effort to exclude individuals enjoying some degree of independent, especially hereditary prestige from the sort of governmental functions which might have made that prestige dangerous to the crown." [23] Louis XIV was not the first monarch to institute such a policy, but he was more successful in implementing it than were his predecessors and successors. In fact, the nobility under the leadership of the high robe regrouped after Louis XIV's death and began to exercise greater political influence. It must nevertheless be recalled that Louis XV never failed to have a decree registered, even though some of his decrees generated opposition from the magistrates.

Clergy. A slightly smaller group than the nobility, Sée estimates the clergy to comprise about 1.8 per cent of the population in the early eighteenth century.[24] Their collective income, however, was considerable. Part of their income was derived from ownership of land, both urban and rural,[25] but even more lucrative was the revenue from tithes.[26]

By the eighteenth century, the high clergy were made up almost entirely of noblemen, and they lived in a manner nearly indistinguishable from that of the wealthy nobility.[27] Many of the lower clergy, upon whom the burden of gratuitous giving fell with inordinate severity, were poverty-striken. Their way of life resembled that of the peasants whom they served with greater devotion than did the more opulent clerics.

Commoners. Within the third estate, the bourgeoisie have attracted the most attention. This class, of course, was hardly homogeneous. An occupational distinction can be made between those engaged in the business and financial world and those who were attracted to the professions.[28] Economically and socially, the most prominent among the business group were the financiers and great merchants (*négociants*), who had amassed huge fortunes and lived in a style comparable to that of the wealthy upper nobility. Indeed, when families of the upper nobility discovered that their resources were insufficient to maintain their lavish mode of existence, they often sought to arrange marriages that would link them with rich financiers and merchants.

Prestige among the business and commercial groups of the bourgeoisie varied according to wealth, declining down the scale to the small shopkeeper, who might not even be regarded as a member of the bourgeois class, especially if he had to do manual labor as part of his shopkeeping chores.

Among the professions, the *avocats* and *procureurs* were the most prestigious (unless the eighteenth-century intellectuals are classified as part of the bourgeoisie). This legal group was followed by physicians and surgeons, law clerks, and assistants. Interestingly enough, some professional people tended to "live as noblemen." After they had accumulated wealth, they often retired from professional life and lived on the income from their investments.[29]

The artisans also formed a distinguishable but not homogeneous group. Significant differences in income and working conditions were to be found between masters and journeymen, and the interests of the two groups were often incompatible. Although the master always had the more prestige, in the eighteenth century the economic regulations of the government[30] enhanced his position even further. A journeyman could not leave his master without written consent, or he would be fined 100 livres. Journeymen were also forbidden to join "brotherhoods" or hold meetings and "intrigue for the sake of getting one another positions with certain masters, or for the sake of leaving them, or in order to prevent masters in any way from selecting their own workmen, whether they be Frenchmen or foreigners."[31]

Unlike land tenure in other countries of Western Europe, a sizable proportion of the agricultural land was owned by the peasants themselves, ranging from about 20 per cent in the western provinces to about 50 per cent in parts of the south and east. The individual holdings, however, tended to be very small and were encumbered with the remains of feudal dues and taxes which were collected by the lords of the manors. Thus, only a small minority of the peasants could earn a living by working entirely on their own land. Most of them had either to work part time as day laborers or to serve as tenant farmers (*métayers*) on land owned by the nobility, the clergy, and the bourgeoisie.[32] By the eighteenth century, industry had begun to spread to the countryside, providing the peasants with alternative forms of employment. This development even gave a few of the wealthier and more enterprising peasants an opportunity to move into merchant roles.[33]

Government Enforcement of Norms Relating to Style of Living. The French government guaranteed special rights to the nobility and the clergy. Compared with the central decision makers and the bureaucracy, the nobility did not wield a great deal of political power, but they did enjoy a wide range of rights and privileges, which were enforced by the government. Among these were their right to collect the old manorial dues[34] and their privilege of exemption from militia service and from the obligation to quarter troops. They also held a number of honorific rights.[35] From the point of view of this study, however, the privilege of tax exemption was of most consequence. This involved exemption from the taille, the most profitable tax levied by the French government.[36] But tax exemptions extended beyond the taille;[37] indeed, it was not until the capitation in 1695, followed by the *dixième* (1710), that a tax was collected without regard to rank. And even when these and later taxes were levied upon them, the nobility managed to pay less than what the government had anticipated. The *dixième,* for example, was abolished in 1717, and there was a progressive easing of the impact of the capitation on the privileged.[38]

In return for these privileges, the nobility undertook certain obligations. Important for this study is the fact that noblemen were expected to refrain from participating in trade and commerce. As Ford points out, ". . . it is worth noting that in the eighteenth century, a nobleman still lost his noblesse and that of all progeny not yet conceived . . . if he adopted any manual craft save the famous exception of glassmaking or if he entered 'for sordid gain' into either retail commerce or the exploitation of another party's land." [39] Specific individuals were given exemption from this restriction in grants of privilege, and some were given permission to purchase stock in royal trading companies. The former exemption affected a very small portion of the noble class, while the latter, although a wholesale exemption, did not lead to significant numbers of the nobility subscribing to stock issues.[40]

Like the nobility, the clergy enjoyed important privileges under the *ancien régime.* They had their own system of courts, and they escaped the most onerous taxes. Indeed, they were even more successful than their noble brethren in easing the burden of the new taxes which were imposed in the eighteenth century. Although they made a "gratuitous gift" to the monarch every five years in an amount suggested by royal authority, this contribution was much smaller than the tax they would ordinarily have paid on their property holdings.

CHINA. The main echelons of social stratification in Manchu China consisted of the imperial nobility, the gentry, and the commoners. The latter group was made up of the peasants, artisans, and merchants.[41] Among the privileged classes, the gentry are of major concern, although mention will be made of the nobility.

Nobility. In theory, the hereditary nobility ranked at the top of the social ladder.[42] The largest segment of the nobility was the imperial clansmen, who were divided into twelve grades and who numbered over 40,000 in the last quarter of the sixteenth century. The nonimperial nobility, which were a smaller group consisting of nine ranks, had been awarded noble status for outstanding service to the regime. The hereditary nobility of China, however, did not enjoy the prestige and influence of the nobility in other countries. As a rule, the hierarchy of noble ranks was governed by rules of declining descent, that is, the son inherited the rank immediately below that of his father. When the sons of a nobleman reached the lowest grade, the title ceased to be a hereditary right. Although some opportunities for government service were eventually opened up for the nobility, actual appointments to office did not keep pace with the demand, and most of them lived a parasitic existence. The imperial clansmen were systematically excluded from policy-making roles, and they were not permitted to engage in political activity.

Gentry. Of greater importance socially and politically were the gentry, i.e., individuals who had ever held public office, whether through civil service examination or purchase (the official-gentry), and the holders of degrees through examination or purchase who aspired to office (the scholar-gentry). During the first half of the nineteenth century, the gentry numbered about 1,095,000, and, together with their families, totaled 5,500,000 people, or 1.3 per cent of the population. The comparable figures during the last part of the nineteenth century list 1,444,000 gentry and approximately 7,200,000 when their families are included—1.9 per cent of the population.[43] While in a technical sense only the official or the degree-holder himself was a member of the gentry class, the prestige and privileges of gentry status were shared by the members of his family—a transfer of rights that was reinforced by legal sanction. Indeed, it was legally possible for certain relatives of an office-holder to receive an honorary official title through bestowal, and these titles carried with them many of the legal privileges that accrued to regular officials. Thus, as in France, people were able to move upward into the aristocratic class, which grew both in absolute numbers and in proportion to total population.

There were, of course, significant gradations within the gentry class, depending upon the type of office held, the quality of the civil service or academic degree, and, to some extent, whether gentry status had been achieved through examination or through purchase. In the case of the office held, the status of the official varied with the relative importance of the position—whether it was a high-ranking, middle-range, or minor post. The hierarchical ordering of gentry status based upon the quality of the degree ranged from the holders of the first degree (who were really undergraduates subject to periodic examinations and for whom there was little opportunity for government appointment), to students at the Imperial Academy who might eventually be selected for minor positions, to those who had passed the provincial examination which entitled them to appointment eventually to a minor post, and, finally, to those students who had passed the metropolitan and palace examinations, which put them automatically into the rank of officialdom.[44] Although those who had purchased gentry status assumed the rights and privileges of the class, their position was apparently not as prestigious or as influential as that of scholars who had won their badges through examination. As a rule, the highest political posts were reserved for individuals who had risen through examination.

While all members of the gentry enjoyed prestige in the society, only a tiny minority of them were able to hold public office.[45] In the latter part of the nineteenth century, the office-holding group numbered only 2 per cent of the gentry. Another 12 per cent were eligible to hold office but received no appointments, while 86 per cent had to be content to serve as leaders in their local areas, performing as teachers, landowners, and merchants. Those gentry who were fortunate enough to become government officials exercised important power in the territories where they served, but they wielded little influence in the leading policy-making decisions of the government. To be influential at the policy level, an individual had to be a member of the advisory councils at the center, and even these officials, as we have seen, were relatively impotent against the will of a strong monarch.

Commoners. The peasants, who constituted about 80 per cent of the population, lived in tiny villages and clung to the security of their kinship groups. Since they were regarded as primary producers of wealth, they were ranked above the merchants and artisans in the social scale and were the objects of little discriminatory legislation. The civil service examinations were open to members of the peasant class, but only a tiny fragment managed to secure the necessary education, though appointment to a government post was a common aspiration. The majority of the peasants were proprietors of the land they cultivated, and they were free to sell it. Many peasants, however, lived on the borderline of tenancy and were forced to make frequent trips to the moneylender. The large landowners ranked higher on the social scale than their impecunious neighbors and wielded considerable influence in their localities.

Occupying an inferior social position were the artisans and merchants. The artisans, after serving a long period of apprenticeship, worked as small craftsmen in their homes or shops and took out membership in the craft guilds. The merchants were traditionally looked down upon as manipulators rather than producers of wealth, and they were often marked for discriminatory legislation. Although under the Manchu regime the merchants suffered from fewer legal disabilities than they had in earlier times, they still sat uncomfortably on the low rungs of the social ladder, despite the size of their fortunes, and they usually aspired to become landowners and to have their sons enter the government service.

Government Enforcement of Norms Relating to Style of Living. As in France, the high status groups in China enjoyed important privileges and exemptions which were enforced by the government. The nobility, for example, held positions that were directly inheritable by law, even though many of them were not perpetually so. Moreover, their homes, carriages, and clothing were prescribed by government decree so that their style of life would conform with their rank-order in society.[46] The nobles were beyond the jurisdiction of ordinary legal processes, and they could not be arrested without the consent of the emperor.[47]

Many of these privileges and immunities applied to government officials and the other members of the gentry class.[48] Scholar-officials, for example, were not subject to ordinary legal procedures and could not be arrested or punished without imperial sanction. When officials became involved with commoners in disputes, the punishment of the humbler citizen would fluctuate in severity according to the rank of the official. When such disputes reached the courtroom, the government official was not required to appear with the opposing party if the opponent happened to be a commoner. The gentry, including those who held no official office, were protected from harassment by administrative officials, and were exempted from humiliating forms of punishment. Commoners were forbidden to insult members of the gentry, and they were not entitled to involve the gentry as witnesses in law suits. The gentry, in addition, were awarded subsidies for further study, through which they might improve their occupational status, and when famine struck, the needy members of the gentry class were given special consideration. Since sumptuary laws regulated the type of clothing and the design and decoration of homes according to social rank, craftsmen who made articles for customers whose status did not entitle them to the use of such commodities were severely punished—a condition that tended to restrain artisans from dealing with potential customers of uncertain social station.[49]

Even more significant were the monetary privileges enjoyed by members of the gentry.[50] They were exempted from all personal taxes (such as the head tax), and they and their families were not required to perform compulsory labor service. For a time the gentry were legally exempt from a portion of the land tax, and even after they became fully liable for this assessment, they were often permitted by the government to delay payment. They were also reluctant to pay the extra surcharges, for which commoners were liable. Moreover, when scholar-officials served as administrators in the various localities, they were in a position to divert large portions of the local revenue for their own use—a practice so commonly followed that the superior authorities frequently overlooked it. As a result of these monetary perquisites, many of the scholar-officials were able to amass large amounts of capital which they sought to invest in promising undertakings.

In return for their privileged status, the members of the gentry class were expected to render service to the community, and they were legally obligated to refrain from engaging in certain mercantile activities.[51] The occupation of the trader and the status of the merchant were, as we have seen, traditionally low in the social hierarchy, and Manchu law forbade the gentry from becoming brokers and port merchants and from engaging in other forms of business. When the lowly holders of the first degree were forced, from economic necessity, to engage in trade and other menial occupations, the government in the early nineteenth century issued a series of decrees prohibiting them from earning their living as merchants' bookkeepers, clerks of local irrigation projects, petty local brokers, and so on.[52] During the nineteenth century, however, when contact with the West was accelerated, business activities began to command the attention of the gentry.[53] Some members of the scholar class became active in the salt monopoly, the foreign trade monopoly, and moneylending. They were nevertheless reluctant to identify themselves as merchants or businessmen, often operating under assumed names. Indeed, it is difficult to determine whether the gentry who engaged in business were "regular" gentry turned merchant, or merchants who had bought their way into the gentry class in order to gain social prestige or official protection for their business ventures. Despite the increased business activity on the part of the gentry, however, it is important to realize that "only a very small portion of the entire gentry group can be said to have depended on business as their major source of income." [54]

The official regulations which placed the upper classes in a favorable position were, by the same token, applied adversely to people of lower station, especially those engaged in mercantile activities. As we have seen, the merchants, in contrast with the gentry, were often subjected to severe tax assessments. Moreover, the regime sought to prevent the peasants from moving into merchant roles. In 1727, for example, the emperor issued a decree emphasizing the importance of agriculture as a calling, and he admonished the peasants not to leave their fields for the profits to be derived from trades and crafts.[55]

JAPAN. Social classes in Tokugawa Japan were rank-ordered as follows: imperial nobility (*kuge*), the military aristocracy (daimyo and samurai), priests, peasants, artisans and merchants, and outcasts. During this period under discussion, the imperial nobility were of little political or economic consequence, and the priests and outcasts may also be safely excluded from this analysis.[56] Within each of the remaining classes there were complex gradations based largely upon income or type of occupational specialty.

Military Aristocracy. The daimyo, numbering about 265 at the end of the era, were the feudal lords whose domains produced at least 10,000 *koku* of rice.[57] Within the daimyo category, the lords were ranked according to the productivity of their fiefs. As we have already noted, they had a relatively free hand in the governing of their territories, and they financed their administration by the tax revenue collected from the peasants and by the profits derived from their own or licensed commercial enterprises.

Ranking below the daimyo were the samurai, or warrior-retainers, who numbered about 350,000. When samurai families were included in this category, the figure reached about 2,000,000, or 5 to 6 per cent of the population.[58] In return for their loyalty and service to the daimyo, most of the samurai received stipends in rice, which determined the social distinctions within the warrior class. The high-ranking knights, for example, served as trusted lieutenants of their lords and received allotments commensurate with the importance of their roles, while the lower-ranking samurai earned less pay for their work as foot soldiers or guards. The long era of isolation and peace, however, rendered the samurai superfluous in their military roles, and, engaging in little or no productive labor, they became a heavy burden upon the social order.

Commoners. The peasants, who comprised about 80 per cent of the population,[59] were ranked higher than the artisans and merchants because they were the main producers of rice. They owned their own land, but they were forbidden by official regulations to sell it. The peasants carried most of the tax burden and bowed in humble submission before the daimyo and samurai.

Although the merchants were officially ranked low in the social hierarchy, being regarded as nonproductive people economically and lacking respectable ancestry, their numbers increased rapidly (more than any other social class) as the Japanese economy developed. Despite their subordinate position, they performed in an important role, serving as middlemen who converted the rice of the daimyo and samurai into negotiable currency and supplying the military class with the necessities and luxuries of life.

Government Enforcement of Norms Relating to Style of Living. The daimyo and samurai enjoyed a wide range of privileges and immunities which were denied to the subordinate social classes and which were enforced by official decree.[60] In terms of social distinction, they were permitted to use surnames, to wear two swords, to don colored robes appropriate to their rank, and to exercise the privilege of hunting and riding. Strict rules governed the forms of address, type of residence and costume, and the order of precedence on ceremonial occasions and during the journeys to Edo. Although the members of the military class were subject to financial assessments by the shogunate, the vast majority were exempt from ordinary taxation and from other burdens that were imposed upon commoners, especially the peasants. Moreover, no member of the military aristocracy was to "engage in trade [or] to lay in a stock of goods with a view to making profit out of them." [61]

The exalted position of the daimyo and samurai was carried over into the legal code. Their laws of marriage were separate from those of the commoner, and, according to the official code, "all offences [were] to be punished in accordance with social status." [62] The law permitted the warriors to "cut down" commoners who were guilty of insulting speech or rude behavior. An offense committed by an ordinary citizen was classified as a "crime," while the same offense committed by a samurai was listed as an "excess." When incarceration became necessary, an ordinary samurai went to a special prison from which commoners were excluded, while the higher lords put themselves in the custody of fellow-daimyo at their residences. The members of the military aristocracy received lighter sentences than did the peasants and merchants, and for a crime that would result in the death sentence for a commoner, the samurai would often be permitted to commit suicide or to go into exile.

ENGLAND. The English government did not exercise tight controls over the people in such important matters as taxation, and its agents made no elaborate censuses or enrollments of the population. For this reason, precise data on English social classes do not become available until around the nineteenth century, and social analysts interested in earlier periods have to rely upon the estimates of demographers and other scholars for their breakdowns. [63] From estimates of occupational groupings in 1690-1696, it is possible to divide the population into the orthodox categories of nobility, clergy, lesser aristocracy, and various gradations of commoners.

Nobility. The nobility in England were a much more strictly defined social group than was the case in France. Apart from the princes of the royal blood, they consisted solely of a small clique of landed magnates who enjoyed the hereditary right to receive a summons from the king to attend the Great Council (House of Lords). The members of the family of an earl or baron were not included in the noble class; noble privileges and obligations extended only to the person who actually held the peerage, and, upon his death, to his eldest son under the principle of primogeniture. In 1690, there were only 160 of these temporal lords—an exceedingly microscopic group when compared with a population of 5,500,000. Even if we assume that each peer had a family of as many as six other members, the group with noble kinship accounts for only 960 people, or 0.0002 per cent of the inhabitants of the country.[64]

Clergy. The clergy were also a class apart, consisting of 26 spiritual lords, 2,000 eminent clergymen, and 8,000 of the lesser, impecunious variety. Together with their families and indoor servants, they numbered about 52,500, or nearly one per cent of the population. Although there was always a wide economic gap between the upper and lower clergy, the position of the ecclesiastical class improved during the eighteenth century so that the size of the well-to-do group expanded.[65]

Lesser Aristocracy. The line between noblemen and commoners in English society was tightly drawn, but links between the two classes were provided by the baronets and the knights, who would in most countries have been included in the nobility. The baronets were a special class of hereditary knights created by James I, while the knights had been the lesser landowners in the noble class who had elected to separate themselves in parliament from the great barons and to make common cause with the mercantile interests of the towns. At the end of the seventeenth century, after social ranks in these two categories had been widely distributed, the baronets numbered only 800 and the knights 600. If these title-holders had families as large as six other members, the entire group would have constituted 8,400 people, or 0.15 per cent of the total population.[66] While this group enjoyed considerable social prestige, they could claim few legal rights attributable to their social station.

Closely linked with the knights were the landed gentry, who would very likely have been ranked as part of the nobility on the Continent. In 1690, there were 3,000 "esquires" and 12,000 "gentlemen," who with their families and servants numbered approximately 126,000 individuals. Along with the peers and those who held lesser titles, the gentry formed the social aristocracy of England, setting the tone for the upper echelons of the rising bourgeoisie. It was from this gentry class that the justices of the peace were largely drawn, and many merchants aspired to purchase land and to become prestigious gentlemen of the countryside.

Commoners. Beneath the baronets, knights, and squire-gentry, the "third estate" constituted a variegation of socioeconomic groupings. As was done in the analysis of France, it will be helpful to examine the segments of this estate by grouping them into "business-commercial-industrial" and "professional" categories. The former group embraced a wide range of individuals from the wealthy merchants, whose prestige and influence in the society were rapidly growing, down to the more humble handcraftsmen, as shown in Table 5.1.

TABLE 5.1. PEOPLE ENGAGED IN BUSINESS, COMMERCE, AND INDUSTRY

Number of Individuals	Occupation	Total Number (including family members and indoor servants)	Proportion of Total Population
2,000	Eminent merchants and traders by sea	16,000	0.29%
8,000	Lesser merchants and traders by sea	48,000	0.87
50,000	Shopkeepers, tradesmen, innkeepers	225,000	4.09
60,000	Artisans and handcraftsmen	240,000	4.36
120,000	Total	529,000	9.62

As the craft system began to disintegrate, a chasm developed between the masters, many of whom had accumulated wealth, and the journeymen and apprentices. The journeymen found it increasingly difficult to rise to the status of master, and many of the apprentices began to flee from their establishments to seek more favorable work opportunities.

The breakdown of the professional group is given in Table 5.2. People who held top positions in the civil service enjoyed prestige comparable with that of military officers, and ranked next to the

TABLE 5.2. PEOPLE ENGAGED IN PROFESSIONAL WORK

Number of Individuals	Occupation	Total Number (including family members and indoor servants)	Proportion of Total Population
5,000	Upper Civil Service	40,000	0.73%
9,000	Army and Navy officers	36,000	0.65
10,000	Lawyers	70,000	1.27
15,000	Liberal Arts and Sciences	75,000	1.36
5,000	Lower Civil Service	30,000	0.54
44,000	Total	251,000	4.56

squires and upper clergy in social distinction. Many of the lawyers were also ranked high on the social scale, as they purchased land and founded country families.[67]

The rank-order of statuses in agriculture ranged from the gentry (whom we have already considered) through the various gradations of freeholders, down to the tenant farmers and agricultural laborers. The upper group of freeholders, whose holdings were large enough to enable them to lease to tenants and whose income afforded a grand style of life and the parliamentary franchise, numbered about 40,000. The figure rose to 280,000 when their families and servants were included. The lesser freeholders and their families numbered about 660,000, and many of them lived on the fine edge of poverty. This group rapidly diminished in size as the smaller farms were sold under the enclosure movement, and many of these freeholders left their fields to make their living in other occupations. The tenant farmers, who leased their land from the more prosperous agriculturalists and paid an annual rent, numbered about 750,000, including the members of their families. At the bottom of the rural social scale were the farm laborers, who, hired by the year or by the day, often lived in small cottages on the commons.[68]

The remainder of the "third estate" was comprised of ordinary soldiers and seamen, nonagricultural laborers and out-servants, and vagrants. The people in this class made up about one-third or more of the total population.

Government Enforcement of Norms Relating to Style of Living. The holders of the peerage were men of great wealth, prestige, and political power, and at times some of them strongly resisted the king's policies. They had the right as individuals to demand an audience with the sovereign, and to consult with and to be consulted by him on public matters. As councilors of the king, they held seats in the exclusive House of Lords, which had the power to approve, modify, or block legislation. In this chamber they were entitled to the use of proxies. When accused of committing a crime, the noblemen were not within the jurisdiction of the ordinary courts or subject to the penalties imposed upon ordinary offenders, but claimed the right to be tried by their peers. Having committed a felony like housebreaking or highway robbery, they might receive the "benefit of clergy" for the first offense—a privilege that enabled them to commit one crime and go free, while a commoner would certainly be hanged for the same offense. In any event, they escaped the burning of the hand, which was performed on commoners. A peer enjoyed freedom of arrest in civil actions, and, while an ordinary citizen got a subpoena to appear in court, he received a less demanding "Letter Missive." He was also exempted from jury service—a release that gave him more time to exercise the privilege of shooting deer in the royal forests.[69] Despite their many legal privileges, however, they were not immune from the payment of taxes. From early times they had owed feudal dues to their monarch, and the direct taxes which he sought increasingly to impose upon his subjects fell upon the peers as well, usually according to their rank. Also important from the viewpoint of this monograph is the fact that there were no prescriptions against the English upper classes having connections with commerce and industry.

As members of a high calling, the clergy also enjoyed certain privileges in the society. The spiritual lords—archbishops and high-ranking bishops—claimed seats in the House of Lords and were eligible for most of the rights that were granted to its noble members. The remainder of the ecclesiastical class had their own representative assemblies at Canterbury and York, and until 1664 these convocations cherished the right to levy taxes upon the clergy as a group. Besides being exempt from jury duty and military service, the members of holy orders were not subject to the judgment of the secular courts in criminal matters (except possibly for treason) but fell under the control of a special set of ecclesiastical courts, which meted out lighter punishment than did the ordinary state courts.

It is important to point out that the squire-gentry class, which formed the bulk of the lesser social aristocracy, did not have the legal rights and duties of the nobility and clergy. Although accorded deference by the lower classes, the country squires enjoyed few special rights and privileges except for those granted by the highly restricted franchise. Legally, they belonged to the "third estate"; socially, they were aristocrats.

Summary

In the analysis of the government's contribution to the satisfaction of the pattern-maintenance functional requisite in the four societies, the empirical data do not yield striking patterns of similarity and difference. With regard to the enforcement by government of norms defining criminal behavior, the most significant difference occurs in the contrast between China and the other three cases. In China, the government appears to have been less involved in the enforcement of these types of norms, relying more heavily upon kinship and other nongovernmental structures in the community to detect and punish criminal acts.

In all four societies, the government enforced norms that helped to define social class. The most observable difference among the cases is the degree to which the highly prestigious classes in France and China enjoyed certain privileges and immunities which enabled them to escape the heavy burdens of taxation and kept them from undertaking business ventures. In the following section on integration, however, we shall see that when social class is defined in part by legal norms, the government necessarily becomes involved in the problems of movement among the various classes, and that in this realm significant differences among the four societies emerge with striking clarity.

THE INTEGRATION FUNCTIONAL REQUISITE

The three functions already discussed are established as requisites for any social system at the societal level primarily because each involves activities that must be undertaken if the social system is to deal adequately with its environment. The rationale for the proposition that integration is also a functional requisite, however, is quite different. In its simplest form it is based upon two assumptions. First, there must be role differentiation in any social system if it is to meet successfully the requirements of the other three requisites. (Hence, role differentiation is an *analytical structural requisite* of any social system.)[70] Second, if interdependent roles are differentiated, they must somehow be integrated, and there must be some concrete structures which contribute to integration.[71] Our concern with the integrative requisite involves the extent to which government contributes to the satisfaction of the integrative function.

Our specific interests in integration may best be identified by focusing attention upon the criteria by which roles (or structures) are differentiated. In this study we are mainly interested in three of these criteria: (1) differentiation on the basis of occupational specialization; (2) differentiation on the basis of prestige; and (3) differentiation on the basis of generation.[72] The relationships among roles that are differentiated along any of these lines are to some degree governed by a set of norms. We are concerned with the question of whether the government plays an important part in securing compliance with these norms.

We shall also take a brief glance at what might be called the integration of roles differentiated on the basis of geographic location. In considering this aspect of the problem, however, we are not dealing with the enforcement of norms governing role relationships. Instead, our attention is turned toward certain activities of government that are designed to facilitate (or inhibit) the movement of commodities from one section of the country to another, and this basically affects the relationships among interdependent roles in different geographic areas.

Integration of Roles Differentiated on the Basis of Occupational Specialization

Durkheim's classic work, *The Division of Labor,* which we have relied upon for the distinction between social control for pattern maintenance and social control for integration, deals mainly with the problem of integrating roles that are differentiated on the basis of full-time occupational specialization. In the study of modern societies, Durkheim concentrates his attention upon the institution of contract (and, implicitly, on the market) to seek clues as to how integration is achieved. The mutual advantage gained by each party to a contractual exchange, he argues, is not the factor that contributes most significantly to this integration. Integration is achieved, rather, through the body of norms and precepts that provides the context within which contracts are negotiated. These norms define such important matters as what constitutes fraud, who may engage in contractual relationships, and what goods and services are to be subject to contractual exchange. These matters, it should be emphasized, are not covered by the terms of the contract itself; they exist prior to and independently of any specific contractual relationship. They constitute the *noncontractual aspects of contract.*[73]

Durkheim points out how the norms and precepts which underly the noncontractual aspects of contract may be enforced by a number of different structures. Obviously, the government is one of the enforcement mechanisms, but not all of these norms are supported by legal sanctions. Professional or trade organizations themselves may be significantly involved, as, conceivably, might be religious organizations, although Durkheim pays little attention to the latter.

ENFORCEMENT OF NORMS BY GOVERNMENT. The most common propositions concerning the political conditions of economic growth at the beginning of industrialization tend to treat the problem of the normative context of interaction among occupational specialists merely as an aspect of the general problem of maintaining law and order. A formulation of this sort, however, makes it difficult to recognize that government may make a very significant contribution to pattern maintenance, while making only a minor contribution to integration. Nor does it allow one to investigate the range within which the government's contribution to the integration requisite through the enforcement of norms that make up the noncontractual aspects of contract may vary. We raise this latter problem, but, unfortunately, our cases provide only a small amount of information as to possible solutions. For this reason, a brief review of the case data will be sufficient.

France. In France, many of the governmental regulations were norms that could be classified as noncontractual aspects of contract. These norms, of course, were enforceable in courts of law and/or by government administrative action. As pointed out earlier, grants of privilege could create monopoly rights which limited the kinds of contracts that both the receiver of the grant and his potential competitors might enter into. The grantee, for example, might be compelled to sell his products only to designated distributors. At the same time, his potential competitors would not be permitted to enter into relationships that would enable them to produce the same products in the area covered by the grant.

In addition to legal norms supported by government, probably many nonlegal norms were also involved, and there were many conflicts involving contractual relationships which were settled outside the courts. The problem, of course, is to determine the relative importance of the government and nongovernmental structures in the enforcement process. While no direct evidence is available on this point, some indirect evidence suggests that in France the government was more involved than it was in any of the other three cases. It will be worthwhile, perhaps, to glance briefly at this evidence.

First, in France, many of the regulations that would ordinarily be classified as noncontractual aspects of contract were matters of public rather than private law. The government would take the alleged offenders into court, and hence the potential litigants had no alternative but to go to court.[74] Second, special provision was made in the courts to give priority to commercial cases, and thus inordinate delay in getting their cases on the court calendar did not serve as motivation for businessmen to settle their cases privately.[75] Third, we know that there were several professions in *ancien France—avocats, procureurs, chandeliers* (notaries), for example—who devoted a great deal of time to drawing up contracts and handling commercial cases in the courts. Nef makes an interesting comment:

As readers of that charming play of Alfred de Musset, *Le Chandelier,* will remember, the notary has occupied a position in French life only less important than the priest. In the late sixteenth and seventeenth centuries, as in more recent times, he visited the poor sick man who wanted to make his will, as well as the rich town merchant who wanted to draw up an agreement for leasing a house, a mill, or a farm in the suburbs. To enter into a contract without the assistance of a notary seemed as strange to most Frenchmen as to die without the consolation of the sacrament. Every detail of the contract was written into the notary's book, so that it could be examined at any time. Tens of thousands of these books have come down to us, and a large proportion of them are now stored in various French archives. . . . [These] books gave a formality and even a sanctity to all agreements that they never had when they were a matter of private arrangements between individuals without such elaborate intervention by a public official. The notarial system helped to make the evasion of the apprenticeship regulations more difficult than in England, where no systematic and detailed records of apprenticeship contracts were kept.[76]

A fourth and final point which suggests that government was significantly involved in the enforcement of norms governing the noncontractual aspects of contract may be presented as a chain of reasoning from other types of evidence. The officials who handled many of the commercial cases held offices that had been purchased. Part of their income from these offices was derived from the fees they received; the more fees they collected, the more valuable was the office. It is reasonable to assume, therefore, that the government, which was heavily dependent upon the sale of offices as a source of revenue, would actually *encourage* the settlement of disputes in court in order to increase the value of the offices and hence the price it could sell them for. At the moment, however, it is impossible to test this proposition from information available in the secondary sources.

China. In China, the government played only a secondary role in enforcing norms relating to the noncontractual aspects of contract.[77] Except for marriage, there was no formal contract law, and conflicts were decided in accordance with custom. Disputants were extremely reluctant to make use of the government's courts in settling their conflicts for several reasons. Court proceedings resulted in loss of "face," and resort to the courts was looked upon as an admission of declining moral virtue and weakened character. Since the local magistrates were often unfamiliar with the customs of the area and were usually more concerned with collecting "squeeze" from the contending parties than with dispensing justice, the disputants were motivated to resolve their difficulties by other means. Moreover, the government itself did not encourage formal appeals to the law, establishing heavy penalties in order to discourage them. When the government did intervene, it did so only when a case that could not be settled outside the courts was referred to them. According to a folk saying, "To enter a court of justice is to enter a tiger's mouth." Sinologists are agreed that the overwhelming majority of cases involving commercial matters were settled without being submitted to the governmental authorities.

This meant, of course, that disputes were handled by nongovernmental structures.[78] Within the family, such cases were settled by the family council, and conflicts between members of different families would be arbitrated by the village headman or the elders. Only when these attempts at arbitration failed were the cases submitted to the magistrates and the courts. The same course of action was followed by the guilds. These organizations had their own special courts, resembling to some extent the courts of the "law merchant," and guild members were required to submit their disputes to the guild rather than to take them directly to the magistrate. If a guild member bypassed the guild and took his grievance directly to a government court, he could be severely punished by his trade organization. Even appeals through channels to the courts were exceedingly rare. As in the case of interfamilial disputes, cases involving members of different guilds were usually resolved by *ad hoc* arbitration committees composed of merchants. Even when a guild referred a case to the magistrate, the latter would often send it back to the members for a final attempt at arbitration. If a conflict, of course, resulted in a disturbance of the peace, the political authorities would step in, treating the matter as a criminal case.

It is possible, however, that the Chinese government was more directly involved in supporting the norms relating to the noncontractual aspects of contract than we have indicated. The penal code, for example, was filled with regulations governing commercial transactions, and when merchants negotiated business deals in violation of the official rules, they were committing criminal acts and were subject to varying degrees of penalty.[79] It is unlikely that all serious cases of this sort were kept out of the official courts. Moreover, as we have seen, some of the economic enterprises in China were state-owned and state-managed. This meant that these state administrative units must have been entering into business relationships with each other, and that disputes over their mutual dealings were likely to have arisen. Such disputes would naturally have to be ironed out by government officials under what is generally understood to be a system of administrative law. On this aspect of economic litigation we have found no data, and it remains a researchable but nonresearched area of Sinology.

Japan. Unlike China, Japan developed recognizable forms of contract law, and the government was as a rule interested in having contract obligations fulfilled.[80] As was the situation in China, however, there were strong pressures upon Japanese litigants to resolve their difficulties outside the formal courts.[81] It was considered disreputable for rural villagers to resort to the courts; they were expected to iron out their differences by employing conciliation councils, heads of families, or the local sages as arbitrators. Indeed, it was a black mark upon the administrative record of the village headman if he were not successful in hammering out agreement, and for this reason he usually did his best to bring the disputants together. From time to time, the Edo government itself issued decrees urging the people to settle such matters as disputes over money loans by private agreement.[82] Subtle pressures exerted by members of the business community were usually sufficient to prevent violation of certain contracts, for an individual who committed the breach would lose his credit standing. In point of fact, oral contracts apparently were seldom broken.[83]

Despite the fact that merchants and other entrepreneurs were strongly encouraged to settle their disputes out of court and often ran the risk of having to compromise valid claims if they entered a courtroom, the government nevertheless assumed an important role in the enforcement process. As Tokugawa society began to struggle with the nascent forces of commercialism, the claims of the commercial interests grew difficult to ignore, and government courts were called upon to settle a rapidly increasing number of cases involving merchants, brokers, and debtors. This was especially true when conflicts arose among people of diverse jurisdictions and among individuals in the larger towns and cities where the bonds of tradition were somewhat looser.[84] We have already noted that the courts were particularly active in settling "main suits" where contractual obligations involving security but not interest were at stake. The shogunal authorities also devoted special attention to disputes concerned with land and irrigation rights, to which they usually gave full protection. In handling litigation arising from commercial transactions, the administrative authorities or "judges" tended to rely upon official decrees and upon precedents that were gradually grouped into regularized patterns.[85] In this way there developed a form of case law in which contests were decided according to social traditions or according to the "reason" of the officials hearing the disputes. As Henderson points out, the shogun's response to the merchants' demands for legal redress "caused the growth of a hierarchy of differentiated procedures, in some ways similar to the formulary system of the English common law, for the handling of cases in accordance with the political evaluation of plaintiffs and their claims by the Shogunate." [86]

England. The fact that the English crown was unable to regulate economic activities effectively meant that the government, especially in the eighteenth century, was not involved in many of the types of cases in which the French government became involved. This statement, however, does not permit us to assume that the government did little to enforce the noncontractual aspects of contract.

As in France, much of the English substantive law relating to problems of integration among occupational specialists was the *law merchant*. This body of law developed in Italy during the Middle Ages and spread into northern and western Europe. From early times, it was administered in special courts, the judges of which were sometimes chosen by the merchants themselves.[87] These courts, however, were not extragovernmental bodies, but were typically under the supervision of a municipality. More rarely, they might operate under royal charter.[88] By the end of the sixteenth century, the law merchant in England had largely been absorbed into the common law and was being administered by the common law courts. Thus, it is clear that the government was structurally equipped to make a significant contribution to integration among the various interdependent specialists. But the degree to which other nongovernmental structures were significantly involved cannot be determined from secondary sources. The government, of course, was not as active as it was in France in dragging merchants and artisans into court. Moreover, there are some hints (in Holdsworth,[89] for example) that pressures were operating to keep merchants out of court and to push them into private arbitration proceedings. Available evidence, however, does not permit precise comparison with France.

CURRENCIES. In addition to supporting norms that define the non-contractual aspects of contract, the government can in another way contribute to the integration of roles differentiated on the basis of occupational specialization. We noted in the section on goal attainment (Chapter 4) that the government in Japan and England provided a more stable monetary system than did the government in France and China, and that this had important implications for the creation of credit. At this stage of the analysis, however, we must recognize that a stable and standardized currency also facilitates exchange among occupational specialists. Fred W. Riggs uses the term *currency* to mean much more than a monetary system.[90] Following his lead but employing a more restricted definition, we define currency as the units in terms of which exchange takes place. Hence, one must consider physical units besides monetary units, and this introduces the problem of the standardization of weights and measures.

In France and China during the traditional stage, there was little standardization of weights and measures on a national scale.[91] Before adopting the metric system at the time of the revolution, France had to put up with a seemingly infinite variety of measurement standards. It was not that the central government ignored the problem; on the contrary, government leaders made repeated attempts to impose a standardized system on the country. But in this field, the efforts of the political authorities in Paris invariably ended in failure. Even such an economic rationalist as Colbert was unable to bring about significant reform. Different standards of measurement persisted in each of the provinces, and even in the same local area. People in different occupations—as, for example, masons and tailors—often employed different units. In 1671, the attempt to make weights and measures uniform in just the ports of the country was unsuccessful.

Lack of order was also characteristic of the system of weights and measures in China. Several emperors attempted to introduce nationwide standards, but the task proved to be more difficult than building the great wall or taming the mighty rivers. Each province and each city used different standards of measurement, and even within a local area the unit was likely to have diverse values. In Hangchow in the nineteenth century, for example, there were 17 different measures attached to the *catty* (a unit of weight), and these varied from 16 to 24 ounces. Throughout the entire country, the value of the catty varied all the way from 12 to 42.5 ounces.

In Japan and England, the situation appears to have been much less chaotic.[92] The Japanese, for example, were fortunate in having been able to establish relatively uniform standards of measurement during the hegemony of the Fujiwara clan beginning in the middle of the ninth century, and the system was improved upon by the Tokugawa shoguns. Dry and linear measures tended to conform to standards set by the central government, and after 1630 all scaling instruments in the country fell under the control of a single family which operated under commission by the shogun and which made it a practice to inspect scaling machines periodically.

England was a pioneer in the unification of weights and measures in Europe. Efforts at standardization achieved notable success as early as the fourteenth century, and such units as the Winchester bushel and yard of Elizabeth received fairly wide acceptance. These facts should not be taken to imply that a single system of weights and measures prevailed throughout the United Kingdom or even in England. But from his comparison, Heckscher concludes that England was far ahead of France in the uniformity of measuring units, so much so that the reformers at the time of the French revolution looked to England as a model.

SUMMARY. It is difficult, if not impossible, to compare the contribution of the four governments to the satisfaction of the integrative requisite with reference to the norms that govern the relationships among occupational specialists. There can be little doubt that the government was most active in France. If we were to guess at the comparative ranking of the other three cases, we would be inclined to list them in the following order: England, Japan, and China. Our direct evidence suggests that the English courts were active, though not as much as in France. Japan appears to have developed a form of contract law, which was unusual in that part of the world, and the businessmen of the cities apparently made some use of the courts. The low rank-order in the case of China may stem from the lack of data in secondary sources, especially the data relating to the Public Works Code and the relationships among government officials who were managing official enterprises.

The situation is quite different on the matter of the standardization of weights and measures. The Japanese and English governments were remarkably successful for the times, while repeated efforts of the French and Chinese governments were almost totally for naught.

Integration of Roles Differentiated on the Basis of Prestige

Differentiation on the basis of prestige involves primarily the patterns of social stratification in a society. The integration problem focuses attention upon the relationship among the social classes. The particular aspect of the integration problem that is important to this study relates to social mobility. In any society which has significant class differences, the problem of integration will be related in part to the channels of movement up and down the social hierarchy and the norms governing such movement.

A society, of course, may structure the pattern of movement from one class to another in many different ways. These can range from the classical Indian caste system in which there was no appreciable movement of individuals from one caste to another, to a society which is characterized by considerable movement in both directions. According to our analysis, the only general requirement of the traditional society is that the channels of mobility and the acceptable techniques of movement (up and down) are known and remain fairly constant over time.[93]

Our attention was drawn to the relationships among social classes primarily because of the important role of a particular social class— the merchant-entrepreneur group—in the cases of take-off during the nineteenth century. This study is mainly concerned with three aspects of this integration problem: (1) the patterns of mobility into and out of the merchant-entrepreneurial class in traditional societies; (2) the norms that governed this movement; and (3) the degree to which the sanctions which supported these norms were legal (as contrasted with nonlegal) sanctions.

FRANCE. Many of the facts concerning social stratification that are necessary for a discussion of mobility in France have already been presented in the treatment of pattern maintenance. It will be useful, however, to review briefly those points that are salient to the problem of upward and downward movement among the social classes. First, it must be emphasized that the status of the nobility— including their rights, duties, powers, and disabilities—were recognized and guaranteed by law, and the circumstances under which an individual might lose his noble status were also established by law.

Second, all of the sons of noblemen enjoyed noble rank and claimed membership in the nobility. Third, there existed clear channels of mobility by which the members of the bourgeoisie could achieve noble status, and to a significant degree these channels were created by the government through such devices as the direct sale of letters of nobility and the sale of offices which carried titles with them.

The monarch could ennoble any person simply by issuing letters patent. This practice probably originated as a reward for services rendered to the crown, but from the sixteenth century onward it became increasingly the practice of the monarch to sell patents of nobility as a means of raising state revenue. At the time of Louix XIV, a title could be purchased for as little as 6,000 livres.[94] Some of the titles that were sold, however, were of varying "quality," and those carrying higher prestige commanded a higher price.[95]

A second way in which an individual might become a nobleman was by purchasing an office that carried with it a title of nobility. These offices included positions in the parlements, numerous municipal posts, and many appointments in the central government.[96] Precise figures are not available on the number of "titled" offices which were sold, but, judging from the amount of revenue collected from this source, the figure must have been high. Within the king's government there were over 900 secretaries to the monarch and 740 offices of finance, all of which carried titles and were available for sale.[97] Between 1732 and 1742, 1,207 payments for ennoblement or confirmation were made in the Paris area alone. The provincial records in the first half of the eighteenth century record an ennoblement for almost every month of every year. In Bordeaux in August 1733, for example, royal letters of ennoblement were registered for a shipper, a wholesaler, a lawyer, and a merchant.[98] This heavy traffic in offices and titles continued until the revolution. Egret estimates that among the 943 parlementaires who received their appointments between 1774 and 1787 and were still in office in 1790, 394 were former *roturiers*.[99] Although many offices were created and sold, there apparently were not always enough of them at proper prices to meet the demand; at times, the titles were rented.[100]

A third method of securing a title was through the purchase of the estate of a nobleman and the titles, rights, and privileges that accompanied it. Transactions of this sort, however, were prohibited by law in 1579. While enterprising individuals devised ways to circumvent the prohibition, the purchase of estates was never as important a ladder of mobility as was the direct purchase of titles and/or offices.[101]

A fourth technique for achieving noble status was through intermarriage. If a wealthy roturier was unable to secure a title for himself, he might at least provide one for his grandsons by marrying his daughter into a noble family. This practice created a veritable "husband market" in Paris, and the prices for husbands in the various noble ranks were well known. For a minimum dowry of 35,000 livres during the time of Louis XIV, a family of the third estate could contemplate buying into the lower ranks of the nobility; a dowry of about 200,000 livres could finance a marital union with the finest noble families of France.[102] This husband market was sustained by the complementarity of interests of the bourgeoisie who desperately wanted the prestige of affiliation with a noble family, and the interests of noble families who were equally desperate for money and who found it necessary to *manure* their titles. The value of dowries rose even higher in the eighteenth century—a development that resulted not so much from the declining supply of potential husbands as from the increased demand of wealthy commoners for noble status.

It is difficult, of course, to get a precise accounting of the number of commoners who became ennobled through one kind of purchase or another. Clearly, only a small percentage of the third estate ever managed to be awarded titles. But there can be little doubt that a significant proportion of the bourgeoisie who had accumulated sufficient wealth did succeed in becoming ennobled. Pontchartrain reputedly told Louis XIV: "Sire, every time it pleases your majesty to create an office, God creates a fool to buy it." Three types of "fools" were engaged in such transactions: the nobleman who was on the lookout for an income-producing investment, the wealthy businessman, and the rich peasant.

Numerically speaking, the wealthy business group, which was not the most prestigious in the third estate, was the most significant in the purchase of social respect.[103] A contemporary French observer, cited by Nef, attests to the great pressure to purchase offices and to the success in this endeavor of those who had achieved wealth:

The French have long since entertained a very disparaging opinion of commerce, which they consider suited only to debased souls. . . . This is the opinion which the majority of Frenchmen hold and especially those of the *tiers état*, who have means and desire to elevate their children to the most honorable stations. . . . They have ambitions to acquire the offices of justice which the state in its need has created in great numbers, so that the majority of those who are rich and have means to carry on commerce abandon it, in order to acquire such positions for their children. . . . It is for this reason that for the maintenance of trade there remain only those of low estate. . . . Whenever, from that small number of Frenchmen who are engaged in foreign commerce, some one amasses a fortune, which is the very moment when he is the most capable of pursuing foreign trade, he abandons it in order to place his children in some office of state.[104]

For the rich member of the bourgeoisie, however, the purchase of offices and titles was often only a first step in achieving the position and prestige he desired. His next objective was to purchase land, perhaps a landed estate which traditionally carried a title with it.

Although some empirical data are lacking, several conclusions may be supported from existing evidence: (1) The values and manner of living of the nobility offered great appeal to the wealthy members of the French bourgeoisie during the seventeenth and eighteenth centuries.[105] (2) The channels of upward movement were sufficiently open to permit wealthy commoners to aspire to noble status. (3) Significant numbers from the richer segment of the bourgeoisie managed to secure titles, either for themselves or for their sons.[106]

CHINA. The government of Manchu China greatly influenced the system of social stratification and the patterns of mobility in the society. The rights and privileges of the gentry class, which were widely sought after, were written into law and were for the most part strictly enforced. The government also made some legal provision for depriving individuals of their academic titles and official posts. More important, however, is the fact that the Peking authorities were able to regulate the flow of people into the ranks of the gentry, thereby determining the size and composition of that class.[107]

The most orthodox method of achieving gentry status was by successfully completing the civil service examinations. The candidates who sat for these examinations were selected on a quota basis, and by adjusting the quotas the government was in a position to affect upward movement to prestigious rank. Although, up to the end of the Sung dynasty (1270), merchants, artisans, and their families had been prohibited from taking the examinations, its successors—especially the Manchu rulers—were much more permissive, removing many of the legal restrictions upon upward mobility. Imperial decrees in the early eighteenth century, for example, provided that in three or four generations even the descendants of the declassed would be eligible to take the examinations.[108] From time to time, the regime would allocate separate quotas for particular regions or occupational categories, thereby enhancing the opportunities for certain groups to rise socially and economically. Under the Manchus, the salt merchants were a favored group, special examination quotas being set up for their children. These quotas, which had been established early in the Manchu era, were increased in 1858 in recognition of the merchants' contribution to the military fund for fighting the Taiping rebels.[109] The data presented by Ho indicate that the academic success of the salt merchant group was disproportionately high.[110] By the same token, of course, the government was able partially to close off the channels of mobility to certain segments of the population and to particular geographic areas by restricting the examination quotas.

A second avenue leading to gentry status was through the purchase of academic titles and public offices. As we have seen, the sale of social status was a conspicuous feature of the entire Manchu period, but it became increasingly frequent at the time of the Taiping rebellion, thus opening a wider path to those who had wealth. In the pre-Taiping period, approximately one-third of all the gentry had purchased their status; in the period after 1850, the proportion had risen to 36 per cent, while at the same time the number of members admitted to the gentry class had increased significantly.[111]

One of the striking features of the mobility patterns in China is the fact that a significantly large number of those who entered the gentry class were "newcomers," that is, commoners whose families in *recent generations* had produced no persons of rank. Out of a nineteenth-century sample of 2,146 cases studied by Chang, 35 per cent were in the "newcomer" category.[112] According to Ho's analysis, approximately 43 per cent of the people who held the highest degree between 1469 and 1892 were from commoner families.[113] Nevertheless, the elite group of official families produced a disproportionately large number of candidates who were successful in examinations, but the people of commoner background, once they were awarded posts, were relatively successful in winning even higher official rank.[114]

Opportunities for the upward movement of impecunious commoners probably became somewhat restricted with the growing tendency to purchase gentry status rather than to rely upon the examination route. The curtailment of examination quotas, for example, was likely to reduce the probability of an individual in poor circumstances achieving high rank.[115] Under these circumstances, the members of the merchant class, who usually had amassed more wealth than other social groups, were in a better position to move upward. In the first place, their wealth was sufficient to provide their children with an "intellectual" home environment and access to formal schooling so that they would stand a better chance of passing the civil service examination. In the second place, the members of merchant families were likely to be the ones with sufficient resources to buy their way to prestigious status.

In any event, there can be little doubt that a considerable number of people with merchant backgrounds entered the gentry class. Chang has analyzed the economic position of approximately 5,000 gentry members during the years 1796-1908, and he notes that the proportion of merchants in the group varied between 2 and 3 per cent.[116] According to Ho, 300 or fewer transport and factory merchant families produced 347 high-ranking and middle-ranking degree-holders between 1646 and 1802, while in roughly the same period 140 members of these families purchased their way to officialdom.[117] There was great pressure within the merchant group for advancement to gentry status. According to one tale, the head of a merchant family, upon hearing that his son had passed the civil service examination, uttered the sigh: "Now we can get ourselves out of this trade business!" [118] Merchants would aspire to gentry status, and, once this status had been achieved, the mercantile element of the family tended to become less prominent.[119]

Although the institutions for vertical mobility were clearly operative in Manchu China, there were few mechanisms working effectively to retain successful families at high status levels and to prevent them from moving downward in the social scale.[120] Rights of inheritance, for example, existed only in narrow scope, and were further attenuated during the years of Manchu rule.[121] This meant that even the sons of office-holders had either to pass the civil service examination in their own right or to purchase their way to public office. Newcomers to the gentry class tended to take over the values of the traditional elite, preferring leisure and the pleasures of lavish consumption to productive endeavors.[122] Mobility based upon the achievement in civil service examinations, the limited number of offices passed on by inheritance, the gradual diminution of wealth resulting from equal division of property, bankruptcy as a consequence of high living, and failure to provide adequate education for offspring—all of these factors helped to promote the downward movement of successful families in the course of several generations.[123] The decline of families that had once eaten the fruits of gentry status naturally made room for aspiring individuals who had enough competence to pass the examination or enough money to buy their titles so that they and their families could climb the ladder to social and economic success.

JAPAN. The shogunate sought to maintain the integrity of the daimyo-samurai group by freezing class relationships, and, according to Honjo, it was virtually impossible at the beginning of the Tokugawa period for people to move from one class to another.[124] While as a matter of practical policy the Tokugawa rulers did little to prevent the lower classes from intermingling or to hold rich merchants at the bottom of the social ladder, they consistently attempted to keep the samurai as a distinct and superior group.[125] According to the official decrees, they alone were to be accorded the privilege of wearing two swords, and the lower social groups were not permitted to marry into the samurai ranks and were not to be eligible for titles and honors.[126] As far as the shogunate was concerned, the task of civil administration was to rest exclusively in the hands of the daimyo and samurai. Perhaps the best index of the government's attitude toward the preservation of daimyo-samurai status was its policy toward the debts accumulated by the members of the upper class when they became pressed financially. In an attempt to safeguard them, the shogunate occasionally repudiated their debts and sometimes loaned them money from its own resources.

Internal developments within Japan, however, encouraged the rise and growth of the merchant class, which came to perform an indispensable role in the society. Even before the Tokugawa era, the samurai had moved to the castle towns within the daimiates, and the merchants had begun to furnish them with supplies. After the rise of the Tokugawa, the merchants engaged in the important activity of supplying goods and services to the daimyo and samurai who were forced to journey to and reside periodically in the capital at Edo. Since the members of the upper class, whose income was in rice, came increasingly to need some form of easily negotiable currency to meet their expenses, they were forced to enter into commercial relations with merchants and brokers who eagerly took on the job of converting the rice into monetary currency. The common practice was for the daimyo to establish rice warehouses in places like Osaka and Edo and to put financial agents (usually merchants-brokers) in charge of them.

The merchants also became important in the Tokugawa economy as creditors to the daimyo and samurai whose incomes were insufficient to meet their contributions to the shogun and the cost of their travel to and residence in Edo. When a daimyo made these periodic visits, he took many of his samurai with him, he maintained an expensive residence in Edo as well as in his home territory, and he and his party often indulged in extravagant living while in the capital. Expenses of this sort became increasingly heavy to bear, especially in view of fluctuations in the price of rice. As a rule it took about half of a daimyo's income to maintain himself and his entourage in Edo, besides the cost of travel back and forth.[127] According to one writer, the samurai spent about 10,000,000 ryo annually in Edo—an amount roughly equal to one-third of the total rice crop for the entire country.[128]

Faced by financial difficulties, the daimyo and samurai fell heavily in debt to the merchants and rice brokers. According to an account of the situation in the seventeenth century, the debts of the feudal lords exceeded the amount of money in circulation in all the provinces by 100 times.[129] At one time in the early decades of the nineteenth century, three-fourths of the rice transported to markets by the daimyo went to the Osaka merchants as interest on debts which aggregated 60,000,000 ryo.[130] The government, of course, often introduced measures to ease the financial pressure upon the military class, sometimes going so far as to repudiate officially the daimyo-samurai debts to the merchant class.[131] Such a policy worked great hardship upon the merchants, some of whom went bankrupt as a result of their uncollectable loans. Very often, however, the financial interests were able to exert pressure to discourage the repudiation of honest debts. When the daimyo or samurai refused to meet their obligations, the merchants would march to their residences to serve notice upon the debtors, and they usually refused to make any more loans to borrowers who had already defaulted in their payments. Indeed, the merchants cooperated in supplying each other with lists of poor financial risks.

Under these circumstances, some of the businessmen in the cities and towns amassed considerable wealth as they carried on their activities as ordinary merchants, commercial agents, and moneylenders, or as speculators who bought and sold rice or changed money. It was estimated that toward the end of the Tokugawa era, about 70 per cent of the national wealth was represented in Osaka.[132] The successful merchants of the cities tended to live luxuriously in their mansions, catering to extravagant tastes, patronizing literature and the arts, and fostering the development of a polished, bourgeois culture.[133] Other classes, including both warriors and peasants, began to envy the growing power of the merchants and to ape their style of living. By the mid-point in the Tokugawa era, some daimyo and samurai were even willing to enter the homes of merchants in order to plead for money, or to entertain them in restaurants in the hope of being able to negotiate loans.

A number of contemporary writers testify to the growing power and influence of the merchant class. According to one report, the "anger of the wealthy merchants of Osaka has the power of striking terror into the hearts of the daimyo." [134] In 1816, another writer lamented that "notwithstanding the fact that the *samurai* ought to be the rulers and the merchants the ruled, it appears that the chonin [townsmen] have now become virtual rulers." [135] The fact that the shogunate and the daimyo were unable to control the merchants was stated rather succinctly in a personal letter sent to the Shogun Yoshimune:

In these circumstances the social standing of the samurai has been greatly lowered of late years, and it is often difficult to distinguish a samurai from a certain class of merchants. Much of the samurai's authority over the commercial has been lost, and some samurai think that they can only live with the aid of the rich merchants, while many merchants declare that the samurai can do nothing without their favours.[136]

In view of their economic power it is not surprising that the merchants began to rise in the social scale, especially during the closing decades of Tokugawa rule. It is important to observe, however, that the number who were actually able to enter the samurai class was probably very small, and even those who managed to attain this status continued for the most part to perform in their merchant roles.[137] Although the merchants began illegally to purchase samurai status, lending money to the daimyo in return for privileges, the most common method of climbing the social ladder was for them to win official appointment by the shogun or individual daimyo as special merchants, business agents, managers of monopolies, or financial advisers. In return for such service, merchants were often privileged to have surnames and to wear the double blades, flashy costumes, and other badges of social distinction. When a merchant was employed by a daimyo as keeper of the warehouse, he was likely to become a powerful financial figure in the daimiate. Occasionally a merchant might rise to the formal rank of retainer. As we have seen, the merchants were active in the reclamation of land, but in many instances they were more interested in achieving the status of landowner than they were in actually plowing the fields.

In sharp contrast with France and China, the merchants of Japan were prompted to continue and to succeed in their roles as merchants.[138] Given the closed nature of Japanese society, the majority of them could nurture little hope that they could become actual members of the upper class. It was virtually impossible for them to become daimyo; their only hope was to have a son or daughter married to someone in a higher social stratum. But while such a union might increase their prestige and provide useful social "connections," it did not give them bona fide membership in the warrior class. Again in sharp contrast with China, the Japanese merchant could not aspire to rise through the purchase of land, for such transactions were illegal, and a merchant who invested heavily in agricultural operations would be inviting confiscation by the central authorities.

Although it was difficult for merchants to move upward into full membership in the samurai class, the hard-pressed warriors tended to move into closer association with the merchants or even to enter the business world directly on their own.[139] It was to be expected that impoverished samurai would seek an alliance with wealthy merchant families which yearned for social prestige, and in many instances they pushed aside their eldest sons and adopted the sons of merchant families. Apparently many samurai were willing to relinquish their superior status entirely and to descend into the productive and commercial world, engaging in the manufacture of sandals, sandal straps, silk, or lanterns in their home provinces or actually performing in merchant roles. Moreover, under the prevailing rules of primogeniture, the members of the family who were disinherited tended to drift to the cities, where they undertook professional work or entered the business world.[140] According to one limited report for the period 1818-1829, no less than 48 out of 250 merchant families were able to boast of samurai ancestors.[141] Thus the superior samurai class tended to feed into the merchant group, providing it with fresh ideas and new administrative resources.

The merchant class was also refurbished by the more enterprising elements of the peasant community.[142] The long era of peace under the Tokugawa helped to precipitate an expansion in agriculture, with a shift from subsistence to commercial farming. This led to the establishment of locally based industries, usually sponsored and administered by landlord families and manned by less well-to-do peasants. This commercial and industrial activity in the countryside provided the wealthier farmers with investment opportunities besides agriculture, and they, along with merchants in the nearby cities, began to engage in such activities as brewing, textile manufacturing, and the marketing of food products. In the early part of the nineteenth century, the shogun and the daimyo began to sell surnames and other symbols of distinction to some of the wealthier peasants and even to appoint them to administrative posts.

The rural areas that enveloped the urban centers were especially vulnerable to mercantile influence.[143] Despite the government's attempt to keep the peasants in village agriculture, many of them were hired by merchants to become tradesmen, or were prompted to move to the cities in the hope of gaining alternative employment. In some instances, the eldest sons of peasant families would relinquish their inheritance and migrate to the urban areas to enter a business or take up a trade. Occasionally, farm families were successful in arranging marriages with merchant families of the city, or in adopting the sons of wealthy businessmen. Even many of the people who remained in the rural areas or returned to their villages from the city began increasingly to engage in petty trade, turning away from the plow to more promising types of employment. A small, isolated report from Sendai during the 1750's provides an interesting if not typical picture of social developments in the countryside. Out of a total of 100 farmers, about 50 entrusted the job of farming to their wives and children and engaged in trade and industry themselves. The remaining members of the sample were involved both in farming and trade.

Thus the relatively closed social system in Tokugawa Japan prompted the merchants to focus their energies upon commercial and industrial activities without being very much enticed by the prospect of careers in the civil service or by the hope of becoming large-scale landowners through legal purchase. Moreover, the ranks of the entrepreneurial class were increasingly being replenished by the influx of lower samurai and prosperous peasants—energetic people who often possessed organizing skill and experience. As in the case of England but unlike France and China, the system of single inheritance (usually the eldest son) forced the male family members who did not share significantly in the property distribution to search for alternative forms of employment. Many of them drifted to the city, becoming merchants, artisans, or ordinary workers.

ENGLAND. In considering the patterns of mobility in the English class system, it is important to note that the policies of the government contributed to the restriction of the nobility to a very small group. During their early struggles for more funds, the English rulers sought to expand the tax base by summoning the knights of the shires to parliament. These lesser nobles resisted the financial schemes of the monarchy, and eventually they separated themselves from their more wealthy and more powerful kinsmen, entering into common cause with the burgesses and other mercantile elements of the realm. Thus the nobility in England came to be defined on a very restricted basis, and the knights and squires, though high in the social scale, were not technically regarded as members of the noble class. The size of the nobility was also limited by the fact that the legal privileges of a peer did not extend to the members of his family; they were relegated to the class of commoners, except for the eldest son *after* he had inherited the title. A system of rank-orders that assigned fewer than 200 members to the noble class did not provide much room for large numbers of individuals to move upward into the peerage. This was also true of such honored non-noble ranks as the baronetcies and knighthoods. Even after a particularly venal period in English history, the former numbered only 800 by 1690, and the latter 600—a supply so limited that only a minute proportion of the wealthy merchants ever stood much chance of being awarded these honors.

The narrow range of opportunities to move upward into the noble class can be seen from a brief examination of the peerage under the early Stuarts, who were notorious for the sale of titles and offices.[144] The number of peerages, which was listed at 59 by the end of Elizabeth's reign, was increased by 62 under James I and by another 65 under Charles I. Thus, during a period of 46 years, when there was a larger influx into the noble class than had hitherto been the case, only 127 individuals were awarded peerages, and probably only a minority were purchased.

Roughly the same pattern obtained in the creation of titles that did not carry noble rank. Whereas fewer than 900 knights bachelors and 11 Knights of the Bath had been awarded during Elizabeth's reign, her successor created more than 2,000 knights bachelors and at least 126 Knights of the Bath. These and other orders represented some of the "purchasable dignity" of the era, and many of the people who were dubbed with the sword were wealthy merchants who had bought their way into the social world. But, when compared with the wholesale distribution of ranks in France and China, the English system of social stratification provided places at the top for only a relatively small number of individuals.

Attracted by the social prestige that accompanied land ownership, however, some merchants aspired to move into the gentry class by purchasing manor estates and establishing "country families," especially during the Hanoverian period.[145] As perceptive an observer of social trends as Daniel Defoe noted the upward social movement of prosperous merchants: "Trade is so far here from being inconsistent with a gentleman, that . . . trade in England makes gentlemen . . . ; for, after a generation or two, the tradesman's children, or at least their grandchildren, come to be as good gentlemen, statesmen, parliamentmen, privy-counsellors, judges, bishops, and noblemen, as those of the highest birth and the most ancient families. . . ."[146] In considering this aspect of vertical mobility in the English class system, however, two important points must be kept in mind: (1) the merchants who succeeded in planting themselves in the countryside were probably only a small proportion of the entire merchant-entrepreneurial group, the majority being content to amass wealth in their urban habitats; and (2) even those who succumbed to the call of the countryside did not divest themselves of their capitalist roles. They soon perceived that the money they put into the land was a sound investment, and they used their profits from trade to introduce new agricultural methods in order to derive profits from the soil. In England, preoccupation with trade, investments, and profit was not a badge of dishonor. At the funerals of merchants who had been knighted, the symbols of their mercantile association were displayed as much as their emblems of knighthood.

Not only did most of the merchants-entrepreneurs continue to perform in their business roles, but their ranks were continually being nourished by recruits from other social classes. To some extent this was facilitated by intermarriage, against which there was no legal restraint. The country gentlemen, attracted by the wealth of the merchants and entrepreneurs, were often willing to have their sons and daughters marry into families of commerce, so that their offspring would be amply provided for and they themselves might get a financial interest in business.[147] Perhaps even more significant was the apprenticeship of the younger sons of the rural aristocrats to prosperous businessmen in the industrial centers. Indeed, under the Statute of Artificers, only those parents whose income and possessions exceeded a prescribed minimum were entitled to apprentice their sons in a trade or craft. A great many of the apprentices were the younger sons of the landed gentry, some of whom aspired to become officials in the firm or to win the affections of the master's daughter.[148] As early as 1633-1635, there were within the City of London no fewer than 900 families which were descended from the rural gentry, and the great majority of these people were engaged in trade.[149]

The lure of wealth as a means of achieving social prestige also attracted into the business class large numbers of people from the professions, from other occupations classified as "middle class," and from less prestigious trades and callings.[150] Scholars who had been educated in humanistic disciplines turned to a study of the physical sciences; some scientists who had been trained along traditional lines shifted their interests to technology; and lawyers, civil servants, and military officials entered the business world, where they found greater opportunity for advancement than existed in their own professions. Even some individuals from humble and nonprestigious callings managed to scrape together enough capital to start a small business, and then to develop it into a large-scale undertaking. The economic history of England records an impressive number of hairdressers, innkeepers, schoolteachers, and people of similar station nursing along their business enterprises which eventually earned for them huge fortunes.

This brief discussion of interclass movement in English society entitles us to make several tentative observations: (1) Although merchants and entrepreneurs were attracted by peerages and titles, relatively few of these ranks were open to them. (2) While some prosperous merchants bought manors and achieved gentry status, they probably constituted only a small proportion of the merchant-entrepreneurial class, and even they did not usually close the door to the business world but invested their money in capitalist farming. (3) The real links between the aristocracy and the business class were forged by the marriage of daughters and younger sons of the nobility and gentry to the children of businessmen, and by the movement of younger sons of the nobility and gentry into trade and manufacture through apprenticeship. (4) The ranks of the merchant-entrepreneurial class were also infused with new talent from the professions and from the less prestigious occupations.

SUMMARY. When it comes to the integration of roles that are differentiated on the basis of prestige, the major patterns of difference and similarity between the two sets of cases stand out quite clearly. In France and China, the policies of government made it possible for—and even encouraged—the wealthy, successful merchants and manufacturers to use their wealth to purchase their way into the prestigious classes, and then to divest themselves of their mercantile roles. In Japan and England, on the other hand, laws and government policies tended to prevent significant numbers of merchants and manufacturers from acquiring noble status. Not only did these entrepreneurial groups continue to perform in the business world, but also their ranks were swelled by members from other social classes.

Integration of Roles Differentiated on the Basis of Generation

In every society, certain rights and duties accrue to people in different age groups or "generations." This situation gives rise to a set of integrative problems concerning the relationships among generations.[151] Among the most important of these relationships—and the only one of interest in this study—is the way in which the rights, privileges, and powers associated with property are passed on from one generation to the next. Our study is specifically focused upon two types of norms governing inheritance: (1) the degree to which an individual was able to bequeath his property to anyone he chose (testamentary freedom); and (2) the degree to which the laws of inheritance influenced the concentration of property or its relatively equal distribution.

FRANCE. No brief treatment of the French laws governing inheritance can do justice to the profusion of practices that prevailed under the *ancien régime*. Even though our attention is limited to the two items listed above, it is difficult not to be misleading in a summary statement.

Two main bodies of law governed inheritance in France before the revolution.[152] In the north, the Germanic customary law placed great emphasis upon the family—its integrity and responsibilities. It viewed the most important property as being owned by the family as perpetual proprietor. The collective rights of the family were protected against the private interests of the head of the family, who was regarded as the temporary administrator of family property. With this view of property ownership and control, it is not surprising that the testamentary freedom of an individual was severely limited; each survivor in the family had claims on the property and had the right to be supported by its income. Where the customary law prevailed, there tended to be a relatively equal division of wealth among the heirs.

Under the written law, an individual had greater freedom to dispose of his estate as he wished. However, he was forced by the law to take care of his children, providing them with half (in some places, a third) of his estate. The effect was to distribute rather than to concentrate property ownership, but the distribution of the property was on a more unequal basis than it was in the north.

During an earlier period of French history, the canonical courts held jurisdiction over many inheritance matters. By the end of the fifteenth century, however, these religious courts had been largely displaced by government courts, and for this reason the enforcement of the laws of inheritance may properly be viewed as an activity of government.[153]

In summary, then, it may be stated that French law placed strict limits upon the freedom of an individual to dispose of his estate as he liked, particularly in the northern part of France. All survivors inherited some property—in relatively equal amounts in the north, and in potentially less equal amounts in the south.[154]

CHINA. Early in their history, the Chinese abandoned the principle of primogeniture, and an inheritance system based upon equal division of property among the sons of the family became the established norm.[155] As in the customary law of France, emphasis was placed upon the family as a group which could survive only through the transfer of its patrimony intact from one generation to the next. For this reason the head of the family was regarded as holding the family property in his stewardship, and he was expected to hand it down to all of the male heirs. In other words, his testamentary freedom was severely restricted. As in most societies, the Chinese made a distinction between real property and "movable" or personal property. Even in the case of the latter, the greater part was distributed among the sons.

Although poorer families were often unable to follow the principle of equal division of family property, the principle itself was deeply rooted in the customs and statutes of the society and was widely practiced by well-to-do families. When the parents decided to distribute the family property before they died, they might choose to live with one of their sons, in which case it was customary to bequeath that son an extra slice of the estate. If the parents elected to live by themselves after having divided their property, the remainder of the estate was equally divided among the male heirs after their death.

The Chinese system of inheritance meant that the younger sons were not required to leave the family acreage and shift for themselves, but could remain at home and work the land in which they had a stake. But the fact that the property of the father was divided among all of his sons tended to prevent any one of them from accumulating a large block of property from which he might develop a significant amount of investment capital.

JAPAN. Unlike France and China, the inheritance system in Japan was as a rule based upon the principle of primogeniture.[156] While there was some deviation from the prevailing pattern, in the vast majority of cases bequests were settled upon the eldest son, or at least upon a single heir. In families whose property holdings were small, the master of the family was forbidden by law to distribute any part of the inheritance among his younger sons. When the family head died without making a will, his property was handed over to a single heir. Exceptions which violated the primogenitary principle usually required the agreement of the family members and permission from the local government authorities. The head of the family in certain areas exercised discretionary power to disinherit the male heir (usually on physical or mental grounds, or because he had misbehaved), and to bequeath his property to one of his younger sons.

In some instances the head of a family might undertake the difficult task of creating a branch family with his eldest son, designating one of his younger sons as his successor in the main family. When he desired to establish a branch family with one of his sons, he would so notify the local officials and attempt to gain approval for the partition. The creation of branch families was frequently discouraged and was usually restricted according to the customary number of families or houses already in existence in a village. In other words, a family head was sometimes unable to establish a branch family until one of the existing families had been discontinued or had moved away.

One might expect that the creation of a branch family would result in a serious depletion of the family patrimony. This, however, was frequently not the case. Although in some areas the amount apportioned from the family estate for this purpose was left to the discretion of the family head, it was never more than one-third or one-fourth of the total inheritance, and most of the time it was much less. Indeed, local villagers often resisted the allocation of respectable amounts of property for the new family. In financing the establishment of a branch family, the family head sometimes relied upon the portion of his estate that he had purchased, leaving the part that he had inherited to the succeeding head of the main family.

In summary, then, the prevailing practice in Japan was for the head of the family to leave his estate to his eldest son, and, in any event, to designate only a single heir. This meant that an individual inherited large blocks of property intact, and that the sons who were not eligible to succeed to the family headship were forced to look out for themselves unless a branch family were created for them. It must also be noted that government played an active role in the inheritance process. The family head was required to make known his intentions to local officials in the matter of bequests and to secure their approval for exemption from the rules of primogeniture. And, as we have seen, the poorer families in some territories were not permitted legally to divide their property among several heirs.

ENGLAND. Unlike France and China, the English people had no concept of property ownership by the family as a collectivity.[157] By the thirteenth century, the rule of primogeniture had been widely established throughout the kingdom, and its influence was still being felt during the period under examination. Although in the sixteenth and seventeenth centuries the head of the family gained a measure of testamentary freedom which enabled him to disinherit his heir, the law still recognized the succession of land and other immovable property that were entailed to the eldest son. Moreover, when a property-owner died intestate, the eldest son held prior rights in the inheritance of real property. Also he would not necessarily be excluded from the heirship of personal property, which was distributed more widely among the survivors. These provisions assume considerable importance in view of the fact that wills were not officially sanctioned until the middle of the sixteenth century and were infrequently made out during much of this period. Under these circumstances, the feudal rules of inheritance, which favored the eldest son, tended to obtain. Thus, even though the property-owner had a wider range of testamentary discretion than in earlier times, the rules of primogeniture were still recognized both in law and in custom, especially in the disposition of land and certain chattels.

Despite the inroads of statutory law and the ruses of the lawyers upon the traditional rules of inheritance by primogeniture, however, there was a distinct tendency on the part of property-owners of all social classes to settle the bulk of their estates upon a single heir. The nobility, for example, usually bequeathed most of their property to their eldest sons. While many wealthy people left some of their property to all of their children, the biggest share of the landed estates or the family businesses went to their eldest sons. Even when the eldest son was not the principal beneficiary, the legator was strongly inclined to devise a large portion of his estate upon one son rather than to distribute it equally among all of them. In this way the large owners of property sought to keep their holdings relatively intact and within the grasp of a responsible member of the family from one generation to the next.

SUMMARY. In the integration of roles differentiated on the basis of generation, the patterns between the two sets of cases are unmistakably distinct. In France and China, inheritance was diffused more or less equally along a number of survivors. In Japan and England, on the other hand, the inheritance system tended to concentrate property in the hands of a single heir. It should also be observed that in all four cases the prevailing patterns of inheritance were fixed by both customary and statutory law, that government officials were involved in the enforcement of inheritance norms, and that disputes over the disposition of estates could *ultimately* be taken to the government courts.

Roles Differentiated on the Basis of Geographic Location

Although the concept "differentiation on the basis of geographic location" presents some methodological problems, we shall not digress to analyze them here. Instead, we shall simply use this as a rubric to call attention to some activities of government that have important integrative implications.

In the discussion of taxation in Chapter 4, we noted that the government in France and China imposed what was in effect a system of internal tariffs, whereas the government in Japan and England did not. The traites in France and the likin in China were taxes upon goods in transit from one section of the country to another, and hence were barriers to trade. In considering the contribution of government to the satisfaction of the integrative functional requisite, these taxes were important because they tended to reduce the size of the area in which interdependencies among differentiated roles could develop.

In the case of France, however, we must note something more than just the system of internal tariffs. France in the seventeenth and eighteenth centuries had inherited from the Middle Ages a great variety of onerous tolls on river and road transport which had been levied by the great vassals and by ordinary private landowners. The number and extent of these tolls were indeed noteworthy. On the Loire from Roanne to Nantes, for example, there was on the average a toll station every five miles. Similar barriers were located on the other major rivers. The fees charged were hardly nominal. In the sixteenth century, a load of salt which was worth 25 *écus* and which was being carried from Nantes to Nevers was assessed 100 *écus* in fees alone. The fact that transport did not desert the rivers for the roads—even the better roads—suggests that the toll-collecting privileges of the landowners were diligently exploited.[158]

It is in the context of these private tolls that one must consider the fees on transport levied by the state itself. For certain administrative purposes, *ancien France* was divided into three parts—the *cinq grosses fermes,* the *provinces réputées étrangères,* and the *provinces à l'instar de l'étranger.* The third group was separated from the rest of the kingdom by tariff walls, but these provinces could trade freely with the rest of the world. The *provinces réputées étrangères* were separated from both the *cinq grosses fermes* and the remainder of France by both import and export barriers.

For a period of several centuries, the government made many attempts to rationalize or abolish the private tolls and to remove or reduce the public tariffs. But even Colbert, who had visions of a uniform economic policy for the entire country, could do little to eliminate the private fees, and the huge appetite of the central government for revenue frustrated plans to reduce the state-imposed duties. Significant reforms had to wait until the *ancien régime* was overthrown by the revolution.[159]

As we have already noticed, the Chinese government had traditionally levied duties on the movement of goods from one section of the country to another. In the middle of the nineteenth century, however, the political authorities introduced the likin, a greatly expanded transit tax.[160] The number of collection barriers rapidly multiplied, many of them without Peking's authorization. Along a portion of the Grand Canal, the intervals between stations averaged only ten miles, and in a part of Kiangsu province south of the Yangtze River no less than 250 barriers were in operation.[161] Although the original rate of the tax was only one-tenth per cent of the value of the merchandise, the levy was subject to abuse, and collection officials were not reluctant to impose extra charges which merchants were usually willing to pay rather than have their goods delayed enroute. The assessment on goods in transit meant that the total levy would be considerable if the shipments were destined to travel through several provinces. Very often large entrepreneurs or guild organizations sought to commute the likin charges to a lump payment of cash, and whenever possible they tried to pass on the burden of taxation to the consumer.

In comparison with France and China, Japan during the Tokugawa period had relatively few toll roads and similar obstructions to trade.[162] By the time the Tokugawa took command, most of the octroi stations had been abolished. Although some of the local daimyo erected commercial barriers, none existed in the shogun's territories, which included the important cities and towns. The movement of the feudal lords to and from Edo and the need to enter into commercial negotiations tended to encourage the removal of impediments to trade and the growth of wider market areas.

While there were perhaps more road tolls in England than there were in Japan, it is important to note that they were very different from those that prevailed on the continent. The old feudal tolls on roads and bridges in England were, with minor exceptions, fees levied for the purpose of maintenance. In other words, they were payments for services rendered and not, as in France, exorbitant charges for personal profit. Even these tolls tended to disappear during the period with which we are concerned, but another type of charge soon became prominent. By the middle of the eighteenth century, parliament was increasing its authorization of turnpike trusts which were allowed to raise capital for road building and road repairs and to charge fees in order to cover the costs.[163] A discussion of these turnpikes, however, is more appropriately presented in the next chapter.

More important than the feudal type of road tolls were the dues levied by towns on the use of the roads which ran through their boundaries. Although they were more than a mere nuisance, they were never a hindrance to trade to the extent that the road and river tolls were in France.[164]

Again in contrast with France, a system of internal tariffs never took root in England. Even the trade between England and Scotland became free after the Act of Union (1707), while customs barriers between England and Ireland were for the most part erased in 1800.

Thus it is quite apparent that in France and China, the government itself, through its system of taxation, limited the development of patterns of exchange among roles that were separated geographically. In Japan and England, the government did not engage in such money-raising schemes and tended to suppress those individuals who sought to exact tolls on the transport of merchandise solely for private profit.

SUMMARY

Marked differences do not appear among the four cases with respect to the contribution of government to the satisfaction of the pattern-maintenance functional requisite. In all four societies, there existed legal norms that partially defined social class and bestowed certain rights, privileges, powers, and obligations on the basis of membership in specific social groups. The differences in the types of bestowals were not distinctive except for the significant fact that liberal tax exemptions were made available to the upper classes in France and China. When it came to the enforcement of norms that defined criminal behavior, the case of China stands out from the rest because the government was not so heavily involved in this aspect of the social-control process.

China again deviates from the other three cases in one segment of the integrative functional requisite. The government in China did not become significantly involved in that aspect of the social-control process which is geared to the enforcement of norms governing the non-contractual aspects of contract. In France, Japan, and England, on the other hand, there had developed during the traditional stage of economic growth a system of commercial laws which was enforceable in government courts.

Although exact comparisons are difficult to make, it seems that the success of the government in facilitating exchange through the standardization of weights and measures was more notable in Japan and England than in France and China. This, of course, affected the size of the area over which the interdependence of roles developed.

The data on the integration among roles differentiated on the basis of prestige and on the basis of generation reveal important similarities and differences among the four societies. In France and China, the government actually encouraged upward movement into the more prestigious strata of the society. This was done in France through the sale of offices and titles, and in China through the establishment of an examination system and the sale of academic degrees and offices. By contrast, the government in Japan and England effectively prevented the movement of large numbers of people into the most prestigious classes of society and, indeed, actually contributed to downward mobility in the upper classes.

Also observable are differences in the laws of inheritance which governed the relationships among roles differentiated on the basis of generation. The inheritance system in France and China tended to distribute estates among relatively large numbers of heirs, while in Japan and England the rule of primogeniture tended to keep property holdings intact by passing them on to fewer beneficiaries.

We must note, further, that the system of internal tolls and tariffs in France and China had an effect on the integration of roles differentiated on the basis of geographic location by restricting the area over which interdependence of roles could develop. In Japan and England, on the other hand, such restrictions were not of great consequence.

With this chapter we have concluded the comparative empirical treatment of the four cases when their economies were in the traditional stage of economic development. Some obvious patterns have emerged from this analysis, but these become even more prominent when considered in the light of the Japanese and English cases during the take-off stage of economic development.

NOTES

1. See, for example, Joseph J. Spengler, "Bureaucracy and Economic Development," in Joseph LaPalombara (ed.), *Bureaucracy and Political Development,* pp. 205-206; Peter T. Bauer and Basil S. Yamey, *The Economics of Under-developed Countries,* pp. 163-164.

2. Émile Durkheim, *The Division of Labor in Society,* pp. 68-69. We use *norm* as a generic term, whereas Durkheim uses *law* or *juridical rule.*

3. We make some distinctions that Durkheim does not make. Where they are relevant, they will be discussed. See below, pp. 193-195.

4. These sanctions are discussed in detail in Holt's forthcoming work on primitive societies, Chapter 4.

5. We recognize, of course, that a great deal of the social-control process which supports societal norms operates at a micro-level (small-group level) and thus falls outside of our consideration. However, we maintain that intersocietal differences in the *amount* of the *social-control burden* that is carried by small

groups can be accounted for in terms of the macro-structuring of the social and cultural systems at the societal level. See Holt's forthcoming work on primitive politics, Chapters 4 and 5.

6. The discussion of the theories that relate to the empirical data presented in this study is to be found in Chapter 7, pp. 313-314.

7. Spengler, "Bureaucracy and Economic Devlopment," p. 205.

8. Apparently Spengler makes no distinction between the pattern-maintenance and the integration aspects of *law and order,* as we do.

9. James F. Stephen, *A History of the Criminal Law of England,* Vol. I, pp. 415-416, 467-468; Harold Potter, *An Historical Introduction to English Law and Its Institutions,* pp. 1-74.

10. See below, pp. 191-192.

11. See Harold S. Quigley, *Japanese Government and Politics,* pp. 13-16; George B. Sansom, *Japan, A Short Cultural History,* pp. 444-446, 445-463; John H. Wigmore, "Materials for the Study of Private Law in Old Japan," *Transactions of the Asiatic Society of Japan,* Vol. 20, Supplement, 1892. Part I, pp. 71-94; Dan F. Henderson, "Some Aspects of Tokugawa Law," *Washington Law Review,* Vol. 27, 1952, p. 105. See also J. Carey Hall, "Japanese Feudal Laws," *Transactions of the Asiatic Society of Japan,* Vol. 38, Part IV, 1911, pp. 269-331; Vol. 41, Part V, December 1913, pp. 683-804; Dan F. Henderson, *Conciliation and Japanese Law: Tokugawa and Modern,* Vol. I, p. 77.

12. See H. C. Hu, *The Common Descent Group in China and Its Functions,* pp. 53-63; T. T. Ch'ü, *Law and Society in Traditional China,* pp. 40-41; E. H. Parker, *China,* pp. 310-314; Ernest Alabaster, *Notes on Chinese Law and Practice Preceding Revision, passim.*

13. The distinction we are making between a norm and a precept is common in the social sciences. A precept describes behavior that is desirable; a norm prescribes behavior that is compulsory in the sense that failure to comply should result in the application of severe sanctions. See, for example, George C. Homans, *The Human Group,* pp. 122-124. The generic term that we employ to include both norm and precept is *directive.* See Ethel Albert, "The Classification of Values: A Method and an Illustration," *American Anthropologist,* Vol. 58, No. 2, April 1956, pp. 221-248.

14. It should be remembered that a tension-management process, as well as a social-control process is relevant to pattern maintenance. Activities relating to tension management are those controlling the development of situations that enhance the propensity of an individual to violate norms. In any society with a rigid stratification system, there is likely to be a set of pattern-maintenance activities that control some of the tension which develops among the classes. This problem is discussed indirectly in connection with social mobility. (See below, pp. 202-216.) It is treated explicitly in Chapter 6.

15. For a good summary treatment of social classes in *ancien France,* see Phillippe Sagnac, *La formation de la société française moderne,* Vol. II, pp. 39-75; Henri Sée, *Economic and Social Conditions in France during the Eighteenth Century,* pp. 14-136; Georges Lefebvre, *The Coming of the French Revolution,* pp. 7-19, 35-44, 83-96, 113-124. The most detailed treatments are found in works which concentrate upon a single region, but which are for this reason of less general applicability. See Gaston Roupnel, *La ville et la campagne au XVIIe siècle,* and Pierre Goubert, *Beauvais et le Beauvaisis de 1600 à 1730,* especially, pp. 85-356.

16. Sée, *Economic and Social Conditions in France during the Eighteenth Century,* pp. 87-88. Sée takes his estimates from the Abbot Coyer and the Marquis de Bouillé.

17. Franklin L. Ford, *Robe and Sword*, pp. 27-31. Ford's estimate is for the year 1715.

18. For a discussion of population, see below, pp. 320-326.

19. See below, pp. 188-192.

20. From an early time, this applied to natural sons as well as to legitimate sons. See Jean-Richard Bloch, *L'anoblissement en France au temps de François 1ᵉʳ*.

21. See Ford, *Robe and Sword*, pp. 32-33 for details.

22. Paul Ardaschev draws a distinction between the *noblesse de l'épée* and the *noblesse d'état*. The *noblesse de la robe*, consisting of the magistrates of the courts, were a subcategory of the latter. (*Les intendants de province sous Louis XVI*, pp. 2-10.)

23. Ford, *Robe and Sword*, pp. 6-7.

24. Sée, *Economic and Social Conditions in France during the Eighteenth Century*, p. 6.

25. Sée estimates that the clergy owned about 6 per cent of the land in France, and that their income from urban property was greater than their income from rural property. (See p. 3 of his book, note 24 above.)

26. Some of the high clergy also held lucrative secular positions. See Sagnac, *La formation de la société française moderne*, Vol. II, pp. 39-47, and Sée, *Economic and Social Conditions in France during the Eighteenth Century*, pp. 67-69.

27. See Sagnac (note 26, above), Vol. II, pp. 40-44; and Sée (note 26 above), pp. 64, 69.

28. Elinor Barber, *The Bourgeoisie in 18th Century France*, pp. 20-33.

29. Sagnac, *La formation de la société française moderne*, Vol. II, pp. 57-70; Sée, *Economic and Social Conditions in France during the Eighteenth Century*, pp. 200-207.

30. See above, pp. 102-103.

31. Sée, *Economic and Social Conditions in France during the Eighteenth Century*, p. 186, quoting letters patent of January 1749.

32. *Ibid.*, pp. 14-24.

33. *Ibid.*, pp. 34-36; 163-165.

34. Ford, *Robe and Sword*, pp. 28-29; Henry S. Maine, *The Early History of Institutions*, pp. 122-124; Alexis de Tocqueville, *The Old Regime and the French Revolution*, pp. 28-31.

35. Sée, *Economic and Social Conditions in France during the Eighteenth Century*, pp. 88-89.

36. *Ibid.*, p. 88; and Ford, *Robe and Sword*, pp. 27-28. See Roland Mousnier, *La vénalité des offices sous Henry IV et Louis XIII*, pp. 411-412 for more detail in identifying those who enjoyed exemption. For one region in France, Roupnel lists all the positions that carried exemption from the taille. See *La ville et la campagne*, pp. 128-130.

37. See Mousnier (note 36 above), p. 413 for a discussion of the exemptions of the nobility and clergy from the gabelle.

38. Ford, *Robe and Sword*, p. 197; Sée, *Economic and Social Conditions in France during the Eighteenth Century*, p. 62.

39. Ford, *Robe and Sword*, p. 25. Other acts that led to loss of noble status are of little consequence to this study.

40. Charles W. Cole, *French Mercantilism*, pp. 7-8, and *Colbert and a Century of French Mercantilism*, Vol. II, pp. 4-6. There is no doubt, of course, that some of the wealth of the nobility, particularly of the nobility of the robe, was invested in commerce and industry. Two comments, however, may be

offered on this investment. First, only a small fraction of the total wealth of the nobility was invested in these outlets. Ford's report on the wealth of a parlementaire inventoried at his death indicates that out of a total estate valued at 411,755 livres, less than 50,000 livres could conceivably have been invested in commerce and industry. (See *Robe and Sword*, p. 169.) Second, the investments that were made tended to be personal loans; the nobility themselves took little entrepreneurial risk.

41. There was also an outcast class of "mean people"—prostitutes, actors, criminals, slaves—who need not concern us in this study.

42. See P. C. Hsieh, *The Government of China, 1644-1911*, pp. 52-53; P. T. Ho, *The Ladder of Success in Imperial China*, pp. 21-24.

43. C. L. Chang, *The Chinese Gentry*, pp. 113, 139-141. For the transfer of gentry privileges to family members, see T. T. Ch'ü, *Local Government in China under the Ch'ing*, pp. 177-180.

44. Ho, *The Ladder of Success in Imperial China*, pp. 24-29.

45. Robert M. Marsh, *The Mandarins: The Circulation of Elites in China*, p. 15.

46. *Ibid.*, p. 51. See also Ch'ü, *Law and Society in Traditional China*, p. 141.

47. Ch'ü, *Law and Society in Traditional China*, p. 177.

48. *Ibid.*, pp. 177, 183-184; Chang, *The Chinese Gentry*, pp. 35-42. See also Ch'ü, *Local Government in China under the Ch'ing*, pp. 173-175; Alabaster, *Notes on Chinese Law and Practice Preceding Revision*, pp. 43-44.

49. Ch'ü, *Law and Society in Traditional China*, p. 151.

50. Chang, *The Chinese Gentry*, pp. 37-40; Ch'ü, *Law and Society in Traditional China*, pp. 185-190.

51. C. L. Chang, *The Income of the Chinese Gentry*, pp. 149-195.

52. P. T. Ho, "Aspects of Social Mobility in China, 1368-1911," *Comparative Studies in Society and History*, Vol. I, No. 4, June 1959, p. 342.

53. See Masaya Sasaki, "Seidai Kanryō no Kashoku ni tsuite" (Accumulation of Wealth by Bureaucrats during the Ch'ing Period), *Shigaku Zasshi*, Vol. 63, No. 2, February 1954, pp. 22-57.

54. Chang, *The Income of the Chinese Gentry*, p. 152.

55. See T. I. Pêng (ed.), *Chung-kuo chin tai shou kung yeh shih tsŭ liao 1840-1949* (Historical Materials on China's Modern Handicraft Industries), Vol. I, p. 419.

56. For a statistical comparison of status groups, see Henderson, *Conciliation and Japanese Law*, Vol. I, p. 27. On the socioeconomic breakdown in one fief, see Neil S. Smith (ed.), *Tokugawa Japan*, p. 31.

57. On the social gradations within the daimyo class, see John W. Hall, *Tanuma Okitsugu, 1719-1788*, pp. 24-25.

58. See Smith, *Tokugawa Japan*, p. 33; Edwin O. Reischauer and John K. Fairbank, *East Asia, the Great Tradition*, p. 606; Takao Tsuchiya, *The Development of Economic Life in Japan*, p. 22; Harry D. Harootunian, "The Economic Rehabilitation of the Samurai in the Early Meiji Period," *Journal of Asian Studies*, Vol. 19, No. 4, August 1960, p. 433. Z. Itani puts the number of samurai households at 400,000. ("The Economic Causes of the Meiji Restoration," *Transactions of the Asiatic Society of Japan*, Vol. 17, Second Series, December 1938, p. 195.)

59. See Smith, *Tokugawa Japan*, pp. 32-33; Takao Tsuchiya, "An Economic History of Japan," *Transactions of the Asiatic Society of Japan*, Second Series, Vol. 15, December 1937, p. 151.

60. See Wigmore, "Materials for the Study of Private Law in Old Japan," Part I, pp. 38, 91; Eijiro Honjo, *The Social and Economic History of Japan*,

pp. 191-192; Eijiro Honjo, "Changes of Social Classes in the Tokugawa Period," *Kyóto University Economic Review,* Vol. 3, No. 1, July 1928, pp. 57-60.

61. See Hall, "Japanese Feudal Laws," *Transactions of the Asiatic Society of Japan,* Vol. 38, Part IV, p. 315.

62. Sansom, *Japan, A Short Cultural History,* p. 463. See also Henderson, "Some Aspects of Tokugawa Law," p. 95; Wigmore, "Materials for the Study of Private Law in Old Japan," Part I, p. 91; S. Ogawa, "Prisons and Prisoners," in S. Okuma, *Fifty Years of New Japan,* Vol. I, pp. 305-307.

63. The estimates used in this monograph are from Gregory King for the period 1690-1696, as reported in Gilbert Slater, *The Growth of Modern England,* pp. 592-593.

64. King's figures on the make-up of the lordly families include indoor servants, and he lists the average family size at forty. Even this, however, is only 0.001 per cent of the population.

65. George M. Trevelyan, *English Social History,* pp. 177, 358-360.

66. King's estimates of this group, including indoor servants, is 20,600 individuals, which is still only 0.36 per cent of the total population.

67. Trevelyan, *English Social History,* pp. 126-127.

68. See Ephraim Lipson, *The Economic History of England,* Vol. II, pp. 371-395.

69. On the privileges of the peerage, see Luke O. Pike, *A Constitutional History of the House of Lords,* pp. 235-278.

70. Marion J. Levy, Jr., *The Structure of Society,* pp. 299-348.

71. *Ibid.,* p. 387.

72. *Ibid.,* pp. 306-327, 343-348.

73. See Durkheim, *The Division of Labor in Society*; Talcott Parsons, *The Structure of Social Action,* pp. 311-314; Talcott Parsons and Neil J. Smelser, *Economy and Society,* pp. 104-105.

74. It is interesting to point out that Durkheim, in the preface to the second edition of *The Division of Labor in Society* (reprinted in all subsequent editions), lamented the degree of government control of the guilds.

75. Cole, *Colbert and a Century of French Mercantilism,* Vol II, pp. 429-430.

76. John U. Nef, *Industry and Government in France and England, 1540-1640,* pp. 22-23.

77. See Hsieh, *The Government of China, 1644-1911,* pp. 215-230; Parker, *China,* pp. 310-312.

78. See Hsieh (note 77, above), pp. 215-230; Abram Lind, Jr., *A Chapter of the Chinese Penal Code*; Sidney D. Gamble, *Peking: A Social Survey,* pp. 165, 194; Sybille Van der Sprenkel, *Legal Institutions in Manchu China: A Sociological Analysis,* pp. 95, 112; "Chinese Gilds and Their Rules," *The China Review,* July-August, 1883, pp. 5-9.

79. See Lind, *A Chapter of the Chinese Penal Code.*

80. Robert N. Bellah, *Tokugawa Religion: The Values of Pre-Industrial Japan,* p. 24.

81. See Wigmore, "Materials for the Study of Private Law in Old Japan," Part I, pp. 71-94.

82. See *ibid.,* Part III, p. 377.

83. Smith, *Tokugawa Japan,* p. 85.

84. Wigmore, "Materials for the Study of Private Law in Old Japan," Part I, pp. 78, 181.

85. Henderson, *Conciliation and Japanese Law,* Vol. I, pp. 7-8, 103-106, 123. See also Hall, "Japanese Feudal Laws," *Transactions of the Asiatic Society of Japan,* Vol. 38, Part IV, pp. 299-304, 315; Vol. 41, Part V, pp. 700-701.

86. Henderson, *Conciliation and Japanese Law,* Vol. I, p. 13.

87. See William Mitchell, *An Essay on the Early History of the Law of Merchant*, pp. 66-77.

88. William S. Holdsworth, *A History of English Law*, Vol. I, p. 569; Vol. V, pp. 69, 94-95, 116-118, 140-148. See also Potter, *An Historical Introduction to English Law and Its Institutions*, pp. 48-50, 178-204. For a discussion of the later period, see Karl N. Llewellyn, "Across Sales on Horseback," *Harvard Law Review*, Vol. 52, No. 5, March 1939, pp. 725-746; "The First Struggle to Unhorse Sales," *ibid.*, Vol. 52, No. 6, April 1939, pp. 873-904.

89. Holdsworth, *A History of English Law*, Vol. I, p. 571.

90. Fred W. Riggs, *Social Change and Political Development*, pp. 133-173.

91. On France, see Marcel Marion, *Dictionnaire des institutions de la France au XVIIe et XVIIIe siècles*, pp. 373-376; Eli F. Heckscher, *Mercantilism*, Vol. I, pp. 111-117. On China, see Hosea B. Morse, *The Trade and Administration of the Chinese Empire*, pp. 170-174.

92. On Japan, see Yosoburo Takekoshi, *The Economic Aspects of the History of the Civilization of Japan*, Vol. II, pp. 476-478. On England, see Heckscher, *Mercantilism*, Vol. I, pp. 114-117; John Perry, *The Story of Standards*, pp. 11-12, 33-42.

93. We suggest that the rigidity of the Indian type of caste system can be maintained over time only if it is supported by a set of reciprocal rights and duties, such as those involved in the Hindu jajmānī system. For some interesting comment on this point as it applies to eighteenth-century France, see Barber, *The Bourgeoisie in 18th Century France*, pp. 99-140.

94. Sée, *Economic and Social Conditions in France during the Eighteenth Century*, pp. 83-84.

95. These differences were appreciated by those aspiring to acquire titles. For an interesting case, see Roupnel, *La ville et la campagne*, pp. 131-132.

96. Ford, *Robe and Sword*, pp. 107-123; Sée, *Economic and Social Conditions in France during the Eighteenth Century*, pp. 84-85; Mousnier, *La vénalité des offices sous Henry IV et Louis XIII, passim*.

97. See Sée (note 96, above), pp. 84-85.

98. Ford, *Robe and Sword*, p. 208.

99. Jean Egret, "L'aristocratie parlementaire française à la fin de l'Ancien Règime," *Revue historique*, Vol. 76, No. 208, July-September 1952, pp. 1-14.

100. Albert Babeau, *Les bourgeoisie d'autrefois*, p. 375, especially note 4.

101. Sée, *Economic and Social Conditions in France during the Eighteenth Century*, p. 85. For an earlier period, see Bloch, *L'anoblissement en France au temps de François Ier*.

102. Babeau, *Les bourgeoisie d'autrefois*, pp. 149 ff.

103. See Mousnier, *La vénalité des offices sous Henry IV et Louis XIII*, pp. 519-522; R. B. Grassby, "Social Status and Commercial Enterprise under Louis XIV," *The Economic History Review*, Vol. 13, No. 1, Second Series, August 1960, pp. 19-38; David S. Landes, "French Entrepreneurship and Industrial Growth in the Nineteenth Century," *The Journal of Economic History*, Vol. 9, No. 1, May 1949, pp. 52-54; Warren C. Scoville, "The French Economy in 1700-1701: An Appraisal by the Deputies of Trade," *The Journal of Economic History*, Vol. 22, No. 2, June 1962, pp. 246 ff.

104. Quoted in John U. Nef, "The Industrial Revolution Reconsidered," *The Journal of Economic History*, Vol. 3, No. 1, May 1943, p. 10.

105. See Barber, *The Bourgeoisie in 18th Century France*, p. 57. Lefebvre comments: "For centuries the bourgeois, envious of the aristocracy, aimed only at thrusting himself into its ranks." (*The Coming of the French Revolution*, p. 40.)

106. It should be pointed out that a complete treatment of integration among

social classes would not stop, but would only begin, with a discussion of mobility. From the point of view of integration, it is not the movement among classes that is of particular importance, but rather the kind of linkages created by different types of mobility. For example, kinship linkages are created between the aristocracy and the middle class when one brother buys a title, or when a daughter is married to a man with a title. The kinds of mobility existing in France in the seventeenth and eighteenth centuries provided this type of kinship linkage among social classes. In England, kinship linkages were created by the fact that second sons of the nobility did not inherit a title, and thus moved downward on the mobility ladder. Either of these types of linkage is an acceptable solution to the problem of relationships among social classes. In this study, we are not interested in the range of acceptable solutions which are possible, but only in the implications of certain solutions for the problem of developing industrialization.

107. In considering the problem of social mobility in traditional China, it is well to keep in mind that the studies are few in number and the samples are small; hence, any generalizations must be regarded as probable tendencies.

108. Ho, "Aspects of Social Mobility in China, 1368-1911," pp. 333, 336.

109. Chang, *The Chinese Gentry*, p. 82.

110. Ho, *The Ladder of Success in Imperial China*, pp. 83-85.

111. See above, pp. 136-137. For an account of the sale of magistrates' offices, see Ch'ü, *Local Government in China under the Ch'ing*, pp. 18-21.

112. See Chang, *The Chinese Gentry*, pp. 214-215.

113. Ho, *The Ladder of Success in Imperial China*, p. 121.

114. Marsh, *The Mandarins*, pp. 187-188.

115. See Ho, *The Ladder of Success in Imperial China*, pp. 182-183, 190.

116. See Chang, *The Chinese Gentry*, pp. 217-218 and Table 39.

117. P. T. Ho, "The Salt Merchants of Yang-chou: A Study of Commercial Capitalism in Eighteenth-Century China," *Harvard Journal of Asiatic Studies*, Vol. 17, No. 1-2, June 1954, p. 165.

118. Ho, *The Ladder of Success in Imperial China*, p. 27.

119. *Ibid.*, pp. 77-78.

120. *Ibid.*, p. 257.

121. *Ibid.*, pp. 149-153.

122. *Ibid.*, pp. 142, 154-159.

123. *Ibid.*, pp. 165-166. See also Marsh, *The Mandarins*, pp. 159-160.

124. Honjo, *The Social and Economic History of Japan*, pp. 189-190.

125. Reischauer and Fairbank, *East Asia: The Great Tradition*, pp. 602-603.

126. Takaharu Mitsui, "Chōnin's Life under Feudalism," *Cultural Nippon*, Vol. 8, No. 2, June 1940, p. 76.

127. Tsuchiya, "An Economic History of Japan," p. 229. Some estimates are as high as 80 per cent. (See Henderson, *Conciliation and Japanese Law*, Vol. I, p. 33.)

128. Kee I. Choi, "Tokugawa Feudalism and the Emergence of the New Leaders of Early Modern Japan," *Explorations in Entrepreneurial History*, Vol. 9, No. 2, December 1956, p. 75.

129. Sho Sawada, "Financial Difficulties of the Edo Bakufu," *Harvard Journal of Asiatic Studies*, Vol. 1, No. 3-4, November 1936, p. 309.

130. Tsuchiya, "An Economic History of Japan," p. 203.

131. See Matsuyo Takizawa, *The Penetration of Money Economy in Japan*, pp. 94-95; Honjo, *The Social and Economic History of Japan*, pp. 40-42, 125-127.

132. See Eijiro Honjo, "From the Tokugawa Period to the Meiji Restora-

tion," *Kyōto University Economic Review,* Vol. 7, No. 1, July 1932, p. 48. In 1840 the outstanding debt of the Choshu daimyo was seventeen times his annual revenue. (Choi, "Tokugawa Feudalism," p. 77.)

133. Honjo, *The Social and Economic History of Japan,* pp. 262-265; Mitsui, "Chōnin's Life under Feudalism," pp. 77-80, 92-93; Robert J. Smith, "Pre-Industrial Urbanism in Japan: A Consideration of Multiple Traditions in a Feudal Society," *Economic Development and Cultural Change,* Vol. 9, No. 1, Part 2, October 1960, pp. 241-254; Marion J. Levy, Jr., "Some Aspects of 'Individualism' and the Problem of Modernization in China and Japan," *ibid.,* Vol. 10, No. 3, April 1962, pp. 237-239. See E. Herbert Norman, *Japan's Emergence as a Modern State,* pp. 54-67.

134. Quoted in Honjo, *The Social and Economic History of Japan,* p. 201.

135. Quoted in Eijiro Honjo, *Economic Theory and History of Japan in the Tokugawa Period,* p. 15.

136. Quoted in Takekoshi, *The Economic Aspects of the History of the Civilization of Japan,* Vol. II, p. 359.

137. See Honjo, *The Social and Economic History of Japan,* pp. 80-81, 206, 209-210, 259; Reischauer and Fairbank, *East Asia, The Great Tradition,* p. 634; Takizawa, *The Penetration of Money Economy in Japan,* pp. 100-101.

138. See Marion J. Levy, Jr., "Contrasting Factors in the Modernization of China and Japan," in Simon S. Kuznets, Wilbert E. Moore, and Joseph J. Spengler, *Economic Growth: Brazil, India, Japan,* p. 523.

139. See Honjo, *The Social and Economic History of Japan,* pp. 202-205; Tsuchiya, "An Economic History of Japan," p. 236; Takizawa, *The Penetration of Money Economy in Japan,* p. 130; Hall, *Tanuma Okitsugu, 1719-1788,* p. 10. See also Eijiro Honjo, "The Decay of the Samurai Class," *Kyōto University Economic Review,* Vol. 2, No. 1, July 1927, pp. 38-51.

140. See Hall, *Tanuma Okitsugu, 1719-1788,* p. 7.

141. Honjo, *The Social and Economic History of Japan,* p. 204.

142. See Edwin O. Reischauer, "Japanese Feudalism," in Rushton Coulborn, *Feudalism in History,* p. 48; Reischauer and Fairbank, *East Asia, The Great Tradition,* pp. 627-630, 640-641; Thomas C. Smith, *The Agrarian Origins of Modern Japan,* pp. 177-178.

143. See Honjo, *The Social and Economic History of Japan,* pp. 129-130, 170-172, 207-208.

144. See Charles R. Mayes, "The Sale of Peerages in Early Stuart England," *The Journal of Modern History,* Vol. 29, No. 1, March 1957, pp. 21-37. See also Lawrence Stone, "The Inflation of Honours, 1558-1641," *Past and Present,* No. 14, November 1958, pp. 45-70.

145. Richard H. Gretton, *The English Middle Class,* pp. 83-90, 111; Frederick C. Dietz, *An Economic History of England,* p. 196; S. T. Bindoff (ed.), *Elizabethan Government and Society,* p. 168.

146. Daniel Defoe, *The Complete English Tradesman,* Vol. I, p. 246.

147. On the movement of the aristocracy into the merchant class, see Ray B. Westerfield, *Middlemen in English Business, Particularly Between 1660 and 1760,* pp. 400-403; Defoe, *The Complete English Tradesman,* Vol. I, pp. 227-240. See also Lawrence Stone, "Marriage among the English Nobility in the 16th and 17th Centuries," *Comparative Studies in Society and History,* Vol. 3, No. 2, January 1961, pp. 196-197.

148. Trevelyan, *English Social History,* p. 126; Gretton, *The English Middle Class,* p. 104; David Mathew, *The Social Structure in Caroline England,* pp. 40-45. Unlike France and China, the English gentry did not regard it as a social disaster if their younger children migrated to the city to take up a trade.

149. Westerfield, *Middlemen in English Business*, p. 411. See also Walter E. Minchinton, "The Merchants in England in the Eighteenth Century," *Explorations in Entrepreneurial History*, Vol. 10, No. 2, December 1957, pp. 62-71.

150. Thomas S. Ashton, *The Industrial Revolution, 1760-1830*, p. 17.

151. Levy, *The Structure of Society*, pp. 324-328.

152. This treatment is taken largely from Phillippe Sagnac, *La législation civile de la révolution française*, pp. 214-216. See also Evelyn Cecil, *Primogeniture: A Short History of Its Development in Various Countries and Its Practical Effects*, pp. 90-107.

The dividing line coincided essentially with the line separating the dialect *Oc* from the dialect *Oïl* (*langue d'Oc* and *langue d'Oïl*). See A. Esmein, *Cous élémentaire d'histoire du droit française*.

Customary Law

Written Law

153. Jean Brissaud, *A History of French Private Law*, p. 494.

154. Henry S. Maine, *The Early History of Institutions*, contains an interesting discussion of French inheritance. See also Eyre Lloyd, *The Succession Laws of Christian Countries*, pp. 8, 20-25.

155. Martin C. Yang, *A Chinese Village: Taitou, Shantung Province*, pp. 81-85; Norman Jacobs, *The Origin of Modern Capitalism in Eastern Asia*, pp. 149, 155-157.

156. See Wigmore, "Materials for the Study of Private Law in Old Japan," Part I, p. 39, Part V, pp. 79-109; Smith, *The Agrarian Origins of Modern Japan*, pp. 37-41; Jacobs, *The Origin of Modern Capitalism in Eastern Asia*, pp. 150-151, 154-155, 157-159.

157. On the English system of inheritance, see Evelyn Cecil, *Primogeniture*, pp. 26-53; Frederick Pollock and Frederick W. R. Maitland, *The History of English Law before the Time of Edward I*, Vol. II, Book 2, pp. 260-363; Potter, *An Historical Introduction to English Law and Its Institutions*, pp. 538-547; H. J. Habakkuk, "Family Structure and Economic Change in Nineteenth-Century Europe," *The Journal of Economic History*, Vol. 15, No. 1, Part 1, 1955, p. 11.

158. Heckscher, *Mercantilism*, Vol. I, pp. 79-81.

159. *Ibid.*, pp. 89-109.

160. See Edwin G. Beal, Jr., *The Origin of Likin* (*1853-1864*).

161. Morse, *Trade and Administration of the Chinese Empire*, p. 107.

162. See George Sansom, *A History of Japan, 1615-1867*, p. 124; *Japan, A Short Cultural History*, p .359; Smith, *Tokugawa Japan*, p. 53; Reischauer and Fairbank, *East Asia, the Great Tradition*, pp. 637-638.

163. Heckscher, *Mercantilism*, Vol. I, pp. 46-49.

164. *Ibid.*, pp. 50-51. Navigation on English rivers was apparently more hampered by water mills and weirs than by tolls.

CHAPTER 6

The Take-Off Stage: Japan and England

AS THE TECHNIQUES OF INDUSTRIAL PRODUCTION BECAME AVAIL-able in Japan and England either through invention or importation, they were fitted with relative speed and ease into the economies of these two countries. Japan by the 1890's and England by the 1790's had achieved rates of economic growth that brought their economies into the take-off stage of economic development. In this exploratory study, we are primarily concerned with the formulation of hypotheses concerning the prerequisites of take-off, and hence the main empirical focus is on four societies whose economies were in a traditional stage of economic growth. The analysis of the take-off stage in this chapter is not presented for the purpose of building an empirical foundation for the development of hypotheses, but is nevertheless important to the study for two reasons. First, some of the patterns that emerged from our examination of the four societies when their economies were in the traditional stage can be illuminated by outlining the patterns which characterize the take-off stage. Second, since the analytical framework presented in Chapter 2 was devised for the analysis of societies at all stages of economic development, treatment of the take-off stage will enable the reader to see how the framework may be applied to countries at two different levels of economic progress.

Because the purpose of this chapter is different from the preceding ones, it will not be necessary to present as much empirical detail. Our intention will be better served by painting the picture with broad strokes which will highlight the major patterns but deliberately ignore some of the interesting particulars. Since this discussion, however, must treat all of the topics handled in the previous chapters, it will be useful to follow the same format of the earlier analysis. The first section, which parallels Chapter 3, will be an overview of the structures of government and the procedures of governing. The succeeding four sections will deal with the government's contribution to the satisfaction of the four functional requisites, thus paralleling the treatment in Chapters 4 and 5.

STRUCTURES OF GOVERNMENT AND PROCEDURES OF GOVERNING: AN OVERVIEW

Either shortly before or during the first decades of the period we have defined as the take-off stage of economic development, important changes were taking place in the structure of government in both Japan and England that were closely associated with certain developments in the functions of government and with important changes in the procedures of governing. These changes were especially obvious in Japan, where they were closely linked with the sudden and dramatic events of the Meiji Restoration. In England, the changes were much more evolutionary; their genesis can be traced farther back in history, and the culmination was much slower. Despite a longer period of evolution, however, the trends are clear and the changes were significant.[1]

Japan

We have already noted that in the eighteenth century important economic and social forces were beginning to erode the foundations of Tokugawa feudalism. Partly as a result of their obligations to the shogunate, the daimyo and samurai had fallen heavily into the debt of the merchants, whose influence and prestige were correspondingly enhanced. As their economic situation worsened, some lords and warriors began to foster the growth of industry and trade in their han. A few samurai were even willing to sacrifice their prestigious status in society in order to take on commercial and entrepreneurial roles.

As Japan moved into the nineteenth century, the shogun's government was proving itself to be more and more ineffective in handling its affairs. Not only was it unable to solve the financial crises which continually plagued Japan, but after 1853-1854 it was incapable of resisting the penetration of the country by Western powers. The economic situation became more chaotic, the samurai became more impoverished, and the peasants grew increasingly restive in the countryside. Moreover, with the opening of the country to the West, many Japanese citizens began to exhibit hostility toward the foreigner. In the 1860's dissident elements, especially among the samurai, mobilized their forces in a series of direct challenges to the shogun and his clansmen. Beset by these internal problems, the Tokugawa rulers soon discovered that their system of controls no longer operated with characteristic subtlety and effectiveness; indeed, in 1862 they were even forced to modify the rules governing compulsory residence in Edo. On a number of occasions during this difficult period, the Tokugawa leaders had to order their troops into the field in order to suppress the revolts of samurai and other unruly groups. That they no longer possessed superior military strength over their internal foes became clear in 1866, when a coalition of the Satsuma and the Choshu clans brought a humiliating defeat to the shogun's armies.

In 1867-1868, the Meiji Restoration, which was engineered largely by samurai of lesser rank, terminated the long period of Tokugawa rule and ushered in a new system whose authority structure of policy making was more highly resolved and in which the controls of the central government extended into all sections of the country. To begin with, the emperor was "restored" to his traditional role as the head of state. Although, as in the past, he was not permitted to wield actual power, he was held up as the focal point of civic loyalty for the entire nation. The Meiji rulers were fortunate in being able to convert invigorated reverence for the monarch into feelings of obligation toward the Japanese state and the new central government. By 1871, for example, the feudal lords had been persuaded (or forced) to surrender their fiefs to the imperial throne—an important step in the abolition of feudal forms and in the establishment of central authority.

Although they operated ostensibly as advisers to the emperor, the real rulers of Japan were a small group of samurai from the four clans (especially from the Satsuma and the Choshu) which had been instrumental in overturning the Tokugawa. During the difficult period of transition, this group of elder statesmen held the most important posts in the government and served as the chief advisers to the emperor, who consulted them on all important problems of state. This pattern of oligarchical rule was clear from the beginning, but it was not until after 1900 that the specific title of *genrō* was applied to the new generation of elder statesmen, some of whom had served their political apprenticeship under the old Restoration leaders. The genro, as well as its unnamed predecessor, was an extralegal body, but its members had the final word on all policy matters affecting the country as a whole.

For two decades following the Restoration, the Meiji oligarchs experimented with a number of governmental institutions, from which more specialized structures emerged in the 1880's.[2] During this period of adjustment and experimentation, the new political leaders operated through a council of state, which passed through several reorganizations and appeared each time with a new name. This body—under whatever name—formulated general policy and supervised its execution. Several administrative departments (including, after 1873, the Department of Home Affairs) carried out their activities under its close supervision. One section of the council was presumably to act as a deliberative assembly, but it proved to be ineffective in this role. In 1875, the political authorities established a Supreme Court, but this agency was largely subordinated to the council through the Department of Justice. Thus, by controlling the council of state, the small group of Meiji leaders managed to dominate important decision-making units throughout the government.

In the 1870's and 1880's, however, this arrangement encountered the opposition of dissident groups who demanded greater representation in the system. Finally, in 1881 the government promised to create a representative parliament at the end of the decade. In anticipation of this event, the Meiji leaders proceeded to establish a number of governmental forms that would enable them to retain much of their power. In 1885, they set up a cabinet, which was based upon the Prussian model, and three years later they made provision for a permanent Privy Council. Thus, in the period between 1868 and 1890, when the parliament (Diet) came into being, the Japanese rulers had greatly increased the resolution of the authority structure of policy making, compared with the Tokugawa system. The men who had carried out the Restoration held the key posts in the agencies of government, and they determined policies which no group could effectively veto. This is not to say that their policies were universally applauded; dissenting leaders occasionally resigned from the governing councils, and it was from the ranks of the opposition that the demand for the establishment of a parliament arose. But until the Diet went into operation in 1890, opposition groups generally lacked formal machinery for organized action within the central government.

With the promulgation of the Meiji Constitution in 1889, Japan's political institutions achieved more stable form. It would be erroneous to assume, however, that the new charter created an effective base of power for groups that could veto the policies of the oligarchy. Although there was sharper distinction among the executive, legislative, and judicial branches of government, the authority of the executive stood out most clearly. According to the letter of the constitution, the powers of government in all three spheres resided in the person of the emperor, who could, for example, issue legislative decrees without the consent of the parliament. This recognition of sweeping imperial authority meant that power was concentrated in the hands of the emperor's ministerial advisers acting in his behalf and with his seal.

One would expect that if any group were to have served as a restraint upon the executive, it would have been the Diet. This body, however, was severely limited in its capacity to block the policies of the oligarchy. Because the House of Peers—the second chamber—was composed largely of members of the recently created nobility and imperial appointees, it had close ties with the executive branch. The House of Representatives, on the other hand, was somewhat more sensitive to mass opinion, and, of all the agencies of government, it was most likely to oppose the rule of the oligarchs. This chamber, however, suffered from certain structural weaknesses which hampered its effectiveness: parliament met infrequently, and executive officials were entitled to exercise ordinance powers when it was not in session; the House of Peers enjoyed virtually equivalent authority and could block the measures approved by the Representatives; if the first chamber refused to approve the government's budget, the executive branch was not thrown into chaos, since the budget of the previous year could be applied; and, if the lower house persisted in its opposition to the government's policies, the Premier could dissolve the Diet, and the individual members of the House would be faced with the cost of an election campaign, as well as with the possibility of defeat.

Despite these weaknesses, however, the House of Representatives could embarrass the government and delay the implementation of the policies it desired. To obviate this difficulty, the Premier and his fellow-oligarchs devised techniques for building up majority support for their programs.[3] They were frequently able to capitalize on the mutual suspicions among the political parties and the factionalism within them, winning support by the judicious distribution of administrative patronage. They also engaged in the purchase of Diet members' votes, especially for the passage of finance measures. Prime Minister Yamagata, for example, set up a special fund from which he paid certain members of the House each time a government bill was passed. The ultimate technique employed by the imperial ministers, however, was to have the emperor issue a rescript urging cooperation between the Diet and the government; such a message from the palace was all that was needed to silence immediately the most vigorous opposition to a ministry.[4]

The Meiji rulers also developed more reliable enforcement machinery for carrying out their policies on a country-wide basis. In the 1880's, they laid the groundwork for the establishment of a professional civil service along Prussian lines and, although personal connections were still helpful in securing appointments, merit examination gradually became the main basis for recruitment.[5] Tokyo Imperial University served as the chief training ground for the national bureaucracy. Before very long, a system of classification and remuneration scales was introduced.

During the early years of the Meiji period, the units of local government were gradually brought under the canopy of central control.[6] As already noted, many feudal lords were persuaded and the rest ordered to turn over their lands to the emperor. Within a few years new prefectures had absorbed the old han. Through this transformation, the units of local government were largely stripped of their autonomy and were administered by agents of the central government who carried out the instructions of the Home Minister. The wide decision latitude enjoyed by the authorities in Tokyo enabled them to issue ordinances which gave significant authority to their agents in the countryside. Moreover, the central authorities held tight rein over public finance, so that the local governments were dependent to a large extent upon the national treasury. A censorate with itinerant inspectors kept a watchful eye on functionaries at all levels of the bureaucracy, reporting cases of unlawful conduct or negligence in the enforcement of decrees issuing from the center.

These administrative controls were reinforced by an extensive police organization, which also operated under the control of the Home Minister. Should the need arise, the central government could also rely upon the services of a national conscript army, which dramatically asserted its effectiveness in 1877 when it put down the rebellion of the Satsuma warriors.

In sum, the changes that occurred in the structures of government and in the procedures of governing after the Restoration in Japan are noteworthy and striking. Within a few years, the authority structure of policy making became highly resolved, and the new rulers assumed command of a reliable bureaucracy, regularly inspected by the censorate to see that their edicts were enforced. Moreover, they were able to employ on a national scale the army, the police, and an expanded system of courts against individuals and groups that put up resistance against their policies. In other words, they not only had a reliable enforcement mechanism but also had in their repertory a wide range of techniques for securing compliance. Indeed, Louis XIV and the most powerful Manchu emperor would have had good reason to be envious of the government of Meiji Japan.

England

The generation that lived in Japan during the last thirty years of the nineteenth century witnessed dramatic changes in government which were a reflection of a basic transformation of Japanese society. In considering the English scene, a British historian has pointed out that "in the last third of the eighteenth century one generation in England saw the rise of modern party politics and a revolution in administration that produced, at a stage or so removed, modern executive government in the parliamentary setting. . . ." [7] But many of the changes in England were so subtle that even contemporary observers were not always aware of some of the developments or their implications, since the patterns did not become set until the last half of the nineteenth century. [8]

In examining the modifications in English government from the end of the eighteenth to the middle of the nineteenth century— changes that greatly increased the resolution of the authority structure of policy making and the reliability of the enforcement instrument—it is necessary to review briefly some of the constitutional and structural developments which began a century earlier. The long struggle between parliament and the crown was constitutionally settled by the bloodless revolution of 1688-1689, which established the principle that the authority of the legislative body was superior to that of the monarch. Under this principle, the House of Commons tightened its hold over the public purse, asserting its right to sanction the expenditure of government funds, although it continued to grant to the executive large sums of money which could be spent without a detailed accounting to the House. Moreover, from this time onward, the king was entitled to act only through his ministers, who gradually declared their independence from the throne and who themselves fell increasingly under the political control of parliament.

The capacity of the ministers to institute policies independently of the royal will was enhanced by the evolution of the cabinet, which was visible in embryonic form in the reign of Charles II. When the first two Georges gave up the practice of attending cabinet meetings, an inner grouping of ministers began to develop a measure of solidarity as they hammered out policy among themselves before taking it to the monarch. With the king being effectively removed from the cabinet, a new leadership position emerged, and early in the eighteenth century the role of the First Minister became recognizable. Under the leadership of Robert Walpole (1712-1742), the cabinet continued to develop its autonomy, and the First Minister asserted his claim to a decisive voice in selecting his cabinet colleagues.

While the ministers were nurturing their independence from the palace, the members of parliament were gradually bringing the ministers themselves under the umbrella of legislative control. As early as the reigns of William III and Queen Anne, it was recognized that executive policies enjoyed smoother passage when the ministers of the crown were chosen so as to represent the majority interests in parliament. By the end of the eighteenth century, cabinets were being put together so that they could command the backing of the legislative assembly on at least the major policy issues. One should not get the impression, however, that majority support in parliament was based upon the tight control of a disciplined political party, or that the cabinet felt obliged to resign if it were defeated in the House of Commons. These developments were still almost a century away. In the eighteenth and early nineteenth centuries, cabinet government was largely coalition government; it was necessary for the ministers to build up their majorities by winning the support of certain blocs and a collection of independent members. A contemporary analysis in 1788 identified six major groupings in the House of Commons.[9] Interestingly enough, in this list the terms "Whigs" and "Tories" were not even used. The "Party attached to Mr. Pitt," which commanded 52 votes, was identified along with the "Opposition to the present [Pitt] Administration," which included the "Party attached to Mr. Fox" (138 votes) and the "Remnants of Lord North's Party" (17 votes). Besides these groups, there were several small factions attached to powerful individuals, a tiny band of neutrals, and two major groupings—the "Party of the Crown" (185 votes) and the "independent or unconnected Members of the House" (108 votes). The "Party of the Crown" was composed of those members who would support any administration if the Prime Minister were not too unpopular, while the independent faction tended to attract many of the country gentlemen.

This complex line-up of political forces is indicative of the problems faced by a Prime Minister in his efforts to build up support for his government. On most issues, he could count on the allegiance of his own Party and usually on the "Party of the Crown." But in order to broaden this strength into a workable majority, he had to win over powerful individuals, who might carry with them a scattering of votes, and a sufficient number of independents. To gain the needed leverage in parliament, the government could bestow special favors and even purchase the votes of House members with public funds.

As repugnant as these tactics may have been to some eighteenth-century reformers, they served to enhance the ability of the cabinet to command a majority in parliament and thus to increase the resolution of the authority structure of policy making. From his position as First Lord of the Treasury, the successful Prime Minister knew how to employ the funds at his disposal and to use to best advantage the parliamentary undersecretaries of the Treasury, the forerunners of the modern party whips.

While it is possible to detect a form of cabinet government within a parliamentary milieu operating at the end of the eighteenth century, the full development of the system had to wait for the reform of parliament, the expansion of the franchise, and the development of modern political parties. Although there was considerable agitation for reform in the late eighteenth and early nineteenth centuries and some reform bills were even presented to the House of Commons, little was accomplished until the passage of the Reform Act of 1832. This measure swept away the rotten boroughs and provided for a modest extension of voting privileges. Moreover, in the struggle over the enactment of the reform, one is able to observe the ineffective resistance of the House of Lords—a signal of its waning power.

Thus, by the mid-1840's, the authority structure of policy making was relatively highly resolved, compared with the situation of a century earlier. Its resolution, however, was to increase much more during the next decades, with the appearance of disciplined parties. In the 1830's and 1840's there remained small groups that could effectively veto certain policies. As an obvious example, the House of Lords, which was controlled by a tiny fraction of the population, maintained its veto power over legislation until 1911. In addition, small minority interests that were entrenched in the House of Commons could block government action unless their demands were met. The power of these groups—and even the power of specific individuals—was especially apparent when Parliament was considering bills to authorize the construction of canals and railways. A country gentleman occupying his seat in the Commons often was in a position to obstruct the passage of a canal bill until the company agreed to bypass his lands. Some of the landed aristocracy resisted the railways and their "infernal machines" because they might mar the beauty of the countryside or disturb the fox hunting. While consideration of many transportation bills by parliament was often perfunctory, there were nevertheless large numbers of contested cases which resulted in long and costly delays. In 1845, for example, the hearings on railway projects designed to connect London and York lasted for seventy days. Earlier, it had cost the promoters of the Liverpool-Manchester Railway £70,000 before they were able to win parliamentary approval.[10] Even though the authority structure of policy making was more highly resolved than it had been in the previous century, the difficulties encountered by many railway companies seeking parliamentary sanction for their projects indicate that there was still room for a further increase in its resolution.[11]

Not only was there a transformation in parliament and the executive and in the relations between these two units of government, especially when compared with the Tudor-Stuart periods, but there also occurred significant changes in the administration of the central government's affairs. During the long ministry of William Pitt (1784-1802), for example, the number of sinecures in the civil service was drastically reduced, the old fee collectors were gradually being replaced by salaried officials, and small offices with underworked staffs were consolidated and the work loads augmented without commensurate increases in pay.[12]

These changes, which greatly improved the efficiency and effectiveness of the central administration, did not come about as a result of dramatic legislative action or sweeping executive decrees. They stemmed, rather, from Pitt's vigorous efforts to reduce the cost and increase the efficiency of government. He diminished the number of sinecures typically by refusing to appoint a successor when an officeholder died, and he consolidated the work of the tax office (responsible for the land tax) and combined a number of offices that handled the collection of customs duties. He even brought the civil list under the scrutiny of parliament, which began to earmark funds for specific purposes rather than to appropriate lump sums to be spent without direction.

By 1800, there began to emerge within the central executive a number of departments charged with specialized responsibilities and with larger full-time staffs. In 1782, the secretariat was divided into two parts, one of which became the Foreign Office and the other the Home Office. The latter served as the parent agency for the administration of many governmental activities, chiefly domestic in nature, and from it a variety of other administrative bodies were later developed. Similar specialization took place within the military establishment, the Treasury, and other segments of the executive—a process that was to continue well into the nineteenth century. In 1840, for example, the Board of Trade began to supervise the regulation of railway companies, and in later years it undertook the regulation of navigation, the supervision of weights and measures, and the registration of joint stock companies.

Along with the development of specialized government agencies there was a substantial growth in the size of administrative staffs.[13] As early as 1797, a total of 15,884 civil servants were employed in 53 national agencies in the United Kingdom. By 1832 the number of employees in the national civil service had risen to 21,305, and by 1851 the figure was 39,147.[14]

The reforms begun by Pitt were continued into the nineteenth century, and under the new rules civil servants were excluded from politics and were forbidden to hold financial interests in firms handling government contracts. In an effort to weed out the incompetent, the government by the middle of the century had introduced a system of examinations in recruiting for certain offices; in some cases, appointees had to serve a period of probation before they could receive permanent appointments.[15]

The central government, however, still relied heavily upon local administrators to handle many problems, and it began in the nineteenth century to reorganize local government in piecemeal fashion. In the course of this reorganization, many of the responsibilities hitherto assumed by the justices of the peace were taken over by the local councils and authorities, which usually employed competent salaried officials to carry out their activities. As time went on, the central government came to exert considerable *administrative* control over the units of local government. The administration of the Poor Law of 1834 affords a good illustration of the tighter controls imposed by the authorities in Westminster. The act provided for the establishment of local boards of guardians, which bore no responsibility whatever to other officials in their localities; they answered only to a central board of commissioners. In this way, the central government, while still making use of local officials, established new and more effective mechanisms for controlling them.

Even more important, however, were the steps taken by the central government to free itself from dependence upon local officials for the enforcement of its statutes and regulations. The Factory Act of 1802 was of little consequence because enforcement was left in the hands of the local justices of the peace and a clergyman appointed for that purpose. But when the government sought to regulate child labor in textile factories in the 1830's, it provided for the appointment of central inspectors who successfully enforced the act. This, according to Lunt, "was the first indication of a tendency, which later became pronounced, to take control of local affairs away from incompetent local officials and give them to the central government." [16]

Summary

The changes in the structures of government and the procedures of governing that occurred in Japan just before and during the take-off period of economic development were part of a sudden but relatively bloodless revolution. In England the changes took place over a much longer period of time and were in good part evolutionary and subtle. Nevertheless, from the standpoint of this study, the similarities are impressive. In both countries, the authority structure of policy making became significantly more resolved, though the pace of change was much quicker in Japan. In both countries, too, the effectiveness of the enforcement instrument was greatly increased, and the techniques available to secure compliance were markedly expanded. Local government units also came increasingly under the administrative supervision of the central government.

The framework of this study has emphasized the similarities between developments in Japan and England. It may also be noted that there were important differences. In England the changes occurred in a structural context that, over a period of decades, increased the accountability of the governors to the governed. In Japan, despite the establishment of a parliament later in the period, the lines of accountability were more blurred and less effective. There were obvious differences in the institutional and structural settings of the two countries that made it possible for a democratic system to develop in England, whereas in Japan the trend toward a democratic polity was reversed in the 1930's and did not change direction again until after World War II. Over the range that is observable in the contrast between Japan and England, however, these differences do not appear to be significant for the purposes of the present study. It must be remembered that in England, even after 1832, the vast majority of citizens were not permitted to vote, and the English polity could not yet be called democratic.

With this overview of the structural and procedural developments, we can now go forward to an analysis of the functions of government in Japan and England during the take-off period of economic development.

THE ADAPTIVE FUNCTIONAL REQUISITE

As noted above,[17] the adaptive functional requisite concerns the adjustment of the social system to its nonhuman environment. Especially pertinent are the processes of production, resource allocation, and resource management. The analysis of Japan and England in the traditional stage of economic development indicated that the government in these two countries made a relatively small contribution to the satisfaction of the adaptive requisite. During the take-off stage of economic development, however, a different pattern predominated.

Japan

Japan is often taken as a model of a "latecomer" to industrialization, where the government was heavily involved in the process of resource allocation and to a lesser degree in the process of resource management. The extent of government involvement in resource allocation is indicated by Rosovsky's study which points out that the mean government share of gross domestic fixed-capital formation from 1887 to 1896 was 42.5 per cent, and that the proportion was higher in later decades.[18] The range of modern industries in which the government was prominent was wide. As Allen points out, "there was scarcely any important Japanese industry of the Western type during the later decades of the nineteenth century which did not owe its establishment to State initiative." [19]

The most conspicuous contribution that the Japanese government made to the satisfaction of the adaptive functional requisite was through the establishment of industrial concerns with public funds and through the direct management of certain firms by the state.[20] All railroad construction prior to 1881 was carried out by the government, and again in 1892 it embarked upon a railway-building program. Even most of the private lines that were built in the 1880's and 1890's were in 1907 absorbed into the government's virtual railway monopoly. The government also built—or took over from the feudal regime—and operated certain shipyards, port facilities, mines, arsenals, steel works, engineering concerns, irrigation and drainage works, and the telegraph system. In addition to firms in these industries, which could be classified as either heavy industries or social overhead capital industries, the government established and managed a few textile mills[21] and factories for the manufacture of glass and construction materials. These concerns were "model" establishments and pilot schemes designed to introduce native entrepreneurs to new industrial processes. In the period from 1868 to 1881, according to Smith, the Japanese government invested ¥34,653,461 in its own enterprises, or about 5.5 per cent of the revenue from ordinary taxation.[22]

It is important to point out, however, that in 1881—still very early in the take-off period—the government began to withdraw from the ownership and management of many of these enterprises.[23] The sales to private buyers included a number of model factories, textile mills, mines, and certain shipbuilding installations. In listing the firms to be placed on the market, the government was careful to retain ownership of the railways, the telegraph system, a shipyard, and a number of key enterprises supplying military needs. By relinquishing the bulk of its holdings, the government became less involved in the process of resource management and more specialized in its involvement in resource allocation. Public ownership in the Japanese economy did not increase significantly again until the 1930's.

While the establishment and operation of a large number of industrial firms by the government typically captures the attention of the scholar and is used as a primary illustration of the government's role in the Japanese economy during the take-off period, public expenditures for military durables represent quantitatively a more significant direct government contribution to gross domestic fixed-capital formation. According to Rosovsky, whose figures are indeed impressive, military investment as a proportion of total investment by the *central* government in the period from 1875 to 1900 never fell below 30 per cent, and ranged as high as 83 per cent. The mean during this period was 57 per cent.[24] This is dramatic testimony to the fact that the central government's involvement in resource allocation vis-à-vis capital formation was primarily in relationship to its military expenditures.

Another important form of government involvement in resource allocation was through the subventions paid to private enterprises. Shipbuilding and shipping companies, for example, were heavily subsidized through direct annual grants, the gift of vessels, guaranteed dividends, cheaply rented yards, postal contracts, and loans at low interest rates.[25] In the 1870's, the government purchased textile machinery for resale to private concerns on "installment loans" without interest, and sizable portions of these debts were never repaid.[26] By the same token, the government provided assistance to settlers in Hokkaido, sold land at low cost, and provided firms with exemption from business and income taxes for stipulated periods so as to attract capital into desired areas. During the period when private firms were engaged in railroad-building, the government donated the land and guaranteed a profit of 8 per cent for designated time periods.[27]

It must be recognized that a subsidy to a given industry or firm represented government involvement in resource allocation that was in fact greater than that indicated by the size of the subsidy itself. Rosovsky makes this point very clearly:

> How can one evaluate the effect of subsidy of, e.g., ¥100,000 to a Mitsubishi shipyard? If it is taken only at face value, an understatement will almost certainly result. A subsidy is an official vote of confidence in an enterprise: It may mean additional investment funds from private sources, better banking accommodations, and perhaps even a larger share of the private market.[28]

In short, a government subsidy may be taken by private investors to be a vote of confidence by the government in a firm, and this is very likely to reduce the risks of investment—a development that serves to attract private funds.

While the involvement of government in the process of resource allocation was of major importance, its involvement was not nearly so significant in the process of resource management. As already indicated, the government very early in the take-off stage largely abandoned its policy of building and managing economic enterprises and sold the bulk of its holdings to private individuals and groups. Railroads remained the major industry in which the government was actively engaged in resource management through public ownership.

During the take-off period in most societies, the corporate form of business organization becomes a conspicuous feature of the economy, and as a rule the regulation of corporations by the government tends to limit the decision latitude of the managers. For this reason it is advisable to regard such regulation as government involvement in resource management.

In Japan, however, government regulation of corporations and other forms of business activity was not of striking importance.[29] The promoters of an enterprise were legally required to draw up articles of association and to register with the government. The object of the firm was to be clearly stated, property holdings were to be publicized, stock was not to be sold below par value, an enterprise was not supposed to purchase issues of its own stock, and stockholders were to be consulted on major company decisions. In addition, corporations were to send financial reports to the Ministry of Finance, and their operations were to be checked periodically by inspectors appointed by the courts.

Although these requirements were listed on the statute and ordinance books, most of them were openly evaded. There was nothing to prevent corporations from going beyond the original purpose stated in the registration, and property interests were not publicly disclosed. Business enterprises circumvented the regulations applying to stock issues simply by setting up subsidiary organizations, and they gave their stockholders virtually no voice in the management of the firms. Inspectors were usually selected from the "inside" rather than by the courts, and the government was particularly lax in checking the financial reports of *zaibatsu* companies.

Financial institutions like banking and insurance companies were subject to more stringent laws. The government prescribed general standards of operation, and it clothed the Minister of Finance with broad authority to alter and enforce them. Thus the Minister was expected to approve the articles of association of these companies; to sanction changes in capitalization, the portfolios of savings banks, location of offices, and so on; to authorize mergers; and even to dissolve them or take them over. The enforcement of these regulations, however, depended upon the individual who headed the Ministry, as well as upon high civil servants who held responsibility when there was a rapid turnover of ministers. Available evidence indicates that supervision tended to be weak, especially in the case of the large zaibatsu financial institutions, and that violations of the stated rules were frequent. But even if they were enforced, they were more related to resource mobilization than to resource management.

Other regulations governing business were at best only incidentally related to resource management. Until about 1900, for example, the government was effectively engaged in restricting the business activities of foreigners, especially in the ownership of land and the direct operation of mines. In some instances, the political authorities influenced the selection of officials in privately owned companies. It is far from clear, however, that minor restrictions on *who* should manage resources had much effect on *how* they were managed.

It should be observed that the Meiji government, whether through indirect influence or regulatory statute, did not intervene to prevent corporations from organizing themselves into partnerships and interlocking directorates, or from entering into sole agency contracts. Large firms did not encounter resistance from the government when it came to matters of prices, output, marketing, and other business practices. Apart from general laws relating to property and contracts, the corporations were free to hire their workers as they saw fit. Government regulation of working conditions for women, children, and men engaged in mining did not appear until after the turn of the century, and even then the attempts did not greatly restrict the decision latitude of private managers. The Mining Act of 1905 was little more than a feeble beginning, and the Factory Act of 1911 did not go into force until 1916. Direct government regulation of the economy grew more frequent during and after World War I, as the political leaders sought to regulate profits, the price of rice, and conditions of employment. But wholesale intervention by the government did not occur until the 1930's.

England

England is frequently cited as an example of a society that moved into and through the industrial revolution with a minimum of direct government involvement in economic activities. The traditional view emphasizes the small expenditure of public funds in industrial enterprise, the absence of government ownership, the lack of effective regulation of the economy, and the introduction of free trade. The analysis employed in the present study, however, leads away from such an orthodox interpretation. Our conceptual scheme, for example, views resource allocation and resource mobilization as aspects of two different functional requisites—adaptation and goal attainment, respectively—and thus forces one to examine these two processes separately. When this analytical distinction is made and the analysis is adjusted to make a comparative fit between the English and Japanese cases, the contribution of English government to the satisfaction of the adaptive functional requisite takes on added significance. One reason why the contribution of the government looms large is because it was so actively involved in the allocation of what were essentially private resources.

On this subject, the work of Gayer, Rostow, and Schwartz on investment in England after 1790 is particularly instructive.[30] Their study indicates that, in the period from 1790 to 1793, the "building of canals and of turnpikes, and the enclosing of farm lands constituted major forms of enterprise at home." [31] From 1794 to 1801, investment in these enterprises continued to be significant, while additional large-scale investment was poured into docks and other harbor facilities.[32] Investment in canals, enclosures, and railways tended to decline after 1801, with enclosures attracting very little capital during the agricultural distress following the Napoleonic wars. In 1826, however, investments in railroads began to rise dramatically, although the amount was still small compared with a decade later.[33] In 1837, a construction boom developed in shipbuilding, which reached its peak in 1840.[34]

Attention is drawn to investment in these enterprises not only because of its proportional importance in the total economy, but also because of the government's role in this type of investment. Before capital could be invested in turnpikes, canals, railways, and most enclosures and harbor facilities, the promoters of each undertaking had to secure authorization by an act of parliament. In the case of projects related to transportation, for example, the act designated a specific company to carry out the project and granted special privileges to the firm. Canal and railway companies were given authority to secure the right of way for their transportation ventures, and they were awarded monopolistic or semi-monopolistic entitlements. The act of parliament also set the maximum amount of capital which a firm could raise in financing its project.

The capital outlays for enterprises of this sort were substantial. Between 1788 and 1796, for example, parliament approved 128 separate acts which authorized the investment of approximately £13,-000,000 in canals and navigation facilities.[35] Although the figures were lower during the wars with France, parliament nevertheless sanctioned a number of large undertakings. In 1799, the West India Dock Company was permitted to raise £500,000—£600,000 if it were needed—for the development of the Port of London. A year later, parliament approved the creation of the London Dock Company, with a capital of £1,200,000.[36]

When in the 1820's the canal system had been largely constructed and investment in this form of transportation was no longer significant, the railway industry became a promising outlet for savings. Before long, parliament authorized the expenditure of capital for railway construction far in excess of what had been sanctioned for the building of canals. Between 1825 and 1839, parliament passed 98 different railway acts; between 1832 and 1837, it authorized the expenditure of nearly £50,000,000.[37]

Through these acts of parliament, the English government was allocating resources among (potential) firms in the same industry by authorizing a specific company to undertake a given project and by granting it monopolistic (or semi-monopolistic) privileges. Even more important for the purposes of this study, however, the government by this action was allocating resources among different industries in a subtle but effective manner. Until the mid-1820's, joint stock companies whose existence was not specifically authorized (by acts of parliament or by royal charter) were illegal. Although they were legal after that time, they did not become numerous until the appearance of general limited liability in the 1850's. By authorizing the creation of joint stock companies with limited liability for canals, dock construction, and railways, the government was in effect channeling into these industries capital resources which private investors might have preferred to invest elsewhere, if they had been legally entitled to do so.

It is impossible from secondary sources to estimate the proportion of total gross capital formation which took place in the industries requiring this type of government sanction. We suspect, however, that if such an analysis could be made, the contribution of the English government to the satisfaction of the adaptive requisite during the take-off period would begin to resemble that of the Japanese.

That this similarity between the Japanese and English cases has not commanded the attention of scholars is perhaps due to the fact that public funds were not so obviously employed in England as they were in Japan. It may be, however, that more government revenues were employed in England than is ordinarily recognized. References to the use of public funds are scattered throughout the secondary sources, and one begins to suspect that a careful investigation of primary sources might reveal even more. It is significant, for example, that in 1837 the Manchester-Liverpool railway[38] sought authorization to borrow £400,000 from the Exchequer Loans Commissioners, but the major secondary sources do not consider this request important enough to indicate whether the loan was granted.[39] Parliament did, however, authorize a £400,000 loan in 1837, and it seems likely that the Exchequer Loans Commissioners granted it. This railway company had already received a government loan for £100,000 a decade earlier.[40]

Public funds were also used in canal construction. The government built and operated two canals in Scotland,[41] and it provided some subsidies to canal companies in the form of tax concessions, although it is difficult to estimate the amount.[42] In the second and third decades of the nineteenth century, an average of £1,000,000 of public money was invested per decade in harbor facilities.[43]

Since scholars have tended to focus their attention upon the government's role in financing undertakings other than railways and canals, greater specificity of treatment is possible. In the eighteenth century, the construction and maintenance of roads was the responsibility of the local parishes whose citizens had long been expected to put in six days of compulsory labor each year. Prior to 1750, private gifts of money, income from grants of land, and similar private sources of revenue were important in the financing of roads. After 1750, however, these sources of funds became much less important because the state supplied a more regular basis of finance. At this juncture, parliament began to authorize the creation of turnpike trusts which borrowed capital, built the roads, and collected tolls in order to repay their debts.[44] The promoters of these trusts were usually the local landlords, clergy, merchants, and other civic leaders. Between 1751 and 1790, about 600 special highway acts were passed by parliament, and within three decades 1,100 turnpike trusts were operating nearly 21,000 miles of road.[45] In 1803, an act of parliament provided that half the cost of any new road-building in Scotland would be borne by the state if the property-owners supplied the remainder. The following year the counties were given the right to contribute the local share from the rates, so that virtually all the funds going into new roads were public funds.[46] New statutes in the

1830's funneled more public funds into road-building, standardized the regulations to a greater extent, and made it easier for the central government to force local officials to maintain the roads in good repair.[47]

While it is not surprising that the government at the beginning of the industrial revolution increased its involvement in road-building, other cases of public support suggest that much scholarly writing has underestimated the role of the English government in financing commercial and industrial development. In the shipbuilding boom of the 1830's, for example, the capital expenditure on the merchant marine followed closely upon the first of the mail subsidies which the government provided in 1830.[48] In the first two decades of the industrial revolution, there was another expenditure by the English government which contributed significantly to capital formation, namely, military appropriations. We have noted that Rosovsky includes certain military items, such as ships, barracks, permanent fortifications, and munitions (but not ammunition) as capital formation, and we accept his argument for including these expenditures.[49]

The identification of specific military expenditures to be included as capital formation would be the subject of a monograph in its own right, and cannot be undertaken in this study. There are indications, however, that during the period from 1790 to 1815 large sums of money were involved. Even before the outbreak of war in 1793, Pitt supported appropriations for the building of naval ships. In 1784, for example, he earmarked for this purpose £2,500,000 out of a total government revenue of £25,000,000.[50] After it became apparent that the war would not be terminated quickly, government expenditures for the navy were greatly increased. Between 1797 to 1815, the budget for naval supplies was never below £10,000,000, and eventually reached a high point of £20,000,000. The mean during this period was approximately £17,000,000.[51] It is, of course, impossible to say what proportion of these expenditures could be classified as capital formation under Rosovsky's definitions. But it is important to note that the total tonnage of fighting ships almost doubled from the outbreak of war to the peak which was reached in 1809.[52]

In order to make the English figures comparable with those of Japan, it would be necessary to add to the expenditures of the central government the money spent by local government units. Unfortunately, we have been able to find no estimate of the total spending by these units that might have contributed to capital formation. The literature simply makes isolated references to spending on projects that would be classified largely as social overhead capital.[53]

It is desirable to have an analysis of capital formation in England which is comparable to Rosovsky's analysis of Japan, but the kind of statistical detail necessary is not available. However, we have the strong impression that if private capital formation were computed as a residual (as Rosovsky computes it), if appropriate military and local government expenditures were included, and if the government allocation of private resources were taken into account, the degree of government involvement in resource allocation in England would be comparable to what it was in Japan.

To complete the discussion of the contribution of the English government to the satisfaction of the adaptive functional requisite, we must treat its involvement in the process of resource management. Compared with Japan, resource management in England through direct government ownership was inconsequential. Some account must be taken, however, of government regulations that restricted the decision latitude of private managers. With the abolition in the latter part of the eighteenth century of many of the old regulations (which, as was pointed out in Chapter 4, were not particularly significant because they were not enforced effectively), a new type of regulation made its appearance. The acts of parliament authorizing canal and railway companies not only granted privileges but also imposed certain restrictions. As a rule, these acts placed limits upon capitalization, and they regulated the dividends which could be paid and the fares which could be charged. The parliamentary statutes applying to railways attempted to standardize some of the track gauge, to eliminate discriminatory practices, to fix passenger and freight rates, and to require the use of safety devices on the trains. In 1838, provision was made for the railways to carry mail at reasonable charges, and the executive was authorized to use some powers of compulsion. A regulation in 1844 required the roads to operate a certain number of third-class passenger trains at a fare of one penny per mile. Parliamentary sanction was needed for the development of continuous routes, the amalgamation of existing lines, and the formation of traffic pools and working agreements among operating companies.[54]

In the 1840's, the controls exercised through the original acts of authorization were reinforced by regulatory powers given to executive agencies. The Board of Trade, for example, became a public watchdog over the railways, receiving authority to gather reports on railway rates, traffic, and accidents. Moreover, new roads could not be opened until they were inspected by the Board's agents. The Act of 1845, which became the basis of modern railway legislation, authorized the submission of bylaws to the Board of Trade, the collection of statistical data, and the revision of the toll clauses for all existing and future railways. It also limited profits to 10 per cent and required the roads to provide regular types of service. Although the government tried to establish a separate board of railway commissioners, the plan met with opposition and was discontinued. The Board of Trade and the courts continued to be the main structures for enforcing the regulations until a special commission with judicial powers was established in 1873.[55]

Besides increasing its control over the railways in the nineteenth century, the government continued its regulation of shipping companies. Although these companies were gradually freed of the restrictions of the old navigation laws, they were still subject to regulations designed to insure the seaworthiness of ships and the safety of passengers and crews.[56]

Beginning largely in the 1830's, the government enacted factory legislation which limited the discretionary authority of firm owners and managers in minor respects, and it thus became involved in resource management. These factory regulations, however, are more important from the perspective of pattern maintenance and integration and merit discussion under those headings.

More significant were the restrictions which the government placed upon joint stock companies when certain types of these companies were legalized in the mid-1820's. The corporations, however, did not become a widely used form of business organization until after parliament had authorized general limited liability in the 1850's, although there was some increase in the number of companies following the passage of the Regulatory Act of 1844.[57] Since these laws received approval midway in the nineteenth century, they fall outside the scope of this review of the take-off period.

Summary

For two countries whose governmental roles during the early stages of industrialization have customarily been viewed as being so different, there are striking similarities between Japan and England in the contribution of government to the satisfaction of the adaptive functional requisite. In the first place, the government in both countries was significantly involved in the process of resource allocation. In both countries, for example, expenditures for military durables were an important part of the total budget. In both countries, too, the government was an important allocator of resources in the civilian economy, and in each case the major emphasis was on the creation of social overhead capital. The building of roads, canals, harbor facilities, and railroads and the enclosures of agricultural land received great attention in England, while in Japan the government was involved in the construction of railroads and harbor facilities. We recognize, of course, that the institutional context of government involvement in the process of resource allocation was different in the two countries, and that in Japan public funds were employed to a greater extent as investment resources in the civilian economy than was the case in England, although in the latter country they were more significant than is usually recognized. But it must be emphasized that these differences are differences in procedures or in resource mobilization; they are not differences in the contribution of the government to the satisfaction of the adaptive requisite. The government in England, for example, was *allocating resources* by making canal and railway firms virtually the only outlet for the investment of small sums in joint stock companies, just as clearly as the Japanese government was allocating resources when it poured its public revenue into the railways.

While the government's involvement in the process of resource allocation was significant in both countries, its involvement in the process of resource management was not nearly so great, especially in the case of England. The Japanese govenment divested itself of the bulk of its holdings very early in the take-off period, and the English government during this era was never the owner and manager of industrial firms. The operation of the railroads by the Japanese government was paralleled in England by significant government regulation, but this regulation was not as important as the direct management in Japan. In both countries, however, the bulk of resources were privately managed in the take-off period.

While striking similarities appear between Japan and England in the areas of resource allocation and resource management, the discussion suggests that there were some differences between the two cases in the involvement of the government in resource mobilization. This process is related to the goal-attainment functional requisite, to which we shall now turn our attention.

GOAL ATTAINMENT

In Chapter 5, the treatment of the goal-attainment functional requisite focused upon the analysis of the government's involvement in the process of resource mobilization and of credit creation. In this section we shall review briefly the involvement of government in this process during the take-off stage of economic development.

Japan

Shortly after coming to power, the new Meiji government set about to revise the tax system and to establish it on a national basis. Agriculture was still the main industry, and the land tax was the major source of revenue. In 1873, the central authorities turned their attention to a complete revision of the old Tokugawa levy upon land,[58] changing the basis of the tax from crop yield to a uniform levy upon land value as determined by an official nation-wide assessment. In its initial form, the tax rate was 3 per cent, and the tax obligation was henceforth to be paid in money rather than in kind. It was anticipated that this tax would cost the peasant approximately half of his crop, an amount customarily paid out under the old system. The land tax was by far the main source of public revenue during the early decades of the Meiji system, supplying 94 per cent in 1873 and an average of 78 per cent in the period from 1868 to 1881.[59]

Next to the assessment on land, the most lucrative source of public revenue was a series of indirect taxes upon consumer goods.[60] These consisted of ordinary levies on liquor, sugar, soy, confections, textiles, and similar commodities, and on tobacco and salt through fiscal monopolies. The operation of these monopolies can be illustrated by the case of tobacco. Although the government had levied a tobacco tax upon wholesalers and retailers since 1875, the government in 1898 began to force the producers of leaf tobacco to sell their crops to the state, which then sold the tobacco to the manufacturers and retailers who had paid registration fees and business taxes. A similar salt monopoly replaced the tax on salt in 1904. In the period 1893-1894, taxes on consumption accounted for 20.4 per cent of the national and local revenues, while the land tax, including local taxes on houses, produced 61.4 per cent.

The mercantile and industrial classes carried a relatively light tax burden, contributing only 13.3 per cent of the national and local revenue in the period 1893-1894. The government did not enact a personal income tax until 1887, and the low rate of the assessment produced only small returns. When this tax was increased in 1899, company profits and interest received from bonds were exempted from the progressive rates. In 1896, a tax on business turnover and capital was applied to twenty-four different kinds of business enterprises whose receipts exceeded ¥1,000 annually. Even with these and other miscellaneous assessments, however, the taxes upon business and industry brought in only modest returns. According to one estimate of the situation in 1908, the farmer paid out 28 per cent of his income in land, personal income, and business taxes, while merchants and industrialists surrendered only 14 per cent of their incomes.[61]

The new government not only devised a national system of taxation but also established tighter, more efficient methods of collection. When a taxpayer became delinquent in his payments, his property could be seized and sold to make up the deficit. In proceedings of this sort, the claims of the government took precedence over those of other creditors.

The revenues of the Meiji government, however, usually failed to keep up with its obligations, and the deficits, often staggering in size, were in large part made up by borrowing.[62] Since foreign loans were of little consequence until after 1900, most of the debt was carried internally. The money loaned to the government by domestic sources was derived through several means: the issuance of paper money, the floating of government bonds, official loans from state banks, and "forced loans" exacted from rich merchants and other wealthy citizens.[63] Through these techniques the government was able to borrow money from the people against the revenue from future taxes and to funnel the nation's resources into investments that were deemed to be most appropriate.

The new Meiji government also developed efficient mechanisms for collecting private savings and directing the flow of investment capital into officially approved channels. This was done largely through the development of a system of banks and other financial institutions which facilitated the creation of credit. Since there was no public securities market, small investors were stimulated to put their savings in bank deposits.[64] Moreover, many of the bigger investors, though conservative about putting their money directly into industrial undertakings, were quite willing to invest in banking operations.[65]

From the beginning of the Meiji era, the government's relationship to the banking system was an extremely close one.[66] At first, the government encouraged the establishment of a number of private exchanges and gave them money to get under way. Then it issued regulations which permitted the formation of national banks. These were allowed to operate for the duration of their charters, and then most of them became ordinary private banks. Many of the daimyo and the more enterprising samurai invested their government pensions in banking firms.

The banking system became more centralized in its organization in 1882, with the establishment of the Bank of Japan which served as the core of the system and had the sole right to issue bank notes. Gradually the private banking institutions were brought under closer government regulation, often through their relations with the huge state banks. In the case of the larger private banks, the Ministry of Finance reserved the right to appoint the principal officials. The government also either created or sanctioned the establishment of a number of special banks whose purpose was to make long-term credit available for certain types of economic activity. The Yokohoma Specie Bank, for example, was set up to help finance foreign trade and to mobilize holdings of domestic metal currency. Other specialized credit institutions included the Japan Hypothec Bank, the Industrial Bank of Japan, the Hokkaido Development Bank, agricultural and industrial banks, and the Oriental Development Company. In addition, a postal savings system was established for the purpose of accumulating the savings of private investors. By 1907, the number of ordinary banks and their branches had reached 4,563, with a capitalization of ¥444,209,000, while the number of savings banks stood at 519 with a capitalization of ¥73,453,600. The amount of deposits in postal savings was ¥92,922,291.[67] Thus, by fostering the development of an elaborate banking and credit system, the Meiji leaders were able to facilitate the mobilization and concentration of individual savings.

A government also becomes involved in the process of resource mobilization when it facilitates the establishment of joint stock companies. In this respect the government of Japan made a noteworthy contribution.[68] From the very beginning of the Meiji era, the government fostered the development of joint stock enterprises, protecting and often subsidizing firms to help them get started. It circulated publications explaining the joint stock system, and it used its powers of persuasion to encourage individuals to establish companies. At times the Meiji rulers even set up a competitor for an existing company and awarded subsidies to both. As a result of the encouragement given by government, joint stock companies were established in such fields as the railway industry, shipping, banking, insurance, commodity exchange/brokerage, paper-making, harbor construction, and sugar and oil refining. Between 1895 and 1898, the number of firms more than trebled, reaching a total of 7,044. After the turn of the century, the government even took steps to organize joint stock companies in agriculture in order to facilitate the raising and sale of farm produce and the development of rural credit.

As we noted in Chapter 4, a stable currency is indispensable for a healthy system of credit. Shortly after having installed themselves in office, the Meiji rulers began to address themselves to the problem of making their currency uniform and more stable.[69] After assaying the old coins and finding them debased, they decided to mint new gold and silver currency. Although the gold standard was technically adopted in 1871, silver remained very much in use, and within a few years it became the virtual standard of value. After the country had experienced difficulty in establishing parity between gold and silver and had suffered from the depreciation of paper money, the government adopted a tight financial policy. Public expenditures were curtailed, taxes were increased, and a sinking fund was created to pay off some of the debt represented by note currency. The establishment of the Bank of Japan, stricter control over foreign exchange through the Yokohama Specie Bank, and some regulation of private banking helped to put the financial structure on a firmer foundation. These policies eventually brought a good measure of stability to the monetary system, and in 1897 the country was solidly on a gold standard, using the Chinese indemnity as a gold reserve fund.

England

The eighteenth century was for England a period of foreign wars, and the problem of financing them seriously strained the national budget. Virtually every cabinet was faced with the task of improving the usual sources of revenue while continually searching for new ones. The government's financial difficulties worsened during the time of the French wars (1793-1815), which cost more than all the previous conflicts the English had waged with foreign enemies.

It is hardly necessary at this point to examine each of the numerous taxes which were collected in England by the end of the eighteenth century. A summary examination of a typical peacetime budget in the 1890's and a large wartime budget after the turn of the century should suffice. In 1892, the principal direct tax was still the assessment on agricultural land, which was levied at the rate of four shillings in the pound (2 per cent), yielding about £2,000,000. The total revenue from all direct taxes (including, for example, levies on houses, post horses, coaches, and property sold at auction) was £3,-837,000. Indirect taxes were imposed on a large number of items, especially consumer goods like salt, sugar, alcoholic beverages, tobacco, candles, and soap but including also a few producers' goods such as iron bars, raw silk, and leather. These taxes produced about £12,158,783 for the public treasury. In addition, almost £1,000,000 were collected from stamp duties.[70]

During the long war, the government greatly increased the rates of many of the old taxes and introduced a number of new levies, the most notable of which was the income tax. In 1815, the yield from direct taxes was slightly more than £25,000,000, about half of which —£14,600,000—came from the income tax. The returns from the land tax had fallen to £1,200,000, largely as a result of the revision which had been made in 1798. Producing revenue amounting to about £6,500,000 were the taxes on houses, which included not only the window tax and a levy on establishments and inhabited houses but also assessments on manservants, saddle and carriage horses, dogs, hair powder, armorial bearings, and other items.

The revenue from indirect taxes was more lucrative, totaling £38,-000,000. In the list of taxable items, consumer goods were by far the most prominent. Most of the enormous increase in yield, when compared with 1792, was derived from existing taxes rather than from an augmentation of articles subject to taxation. (In its struggle to gain new revenue, the government did, however, search for new items to be taxed. Levies on plum puddings, raisins for dessert, and currant dumplings yielded £307,000.) The income from stamp duties had risen to over £2,500,000.[71]

During the two decades following the war, the government repealed many taxes and reduced the rates on several others. For example, it abolished the income tax, which, as we have noted, had been the largest single source of revenue during the later war years. (It was not imposed again until 1842, and then at a much lower rate.) Although some taxes on consumer goods disappeared in the 1820's and 1830's, the emphasis was primarily on the repeal of taxes on "commerce." Levies on producers' goods became even less significant in the budget, and the government did away with some stamp duties on documents required for commercial transactions.[72] It also greatly reduced the house tax.

In sum, then, it is clear that taxes on consumer goods provided the bulk of the revenue throughout this period. Taxes on agricultural land were much less important after the opening years of the nineteenth century, while the income tax was used only as an emergency war-time measure.

Although the tax systems of Japan and England in peacetime were similar in that the burden was carried mainly by citizens who had a low propensity to save, the banking systems of the two countries were apparently very different. The Bank of England, chartered in the seventeenth century, remained throughout the take-off period as an important lender to the government and did not figure significantly in the direct financing of industrial undertakings, although it did aid in the financing of large commercial operations.[73] All the other banks in England were private concerns which were regulated by the government largely through general laws applicable to partnerships and by the specific proviso that there could be no joint stock banks except for the Bank of England. It would be erroneous to assume, however, that the government was not involved in resource mobilization for industrial development through the banking system. Many of the country banks which grew up in England during the last half of the eighteenth century—there were more than 500 of them—were established by individuals who were responsible for the collection of certain government revenues. Very often the funds they loaned out for industrial and commercial purposes were the money they had collected in taxes. How this was done is a fascinating case illustrating how the government, without intent, became deeply involved in resource mobilization for industrial development. In his study, Pressnell discloses the three stages through which money passed from the tax-payer to the Exchequer:

First, the taxes were collected locally; next, they were sent to an agent in London; finally, the London agent paid the tax proceeds into the appropriate government department, probably by Bank of England paper.

Taxes were collected in a variety of media, but were usually sent to the capital by bills and drafts on London houses. In procuring these means of remittance revenue officials were, in effect, acting as discounters. Equally, by slackness in actual payment, they were engaging in a species of deposit banking; they secured time, at the government's expense, in which to use public money for private profit. This delay in payment might occur both before and after the money was dispatched to London; in either case the government funds increased the resources of private individuals. Locally they added directly to cash reserves and thereby to the ability to expand private credit; in London they performed a similar function—for the extent of provincial bill drawing depended upon the funds available with a London agent—or they might be invested in government securities.[74]

The time delay between collection and remittance might be considerable, for the revenue from land taxes and stamp duties was usually not sent forward for a year or more after it had been collected.[75] The men who received and held public funds derived from taxation invested them in commercial, industrial, and agricultural enterprises.[76] At the same time, the government was regularly borrowing from the Bank of England against the anticipated revenue from the land and malt taxes[77]—money that at least in part had already been collected and was being used for private gain. The use of public funds by private bankers was an excellent example of government resource mobilization and the private allocation of these same resources.

Such practices by country banks were not important after 1821, but other funds were made available to private banks. In 1826, parliament authorized joint stock banking beyond a sixty-five-mile radius of London. At the same time the Bank of England began to establish note-issuing branches in the provinces.

As already indicated, the fostering of joint stock enterprises by government involves it in the process of resource mobilization. The English government, however, did not make a notable contribution to the development of corporate forms of business enterprise until the middle of the nineteenth century. The Bubble Act of 1720 rendered illegal any joint stock company that was not specifically authorized, usually by an act of parliament. Although there was some relaxation of these restrictions in the 1820's, limited liability—the feature that is most significant for resource mobilization—did not become well established until the 1850's.[78] However, parliament did authorize by special acts the formation of many limited liability joint stock companies, especially for developing canals and railways, and between 1790 and 1850 large amounts of capital were poured into these organizations.

During this period, the English government took steps to improve facilities for the creation of credit by tackling its currency problems. By the middle of the eighteenth century, the circulating coins of the realm were in poor condition. In 1774, parliament approved the recoinage of the worn gold coins and authorized the public treasury to bear the cost. Since the recoinage did not apply to silver, the government's action in effect put England on the gold standard and put the standard coinage in good order.[79]

The next important change in the currency occurred after 1797, when the Bank of England was forced to suspend cash payments. Within a few years, notes had in large part replaced coins as a circulating medium, and by the end of the war checks were coming into more common use. It should be observed that there was no significant overissue of paper, which would have rendered it worthless like the American continental or the French *assignat,* and would thus seriously have restricted credit creation.[80] Although inflation developed during the war, the rise in prices was not as great as one might have expected, especially in view of the fact that the government financed such a high proportion of its wartime budget through borrowing.

Summary

In considering the contribution of the Japanese and English governments to the goal-attainment functional requisite during the take-off stage, a number of similarities become evident. Either prior to or during the take-off period, the governments of the two societies increased the effectiveness and efficiency of their systems of tax collection. It should also be noted that in both countries the major portion of the tax burden fell upon people who had a low propensity to save.

There were, however, some important differences in the involvement of government in the resource-mobilization process. Compared with Japan, the government of England was much less involved in this process during peacetime, and this was especially true with respect to the mobilization of resources that would find their way into the new industrial undertakings. But while this significant difference must be recognized, the data of this study suggest that typically the role of the English government is underestimated owing to the neglect of three factors: (1) the use of public funds for investment by country bankers; (2) the spending by local units of government; and (3) the loans by the government to certain important enterprises.

When it comes to the creation of credit, the Japanese government was more directly involved in banking and in the creation of credit through the bank system. The governments of both countries, however, took similar steps to reform the coinage and to put the monetary system on a more solid foundation.

In goal attainment, then, the similarities between the two societies are not as striking as they were in the adaptive functional requisite. Closer parallels emerge again, as we shall see in the next section, in the pattern-maintenance functions of the two governments.

PATTERN MAINTENANCE

The pattern-maintenance functional requisite is concerned with maintaining conformity with the values prescribed by the cultural (belief-value) system. As pointed out in Chapter 2, three processes are of particular importance: (1) a social-control process which involves the application of sanctions to secure compliance with the basic norms of the value system; (2) an enculturation process by which values are passed on from one generation to the next; and (3) a tension-management process by which the propensity to violate norms is diminished.

The analysis of the pattern-maintenance functional requisite in the take-off stage of economic development is more difficult than during the traditional stage, because during the take-off period the shifts in the structure and content of the cultural system are much more rapid. Changes in beliefs, especially concerning science and technology, are of course crucial in the general picture of societal change, but they are a less important consideration when attention is focused specifically upon the functions of government.[81]

Changes in values also enter into the picture, but in the analysis of the Japanese and English cases changes in the *structure* of the value system—as contrasted with substantive changes in values—were of even greater importance. A thorough elaboration of this point is beyond the scope of the present study, but a few illustrations will help to clarify what we mean by changes in the structure of the value system.

One type of change in the structuring of values occurs when a conflict develops between two values that at a previous time could be realized simultaneously. For example, one of the deeply rooted values in England was the independence of the laboring man. He was regarded as a "free agent" who could bargain to work in a factory or other establishment for as many hours a day as he wished.[82] There was also a deeply held value that children who were employed should not be unduly exploited. Cruelty to apprentices could, for example, be treated as a criminal act.[83] In the early eighteenth century, these two values did not as a rule compete with each other and could be achieved simultaneously. The situation changed, however, with the development of the factory system. To restrict the working hours of a juvenile employee to ten per day could be regarded as preventing the undue exploitation of child labor. But if such a restriction were to limit the operation of a factory to ten hours per day, it also prevented the adult male from freely bargaining to work twelve hours. Hence, the two values came into sharp conflict, and their simultaneous achievement was no longer possible. Under these circumstances, one of the values has to be given priority over the other, and some hierarchical relationship between the two tends to emerge. This is what is meant by a change in the structure of the value system.

Another type of structural change in the value system is the shift of an official policy directive from a precept to a norm, or vice versa. In Chapter 2, a norm was defined as a directive to which obedience is compulsory, while a precept is a directive to which conformity is desirable but not compulsory. Thus "love thy neighbor" is a precept; "thou shalt not kill" is a norm. In 1848, parliament passed a public health act which granted to local governments certain powers over sanitation. It seems likely that, prior to 1848, good sanitation was a value and that certain practices were considered to be undesirable but not illegal. These practices, however, were to be more strictly controlled under the 1848 law, and the change represented a shift from a precept to a norm—a structural change in the value system.

It is these changes in the structuring of the value system that make the analysis of pattern maintenance more difficult to handle, both conceptually and empirically, during the take-off stage. In this section, however, we shall have to ignore these complexities and present a straightforward empirical treatment of government involvement in the three relevant processes.[84]

The Social-Control Process

In both Japan and England during the take-off stage, there was a notable increase in the size and operation of the police force. By

1880, the Japanese had largely completed the organization of a national police force, which, except for the separate organization in Tokyo, was directed by the central Police Bureau in the Home Ministry.[85] The lines of authority ran from the Home Minister and the Police Bureau to the prefectural governors who were responsible for the police within their territories and who were entitled to call for the aid of military forces should the need arise. Following the pattern established by the Tokugawa, the Meiji rulers set up a censorate which had as one of its responsibilities the dispatching of inspectors and secret agents to all sections of the country to check on the operation of the police system and to investigate alleged plots and violations of the law. In the 1880's, a special branch of political police emerged and they fell under the direct supervision of the central government. The extent of the police establishment is indicated by the fact that, shortly after the turn of the century, there were in Japan 31,454 ordinary policemen, 1,855 police sergeants, and nearly 200 superior officers.

Over a period of several decades, the new regime also issued a variety of edicts and regulations that increased the involvement of government in the social-control process and granted to the police extensive powers of enforcement. It is interesting to observe that, while the Japanese had prolonged disagreements over the civil code and the commercial code, they had much less trouble in formulating the penal code.[86] The first written code, which was strongly influenced by the Chinese, was promulgated in 1870, and a new code, modeled after that of France, went into effect in 1882. Under the penal code and other official enactments, the police were entrusted with the ordinary task of providing security against wrongdoers and individuals contemplating unlawful acts. The police were also authorized to intervene in labor-management disputes, to control the use of firearms, to prevent smoking among young people, and to restrain any person in the interest of preserving public peace and order. In the 1870's and 1880's, when political parties were being organized to resist the policies of the oligarchy and to agitate for a measure of popular government, the regime promulgated a series of press laws and "peace preservation" statutes. Under these enactments, the police were authorized to censor printed materials believed to be unreasonably critical or otherwise harmful to the government, and to observe political meetings, disbanding them if they thought it wise to do so. Restrictions were placed upon the organization of political parties, and groups holding public meetings were required to secure permission in advance—approval that would be withheld if the police felt that the gathering might disturb the "public peace." Prefectural governors were entitled, through the police, to order anyone who was committing violent acts or stopping other people from carrying out their duties to take up some form of lawful employment. In Meiji Japan, the executive had the power to issue police ordinances for the preservation of order and the promotion of the general welfare, so long as these edicts did not conflict with existing law.

As in Japan, the English government during the early decades of the nineteenth century took steps to create an effective police establishment.[87] Prior to the development of a professional police system, the local areas had to depend upon petty constables who were obligated to serve without pay (except for certain fees) under appointment by the justices of the peace. This arrangement was particularly ineffectual in the growing metropolitan areas.[88]

The first step in the development of a modern, paid police force was taken in 1829 by Sir Robert Peel, who secured the establishment of the Metropolitan Police for the London area, an organization that was subject to the Home Minister. In 1835, parliament required the boroughs to hire paid, permanent constables who carried out their duties under the supervision of the local councils. Four years later, in 1839, the justices of the peace in the countryside were empowered to develop a paid constabulary for their counties. Since many counties did not take advantage of the parliamentary authorization, however, the government in 1856 secured the passage of legislation forcing the counties to set up police establishments. These police forces also fell under the ultimate control of the Home Minister, who enforced his authority through a system of royal inspectors. Thus, with the creation of a modern police arrangement, the use of the armed forces to restore order was reserved for extreme emergencies.

Improvement in criminal detection was accompanied by greater specialization in the trying of criminal cases at the local level. With the creation of a more effective police force, for example, as well as the development of local administrative bodies, the justices of the peace were relieved of many of their traditional burdens, and were in a position to devote more time to the hearing of cases which fell within their jurisdiction. Periodic reorganization of the court system helped to make it more uniform and more efficient in the trying of criminal offenses.

While both governments were becoming more involved in the social-control process through the creation of a police force, they were withdrawing from the enforcement of the norms that bestowed certain rights, privileges, disabilities, and liabilities on specific social classes. In Japan, shortly after the Restoration, a series of decrees destroyed the legal basis of social distinctions and privileges.[89] The *eta* (outcast class) were elevated to the status of commoners, ordinary folk were entitled to use their own surnames, intermarriage between peers and commoners was sanctioned, and a ban was placed on the wearing of swords. Even more important, the regime abolished the regulations that had tied occupation to social position. In 1871, the members of the Tokugawa military class were given the freedom to pursue any occupation, and in the following year the same right was extended to farmers. Although some legal distinctions were carried forward by the creation of a new peerage, whose members were favored in the post-Restoration schedule of punishments and whose sons were encouraged to go abroad and were given opportunities for education at a special school for the nobility,[90] only a comparatively small number of families was affected.

In England, there were few legal privileges held by members of classes other than the small group of noblemen. Most notable among these privileges were the special voting rights of certain classes, which were partly swept away by the Reform Act of 1832, and more completely in 1867. In securing the enactment of the Reform statute, the government, with the acquiescence of the monarch, threatened to "pack" the House of Lords if the members blocked the measure—an indication of the decline in the power of the nobility, which, however, did not lose their authority to veto legislation until 1911.

Although not defined in terms of social class, certain legal restraints, based upon religious tests, had been applied since the seventeenth century to religious minorities—Catholics, Protestant Dissenters, Jews, Quakers. These laws had had the effect not only of restricting religious liberty but also of denying members of these groups of the right to hold civil, military, and corporate posts, or to take seats in parliament. In a series of laws beginning in 1828 and continuing for more than two decades, parliament removed many of the restrictions on religious worship and abolished the civil disabilities so that individuals who had suffered discrimination could claim the same rights enjoyed by other citizens.

Thus, in summary, government in both Japan and England during the take-off period became more deeply involved in the social-control process through the establishment of sizable police forces. At the same time, however, a number of decrees and other legislative acts changed the legal norms that applied specifically to certain social classes or members of religious groups.

The Enculturation Process

In the chapters dealing with the traditional stage of economic development, no mention was made of the government's involvement in the enculturation process. This was ignored because it did not appear to be significant in any of the four cases, and the differences that did exist provided no basis for discriminating in meaningful fashion among the four societies. During the take-off stage, however, the government became much more involved in the enculturation process through its contribution to and regulation of education, especially at the elementary level.[91]

The development of a public-supported system of elementary education proceeded much faster in Japan than it did in England. In pre-Restoration Japan, education had been the privilege of the few, and anything more than the rudiments had been enjoyed largely by the offspring of the samurai and well-to-do commoners. When the Meiji leaders assumed control, they proceeded to lay the foundation for a system of compulsory primary school training.[92] In 1871, they established a Department of Education. In the following year they unfolded a plan of compulsory education at the elementary level—at first for a period of sixteen months, which was extended to four years in 1886 and later to six years. At this time, the budget of the Department of Education was ¥800,000, one-eighth of which was allocated for the training of Japanese students abroad. The central government also financed the use of several thousand Western experts who assisted in the development of the educational system at all levels. The cost of the primary schools was borne by the local units of government, usually supplemented by grants from the central or prefectural treasuries.

Although at first progress was slow, owing to the shortage of buildings, teachers, and instruction materials, as well as to the uncertainties of reorganization, the educational system toward the end of the century made rapid advances. Shortly after 1900, there were 27,-000 primary schools giving at least rudimentary training to 5,000,000 children. By 1910, 98 per cent of the children in the six to thirteen age bracket were registered in primary schools, with an average daily attendance of 93 per cent. During this period, the government also established secondary schools, teacher training colleges, technical institutes, a number of state universities, and a program of business and vocational education.

Until well into the nineteenth century, there was little support in England for the view that the government should play an active role in providing educational facilities for its citizens or should undertake the regulation of elementary education.[93] The central government first appropriated financial aid for elementary education in 1832-1833, shortly after the passing of the Reform Act, when it granted a sum "not to exceed £20,000" annually to assist private groups in the building of schoolhouses for the poor. This was soon followed by other legislation which had an effect upon education. The Factory Act of 1833, for example, stipulated that juvenile factory workers were to spend three days a week in some type of school. Similarly, the Poor Law of 1834 required that all children in a workhouse were to receive at least four hours of instruction each day.

Although the size of state grants to education was increased in the 1840's and the amended factory acts tended to strengthen the educational requirements for youngsters, England was slow in developing a system of public-supported elementary education. The Elementary Education Act of 1870 provided for the establishment of local school boards which were authorized to levy a rate in support of schools and to compel attendance on the part of children between the ages of five and thirteen. Even this Act, however, did not establish free, compulsory education in England. Compulsory school attendance was not made universal until 1880, and it was not until 1891 that, for all practical purposes, parents were entitled to send their children to elementary schools at public expense.

Before these acts were passed, school attendance was the privilege of only a small minority. The Royal Commission, under the chairmanship of the Duke of Newcastle, reported in 1861 that only one child in 7.7 was attending school of any kind, and that 19 per cent of those counted as school attenders spent no more than 50 days a year in the classroom.[94]

The Tension-Management Process

The structural changes occurring during the take-off stage of economic development are likely to increase the propensity of certain groups within the society to violate the basic norms. For example, the occupants of roles that are rapidly losing their power in the society, or showing signs of losing their prestige and privilege, may be tempted to seek to maintain their influence by resorting to extreme action outside the accepted normative patterns. Some roles will even disappear, and the occupants of these roles are likely to engage in destructive behavior in an effort to prevent the changes that threaten their position. The tension-management process is concerned with activities that are designed to reduce the propensity of individuals and groups to violate the fundamental norms of the society.

During the take-off stage, the government in both Japan and England became more actively involved in the tension-management process.[95] In Meiji Japan, the powerful and prestigious roles occupied by the daimyo and samurai under the Tokugawa were undergoing rapid change, and the members of the military class had a great deal to lose. The extent of the disaffection of many of the warriors was indicated by the disorders which plagued the Restoration government and culminated in the Satsuma revolt in 1876-1877.

Soon after the downfall of the Tokugawa, however, the Meiji rulers began to make concessions to the elite of the old regime. They appointed large numbers of warriors to posts in the new state administration. Perhaps even more important, they assumed responsibility for giving the daimyo and samurai annual pensions which amounted to a percentage of the stipends they had been accustomed to receiving under the feudal system. But this financial outlay from the public treasury was apparently more than the new government could afford, and in 1873 it offered to commute the pensions to government bonds. By 1876, the government was in a sufficiently strong position to make the commutation of pensions compulsory.[96] Significantly enough, the Satsuma uprising broke out shortly after the announcement of this policy, but by this time the government had developed the means to suppress disorders by superior armed force.[97]

In England, where the pace of change was slower, a smaller number of roles and role occupants were suddenly threatened by the policies of the government. But, despite this fact, the government awarded pensions and subsidies to individuals who had been removed from lucrative but fairly useless posts. Since there was no general policy of paying subsidies and pensions to entire classes of people, it is difficult to estimate how much public revenue actually went into this kind of support. It is possible, however, to offer a few examples.

When the sinecure offices of the auditors of the imprests were abolished in 1785, the individuals who held these posts were paid £7,000 annually for the rest of their lives. When a man employed in the postal system was forced to abandon his packet boat service, the government awarded him compensation amounting to £400 a year. The literature discloses many other instances of such subsidies.[98]

As industrialization spreads more widely throughout the countryside, many of the traditional roles in handicraft and home-employment industries become vulnerable, and ordinary people who occupy these roles are likely to feel threatened and grow restive. In England during the late eighteenth and early nineteenth centuries, this was reflected in such behavior as the smashing of machinery,[99] indicating an increase in the propensity to invade the rights of property-owners by violence. While the Japanese managed to link their traditional and modern economies with amazing smoothness, there were nevertheless frequent disturbances among the peasants (often led by disgruntled samurai) that were partly related to the rapid pace of economic and social change.[100] Even before the Restoration, peasant disorders broke out in localities where the primitive factory system was beginning to take root. After the Meiji rulers had seized power, they encountered open resistance to their policies of innovation. According to Inouyé, "people generally disliked the railway because of the heavier burden it would throw upon their shoulders by causing additional taxes, and the innkeepers and goods-carriers living along the line feared that it would deprive them of their occupation." In treating the complaints of the dissidents during this period, scholars list the importation of cotton fabrics and yarns which threatened the subsidiary industry of the peasants, the enactment of conscription, the land survey and the land tax, the dispossession of the peasants from their lands, the loss by farmers of usufract of common fields, competition with foreign entrepreneurs in Japan, and similar grievances.

In both countries, the government usually responded to these outbreaks of violence by dispatching troops or the newly established police forces to the scene. This method of handling the infringement of norms was, of course, an aspect of social control, which has already been discussed in this chapter. But eventually the governments of the two societies sought to reduce the propensity to violate norms by introducing ameliorative welfare legislation, which dissident elements of the population were demanding.

Early in the Meiji era, the Japanese government introduced modest schemes for the relief of disabled veterans and hardship cases, and it inaugurated a plan for the storage of grain in anticipation of famine emergencies.[101] Throughout much of this period, the government also attempted to maintain a fairly high price for rice, which was so important in the economy of the countryside.[102] After the Sino-Japanese war (1895), the number of urban wage-earners increased rapidly, and groups began to agitate for the formation of trade unions. It was partly in response to the growth of such movements that the political authorities enacted peace preservation laws, some features of which hampered for a time the organization of workers' societies. At the same time, however, government leaders often took the initiative in introducing welfare legislation, even though financial and industrial interests in the country usually opposed their programs.

The early forms of factory legislation, which were introduced in the 1870's, were designed to provide accident compensation for workers in government factories.[103] During the next two decades, the government conducted a number of surveys of factory conditions and drafted several bills to promote the welfare of laboring people. These measures, however, met with such resistance from factory owners that they were never enacted into statute, although regulations were applied to the mining industry during this period. In 1910, the Meiji government drew up another factory bill which was to regulate the age level and working hours of laborers, but when the cotton spinners objected to the prohibition of night work for women and children, it amended the bill and submitted it again the following year. Although the Factory Act of 1911 did not go into effect for five years, it was a landmark in Japanese social legislation—the forerunner of more comprehensive statutes which were promulgated in subsequent years, especially in 1926.[104]

Besides introducing welfare measures, the government also widened the scope of political representation in the system, thereby submitting to the demands of groups that were growing increasingly vocal. The Diet provided something of a forum for the airing of dissident opinions, and increased pressure upon the oligarchy resulted in several extensions of the franchise, culminating in the promulgation of the Manhood Suffrage Act in 1925. Gradually, too, the political authorities gave *de facto* recognition to the existence of trade unions, which eventually won legal status.

As in Japan, the government of England ultimately embarked upon programs of welfare legislation. Parliament approved a series of laws regulating working conditions in factories and mines, it established state employment exchanges, and it revised the system of public relief not only to distribute aid to the needy more effectively but also to help make workers more mobile, freeing them from their local parishes so that they no longer had to compete with public subsidized labor. Much of this type of legislation, however, may be more appropriately related to the integration functional requisite and will be discussed below.

In addition to promulgating welfare measures, the government of England broadened the span of representation in the political system. Through the expansion of the suffrage in 1832 (and again in 1867 and 1884), direct representation in the House of Commons was provided for more segments of the society which were growing noticeably restless without it. In line with this trend, the political leaders over a period of years removed the civil disabilities which had denied certain rights to Catholics, Protestant Dissenters, and other minority groups. In 1824-1825, the government also abolished restrictions on the organization of trade unions, permitting their members to agitate for better wages and hours so long as they did not resort to violent methods. In the terms of this study, these sorts of activities by government are an aspect of tension management, since the propensity to violate basic norms of the society will tend to be inversely proportional to the degree of involvement and participation in the political system.

Summary

During the take-off stage, the government in Japan and England increased in markedly similar ways its contribution to the satisfaction of the pattern-maintenance functional requisite. Among the most striking similarities was the development of a professional police force under the ultimate control of the central authorities, with the result that government was increasingly involved in the enforcement of norms defining criminal behavior. Also important was the general abolition of legal norms that defined social class or imposed disabilities upon certain groups in the society.

As a country enters the take-off stage, the government becomes more deeply involved in the enculturation process. It has long been recognized that the development of the factory system tends to disrupt the family structure, thus diminishing its capacity to socialize the children. The support and regulation of elementary education by government represents its greater involvement in the process of enculturation. In the two cases under examination, however, the government of Japan gave more support to public education than did the government of England.

It is also in the take-off stage that there is an observable increase in the involvement of government in the tension-management process. In both Japan and England, the government paid subsidies to individuals who occupied positions of prestige and/or power, and thus reduced their propensity to hinder the social changes which threatened to erode their influence. While this type of activity was prominent in the early phase of the take-off period, a few decades later the government resorted to other kinds of conciliatory measures. Political representation, for example, was broadened in both societies, and welfare legislation was introduced to improve conditions of employment and to provide public relief. All of these activities marked an increase in the involvement of government in the tension-management process.

INTEGRATION

In considering the contribution of government to the satisfaction of the integration functional requisite in Chapter 5, we concentrated our attention upon the degree to which legal sanctions were used to enforce those norms that govern the relationships among roles differentiated on the basis of (1) occupational specialization, (2) prestige, and (3) generation. In this chapter, we shall present a brief treatment of the same topics, and we shall also discuss how the government was involved in processes of integration other than that of social control.

Roles Differentiated on the Basis
of Occupational Specialization

In Tokugawa Japan, commercial law was only partially developed. Other structures besides the government were significantly involved in the enforcement of contracts which linked various occupational specialists, as well as in the enforcement of norms that established the context within which contracts were negotiated.

After the Restoration, the Meiji rulers set about to formulate a civil code and a commercial code. Although frequent disagreements caused the promulgation of the two codes to be postponed, it was widely recognized that bills of exchange, promissory notes, business firms, and bankruptcy should be regulated. Therefore portions of the code dealing with these matters were put into effect before the whole document was sanctioned.[105]

The civil and commercial codes made important stipulations which involved the government in enforcing both the contractual and the noncontractual aspects of contract.[106] For example, they set forth detailed regulations governing contracts and bankruptcy, and these were usually enforced through the courts or through some form of administrative action. Unless contracts followed the official rules, disputes over them were not admissible in the courts. The bankruptcy regulations were especially punitive, and the courts played an important part in enforcing them. Under the new legal arrangement, custom was enforced through the judicial machinery; when the provisions of the codes were not applicable, custom was to be applied. Thus a whole body of pre-Restoration nonlegal norms was transformed into legal norms. As in the days of the Tokugawa, the courts encouraged conciliation between disputants, but in such cases the courts themselves were usually involved. The judges, for example, often presided over the mediatory proceedings, and a litigant who was tardy or who failed to attend was subject to punishment according to court rules. The courts in civil suits were also entitled to apply sanctions to parties who had fled or had otherwise failed to respond to a summons. A private suit that was incidental to a public action was tried in a criminal court. Following the practice of the Tokugawa period, the courts often gave special consideration to cases involving commercial transactions. The most urgent cases were given priority on the docket and were subject to quicker appeal than were ordinary suits.

Increased government involvement in the enforcement of norms relating to occupational specialists was also brought about by the creation of a special Court of Administrative Litigation (1890), which handled disputes between private individuals and government agencies.[107] It had jurisdiction over suits dealing with the imposition of taxes and fees, the recovery of back taxes, and the refusal or annulment of business licenses. This jurisdiction also extended to disputes arising out of irrigation and public works and boundary disagreements over private and public lands. An aspect of all these matters is related to integration.

England, as was noted in Chapter 5, was far ahead of Japan in the development of commercial law, as the law merchant came to be administered through the regular court system. By the beginning of the take-off period, the common law courts were rendering decisions which contributed to the substance of commercial law. In the early years of the nineteenth century, however, the rapid growth of commercial and industrial activity gave rise to new problems, many of which could not easily be handled by following old precedents. Under these circumstances, statutory enactments began to assume added importance in the development of commercial law. For example, the rules governing bankruptcy were modified, and laws were passed to facilitate the use of negotiable instruments.[108]

In the nineteenth century, the increase in litigation over commercial and other civil matters revealed a number of shortcomings in the English legal system. One weakness was the lack of machinery to permit ordinary citizens to settle minor claims in civil suits with dispatch and at small cost. The establishment of the county courts in 1846 helped to remedy this difficulty, making it possible for individuals to have certain types of contracts enforced.[109]

From the viewpoint of this study, the most striking inadequacy was the frequent conflict between equity and the common law. It was possible for a litigant to have a clearly established claim that would have been settled in his favor in equity proceedings but would have been decided against him in a court of common law.[110] Such a situation might not have been of great consequence if the jurisdiction of the two court systems had been clearly defined. Unfortunately, however, this was not the case. A claimant might not discover that he was seeking remedy in the wrong court system until his suit had reached the highest court of appeal. He might then be told that if he desired justice, he would have to start proceedings all over again in the court deemed proper by the House of Lords. This deficiency was not rectified until the court system was reorganized by the Judicature Act of 1873 and succeeding statutes.

Thus, in comparison with Japan, the English had entered the take-off period with a more developed system of commercial law and of courts equipped to resolve disputes arising under the law. But toward the end of the take-off stage, the English system probably tended to lag behind its Japanese counterpart, especially in terms of providing clear-cut channels for handling litigation in commercial cases on the basis of an unambiguous set of principles.

In Chapter 2, it was argued that two processes, besides a social-control process, are relevant to the satisfaction of the integration functional requisite: (1) an information process by which the needs of interdependent roles become known to one another; and (2) a coercive process through which the occupants of roles of greater power can force the occupants of roles with less power into behavior that may be integrative for the social system as a whole.

During the take-off period, government in both Japan and England became more deeply involved in the information process of integration through many of the activities we have already noted. The development of the railroads and the telegraph in Japan and England and the emphasis on highway improvement in the latter country greatly improved the channels of information among interdependent roles that were growing increasingly differentiated and which were often geographically removed from each other. The government also devoted attention to major improvements in the postal service.[111]

The government's involvement in the coercive process is somewhat more interesting from a theoretical standpoint. If a society is to be successful in achieving take-off, sizable numbers of people will be forced to relinquish their old roles and to take on new ones under conditions to which they strenuously object. In both Japan and England, for example, many workers had to abandon their traditional cottage industries and take jobs in workshops or factories owing to the fact that the role occupied by the modern entrepreneur was more powerful than that of the employee. In the enclosure movement in England, one can see an excellent illustration of the coercive process in operation.[112] Although we contend that coercion is to some degree involved in satisfying the integration requisite, especially in periods of rapid social change, we recognize that if the disparity in power among interdependent roles becomes too great and the coercion applied becomes excessive, the use of coercion is likely to be so disruptive of the society that economic development may be inhibited.

Toward the end of the take-off period, the government in both Japan and England began to intervene in an effort to minimize the effect of the employer's advantage over his employees. In this respect it is worth noting that most of the early factory legislation protected women and children—those workers whose bargaining position was weakest and who were therefore especially vulnerable to coercion—by making certain conditions of employment not subject to contract. Consider, for example, the Japanese Factory Act of 1911, which went into effect in 1916.[113] Although this legislation had serious loopholes, it forbade the employment in certain industries of children below the age of ten, and it provided for a reduction of working hours for women and children from fourteen hours per day to twelve over a fifteen-year period. In addition, the law made it illegal for employers to hire people with contagious diseases or women in an advanced stage of pregnancy.

Similarly in England, the Factory Act of 1833 removed from the area of legitimate contract any terms that called for the employment of children below a certain age level or the hiring of women and juvenile workers beyond a stipulated number of hours each day. Legislation requiring the installation of safety devices on machinery for the protection of laborers may also be viewed as an attempt by government to reduce the effect of the more powerful roles of owners/managers vis-à-vis those of the employees. In England, as in the case of Japan, the removal of the ban on the organization of working-men's associations may be regarded as an act by government that tended to reduce somewhat the disparity in power between the employer's role in a large firm and that of the worker.[114]

Roles Differentiated on the Basis of Prestige

As was indicated in the section on pattern maintenance, the government in Restoration Japan abolished many of the norms that had helped to define social classes. In England, such action was not so important, since fewer of these kinds of laws existed. Indeed, the most comparable action by the English government applied to religious and other minorities when it removed civil disabilities and extended voting privileges. If social classes are not defined by legal norms, the government will play a smaller direct role in the mobility between classes. For example, it cannot by decree transform a role that is defined as "lower" class into a "middle" class role, nor can it by decree elevate masses of people from a "middle" class position to the "upper" class. Thus, to the extent that the government in the take-off stage reduces the legal norms defining a social class, it also diminishes its contribution to integration among roles that are differentiated on the basis of prestige. But if, in addition, the government takes steps to reduce the efficacy of the nonlegal norms and precepts that define social class, it becomes involved in another way with the relationships among these roles.

For example, as universalistic criteria are applied more frequently in the recruitment of role occupants—in other words, as the norms and precepts that govern a particular role become more related to competence and less related to *who* the person is—certain structures in the society assume added importance in the upward or downward movement of the population. Especially significant are those structures that train people in the skills they need to have in order to occupy new roles. Thus, the government, in promoting training programs for potential role occupants who are recruited because of their ability to perform in those roles, becomes involved in the relationships among the roles.

As noted in the section on pattern maintenance, the government in Japan and to some degree in England became more involved in education during the take-off period. Besides establishing a system of public schools at the elementary level, the government of Japan sponsored programs of technical education. In order to train personnel in modern industrial methods, it imported large numbers of Western experts in a variety of fields, it sent students abroad for special schooling, and it founded and financed technical institutes.[115] In England, however, the government lagged behind in its support of public education. It is our contention that this tended to inhibit mobility into crucial roles which were developing under the impact of industrialization. In more technical language, we hypothesize that the government's support of education in England was high enough to meet the requisite of take-off but not the prerequisite for drive to modernity. This is one of the reasons for England's later economic stagnation.

Roles Differentiated on the Basis of Generation

As pointed out in Chapter 5, inheritance in Tokugawa Japan and Tudor-Stuart England was based on the principle of primogeniture, which tended to concentrate wealth and to restrict the growth of population. This principle persisted throughout the take-off period, though in somewhat attenuated form. In Japan, for example, the eldest son—unless he was incapacitated or unworthy—succeeded to the headship of the family, and he inherited by law at least one-half of the estate.[116] Moreover, the inheritance tax law of 1905 provided for higher exemptions and lower tax rates in the case of an individual who succeeded to the headship of a house. In England, a property owner enjoyed testamentary freedom, and he had no legal obligation to remember any of his children when he made out his will.[117] In case he died intestate, however, a legal distinction was made as to the type of property that would be distributed to his heirs. The land was given to the eldest son, or to the second son if the eldest had died without leaving issue. The widow received one-third of the personal property, while the remaining two-thirds was divided equally among the children.

While the institution of primogeniture was important in the pre-take-off stage of economic development, it becomes less significant during the take-off period. By this time, other structures (like a banking system) have been developed to mobilize resources and to maintain adequate concentrations of capital. Moreover, economic growth is rapid enough so that larger supplies of wealth can be accumulated despite increases in population. Indeed, the growth in population during the take-off stage may work to the advantage of the economy by providing recruits for factory jobs and by providing a mass market for the products of industry.

Summary

In the realm of integration during the take-off stage, interesting parallels again emerge in the contribution made by government in both Japan and England to the satisfaction of a functional requisite. In both countries, the government became more involved in the development and enforcement of commercial law. In both countries, too, the government removed most of the laws defining social class (except for laws which established or maintained a peerage), thus facilitating the shift from particularistic to universalistic criteria in the recruitment for crucial roles in the society. By fostering a system of education, the government also increased the opportunity for individuals to acquire the necessary skills for them to compete for the occupancy of these roles, although in this regard the government of England lagged behind Japan in developing an educational system, and this deficiency may have exacerbated certain economic problems which England faced in the succeeding stage of economic development.

THE TAKE-OFF STAGE IN JAPAN AND ENGLAND: A SUMMATION

This survey of the take-off period in Japan and England was not intended to serve as a basis for developing the hypotheses, which are to be listed in the next chapter. Its purpose, rather, was to indicate how the conceptual framework would cope with the analysis of another stage of economic development, and to highlight by contrast some of the patterns which emerged from the examination of the traditional stage.

Shortly before reaching the take-off stage, both Japan and England were already undergoing changes in the structures of government and in the procedures of governing. Within a generation these changes had led to a great increase in the resolution of the authority structure of policy making and to the development of a more reliable and effective mechanism for enforcing central decisions. These modifications made possible the most observable shift in the functions of government—the marked increase in the government's contribution to the satisfaction of the adaptive functional requisite. In both countries, this shift manifested itself through an increase in the involvement of government in the process of resource allocation, and the effect in each case was a heavy allocation of resources to the military establishment and a build-up of social overhead capital. In neither country, however, was there a great deal of government involvement in the process of resource management. The ownership and management of some firms by the Japanese government for a short time should not obscure the fact that, during most of the take-off period, the only major industry dominated by government management was railroading. To some extent this was paralleled in England by the regulation of the railroads, especially after 1844.

Some significant differences between Japan and England occur in the contribution of the government to the goal-attainment functional requisite, especially in the process of resource mobilization. Although solid statistical evidence is not available, it seems likely that the revenue collected by the Japanese government represented a higher proportion of the gross national product than was true of England. Also it is clear that the government in Japan was more involved in the banking system and in the development of joint stock companies. But if one bears in mind the heavy taxation and expenditures by the English government for military purposes during the first two decades of the take-off period and the private allocation of funds that had been mobilized by the government of England, the patterns in the two countries appear to be somewhat more congruent than is usually perceived. The government in the two countries, it must also be recalled, undertook significant reforms of the currency either just before or early in the take-off stage.

Remarkable parallels are observable in the increased contribution by government to the satisfaction of the pattern-maintenance and integration functional requisites. Evident in both Japan and England were such developments as the creation of professional police forces, the repeal of laws defining social class, the payment of subsidies to individuals who had much to lose from widespread reform and who were in a position to resist changes, the fostering of public education, and the eventual introduction of welfare legislation designed to improve working and living conditions.

The rapid development of commercial law in Japan put that country at least on a par with (or perhaps even ahead) of England in the enforcement of norms that defined the relationships among roles differentiated on the basis of occupational specialization. Moreover, through the support of education the government in both countries took steps to widen the opportunities for people to become trained for the important roles in the new industrial society. The principle of primogeniture remained, although in somewhat diluted form, a recognizable feature of inheritance in the two countries.

The differences between the two cases are perhaps most striking in the greater encouragement and support that the Japanese government gave to public education. The slowness of England in developing an adequate system of primary training, we hypothesize, had significant consequences for the drive to modernity stage of economic development in that country.

As we proceed to the systematic formulation of hypotheses in Chapter 7, it is important to recognize that just before and during the take-off stage the governments of Japan and England began to resemble more closely those of France and China in the traditional stage, as they increased their contributions to the satisfaction of the adaptive functional requisite and facilitated the application of universalistic criteria in recruiting occupants for certain roles. Partly on the basis of this evidence, we are inclined to emphasize the *sequence* of particular developments if take-off is to be successfully achieved. The details of this argument, however, will appear in the next chapter.

NOTES

1. It should be remembered that this analytical framework makes a distinction between *prerequisites* and *requisites*. (See above, pp. 44-45.) Prerequisites must be fulfilled before an economic stage can begin; requisites must be fulfilled before an economic stage can be completed. Thus in this chapter we shall be dealing with the requisites for take-off and the prerequisites for the drive to modernity. If we were using the empirical findings in the take-off period as a basis for developing hypotheses, the logic of our exploratory research design would lead us to include the case of a society that had

experienced great difficulty in completing take-off and in moving into the drive to modernity stage. In some respects, England conforms to this requirement, and in this discussion we shall refer to certain functions, in the satisfaction of which the English government needed to make a more significant contribution in order to facilitate the drive to modernity. These failures, however, will not be explored in detail; they will be discussed more fully in future publications.

2. See Walter W. McLaren, *A Political History of Japan during the Meiji Era, 1867-1912*, pp. 58-71, 112-122, 182-200.

3. See Robert A. Scalapino, *Democracy and the Party Movement in Prewar Japan: The Failure of the First Attempt*, pp. 165-178; McLaren, *A Political History of Japan during the Meiji Era, 1867-1912*, pp. 213-222, 257-262.

4. Japanese political institutions came closer to the "parliamentary model" in the 1920's. The older members of the genro died; the government expanded the franchise; and parties grew stronger and more influential in the Diet, becoming the basis for a number of cabinets. This trend, of course, was reversed in the 1930's.

5. See M. Inoki, "The Civil Bureaucracy: Japan," in Robert E. Ward and Dankwart A. Rustow, *Political Modernization in Japan and Turkey*, pp. 288-295.

6. See McLaren, *A Political History of Japan during the Meiji Era, 1867-1912*, pp. 72-132.

7. John Norris, *Shelburne and Reform*, p. xi.

8. An excellent treatment of English government and politics in the middle of the eighteenth century is found in Lewis B. Namier, *The Structure of Politics at the Accession of George III*, Vol. I and II. A general history of the period from 1760 to 1815 is J. Steven Watson, *The Reign of George III, 1760-1815*. For the later era, see Llewellyn Woodward, *The Age of Reform, 1815-1870*.

9. Lewis B. Namier, *Personalities and Powers*, pp. 31-32.

10. Abbott P. Usher, *An Introduction to the Industrial History of England*, p. 461; L. C. A. Knowles, *The Industrial and Commercial Revolutions in Great Britain during the Nineteenth Century*, p. 255; W. T. Jackman, *The Development of Transportation in Modern England*, pp. 497-506.

11. It is our speculation that the authority structure of policy making was not resolved to a point that enabled it to facilitate take-off optimally, and that some of the economic problems encountered by England in the twentieth century are in part the consequence of this lack of adequate resolution. In more technical terms, we are suggesting that a relatively high resolution of the authority structure of policy making is a requisite for take-off, and that an even higher degree of resolution is a prerequisite for the drive to modernity stage. England met the requisite and the prerequisite marginally.

12. See Watson, *The Reign of George III, 1760-1815*, pp. 283-288.

13. Emmeline W. Cohen, *The Growth of the British Civil Service, 1780-1939*, pp. 34-35. For an over-all treatment of the period that we are concerned with, see especially pp. 45-71, 110-136.

14. Frederic A. Ogg, *English Government and Politics*, p. 225. These figures include civil servants employed in Irish offices. To be strictly comparable, the 1797 figure would have to be 16,267. (See Cohen, *The Growth of the British Civil Service, 1780-1939*, p. 23.)

15. It was not until the decades from 1850 to 1880, however, that a true merit system was firmly established. During this period, the government created a Civil Service Commission which eventually assumed control of the entrance requirements for public service. A widespread system of qualifying examinations was also set up to facilitate recruitment and division of labor. In addition,

the Treasury assumed responsibility for supervising and coordinating administration among the various departments.

16. W. E. Lunt, *History of England,* pp. 683-684.

17. See pp. 51-52, 100.

18. Henry Rosovsky, *Capital Formation in Japan, 1868-1940,* pp. 23-24 and Table 9 on pp. 25-26. These figures include relevant military expenditures. Excluding the military expenditures, the figure is 33.5 per cent. We accept Rosovsky's argument that expenditures for ships, barracks, fortifications, munitions (except ammunition)—in general, all military durables—should be included in capital formation. (See *ibid.,* pp. 15-16, 22-23.) It should also be pointed out that Rosovsky computes his private/public ratio by treating private expenditures as a residual. His formula for private investment is:

Total Production of Capital Goods — Government Purchases — Exports + Imports = Private Investment [p. 23].

He recognizes that this formula may understate the role of private investment. If one were to make a study of capital formation in England from 1790 to 1840 that would be comparable to Rosovsky's analysis of Japan, it would be necessary to use the same formula.

19. George C. Allen, *A Short Economic History of Japan, 1867-1937,* p. 30.

20. For a listing of government-owned concerns, see J. Fujii, *Outline of Japanese History in the Meiji Era,* pp. 512-513. See also Y. Horie, "Government Industries in the Early Years of Meiji," *Kyōto University Economic Review,* Vol. 14, No. 1, January 1939, pp. 67-87.

21. See, for example, K. Ohara, *Japanese Trade and Industry in the Meiji-Taishō Era,* p. 332.

22. Thomas C. Smith, *Political Change and Industrial Development in Japan: Government Enterprise, 1868-1880,* p. 69. This is a conservative estimate, since for the first decade it includes only those government concerns that fell under the jurisdiction of the Department of Industry.

23. See *ibid.,* pp. 86-100, especially pp. 90-91; E. Herbert Norman, *Japan's Emergence as a Modern State: Political and Economic Problems of the Meiji Period,* pp. 127-133.

24. Rosovsky, *Capital Formation in Japan, 1868-1940,* pp. 25-26 (Table 9). The table includes the total expenditures by the central government for investment in railroads and the military establishment. These figures clearly indicate that the direct government involvement in resource allocation was to a large extent involvement in railway building and in equipping the armed services. Capital for the rest of the economy must have come primarily from private sources.

25. John E. Orchard, *Japan's Economic Position: The Progress of Industrialization,* p. 88. See also Nurul Islam, *Foreign Capital and Economic Development: Japan, India, and Canada: Studies in Some Aspects of Absorption of Foreign Capital,* p. 197.

26. See Ohara, *Japanese Trade and Industry in the Meiji-Taishō Era,* pp. 329-330.

27. Orchard, *Japan's Economic Position,* p. 80.

28. Rosovsky, *Capital Formation in Japan, 1868-1940,* p. 22.

29. This material is drawn from U.S. Department of State, *Report of the Mission on Japanese Combines,* pp. 21-27, 53-59; William W. Lockwood, *The Economic Development of Japan: Growth and Structural Change, 1868-1938,* pp. 220-221, 288, 322, 531-532, 553-566; R. Ishii (ed.), *Japanese Legislation in the Meiji Era,* pp. 593-706; K. Shibusawa (ed.), *Japanese Society in the Meiji Era,* pp. 104-106, 121-129, 155-156, 161-162.

30. Arthur D. Gayer, W. W. Rostow, and Anna J. Schwartz, *The Growth and Fluctuation of the British Economy, 1790-1850,* Vol. I and II.

31. *Ibid.,* Vol. I, p. 14.

32. *Ibid.,* p. 35.

33. *Ibid.,* pp. 186, 254-255.

34. *Ibid.,* p. 286.

35. *Ibid.,* pp. 14, 35.

36. *Ibid.,* p. 35. Between 1799 and 1815, capital investment authorized by parliament for London docks amounted to nearly £15,000,000. See Phyllis Deane, "Capital Formation in England before the Railway Age," *Economic Development and Cultural Change,* Vol. 9, No. 3, April 1961, p. 364.

37. Gayer *et al., The Growth and Fluctuation of the British Economy, 1790-1850,* Vol. I, p. 254.

38. This was the first line to link two major metropolitan centers. The success of this venture helped to stimulate the boom in railway construction.

39. Jackman, *The Development of Transportation in Modern England,* p. 530; John H. Clapham, *An Economic History of Modern Britain,* Vol. I, p. 384.

40. Harold Pollins, "The Finances of the Liverpool and Manchester Railway," *The Economic History Review* (2nd series), Vol. 5, No. 1, 1952, p. 96.

41. Knowles, *Industrial and Commercial Revolutions in Great Britain during the Nineteenth Century,* pp. 243-244. They were built so that ships could avoid the hazards of the rocky coast.

42. Jackman gives one example of such a subsidy in *The Development of Transportation in Modern England,* p. 491.

43. Deane, "Capital Formation in England before the Railway Age," p. 364.

44. Jackman, *The Development of Transportation in Modern England,* pp. 216-236.

45. George M. Trevelyan, *English Social History: A Survey of Six Centuries, Chaucer to Queen Victoria,* p. 382; Frederick C. Dietz, *An Economic History of England,* pp. 298-299.

46. Clapham, *An Economic History of Modern Britain,* Vol. I, p. 95.

47. Jackman, *The Development of Transportation in Modern England,* pp. 227-265.

48. S. Pollard, "Laissez-faire and Shipbuilding," *The Economic History Review,* Vol. 5, No. 1, Second Series, 1955, p. 111. The author suggests that government mail subsidies were an important aspect of the development of English shipping during the nineteenth century, and that, if other industries were carefully examined, scholars would find that the role of government was much greater than is typically supposed.

49. See above, pp. 246-247.

50. Herbert Richmond, *Statesmen and Seapower,* p. 158.

51. These figures have been compiled from William L. Clowes, *The Royal Navy: A History from the Earliest Times to the Present,* Vol. IV, p. 153; Vol. V, p. 9.

52. Clowes, *The Royal Navy,* Vol. IV, p. 153; Vol. V, p. 10. The expenditures on military durables certainly had a stimulating effect on capital-goods industries. (See Thomas S. Ashton, *Iron and Steel in the Industrial Revolution,* pp. 128-161.) While noting the effect of war purchasing on the growth of the iron and steel industry, Ashton tends to de-emphasize it. He wants no part of what he calls the "heresy that war may be productive of national wealth" (p. 152).

53. For example, see Deane, "Capital Formation in England before the Railway Age," p. 360.

54. See Knowles, *Industrial and Commercial Revolutions in Great Britain during the Nineteenth Century*, pp. 253-275; Usher, *An Introduction to the Industrial History of England*, pp. 443-468; Clapham, *An Economic History of Modern Britain*, Vol. I, pp. 387-393.

55. In addition to works cited in note 54, see Jackman, *The Development of Transportation in Modern England*, pp. 572-593.

56. Knowles, *Industrial and Commercial Revolutions in Great Britain during the Nineteenth Century*, pp. 291-305.

57. On business organization and regulation, see Bishop C. Hunt, *The Development of the Business Corporation in England, 1800-1867;* Armand B. DuBois, *The English Business Company after the Bubble Act, 1720-1800.*

58. See Ishii, *Japanese Legislation in the Meiji Era*, pp. 176-186; Norman, *Japan's Emergence as a Modern State*, pp. 138-144.

59. Lockwood, *The Economic Development of Japan*, p. 98; Smith, *Political Change and Industrial Development in Japan*, p. 74. To the degree that the government's propensity to invest was greater than that of the people who were paying taxes, taxation became a form of "forced saving."

60. This discussion of excise, business, and income taxes is taken from Ishii, *Japanese Legislation in the Meiji Era*, pp. 238-241; 450-459; Lockwood, *The Economic Development of Japan*, pp. 521-525; and M. Matsukata, "Japan's Finance," in Shigénobu Okuma, *Fifty Years of New Japan*, Vol. I, pp. 367-372.

61. Lockwood, *The Economic Development of Japan*, p. 26.

62. See Smith, *Political Change and Industrial Development in Japan*, pp. 72-77.

63. For an example of forced loans, see Eijiro Honjo, *The Social and Economic History of Japan*, pp. 139-140.

64. See Lockwood, *The Economic Development of Japan*, p. 222.

65. See Norman, *Japan's Emergence as a Modern State*, pp. 111-114.

66. On the development of the Japanese banking sysem, see Hubert F. Schiffer, *The Modern Japanese Banking System;* Y. Shibusawa, "The Development of Banking in Japan," in Okuma, *Fifty Years of New Japan*, Vol. I, pp. 486-532.

67. M. Matsukata, "Japan's Finance," in Okuma, *Fifty Years of New Japan*, Vol. I, pp. 386-387.

68. See Y. Shibusawa, "Joint-Stock Enterprise in Japan," in Okuma, *Fifty Years of New Japan*, Vol. I, pp. 465-485; Ishii, *Japanese Legislation in the Meiji Era*, pp. 697-701.

69. For treatments of their monetary policies, see T. Kato, "Development of the Monetary System," in K. Shibusawa, *Japanese Society in the Meiji Era*, pp. 181-235; Jerome B. Cohen, "Financial Development," in Hugh Borton, *Japan*, pp. 129-132.

70. Stephen Dowell, *A History of Taxation and Taxes in England*, Vol. II, pp. 206-207.

71. *Ibid.*, Vol. II, pp. 249-258. Only 35 per cent of the cost of the war was financed through taxation; borrowing accounted for the rest.

72. *Ibid.*, Vol. II, pp. 262-323, especially pp. 275-287.

73. On the Bank of England, see John H. Clapham, *The Bank of England*, Vol. I and II. The short-term credit granted by the Bank of England through its discounting practices was particularly significant during the war. In 1807, the commercial paper held by the Bank under discount totaled £ 13,250,000. (*Ibid.*, Vol. II, p. 11.) Clapham says, ". . . the Bank treated the discounting

of good commercial paper as a duty little less binding than its duty to the state" (*ibid.*, Vol. II, p. 15).

74. L. S. Pressnell, *Country Banking in the Industrial Revolution*, pp. 56-57.

75. *Ibid.*, pp. 57-58.

76. It should be pointed out that the banker himself did not need to be the collector of the revenue in order to use public funds for investment purposes. It was only necessary for the revenue officials to keep their accounts in his bank or to accept his notes. (See Pressnell, *Country Banking in the Industrial Revolution*, p. 61.)

77. Clapham, *The Bank of England*, Vol. I, p. 174.

78. See H. A. Shannon, "The Coming of General Limited Liability," *Economic History*, Vol. 2, No. 6, January 1931, pp. 267-291; Hunt, *The Development of the Business Corporation in England, 1800-1867*, pp. 14-144.

79. Clapham, *The Bank of England*, Vol. I, pp. 175-176.

80. *Ibid.*, Vol. II, pp. 4-15.

81. John U. Nef, *Cultural Foundations of Industrial Civilization*, especially pp. 50-80, 149-155.

82. Neil J. Smelser, *Social Change and the Industrial Revolution*, pp. 266-267.

83. *Ibid.*, pp. 269-270.

84. We have introduced this brief discussion of the structure of the value system in order to anticipate some of our work in the future. At a higher level of generalization than we are concerned with in this chapter, we suspect that the extent of the government's contribution to the satisfaction of the pattern-maintenance functional requisite varies according to certain structural characteristics of the cultural system. More particularly, some of the increase in the government's contribution to the satisfaction of the pattern-maintenance requisite, which we shall note, is due to changes that have taken place in the structure of the cultural system.

85. On the organization and powers of the police, see Ishii, *Japanese Legislation in the Meiji Era*, pp. 241-263; K. Oura, "The Police of Japan," in Okuma, *Fifty Years of New Japan*, Vol. I, pp. 281-295. Some of the regulations governing the police may be found in Walter W. McLaren, "Japanese Government Documents," *Transactions of the Asiatic Society of Japan*, Vol. 42, Part 1, 1914, pp. 256-257, 264-268, 299-301, 305. For examples of the "peace preservation" laws, see pp. 495-504. Examples of press regulations are found on pp. 539-550.

86. Strictly speaking, the introduction of a new penal code is a matter that relates to the cultural system rather than to the social system. However, if the changes involve a shift from precepts to norms and/or a shift from nonlegal to legal norms, these will result in an increase in the participation of the government in the social-control process.

87. K. B. Smellie, *A Hundred Years of English Government*, p. 81; Hannis Taylor, *The Origin and Growth of the English Constitution: An Historical Treatise*, Vol. II, pp. 576-577.

88. W. L. Melville Lee, *A History of Police in London*, pp. 196-216.

89. See Shibusawa, *Japanese Society in the Meiji Era*, pp. 50-51, 104-105.

90. See Fujii, *Japanese Legislation in the Meiji Era*, pp. 339-340.

91. Smelser emphasizes the development of specialized educational structures in England during the 1830's and the involvement of these structures in what we have called the enculturation process. However, he employs different terminology. (See *Social Change and the Industrial Revolution*, pp. 294-297.)

92. This section on Japanese education is drawn from K. Shibusawa, *Japa-*

nese Life and Culture in the Meiji Era, pp. 294-303; R. P. Dore, "Education: Japan," in Ward and Rustow, *Political Modernization in Japan and Turkey,* pp. 176-189; Lockwood, *The Economic Development of Japan,* pp. 510-512.

93. For a treatment of elementary education in England during the nineteenth century, see John W. Adamson, *English Education, 1789-1902,* pp. 13-42, 123-154, 236-257, 347-386; S. J. Curtis and M. E. A. Boultwood, *An Introductory History of English Education since 1800,* pp. 54-79.

94. Education is related not only to the pattern-maintenance functional requisite but also to the integration requisite. For further comments, see below, pp. 280-281.

95. We did not treat the involvement of government in the tension-management process in the traditional stage of economic development because all of the governments seem to have been involved, and there appears to be no significant differences among the four cases.

96. Many of the daimyo and some of the more resourceful samurai invested the money from these subsidies in banking and other business undertakings.

97. See Norman, *Japan's Emergence as a Modern State,* pp. 93-98.

98. Watson, *The Reign of George III,* pp. 284-285.

99. See Paul J. Mantoux, *The Industrial Revolution in the Eighteenth Century: An Outline of the Beginnings of the Modern Factory System in England,* pp. 398-408. The Luddite movement is an illustration of the mass disorders of this period.

100. See, for example, Nobutaka Ike, *The Beginnings of Political Democracy in Japan,* pp. 73, 79, 85, 144, 160-165; Norman, *Japan's Emergence as a Modern State,* pp. 69-80, 149-153, 160-165; Masaru Inouyé, "Japanese Communications: Railroads" in Okuma, *Fifty Years of New Japan,* Vol. I, p. 431. According to Norman, the number of peasant revolts during the first decade of the Meiji era was more than 190.

101. Ishii, *Japanese Legislation in the Meiji Era,* pp. 558-559.

102. See Norman, *Japan's Emergence as a Modern State,* p. 161.

103. For a sketch of early industrial legislation, see Fujii, *Outline of Japanese History in the Meiji Era,* pp. 453-455.

104. Because these acts regulated the relationships among interdependent roles, they also have an integration aspect, which will be treated below, pp. 279-280. Except for the Health Insurance Act, which was enacted in 1926 and which provided confinement, sickness, and death benefits for workers in factories and mines, most of the legislation of the 1920's was more important from the viewpoint of integration rather than pattern maintenance. It will be discussed briefly in the next section.

105. See Fujii, *Outline of Japanese History in the Meiji Era,* pp. 249-254; Arthur T. von Mehren (ed.), *Law in Japan: The Legal Order in a Changing Society,* pp. 31-32.

106. See Ishii, *Japanese Legislation in the Meiji Era,* pp. 305-320, 491-524, 609-660, 696-706.

107. *Ibid.,* pp. 475-477.

108. See William S. Holdsworth, *A History of English Law,* Vol. XIII, p. 385.

109. Smellie, *A Hundred Years of English Government,* pp. 78-79.

110. Holdsworth, *A History of English Law,* Vol. I, p. 635.

111. On the development of the postal service in Japan, see Shibusawa, *Japanese Society in the Meiji Era,* pp. 378-379, 394-397. The English postal system is treated in Jackman, *The Development of Transportation in Modern England,* pp. 323-377.

112. See Karl de Schweinitz, Jr., "Economic Growth, Coercion, and Freedom," *World Politics,* Vol. 9, No. 2, January 1957, pp. 166-192.

113. *Japan Yearbook,* 1917, pp. 293-294.

114. Although in Japan labor organizations gained a measure of freedom, this development was not as significant as it was in England.

115. See, for example, Ohara, *Japanese Trade and Industry in the Meiji-Taishō Era,* pp. 288-291.

116. See Ishii, *Japanese Legislation in the Meiji Era,* pp. 685-695; Lockwood, *The Economic Development of Japan,* p. 220, footnote 93.

117. Leonard Courtney, *The Working Constitution of the United Kingdom,* pp. 250-255.

CHAPTER 7

The Major Hypotheses

THE EMPIRICAL ANALYSIS OF OUR FOUR CASES WAS NOT PRESENTED in order to provide an "explanation" of why England and Japan managed to achieve take-off quickly after the techniques of industrial production became known, while France and China lagged behind. Rather, our purpose for undertaking the empirical studies was to provide a groundwork for generating hypotheses concerning the political basis of economic development which can be tested in future, rigorously designed research. This, however, is not the ideal way of developing hypotheses. It would be far more desirable to deduce them from existing theories so that the test of the hypotheses would constitute a partial test of the theories themselves. This is the ideal *deductive-inductive* procedure of science. But scholars who labor in the vineyard of social science theory know that conditions are often far from ideal. Few theories in the social sciences have sufficient deductive power to permit the researcher to adopt this ideal procedure. This exploratory study for the purpose of developing hypotheses is an approach that enables one to proceed with his research, in spite of the weaknesses of social science theory, without falling into the trap of trying to develop hypotheses entirely from armchair hunches.

It must be pointed out, however, that there are three marked weaknesses of empirically generated hypotheses, especially when they have been derived from a very small number of cases. (1) There is always a probability that the patterns of similarity and difference which emerge from the analysis are idiosyncratic. (2) The scholar has little notion of the level of generality of the hypotheses. (3) It is difficult to develop a research design which can test such hypotheses and at the same time be useful in the testing of a significant theory. We have attempted to overcome these problems as much as possible

292

by introducing a special step in the development of the hypotheses. We shall first examine the patterns of similarity and difference which emerge from the data and formulate the hypotheses that are most consistent with these patterns. Next, we shall examine these empirically generated hypotheses in relationship to a number of social science theories from which the hypotheses could conceivably have been deduced. Finally, we shall modify the hypotheses so that they are consistent both with the empirical data of the exploratory study and with the theories we have examined. Where the theoretical argument is particularly complex, the two forms of a given hypothesis will be kept distinct by labeling the empirically generated form as the *preliminary hypothesis*. The hypothesis that has been modified in light of relevant theories in the social sciences and is therefore ready for testing will be designated as the *final hypothesis*.

THE ADAPTIVE FUNCTIONAL REQUISITE

In France and China, the government made a major contribution to the satisfaction of the adaptive functional requisite. A significant amount of resource allocation by government occurred in France through the device of grants of privilege, and in China through direct ownership and support by the state. In both France and China, too, the government's regulation of production processes, its specifications for manufactured products, and its attempts at quality control were important contributions to the satisfaction of the adaptive requisite, which tended to reduce the contribution made by nongovernmental structures.

The situation in Japan and England during the traditional stage was in marked contrast to that of France and China. Government ownership of the means of production was insignificant. The perpetually embarrassed government treasuries did not have sufficient capital for use in the support of industry and commerce. While regulations were issued in great numbers, they were of little functional consequence because they were not enforced with telling effect. Indeed, the fact that the governments of Japan and England made such a slight contribution to the satisfaction of the adaptive requisite was not the result of any explicit decision to leave this domain to nongovernmental structures. It was, rather, the result of certain procedures of governing that seemingly made it impossible for the government to act effectively. The authority structure of policy making was not resolved in Japan and England—that is, within the central policy-making structure itself, there existed powerful veto groups, any one of which could block the issuance of authoritative directives (England), or which led to the promulgation of conflicting and confusing directives (Japan). Moreover, the regulations that might be issued could not be consistently and persistently enforced because the enforcement structures were not reliable. In France and China, by contrast, the authority structure of policy making was highly resolved, and the enforcement structures were more reliable.

These patterns suggest the following:

Preliminary hypothesis: A government that does not contribute significantly to the satisfaction of the adaptive functional requisite during the traditional stage is a prerequisite for take-off.

Some Economic Theoretical Underpinnings

If this hypothesis is examined in the light of a popular theory on economic development, an interesting problem emerges. A body of economic growth theory—the theory of the *big push*—may suggest a different conclusion. This theory holds that a major, concerted effort is necessary if take-off is to be achieved, and that government is the agency that can provide the necessary impetus and coordination. Rosenstein-Rodan, one of the major big push theorists, states the central proposition as follows:

"There is a minimum level of resources that must be devoted to . . . a development program if it is to have any chance of success. Launching a country into self-sustaining growth is a little like getting an airplane off the ground. There is a critical ground speed which must be passed before the craft can become airborne. . . ." Proceeding "bit-by-bit" will not add up in its effects to the sum total of the single bits. A minimum quantum of investment is a necessary though not sufficient condition of success.[1]

There are three basic assumptions on which the theory of the big push rests. First, it assumes that there are certain discontinuities in the production functions that give rise to increasing returns and technological external economies. Second, it assumes that allocation of investment occurs in an imperfect market; pecuniary external economies, which are common and all-pervasive, make it impossible for the price mechanism to lead to an optimum solution of investment allocation. Third, it assumes that not only the investment market but all markets are much less perfect in underdeveloped than in developed countries and that, therefore, the price mechanism cannot guide the economy toward an optimal solution.[2]

Rosenstein-Rodan does not hold that all indivisibilities give rise to external economies, nor that all external economies derive from indivisibilities. It is, however, those indivisibilities that do give rise to external economies which particularly interest him. He emphasizes three types of indivisibilities:

First, there is indivisibility in the production function, especially indivisibility in the supply of social overhead capital. . . . Second, there is indivisibility of demand (complementarity of demand). . . . Third, there is indivisibility (kink) in the supply of savings. . . .

In one way, the first indivisibility is fundamental. If it did not exist, the others would not arise. Linear homogeneous production functions are basic in this sense, but they are completely unrealistic. They imply no economies of scale or of agglomeration, no entrepreneurship, no phenomenon of minimum quantum or threshold, so that they threaten to obscure the nature of the economic process and the risks involved rather than throwing light on it. In reality there are indivisibilities in the production function. They create not only non-constant returns but also risks of investment and imperfect markets which give rise to the indivisibility (complementarity) of demand.[3]

When the decision environment is marked by the externalities described by Rosenstein-Rodan, some degree of centralization in resource-allocating decisions is necessary if such decisions are to lead to effective allocation. For many theorists who subscribe to the theory of the big push, a central government is the structure *par excellence* which can provide for the necessary centralized economic decision making.

It would appear from the analysis made in the present study that the government in France and China was well suited structurally for providing the effective, centralized decisions required by the theory of the big push. In comparison with government in Japan and England, it was organized to plan economic development so as to cope with the indivisibilities that Rosenstein-Rodan holds to be so important. This was particularly true of the indivisibility that he regards as the most significant—"indivisibility in the production function, especially indivisibility in the supply of social overhead capital." Indeed, in the pre-industrial period in France and China, we find notable instances where the government made it possible to embark upon and to complete projects in which the capital requirements were lumpy. Such examples as the Chinese irrigation and flood control systems and the French Languedoc canal and the eighteenth-century highway system immediately come to mind. It should also be pointed out that, according to our analysis, government in England and Japan at the time of take-off increased its contribution to the adaptive functional requisite by increasing involvement in the process of resource allocation. In other words, at the time of take-off, government in England and Japan began to contribute to the satisfaction of the adaptive functional requisite in a manner more similar in many ways to government in traditional France and China than to government in traditional England and Japan.

The problem can be stated succinctly: When the technology of industrialization becomes available to a traditional economy (either domestically or through import), does the probability of achieving take-off increase as the government makes a significant contribution to the satisfaction of the adaptive functional requisite? Our analysis suggests that the answer to this question is *no;* it suggests that there may be some preconditions that must be satisfied before take-off can be achieved, and that these preconditions can best be met if government makes only a minimal contribution to the satisfaction of the adaptive functional requisite. When government becomes heavily involved in resource allocation too early, the probability of achieving take-off is reduced.

Of the various possible preconditions, two of them that are relevant to the argument at this point may be stated in the form of testable propositions:

No. 1. At the time the technology of industrialization becomes available, there must be a minimum level of per capita wealth in the society which can be mobilized for increased investment. (It should be noted that we have raised two separate problems here: [a] the necessity of a certain level of wealth and [b] the requirement that this wealth be mobilizable. The latter will be of no further concern at this stage of the discussion, since it is a problem of goal attainment and not an adaptive problem.)[4]

No. 2. This necessary minimum level of wealth is most likely to be achieved if there is a slow but continual process of economic growth (in terms of product per capita) before the introduction of the capital-intensive techniques of industrial production.

These two propositions enunciate certain economic prerequisites of take-off. If they are valid, one would anticipate that England and Japan would have experienced moderate economic growth rates (below the level we have defined for take-off during the five or ten decades before take-off), that France would not have experienced such growth until sometime after 1789, and that China would not have experienced such growth prior to 1911. Assuming this situation to be the case, it bears an interesting relationship to our previous analysis.[5]

For purposes of argument we are suggesting that, in the period before the introduction of the techniques of industrial production into a society, increasing returns and external economies are not very important, and that, in most projects for which this is not the case, the marginal return on investments is below the average for all industries in the economy. In other words, we contend that significant externalities, increasing returns, and indivisibilities are absent from the decision-making environment.

Classical economists would hold that under these environmental conditions resource allocation would not be as close to optimality in China and France as in a perfectly competitive economy. But this is not particularly helpful to our case for two reasons: (1) the traditional economies in England and Japan were not close enough approximations to the perfectly competitive economy; (2) we are not interested in the problem of the optimal allocation of resources and deviations from optimality, but rather in the question of whether the resource-allocating mechanism was effective enough (even though far from optimal) to provide for a certain minimal level of economic growth.

Theories of the relative efficiency of centralized versus decentralized decision structures (particularly those of Leonid Hurwicz)[6] are more central to our concern than those of an ideal competitive market economy versus a command economy. In order to indicate their relevance, however, it is necessary to link our description of the centralized structures in France and China and the decentralized structures in England and Japan with Hurwicz' definition of centralization and decentralization.

To the degree that the government in France and China contributed to the satisfaction of the adaptive functional requisite, the resource-allocation process in these countries was centralized. Our description of the decision structure has emphasized authority relationships. Government regulation in France and China may be treated as a constraint on the decision latitude of a private entrepreneur in a regulated industry. In any decision model focusing at the firm level, the regulations might be treated as an environmental limit. This kind of definition of centralization, however, provides little basis for addressing oneself to the problem of the relative efficiency of centralized versus decentralized decision structures.

Hurwicz' concept of decentralized decision structures is based not upon authority relationships, but upon information flow. Two concepts are central to his definitions: *operationality* and *anonymity*. A decision structure is operational if no decision unit (plant, firm, government) receives *internal* information about any other unit. Internal information is defined to include such things as productivity, cost, and consumer-preference data, but to exclude information that can be deduced from the market behavior of a firm.[7] Anonymity is maintained in the decision structure if (1) proposals are symmetric as between units other than the sender. (If, for example, a proposal from unit *three* creates the option that unit *one* may take alternative A and unit *two* may take alternative B, it must also create the option that unit *one* may take alternative B and unit *two* may take alternative A.) (2) The response to a set of messages must be dependent upon their content, not on the origin (sender).[8] Any decision system that has the characteristics of operationality and anonymity is decentralized.[9]

Hurwicz introduces two other useful concepts—decomposable and nondecomposable decision-making environments. In explaining the meaning of these terms, he finds it useful to distinguish between production and consumption decisions. From the production side, an environment is decomposable if the productivity of a given production unit is not dependent upon the level of activity of any other unit. From the consumption side, an environment is decomposable if the level of satisfaction of a given consumer is not dependent upon the level of consumption of any other consumer. In a decomposable environment, centralized decision making is informationally less efficient than decentralized decision making.[10]

The role that the central government in France and China played in the satisfaction of the adaptive functional requisite made the resource-allocating process centralized in precisely the Hurwicz sense. The regulation of industry violated the operationality rule. The government (a unit) had internal information about other units. Grants of privilege and government ownership and support of certain economic activities violated the anonymity rule. A proposal between a privileged or government-owned firm and a completely private firm in the same industry was not likely to be symmetric. The response to a proposal was likely to be dependent upon whether or not a firm was privileged or government owned/supported. Clearly, all of the requirements for a decentralized decision system in Hurwicz' definition were violated in the cases of France and China. In Japan and England the decision system, although certainly not perfectly competitive, was much less centralized than in France and China.

When the central government makes a significant contribution to the satisfaction of the adaptive requisite, resource-allocating decisions are far more likely to be made centrally than when nongovernmental structures are involved. In the next few paragraphs we shall focus attention not simply on the fact of government involvement in France and China, but on the consequences of the centralized resource-allocating mechanism that was associated with government involvement.

Hurwicz shows that decentralized allocation will be more efficient than centralized allocation when the environment is decomposable. We must, however, direct our attention to the question of whether the centralized decision structure in France and China was so much less efficient than the decentralized structure in Japan and England that the probability of growth in the traditional economy was significantly reduced.

When externalities, "public" goods, indivisibilities, and increasing returns are relatively insignificant in the decision environment, all of the information necessary for a decision that will contribute to an optimal allocation of resources is available to a decision maker in an autonomous, decentralized unit. Thus, theoretically no possible information advantage is gained by centralizing the decision making. There are, however, costs involved in centralization: (a) the capital cost of building the communications network; (b) the labor costs involved in operating the communication network; and (c) the loss of information during the transfer of information—perhaps the most significant cost, although it may be the most difficult to measure. In addition to these costs, the time delays involved in a centralized decision-making structure may lead to additional inefficiencies.

Through grants of privilege and/or government ownership-support, the government is involved in the allocation of resources in an environment which holds no advantage for centralization and which involves the sorts of costs discussed above. Grants of privilege, government ownership, and other forms of government support, however, create still another kind of problem. Dealings with a privileged or a government-owned unit will in many instances be different from dealings with an entirely private unit. For example, a distributor might be required to purchase a certain amount of goods from such a unit at a specified price (a violation of the anonymity requirement). The number of his alternative choices is thus restricted. This would not necessarily lead to inefficiency (indeed, it might even contribute to efficiency) if only the less desirable alternatives were excluded, since the cost of examining the alternatives would be reduced. However, in the environment we have assumed to exist, the centralized decision maker has no information concerning this problem that is not available to the local unit. Since there are information loss and time delays involved in centralization, the constraints placed upon the local decision makers are likely to exclude some of the more desirable alternatives.

It seems likely that the centralized decision structure in the environment we have assumed to exist in the traditional economy cannot optimize for the economy as a whole. Our case, however, demands something more. We hold that the centralized structure is a crucially less efficient resource allocator and resource manager than the decentralized structure. It is such an inefficient resource allocator that it tends to prevent the slow per capita growth which we hypothesize is an economic prerequisite for take-off. Although nothing thus far presented would support this contention, it is important to notice two characteristics of a centralized decision structure that may be particularly inhibiting in a traditional economy. The first is the absence of an *iterative feedback system with a short time lag*. The second is the excessive *aggregation of information* as it moves toward the center of the centralized decision structure. Both of these are of great significance in the traditional economy because of the absence of a technology that can to some degree mitigate their consequences.

An iterative feedback system with a short time lag has two essential features: (1) Information on each small increment of change becomes available quickly to the decision maker; and (2) there is a good "memory," in which is stored information on previous decisions and their consequences, and there is quick access to this memory. We can illustrate the way in which such an iterative feedback system operates by listing some of the main characteristics of decision making in a decentralized system operating in a decomposable environment.

(1) The authoritative decision maker in a decentralized system has control over only a small portion of the total resources of an economy or of an industry.

(2) In most situations he has at any given moment only a small amount of resources to allocate in relationship to his total investment.

(3) His choice of alternatives, therefore, is typically limited to courses of action like those he is already following. Any changes he makes are likely to involve only a few of the many elements over which he has some control—that is, he can manipulate at any one time only a few variables.

(4) By definition, the authoritative decision maker in a decentralized structure is "closer" to the direct consequences of a decision for him than is a decision maker in a centralized structure. He receives information (feedback) on the consequences of his decisions relatively fast. Because in any single decision he has varied only a few of the elements under his control and has thus changed the status quo only slightly, he has a good information base for determining the effect of change in one (or a few) variables. Through long experience, the decision maker is able to build up knowledge on how each of the variables under his control affects progress toward his objectives. In other words, he can build up a good memory on the consequences of change in specific variables.

(5) It is likely, too, that the communication system in a decentralized structure is more reliable than that in a centralized structure. This is probably true not only because messages must travel greater distances in a centralized structure, but also because there is less redundancy in the centralized structure.[11] For an illustration, let us place six fictitious entrepreneurs in charge of six textile plants in southern France. If they are all under the control of a central decision maker in Paris, the messages from all six plants will likely travel through a single channel on their way to Paris. If that channel is suddenly broken, the messages from all of the plants will fail to reach their destination. If, by contrast, the six entrepreneurs are independent, a break in a channel that links the plant with the decision maker could cut off only one-sixth of the total amount of relevant information.

In summary, then, the process of change in a decentralized structure may be visualized as trial-and-error learning, with trials occurring with great frequency and with error being quickly detected after each trial.[12]

In a centralized structure, on the other hand, it takes longer for feedback to reach the authoritative decision maker (greater lag). Because the resources under his command are greater, more variables will be affected by a single decision, and each decision is likely to involve a greater change from his initial position. Since no information is generated directly on the effects of a change in any one of the variables, it is difficult to develop memory which contains this kind of information. When the environment is decomposable, there will be a less adequate information base from which to evaluate feedback than there would be in a decentralized structure.

This leads to the second characteristic of a centralized decision structure—*the aggregation of information.* The channels of the information network tend necessarily to narrow as they reach the center. This causes the information bits to agglutinate. Information that reaches the central decision maker tends to be aggregate information. He may learn of the aggregate effects of his decision, but he does not receive the information necessary to discover the effects of change in a specific variable. Thus it becomes difficult to put into memory the information which identifies the specific variable to be manipulated and which is needed to develop a strategy for reaching objectives. For example, it may be difficult for a centralized decision maker to deal with problems that concern *product mix,* because the aggregated information in memory does not provide him with the detailed information necessary for a rational decision.

Adequate feedback and aggregated information are problems in any centralized decision structure, but they are of particular consequence in a traditional economy because of the low level of technology. Communication was slow in prerevolutionary France and in Manchu China. Messages took days or even weeks to reach Paris or Peking. This delay in communication, as well as the aggregation of information that occurred, meant that months or years were likely to pass before the consequences of the given course of action would be known to the decision makers, and it would take even more time until they had the necessary information to know what to do about these consequences.

This theory on the relative efficiency of centralized and decentralized decision-making processes in a decomposable environment (externalities and indivisibilities are absent) appears to be relevant to the empirical data produced by this study. But the hypothesis that would be derived from the theory is different from that which has been generated from the empirical data. The hypothesis derived from the theory may be stated as follows: *Any highly centralized decision structure involved in adaptive processes in a traditional economy will be so inefficient as to reduce significantly the probability of maintaining the slow but steady increases in product per capita that were assumed to be an economic prerequisite of take-off.* The hypothesis developed from the empirical data held that *a government that contributes significantly to the satisfaction of the adaptive functional requisite would significantly decrease the probability of maintaining slow but steady increases in product per capita.*

It should be noted that the difference between these two formulations is very important when viewed in terms of the conceptual framework of this study. The former statement refers to a procedural characteristic, while the latter deals with a structural-functional characteristic. The two formulations may be linked, however, by the introduction of two additional propositions which serve to connect the procedural characteristic of centralized resource allocation with the structural-functional characteristic of a major contribution by government to the satisfaction of the adaptive requisite.

The first of these propositions is that it is highly improbable that any nongovernmental structure can make centrally for the entire economy the wide range of detailed decisions which were made by the government in France and China. This proposition seems reasonable; if there were a single monopolistic firm or association of firms with such a wide competence, it would either have to be completely regulated by government or it would very likely become government.

The second proposition is that any significant contribution by government to the satisfaction of the adaptive functional requisite will probably involve highly centralized decision-making procedures.[13] This is less reasonable than the first proposition. The Lerner-Lange theories of socialist decision making indicate how governmental resource-allocating decisions can be decentralized. Although it might be very difficult to employ these procedures in a traditional economy, it is conceivable that local government units might in the aggregate make a significant contribution to the satisfaction of the adaptive functional requisite, and yet the decision-making structure would be decentralized.[14]

The Hurwicz theory of decision making suggests that we should develop a hypothesis focused upon a *central* government which employs highly centralized decision-making procedures with regard to resource allocation. The contribution that the government makes to the satisfaction of the adaptive functional requisite would be important only because of the decision-making procedures associated with resource allocation by the central government. There are, however, some noneconomic theories which indicate that the government's contribution to the satisfaction of the adaptive requisite is important regardless of the type of decision-making procedures associated with it.

Some Noneconomic Theoretical Underpinnings

The discussion thus far has centered upon economic theories that are compatible with the empirical findings. If economic factors were the only consideration, one could probably find among them several alternatives to the two preconditions for take-off listed on page 296. For example, if a period of economic growth before take-off is necessary merely to provide mobilizable capital when the techniques of industrialization become available, a massive foreign aid program might be one alternative—an alternative that would probably involve a great governmental contribution to the satisfaction of the adaptive functional requisite. Besides the body of economic theory, however, there are other theories—or rudiments of theory—that are also related to our first hypothesis. These can best be introduced by stating in propositional form two additional preconditions for take-off which should be listed along with the two already discussed.

No. 3. When the techniques of industrial production are introduced into a society, there is a need not only for mobilizable capital but also for rapidly increasing numbers of entreprenuers. The probability of achieving take-off at the time when the techniques of industrial production become available is greatly enhanced if the traditional economy has provided a reservoir of people who possess both entrepreneurial skills and motivation.

No. 4. The probability of achieving take-off will decrease as the normatively preferable ways of achieving individual goals and the actual achievement of these individual goals tend to reduce the available supplies of capital and/or entrepreneurial talent. In other words, take-off will be facilitated if there are structures in the society that tend to "align" individual goals and the means acceptable for reaching them with the societal goal of rapid economic growth.[15] Adam Smith was referring to one of these "aligning structures" when he wrote of the "invisible hand."

The noneconomic theories which might serve to relate the hypothesis (that the government should not make a significant contribution to the satisfaction of the adaptive requisite) to either or both of these propositions are not as elaborate or as rigorous as the economic theories just discussed. They may, however, be of equal or even greater importance.

Here the work of Fred W. Riggs seems especially applicable. He views modernization as change from a society with a "fused" social system to a society with a "diffracted" social system. He also identifies a transitional type, which he labels "prismatic." The identifying characteristic of the fused system is that there is little role differentiation, while in the diffracted system there is "super-differentiation." The terminology is adopted from the study of optics: the analogy is with fused light and diffracted light. Riggs employs the same analogy in using the term *prismatic* to refer to the period of turbulence through which a diffracting society passes. This, however, is not a conceptualization of social change in which the transitional (prismatic) society is viewed simply as the mid-point between two extremes, and for this reason it differs from the conceptualization discussed briefly in Chapter 1. The prismatic system has features which are shared with neither extreme, and Riggs conceives of the course of modernization from a fused system to a prismatic system as differing markedly from the evolution of a prismatic system to a diffracted system.[16]

In Riggs' conceptualization, social change from the fused system to the prismatic system is comparable to our conceptualization of the change from a traditional economy to that of the take-off stage. In his view of the fused society, Riggs emphasizes the importance of the role of power-holders. Because of the absence of effective structures through which other elites—economic, religious, educational, and so on—can hold them accountable, those who hold power control a disproportionate amount of the wealth and command a disproportionate amount of the prestige and deference in the society. In other words, there is an *agglutination* of values around the power-holders, and this tends to restrict differentiation, particularly among the various elites.[17]

Riggs' theories have important implications for the problems identified in propositions No. 3 and No. 4. There is some evidence to indicate that, in the early stages of economic development, ethnic and religious minority groups supply an inordinate amount of the entrepreneurial talent. Hagen, for example, draws attention to the role of the Nonconformists in the United Kingdom, the "Old Believers" in Russia, and the Antioqueños in Colombia.[18] Given the typical emphasis upon particularistic criteria of recruitment in a society with a fused social system, one would expect members of these minority groups to be excluded from significant power-holding roles, and hence from strategic posts in the government. If the government is making a significant contribution to the satisfaction of the adaptive functional requisite (and thus government officials are making the important entrepreneurial decisions), the exclusion of these minority groups from government office will tend also to exclude from entrepreneurial roles those individuals who are the most motivated and perhaps the most qualified.

Even if the government is less actively involved and merely "regulates" the economy rather than directly managing it, members of ethnic and religious minority groups who are successful entrepreneurs are likely to suffer most from rigorous enforcement of the regulations.

This leads to the second proposition, which deals with the alignment of individual goals with those of the total society. In a traditional economy where the government contributes significantly to the adaptive functional requisite through regulation and control (as opposed to direct ownership and management), the talented, aggressive, and pecuniarily motivated—to use adjectives that typically describe the successful entrepreneur—may regard as the most desirable those government jobs that involve them in economic regulation. Under these circumstances, the road to wealth is paved with the tribute they are able to collect from entrepreneurs who need their favor in order to carry on their business activities. Such individuals operating from within the government bureaucracy are not apt to invest their accumulated wealth in domestic business concerns. They are more likely to invest it in land or to put it in a foreign bank. In such a system, the members of ethnic and religious minorities who may have the highest propensity to invest are the most vulnerable to exploitation.

This line of argument can be expanded to provide some linkage between the functions of government and the procedures of governing. The agglutination of values, which Riggs identifies as being a conspicuous feature of the fused social system, tends to impair the differentiation and specialization of roles that are necessary to modernization. But if the authority structure of policy making in the government is not highly resolved and if the enforcement machinery is not effective, the likelihood that so many values will agglutinate around the power-holders is reduced. Hence, role differentiation is able to develop more easily, and larger supplies of experienced entre-preneurs emerge.[19]

The hypothesis on the government's contribution to the adaptive functional requisite, which was developed on the basis of certain theories that were related to the data, may now be stated as follows:

Final hypothesis: A government (particularly a central govern-ment) that does not contribute significantly to the satisfaction of the adaptive functional requisite is a prerequisite for take-off.

The theories which were considered in the development of this hypothesis reveal a number of propositions that serve as a basis for this hypothesis. These propositions may in themselves be regarded as hypotheses for further testing and research.

(A) In order for an economy to move into the take-off stage, a society must have, at the time when the techniques of industrial pro-duction become available, the following elements: (1) a certain mini-mal level of wealth which can be mobilized for investment, (2) a minimal level of entrepreneurial talent, and (3) an alignment of indi-vidual goals and the acceptable ways of reaching these goals with the societal goal of rapid economic growth.

(B) A central government that makes a significant contribution to the satisfaction of the adaptive functional requisite will with a high probability employ centralized decision-making procedures in allo-cating the society's resources.

(C) In a traditional economy, centralized decision-making proce-dures of resource allocation are likely to be so inefficient that they will impede the slow but steady economic growth in the traditional society.

(D) The absence of slow but steady growth per capita in the tradi-tional economy reduces the probability that there will be an adequate level of mobilizable wealth when the techniques of industrial produc-tion become available.

(E) A disproportionate number of entrepreneurs in the traditional and early take-off economies come from religious and/or ethnic mi-nority groups, far in excess of the size of these groups among the entire population.

(F) A decentralized decision-making structure for allocating and managing resources in a traditional economy increases the number of individuals who gain entrepreneurial experience.

(G) A government that makes a significant contribution to the satisfaction of the adaptive functional requisite tends to reduce the number of skilled and motivated entrepreneurs who are available when the techniques of industrial production are introduced: (1) by excluding members of ethnic and religious minority groups from entrepreneurial roles, (2) by reducing the number of individuals who gain entrepreneurial experience, and (3) by reducing the probability that there will be an alignment of individual goals and the acceptable means for reaching these goals with the societal goal of rapid economic growth.

At the time when the techniques of industrial production become available, some of the features that characterized the decision environment of the traditional economy begin to change. Of special significance is the fact that externalities, increasing returns, and indivisibilities become important in the environment of decision making with reference to the allocation of resources. Although the treatment of the take-off stage in Japan and England was designed to illustrate the application of the analytical framework to that phase of development rather than to serve as a basis for the development of hypotheses, it is difficult to resist making a few preliminary observations.

At the time of take-off, it becomes important for the government to increase its contribution to the satisfaction of the adaptive requisite and to centralize its decision making in matters related to resource allocation. It seems equally important, however, for the government to be only minimally involved in the process of resource management. We would argue, for example, that when the Japanese government divested itself of the ownership and direct management of certain firms, it was facilitating the achievement of take-off. The brief survey of the Japanese and English cases during the take-off period suggests that where significant nondecomposabilities exist in the environment of decision making concerned with resource allocation, the government should become involved in the resource-allocation process and should centralize the decision making. In this regard it is important to note that when the English government conferred special privileges on canal and railway companies, it was centralizing its resource-allocating decisions in precisely the sense in which Hurwicz defines centralization. But in a system that has to cope with decomposabilities, decision making in the area of resource management should be left in the hands of private managers. Part of this argument, however, is closely related to the treatment of goal attainment, and will be discussed in connection with that function.

THE GOAL-ATTAINMENT FUNCTIONAL REQUISITE

The two aspects of goal attainment which we examined in Chapter 5 were the mobilization of societal resources through taxation and other devices, and the creation of credit. In France and China, the government raised proportionately much more revenue than was raised in Japan and England. Furthermore, the most prestigious groups whose wealth was largely in land tended to avoid carrying much of the tax burden, while those who were economically the most active bore a heavy share of the tax load. In both England and Japan, commercial and manufacturing interests escaped with relatively light taxes.

As a preliminary hypothesis, the empirical data suggest that in the traditional stage a government that makes a relatively small contribution to the satisfaction of the goal-attainment functional requisite through direct resource mobilization, and which tends not to mobilize resources by taxing commercial and manufacturing interests, is a prerequisite for take-off. This hypothesis can be related directly to the theory of the relative efficiency of centralized and decentralized resource allocation discussed in the previous section. Resources that in Japan and England were allocated by private, local entrepreneurs were in France and China collected by the government and centrally allocated. Why such a system might lead to less efficient resource allocation has already been discussed. In addition, however, attention must be drawn to the possibility that the marginal propensity of the government to consume will be different from that of citizens from whom taxes are collected. There was no way of estimating what these differences were in the four cases considered in this study, and we can do nothing but draw the attention of the reader to this point. Perhaps it may be examined in detail in future studies.

One of the measures of the government's involvement in economic development is its contribution to capital formation.[20] This, however, is not a measure that can be well accommodated by the conceptual framework employed in this study. For government to contribute to capital formation, as this is typically measured, it must be involved in two processes—resource mobilization and resource allocation—each relating to a different functional requisite. Our framework tends to keep these two separate and forces us to look not at two alternatives (public and private capital formation) but at the four alternatives which are identified in Table 7.1:

TABLE 7.1. RESOURCE MOBILIZATION

	I Private	II Government
A. Private	IA	IIA
B. Government	IB	IIB

RESOURCE ALLOCATION

IA representing private capital formation (private mobilization and private allocation) and IIB representing public capital formation (government mobilization and government allocation) are the commonly considered alternatives. But we must also consider IIA (government mobilization and private allocation) and IB (private mobilization and government allocation). A government that mobilizes resources through taxation, places public revenues in an investment bank, and then manages the bank like a private entrepreneur—letting the *market* make the investment decisions—is an example of IIA. A government that directs the investment of privately mobilized capital, eliminating or greatly restricting the discretionary authority of the private investor, is an example of IB.

This type of breakdown aids in the interpretation of the empirical data. We are suggesting that the heavy role of the French and Chinese governments in mobilizing the societal resources inhibited to some extent the satisfaction of the prerequisites for take-off because these resources were centrally allocated. Thus the kind of resource mobilization is significant partially because it is empirically related to the kind of resource allocation that is employed.

This breakdown also sheds some interesting light on the take-off. Japan and England are sometimes represented as polar opposites in government involvement in the economy at the time of take-off. If one simply compares the government's share in capital formation in these two countries, this position can to some degree be supported. But the four-way breakdown in this analysis calls attention to a more significant phenomenon. Although the government in England was perhaps not as important a resource mobilizer as the government in Japan, it did allocate resources through legislation that created joint stock companies in some industries and effectively prohibited them in others. In other words, the resources it allocated were private, not government, resources. By this form of action, the English government centralized the resource-allocating decision structure according to the way that we have defined centralization. (Both operationality and anonymity were violated.) As one compares the contribution of the Japanese and English governments to the adaptive functional requisite through their involvement in resource allocation during the take-off stage, he finds patterns of striking similarity. The differences appear more with regard to the resource-mobilization process of goal attainment. But even here the differences are not so great when account is taken of the high levels of taxation in England during the great war, the private investment of publicly mobilized funds, and some provision for joint stock companies. The analysis of the private and public contributions to capital formation uncovers some differences between the Japanese and English cases but fails to reveal wider basic similarities.

This brief discussion of the take-off period has been introduced here merely to enable us to place our hypothesis in perspective. We are hypothesizing that in the traditional stage the degree of governmental contribution to goal attainment through resource mobilization is relevant when such mobilization affects the resource-allocating process. If resource allocation and resource mobilization are treated as conceptually separable processes, we suggest that in meeting the prerequisites for take-off there are rather wide limits to the government's contribution to goal attainment through involvement in resource mobilization,[21] but narrow limits to the government's contribution to the adaptive requisite through resource allocation.

The creation of credit was the second aspect of goal attainment which commanded attention in Chapter 5. Normally, one associates government and credit creation with national banks and similar lending agencies. Among our four cases in the traditional stage, however, there was only one national bank—the Bank of England—and it served as a source of credit largely for the government itself, not for private entrepreneurs. Only in France was the government a significant source of long-term credits for private industrial undertakings, and then largely for the Royal Manufacturers.

The government in Japan and England, however, made an obvious contribution to credit creation through the establishment and maintenance of a relatively stable currency. The government in France and China, on the other hand, not only failed to aid in the stabilization of the currency but also deliberately manipulated the value of the coin of the realm. Such activities inhibit private credit creation, especially the provision of long-term industrial credits. People with disposable liquid assets are not only tempted to engage in currency speculation, but they also are discouraged from making long-term loans which might be repaid with currency worth only a fraction of the original debt.

It might be argued that the currency devaluation which was so prevalent in France and China (and to a somewhat lesser extent in Japan) may actually lead to increased investment because it will encourage the conversion of liquid assets into tangible property. But the pressures were for the purchase of real estate and not for investment in productive capital. We must also remember that the intrinsic value of the coins themselves was considerable, and that profit could be made simply by hoarding the coins until their intrinsic value exceeded their official value.

Before stating the final hypothesis, let us point out that the patterning of data on goal attainment among the four cases is very closely related to the problem discussed under adaptation. If central resource allocation in the traditional economy is so much less efficient then decentralized resource allocation, any activity that tends to discourage the former and encourage the latter will contribute to economic growth. This is precisely what happened in the cases of the governments of Japan and England, as contrasted with France and China. The Japanese and English did not unduly tax money out of the hands of those most likely to invest, while they did maintain a monetary system that encouraged the private creation of credit and thus increased the amount of disposable capital.

Final hypothesis: There are wide limits to the tolerable range of variation in the government's contribution to the satisfaction of the goal-attainment requisite as a prerequisite to take-off. There are, however, certain qualifications:

(1) If a significant government contribution to the satisfaction of the goal-attainment requisite increases the probability that resource allocation will be centralized, it decreases the probability of achieving take-off.

(2) If the government, through resource mobilization, lowers the propensity to invest in the economy, it reduces the probability of achieving take-off.

(3) If the government takes any action that impedes the operation of private credit creation without increasing proportionately its own credit creation, it reduces the probability of achieving take-off.

PATTERN MAINTENANCE

One of the prerequisites of economic growth, which has been discussed in the economic literature from the time of the classical economists down to the present-day scholars, is that the government must maintain law, order, and a modicum of security. We include these activities within the general rubric of pattern maintenance. The question raised earlier was whether or not there are structural alternatives to government which can enforce the norms defining criminal behavior (maintain order) and which also meet the prerequisites for takeoff. Since the four cases provide few clues, we shall have to be content to discuss some of the theoretical reasons why our answer is in the negative.

There is no doubt that the norms defining criminal behavior can under certain conditions be supported effectively by nongovernmental structures. In Chapter 5, we identified three basic sanctions which, in addition to legal sanctions, may operate on the societal level. They are retaliation-compensation, withdrawal of reciprocity, and supernatural sanctions. Although none of these is defined in terms of a specific social structure (except that government is, by definition, not involved), each requires relatively specific kinds of social structuring if it is to be effective. Most significantly, certain kinds of kinship structures and certain types of community structures are necessary. For example, retaliation-compensation is most effective if each individual belongs to a specific kin or community vengeance group, which is defined in such a way as to avoid significant overlapping membership. The vengeance group must be (1) clearly *visible,* (2) a prime object of loyalty for its members, (3) localized territorially, and (4) larger than an extended family.

The development of industrialization tends to break down such a kin or territorial group, and retaliation-compensation ceases to be an effective sanction. A similar kind of argument applies to both supernatural sanctions and to withdrawal of reciprocity. Industrialization tends to destroy the kinds of social structuring which are necessary if these types of sanctions are to be effective. If conformity to the norms governing criminal behavior is to be maintained, legal sanctions that involve government must be employed. The question we are concerned with is whether the government must be involved before takeoff, or whether it can effectively step in (if it has not previously been involved) at the beginning of the take-off period when the other structures are breaking down. The final hypothesis, derived more from theoretical considerations than from the data, is that a significant contribution by government to the satisfaction of the pattern-maintenance functional requisite is either a prerequisite or a requisite for take-off.

A clearer patterning of the data occurred with respect to the enforcement of norms that defined the rights, privileges, powers, and disabilities of members of various prestige groupings. In all four cases the government attempted to enforce certain of these norms. The most notable difference was the existence of certain legal prohibitions against direct participation in commerce and manufacturing by the most prestigious classes in France, while in England there was no such restriction. The data on China and Japan are more difficult to interpret. In both countries there were restrictions similar to those that existed in France and in both countries they were violated with some frequency. In China, however, the gentry who engaged in commercial activities usually did so behind the scenes and under assumed names. In Japan, by contrast, the daimyo and samurai openly engaged in commercial and industrial enterprises. Moreover, because of the difference in inheritance laws, younger sons of the military aristocracy in Japan tended to move to the cities and towns and take up the new forms of employment.

No extended discussion of theory is necessary to place these data in adequate perspective. Any action of government that tends to reduce the funds available for investment will impede economic growth. Since a disproportionate amount of wealth was held by the most prestigious classes in France and China, the restrictions placed upon their commercial activity were probably of some consequence. The more general final hypothesis may be stated in this way: A prerequisite for take-off is a government that does not enforce norms severely restricting the investment outlets for those classes that hold a large portion of the potential investment capital.

INTEGRATION

The contribution of government to the satisfaction of the integration requisite was discussed largely with reference to integration among roles differentiated on the basis of (1) occupational specialization, (2) prestige, and (3) generation.

Integration Among Roles Differentiated on the Basis of Occupational Specialization

Only slight patterning of the four cases appeared in the degree to which conflicts among businessmen were settled in government courts. Standing out notably was the French case, in which there was the greatest probability that conflicts among merchants and manufacturers would be settled in formal court proceedings. In England, the common law courts took over many of the responsibilities previously handled by the law merchant and the special system of local courts which administered it. Because there were fewer regulations and restrictions than in France and because many of those that were issued were not enforced, the English government did not have reason to be involved in as many commercial cases as did the French government.

In both Japan and China, there were strong cultural and social pressures upon mercantile litigants to settle their disputes through arbitration and through the medium of nongovernmental structures. The government in both countries openly discouraged contesting parties from bringing their private commercial disagreements into the courtroom. There is some reason to believe that the Japanese merchants, especially those in the cities and towns who were less restrained by social bonds, resorted voluntarily to legal action more often than the merchants of China. Japan developed a relatively sophisticated form of contract law, and court procedures made special provision for the handling of matters involving money and credit. In China, however, more commercial transactions were regulated by the government, and, to the degree that these were enforced, cases of alleged violations could end up in the courts. It is likely, too, that disputes would arise among state enterprises, and, while there is a paucity of information on this subject, such conflicts would probably have to be ironed out according to precedents brought together under a system of "administrative law."

In England after the sixteenth century, the courts of the law merchant and the common law courts provided a governmental structure which merchants could use in settling their disputes. However, it seems impossible to determine the extent to which cases were settled privately as an alternative to the courtroom process. But in all probability the courts in England were used more than they were in Japan and China, although there is some question about the latter because of the absence of information on litigation among government-owned and/or -operated firms.

These data do not clearly suggest any hypothesis. We might point out, however, that the very significant contribution by government in the case of France was more inhibiting to satisfying the prerequisites for take-off than was the lesser contribution of government in, for example, Japan. A brief discussion of the kind of theory which would be compatible with this interpretation may be useful at this point.

Implicit throughout E. Adamson Hoebel's work in jurisprudential theory[22] is the notion that the individuals who occupy the roles of judges and make crucial decisions on the interpretation and application of legal norms (indeed, at times establishing new legal norms) are drawn from the most conservative segments of society. Reflecting upon this idea, Hoebel introduces an even more elucidating term than conservative. He speaks of the *preservators* of culture. Although this is hardly a well-developed theory, it sheds some light upon our empirically generated hypothesis. If judges are in fact recruited from social groups that are the most interested in *preserving* existing values, the energetic and enterprising merchants and manufacturers in the traditional economy will probably find themselves out of tune with the values of the judges and the conservative interests they represent. In other words, if a dispute is settled in court, it is likely to be resolved on the basis of values that are inimical to the interests of the economically active segments of the population. When such disputes are settled privately, however, with merchants and manufacturers (or people drawn from this class) acting as mediators, it is more probable that the case will be decided according to the best interests of the mercantile class.

The English case represents something of an exception to this generalization. Not only was the law merchant absorbed into the common law, but also a significant number of the common law judges came from the middle class. Hence the courts were not the *preservators* of aristocratic values, as they were, for example, in France, where all the judges were members of the nobility.

If an interpretation of this sort has any validity, the curious student is led to explore the conditions under which less prestigious elements of the society tend to be *represented* in judicial positions. Although such an investigation is very tempting, it lies beyond the scope of this monograph.

The point was also made in Chapter 5 that a government contributes to the integration among roles differentiated on the basis of occupational specialization if it provides for the necessary *currencies*—that is, standardized units in terms of which exchange can take place. The government in Japan and England went much farther than its counterpart in France and China in providing some standardization of weights and measures on a nation-wide basis. This action facilitated the expansion of the area in which role interdependencies could develop, and thus contributed to the enlargement of the market for many goods. The theories suggesting that relatively large markets in the traditional economy are a prerequisite for take-off are presented below in the section which treats the integration of roles differentiated on the basis of geographic location. Here a different point is worth some consideration. It is paradoxical that the Japanese and English governments, which were ineffective in almost all other phases of economic regulation, were much more successful than the French and Chinese governments in providing some standardization of weights and measures. The difficulties experienced by most governments in their attempts at standardization as late as the twentieth century are testimony to the complexity of the task and indicate that techniques which are ordinarily successful in enforcing other kinds of regulations often do not suffice to rationalize and unify weights and measures. In a preindustrial society, we speculate, standardization is possible only over those areas within which there is significant exchange. In France and China, therefore, the activities of government that restricted trade and commerce doomed their efforts to regulate weights and measures. The success of Japan and England did not result from any esoteric method of enforcement, but was due to the fact that standardization was a much easier task in these two societies. It must be recognized, however, that the early success of the Japanese in this area was facilitated by the ingenious techniques of control which the shogun managed to employ.

The hypothesis which emerges from the data and which is supported by additional theories to be presented below may be stated in this form: A government that contributes to the satisfaction of the integration functional requisite by providing the necessary currencies if role interdependencies are to develop over a large area is a prerequisite for take-off.

*Integration Among Roles Differentiated
on the Basis of Prestige*

One of the most striking differences between the two sets of cases is to be found in the governmental activities relating to the stratification system in the society. In France and China not only was there mobility from commercial and manufacturing groups into the most prestigious classes of the traditional society, but also the channels of upward movement were provided and reinforced by the government. The sale of titles and offices in France and the sale of academic degrees and offices in China provided a ladder of mobility which many could climb and which many more could aspire to climb. The absence of government restrictions on the sale of land to merchants and manufacturers also permitted individuals who had accumulated capital from business adventures to acquire this most revered form of wealth.

In Japan and England, on the other hand, there were severe and effective restrictions upon movement into the aristocracy. In neither country did the sale of titles and offices reach a significant magnitude, and in Japan there were laws that prohibited the alienation of land and especially restricted its sale to merchants.

The preliminary hypothesis suggested by these data is that a government which prohibits (or severely restricts) the movement of merchants and manufacturers into the most prestigious classes of the traditional society is a prerequisite for take-off.

The theory relevant to this hypothesis is again related to the conditions necessary to achieve the slow and sustained economic growth in the traditional economy. The investment necessary to generate this growth will most probably come from merchants or manufacturers (or, in some instances, from the more prosperous peasants). Whenever possible, the most successful merchants/entrepreneurs will seek to move into the high status groups of the traditional society, which are less inclined toward saving and productive investment.[23] The implication of this tendency grows more serious for economic growth as the technology of industrialization becomes available and the technological prerequisites for take-off are met. Rosenstein-Rodan has stated the problem clearly:

A high minimum quantum of investment requires a high volume of savings, which is difficult to achieve in low income, under-developed countries. There is a way out of this vicious circle. In the first stage when income is increased due to an increase in investment which mobilizes additional latent resources, mechanisms must be provided which assure that in the second stage the marginal rate of savings is very much higher than the average rate of savings.[24]

It was suggested earlier that opportunities for upward mobility of people who have accumulated wealth into strata that are economically inactive tend to make it difficult to provide the kind of mechanisms Rosenstein-Rodan is writing about.

The preliminary hypothesis does not have to be revised. However, it is based upon three propositions which should also be examined:

(1) The most probable pattern of middle-class mobility into the prestigious classes of the traditional society involves the exchange of wealth for prestige.

(2) The marginal propensity to consume is greater among the aristocratic classes than among commercial and manufacturing groups.

These propositions, if true, indicate why severe restrictions upon movement into the aristocratic classes may be a prerequisite for take-off. They do not, however, provide any basis for asserting that restrictions upon upward movement must be governmental. This aspect of the problem requires an additional proposition.

(3) In traditional societies, if nonprestigious groups are allowed to accumulate wealth to the point that many individuals become richer than people in the high-status classes, only legal norms will successfully prevent them from moving into the most prestigious stratum of the society—that is, only government action can prevent them from exchanging wealth for prestige.[25]

Integration Among Roles Differentiated on the Basis of Generation

In all four cases, government was involved in the integration among roles differentiated on the basis of relative age. Differences were procedural—that is, there were differences in the way in which the government contribution was made. In Chapter 5 attention was concentrated upon laws of inheritance. In France and China, these laws generally required an individual to distribute his estate among his immediate survivors more or less equally. In Japan and England, however, the laws of inheritance tended to force the bulk of the deceased's estate into the hands of a single survivor.

This suggests the preliminary hypothesis that the laws of inheritance must not force a relatively equal distribution of property among several heirs. Ideally, government should require that the estate of the deceased should be kept intact, and should be used to support only one survivor.

There are two theories in the social sciences—one economic, the other demographic—that relate to this hypothesis. A body of economic theory holds that the propensity to save varies directly with size of income, and that the curve is convex. Therefore, in any economy whose rate of saving is below a certain point, the total savings

TABLE 7.2. PROPENSITY TO SAVE

(at a given national income level) will be greater if that income is maldistributed than if it is equally distributed. Laws of inheritance which concentrate the deceased's estate into the hands of one individual will contribute to an unequal distribution of income.

In the traditional economy, however, it is not only the total supply of savings that is significant. In the typical, traditional economy there are few structures that serve to concentrate small amounts of savings from individuals so that they add up to the larger chunks of capital needed for important investments. Direct investment from an individual's own savings is far more significant than it is during the later stages of economic growth. Thus devices that tend to concentrate capital and earning power within a small segment of the population will help to contribute to an increase in investment. Under these conditions, it is easier to meet the economic prerequisites of take-off discussed above, namely, (1) slow, but marked, growth per capita for several decades; and (2) concentration of capital in such a way that it will be available for investment in new industrial techniques.

In considering this position, two problems must be carefully examined: (1) if the propensity-to-save curve is only slightly inclined and only slightly convex, the concentration of wealth will have little effect on the level of investment; and (2) it is possible that propensity-to-save at a given income level varies so greatly from class to class that aggregate figures will have little relevance to the problem under consideration.

The demographic theory relating to this hypothesis appears to have great deductive power and directly reinforces the economic theory. Kingsley Davis and Judith Blake have presented a conceptual framework for the study of social, cultural, and psychological factors affecting birth rates and population growth.[26] The most significant of the social-structural factors limiting population growth in preindustrial societies is the enforcement of norms of inheritance that restrict the estate of the deceased to a single heir who is not responsible for providing livelihood for all other next of kin. The effect of this kind of inheritance regulation is to delay the marriage age of other sons, since they cannot get married until they have accumulated the capital and developed the earning power necessary to support a family.

We suggest that the laws of inheritance in England and Japan tended to delay marriage age, thus acting as a check on population growth, while in France and China the inheritance laws tended to operate in an opposite manner. We would anticipate that population growth will tend to approach a Malthusian limit in France and China, because there were no significant social-structural checks to prevent increases in national income from being deployed to support a larger population. In France and China it would thus be difficult for increases in gross national product (GNP) to be reflected in growth in product per capita, which would be necessary to meet what we have postulated as an economic prerequisite for take-off. In England and Japan, on the other hand, the laws of inheritance tended to delay the marriage age and consequently to restrict birth rates to something well below the Malthusian limit. Increases in GNP could well be reflected in an increase in product *per capita*.

While population data for the centuries we are interested in are not noted for their reliability, they are at least consistent with our interpretation. In Table 7.7 (based on data in Tables 7.3, 7.4, 7.5 and 7.6) index figures of population change are graphed. In China, the population growth from about 1740 to 1850 was enormous. During this period there were remarkable increases in agricultural production due in large measure to the development and rapid dissemination of faster maturing rice (which made multiple cropping possible) and the spread of new world crops (which made it possible to bring previously unproductive lands under cultivation).[27] This rate of population growth suggests that increased production led directly and immediately to increased population, so that increases in GNP were not significantly reflected in growth per capita.

TABLE 7.3

POPULATION OF FRANCE[1]

Year	Population	Years between Statistics	Average Decade Increase	Percentage Increase for Decade
1600	16,000,000?[2]			
1650	18,000,000?[2]	50	400,000	2.5%
1680	21,899,221[3]	30	1,299,740	7.2%
1700	20,402,660[4]	20	−748,281	−3.4%
1710	18,833,330[3]	10	−1,569,330	−7.7%
1715	18,000,000	5	−1,666,660	−9.2%
1750	21,000,000?[2]	35	571,430	3.2%
1762	21,769,163	12	640,970	3.1%
1766	23,100,000[2]	4	3,327,090	15.3%
1770	24,500,000	4	3,500,000	15.2%
1784	24,800,000	14	214,290	.87%
1789	26,300,000[2]	5	3,000,000	12.1%
1801	27,349,003	12	874,170	3.3%

[1] All figures from Maurice Block, *Statistique de la France*, Vol. I, unless otherwise noted.
[2] Joseph H. Spengler, *France Faces Depopulation*.
[3] Estimated from periodical growth rates and population increases or decreases in Spengler, *France Faces Depopulation*.
[4] Averaged estimate of two figures given for the same period, 19,669,320 from Block and 21,136,000 from Spengler.

The Japanese statistics are in striking contrast with those of China. During the Tokugawa period, there seems to have been a significant increase in agricultural production due to tremendous increases in the land under cultivation, new varieties of rice and other crops, and improved agricultural techniques.[28] There also seems to have been a significant increase in income from nonagricultural sources. The population, however, grew little, particularly after 1730. We interpret this to be in marked contrast to the Chinese case and a clear indication that some non-Malthusian checks on population growth were in operation.[29] Increases in GNP were reflected in increases in product per capita.

The French and English data do not provide such clear-cut conclusions. The French curves reveal generally steady increases in population, except for the period 1680-1715 when a combination of war, famine, abnormally cold winters, and Huguenot emigration contrib-

TABLE 7.4

POPULATION OF ENGLAND AND WALES[1]

Year	Population	Decade Increase	Percentage Increase for Decade
1603	5,000,000[2]		
1625	5,500,000[2]		
1660	5,500,000[2]		
1700/1	5,740,000	240,000	4.4%
1710/1	5,710,000	−30,000	−.5%
1720/1	5,842,000	132,000	2.3%
1730/1	5,924,000	82,000	1.4%
1740/1	5,997,000	73,000	1.2%
1750/1	6,292,000	295,000	4.9%
1760/1	6,634,000	342,000	5.4%
1770/1	7,197,000	563,000	8.5%
1780/1	7,696,000	499,000	6.9%
1790/1	8,392,000	696,000	9.04%
1800/1	9,193,000	801,000	9.5%

[1] All figures, unless otherwise cited, represent averages of the population figures presented in B. R. Mitchell and Phyllis Deane, *Abstract of British Historical Statistics*, Cambridge University Press: Cambridge, 1962.
[2] A. M. Carr-Saunders, *Population*.

uted to an actual decrease in population. The English population remained rather steady from 1600 until the second decade of the eighteenth century. Population growth began about 1715 and continued throughout the century, with the rate of growth increasing after 1760. These figures do not necessarily refute the Davis-Blake thesis. A detailed analysis suggests that this increase was due not to an increase in births, but to a decrease in the death rate[30]—a factor that could not in the short run have been affected by marriage age. It should also be pointed out that, although the population in England was growing after 1715, there was still a significant increase in product per capita.

The economic and demographic theories just reviewed reinforce the hypothesis in the preliminary form as it was developed from the empirical study. In its precise final form, it would hold that a govern-

TABLE 7.5

POPULATION OF CHINA[1]

Year	Population	Decade Increase	Percentage Increase for Decade
1600	150,000,000		
1650	131,250,000[2]	−375,000	−.25%
1700	150,000,000	−375,000	−.25%
1741	143,411,559	−164,711	−.109%
1751	181,811,359	38,399,800	24.9%
1761	198,214,555	16,403,196	9.0%
1771	214,600,356	16,385,801	8.2%
1781	279,816,070	65,215,714	30.3%
1791	304,354,160	24,538,090	8.8%
1801	297,501,548	−6,852,612	−2.3%
1811	358,610,039	61,108,491	20.8%
1821	355,540,258	−3,069,781	−8.6%
1831	395,821,092	40,280,834	11.3%
1841	413,457,311	17,636,219	4.5%
1850	429,931,034	16,473,723	4.0%

[1] All figures from P. T. Ho, *Studies on the Population of China, 1368-1953*, unless otherwise noted.
[2] Estimated from periodical growth rates and population increases or decreases in Ho.

ment that does *not* enforce norms of inheritance which distribute the estate of the deceased more or less equally among several heirs is a prerequisite for take-off. But there are a few additional questions which need to be answered. Our data and the supporting theories shed little light on the question of whether the norms governing the relationship among roles differentiated on the basis of generation must be legal norms. If the answer to this question is *no*, we would make no modification in our hypothesis. If the answer is *yes*, however, we could make it more restrictive by holding that the govern-

TABLE 7.6

POPULATION OF JAPAN[1]

Year	Population	Years between Statistics	Average Decade Increase	Average Percentage Increase for Decade
1600	18,000,000			
1650	21,500,000[2]	50	700,000	3.8%
1700	25,000,000	100	700,000	3.8%
1721	26,065,000	21	507,140	2.03%
1726	26,489,000[3]	5	848,000	3.3%
1731	26,921,000[3]	5	864,000	3.3%
1744	26,153,450	13	−590,420	−2.2%
1750	25,917,830	6	−392,700	−1.5%
1756	26,062,000	6	240,280	.9%
1762	25,921,458	6	−234,340	−.9%
1768	26,252,057	6	550,980	2.1%
1774	25,990,457	6	−436,000	−1.7%
1780	26,010,600	6	33,570	.13%
1786	25,086,466	6	−1,540,220	−5.9%
1792	24,891,441	6	−325,040	−1.3%
1798	25,471,033	6	965,990	3.9%
1804	25,621,957	6	251,540	.98%
1822	26,602,110	18	54,470	.2%
1828	27,201,400	6	998,820	3.7%
1834	27,063,907	6	−229,160	−.8%
1846	26,907,625	12	−130,240	−.5%
1852	27,201,400	6	489,630	1.8%

[1] All figures from Irene B. Taeuber, *The Population of Japan*, unless otherwise noted.

[2] Estimated from periodical growth rates and population increases or decreases listed in Taeuber.

[3] Ayanori Okasaki, *Histoire du Japon: L'Economie et la Population*.

ment must support norms of inheritance that tend to concentrate wealth in the hands of a single (or small number) of heirs.

Integration Among Roles Differentiated on the Basis of Geographic Location

One of the striking differences between the two sets of cases emerges from the data concerning the existence of barriers to inter-re-

TABLE 7.7. INDEXED RATES OF POPULATION GROWTH

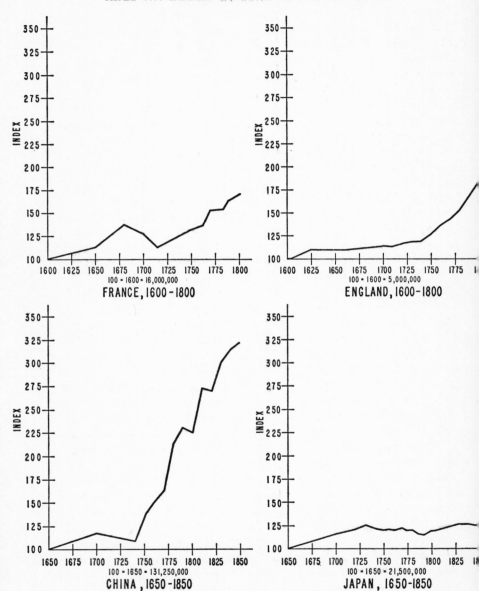

gional trade. Japan and England were relatively free from such restrictions, while the government in both France and China imposed taxes on the transport of goods. In addition, inter-regional trade in France was encumbered by privately levied tolls which the government seemed powerless to abolish. This was one of the few areas of regulation in which the French government was the least effective of the four cases analyzed.

This study treats these barriers to trade as actions by government that facilitate or inhibit the expansion of the geographic area over which role interdependencies will tend to develop. Two economic "laws" suggest the hypothesis that a wide area within which roles can become interdependent facilitates the achievement of take-off; these are the law of comparative advantage and the law of increasing returns to scale. In a country which has regional diversities in the conditions of production, increases in productivity will be facilitated as these regions are able to specialize in the production of commodities in which they enjoy a comparative advantage and to exchange these commodities for other goods produced elsewhere. To the degree that a government, through the assessment of import and export duties within the regions of a country, impedes specialization, it reduces the probability that slow but steady increase in product per capita will occur during the traditional stage of development—the growth that we have hypothesized is an economic prerequisite for take-off.

With regard to increasing returns to scale, a different argument has to be made. We have suggested that increasing returns are not of great consequence for an economy in the traditional stage, but that they grow more significant as the techniques of industrial production become available. The advantages of increasing returns to scale, however, will not be manifested unless there is a relatively large market to absorb the growing quantities of the less expensive products. Where inter-regional trade has been relatively unrestricted for decades, it will be easier to exploit the economies of scale which are inherent in an industrial technology.

But too much emphasis must not be placed on increasing returns to scale during the take-off period; they appear to become far more important in the later stages of economic growth. At the beginning of the take-off period, the existence of a large free-trade area within which role interdependencies can develop takes on importance, rather, because regional comparative advantages grow more significant as a result of the use of industrial technology and the improvement in transportation facilities.

Granted that a large market area is desirable, the question still arises whether a wide free-trade territory can exist in a traditional economy unless the government actually prohibits the development of trade barriers. Our answer is that in such a society parochial interests are likely to be so strong that locally established impediments to trade will be erected unless the central government effectively restricts such activities.

A single final hypothesis is supported both by the empirical data and by economic theory: A government that acts to prevent the establishment of barriers limiting the area within which role interdependencies can develop is a prerequisite for take-off.

INTERRELATIONSHIPS AMONG THE HYPOTHESES

Some scholars will object to the use of the term *prerequisites* in the statements of the hypotheses on the ground that they imply that if one of the prerequisites is not satisfied, take-off cannot be accomplished even though all the remaining prerequisites are met. It must be emphasized that we found the concept *prerequisite* a useful heuristic device which enabled us to concentrate upon certain outstanding patterns. But our concept of prerequisite is essentially a probability concept. This notion was implied at the very outset of the study, when in Chapter 2 we spoke of alternative prerequisites. We also explicitly recognize the theoretical possibility that if most of the factors we have listed as prerequisites are present, take-off might be achieved even though one of them may be absent. We do not wish, however, to explore the implications of this possibility, because there are reasons to suppose that the existence of certain prerequisites increases the probability that others will also be present. If this is the case, it is unlikely that all the prerequisites but one would be present.

If each of the hypotheses suggested above was a necessary condition for take-off (within a specified probability range) and each was independent of the others, it would indeed be difficult for a society to satisfy the prerequisites for take-off. And if such were the case, there could never be a well-integrated theory concerning the political prerequisites for take-off, because the several propositions could not be linked empirically.

It is more interesting theoretically if hypotheses are interrelated—if the existence of the conditions specified in one would give rise to, or were determined by, the conditions specified by in another, or if several sets of conditions were determined by the same factor. There is some reason to suppose that the hypotheses which emerge most clearly from the data in this exploratory study are interrelated.

The most striking similarities which link France and China and differentiate them from Japan and England are (1) a significant government contribution to the adaptive requisite (particularly involvement in resource-allocation and resource-management, (2) a system of burdensome taxation which tended to exclude the most prestigious landed interests and to fall heavily upon the economically most active segment of the population, (3) a highly resolved authority structure of policy making, (4) a reliable policy-enforcement instrument, (5) a fairly wide range of techniques for securing compliance, (6) government-established channels of mobility into the most prestigious classes, (7) an inheritance system that inhibited the concentration of wealth, and (8) restrictions that discouraged the most prestigious classes from investing in commerce and manufacturing.

For a government to maintain high rates of taxation and to engage in close regulation of economic activity, it must necessarily have a relatively well-resolved authority structure of policy making, reliable enforcement machinery, and a range of techniques for securing compliance. This much is obvious, and was discussed in the first section of this chapter. Further linkages among our hypotheses, however, can be made only if we introduce some additional propositions that do not emerge from the data of the study.

A central government is confronted by certain limits beyond which it cannot go in seeking to impose heavy taxes and detailed economic regulations, especially as it meets opposition from people in the local communities. Stringent measures introduced by the central authorities increase what might be called the *propensity to revolt* in the society. There are, however, two conditions that tend to make heavy tax burdens and tight economic regulation more tolerable over the long run: (1) The effects of such policies are somewhat mitigated if local interests are represented in the central decision structure, and have consented to regulatory and tax measures and have been able to block policies that they oppose most strongly. (2) Potentially unpopular policies imposed by the central government also become more tolerable if significant numbers of the victims of these policies can expect to gain some benefits from the system that taxes and regulates them.

The first condition is rarely possible in a traditional society. The great diversity of local interests and the relative importance of local as compared with national concerns make it extremely difficult to have local interests represented in a central policy-making structure (or with veto power over policies), and still have an authority structure that is highly resolved. Indeed, it is our contention that if the authority structure in a traditional society is highly resolved, only a few interests are likely to be represented in policy making, and that there will be a strong tendency for the central authorities to tax and to regulate those interests that are not represented. The taxes will tend to include high levies on visible commercial and industrial wealth and on the long-distance transport of bulk goods. Wide representation in a highly resolved authority structure does not become possible until the development of the modern disciplined party system in a relatively homogeneous society, where national political interests take precedence over local concerns.

The second alternative—where large numbers of the taxed and regulated groups can reap benefits from the system—is feasible in a traditional society. This alternative merely requires that the government open up the channels of mobility so as to make possible the acquisition of prestige but not the acquisition of power. Strong opposition to the central government, which increases the cost of enforcement and threatens the effectiveness of policies, is less likely to come from those people who have good prospects for upward mobility in the society and sufficient opportunity to share in its prestigious positions.

When the central rulers of a traditional society sell titles and powerless offices, two obvious complementary needs are met—the government's need for funds and the merchants' and manufacturers' need for status and prestige. But the government may be gaining more than the mere receipt of revenue; it may also be buying off potential opposition of a dangerous sort. Indeed, we are suggesting that the ruling group may have to provide upward mobility into the prestigious classes so that it will be able to tax and regulate economic activities over long periods of time.

It may also be that the ruling group will have to encourage regionalism through such policies as the erection of trade barriers in order to reduce the likelihood that deviants in various sections of the country will unite into a cohesive opposition. "Divide and rule" may be more than a possible strategy; it may be a highly probable one.

This is the negative case in which some of the factors that inhibit take-off are interrelated. Stated positively, the formulation would suggest that if local interests are represented in central policy making and can *veto* the enforcement of policies to which they object, the propensity to revolt will remain relatively low, and it is not necessary for the government to provide mobility into the most prestigious classes. More than this, if merchants and manufacturers are able to accumulate wealth in sizable proportions, they can be kept out of the most prestigious classes *only* if the norms that block their upward mobility are legal norms enforced by the government.

Further linkages among our hypotheses seem reasonable. To go back to the negative case, we are hypothesizing that if a government is to tax heavily and to control the economy in minute detail, it must distribute prestige to those who are tightly squeezed and in a position to be potentially an effective opposition. In other words, it must *sell prestige;* it must not *sell power.* Indeed, if the central government is to continue its restrictive policies, it must thwart the development of competing power centers which it cannot dominate. If it fails in this objective, these power centers will either tend to become represented in the policy-making structure (and, hence, the authority structure of policy making will cease to be resolved), or they are likely to revolt.

An inheritance system which splits up an estate will help to limit the build-up of such power centers. The family whose aspirations to *purchase prestige* are satisfied in one generation may, if its wealth continues to accumulate, try to *buy power* in the next generation. The probability of such a development is less if the inheritance laws dilute rather than concentrate wealth, and if the members of the prestigious classes are not permitted to invest in those sectors of the economy where profits are potentially the greatest.

But an inheritance system that dilutes rather than concentrates wealth among the heirs has two consequences for economic growth: (1) It tends to push population expansion near the Malthusian limits, and (2) it tends to reduce the marginal propensity to save in the economy.

Returning to the positive case, we suggest that the inability of a government to tax business wealth and the movement of goods encourages the growth of trade and the expansion of markets. This makes it possible for the government to standardize weights and measures, which in turn further facilitates an expansion of the market area. Furthermore, inheritance laws that tend to concentrate wealth place checks upon the growth of population and increase the marginal propensity to save. In the short run, such laws may not affect the authority structure of policy making, which may continue to reflect various interests and remain relatively unresolved. It is possible, however, to speculate about changes in the long run. If the prestigious classes can invest in productive enterprise, their economic interests become more compatible with those of the merchants and manufacturers, especially when there is downward mobility from the noble families into the business groups and when the older commercial wealth begins to find an outlet in the new techniques of an industrial economy. We would then expect to find a gradual change to a more highly resolved authority structure of policy making. If this occurs while the techniques of industrial production are being introduced, one of the requisites for take-off will have been met.

But change occurs differently in the negative case. When the government can no longer *sell prestige* effectively, it may be faced with a revolutionary situation which could result in violent change. However, even if this coincides with the availability of industrial technology and even if representatives of the active economic interests come to power, they are unlikely to be able to pursue policies that will lead directly to take-off because certain prerequisites for take-off will not have been met.

These last few paragraphs have taken us beyond the intended limits of this monograph, and we shall close where we began—on a methodological note. We have attempted to formulate some hypotheses by an empirical comparative analysis, and we have checked and modified these hypotheses in accordance with the generalizations of relevant theory in the social sciences. As a final step, we have sought to link these hypotheses by introducing a set of additional propositions. Taken together, all of these propositions will hopefully provide the broad outline of a theory on the political prerequisites for economic take-off.

We do not claim, of course, that we have in any sense tested these hypotheses, but we offer them in the conviction that hypotheses which have been systematically developed and theoretically justified deserve to be tested in carefully designed empirical research. We are reminded of the admonition of a wise old social scientist: "We *must* have hypotheses—good ones if possible; but bad ones are better than none at all."

NOTES

1. P. N. Rosenstein-Rodan, "Notes on the Theory of the 'Big Push'," in Theodore Morgan, George W. Betz, and N. K. Choudhry, *Readings in Economic Development*, p. 143. The author quotes the first two sentences from MIT, Center for International Studies, *The Objectives of the United States Economic Assistance Programs*, p. 70.

2. *Ibid.*, pp. 143-144. For a discussion of the differences between pecuniary and technological external economies, see Tibor Scitovsky, "Two Concepts of External Economies," in Morgan *et al.*, *Readings in Economic Development*, pp. 119-128; Francis M. Bator, "The Anatomy of Market Failure," *Quarterly Journal of Economics*, Vol. 72, No. 3, August 1958, pp. 351-367.

3. Rosenstein-Rodan, "Notes on the Theory of the 'Big Push'," p. 145. When reading this quotation, it will be helpful to remember that an economic good is indivisible to the degree that the economic value of a fraction of it is less than the arithmetic value of that fraction. Arithmetically, two halves equal one, but two half-blast-furnaces are hardly equal to one. For an excellent analysis of the controversy among economists in the field of resource allocation, see Hollis B. Chenery, "Comparative Advantage and Development Policy," in Morgan *et al.*, *Readings in Economic Development*, pp. 158-186.

4. For some interesting observations on the different organizations that can be actively involved in resource mobilization at the beginning of industrialization, see Alexander Gerschenkron, *Economic Backwardness in Historical Perspective*, pp. 13-16, 90-118.

5. Perhaps it will never be possible to support this assumption with adequate empirical evidence. The best data are available for England, and they do indicate growth in per capita product from the end of the seventeenth century. (See Phyllis Deane and W. A. Cole, *British Economic Growth, 1688-1959*, pp. 80-81.) On Japan, there is strong inferential evidence to support the proposition that there was growth in per capita product through the last half of the Tokugawa era. (The evidence presented in Thomas C. Smith, *The Agrarian Origins of Modern Japan*, [on the increases in land under cultivation, new varieties of crops, and the expansion in commerce and manufacturing during a period of relatively stable population], supports this contention.) For China, the population growth was so great that it is difficult to conclude that there was any significant increase in product per capita. (See below, pp. 321-325.) On France, the authorities are not in agreement. We tend to follow C. E. Labrousse, *La crise de l'économie française à la fin de l'ancien régime et au début de la revolution*.

6. Leonid Hurwicz, "Optimality and Informational Efficiency in Resource Allocation Processes," in Kenneth J. Arrow *et al.*, *Mathematical Methods in the Social Sciences*, pp. 27-46; "Conditions for Economic Efficiency of Centralized and Decentralized Structures," in Gregory Grossman (ed.), *Value and Plan: Economic Calculation and Organization in Eastern Europe*, pp. 162-175.

7. Hurwicz, "Conditions for Economic Efficiency of Centralized and Decentralized Structures," p. 169.

8. *Ibid.*, pp. 169-170.

9. Hurwicz, "Optimality and Informational Efficiency in Resource Allocation Processes," pp. 36-41. The perfectly competitive economy is decentralized in precisely this sense.

10. Hurwicz, personal communication. It might be noted further that the decision environment is decomposable when externalities, "public" goods, indi-

visibilities, and increasing returns are absent. (A "public" good is present if an additional customer can be served with no additional output of a good or service. For example, an additional consumer of music from a radio station may be served with no additional output from the station.)

11. William H. Pierce, "Redundancy in Computers," *Scientific American,* Vol. 210, No. 2, February 1964, pp. 103-105.

12. The iterative feedback system with short time lag has many of the characteristics of *incrementalism,* as discussed in Robert A. Dahl and Charles E. Lindblom, *Politics, Economics, and Welfare,* pp. 82-85. For further treatment, see Albert O. Hirschman and Charles E. Lindblom, "Economic Development, Research and Development, Policy Making: Some Converging Views," *Behavioral Science,* Vol. 7, No. 2, April 1962, pp. 211-222. It must be emphasized that the characteristics of decentralized decision making being treated in this section hold only if the environment is decomposable.

13. It is important to draw attention to what these two propositions involve methodologically. Our basic conceptual framework established two main categories of analysis—functions of government (or, more generally, the pattern of alternative concrete structures that may contribute to the satisfaction of any given functional requisite) and procedures of governing. There is no logical link between these two categories of analysis; that is, one cannot logically derive any characteristics of the decision-making procedures related to any functional requisite simply by knowing the pattern of concrete structures that in any given case contributes to the satisfaction of any given functional requisite, or vice versa. We do, however, anticipate that there is a set of empirical propositions that will link these two categories of analysis, and that this set will be a significant part of a more general theory.

14. The range of alternative ownership and allocation models is, of course, far greater than we have suggested. See P. J. D. Wiles, *The Political Economy of Communism,* especially Chapters 1 and 4. We have greatly benefited from our conversations with Robert Merrill, whose work on the early introduction of Western techniques of production among the New Zealand Maori suggests a model for decentralized, public resource allocation in a traditional economy which is beginning to modernize.

15. The use of the term "societal goal" in this context does not do full justice to our theoretical framework. Three comments should be made: (1) Technically, within our framework the problem of the "alignment" of individual and societal goals is a problem of the cultural system and not of the social system. It represents an aspect of the environment of the social system to which the social system must adjust in a particular way if take-off is to be achieved. (2) In our framework the possibility is held open that the state of the social system at a future time may be the result of certain unanticipated consequences and thus may bear little relationship to the explicit societal goals at the beginning of a period of change. Therefore, in addition to being concerned about the "alignment" of individual and societal goals when a societal goal is rapid economic growth, we must also take into account the possibility that rapid economic growth may be achieved even when it is not an explicit societal goal. (3) When we speak of the "alignment" of individual and societal goals, we do not mean to imply that this demands an acceptance on the part of individuals of these goals, or even a common perception of them.

16. Fred W. Riggs is a social theorist who is continually modifying and improving his theories. While this is certainly an admirable quality, it does complicate the problem of adequate citation. The best statement of his position from the point of view of this study is contained in an unpublished monograph, *Social Change and Political Development,* especially Part I, pp. 13-24.

17. *Ibid.*, p. 16.

18. Everett E. Hagen, *On the Theory of Social Change*, p. 28-29.

19. This proposition must be interpreted in relationship to the previous discussion of mobility. See below, pp. 318-319, 329, 331.

20. See, for example, Henry Rosovsky, *Capital Formation in Japan, 1868-1940*, pp. 23-26.

21. At later stages, we hypothesize, there are much more severe restraints upon the limits of the government's contribution to goal attainment through involvement in resource mobilization.

22. E. Adamson Hoebel, *The Law of Primitive Man*.

23. There are perhaps some exceptions to the proposition that the most prestigious groups in a traditional society are not as oriented toward saving and investment as are the merchants and manufacturers. But it should be noted that even in England, where the nobility and gentry did make significant investments, they frequently borrowed their capital from merchants.

24. Rosenstein-Rodan, "Notes on the Theory of the 'Big Push'," p. 149.

25. Attention must be called to some of the theoretical implications of these propositions. We recognize that universalistic (as opposed to particularistic) criteria of recruitment are an important feature of a modern society. It is our contention, however, that in the traditional stage of economic development rigid particularistic criteria for recruitment into the society's most prestigious positions may actually facilitate the achievement of take-off. In other words, we are suggesting that an open-class system (like that of France and China), even though it may appear to be more modern because of the greater use of universalistic criteria, may inhibit a society in its important first steps along the path to modernization. During the take-off period, however, the situation changes. At this stage, it becomes important for the entrepreneurial roles to take on added prestige and for universalistic criteria to be employed in the recruitment of occupants for these roles. It also becomes necessary for the government, through such devices as the financing of public education, to provide opportunities for people to acquire the skills they need in order to occupy the roles that are important in the economy.

26. Kingsley Davis and Judith Blake, "Social Structure and Fertility: An Analytic Framework," in Seymour M. Lipset and Neil J. Smelser (eds.), *Sociology: The Progress of a Decade*, pp. 356-377.

27. P. T. Ho, *Studies on the Population of China, 1368-1953*, pp. 167-195.

28. Smith, *The Agrarian Origins of Modern Japan*, pp. 97-101.

29. There is some disagreement here with Taeuber, who holds that the Japanese population did not grow because it was at the Malthusian limit. (See Irene B. Taeuber, *The Population of Japan*, pp. 20-23.)

30. Marcel R. Reinhard and André Armengaud, *Histoire général de la population mondiale*, graphique 17, p. 157.

Epilogue

ALTHOUGH THE EXPLORATORY STUDY HAS NOW BEEN COMPLETED and the hypotheses have been developed, we have in a sense just reached the beginning. It is only the beginning because it was our intention to develop hypotheses worthy of being tested in field research in contemporary developing countries. There are, of course, some scholars who argue that the early industrialization experiences of the previous century are so different from those of the present day that hypotheses derived from a study of the former are not particularly relevant to the latter. If one is interested exclusively in the policy implications of research in development, this view has some merit. However, we are primarily interested in trying to develop a general theory on the political basis of economic development. In science that does not emphasize the applied side, generality is a desideratum, and hence we are interested in a theory that will apply to both historical and contemporary cases.

This point is so important that it deserves brief elaboration. A theory of economic development would be a special theory of social change, while a theory concerning the political basis of economic development would be a special theory of economic development. It is at this last level of generality that we are aiming. Although it might be possible to develop subtheories applicable to historical and contemporary cases, respectively, we are not concerned with this problem at the present time. We recognize, of course, that a theory which applies to a limited class of contemporary developing countries will be of greater interest to political advisers who are immediately concerned with events in such countries than would a general theory of social change. But the scientist, in contrast, is more interested in a broader picture of social change.

A critic, even though he accepts this view, may still argue that since our hypotheses apply only to historical cases we have missed the mark. This criticism we are unable to answer at the present moment, and its validity will not be known until the proposed field research has been undertaken. Before we proceed any further, however, it will be worthwhile to examine the position of those who emphasize the difference between the historical and contemporary cases of modernization. Mason has presented such an argument very clearly. He makes three major points:

1. The technology which developing nations are able to borrow from the West is more capital-intensive and comes in larger minimal units than did the technology of a century or more ago. In an economy at the take-off stage today, externalities and indivisibilities are of greater consequence than they were in the eighteenth and nineteenth centuries.[1]

2. In the developing countries of the twentieth century, government stands in a different position as a source of funds for investment than it did in the nineteenth century. Not only is government able to mobilize resources through its tax power, but government securities are (except for direct investment) the major outlet for private savings. Moreover, whatever foreign aid may be available is usually funneled through some government agency.[2]

3. The people in developing countries have a vision of a better way of life economically. They can, in effect, sense the potentialities of their own future by looking at life in advanced countries. They may develop expectations to reach certain economic goals which are quite different from the popular expectations developed in eighteenth-century England and nineteenth-century Japan, and which require the vigorous participation of the government in economic matters (regardless, we might add, of the rationality of such participation).[3]

The existence of these factors leads Mason to conclude that centralized resource mobilization, resource allocation, and resource management by government must play a far more important role in contemporary societies than they did in the earlier cases.

If the prerequisites for take-off have not been met (which is the case in many developing countries today), the implication of our (untested) theory is that the government's contribution to the adaptive functional requisite should remain minimal. At this stage, there are activities that government should be undertaking, but they are related to the other functional requisites. Indeed, the hypotheses suggest that considerable government involvement in the adaptive area at this juncture is likely to delay development. To the degree that Mason and other scholars advocate a major government effort in economic planning and resource allocation for countries that have not yet satisfied the prerequisites for take-off, we have a contrary position. We simply argue that until certain conditions have been met, it will not be too rewarding to attempt to force the introduction of sophisticated techniques of industrial production. Some new technology may well be developed domestically or imported, but it should not be a technology requiring an elaborate, centralized decision-making structure.

But we do not mean to imply that the most efficacious way of achieving take-off in the twentieth century is to mimic in every detail the patterns established by Japan and England. We would not maintain, for example, that a society which does not have a system of primogeniture would have to introduce new inheritance laws and then wait for a hundred years before trying to introduce the techniques of industrial production. There may be alternative ways of achieving an initial concentration of wealth in the hands of people who are most likely to funnel it into industry. Other methods are also available for controlling the growth of population. The widespread use of intra-uterine devices of birth control, for example, may possibly accomplish this objective. We do suggest, however, that the introduction and wide dissemination of such techniques would require participation by government. In other words, we are hypothesizing that it is probably desirable for the government to make similar contributions to the satisfaction of the various requisites in the twentieth century as it did in the successful cases of take-off in the nineteenth century. But the procedures of governing—the manner in which the contribution is made—may very well differ.

Although we did not undertake a detailed analysis of the take-off stage within a proper exploratory research design, it seems appropriate to make a few preliminary comments about the possible similarity between nineteenth- and twentieth-century cases. The brief survey of Japan and England during take-off suggests that in this stage the contribution by government to the satisfaction of the adaptive and goal-attainment requisites should increase through its greater involvement in the process of resource mobilization and the process of resource allocation (but not resource management). This analysis, however, does not suggest the kind of deep government involvement in the economy that is advocated by Mason and others. Some of the important differences are worth noting. Mason's crucial point rests on the assumption that, compared with an earlier time, external economies and indivisibilities are more significant for present-day modernizing economies because of the nature of contemporary technology. While this is a factual question which cannot be examined in detail here, several questions may be raised. In comparison with the last century, the range of industries and the range of problems involving production and distribution to which an industrial technology can be applied are also far greater today. When one considers the enormously wide choice of industries to which a modern technology is applicable, it is difficult to assert flatly that the capital requirements are lumpier than they were a century ago. But even if the trend is in that direction, the numerous exceptions may be as significant as the trend.

There is, of course, little doubt that a steel mill today demands a larger initial capital investment than was required fifty or a hundred years ago. It is also likely that the amount of capital required for such a plant today would be extremely difficult to raise from private sources in most developing countries. There may be some doubt, however, that an economy at the beginning of the take-off period should be building a steel mill at all. This assertion is made despite the fact that it might be possible to cite, on a technological and economic basis, powerful reasons for constructing a massive steel complex. If such a plant is to be built in a contemporary developing area, we concede that it will probably have to be built, owned, and managed by the government. We also concede that it is *theoretically possible* to establish an institution like the autonomous public corporation, through which the government is able to own the means of production without having political considerations unduly hampering the management. But the *probability* that in a developing area such a sophisticated organization will be able to keep politics out of management is very small. In other words, we suggest that government ownership of large industrial complexes in developing countries will necessarily involve government deeply in the process of resource management, and that political considerations will tend to supersede economic criteria in the decision-making process. This situation is likely to result in levels of efficiency below those predicted by individuals who base their judgment entirely on economic and technological factors.

Perhaps it would be wiser to encourage the introduction of a much less capital-intensive technology. This would make it possible for decisions concerning resource management to be made through decentralized structures by private individuals, even though the government may have been involved in resource mobilization and resource management.

This alternative suggestion leads to another speculative observation. It may be that, even with all of the scientific and technological sophistication of the Western world, the technology most appropriate for developing societies is not yet available—indeed, has not even been invented. The present study suggests that in developing societies the constraints which the traditional social structure places upon the introduction of new forms of social organization are so great that it might be better in the long run to invent a technology which can be satisfactorily employed by existing structures or by structures that can be easily established, rather than to try to develop entirely new structures which are designed to employ available technology.[4]

This is a fundamentally different position from that of Mason, who in effect says: "Create in the developing areas the structures that are able to employ the advanced technology which the West has made available for import." We would emphasize the development of technology that, with a reasonable probability, can be made to work within the social structuring which is likely to exist or can be established in the developing areas. One of the main tasks of the social scientist is to determine the limits that the existing social structures place upon the range of possible changes in that social structuring.

In some respects, this book is a prolegomenon to a research proposal. We have indicated what we want to do, but we have not shown how we propose to do it. In indicating the type of research anticipated, we list as the first item on the research agenda the testing of the hypotheses which have been developed. We are not interested in further macro-studies for this purpose but prefer to develop research designs which will enable us to test each hypothesis. Perhaps it will be helpful if we explain our objectives somewhat more in detail. A major part of our conclusions turned on the hypothesis concerning the relative efficiency of centralized and decentralized decision structures. Although there is formal proof that under certain conditions a decentralized structure is more efficient than a centralized structure and that under other conditions the opposite is true, the proof assumes that specific factors remain constant. It assumes, for example, that entrepreneurial talent is equally available at both the local and central points. In some settings, however, this may not be the case; more talent might be available in the central structure than in the local structures.

This deficiency is to a large extent overcome in field settings, for it is possible to explore the effects of factors which are held constant in the formal proof. There is, for example, a developing country which has two different public-works programs. In one, the decision structure is very decentralized; in the other, operating in a different part of the country, the decision structure is highly centralized. Such a setting provides an intriguing field opportunity for examining the basic hypothesis dealing with the relative efficiency of centralized and decentralized decision making.

It is also possible to find developing countries that are adjacent and have somewhat similar cultural backgrounds but differing inheritance systems and/or different laws controlling social mobility. There are also developing countries that have changed their inheritance laws so as to replace equal distribution of property with rules of primogeniture. Areas such as these provide challenging settings for the testing of the hypotheses suggested by this study.

As a second item on the research agenda, more exploratory studies are needed to develop hypotheses concerning the take-off, the drive to modernity, and the modernity stages of economic development.

Future research, in other words, must have a dual emphasis: first, on the comprehensive exploratory study for the formulation of hypotheses; and, second, on the detailed experimental study to test the hypotheses. Both kinds of research involve the use of the comparative method and require that societies be selected for study, not because of any intrinsic interest in a given country, but in order to secure the desired variation in factors that cannot be manipulated directly.

NOTES

1. Edward S. Mason, *Economic Planning in Underdeveloped Areas: Government and Business*, pp. 46-47. Perhaps the most systematic attempt to compare nineteenth-century and twentieth-century cases of modernization is found in Simon Kuznets, "Underdeveloped Countries and the Pre-Industrial Phase in the Advanced Countries: An Attempt at Comparison," in *Proceedings of the World Population Conference*, pp. 947-969. This comparison, however, does not deal systematically with any of the political concerns that have been of interest in this monograph.

2. Mason, *Economic Planning in Underdeveloped Areas*, pp. 48-49.

3. *Ibid.*, pp. 47-48. The notion of a "demonstration effect" is not new in the literature of economic development. Marx himself referred to the peoples in nonindustrialized countries seeing the vision of their own future in the industrially developed states. For a contemporary comment, see Gottfried Haberler, "Critical Observations on Some Current Notions in the Theory of Economic Development," in Theodore Morgan, George W. Betz, and N. K. Choudhry, *Readings in Economic Development*, pp. 233-234.

4. See Richard C. Jordan, "New Techniques for Temperature Control of Perishable Goods in Transport and Storage Applicable to the Less Developed Areas," *Science, Technology and Development,* Vol. V, "Transportation," February 1963, pp. 120-133. Jordan's discussion of new techniques for the refrigeration of perishable goods in transit and storage draws attention to such techniques as the use of liquid gases as coolants. Although, on the basis of his primarily technical treatment of the problem, it is difficult to draw comparative economic conclusions, one might wish to explore the capital requirements of a system employing liquid nitrogen in comparison with an ice system or a salt and ice system, such as were developed in the United States years ago.

Two additional implications of Jordan's discussion are worth parenthetical comment: (1) The skill requirements for operating a liquid nitrogen system are quite different from those of an ice and salt system. The former requires highly skilled people in a central plant (which can serve a wide area) and a low level of skill on the part of people who are actually using the cooling equipment. The latter requires people of intermediate training, and the skill has to be widely disseminated throughout the system. The training problem for the operation of the nitrogen system is probably easier to solve in a developing country than is the training problem for the operation of the ice and salt system. (2) The potential returns from capital invested in food preservation might be very great indeed because of the enormous food loss due to spoilage in tropical areas, the overconsumption that occurs during harvest seasons, and the indirect loss that results from sickness caused by the consumption of spoiled food.

The Changing Soviet Polity, 1930-1964

IN OUTLINING THE CONCEPTUAL FRAMEWORK IN CHAPTER 2, WE AD-
vanced the claim that it can be applied to the analysis of any society
at any stage of economic development. The empirical analysis thus
far, however, has dealt only with the traditional economies of four
societies and briefly with the early part of the take-off stage in two
of these societies. It was not the purpose of this study to explore
every stage of economic development, but the analytical framework
will probably take on added meaning if we can indicate, at least in a
tentative way, how it might be applied to a society at later stages.

For this purpose we have selected the Soviet Union during the
period from 1930 to 1964. The analysis is based on the assumption
that from 1930 until the early 1950's the Soviet economy was in the
drive to modernity stage of economic growth, and that by the mid-
1950's the economy had begun to exhibit characteristics that, according to our definition, are indicative of a modern economy.[1] If
our framework has general applicability, it should call attention to
some important differences in the functions of government and in the
procedures of governing during these two periods. The kind of comparison we are making in this appendix, it must be observed, differs
from that undertaken in the previous chapters. Instead of comparing
several countries in the same stage of economic development, we are
comparing certain features of political and economic organization in
one society at different stages. In order to underline certain conclusions, however, we shall suggest some comparisons between the Soviet Union and the United States during similar periods of economic
development.

For purposes of analysis, we are assuming that the Soviet economy
from the late 1920's until the early 1950's successfully passed
through the drive to modernity stage of economic development and

must, of course, have satisfied the requisites for that stage. We further assume that the Soviet economy is moving well into the modern stage, at this writing (1965), and is beginning to satisfy the requisites for the modern stage.

FUNCTIONS OF GOVERNMENT AND PROCEDURES OF GOVERNING, 1930-1953

By almost any definition, a totalitarian society is a society in which the government makes a major contribution to the satisfaction of *all* of the functional requisites. Although there are few differences in the functions of government in the two periods under consideration here, the differences that do emerge are significant. We shall begin this analysis by reviewing briefly the wide-ranging functions of government in Stalin's Russia.

Functions of Government

In any Communist society, the government, as owner and manager of most of the means of production, will make a major contribution to the satisfaction of the adaptive functional requisite. The Soviet economy of the 1930's and 1940's was a rigid command economy. In accordance with a centrally designed plan, the government laid down detailed instructions concerning what was to be produced and in what quantities, the production processes to be employed, and the prices to be charged. It was thus deeply involved in the processes of resource allocation and resource management.

Similarly, in the satisfaction of the goal-attainment functional requisite, the government was the primary structure involved in the process of resource mobilization. Indeed, the political authorities set about to control or even suppress any nongovernmental structure (such as a religious organization) that might claim to set goals for the society as a whole and sought to mobilize resources in an effort to achieve those goals. Under the direction of the Party oligarchy, the government established explicit societal goals, outlining in its plan the objectives that were to be sought in virtually every field of endeavor.

The government also made a major contribution to the satisfaction of the pattern-maintenance functional requisite, being involved in the processes of social control, of enculturation, and of tension management. The police, the army, the ministries or committees of control, and similar agencies were diligent in their efforts to compel obedience to the official norms and to impose severe punishments upon violators. The political authorities, however, did not rely solely upon the instruments of raw coercion to force an unwilling citizenry to comply with their edicts. They developed, under tight state control, a system of formal education through which the young people, from nursery school onward, were indoctrinated with the values deemed praiseworthy by the Soviet elite (the enculturation process). The government was also involved in the process of tension management. Prolonged structural unemployment was, by and large, eliminated (or made less obvious), and pension plans and schemes for medical care were initiated and administered by the government.

In Stalin's Soviet society, where so many diverse activities had to be coordinated and geared into a unified set of patterns, the government made a major contribution to the satisfaction of the integrative functional requisite. The national economic plan—which specified the source of supplies for each producer as well as the outlet for the commodities he produced—made the government the most important concrete structure in integrating roles differentiated by occupational specialization. The government was also deeply involved in the integration of roles differentiated on the basis of prestige when it poured resources into free, public education. More spectacularly, the political authorities could precipitate the rise or fall of particular individuals or social groups by intensifying the purge or by regulating admissions to Party membership. It could affect the relative position in society of large groups of people by drastically adjusting the wage scales, by instituting forced loans, and by confiscating property directly or by changing the value of the currency.

Even this brief review indicates how the government in Stalin's Russia made a major contribution to the satisfaction of all four of the functional requisites. More interesting for the point of view of this study, however, are the special procedures of governing which were employed in the Soviet Union during the 1930's and 1940's.

Procedures of Governing

In any dictatorial form of government, one ordinarily expects to find the authority structure of policy making highly resolved. Although the perfect monolithic state, where all decisions are made by a single individual, is largely a figment in the minds of theorists and polemicists, it must be admitted that there was much in Stalin's Russia to give rise to the image.[2]

In the political realm, it is widely understood that major policy decisions were made either by Stalin himself or in collaboration with his colleagues in the Party's Politburo/Presidium; Communist organizations lower in the scale were little more than administrative mechanisms in the hands of the central authorities in Moscow, whose decisions they were expected to carry out in detail and with dispatch.

In the economic sphere, policy decisions followed similar centralized patterns. Political leaders in the Politburo/Presidium determined the basic priorities of the economic plan, that is, what proportion of the economic product should be allocated to the armed services, for investment in heavy industry, and for the development of consumer-goods industries. After the general priorities had been established, the Communist leaders turned over the information to the Council of Ministers in the government which worked out the broad outlines of the economic plan. These outlines were then submitted to a national economic agency called *Gosplan,* a "general staff" of economists and planners who were responsible for translating the general outlines and statements of priorities into a detailed economic blueprint for the entire society. After consulting with regional and local functionaries, Gosplan proceeded to draw up plans which specified not only the production goals for the important nation-wide industries, but also the targets for each firm within a given industry. In other words, for the significant economic enterprises in the country, Gosplan collaborated with lower government agencies to determine such matters as the type and sources of their supplies, the amount and kinds of labor to be used, the prices to be charged for their products, the methods of distribution to be employed, and the way in which profits were to be expended.

Under the Stalin regime, the Council of Ministers embraced a number of industrial ministries, each of which was headed by a minister who was in charge of all of the operations of his particular industry throughout the entire country. In this capacity, the minister had authority to issue orders to the important individual firms and other organizations that were related to his industry, regardless of the section of the country in which they happened to be located. The local plant director was given little administrative discretion in the management of his enterprise, and regional Party officials had only a small voice in economic matters involving industry, although they played a more important role in handling agricultural affairs.

To make policy is one matter; to have policies faithfully and fully executed is another. After he had firmly established himself at the summit of Soviet power, Stalin employed a number of bureaucracies to implement his policies, and he devised a number of techniques to make these instruments of enforcement reliable and effective, if not entirely efficient. There were four major, distinct but interlocking hierarchies that had emerged by the mid 1930's—the Communist Party apparatus, the government or state bureaucracy, the police organization, and the military establishment. Each of these bureaucracies had a general area of competence; all were ultimately responsible to Stalin, who manipulated them by controlling the leader in charge of each structure. Within some of these organizations there were sub-bureaucracies that were responsible to the topmost echelon of a given hierarchy. For example, the Party apparatus had, in addition to the lineup of Communist secretaries, an organization of control commissions which checked the operation of the Party bureaucracy. Similarly, the hierarchy of state functionaries was under the watchful eye of officials both in the Commissariat/Ministry of Soviet Control and in the Procuracy. The four great power bureaucracies also operated through and were partially checked by mass organizations, such as the trade unions, cooperatives, youth groups, and other tightly directed societies. But a consideration of these factors is not necessary to the general argument of this analysis. The purpose will be served simply by analyzing the techniques Stalin employed to maintain the four major organizations as faithful executors of his policies. We can begin by discussing three significant characteristics of these bureaucracies and/or characteristics of the relationships among them.

First, it should be observed that, although each of the hierarchies of power had a general sphere of competence, the lines of jurisdiction between them were ambiguously drawn and the boundaries of their responsibility were dimly marked. This situation was due in part to the nature of the tasks assigned to them. The police, for example, shared responsibility with the army in security matters, and through the management of certain projects manned by forced labor they engaged in economic activities of the type which usually fell under the administration of the state bureaucracy. Through the Commissariat/ Ministry of Soviet Control and the Procuracy, the government bureaucracy had important surveillance and law-enforcement tasks which brought it into the domain of the police agencies. The Party hierarchy, of course, enjoyed such a broadly defined sphere of competence that its activities to some degree overlapped those of virtually every other organization. The blurred and confused lines of jurisdiction were a result not only of the overlapping nature of the assigned tasks but also of the duplicating roles of individual functionaries who in some cases held posts in more than one hierarchy. When this happened, the people involved had at least two chains of command through which they could receive orders and send in reports. Thus, at times it was not entirely clear in what capacity an individual might be acting.

In Chapter 2, we used the term *clarification* to identify the situation in which the jurisdiction of the parallel bureaucracies is rigorously defined. Using this terminology, we would say that the relationships among the various bureaucracies in the Soviet Union under Stalin were markedly *unclarified*.

In addition to the purposive overlapping of jurisdiction among the four hierarchies, there was designed ambiguity in the authority and responsibility of offices within a given bureaucracy. To be sure, a functionary would be aware of some of the obvious tasks assigned to him, but he could never be entirely certain of what his responsibilities were. The "job description" of the Communist secretary in a factory, for example, was sufficiently vague so that it was difficult for him to know at what point his orders to "check" the operation of the factory would interfere with the "management" of the enterprise, an invasion he was ordinarily expected to avoid. Under these circumstances, the secretary might on one occasion be severely reprimanded by his superiors for having meddled in the affairs of the factory manager, and shortly thereafter be rebuked for his lack of diligence in uncovering weaknesses in the administration of the firm.[3] In other words, a functionary performing under ambiguous instructions in any of the bureaucracies was vulnerable to censure or even arrest for doing what he did not realize was forbidden, or for neglecting what he did not know was required.[4]

As significant as the obscure boundaries of competence among the major hierarchies and the ambiguous job descriptions of offices within the hierarchies was a third characteristic of these powerful bureaucracies: the important power relationships within and among them tended to be personal in nature. Personal allegiances to powerful or potentially powerful leaders tended to become crucial and, in evaluating an individual's performance, his superiors were likely to consider personal loyalty ahead of merit or achievement in office.[5]

Until his death in March 1953, Stalin was in personal command of this network of interlinked authorities. He attempted to preserve his position of dominance and to make sure that his policies would be carried out by pitting one organization against another, thereby stimulating competitive uncertainty among his chief subordinates while reserving ultimate decision making on major issues to himself. At the same time he made certain that he did not become entirely dependent upon a single hierarchy of power. The overlapping jurisdictions, the ambiguous specification of duties, and the ties of personal obligation enabled each organization to scrutinize the activities of the others and to report to Stalin and his henchmen any ineptitude or lack of diligence which might impede the march toward officially designated objectives.

With the various bureaucracies under his command, Stalin was able to shift his primary reliance from one hierarchy to another according to his diagnosis of the situation. During the purges in the late 1930's, for example, the police organization was employed to remove "undesirable" elements from the Party, the government agencies, and the army, but eventually the purge was directed against police officials themselves. While the regime was forced to depend upon the army during World War II, the demotion of a number of military heroes after the defeat of Germany and Japan signified a relative decline in the influence of the armed forces. Similarly, in 1952, the police apparatus had fallen within the orbit of criticism, while the appointment of leading officials from the state bureaucracy—especially from the economic agencies—to the enlarged Presidium of the Party marked their growing contribution. That economic planners and police officials sat in high Communist councils along with functionaries who had worked their way up through the Party apparatus was an indication of the multiple chains of command, each of which provided access to important positions of power in the Soviet system.

The patterns of organization and procedure of the Stalin dictatorship have often been compared with those of a large army under the control of a powerful general who selects the members of his general staff and operates through a network of rigidly structured subordinate commands. The analogy, however, is somewhat misleading, for the essential features of the Soviet system under Stalin appear more in contrast with than in resemblance to military organization. The Stalinist type of dictatorship is characterized by multiple chains of command rather than the single line of authority regarded as ideal in modern military organization. Moreover, in a military establishment the responsibilities attached to specific offices are specifically laid out, and the sphere of competence of any office is ideally regarded as inviolate. The bureaucracies in Stalin's Russia, on the other hand, were designed to enable top political leaders to bypass the formal chains of command. The dictator, for example, could use the hierarchy of police agencies to intervene in the operations of the Party apparatus or the government bureaucracy, or he could employ the military hierarchy to invade the jurisdictional realm of the police. It was also possible for him to circumvent a given chain of command by utilizing the intricate network of personal connections and allegiances.

In using these enforcement instruments, Stalin and his lieutenants had a wide range of techniques at their disposal to insure that their directives would be followed. For example, the political authorities were in a position to influence the hierarchy of orders and prestigious positions in the society, and individuals who refused to comply with official demands could fall from positions of high status as rapidly as the subservient could rise.

In this analysis we are especially interested in the techniques used to secure compliance with government edicts that were aimed to increase rapidly the levels of industrial productivity. At the beginning of the industrialization drive, the Soviet regime instituted an incentive system, which involved a vicious combination of negative sanctions and positive rewards—the "stick and the carrot." Probably few regimes in history have made as much use of the stick to compel obedience as did Stalin and his henchmen. Its use was made evident through the arbitrary powers exercised by the police, the ruthlessness of the periodic purges, the brutalities of compulsory collectivization, the forced labor camps, and the directed migration of minority peoples. In agriculture, which was marked out to provide the bulk of the capital for the forced-draft industrialization, the regime forced the peasants to sell much of their produce at minimum prices (perhaps below opportunity costs), and it drafted farm labor into industry.

Stalin's administration was especially characterized by the use of coercive methods to insure labor discipline in the factories and workshops. As World War II approached, such behavior as absenteeism, tardiness, slovenly work, changing jobs without the permission of the plant directors, and even the accidental damaging of machinery were listed as criminal acts for which severe punishment was often meted out. The factory manager, too, was not immune, since the failure of his enterprise to achieve its production goals could lead to charges of gross negligence in administration. By the time of Stalin's death, a large proportion of Soviet workers and peasants had probably either experienced the "stick" themselves or had relatives or friends who had suffered the wrath of the regime. Those who were found guilty of criminal acts, of course, were not lost to the labor force; millions were shipped to the forced labor camps where they were compelled to drain their energy into the construction of the state's grand projects.[6]

All was not coercion and terror, however. The carrot was dangled before the noses of managers, workers, and to some degree the peasants. Material rewards and social prestige were granted to those who were industrious and systematic in carrying out their assignments. Under this incentive system, separate industries and particular tasks within an industry were graded and differentially rewarded in accordance with the priorities established by the regime. The system, moreover, was based for the most part upon the *quantity* of output realized within a set span of time. In addition to such perquisites as housing, the use of an automobile, and allowances for travel, the manager of an enterprise who had exceeded its production norms received lucrative bonuses for himself and his administrative staff; successful managers in some industries were able to double their ordinary salaries. By the same token, most factory workers were employed under the "piecework" system and were paid higher wages when they overfulfilled their output quotas. Rates were set so that highly skilled laborers would earn three or four times more than their less skilled colleagues. In the countryside, the peasants too were paid according to the type of task and their level of performance, but the low prices the collective farms were given for their produce tended to make the general wage scales much lower than they were in the factories and workshops. Stalin's incentive system did not as a rule distribute added remuneration widely among the working population. The Stakhanovite workers, for example, constituted a relatively small elite, whose incomes were far in excess of the pay received by ordinary folk.

In general, then, Stalin's formula for stimulating productive effort was to deal harshly with those who were lackadaisical, negligent, or otherwise did not perform well, and to reward those who produced in quantity. The rewards, of course, did not permit luxurious living except for the favored few. Consumer goods were usually very scarce. The standard of living for the vast majority of citizens was low. Failure to meet his output norms probably made it difficult for an ordinary worker to provide adequate supplies of food and clothing for himself and his family. This incentive system was an important factor in enabling the regime to concentrate upon its priorities and in stimulating the industrial labor force, a significant portion of which had been recruited from the rural areas and was not accustomed to the routine and discipline of the factory system.

Conclusions

Stalin's dictatorship will long be remembered for its cruelty and terror. But in the analysis of the present study, this observation is rather beside the point. We must recognize that it was as successful economically as it was reprehensible morally. From the early 1930's until the death of Stalin, average economic growth rates of approximately five per cent per capita annually were maintained without interruption, except for the period of the German occupation. Such rates of growth over a substantial period of time were until more recently unparalleled in the world's economic history.[7] Thus, we have no alternative but to conclude that in the case of the USSR the political requisites for the drive to modernity stage were well satisfied by a government that assumed major responsibility for satisfying all of the functional requisites and which centralized to a high degree all of the significant and many of the minor decisions in a highly resolved authority structure of policy making. The mammoth bureaucracies with overlapping jurisdictions, each checking the others, might have appeared to be inefficient, but they nevertheless served their purpose in carrying out the orders of the regime without at the same time gaining sufficient strength to be able to challenge the dictator himself. The liberal use of raw coercion and terror and a system of positive rewards that held out promise to many but granted returns to only a few proved successful in creating a hard-working and disciplined labor force. The Soviet experience suggests that an economy organized and operated on principles that are very different from those of a capitalist economy can meet the requisites for the drive to modernity stage of economic development. We will argue, however, that the requisites for the modern stage differ in significant ways, and what appears to have been reasonably successful in Stalin's Russia may be self-defeating in the society of his successors.

FUNCTIONS OF GOVERNMENT AND PROCEDURES
OF GOVERNING, 1953-1964

By the end of the Stalin era, the economy of the Soviet Union was beset by serious problems, some of which had been visible in rudimentary form for some time. Agricultural production was lagging badly, reflecting the low priority it had had in the general scheme of Soviet investment and planning. In the industrial sector of the economy, the highly centralized planning machinery often turned out directives that failed to take account of the unique problems of the local areas, sometimes resulting in ludicrous inefficiencies which the local plant management clearly recognized but could not ameliorate because of its limited authority. There were indications, too, that problems of inter-industry supply were growing more frequent and more severe and no longer yielded to ordinary types of solutions. That the Soviet economy was undergoing serious strain was indicated in 1956-1957 when the control figures of the sixth Five-Year Plan had to be scaled down and the plan itself eventually scrapped.

In the years that followed, Soviet economists began to examine the working mechanism of their economic machine, and they pointed out a number of weaknesses. There was a need, many felt, for objective measures to gauge the efficiency of production. Some specialists stressed the importance of revising the system of incentives. Of even greater significance was the demand of several prominent economists that a more efficient balance be struck between production and consumption by paying greater heed to the needs and demands of the potential purchaser. All of these problems have been given some attention during the post-Stalin era, with the result that the regime has reorganized the economic structure on several occasions and has instituted a number of experiments in planning and factory administration, as well as in the distribution of certain types of commodities.

Within one decade after the death of Stalin, it was possible to observe significant changes in the functions of government and in the procedures of governing in the Soviet Union. By 1965, the structuring of the society and the procedures used in the formulation and enforcement of policies were in several important respects different from those that had prevailed in 1950. According to our analysis, the patterns that existed under Stalin did not meet the requisites of a modern economy, while the new patterns—if they become firmly entrenched—have a greater probability of doing so. The argument will perhaps be presented most effectively by treating, as a first step, changes in the functions of government as these become apparent through an analysis of reorganizations of the economy, and then by moving on to a consideration of modifications in the procedures of governing.

Functions of Government

Under Stalin's successors, the government of the USSR has continued to make a major contribution to the satisfaction of all four functional requisites. Worthy of consideration, however, are some of the changes in the contribution by government to the satisfaction of the adaptive and integrative requisites.

Reference has already been made to the main features of industrial organization under Stalin. The planning and administration of the economy was centralized in Moscow, where each major industry was headed by a powerful minister who was a member of the Council of Ministers. A minister who was in charge of a given industry managed a huge horizontal monopoly, which embraced all of the firms in that industry. Also under the jurisdiction of his ministry was a network of service and supply facilities so that the factories and other installations would not be dependent upon other ministries for certain ancillary services. Under this system, the manager of an enterprise was regarded as an administrative employee of the ministry, who was bound by the directives from Moscow, being allowed little administrative discretion in the operation of the concern.[8]

All of the major and many of the minor decisions were bucked up by the hierarchy, and the ministries in Moscow were often threatened with burial in the avalanche of paperwork which flowed in from the provinces. Delays were frequent both in making decisions and in relaying them to the local managers. There was also a tendency for the central authorities to respond to specific local problems with general decrees which ignored the unique local conditions that may have given rise to the problems in the first place.

From the viewpoint of this study the problems of inter-industry supply were of particular consequence. The central plan made provision for the transfer of the products of one industrial ministry to the various enterprises that needed them and which fell under the jurisdiction of other ministries. This complex pattern of organization created difficult problems of procurement which can be illustrated by a simple example. If the supply of copper wire delivered to a tractor factory was inadequate for the number of tractors being manufactured at the plant, the manager was not entitled to negotiate directly with the firm producing the needed item, even though it might be located nearby. Instead, he would have to send his requisition up through the chain of command so that it would eventually reach the ministerial echelon. When the manager's request for more wire came up for action, an official in the minister's office would have to get in touch with the ministry that was in charge of the plants that were producing copper wire, and through this agency he would attempt to get delivery of the necessary supplies. Needless to say, a factory manager who was forced to run the hurdles through this bureaucratic maze encountered many frustrating delays. Small wonder that he was tempted to set up his own facility for producing wire, regardless of the economic cost, or that he was prompted to use his "influence" or to enter into illegal barter in an effort to secure the supplies and keep his assembly line in operation.

Stalin's heirs began to experiment with fresh solutions for their economic problems in 1955, after Malenkov's resignation as Chairman of the Council of Ministers, when they proceeded to transfer huge segments of industry to the administrative authority of the fifteen republics. At that time, a substantial number of economic enterprises were shifted from the direct operational control of the Moscow authorities, but the basic production units continued to operate within the framework of the ministerial system.

A more drastic reorganization of industry occurred in 1957. This was in part an outgrowth of Khrushchev's struggle with the so-called "anti-Party faction," whose main base of strength was in powerful industrial ministries in Moscow. Although the political aspects of this reform are important in a study of the succession struggle, they are largely outside the scope of this analysis, which must be focused upon the economic content of the reorganization. In May 1957, at the behest of Khrushchev, the Supreme Soviet enacted a statute which replaced the majority of the heavy industrial ministries with slightly more than 100 regional economic councils (*sovnarkhozes*). Each economic council was divided into specialized branch and operational directorates and supervised, within the confines of the national economic plan, the working of the major factories and construction enterprises within the region. After the general outline of the national plan had been drawn up by the political and economic leaders in

Moscow, the economic council was authorized to consult with the managers of its enterprises and then to prepare a preliminary version of the region's plan to be sent on to the authorities at the republic level. This initial plan for the region could, of course, be modified and set in final form by the superior economic agencies. Once the final control figures had been decided upon, however, the *sovnarkhoz* was responsible for seeing to it that the targets were met by the enterprises under its supervision. It had some discretion in determining how the quotas could best be realized, and it had a fairly wide range of administrative choice in directing any enterprises that were not included in the official plan. The economic councils were given authority to appoint factory managers, to shift personnel between enterprises, to allocate and redistribute materials and supplies among them, to alter the quotas of a particular establishment, and to arrange the delivery of raw materials and finished products to other sections of the country. They were also authorized to encourage the introduction of new machinery, processes, and techniques into their factories and workshops. Within a short time after the enactment of this reorganization, enterprises operating under the direction of the regional economic councils were producing 74 per cent of the industrial output of the country and employing 73 per cent of the industrial workers.[9]

The 1957 reorganization was no panacea for the economic ills of the country. If it helped alleviate some problems of inter-industry supply and made the decision-making apparatus somewhat more responsive to local differences, it also created new problems of *inter-regional* supply. Shortly after the reorganization, the Moscow rulers began to detect "parochial tendencies" among the *sovnarkhozes,* which tended to place their own needs ahead of their obligations to other territories in the commonweal. According to the complaints which were voiced, some *sovnarkhoz* officials were absorbed in trying to make their own regions self-sufficient, and were inclined to delay or even to avoid shipping materials to other regions, despite their obligations under the national plan to make these deliveries.

In light of this developing autarchy and "localism," the regime has at various times restructured the planning and administrative machinery in an effort to bring about better coordination and to make the local units more responsive to the demands of the center. In 1960, for example, a coordinating *sovnarkhoz,* superior to the small regional *sovnarkhozes,* was established at the republic level in three of the large republics (the R.S.F.S.R., the Ukraine, and Kazakhstan), whose numerous regional *sovnarkhozes* had created problems of inter-regional relations.[10] If the republic *sovnarkhoz* in the R.S.F.S.R. was at all representative of the others, these new councils concerned themselves not only with coordinating the activities of the subordinate regional *sovnarkhozes* but also with filling in the details in the national plan, especially in the field of materials supply.

The establishment of republic *sovnarkhozes* in three republics proved to be only the first in a series of attempts to coordinate industrial activities over wider areas of coverage. The next step was taken in May 1961, when the regime set up 17—later increased to 18 —large economic regions. Embracing a number of ordinary regional *sovnarkhozes,* each of the new (and larger) economic regions, with two exceptions, had a planning and coordinating council which was to foster specialization in production and to help relate the work of the industrial branches and the regional *sovnarkhozes* to each other.[11]

The Soviet rulers proceeded to give their planning and administrative machinery another overhaul in November 1962 when they reduced the number of ordinary regional *sovnarkhozes* from more than 100 to about 40.[12] The four Central Asian republics, for example, were consolidated into one large economic region. At the same time, the regime established a Council of the National Economy—a *sovnarkhoz* at the All-Union level, called *Sovnarkhoz* USSR—which was to be responsible for carrying out the annual plan. Gosplan was given responsibility for long-term planning. As a result of this reorganization, the operation of the construction industry was taken away from the *sovnarkhozes* and given over to a revamped central agency, the USSR State Committee for Construction Affairs (*Gosstroi*). Special state committees were set up for the various branches of industry, and these assumed responsibility for the introduction of new machinery and production processes.

Another new organization, the Supreme Council of the National Economy, was created in March 1963 for the purpose of coordinating the work of the other central agencies.[13] At the same time, the regime reorganized a number of the state committees for branch administration and production, many of which appeared to resemble in some respects the old industrial ministries.

Thus, by 1965, the system of industrial planning and administration had experienced nearly a decade of almost continual reorganization and was structured according to the following pattern.[14] At the top, immediately responsible to the Council of Ministers, was the Supreme Council of the National Economy. This agency coordinated the work of the USSR Gosplan, the USSR Sovnarkhoz, the USSR Gosstroi, and the various branch and production state committees. Equipped with superior legal powers over other bodies, the Supreme Council was responsible for seeing to it that industrial quotas were met, that material, manpower, and investment resources were used efficiently, and that production costs were lowered.

The USSR Gosplan, a union-republic agency, was charged with formulating the country-wide plan on the basis of the plans that had been drawn up at the republic level. Attached to the central Gosplan was a number of state committees whose chairmen were members of the agency: the committees for Heavy, Power, and Transport Machine Building; Chemical and Petroleum Machine Building; Truck-and-Tractor and Farm Machine Building; and similar industrial organizations. These committees, in collaboration with Gosplan, were responsible for developing new technology in the specialized enterprises under their jurisdiction.

The USSR Sovnarkhoz, also a union-republic organ, was responsible for putting the economic plans into effect in the most efficient way, and for fulfilling the material and supply targets for the national economy. In order to achieve these objectives, it worked not only through the central ministries and agencies but also through the large inter-regional economic councils, the councils of ministers in the several republics, and the ordinary regional *sovnarkhozes*.

Another union-republic agency, the USSR State Committee for Construction Affairs, planned and carried out the major construction projects in the Soviet Union. Attached to it were such state committees as the building materials industry; civil construction and architecture; and construction, road, and communal machine building. Each republic, except those republics in Central Asia, had a ministry of construction which supervised the state trusts and administrations that did construction work on a contract basis.

Below these central agencies were the 18 major economic regions into which the country was divided.[15] Some of these regions embraced several republics, and each of them had an economic council or a planning agency which was concerned with the operation of enterprises and organizations within its area, approving and correcting their plans and supervising their production.

The three large republics, which included within their territory a number of major economic regions, had a supervisory economic council operating at the republic level, and its task was to coordinate the work of the councils within the boundaries of the republic. A few of the republics each constituted a single economic region, and in such a case the *sovnarkhoz* operated directly under the control of the republic council of ministers. The four Central Asian republics, as we have already observed, formed a single economic region, with an over-all *sovnarkhoz* working in a supervisory capacity. Similarly, three republics were united to form the Transcaucasus region.

Thus, in the years after 1957 the Soviet rulers instituted a number of major overhauls of their economic machine, searching for the proper blend of local autonomy and centralized controls. It is quite likely, however, that the problem of securing a "proper" balance between centralized and decentralized decision making cannot be solved simply by tinkering with the administrative structure and establishing another pattern of administrative organization. As a result of the experimentation with new planning agencies and operational councils, the Soviet economy was more administratively regionalized than it had been in Stalin's day, but trends toward recentralization appeared from time to time. The uncertain movement back and forth between the poles of centralism and localism led to great confusion and to overlapping boundaries of administrative jurisdiction. At a meeting of the Supreme Soviet in December 1964, a deputy from Leningrad cited the illustration of the Izhorsky Plant which was under the authority of nine state committees, four economic councils, and two state planning committees; no less than 70 different officials were entitled to issue orders to the firm. Such complex administrative arrangements, he pointed out, had required the executives from Leningrad enterprises to spend more than 500,000 hours on business trips to Moscow in order to discuss matters with central authorities.[16]

From 1957 to 1964, the attempts of the Soviet leaders to strike an appropriate balance between centralization and decentralization failed because, within the limits they set for themselves, there was no real solution to the problem. What they needed was either a mechanism that would provide central decision makers with all of the information necessary for rational planning and the means for processing the information efficiently, or some machinery that would link the goals of the local decision makers with those of the economy at large and provide local officials with the information necessary to achieve their goals. As will be indicated later, it is our contention that the first alternative is impossible in a modern economy. Initial steps in the direction of the second alternative were taken by the regime in 1964. Before we examine these important changes, it will be helpful to glance at some of the earlier discussion of economic matters which was taking place in the Soviet Union.

In the years following Stalin's death, Soviet economists had voiced some criticisms of the way in which the economy was being planned and managed. In 1962, many of them became less guarded in their suggestions of how the economic system might be improved, and a vigorous debate ensued over the substantive issues. Indeed, the press eventually opened its columns to the economists so that they might present their views, and then the editors invited comments from readers on the solutions proposed by the economic specialists.

Under the intellectual leadership of such economic experts as Yevsei G. Liberman, Vasily S. Nemchinov, and V. Cherniavski, industrial planners and business executives at various levels began to agitate for radical changes in the basic approach to planning. Some of the major suggestions were the following:

1. There must be adopted a sensitive indicator of economic performance which can be applied to plants and factories. Such an indicator must take account of all costs of operation, including interest charges on the capital that has been provided by the government. Liberman particularly argued that profit, calculated in relation to fixed and working capital, is the best index of economic performance and should be accepted throughout the Soviet economy.[17]

2. Capital should be invested in those areas where the payoff is likely to be the greatest. Unnecessary investments in an enterprise—such as the needless stockpiling of machinery and materials—should be penalized.[18]

3. There should be introduced a flexible decision system which will respond sensitively to consumer demand and which will reflect scarcities of supply.[19]

4. A wider range of operational responsibility must be granted at the local and factory levels, since certain types of industrial enterprise do not perform efficiently under centralized planning. Factory managers, for example, should be given a range of choice in determining whether their bonus funds should be expended for salaries, apartments for workers, or new machinery and industrial techniques. Nemchinov put the matter in this way:

No superior agency can know the internal production resources and conditions as well as the enterprise itself does. With centralized planning, it is therefore particularly important to observe the degree of centralization necessary for ensuring enough scope for lower-level planning and local initiative. And no increase in the number of plan indicators will ensure rational economic relations between the center and the localities, between central planning agencies and the enterprises.[20]

He went on to suggest that plants should send in bids to the superior planning committee, which would then grant the contract to the factory that is able to promise the most efficient production on the most favorable terms. Factories, on the other hand, would be permitted to refuse to produce certain commodities if the directors felt that there were more profitable ways of employing their resources.

One of the reasons for this suggestion was the recognition that, with the increased availability of consumer goods, the consumer had acquired new wants and more discriminating tastes. Some commodities that had been produced during the mad scramble to meet purely quantitative targets remained unsold on the warehouse shelves, even after extensive advertising campaigns. To remedy this problem some economists were suggesting that production should be tied directly to consumer demand—that certain goods under certain circumstances should be freely bought and sold.[21]

All of these developments—the concern with objective indicators of economic performance, the enunciation of the need for a decision system that would both reflect relative scarcities and respond to consumer demand, the desire for an incentive system that would provide the highest rewards for those whose investment contributed most to the total economy, and the recognition that certain crucial information was peculiarly available to enterprise management—pointed in the direction of a solution which was for the Soviet Communists a radical one: the introduction of a market system to aid in the making of difficult economic decisions.

Although it was possible to detect as early as 1958 rudimentary price-making markets operating in the interstices of Soviet economic life, a dramatic step was taken in mid-1964. The political and economic leaders authorized an experiment in local planning and marketing in two large clothing firms, the Bolshevichka (Bolshevik) production association in Moscow and the Mayak (Beacon) association in Gorky.[22] Under this new scheme, the two establishments formulated their own production plans on the basis of orders and contracts negotiated with retail trade organizations. The contracts provided for the quantity, quality, style, and delivery schedules of the finished product, and the directors of the associations bore full responsibility for carrying out the terms of their agreements. They also contracted directly for their raw materials and other supplies, and they enjoyed considerable autonomy over wage matters and the distribution of bonuses. The officials of these firms informed the economic councils of their planning decisions, and their report indices were confined to the proportion of output *sold* on orders and the percentage of profit. By the autumn of 1964, the regime had signaled its approval of the methods of operation in these two enterprises by announcing that the experiment had been a marked success.

This was the cue for the new form of local administration to be extended to other firms.[23] In a matter of weeks, the system had been introduced on a large scale in the textile and shoe and leather trades, and it was anticipated that in less than a year one-third of the enterprises in these fields—especially those in the major cities—would be operating under the scheme. This meant that, contrary to the rigidly centralized practices of the Stalin period, hundreds of Soviet factories would then gear their production to consumer demand as reflected by trade orders, they would purchase their raw materials as they chose, they would negotiate their prices with retail trade associations, they would fix their own wage and bonus funds, and they would gauge their efficiency on the basis of the output they were able to sell and the percentage of profit they were able to make. If the present trend is permitted to continue, the innovations in local management will be extended to other important branches of the consumer-goods industry, and possibly even to other sectors of the economy.[24]

These developments in the industrial sector of the economy were paralleled to some extent in agriculture. During the period from 1953 to 1958, the agricultural policies of the post-Stalin rulers fitted into a reasonably consistent pattern. In the years from 1958 to 1963, however, the field of agriculture was hit by frequent reorganizations and "crash" programs which reflected vacillation and sudden shifts in emphasis. Not until 1963-1964 did the regime show signs of returning to programs more congenial with those instituted during the early years of the post-Stalin era. In general, the Communist leaders since Stalin's death have been attempting to improve the productivity of the farms by (1) striking an appropriate balance between central controls and local initiative in the planning field and (2) improving and extending the system of incentives in order to increase the output of the peasants.

Beginning in March 1955, the Soviet rulers sought to give the collective farm organizations greater leeway in planning the details of their production. The official plan was to specify only the delivery targets, leaving it to the authorities on an individual farm to determine in what manner the quotas were to be met. The officials of the district executive commitees, however, retained the right to scrutinize the plans which were formulated by the collective farms and to modify them in any way that seemed appropriate. Subsequent reorganizations of the agricultural hierarchies, which usually tended to strengthen the Party's hold over the farms, diminished the effectiveness of the 1955 experiment, and the collective farm officials for the most part did not enjoy much discretion in planning their work. According to a statement by the Minister of Agriculture in 1964, the executive committees in the districts frequently intervened in the planning process and made additional assignments to the farms.[25]

In an effort to reduce the authority of district agricultural officials and to reaffirm the position of the farm managers in planning their crops, the Party's Central Committee in March 1964 ordered a return to the 1955 statute and deprived the district executive committees of their right to review and modify the plans of the collective farms. According to the new decree, when disagreements arose between the farm directors and the officials of the state agricultural agencies at the local level, the ultimate decision was to rest with the governing boards of the farms.[26] Whether this attempt to give to the local farm management wider areas of choice in meeting its assignments will be any more successful than the 1955 experiment remains a question for the future. But the 1964 decree, which provided stronger legal support for the farm chairmen, represented a tendency (similar to the trend in consumer-goods industry) to devolve more operational responsibility upon the collective farms themselves. The prevailing economic thought in industry was reflected by demands that an adequate profit system be instituted as an index for evaluating the work of the farms, and that adequate credit be given for the introduction of new machinery.[27]

In seeking to improve the incentive system in agriculture, the regime attempted, especially in the period from 1953 to 1958, to increase the prices of farm commodities and thereby to augment the incomes of the collective and state farmers. In 1953, for example, the Communist authorities increased the prices paid by the state for the obligatory deliveries of a large number of agricultural items and for the over-quota purchases by the state. Five years later, in 1958, the above-quota purchases were abandoned in favor of a one-price system of state procurement, with certain regional differences, and the scales of remuneration (compared with the old system) worked to the distinct advantage of the farmers. Early in the same year, the compulsory deliveries of produce from the private garden plots were abolished. The upgrading of prices for livestock and livestock products was especially noticeable during this period, and the workers in animal husbandry were ranked among the elite of agricultural workers in the USSR. The uneven record of procurement, which was marked by frequent cases of corruption and falsified reporting, resulted in the establishment of a tighter organization early in 1961. At that time, a State Procurement Committee was set up to supervise through its subordinate agencies the delivery of farm products on the basis of contracts. An army of procurement inspectors was given authority to supervise the fulfillment of the plans and contractual obligations of the farms. In the case of farms that were not living up to the terms of their contracts, the procurement officials were authorized to terminate or restrict the cash advances given to the collective farms by the state bank and to curtail the bank credits issued to the state farms.[28]

In addition to raising agricultural prices, the Soviet leaders sought to stimulate productivity on the farms through the use of additional monetary incentives. In 1956, the regime introduced a program of advance cash payments under which deserving farmers could get some remuneration without having to wait for the division of kolkhoz earnings at the end of the year. This experiment was undertaken by a great many of the collective farms, although some of them had difficulty in balancing their books after a poor harvest. After 1958, attempts were made to encourage the farms to move toward a guaranteed monthly cash wage system. For the most part, however, the traditional labor-day system of remuneration remained prevalent, and wage incentives were confined to high payments to farmers who had achieved outstanding quotas of output.

When the regime desires to improve the effectiveness of the incentive system, it has traditionally granted concessions to the farmers in the cultivation of their private garden plots and in the raising of private herds of livestock. In 1953, for example, the tax paid by the peasants on their private allotments was reduced, as were the quotas of compulsory deliveries to the state of produce grown on the garden plots. This type of compulsory delivery, as we have already seen, was abolished in January 1958. The concessions to the private sector were narrowed considerably during the late 1950's. Thus, in 1956 a decree authorized reductions in the size of private plots when peasants had not spent enough of their time on the collective fields. The emphasis on the reduction of the plots and the sale of private herds to the collective continued during 1959 and 1960. The trend, however, was dramatically reversed in 1964 when a series of statutes, issued first in the Ukraine, ordered that private plots be restored to their pre-1955 size, before they had been curtailed by restrictions. Even people who were not resident on collective farms were to have their plots returned to them, and people whose collective farms had been converted into state farms were to retain their private gardens. Similar encouragement was given to private individuals to own their own livestock. Taxes on private herds were eliminated. Party and state officials were ordered to help ordinary citizens to acquire livestock and to make sure that fodder and pasture would be available to them.[29]

These changes in the organization of Soviet industry and agriculture and the new decision-making procedures which were introduced in the course of the decade from 1955 to 1965 modified the contribution of the government to the satisfaction of both the adaptive and the integrative functional requisites. The immediate effect of the 1957 reorganization was to increase the degree of operational responsibility of regional planners and factory managers. Plant directors who were interviewed by the authors in the autumn of 1958 testified that they enjoyed a wider range of discretionary authority at the administrative level, and they were fond of citing numerous examples to underline the point. The system of regional *sovnarkhozes* established in 1957, however, created such pressures toward autarchy that the regime reintroduced centralized controls in one form or another. The trend toward recentralization was reversed to a great extent by the innovations in 1964 and early 1965, which increased once again the discretionary authority of local managers by permitting them to make contracts directly with supply and retail organizations and to use estimated profits as the basic criterion for decision making. A similar program in agriculture gave farm managers greater freedom to plan their crops and created incentives for individuals to develop their private plots and to own their livestock.

Although the central authorities in Moscow will certainly continue to be the most important resource allocators in the economy as a whole, they appear in the 1960's to be less significant than they were under Stalin's system. As factories are increasingly allowed to accept orders directly from retailing organizations, and as plant managers are given more freedom in fulfilling these orders without having to adhere to detailed instructions from Moscow or the regional *sovnarkhozes,* the central government becomes less involved in the process of resource management.

Modifications in the contribution by government to the satisfaction of the integrative functional requisite were even more striking. Of primary importance under Stalin was the integrative process of social control. The supply and delivery directives of the official central plan were in reality *norms,* and the government could resort to the use of violent sanctions if the norms were not observed. Workers could be coerced into behavior that was deemed by the government to be the most integrative for the system as a whole.

The innovations of 1964-1965 have wrought distinctive changes in this pattern. The firms that were allowed to make their own contracts for supplies and deliveries were now outside the detailed control of the central plan. The old norms no longer applied; the information process of the integrative requisite now assumed greater importance. A market—at least a limited market—had been created, and the information generated in that market aided in the satisfaction of the integrative requisite. Information concerning the relative needs of potential customers had replaced the directives of the central plan, and those firms that could produce the desired products at the lowest price received the orders. Equally important, supplies moved to the factories on the basis of the orders issued by the managers.

In the Soviet context, one can speak of an increase in the discretionary authority of the plant administrator under the new system. But from a broader point of view, their discretionary authority, which was once limited by the central planners, was now limited by the impersonal forces of the market. If the new system were to operate efficiently, the decision-making apparatus at the plant level would have to be *preprogramed* to respond in a given way to the information that is generated in the market. To the degree that it is preprogramed, the government makes a smaller contribution to the satisfaction of the integrative functional requisite.

We had best leave this line of argument for the moment in order to examine briefly some of the changes in the procedures of governing in post-Stalin Russia. It will be necessary for us to return to this aspect of the analysis in the concluding section, where we shall indicate how the new patterns, in sharp contrast with the older patterns, met the requisites of the modern stage of economic development.

Procedures of Governing

The governing methods and the techniques of control which were employed by Khrushchev and his associates were markedly different from those utilized by Stalin. One of the major differences in their methods of rule stems from the fact that Khrushchev sought to govern primarily through the Communist Party apparatus, in which he had carved out his career and through which he had risen to power. During the succession struggle, his political strength was rooted in the Party organization, while that of his opponents was closely linked with the other major bureaucracies, especially the police and the government administration. Instead of playing one bureaucracy against another and alternating reliance upon them as Stalin did, Khrushchev increased his hegemony over the Party hierarchy and extended its influence into other sectors of the society. Besides attempting to remove his rivals from the contest, he tried to diminish the bases of their support so that the probability of future challenges to his power would be reduced. In the course of this struggle, Khrushchev set about to make the competing hierarchies of power more subordinate to the will of the Party apparatus, a strategy that for a time met with considerable success. In the decade from 1953 to 1963, for example, the Party reasserted its authority over such powerful bureaucracies as the police (after Beria's downfall), the armed forces (after Zhukov's ouster), and the state administration (during the various phases of industrial reorganization). By the end of 1958, Khrushchev had secured the appointment of several of his supporters to membership in the Party Presidium, which fell under the domination of leaders from the Communist apparatus. The police no longer had direct representation in this policy-making agency, and the economic planners and industrial administrators had a weakened voice in this important body.

How Khrushchev relied upon the Party as the primary instrument of his rule can be seen in the role assigned to the Party apparatus under some of the industrial reorganizations and reshuffles. In the program of administrative decentralization of factories in 1957, for example, most of the heavy industrial ministries were dismantled and many of the powerful economic planners and administrators were transferred to regional economic councils throughout the country, where they came under the scrutiny of the regional Party secretaries. The establishment of industrial administration on a more regional basis afforded the regional Party organizations somewhat greater control over economic affairs and gave the secretaries added influence in certain types of economic decisions.

Agriculture had been Khrushchev's special responsibility in the Politburo-Presidium even before Stalin's death, and with his new assignment as First Secretary he wasted little time in expanding the Party's controls into the rural areas. In the autumn of 1953, for example, the political departments of the machine and tractor stations were eliminated, and responsibility for supervising the collective farms was handed over to the district Communist secretaries, who commanded squads of agents in carrying out their administrative and control activities.[30] Moreover, the amalgamation of the farms into larger units enabled the Communist leaders to establish their organizations on a higher proportion of the kolkhozes and to install Party members as directors of the collective farms. A number of recruitment campaigns during the post-Stalin era led to the transfer of thousands of Communist functionaries to the countryside to help supervise the operation of the farms. The restructuring of the administrative machinery in agriculture since the turn of the decade gave added responsibilities to officials in the Party apparatus, from the leading secretary at the republic and regional levels down to the Communist organizers in the local territories. That the Party was a central arch in the economic edifice was indicated in November 1962 when the organization, up to the level of the republics, was split into two specialized and independent sectors, one to be concerned with agriculture and the other to be involved in the industrial sphere. After Khrushchev's fall from grace, his successors decided to merge the agricultural and industrial structures of the Party into cohesive territorial units again.

When a comparison is made between the Khrushchev period and the Stalin era, a second distinction quickly emerges: under Khrushchev, there was a reduction in the visible use of raw coercion and terror as instruments of control. After Stalin's death, amnesties were granted to designated types of prisoners and from 1953 to 1957 large numbers of inmates were released, the prison camps were to some extent reorganized, and the police were deprived of some of the authority they had once wielded. Between 1953 and 1958, the political and legal authorities studied the outdated criminal code, and eventually a revision of the code was enacted into statute—an improvement over the judicial practices of the Stalin period, though not as much as some of the Soviet jurists desired. The doctrine of analogy was formally abolished, defendants were given some procedural guarantees, crimes were defined somewhat more precisely, and the courts were recognized as the legitimate agencies for determining guilt and imposing sentences. An edict in 1956 abrogated the decrees of the Stalin era that had sanctioned "exceptional procedures" of investigation and interrogation in cases of alleged "terrorism." As a result of the repeal of certain decrees which had been enacted in the late 1930's and early 1940's, the penalties for violations of labor discipline were reduced in severity. Thus, it was no longer a crime to change jobs without permission or to be late for or absent from work. These reforms in the legal system continued in a liberal direction until about 1961-1962, representing a significant shift away from the arbitrary procedures and brutalities of Stalinism. During 1961-1962, however, a counter-trend began to develop, as some Communist leaders criticized the leniency of sentences and the pampering of criminals, especially in cases involving economic crimes.[31] At the same time the regime instituted harsher methods of apprehension and punishment, extending the death penalty to certain economic offenses and to specified types of assault.

In pointing out the decreased reliance upon terror during the Khrushchev era, we do not wish simply to give the impression that raw coercion and terrorist methods were less important. We are suggesting further that official pressure was more subtle and less overt. Although factory workers who had violated labor discipline were no longer committing crimes in a technical sense, they were nevertheless still subject to punitive action. In place of severe punishment by the police and the courts, the regime authorized plant managers to impose fines upon delinquent laborers, to deprive them of bonus benefits, to dismiss them with adverse notations in their labor records, or to institute proceedings in one of the "popular assembly" courts.

Through these popular assemblies—the "antiparasite" courts and the comrades' courts—the regime attempted to exert the pressure of public opinion upon potential offenders. The purpose of these instruments of control was to detect an "antisocial" individual before he committed a serious crime, and to make him painfully aware of the civic intolerance toward violations of socialist norms. These assemblies, which were not regarded as regular courts and hence were not bound by ordinary legal procedures, handled cases of citizens who had allegedly violated labor discipline, avoided "socially useful" work, lived on unearned income, or engaged in illegal business activities. They were authorized to sentence the accused to varying degrees of punishment, ranging up to termination of employment and exile to another region for five years. Besides the popular assemblies, the regime also established a system of voluntary people's militia (*druzhiny*), which were made up of young aktivists who assisted the regular police in directing traffic, maintaining order in the streets, combatting delinquency, and unearthing economic crimes and other forms of antisocial behavior. It is important to note that these forms of mass participation in social control—the antiparasite courts, the comrades' courts, and the people's militia—were dominated by the Communist Party. One of the distinctive features of the post-Stalin era has been the use of group pressure, which can be manipulated by the Party aktivists, to encourage citizens to conform to the basic norms of the society. Thus the regime sought to develop socially based substitutes for the openly oppressive social-control methods employed by Stalin.

The Khrushchev period was also distinct from the Stalin era in the greater reliance that was placed upon incentives as a means of influencing human behavior. Stalin's successors sought to replace the compulsory draft of young workers with more voluntary recruitment methods, and in their effort to entice a supply of labor into the underdeveloped areas of the country, they offered wage supplements, travel grants, holiday benefits, and similar inducements. By the same token, the regime cut the retail prices of food and manufactured items from time to time (although the prices of certain staples were substantially raised in the later months of Khrushchev's rule); it discontinued the compulsory state loan; and it eliminated tuition fees for students in secondary and higher education. Throughout most of the post-Stalin era, increased allocations were made for new housing construction and for repairing the old units, and larger supplies and a wider variety of consumer goods were made available for sale in the shops— programs that helped to make the system of monetary incentives more meaningful and more workable.

In line with their policy of trying to entice their citizens with more carrots rather than to coerce them with sticks, Khrushchev and his colleagues tried to extend the system of material incentives in industry and especially in agriculture, and to distribute material rewards more widely throughout the population. Indeed, some attempts were made to reduce the disparity between high- and low-paid workers by diminishing the size and increasing the number of bonuses, by upgrading the rates for certain types of piecework, and by raising the wage scales of disadvantaged citizens. The regime, for example, adopted a minimum wage for factory workers and introduced a pension scheme for farmers; it reduced taxes for lower income groups; it shortened the work week in many industries; and it increased retirement and disability pensions, especially for workers in hazardous occupations. As pointed out earlier, the economists and other specialists have strongly urged that the incentive system be adjusted so that the goals of individual factories and farms can be geared with the objectives of the over-all economy.

In sum, then, the procedures of governing employed by Khrushchev differed from Stalin's methods of rule in several important respects. Khrushchev relied primarily upon the Party apparatus as an instrument of control, and he sought to extend its influence into other spheres, especially into the economic sector. After Stalin's death, there was a noticeable reduction in the use of physical coercion to achieve conformity with the basic norms. Instead of relying so heavily upon the police and the ordinary courts to enforce compliance, the Khrushchev regime turned to more subtle techniques and, through such agencies as the antiparasite courts, the comrades' courts, and the people's militia, it sought to confront dissidents with the wrath of their peers. It also attempted to stimulate workers and farmers to produce more by making the incentive system more broadly based, by developing a number of welfare schemes, and by increasing the availability of consumer goods.

Khrushchev's successors have inherited all of the problems that plagued him. As yet there is no reason to believe that, in addressing themselves to these problems, they will ignore the imperatives of advanced industrialization and return to the procedures of governing employed by Stalin. Although firm documentary evidence is lacking, it is possible—perhaps even likely—that some of the Soviet leaders who had risen to positions of authority under Khrushchev's patronage were actually concerned about the effect of his policies on the economic development of the country. They may have been disturbed by the erratic behavior of the First Secretary, his vacillating policies and "harebrained" schemes, his intrusion of the Party apparatus far into economic sphere, and the unpredictability of administration occasioned by his frequent tinkering with the planning machinery and the still conflicting lines of jurisdiction. In other words, we are suggesting that Khrushchev's ouster may have been partly due to the fact that he was incapable of carrying to fruition some of the policies he had helped to set in motion.

CONCLUSIONS

Although the analysis of the Soviet Union during parts of two different stages of economic development does not conform to the requirements of the basic model of this exploratory study, we shall suggest in a general way the propositions that appear to be compatible with the data. These hypotheses stand out more clearly when we call brief attention to some contrasts and similarities between the USSR and the United States in the same stages of economic development. It must be remembered, however, that the purpose of this appendix is not to develop hypotheses for testing in field research, but merely to illustrate how the basic framework might be applied to the studies of societies at later stages of economic evolution.

We have indicated the major contribution made by the central government in the Soviet Union to the satisfaction of all of the functional requisites during the drive to modernity stage. This pattern, of course, stands in striking contrast to the American pattern during a comparable stage of economic development (from the 1890's to the mid-1920's). The contrast suggests that in meeting the requisites for the drive to modernity stage a wide variation is possible in the functions of government if the prerequisites of this stage have been met.[32]

The principal reason for the wide variation is that economic decisions are relatively simple at this stage of development. The basic steps toward industrialization have already been taken, and a fair stock of overhead capital has been accumulated. The cream of the natural resources is usually still available for exploitation. Many of the potential economies of scale are fairly obvious. At the same time, the pattern of inter-industry relations is not complex. In a large economy, the "block-triangular" input-output matrix may be common. (See pp. 46-47.) If this is the case, large sectors of the economy may be able to operate in relative isolation from other large sectors.

In the drive to modernity stage, the government may play a very active part in mobilizing capital (goal attainment), in allocating and managing resources (adaptation), and in integrating interdependent, specialized units in the economy (integration). If this pattern prevails, the decision procedures are likely to be centralized, and great advantage will be taken of the external economies (both technological and pecuniary). Inefficiencies are almost certain to be present, particularly in situations where the environment is decomposable. But even in these cases, the number of meaningful alternatives is apt to be limited, and hence the central decision maker will not suffer disastrously from a system that is informationally inefficient.

The government, in the drive to modernity stage, may alternatively play only a minor part in satisfying these requisites. In this case, an acceptable level of centralization which is needed to take advantage of external economies may be achieved by private firms and trade organizations in a manner that was not possible during the take-off stage. Even small entrepreneurs will in many instances benefit simply from the expansion of the entire economy, and some will see investment opportunities that take advantage of the social overhead capital which has been provided.

Our analysis suggests, however, that in the modern stage there is much less toleration in the variation of the functions of government. As the economy approaches modernity, fundamental economic decisions grow increasingly complex. This can be illustrated by the Soviet economy after the period of postwar rehabilitation. There eventually developed a rapidly growing demand for a wide range of products of high quality. New industries like plastics and electronics had to be developed or vastly enlarged, and not a few but many kinds of steel were needed and had to be scheduled for production in the appropriate proportions. Thus, a new and broadened range of investments had to be made at a time when the obvious economies of scale and comparative regional advantages had already been exploited.

These types of economic decisions are largely related to the processes of resource management and resource allocation and involve the adaptive functional requisite. But in a modern economy, problems involving the integrative functional requisite are even more difficult to solve. The modern stage of economic development, it will be recalled, was defined in terms of a high degree of inter-industry interdependence. Thus, the large variety of high-quality products of the modern economy must be widely distributed. If an intermediate product is not at the proper place when it is needed, the dislocation can ramify quickly throughout the entire economy.

At the modern stage of development, universalistic criteria of recruitment in the economy become an important requirement if the economic system is to operate efficiently. Individuals who are responsible for making the difficult economic decisions must obviously be trained to make these decisions properly. The problem of training specialists has grown more serious in the Soviet Union since 1957 as a result of the restructuring of planning and economic management. The devolution of operational responsibility, especially the 1964 scheme which placed certain factories outside the detailed control of the central plan, has tended to give local managers more freedom to make significant economic decisions.

As the basic units of the economy became more interdependent, a more sophisticated and efficient information system is needed. From our cursory examination, it appears doubtful that the acceptable levels of informational efficiency can be reached in a highly centralized system such as existed in Russia under Stalin. We would hypothesize that in the modern stage a certain degree of decentralization is necessary, and that the increased reliance in the Soviet Union upon a type of market mechanism is significant primarily because it involves a decentralized information system.[33] As noted earlier (pp. 366-367), when a plant manager responds in an appropriate way to the information generated by the market, it is the market and not the government that is making the decision. Under these circumstances, the structures involved in the market make the contribution to the satisfaction of the integrative requisite which was previously made by the central government.

The suggestion that in the modern stage (as contrasted with the drive to modernity stage) there is a smaller tolerable range of variation in the contribution by government to the satisfaction of the four functional requisites is also supported by developments in the United States. In that country the period of the late 1920's and early 1930's can be viewed as an era of transition from one stage to the next. The economic troubles encountered during this period are comparable in our scheme to those faced by the Soviet Union in the 1950's and early 1960's. But if the economic troubles in the USSR were due in part to a government that did "too much," those in the United States were partly due to a government that did "too little." We would associate the breakdown of the economic machine in the early

1930's with a government that did not make a significant enough contribution to the satisfaction of the adaptive, pattern-maintenance, and integrative functional requisites to meet the demands of a modern economy. Much of the legislation in the United States from 1930 onward may be regarded as increasing the government's contribution to these three functional requisites.

In considering the functions of government, then, we hypothesize that all societies will tend to look more alike as their economies enter the modern stage. However, since the range of procedures that is compatible with these functions also increases, growing similarities in the functions of government do not necessarily imply a convergence on some dictatorship-democracy dimension. But it must be observed that some procedures that are highly successful in the drive to modernity stage of development may impede economic growth in the modern stage. It will be useful to examine briefly some of these procedures that appear to have emerged from the study of the Soviet Union.

Few would question the gross effectiveness of Stalin's techniques of control. His methods of rule helped him to remain in power for more than two decades and made it possible for him to enforce his decrees throughout the country. But the technique of playing one hierarchy off against another had certain imperatives that would prove to be too costly at a later stage: it required patterns of overlapping jurisdiction; it led to a dependence upon personal loyalties; and to be effective it required a certain amount of capriciousness in the system which made it difficult for an individual to predict when or for what reasons the terror might victimize him. Although these problems continued to plague the post-Stalin rulers, it is probable that Khrushchev's reliance upon the Party as the major instrument for governing, coupled with the reduction in the use of terror, tended to make for a greater measure of regularity and predictability than was true of the Stalin era. It seems likely that Khrushchev's successors will push further in this direction.

Besides requiring sharply defined areas of jurisdiction, a modern economy demands that much greater reliance be placed upon universalistic criteria of recruitment. Officials in the economic bureaucracy must be chosen for qualities that are germane to "proper" decision making. If personal loyalties dictate appointments to crucial economic posts, the probability that the most competent individuals will be drawn into the system is reduced.

The incentive system which proved so successful in Russia during the drive to modernity stage also showed serious signs of weakness by the 1950's. The problem of how to stimulate greater effort from the working population may be clarified if we examine the conditions under which the heavy use of the stick will probably be effective, and then glance at some of the difficulties involved in dangling the carrot effectively.

In the drive to modernity stage of economic development, the unskilled and semiskilled laborers are of great quantitative importance. Workers of this type can usually be kept hard on the job by physically coercive methods. However, the skilled technician, who is so important in the modern stage, is apt to respond less favorably to such techniques of compulsion. For the regime to treat a worker harshly or to send him to prison as an "example" to his fellows may be an effective sanction when labor is cheap and training programs are of short duration. But the man who had undergone several years of expensive preparation for his job cannot easily be replaced, and the costly investment in his training cannot be written off cheaply.

There is also in the modern economy less use for prison labor. In the drive to modernity stage, when an economy is still relatively poor in capital goods, certain large-scale projects can successfully employ slave laborers who work with picks and shovels. The situation is radically changed, however, when power shovels and bulldozers become more readily available in the modern economy. When huge earthmoving machines are introduced in large numbers, it is a mark of inefficiency to use manpower on pick-and-shovel jobs, especially if the manpower consists of forced workers who require the use of custodial personnel. It would also seem unwise to put slave laborers in charge of scarce and expensive machinery, for they may be strongly tempted to destroy the equipment as an act of revenge against their captors. Thus, it would appear that in the advanced technological setting of a modern economy, the use of the stick to discourage inefficient practices and to provide motivation for increased productivity tends to be self-defeating.

When the stick loses some of its effectiveness, more reliance has to be placed upon the carrot. The monetary incentives under Stalin were based upon piecework wages, with premium rewards for the overfulfillment of production quotas. While this system harbored many weaknesses, it was a factor in motivating industrial workers, many of whom had migrated to the cities from the rural areas and were not accustomed to the rigor and regimentation of the assembly line. For a variety of reasons, consumer goods were usually very scarce during the Stalin era, and living standards remained low. Failure to meet production quotas meant that workers would not only be denied access to luxury items, but that they would very likely experience difficulty in providing the necessities of life for themselves and their families. However, by the mid-1950's, the carrot of Stalin's day was becoming a trifle moldy. Levels of living were considerably higher than they had been twenty years earlier. Workers could at least exist without bonus payments. As it became easier to acquire the essentials for living, consumers grew more discriminating in their wants and tastes, taking critical note of style and quality in their purchases. Certain consumer items, especially those of poor quality and unattractive design, gathered dust in the shops, while other goods were in high demand and not available for purchase by ordinary citizens. Under these conditions, some workers had less motivation to work hard in order to meet or to surpass their quotas. The goods they wanted to spend their earnings on were not to be found in the warehouses and stores. Moreover, there was little incentive for them to set their wages aside for future purchases, since the government's record of currency devaluation and confiscation of savings hardly inspired confidence.

It is our suggestion that workers in such a situation might tend to opt for leisure time. Rather than pouring their efforts into piecework that would enable them to accumulate funds they could not exchange for desired consumer goods, they might choose to conserve their time and energy for low-cost recreation. If this were the case, productivity would obviously suffer.

For the wage system to stimulate labor productivity at levels anticipated by the regime, more consumer goods that would appeal to potential purchasers would have to be made available. In order to secure money to buy these goods, however, workers would have to be more diligent in their jobs. Productivity would thus increase. But to provide larger supplies of consumer items, the Soviet rulers would have to shift some investment from heavy industry (and armaments) into consumer-goods industry. More important for our analysis, sensitive indicators of consumer demand would have to be developed. At this point, the decentralization of certain types of economic decisions becomes important not only to facilitate the integration of specialized producing units, but also in order to register consumer preferences and to translate them into decisions concerning production and distribution. Failure to do this would seriously undercut the whole system of industrial incentives.[34]

The predictive implications of this discussion are fairly clear. Some degree of decentralized economic decision making is likely to remain a feature of Soviet life in the foreseeable future; indeed, it will probably expand not only into other consumer-goods industries but also into certain segments of heavy industry. Increased reliance upon the market, however, will generate crucial problems for the regime. Will the manufacturers of consumer durables, for example, be permitted to bid for orders, and then to purchase steel in quantities sufficient to fill these orders? An affirmative answer to this question could have the effect of inflating the price of steel and of thereby reducing the amount of war material which can be purchased for a ruble. Powerful forces in Soviet life would undoubtedly oppose such a development, and as greater reliance is placed upon the market, we would anticipate attempts to insulate the military sector of the economy from the consumer sector.

Our analysis also suggests that a return to the overt terror and oppression of the Stalin period is unlikely because of its adverse effects upon economic growth rates.

It is obviously impossible to attach a probability figure to these somewhat speculative predictions. The work of this study, however, leads us to conclude that if these predictions turn out to be wrong, the Soviet economy will face serious difficulties, not the least of which will be a significant decline in growth rates. In other words, there appear to be only two alternative lines of development in the immediate future: (1) increased reliance in the economic sphere upon decentralized decision making, administrative predictability, universalistic criteria of recruitment, and positive incentives to link the goals of individuals with those of the society, or (2) major economic dislocations which will lead to a decline in growth rates. These speculative predictions are made, of course, within the confines of the basic framework which were discussed in the Prologue and Chapter 2. We are assuming that no nonpolitical factor will impede growth, and that the international factors will remain within certain constraints. Most particularly, the predictions would have to be revised if the international situation deteriorated drastically. If a general war breaks out, of course, all bets are off.

NOTES

1. We have no input-output table of the Soviet economy to support this assumption. It is based, rather, upon reports of the problems confronting the Soviet economy in the period shortly before Stalin's death until the economic reorganization in 1957. These reports suggest that problems of inter-industry relationships were becoming increasingly severe.

2. The basic framework of this analysis was presented for a popular audience by the authors in *Soviet Union: Paradox and Change,* pp. 1-34, 207-231. Readers who are interested in more historical detail than is given in the present chapter may consult such works as Merle Fainsod, *How Russia is Ruled;* Leonard Schapiro, *The Communist Party of the Soviet Union;* John A. Armstrong, *The Politics of Totalitarianism: The Communist Party of the Soviet Union from 1934 to the Present;* Herbert McClosky and John E. Turner, *The Soviet Dictatorship.*

3. Ambiguous job descriptions of this sort might lead to the feelings of insecurity which Blau observed in "Section A" of the agency he studied, or which Pye reported in the Burmese bureaucracy. An administrative official whose job is not clearly defined is likely to perform his tasks with extreme caution, handling only those matters that are obviously required of him and leaving border-line problems to someone else.

4. Fuzziness of obligation was extended to the ordinary citizen through such devices as the rule of "analogy," under which an individual who had not violated any existing law could nevertheless be punished by having the judicial authorities apply an "analogous" statute.

5. On this point, see Barringtom Moore, Jr., *Terror and Progress USSR: Some Sources of Change and Stability in the Soviet Dictatorship,* pp. 16-21.

6. Besides these means of physical coercion, the regime employed other techniques of control. For example, the Communist leaders sought to indoctrinate the masses and to "engineer consent" through the establishment and maintenance of a far-flung and penetrating communication system, through the control of popular education, and through the strict regulation of all institutions for the exchange of ideas. These devices for the reinforcment of the status quo are, of course, well known, and need not be treated here. In this discussion, the aim is to focus attention upon only those procedures of governing that are relevant to the main theses of our study.

7. Peter J. D. Wiles, *The Political Economy of Communism,* p. 253.

8. See Alec Nove, *The Soviet Economy,* pp. 67-69.

9. Paul H. Cook, "The Administration and Distribution of Soviet Industry," in Joint Economic Committee, Congress of the United States, *Dimensions of Soviet Economic Power,* Part III, p. 191.

10. Herbert S. Levine, "Recent Developments in Soviet Planning," in *ibid.,* Part I, p. 53.

11. *Ibid.,* p. 55. See also *Ekonomicheskaya gazeta,* May 28, 1961, condensed and translated in *Current Digest of the Soviet Press,* November 8, 1961, Vol. XIII, No. 41, pp. 16-17.

12. *Pravda,* November 24, 1962, translated in *Current Digest of the Soviet Press,* December 26, 1962, Vol. XIV, No. 48, pp. 12-15; *Sovetskaya Rossia,* December 28, 1962, translated in *ibid.,* February 6, 1963, Vol. XV, No. 2, pp. 14-16.

13. See *Vedomosti Verkhovnovo Soveta SSSR,* February 22, 1963, translated in *Current Digest of the Soviet Press,* March 27, 1963, Vol. XV, No. 9, pp. 3-4.

14. See G. Mironov, *Ekonomicheskaya gazeta,* November 23, 1963, condensed and translated in *Current Digest of the Soviet Press,* February 12, 1964, Vol. XVI, No. 3, pp. 3-5. Other articles follow on pp. 5-8.

15. See *Ekonomicheskaya gazeta,* May 28, 1961, condensed and translated in *Current Digest of the Soviet Press,* November 8, 1961, Vol. XIII, No. 41, pp. 16-17.

16. Supreme Soviet Deputy G. I. Popov, *Pravda,* December 11, 1964, condensed and translated in *Current Digest of the Soviet Press,* January 13, 1965, Vol. XVI, No. 51, p. 12.

17. See, for example, I. Malyshev, *Izvestia,* February 7, 1964, translated in *Current Digest of the Soviet Press,* March 11, 1964, Vol. XVI, No. 7, pp. 26-27. Important articles by Liberman may be found in *Pravda,* September 9, 1962, translated in *ibid.,* October 3, 1962, Vol. XIV, No. 36, pp. 13-15; *Ekonomicheskaya gazeta,* November 10, 1962, translated in *ibid.,* December 5, 1962, Vol. XIV, No. 45, pp. 17-19.

18. See, for example, R. Belousov, *Pravda,* November 13, 1964, translated in *Current Digest of the Soviet Press,* December 9, 1964, Vol. XVI, No. 46, pp. 3-4; V. Trapeznikov, *Pravda,* August 17, 1964, translated in *ibid.,* September 9, 1964, Vol. XVI, No. 33, pp. 13-15.

19. See, for example, *Pravda,* May 16, 1964, translated in *Current Digest of the Soviet Press,* June 10, 1964, Vol. XVI, No. 20, pp. 11-12.

20. *Kommunist,* No. 5, 1964, translated in *Current Digest of the Soviet Press,* May 27, 1964, Vol. XVI, No. 18, p. 3. For the views of an important plant manager, see M. Alexeyev, *Pravda,* December 7, 1964, translated in *ibid.,* January 6, 1965, Vol. XVI, No. 50, pp. 13-14.

21. See, for example, M. Denisov, *Izvestia,* January 11, 1964, condensed and translated in *Current Digest of the Soviet Press,* February 5, 1964, Vol. XVI, No. 2, p. 32; O. Volkov, *Pravda,* August 23, 1964, condensed and translated in *ibid.,* September 23, 1964, Vol. XVI, No. 35, p. 20. These ideas were aimed at certain perceived weaknesses of the existing system. Plant managers were driven to produce huge amounts of commodities, even though the style was drab and the quality was low, so that they could meet their quotas and secure their bonuses. Yet consumers refused to purchase many of these items. Moreover, there was little incentive for factory directors to install new machinery, to introduce new technological processes, or to change the style of their products, for such policies were likely to lower their output over the short run.

22. See K. Michurin, *Pravda,* May 17, 1964, condensed and translated in *Current Digest of the Soviet Press,* June 10, 1964, Vol. XVI, No. 20, p. 13; M. Kuznetsova, *Pravda,* October 4, 1964, condensed and translated in *ibid.,* November 4, 1964, Vol. XVI, No. 41, pp. 12-13.

23. See *Current Digest of the Soviet Press,* November 11, 1964, Vol. XVI, No. 42, pp. 6-10.

24. See A. N. Kosygin, Speech to Supreme Soviet, *Pravda,* December 10, 1964, translated in *Current Digest of the Soviet Press,* December 30, 1964, Vol. XVI, No. 49, pp. 3-13, especially p. 11.

25. L. P. Volovchenko, Report to the Central Committee, *Pravda,* February 11, 1964, condensed and translated in *Current Digest of the Soviet Press,* March 4, 1964, Vol. XVI, No. 6, p. 14.

26. See Resolution of Central Committee, *Pravda,* March 24, 1964, translated in *Current Digest of the Soviet Press,* April 15, 1964, Vol. XVI, No. 12, pp. 10-11. See also *Pravda,* January 5, 1965, condensed and translated in *ibid.,* January 27, 1965, Vol. XVII, No. 1, pp. 12-14.

27. See, for example, L. Kassirov, *Pravda,* January 22, 1965, translated in

Current Digest of the Soviet Press, February 10, 1965, Vol. XVII, No. 3, pp. 10-11.

28. See *Pravda,* February 26, 1961, translated in *Current Digest of the Soviet Press,* March 22, 1961, Vol. XIII, No. 8, pp. 7-9.

29. See *Current Digest of the Soviet Press,* November 25, 1964, Vol. XVI, No. 44, p. 3.

30. Leonard Schapiro, *The Communist Party of the Soviet Union,* p. 578.

31. See Procurator-General R. A. Rudenko, *Izvestia,* May 7, 1961, in *Current Digest of the Soviet Press,* May 31, 1961, p. 21; *Pravda,* July 6, 1961, in *ibid.,* August 2, 1961, pp. 28-29.

32. If forced to push our analysis further, we would hypothesize that this wide range of tolerable variation applies especially to the contribution by government to the satisfaction of the adaptive and integrative functional requisites. Although a comparison of the Soviet and American experiences suggests that it should also apply to the tension-management process of pattern maintenance, we suspect that the limited involvement of the American government in this process during the drive to modernity stage is atypical. The extraordinary richness of natural resources in the United States and the influx of adults from Europe into the economy made the small involvement of the government in the tension-management process tolerable.

33. This hypothesis brings us into disagreement with Peter Wiles, *The Political Economy of Communism,* pp. 193-203, especially p. 194. Wiles argues that the modern computer makes "perfect computation" possible and that "perfect computation" can be as efficient as "perfect competition" since the administrative costs of the former are roughly equal to those involved in seeking an approximation of the latter. There is, of course, little evidence to draw upon either to support this speculation or the opposite view. In taking his position, Wiles tends to neglect some considerations. One of these is the loss of information efficiency that stems from equal deviations from perfect computation and perfect competition respectively. It is our contention that in a system of centralized computation even minor mistakes would ramify widely throughout the economy and their effects would be multiplied. In terms of the framework presented in Chapter 2, we are suggesting that the lag in the feedback system would be relatively large, and that it would be difficult to eliminate all cases of positive feedback. By contrast, deviations from perfect competition, although they would ramify, would tend not to multiply. The feedback system would iterate more rapidly, and the possibility of positive feedback is reduced. In other words, we are speculating that deviations from perfect computation are likely to have more deleterious effects than equal deviations from perfect competition.

34. The analysis of events in post-Stalin Russia provides a context for illustrating the differences between a psychological and a sociological explanation, as discussed in Chapter 1. We do *not* argue that Khrushchev carefully analyzed the requisites for a modern economy and then proceeded to introduce modifications in the existing system. Indeed, in the industrial reorganization of 1957 it is likely that political considerations linked with his struggle for power were more important than personal motivations based upon economic analysis. We do argue, however, that serious economic difficulties are likely to arise unless the functions of government and the procedures of governing conform to the requisites of the modern economy. The decisions of individuals that bring the pattern into an acceptable range may be prompted by a variety of motivations. But major economic troubles will tend to give rise to continual change until acceptable forms are developed—unless, of course, the social structuring

of the system during the previous period, or unless changes in the environment of the social system, do not make the development of such forms probable. According to the position taken in this monograph, the important thing to explain is *why* one form persists while another form is merely transient. This difference cannot be accounted for merely by considering the motivation of the decision makers.

Bibliography

In order to increase the usefulness of the bibliography, the major works have been listed under eight different headings:

I. Methodology
II. Economic and Political Development; General Economic History.
III. France
IV. China
V. Japan
VI. England
VII. Soviet Union
VIII. Miscellaneous

A few items have been listed under two different headings. The miscellaneous section includes works that are only of incidental interest, but since they have been cited in footnotes, they are included in the bibliography. We have made no attempt in this bibliography to provide a complete inventory of all relevant works. Only those that have been of direct use in this monograph have been listed.

I. WORKS OF GENERAL METHODOLOGICAL INTEREST

Albert, Ethel, "The Classification of Values: A Method and an Illustration." *American Anthropologist,* Vol. 58, No. 2 (April, 1956), pp. 221-248.

Almond, Gabriel A., "Comparative Political Systems." *Journal of Politics,* Vol. 18, No. 3 (August, 1956), pp. 391-409.

Almond, Gabriel A., "A Developmental Approach to Political Systems," *World Politics,* Vol. 17, No. 2 (January, 1965), pp. 183-214.

Almond, Gabriel A., "Introduction: A Functional Approach to Comparative Politics," in G. A. Almond and J. S. Coleman, eds., *The Politics of Developing Areas,* Princeton, 1960.

Almond, Gabriel A., "Political Systems and Political Change." *American Behavioral Scientist,* Vol. 6, No. 10 (June, 1963), pp. 3-10.

Almond, Gabriel A., and James S. Coleman, *The Politics of Developing Areas,* Princeton, 1960.

Almond, Gabriel A., and Sidney Verba, *The Civic Culture,* Princeton, 1963.

Apter, David E., *The Gold Coast in Transition,* Princeton, 1955.

Apter, David E., *The Political Kingdom in Uganda,* Princeton, 1961.

Arrow, Kenneth J., Samuel Karlin, and Patrick Suppes, eds., *Mathematical Methods in the Social Sciences,* Stanford, 1960.

Ashby, W. Ross, *An Introduction to Cybernetics,* London, 1964.

Barna, Tibor, ed., *The Structural Interdependence of the Economy,* New York, 1956.

Bator, Francis M., "The Anatomy of Market Failure." *Quarterly Journal of Economics,* Vol. 72, No. 3 (August, 1958), pp. 351-367.

Black, Max, ed., *The Social Theories of Talcott Parsons,* Englewood Cliffs, N.J., 1961.

Blau, Peter M., *The Dynamics of Bureaucracy,* Chicago, 1955.

Brodbeck, May, "Methodological Individualisms: Definitions and Reduction," *Philosophy of Science,* Vol. 25, No. 1 (January, 1958), pp. 1-22.

Chenery, Hollis B., and Paul G. Clark, *Interindustry Economics,* New York, 1959.

Coser, Rose L., "Authority and Decision-making in a Hospital: A Comparative Analysis," in James D. Thompson, *et al.,* eds., *Comparative Studies in Administration,* Pittsburgh, 1959.

Dahl, Robert A., and Charles E. Lindblom, *Politics, Economics, and Welfare,* New York, 1953.

Deutsch, Karl W., *The Nerves of Government,* London, 1963.

Deutsch, Karl W., "Social Mobilization and Political Development." *American Political Science Review,* Vol. 55, No. 3 (September, 1961), pp. 493-514.

Durkheim, Émile, *The Division of Labor in Society,* New York, 1933.

Easton, David, "Classification of Political Systems." *PROD,* Vol. 1, No. 1 (September, 1957), pp. 3-7.

Eisenstadt, S. N., *From Generation to Generation,* Glencoe, 1956.

Eisenstadt, S. N., *The Political Systems of Empires,* New York, 1963.

Erikson, Erik H., *Childhood and Society,* New York, 1950.

Faucheux, Jean, *La décentralisation industrielle,* Paris, 1959.

Freeman, Linton C., and Robert F. Winch, "Societal Complexity: An Empirical Test of a Typology of Societies." *American Journal of Sociology,* Vol. 62, No. 5 (March, 1957), pp. 461-466.

Frey, Frederick W., "Political Development, Power, and Communications in Turkey," in Lucian W. Pye, ed., *Communications and Political Development,* Princeton, 1961, pp. 298-326.

Gluckman, Max, *Order and Rebellion in Tribal Africa,* New York, 1963.

Gross, Llewellyn, ed., *Symposium on Sociological Theory,* Evanston, 1959.

Grossman, Gregory, ed., *Value and Plan: Economic Calculation and Organization in Eastern Europe,* Berkeley, 1960.

Hagen, Everett E., *On the Theory of Social Change,* Homewood, Ill., 1962.

Hayek, F. A., "The Use of Knowledge in Society." *The American Economic Review,* Vol. 35, No. 4 (September, 1945), pp. 519-530.

√ Hempel, Carl G., "The Logic of Functional Analysis," in Llewellyn Gross, ed., *Symposium on Sociological Theory,* Evanston, 1959.

Hoebel, E. Adamson, *The Law of Primitive Man,* Cambridge, Mass., 1954.

Hogbin, Herbert Ian, *Social Change,* London, 1958.

Homans, George C., *The Human Group,* New York, 1950.

Homans, George C., and David M. Schneider, *Marriage, Authority, and Final Causes,* Glencoe, 1955.

Hurwicz, Leonid, "Conditions for Economic Efficiency of Centralized and Decentralized Structures," in Gregory Grossman, ed., *Value and Plan,* Berkeley, 1960, pp. 162-175.

Hurwicz, Leonid, "Optimality and Informational Efficiency in Resource Allocation Processes," in Arrow, *et al.,* eds., *Mathematical Methods in the Social Sciences,* Stanford, 1960, pp. 27-46.

Katz, Elihu, "The Two-Step Flow of Communication: An Up-to-Date Report on a Hypothesis." *Public Opinion Quarterly,* Vol. 24, No. 1 (Spring, 1957), pp. 61-78.

Katz, Elihu, and P. F. Lazarsfeld, *Personal Influence,* Glencoe, 1955.

Krislov, Samuel, "The Perimeters of Force," unpublished paper read at the annual meeting of the American Political Science Association, 1963.

Kroeber, A. L., and Talcott Parsons, "The Concepts of Culture and of Social System." *American Sociological Review,* Vol. 23, No. 5 (October, 1958), pp. 582-583.

Leach, Edmund R., *Rethinking Anthropology,* London, 1962.

Leontief, Wassily, "The Structure of Development." *Scientific American,* Vol. 209, No. 3 (September, 1963), pp. 148-167.

Levi-Strauss, Claude, *Les structures élémentaires de la parenté,* Paris, 1949.

Levy, Marion J., Jr., "Contrasting Factors in the Modernization of China and Japan," in Simon S. Kuznets, Wilbert E. Moore, and Joseph J. Spengler, *Economic Growth: Brazil, India, Japan,* Durham, N. C., 1955, pp. 496-536.

Levy, Marion J., Jr., "Some Aspects of 'Individualism' and the Problem of Modernization in China and Japan." *Economic Development and Cultural Change,* Vol. 10, No. 3 (April, 1962), pp. 225-240.

Levy, Marion J., Jr., *The Structure of Society,* Princeton, 1952.

Lipset, Seymour M., and Neil J. Smelser, eds., *Sociology: The Progress of a Decade,* Englewood Cliffs, N. J., 1961.

Lounsbury, F. G., "Review of R. Needham's *Structure and Sentiment.*" *American Anthropologist,* Vol. 64, No. 6 (December, 1962), pp. 1302-1310.

Maddick, Henry, *Democracy, Decentralization and Development,* Bombay, 1963.

Martindale, Don, *The Nature and Types of Sociological Theory,* Boston, 1960.

Martindale, Don, *Social Life and Cultural Change,* Princeton, 1962.

Merton, Robert K., *Social Theory and Social Structure,* Glencoe, 1957.

Moore, Wilbert E., *Economy and Society,* Garden City, N. Y., 1955.

Moore, Wilbert E., *Social Change,* Englewood Cliffs, N. J., 1963.

Morse, Chandler, "The Functional Imperatives," in Max Black, ed., *The Social Theories of Talcott Parsons,* Englewood Cliffs, N. J., 1961, pp. 100-152.

Needham, Rodney, *Structure and Sentiment: A Test Case in Social Anthropology,* Chicago, 1962.

Nordskog, John E., ed., *Social Change,* New York, 1960.

Parsons, Talcott, *The Social System,* Glencoe, 1951.

Parsons, Talcott, *The Structure of Social Action,* Glencoe, 1949.

Parsons, Talcott, and Edward Shils, eds., *Toward a General Theory of Action,* Cambridge, Mass., 1951.

Parsons, Talcott, and Neil J. Smelser, *Economy and Society,* Glencoe, 1956.

Pierce, William H., "Redundancy in Computers." *Scientific American,* Vol. 210, No. 2 (February, 1964), pp. 103-112.

Polanyi, Karl, Conrad M. Arensberg, and Harry W. Pearson, eds., *Trade and Market in the Early Empires,* Glencoe, 1957.

Pye, Lucian W., *Politics, Personality, and Nation Building: Burma's Search for Identity,* New Haven, 1963.

Ray, Donald P., ed., *Trends in Social Science,* New York, 1961.

Riggs, Fred W., *Administration in Developing Countries: The Theory of Prismatic Society,* Boston, 1964.

Riggs, Fred W., *Social Change and Political Development,* unpublished monograph.

Riggs, Fred W., "The Theory of Developing Polities." *World Politics,* Vol. 16, No. 1 (October, 1963), pp. 147-171.

Rosovsky, Henry, *Capital Formation in Japan, 1868-1940,* New York, 1961.

Sahlins, Marshall D., and Elman R. Service, eds., *Evolution and Culture,* Ann Arbor, 1960.

Schapera, I., *Government and Politics in Tribal Societies,* London, 1956.

Scitovsky, Tibor, "Two Concepts of External Economies," in Theodore Morgan, *et al.,* eds., *Readings in Economic Development,* Belmont, Calif., 1963, pp. 119-128.

Shils, Edward A., "The Macrosociological Problem," in Donald P. Ray, ed., *Trends in Social Science,* New York, 1961.

Shils, Edward A., and Morris Janowitz, "Cohesion and Disintegration in the Wehrmacht in World War II." *Public Opinion Quarterly,* Vol. 12, No. 2 (Summer, 1948), pp. 280-315.

Smelser, Neil J., *Social Change in the Industrial Revolution,* Chicago, 1959.

Smith, Michael G., *Government in Zazzau, 1800-1950,* London, 1960.

Snyder, Richard C., H. W. Bruck, and Burton Sapin, *Foreign Policy Decision-Making,* New York, 1962.

Sorokin, Pitirim, *Social and Cultural Dynamics,* 4 vols., New York, 1937.

Steward, Julian H., *Theory of Culture Change,* Urbana, 1955.

Thompson, James D., *et al.,* eds., *Comparative Studies in Administration,* Pittsburgh, 1959.

Udy, Stanley H., Jr., *Organization of Work,* New Haven, 1959.

Vallance, T. R., "Methodology in Propaganda Research." *Psychological Bulletin,* Vol. 48, No. 1 (January, 1951), pp. 32-61.

Wallace, Anthony F., *Personality and Culture,* New York, 1961.

Weber, Max, *The Theory of Social and Economic Organization,* Glencoe, 1947.

Wiener, Norbert, *Cybernetics,* New York, 1961.

Wiles, Peter J. D., *The Political Economy of Communism,* Cambridge, Mass., 1962.

II. POLITICAL AND ECONOMIC DEVELOPMENT; GENERAL ECONOMIC HISTORY

Almond, Gabriel A., and James S. Coleman, *The Politics of Developing Areas,* Princeton, 1960.

Apter, David E., *The Gold Coast in Transition,* Princeton, 1955.

Apter, David E., *The Political Kingdom in Uganda,* Princeton, 1961.

Bator, Francis M., "The Anatomy of Market Failure." *Quarterly Journal of Economics,* Vol. 72, No. 3 (August, 1958), pp. 351-367.

Bauer, Peter T., and Basil S. Yamey, *The Economics of Underdeveloped Countries,* Chicago, 1957.

Binder, Leonard, *Iran: Political Development in a Changing Society,* Berkeley, 1962.

Blodgett, Ralph A., and Donald L. Kemmerer, *Comparative Economic Development,* New York, 1956.

Cairncross, A. K., "Review of Rostow's *The Stages of Economic Growth.*" *The Economic History Review,* Vol. 13, No. 3 (April, 1961), pp. 450-458.

Chenery, Hollis B., "Comparative Advantage and Development Policy," in Theodore Morgan, *et al.,* eds., *Readings in Economic Development,* Belmont, Calif., 1963, pp. 158-186.

Clark, Colin, *The Conditions of Economic Progress,* London, 1951.

Clough, Shepard B., *The Economic Development of Western Civilization,* New York, 1959.

Davis, Kingsley, and Judith Blake, "Social Structure and Fertility: An Analytic Framework," in S. M. Lipset and Neil J. Smelser, eds., *Sociology: The Progress of a Decade,* Englewood Cliffs, N. J., 1961, pp. 356-377.

Gerschenkron, Alexander, *Economic Backwardness in Historical Perspective: A Book of Essays,* Cambridge, Mass., 1962.

Habakkuk, H. J., "Review of Rostow's *The Stages of Economic Growth.*" *The Economic Journal,* Vol. 71, No. 283 (September, 1961), pp. 601-604.

Haberler, Gottfried, "Critical Observations on Some Current Notions in the

Theory of Economic Development," in Theodore Morgan, *et al.*, *Readings in Economic Development*, pp. 231-239.

Hammond, John, and Barbara Hammond, *The Rise of Modern Industry*, New York, 1926.

Heaton, Herbert, *The Economic History of Europe*, New York, 1936.

Hirschman, Albert O., *The Strategy of Economic Development*, New Haven, 1958.

Hirschman, Albert O., and Charles E. Lindblom, "Economic Development, Research and Development, Policy Making: Some Converging Views." *Behavioral Science*, Vol. 7, No. 2 (April, 1962), pp. 211-222.

Hoselitz, Bert F., "Levels of Economic Performance and Bureaucratic Structures," in Joseph LaPalombara, ed., *Bureaucracy and Political Development*, Princeton, 1963, pp. 168-198.

Hoselitz, Bert F., *Sociological Aspects of Economic Growth*, Glencoe, 1960.

Hoselitz, Bert F., "Theories of Stages of Economic Growth," in Bert F. Hoselitz, *et al.*, *Theories of Economic Growth*, Glencoe, 1960, pp. 193-238.

Hoselitz, Bert F., Joseph J. Spengler, J. M. Letiche, Erskine McKinley, John Buttrick, and Henry J. Bruton, *Theories of Economic Growth*, Glencoe, 1960.

Jordan, Richard C., "New Techniques for Temperature Control of Perishable Goods in Transport and Storage Applicable to the Less Developed Areas," *Science, Technology and Development*, Vol. 5 (February, 1963), pp. 120-133.

Kautsky, John H., ed., *Political Change in Underdeveloped Countries: Nationalism and Communism*, New York, 1962.

Kerr, Clark, John T. Dunlop, Frederick Harbison, and Charles A. Myers, *Industrialism and Industrial Man*, Cambridge, Mass., 1960.

Kuznets, Simon S., "Notes on the Take-off," in Theodore Morgan, *et al.*, eds., *Readings in Economic Development*, Belmont, Calif., 1963.

Kuznets, Simon S., *Six Lectures on Economic Growth*, Glencoe, 1960.

Kuznets, Simon S., "Underdeveloped Countries and the Pre-Industrial Phase in the Advanced Countries: An Attempt at Comparison," *Proceedings of the World Population Conference*, United Nations Organization, New York, 1954.

Kuznets, Simon S., Wilbert E. Moore, and Joseph C. Spengler, *Economic Growth: Brazil, India, Japan*, Durham, N. C., 1955.

Lane, Frederic C., and Jelle Riemesma, eds., *Enterprise and Secular Change: Readings in Economic History*, Homewood, Ill., 1953.

LaPalombara, Joseph, ed., *Bureaucracy and Political Development*, Princeton, 1963.

LaPalombara, Joseph, "Bureaucracy and Political Development: Notes, Queries, and Dilemmas," in Joseph LaPalombara, ed., *Bureaucracy and Political Development*, Princeton, 1963, pp. 34-61.

Leontief, Wassily, "The Structure of Development." *Scientific American*, Vol. 209, No. 3 (September, 1963), p. 148-167.

Levy, Marion J., Jr., "Some Social Obstacles to 'Capital Formation' in 'Underdeveloped Areas,'" in National Bureau of Economic Research, *Capital Formation and Economic Growth*, Princeton, 1955, pp. 441-520.

Maine, Henry S., *The Early History of Institutions*, New York, 1875.

Mason, Edward S., *Economic Planning in Underdeveloped Areas: Government and Business*, New York, 1958.

Millikan, Max F., and Donald L. Blackmer, eds. *The Emerging Nations: Their Growth and United States Policy*, Boston, 1961.

Morgan, Theodore, George W. Betz, and N. K. Choudhry, eds., *Readings in Economic Development*, Belmont, Calif., 1963.

National Bureau of Economic Research, *Capital Formation and Economic Growth*, Princeton, 1956.

Nef, John U., *Cultural Foundations of Industrial Civilization*, New York, 1960.

Ohlin, Goran, "Reflections on the Rostow Doctrine." *Economic Development and Cultural Change*, Vol. 9, No. 4 (July, 1961), pp. 648-655.

Polanyi, Karl, Conrad Arensberg, and Harry W. Pearson, eds., *Trade and Market in the Early Empires*, Glencoe, 1957.

Pye, Lucian W., ed., *Communications and Political Development*, Princeton, 1961.

Pye, Lucian W., *Politics, Personality, and Nation Building: Burma's Search for Identity*, New Haven, 1963.

Reinhard, Marcel R., *Histoire de la population mondiale de 1700 à 1948*, Paris, 1949.

Reinhard, Marcel R., and André Armengaud, *Histoire général de la population mondiale*, Paris, 1961.

Riggs, Fred W., *Administration in Developing Countries: The Theory of Prismatic Society*, Boston, 1964.

Riggs, Fred W., *Social Change and Political Development*, unpublished monograph.

Rosenstein-Rodan, P. N., "Notes on the Theory of the 'Big Push,' " in Theodore Morgan, *et al.*, eds., *Readings in Economic Development*, Belmont, Calif., 1963, pp. 143-150.

Rostow, W. W., *The Stages of Economic Growth*, Cambridge, 1960.

Rostow, W. W., "Take-Off into Self-Sustained Growth," *Economic Journal*, Vol. 66, No. 261 (March, 1956), pp. 25-48.

Schweinitz, Karl de, Jr., "Economic Growth, Coercion, and Freedom." *World Politics*, Vol. 9, No. 2 (January, 1957), pp. 166-192.

Smelser, Neil J., *Social Change in the Industrial Revolution*, Chicago, 1959.

Spengler, Joseph J., "Bureaucracy and Economic Development," in Joseph LaPalombara, ed., *Bureaucracy and Political Development*, Princeton, 1963, pp. 199-232.

III. FRANCE

Ardaschev, Paul, *Les intendants de province sous Louis XVI*, Paris, 1909.

Babeau, Albert, *Les bourgeoisie d'autrefois*, Paris, 1886.

Babeau, Albert, *La Province sous l'ancien régime*, 2 vols., Paris, 1894.

Ballot, Charles, *L'introduction du machinisme dans l'industrie française*, Lille, 1923.

Bamford, Paul W., "Entrepreneurship in Seventeenth and Eighteenth Century France: Some General Conditions and a Case study." *Explorations in Entrepreneurial History*, Vol. 9, No. 4 (April, 1957), pp. 204-213.

Barber, Elinor G., *The Bourgeoisie in 18th Century France*, Princeton, 1955.

Bardoux, A., *La bourgeoisie française (1789-1848)*, Paris, 1893.

Baudet, Jacques, *Le monde des affaires en France de 1830 à nos jours*, Paris, 1952.

Beaulier, E. P., *Les Gabelles sous Louis XIV*, Paris, 1903.

Behrens, Betty, "Nobles, Privileges and Taxes at the End of the Ancien Regime." *The Economic History Review*, Vol. 15, No. 3 (April, 1963), pp. 451-475.

Beik, Paul H., *A Judgment of the Old Regime*, New York, 1944.

Bickart, Roger, *Les parlements et la notion de souveraineté nationale au XVIIIe siècle*, Paris, 1932.

Bloch, Jean-Richard, *L'anoblissement en France au temps de François, 1er*, Paris, 1934.

Bloch, Marc, *Esquisse d'une histoire monétaire de l'Europe,* Paris, 1954.

Block, Maurice, *Statistique de la France comparée avec les autres états de l'Europe,* 2 vols., Paris, 1860.

Boissonnade, P., *Colbert, le triumphe de l'étatisme, la fondation de la suprématie industrielle de la France, la dictature du travail (1661-1683),* Paris, 1932.

Bonnet, Pierre, *La commercialisation de la vie française du premier empire à nos jours,* Paris, 1929.

Borrelli de Serres, Léon Louis, *Recherches sur divers services publics du XIIIe au XVIIe siècle,* Paris, 1895.

Boulainvilliers, Henri, *Histoire de l'ancien gouvernement de la France,* Amsterdam, 1927.

Brissaud, Jean, *A History of French Private Law,* Boston, 1912.

Cameron, Rondo E., "Economic Growth and Stagnation in France, 1815-1914." *The Journal of Modern History,* Vol. 30, No. 1 (March, 1958), pp. 1-13.

Cameron, Rondo, E., *France and the Economic Development of Europe, 1800-1914,* Princeton, 1961.

Cecil, Evelyn, *Primogeniture: A Short History of Its Development in Various Countries and Its Practical Effects,* London, 1895.

Chabert, A., *Essai sur les mouvements des revenus et de l'activité économique en France de 1789 à 1820,* Paris, 1949.

Chevallier, Jean Jacque, *Histoire des institutions politiques de la France de 1789 à nos jours,* Paris, 1952.

Clamageran, J. J., *Histoire de l'impôt en France,* Paris, 1868.

Clapham, John H., *The Economic Development of France and Germany, 1815-1914,* Cambridge, 1948.

Cole, Charles W., *Colbert and a Century of French Mercantilism,* 2 vols., New York, 1939.

Cole, Charles W., *French Mercantilism,* New York, 1943.

Coleman, D. C., "Economic Problems and Policies," in F. L. Carsten, ed., *The New Cambridge Modern History,* Vol. V, Cambridge, 1961, pp. 19-46.

Dareste de La Chavanne, M.C., *Histoire de l'administration en France et des progrès du pouvoir royal, depuis de règne de Philippe-Auguste jusqu'à la mort de Louis XIV,* Paris, 1848.

D'Avenel, Vicomte Georges, *Histoire de la fortune française,* Paris, 1927.

De Vidaillan, M., *Histoire des conseils du roi depuis l'origine de la monarchie jusqu'à nos jours,* 2 vols., Paris, 1856.

Doolin, Paul R., *The Fronde,* Cambridge, Mass., 1935.

Doucet, Roger, *Les institutions de la France au XVIe siècle,* Paris, 1948.

Dubuc, Pierre, *L'intendance de Soissons sous Louis XIV, 1643-1715,* Paris, 1902.

Egret, Jean, "L'aristocratie parlementaire française à la fin de l'Ancien Régime." *Revue historique,* Vol. 76, No. 208 (July-September, 1952), pp. 1-14.

Esmein, A., *Cours élémentaire d'histoire du droit française,* Paris, 1925.

Ford, Franklin L., *Robe and Sword,* Cambridge, Mass., 1953.

Fréville, Henri, *L'intendance de Bretagne (1689-1790),* 3 vols., Rennes, 1953.

Gaullieur, Henri, *The Paternal State in France and Germany,* New York, 1898.

Gille, Bertrand, *Affaires et gens d'affaires, recherches sur la formation de la grande entreprise capitaliste (1815-1848),* Paris, 1959.

Glasson, Ernest Désiré, *Histoire du droit et des institutions de la France,* 8 vols., Paris, 1887-1903.

Glasson, Ernest Désiré, *Histoire du droit et des institutions politiques, civiles et judiciaires de l'Angleterre comparés au droit et aux institutions de la France depuis leur origines jusqu'à nos jours,* 6 vols., Paris, 1882, 1883.

Goubert, Pierre, *Beauvais et le Beauvaisis de 1600 à 1730,* Paris, 1960.

Grassby, R. B., "Social Status and Commercial Enterprise under Louis XIV." *The Economic History Review,* 2nd series, Vol. 13, No. 1 (August, 1960), pp. 19-38.

Green, Frederick C., *The Ancien Régime,* Edinburgh, 1958.

Greenlaw, Ralph, W., ed., *The Economic Origins of the French Revolution: Poverty or Prosperity,* Boston, 1958.

Habakkuk, H. J., "Family Structure and Economic Change in Nineteenth-Century Europe," *The Journal of Economic History,* Vol. 15, No. 1, Part 1 (1955), pp. 1-12.

Hauser, Henri, "The Characteristic Features of French Economic History from the Middle of the Sixteenth to the Middle of the Eighteenth Century." *The Economic History Review,* Vol. 4, No. 3 (October, 1933), pp. 257-272.

Hauser, Henri, *Les débuts du capitalisme,* Paris, 1927.

Hauser, Henri, *La pensée et l'action économiques du Cardinal de Richelieu,* Paris, 1944.

Hauser, Henri, *Travailleurs et marchands dans l'ancienne France,* Paris, 1920.

Heckscher, Eli F., *Mercantilism,* 2 vols., London, 1955.

Hoselitz, Bert F., "Entrepreneurship and Capital Formation in France and Britain since 1700," National Bureau of Economic Research, *Capital Formation and Economic Growth,* Princeton, 1955, pp. 291-337.

Institute de Science Économique Appliquée, "La croissance économique française," in Milton Gilbert, ed., *Income and Wealth,* Series III, Cambridge, 1953, pp. 45-100.

Johnson, Allen, *The Intendant as a Political Agent under Louis XIV,* Lowell, Mass., 1889.

Joubleau, Felix, *Études sur Colbert,* 2 vols., Paris, 1856.

King, James E., *Science and Rationalism in the Government of Louis XIV, 1661-1683,* Johns Hopkins University Studies, Baltimore, 1949.

Labrousse, C. Ernest, *La crise de l'économie française à la fin de l'ancien régime et au début de la révolution,* Paris, 1944.

Landes, David S., "French Entrepreneurship and Industrial Growth in the Nineteenth Century." *The Journal of Economic History,* Vol. 9, No. 1 (May, 1949), pp. 45-61.

Lavisse, Ernest, *Histoire de France depuis des origines jusqu'à la révolution,* Vols. V, VI, VII, VIII, IX, Paris, 1911.

Lefebvre, Georges, *The Coming of the French Revolution,* New York, 1947.

Levasseur, M. E., *La France industrielle en 1789,* Paris, 1865.

Levasseur, Emile, *Histoire des classes ouvriers et de l'industrie en France de 1789 à 1870,* 2 vols., Paris, 1903, 1904.

Lucay, Charles, *Des origines du pouvoir ministeriel en France,* Paris, 1881.

Lüthy, Herbert, *La banque protestante en France de la révocation de l'édit de Nantes à la revolution,* 2 vols., Paris, 1959, 1961.

Marion, Marcel, *Dictionnaire des institutions de la France au XVIIe et XVIIIe siècles,* Paris, 1923.

Martin, Germain, *La grand industrie sous le règne de Louis XIV, 1660 à 1715,* Paris, 1899.

Martin, Germain, *La grande industrie en France sous le règne de Louis XV,* Paris, 1900.

Mourre, Baron Charles, *D'où vient decadence économique de la France?* Paris, 1899.

Mousnier, Roland, "Le Conseil du Roi de la mort de Henri IV au gouvernement personnel de Louis XIV," *Étude d'histoire moderne et contemporaine,* 1947, pp. 29-67.

Mousnier, Roland, *La vénalité des offices sous Henri IV et Louis XIII,* Rouen, n.d.

Nef, John U., "The Industrial Revolution Reconsidered." *The Journal of Economic History,* Vol. 3, No. 1 (May, 1943), pp. 1-31.

Nef, John U., *Industry and Government in France and England, 1540-1640,* New York, 1957.

Normand, Charles, *La bourgeoisie française au XVIIᵉ siècle: la vie publique; les idées et les actions politiques, 1604-1661,* Paris, 1908.

Nussbaum, Frederick L., *The Triumph of Science and Reason,* New York, 1953.

Pagès, George, "Essai sur l'évolution des institutions administratives en France du commencement du XVIᵉ siècle à la fin du XVIIᵉ," *Revue d'histoire moderne,* Vol. 7, No. 1, pp. 2-76; No. 2, pp. 113-137, 1932.

Pagès, George, "Le gouvernement et l'administration monarchique en France à la fin du règne de Louis XIV," (in four parts), *Revue bimensuelle des cours et conférences,* Vol. 38, No. 1, pp. 1-9, No. 4, pp. 289-297, No. 7, pp. 610-619, No. 8, pp. 703-712, 1936.

Pagès, George, *La monarchie d'ancien régime en France,* Paris, 1946.

Palm, Franklin C., *The Economic Policies of Richelieu,* Urbana, 1922.

Ranum, Orest A., *Richelieu and the Councillors of Louis XIII,* Oxford, 1963.

Ricard, Louis, *Les institutions judiciaires et administratives de l'ancienne France et spécialement du Bailliage de Gex,* Paris, 1886.

Roupnel, Gaston, *Histoire de la campagne française,* Paris, 1932.

Roupnel, Gaston, *La ville et la campagne au XVIIᵉ siècle,* Paris, 1955.

Rubichon, M., *Du mecanisme de la société en France et en Angleterre,* Paris, 1837.

Sagnac, Phillippe, *La formation de la société française moderne,* 2 vols., Paris, 1945, 1946.

Sagnac, Phillippe, *La législation civile de la révolution française,* Paris, 1898.

Sagnac, Phillippe, "Louis XIV et son administration." *Revue d'histoire politique et constitutionnelle,* Vol. 3, No. 1 (January, 1939), pp. 23-47.

Sargent, Arthur J., *The Economic Policy of Colbert,* New York, 1899.

Scoville, Warren C., "The French Economy in 1700-1701: An Appraisal by the Deputies of Trade." *The Journal of Economic History,* Vol. 22, No. 2 (June, 1962), pp. 231-252.

Scoville, Warren C., *The Persecution of the Huguenots and French Economic Development, 1680-1720,* Berkeley, 1960.

Sée, Henri, *Economic and Social Conditions in France during the Eighteenth Century,* New York, 1927.

Sée, Henri, *Histoire économique de la France, le moyen age et l'ancien régime,* Paris, 1948.

Sée, Henri, *Histoire économique de la France, les temps modernes, 1789-1914,* Paris, 1951.

Spengler, Joseph J., *France Faces Depopulation,* Durham, N. C., 1938.

Spooner, Frank C., *L'économie mondiale et les frappes monetaires en France, 1493-1680,* Paris, 1956.

Taine, Hippolyte A., *The Ancient Régime,* New York, 1896.

Tilley, Arthur, *Modern France: A Companion to French Studies,* Cambridge, 1922

Tocqueville, Alexis de, *The European Revolution and Correspondence with Gobineau,* New York, 1959.

Tocqueville, Alexis de, *The Old Regime and the French Revolution*, New York, 1955.

Wolf, John B., "The Reign of Louis XIV: A Selected Bibliography of Writings since the War of 1914-1918." *The Journal of Modern History*, Vol. 36, No. 2 (June, 1964), pp. 127-144.

Zeller, Gaston, *Les institutions de la France au XVIᵉ siècle*, Paris, 1948.

IV. CHINA

Alabaster, Ernest, *Notes on Chinese Law and Practice Preceding Revision*, Shanghai, 1906.

Auber, Peter, *China: An Outline of its Government, Laws, and Policy*, London, 1834.

Backhouse, Edmund, and J. O. P. Bland, *Annals and Memoirs of the Court of Peking (From the 16th to the 20th Century)*, New York, 1914.

Balazs, E., "The Birth of Capitalism in China." *Journal of the Economic and Social History of the Orient*, Vol. 3, Part 2 (August, 1960), pp. 196-216.

Beal, Edwin G., Jr., *The Origin of Likin (1853-1864)*, Chinese Economic and Political Studies, Harvard University, Cambridge, Mass., 1958.

Brunnert, H. S., and V. V. Hagelstrom, *Present Day Political Organization of China*, Shanghai, 1912.

Burgess, John S., *The Guilds of Peking*, New York, 1928.

Carlson, Ellsworth C., *The Kaiping Mines (1877-1912)*, Chinese Economic and Political Studies, Harvard University, Cambridge, Mass., 1957.

Chan, Raymond L., *An Outline of Inter-governmental Relations in China*, Harvard Graduate School of Public Administration, Cambridge, Mass., 1943.

Chang, Chung-li, *The Chinese Gentry: Studies on Their Role in Nineteenth-Century Chinese Society*, Seattle, 1955.

Chang, Chung-li, *The Income of the Chinese Gentry*, Seattle, 1962.

Chen, Shao-kwan, *The System of Taxation in China in the Tsing Dynasty, 1644-1911*, Studies in History, Economics and Public Law, Columbia University, New York, 1914.

Chen, Sih-gung, *Modern China: A Political Study*, Oxford, 1919.

Cheng, Yu-kwei, *Foreign Trade and Industrial Development of China*, Seattle, 1956.

Chi, Ch'ao-ting, *Key Economic Areas in Chinese History*, London, 1936.

"Chinese Guilds and Their Rules." *The China Review* (July-August, 1883), pp. 5-9.

Ch'ü, T'ung-tsu, *Law and Society in Traditional China*, Paris, 1961.

Ch'ü, T'ung-tsu, *Local Government in China under the Ch'ing*, Cambridge, Mass., 1962.

Dibble, Vernon K., and P. T. Ho, "The Comparative Study of Social Mobility (Debate)." *Comparative Studies in Society and History*, Vol. 3, No. 3 (April, 1961), pp. 315-327.

Douglas, Robert K., *Society in China*, London, 1901.

Edkins, Joseph, *The Revenue and Taxation of the Chinese Empire*, Shanghai, 1903.

Eisenstadt, S. N., "Political Struggle in Bureaucratic Societies." *World Politics*, Vol. 9, No. 1 (October, 1956), pp. 15-36.

Fairbank, John K., *Chinese Thought and Institutions*, Chicago, 1957.

Fairbank, John K., Alexander Eckstein, and L. S. Yang, "Economic Change in Early Modern China: An Analytic Framework." *Economic Development and Cultural Change*, Vol. 9, No. 1 (October, 1960), pp. 1-26.

Fairbank, John K., *et al.*, "The Influence of Modern Western Science and

Technology on Japan and China." *Explorations in Entrepreneurial History,* Vol. 7, No. 4 (April, 1955), pp. 189-204.

Fei, Hsiao-t'ung, *China's Gentry: Essays in Rural-Urban Relations,* Chicago, 1953.

Fei, Hsiao-t'ung, "Peasantry and Gentry: An Interpretation of Chinese Social Structure and Its Changes." *American Journal of Sociology,* Vol. 52, No. 1 (July, 1946), pp. 1-17.

Fei, Hsiao-t'ung, and C. I. Chang, *Earthbound China: A Study of Rural Economy in Yunnan,* Chicago, 1945.

Feuerwerker, Albert, *China's Early Industrialization: Sheng Hsuan-huai (1844-1916) and Mandarin Enterprise,* Cambridge, Mass., 1958.

Gamble, Sydney D., "A Chinese Mutual Savings Society." *Far Eastern Quarterly,* Vol. 4, No. 1 (November, 1944), pp. 41-52.

Gamble, Sidney D., *Peking: A Social Survey,* New York, 1921.

Goodnow, Frank J., *China: An Analysis,* Baltimore, 1926.

Grantham, Alexander E., *Manchu Monarch: An Interpretation of Chia Ch'ing,* London, 1934.

Gray, John H., *China, A History of the Laws, Manners and Customs of the People,* 2 vols., London, 1878.

Ho, Ping-ti, "Aspects of Social Mobility in China, 1368-1911." *Comparative Studies in Society and History,* Vol. 1, No. 4 (June, 1959), pp. 330-359.

Ho, Ping-ti, *The Ladder of Success in Imperial China: Aspects of Social Mobility, 1368-1911,* New York, 1962.

Ho, Ping-ti, "The Salt Merchants of Yang-chou: A Study of Commercial Capitalism in Eighteenth-Century China." *Harvard Journal of Asiatic Studies,* Vol. 17, Nos. 1 and 2 (June, 1954), pp. 130-168.

Ho, Ping-ti, *Studies on the Population of China, 1368-1953,* Cambridge, Mass., 1959.

Hsiao, Kung-ch'üan, *Rural China: Imperial Control in the Nineteenth Century,* Seattle, 1960.

✓ Hsieh, Pao-chao, *The Government of China, 1644-1911,* Johns Hopkins University Studies in History and Political Science, New Series, No. 3, Baltimore, 1925.

Hsü, Francis L. K., "Social Mobility in China." *American Sociological Review,* Vol. 14, No. 6 (December, 1949), pp. 764-771.

✓ Hu, Ch'ang-tu, "The Yellow River Administration in the Ch'ing Dynasty." *Far Eastern Quarterly,* Vol. 14, No. 4 (August, 1955), pp. 505-513.

✓ Hu, Hsien-chin, *The Common Descent Group in China and Its Functions,* New York, 1948.

Hucker, Charles O., *The Traditional Chinese State in Ming Times (1368-1644),* Tucson, Ariz., 1961.

Jacobs, Norman, *The Origin of Modern Capitalism in Eastern Asia,* Hong Kong, 1958.

Jernigan, Thomas R., *China's Business Methods and Policy,* London, 1904.

Jones, Fred O., "Tukiangyien: China's Ancient Irrigation System." *Geographical Review,* Vol. 44, No. 4 (October, 1954), pp. 543-559.

Kirby, E. Stuart, *Introduction to the Economic History of China,* London, 1954.

Kroker, Edward, "The Concept of Property in Chinese Customary Law." *Transactions of the Asiatic Society of Japan,* Vol. 7, 3rd Series (November, 1959), pp. 123-146.

Leong, Y. K., and L. K. Tao, *Village and Town Life in China,* London, 1915.

Levy, Marion J., Jr., "Contrasting Factors in the Modernization of China and

Japan," in Simon S. Kuznets, Wilbert E. Moore, and Joseph J. Spengler, *Economic Growth: Brazil, India, Japan,* Durham, N. C., 1955, pp. 496-536.

Levy, Marion J., Jr., "Some Aspects of 'Individualism' and the Problem of Modernization in China and Japan." *Economic Development and Cultural Change,* Vol. 10, No. 3 (April, 1962), pp. 225-240.

Levy, Marion J., Jr., and K. H. Shih, *The Rise of the Modern Chinese Business Class,* Institute of Pacific Relations, New York, 1949.

Li, Chuan-shih, *Central and Local Finances in China: A Study of the Fiscal Relations between the Central, the Provincial, and the Local Governments,* Columbia University Studies in History, Economics and Public Law, New York, 1922.

Lind, Abram, Jr., *A Chapter of the Chinese Penal Code,* Leiden, 1887.

Liu, Kwang-ching, "Administering a Steam-Navigation Company in China, 1862-1867." *The Business History Review,* Vol. 29, No. 2 (June, 1955), pp. 157-188.

Liu, Kwang-ching, "Financing a Steam-Navigation Company in China, 1861-62." *The Business History Review,* Vol. 28, No. 2 (June, 1954), pp. 154-181.

Liu, Kwang-ching, "Steamship Enterprise in Nineteenth-Century China." *Journal of Asian Studies,* Vol. 18, No. 4 (August, 1959), pp. 435-455.

Liu, Ta-chün, *China's Industrial Development,* Institute of Pacific Relations, Data Paper 257, Honolulu.

Liu, Ta-chün, *China's Industries and Finance,* Chinese Government Bureau of Economic Information, Shanghai, 1927.

Lockwood, William W., "Japan's Response to the West—The Contrast with China." *World Politics,* Vol. 9, No. 1 (October, 1956), pp. 37-54.

Macgowan, D. J., "Chinese Gilds or Chambers of Commerce and Trade Unions." *Journal of the North China Branch of the Royal Asiatic Society,* Vol. 21 (1886), pp. 133-192.

✓ Marsh, Robert M., "Bureaucratic Constraints on Nepotism in the Ch'ing Period." *Journal of Asian Studies,* Vol. 19, No. 2 (February, 1960), pp. 117-133.

Marsh, Robert M., *The Mandarins: The Circulation of Elites in China,* New York, 1961.

Marsh, Robert M., "The Venality of Provincial Office in China and in Comparative Perspective." *Comparative Studies in Society and History,* Vol. 4, No. 4 (July, 1962), pp. 454-466.

Martin, R. Montgomery, *China: Political, Commercial, Social,* 2 vols., London, 1847.

Mayers, William F., *The Chinese Government,* Shanghai, 1886.

Michael, Franz, "State and Society in Nineteenth-century China," *World Politics,* Vol. 7, No. 3 (April, 1955), pp. 419-433.

Morse, Hosea B., *The Gilds of China,* New York, 1932.

Morse, Hosea B., *The Trade and Administration of the Chinese Empire,* Shanghai, 1908.

Nagano, Akira, *Development of Capitalism in China,* Japan Council of the Institute of Pacific Relations, Tōkyō, 1931.

Needham, Joseph, *Science and Civilization in China,* Cambridge, 1956.

Negishi, Tadashi, *Chūgoku no Girudo* (Guilds of China), Tōkyō, 1953.

Orchard, John, "Contrasts in the Progress of Industrialization of China and Japan." *Political Science Quarterly,* Vol. 52, No. 1 (March, 1937), pp. 18-50.

Parker, E. H., *China: Her History, Diplomacy, and Commerce from the Earliest Times to the Present Day,* New York, 1917.

Pêng, Tsê-i, ed., *Chung-kuo chin tai shou kung yeh shih tzŭ liao (1840-1949)*

(The Historical Materials on China's Modern Handicraft Industries), 4 vols., Peking, 1957.

Reischauer, Edwin O., and John K. Fairbank, *East Asia: the Great Tradition,* Boston, 1960.

Sasaki, Masaya, "Seidai Kanryō no Kashoku ni tsuite" (Accumulation of Wealth by Bureaucrats during the Ch'ing Period). *Shigaku Zasshi,* Vol. 63, No. 2 (February, 1954), pp. 22-57.

Shih, Kuo-hêng, *China Enters the Machine Age: A Study of Labor in Chinese War Industry,* Cambridge, Mass., 1944.

Shou, Ching-wei, *Democracy and Finance in China: A Study in the Development of Fiscal Systems and Ideals,* Columbia University Studies in History, Economics, and Public Law, New York, 1926.

Smith, Arthur H., *Village Life in China: A Study in Sociology,* New York, 1899.

Sun, E-tu Zen, and John de Francis, *Chinese Social History,* American Council of Learned Societies, Washington, D.C., 1956.

Swart, K. W., *Sale of Offices in the Seventeenth Century,* The Hague, 1949.

Ta Ch'ing hui-tien shih-li (The Collected Institutes of the Ch'in Dynasty, Cases and Precedents), Li Fan Yuan, Chuan 983, Kuang Hsü Edition, 1899, United States Library of Congress microfilm copy.

Tayler, John B., *Farm and Factory in China: Aspects of the Industrial Revolution,* Student Christian Movement, London, 1928.

Van der Sprenkel, Sybille, *Legal Institutions in Manchu China: A Sociological Analysis,* London School of Economics, Monographs on Social Anthropology, No. 24, London, 1962.

Vinacke, Harold M., *A History of the Far East in Modern Times,* New York, 1950.

Vinacke, Harold M., *Problems of Industrial Development in China: A Preliminary Survey,* Princeton, 1926.

Wagel, Srinivas R., *Chinese Currency and Banking,* Shanghai, 1915.

Wagel, Srinivas R., *Finance in China,* Shanghai, 1914.

Wang, Y. C., "Free Enterprise in China: The Case of a Cigarette Concern, 1905-1953." *Pacific Historical Review,* Vol. 29, No. 4 (November, 1960), pp. 395-414.

Wang, Y. C., "Western Impact and Social Mobility in China." *American Sociological Review,* Vol. 25, No. 6 (December, 1960), pp. 843-855.

Williams, Edward T., *China, Yesterday and Today,* New York, 1927.

Williams, S. Wells, *The Middle Kingdom,* 2 vols., New York, 1883, 1900.

Wu, James T. K., "The Impact of the Taiping Rebellion upon the Manchu Fiscal System." *Pacific Historical Review,* Vol. 19, No. 3 (August, 1950), pp. 265-275.

Wu, C. F., *Chinese Government and Politics,* Shanghai, 1934.

Yang, Lien-shêng, *Money and Credit in China: A Short History,* Cambridge, Mass., 1952.

Yang, Lien-shêng, *Studies in Chinese Institutional History,* Cambridge, Mass., 1961.

Yang, Martin C., *A Chinese Village: Taitou, Shantung Province,* New York, 1945.

V. JAPAN

Allen, George C., *A Short Economic History of Modern Japan, 1867-1937,* London, 1946.

Allen, George C., and Audrey G. Donnithorne, *Western Enterprise in Far Eastern Economic Development: China and Japan*, London, 1954.

Beasley, W. G., "Feudal Revenue in Japan at the Time of the Meiji Restoration," *Journal of Asian Studies*, Vol. 19, No. 3 (May, 1960), pp. 255-271.

Bellah, Robert N., *Tokugawa Religion: The Values of Pre-Industrial Japan*, Glencoe, 1957.

Borton, Hugh, *Japan's Modern Century*, New York, 1955.

Choi, Kee Il, "Tokugawa Feudalism and the Emergence of the New Leaders of Early Modern Japan." *Explorations in Entrepreneurial History*, Vol. 9, No. 2 (December, 1956), pp. 72-90.

Cohen, Jerome B., "Financial Development," in Hugh Borton, ed., *Japan*, Ithaca, 1950, pp. 127-143.

Craig, Albert M., *Chōshū in the Meiji Restoration*, Cambridge, Mass., 1961.

Crawcour, Sydney, "The Development of a Credit System in Seventeenth-Century Japan." *The Journal of Economic History*, Vol. 21, No. 3 (September 1961), pp. 342-360.

Dickson, Walter G., *Japan*, New York, 1901.

Dore, R. P., "Education: Japan," in Robert E. Ward and Dankwart A. Rustow, *Political Modernization in Japan and Turkey*, Princeton, 1964, pp. 176-204.

Fairbank, John K., *et al.*, "The Influence of Modern Western Science and Technology on Japan and China." *Explorations in Entrepreneurial History*, Vol. 7, No. 4 (April, 1955), pp. 189-204.

Fujii, Jintaro, ed., *Outline of Japanese History in the Meiji Era*, Tōkyō, 1958.

Griffis, William E., *The Mikado's Empire*, New York, 1886.

Gubbins, J. H., "The Feudal System in Japan under the Tokugawa Shōguns." *Transactions of the Asiatic Society of Japan*, Vol. 15 (1887), pp. 131-142.

Gubbins, J. H., "Some Features of Tokugawa Administration." *Transactions of the Asiatic Society of Japan*, Vol. 50 (December, 1922), pp. 59-77.

Gubbins, J. H., *The Making of Modern Japan*, London, 1922.

Hall, J. Carey, "Japanese Feudal Laws." *Transactions of the Asiatic Society of Japan*, Vol. 38, Part 4 (1911), pp. 269-331.

Hall, J. Carey, "Japanese Feudal Laws." *Transactions of the Asiatic Society of Japan*, Vol. 41, Part 5 (December, 1913), pp. 683-804.

Hall, John W., "The Castle Town and Japan's Modern Urbanization." *Far Eastern Quarterly*, Vol. 15, No. 1 (November, 1955), pp. 37-56.

Hall, John W., "The Nature of Traditional Society: Japan," in Robert E. Ward and Dankwart A. Rustow, *Political Modernization in Japan and Turkey*, Princeton, 1964, pp. 14-41.

Hall, John W., *Tanuma Okitsugu, 1719-1788: Forerunner of Modern Japan*, Cambridge, Mass., 1955.

Hall, John W., "The Tokugawa Bakufu and the Merchant Class." *Occasional Papers*, Center for Japanese Studies, Ann Arbor, No. 1, 1951, pp. 26-33.

Harootunian, Harry D., "The Economic Rehabilitation of the Samurai in the Early Meiji Period." *Journal of Asian Studies*, Vol. 19, No. 4 (August, 1960), pp. 433-444.

Henderson, Dan F., *Conciliation and Japanese Law: Tokugawa and Modern*, 2 vols., Seattle, 1965.

Henderson, Dan F., "Some Aspects of Tokugawa Law." *Washington Law Review*, Vol. 27, No. 1 (February, 1952), pp. 85-109.

Honjo, Eijiro, "The Agrarian Problem in the Tokugawa Regime." *Kyōto University Economic Review*, Vol. 1, No. 2 (December, 1926), pp. 75-93.

Honjo, Eijiro, "Changes of Social Classes in the Tokugawa Period." *Kyōto University Economic Review*, Vol. 3, No. 1 (July, 1928), pp. 56-74.

Honjo, Eijiro, "The Commoner Class of the Tokugawa Period." *Kyōto University Economic Review,* Vol. 8, No. 2 (December, 1933), pp. 38-47.

Honjo, Eijiro, "The Decay of the Samurai Class." *Kyōto University Economic Review,* Vol. 2, No. 1 (July, 1927), pp. 38-51.

Honjo, Eijiro, *Economic Theory and History of Japan in the Tokugawa Period,* Tōkyo, 1943.

Honjo, Eijiro, "On the Finance of the Tokugawa Government." *Kyōto University Economic Review,* Vol. 6, No. 2 (December, 1931), pp. 16-33.

Honjo, Eijiro, "The Importance of *Goyōkin* or Forced Loans in the Meiji Restoration." *Kyōto University Economic Review,* Vol. 8, No. 1 (July, 1933), pp. 18-35.

Honjo, Eijiro, "The New Economic Policy in the Closing Days of the Tokugawa Shōgunate." *Kyōto University Economic Review,* Vol. 4, No. 2 (December, 1929), pp. 52-75.

Honjo, Eijiro, *The Social and Economic History of Japan,* Kyōto, 1935.

Honjo, Eijiro, "From the Tokugawa Period to the Meiji Restoration." *Kyōto University Economic Review,* Vol. 7, No. 1 (July, 1932), pp. 32-51.

Horie, Yasuzo, "The Development of the Domestic Market in the Early Years of Meiji." *Kyōto University Economic Review,* Vol. 15, No. 1 (January, 1940), pp. 42-59.

Horie, Yasuzo, "The Feudal States and the Commercial Society in the Tokugawa Period." *Kyōto University Economic Review,* Vol. 28, No. 2 (October, 1958), pp. 1-16.

Horie, Yasuzo, "Government Industries in the Early Years of the Meiji Era." *Kyōto University Economic Review,* Vol. 14, No. 1 (January, 1939), pp. 67-87.

Horie, Yasuzo, "An Outline of the Rise of Modern Capitalism in Japan." *Kyōto University Economic Review,* Vol. 11, No. 1 (July, 1936), pp. 99-115.

Horie, Yasuzo, "The Problem of the Modernization of Japan." *Kyōto University Economic Review,* Vol. 26, No. 1 (April, 1956), pp. 1-12.

Hubbard, Gilbert E., *Eastern Industrialization and Its Effect on the West, with Special Reference to Great Britain and Japan,* London, 1935.

Ike, Nobutaka, *The Beginnings of Political Democracy in Japan,* Baltimore, 1950.

Inoki, Masamichi, "The Civil Bureaucracy: Japan," in Robert E. Ward and Dankwart A. Rustow, *Political Modernization in Japan and Turkey,* Princeton, 1964, pp. 283-300.

Inoue, Junnosuke, *The Economic and Industrial Development of Modern Japan,* Japan Council, Institute of Pacific Relations Data Paper No. 14, Tōkyō, 1929.

Inouyé, Masaru, "Japanese Communications: Railroads," in S. Okuma, *Fifty years of New Japan,* Vol. I, London, 1910, pp. 424-446.

Ishii, Ryosuke, ed., *Japanese Legislation in the Meiji Era,* Tōkyō, n.d.

Islam, Nurul, *Foreign Capital and Economic Development: Japan, India, and Canada: Studies in Some Aspects of Absorption of Foreign Capital,* Tōkyō, 1960.

Itani, Zenichi, "The Economic Causes of the Meiji Restoration." *Transactions of the Asiatic Society of Japan,* 2nd series, Vol. 17 (December, 1938), pp. 193-207.

Jacobs, Norman, *The Origin of Modern Capitalism in Eastern Asia,* Hong Kong, 1958.

Japan Yearbook, Tōkyō, 1917.

Johnston, Bruce F., "Agricultural Productivity and Economic Development in Japan." *Journal of Political Economy,* Vol. 59, No. 6 (December, 1951), pp. 498-513.

Kato, T., "Development of the Monetary System," in K. Shibusawa, ed., *Japanese Society in the Meiji Era,* Tōkyō, 1958.

Kinoshita, Yetaro, *The Past and Present of Japanese Commerce,* New York, 1902.

Levy, Marion J., Jr., "Contrasting Factors in the Modernization of China and Japan," in Simon S. Kuznets, Wilbert E. Moore, and Joseph J. Spengler, *Economic Growth: Brazil, India, Japan,* Durham, N. C., 1955, pp. 496-536.

Levy, Marion J., Jr., "Some Aspects of 'Individualism' and the Problem of Modernization in China and Japan." *Economic Development and Cultural Change,* Vol. 10, No. 3 (April, 1962), pp. 225-240.

Lockwood, William W., *The Economic Development of Japan: Growth and Structural Change, 1868-1938,* Princeton, 1954.

Lockwood, William W., "Japan's Response to the West—The Contrast with China." *World Politics,* Vol. 9, No. 1 (October, 1956), pp. 37-54.

McLaren, Walter W., *A Political History of Japan during the Meiji Era, 1867-1912,* New York, 1916.

McLaren, Walter W., "Japanese Government Documents." *Transactions of the Asiatic Society of Japan,* Vol. 42, Part I (1914).

Matsukata, M., "Japan's Finance," in S. Okuma, *Fifty Years of New Japan,* Vol. I, London, 1910, pp. 359-389.

Mitsui, Takaharu, "Chōnin's Life under Feudalism." *Cultural Nippon,* Vol. 8, No. 2 (June, 1940), pp. 65-96.

Morris, Morris D., "The Problem of the Peasant Agriculturalist in Meiji Japan, 1873-1885." *Far Eastern Quarterly,* Vol. 15, No. 3 (May, 1956), pp. 357-370.

Moulton, Harold G., *Japan: An Economic and Financial Appraisal,* Washington, D.C., 1931.

Murdoch, James, *A History of Japan,* Vol. III, London, 1926.

Norman, E. Herbert, *Japan's Emergence as a Modern State: Political and Economic Problems of the Meiji Period,* New York, 1940.

Ogawa, S., "Prisons and Prisoners," in S. Okuma, *Fifty Years of New Japan,* Vol. I, London, 1910, pp. 296-319.

Ohara, Keishi, ed., *Japanese Trade and Industry in the Meiji-Taishō Era,* Tōkyō, 1957.

Okawa, Kazushi, *The Growth Rate of the Japanese Economy since 1878,* Tōkyō, 1957.

Okuma, Shigénobu, ed., *Fifty Years of New Japan,* 2 vols., London, 1910.

Ono, Yeijiro, "The Industrial Transition in Japan." *Publications of the American Economic Association,* (January, 1890).

Orchard, John E., "Contrasts in the Progress of Industrialization of China and Japan." *Political Science Quarterly,* Vol. 52, No. 1 (March, 1937), pp. 18-50.

Orchard, John E., *Japan's Economic Position: The Progress of Industrialization,* New York, 1930.

Oura, Kanétaké, "The Police of Japan," in S. Okuma, *Fifty Years of New Japan,* Vol. I, London, 1910, pp. 281-295.

Pelzel, John C., "The Small Industrialist in Japan." *Explorations in Entrepreneurial History,* Vol. 7, No. 2 (December, 1954), pp. 79-93.

Quigley, Harold S., *Japanese Government and Politics: An Introductory Study,* New York, 1932.

Ranis, Gustav, "The Community Centered Entrepreneur in Japanese Development." *Explorations in Entrepreneurial History,* Vol. 8, No. 2 (December, 1955), pp. 80-98.

Reischauer, Edwin O., "Japanese Feudalism," in Rushton Coulborn, *Feudalism in History,* Princeton, 1956, pp. 26-48.

Reischauer, Edwin O., and John K. Fairbank, *East Asia: The Great Tradition,* Boston, 1960.

Rosovsky, Henry, *Capital Formation in Japan, 1868-1940,* New York, 1961.

Rosovsky, Henry, "Japanese Capital Formation: The Role of the Public Sector." *The Journal of Economic History,* Vol. 19, No. 3 (September, 1959), pp. 350-373.

Sansom, George B., *A History of Japan, 1334-1615,* Stanford, 1961.

Sansom, George B., *A History of Japan, 1615-1867,* Stanford, 1963.

Sansom, George B., *Japan: A Short Cultural History,* New York, 1962.

Sawada, Sho, "Financial Difficulties of the Edo Bakufu." *Harvard Journal of Asiatic Studies,* Vol. I, Nos. 3 and 4 (November, 1936), pp. 308-326.

Scalapino, Robert A., *Democracy and the Party Movement in Prewar Japan: The Failure of the First Attempt,* Berkeley, 1950.

Schiffer, Hubert F., *The Modern Japanese Banking System,* New York, 1962.

Sheldon, Charles D., *The Rise of the Merchant Class in Tokugawa Japan, 1600-1868,* Monographs of the Association of Asian Studies, New York, 1958.

Shibusawa, Keizō, *Japanese Life and Culture in the Meiji Era,* Tōkyō, 1958.

Shibusawa, Keizō, ed., *Japanese Society in the Meiji Era,* Tōkyō, 1958.

Shibusawa, Y., "The Development of Banking in Japan," in S. Okuma, *Fifty Years of New Japan,* Vol. I, London, 1910, pp. 486-532.

Shibusawa, Y., "Joint-Stock Enterprise in Japan," in S. Okuma, *Fifty Years of New Japan,* Vol. I, London, 1910, pp. 465-485.

Shiraishi, Bon, "Merchants of Osaka." *Japan Quarterly,* Vol. 5, No. 2 (April-June, 1958), pp. 169-177.

Smith, Neil S., ed., *Tokugawa Japan* (1), London, 1937.

Smith, Robert J., "Pre-Industrial Urbanization in Japan: A Consideration of Multiple Traditions in a Feudal Society." *Economic Development and Cultural Change,* Vol. 9, No. 1, Part 2 (October, 1960), pp. 241-254.

Smith, Thomas C., *The Agrarian Origins of Modern Japan,* Stanford, 1959.

Smith, Thomas C., "Introduction of Western Industry to Japan during the Last Years of the Tokugawa Period." *Harvard Journal of Asiatic Studies,* Vol. 11, Nos. 1 and 2 (June, 1948), pp. 130-152.

Smith, Thomas C., "Landlords and Rural Capitalists in the Modernization of Japan." *The Journal of Economic History,* Vol. 16, No. 2 (June, 1956), pp. 165-181.

Smith, Thomas C., "The Land Tax in the Tokugawa Period." *Journal of Asian Studies,* Vol. 18, No. 1 (November, 1958), pp. 3-20.

Smith, Thomas C., *Political Change and Industrial Development in Japan: Government Enterprise, 1868-1880,* Stanford, 1955.

Taeuber, Irene B., *The Population of Japan,* Princeton, 1958.

Taeuber, Irene B., "Urbanization and Population Change in the Development of Modern Japan." *Economic Development and Cultural Change,* Vol. 9, No. 1, Part 2 (October, 1960), pp. 1-28.

Takekoshi, Yosoburo, *The Economic Aspects of the History of the Civilization of Japan,* 3 vols., London, 1930.

Takizawa, Matsuyo, *The Penetration of Money Economy in Japan,* New York, 1927.

Tsuchiya, Takao, *The Development of Economic Life in Japan*, Tōkyō, 1937.

Tsuchiya, Takao, "An Economic History of Japan." *Transactions of the Asiatic Society of Japan*, 2nd Series, Vol. 15 (December, 1937).

U.S. Department of State, *Report of the Mission on Japanese Combines*, Publication 2628, Far Eastern Series 14, Part 1, Washington, D.C., 1946.

Vinacke, Harold M., *A History of the Far East in Modern Times*, New York, 1950.

von Mehren, Arthur T., ed., *Law in Japan: The Legal Order in a Changing Society*, Cambridge, Mass., 1963.

Ward, Robert E., and Dankwart A. Rustow, *Political Modernization in Japan and Turkey*, Princeton, 1964.

Wigmore, John H., "Materials for the Study of Private Law in Old Japan." *Transactions of the Asiatic Society of Japan*, Supplement to Vol. 20, Part I (1892).

Yanaga, Chitoshi, *Japan since Perry*, New York, 1949.

VI. ENGLAND

Abrams, M. A., "The English Gold- and Silver-Thread Monopolies, 1611-1621." *Journal of Economic and Business History*, Vol. 3, No. 3 (May, 1931), pp. 382-406.

Adamson, John W., *English Education, 1789-1902*, Cambridge, 1930.

Ashley, Maurice, *England in the Seventeenth Century [1603-1714]*, Harmondsworth, Middlesex, 1952.

Ashley, William, *The Economic Organization of England: An Outline History*, London, 1949.

Ashton, Thomas S., *Economic Fluctuations in England, 1700-1800*, London, 1959.

Ashton, Thomas S., *The Industrial Revolution, 1760-1830*, London, 1948.

Ashton, Thomas S., *Iron and Steel in the Industrial Revolution*, Manchester, 1951.

Aspinall, Arthur, "The Cabinet Council, 1783-1835," *Proceedings of the British Academy*, 1952, pp. 144-252.

Aylmer, G. E., *The King's Servants: The Civil Service of Charles I*, New York, 1961.

Barcroft, John H., *Buckingham and the Central Administration, 1616-1628*, unpublished PhD thesis, University of Minnesota, 1963.

Baumer, Franklin, *The Early Tudor Theory of Kingship*, New Haven, 1940.

Beresford, M. W., "The Common Informer, The Penal Statutes and Economic Regulation." *The Economic History Review*, 2nd Series, Vol. 10, No. 2 (December, 1957), pp. 221-238.

Bindoff, S. T., ed., *Elizabethan Government and Society*, London, 1961.

Black, Eugene C., *The Association: British Extra-Parliamentary Organization, 1769-1793*, Cambridge, 1963.

Bowden, Witt, *Industrial Society in England Towards the End of the Eighteenth Century*, New York, 1922.

Briggs, Milton, and Percy Jordan, *Economic History of England*, London, 1957.

Bryant, Arthur, *The Years of Endurance, 1793-1802*, New York, 1942.

Buer, Mabel C., *Health, Wealth, and Population in the Early Days of the Industrial Revolution*, London, 1926.

Cameron, Rondo E., *France and the Economic Development of Europe, 1800-1914*, Princeton, 1961.

Carsten, F. L., ed., *The New Cambridge Modern History,* Vol. V, Cambridge, 1961.

Caspari, Fritz, *Humanism and the Social Order in Tudor England,* Chicago, 1954.

Cecil, Evelyn, *Primogeniture: A Short History of Its Development in Various Countries and Its Practical Effects,* London, 1895.

Chambers, A. M., *A Constitutional History of England,* London, 1909.

Cheyney, Edward P., *An Introduction to the Industrial and Social History of England,* New York, 1920.

Chrimes, Stanley B., *English Constitutional History,* London, 1953.

Christie, Ian R., *Wilkes, Wyvill and Reform,* London, 1962.

Clapham, John H., *The Bank of England,* 2 vols., Cambridge, 1944.

Clapham, John H., *An Economic History of Modern Britain,* 3 vols., Cambridge, 1926, 1932, 1938.

Clark, G. N., *The Seventeenth Century,* London, 1929.

Clark G. N., *The Wealth of England from 1496 to 1760,* London, 1946.

Clowes, William L., *The Royal Navy: A History from The Earliest Times to the Present,* London, Vol. IV, 1899, Vol. V, 1900.

Cohen, Emmeline W., *The Growth of the British Civil Service 1780-1939,* London, 1941.

Court, William H. B., *A Concise Economic History of Britain from 1750 to Recent Times,* Cambridge, 1954.

Courtney, Leonard, *The Working Constitution of the United Kingdom,* New York, 1908.

Cunningham, William, *The Growth of English Industry and Commerce in Modern Times,* Cambridge, 1919.

Cunningham, William, *The Progress of Capitalism in England,* Cambridge, 1925.

Curtis, S. J., *History of Education in Great Britain,* London, 1951.

Curtis, S. J., and M. E. A. Boultwood, *An Introductory History of English Education since 1800,* London, 1962.

Davis, H. W., *The Age of Grey and Peel,* London, 1929.

Deane, Phyllis, "Capital Formation in Britain before the Railway Age." *Economic Development and Cultural Change,* Vol. 9, No. 3 (April, 1961), pp. 352-368.

Deane, Phyllis, and W. A. Cole, *British Economic Growth, 1688-1959: Trends and Structure,* Cambridge, 1962.

Defoe, Daniel, *The Complete English Tradesman,* 2 vols., Oxford, 1841.

Derby, T. K., "The Repeal of the Apprenticeship Clauses of the Statute of Apprentices." *The Economic History Review,* Vol. 3, No. 1 (January, 1931), pp. 67-87.

Dicey, Albert V., *The Privy Council,* London, 1860.

Dietz, Frederick C., *An Economic History of England,* New York, 1942.

Dowell, Stephen, *A History of Taxation and Taxes in England: From the Earliest Times to the Year 1885,* 2 vols., London, 1888.

DuBois, Armand B., *The English Business Company after the Bubble Act, 1720-1800,* New York, 1938.

Elton, Geoffrey R., *The Tudor Revolution in Government: Administrative Changes in the Reign of Henry VIII,* Cambridge, 1953.

Emden, Cecil, *The People and the Constitution, Being a History of the Development of the People's Influence in British Government,* Oxford, 1956.

Fitzroy, Almeric W., *The History of the Privy Council,* London, 1928.

Flinn, M. W. *An Economic and Social History of Britain, 1066-1939,* London, 1961.

Frischauer, Paul, *England's Years of Danger,* London, 1938.

Gayer, Arthur D., W. W. Rostow, and Anna Jacobson Schwartz, *The Growth and Fluctuation of the British Economy, 1790-1850,* 2 vols., Oxford, 1953.

Gibbins, Henry De B., *Industry in England: Historical Outlines,* New York, 1906.

Giffen, Robert, *Economic Inquiries and Studies,* 2 vols., London, 1904.

Gras, N. S. B., *An Introduction to Economic History,* New York, 1922.

Gretton, Richard H., *The English Middle Class,* London, 1917.

Gretton, Richard H., *The King's Government: A Study of the Growth of Central Administration,* London, 1913.

Gross, Charles, *The Gild Merchant,* London, 1890.

Habakkuk, H. J., "Economic Functions of English Landowners in the Seventeenth and Eighteenth Centuries." *Explorations in Entrepreneurial History,* Vol. 6, No. 2 (December, 1953), pp. 92-102.

Habakkuk, H. J., "Family Structure and Economic Change in Nineteenth-Century Europe." *The Journal of Economic History,* Vol. 15, No. 1, Part 1 (1955) pp. 1-12.

Hammond, John, and Barbara Hammond, *The Rise of Modern Industry,* New York, 1926.

Heckscher, Eli F., *Mercantilism,* 2 vols., New York, 1955.

Hoffmann, Walther G., *British Industry, 1700-1950,* Oxford, 1955.

Holdsworth, William S., *A History of English Law,* 13 vols., London, 1903-1952.

Hoselitz, Bert F., "Entrepreneurship and Capital Formation in France and Britain since 1700." National Bureau of Economic Research, *Capital Formation and Economic Growth,* Princeton, 1955, pp. 291-337.

Hughes, Edward, *Studies in Administration and Finance, 1558-1825: With Special Reference to the History of Salt Taxation in England,* Manchester, 1934.

Hunt, Bishop Carleton, *The Development of the Business Corporation in England, 1800-1867,* Cambridge, Mass., 1936.

Jackman, W. T., *The Development of Transportation in Modern England,* London, 1962.

Jane, Lionel C., *The Coming of Parliament: England from 1350 to 1660,* London, 1905.

Jenks, Leland, *The Migration of British Capital to 1875,* New York, 1927.

Jordan, Wilbur K., *Philanthropy in England, 1480-1660: A Study of the Changing Pattern of English Social Aspirations,* London, 1959.

Kallett, J. R., "The Breakdown of Gild and Corporation Control over the Handicraft and Retail Trade in London." *The Economic History Review,* 2nd Series, Vol. 10, No. 3 (April, 1958), pp. 381-394.

Knowles, L. C. A., *The Industrial and Commercial Revolutions in Great Britain during the Nineteenth Century,* London, 1921.

Kramer, Stella, *The English Craft Gilds and the Government: An Examination of the Accepted Theory Regarding the Decay of the English Craft Gilds,* New York, 1905.

Lee, W. L. Melville, *A History of Police in England,* London, 1901.

Levy, Hermann, *Monopolies, Cartels, and Trusts in British Industry,* London, 1927.

Lipson, Ephraim, *The Economic History of England,* 3 vols., London, 1929, 1931.

Llewellyn, Karl N., "Across Sales on Horseback." *Harvard Law Review*, Vol. 52, No. 5 (March, 1939), pp. 725-746.

Llewellyn, Karl N., "The First Struggle to Unhorse Sales." *Harvard Law Review*, Vol. 52, No. 6 (April, 1939), pp. 873-904.

Lloyd, Eyre, *The Succession Laws of Christian Countries, with Special Reference to the Law of Primogeniture as it Exists in England*, London, 1877.

Lovell, Michael C., "The Role of the Bank of England as Lender of Last Resort in the Crises of the Eighteenth Century." *Explorations in Entrepreneurial History*, Vol. 10, No. 1 (October, 1957), pp. 8-21.

Lunt, W. E., *History of England*, New York, 1928.

Maitland, F. W., *Justice and Police*, London, 1885.

Mantoux, Paul J., *The Industrial Revolution in the Eighteenth Century: An Outline of the Beginnings of the Modern Factory System in England*, New York, 1962.

Mathew, David, *The Social Structure in Caroline England*, Oxford, 1948.

Mathieson, William L., *England in Transition*, London, 1920.

Mayes, Charles R., "The Sale of Peerages in Early Stuart England." *The Journal of Modern History*, Vol. 29, No. 1 (March, 1957), pp. 21-37.

Meredith, Hugh O., *Outlines in the Economic History of England: A Study in Social Development*, London, 1930.

Minchinton, W. E., "The Merchants in England in the Eighteenth Century." *Explorations in Entrepreneurial History*, Vol. 10, No. 2 (December, 1957), pp. 62-71.

Mitchell, B. R., and Phyllis Deane, *Abstract of British Historical Statistics*, Cambridge, 1962.

Mitchell, William, *An Essay on the Early History of the Law of Merchant: Being the Yorke Prize Essay for the Year 1903*, Cambridge, 1904.

Moffit, Louis W., *England on the Eve of the Industrial Revolution: A Study of Economic and Social Conditions from 1740 to 1760, with Special Reference to Lancashire*, New York, 1925.

Mosse, George L., *The Struggle for Sovereignty in England: From the Reign of Queen Elizabeth to the Petition of Right*, East Lansing, Mich., 1950.

Namier, Lewis B., *Personalities and Powers*, London, 1955.

Namier, Lewis B., *The Structure of Politics at the Accession of George III*, 2 vols., London, 1957.

Neale, John E., *Elizabeth I and Her Parliaments, 1559-1581, 1584-1601*, 2 vols., New York, 1953, 1958.

Nef, John U., *Industry and Government in France and England, 1540-1640*, New York, 1957.

Nef, John U., "The Progress of Technology and the Growth of Large-Scale Industry in Great Britain, 1540-1640." *The Economic History Review*, Vol. 5, No. 1 (October, 1934), pp. 3-24.

Norris, John, *Shelburne and Reform*, New York, 1963.

Ogg, Frederic A., *English Government and Politics*, New York, 1947.

Pares, Richard, *King George III and the Politicians*, Oxford, 1953.

Pares, Richard, *Limited Monarchy in Great Britain in the Eighteenth Century*, London, 1957.

Percy, Eustace, *The Privy Council under the Tudors*, Oxford, 1907.

Perry, John, *The Story of Standards*, New York, 1955.

Pike, Luke O., *A Constitutional History of the House of Lords*, London, 1894.

Pollard, A. F., "Council, Star Chamber and Privy Council under the Tudors: I, the Council; II, The Star Chamber." *English Historical Review*, Vol. 37, No. 147 (July, 1922), pp. 337-360.

Pollard, A. F., "Council, Star Chamber and Privy Council under the Tudors: III, The Privy Council." *English Historical Review*, Vol. 38, No. 149 (January, 1923), pp. 42-60.

Pollard, S., "Laissez-faire and Shipbuilding." *The Economic History Review*, 2nd Series, Vol. 5, No. 1 (1955), pp. 98-115.

Pollock, Frederick, and Frederick W. R. Maitland, *The History of English Law before the Time of Edward I*, 2 vols., Boston, 1899.

Pollins, Harold, "The Finances of the Liverpool and Manchester Railway." *The Economic History Review*, 2nd Series, Vol. 5, No. 1 (1952), pp. 90-97.

Potter, Harold, *An Historical Introduction to English Law and Its Institutions*, London, 1947.

Pressnell, L. S., *Country Banking in the Industrial Revolution*, Oxford, 1956.

Pressnell, L. S., "Public Monies and the Development of English Banking." *The Economic History Review*, 2nd Series, Vol. 5, No. 3 (1953), pp. 378-397.

Pressnell, L. S., ed., *Studies in the Industrial Revolution*, London, 1960.

Price, William H., *The English Patents of Monopoly*, New York, 1906.

Read, Conyers, "Factions in the English Privy Council under Elizabeth." *Annual Report of the American Historical Association*, Vol. 1 (1911), pp. 111-119.

Read, Conyers, *The Government of England under Elizabeth*, Washington, D.C., 1960.

Reid, William S., *Economic History of Great Britain*, New York, 1954.

Richards, R. D., "Early English Banking Schemes." *Journal of Economic and Business History*, Vol. 1, No. 1 (November, 1928), pp. 36-76.

Richards, R. D., "The Pioneers of Banking in England." *Economic History*, Series No. 4 (January, 1929), pp. 485-502.

Richmond, Herbert, *Statesmen and Sea Power*, Oxford, 1946.

Rogers, James E. T., *Six Centuries of Work and Wages: The History of English Labour*, London, 1886.

Roskell, John S., *The Commons in the Parliament of 1422: English Society and Parliamentary Representation under the Lancastrians*, Manchester, 1954.

Shannon, H. A., "The Coming of General Limited Liability." *Economic History*, Vol. 2, No. 6 (January, 1931), pp. 267-291.

Slater, Gilbert, *The Growth of Modern England*, London, 1932.

Smellie, K. B., *A Hundred Years of English Government*, London, 1950.

Smith, Lacey B., *Tudor Prelates and Politics, 1536-1558*, Princeton, 1953.

Stephen, James F., *A History of the Criminal Law of England*, 3 vols., London, 1883.

Stone, Lawrence, "The Inflation of Honours, 1558-1641." *Past and Present*, No. 14 (November, 1958), pp. 45-70.

Stone, Lawrence, "Marriage among the English Nobility in the 16th and 17th Centuries." *Comparative Studies in Society and History*, Vol. 3, No. 2 (January, 1961), pp. 182-206.

Stone, Lawrence, "The Nobility in Business." *Explorations in Entrepreneurial History*, Vol. 10, No. 2 (December, 1957), pp. 54-61.

Stone, Lawrence, "State Control in Sixteenth-Century England." *The Economic History Review*, Vol. 17, No. 2 (1947), pp. 103-120.

Supple, Barry, *Commercial Crisis and Change in England, 1600-1642: A Study in the Instability of a Mercantile Economy*, Cambridge, 1959.

Swart, K. W., *Sale of Offices in the Seventeenth Century*, The Hague, 1949.

Tanner, Joseph R., *English Constitutional Conflicts of the Seventeenth Century, 1603-1689*, Cambridge, 1937.

Taube, Edward, "German Craftsmen in England during the Tudor Period." *Economic History*, Vol. 3, No. 14 (February, 1939), pp. 167-178.

Tawney, R. H, "The Rise of the Gentry, 1558-1640." *The Economic History Review*, Vol. 11, No. 1 (1941), pp. 1-38.

Taylor, Hannis, *The Origin and Growth of the English Constitution: An Historical Treatise*, 2 vols., New York, 1898.

Trevelyan, George M., *English Social History: A Survey of Six Centuries, Chaucer to Queen Victoria*, London, 1942.

Trevor-Roper, H. R., *The Gentry, 1540-1640*, London, 1953.

Turner, Edward R., *The Cabinet Council of England, 1622-1784*, Baltimore, 1930.

Turner, Edward R., *The Privy Council of England in the Seventeenth and Eighteenth Centuries, 1603-1784*, 2 vols., Baltimore, 1927, 1928.

Usher, Abbott P., *An Introduction to the Industrial History of England*, New York, 1920.

Walcott, Robert, Jr., *English Politics in the Early Eighteenth Century*, Cambridge, Mass., 1956.

Ward, A. W., G. W. Prothero, and Stanley Leathes, *The Cambridge Modern History*, Vol. V, New York, 1912.

Watson, J. Steven, *The Reign of George III, 1760-1815*, London, 1960.

Westerfield, Ray B., *Middlemen in English Business, Particularly between 1660 and 1760*, New Haven, 1915.

Wilson, Charles, "The Entrepreneur in the Industrial Revolution in Britain." *Explorations in Entrepreneurial History*, Vol. 7, No. 3 (February, 1955), pp. 129-145.

Wingfield-Stratford, Esmé, *The Squire and His Relations*, London, 1956.

Woodward, E. Llewellyn, *The Age of Reform, 1815-1870*, Oxford, 1962.

Wormuth, Francis D., *The Royal Prerogative, 1603-1649: A Study in English Political and Constitutional Ideas*, Ithaca, N. Y. 1939.

Zeeveld, William G., *Foundations of Tudor Policy*, Cambridge, Mass., 1948.

VII. SOVIET UNION

Armstrong, John A., *The Politics of Totalitarianism: The Communist Party of the Soviet Union from 1934 to the Present*, New York, 1961.

Dimensions of Soviet Economic Power, Joint Economic Committee, 87th Congress of the United States, Second Session, Washington, D.C., 1962.

Fainsod, Merle, *How Russia is Ruled*, Cambridge, Mass., 1963.

Holt, Robert T., and John E. Turner, eds., *Soviet Union: Paradox and Change*, New York, 1962.

Inkeles, Alex, *Public Opinion in Soviet Russia: A Study in Mass Persuasion*, Cambridge, Mass., 1958.

McClosky, Herbert, and John E. Turner, *The Soviet Dictatorship*, New York, 1960.

Moore, Barrington, Jr., *Terror and Progress USSR: Some Sources of Change and Stability in the Soviet Dictatorship*, Cambridge, Mass., 1954.

Nove, Alec, *The Soviet Economy*, London, 1961.

Schapiro, Leonard, *The Communist Party of the Soviet Union*, New York, 1962.

Wiles, Peter J. D., *The Political Economy of Communism*, Cambridge, Mass., 1962.

VIII. MISCELLANEOUS

Berkowitz, Leonard, *Aggression: A Social Psychological Analysis*, New York, 1962.

Cameron, Norman and Ann Magaret, *Behavior Pathology*, Cambridge, Mass., 1951.

Duverger, Maurice, *Political Parties, Their Organization and Activity in the Modern State*, New York, 1959.

Holt, Robert T., and Robert W. van de Welde, *Strategic Psychological Operations and American Foreign Policy*, Chicago, 1960.

Lane, Robert, *Political Life*, Glencoe, 1959.

Shils, Edward, "Further Observations on Mrs. Huxley." *Encounter*, Vol. 17, No. 4 (October, 1961), pp. 44-49.

Index

adaptive functional requisite, 19, 51–52, 100–126, 245–257, 293–308, 329, 337, 373
aggregation of information, 302
agricultural organization: Soviet Union, 362–366
aides, 129
Allen, George C., 245
allocation, 299
Almond, Gabriel A.: concept of modern political system, 8–19; critique of, 12–19
anonymity, 298, 311
antiparasite courts, 369–370
Apter, David E., 20–24
aristocracy: England, 188–189; Japan, 186–188, 209 (*see also* gentry; nobility)
augmentations, 132
autarchy, 356
authority structure: clarification of, 58, 348; hypothesis concerning, 329; reliability of, 57–58; resolution of, 57–58; Soviet Union, 345 (*see also* specific country)
authority system: hierarchical, 22–23; pyramidal, 22–23

banking: China, 137–138; England, 156–157, 262–263; France, 131–132; Japan, 144–145, 258–259
Bank of England, 157–158, 262, 263
big push: theory of, 294–295
Blau, Peter, 32
Board of Trade, 255
Boissannade, P., 102
Buganda, 22–24
Burma, 24, 26–27

Cairncross, A. K., 41
capital-intensive technology, 337, 339
capitation, 129, 130, 181
Censorate, 77, 110
centralization, 310–311, 358–359, 372–375
centralized decision structure, 301–303, 307, 340
Chang, Chung-li, 206
Chen, Shao-kwan, 107
Cherniavski, V., 360
China: adaptive requisite, 105–111; authority structure, 81–82; banking, 137–138; bureaucracy, 78–82, 182–185; commercial law, 196–198; creation of credit, 137–139; criminal law, 176–177; enforcement practices and procedures, 110–111; goal attainment, 132–139; government regulation

of economic enterprises, 107–110; government support of economic endeavor, 105–107; inheritance, 217–218; internal tariffs, 221–222; level of technology, 67; monetary system, 138–139; non-tax revenue, 136–137; procedures of governing, 75–82; resource allocation, 105–107; resource management, 107–111; resource mobilization, 132–139; role of emperor, 75–76; sale of office, 136–137; social mobility, 205–208; social stratification, 182–186; structure of government, 75–82; taxes, 133–136
civil service (*see* specific country, bureaucracy)
clergy; England, 189, 192; France, 179
coercive process, 54, 279–280
Colbert, Jean-Baptiste, 70, 101–103, 129
Cole, Charles W., 102
commercial law, 315–316: China, 196–197; England, 199–200; France, 195–196; Japan, 198–199, 277
commoners: China, 183–184; England, 189–190; France, 179–181; Japan, 187
communication channels, 59
communication process, 53
comparative method, 2–5
compliance, techniques of securing, 58
comrades' courts, 369–370
conseil d'état, 70
conseil des dépêches, 70
conseil des finances, 70
conseil des parties, 70
consociational system, 20–21, 22
consummatory values, 22–23
corvée, 133
Coser, Rose L., 32
Council of Ministers, 346, 358
council of state (*Gorōju*), 84
courts, common law, 124–125
creation of credit, 311–312 (*see also* specific country)
criminal law (*see* specific country)
cultural system, definition of, 54–55
currencies, 200–202, 317

daimyō, 83–116 (*see also* Japan, nobility)
decentralization, Soviet Union, 360–362
decentralized decision making, 298, 301, 359, 367, 378
decomposability, 298, 302
Deutsch, Karl, 58
Diet, 236–237

differentiation, structural, 8–10; **16**
diffracted social system, 305
diminutions, 132
district magistrate, 78–79
dixième, 129–130, 181
drive to modernity stage, 45–49, 352, 343–352
Durkheim, Émile, 172

economic planning (*see* planning, economic)
education: England, 271–272; Japan, 270–271
Egret, Jean, 203
emergent explanation, 27–28
enculturation process: general, 53, 64, n. 39, 344–345; England, 271–272; Japan, 270–271
England: adaptive requisite, 118–126, 249–256; authority structure, 91, 241; bureaucracy, 242–244; canals, 250–252; commercial law, 199–200; criminal law, 175–176; customs duties, 151; enforcement practices and procedures, 122–126; functions of government, 88–94; goal attainment, 260–264; government regulation of economic enterprises, 119; government support of economic endeavor, 118–119; grants of privilege, 118–119; inheritance, 219–220; internal tariffs, 222, 223; joint stock company, 251–252, 263–264; level of technology, 67–68; military expenditures, 253; procedures of governing, 239–244; railroads, 251–254; resource allocation, 118–119, 250–255; resource management, 254; sale of office, 154; social control process, 268–269; social mobility, 213–216; social stratification, 188–192; structure of government, 239–244; taxes, 147–153; turnpike trusts, 252
entrepreneurs, 304, 307–308
Erikson, Erik H., 29–30
Exchequer Loans Commissioners, 252
exploratory study, 3–5
externalities, 297, 299, 308
extragovernmental process, 57–59

factory legislation: England, 274–275; Japan, 273–274
farmers, England, 191
feedback, 58, 300–301
"fifteenth", 148
France: adaptive requisite, 100–105; authority structure, 72, 75, 96, n. 11; banking, 131–132; bureaucracy, 72–78; commercial law, 195–196; creation of credit, 131–132; criminal law, 174–175; enforcement practices and procedures, 103–108; goal attainment, 127–132; government regulation of economic enterprises, 102–103; government support of economic endeavor, 101–

102; inheritance, 216–217; internal tariffs, 220–221; level of technology, 67–68; monetary system, 131–132; non-tax revenue, 130–131; procedures of governing, 69–75; resource allocation, 101–102; resource management, 102–105; resource mobilization, 127–131; sale of titles, 130–131; social mobility, 202–205; social stratification, 178–182; structures of government, 69–75; taxes, 127–130
Fronde, 72
Fulani, 15
function, definition of, 50–51
functions of government, 50–56, **61**
fused social system, 305

gabelle, 101, 128
gain, 65, n. 57
genrō, 235
gentry: China, 182–183, 184–185, 205–208; England, 189, 214–215
Germany, 30–31
Ghana, 23
goal-attainment functional requisite, 52, 127–145, 257–264, 309–312, 373, 127–159
Gosplan, 358
governmental processes, 57
Grand Council, 76
Grand Secretariat, 76
grants of privilege, 101, 112 (*see also* specific country)
guilds: China, 109–111, 197; England, 119–121; France, 103–104; Japan, 114, 117–118

Hansen, Alvin, 62, n. 24
hatamoto, 85
Hausa, 15
Ho, Ping-ti, 206
Hoebel, E. Adamson, 316
Honjo, 208
House of Commons, 90, 120, 239–**240**
House of Lords, 90, 241
House of Peers, 237
House of Representatives, 237
Hsiao, Kung-ch'üan, 81
Hucker, Charles O., 106
Hurwicz, Leonid, 297–298

incentive system, 350–351, 353, **364**, **376–377**
increasing returns, 297, 299, 308
indivisibilities, 295, 297, 299, 308
industrial ministries, 346, 354–355
information networks, 58–59
information process, 278–280, 366
inheritance system, 216, 219–220, **281–282**, 320–321, 329, 338
input functions, 9
inspecteurs des manufactures, **73**, **103**
inspecteurs généraux, 103

instrumental values, 22–23
integrative functional requisite, 19, 53, 171, 193–223, 276–282, 314–328, 345, 355–357, 366, 373
intendants, 72–73, 97, n. 18, 174–175
interest aggregation, 9, 11
interest articulation, 9–11, 13–14
interest groups, 11
internal tariffs: China, 221–222; England, 222–223; France, 220–221; Japan, 222

Japan: adaptive requisite, 111–118, 245; authority structure, 85, 237; banking, 144–145, 248–249; bureaucracy, 86–88, 238–239; cabinet, 237; commercial law, 198–199; council of state, 236; creation of credit, 144–146, 260; criminal law, 176; Japan, enforcement practices and procedures, 115–118; functions of government, 82–88; goal attainment, 139–146, 257–260; government regulation of economic enterprises, 113–115; government support of economic endeavor, 110–113, 245–248; inheritance, 218–219; integration, 276–277, 279–282; internal tariffs, 222; joint stock companies, 248–249, 259–260; level of technology, 67; monetary system, 144–145; non-tax revenue, 142–144; procedures of governing, 82–88, 234–239; resource allocation, 110–113, 245–248; resource management, 113–118, 245–248; resource mobilization, 139–144, 257–264; social control process, 267–268; social mobility, 208–213; social stratification, 186–188; structure of government, 234–239; taxes, 140–142
joint stock company (*see* specific country)
justices of the peace, 93–94, 125, 175, 243

Katz, Elihu, 11
Khrushchev, Nikita S., 353, 367–368
King's Bench, Court of the, 175
Kuznets, Simon, 42–43, 50

lag, 58–59, 65, n. 57
land tax, 133, 140, 257
Liberman, Yevsei G., 360
li-chia, 79–80
lieutenants généraux de police, 73, 103
likin, 135, 220–222
load, 65, n. 57
Lords Lieutenant, 92

macro-analysis, 56
Malenkov, Georgi M., 355
Manchester-Liverpool railway, 252
Mandate of Heaven, 77
market system, 361
Martin, Germain, 101
Mason, Edward S., 337, 338, 340
Meiji Restoration, 234–235
memory, 59

merchants: China, 184, 197, 205–208; England, 148, 189–191, 199–200, 214–215; France, 180, 195–196; Japan, 146, 187, 198–199, 208–213
military establishment, 347
mobilization system, 20–22
modern economy, 45–49, 343, 353–378, 360, 367, 374
modernizing autocracy, 20–22
monetary system (*see* specific country)
Mousnier, Roland, 130

nakama, 117
nation-building, 24–27
Nef, John U., 124, 130, 196, 204
Nemchinov, Vasily S., 360
nobility: China, 182; England, 188–189, 191–192, 213–214; France, 75, 178–179, 181–182, 202–205; Japan, 186 (*see also* aristocracy)
nondecomposability, 298

office, sale of: China, 205–208; England, 213–214; France, 202–205
operationality, 298, 311
output functions, 9, 12

Pagès, George, 71
pao-chia, 79–80
parlements, 73–74, 203
Parsons, Talcott, 51, 56
party system, 11
pattern-maintenance functional requisite, 51, 171–193, 225, n. 14, 313–314, 344
peasants: China, 183–184; France, 180–181; Japan, 187, 211–213 (*see also* farmers)
Peel, Robert, 268
perfect competition, 381
perfect computation, 381
piecework, 351
Pitt, William, 242–243
planning, economic, 346–347
police: England, 268; Japan, 267–268; Soviet Union, 344, 347, 349, 369
policy-enforcing process, 57
policy-making process, 57
Politburo, 346
political communication, 9, 11–12
political modernization: process of, 19–33; theory of, 7–19
political recruitment, 9, 10, 15
political socialization, 9, 10, 14–15
political systems: modern, 7–19; primitive, 15
population growth, 321–325
post-modern economy, 48–49
prerequisites, 44, 284, n. 1
Presidium, 346, 349
Pressnell, L. S., 262
prime minister, 240

prismatic society, 305
Privy Council, 89, 91–92, 122–125, 175
procedures of governing, 56–61, 371 (see also specific country)
production, processes of, 52
product mix, 302
propensity to revolt, 329
propensity to save, 320
psychological conceptualizations, 24–33
public corporation, 339
public goods, 299
Pye, Lucian W., 20, 24–27

receveurs des tailles, 128
receveurs généraux, 128
reciprocity, withdrawal of, 172–173
reductive explanation, 27–28
registration, 74
remontrance, 74
repressive sanctions, 64, n. 42
requisites, 284, n. 1
resource allocation, process of, 52, 297, 303, 307, 309–310, 329, 337, 344, 373 (see also specific country)
resource management, process of, 52, 329, 337–340, 344, 346–347, 373 (see also specific country)
resource mobilization, process of, 52, 263, 309–311, 337–344 (see also specific country)
restitutive sanctions, 64, n. 42
retaliation-compensation, 172–173, 313
Richelieu, Cardinal, 71
Riggs, Fred W., 200, 305, 306
Rosenstein-Rodan, P. N., 294, 295
Rosovsky, Henry, 245
Rostow, W. W., 40
rule adjudication, 9, 13–16
rule application, 9, 13, 16
rule making, 9, 13, 16

sale of office (see office, sale of)
sale of titles (see titles, sale of)
salt tax, 134
sanctions: legal, 172–173; nonlegal, 172–173; repressive, 172, 173; restitutive, 172
sankin-kōtai system, 86
Sansom, George B., 84
Schapera, I., 18
scholar-gentry, China, 182–183
secular political system, 8, 10, 35
Sée, Henri, 179
Smith, M. G., 15–16
social class, norms that apply to, 177–193

social-control process, 53, 171–200, 224, n. 5, 225, n. 13, 267–270, 344, 350–352, 366–371, 376–378
socialization, 64, n. 39
social mobility, 202–216, 229, n. 93, 229, n. 106, 318–319, 341
social stratification, 177–193, 315–316 (see also specific country)
social system, definition of, 54–55
societal functions, 17–19
sociological conceptualization, 20–24, 27–33
Soviet Union: bureaucracy, 347–349, 367–369; functions of government, 344–345, 354–367; procedures of governing, 345–351, 367–372
sovnarkhozes, 355–358, 365
Spengler, Joseph J., 174
stages of economic growth, 40–50, 60–61
stagnation, economic, 63, n. 24
Stalin, Joseph, 345, 346, 347, 348
Statute of Artificers, 121–122
Statute of Monopolies, 120
style, 8, 10–12
subdélégués, 73
supernatural sanctions, 172–173
Supreme Council of the National Economy, 358

taille, 101, 127
take-off, 41–44, 44–45, 49, 62, n. 12, 233–284, 296, 304, 307, 309, 338
taxation (see specific country)
tax farmers, 129
tension-management process, 19, 53, 225, n. 14, 271–274, 344–345
"tenth", 148
theocratic political system, 8, 10
third estate, France, 179–181
titles, sale of: China, 205–208; England, 213–214; France, 202–205
totalitarian system, 13–14
traditional economy, 49
traditional society, 44–45
traites, 129, 220–221
tribute tax, 140

Udy, Stanley H., 16

vingtième, 130

Wakadoshiyori, 84
Walpole, Robert, 240
weights and measures: China, 200–201; England, 201; France, 200; Japan, 201
Wigmore, John H., 84

Reasoning & Writing Well

A Rhetoric, Research Guide, Reader, and Handbook

THIRD EDITION

Betty Mattix Dietsch
Marion Technical College
Marion, Ohio

Boston   Burr Ridge, IL   Dubuque, IA   Madison, WI   New York
San Francisco   St. Louis   Bangkok   Bogotá   Caracas   Kuala Lumpur
Lisbon   London   Madrid   Mexico City   Milan   Montreal   New Delhi
Santiago   Seoul   Singapore   Sydney   Taipei   Toronto

McGraw-Hill Higher Education

A Division of The **McGraw-Hill** Companies

REASONING AND WRITING WELL:
A RHETORIC, RESEARCH GUIDE, READER, AND HANDBOOK

Published by McGraw-Hill, a business unit of The McGraw-Hill Companies, Inc.,
1221 Avenue of the Americas, New York, NY, 10020. Copyright © 2003, 2000, 1998 by
Betty Mattix Dietsch. All rights reserved. No part of this publication may be reproduced
or distributed in any form or by any means, or stored in a database or retrieval system,
without the prior written consent of The McGraw-Hill Companies, Inc., including, but
not limited to, in any network or other electronic storage or transmission, or broadcast
for distance learning. Some ancillaries, including electronic and print components, may
not be available to customers outside the United States.

This book is printed on acid-free paper.

1 2 3 4 5 6 7 8 9 0 DOC/DOC 0 9 8 7 6 5 4 3 2

ISBN 0-7674-3000-X

Executive editor: *Lisa Moore*
Senior development editor: *Renee Deljon*
Senior marketing manager: *David S. Patterson*
Senior media producer: *Todd Vaccaro*
Project manager: *Karen Nelson*
Production supervisor: *Susanne Riedell*
Senior designer: *Jenny El-Shamy*
Lead supplement producer: *Marc Mattson*
Typeface: *10/12 Berling Book*
Compositor: *G&S Typesetters*
Printer: R. R. Donnelley & Sons Company

Dietsch, Betty M.
    Reasoning and writing well : a rhetoric, research guide, reader, and handbook / Betty
Mattix Dietsch.—3rd ed.
    p. cm.
Includes bibliographical references and indexes.
ISBN 0-7674-3000-X (softcover : alk. paper)
    1. English language—Rhetoric.   2. English language—Grammar—Handbooks,
manuals, etc.   3. College readers.   4. Report writing.   5. Reasoning.   I. Title:
Reasoning and writing well.   II. Title.
PE1408.D5437 2003
808'.042—dc21   2002026485

www.mhhe.com

To my former students, with thanks.

Topic examples: 172   149 disc
                11

Transitions: 81

Contents in Brief

A Note to Instructors   xxxix

RHETORIC AND RESEARCH WRITING GUIDE

PART 1. The Writing Situation and Early Stages of the Writing Process   1

1   Writing in Context   3
2   Different Voices for Different Occasions and Audiences   12
3   Prewriting: Discovering Ideas   24
4   Drafting: Exploring Ideas   32

PART 2. Revision Workshop: Later Stages of the Writing Process   47

5   Revising, Editing, and Proofreading: An Overview   49
6   Revision and Accuracy: Beginning to Think Critically   66
7   Revising Paragraphs   78
8   Editing: Styling Sentences   92
9   Editing: Improving Word Choice   108

PART 3. Options for Organization   121

10   Narration: Recounting Events   123
11   Description: Conveying Impressions   138
12   Process Analysis: Explaining How   151
13   Illustration: Showing with Examples   163
14   Classification: Grouping and Dividing   173
15   Comparison and Contrast: Explaining Likeness and Difference   186
16   Definition: Identifying Basic Characteristics   200
17   Cause and Effect: Explaining Why   215

PART 4. Critical Thinking, Evaluation, and Argument   227

18   Problem Solving   229
19   Shaping an Effective Argument   243
20   Detecting Fallacies   273

PART 5. Research Writing   287

21   Preliminary Considerations for Research   289
22   Primary Research: Observation, Interviews,and Surveys   295
23   Secondary Research: Locating Print and Electronic Sources   316
24   Documenting Sources   339
25   Using Sources and Writing a Research Paper   378

PART 6. Reading and Writing about Essays, Fiction, Plays,and Poetry   409

26   Reading and Responding to Essays   411
27   Reading and Responding to Short Stories, Novels, and Plays   428
28   Reading and Responding to Poetry   450

PART 7. Essay Exams, Employment Writing, and Oral Presentations   465

29   Writing Effective Essay Exams   467
30   Employment Writing for the Twenty-First Century   477
31   Oral Presentations   520

THE READER   545

THE HANDBOOK: A GUIDE TO GRAMMAR, PUNCTUATION, MECHANICS, AND USAGE   733

Credits   C-1
Index of Authors and Titles   I-1
Subject Index   I-4

Contents

A Note to Instructors   xxxix

RHETORIC AND RESEARCH WRITING GUIDE

PART 1 The Writing Situation and Early Stages of the Writing Process   1

CHAPTER 1 Writing in Context   3

Why Learn to Reason and Write Well?   3

What Is the Rhetorical Situation?   4

    Occasion   4

    Purpose   4

        The General Purpose   4

        The Specific Purpose   5

    Topic   5

        [Box] Selecting a Topic   6

    Audience   6

    The Voice of the Writer   6

        [Box] Questions to Assess Audiences   7

        How Should a Writer's Voice Sound?   7

        Word Choice and Voice   7

        [Box] Key Point: What Makes Writing Effective?   7

What Is the Writing Process?   8

A Word of Encouragement   8

        [Box] The Four Stages of the Writing Process   9

Summary   9

Key Terms   10

Practice   10

Ten Ideas for Writing   10

CHAPTER 2 Different Voices for Different Occasions and Audiences   12

The Writer's Voice   12

Workplace Case Study: A Series of Collection Letters   13

How Casual Conversation Differs from Focused Writing   14

Standard and Nonstandard Usage   14
    Standard Usage   14
    Nonstandard Usage   15
        Dialect and Regionalism   15
        Where Can I Find Keys to Usage Labels and Abbreviations?   15
            What If Dictionaries Disagree?   15
    Three Vocabularies   15
        [Box] Levels of Formality   16

Three Levels of Formality   16
    Informal Standard English   16
        Watch the Pronouns   17
        Mixing Levels of Formality   17
    Professional English   17
        [Box] Levels of Formality in the Workplace   18
    Formal English   18

Three Common Concerns That Affect Voice   19
    Out-of-Place Colloquialisms   19
    Switching Pronouns in Mid-Sentence   20
    Inappropriate Prescriptive Tone   20

Three Crucial Questions for Achieving an Appropriate Voice   21

Summary   22

Key Terms   22

Test Yourself   22

Practice   22

Test Yourself Answers   23

CHAPTER 3 Prewriting: Discovering Ideas   24

Overcoming Anxiety   24

Finding a Topic and Ideas by Prewriting   25
    Freewriting   26
    Clustering   26
    Brainstorming   27
    List-Making and Scratch Outlining on a Computer   28
        [Box] Computers and Outlining Tip   29
    Questioning   29
    Combining Invention Techniques   29

Gathering Information   30
    Reading Literature and Doing Research   30
    Keeping a Journal   30

Summary   30

Key Terms   31

Practice   31

Ten Ideas for Ten-Minute Writings   31

CHAPTER 4 Drafting: Exploring Ideas   32

Fleshing Out Your Prewriting Notes   32
When Ideas Disappear   33

Focusing an Exploratory Draft   33
Narrowing a Topic   33
Case Study: Nita Narrows Her Topic   34
Writing a Purpose Statement   34
Writing a Thesis Statement   35
Where Should the Thesis Statement Go?   36
[Box] Drafting a Thesis Statement   35
Omitting a Thesis Statement   36

Drafting an Introduction   36
Begin with an Anecdote That Sets the Scene   37
Overuse of the Pronoun "I"   37
[Box] Dietsch's "I" Rule   37
Begin with a Description   38
Begin by Stating a Problem   38
Begin with a Surprising Statistic or Striking Bit of History   39
Begin by Disputing a Common Belief or Defying a Stereotype   39

Seven Basic Ways to Organize a Draft   39
[Box] The Seven Basic Orders   40
Chronology   40
Spatial Order   40
Order of Importance   40
Order of Generality   41
Order of Formation   41
Order of Complexity   41
Order of Materiality   41

Writing an Effective Conclusion   42
End with a Reference to a Benefit   42
End by Referring Back to the Thesis   42
End with a Personal Response   42
End on a Note of Optimism   43
End with an Unexpected Twist   43

Drafting on a Computer   43
[Box] Tips for Maintaining Security of Computer Files   43

A Note of Reassurance and a Brief Review   44

Summary   44
[Box] Guidelines: Tips for Drafting Successfully   45

Key Terms   46

Ten Ideas for Ten-Minute Writings   46

PART 2 Revision Workshop: Later Stages of the Writing Process   47

CHAPTER 5 Revising, Editing, and Proofreading: An Overview   49

How Do You Become Your Own Editor?   49

Revision: Stage Three of the Writing Process   50

Five Major Steps of Revision   50
    Step 1. Acknowledge the Need for Revision   50
    Step 2. Look at the Big Picture   50
    Step 3. Reread and Mark the Draft   50
        [Box] Tools for Revision   51
    Step 4. Revise and Refine   51
    Step 5. Let the Draft Cool, Then Check the Focus   51
        [Box] Tips for Revising with a Computer   52

Refocusing a Draft   53
    Focusing the Title   53
    Outlining   53
    Finding a Fresh Perspective   53
        [Box] Formal Outlines   54

Clarifying the Draft   55
        [Box] Checklist: Listening to Your Written Voice   55
    Revising Sluggish Openings   55
    Revising the Body   56
        [Box] Checklist: Revising Paragraphs   56
    Revising the Conclusion   56
    Case Study: A Series of Student Outlines and Drafts   56

Editing and Proofreading: Stage Four of the Writing Process   59

Major Tasks in Editing and Proofreading   59
    Marking the Revised Draft   59
    Making Sentences Clear and Concise   60
    Finding Fresh Language   60
        [Box] Pruning Extra Words   60
    Create a Simile or Metaphor   61
    Experiment with Alliteration and Rhyme   61
        [Box] Editing and Proofreading On-Screen   62
    Experiment with Old Sayings   62

Proofreading Effectively   62

Peer Review: Helping to Improve Each Other's Writing   63
        [Box] Suggestions for Peer Review   64

Hang in There!   64

Summary   65

Key Terms   65

Practice 65

CHAPTER 6 Revision and Accuracy: Beginning to Think Critically 66

Why Is Accuracy Important? 66
    Case Study: Why Have Newspapers Lost Credibility? 67

How Can Fact Be Determined? 67

Inferences Are Unproven 68

Value Judgments and Point of View 69

Listening to the Tone of Writing 70
    [Box] Characteristics of Facts, Inferences,
      and Value Judgments 70

Four Ways Misinformation Arises 70
    Expert Opinion Occasionally Changes 70
    A Small Survey Is Inadequate Proof 71
    Facts Are Overstated 71
    Stereotyping Shuts Out Fact 71

Writing Responsibly 72
    Limiting Generalizations 72
    Using Absolute Terms Accurately 73
    Identifying Inferences and Other Opinions 74

Revising for Accuracy 74
    [Box] Checklist: Revising for Accuracy 75

Summary 75

Key Terms 75

Test Yourself 76

Practice 76

Test Yourself Answers 77

CHAPTER 7 Revising Paragraphs 78

Elements of an Effective Paragraph 78
    The Topic Sentence 78
    Support Sentences 79
    A Concluding Sentence 79

Qualities of Effective Paragraphs 80
    Clarity 80
    Interest 80
    Unity 80
    Coherence 81
      Signpost Transitions 81
        [Box] Common Signpost Transitions 81
      Embedded Transition 82
      Parallelism 82
    Completeness 82

Prewriting and Drafting Paragraphs   83

Narrowing a Topic Sentence   83

Positioning the Topic Sentence   83
    The Topic Sentence at the Beginning   84
    The Topic Sentence in the Middle   84
    The Topic Sentence at the End   84
    Unifying a Paragraph without a Topic Sentence   85
    Adjusting Paragraph Length   85
        [Box] Guidelines: Dividing Long Paragraphs   86

Organizing and Developing Paragraphs   86
    Narrative Paragraphs   86
    Descriptive Paragraphs   87
    Process Analysis Paragraphs   88
    Illustration Paragraphs   88
    Comparison or Contrast Paragraphs   89
    Paragraphs of Definition   89
Transitional Paragraphs   90

Summary   90

Key Terms   90

Practice   91

CHAPTER 8 Editing: Styling Sentences   92

Effective Use of Verbs   93
    Favoring the Active Voice   93
        [Box] Guidelines: When Should You Use
          the Passive Voice?   93
    Replacing Forms of *Be*   94

Sentence Variety   94
    The Simple Sentence   94
    The Compound Sentence   95
        Coordinating Conjunctions   95
          [Box] Punctuating Compound Sentences   96
        What Are Comma Splices and Fused Sentences?   96
    The Complex Sentence   97
        Adjective Clauses   97
          [Box] Distinguishing *Who, Whom, Which,* and *That*   98
        Adverb Clauses   98
          [Box] Punctuating Sentences with Adverb Clauses   98

Parallelism: A Balancing Act   99
    Parallelism with Items in a Series   99
        Parallel Adjectives   99
        Parallel Prepositional Phrases   99
        Parallel Subordinate Clauses   100
    Parallelism with Items in Pairs   100

Parallel Nouns   100
Parallel Verbs   100
Parallel Phrases   100
Parallelism with Comparisons   101
Parallelism with Correlative Conjunctions   101
[Box] Punctuating Sentences with Parallel Structures   101
Chopping out Deadwood   102
References to Self   102
Prepositional Phrases   103
Adjective Clauses   103
Sentence Style   104
Periodic Sentences   104
Sentence Length   104
Position of Words within Sentences   105
Summary   105
Key Terms   106
Test Yourself   106
Practice   106
Test Yourself Answers   107

CHAPTER 9 Editing: Improving Word Choice   108
Word Meanings: Denotation and Connotation   108
Negative and Positive Words   109
Focusing on the Positive   109
[Box] Improving Your Choice of Words   110
Do Euphemisms Have a Place?   110
Inclusive Language   111
Replacing Sexist Terms with Gender-Free Terms   111
[Box] Replacing Sexist Terms   112
Replacing Offensive Terms with Respectful Terms   112
[Box] Replacing Offensive Terms   113
Technical Jargon   113
[Box] Avoiding Jargon   114
Trite Language and Clichés   114
Making the Message Clear and Appropriate   115
Making Abstractions Concrete   115
Moving from General to Specific   116
Scholarly or Everyday Words?   116
[Box] For Your Reference: Essays on Language Use
in the Reader   117
Summary   118
Key Terms   118

Test Yourself 118

Practice 119

Test Yourself Answer 119

PART 3 Options for Organization 121

CHAPTER 10 Narration: Recounting Events 123

Purpose of Narration   123
    Workplace Case Study: "Spencer's Letter"   124

Elements of Narration   124
  The Why   124
  Point of View in Narration   125
    First-Person Narration   125
    Mixing Writing Strategies   126
    Third-Person Narration   126

Writing a Narrative Paper   127
  Prewriting   127
    [Box] Movement in a Narrative   127
  Drafting an Introduction   127
    Opening with Action   128
    Opening with a Quotation   128
    Opening with a Comparison   128
  Organizing a Narrative Paper   128
  Developing the Narrative Paper   129
    Dialogue   129
    Concrete Details and Action Verbs   129
    Building Suspense   130
  Writing a Conclusion   130
    Ending with a Hint or a Hope   130
    Ending with a Surprise   130
    Ending with a Reaction   130

Writing a Narrative Report   131

Revising a Narrative   131
    [Box] Checklist: Revising a Narrative   132
    Two Student Papers: Narration   132
    [Box] For Your Reference: Narrative Essays in the Reader   134

Summary 135

Key Terms 135

Practice 135

Thirty Ideas for Narrative Papers 136

CHAPTER 11 Description: Conveying Impressions 138

What Exactly Is Description?   138

Purpose of Description   139

Creating a Dominant Impression   139
    Subjective and Objective Description   139
Writing a Paper of Description   140
    Prewriting   140
    Determining the Dominant Impression   141
    Selecting a Vantage Point and Transition   142
    Drafting an Introduction   142
    Organizing and Developing a Description   143
    Writing a Conclusion   144
    Revising a Description   144
        [Box] Checklist: Revising a Description   145
        Two Student Papers: Description   145
        [Box] For Your Reference: Descriptive Essays
            in the Reader   147

Summary   148

Key Terms   148

Practice   148

Thirty Ideas for Descriptive Papers   149

CHAPTER 12 Process Analysis: Explaining How   151
What Is Process Analysis?   151
    Directions for Procedures   152
        Use Second Person for Clarity   152
            Workplace Case Study: Ethan Solves the Office
            Lounge Problem   152
    Process Descriptions   153
        Using First Person   153
        Using Third Person   153
Transition in Process Analysis   154
        [Box] Transitions to Clarify a Process   154
Writing a Process Paper   154
    Selecting a Topic and Prewriting   155
    Drafting an Introduction   155
        Generalization Followed by Restriction   155
        Historical Opening   155
        Combining Second Person with Third Person   156
    Developing a Process Paper   156
    Writing a Conclusion   157
    Revising a Process Paper   157
        [Box] Checklist: Revising a Process Paper   157
        Two Student Papers: Process Analysis   157
        [Box] For Your Reference: Process Analysis Essays in
            the Reader   160

Summary   160

Key Terms   160

Test Yourself   161

Practice   161

Test Yourself Answers   161

Thirty Ideas for Process Papers   161

CHAPTER 13 Illustration: Showing with Examples   163

Purpose of Examples   163

Elements of Illustration   164

Writing a Paper of Illustration   164

    Prewriting   164

    Organizing and Developing a Paper of Illustration   165

        Order   165

        Relevant, Accurate, and Sufficient Examples   166

        Weaving Examples with Explanation   166

    Writing a Conclusion   167

    Revising a Paper of Illustration   167

        [Box] Checklist: Revising a Paper of Illustration   168

        Two Student Papers: Illustration   168

        [Box] For Your Reference: Illustration Essays in the Reader   170

Summary   171

Key Terms   171

Practice   171

Thirty Ideas for Papers of Illustration   171

CHAPTER 14 Classification: Grouping and Dividing   173

Purpose of Classification   173

What Is the Basis of Classification?   173

Writing a Paper of Classification   174

    Shaping a Topic to the Purpose and Audience   174

        [Box] Guidelines: Classification   175

    Prewriting with the "Because" Technique   175

    Organizing a Classification Paper   176

    Drafting a Thesis Statement   176

    Developing Main Points and Embedding Transitions   176

        [Box] Four Kinds of Embedded Transitions   177

        Student Essay with Main Points in the Thesis   177

    Making Main Points Parallel   178

    Writing a Conclusion   179

    Revising the Paper   179

        [Box] Checklist: Revising Classification Papers   179

        Two Student Papers: Classification   179

[Box] For Your Reference: Classification Essays
in the Reader   181

Summary   182

Key Terms   182

Test Yourself   182

Practice   183

Test Yourself Answers   183

Thirty Ideas for Classification Papers   184

**CHAPTER 15 Comparison and Contrast: Explaining Likeness
and Difference   186**

Purpose of Comparison or Contrast   186
Determining a Purpose   187
Selecting a Suitable Topic   187

Transition in Comparison or Contrast Papers   187

Pitfalls to Avoid in Comparison or Contrast Papers   188

Analogy: A Special Kind of Comparison   189

Writing a Paper of Comparison or Contrast   190
Gathering Information and Prewriting   190
Organizing a Paper of Comparison or Contrast   191
Drafting an Introduction   192
Developing a Comparison or Contrast Paper   193
Writing a Conclusion   194
Revising a Paper of Comparison or Contrast   194
[Box] Checklist: Revising a Paper of Comparison
or Contrast   194
Two Student Papers: Comparison   194
[Box] For Your Reference: Comparison and Contrast Essays
in the Reader   197

Summary   197

Key Terms   197

Test Yourself   198

Practice   198

Test Yourself Answers   198

Thirty Ideas for Comparison or Contrast Papers   198

CHAPTER 16 Definition: Identifying Basic Characteristics   200

Purpose of Definition   200

Formal Sentence Definition   200
[Box] Writing a Sentence Definition   201

Extended Definition   202

Consulting Sources   202
Documenting Sources   202
Guidelines for Using Extended Definitions   203
Writing a Paper of Extended Definition   203
Narrowing a Topic and Prewriting   204
Drafting a Special Kind of Introduction   204
Establishing Transition   204
Developing an Extended Definition   205
Operational Definition   205
Defining by Comparison   206
Defining by Synonym   206
Defining by Negation   206
Weaving Example with Explanation   206
Including a Dictionary Definition   207
Writing a Conclusion   207
Closing with a Formal Sentence Definition   207
Alluding to an Opening Quotation   207
Ending with a Personal Lesson   208
Revising a Paper of Definition   208
[Box] Checklist: Revising Extended Definitions   208
Two Student Papers: Definition   209
[Box] For Your Reference: Definition Essays in the Reader   211

Summary   *211*

Key Terms   *212*

Practice   *212*

Possible Answer for Writing a Sentence Definition   *213*

Thirty Ideas for Papers of Definition   *213*

CHAPTER 17 Cause and Effect: Explaining Why   215

Purpose of Causal Analysis   215
Workplace Case Study: The Accident   216

What Is Causal Analysis?   216
[Box] Steps in Causal Analysis   217
A Reversed Chain of Cause and Effect   217
Logical Principles of Cause-and-Effect Relationships   217
Two Fallacies to Avoid in Analyzing Cause and Effect   218

Writing a Paper Analyzing Cause and Effect   218
Planning a Cause-and-Effect Paper   218
Drafting an Introduction   220
Developing a Paper Analyzing Cause and Effect   220
Writing a Conclusion   220
Revising a Cause-and-Effect Paper   221
[Box] Checklist: Revising a Cause-and-Effect Paper   221

Two Student Papers: Cause and Effect   221
[Box] For Your Reference: Cause-and-Effect Essays
   in the Reader   223

Summary   *223*

Key Terms   *224*

Practice   *224*

Thirty Ideas for Papers of Cause and Effect   *225*

PART 4 Critical Thinking, Evaluation, and Argument   227

CHAPTER 18 Problem Solving   229

Dewey's Method of Problem Solving   229

How Can One Be Objective?   230
   Workplace Case Study: Writing a Company Policy   231

Writing a Problem-Solving Paper   231
   Selecting a Topic and Prewriting   231
   Making an Outline   232
      [Box] Transition in a Problem-Solving Paper   233
   Drafting an Introduction   233
   Identifying Criteria   234
      What Are Criteria   234
      Stating Criteria   234
   Proposing and Evaluating Alternatives   235
   Writing a Conclusion   236
   Revising a Problem-Solving Paper   236
      [Box] Checklist: Revising a Problem-Solving Paper   237
      Two Student Papers: Problem-Solving   237
      [Box] For Your Reference: Problem-Solving Essays
         in the Reader   239

Summary   *239*

Key Terms   *240*

Practice   *240*

Thirty Ideas for Problem-Solving Papers   *241*

CHAPTER 19 Shaping an Effective Argument   243

Purpose of Argument   243

Three Classic Appeals Used in Argument   243
   Workplace Case Study: "You Got a Tiger by the Tail!"   244
   The Logical Appeal   245
      Established Truths   245
      Primary Sources   245
      Statistics   245
      Expert Opinion   246

Personal Experience   246
Important Considerations   246
The Ethical Appeal   246
The Emotional Appeal   247
Using the Three Appeals   247
[Box] Guidelines for Using Persuasive Appeals   247

Understanding Opposing Views and Overcoming Objections   247
[Box] Questions to Analyze an Audience   248

Writing a Classic Argument Paper   248
Selecting a Topic   249
[Box] Criteria for Selecting an Argument Topic   250
Gathering Information and Prewriting   250
Drafting a Controlling Question   251
Searching for Reliable Sources   251
Note-Taking and Critical Reading   251
Making Con/Pro Lists   252
Stating a Position   252
Writing a Proposition   252
Taking a Position of Compromise   252
Writing a Focused Title   253
Planning the Shape of an Argument   253
Direct or Indirect Order: Early or Delayed Thesis?   254
Direct Approach   254
Indirect Approach   254
[Box] Factors to Consider in Planning an Argument   255
Presenting Opposing Viewpoints   255
Block and Alternating Organization   255
[Box] Labeling Points of View   257
Drafting a Neutral Introduction   258
Finding Common Ground   258
Acknowledging and Clarifying Points of Agreement   259
Refuting Opposing Points   259
Dodging Fallacies   260
Writing a Conclusion   260
Revising an Argument   261
[Box] Checklist: Revising an Argument   261
Two Student Papers: Classic Argument   261
[Box] For Your Reference: Argumentative Essays
in the Reader   269

Summary   269

Key Terms   269

Practice   270

Thirty Ideas for Papers of Argument   271

CHAPTER 20 Detecting Fallacies   273

Logical Fallacies   274
  Card Stacking   274
  Either/or Fallacy   274
  False Analogy   275
  Red Herring   275
  Begging the Question/Circular Argument   275
  Hasty Generalization   276
  Non Sequitur   276
    Workplace Case Study: Non Sequitur—
    A Grocer's "Mistake"   277
  The Post Hoc Fallacy   277
Emotional Fallacies   278
  Argumentum ad Hominem/Straw Man   279
  Bandwagon   280
  Plain Folk Appeal/*ad Populum*   280
  Status Appeal   280
  Scare Tactics   281
  Testimonial and Improper Appeal to Authority   281
  Glittering Generalities   282
    [Box] Checklist: Using Appeals in Writing   282
Dealing with Fallacies   282
Summary   283
Key Terms   283
Test Yourself   284
Practice   284
Test Yourself Answers   286

PART 5 Research Writing   287

CHAPTER 21 Preliminary Considerations for Research   289

Primary and Secondary Research   289
  The Path to Objectivity   290
  Fact or Idea?   291
Scheduling Research Tasks   292
  Is a Schedule Really Necessary?   292
  Will the Internet Cut Research Time?   292
    [Box] Tentative Five-Week Schedule for
    Secondary Research   293
A Note of Encouragement   293
Summary   294
Key Terms   294
Practice   294

CHAPTER 22 Primary Research: Observation, Interviews, and Surveys   295

Observation   295
   Selecting a Site   296
   Preparing to Observe   296
   Keeping a Log   296
      [Box] Checklist: Maintaining Objectivity   297

Interviews   298
   Types of Interviews   298
      Informational Interviewing   298
      Unstructured Versus Structured Interviews   298
   Types of Questions   299
      [Box] Guidelines for Interviewing   300

Surveys   300
   Planning a Survey   300
   Representative and Random Samples   301
      [Box] Checklist for Planning a Survey   301
   Constructing a Questionnaire   302
   Distributing Questionnaires   302
      [Box] Guidelines for Constructing Questionnaires   303
      Workplace Case Study: Cindy Surveys Dress Codes for Bank
         Employees   303
   Drawing Conclusions from a Survey and Interviews   305

Making an Outline   305

Writing a Primary Research Paper or Report   305
   Organizing and Interpreting Findings   306
   Observation   306
   Interviews and Surveys   306
   How Research Papers and Research Reports Differ   307
      Student Paper Based on Observation   308
      Student Report Based on Reading and Observation   309

Summary   313

Key Terms   313

Thirty Ideas for Observation, Interviewing, and Surveys   313

CHAPTER 23 Secondary Research: Locating Print
            and Electronic Sources   316

Determining the Aim or Purpose   316
   Informative Research Papers   316
   Problem-Solving Research Papers   317
   Research Papers of Argument   317

Selecting an Appropriate Topic   317
      [Box] Where to Find Possible Topics   318

Limiting the Topic   318
   Starting Points   318

[Box] Tips for Using Key Words Online to Narrow
   a Topic   319
Writing a Controlling Question   319
   Case Study: Flora Narrows a Very Broad Topic   319
Selecting Suitable Sources   320
   [Box] Checklist: Previewing Sources   321
Making a Working Bibliography   321
   How to Begin   321
   [Box] Never Postpone Noting a Source   322
Finding and Evaluating Print and Electronic Sources at the Library   322
   Finding Your Way around the Library   323
      [Box] Guidelines: How to Make a Working Bibliography   323
   Preliminary Reading: General References   323
   Electronic Central Catalog   324
   Periodical Indexes and Abstracts   324
      General Indexes   324
      Specialized Indexes   324
      Government Publications   325
   Bibliographies   325
      [Box] Tip: Don't Overlook Library Sources on CD-ROM   325
   Finding Print Sources   325
   Skimming Sources and Evaluating Content   326
   A Precaution   326
   Borrowing Materials from Other Libraries   326
      Online Catalogs for Regional Networks   326
      [Box] Guidelines for Evaluating Sources   327
   Requesting Materials via OCLC   327
Finding and Evaluating Internet Sources   328
   Using Online Directories and Search Engines   328
      Online Directories   328
      Search Engines   328
      [Box] Seven Tips for Searching the Internet   329
   Evaluating Web Sites   329
      Clues to Sponsors of Web Sites   329
      [Box] Avoid Plagiarizing Online Materials   330
      Free or for-a-Fee?   331
   Evaluating the Reliability of Internet Sources   331
      Check for a Monitor   331
      Watch for Credentials   331
      Notice the Tone   331
      Notice Dates   331
      [Box] How to Find Web Page Dates   332
      Evaluate the Coverage   332
      [Box] Guidelines for Evaluating the Reliability of
         Web Sites   332

Preserving Online Source Information   333
How Much Source Data Do You Need?   333
[Box] Save Your Internet Sources After Turning in a Paper   333
Balancing Library and Internet Sources   334
[Box] Directory for Internet Research   334

Summary   336

Key Terms   337

Practice   337

Thirty Ideas for Research   338

CHAPTER 24 Documenting Sources   339

What Is Documentation?   339

What Is Plagiarism?   339
[Box] Frequently Asked Questions: Source Information   340

Which Documentation Style Is Appropriate?   341

MLA Style of Documentation   341
[Box] Chapter 24 MLA Style Directory   342
Parenthetical Citations: MLA Style   342
One Author   342
Two or More Works by the Same Author   343
Two or More Authors   343
Works by Two Authors with the Same Last Name   343
Entire Work   343
One-Page Articles   344
Source with No Author Given   344
Corporate Author   344
Indirect Source   344
Quotations by Two or More Authors in One Sentence   345
Two or More Sources in One Citation   345
Work of More Than One Volume   345
Literary Works   345
Nonprint Sources   346
Long Quotations   346
Punctuation   346
Using Notes with MLA Parenthetical Citations   346
Content Notes   346
Bibliographic Notes   347

Preparing a List of Works Cited: MLA Style   347
[Box] Recommended Abbreviations for MLA Works
Cited Entries   348

1. Sample MLA Entries for Books   349
1.1 A Book by One Author   349
1.2 Two or More Books by One Author   349

1.3 A Book by Two or Three Authors   350
1.4 A Book by Four or More Authors   350
1.5 Corporate Author: A Book by a Group   350
1.6 Second or Later Edition of a Book   350
1.7 A Work in a Compilation, Anthology, or Collection   350
1.8 A Book by an Anonymous Author   351
1.9 A Book with an Editor or Editors   351
1.10 A Book with an Author and an Editor   351
1.11 A Book in Volumes   351
1.12 An Article from a Reference Book   351
1.13 An Introduction, Preface, Foreword, or Afterword   351
1.14 A Translation or Edited Edition   352
1.15 A Pamphlet   352
1.16 Government Publications   352
1.17 Sacred Writings   352

2. Sample MLA Entries for Articles   352
2.1 Journal Article with Continuous Paging   353
2.2 Journal Article with Each Issue Paged Separately   353
2.3 Article from a Daily Newspaper   353
2.4 Article from a Monthly Magazine   354
2.5 Article from a Weekly Newspaper or Weekly Magazine   354
2.6 An Anonymous Article   354
2.7 Review   354
2.8 Abstract and a Review   354
2.9 An Editorial   355
2.10 A Letter to the Editor   355
2.11 Newsletter Article   355

3. Sample MLA Entries for Miscellaneous Print and
Non-Print Sources   355
3.1 Television or Radio Programs   355
3.2 Sound Recordings   356
3.3 Film or Video Recording   356
3.4 Interviews   357
3.5 Cartoon   357
3.6 Legal References   358

4. Sample MLA Entries for Electronic Sources   358
4.1 Online Database, Scholarly Project, Professional and
Personal Sites   358
[Box] MLA Style: Documenting Electronic Sources   359
4.2 Online Book   360
4.3 Online Poem, Short Story, or Other Short Work
within a Work   360
4.4 Online Article in a Scholarly Journal   360
4.5 Online Article in a Newspaper   361
4.6 Online Article in a Magazine   361

4.7 Online Abstract   361
4.8 Online Article from a Newsletter   361
4.9 Posting to a Discussion Group   361
4.10 E-Mail Communication   362
4.11 Periodical Published on CD-ROM   362
4.12 Nonperiodical Publication on CD-ROM   362
4.13 Publication on CD-ROM or Diskette   362
4.14 Article from an Online Service   363
4.15 A Work in More than One Publication Medium   363
4.16 Other Electronic Sources   363

APA Style of Documentation   363

Parenthetical Citations: APA Style   363
        [Box] Chapter 24 APA Style Directory   364
Single Author   364
Two or More Works by the Same Author   364
Two or More Authors   364
Works by Two Authors with the Same Last Name   365
Source with No Author Name Given   365
Groups as Authors   365
Secondary Source   365
Two or More Sources in One Citation   365
Personal Communications   365
Long Quotations   365

Preparing a Reference List: APA Style   366

A. APA Entries: Periodicals   366
1. Journal Article with Two Authors and Continuous Paging   367
2. Journal Article with Each Issue Paged Separately   367
3. Magazine Article   367
4. Anonymous Article   367
5. Daily Newspaper Article Continued to Other Pages   367
6. Newsletter Article   367
7. Editorial   367
8. Letter to the Editor   368
9. Abstract and Review from a Secondary Source
   (print periodical)   368

B. APA Entries: Books, Brochures, and Government Publications   368
10. A Book by One Author   368
11. Two or More Books by One Author   369
12. A Book by Two or More Authors   369
13. A Book by an Unknown Author   369
14. Book, Revised or Later Edition   369
15. Article or Chapter in a Book   369
16. A Work in an Anthology   369
17. Published Interview   370

18. Review   370
19. Dictionary or Encyclopedia   370
20. Chapter in a Volume in a Series   370
21. Brochure, Corporate Author   370
22. Government Publications with a Group Author   371
C. APA Entries: Audiovisual Media   371
23. Motion Pictures   371
24. Television Broadcasts   371
25. Music and Audio Recordings   372
D. APA Entries: Internet and Other Electronic Sources   372
Internet Articles Based on a Print Source   372
Periodicals on the Internet   373
26. Article in a Journal   373
27. Article in a Magazine   373
28. Article in a Newspaper   373
29. Article in an Internet-Only Newsletter   373
30. Abstract   373
Nonperiodical Documents on the Internet   374
31. Chapter or Section in an Internet Document   374
32. Online Anthology   374
33. Collection of Short Stories from a Book   374
34. Document Available on University Program or Department
Web Site   374
35. Online Encyclopedia   374
36. Professional Site or Personal Site   375
37. Message Posted to an Online Forum or Discussion Group   375
38. E-Mail   375
Nonperiodical Publications on CD-ROM   375
39. CD-ROMs   375
40. Daily Newspaper Article, Electronic Version Available by
Search   375
41. Material from an Electronic Database   376
42. Computer Software and Computer Programs   376
Summary   376
Key Terms   376
Practice   376

CHAPTER 25 **Using Sources and Writing a Research Paper**   378
Workplace Case Study: Tracking the Truth   378
Research Reading   379
Examining Dates and Credentials   379
[Box] Checklist for Examining Sources and Credentials   379
Using Tentative Words to Discuss Findings and Theories   379
[Box] Tentative Words Commonly Used in Research   379
Recognizing Information That Must Be Acknowledged   380

Restating Common Knowledge   381
Acknowledging Everything Else   381
Stating Your Own Ideas and Conclusions   381
[Box] Tips for Compiling a List of Sources   382
Note-Taking, Summarizing, Paraphrasing, and Quoting   382
Note-Taking and Critical Reading   382
Summarizing   383
Paraphrasing   384
[Box] Guidelines: Writing Summaries and Paraphrases   385
Using Quotations   385
Making Changes in Quotations   386
Ellipsis   386
Brackets   387
Quotation within a Quotation   387

Making a Working Outline   387
[Box] Questions for Developing a Thesis
and an Outline   388

Drafting a Research Paper   388
Drafting a Thesis and Introduction   388
Using Signal Phrases to Integrate Quotations into the Text   390
Weak Phrases   390
Short Quotations   390
[Box] Verbs in Signal Phrases   391
Block Quotations   391
Inserting Explanatory Notes   392
Writing a Conclusion   392

Revising, Editing, and Formatting   393
Revising   393
[Box] Checklist: Revising Source-Based Papers   393
Checking Documentation   393
[Box] Checklist: Using Parenthetical Citations   394
Editing and Proofreading   394
Using an Appropriate Format   394
Margins and Indentations   394
MLA Style Heading, Title, and Page Numbering   395
APA Style Headings, Title, and Page Numbering   395
Sample Student Research Paper: MLA Style   396

Summary   406

Key Terms   406

Test Yourself   406

Practice   407

Test Yourself Answers   408

PART 6 Reading and Writing about Essays, Fiction, Plays, and Poetry 409

CHAPTER 26 Reading and Responding to Essays 411

What to Expect in Essays 411
   Purpose of Essays 412
   Characteristics of Personal Essays 412
   Characteristics of Formal Essays 413
   Point of View and Voice 413
   Figurative Language 414
   The Power of Plain Words 414

Critical Reading 416
   Evaluating What You Read 417
   A Strategy for Critical Reading 417

Writing a Paper of Reaction or Essay Exam Answers 419
   Two Types of Reactions 419
      A Commentary 419
         [Box] Tasks in Responding to Readings 420
      An Argument 420
   Prewriting and Outlining 421
   Drafting 421
      Writing a Commentary 421
         [Box] Working Outline for a Paper of Reaction 422
      Planning an Argument 422
   Revision and Editing 422
         [Box] Checklist for Revising a Reaction Paper 423
         Student Paper: Reaction 423

Summary 424

Key Terms 425

Practice 425

Thirty Ideas for Reaction Papers 425

CHAPTER 27 Reading and Responding to Short Stories, Novels, and Plays 428

The Human Condition 428

What Is the Role of the Reader? 429
   What Are the Major Characteristics of Novels? 429
   How Do Short Stories Differ from Novels? 429
   How Does Reading a Play Differ from Reading a Novel? 430

Reading and Taking Notes 431
   How to Start Prewriting 431
   Getting Ready to Draft 432

Elements of Literature 432
   Point of View 432
   Setting 433

Plot   433
  Foreshadowing   434
Characters   434
Symbolism   435
Irony   435
Theme   435
Figurative Language and Literary Devices   436
Preparing an Analysis of Literature   436
  [Box] Tentative Words for Interpreting Literature   437
  Writing about Point of View   437
    [Box] Checklist: Questions for Analyzing Point of View   438
  Writing about Setting   438
    [Box] Checklist: Questions for Analyzing Setting   439
  Writing about Plot   439
    [Box] Checklist: Questions for Analyzing Plot   440
  Writing about Character   440
    [Box] Checklist: Questions for Analyzing Character   441
  Writing about Symbols   441
    [Box] Checklist: Questions for Interpreting Symbols   442
  Writing about Irony   442
    [Box] Checklist: Questions for Detecting Irony   443
  Writing about Theme   443
    [Box] Checklist for Questions to Identify Clues to Theme   444
Revising   444
    [Box] Checklist for Revising an Analysis of Literature   444
    Student Paper: Literary Analysis   445

Summary   447
    [Box] For Your Reference: Short Stories and Narratives
      in The Reader   447

Key Terms   447

Twenty-Five Ideas for Papers of Literary Analysis   448

CHAPTER 28 Reading and Responding to Poetry   450
How Can a Reader Get Hold of a Poem?   451
  ARTHUR GUITERMAN, On the Vanity of Earthly Greatness   451
  CARL SANDBURG, Grass   452

Reading Narrative Poems   453
  COUNTÉE CULLEN, Incident   453

Reading Lyric Poems   454
  Special Effects with Words   454
  Imagery in Lyric Poems   455
    JOSO, The Barley Field   455
    SORA, The Barley Field   455

EMILY DICKINSON, [I Taste a Liquor Never Brewed] 456

ARCHIBALD MACLEISH, *Ars Poetica* 457

The Mysterious Fact of Poetic Energy 458

Preparing an Analysis of a Poem 459

Developing Your Analysis 459

Organizing the Paper 459

[Box] Tips for Analyzing a Poem 460

[Box] Guidelines: Organizing and Developing
a Poetic Analysis 461

Revising an Analysis of a Poem 461

[Box] Checklist: Revising an Analysis of a Poem 461

Student Paper: Analysis of a Poem 462

WILLIAM WORDSWORTH, [I Wandered Lonely as a Cloud] 462

Summary 463

Key Terms 463

Practice 463

**PART 7 Essay Exam Writing, Employment Writing,
and Oral Presentations 465**

CHAPTER 29 Writing Effective Essay Exams 467

Preparing for Exams 467

Time Management 467

Setting Priorities and Scheduling 468

Timesavers 468

Reviewing for Essay Exams 469

Predicting Essay Exam Questions 470

Open Book Exams 471

Two Types of Essay Questions 471

Taking Essay Exams 472

[Box] Tips for Writing Essay Answers 472

Writing Complete Essay Exam Answers 473

Understanding the Question 473

[Box] Writing Strategies Suggested by Key Phrases 474

Drafting Complete Essay Answers 474

Paragraph Essays 474

[Box] Precautions for Writing Complete Essay Answers 475

Sample Paragraph Essay 475

Long Exam Essays 475

Summary 475

Key Terms 476

Practice 476

CHAPTER 30 Employment Writing for the Twenty-First Century   477

I. Writing an Effective Résumé   477

Reasons Résumés Are Culled   478

Two Popular Styles of Printed Résumés   478
   The Chronological Résumé   478
   The Functional Résumé   479

Research and Prewriting for a Résumé   479
   Gaining an Overview of a Career Field   479
   Identifying Employers' Needs   480
   Identifying Qualifications   480
      Workplace Skills   481
      Academic Skills   481
      Personal Skills   482
      Personal Qualities and Work Habits   483

Drafting a Résumé   483
   The Basic Job Objective   484
   The Service-Oriented Job Objective   484
      [Box] Service-Oriented Objectives   485
   Grouping and Sharpening Skills   485
      Combining Skill Groups   486
      Adding Actions Verbs   486
      [Box] Action Verbs for Résumés   486
      Citing Accomplishments   486

Education   488

Work Experience   488
      [Box] Frequently Asked Questions About
      Work Experience   488

Other Information on a Résumé   489

Organizing Résumés   489
   Organizing a Chronological Résumé   490
   Organizing a Functional Résumé   492
      Case Study: Mark Focuses His Functional Résumé   495
   Scannable Résumés   495
      Keyword Summary   495
      [Box] A Keyword Summary   496
      Editing and Printing   496
   E-Mail Résumés   496
      Preparation   496
      Internet Posting   496

Formatting a Printed Résumé   497

Revising, Editing, and Proofreading a Résumé   497
   Checking Layout and Order   497
      [Box] Checklist: Revising Layout, Order, and Emphasis   498

Adjusting Length of Printed Résumés   498
Scrutinizing Word Choice   499
Eagle-Eyed Proofreading   499
    Consistent Punctuation   500
    Other Problems   500
        [Box] Checklist: Editing and Proofreading a Résumé   500
A Note of Encouragement   500
        [Box] Internet Career Directory   501
II. Writing Letters and Other Correspondence for Employment   501
Writing E-Mail Messages   502
Writing an Effective Cover Letter for a Résumé   502
        [Box] Guidelines for Email Messages   503
    Effective Introductions   504
        The Name Opening   504
        The Creative Opening   504
        The Summary Opening   505
        The Question Opening   505
    The Body of the Letter   505
    How to Handle the Salary Question   506
    Effective Conclusions   506
        [Box] Checklist: Effective Conclusions   507
    Other Considerations   507
        E-Mail Cover Letters   507
            [Box] Checklist: Revising a Cover Letter   508
    Revising a Cover Letter   508
Format for a Business Letter   508
Packaging Job Search Documents   511
Providing a List of References   511
        [Box] Guidelines: Compiling a List of References   512
Writing a Letter of Appreciation   512
        Workplace Case Study: Connect the Dots   514
Writing a Letter of Acceptance   514
Writing a Letter of Refusal   515
Writing a Letter of Resignation   516
Summary   518
Key Terms   518
Practice   519

CHAPTER 31 Oral Presentations   520
Whether Speaking to Six or to Sixty . . .   520
How Do Writing and Speaking Differ?   521
    Writing and Speaking: Comparing Two Types of
        Rhetorical Situations   521

Presenting Versus Reading   521
[Box] Preparing a Paper for Oral Presentation   522

Four Types of Oral Presentations   523

Planning an Extemporaneous Presentation   524
Preview the Setting   524
Assess the Audience   524
Case Study: Murphy's Law in Action   525
Consider the Occasion   525
Define the Purpose   525
Select an Appropriate Topic   526
Get Off the Beaten Path   526
Link the Topic to the Audience   526
Role-Play   527
Case Study: Finding a Link to the Audience   527
Audience Analysis: Make a Brief Written Plan   527

Credibility, Organization, and Development   528
Considering Credibility   528
Organizing an Informative Presentation   528
Organizing a Persuasive Presentation   529
Considering Ethics, Logic, and Emotion   529
Choosing the Right Words   529
Improving Transition   530

Options for Introductions and Conclusions   530
Introductions   530
Refer to the Occasion   530
Offer an Anecdote or Example   531
Provide an Unfamiliar Fact or Bit of History   531
Give Surprising Statistic or Opinion   531
Ask a Question   531
Find an Apt Quotation   531
Use Humor   532
[Box] Guidelines for Using Humor   532
Conclusions   532
Summarize   532
End with a Quotation   533
Loop to the Introduction   533
Pose a Challenge or Question   533
Call for Action   533
Refer to the Future   533

Preparing Notes and Audiovisuals   533
Notes on Paper or Cards?   534
[Box] Tips for Making Note Cards   534
Creating Effective Audiovisuals   534
[Box] Guidelines for Planning Audiovisuals   535

Practicing a Presentation   535
    Using Audiovisuals   536
    Revising Note Cards   536
    Improving Eye Contact, Posture, and Gestures   536
        Eye Contact   536
        Gestures   536
    Improving Vocal Variety   537
        Volume   537
        Rate   537
        Articulation   538
        Pitch   538

Giving a Presentation   538
    Arrive Early   538
    Take a Deep Breath . . .   539
    Don't Apologize Unnecessarily   539
    Adapt to the Audience   539
    End Purposefully and Gracefully   539
    Be Prepared for Questions   540
        Student Sample: Persuasive Presentation   540

Summary   541

Key Terms   541

Practice   542

Thirty Ideas for Oral Presentations   542

THE READER   545

Reader Contents   547
        [Box] Alternate Contents: The Readings by Theme   549

Introduction to the Reader   553
    How Do Essays and Short Stories Differ?   553
    Critical Reading   553
    Second Guessing   554

Narration: Recounting Events   555

DAVID BANK, Rosetta Disk Is Foundation's Gift to Future Linguists   555

CARSON MCCULLERS, Home for Christmas   559

JEAN HOUSTON, The Art of Acknowledgement   563

PHILIP WEISS, How to Get Out of a Locked Trunk   567

Description: Conveying Impressions   572

SUE HUBBELL, Caterpillar Afternoon   572

EUDORA WELTY, One Writer's Beginnings   576

JOHN CIARDI, Dawn Watch   579

LIANE ELLISON NORMAN, Pedestrian Students
and High-Flying Squirrels   583

Process Analysis: Explaining How   586

    EUELL GIBBONS, How to Cook a Carp   586

    NOEL PERRIN, Falling for Apples   590

    CAROL CARTER, Write Your Own Success Story   594

    MARYA MANNES, How Do You Know It's Good?   600

Illustration: Showing with Examples   606

    ETHLIE VARE and GREG PTACEK, Introduction of *Mothers of Invention*   606

    JASON VEST, WARREN COHEN, and MIKE THARP, Road Rage   609

    ANDREA LEE, Black and Well-to-Do   615

    HOLMAN W. JENKINS, JR., Uptight Is Back in Style   618

Classification: Grouping and Dividing   621

    KATHLEEN FURY, It's Only a Paper World   621

    NORMAN BROWN, Mind Over Munchies   624

    LISA DAVIS, Where Do We Stand?   629

    JAMES T. BAKER, How Do We Find the Student?   632

Comparison–Contrast: Exploring Likeness and Difference   636

    PHILLIP LOPATE, A Nonsmoker with a Smoker   636

    NEAL PEIRCE, Americans: Conservationists or Champion Land Hogs?   640

    AMY TAN, Mother Tongue   643

    DEBORAH TANNEN, Women and Men Talking on the Job   649

Definition: Identifying Basic Characteristics   655

    DAVID RAYMOND, On Being 17, Bright, and Unable to Read   655

    WILLIAM RASPBERRY, The Handicap of Definition   659

    BARBARA JORDAN, Becoming Educated   662

    LAURENCE SHAMES, The Sweet Smell of Success Isn't All That Sweet   665

Cause and Effect: Explaining Why   668

    BARBARA EHRENREICH, Spudding Out   668

    ANNE ROIPHE, Why Marriages Fail   671

    NICHOLAS GAGE, The Teacher Who Changed My Life   675

    ELISABETH KÜBLER-ROSS, The Emotional Quadrant   680

Shaping an Effective Argument   683

    MIKE ESKENAZI, The New Case for Latin   683

    ANDREA SACHS, When the Lullaby Ends   686

    AMITAI ETZIONI, Working at McDonald's   689

RICHARD M. RESTAK, The Other Difference between Boys and Girls   693

C. S. LEWIS, We Have No "Right to Happiness"   698

Short Stories   703

URSULA HEGI, Doves   703

CHARLES BAXTER, Scheherazade   707

KATE CHOPIN, The Story of an Hour   711

JOHN UPDIKE, Still of Some Use   714

Creation Narratives   719

Introduction: The Search for Our Beginnings   719

PIMA INDIAN LEGEND, The Well-Baked Man   721

GENESIS 1–2 from the Torah   723

GENESIS 1–2 from the Bible (King James Version)   726

The Koran   730

Selected Verses from the Koran   730

THE HANDBOOK: A Brief Guide to Grammar, Punctuation, Mechanics, and Usage   733

[Box] Handbook Directory   734

Introduction   H-1

What Is the Best Way to Use This Handbook?   H-1

Should a Writer Ever Break a Rule?   H-1

1. Punctuation   H-2

1a. Comma   H-2

1b. Semicolon   H-4

1c. Colon   H-5

1d. Apostrophe   H-6

1e. Dash   H-7

1f. Parentheses   H-8

1g. Brackets   H-9

1h. Hyphen   H-9

1i. Slash   H-10

1j. Quotation Marks   H-11

1k. Italics (underlining)   H-13

1l. Ellipses   H-14

1m. Period   H-15

1n. Question Mark   H-16

1o. Exclamation Point   H-16

2. **Capitalization**   H-16

3. **Abbreviations**   H-19

    3a.   General Guidelines for Using Abbreviations   H-19

    3b.   Common Abbreviations and Reference Terms   H-20

4. **Numbers**   H-21

5. **Grammar and Usage**   H-23

    5a.   Sentence Fragments   H-23

    5b.   Comma Splices and Fused (Run-On) Sentences   H-25

    5c.   Pronouns   H-26

    5d.   Verbs   H-31

    5e.   Use *Like* Correctly   H-37

    5f.   Modifiers   H-37

6. **Spelling**   H-39

    6a.   Spelling Tips   H-39

    6b.   Association Aids to Improve Spelling   H-40

    6c.   Other Spelling Aids   H-41

    6d.   Six Ways to Improve Spelling   H-42

7. **Glossary of Usage**   H-44

Credits   C-1

Index of Authors and Titles   I-1

Subject Index   I-4

LIST OF FIGURES

    Figure 3.1   Clustering   27

    Figure 14.1   Classification of Buckeye fans   174

    Figure 19.1   Ways to organize an argument   256

    Figure 21.1   Path to objective research   291

    Figure 30.1   Chronological resume   490

    Figure 30.2   Functional resume (no paid experience)   492

    Figure 30.3   Functional resume (part-time experience)   494

    Figure 30.4   Cover letter with creative opening   509

    Figure 30.5   Cover letter with summary opening   510

    Figure 30.6   Letter of appreciation   513

    Figure 30.7   Abbreviated letter of acceptance   515

    Figure 30.8   Abbreviated letter of refusal   516

    Figure 30.9   Abbreviated letter of resignation   517

A Note to Instructors

Reading, critical thinking, and writing skills are cornerstones of an education—not just for the elite but for everyone who aspires to attain a college degree. A fourth cornerstone, oral presentation skills, has been identified recently by many colleges and universities and added to their graduation requirements. These skills serve as the foundation of a successful career as well as a solid higher education: To gain credibility in the workplace, employees need to be able to present their ideas cogently and convincingly, both in writing and speaking.

To help students meet and exceed the requirements of their schools and employers, *Reasoning and Writing Well* is a practical and comprehensive process-based rhetoric that demystifies the art of writing well. This book emphasizes not only analytical reading and thinking but also accuracy and ethics. The central goals of *Reasoning and Writing Well* are to enable students to

- Write with a purpose or an aim that considers the rhetorical situation
- Write clearly, concisely, and accurately
- Use language appropriately and correctly
- Develop an awareness of their voices as writers
- Research a topic using a variety of print and electronic sources, including the Internet
- Document sources correctly
- Read and think critically
- Analyze and evaluate logically and objectively
- Give a presentation before an audience
- Appreciate the value of effective writing and speaking

The philosophy of *Reasoning and Writing Well,* Third Edition, is based on my belief that students at all levels of preparedness can be motivated to do their best through encouragement and clear instruction in plain English. My philosophy has been shaped by experience in the workplace, graduate education at Ohio State University, over twenty years of college teaching and curriculum development, participation in Toastmasters International, research, and professional writing. Employers, editors, reviewers, and students have all influenced this book's content.

PROVEN FEATURES

Four books in one, *Reasoning and Writing Well* provides exceptionally comprehensive coverage and abundant learning aids. Its proven features include the following.

Students like it. Students consistently comment that the tone of the book is friendly, respectful, and encouraging and that its explanations are clear and its examples helpful. Students especially like the lists of Ideas for Writing that conclude chapters.

In-depth coverage of rhetorical strategies. The rhetorical situation is introduced in chapter 1 and reinforced throughout the book, including in related activities. Students are asked to consider elements of the rhetorical context such as audience, purpose, and occasion. Separate chapters cover each major method of development and progress from prewriting to proofreading, providing step-by-step instruction for each stage of the writing process. Student papers model each rhetorical mode.

The writing process. After the two opening chapters on the rhetorical situation, part 1 covers the early stages of the writing process: prewriting (chapter 3) and drafting (chapter 4). In part 2, chapters 5 through 9 cover the later stages of revision, editing, and proofreading. These early chapters include clear, specific help for focusing ideas with topic sentences, thesis statements, controlling questions, purpose statements, and outlines. Many examples of formal, scratch, and working outlines are provided. Students are advised of the recursive nature of the writing process and encouraged to return to the early stages of the process as necessary.

A unique revision workshop. *Reasoning and Writing Well* offers extensive, and intensive, coverage of revision, with five chapters focused on this important skill in the Revision Workshop, part 2. Chapter 5 provides an overview of revising, editing, and proofreading. Chapter 6 introduces students to critical thinking in the context of revision by focusing on accuracy in writing. Individual chapters then cover revising paragraphs (chapter 7), editing sentences (chapter 8), and improving word choice (chapter 9).

Critical thinking, problem solving, and argument. Four chapters focus on critical thinking, including the related skills of evaluation, problem solving, and argument—the most comprehensive coverage of these important academic and workplace skills available in a four-in-one composition text. Early in the book, chapter 6, Revision and Accuracy, sets forth criteria for evaluating so-called *facts*, using inferences, and avoiding hasty generalizations and absolute terms.

Part 4, Critical Thinking, Evaluation, and Argument, covers practical strategies for organizing problem-solving papers, shaping effective arguments, and identifying fallacies. Chapter 18 explains Dewey's version of the scientific method and applies problem solving to report writing and research papers. Chapter 19 explains the classic appeals of logos, ethos, and pathos and shows how these appeals can form the basis for effective argument. Chapter 20 explains how to recognize common logical and emotional fallacies. In part 6, chapter 26 includes instruction for critical reading.

Comprehensive research and documentation coverage.

The five chapters forming part 5 of *Reasoning and Writing Well* provide thorough support for students who are writing research-based papers. Chapter 22 covers observation, interviews, and surveys and includes a sample questionnaire and student report of findings. Chapter 23's coverage includes extensive help for conducting research on the Internet. Chapter 24 presents separate sections on the latest Modern Language Association (MLA) and American Psychological Association (APA) formatting guidelines and documentation models. Chapter 25 explains and shows how to use sources to write research-based papers. It includes a new sample student outline and research paper in MLA style on the subject of workers' compensation. Throughout part 5, step-by-step instructions and numerous examples help students through every stage of writing a research paper.

Integrated coverage of writing on a computer.

Reasoning and Writing Well offers numerous tips and precautions that give students helpful "insider" information and alert them to possible pitfalls in writing on a computer. Two Web site directories (one in chapter 23 on Internet research, the other in chapter 30 on career resources) provide quick, handy information about help available online.

Plentiful student models.

Exemplary but realistic models of student writing appear throughout the book. Dozens of introductions, conclusions, outlines, and complete papers illustrate various rhetorical strategies and techniques for writing from sources.

Exceptional learning resources and study aids.

In addition to many essay assignments, *Reasoning and Writing Well* includes a wealth of resources for individual and collaborative learning: hundreds of suggested writing topics, numerous guides to generating topic ideas, and abundant practice activities. Role plays, case problems, peer review exercises, and small-group discussion guides help students strengthen their understanding of concepts and processes, analyze situations, and explore other points of view. Figures and tables, boxed guidelines and checklists, chapter summaries, and "Test Yourself" exercises also help students to deepen their understanding while strengthening their skills.

Incremental, yet flexible organization. Parts and chapters in *Reasoning and Writing Well* appear in a logical sequence, with parts 1 and 2 following the steps of the writing process and parts 3 through 6 moving from less difficult to more difficult concepts and projects. Each section of the reader follows the same progression from less to more difficult, with selections progressing from least to most challenging. The chapters are freestanding, however, and can be used in whatever order and combination individual teachers deem appropriate. That is, instructors can quickly select what they need from the book and adapt it to a wide variety of teaching and learning situations.

A separate Reader, organized by rhetorical modes. Forty-five engaging essays, short stories, and creation narratives, representing diverse authors and points of view, make up the Reader. Eudora Welty, C. S. Lewis, Elisabeth Kübler Ross, Amy Tan, Barbara Jordan, and John Updike are among the authors included. An alternate table of contents organized by thematic groupings appears at the start of the reader to ensure its flexibility.

Three chapters on writing about literature. Focusing on essays, short stories, drama, and poetry, chapters 26, 27, and 28 explain the elements of each major genre and common literary devices. These chapters also teach students how to analyze literature, take and defend a position on a literary work, and write papers that analyze and respond to literature. In all, part 6 provides a solid introduction to the study of literature.

Preparing for and writing essay exams. Chapter 29 focuses on studying for and writing essay exams. Related issues, such as time management and study techniques, are explained, and practical tips and examples appear throughout the chapter.

Writing for employment. Chapter 30 provides up-to-date guidelines not only for preparing print, scannable, and electronic résumés but also for writing various types of business correspondence, including e-mail. Students learn how to analyze the needs of employers and to represent themselves appropriately. This chapter also includes numerous examples and models, as well as an Internet Career Directory.

Workplace Relevance. Sixteen case studies, most based on real incidents in the workplace, offer insight into writing situations and provide topics for writing. Workplace examples and case problems offer opportunities for discussion and writing.

Concise Handbook. Students can find quick answers to common questions about grammar, punctuation, mechanics, spelling, and usage and can refer to numerous examples. The handbook also refers to related chapters in the rhetoric that explain punctuation, sentence structure, and usage. To supplement the Handbook, grammar worksheets are provided in the instructor's manual, *The Idea Book*, that accompanies *Reasoning and Writing Well.*

NEW FEATURES

The third edition of *Reasoning and Writing Well* has been revised from cover to cover. The overall result is a more streamlined text that offers the most up-to-date coverage of such evolving topics as research, documentation styles, employment writing, and Internet use and resources. Among the many improvements are the following highlights:

Expanded coverage of the rhetorical situation. One entire chapter (chapter 1) explains rhetorical situation, and chapter 2 focuses on what is perhaps the most important element of any writing situation: audience. The rhetorical situation is now emphasized throughout the book.

Two Internet directories. This edition provides two new Internet directories: one in chapter 23 for Internet research, the second in chapter 30 for career resources.

Expanded and updated coverage of the Internet. The third edition also contains more timely tips and additional instruction for students conducting research on the Internet, including detailed criteria for evaluating online sources. In addition, the number of documentation models for online sources has been increased in both the MLA and the APA style sections.

New chapter on oral presentations. Part 7 now includes a full chapter on public speaking that includes topics such as managing anxiety, adapting a paper for oral presentation, and incorporating audio-visuals into presentations. Students learn how to engage an audience and present points with conviction so that they gain confidence and skill in presenting their ideas orally.

Revised Reader. Over 30% (16) of the 45 reading selections are new to this edition. In addition to many new essays and short stories (by noted authors such as Kathleen Fury, Deborah Tannen, William Raspberry, Barbara Ehrenreich, and Kate Chopin), the Reader now also includes creation narratives drawn from the Pima Indians, the Bible (King James Version), the Torah, and the Koran. The discussion questions accompanying selections retained from the previous edition have been revised to focus on rhetorical considerations.

Expanded and updated research coverage. The third edition of *Reasoning and Writing Well* provides specific coverage to help students avoid plagiarism; provides thoroughly revised APA coverage based on the recently published fifth edition of the APA's *Publication Manual* (2001), including a significantly increased offering of documentation models for electronic sources; provides updated MLA coverage; and offers expanded discussions of conducting Internet research.

An exemplary new student research paper (in MLA style) on the topic of workers' compensation appears in chapter 25, modeling such research writing skills as summarizing, paraphrasing, integrating short and long quotations, and preparing an extensive works cited list of both print and electronic sources.

Finally, the format of the MLA and APA sections has been changed for greater ease of use. Each section now opens with a directory of contents. Contrasting color strips mark the edges of the sections' pages so that students can locate and distinguish between them easily.

New part-opening photos and more visuals throughout. To make the book more visually appealing for students, the third edition offers an updated interior design that includes new part-opening photographs, more boxes, and more cartoons. Additional illustrations also appear throughout the book to enhance its appearance and improve its readability.

New workplace case studies, case problems, and activities. Updated activities appear throughout the book to ensure currency, increase student interest, encourage critical thinking, and stimulate topic ideas.

New margin notes and other cross-references. Cross-references are provided in the margins for greater visibility and easier reference. New reference boxes in chapters 10 through 17 (covering methods of development), 19 (argumentation), and 27 (reading and responding to fiction) direct students to corresponding essays and stories in the Reader.

Improved Handbook. Both the content and format of the Handbook have been revised. A new introduction and directory of contents precede the explanation and examples. A simplified numbering system identifies the sections of the handbook, and expanded coverage of verbs, including a new explanation of the four basic forms of a verb, and all four forms are shown for 70 irregular verbs.

Revised and expanded *Idea Book.* This unusually robust instructor's resource manual has been thoroughly revised to reflect all of the changes in the textbook, as well as expanded and enhanced in numerous ways. Elements new to the *Idea Book* include:

- A new model syllabus, making four in all
- A new directory of Internet resources for preventing and detecting plagiarism
- New grammar worksheets
- Page references to corresponding rules in the handbook added to all grammar worksheets

- Several evaluation forms for oral presentations and speech plans for students
- More quizzes
- More worksheets for collaborative activities

PRINT AND ELECTRONIC SUPPLEMENTS

The Idea Book. An unusually comprehensive resource for instructors with varying levels of experience, the instructor's manual to accompany *Reasoning and Writing Well* contains resources such as lesson plans, teaching objectives, supplemental assignments, answers to exercises, grammar worksheets, transparency masters, guides to working with the selections in the reader, a bank of quizzes, sample syllabi, and numerous activity worksheets.

Instructor CD-ROM. The CD-ROM contains the entire *Idea Book* in a portable electronic format. Most of the *Idea Book*'s content is also provided in electronic format in the instructor's area of the text's Online Learning Center (see below).

Online Learning Center. The *Reasoning and Writing Well* Web site provides a wealth of resources for instructors and students, and is compatible with most online course management systems, such as WebCT and BlackBoard (for more information, see the related description in the next section).

For students, the site provides 500 interactive grammar, punctuation, and editing exercises, as well as interactive activities focused on skills such as critical reading and evaluating Web sites. Chapter-by-chapter links are also provided, offering easy access to sites whose URLs are printed in the text, hypertext definitions of key terms, and interactive student models.

For instructors, the Online Learning Center provides all of the content of the instructor's manual (*The Idea Book*) as well as all of the non-Web-based content of the instructor's CD-ROM, excluding answers to exercises, quizzes, and tests. The instructor's area of the OLC also provides links to a wide array of online resources for composition teachers.

MCGRAW-HILL'S RESOURCES FOR ONLINE COURSE DELIVERY AND DISTANCE EDUCATION

Compatibility with Online Course Management Systems. The online content of *Reasoning and Writing Well*, Third Edition, is supported by WebCT, Blackboard, eCollege.com, and most other online course systems.

PageOut. McGraw-Hill's own PageOut service is available to help you get your course up and running online in a matter of hours—at no cost. Additional information about the service is available online at <http://www.pageout.net>.

AllWrite! Available online or on CD-ROM, *AllWrite* offers over 3,000 exercises for practice in basic grammar, usage, punctuation, spelling, and techniques for effective writing. The popular program is richly illustrated with graphics, animations, video, and Help screens.

Webwrite. This online product, available through our partner company MetaText, makes it possible for writing teachers and students to, among other things, comment on and share papers online.

For further information about these and other electronic resources, contact your local McGraw-Hill representative, visit the English pages on the McGraw-Hill Higher Education Web site at <www.mhhe.com/catalogs/hss/english/>, or visit McGraw-Hill's Digital Solutions pages at <www.mhhe.com/catalogs/solutions>.

A NOTE OF APPRECIATION

This book could not have been written without the generosity of the many students who have contributed their work. Heartfelt gratitude is also extended to my Marion Technical Community College colleagues Professors Nancy Gilson and Leslie Weichenthal, and librarians David Evans and Nannette White. Also lending expertise, as well as encouragement, were family members George, Neil, Scott, Jeanne, Julie, and Christine. My thanks also go to the reviewers who helped us develop this new edition of *Reasoning and Writing Well:* Robert Barnett, University of Michigan at Flint; Joyce Cherry, Albany State University; Gay Church, Northern Virginia Community College—Manassas; Barbara Cruz, San Antonio College; Michel A. de Benedictis, Miami-Dade Community College; Gretchen E. DiGeronimo, Becker College; Helen Groves, University of Louisiana at Monroe; Tracy Haney, Walla Walla Community College; Sarah Harrison, Tyler Junior College; Michael J. Hricik, Westmoreland County Community College; Glenn D. Klopfenstein, Passaic County Community College; Michael Mackey, Community College of Denver; Miles S. McCrimmon, J. Sargeant Reynolds Community College; Shirley Nelson, Chattanooga State Technical Community College; Dr. Jeanie Page Randall, Austin Peay State University; Mary H. Sims, Ball State University; Ron Sudol, Oakland University.

Still deeply appreciated, too, are the comments and suggestions of the reviewers who helped guide the development of this text's first and second editions: Martin T. Baum, Jamestown Community College; Patricia Blaine, Paducah Community College; Brian Cotter, Chattanooga State Technical Community College; Julie Ann Doty, Southeastern Illinois College; Joel B. Henderson, Chattanooga State Technical Community College; Linda Jarvis, Kilgore College; Dorothy

Lockridge, Chattanooga State Technical Community College; Bill H. Lamb, Johnson County Community College; Robert Lesman, Northern Virginia Community College; Sharon Poat, Paducah Community College; Bonnie C. Plummer, Eastern Kentucky University; Jonah Rice, Southeastern Illinois College; Lana Richardson, Northeast Mississippi Community College; Deneen M. Shepherd, St. Louis Community College at Forest Park; Phillip Sipiora, University of South Florida; and Marilyn Terrault, Macomb Community College. I also wish to extend special thanks to Matt Smith and the many instructors at Chattanooga State Technical Community College for keeping teaching journals, offering encouragement, and supporting this text through all of its editions.

Betty Mattix Dietsch
Marion, OH

Rhetoric and Research Writing Guide

The Writing Situation and Early Stages of the Writing Process

Part 1

CHAPTER 1

Writing in Context

Freedom to be your best means nothing unless you're willing to do your best.

—Colin Powell, *Priorities*

In an age of remote controls, fast food, and instant messaging, many Americans have come to expect instant results by expending little effort. But learning to write well is neither quick nor effortless. Discovering ideas, drafting, revising, and proofreading take considerable time and energy. For students who have become habituated to learning only enough to pass a multiple-choice test, college and workplace writing will pose quite a challenge. That's the bad news; read on for the good news.

WHY LEARN TO REASON AND WRITE WELL?

Various surveys have found that white collar workers spend from 10 to 70 percent of their time writing. For example, a study conducted at California State University at Chico found that technical graduates, "regardless of their job duties, all spend half or more of their career time writing." Skill in writing is crucial for succeeding in college and for advancing a career.

Whether you relish or dread writing or range somewhere in between, *Reasoning and Writing Well* will guide and encourage you to do your best. You'll learn shortcuts to ease the tasks of transferring thoughts from mind to paper and of developing ideas. You'll sharpen both your thinking and writing skills, refining your ability to reason logically, solve problems, write persuasively, and conduct research. As you expand your repertoire, you will be better prepared to write not only college papers but also the letters and documents required on the job. You will learn how to consider a given writing situation and to draft and revise accordingly. You won't be like Calvin who has confused the purpose of writing and misjudged his audience.

CALVIN AND HOBBES © Watterson. Reprinted with permission of Universal Press Syndicate. All rights reserved.

WHAT IS THE RHETORICAL SITUATION?

Every piece of writing has a context or circumstance surrounding it—referred to as the *rhetorical situation*. Basically, this term refers to the way words are used in regard to five elements: the *occasion, writer's purpose, topic, audience,* and *writer's voice.* All five elements of the rhetorical situation influence the effectiveness of writing. (Purpose and audience, in particular, will be emphasized in the chapters to come.) If a writer neglects any of the elements, the writing may ramble, go astray, or miss the mark. The primary goal—to communicate—will not be attained.

Occasion

The occasion is the event, condition, or need that causes you to write. You may write an apology for hasty words, a thank you for a birthday gift, or an e-mail to a friend to keep in touch. On the job your writing may spring from a client's need, a problem with a supplier, or another complication that requires a written response. Or your job may require regular record keeping and reporting. Different occasions call for different writing strategies. To consider the occasion of your writing, ask yourself "What is expected?" "What is appropriate?"

Purpose

Purpose refers to a writer's motive, or reason for writing, which can be stated or implied. Purpose has two aspects: general and specific.

The General Purpose   Writing has four general purposes: *to inform, to persuade, to express,* and *to entertain.* More often than not, these general purposes are combined in various ways. For example, most writing is intended to inform, but it also has a secondary persuasive element: to convince the reader that it is factual and reliable. Other writing is primarily persuasive, designed to argue a point and secure agreement, yet it is also informative. The degree of persuasion varies according to the occasion, purpose, and audience.

Some writing is primarily expressive, allowing the writer to reveal feelings and opinions, usually recalling experience. Expressive writing often takes the form of personal essays, journal writing, diaries, poetry, fiction, or plays. Yet writing may also be expressive to a lesser extent in a business letter, report, or proposal, depending upon the rhetorical situation.

Although some humorous writing seems intended merely to entertain, it may also make a serious point. The clever use of humor can advance a point, as in the writing of Mark Twain. Former President Ronald Reagan used humor in his speeches to sway the audience to his way of thinking. A light-hearted approach captures the attention of readers and makes them more willing to listen. To be successful, humor must not be heavy-handed or derisive—otherwise, it may backfire.

The Specific Purpose   To be clear, writing should have a specific purpose. In the introduction to *Watch Your Language*, Theodore M. Bernstein states the specific purpose that directed the *New York Times* during his seven years as the assistant managing editor. The first sentence below states the guiding editorial philosophy of this newspaper. The second gives a valuable tip for assessing audience.

> Today we think it well to make each issue as nearly self-sufficing as is reasonable so that the reader does not feel the need for a research staff to help him understand the day's news. Perhaps the best slogan a newspaper could post in its city room would be this: "Keep two readers always in mind: the high school sophomore and the man who has been marooned on a desert island for three months." Both of them, for different reasons, have to be told what it is all about.

Your instructor may assign a general purpose for a paper, but usually you will choose the topic, the specific purpose, and the audience. Jotting down your specific purpose and audience early will help you to select, sort, and shape ideas so that they unite and flow toward a conclusion that is appropriate for the rhetorical situation.

Topic

In the workplace, as well as daily life, topics for writing spring from real situations—perhaps late payment of a bill, an incorrect shipment, or a progress report for a contractor. Then you have a specific rhetorical situation to respond to and little, if any, need to narrow the topic. If you have work experience, you may be able to base college papers on topics from those experiences. If not, you might draw from other experience, such as travel, hobbies, or unusual events or people, always remembering to limit a broad topic to one specific purpose.

Whether you draw details from your own experience or research, or seek answers at the library or on the Internet, this book will show you how to proceed. Because the Internet has so greatly affected research and writing opportunities for students and other readers, this book develops the topic at length in chapter 23.

SELECTING A TOPIC

The first guideline for successful college writing is to *select a topic you care about.* The second is to *narrow the topic* so that you can focus the paper on one main idea and develop it well for your audience.

Audience

The writer's *audience* is the reader. To accomplish your purpose, you should recognize, respect, and respond to your readers' needs. Knowing characteristics of their backgrounds, interests, and viewpoints will help you to choose a suitable topic and devise an appropriate writing strategy. The more you can learn about the person or group who will be reading your writing, the more effective you can make it. *Writing that is addressed to no one in particular will lack a sense of purpose.*

In the workplace, your readers are probably people you have met or talked to on the telephone or communicated with via e-mail. These readers may be customers, wholesalers, service personnel, or others. In the classroom your instructor may assign an audience or suggest you write for an audience of your classmates. Otherwise, you might visualize a typical reader and write directly to him or her. If puzzled, ask yourself, "Who would be likely to read this writing?"

A helpful strategy for your audience is to deliberately shift your perspective from writer to reader. Try to put yourself into the reader's role—to feel and think as the reader might. In "Don't Blame the Editors," Sloan Wilson explains this dual role of writer/reader:

> Each of us is both writer and reader, and no reader has mercy for dullness. My editor who as politely as possible had told me that my work was boring, had learned to speak for millions of readers, and I was grateful to him for making me clean up my act before putting it before the world's sleepy eyes. . . . Those listeners would start getting restless if I confused them; they demanded clarity above all else.

See chapter 2. If a writer ignores readers and neglects their needs, they will respond by ignoring the writing. A keen awareness of how readers think and feel will assist you in shaping your writing purpose and in finding an appropriate *voice.*

The Voice of the Writer

The *writer's voice*, the sound behind the words, is an important part of the rhetorical situation and affects how the audience will respond to a piece of writing. Your written voice is influenced not only by your knowledge, experience, beliefs, and biases but also by how you feel about the act of writing, the reader, and the topic. For example, your written voice may sound confident or unsure, encouraging or critical, or approving or sarcastic. Actually, a writer has many voices

QUESTIONS TO ASSESS AUDIENCES

1. ***To whom am I writing?*** What do I know about the age, gender, education, social class, economic status, interests, and attitudes of the readers? How should these characteristics influence my writing?

2. ***Why will they read this piece of writing?*** How can they benefit? Will they gain information? Be entertained? What else?

3. ***How much do they need or want to know?*** How much can I assume they already know about the subject? What terms should be defined? How much should I say?

4. ***How might they feel about the subject?*** How will their feelings affect my word choice and strategy?

5. ***How will they react to my point of view?*** How should their probable reaction affect my approach to the topic?

that vary according to each rhetorical situation. To adapt your writing voice to a rhetorical situation, you might begin by asking yourself three questions:

- How much do I know about the topic? Will I need to do research?
- Can I write objectively about the topic?
- What level of formality is appropriate for the audience and occasion?

See page 16.

How Should a Writer's Voice Sound? To be respected by your readers, you need a written voice that not only serves your purpose but also reflects preparation, sincerity, integrity, and (at times) empathy for the audience. Readers expect competence and trustworthiness, and they are usually quick to recognize incompetence, insincerity, arrogance, or dishonesty.

To better understand voice in writing, think about what you do when chatting with a friend face to face. You automatically adapt your voice to the occasion. Your tone is pleasant and friendly. You welcome your friend by your manner *and* your words. When writing informally, you might think of the reader as a friend and use a similar tone. Of course, not all writing carries the mark of a writer's personality.

In between the conversational voice and the academic voice, there are different voices that vary in the degree of formality. For college essays, you will be expected to have a clear, knowledgeable voice, not academic but not too informal either. For research papers, teachers often expect an *academic voice*.

Word Choice and Voice Seasoned writers select words that are appropriate for the occasion, purpose, and audience. They also listen to the meaning and the

> ### KEY POINT: WHAT MAKES WRITING EFFECTIVE
>
> Effective writing is focused, fresh, and appropriate. The purpose and organization are clear; words and sentences reflect a sense of style; words mean what they are intended to. Spelling observes standard usage; grammatical structures fit the ideas they house; and punctuation makes relationships clear.

See chapters 2 and 9. music of the words. Precise words specify exactly what you mean. Little surprises in sounds dispel dullness and delight the reader. To evaluate the voice of your writing, read it aloud. How does it sound?

To help you avoid needless frustration and learn how to start writing easily, here is an overview of the writing process.

WHAT IS THE WRITING PROCESS?

Although not a set procedure, the writing process has been observed as having five distinct stages. Writers often shuttle back and forth between stages. Rarely is writing a neat linear procedure, even though it may seem so if you have thought long about a subject. In general, every writing process includes prewriting, drafting, revision, and editing/proofreading. Part 1 of this book focuses on the early stages of writing—prewriting and drafting. Part 2 focuses on concerns that arise during revision and editing.

Although there is no one way to write, there are ways to make writing easier and more effective, and you will find them as you traverse through this book. An excellent way to gain confidence is to dispel any myths you may have heard about writing processes. Then you will be less likely to become entangled in the "perfect draft" approach, expecting to perfect each sentence the first time. This method is tedious and exasperating. Those who use it proceed at a snail's pace.

Nor will you be lulled by the false belief that inspiration alone can transform a first draft into a final draft without several revisions. High-quality papers require much more than an hour or two of effort. They require considerable thought and multiple revisions.

A WORD OF ENCOURAGEMENT

If you consider how much you already know about the process of writing and the English language, you should be encouraged. You are not attempting to learn something completely new. As you write, you'll recover much that now lies

THE FOUR STAGES OF THE WRITING PROCESS

PREWRITING

This first stage of writing is simply setting forth ideas in whatever shape or form that is handy for you—fragments, lists, or sentences. The purpose of prewriting is to get ideas down on paper (or a disk).

DRAFTING

In the second stage of writing, you transform ideas into sentences in a semi-organized manner. Here the purpose is to let your ideas develop, expand, and form links. Drafting is primarily a stage of discovery and exploration.

See chapters 5, 6, 7.

REVISION

Although revision is classified as the third stage of writing, it is ongoing—recurring whenever needed. During revision your goal is to rethink ideas, refine, and develop them. You may drastically reorganize the draft. During this time, you reshape ideas—expanding, deleting, and clarifying.

See chapters 5, 8, 9.

EDITING/PROOFREADING

The final stage requires examining ideas, details, words, grammar, and punctuation—attending to matters *within each sentence*. Here the emphasis is not only on accuracy and correctness but also on clarity.

forgotten in your memory files. Whether words flow from your fingers or each syllable is a struggle, the key is not to compare yourself to others, but to evaluate your own achievement step by step. There is a tiny lesson in each mistake. Master these mini-lessons, and you will make steady progress.

Anything worth achieving is seldom a snap. And writing is no exception; you may need intensive practice. But keep in mind that you will be building on what you already know. If you are already proficient in grammar, punctuation, and mechanics, college writing may be easier than you expect, for you'll be able to focus on developing and organizing your ideas and research findings.

Summary

Writing well is a skill you can learn. To write effectively, a writer must consider the rhetorical situation, which has five elements: the occasion, purpose, topic, audience, and writer's voice. The occasion refers to the situation or event that prompts the writing.

The *general* purpose of writing may be primarily to inform, to persuade, to express, or to entertain. The *specific* purpose involves responding to a certain need for writing. The topic is the subject.

The audience is the reader. The writer's voice is the sound of the words on paper, and it influences the reaction of the reader. Awareness of the four stages of writing—prewriting, drafting, revision, and editing and proofreading—can forestall frustration and increase efficiency. Prewriting before (and possibly during) drafting can save time in the long run. The chief purpose of drafting is to get ideas on paper. Revision refines the larger aspects of a draft; editing refines sentences; and proofreading catches mistakes or other unintended problems.

Take heart! In learning to write better, you are honing a skill that will multiply your chances for success whenever and wherever you communicate.

Key Terms

audience	prewriting	rhetorical situation
drafting	purpose	writer's voice
editing/proofreading	revision	writing process
occasion	rhetoric	

Practice

Case Problem: Responding to a Rhetorical Situation

Directions: Last night you went to a party off campus. Three students spray-painted parked cars, but you just watched. Soon the police arrived, sirens screaming. The culprits threw down their paint cans and blended into the crowd. One can rolled up to your feet, so you tossed it into the nearest trash can. Police questioned bystanders and noticed an orange smudge on your index finger. They handcuffed you and three guys who had a fine mist of paint spray on their faces (the wind was blowing) and took you to the station. The three confessed; you were released. In a letter how would you tell the following persons of the incident?

1. Your guidance counselor
2. Your best friend, who is doing her student teaching in a nearby town
3. Your parents

Ten Ideas for Writing

Directions: Identify and discuss an interesting object, event, pastime, or thought. Perhaps the suggestions below will foster an idea.

1. My ideal job
2. A memorable concert
3. An interesting one-day trip

4. Thoughts of a people watcher
5. A great moment in . . .
6. My favorite pet
7. An unusual experience
8. My earliest memory
9. Hiking in the spring
10. How to make homemade ice cream (or something else)

CHAPTER 2

Different Voices for Different Occasions and Audiences

> True ease in writing comes from art, not chance,
> As those move easiest who have learn'd to dance.
> Tis not enough no harshness gives offence—
> The sound must seem an echo to the sense.
>
> —Alexander Pope (1688–1744)
> *Essay on Criticism*

Alexander Pope knew that for writing to be effective, it should be appropriate for the audience, and the sound should be consistent with the meaning. These two guidelines apply not only to poetry but also to letters, reports, and college papers. A carelessly worded message may carry a negative tone that will undermine the purpose and antagonize readers.

In the workplace and in college classes, you will be expected to write appropriately according to the occasion, purpose, reader, and topic. To fulfill this expectation, you observe conventional rules of usage and grammar and use an appropriate voice for the rhetorical situation.

THE WRITER'S VOICE

Voice is the presence of the writer as perceived by the reader. Behind the words of every piece of writing is the distinctive sound of the writer's voice. This voice—which radiates from word choice, phrasing, and sentence style—reveals an attitude toward the reader and the topic. The writer's voice is like a mirror that reflects not only the writer's authority on a topic but also the mind-set and personality.

As writers develop proficiency, they listen to the voice of their writing. They consider not only the literal meanings of the words but also the shadowy nuances—the subtle shades of meaning and feeling that accompany words. Some words sound prickly; others crack like a whip. Some are as soft and soothing as a lullaby. A writer's choice of words, level of formality, and attitude greatly influence how the audience perceives the message.

A writer has many voices; for example, let's listen to the three different voices in this series of collection letters.

WORKPLACE CASE STUDY

A Series of Collection Letters

Just as the occasion and status of the reader change in each stage of the collection process, so too the writer's voice changes. As the urgency for payment escalates, the concern for the customer's feelings lessens. (Company policies vary.)

Stage 1. Cheery Reminder
(Assumption: Customer overlooked and will pay.)

Are you enjoying that lovely walnut desk you purchased on April 12? Will you please look around on it for your bill—which seems to have been overlooked.

Your payment is now six weeks overdue. If payment has already been mailed, please disregard this reminder. If not, take a minute to write a check for $55.00, the amount of your first month's payment.

Stage 2. Firm Request for Payment
(Assumption: Pressure needed to collect.)

For many years, you have been one of our preferred customers. We appreciate your patronage and your promptness in sending past payments. You have been fair and responsible; you have kept your credit in mint condition.

But now that A-1 rating has begun to slip away. You are two months behind on the walnut desk, purchased April 12. To protect your credit rating, stop by and pay the $110 (two payments) this week.

Stage 3. Demand
(Assumption: Warning needed to motivate payment.)

Your credit rating is in serious danger! The payments on the desk, bought April 12, are three months overdue. To clear this obligation and avoid dealing with a collection agency, send payment of $165 today.

If you are unable to clear the entire obligation, we would like to help you. To discuss an alternative payment plan, call us at (800) 555-9891.

Stage 4. Ultimatum
(Assumption: Customer may not pay.)

Unless payment is made within TEN DAYS of the above date, your bill will be turned over to a collection agency. A payment of $220 will clear your obligation for the desk, purchased April 12.

YOU CAN STOP THIS ACTION! Call us now at (800) 555-9891.

HOW CASUAL CONVERSATION
DIFFERS FROM FOCUSED WRITING

Although a speaker uses various voices in casual conversation, the spoken voice tends to be more friendly and less purposeful than the written voice, particularly in focused writing. Casual conversation ambles along at a leisurely pace, often wordy and repetitive at times, perhaps punctuated by witticisms. Often fragmented and abbreviated, it may become sidetracked and never get to the point. The speaker may omit transitions and significant information. When this happens, the listener may frown, raise an eyebrow, or ask a question. Then the speaker has the opportunity to backtrack and explain.

In contrast, even when focused writing is informal, it has a logical order—steadily advancing toward the point to be made. Since few writers have the chance to observe nonverbal feedback or to ask questions of the reader, they must exert more effort than conversationalists to be clear, complete, and diplomatic. To be effective, writing must be more specific, concise, and thorough than casual conversation. The writer must carefully monitor words to refrain from offending. The writer's voice should sound knowledgeable, kind, and trustworthy.

STANDARD AND NONSTANDARD USAGE

With each technological advance, new words flow out over the airwaves and into cyberspace. Dictionary publishers scramble to keep up with the flood of new words by bringing out revised editions every few years. To maintain a semblance of order, they classify words in various ways according to usage. All dictionaries have two broad categories of usage—standard and nonstandard.

Standard Usage

To sound knowledgeable, a writer needs a command of standard usage. Most English words are standard usage, meaning they are widely accepted by educated speakers and writers. These words follow conventional spellings and rules of grammar. Standard usage varies widely, ranging from informal to formal words.

If a word in the dictionary has no usage label, then it is standard. Note that some words have several meanings, both standard and nonstandard. So if you use the word, be sure to apply it in the context you intend. Some dictionaries provide examples showing standard usage. If a word is used primarily in conversation, it will be labeled *colloq.* or *colloquial.*

Sometimes the status of words changes; a word can gain or lose acceptance or acquire new meanings. For example, the word *punk* has several colloquial or slang meanings, but once *punk* was used to refer to a style of dress and music, it became standard English. Often language is a mixture of the informal and formal, technical and nontechnical.

Nonstandard Usage

Although nonstandard words are sometimes used to lend a sense of realism to poetry and fiction, they are generally inappropriate in college and workplace writing. In fact, Bloomberg, the financial news and data company, filters electronic messages written by anyone who uses the company's desktop terminals. When profanity or ethnic, racial, or gender slurs are typed, a warning appears, and the user must reword the message before it can be sent.

See chapter 30 for e-mail.

Dialect and Regionalism Words that are limited to a geographic area are identified as *dialect* or *regional*. Dialect is the natural way some folks talk, using colloquialisms such as "hit the road," regionalisms such as "down the road a piece," and fractured grammar such as "didn't never" or "them books." This usage can be difficult to understand; sometimes it is nonstandard. Although dialect is incorporated into some writing to suggest regional or informal speech, it should be avoided in academic papers and business writing.

Where Can I Find Keys to Usage Labels and Abbreviations?

The keys to usage and abbreviations are usually located in the introduction of a dictionary. Here are nonstandard usage labels and their common abbreviations:

N.S. or nonstd.	= nonstandard
substand.	= substandard
dial.	= dialect
vul.	= vulgar (common)

What If Dictionaries Disagree? Since the spelling and the status of a word can change in a relatively short time, consult an up-to-date dictionary. Even then dictionaries may not agree on the status of a word. For example, *complected* is listed as "regional dialect" or "substandard" in several dictionaries, whereas *Merriam-Webster's Collegiate Dictionary*, 10th edition (1999) states, "Not an error, nor a dialectal term, nor nonstandard—all of which it has been labeled—*complected* still manages to raise hackles."* If you are trying to decide whether or not to use a word of questionable status, it is safer to be conservative. Avoid it lest the reader, unaware of the diversity in opinion, regard the word as an error.

Three Vocabularies

A factor that complicates word choice for beginning writers is that most of us have three distinct vocabularies that have varying levels of formality—one for speaking, one for writing, and one for reading. The spoken vocabulary is the smallest and least formal; rough drafts are often written at this level. The vocabulary

---

*By permission. From *Merriam-Webster's Collegiate® Dictionary*, Tenth Edition © 1999 by Merriam-Webster, Inc.

for writing lies somewhere in between those of speaking and reading. Your final draft, after being revised several times, should contain this middle level, which uses standard words and grammar.

The reading vocabulary is the largest, most specific, and most formal. Sometimes students pull words from this vocabulary or use a word found during research but do not look up the meaning. This practice can result in confusion and error. Awareness of the different levels of formality and your own three distinct vocabularies can help you select an appropriate voice for each rhetorical situation.

THREE LEVELS OF FORMALITY

In workplace and college writing, three levels of formality—Informal English, Professional English, and Formal English—are used. All three levels follow the conventional rules of grammar. The level a writer selects depends upon the rhetorical situation. The level of formality influences the sound of the writer's voice.

LEVELS OF FORMALITY			
Nonstandard	Informal English	Professional English	Formal English
Least Formal			Most Formal
(nonstandard grammar)		Standard grammar	

Informal Standard English

Although Informal Standard English may include a well-placed fragment, the verb forms, pronoun agreement, and other grammatical structures are always standard. Dictionary entries usually label informal words, but not always in the same way; you may find either of two labels to denote *informal* usage:

inf. = informal

colloq. = colloquial (conversational or casual)

Informal Standard English is the language of conversation. You read Informal Standard English in many popular magazines, novels, short stories, poems, comics, ads, newspaper articles, and other writing. A *Wall Street Journal* article entitled "In 24-Hour Workplace, Day Care Is Moving to the Night Shift" uses Informal Standard English in the opening paragraphs:

> There are plenty of places to sleep at the Children's Choice Learning Center here, but nine-year-old Najah Finch isn't napping. Wearing a pink "I am Boy Crazy" T-shirt, she cartwheels around the floor, breaks for juice and popcorn, then settles down at the TV for a Muppet video. Najah's mom isn't due to pick her up for another three hours.
> At 3:30 a.m.

—Barbara Carton

Did you note the conversational voice and the fragment "At 3:30 a.m."? Other clues to informality include the contraction *isn't* and the colloquial use of *mom* (mother). There are different varieties of Informal Standard English. Many business letters and printed materials require all sentences to be complete. The voice may be a bit more formal as in Stuart M. Berger's *What Your Doctor Didn't Learn in Medical School:*

> The word *hypoglycemia* is the kind of six-syllable medicalese word that my patients hear and tell me: "That's Greek to me, doctor." Well, in the case of this word, it really is Greek! But just in case your ancient Greek is a tad rusty, let's review: *hypo* means "too little"; *gly* is the Greek root for "sugar"; and the suffix *-emia* means "of the blood." String them together, and you have "too little sugar in the blood." (The disease is the polar opposite of diabetes, which creates too much sugar in the blood.)

Watch the Pronouns   Did you notice Dr. Berger's use of the first-person (*me*) and second-person (*your*)? This usage is typical of Informal Standard English. Although Professional English and Formal English sometimes include the first person [*I, me, mine, we, our, us*], it is only for a good reason. As a rule, these two levels do not include second person when written. In an oral presentation, second person is desirable since you will be talking directly to an audience—and you will probably mix levels of formality.

See page H-26 in the handbook.

Mixing Levels of Formality   Once in a while, a writer may mix levels of formality for a special effect, but only for a purpose. Making a switch *between* paragraphs, as Barbara Carton did, is easier than doing so within a paragraph, which requires more transition. As a rule, it is better (and certainly easier) to use just one level of formality in business writing and academic papers.

Professional English

Professional English marks a writer as well-educated and knowledgeable. Certain audiences in the professional world (of business, higher education, and literature, for example) expect a more serious, reserved, and authoritative voice than that found at the informal level. Some writers call this level Edited American English. Actually, the term *level of formality* is somewhat misleading. *Range of formality* would be more accurate, but no one calls it that. Professional English contains the most words, so it goes *unlabeled* in all dictionaries.

The hallmarks of Professional English are complete sentences, correct grammar, and standard word choice. This level of usage is found in many newspaper articles, textbooks, business reports, annual reports to stockholders, and much academic writing, including research papers. In the article on twenty-four-hour day care, Barbara Carton's voice changes in the fourth paragraph, where she switches to Professional English. (Note that there are no contractions or informal words.)

> As more single parents and working couples cope with a 24-hour economy, day care is making an uneasy transition to night care. Employers are building round-the-clock centers to attract and keep employees. State and local governments are also supporting extended-hour and night-care initiatives, partly because they feel obliged to help the single mothers they sent to work under welfare reform.

LEVELS OF FORMALITY IN THE WORKPLACE		
Informal Standard	*Professional English*	*Formal English*
memos	memos, e-mail	legal notices, letters
customer letters	bulletins	proposals
newsletters	newsletters, letters	laws, statutes
sales talks	bids, proposals	legal documents
letter reports	professional reports	technical reports
informal speeches	presentations	formal speeches
conversation	policies	policies
newspaper articles	contracts, forms	contracts, forms
e-mail	manuals	technical documents

Formal English

You may be familiar with Formal English. If enrolled in prelaw, paralegal, education, premed, nursing, data processing, engineering, or other such programs, you may read Formal Technical English in your textbooks. Or you may work in a profession where it is spoken and written daily.

Formal English may include foreign phrases, literary allusions, and specialized or technical terms unknown to the average reader. The sentence structure tends to be long and complex, written in third person. All of these characteristics tend to make the voice of the writer impersonal.

Formal English usually goes unmarked in dictionaries, but archaic words and foreign phrases are labeled. If you find the following labels, you will know the words are formal:

arch.   = archaic (antiquated or rarely used)

obs.   = obsolete (used chiefly before 1775)

poetic   (found in poetry)

Formal English is primarily written. It is the language of technical manuals, some college textbooks, classical literature, professional journals, formal reports, many insurance policies, legal and government documents. The following passage from a legal decision written by former U.S. Supreme Court Chief Justice Earl Warren is easier to understand than many other legal documents:

> The plaintiffs contend that segregated public schools are not "equal" and cannot be made "equal," and that hence they are deprived of the equal protection of the laws. Because of the obvious importance of the question presented, the Court took jurisdiction. Argument was heard in the 1952 Term, and reargument was heard this Term on certain questions propounded by the Court.

> **The School Segregation Decision of 1954**
> ***Brown versus Board of Education of Topeka, Kansas***
> **347 U.S. 487–496 (May 17, 1954)**

THREE COMMON CONCERNS
THAT AFFECT VOICE

Just as the level of formality should be appropriate for each occasion and audience, so too should the writer's voice. Although colloquialisms may give an air of casual friendliness, they are inappropriate for much college writing.

Out-of-Place Colloquialisms

As you edit your college essays, watch for out-of-place colloquialisms. A sudden, unnecessary downshift to informality is jarring for the unsuspecting reader. Such shifts need to be made carefully and only for a sound reason. To help you avoid some common colloquialisms, consider the following lists:

Colloquial	*Standard*
He cleared the *stuff* out of his desk.	He *cleared out* his desk.
The client *really wants* to sell.	The client *is eager* to sell.
She got a *good deal* on her car.	Her Ford Escort was a *bargain*.
Jim is in *a lot* of trouble.	Jim has *many* problems.
I'd hate to see her do that.	*I would prefer* she not do that.
Erin is an *awfully* good doctor.	Erin is a *very* good physician.
Jason added his *two cents' worth*.	Jason added his *opinion*.
Alright, I'll go.	*All right, I will go.*
When did Sue *get* married?	When *was* Sue *married*?
He takes his *kids* to the office.	He takes his *children* to the office.

Other colloquial expressions to avoid in expository writing are listed below, along with standard alternatives:

Colloquial	*Standard*
looking to	planning to
seeing as	since, because
sort of	rather, somewhat
headache	problem, concern
a couple of	two
fight (verbal)	argument, quarrel
really good	very good, excellent
mad	angry, upset
ballpark figure	estimate
stuff	items, articles, materials

Many unsuspecting writers misuse the term *great*, when they mean excellent, elated, or happy: "She's a great dancer." "We were feeling great." The standard meanings of *great* include "very large in size," "large in quantity or number," and "extensive distance or time." Only *informally* does *great* mean "wonderful" or "excellent." If you are unsure of the status of a word, consult a dictionary.

Switching Pronouns in Mid-Sentence

When students write the way they talk, they may switch from first-person to second-person pronouns unnecessarily. An abrupt shift in person changes the point of view, which is distracting to the reader. Consider this student's rough draft:

> Years ago *I* would start my vegetable plants from seed because it was much cheaper and *you* could get a jump on the season. But as *I* expanded my garden, more and more plants were needed, too many to grow from seed. So *I* would go to garden centers, which is exciting. *You* can select from dozens of kinds and dream of big, red, ripe tomatoes.

These unnecessary shifts in person could be easily remedied by deleting each *you* and replacing it with an *I*. If you have this concern, beware of using *you* in academic writing except in process papers and business letters. Then use *you* correctly for a purpose.

See page H-26.

Inappropriate Prescriptive Tone

A prescriptive tone lends authority to a statement. Prescriptive language is appropriate for giving directions, establishing rules and laws, and issuing commands. Just as a doctor prescribes medicine, a prescriptive writer offers advice, makes suggestions, or requests the reader to do something. Unnecessary prescription intrudes and irritates. You can usually identify prescriptive language by the words *must*, *should*, *ought*, or *need*. Sometimes appropriate prescription is implied, as in the first two examples that follow:

Appropriate:

Process paper: First, *detach* all the parts from their plastic frames.

Persuasive speech: On the eve of the November election, *set* your alarm clock so that you can cast your ballot and fulfill your civic duty.

Business etiquette manual: The boss *should* issue the first invitation to a lunch, dinner, or party.

But prescription can be unnecessary and inappropriate. As you read the two examples below, listen to the difference in tone. [Here the descriptive example is preferable. Prescription is unnecessary.]

Inappropriate:

Prescriptive: Setting goals *should* be a person's most important objective in life. (The student writer projects her priority onto everyone.)

Descriptive: Setting goals is an important part of my life.

In college papers you may be expected to use prescription to explain a process or argue a belief. For a report or other rhetorical situation, you may be expected to write a recommendation. Any prescriptive or descriptive language should be worded appropriately according to the occasion, purpose, audience, and topic.

THREE CRUCIAL QUESTIONS FOR ACHIEVING AN APPROPRIATE VOICE

In college and on the job, you will be writing for many different audiences via e-mail, letters, reports, papers, and other documents. All of these pieces will require different voices, tailored according to each occasion and audience. To achieve an appropriate voice, you might first consider three important questions:

- **Who will be reading the writing?** What are the primary interests and characteristics of the audience? Adjust your written voice to their culture, occupation, gender, expectations, and educational level.

- **Why will they be reading this writing?** The motivation of the audience will influence how you shape your purpose and voice. Think in terms of advantages: how can they benefit? What words and approach will be effective and appropriate?

- **Can I write objectively about this topic?** Read your writing aloud. Does it sound fair and unbiased? Do the words say what you intend? Is the tone pleasing and suitable for the occasion and the audience?

Summary

Voice is the result of all the stylistic decisions a writer makes, including level of formality. Writers are expected to find an appropriate voice for the rhetorical situation. Focused writing is more orderly, concise, and complete than casual conversation.

Words are classified as either nonstandard or standard usage. Standard usage comprises three levels of formality: Informal Standard English, Professional English, and Formal English. In the workplace, standard usage is expected, and all three levels are used at various times. Sometimes language is a mixture of informal and formal words. For college papers, use a level of formality that is appropriate for the assignment.

For workplace and college writing, avoid *unnecessary* colloquialisms, switches in person, and prescription.

Key Terms

archaic	Informal Standard English	prescriptive tone
colloquial	level of formality	Professional English
dialect	nonstandard usage	standard usage
Formal English	obsolete	voice

Test Yourself

Identifying the Level of Formality

Directions: Identify the level of formality of each example and then check your answers with those at the end of the chapter.

1. "For ten years after finishing college, I made my living running around in short pants in drafty arenas across America, as a professional basketball player. The rhythm of the road—a drive, a flight, a performance, a hotel, a sleep . . . provided a frame through which I saw America and myself. For the past seventeen years, I have crisscrossed America as a politician, a United States senator from New Jersey, following the familiar rhythm— a drive, a flight, a performance. . . ."

    —Bill Bradley, *Time Present, Time Past*

2. Some editors may use the phrase "We can't use it right now" merely to soften the letdown, and many writers take the words as literal truth. However, some editors may mean the phrase literally, so if an editor writes, "We can't use it right now," write back and ask, "When can you use it?" If you receive encouragement from an editor, ask "If I changed the ending (or whatever change the editor suggests), would you be interested in seeing it again?"

    —Kenneth Atchity, "Dealing with Rejection"

3. Linda Ronstadt: "When we were little, we spoke Spanish at home. . . . My Spanish is very rudimentary—child's Spanish, really. But I sing in Spanish, and my new album is all Spanish *canciones* [songs], and I sing two songs in the movie *The Mambo Kings*."

    —James Brady, "In Step with: Linda Ronstadt"

4. "Between eye-wiping and nose-blowing, I told him, 'I don't ever want another dog. It hurts too much. . . .' 'You're right about the hurt, son,' he answered, 'but that's the price of love.'"

    —Fred Bauer, "The Price of Love"

5. To every thing there is a season, and a time to every purpose under the heaven: A time to be born, and a time to die; a time to plant, and a time to pluck up that which is planted; . . .

    —Ecclesiastes 3:1,2 KJV

Practice

Rewriting Colloquialisms and Contractions

Directions: When you find colloquialisms or contractions below, rephrase the sentence into Professional English. If the sentence is already Professional English, mark with a C.

1. Tasha is looking to buy a new car.
2. Seeing as Michael has the lead in the senior play, he will be staying after school for the next several weeks.
3. Around 11:30 I'll stop by your office so that we can go to lunch.
4. Tara and Jeanne had a fun time at the flea market.
5. Yesterday Lance had a client who was a big headache.
6. In the employees' lounge are some awfully good cinnamon rolls.
7. That's a ballpark figure.
8. He made a lot of punctuation errors in that letter.
9. I heard Scott and Julie got married last week.
10. Brent bought a really good sound system.

Groups: Levels of Formality for Different Audiences

Directions: Read the case problems below. Then decide which level of formality would be best for each audience.

1. You are a newspaper reporter interviewing Colin Powell for a feature in the Sunday paper about his career. Which level of formality will you use?
2. You are a systems analyst, and your boss has assigned a systems project. He has asked for weekly memo reports. What level of formality will you use?
3. You are writing a cover letter to mail with your resume. What level of formality will you use?
4. You are writing a television commercial for antifreeze. You want to appeal to everyone who drives a car, so have decided to feature a mechanic at a local garage. Which level of formality will you use?
5. Imagine you are a physician writing an article that describes a new treatment for cancer. The article will appear in a medical journal that is read primarily by other doctors. What level of formality will you use?

Test Yourself Answers

1. *Professional*
2. *Informal*
3. *Professional*
4. *Informal*
5. *Formal*

CHAPTER 3

Prewriting

Discovering Ideas

*A writer needs three things, experience, observation, and imagination,
any two of which, at times any one . . . , can supply the lack of the others.*

—William Faulkner
Writers at Work: First Series

Your experience, observation, and imagination can fuel your writing. You can take amusing, unusual, or perhaps ordinary incidents and transform them—after thoughtful reflection—into essays. Just ask yourself, "How did this experience influence me? What did I learn about life?" Questions like these start you thinking so that you can draw a conclusion about the incident or event.

Still, some students are reluctant to write because they don't know how to begin. The prewriting techniques explained in this chapter can help anyone start writing quickly. They can also help to divert the flood of anxiety that sometimes overwhelms writers.

OVERCOMING ANXIETY

When an instructor assigns a paper, does your stomach contract into a tight knot? If it does, remember that you are not alone. Some writers carry a heavy bundle of anxiety that impedes the effectiveness of their writing. One student confided, "I don't know what's the matter, but when I walk into this classroom, I become so frightened." When asked if she was afraid of the instructor, she smiled and said, "No, but if I don't get over this feeling, I'll have to drop the course." Yet she came to every session and did excellent work. Late in the quarter, during a practice assignment, she confided the source of her anxiety:

> Finally, I've realized why I was so scared of this class. I was haunted by the memory of a high school literature class where we had to memorize poetry. I had learned my poem well, but when my turn came to stand and recite, I drew a blank. I could

not remember a word. The teacher became angry and bawled me out in front of the class. It's taken me fifteen years to exorcise this old ghost.

Professional writers also experience fear of writing. Novelist Anna Quindlen, author of *Black and Blue*, *One True Thing*, and *Object Lessons*, writes

> I have never sat down in front of a blank screen and not had that moment of terror that says, "It's not going to be good, it's not going to come out right, it's too hard, it'll take too long." . . . you always have this vision in your mind of how ideally [the book] is going to be when it's done. The final project never conforms to the vision. It's never quite as broad, or as sweeping, or as meaningful. So you try to get as close to the vision as possible. And when you're done and you have gotten some-what close, then that's a satisfying feeling.

Insecurity never vanished for John Steinbeck, the prolific American novelist and Nobel Prize winner. In a letter, Steinbeck wrote, "I suffer as always from the fear of putting down the first line [of a book]. It is amazing the terrors, the mag-ics, the prayers, the straitening shyness that assails one. . . . A strange and mystic business, writing." Later, as Steinbeck was about to finish a book, he again became apprehensive over whether or not he had achieved his purpose. He described his fear as being "as natural as breathing."

By acknowledging fear and finding the cause, you, too, can control it. Once you begin to prewrite and pace yourself throughout the writing process, chances are your fear will shrink. Dana White described how she manages fear and as-sumes responsibility for her writing:

> When I do not achieve as high a grade as expected, fear begins to creep in. For a while I feel inadequate. Then I become more positive as I begin to analyze why I did not reach my goal. Maybe it was poor timing, or I did not put my whole self into my writing. For whatever reason, I do not place the burden on anyone else; it always falls on my shoulders. By realizing my mistakes, I start to alleviate them. I work hard to overcome these problems so that my fear does not keep me from doing what I want to accomplish.

Criticism is a fact of life for all of us. Professional writers, too, encounter crit-icism. Not every manuscript is published, nor are published pieces always re-ceived kindly by critics. The best way to dull the pain of criticism is to view er-rors and comments as a doorway to revision. Then they become opportunities to learn.

FINDING A TOPIC AND IDEAS BY PREWRITING

Prewriting, the first stage of the writing process, is a time of discovery—you unearth ideas. Prewriting can condense swirling mists of thoughts into words on paper. You uncover raw material to shape and polish later. There is no need to think about order or correctness—*the objective is to produce as many ideas as possible.*

You can prewrite whenever and however you like—on paper, at a keyboard, or with a tape recorder. Mystery novelist Agatha Christie often paused while washing dishes to jot down notes. One student keeps a tape recorder in his car to record insights. When ideas are elusive, some writers like to walk along a quiet street or path to let their thoughts settle. Yet it is essential to pin down ideas before they flit away.

The six invention techniques in this chapter are ways to jump-start ideas. By trying all six techniques, you can find out which ones work best for you. All can be done on a computer or with pen and paper, whichever is more comfortable.

Freewriting

Freewriting is uncensored writing, often in sentence form. Freewriting enables anyone to start writing immediately. It may work well for writers whose thoughts flee at the sight of a fresh sheet of paper, for you can write anything. To freewrite, just empty whatever bits and pieces of ideas are in your mind out onto the paper. Here is an example:

> What to write? There's so much debris in my mind. Clutter. The files are overflowing—it's no wonder I can't find anything to write about. What is significant? Let's see. Life is significant—very, very, very much so. Yet some individuals toss it away so lightly. Just last week in our town, two guys in their twenties carried out a suicide pact. They had been drinking and doing drugs. A bartender overheard them planning the night before. But he didn't tell anyone. Probably thought they were just talking—old saying, you know, that those who talk about it won't. But the truth is they often do. How sad—only one chance and they throw it away. They jump into eternity without a parachute, not knowing where they will land.

This freewriting sample has unearthed three general topics: the value of life, suicide, and the possibility of another life after death. The writer might go on to take one of these three topics as the subject for a second round of freewriting. Freewriting in this way is called *focused freewriting* because rather than starting with whatever is on his or her mind, the writer has already established a focus for freewriting.

Note that freewriting may not be the best technique for writers who are under time constraints: it may take much longer than other techniques. To avoid a time trap while freewriting, set a timer for ten minutes. Shut off your conscious editor and write quickly. When the timer rings, stop, examine your catch, and develop whatever seems promising.

Clustering

Clustering, devised by Gabriele Rico, is uncensored brainstorming combined with doodling. Clustering produces an overview of a subject, suggests specific topics, and yields related details. To begin, take a fresh sheet of paper and write a

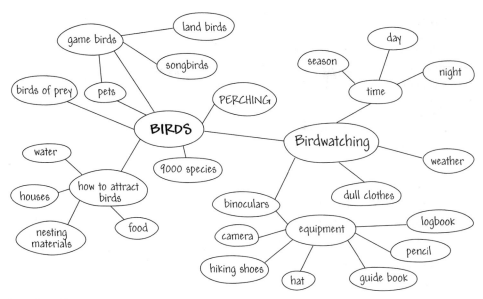

Fig. 3.1 Clustering

general subject in the center. Then circle the word. As each new thought bursts forth, jot it near the word that prompted it. Circle the new word. Next, draw a line between the two. Repeat the procedure. The sample cluster (fig. 3.1) began with the subject of birds. That central idea branched out, leading to the specific topic of birdwatching.

Brainstorming

An efficient way to start your mind moving is to brainstorm, either alone or in groups. Brainstorming captures ideas as they flit by, either as words, phrases, or fragments. You can use this technique in a group or alone. *The secret of success in brainstorming is to think fast and forgo criticism.* Remarks such as "That's no good" or "That won't work" dampen enthusiasm and dam the stream of ideas. In brainstorming, all ideas are respected and recorded, no matter how wild.

Brainstorming is often used to create a new product, to improve an existing product, or to solve a problem. You can use this technique to find a topic for a paper, to narrow a topic, and to find supporting details. In a group one person can record responses while others contribute. It is helpful to use a chalkboard because the sight of ideas may trigger others, related but different.

Alone you can talk into a tape recorder without the distraction of making notes. Or you can write a general topic at the top of a sheet of paper and start jotting down possible ways to narrow it, as in this example:

Water Gardens

half barrels	landscaping a small pond	choosing fish and snails
molded ponds	selecting water plants	preventing algae
dig your own	building a waterfall	cost of materials
amount of labor	installing a fountain	legal liability

After you narrow your topic down to one aspect of water gardens, you can start listing possible supporting details.

List-Making and Scratch Outlining on a Computer

List-making can be a boon when you know so much about a topic you feel overwhelmed. With a list you can narrow a broad range of possibilities. To quickly capture and organize ideas, try list-making and scratch outlining, using a computer. Place your topic at the top of the screen or page. Then list details that might be relevant. If you sort details as you write, place each group in a short column. Before you start revising the list, make a backup copy.

Then reread and sort the details. If you spy an item that does not belong, simply delete it from the screen but *not* from your backup medium. That way you can go back to your original if needed. The example below shows a student's quick listing of ideas.

received two baby Pekin drakes as a gift

ducks were noisy, affectionate, intelligent when older

quacking to call me when hungry

ducks will not obey

locked them in the yard while my friends went to the woods

grew fast—ugly awkward stage—changes

Dad was angry—they polluted the horse trough

lesson learned: no eggs, no income

Lists often have no apparent order. When you start placing ideas in order, you are beginning a *scratch outline*. This primitive outline is simply a revised list that herds ideas into a tentative order. To develop a scratch outline, first scan your details, looking for some logical order. This may be a chronological sequence or a grouping of ideas according to topics.

As you categorize the groups, place the headings at the top of columns. The headings will become your main points. Now recopy your points into one column, leaving several spaces between items so that you can insert related details. Your scratch outline will enable you to organize your paper. The scratch outline that follows groups details from the previous list under topical headings in chronological order.

Scratch Outline: A Child's Lesson in Economics

1. Intro: gift of two noisy newborn Pekin drakes
2. Duck adolescence: feeding, digging worms, fast growth, ugly awkward stage. Changes.
3. Duck habits: Dad didn't like polluting the horse trough. Ducks will not obey.
4. Duck maturity: sleek, affectionate, intelligent. Quacking at the back gate to call me when they were hungry. Locking them in yard while my friends and I went to the woods. How ducks escaped and found us.
5. Conclusion: no eggs, no income, the fate of my beloved pets

---

COMPUTERS AND OUTLINING TIP

Check your word-processing program to see if it has an integrated outline function. This function allows you to develop and reorganize an outline easily. This way you can start a scratch outline and quickly move to a working outline.

Questioning

To use questioning at its best, try projecting yourself into the role of a reporter. What questions could you ask to elicit information from other people? Then try the questions on yourself. Whenever your writing stalls, ask questions to restart the flow of details. The traditional "five W's and an H" (who? what? when? where? why? how?) can be expanded to full-fledged questions:

- Who was involved?
- What happened?
- When did it happen?
- Where did it happen?
- Why did it happen?

- How did it happen?
- What will be its effect?
- What can be learned?
- What is the subject like or unlike?
- How has it changed over time?

Combining Invention Techniques

As you prewrite, play around with ideas. Many writers find that combining invention techniques is even more productive than using one technique alone. For instance, while clustering, you might try asking yourself brief questions to increase the flow of ideas: What? Where? What next? What else should be said? Who? How? What else? What is interesting? Funny? When? Why? So what? What does the reader need to know?

GATHERING INFORMATION

All of the discovery techniques mentioned here are useful for gathering ideas from your personal experience. But for most college work, you will need other methods of gathering information.

Reading Literature and Doing Research

You can gather ideas for writing by reading literature. Chapter 26 gives tips for reading essays critically and reacting in a paper. Chapter 27 explains how to analyze short stories, novels, and plays and write a paper of analysis. Chapter 28 suggests a way to experience a poem, look at its parts, appreciate its artistry, and write a short paper.

Many college classes require research. Chapter 22 explains how to gather information through observation, interviews, and surveys. Chapter 23 explains how to locate sources in the library and on the Internet. Usually, information gained from printed sources is stored on note cards or on a computer using note taking software. Other data and ideas are often stored in a journal.

Keeping a Journal

Some instructors require that students keep a journal to store reactions to essays, fiction, and poetry or other ideas for writing. Journals are also useful for recording observations, impressions, and incidents when you conduct firsthand research. For example, a student who worked in a restaurant researched nonverbal communication in her workplace. By smiling and lightly touching patrons as she served them, she found that her tips nearly doubled. The daily notes she kept in her journal provided the material for her report.

In some ways a journal is similar to a diary, but journals often include a wider range of material. A journal can be a private account of conversations, events, perceptions, reactions, or anything else a writer cares to record. Some writers save quotations, funny stories, or poems. Any of these items may prove valuable for later writing.

Summary

Prewriting is a practical way to manage fear of writing. When a writer faces fear and starts prewriting, progress begins. Prewriting is the first stage of the writing process, an opportunity to discover ideas and write them down. Six common invention techniques, useful in prewriting, are freewriting, clustering, brainstorming, list-making, scratch outlining, and questioning.

You may also gather information for writing from reading literature and doing research. Journals are valuable for storing observations and ideas for later writing, when you can shape journal excerpts according to your purpose and audience.

Key Terms

brainstorming	freewriting	questioning
clustering	list-making	scratch outline

Practice

Case Problems: Brainstorming in Small Groups

Directions: Choose one of the cases below or devise one of your own. Appoint a recorder to jot down what is said while the others brainstorm possible solutions. Remember to hold off on evaluation.

1. Many personnel in your office pack their lunches. Lately food and beverages have been disappearing from the break room refrigerator. What might be done?

2. Imagine you are a group of citizens concerned about the number of accidents that have occurred in your residential neighborhood because of speeding and failure to observe stop signs. What alternatives might be tried?

3. A neighbor has become overly friendly. When you moved into the neighborhood, she offered to babysit your children in her home, which she has done occasionally, refusing a fee. On your birthday, she baked you a cake. Now she has started coming to your front door, entering without knocking, and wandering about your house until she finds you. What can you do?

Ten Ideas for Ten-Minute Writings

Directions: Freewrite for ten minutes about anything you wish. The suggestions below may be helpful.

1. I wonder . . .
2. Tomorrow . . .
3. I can't . . . but I can . . .
4. Once I . . . but now . . .
5. When I see . . . , I remember . . .
6. Write a short poem.
7. Happiness is . . .
8. Summarize your worst mistake. What have you learned from it?
9. What would you most like to do? How might you do it?
10. Sketch a career plan. What training or education will you need?

CHAPTER 4

Drafting: Exploring Ideas

Writing and rewriting are a constant search for what it is one is saying.
—John Updike

Drafting, the second stage of the writing process, is the time to rummage through ideas accumulated during prewriting and unfold them into sentences and paragraphs. It can be exciting—hours may seem like minutes. You may glance at an old idea and suddenly see it in a new light. You may devise a delightful comparison or find a bit of irony or an unusual twist. You may grope for words and settle for temporary substitutes. Regardless, keep writing. The purpose of the draft is to expand ideas on paper as quickly as possible without interruption by an internal censor or other noise.

Fleshing Out Your Prewriting Notes

Before you begin to write, find a secluded spot. Resolve to ignore the telephone or other distractions. Do whatever you can to ensure privacy. To start a first draft, you need a block of uninterrupted time, at least an hour, when your mind is keen. Start wherever you wish—beginning, middle, or end. That way, there is no worry about wording a thesis statement, supplying transitions, or other concerns. There is no need to correct or do anything that will disrupt your concentration. Just glance at your prewriting notes whenever you need more ideas.

Perhaps the best advice is to let ideas go where they will. Don't worry if your first draft wanders into byways. Unnecessary details and mistakes may litter the path of your main idea. That's all right. This draft is for your eyes only. It lets you explore. You can rearrange and clean up later. If your inner censor will not allow you free rein, then circle suspicious spellings or mark questionable words, but move on quickly. If a word or idea eludes you, just draw a short line and keep on writing. Carefree, you will be more apt to experience the fun of discovering what you know as you write.

When Ideas Disappear

As you roam the hills and valleys of your memory, collecting bits of experience (incidents, anecdotes, examples, and other specific details) for your exploratory draft, sometimes there is little to find. That may be the time to stop and take an exercise break. Whether you do isometrics or pushups, jog in place, or ride an exercise bike, the deep breathing and increased blood flow will decrease muscle tension and fatigue. Refreshed, you can return and restart. To focus and find more material, try asking yourself questions:

- What might readers like to know?
- How might readers feel about the topic?
- How do I feel about the topic? Why?
- What else needs to be said?

Or if you find that you are completely blocked, a break may be the only solution. Before you stop, schedule a specific time to resume writing.

FOCUSING AN EXPLORATORY DRAFT

Some writers do much of their prewriting and drafting mentally before they ever start to write. They have a distinct sense of purpose and audience and are often able to focus their exploratory draft surprisingly well. A clear central idea unifies the material so that it progresses in a logical way and fulfills the purpose. Other writers know their general topic but circle aimlessly around it, unsure of the central point they will make. Pausing to limit the topic and write a thesis statement, however, can establish a direction for writing.

Narrowing a Topic

When you narrow a topic, you focus on a segment that you can develop well. You write more about less. If you find yourself rambling or lost while exploring your topic, stop and consider the range you are covering. Is the topic too broad? Can it be covered adequately in the required number of words? To be manageable, a topic should be whittled down to fit the assignment and the rhetorical situation. The pyramid below shows how a very broad topic (top of the pyramid) can be narrowed.

Ohio

touring Ohio

touring the Ohio River

steamboats on the Ohio River

my steamboat ride on the Ohio River

NITA NARROWS HER TOPIC

Nita Jones wishes to research solar energy. Over the years she has read a few articles on the subject, but she wonders what has been discovered recently. She suspects that her general readers are also hazy about the topic. And they may not care one way or the other. She asks several of her classmates and verifies both inferences. How can she interest them in the topic? How might they benefit from reading about it? She writes down these questions and starts a list to narrow the topic.

Question: How might readers benefit by learning more about solar energy?

Narrowing: general-to-specific

solar energy

practical applications for solar energy

solar heating for homes

solar heating during construction of new homes

solar heating for existing homes

As Nita reviews her list, she realizes that every reader is a potential homeowner. At first she considers discussing applications for new home construction, but then she thinks about budget constraints. Few of her readers will be building their first home. Most will buy older homes and repair or remodel them. At this point, she briefly describes her audience and writes a purpose statement.

Audience: College students who are potential buyers of existing homes and who are interested in comfort at a reasonable cost.

Purpose: To inform the reader of solar heating applications for existing homes and to evaluate practicality.

Thesis statement: Solar heating installations can reduce fuel bills and improve the value of an older home.

Writing a Purpose Statement

Stating your purpose on paper is a quick, preliminary step to drafting. This way you pin down your main idea. A purpose statement provides the foundation for your thesis statement, which can be written later. First, jot down a brief description of your readers. This step will help to clarify your approach to the topic and the perspective you will take:

Audience for a letter to the editor: Readers of the local paper who have never ridden a steamboat on the Ohio River.

Audience for a paper on litter control: Voters who are concerned about the numerous cans and bottles littering city streets, roads, and highways.

Second, start writing the purpose statement. There are just two basic parts: general purpose and specific purpose.

Purpose: To *inform* readers about the *scenic beauty of the Ohio River banks and islands, the convenience of the steamboat trip, and the reasonable cost.*

Purpose: To *persuade* readers *to vote for a bill requiring deposits on and recycling of all beverage cans and glass bottles.*

See Chapter 1 for "Purpose."

Writing a Thesis Statement

A thesis statement is similar to a topic sentence. Just as a topic sentence states the main idea of a paragraph, so too *the thesis states the main idea of a paper.* Both the topic sentence and the thesis statement act as a contract—a promise the writer makes to the reader. When the writing is effective and complete, the promise is kept.

A thesis can be stated in just one sentence. In some writing, the thesis extends over several sentences. A thesis statement performs four specific tasks:

Four Tasks of a Thesis Statement

1. Identify the subject
2. State a claim, an approach, or an attitude
3. Suggest the direction of the writing
4. Set the tone

The following one-sentence thesis, from a paper by student Michele Flahive, contains three parts. Her thesis demonstrates the four tasks:

Thesis: For the dedicated player, the challenge, the enjoyment, and the camaraderie make softball a game worth playing.

Topic: Playing softball

Claim: For the dedicated player, softball is worth playing.

Direction: The focus is on three main points—*challenge, enjoyment,* and *camaraderie*—in that order.

Tone: Middle level of formality

The sooner you can write a tentative thesis statement, the fewer drafts you are likely to need.

Where Should the Thesis Statement Go? Usually, the thesis statement is placed in the introduction, often in the opening paragraph of short papers.

DRAFTING A THESIS STATEMENT

An easy way to draft a three-part thesis is to make a list and fill in the blanks:

Topic: _____

Main points: _____

_____

_____

Thesis statement: _____

_____

For Practice: Choose a topic that can be divided into three parts. For example, "Three reasons I chose _____ College/University." Write the topic in the first blank. Second, think of reasons and list them in the blanks for main points. Third, condense and combine the reasons to make a complete sentence. Even if this tentative thesis doesn't seem quite right, it can still act as a controlling idea and help you organize an exploratory draft. (For more on a three-part thesis, see chapter 14.)

Sometimes it appears at the beginning but more often at the end of the opening paragraph. There it can forge a tight link to later paragraphs. In research or other long papers, the introduction may contain two or more paragraphs. In that case, the thesis sentence generally appears at the end of the introduction.

Omitting a Thesis Statement   Some kinds of writing have a thesis that is never specified but is clearly implied. The omission is not a lapse; careful planning and considerable skill are required to keep the controlling idea apparent without stating it openly. Omission of a thesis sentence is hazardous for a budding writer, especially for the kinds of writing often done in college. Most instructors expect an explicit thesis.

Dozens of examples of thesis statements written by students can be found in parts 2, 3, 4, and 5. You can find these examples and explanations within the chapters as well as in the sample papers.

DRAFTING AN INTRODUCTION

An effective introduction affords a graceful entry into a topic. Whether you draft your introduction first or last, keep your audience in mind. The opening sentence should arouse interest and induce the reader to continue. The writer's voice sets a suitable tone for the writing, inviting the reader to consider the topic. Although a wide array of introductions appear throughout the book, here is a preview of five common types.

Begin with an Anecdote That Sets the Scene

An anecdote, or a brief narrative, can capture the reader's attention. You can begin by first setting the scene. To orient readers and forestall puzzlement, state *when* and *where* the experience happened. Sometimes just a few carefully chosen details will give a sense of time and place:

My Worst Job

When I was sixteen, my cousin suggested I take a job at a dress factory where she worked. Because she liked the people and the wages, I hired on. For a country girl who had never been inside a factory, the first day was overwhelming. Rows and rows of sewing machines whirred while hundreds of women worked at a furious pace. Finding me an empty chair, the trainer demonstrated how to operate the machine and sew a facing on the bodice of a cotton dress. Since I had made my own clothes for years, the task was simple. Outwardly, the power sewing machines somewhat resembled the old Singer at home. But the piece of technology in front of me was as much like my old machine as a Mercedes is like a Model T. Careening around the curves, I hung onto the cloth and somehow guided it under the presser foot. By lunch time, however, I had mastered the machine and the five-minute task that was my only responsibility. Day after day for an interminable week, I repeated that mind-numbing procedure.

***Overuse of the Pronoun* I.**   A successful narrative opening not only provides interest, but also aids in avoiding "I" as the first word in a paper or paragraph. *Using* I *as the first word focuses on the writer, not the needs of the reader.* Usually, there is a more interesting and effective way to open.

In effective business writing, letters should be worded diplomatically to consider the reader's needs. For example, a well-planned application letter for employment focuses unobtrusively on what the writer can do for the company. If, however, most sentences start with *I*, the interviewer may conclude that despite an applicant's skills and experience, a super-size ego is not what the company needs. The following rule will assist you in using first person with discretion.

See chapter 30.

DIETSCH'S "I" RULE
Think twice before using *I* to open a letter, paper, or paragraph. Try to devise a more effective way to begin.

To avoid the use of *I* at the beginning, look at the rest of the sentence. Do you see another word or phrase that can be moved up and placed before *I?* Even one word, such as *yesterday, although,* or *when,* will provide a smoother opening than a reference to yourself. To begin a narrative example, briefly tell when and where the action took place. Often just a phrase of three or so words will do. To help you start, here are some ideas.

Opening Words to Set the Scene

References to Time	**References to Place**
Ten years ago	From my window
When I was a small child	While working as assistant manager at
After I graduated	In the green hills of
In 1932 my grandfather	Near the Bay of Biscayne
Last month my life	On Kelly's Island

Begin with a Description

A few words of artful description at the beginning of a paper can explain, illustrate, or provide a bit of background. In the following introduction, Kenny Patrick sets the scene and informs his classmates about fly fishing, using vivid words to explain his fascination with the sport:

Hooked on a Tradition

Icy water swirls around the wading fly fisherman. With experience gained from thousands of casts, he deposits the tiny brown deer hair fly directly beneath an overhanging branch at the water's edge. His pulse quickens as he gently twitches the tip of the rod. Like a living being, the tiny fly dances across the surface. Suddenly, a bronze torpedo erupts from the depths and snatches the small offering. The fisherman feels the solid pull of a feisty small-mouth bass and sets the hook. With a powerful thrust of its tail, the large fish launches itself into the air. Shaking its head, the bass dislodges the hook. Hands trembling, the fisherman is left with just a memory. Moments like this make fly fishing a frustrating, yet fascinating and educational sport.

Begin by Stating a Problem

Stating a problem can be a practical way to open. The purpose of Janet Edington's paper was to inform pet owners of ways to enhance the safety of animals when transporting them to the vet.

Safety First!

Pet owners are frequently faced with the challenge of transporting their animal friends to the veterinarian. This task can be not only nerve-wracking but also hazardous, particularly if they are transporting a nervous cat or a large animal. In an automobile, an even-tempered pet can swiftly turn into a frightened, hostile enemy. The following suggestions are offered to spare anyone the battle scars I carry today.

Begin with a Surprising Statistic or Striking Bit of History

You may be able to spur a reader's curiosity with a surprising statistic or striking bit of history. The purpose of Kathy Cordle's paper was to inform classmates of a way to kick the tobacco habit that worked for her.

Kicking the Habit

Concern about the hazards of tobacco is not new. In 1604 King James I of England officially condemned the use of tobacco. An 1859 report about the dangers of tobacco stated that of the sixty-eight persons suffering from cancer of the mouth and throat in a hospital in Montpelier, France, all were tobacco users. In the United States during the early 1900s, admonitions such as "Don't smoke, or it will stunt your growth" and "Now that you are expecting, you'll have to lay off smoking" were common.

Begin by Disputing a Common Belief or Defying a Stereotype

The writer who surprises readers with a statement that disputes a common belief or an example that defies a stereotype will grab their attention. In the next paragraph, Paul Giacalone's purpose was to entertain his classmates. He begins by expressing a view that runs counter to the commonly held belief that everyone should love the family dog. His offbeat perspective and critically amused tone surprise readers and hook their curiosity.

The Trials of Tia

Recently my father brought home a very small and very ignorant animal. My parents named it Tia, and they have tried to convince me that it is a dog—I swear it is a rat. Actually, Tia is half rat terrier and half poodle—a strange-looking animal that has not been easy to train. Therein lies the nub of the problem.

SEVEN BASIC WAYS TO ORGANIZE A DRAFT

To be clear and readable, every completed manuscript should have a logical order. As you sort through your prewriting notes and write your first draft, watch for a dominant order to emerge. Look closely at the transitions you have included. Do they refer to time? To location? To cause and effect? Are some points more important than others? Or does your thesis statement contain a clue to a suitable order? The sooner you can find an order appropriate for the rhetorical situation, the fewer drafts you will need. Seven basic orders are commonly used, and combined, to organize writing.

THE SEVEN BASIC ORDERS

1. **Chronology** (time): chronological/reverse chronological
2. **Spatial order** (space): organized by layout, design, direction, or location
3. **Order of importance:** least to most/most to least
4. **Order of generality:** general to specific/specific to general
5. **Order of formation:** whole to parts/parts to whole
6. **Order of complexity:** simple to complex/familiar to unfamiliar
7. **Order of materiality:** concrete to abstract/abstract to concrete

---

Chronology

When dates or events are placed in a natural sequence according to *time*, this arrangement is known as *chronological order*. In process analysis you arrange the steps or stages chronologically. In a research paper, you may combine chronological order with other orders. Narratives usually move forward in chronological order, but not always. A sidewise shift in time may be indicated by transitions such as "meanwhile" or "at the same time."

Résumés are usually organized in *reverse chronological order*. This arrangement presents the most recent experience first, then goes backward, ending with the earliest.

Spatial Order

Unlike chronological order, which moves along a time line, *spatial* order locates details according to layout, design, direction, or place. In "Through a Child's Eyes," the writer describes her father, beginning with his head and moving down to his lap (see page 82). Any of the following spatial orders (or their reverse) might be used in description:

head to toe	outside to inside	clockwise
bottom to top	north to south	circular
left to right	up and down	horizontal

Order of Importance

See "Buckeye Fever" p. 180.

Newspaper articles typically use *most- to least-important* order, beginning with the most important information and leaving the least important details until last. Editors know that readers often read only the first few paragraphs of an article or only the front page section. For other writing, *least- to most-important* order is often used. This order places the emphasis on the final point. You might use least- to most-important order in essays of division, classification, illustration, or argument.

Order of Generality

The order of generality can be used to inform or to convince. An observation, generalization, or basic principle is presented either at the beginning or at the end of the piece of writing. Using the *general-to-specific* order, you begin with the claim, then supply enough specific details to support it. For example, a student wrote, "The magic of a carousel has a way of turning men and women into children again." Then she presented specific details to support her observation. This order can be reversed to *specific to general* with the claim at the end of the writing.

Order of Formation

The order of formation is convenient to describe and explain a complicated topic or to formulate a balanced argument. This comprehensive order can supply a sense of completeness, conviction, and objectivity. Writers often use the *whole-to-parts* order in problem solving or in an argument. They begin with a summary of a problem or an issue, then move on to look at the individual factors or aspects. This way they present an overview before covering all significant alternatives, angles, or parts.

The whole-to-parts order can also be used to explain less complicated topics. For example, a student described an old rocking chair, starting with the overall appearance of the rocker and then going to its parts. He created an image of the old chair before explaining how it functioned in the life of his family. In some writing situations, this order can be reversed to move from *the parts to the whole*.

See page 4.

Order of Complexity

Often an effective way to explain an unusual topic is according to its complexity. Going from *the simple to the complex* or *familiar to unfamiliar* will help to clarify the topic. By starting with what readers already know and accept, you can orient them and establish rapport. Then they will be more comfortable and willing to explore the complex or the unfamiliar. If you were to begin with a difficult concept or highly technical material, some readers might refuse to read further.

Order of Materiality

Using an order of materiality, a writer may arrange details by going from *the concrete to the abstract* or from *the abstract to the concrete*. Concrete words refer to actual physical data about a condition, event, experience, object, animal, or person. Through our five senses, we can perceive evidence of these elements. Most of us are able to see, hear, touch, taste, and smell to obtain firsthand proof that concrete items exist. For example, tears are concrete—we can see them, feel them, even taste them. Sometimes tears indicate sadness, but sadness is an abstraction.

Abstract refers to ideas that have no physical referent; nothing material can prove they exist. We can think and talk about abstractions, but we *cannot* see, hear, taste, touch, or smell them. For example, patriotism, love, and integrity are all abstractions. The only way that we can infer that they exist is to look for

See
page 209.
concrete evidence that *implies* their existence. Jeannine Caudill uses this order in "Mother Love."

Writers of description often move from *the concrete to the abstract*, presenting physical details about a subject first. For example, a writer might briefly describe our national flag before describing its symbolic significance. An essay of definition might use the reverse order, *abstract to concrete*, introducing an abstract concept—such as friendship or bravery—then providing concrete instances and examples.

WRITING AN EFFECTIVE CONCLUSION

Often a first draft does not have a conclusion. The writer may need more time to ponder the meaning of ideas. A few writers, if they have thought long and hard about a topic, may start by writing the conclusion first. The rest of us may have to tug and pull it into shape until it works. An effective conclusion indicates that you have finished what you have to say; it does not rehash opinions or recite the obvious. No new material intrudes. An effective ending flows logically and smoothly from the body, giving a sense of completeness or *closure*. Five basic ways to conclude are described here.

End with a Reference to a Benefit

Sales letters cite the benefits of a product of a plan. A college paper may conclude by referring to a value, advantage, or benefit. Diane Zachman points out the benefits of a good manicure:

> The process of manicuring, when done correctly, gives your nails a vibrant, healthy appearance and keeps them from becoming weak and brittle.

End by Referring Back to the Thesis

To provide a satisfying ending, writers often refer briefly to the thesis. Notice that this device is an allusion, *not* a repetition of the entire thesis. By reworking an old cliché and repeating key points, Nora Lee Corbett is able to establish closure:

Thesis: We raise Leghorn laying hens for their hardiness, longevity, and egg production.

Conclusion: On our farm the chicken comes before the egg. And we have learned over the years that the best chicken according to hardiness, longevity, and egg production is the Leghorn.

End with a Personal Response

Writers sometimes confide their feelings to the reader. Especially at the end of a paper, they may express a sense of sadness, embarrassment, satisfaction, ela-tion, or some other emotion in response to a situation. For example, the student who described her "worst job" concluded with the following:

> On Friday I was still doing the same mind-numbing procedure. By then my hands guided the cloth under the pressure foot with ease, but I knew I could not continue unless I underwent a lobotomy. So at quitting time I picked up my pay-check, inhaled the fresh air of freedom, and left with a light heart, knowing I would never go back.

End on a Note of Optimism

A note of optimism can create a satisfying conclusion. It might be a note of encouragement to yourself or to the reader, or it might be a look toward the future. Sue Taylor concluded "Breaking the Habit" with a congratulatory note to herself:

> Since November 7, I have not had one cigarette. Yes, there are times when I still want one, and I am struggling to drop those extra pounds, accumulated from eating all that candy, but I feel really good about myself. I am a winner!

End with an Unexpected Twist

A conclusion that creeps up on readers, catching them off guard, can surprise and delight. When well done, such an ending seems spontaneous and appropriate. A brief comment or fact can pose an absurdity or profundity that causes the reader to smile or think. Paul Giacalone ended with a twist in his paper about his parents' dog Tia:

> I feel the only solution to this problem is either I go or the dog does. After I discussed this with my parents, they went out and bought me a set of luggage for Christmas.

Although a twist may be appropriate for personal writing, it is rarely appropriate for business writing. Customers, employees, and managers need to know what to expect and need to understand the writer's purpose.

DRAFTING ON A COMPUTER

Almost every semester an agitated student knocks on my office door with a request for more time and a tale of the perils of using a computer. Most stories have a common theme: the failure to provide a backup file. Yet simple precautions can prevent the shock of lost text and erased or defective diskettes or other disasters. Even if you are an experienced user, read on. Overconfidence and fatigue can contribute to this predicament.

TIPS FOR MAINTAINING SECURITY OF COMPUTER FILES

1. *Save files frequently.* Keep in mind that a computer crash or power failure can cause you to lose all material that has not been saved.

2. *Make a backup copy.* Periodically save files to a second storage medium, such as a diskette, CD, or tape or to a server or second computer. Even if you are working at home, saving on your hard drive is not enough. Your work can be lost because of hardware, software, or user errors.

3. *Print out a copy of your draft early.* To safeguard your exploratory draft, print it out at the end of the first session. Do not wait for a completed draft. That way, if you should lose or damage your disk, you still have a copy.

4. *Be extremely careful with copying, cutting, and moving material.* Paste in moved material *immediately*. Otherwise, you run the risk of forgetting about it, copying something else, and losing the first batch. *Double-check* to see that you have taken only what you intended.

5. *Take special precautions in a computer lab.* Lab personnel regularly erase hard drives to keep them from filling up. Then, too, if you save on a hard drive, another student might gain access to your writing, which could prove embarrassing or lead to theft.

A NOTE OF REASSURANCE AND A BRIEF REVIEW

Drafting should bring a sense of adventure and exploration. Drafting is just the second stage in the writing process, not the last. You don't have to get everything right the first time; you will have chances to go back and revise. So focus on your central idea, follow the suggestions given here, and your work should proceed fairly quickly.

Summary

Drafting, the second stage of the writing process, is the time to explore ideas uncovered during prewriting. Write as quickly as you can without interruption and without thought for rules or restrictions. Revision and editing can come later.

A brief description of your audience and a purpose statement will help you focus on the main idea, paving the way for a thesis. A thesis statement identifies

GUIDELINES: TIPS FOR DRAFTING SUCCESSFULLY

1. *Schedule a block of time for writing an exploratory draft.* Start early so that you will have plenty of time to revise, edit, and proofread.

2. *Study your prewriting notes to determine whether or not the topic is adequate for the assignment.*
   a.   Is the topic significant?
   b.   Has it been narrowed adequately?
   c.   Will it interest the audience?
   d.   Are there enough facts, examples, and details for support?
   e.   How can the topic be presented in an interesting way?

3. *Think about how you want your written voice to sound.* Do you want to sound playful? Serious? Amused? Outraged? Or how? Your attitude toward a topic (and perhaps the assignment) will be reflected in your written voice. (See Chapter 2.)

4. *Begin composing anywhere in the exploratory draft.* Write in a way that is comfortable for you.

5. *Double-space and leave wide margins.* Allow room to mark changes and comments on the draft.

6. *After finishing the first draft, leave it for a day, if possible.* If not, leave it for at least an hour while you have lunch or work on another assignment. You need time to distance yourself intellectually and emotionally before revising.

7. *Save all drafts until you receive the graded paper back.* A paper may go astray. Saving drafts helps avoid losing all your work.

the subject; states a claim, an approach, or an attitude; suggests the direction; and sets the tone.

As you find related ideas, you can begin to group them in some logical way, such as chronological order, spatial order, and order of importance. You can also organize ideas from general to specific, whole to parts, simple to complex, easy to difficult, familiar to unfamiliar, and concrete to abstract, or in other logical ways.

To draft an introduction, you might begin with a narrative, a description, a statement of a problem, an interesting fact, a striking statistic, or a bit of history. You could end by stating a benefit, summarizing your ideas, providing a twist, or using another device.

To ensure against lost text when writing on a computer, save files regularly, make a backup copy, and print copies of drafts.

Key Terms

chronology	order of complexity	order of materiality
closure	order of formation	purpose statement
exploratory draft	order of generality	spatial order
narrowing a topic	order of importance	thesis statement

Ten Ideas for Ten-Minute Writings

1. I wish . . .
2. The magic of a music box
3. My favorite fragrance is the smell of . . .
4. If I had my way, . . .
5. My job
6. My earliest memory
7. If I could buy a ticket to anywhere, I would . . .
8. My grandfather's _____ was a tool to him, but for me it is a symbol of his . . .
9. Snails (or what else?) are wonderful creatures because . . .
10. If I had more free time, I would . . .

Revision Workshop: Later Stages of the Writing Process

Part 2

CHAPTER 5

Revising, Editing, and Proofreading: An Overview

A piece of writing is never finished. It is delivered to a deadline, torn out of the typewriter on demand, sent off with a sense of accomplishment and shame and pride and frustration. If only there were a couple more days, time for just another run at it, perhaps then . . .

—Donald Murray
"The Maker's Eye:
Revising Your Own Manuscript"

Professional writers rewrite constantly, perhaps reworking one draft dozens of times. How much a writer revises and edits depends on the rhetorical situation and the deadline. Although most instructors do not expect Donald Murray's level of dedication, they do expect several revisions of papers. Yet too many students skip or skimp on revision, editing, and proofreading—turning in rough drafts. A good way to start revision is to assume the role of an editor.

HOW DO YOU BECOME YOUR OWN EDITOR?

Someone once said that a writer must eventually become his or her own editor. This is even more true today. On the job workers are unlikely to have someone to mark errors and make suggestions—they often work alone at a computer. To start becoming your own editor, evaluate the effectiveness not only of grammar and word choice but also of structure, logic, and development. As you revise, edit, and proofread, ask yourself these two critical questions:

- Is the expression of ideas appropriate for the occasion and the audience?
- Have I fulfilled the purpose?

Revision is concerned with the larger aspects of the draft: the organization and presentation of ideas. The smaller items within the sentence—word choice, grammar, spelling, and punctuation—are treated in the final stages of editing and proofreading. That does not mean you can't jump back and forth between the two stages—work any way you wish. But many writers find it easier and more effective to look at one aspect at a time.

REVISION: STAGE THREE
OF THE WRITING PROCESS

The goal of revision is to rethink and reshape your writing so that it effectively reaches your audience and accomplishes your purpose.

FIVE MAJOR STEPS OF REVISION

Perhaps you revise in a hit-or-miss fashion that, more or less, works for you. But in this chapter you may find a more efficient way to achieve your purpose. The tools, tips, and options should help you save time and increase the quality of your writing. The secret of revision is this: just keep repeating the process as often as needed.

Step 1: Acknowledge the Need for Revision

This first step sounds simple, but some student writers seem to think they have hit the jackpot on their first draft. They refuse to acknowledge the reality that every exploratory draft will need revision. Others think they can merely change a word here and there. But revision is not that quick or easy. No matter how pleased you are with early drafts, keep looking for ways to improve them. After your euphoria wears off, you will find many imperfections.

Step 2: Look at the Big Picture

Print out your draft and read it quickly to ascertain the direction or path of the controlling idea. You cannot do this on-screen, one frame at a time. Ask yourself questions: Is there just one main idea? Does it keep advancing steadily toward the final point? Do you have a final point? Place a check mark wherever the main idea goes astray. If you are unsure about the ending, write "What is my point?" Then select whichever tool you prefer to start work on the draft.

Step 3: Reread and Mark the Draft

Reread your printed draft silently and carefully. Mark it as you go but hold off on any drastic action. Just place parentheses around surplus or doubtful material.

TOOLS FOR REVISION

- **Outline to corral details.** To check the order of dates, events, steps, or paragraphs, an outline is an excellent tool. It may also uncover a potpourri of items to sort out. To focus a research paper, an outline is essential.
- **Sketch or diagram the direction of a draft.** You may prefer sketching to making an outline. Just jot down notes, arrows, and pictures to track the path of the main idea. Or you might draw a chain of cause and effect or a time line to chart the chronology of events. Do whatever works for you.

See chapters 17 & 27.

- **Question.** As you reread a draft, jot brief questions or question marks or ideas in the margins. If you are blocked, bounce ideas off someone face-to-face or by e-mail or telephone. Describing a concern or asking a question will often trigger an answer in your own mind.

In the margins, pencil notes, questions, and possible restatements. Or list ideas on another sheet. If your draft has just one or two paragraphs, use brackets to divide logical units of thought into paragraphs. Recheck and number any changes in their order. Next, start revising on screen.

See "Critical Reading," p. 416, chapter 26.

Step 4: Revise and Refine

Before you start to revise, *rename and copy your draft*—just in case you should change your mind and want to retrieve items you have deleted. Then revise from your marked copy, adding any further ideas on-screen. Keep your eye on clarity. Any passage that seems unclear becomes a candidate for revision. Be prepared to expand, define, cut, splice, summarize, or condense. If you need more information, review your prewriting notes, outline, or diagram or do on-line research. To evaluate writing, ask questions such as these:

- What else needs to be said?
- What else might the audience like to know?
- Do any parts need to be trimmed?
- Are any details insignificant or irrelevant?

Step 5: Let the Draft Cool, Then Check the Focus

After the first revision, let your draft cool for half a day or more, if possible. Your thoughts need to settle, so new ideas can sprout. At least take a break and

TIPS FOR REVISING WITH A COMPUTER

Risky shortcuts while using a computer can devour time and elevate blood pressure. The following advice is based on hard-won wisdom.

1. *Save drafts periodically.* If your word-processing program has an automatic save feature, you may want to set it for every ten minutes or so. Otherwise, you risk loss of text when a power failure occurs or your computer crashes.

2. *Save old drafts.* Save early drafts under different file names, such as *Research 1, Research 2*, and so forth. Place the drafts in *one* file folder to avoid confusion. If you lose your latest draft, then you can go back to the previous one.

3. *Move text without losing it.* Copying text and moving it carries risks. If you copy a section and stop to work elsewhere on screen or answer the telephone, instead of pasting in the copied text, you may forget. Then when you copy again or shut down, the passage is lost. To be safe, do not cut the copied portion until you have inserted it into the new spot.

4. *Take special precautions.* When moving any text, double-check to be sure you have inserted every line back into the manuscript. When moving entries in the works cited list of a research paper, be especially careful.

5. *Submit your latest draft.* It sounds so simple—but one student submitted a six-page formal report with misplaced graphics and omissions. After receiving a C−, he realized he had not submitted the final draft, which had ten pages.

See pages 5 and 6.

do something that requires you to move around. But be sure to set a time to return. Then without looking at your paper, jot down your specific purpose and audience. Has it changed? Continue to ask questions to assess your draft:

- Is there one clear central idea throughout the paper?
- Are paragraphs arranged in a logical order?
- Does each paragraph relate back to the thesis statement?
- Are paragraphs well developed and interesting?
- Does the conclusion flow logically from the body?

The suggestions that follow are based on common problems encountered by student writers. If they don't apply to you, skip on to the next section.

REFOCUSING A DRAFT

As you revise, you may decide to narrow your topic and refocus it. You might try the pyramid method, shown on page 33, or you might focus the title, revise your outline, or look for a fresh perspective.

Focusing the Title

A focused title not only sharpens the topic but also suggests the approach the writer will take. A good title specificies and limits the topic whereas an unfocused title gives only a vague idea of what is to come. Let's consider some examples of titles for research papers:

Unfocused	Focused
The Internet and Education	Using the Internet in the Classroom
Nutrition of the Elderly	Nutrition for the Elderly Who Live Alone

The unfocused titles are so broad that the topics could not be covered adequately in a paper. But the focused titles offer a feasible scope. Achieving an appropriate, focused title can be an integral part of revision.

Outlining

Rather than committing mayhem on a draft, you can save time and effort by testing changes on an outline. Using your scratch outline, refine it into a working outline on screen. Then save and adapt as needed. Print out a copy to keep track of your changes. Some instructors may require a formal outline, particularly with a research paper. You can transform a working outline into a formal outline by following the model on page 54.

If your draft is just not going the way you intend, you might look for a different point of view, a fresh perspective on the topic.

Finding a Fresh Perspective   In one episode of P. M. Brady's comic strip "Rose Is Rose," Pasquale, a preschool child, grew tired of his toys and pleaded for a new one. His father listened, then showed him to the door, hinting there was a big toy outside. Wading through newly fallen snow, Pasquale looked around and asked where the toy was. His father replied that Pasquale was standing in it.

We are all standing knee-deep in ideas for invigorating our writing. And like Pasquale, we often overlook them. Creativity involves taking everyday experience and transforming it. As writers we can benefit by stepping back to get an offbeat view of our lives. Sometimes an ordinary topic can be enlivened by looking at it from an angle the reader does not expect. John Yeoman decided to give an imaginative spin to an experience by writing from the perspective of his two-year-old self in "Babysitting for Grandfather" (see page 55).

FORMAL OUTLINES

Formal outlines may be written in fragments or sentences. How detailed an outline is depends on the writer and the assignment, but here's a word of warning: Shy away from elaborate outlines. You can invest so much time and energy that you may be reluctant to revise. (For examples of outlines, turn to Chapters 15, 17, and 25.) Both topic outlines and sentence outlines use the following format with numerals and letters to distinguish parts and subparts:

I.
  A.
    1.
      a.
      b.
    2.
      a.
      b.
      c.
  B.
    1.
      a.
      b.
    2.
      a.
      b.

II. (Repeat as needed)

III. (Repeat as needed)

POINTERS FOR MAKING OUTLINES

- Begin with a large roman numeral. Follow with a capital letter, then an arabic number.
- For subtopics, use small letters.
- Use periods after each of the above.
- If you have an A, then you need a B. If you have a 1, then you need a 2. Otherwise, the section does not need a letter or number.

Babysitting for Grandfather

Everyone except me was getting ready to go somewhere. Being the youngest of the family and a member in good standing of the club known as "the terrible twos," I was used to receiving a lot of attention. But that night my four-year-old sister, dressed in a lacy white dress and black patent leather slippers, was the center of attention. In her hands, she carried a beautiful bouquet of fresh flowers for her role in a wedding.

Of course, so unusual a perspective as John's will not be appropriate for every writing occasion. When a draft seems dull or lifeless, trying out different perspectives can lead to ideas you might not find otherwise.

CLARIFYING THE DRAFT

After you are satisfied with the focus of the draft and the external order of paragraphs, it is a good idea to check the sound. Read the draft aloud and listen as a reader might. Be critical. How might some readers regard your point of view? How might they perceive your intent? Would they grasp the main point, or might they be distracted or offended by some remark? The following checklist will help you assess your written voice.

See chapters 2 and 9

CHECKLIST: LISTENING TO YOUR WRITTEN VOICE

1. Is your written voice appropriate for the occasion, purpose, and audience?
2. Does your written voice sound knowledgeable?
3. Might the reader take offense at any of the words?
4. Will a synonym improve the sound without changing the meaning?

Revising Sluggish Openings

Have you taken a second look at your thesis statement? Does it require a little tinkering? Does your first sentence capture the attention of your audience? Or do readers have to stumble through unnecessary words, vague generalities, or other nuisances? One common cause of sluggishness is the overuse of the empty expressions *there is*, *there are*, or *it is*. Uproot these toadstools and rephrase the sentence.

To review types of openings, turn to page 36 in chapter 4. Or you might leaf through Part 3 and look at student papers at the ends of chapters. You will see a variety of techniques for effective openings.

Revising the Body

As you check the *internal* order of each paragraph, consider that it should be a logical unit with one central idea. Usually, one sentence—the topic sentence—announces the subject of the paragraph and makes a claim. Supporting sentences provide evidence for the claim. They undergird the topic sentence with explanations, examples, anecdotes, reasons, and facts. If you should find more than one subject to a paragraph, you can either split it into two paragraphs or discard the less important idea. Trim off the fat.

See chapter 7.

Skinny paragraphs may need to be fleshed out with more details. Or you may spot gaps in thought. A transitional phrase, sentence, or even paragraph may be needed to bridge ideas. (To find what you need, turn to the index in the back of this book and look up *transition*.)

CHECKLIST: REVISING PARAGRAPHS

1. Is each paragraph organized around *one* central idea?
2. Does each supporting sentence closely relate to the topic sentence?
3. Is each sentence placed in a logical sequence?
4. Is transition needed to connect any sentences?
5. Does any paragraph need more explanation, examples, or details?

Revising the Conclusion

An effective conclusion gives a sense of completeness. You have made your point and left the audience with something to think about. The ending should flow logically and smoothly from the body and be consistent with the opening. An effective ending does not linger to rehash opinions or recite the obvious. No new material intrudes. To see examples of conclusions, turn to page 42 or to student papers in Part 3.

CASE STUDY

A *SERIES* OF STUDENT OUTLINES AND DRAFTS

Roger Moore's final draft, "People Who Flock to Swap Meets," was revised eight times. The four examples show key points of his progress. From a prewriting list, Roger wrote a first draft, revised it, and decided it was still vague. To focus, he listed his audience and purpose, then transformed the list into a scratch outline. He also renamed the categories of customers and rearranged their order.

SCRATCH OUTLINE
(LEAST- TO MOST-IMPORTANT ORDER)

Audience: classmates

Purpose: to inform the class about why I enjoy attending swap meets

Title: Kinds of People Who Attend Swap Meets

1. **Sightseers:** arrive in late afternoon and up till closing time. They just look around and complain. Want us to unload but they still do not buy. (It takes all kinds.)
2. **Early Birds:** Are there at 4 a.m. Want to buy cheap parts for re-sale. Buy very little. Just drink coffee, get in the way, and razz us.
3. **Buyers:** Come promptly at 8:00 a.m. to find parts they need to fix up old cars at their homes. Tell us stories. Visit. Fun to be with.

From his scratch outline, Roger wrote drafts three and four. Then he tried chronological order, revising his scratch outline into a working outline. To focus the internal order of each paragraph, he used "arrival, purpose, and behavior" to set up the details.

Working Outline (Chronological order)

1. **Early Birds**
   Arrival: 4 a.m.
   Purpose: Buy cheap for resale
   Behavior: Buy little; give us a hard time.

2. **Buyers**
   Arrival: 8:00 a.m.
   Purpose: Find parts they need themselves
   Behavior: Pleasant, polite

3. **Sightseers**
   Arrival: Late afternoon till closing time
   Purpose: Look around
   Behavior: Complaining

FIFTH DRAFT

Swap Meets

Jack, my son, and I have decided there are three types of people who attend swap meets—the early birds, the buyers, and the sightseers. Swap meets are like flea markets, except these swap meets are for car parts only. Set-up times usually start at 4 a.m. This is the time when the early birds

continued

try to buy our car parts. They hope to run across a good deal. They don't buy much.

The buyers don't arrive until 8 o'clock or thereafter. They usually look for hard-to-find parts to fix up an old vehicle they are working on. They take their time and hunt carefully through the boxes and piles of parts. They are serious buyers and do not give us a hard time. Some are almost like old friends—we see them regularly.

Sightseers generally come late in the afternoon, often at closing time. They are always complaining about something. Years ago we used to unload parts so they could see them, but then we noticed they would not buy anything anyway.

Swap meets are enjoyable because Jack and I get together, make a little money, and meet some fine people.

Roger's fifth draft was fairly well developed. Like most early drafts, it needed revision, particularly in the introduction and conclusion. Three more revisions yielded his final draft.

FINAL DRAFT

People Who Flock to Swap Meets

In the summertime my son and I load my panel truck with auto parts every Saturday and head for a swap meet. Swap meets are like flea markets, except these swap meets are for car parts only. At swap meets Jack and I not only make a little money and enjoy the time together but also meet some interesting people. We have found that three types of folks usually attend: the early birds, the buyers, and the sightseers.

The early birds start flocking around the truck as we begin unloading and setting up at 4 a.m., before daybreak. They are usually dealers who are out for a fast buck. They crowd around, getting in the way, hoping to strike a good deal. A few may offer to help unload, but most stand around, drinking coffee and giving us a hard time. Often they make sarcastic remarks in a joking way. They don't buy much.

The buyers don't arrive until 8 o'clock or so. They generally look for difficult-to-find parts to repair an old vehicle they are working on in their spare time. Often they are restoring a classic car in their garage, and they like to tell us about it. We've heard some surprising stories about how much money they made from restoring a junked car. Some of them return regularly; they are almost like old friends. Sometimes they bring their families. They take their time, hunting carefully through boxes and piles of parts. They are serious buyers who ask how much a part costs. If they don't want it, they go on to the next display. Otherwise, they buy.

Sightseers usually come late in the afternoon, often near closing time. It seems they can always find something to complain about. Seldom do they

continued

find what they want, and they often become irritated when we are too busy loading the truck to help them. Some even ask us to unload so that they can look over the rest of the parts! Years ago we tried unloading the parts for them to see, but we noticed they would not buy anything anyway. They just wanted to sightsee.

Despite the little irritations, swap meets are still a good place to spend a leisurely Saturday, visiting with my son and meeting interesting people.

EDITING AND PROOFREADING: STAGE FOUR OF THE WRITING PROCESS

During editing and proofreading, you attend to matters within the sentence. Although editing is a general term meaning to "ready for publication or presentation by amending errors or revising," it is often applied specifically to stage four of the writing process. Proofreading means "discovering small errors and making corrections." Thus the terms overlap somewhat. By delaying editing and proofreading until stage four, writers are free to think about the larger matters of a paragraph. The goal in stage four is to clarify meaning and eliminate grammatical distractions within each sentence so that the writing purpose can be achieved.

MAJOR TASKS IN EDITING AND PROOFREADING

An essential part of editing is looking closely at the meaning of each sentence as well as its structure. Proofreading requires a scrutiny of grammar and punctuation and typing/keyboarding errors. For more intense concentration, many writers separate editing and proofreading. Others combine the two tasks. Regardless, there is one guideline that is certain to be fruitful: Go through your revised printed draft three or more times. Editing and proofreading just once will not catch all the errors.

Marking the Revised Draft

After you have added all your revisions on-screen, save them, then run a spelling check. Next print out a clean, double-spaced copy to edit. Off-screen, you will be apt to notice more problems than on-screen. On the first round of editing, do not disrupt your concentration by consulting a thesaurus, dictionary, or handbook—that can come later. Just mark the spot and go on. Your first task is to find and mark concerns that interfere with clarity, completeness, and accuracy.

Procedure for Effective Editing and Proofreading

1. **Read every word.** After your second silent reading, read aloud to spot omissions, errors, and undue repetition. Listen carefully to the sound of the words. Are they pleasing, accurate, and appropriate?

2. **Mark the draft.** Use brackets to set off wordiness. If you notice an error in spelling or grammar, circle it. Place a check mark by any word or sentence you want to return to. Or devise your own system of marking.

3. **Revise sentences and improve wording.** Write changes on your hard copy. In the margins, list possible synonyms for dubious words. To select the best words, look up the meanings.

4. **Add changes on-screen.** After you finish marking your hard copy, make each change on-screen.

5. **Print out a copy.** If your printed draft is quite messy, make a clean copy. Repeat the editing process as needed.

Making Sentences Clear and Concise

Reading sentences aloud will also help you to evaluate word choice and the placement of ideas. To gain significance, important words should be placed in positions of emphasis—at the beginning or end of a sentence. To edit, underline the important words in your draft, then rearrange the sentence. Simply inverting the sentence and adding a comma will often improve the emphasis, as in this opening of a résumé cover letter:

Draft: I have developed a keen eye for detail, line, and color as an artist.

Revised: As an artist, I have developed a keen eye for detail, line, and color.

If ideas are vague and lightweight, rethink them and restate in more specific words. You might ask yourself, "What do I really intend?" Shorten long rambling sentences by omitting unnecessary phrases, such as *sort of, color of, kind of, number of, in view of* and *type of*. Watch, too, for passive voice of verbs, which adds extra words and numbs ideas. Can you rewrite the sentence so that the subject is doing the action? Another way to clear out wordiness to to combine short related sentences:

Draft: Do you have short, choppy sentences? Are they related? Can they be combined into one sentence?

See
chapter 8.
Revised: If you find too many short, choppy sentences, try combining related ideas into one sentence.

Finding Fresh Language

Specific words, fresh language, and comparison enliven humdrum sentences. By choosing precise nouns and perhaps an adjective, you can create visual images: instead of *flowers*, say *yellow pansies* or *pink iris*. Add power to verbs by refining

PRUNING EXTRA WORDS

Keep sentences clear and vigorous by pruning unnecessary words. Consider these redundancies and their edited counterparts:

Redundant	Edited
absolutely essential	essential
actual truth of the matter	truth
advance warning	warning
cancel out	cancel
connected together	connected
foreign imports	imports
free gifts	gifts
past history	history

them. Instead of *went,* say *hurried* or *drove* through a red light, or *fell* through the ice. Don't try to sneak slang or a pet colloquialism such as *mess up* or *stuff* past the reader by wrapping it in a set of quotation marks. Find a better way to say what you mean.

Create a Simile or Metaphor   Business and technical writing, as well as literature, employs similes and metaphors. These unusual comparisons use familiar images to lead readers to see or understand less familiar images. A *simile* is an explicit (or stated) comparison of two unlike items or ideas, using *like* or *as.* Let's take a look at these student similes:

- "My tires, *smooth as the soles of worn-out tennis shoes,* have tiny cracks in the sidewalls." (Kim Coffey)
- "Spade, whose pedigree was a mystery, had a tail eighteen inches long that *he could use like a whip.*" (John Spillman)

A *metaphor* is a figure of speech that contains an implicit (or suggested) contrast, such as "His last car *was a lemon.*" Notice that such metaphors contain *is* or *was;* they have no other signal words to announce them. Another type of metaphor is just one word, as in some names: Rocky, Angela, Heather, Ruby, and Forest. Verbs, too, can contain metaphors: the motor *purred;* employees *support* their manager's decisions.

Experiment with Alliteration and Rhyme   *Alliteration* is the repetition of the initial (first) consonant sound. In a speech titled "Run-of-the-Mill Miracle," Gary Fenton used *alliteration* in the title (two m's). Later he commented on his

EDITING AND PROOFREADING ON-SCREEN

On-screen editing and proofreading carry the risk of overlooking errors you would normally notice on a printed page. Even after you think your text is error-free, print out a copy and proofread it carefully several times.

1. *As you add each correction on-screen, check it off on the hard copy.* This habit will increase your accuracy.

2. *After you make changes on-screen, read the sentence aloud.* A writer may omit little words or leave extra ones when moving text and revising.

3. *Run a final spelling check right before printing out your last draft.* Last-minute changes can cause errors. If you are not the world's best typist, typos could be lurking in your text.

daughter's birth: "No doubt about it. Having a baby is not easy. If it were, we would refer to it as leisure, not labor (two l's)."

Note too that *leisure* and *labor* also rhyme, as does "No doubt about it." Alliteration and rhyme can be pleasing and emphatic as long as they are not overdone. Alliteration is easy to use; anyone can use it in titles or phrases.

Experiment with Old Sayings   You may be able to revitalize an old saying or cliché by putting a different spin on it. For example, Robin Allen reworked "I never laid a hand on him" to "Sidney was a quiet cat and basically gentle. Even when I gave him a bath, which he hated, *he never laid a paw on me.*" In the paper about "babysitting" for his grandfather, John Yeoman surprises the reader with a revitalized cliché:

What about me? Why couldn't I go? This is when the plot thickened. Someone had to stay home and watch grandfather, or "Popo" as I called him. It was the classic, though crude, method of reverse psychology. Having a limited amount of reasoning ability at age two, I fell hook, line, and baby bottle.

PROOFREADING EFFECTIVELY

No significant piece of writing—whether a college paper, a report to a boss, or a business letter—can be considered complete until it has been carefully proofread at least twice for errors. Three times is better. Lapses in grammatical usage, punctuation, and spelling undercut your credibility as a writer and call into question your commitment to your work. In college these errors may result in lowering your grade; at work they may damage your career prospects. We recommend that you

- ***Correct your graded papers soon after their return.*** Look up words and errors. (Your instructor may use marks and symbols keyed to the chart in the inside back cover of this book. These pages will guide you to the appropriate page in the handbook.) Correct every error. Look up misspelled words and write each one ten times to rivet the correct spelling in your mind.

- ***Keep a list of errors pointed out in your graded papers.*** Make a list of common errors you need to work on. Review regularly. Once you become aware of specific errors, you will be better prepared to avoid them.

- ***Review the word pairs in the Glossary of Usage, H–44.*** These words are commonly confused because they look or sound alike. Examples: *effect/affect*, *ensure/insure*, *all ready/already*, and others.

- ***Learn the rules of standard grammar, punctuation, and spelling.*** Don't ask someone else; you may get bad advice. Take responsibility by learning the rules and carefully checking your own work. On the job you will be glad you did. You might start by memorizing the eight basic rules for using commas, pages H-2 and H-3.

PEER REVIEW: HELPING TO IMPROVE EACH OTHER'S WRITING

Published writers often receive input from writing groups, agents, editors, or reviewers. Peer review in a classroom provides similar help. These reviews enable class members not only to help each other with early drafts but also to sharpen their skill at identifying rough spots in their own writing.

The job of a peer reviewer is to pinpoint problems, not solve them. Revision, editing, and proofreading are the responsibility of the writer. When giving feedback, the reviewer should be tactful. Comments that are overly blunt, unduly critical, or vague can be worse than none at all. Before critiquing, you might ask yourself, "How would I feel if I received this feedback?"

The difference between callousness and tact often lies in the phrasing. Vague reactions such as "I don't like the opening" or "Confusing" or "Dull" are not very helpful. Responses should be fairly specific so that the writer understands where and what the problem is. Responses can be softened in three ways:

1. *Begin with a positive comment about the draft:*
   - This is an interesting topic.
   - That example is well developed (funny or unusual).
   - The anecdote is delightful (or amusing or charming).
   - The spelling is correct.

SUGGESTIONS FOR PEER REVIEW

Writers who are mentally prepared to accept constructive criticism can learn much from peer review. Still, peer responses should not be taken as gospel. As you start to revise, evaluate the quality of each response and extract what is useful.

FOR REVIEWERS

1. Consider one aspect of the writing at a time.
2. Word your comments and suggestions thoughtfully and carefully.
3. Identify concerns tactfully, but don't whitewash.

FOR REVIEWEES

1. Keep an open mind. Be willing to consider suggestions. Ask about comments that seem unclear.
2. Evaluate each suggestion thoughtfully. If in doubt, make an appointment with your instructor or seek help at the campus writing center.

2. *Be tentative.* Offer comments as opinion, not a final decree:
   - This sentence *appears* negative. Is that what you intend?
   - This passage *seems* unclear. What do you mean? (If the person clarifies, say, "That's a good start. Why don't you write it down so you'll have it?")
   - I *wonder* if this part might work better here? (Not "You ramble.")
3. *Ask polite questions:*
   - Where is the thesis? (Not "You don't have a thesis statement.")
   - Have you thought about the ending yet? (Not "There isn't any conclusion.")

HANG IN THERE!

If you feel overwhelmed by this overview of revising, keep in mind that the chapter can be used for reference as you need it. Then too, the other chapters in Part 2 will provide specific help for revision and editing. As you write and revise, you are building skills that are adaptable to a wide array of rhetorical situations in both college and the workplace.

Summary

Revision has five major steps that increase efficiency and save time. To refocus a draft, you can narrow the title, make an outline, and find a fresh perspective. Revising a draft requires taking a close look at both the structure and the meaning. The order should be logical; the expression of ideas, logical, clear, and accurate.

During editing you improve word choice and sentence structure. During proofreading, you correct grammar, punctuation, and spelling.

Peer review can assist in revising and editing. When giving feedback, a reviewer should be tentative, tactful, and helpful.

Key Terms

alliteration	metaphor	revision
editing	peer review	simile
formal outline	proofreading	

Practice

Ideas for Writing

Directions: Describe an incident, experience, or tradition, or use one of these options:

1. The job you would like to have in five years
2. Broken promises
3. An anecdote about a family holiday or vacation
4. An incident at summer camp, school, or work
5. The earliest childhood scene or event that you can recall

Suggestions for Peer Review Practice

1. Reread "Guidelines for Peer Review."
2. Select one of your practice writings to revise and edit.
3. After you finish, find a partner and exchange papers.
4. Write your responses and suggestions on a separate sheet.
5. Return the paper along with the peer review.
6. Question your reviewer about anything you are unsure of.
7. Revise again, using any beneficial suggestions.

CHAPTER 6

Revision and Accuracy

Beginning to Think Critically

Whatever is only almost true is quite false, and among the most dangerous of errors, because being so near truth, it is the more likely to lead astray.

—Henry Ward Beecher (1813–1887)

We live in an era when propaganda, myth, and other misinformation masquerade as truth. Often inaccuracies come from politicians and reporters. They may confuse, misrepresent, and repeat unverified items so often the misstatements gain widespread acceptance. Then too, studies and polls based on invalid samples can gain credence. Other misinformation spreads in various ways, including via the Internet. Eventually, some readers may wonder why telling the truth is important. Why bother to be accurate?

WHY IS ACCURACY IMPORTANT?

Throughout the ages, civilizations have accepted the basic premise that *truth is the cornerstone of trust*. Truth undergirds trust in both social and business relationships. Friendships, marriages, partnerships, and businesses are built on truth and trust. When someone tells lies and those lies come to light, doubt and skepticism shatter trust. Broken promises and contracts lead not only to ruptured relationships but also to legal problems and even financial loss. Our courts take a firm stand on the need for truth in business and trade: fraud, forgery, copyright infringement, slander, and other violations of truth are punishable by law.

Accuracy is synonymous with truth; both are an exact rendering of the facts. As writers, we are obligated to check our facts and examine our claims critically in order to provide the most accurate and up-to-date information possible. Expository writing should be factual and accurate.

WHY HAVE NEWSPAPERS LOST CREDIBILITY?

The *San Jose Mercury News* (16 Dec. 1998) reported that the American Society of Newspaper Editors had begun a three-year project to discover why newspapers have lost credibility. The first study was based on a "national telephone survey of 3,000 U.S. adults . . . 16 focus groups and a 12-page questionnaire completed by newspaper journalists." Nearly 80 percent of the respondents said newspapers over-dramatize some news and emphasize sensational stories. Nearly half (48 percent) said their newspapers ran misleading headlines at least once a week.

More than one third of those contacted had noticed spelling or grammatical errors in their newspapers more than once a week. In fact, 21 percent stated they see errors every day. Factual mistakes in news stories in daily papers were also noticed by 23 percent at least once a week. Of the 31 percent who had been the subject of or interviewed for a news story, nearly one fourth (24 percent) said they had been misquoted; 31 percent found errors.

Another source of displeasure was the use of anonymous sources. More than three fourths of the respondents doubted the credibility of new stories from unnamed sources. A significant number, 45 percent, believed that such stories should not be printed. As a result of these problems, 73 percent now question the accuracy of news.

Concerned with public perception of the media, the *Wall Street Journal* (3 Jan. 2001) printed a letter from the publisher. Reprinted here are the first two points of a section entitled "What We Value":

- **Fairness and accuracy**—There is no substitute in our business for getting the story right, and for putting it in context, for being both accurate and fair.
- **A clear distinction between news and views**—There are places in most any publication, and certainly in every newspaper, for both news and views, for reporting on and analyzing events and trends and for expressing opinions about those events and trends. . . . But we pursue these two missions separately. Our opinions are clearly labeled; our news judgments are arrived at independently.

Whether you write papers, reports, or letters, the two guidelines above can assist you in finding and presenting facts to your audience.

HOW CAN FACT BE DETERMINED?

Statements and claims that have been rigorously tested and finally accepted by authorities in the field are said to be *established facts*. When you think something is probably true, ask whether or not it is an established fact. Can you find reliable research or other evidence to *prove* it? If not, then it is still in the realm of opinion.

In court, sworn evidence and the risk of perjury should keep witnesses truthful. Yet there can still be problems in accuracy. Two eyewitnesses can disagree about the same event. Perhaps one did not see the entire event, or they interpreted it differently. Then too, recollections fade with time. Expert opinion seems to be reliable most of the time, but even experts disagree. Legally, fact is based on three types of evidence:

1. Eyewitness reports sworn under oath

2. Expert opinion by an authority in the field

3. Material evidence (physical items that can be tested)

Without a doubt, material evidence is the most reliable of all. Hair, body fluids, fingerprints, voice prints, tire casts, and other materials can be carefully analyzed. Usually, the results are accurate, but once in a while human error does intrude. Even electronic devices are not foolproof. Temperature and other factors can hinder the performance of equipment, or someone may tamper with photographs, tapes, or other evidence. Determining what is true can be difficult.

INFERENCES ARE UNPROVEN

An *inference* is an assumption—an opinion—that is thought to be true but has not yet been proven. For example, on a subzero morning a neighbor's car fails to start. This is the first time the engine has refused to budge. Since the gas gauge registers half full, he *infers* that the battery is weak. He calls the local service station for a quick charge. After that, the motor starts. A battery check reveals a faulty cell. Thus his inference has been proven to be a fact. Some inferences are tested and discredited.

As long as inferences are reasonable and not presented as facts, they seldom cause problems in writing. But sometimes beginning writers confuse inferences and facts, as in the following example:

> When his owner's red pickup truck approaches his pen, Buck realizes raccoon season must be here. During hunting season, his mind is strictly on tracking coon, but at other times his chief pleasure is chasing cats.

What are the problems here? First, dogs cannot understand the concept of "raccoon season" (although they might associate the truck with hunting). Second, the word *strictly* means 100 percent of the time, and it is doubtful that Buck thought only about one thing. Dogs are easily distracted by noises, other animals, and hunger pangs. The final statement—"his chief pleasure is chasing cats"—is not an established fact but a value judgment.

VALUE JUDGMENTS AND POINT OF VIEW

Lew Wallace's familiar words, "beauty is altogether in the eye of the beholder," point out the elusive nature of value judgments. Too often we regard these opinions as fact. Actually, they are perceptions, which can be illogical and unpredictable. Often we assume other people have (or should have) the same values we cherish. The problem is that value judgments often masquerade as fact.

A *value judgment* is an opinion—an estimate of worth. Frequently, we rate items as bad or good, cheap or expensive, ugly or beautiful. Or we consider actions wrong or right, immoral or moral, according to our own perspective and experience. Yet value judgments are imprecise and variable. They vary from person to person and change with the times. For instance, baseball cards were originally just prizes collected by schoolchildren from packs of bubble gum. Now the cards are valuable and sought by adult collectors. They are regarded from a different point of view.

Point of view refers to the way something is perceived—the perspective. We form value judgments based on our differing points of view. Sinclair Lewis, in his early novel *Main Street*, describes two young women who see the town of Gopher Prairie through very different eyes. The impressions of Carol Kennicott, a city girl from Minneapolis, reveal her point of view:

> She glanced through the fly-specked windows of the most pretentious building in sight, the one place which welcomed strangers and determined their opinion of the charm and luxury of Gopher Prairie—the Minniemashie House. It was a tall lean shabby structure, three stories of yellow-streaked wood. . . . In the hotel office she could see a stretch of bare unclean floor, a line of rickety chairs with brass cuspidors. . . . The dining room beyond was a jungle of stained tablecloths and catsup bottles.

At the same time Bea Sorenson, "bored by farm work," walked along the other side of Main Street, thinking about the "excitements of city life" and the Minniemashie House. Her impression reveals very different judgments and a very different point of view:

> A hotel, awful high, higher than Oscar Tollefson's new red barn; three storied, one right on top of another; you had to stick your head back to look clear up to the top. There was a swell traveling man in there—probably been to Chicago lots of times.

Carol and Bea, coming from varying backgrounds, view the town differently. Later they make value judgments about Gopher Prairie, based on their points of view. Carol thinks: "I must be wrong. People do live here. It can't be as ugly as—as I know it is! I must be wrong." But Bea reasoned that even if she didn't receive a salary of six dollars every week, she would work for much less "to be allowed to stay here."

LISTENING TO THE TONE OF WRITING

A writer's point of view may range from essentially *objective* to highly *subjective* depending on the purpose and the topic. Some writing requires an impersonal voice that presents the facts squarely. The front pages of most American newspapers, for example, carry factual reports in which the writers attempt to relay news stories objectively. The purpose is to report what happened—not to push a particular view. The tone of objective writing is impartial, unslanted, and unbiased; readers seldom get a sense of the writer's opinion or personality.

The purpose of editorial pages is to allow writers to express their individual points of view. In editorials, columns, and letters to the editor, writers interpret facts subjectively, based on their own political, ethical, and economic values. They offer opinions and judgments; they praise and criticize; they urge specific courses of action. Their written voices may convey conviction, indignation, anger, or joy.

See page 6. A degree of subjectivity is inevitable in almost any writing, but it should be controlled and appropriate for the writing situation. Reading your draft aloud will help you to listen to the tone of your written voice. For help in presenting information fairly, clearly, and accurately, see the box below.

CHARACTERISTICS OF FACTS, INFERENCES, AND VALUE JUDGMENTS

Fact	*Inference*	*Value Judgment*
Act, deed, event, state or condition of reality	Assumption, generalization, or decision derived from evidence	Opinion or estimate of worth, an evaluation or rating
Objectively proved by observation, experiment, eyewitness, or expert opinion	Has not been proved; has possibility of being proved or discredited	Cannot be proved; will always be an opinion

---

FOUR WAYS MISINFORMATION ARISES

As we grow up, we hear folk wisdom, propaganda, myths, superstitions, and other inaccuracies presented as fact. Steeped in these beliefs, we tend not to question them, and so we accumulate much misinformation without realizing it. Here are four ways misinformation commonly comes to be accepted as fact.

Expert Opinion Occasionally Changes

We all know that one should not swim for an hour after eating—or do we? This bit of advice was published by the American Red Cross over fifty years ago.

A lifesaving manual claimed that a swimmer who ate immediately before a dip risked stomach cramps or even death. Now the *Journal of Health, Physical Education, and Recreation* disputes the idea of "stomach cramps." A prominent physical educator was quoted as saying, "I have never seen a case of so-called stomach cramps, although I have observed hundreds of thousands of persons swimming immediately after eating." Medical opinions, as well as other expert opinions, sometimes change over the years.

A Small Survey Is Inadequate Proof

Sometimes we hear someone generalize after surveying a few friends or considering a few unusual incidents. It's the old story of "everyone else is getting a new prom dress but me." But a small sample is hardly a reliable survey (see chapter 22).

Overstatement, stereotypic thinking, and generalizing from an unrepresentative sample can lead to the fallacy of hasty generalization. *A hasty generalization is a broad statement, an inference, that lacks sufficient proof.* A hasty generalization can occur when a *trend* or a *tendency* is overstated as if it were true for an entire group or population. Although assumed to be true, a hasty generalization is not an established fact. (This fallacy and others are explained in chapter 20.)

Facts Are Overstated

Unintentional overstatement sometimes occurs. We may not recall exactly what we read or heard and may overstate the facts. Or we may paraphrase, using synonyms that give an impression different from the one we intended. And some people exaggerate without being aware of it. For example, the student who wrote the following paragraph was convinced it was absolutely true:

> Lack of participation by the American people in their government is the number one cause for their loss of control over their own affairs. They say: "I don't care." "My vote doesn't matter." "I didn't have time to vote." These are some of the excuses given for not carrying out one of the most important rights given to the people, the right to vote.

Here a partial truth has been stretched ("number one cause"). This "statistic" is not an established fact. He could have made the statement acceptable by adding one word, *possibly*.

Stereotyping Shuts Out Fact

A writer must be on guard against stereotypes based on gender, race/ethnicity, age, religion, and the like. Stereotyping is pigeonholing, classifying someone or something into a tight little box. A stereotypic belief supposedly typifies a group, place, issue, or event. Although the characteristic attributed to the group may be true for some individuals, it is not true for all. Consider the following statements carefully. Then mark each one true or false.

_____   1. Redheads have quick tempers.

_____   2. Men are stronger than women.

_____   3. Politicians can't be trusted.

If you marked all of the statements true, you have probably grown up hearing these stereotypes presented as fact. If you marked some false, you are to be congratulated on your growing skepticism. If you marked all false, you rate an A. Why are all three statements false? None allows for an exception. These statements are *absolute* or all-inclusive: they claim to apply 100 percent of the time. Think about it. Do *all* redheads in the world have quick tempers? Are *all* men stronger than *all* women? Isn't there even one politician who can be trusted? To further complicate matters, item 2 contains an *undefined term.* What kind of strength are we talking about—physical, emotional, intellectual, or spiritual?

Experienced speakers and writers avoid stereotypic thinking, for it is not only unfair and undiplomatic but also inaccurate. Stereotypes shut out new information that conflicts with old, embedded beliefs. Stereotypic thinking is a quagmire that can lead to charges of sexism and discrimination as well as hurt feelings.

WRITING RESPONSIBLY

Responsible writing presents the truth, and responsible claims are backed by evidence. Readers should not have to grope through a fog of unsupported information to determine the facts. Once you become aware of the slipperiness of fact, you can take three precautions to avoid misstatement: Limit your generalizations, use absolute terms accurately, and identify inferences and opinion.

Limiting Generalizations

To be accurate and useful in writing, generalizations must be factual. If they are overstated and too broad they undermine your credibility. Thus you need to limit, or "qualify." *Qualifiers are words or phrases that modify meanings and allow for exceptions.* Qualified generalizations often serve as topic sentences and thesis statements. The generalizations below were used successfully as thesis sentences in student essays. (Qualifiers are italicized.)

Some outstanding women have graced history with their heroic feats during battle.

In today's hurried pace, the giving and receiving of love is *often* overlooked.

Crash dieting *seems* to be the surefire approach to coping with obesity.

To limit an overly broad generalization, you may need a word such as *may*, *might*, *tend*, *seem*, or *appear* to make your claim acceptable. Other qualifiers refer to number. To indicate a *majority* (more than 50 percent), you can use terms such as the following:

most	largely	overall	chiefly	as a rule
usually	primarily	typically	generally	mainly

To indicate a *minority*, use less specific words. Note, however, that the size of a minority can vary and influence your word choice. If in doubt about the appropriateness of a qualifier, consult two or more good desk dictionaries for fine distinctions in meaning. Terms such as those below can be used to indicate less than 50 percent:

many	rarely	often	several
few	frequently	irregularly	seldom
some	relatively few	sometimes	occasionally

Using Absolute Terms Accurately

Absolute terms are inflexible words that state or imply *none* or *all*. These words mean zero or 100 percent. When you revise, examine every statement that contains an absolute term. Be sure you consider what the word means, not just what you intend. If you overstate a case by misusing an absolute, the reader will be apt to take the literal meaning unless you plant a clue that the statement is ironic or joking. The list below will help you recognize absolute terms:

all	always	everyone	no one
none	never	only	same
every	completely	exact	anything

Can you identify Peppermint Patty's absolute term?

PEANUTS reprinted by permission of United Feature Syndicate, Inc.

Other kinds of words can also be all-inclusive. Verbs and adjectives like the following can also lead to overstatement and misstatement:

is	perfect*	greatest	same
are	unique*	smallest	best
was	worst	opposite	exact

*Something is either perfect or imperfect; unique or not unique. Phrases such as *very perfect* or *rather unique* are incorrect. If in doubt about such usage, check a dictionary.

Identifying Inferences and Other Opinions

In workplace writing and college assignments, you may be asked to "draw a conclusion" (inference) from a set of facts, to "write a reaction" (see chapter 26), or to "interpret facts." To complete such assignments successfully, you need to know how to identify inferences and other types of opinion. Qualifiers like those below indicate inferences:

theory	probably	apparently	seems
conjecture	possibly	it appears	imply
indicate	evidently	suggests	infer

As you revise, check to see that no opinions are presented as facts. For example, a widely held belief that is unproved should be identified as opinion. Phrases such as "a common belief" or "the conventional wisdom" indicate the nature of such statements. Other terms that identify opinion include the following:

current thinking	viewpoint	reaction	perception
appraisal	impression	feeling	folk wisdom
point of view	estimate	prediction	view

REVISING FOR ACCURACY

Whether you write a report, an essay, a research paper, or some other document, double-check every item to be sure it is logical and accurate. In the flurry of pinning down ideas during prewriting and drafting, it is easy to leave out a word, transpose a number, overstate a generalization, or commit some other blunder. Develop the habit of being thorough, of questioning information that doesn't quite ring true or seems suspicious. The checklist below should be helpful:

CHECKLIST: REVISING FOR ACCURACY
1. Are all data established facts?
2. Have inferences, value judgments, and other opinions been qualified?
3. Do any generalizations need to be limited?
4. Are all words accurate?
5. Does the tone sound appropriate?
6. Have any significant facts been omitted? Are any more needed?

Only when we learn to think logically and critically, to analyze carefully our own ideas as well as the ideas of other speakers and writers, can we begin to approach "the whole truth." That is what the writing process is all about.

Summary

Responsible writers present the truth, yet truth is not always easy to recognize. Our courts accept three kinds of evidence as fact: eyewitness accounts, expert opinion, and material evidence. Still, there can be problems with all three kinds.

Inference and value judgment can be mistaken for fact. Inferences are unproved assumptions. Value judgments are evaluations that reflect a writer's point of view. Responsible writers distinguish opinion from fact; they qualify inferences and other forms of opinion. They present facts objectively and accurately, limiting unfounded generalizations. Opinion adds subjectivity to writing. The tone of writing should be appropriate to the situation.

Misinformation can arise in various ways; among these are changes in expert opinion, generalization from a small sample, overstatement, and stereotypes. Sometimes inaccuracy can be avoided by careful word choice. Checking for accuracy is an important element of revision.

Key Terms

absolute	objective	qualifier
established fact	overstatement	stereotype
hasty generalization	point of view	subjective
inference	qualified generalization	value judgment

Test Yourself

Fact, Inference, or Value Judgment?

Directions: Imagine or examine a Red Delicious apple. Then mark F (fact), I (inference), or VJ (value judgment) below. Check your answers with the key at the end of the chapter.

_____ 1. This apple has four bumps (protrusions) on the bottom.

_____ 2. This apple is attractive to the eye.

_____ 3. This apple has a shiny red skin.

_____ 4. This apple will taste good.

_____ 5. This apple contains dark brown seeds. (The apple is uncut.)

Opinion or Observable Fact?

Directions: Write O for opinion or F for observable fact in the blanks. Then check your answers with the key at the end of the chapter.

_____ 1. The fender was *dented*.

_____ 2. Peggy is *pretty*.

_____ 3. The lighting was *adequate*.

_____ 4. The rock is *moss covered*.

_____ 5. The speech was *boring*.

Practice

Collaborative Learning: Fact, Inference, or Value Judgment?

Directions: Mark each item as fact (F), inference (I), or value judgment (VJ). If both fact and inference, mark I; if both fact and value judgment, mark VJ. Discuss any disagreement.

_____ 1. Great Britain is an island, not a continent.

_____ 2. Many exquisite bays line Britain's coast.

_____ 3. The beautiful white cliffs of Dover, overlooking the English Channel, are composed of chalk.

_____ 4. The Isle of Man lies in the Irish Sea.

_____ 5. If you mention hunting to a Brit, he or she will immediately think of fox hunting.

_____ 6. Most Americans are surprised to learn that a subway in London is an underground passageway for pedestrians.

_____ 7. If you want a delicious meal in London, order fish, not steak.

_____ 8. The Tower of London is the most fabulous sight in the city.

———— 9. In the spring after a rain, Paris has a delicate shimmering beauty.

———— 10. The Louvre, the largest art museum and palace in the world, is located on the north bank of the River Seine in Paris.

Test Yourself Answers

Fact, Inference, or Value Judgment?

1. F   4. VJ

2. VJ   5. I

3. F

Opinion or Observable Fact?

Items 1 and 4 are observable facts. The others are opinions.

CHAPTER 7

Revising Paragraphs

There is a poignancy in all things clear,
In the stare of a deer, in the ring of a hammer
in the morning. Seeing a bucket of perfectly lucid water
we fall to imagining prodigious honesties.

—Richard Wilbur, "Clearness," *Ceremony*

Clarity is the heart of effective writing, and well-developed paragraphs are essential for clarity. Opening and concluding paragraphs, discussed in chapter 4, act as a frame for an essay, paper, or report. Body paragraphs focus on making specific points and presenting information in a complete and coherent way. Transitional paragraphs provide connections between different ideas. A single well-developed paragraph by itself may even form a complete brief essay, exam answer, or business communication.

This chapter discusses elements and qualities of successful single paragraphs, as well as body paragraphs within essays, paying special attention to some specific modes of development.

ELEMENTS OF AN EFFECTIVE PARAGRAPH

To be effective, a paragraph must be centered on one idea, and the sentences must flow in a logical sequence. And regardless of whether the paragraph stands alone or comes in the body of an essay (or other piece of writing), it contains certain elements. For clarity, most paragraphs have a topic sentence.

The Topic Sentence

The topic sentence contains the main idea of a paragraph. This sentence tells the reader *what* will be covered and *why*. Some topic sentences also tell *where* or *when*. A basic topic sentence has two essential functions:

1. *To limit the subject to one main idea* that can be developed in the paragraph.
2. *To make a claim, assertion, or statement of opinion.* This part of the topic sentence may be a belief, impression, generalization, or recommendation.

Let's consider a topic sentence that performs both these functions:

Uncle Jake, who came uninvited, was a difficult house guest.

The subject of this topic sentence is "Uncle Jake," and the claim is that he was "a difficult house guest." This topic sentence sets up the expectation that the writer will describe Uncle Jake's behavior. In the body of the paragraph, readers will expect support—examples of what he said and anecdotes of what he did so that they can see for themselves how difficult Uncle Jake was.

Support Sentences

Support sentences explain the main idea of the topic sentence. They supply *evidence* to convince the reader of the soundness of the claim, assertion, or opinion. You might regard the topic sentence as an argument (view) to be proven. The support sentences supply evidence in the form of facts, definitions, reasons, examples, or illustrations to back up the claim in the topic sentence.

The minimum for support sentences is generally three or four; often there are more. As you search for support, keep in mind that *quality* is more important than quantity. A few excellent examples are worth more than a dozen mediocre ones. Established facts, definitions, and valid reasons provide credible evidence. Appropriate illustrations and anecdotes increase readers' interest, understanding, and conviction.

A Concluding Sentence

Besides the two basic parts just discussed—the topic sentence and support sentences—some paragraphs have a third part: a concluding sentence. This final sentence may be a summary of the points made in the support sentences. It can also serve as a *clincher*, providing the paragraph with a sense of completeness by commenting on the subject in an interesting, surprising, or humorous way. In the following student paragraph, the concluding sentence not only alludes to the opening topic sentence but also makes a point.

Climb Aboard!

The magic of a carousel has a way of turning men and women into children again. As they approach the carousel house, their steps and their hearts suddenly become lighter. Tots tug at adult hands, eager to climb aboard this remnant from a fairy tale. The magnificent carousel stands with hundreds of lights reflected in mirrors on the brightly painted rounding boards. Adventurous riders select mounts from rows of prancing horses or from the menagerie of bears, big cats, goats, ostriches, rabbits, a zebra, a giraffe, or a hippopotamus. The timid and the elderly seem to prefer the sedate pace of the two chariots. When all riders are seated, the calliope signals the ride is about to begin. As the carousel gains speed, whirling faster and faster, the riders' faces are transformed by smiles. Their cares seem to disappear as they are charmed by the magic of the carousel.

—**Bonita M. Goings**

QUALITIES OF EFFECTIVE PARAGRAPHS

Effective paragraphs have five distinctive features: clarity, interest, unity, coherence, and completeness. Clarity is of primary importance.

Clarity

Some writing is like bright sunlight. The main idea shines through the words clearly. For writing to be effective, readers must be able to determine the meaning upon a first reading. True, they may need to reread to recall specific details, but the main idea should be apparent the first time.

Clarity is the end result of knowing your purpose, correctly assessing the audience, connecting ideas, selecting appropriate words, and being complete. Important influences on clarity are the level of formality, the voice of verbs, sentence structure, length of sentences and paragraphs, and positions of emphasis (see chapter 8). Careful revision and editing will help to make your paragraphs clear.

Interest

An effective paragraph is worth reading. The topic is significant and the development is interesting. A secret of good essay writing is to remember that readers like to be entertained. Try to capture readers' attention and make them eager to continue. Before beginning a draft, consider how you might stimulate interest. Can you approach your topic in an unusual way? What might readers like to know? Then use action verbs and concrete nouns to help the reader share your impression (see chapter 11).

Unity

To write effective paragraphs, resist the temptation to create thickets of words. Focus on one major idea (in the topic sentence) to unify the paragraph. *All of the other sentences in the paragraph should link to the major idea.* They may support it with examples, facts, statistics, opinion, or reasons. During the drafting stage, don't worry unduly about unity. At that stage your goal is to expand ideas on paper. But when you start to revise, unity becomes a priority. To check the unity of a paragraph, ask yourself three questions:

- What is the purpose (main idea) of the paragraph?
- Does each support sentence assist in achieving the purpose?
- If not, what needs to be deleted or added?

Coherence

You might think of a paragraph as a jigsaw puzzle—each piece must fit. If not, the paragraph lacks coherence; it does not flow smoothly. If words, phrases, or sentences are in the wrong places, they must be rearranged. If there are gaps between ideas, you need to add transitions to provide connections. Other ways of achieving coherence are by repeating key words and by using parallelism.

Signpost Transitions   Like signs on a highway, signpost transitions direct the reader. Usually, these signal words and phrases appear at the beginning of sentences. Just adding a word or phrase to indicate how the material relates to the preceding sentence often makes a paragraph clearer and easier to read. In the following student paragraph, signpost transitions show the passing of *time*.

Playing Possum

While defending an ambush position in Vietnam, I was run over by a tank. Hurt and bleeding, I was left lying in a rice paddy. My buddy, *after* routing the ambush against "Charlie," took off in pursuit, believing I was dead. *After an hour,* which seemed like an eternity, night fell. *A few hours later* the sky was pitch black. There was no moon nor stars, just blackness. Suddenly I heard someone sloshing through the paddy. It was Charlie. *As* I lay there motionless, I heard the Viet soldier rummaging through my Jeep. *After* he finished with the Jeep, he started to strip the dead. *Before* I knew it, he was standing over me. *While* lying there playing dead, trying not to breathe, I was sure he could hear the blood rushing from my wounds. Luckily for me, he was in a hurry and just stripped off my watch, flak jacket, lighter, and cigarettes. *After* he left, I took a big breath and let out a sigh of relief. *Hours later, as* dawn broke, a patrol finally happened across my Jeep and discovered the bodies lying around. Tears came to my eyes *as* I heard a U.S. soldier say, "Medic, this one is still alive!"

—Sonny Dyer

COMMON SIGNPOST TRANSITIONS

- *To show time:* once, years ago, later, soon, now, today, then, before, when, while, after, meanwhile, as, next, first, second, and so forth
- *To add:* too, also, and, another, besides, in addition, furthermore
- *To show difference:* but, yet, however, still, otherwise, even so, although
- *To show similarity:* like, likewise, similarly, both, resemble, identical
- *To show effects or results:* because, for, therefore, as a result, since, thus
- *To emphasize:* in fact, indeed, above all, again, regardless, nonetheless
- *To point out examples:* for example, for instance

See chapter 14.

Embedded Transition   Transition that is placed within a sentence is said to be "embedded." *Key words*, *natural relationships*, *synonyms*, and *pronouns* are four types of embedded transition. Repeating key words, substituting synonyms for words, and using pronouns that refer to key words can help you knit sentences smoothly into a paragraph. Note how the repetition of key words, natural relationships, synonyms, and pronouns help make the following paragraph coherent:

> *My mother* was the eldest of *her* generation—of nine children—and came from a slightly more elevated social station in Jamaica. *She* had a high school education, which *my father* lacked. . . . Before emigrating, *Mom* had worked as a stenographer in a lawyer's office. *Her* mother, Gram McKoy, was a small, lovely woman whose English wedded *African cadence* to *British inflection*, the sound of which is still music to my soul. The McKoys and the Powells both had *bloodlines* common among *Jamaicans*, including *African, English, Irish, Scotch*, and probably *Arawak Indian*. *My father's side* even added a *Jewish strain* from a Broomfield *ancestor*.
>
> **—Colin Powell, *My American Journey***

Parallelism   Parallel structures provide balance in writing and contribute to coherence. Possibly without thinking, you already use parallelism in several ways: for items in a series, coordinate phrases and clauses, compound sentences, and pairs of related sentences (see chapter 8). You may sense that parallelism smooths sentence structure and gives equal emphasis to coordinate ideas. To check the coherence and parallelism of your paragraphs, read them aloud. The ear is often a better detector of imbalance than is the eye. Note the use of parallelism in the following descriptive paragraph by a student:

> **Through a Child's Eyes**
>
> A tall, husky man has long been a very special person in my life. *His hair is the color of bricks in a schoolhouse*, while *his eyes are the color of hickory nut shells*. *Above his eyes* he wears a permanent frown, but *in his smile* I can see his inner warmth peeking through. *When he speaks*, his voice sounds like a semi-truck going through a tunnel at a high rate of speed. The low, gravelly tones echo like a bouncing tennis ball in an empty room. *When he enters a room*, he resembles a bear just waking from its winter slumber. But *when he sits*, a lap appears that would never turn away a child who wished to crawl upon it. When sitting there, I can detect the faint scent of Old Spice. *His big, muscular arms* make me feel safe from any possible harm. *His huge, powerful hands* are *like vise grips*, but when wiping tears away, they are *like soft cotton*. As rough as this man appears *on the outside, on the inside* he is soft and gentle, just like a newborn kitten. . . . This very dear person is my dad.
>
> **—Nancy Smathers**

Completeness

An effective paragraph does not weary readers or waste their time. Details appear for a valid reason: to support the topic sentence. To be complete, a paragraph must supply adequate and appropriate information. But how much is enough? What is suitable? You, the writer, must decide according to each rhetorical situation. Whether your professor assigns a single paragraph or a lengthy paper, you will have to assess the audience and the occasion. You might consider the following points:

- How much are readers likely to know?
- How much more do they need to know?
- Why? How will the information be used?
- Are there enough examples, reasons, or anecdotes to be interesting?
- Is there enough specific support to make my point?

PREWRITING AND DRAFTING PARAGRAPHS

If you are writing a body paragraph in an essay, the topic sentence introduces one segment of your thesis statement (central idea of the essay). Although this chapter shows some body paragraphs, they are explained in part 3. This chapter focuses on single student paragraphs.

Narrowing a Topic Sentence

Beginning writers frequently struggle to whittle down a general topic. Narrowing a topic requires selecting one significant aspect. The problem may be that you know so much, you can't decide where to start. For example, a first attempt might read "I like horses." But you realize the sentence is boring and too broad. Your mind spinning with ideas, you begin to prewrite. Soon you have a list that yields a suitable topic. Your efforts might look like this:

horses
riding horses
riding horses I have owned
my first riding horse

Draft topic sentence: I'll never forget my first horse.

First revision: Pinto was my first riding horse; actually, he was a pony.

Second revision: My first riding horse was actually a pony, but to my five-year-old eyes, Pinto was the finest of horses.

For most topic sentences, a limit of twenty words or so usually works well. A topic sentence that is too long may overwhelm the reader.

Positioning the Topic Sentence

Once you have drafted a topic sentence, your next concern is where to place it in the paragraph. Before positioning the topic sentence, consider its function and the effect you want to obtain. Will you place it at the beginning, the middle, or the end?

The Topic Sentence at the Beginning   Most expository paragraphs follow the direct approach: the topic sentence is placed at the beginning. There the topic receives more emphasis than in the middle, and the reader knows immediately what the writer will explain. Yet topic sentences sometimes wander into odd places. While revising this book, I have been surprised now and then to find a topic sentence huddled in the middle of a paragraph for no apparent reason. Unless I found a reason to leave it there, I yanked it back to the beginning. Check your drafts to see that your topic sentences are in the most effective position for the purpose and audience.

The Topic Sentence in the Middle   Sometimes a writer may wish to take a leisurely path to the main idea. Then the topic sentence may appear in the middle of a paragraph. Placed there, the major idea receives less emphasis than at the beginning or end. In a paragraph of comparison, for instance, a topic sentence might be located midway between the two subjects. There it can identify the purpose and connect the items being compared. Or the topic sentence may be in the middle for other reasons, as in the following paragraph, which describes nonverbal communication:

> Mrs. Clark, who teaches math, is explaining an essential aspect of the subject. She notices that Fred is staring at her with unblinking eyes, his body taut and erect, his feet flat on the floor. She discerns no motion whatever from Fred. Do you think that Fred is listening to the lecture, evaluating what Mrs. Clark is saying? *If you think he is interested, you are wrong.* A young teacher unaccustomed to this posture might fall for it, but a more experienced educator would not. Fred has turned his teacher off and is using a cover-up technique to convince her that he is "all ears."
>
> —Gerard I. Nierenberg and Henry H. Calero
> *How to Read a Person Like a Book*

Placing a topic sentence in the middle of a paragraph does carry a risk, however. The danger is that if readers are impatient or in a hurry, they may skim over the middle and miss the key idea. If the idea is very important, place it at the beginning or end.

The Topic Sentence at the End   At the end of an expository paragraph, the topic sentence acts as a summary, spelling out the controlling idea that is implicit in the sentences that precede it. The following paragraph, for example, builds up to a concluding topic sentence that offers a startling and bleak statistic:

> Many illiterates cannot read the admonition on a pack of cigarettes. Neither the Surgeon General's warning nor its reproduction on the package can alert them to the risks. Although most people learn by word of mouth that smoking is related to a number of grave physical disorders, they do not get the chance to read the detailed stories which can document this danger with the vividness that turns concern into

determination to resist. They can see the handsome cowboy or the slim Virginia lady lighting up a filter cigarette; they cannot heed the words that tell them that this product is (not "may be") dangerous to their health. *Sixty million men and women are condemned to be the unalerted, high-risk candidates for cancer.*

—Jonathan Kozol, "The Human Cost of an Illiterate Society"

A topic sentence at the end of a paragraph requires the reader to look at the support before the main idea. Since the writer takes time to explain the reasons before making the claim, the readers are less likely to reject the assertion. You might also place a topic sentence at the end to let readers know how and why you arrived at a decision.

Unifying a Paragraph without a Topic Sentence

Not all paragraphs have a topic sentence. Nonetheless, the main idea must be clear. In narrative writing topic sentences are often lacking, but a general point will still be strongly implied, as in the following paragraph:

In the spring of 1948, in the first softball game during the afternoon hour of physical education in the dusty schoolyard, the two captains chose teams and, as always, they chose other boys until only two of us remained. I batted last, and first came to the plate with two or three runners on base, and while my teammates urged me to try for a walk, and the players on the field called Easy out, Easy out, I watched the softball coming in waist-high and stepped and swung, and hit it over the right fielder's head for a double. My next time at bat I tripled to center. From then on I brought my glove to school, hanging from a handlebar.

—Andre Dubus, "Under the Lights"

The paragraph has no topic sentence, but its point is clearly implied and might be stated as "Without warning, I had become a good softball player."

Diplomacy may be an excellent reason for omitting a topic sentence. Some business letters, such as a credit refusal, may not state the main idea directly. Instead, the refusal is *implied* in a subordinate clause. Unless there is a good reason to omit a topic sentence, however, include one.

Adjusting Paragraph Length

Reportedly, when Abraham Lincoln was once asked "How long should a man's legs be?" he answered, "Long enough to reach the ground." A similar answer comes to mind when students ask "How long should a paragraph be?" A paragraph should be long enough to cover the central idea well according to the needs of readers and their purpose in reading.

As a general rule, avoid one- and two-sentence paragraphs as well as a series of short paragraphs. These will give your writing a choppy, careless appearance. (In newspapers and magazines, paragraphs tend to be short because they are crammed into columns and look longer than otherwise.) Introductory paragraphs of short papers (500 words or less) usually range from three to five sentences;

GUIDELINES: DIVIDING LONG PARAGRAPHS

1. ***Divide when a paragraph has more than one main idea.*** Divide where the second idea or a shift to another facet of the major idea begins.

2. ***Divide where there is a lapse in time.*** Time provides a natural break. Tip: Look for transitions of time or a shift in verb tense.

3. ***Divide if there is a shift in person of pronouns.*** First, check to see that the shift is necessary. If it is, that may be an excellent spot to divide.

4. ***In dialogue, start a new paragraph for each speaker.***

---

introductions for research papers tend to be longer. Body paragraphs often range from five to eight sentences. Conclusions tend to be rather brief, perhaps three to five sentences. A one-paragraph essay may range from seven to twelve or more sentences.

Complexity of the subject also influences length; difficult subjects tend to require more explanation. If a paragraph becomes quite long, consider the needs of the reader, the purpose of the writing, and the coverage required for clarity. If division is needed, look for a shift from one aspect of an idea to another.

ORGANIZING AND DEVELOPING PARAGRAPHS

You can organize the details in a paragraph by any strategy that is clear and reasonable. Narrative and process paragraphs are generally in *chronological* (time) order with events and steps presented as they naturally occur. Descriptive paragraphs are generally arranged in *spatial* order according to location or design. For example, in describing objects, animals, or people, you might go from head to toe, left to right, outside to inside, or in another direction. (See "Through a Child's Eyes," earlier in this chapter, for an example of spatial order.) Paragraphs may also be organized in other logical or sequential orders, as explained in chapter 4. The student paragraphs that follow are organized according to strategies of narration, description, process analysis, illustration, and comparison/contrast.

Narrative Paragraphs

Narrative paragraphs tell a story or relate an event or anecdote. The writer often sets the scene first, telling *who* or *what*, *when*, and *where*. Description, dialogue, or illustrations may be included to kindle interest and to clarify. Action verbs keep a story moving. Narratives often build suspense and reserve a surprise until the end. They may reveal rather than explain, letting the reader interpret the meaning, or they may direct attention to a social or political concern that has universal relevance (see chapter 10). The following narrative paragraph by student Suzanne Omaits suggests a fear we all might experience:

Home Alone

Quiet holds many sounds. I never knew how many until I found myself alone one Friday night. Was that the wind rubbing a bare branch against the house, I wondered; or was that the front step groaning under someone's weight? I tried not to think about the sound and turned on the television set. But something compelled me to turn in my chair and look over my shoulder at the window. Slowly I turned, dreading what I might see yet afraid not to look. For a moment I froze! Through the fogged glass, I saw a man's face pressed against the window pane, staring at me. Leaping to my feet, I flipped off the lights and TV. Then he began to pound on the window. Realizing he could still see me dimly, I ran to the back room and hid. After a moment I knew I had to get help. Fearfully, I crawled back to the living room to use the telephone. My hands trembled so I could hardly dial. Anxiously, I waited for the familiar voice of my neighbor. Suddenly the pounding stopped. Minutes dragged by until my neighbor arrived. After checking, he assured me the intruder was gone. At that moment a car drove into the driveway. Never was I so glad to hear my parents call, "We're home!"

Descriptive Paragraphs

An effective description has a specific purpose; details are not just a pleasant filler. *Significant* physical details can capture the essence of a person, place, or object. Concrete words reveal perceptions obtained through the five senses: seeing, hearing, touching, tasting, and smelling. A single dominant impression can unify the details. In the next student paragraph, by Michael Schnitzler, the physical details about a chair and how it has been used down through the years yield a dominant impression of an affectionate family.

See chapter 11.

The Old Rocking Chair

In the corner of our living room sits an old wooden rocking chair. The chair is made of solid maple, varnished and trimmed in gold. The arms are worn smooth, as if someone had used the finest of sandpaper on the wood. On the edges of its arms, I can see indentations in the wood where little tykes did their teething. As I rock back and forth, the old chair squeaks and creaks; but the sounds are soothing. This rocking chair has served several purposes. It has helped to console our three children, countless nieces, nephews, and children of friends. It has rocked babies to sleep for naps and at bedtime. With its soothing rhythm, it has comforted and quieted them when they were restless or sick. Now that the children have grown older, the old chair is seldom used. Yet it sits patiently, awaiting the years when it will hold our grandchildren.

Process Analysis Paragraphs

See chapter 12.

Process analysis explains how to do something or how something happens. Chronological order is the clearest way to organize process analysis. Just list steps or actions in sequence as they normally occur. Include enough details for the reader to understand. *If there is a risk during any part of the procedure, give a precaution early.* For conciseness and clarity, use second person (mainly the understood "you"). In the following example, which is directed to someone who has never used a coin-operated car wash, notice how the student writer Kristi Gruber takes an ordinary topic and transforms it into an interesting paragraph:

How to Get the Best Shine from a Coin-Operated Car Wash

Whether your car is a prized possession or a necessary nuisance, it deserves an occasional wash. By following five simple steps, you can make your vehicle sparkling clean in just five minutes. First, vacuum the interior with the hose located outside the entrance of the car wash. Be sure the hose inhales every crumb, pebble, and gum wrapper. Second, drive into the wash cage. Third, before you add coins, read the directions for the wand. Then turn the dial to "Prewash." Add the coins and be ready to work fast. Fourth, spray all the exterior once to break up grime. Fifth, switch to "High Pressure Soap" and grip the wand tightly. As you move around the car, spray the top, hood, sides, wheels, and trunk. Sixth, change the mode to "High Pressure Rinse." To prevent streaking, rinse all suds off. Next, switch to "Spot-free Final Rinse." This final step will prevent water spots and ensure a brilliant shine. If you are very dedicated to your four-wheeled friend, take time to wipe her off with the old bath towel you brought along. After that you will probably head down the highway only to be greeted with a gift from a passing bird!

Illustration Paragraphs

Illustration paragraphs—also called paragraphs of exemplification—present a *series* of examples to support the topic sentence. To maintain unity, every example is closely linked to the controlling idea. As you read the next student paragraph, notice the order of the examples Sharon K. Cleveland used:

The Fearsome Rabbit

Bathsheba was not the typical Easter bunny. Sheba was a Newfoundland flop-eared rabbit. Soon she grew into a fat fur ball. At maturity, she weighed thirty-five pounds—more than my two-year-old nephew! Our guests loved to watch her hop down the hall, then stand on her hind legs while she washed her face. With her long floppy ears hanging down, she had a sad, gentle look, which was deceiving. One day we came home to find her chewing on a camera bag that belonged to my husband. He yelled, "If I didn't love that rabbit so much, she would be dinner tonight!" Soon electrical cords, woodwork, wooden chairs, books, and other objects also bore the marks of her sharp teeth. As Sheba grew older, she developed a mean streak. One day our son, who was six, went near her litter box and came running—Sheba hopping close behind. As she nipped his bare heel, he screamed, "HELP!" After this incident she would hop toward him, and he would leap onto the couch. He had become afraid of her. Soon we took her to a farm that raised rabbits, where she seems fat and happy.

Comparison or Contrast Paragraphs

Comparison includes both similarities and differences, while *contrast* refers to differences only. The key to writing a good comparison or contrast paragraph is first to select two subjects that might make an interesting pair. Then list specific, significant features of each, matching every detail you list for one subject with a corresponding detail for the other. (See chapter 15 for outlines.)

The Eye of the Beholder

This year when the first warm days of April began, I overflowed with energy. I wanted to make our family room as fresh as the spring buds outside. In a frenzy, I started to throw out one piece of junk after another, but each time Jerry would intervene to save a "treasure." First, I discarded a faded, cracked plate; but he rescued his family heirloom. Then I seized the tattered quilt; he returned his comforter for cold nights to its rightful place on the couch. Next I tossed out the stack of old *Time* and *Newsweek* magazines from the coffee table; he retrieved them because he might need a reference for a "current" event. And so it went. Finally, I said, "That sagging old couch we bought at a garage sale simply has to go!" But he objected sharply, "That's my favorite spot to watch football!" Refusing to argue, I stopped. But the first day he goes golfing, I'm calling Goodwill for an immediate pickup. . . . I may keep the plate.

—**Peggy Walker**

Paragraphs of Definition

Sometimes a paragraph of definition is needed to explain the meaning and context of a word. A technical definition may specify the purpose and the function of a part or appliance. A literary definition may specify the root or origin of the word, the part of speech, and the standard meaning—or several meanings in different contexts. During practice writing, student Mark Jones speculated about the meaning and uses of the word *shaft*.

Words are fun to play with and think about. For example, *shaft* as a noun is a pole or long handle of a spear or other weapon. By that definition, an arrow could be considered a shaft, although it would seem strange to say we shafted a deer. The space shuttle might also be called a shaft. A pretty girl can wear a short dress and show a little shaft. The White House has many shafts; there are pillars at the entrance. *Shaft* is also used as a verb, but only in slang. If Bill shafted Al, then Bill did a wrong or injustice to Al. Bill did not hurl an arrow, spear, or space shuttle at Al, although Al has been hurt by Bill's action. *Shaft* is also the name of an old movie starring a super-cool, super-bad bald man named John Shaft. If violent movies about super-cool, bad, bald men are not appealing, then paying three dollars to rent the film and not liking it would be getting the shaft.

Transitional Paragraphs

Sometimes a special paragraph of transition is needed to connect two major ideas. In the middle of an essay or paper, you may need a paragraph of transition to bridge a gap or to direct the reader to a shift in thought. For example, Patty Seigneur wrote a brief transitional paragraph for a paper contrasting two good friends:

> Sue is a wonderful person and friend, but I found myself wanting a friend more like myself. Then I met June. Quickly, she and I became good friends. We both realized how alike we are and how much we enjoy each other's company.

Notice that only one signpost transition, *then*, is used in this transitional paragraph. But the writer repeats key terms and uses pronouns to establish clear *embedded* transition.

Summary

The two basic elements of a standard paragraph are the topic sentence and support sentences. Some paragraphs have a third part, a concluding sentence. The topic sentence identifies the subject and makes a claim about it. The support sentences supply proof. The concluding sentence gives a sense of completeness.

Effective paragraphs have five distinct features: clarity, interest, unity, coherence, and completeness. A topic sentence should be narrowed sufficiently to interest the reader and unify the paragraph. Although most topic sentences are placed at the beginning, they may appear in the middle or at the end of the paragraph. In special circumstances, a paragraph may not have a topic sentence.

Paragraph length is determined by audience, subject, and purpose.

Paragraphs may be arranged according to chronology, importance, complexity, generality, familiarity, emphasis, or some other logical order. A special type is the transitional paragraph, which may serve as a bridge between ideas in an essay.

Key Terms

chronological order	embedded transition	signpost transition
coherence	illustration	spatial order
comparison	narrative	support sentences
concluding sentence	order of importance	topic sentence
contrast	parallelism	transitional paragraphs
dominant impression	process analysis	

Practice

Small Groups: Evaluating Topic Sentences

Directions: Check the sentences that would make *good* topic sentences (just four). Discuss why the other sentences would be ineffective.

———— 1. My motto "play before work" received a severe blow this week.

———— 2. The leftover macaroni and cheese in my refrigerator was covered with green mold.

———— 3. Mary Todd married Abe Lincoln.

———— 4. The older I become, the more I appreciate. . . .

———— 5. Overnight the amaryllis opened one large red trumpet.

———— 6. Mr. Inskeep is my favorite teacher.

———— 7. Computers are necessary for most workplaces.

———— 8. A roommate who is a musician can be exasperating.

———— 9. Cutting the Brazilian rain forest is causing weather problems.

———— 10. Every Thursday night I watch my favorite TV program.

Ideas for Paragraphs

1. How and where to find arrowheads (or lovely shells? what else?)
2. My favorite vacation spot
3. The day I almost drowned
4. Describe a small object you own and its significance
5. Tips for shopping at garage sales (or flea markets or auctions)
6. How to make an unusual salad
7. My first day in school (on the first time I . . .)
8. The raccoons and the water garden (or other animal episode)
9. How to buy a good . . .
10. Why I . . .

CHAPTER 8

Editing: Styling Sentences

Style is the dress of thoughts; and let them be ever so just. . . .
—Lord Chesterfield,
Letter to His Son

In the workplace, employees are expected to be able to write strong, clear sentences at a moment's notice. They may have to dash off e-mail, a memo, a letter to a customer, or a short report. Regardless of the time crunch, rereading and revision are imperative. Otherwise, the message may be unclear, inaccurate, ungrammatical, or offensive.

Styling sentences is a challenging task, but it is the mark of a proficient writer. Effective sentences can be plain or ornate, simple or complex, short or long, depending on the purpose. The design and strength of sentences depend on the topic, the needs of the audience, the occasion for writing, and the voice of the writer. The clarity of sentences depends not only on the sentence pattern and word choice but also on correct punctuation, which is discussed briefly in this chapter, along with sentence structure.

As you revise at the sentence level, you will be trying to clarify, to emphasize major ideas, as well as add interest, variety, and style to your writing. Varying sentence patterns to fit particular ideas will make your writing not only clearer but also more interesting. Repeating the same sentence pattern throughout makes for humdrum writing.

There are other ways to spark vitality into lifeless sentences: Replace passive verbs and forms of *be* with action verbs. Create parallel forms for similar ideas. Eliminate awkwardness and unnecessary words. Condense long phrases and clauses. Vary the length of sentences. Position ideas at strategic points within sentences. Vary your choice of words. Revision can make your sentences strong and interesting. (Word choice is discussed in chapters 2, 6, and 9. See also "Figurative Language" in the index.)

EFFECTIVE USE OF VERBS

Although sentences can do without some parts of speech, a verb is always required. Even nouns can be omitted—leaving a verb to stand alone as a one-word sentence. For example, "Go!" "Heel!" and "March!" are complete sentences. The verbs you select will influence the strength and clarity of your writing.

Favoring the Active Voice

Strong action verbs can invigorate writing. Action verbs show movement and help readers to imagine an activity. For example, *ski, swim,* and *skate* show physical activity whereas *think, know,* and *dream* show mental activity. Action verbs can be written in either the active or passive voice. Usually, the active voice is preferred, for it is direct and concise. Active voice simply means the subject of the sentence is *performing the action,* as in the example below:

Active voice: Johnny *shot* the bear.

However, a verb is in the *passive* voice when the subject *receives the action.* Something or someone else is performing the act or deed. The passive voice consists of a *be* verb and a past participle so that a verb in the passive voice always consists of two (or three) words.

Passive voice: The bear *was shot* by Johnny.

Which sentence do you prefer? Why? You probably noticed that the sentence in active voice gives the sharpest image of the event. Perhaps you noted that the sentence in active voice has just four words, whereas the one in passive voice contains six words. Although passive voice is useful at times, it lessens the impact of a sentence. To make writing clear and direct, experienced writers prefer the active voice in most situations.

GUIDELINES: WHEN SHOULD YOU USE THE PASSIVE VOICE?

1. **The person responsible wishes to remain unknown.**
   Example: The new rule was enacted to tighten security.
2. **The one who does the action is unknown.**
   Example: The oriental rug was made in China.
3. **To place emphasis on an important word.** Passive voice allows the important word to become the subject of a sentence.
   Example: The *needs* of the student should be considered.

Replacing Forms of *Be*

The forms of *be* indicate a state of being or existing here on this planet. They do not show action. Although *be* verbs are sometimes necessary, too many of them tend to make a piece of writing seem wordy and lifeless. The main forms of the verb *be* are *is*, *am*, *are*, *was*, *were*, *be*, *been*, and *being*. To remember them easily, practice saying them in this order:

Say	*Remember*	*Say*	*Remember*
is	(one *i*)	be	(three *b*'s)
am	(two *a*'s)	been	
are		being	
was	(two *w*'s)		
were			

With a little thought, you can often replace a *be* verb with an action verb. Such revision not only shortens the sentence but also strengthens it. The following examples illustrate why action verbs are generally preferred:

> **Be verb:** Sammy Davis, Jr., *was* a famous entertainer who entertained millions with his singing and comedy. (14 words)

> **Action verb:** Sammy Davis, Jr., *entertained* millions with his singing and comedy. (9 words)

SENTENCE VARIETY

Verbs are an essential part of all sentence patterns. The three basic sentence patterns are the simple sentence, the complex sentence, and the compound sentence.

> **Simple:** Interviewers may ask about weaknesses. (independent clause)

> **Compound:** Interviewers may ask about weaknesses, but savvy applicants prepare for this question. (two independent clauses)

> **Complex:** Since interviewers may ask about weaknesses, savvy applicants prepare for this question. (dependent clause + independent clause)

Using all three structures adds interest to your writing, clarifies relationships among ideas, and emphasizes major points.

The Simple Sentence

The simple sentence is the "workhorse" that will pull the load in about 70 percent of your writing. A simple sentence contains a single subject (which may consist of more than one noun) and one or more verbs. The simple sentence is an *independent* clause—one complete thought that can stand alone. At its simplest, such a sentence may consist of only a subject and verb:

- Eagles soar.

More often though, simple sentences will contain other sentence parts, including objects, prepositional phrases and other modifiers, and perhaps additional verbs:

- Eagles build *large nests*. (subject + verb + direct object)
- Eagles build large nests *in isolated places*. (+ prepositional phrase)
- *Most commonly*, eagles build large nests in isolated places. (+ adverbs)
- Most commonly, eagles build large nests in isolated places and *lay two or three eggs*. (+ second verb and object)

The simple sentence is the primary sentence structure. In a piece of expository writing, as many as two thirds of the sentences may have this pattern. When only simple sentences are used, however, writing can become boring, and ideas can seem disconnected. As you revise your drafts, look for ways to expand simple sentences into complex sentences or to combine two simple sentences into a compound sentence. With effective revision, you can clarify related ideas.

The Compound Sentence

Two related simple sentences can be joined to form a *compound* sentence. The compound sentence gives the clauses *equal* rank because both clauses contain important ideas. This means that a compound sentence has two main subjects and two main verbs. If a transition is needed the two clauses are connected by a coordinating conjunction, as italicized in the following examples:

- Geraniums are easy to grow, *for* they are quite hardy.
- Mammoth Cave is the largest cave in the United States, *but* Carlsbad Caverns are the most colorful.
- Minarsi entered the Maine Turnpike at Falmouth, *and* she followed it until Augusta.

Coordinating Conjunctions   Coordinating conjunctions link similar elements, such as clauses, phrases, or nouns. There are just seven coordinating conjunctions to learn. An easy way to remember them is to memorize the acronym *fanboys: f*or, *a*nd, *n*or, *b*ut, *o*r, *y*et, *s*o.

The conjunction you use between clauses in a compound sentence depends on the relationship between the ideas in the two clauses. If the second clause provides additional information, use *and*. If the second clause is in contrast to the first, use *but, or, yet*, or *nor*. If the second clause has a cause-and-effect relationship with the first, use *for* or *so*.

PUNCTUATING COMPOUND SENTENCES

If *both* clauses in a compound sentence are four words or less, you may join them without a comma. If one clause or both have five words or more, you have three options—according to the relationship:

1. **Comma and Conjunction.** Connect two related independent clauses with a *coordinate conjunction* preceded by a comma when transition is needed:
   - The hidden job market consists of an estimated 80 percent of available jobs, *but* most job seekers seem unaware that it exists.

2. **Semicolon.** You can use a *semicolon* between two independent clauses when the connection between the ideas is so close no transition is needed:
   - The hidden job market consists of an estimated 80 percent of available jobs; only 20 percent or so of the available jobs are ever advertised.

3. **Colon.** Use a *colon* to indicate that the second clause of the compound sentence will explain the first:
   - The astute job seeker compiles a packet of employment search documents: the packet can contain an up-to-date résumé, cover letter, thank-you letter, and sheet of references.

What Are Comma Splices and Fused Sentences?   It is incorrect to link independent clauses with only a comma and no coordinating conjunction. The resulting error is called a *comma splice*. If no punctuation whatever is used between two independent clauses in a compound sentence, the error is called a *fused sentence*.

Comma splice: Terrariums are costly at a flower shop, they are inexpensive to make at home.

Correct: Terrariums are costly at a flower shop, *but* they are inexpensive to make at home. (comma and conjunction)

Comma splice: Weather bulletins warned of ice-glazed roads, however, some drivers ignored the warning.

Correct: Weather bulletins warned of ice-glazed roads; however, some drivers ignored the warning. (semicolon)

Fused Sentence: The ordinance won wide support it was passed by a two-thirds vote.

Correct: The ordinance won wide support; it was passed by a two-thirds vote. (semicolon)

While compound sentences are often effective, they should not be overused. Also remember that a compound sentence gives both clauses equal weight. When the idea in one clause is more important, then the two clauses should be combined into a complex sentence.

The Complex Sentence

A *complex* sentence consists of an independent clause and one or more dependent clauses. The complex sentence ranks a major idea and a minor idea. The major idea appears in the independent clause; the minor idea appears in the dependent clause. To the untrained eye, a dependent clause may look like a complete sentence because both have a subject and a verb. But the dependent clause has a word at the beginning that makes the (minor) idea incomplete. Thus *a dependent clause is always a fragment and cannot stand alone.*

Fragments (incomplete ideas)

That has white forepaws

When the doorbell rings

Because McDaniel Motors gives dependable service

Sentences (complete ideas)

- The black cat that has white forepaws is Jeff's.
- When the doorbell rings, my dog barks.
- Because McDaniel Motors gives dependable service, Jason has his car serviced there.

Adjective Clauses Adjective clauses are dependent clauses that refer to nouns or pronouns. These clauses are easy to identify because they always start with one of five relative pronouns: *who, whom, whose, which,* or *that.* (Think: four *w*'s and a *t*.)

Essential: The car *that he prefers* has bucket seats.
The young woman *who is wearing blue jeans* is Mary's sister.

Nonessential: Terry, *who is my brother*, is an avid photographer.
The yellow truck, *which is a Dodge*, represents her life savings.

Did you notice that the sentences with *essential* clauses need no commas? But *the sentences with nonessential clauses require a pair of commas.* These commas act like tiny parentheses to set off extra material, which could be removed. To test whether or not a clause is essential, try covering it with your hand and reading the rest of the sentence. Does the basic meaning of the sentence change? If so, no commas are needed; the clause is essential. If the meaning does not change, set off the extra material (the nonessential clause) with commas.

DISTINGUISHING *WHO, WHOM, WHICH,* AND *THAT*

1. *That* is always used to indicate essential information. Sometimes *that* is omitted for the sake of conciseness if the meaning is clear. *That* can refer to people, animals, or things.
2. *Who* and *whom* refer only to people. *Which* can refer to animals or things. *Who, whom,* and *which* can introduce essential or nonessential clauses.

Adverb Clauses   Adverb clauses, like adverbs, tell *when, where, why, how,* or *under what conditions.* Adverb clauses begin with *subordinating conjunctions.* Some introduce reasons or explanations (*because, since, whereas, although*). After you learn to recognize the common subordinating conjunctions, you will be able to identify adverb clauses easily.

Common Subordinating Conjunctions

when	although	if	as	whether
while	even though	until	as long as	before
where	so that	unless	as though	than
since	because	as if	after	whenever

The adverb clause may come before or after the independent clause in a complex sentence. Let's look at two versions of a sentence with the dependent clause italicized:

- *When the big Doberman snarled,* I slammed the door.
- I slammed the door *when the big Doberman snarled.*

Which sentence do you prefer? Actually, the first sentence has two advantages: (1) the ideas appear in chronological order; (2) the word *I* appears in the middle of the sentence, where emphasis is minimized.

PUNCTUATING SENTENCES WITH ADVERB CLAUSES

1. **Introductory adverb clause.** When a long adverb clause (five words or more) appears at the beginning of a sentence, *place a comma after the clause.* If a misreading is possible, use a comma after a short clause.
2. **Concluding adverb clause.** When an adverb clause appears at the end, in a sequence of two events, no comma is needed.

PARALLELISM: A BALANCING ACT

Grammar rules decree that when two or more parts of a sentence are coordinated, they must be parallel. In other words, you place sentence parts of equal rank in the same grammatical form. Nouns are matched with nouns, active verbs with active verbs, passive verbs with passive verbs, and *be* verbs with *be* verbs. Phrases are matched with phrases, and clauses are matched with clauses. This balance is called *parallelism*.

Undoubtedly, you have used parallelism in your writing without realizing it. You may have chosen parallel forms because they sounded clear or right. Experienced writers use parallelism not only for clarity but also for balance and emphasis. Winston Churchill, John F. Kennedy, and other great speakers used parallelism frequently in their speeches. Kennedy's most famous words, "Ask not what your country can do for you; ask what you can do for your country," serve as a prime example.

As you revise, be alert for instances of faulty parallelism. The next few sections discuss situations where parallelism is required.

Parallelism with Items in a Series

Items in a series require balance, which is called *parallelism*. Regardless of whether the items are single words, phrases, or clauses, all must be parallel: Every item must be matched according to grammatical form.

Parallel Adjectives   In the following example, the three adjectives that follow the pronoun and end the sentence are not only parallel but also alliterative (all start with the same consonant sound of the letter *p*):

> Three factors in the Complainers' view of the world combine to convert useful problem solving into complaining. They find themselves *powerless, prescriptive,* and *perfect.*

—**Robert M. Bramson,** ***Coping with Difficult People***

A writer who was not paying attention to parallelism might have written "without power, prescriptive, and perfect."

Parallel Prepositional Phrases   Among the most famous examples of parallelism in the English language is Abraham Lincoln's statement in the "Gettysburg Address" that ". . . government of the people, by the people, and for the people shall not perish from the earth." Although Lincoln began all three phrases with a different preposition, they are still parallel. When the same preposition applies to all phrases in a series, it may be stated before every item or stated once at the beginning of the first phrase:

- I spend most of my time *at* work, *at* school, or *at* home.
- I spend most of my time *at* work, school, or home.

Parallel Subordinate Clauses   A famous sentence from the Declaration of Independence contains three parallel clauses: "We hold these truths to be self-evident, *that all men are created equal, that they are endowed by the Creator with certain unalienable Rights, that among these are Life, Liberty, and the pursuit of Happiness.*" (All the parallel clauses start with *that* and all contain the verb *are*.)

As you revise, make sure that all items in a series are parallel. Reading your writing aloud can help you to detect nonparallel structures. The final item in the following series is not parallel. Note how it can be corrected:

> **Not parallel:** I enjoy listening to music, taking long walks, and *also like to work crossword puzzles.*
>
> **Parallel:** I enjoy listening to music, taking long walks, and *working crossword puzzles.*

Parallelism with Items in Pairs

When a coordinating conjunction is used, the structures on each side should be balanced, although the degree of parallelism can vary. In *Coping with Difficult People*, Bramson often uses pairs of parallel nouns and verbs, as in the following examples:

Parallel Nouns   The slight variations in the second example make it less parallel:

- "It pays to follow up any *complaint* or *suggestion* with an inquiry about what's happened."
- "Your coping reply should be to ask, 'Is that a *decision* or just your *opinion* at this stage?'"

Parallel Verbs   Notice that to be parallel, verbs *must be the same tense, the same form, and the same voice*. Different tenses should not be mixed. One-word verbs should not be mixed with verb phrases. Passive voice should not be mixed with active voice. The italicized verbs below are parallel:

- The students *are protesting* parking fees and *are requesting* free parking. (Both verbs are present tense and active voice.)
- The students *protested* campus parking fees and *requested* free parking. (Both verbs are past tense, active voice.)

Parallel Phrases   Pairs of phrases in the same sentence should be balanced:

- *For richer or for poorer, in sickness* and *in health* (prepositional phrases)
- *To run a company profitably* and *to treat the environment responsibly* need not be conflicting goals. (infinitive phrases)

Parallelism with Comparisons

Comparisons formed by using *as* or *than* should be parallel: To balance, the two subjects being compared must have the same grammatical form:

- A *spelling check* (noun) is not as accurate as *careful proofreading* (noun).
- For most interviews, *wearing a suit* (gerund phrase) is safer than *wearing casual attire* (gerund phrase).

As you check your comparisons, look for faulty parallelism. Note how the imbalance in the first sentence below can be rectified in two ways:

Not Parallel: It is better *to do* (infinitive phrase) school work throughout a semester than *cramming* (gerund) the night before an exam.

Revised: It is better *to do* school work throughout a semester than *to cram* the night before an exam. (two infinitive phrases)

Revised: *Doing* school work throughout a semester is better than *cramming* the night before an exam. (two gerunds)

Parallelism with Correlative Conjunctions

Correlative conjunctions work in pairs to link words, phrases, or clauses. These conjunctions add grace and emphasis to a sentence by requiring parallel structure. Common correlative conjunctions include these five pairs:

either . . . or	neither . . . nor
not . . . but	not only . . . but also
both . . . and	

PUNCTUATING SENTENCES WITH PARALLEL STRUCTURES

SIMPLE SENTENCES

There is *no comma* before the final conjunction in a simple sentence. In the first set of examples, the parallel structures are italicized:

- The talk was both *interesting* and *inspirational.* (two adjectives)
- David has been outstanding not only *in football* but also *in academic work.* (two prepositional phrases)

COMPOUND SENTENCES

The main subjects and verbs in a compound sentence should be parallel. Note that the final correlative conjunction is preceded by a *comma.*

- *Not* everyone received a bonus, *but* everyone received a raise.
- *Either* he would pay the 96 parking tickets, *or* he would go to jail.

Correlatives need to be in the right place in a sentence to be logical and balanced. Place the correlative right *before* the word or phrase that it modifies:

Not parallel: *Either* you pay the fee for parking *or* a penalty.

Parallel: You pay *either* the parking fee *or* a penalty. (Each correlative precedes an article and a noun.)

Not parallel: *Not only* was the defendant charged with breaking and entering *but also* with resisting arrest.

Parallel: The defendant was charged *not only* with breaking and entering *but also* with resisting arrest. (Both of the correlatives precede a prepositional phrase.)

CHOPPING OUT DEADWOOD

Even the rough drafts of professional writers ramble and repeat. Although Ernest Hemingway's finished writing is sparse and clean, he worked long and hard to bring it to that state. Once Hemingway was questioned about how often he had revised the ending of his novel *A Farewell to Arms*. He said it had taken thirty-nine revisions for him to be satisfied. Revision is also a necessity for student writers, who often find deadwood in their papers. Some common sources of wordiness are discussed in the following sections.

References to Self

Self-confident persons sometimes refer to themselves often during conversation. In writing, however, this tendency should be monitored, lest it give the impression of an oversized ego. If *I* appears at the beginning of a sentence, the writer may be able to invert the sentence. Placing *I* in the middle of a sentence makes the reference to self less noticeable. Delete unnecessary words as long as there is no change in meaning:

Draft: I will graduate on June 12 and will be available for employment after that. (14 words)

Revised: After graduation, June 12, I will be available for employment. (10 words)

When a rough draft has two sequential sentences that begin with *I*, try to combine the sentences and delete one of the *I*'s as well as extra words. Then check the revision to be sure it is clear and complete.

Draft: I use Microsoft Word daily to write letters. I also use Quicken for other tasks. (15 words)

Revised: Daily I use Microsoft Word and Quicken. (7 words)

Still another way to bypass *I* is to substitute *me* or *my* when a reference to self seems necessary.

Draft: I can type accurately, answer the telephone courteously, and perform basic accounting functions, as you requested in your ad for a receptionist. (22 words)

Revised: My keyboarding skills, telephone etiquette training, and experience with accounts payable/receivable should qualify me for your position of receptionist. (20 words)

Instead of overusing first person singular, some people go to another extreme; they completely avoid *I, me, my,* or *mine.* They may resort to stilted phrases such as "the writer" or "the author of this paper." Experienced writers use *I* sensibly and sparingly.

Prepositional Phrases

Another source of wordiness may be unnecessary prepositional phrases in a sentence. If you find more than two prepositional phrases in a sentence, check for wordiness. Although using several prepositional phrases may not affect clarity, there may be a clearer, more concise way to make your point. Consider the following sentences before and after revision:

Draft: A new type of compact, the Stallion II by CMG, was rated the safest in recent collision tests of compacts. (19 words)

Revised: CMG's new Stallion II was rated safest in recent collision tests of compacts. (12 words)

Common phrases such as "this *type of* car" or "this *kind of* oven" or *"in the amount of $10"* may be shortened to "this car" or "this oven" or "$10."

Adjective Clauses

Sometimes there is little justification for an adjective clause, and the sentence can be made more effective by trimming the clause down to an appositive. Or you might substitute an adjective for an adjective clause. Consider the following examples:

Draft: Dr. Goldberg, *who has been our physician since I was a child,* is going to retire. (adjective clause)

Revised: Dr. Goldberg, *our long-time family physician,* is going to retire. (appositive)

Draft: My Appaloosa mare, *which is only two years old,* placed first in the "Best-Trained Horse" trials. (adjective clause)

Revised: My *two-year-old* Appaloosa mare placed first in the "Best-Trained Horse" trials. (adjective)

SENTENCE STYLE

The style of a sentence is influenced by the sentence pattern, the length of the sentence, and the position of the most important idea(s). In addition to the three major sentence patterns discussed earlier, you can use an occasional periodic sentence to provide interest and emphasis.

Periodic Sentences

A periodic sentence affords an opportunity to combine several related ideas into one grand sentence. This sentence pattern builds anticipation and suspense by presenting less important details before the major idea. This means that the major idea always appears just before the period. Although the subject may be placed early in the sentence, *the verb is always delayed*. Periodic sentences provide not only a refreshing change of pace, but also emphasis. Sometimes they are the ideal structure for a concluding sentence. James Herriot uses a periodic sentence at the end of his story "The Strychnine Episode at Darrowby":

> To me, the outbreak is a sad memory of failure and frustration. Fergus was my only cure. But over the years, when I saw the big dog striding majestically in his harness, leading his master unerringly around the streets of Darrowby, I always had one good feeling.

In the final sentence, Herriot builds to a climax, saying in one sentence what someone else might have said in three. Yet the periodic sentence is not an everyday sentence—it should be used for a significant idea. The next two examples of periodic sentences are taken from James Kelly's article "Rocky Mountain High":

- In Sandpoint, Idaho, a favorite refuge of disillusioned Californians, boutiques and craft shops flourish and stores sell wooden tubs for outdoor bathing.
- Of the eight states, Montana, Idaho, Wyoming, Nevada, Utah, Colorado, New Mexico and Arizona, which occupy 863,524 sq. mi., an area considerably bigger than all of Western Europe, Washington [the U.S. government] owns about 80% of the resources and nearly one-half of the land.

Sentence Length

Since Elizabethan times, sentences have been shrinking. In the 1600s the average sentence had about 45 words. One early English writer named Hakluyt actually wrote sentences that averaged 90.5 words. By Victorian times, the average sentence was down to 29 words. Now the average sentence length, according to Rudolph Flesch, is 17 words. ("Average" does not mean you should make every sentence the same length. Vary your sentences to produce variety and a change of pace.)

The length of a sentence is influenced by the kind of idea it houses. Brief sentences emphasize key ideas. Long sentences are like baskets, collecting several less important details. Each type has its place, but neither should be overused. Too many short sentences cause choppiness whereas too many long sentences interfere with clarity.

Position of Words within Sentences

Important words should be placed in *positions of emphasis*, either at the beginning or end of a sentence. Likewise, important sentences are usually placed at the beginning or end of a paragraph. The reader may skim over the middle. Ordinarily, the end position of a sentence or a paragraph carries more emphasis than the beginning; the middle carries the least of all. Of the three examples below, which one do you prefer? Why?

- Snatching a field mouse, the spotted owl swooped down, wings outstretched.
- The spotted owl swooped and snatched a field mouse.
- Swooping with outstretched wings, the spotted owl snatched a field mouse.

The first sentence is anticlimactic and the least interesting. The second sentence is an improvement because the events are in chronological order, and the major action is emphasized. In the third sentence, "swooping with outstretched wings" gives a vivid picture of the action.

Summary

The ability to style sentences that fit the rhetorical situation is the mark of a proficient writer.

Action verbs show movement. They can be written in either the active or passive voice. Usually, active voice is preferred because it is powerful and concise. *Be* verbs refer to a state of being or existing. Both the passive voice and *be* verbs lessen the impact of a sentence and frequently contribute to wordiness.

There are three basic sentence types: simple, compound, and complex. A simple sentence has one independent clause. A compound sentence has two independent clauses, which are equal in rank and parallel. A complex sentence has an independent clause and at least one dependent clause.

In a complex sentence, the dependent clause is either adjectival or adverbial. Adjective clauses begin with a relative pronoun. An essential adjective clause does not need commas. Nonessential clauses are set off by commas. Adverb clauses begin with subordinating conjunctions. A long introductory adverb clause is set off with a comma.

Coordinating conjunctions and correlative conjunctions link sentence elements of equal rank. These conjunctions require parallel structure. To be parallel, similar sentence elements must be in the same grammatical form. If not, the sentence will be unbalanced.

The time to trim wordiness is during revision. Too many references to self, unnecessary prepositional phrases, or other unneeded words slow down the pace of a sentence. Sometimes an adjective clause can be condensed to an appositive, or several ideas can be combined into a periodic sentence.

Sentence style is influenced by the sentence pattern, the length of the sentence, and the position of important ideas. The beginning and end of a sentence are the most prominent positions. For clarity, important ideas should appear in these emphatic positions. Short sentences highlight important ideas. Less important ideas can be combined into long sentences.

Key Terms

action verbs	compound sentence	parallelism
active voice	coordinating conjunction	passive voice
adjective clause	correlative conjunction	periodic sentence
adverb clause	dependent clause	prepositional phrase
be verbs	fragment	relative pronouns
comma splice	fused sentence	simple sentence
complex sentence	independent clause	subordinating conjunction

Test Yourself

Parallelism

Directions: Make the italicized segments parallel. You may have to delete. To check your answers, turn to the end of the chapter.

1. Peach orchards dot the south-central shore of Lake Erie in Ohio, but *grapes are grown* along the eastern shore in New York.
2. Ohio's principal crops are corn, soybeans, and *sometimes wheat is also grown*.
3. Raising soybeans is much more profitable than *to raise corn*.
4. To produce a pound of meat on chickens costs much less than *producing* a pound of meat on beef cattle.
5. Canola, which yields an edible oil, is grown more often than ordinary rape, *yielding a similar oil*.

Practice

Combining Sentences

Directions: Combine the choppy sentences into one well-balanced sentence. Delete any extra words. For help, refer to similar examples in this chapter.

1. Prewriting is the first stage of the writing process. Prewriting is a time of discovery. (*Tip:* Change the first sentence into an appositive and combine with the second.)

2. The subject of a periodic sentence may be placed early in the sentence. The verb is always delayed. (Make a compound sentence.)

3. Engineers and urban planners are designing new highway overpasses. Citizens are urging them to design overpasses that are graceful. They want attractive overpasses.

4. Four concrete bridges in Houston, Texas, were replaced. They were located in the museum district, spanning Route 59. They were replaced with arched bridges, outlined in fiber-optic tubing. (*Tip:* Put the two prepositional phrases referring to location first.)

5. Ohio communities are now consulted about even the color of paint for bridges. The community of Troy, Ohio, chose red to paint its bridge. This color was chosen to represent Troy's annual strawberry festival. (*Tip:* Is the first sentence really necessary?)

Test Yourself Answers

Parallelism

1. *Peach orchards dot the south-central shore of Lake Erie in Ohio, but* vineyards line *the eastern shore in New York. (or another verb)*

2. *Ohio's principal grain crops are soybeans, corn, and* wheat.

3. *Raising soybeans is much more profitable than* raising corn.

4. *To produce a pound of meat on chickens costs much less than* to produce *a pound of meat on beef cattle.*

5. *Canola, which yields an edible oil, is grown more often than ordinary rape,* which yields a similar oil.

CHAPTER 9

Editing: Improving Word Choice

Words play an enormous part in our lives. . . . Words have power to
[mold] . . . thinking. . . . Conduct and character are largely determined
by the nature of the words we currently use to discuss ourselves and the
world around us.

—Aldous Huxley

Selecting words is rather like shopping in an enormous supermarket. But instead of roaming the aisles for groceries, a writer thumbs through the pages of a dictionary or thesaurus or goes online to search for the right words. The supply is plentiful, for the English language has more words than any other language. Whether a writer wants plain bread-and-butter words, sweet words, tart words, tasteless words, kosher words, gourmet words, or playful words—they are all there for the taking, free of charge. Because there are so many words to choose from, a writer has countless opportunities to be creative, whether writing papers, letters, reports, poetry, or short stories. True, some writing offers more opportunities for creativity than expository writing does, but all rhetorical situations afford leeway in phrasing and sentence structure.

Reading widely and often will help you to become more aware of the nuances and subtle meanings of words. Frequent use of a good thesaurus and dictionary during revision will help you maintain an appropriate tone. Your awareness of the delicate distinctions in words will also increase as you study this chapter. Your skill in detecting inappropriate words and in selecting appropriate words will be honed. With regular practice, your writing will become more precise, positive, and appropriate for the rhetorical situation.

WORD MEANINGS: DENOTATION AND CONNOTATION

For years you have been looking up *denotations* in dictionaries. Denotations are the specific, literal meanings of words. If you look up the denotation of *horsecar* in *Merriam-Webster's New Collegiate Dictionary*, you will find it is "1: a streetcar drawn by horses [1833] 2: a car fitted for transporting horses."* Denotations seldom cause confusion when writers know a language well and take time to edit carefully. Denotations seldom change. When they do, the changes often take place over a century or more, as in the example above.

Connotative meanings are more difficult to pinpoint. *Connotations* are the hidden meanings beyond the denotation. These subjective meanings are imprecise associations, the emotional overtones attached to words. Our friends may agree with us on some connotations, but may disagree on others. A further complication is that connotations can change gradually or rather suddenly.

Culture, education, occupation, region, generation, and gender influence one's perception of connotative meanings. Men tend to use some words differently than women usually do. Individual differences also influence thought and style of expression. Thus connotations contribute not only to meaning but also to the tone of writing. Connotations may be positive or negative, depending on the perception of the audience.

NEGATIVE AND POSITIVE WORDS

A negative word or an inappropriate word can contaminate an entire message and cause readers to misunderstand. Or they may become so irritated they stop reading and distort the message. As a safeguard, never send an e-mail, note, memo, or letter without rereading and reconsidering your choice of words. When a situation is sensitive, take a day to mull over the best way to phrase the message.

Focusing on the Positive

During revision, the old adage "Tell them what you can do, not what you can't" is invaluable. Often an idea can be restated indirectly in positive words to soften unpleasant news, as in the examples below:

> **Negative:** We are *out* of the HP Cwi23T tri-color inkjet print cartridges. They will *not* be available for three days.

> **Positive:** The HP Cwi23T tri-color inkjet print cartridges *will* be here in three days.

> **Negative:** I *don't* have my paper finished. I had to work seven days last week.

> **Positive:** Professor James, although I worked seven days last week, I *do* have a typed draft. *May* I have another day to *polish?* Or would you *prefer* the rough draft now?

Courtesy words enhance the tone and effectiveness of messages, oral and written. For example, sprinkling courtesy words at the beginning and end of

---

*By permission. From *Merriam-Webster's Collegiate® Dictionary*, Tenth Edition © 1999 by Merriam-Webster, Inc.

e-mail, memos, and letters helps to create goodwill. Yet we sometimes overlook several positive words that could improve our messages:

advantage	courtesy	help	prompt
appreciate	encourage	invite	save
assistance	enjoy	may	succeed
benefit	glad	please	success
cooperation	gratitude	pleasure	thank you

Positive words tend to elicit pleasant responses whereas negative words risk offending. Some common offenders are found in the list below. The words in the "More Favorable" column will improve the tone of your writing.

IMPROVING YOUR CHOICE OF WORDS

Unfavorable	More Favorable
wrong	incorrect, inaccurate
omitted, forgot	overlooked
failed	missed
mistake	error
advice	suggestion, recommendation
complained	reported
claimed	stated
problem	concern, challenge
deal	bargain, offer, opportunity

If you're struggling to find a positive word, try looking up the negative word in a thesaurus and checking antonyms. Or if you have reason to state a negative idea directly, then you can soften the impact somewhat by using a negative prefix. There are nine common negative prefixes: *non-, un-, im-, in-, dis-, il-, ir-, a-, ab-*. All enable a writer to delete *not*. For example, instead of *not perfect*, you might say *imperfect* or *irregular*.

Do Euphemisms Have a Place?

For the sake of politeness, indirectness and euphemisms are sometimes advisable. Euphemisms are words with overly favorable connotations. Euphemisms are often substituted for unpleasant words, words that might offend or cause pain. For example, the manager who bluntly evaluates work as "poor" or "sloppy" will undermine morale and productivity. But the manager who allows the employee

PEANUTS reprinted by permission of United Feature Syndicate, Inc.

to save face with a euphemism such as "needs to improve" or "can do better" and who encourages with constructive suggestions will have a better chance of motivating. If a euphemism is needed in a touchy situation, that is fine—as long as there is no deception. There is a big difference between tact and deceit.

Over the years, as words lose their favorable connotations, new euphemisms are coined. For example, dealers once sold "used" cars. Later the cars were referred to as "secondhand," but now they are referred to as "pre-owned" or "previously owned." In the 1940s the person who cleaned, maintained the plumbing, and tended the heating system was a "janitor." In the 1960s he or she became a "custodian." In this decade the same job may carry the title of "maintenance engineer."

Connotations of a word can change, becoming either negative or positive. For example, "Dear Madam" was once a polite salutation for a business letter. Now hopelessly outdated, the term is marred by negative connotations. In contrast, the term "Ms." was unpopular in the 1970s, but is now widely accepted in the United States as a polite form of direct address. Along with the acceptance of "Ms." has come a new awareness of sexist language.

INCLUSIVE LANGUAGE

Just as society and culture change, so too does language. One of the biggest changes in the United States in the last forty years has been the recognition that women have the same legal rights that men do. With this legislation has come the idea that language should reflect equality by being gender-free or gender-neutral.

Replacing Sexist Terms with Gender-Free Terms

The Civil Rights Act of 1964 forced the U.S. Department of Labor to revise its *Dictionary of Occupational Titles* to eliminate sexist and ageist terms. Likewise, the Bureau of the Census modified 52 of the 442 categories of work. Newspapers have even changed column titles of advertisements from "Help Wanted—Male" and "Help Wanted—Female" to one column titled "Help Wanted."

Some words carry sexist overtones because they contain the root *man: fire-man, policeman, mailman.* But these forms are gradually being dropped in favor of gender-free counterparts such as firefighter, police officer, and mail carrier. The following list gives other outmoded words and their updated counterparts.

REPLACING SEXIST TERMS

Sexist	*Nonsexist*
man, men (if applied to both sexes)	person, people
average man	average person
chairman	chair, chairperson
male nurse	nurse
girl, gal, chick	woman (adult)
man and wife	husband and wife

Although masculine nouns and pronouns (*he, his, him*) were used for centuries to include women, this usage is also outmoded. One way to avoid this faux pas is by writing in the plural—for example, "players . . . they." But the plural is not always possible. Then one "he or she" or one "his or her" is relatively unobtrusive. Often the best and simplest way is to use gender-neutral words, omitting any reference to gender.

Plural: The *deans* are to bring *their* projected department budgets.

Gender-specific: Every dean should bring *his* projected department budget. (Correct only if all deans are male.)

Gender-free: Every dean should bring *a* projected department budget.

Replacing Offensive Terms with Respectful Terms

An August 2000 survey of U.S. postal workers reported that 43 percent said they had been "cursed at in the workplace." In some other high-stress jobs, crude and disrespectful language is not uncommon. As a result some companies are formulating language codes of ethics. One policy forbids "unwanted, deliberate, repeated, unsolicited profanity, cussing, swearing, insulting, abusive or crude language." Penalties may include counseling or firing, depending on the case.*

Other words discriminate and disrespect on the basis of race/ethnicity, religion, skin color, or other factors. Although some words may not actually be discriminatory, they may be unwise in terms of politeness and the law. While the

---

*Rachel Emma Silverman, "On-the-Job Cursing: Obscene Talk Is Latest Target of Workplace Ban," *Wall Street Journal* 8 May 2001: B14.

definition of verbal harassment varies, we need to be especially careful when mentioning personal attributes, such as body parts, size, attractiveness, ethnicity, and skin color.

The purpose here is to alert you to rapidly changing usage. According to dictionaries and the media, the present usage shown below is current. Probably the best advice is to notice the accepted usage in your geographical area. If you are unsure, the following list can serve as a guide.

REPLACING OFFENSIVE TERMS

Past	*Present*
Indian	Native American, American Indian
Latin	Hispanic American
	Latino/Latina American
	Mexican American, chicano/chicana
Asiatic, oriental	Asian, or specific designations such as Chinese American
colored	person of color
Negro	African American or Black
Anglo-Saxon	European American
	Anglo-American
	White

TECHNICAL JARGON

Technical jargon is the professional or formal language of a trade, profession, or similar group. For example, medical jargon is used daily by pharmacists, physicians, nurses, and technicians. Technical jargon among peers rarely causes problems. But when a message is intended for a layperson, unfamiliar jargon may make the message unclear. At times the resulting confusion could be dangerous.

Perhaps you are wondering when technical jargon is appropriate. The answer seems to hinge upon two questions:

- Can the language be understood by the intended audience?
- Does the language serve a technical purpose?

If the answer to both questions is yes, then use technical jargon, for it does have a valid purpose.

AVOIDING JARGON

Although a brand of hydrocortisone cream is intended for use by the general public, it carries this warning: "For dermatological use only. Not for ophthalmic use." The message would have been much clearer if it had said: "Apply to the skin only. Do not use near or in the eyes."

TRITE LANGUAGE AND CLICHÉS

In everyday casual greetings and small talk, we often hear the same familiar words. Trite, overworked phrases such as the following echo in our ears daily:

richly rewarding	last but not least	in this day and age
each and every	tip of the iceberg	tell you in a heartbeat
to the tune of	ballpark figure	never meets a stranger

Other overused and misused words are *a lot* and *get*. Although *a lot* is frequently heard, it is informal. "Alot" is a common misspelling. Instead, you can use a synonym such as *many, much, several, various, some,* or *considerable*. The word *get* has numerous informal meanings that are unsuitable for college writing, for example, "got married." Say "were married."

Why risk boring or antagonizing the reader with repetitive or outworn words and phrases when fresh ones can be located easily? As you search for suitable words, beware of clichés. Like favorite recordings, clichés become worn from overuse. Although they were once original, clichés have become familiar—now they are ingrained in our daily language. Many of William Shakespeare's brilliantly descriptive lines, written four hundred years ago, are now clichés. How many of the following have you used?

Famous Lines	*Source*
The naked truth	*Love's Labour's Lost*, 5.2.715
Out of the jaws of death	*All's Well That Ends Well*, 3.1.396
A dish fit for the gods	*Julius Caesar*, 1.1.173
Parting is such sweet sorrow	*Romeo and Juliet*, 2.2.184

Perhaps you are familiar with other clichés such as "fresh as a daisy," "happy as a lark," "solid as a rock," or "his bark is worse than his bite." For most conversations and some informal writing, a cliché now and then may be acceptable. In academic and professional situations, however, clichés do not belong except when used creatively for a reason.

MAKING THE MESSAGE CLEAR AND APPROPRIATE

Heads of state are expected, even when speaking informally, to have an excellent command of language. Abraham Lincoln's ready wit and John F. Kennedy's apt rejoinders served them well during casual conversation and interviews. But George Bush, Sr., was not so gifted. For instance, during the Gulf War, the former president habitually used the phrase "the Saddam thing." This careless habit not only trivialized the subject, but also undercut his effectiveness and professional image.

As you examine your written words, read them aloud so that you can hear how they sound. Are they clear and appropriate? Consider the occasion. Who is the audience? What sort of language will they expect? How well you fulfill those expectations will influence not only the clarity and success of your message but also your credibility as a writer.

Making Abstractions Concrete

Thing is a shapeless blob of a word, for it is purely abstract. *Thing* can refer to a monster or a gnat, a flask of poison or a glass of buttermilk, a viper or a star. *Thing* can mean a condition, quality, vegetable, animal, mineral—or any bit of matter on or off this planet. In recent years, *stuff* has also been overused. *Stuff* is an elastic word—frequently used as slang to refer to objects, talk, or actions. ("I picked up some stuff"; "Don't give me that stuff about being too busy.") *Thing* and *stuff* often serve as substitutes for thinking. Shrewd speakers and writers tend to shun these words and limit their use of abstractions.

Abstractions are general words that identify categories, qualities, or ideas. Some abstractions refer to the intangible—concepts undetectable through the senses, such as *honesty, patriotism, fear,* and *courage.* Certainly, these broad terms have their place, but using unexplained abstractions or too many without concrete examples makes language vague and unclear.

Words that represent tangible qualities, objects, or activities are said to be *concrete.* Concrete words describe details that can be perceived through one or more of the five senses. You can see the delicate perfection of a purple crocus, the luminous rings of a lunar eclipse, and the muted hues of a rainbow. You can hear the whir of a hummingbird's wings or the thump of a human heart. You can smell the fragrance of honeysuckle or the pungent odor of an annoyed skunk. You can touch the fur of a baby rabbit or feel the grit of sandpaper. You can taste the sweetness of raspberry jam or the piquancy of horseradish. Concrete words stimulate the imagination and evoke vivid imagery.

As you revise, look particularly for abstract adjectives (*beautiful, terrible, impressive, delicious, unpleasant,* and the like) that can be replaced by concrete sensory words. Because some topics such as sunsets and love have been so popular, it is difficult to find a fresh way to describe them. In that case, you might choose another topic or devise an unusual comparison that uses concrete imagery.

Questions to Find Concrete Words

1. How did *X* look? Size? Shape? Color? Length of hair/coat?
2. Does *X* make a sound? Volume? Rate? Pitch?
3. How does *X* feel? Texture?
4. Does *X* have a fragrance or odor? Pungent? Faint? Pleasant?
5. If *X* is edible, how does it taste? Sweet? Sour? Tangy? Acid? How does it feel on the tongue?

Moving from General to Specific

If your friend tells you she purchased a new car, you have no mental image of the car. To obtain further information, you might ask, "What kind?" She may respond with "a Buick." And so the conversation continues until you learn she has purchased a dark-red, two-door Buick Regal Limited. Although the word *car* is concrete, it is general, lacking descriptive information.

Likewise, other general terms such as *cat, dog,* or *horse* tell very little about a specific animal. For example, do you mean a lion or a domesticated cat? If you mean the latter, is the cat a mixed breed or registered breed? A barn cat or a house pet? Male or female? What age, size, and color is it? Writers need to be specific so that the reader comprehends quickly. Normally, a specific word or phrase is more appropriate than a general word as long as you don't drench the reader with nonessential details.

In the sentences below, note the differences in the effects of general words and specific words:

General: A *dog* went into a *building* and lay down in a *room*.

Specific: A *Dalmation* entered the side door of the *brick firehouse* and stretched out in a corner of the *kitchen*.

General: *Walking* is a good way to enjoy the *wonder of nature*.

Specific: *Hiking* in Sandy Cove Park is a good way to enjoy the *brilliance of an Indiana autumn*.

SCHOLARLY OR EVERYDAY WORDS?

A woman went up to Adlai Stevenson after a speech. Enthusiastically, she said, "Oh, Mr. Stevenson, I think your speech was absolutely superfluous!"

He replied, "Thank you. I think I shall have it published—posthumously."

"Fine!" she said. "The sooner, the better."

Leafing through a thesaurus, some students select scholarly or other unfamiliar words without consulting a dictionary. The results may be disastrous or unintentionally amusing. Even if used correctly, words may be inappropriate for a piece of writing. Novelist Kurt Vonnegut says, "Simplicity of language is not only reputable but perhaps even sacred. The Bible opens with a sentence well within the writing skills of a lively fourteen-year-old: 'In the beginning God created the heavens and the earth.'" Vonnegut recommends simplicity for most writing.

Lewis Thomas, an editor, physician, and contributor to the *New England Journal of Medicine,* used simple language to explain a complicated process in his book *The Lives of a Cell:*

> Everything in the world dies, but we know about it [only] as a kind of abstraction. If you stand in a meadow, at the edge of a hillside, and look around carefully, almost everything you can catch sight of is in the process of dying, and most things will be dead long before you are. If it were not for the constant renewal and replacement going on before your eyes, the whole place would turn to stone and sand under your feet.
>
> There are some creatures that do not seem to die at all; they simply vanish totally into their own progeny. Single cells do this. The cell becomes two, then four, and so on, and after a while the last trace is gone. It cannot be seen as death; barring mutation, the descendants are simply the first cell, living all over again. . . .

Since Thomas is writing for a lay audience, he is careful to select words they will understand. He begins with a statement about death and relates it to his readers. Then he compares the familiar process of death to that of cell division, which is unfamiliar. Because he supports the abstractions with concrete examples, the result is beautifully clear. For most college writing, don't use a long, obscure word when a short, familiar one will do.

As you examine your word choice for college writing, consider how your audience might perceive the message, then revise accordingly. After any revision, reread each sentence to be sure that it says what you mean. Don't use a long word when a short word will do, but do not sacrifice meaning for conciseness. Clarity should remain top priority.

FOR YOUR REFERENCE:
ESSAYS ON LANGUAGE USE IN THE READER

- "Dawn Watch," John Ciardi, page 579
- "Mother Tongue," Amy Tan, page 643
- "The Handicap of Definition," William Raspberry, page 659

Summary

A good command of language makes a positive, lasting impression. Being keenly aware that words have both denotative and connotative meanings can help you improve your word choice. Denotations are the literal, precise meanings that are always defined in the dictionary. Denotations seldom cause confusion.

Connotations are the emotional overtones, the hidden meanings that people attach to words. Negative connotations sometimes interfere with a message because people tend to add meanings. Negative connotations may cause misunderstanding and rupture relationships. Therefore it is important to choose specific words free from undesirable connotations. Positive words improve the tone of writing. Selecting positive words and de-emphasizing negative words is an essential part of diplomatic communication. Euphemisms have a place in communication as long as they do not mislead or deceive.

Sexist language contains gender references with negative connotations. Sexism can be avoided by writing in the plural, by using one unobtrusive *he or she*, and by using gender-neutral language. Other taboo terms referring to ethnicity, religion, skin color, or other personal characteristics should be avoided. Outdated terms can be offensive; instead, use current terms.

Technical jargon should be tailored to the audience. Clichés were once fresh and original, but they have become stale from overuse. Trite, outworn language is unsuitable for most writing in the workplace and in the classroom.

Abstract words may cause misunderstanding when unexplained. *Thing* is the most abstract word of all. *Thing, stuff,* and other vague abstractions should be avoided in writing. Concrete words and examples clarify abstract concepts and provide interest. Simple words are usually preferable to scholarly words. Accurate, precise word choice is necessary to communicate. Don't sacrifice clarity for conciseness.

Key Terms

abstract words	denotation	sexist, sexism
cliché	euphemism	technical jargon
concrete words	gender-free	trite
connotation	gender-neutral	

Test Yourself

Can You Find the Concrete Terms?

Directions: Underline the concrete words in the following excerpt from "Living Like Weasels," by Annie Dillard. Then check your answer against the key at the end of the chapter.

Weasel! I'd never seen one wild before. He was ten inches long, thin as a curve, a muscled ribbon, brown as fruitwood, soft-furred, alert. His face was fierce, small and pointed as a lizard's; he would have made a good arrowhead. There was just a dot of chin, maybe two brown hair's worth, and the pure white fur began that spread down his underside. He had two black eyes I didn't see, any more than you see a window.

Practice

Collaborative Learning: Negative Connotations

Directions: Pretend you have had a mild disagreement with a family member. Later you overhear the person describing the exchange. Which terms below would you dislike? Which would be acceptable? Do your group members agree or disagree? If so, why? (Consult a dictionary if you wish.)

dispute	quarrel	fracas	brawl
bicker	scrap	controversy	altercation
squabble	fight	conflict	hassle
spat	difficulty	argument	beef
tiff	row	disagreement	feud

Write a Description Using Concrete Words

Directions: In one paragraph, write a description. Give concrete details and examples. If you wish, describe one of the following topics:

1. The footwear you are wearing
2. A "white elephant" in your home
3. A vehicle you use or have used
4. A favorite hideaway
5. A family heirloom

Test Yourself Answer

Weasel! I'd never seen one wild before. He was <u>ten inches long, thin as a curve, a muscled ribbon, brown as fruitwood, soft-furred,</u> alert. His <u>face</u> was fierce, <u>small and pointed as a lizard's;</u> he would have made a good <u>arrowhead.</u> There was just <u>a dot of chin,</u> maybe <u>two brown hairs'</u> worth, and the pure <u>white fur</u> began that spread down his <u>underside.</u> He had <u>two black eyes</u> I didn't see, any more than you see a <u>window.</u>

—**Annie Dillard, "Living Like Weasels"**

Options for Organization

Part 3

CHAPTER 10

Narration

Recounting Events

A story has the uncanny ability to raise the spirit out of the flesh like bread rising yeasty in a warm place.

—Thomas Moore, "Introduction"
Best Spiritual Writing 2000

Narration is used not only in fiction writing but also to relay news of a neighborhood or news of a nation, to share research data, to write reports and other documents. Histories, biographies, journals, college papers, magazines, and even advertisements include narratives. Narration is a powerful tool that can captivate an audience—stirring the imagination, eliciting empathy, and lending weight to opinion. This chapter explains techniques of narration, which have a wide range of practical uses.

PURPOSE OF NARRATION

An effective narrative recounts action for a purpose. If the purpose is to entertain and establish camaraderie, then it may not matter whether the account is fiction or fact. But when the purpose is serious—primarily to reflect, inform, or persuade—then the audience expects facts and should receive them. The writer is obligated to put forth the truth.

Narration may be used as a major or minor writing strategy. If major, then the action is most important. For example, medical personnel write reports of patients' progress. Managers keep brief histories of employees' performance. Law enforcement officers write narratives of events prior to an arrest. Although these records may include description as support, narration is the major strategy.

In this chapter the major mode is narration, but examples of mixed strategies are also provided. In the following case study, narration is the major strategy. The case is based on a real incident; it shows how writing can grow out of an actual situation.

WORKPLACE CASE STUDY

SPENCER'S LETTER

One afternoon in his office, Spencer leafed through a singles magazine and paused to read the personal ads in the back pages. One, signed "Golden Girl," sounded tantalizing. He typed up a one-page letter on the office computer, placed it in a company envelope with the printed logo. After writing his name above the company name, he addressed the letter to Golden Girl at Box 312. He attached his own stamp. That evening on the way home, he dropped the letter into a mailbox.

Several days later the letter was returned to the company, but not to Spencer. On the outside of the envelope, the post office had stamped: "Moved. Left no forwarding address." As Spencer's supervisor sorted through a newly arrived pile of mail, he noticed the company envelope and the unusual name of the addressee. He opened and read the letter. The vulgar language and sexual content surprised him.

ACTIVITY

Assume the role of supervisor. You have interviewed Spencer and gained his account of what happened (first paragraph). Write up a brief narrative of the incident in your own words and explain how it affects the company. Make a recommendation for (minor) disciplinary action.

In college you may write narratives not only in English, business, and technical writing classes but also in anthropology, sociology, law enforcement, pre-law, engineering, and other classes.

ELEMENTS OF NARRATION

Every narrative has six basic elements—the *who, where, when, what, why,* and *how* of the event. The point of view from which the story is told also influences its effect on the audience. Who was involved? Where did the action take place? When? What happened? How did it happen? Why did it happen? Who is the narrator? The first four questions come early and easily when the writer sets the scene, giving the necessary background. After that the telling becomes more difficult.

The Why

The *why* of a narrative is the cause or reason or motivation that propels the action. This element may not become entirely clear until you are heavily into revision and reexamining the facts. To explore the *why*, you might ask yourself these questions:

- What set off the chain of events? What or who initiated the action?
- How did the central character react?
- What motivated her or him?
- How did relationships and connections influence events?

Point of View in Narration

Who tells the story and how it is told influences its credibility. Is the writer/ narrator giving a firsthand account or describing it secondhand? How reliable is the narrator? How objective? From which attitude or angle does the narrator regard the subject? The point of view shapes a narrative and influences its reception by the audience.

First-Person Narration   A writer may tell a story from either a first-person or a third-person point of view, depending on the rhetorical situation and the purpose. Whether or not you choose first person (*I, me, my, mine, we,* or *ours*) will depend upon your role. Is it your story or someone else's? Either way, first-person narration will lend a sense of immediacy, giving the reader a front-row seat on the action.

In first-person narration, an observer or a participant tells the story. This eyewitness account is often written in a conversational tone. First-person point of view works well in journals, autobiographies, and personal essays. Barb Bronson uses first person in her essay. The first three paragraphs appear here.

Clipper Ship Mom

Unique and truly American, the clipper ship is a fast-sailing cargo ship whose shipmaster's talents have never been surpassed. My mother reminds me of those early ships and courageous sailors. Whenever the open sea of marriage gave warning of an approaching storm, Clipper Ship Mom would batten down the hatches and set her course in preparation for the rough voyage ahead. As a child, I watched helplessly as Clipper Ship Mom sailed to a hell where my father resided as gatekeeper.

Even when my father was sober, his behavior was unpredictable. Petty, trivial incidents would arouse his raging temper. But whenever he had too many drinks, it was like coming face to face with Satan himself. So many times I wished Mom would take us away to some safe place where we could hide. I also knew Mom had been taught to honor her marriage vows—for better or worse.

When I was fourteen I awoke to an argument which led to my father's yanking my mother to the front yard in her nightclothes and placing a gun to her temple as her five children watched. He told us to say goodbye to our mother; she was going to "meet her maker." Frozen with fear, we clung to each other as tears streamed down our faces. Looking to the heavens above, I whispered a prayer for God to spare her life. He must have heard the prayer, for after a while Dad calmed down and we all went back to bed.

Mixing Writing Strategies   In this excerpt from "Clipper Ship Mom," Barb Bronson mixes strategies. She supports her thesis with comparison, description, and narration. Comparison begins in the title, "Clipper Ship Mom"; continues through the first paragraph; and reappears in the conclusion (see chapter 13). The second paragraph describes and summarizes the problem. The third paragraph narrates an episode.

Third-Person Narration   Writers or narrators who are not involved in a story adopt a third-person point of view. They restrict pronouns to words such as *he, she, it, they,* and *them.* Third-person narration puts distance between the reader and the topic, producing a more detached voice than first person provides. A professional response, such as those found in many business and technical reports or research papers, usually requires third-person point of view. There the goal is to focus on facts and results, not on feelings or opinion. Reporters, biographers, and historians use third person in an objective way for various reasons.

The following third-person narrative recounts a disastrous 1981 accident at the Hyatt Regency Hotel in Kansas City. Think how differently a narrative of the accident by a first-person survivor would have sounded.

> At 7:05 P.M. on Friday, July 17, 1981, the atrium was filled with more than sixteen hundred people, most of them dancing to the music of a well-known band for a tea dance competition, when suddenly a frightening, sharp sound like a thunderbolt was heard, stopping the dancers in mid-step. Looking up toward the source of the sound, they saw two groups of people on the second- and fourth-floor walkways, observing the festivities and stomping in rhythm with the music. As the two walkways began to fall, the observers were seen holding on to the railing with terrified expressions on their faces. The fourth-floor walkway dropped from the hangers holding it to the roof structure, leaving the hangers dangling like impotent stalactites. Since the second-floor walkway hung from the fourth-floor walkway, the two began to fall together. There was a large roar as the concrete decks of the steel-framed walkways cracked and crashed down, in a billowing cloud of dust, on the crowd gathered around the bar below the second-floor walkway. People were screaming; the west glass wall adjacent to the walkways shattered, sending shards flying over 100 ft. (30 m); pipes broken by the falling walkways sent jets of water spraying the atrium floor. It was a nightmare the survivors would never forget.

> —Matthys Levy and Mario Salvadori
> ***Why Buildings Fall Down***

There may be a time when you decide to write in third person about your experience. Perhaps the topic is still hurtful, even heartrending. To gain distance and objectivity, you might write in third-person about yourself, perhaps using a pseudonym. But first consider the nature of the experience. If a recent event has been traumatic, beware. You can become so entangled in emotion that you hit a writing block and lose the point.

WRITING A NARRATIVE PAPER

You have a treasure trove of stories just waiting to be told, some sad, some happy. Perhaps they are family stories, passed down from generation to generation. Prewriting will help you find them. Mull over the episode and consider:

- How did the experience influence me? Am I happier? Wiser? How so?
- What did I gain or learn? Can I find a lesson or moral?
- How might the narrative affect the audience?

Prewriting

The simplest way to start prewriting is to list key events in the order they occurred. Leave two inches or so of space between items to insert related details. After listing key events, jot down significant details about each one. Asking questions can guide you:

- What is the purpose of the narrative?
- Who are the readers? How much do they need to know?
- Does the experience remind me of an event in the public eye? How?
- Is the comparison relevant to my purpose?
- What is the source of tension or conflict? (barrier, problem, decision)

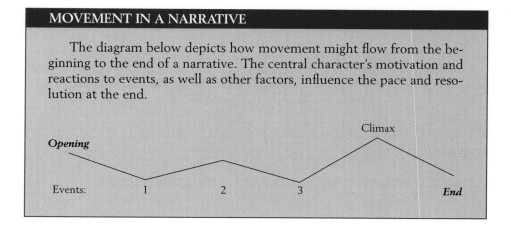

MOVEMENT IN A NARRATIVE

The diagram below depicts how movement might flow from the beginning to the end of a narrative. The central character's motivation and reactions to events, as well as other factors, influence the pace and resolution at the end.

Drafting an Introduction

The purpose of the narrative will guide you in deciding whether to place the thesis at the beginning or end. Does the reader need to know immediately where the main idea is headed? For reasons of clarity and practicality, some rhetorical situations call for an early thesis. Other times the writer may delay the thesis, *laying a foundation to support the point of the narrative* and building to the peak of the action. Then the thesis comes at the end, where it can be stated or implied, depending upon the purpose. To begin a narrative, you may find these questions helpful:

- Where is the best spot to start?
- Should the story be told in first person or third?
- What tone is appropriate?
- What is the source of tension or conflict? (barrier, problem, decision)

The opening usually sets the stage for action. In other words, you identify the central person or character, place, and time. As the action starts rolling, description is usually sparse. Only essential details are shown. Gradually, necessary bits of background appear and conflict or suspense develops.

Opening with Action   To create interest, successful writers often open with an action, weaving in brief glimpses of background as the story proceeds. An *action opening* plunges the reader into a story with no unnecessary details or explanations. Right away the main person or character is faced with a decision or immersed in a predicament that must somehow be resolved. (See "Just a Walk" at the end of the chapter.) Other types of openings reveal the action, problem, or conflict gradually.

Opening with a Quotation   If you find an appropriate quotation that *specifically* relates to your main idea, then you can easily tie it to the beginning of a narrative. Be sure that any explanation does not delay the action unduly. Do not belabor the point of the quotation lest the reader perceive it as talking down. If you want to use a quotation that relates in a *general* way to your main idea, then you may have to look long and hard to connect it adequately.

See chapter 16.

Opening with a Comparison   An unusual comparison in the title or first paragraph can hook the reader and serve as a unifying thread throughout the narrative. An effective comparison is introduced early and alluded to periodically. Sometimes a comparison may involve a symbol rich in connotations; consider the opening paragraph of "Clipper Ship Mom," at the beginning of this chapter. Along with this striking symbol, the writer used water imagery: matrimonial seas, rough seas, tears, and similar images in developing her paper.

Organizing a Narrative Paper

Narratives need a clear progression. Each event, detail, and section of dialogue should advance the narrative point and contribute to the unity. If you can limit the focus early, then it will be easier to decide what to include—and what to omit. Or if the white heat of inspiration seizes you, write down everything, then go back and delete extra details, no matter how interesting. Make sure that every detail helps to establish a coherent design.

In most narratives the action is presented in the order that it occurs. Sometimes, however, a writer may disrupt the chronology by a sudden shift to the past, or *flashback*. For example, you might begin a narrative at a dramatic moment near its chronological conclusion, then flash back to events leading up to this point. Keep in mind, though, that flashbacks are tricky to manage effectively because of the special transition and plotting required. As a novice writer of narrative, you may want to stick to chronological order.

Developing the Narrative Paper

As you develop a narrative, keep in mind the nature of the central character. It is usually advisable to look at people and events from a positive perspective but be realistic. Human beings are a mix of negative and positive traits, and life is a blend of potholes, porcupines, and poppies. The following questions may be helpful to consider:

- Does the main character have a need or compulsion to reach a goal?
- Does the person have an internal or external conflict? A barrier to face?
- What is the person going to do?
- What is the darkest moment—the crisis? (It usually occurs about halfway.)
- How does the central character react?
- Does the person change or learn?

Dialogue   Selected dialogue can enliven a narrative, advance the action, and give clues to the personality of the speaker. It should have the ring of real conversation but move more quickly. Actual conversation often ambles along, backtracks, circles, and pauses. To create realism, copy the way a person talks, perhaps using slang or fragments. Or clip excerpts from actual conversation and shape them into dialogue for your narrative purpose.

When writing dialogue, minimize the use of "he said" and "she said." As long as the identity of the person who is talking is clear, no other identification is needed. Just indent for a new paragraph with each new speaker, no matter how short the exchange is. Set off the dialogue with quotation marks. (See "The Mulberry Tree" on page 132 in this chapter.)

Concrete Details and Action Verbs   The trick to writing an effective narrative is to keep it interesting. Include enough *concrete details* of the setting and action to give life to the story, enabling readers to visualize events and feel as if they know the people involved. Use strong action verbs, specific nouns, and modifiers that will appeal to your readers' senses not only of sight but also of hearing, touch, taste, and smell. But beware of including unnecessary description that may be distracting or boring.

Building Suspense   Another way to keep readers interested is to build *suspense*. You can do this by hinting at something but withholding crucial details in order to reveal them at a strategic moment. You can also build tension by pacing your narrative so that readers are kept wondering what will happen next. By the end, however, all loose threads should be clearly connected and the conflict or problem resolved. This technique is not applicable to most workplace writing.

Writing a Conclusion

Although endings of narratives vary widely, every ending should have a sense of completeness. It should leave readers satisfied, convinced, empathetic, hopeful, amused, thoughtful, or wiser. Usually, the complication, problem, or conflict is resolved at the end. To resolve matters successfully, the writer must tell enough but not too much. If an ending is too long and wordy, it may become tiresome or confusing. Underdeveloped endings may leave readers feeling frustrated or cheated. Readers should not be left hanging without a clue to what happened.

Ending with a Hint or a Hope   Even if the full story remains untold or the conflict is not resolved, there should be a clue so that readers can draw their own inferences. For example, in *Gone with the Wind*, Rhett is leaving Scarlett, and she is agonizing over his departure. Yet the reader is offered a hint and a hope that life will get better. The novel closes with these words:

> She could get Rhett back. She knew she could. There had never been a man she couldn't get, once she set her mind upon him.
> "I'll think of it all tomorrow, at Tara. I can stand it then. Tomorrow I'll think of some way to get him back. After all, tomorrow is another day."

Ending with a Surprise   An unusual incident or twist may bring a story to a satisfying close. The surprise ending contains something the reader does not expect. The surprise may be amusing, embarrassing, enlightening, romantic, or dramatic as long as it is appropriate. To be effective, the unexpected event should grow out of the action, problem, or conflict. For example, Shasta Scharf used a surprise ending that sprang from a key event in "Just a Walk" (at the end of the chapter).

Ending with a Reaction   Sometimes a narrative ends with a brief *reaction*, a focused response or thoughtful commentary. The reaction may mention influences, implications, or consequences of the action. There may be an attempt to explain an underlying motive. Columnists, biographers, historians, novelists, and other writers often explore motives that may have precipitated an event. Or the reaction ending may connect a personal experience to one with universal implications, as in "The Mulberry Tree" later in this chapter.

Writing the ending of a narrative may require painstaking effort. In fact, you may attempt more than one conclusion before finally being satisfied. If in doubt about your ending, try asking these questions:

- What is my narrative point?
- Was there an unexpected result?
- Are there any loose ends to resolve?
- Does the voice of the narrator sound appropriate?
- Does the ending seem complete?

See endings in chapter 4.

Spend time in thought and on revision. The spot where you stop should seem just right, even if it means omitting pet details.

WRITING A NARRATIVE REPORT

A narrative report is written in response to the need for a record of a real situation or event. Before starting to write any report, consider the *purpose* and the *audience.* Why is the report needed? To whom is it directed? Will one person or several read the report? Might it become a public record? Considering these questions will help you judge the amount of detail needed, the level of language expected, and the degree of privacy involved.

Unlike personal narratives and fiction, a narrative report always has *a thesis at the beginning.* Reports do not withhold information to build suspense. In the workplace, the reader immediately needs to know the *purpose and scope,* which is the usual heading of the first section. This section tells why the report is being written and the range it will cover.

The body of a report also has a suitable heading. This major section explains the topic. The conclusion (use a heading) may summarize, recommend, or look to the future. For instance, research reports sometimes mention a need for future research. (See "How Research Papers and Research Reports Differ" in chapter 22. An example of a report appears at the end of that chapter.)

REVISING A NARRATIVE

When revising a narrative, look at the larger items first. Check the shape of the story. Is the setting clear? Does the action flow well, or should some events be rearranged? Is the direction clear, or are more transitions of time and place needed?

Watch for complicated sentences or cumbersome words that slow the pace unnecessarily. When the action is fast-paced, use short sentences. When movement slows, use longer sentences, combining ideas, to reflect the pace (like this one). The checklist that follows will also help you revise.

CHECKLIST: REVISING A NARRATIVE

1. Does the narrative begin at a significant spot?
2. Is the complication, conflict, or problem clear?
3. Is the action arranged in the most effective order?
4. Do major details advance the point of the narrative? Do minor details clearly relate?
5. Does the pace of sentences reflect what is happening?
6. Does the ending give a sense of completion?

TWO STUDENT PAPERS: NARRATION

In the first paper Betty Russell briefly sets the scene before her story starts to unfold. The point of her story appears at the end.

The Mulberry Tree

Mr. Grump's mulberries were big, plump, and tempting. At the edge of his yard stood two large trees, loaded with luscious blue-black mulberries. Although I would not have dreamed of stealing, I picked a few off the grass and ate them; the other kids followed. The berries tasted so good.

There were eight of us—me, Alice, Dorothy, and Shirley, my sisters, and our friends, the four Smith sisters. I was ten years old and they were all younger. We often played at a vacant lot near our homes. There we would fill our cans at the "red haw" (hawthorn) tree. We used the red haws to string for necklaces or for pretend food when we played house.

That afternoon, however, we had taken a different way to the red haw tree, past Mr. Grump's house. When we saw all those big dark berries going to waste underneath the trees, we decide to fill our cans. Then we thanked "Mr. Mulberry Tree" and ran home. Our mother washed the berries and put them in a big bowl for supper. That evening we piled whipped cream on the berries for dessert. We felt so proud because there were enough to treat the whole family.

Two days later all eight girls agreed it was time for more berries and cream. Our parents, thinking the trees were in the empty lot with the red haws, gave permission to go. To our dismay, when we reached the tree, there were no berries on the ground. Even the lower half of the trees were bare of fruit. Lucy Smith and my sister Alice, tomboys of the group, climbed a tree, and started jumping and shaking the branches. Mulberries fell like black rain.

We had started to fill our cans, when suddenly a voice thundered, "What are you kids doing? I'm going to call the police. You are on MY property STEALING my mulberries!"

Within seconds Lucy and Alice slid down from the tree. The other kids were running in different directions. Alice grabbed five-year-old Shirley by the hand, and they ran toward home. I turned to pick up my can and, to my horror, saw

Mr. Grump holding my seven-year-old sister, Dorothy, up by the back of her neck. Her feet dangled in the air.

"Let her go!" I shrieked.

"I'm going to hand you both over to the police," he yelled. He held her with one hand and tried to reach me with the other. We circled—he, trying to reach me, and I, trying to reach Dorothy. But I could not get close enough to grab her without his grabbing me. So I ran up and threw the berries, can and all, in his face. He released his grip on Dorothy, and I snatched her hand.

As we cut across yards and down an alley, we could still hear Mr. Grump yelling. When we reached our yard, we slumped against the back of the garage to catch our breath. Our hearts seemed ready to leap out of our chests. How long we leaned there, I don't know.

Then we sneaked in the house. I hid in the closet under the stairs. Dorothy ran upstairs and hid with Alice under their bed. Shirley ran to the kitchen and clung to Mom like a second skin. When dinner was ready, Mom made us come out of our hiding places and demanded to know what we had done. No one said a word.

For two days we stayed in the house, expecting the police to come any moment and take us away. Our fear and guilt stayed with us for a long time. "Thou shalt not steal" was a commandment we never forgot.

Questions for Discussion

1. What do you learn about the narrator in the first paragraph?

2. What strategy supplements narration?

3. What is the effect of including dialogue?

4. What is the effect of having the commandment in the last line?

5. Does this story remind you of another about a tree with forbidden fruit? What similarities do you see?

The second paper, by Shasta Scharf, is written in the third person. For the concluding paragraph, she shifts to first person for a reason.

Just a Walk

Jimmy was seventeen the day he joined the armed forces. Fresh from the coal mines of West Virginia, with only a sixth-grade education and six weeks' survival training in Massachusetts, he was flown over 9,000 miles to Corregidor. Suddenly, his life became a battleground for survival. The day that General MacArthur left the Philippines, Jimmy shot his first enemy warrior. "This," he said, "was the first time I walked through Hell." As the Japanese took possession of the Philippines, the Bataan Death March began. Jimmy was near the head of the line. For over ninety days, he and the other U.S. soldiers suffered severe malnutrition, dysentery, malaria, and abuse as they walked to a prison camp. This was another walk through Hell. For three years, Jimmy was the camp interpreter. Being the interpreter gave him the chance to send messages to and receive them from the United States Army covertly. The Japanese never knew that "Jimpie," as they called him, was using their equipment for spying.

In 1945 Jimmy and the others left the Philippines via three "Hell Ships." Each ship was designed to hold 200 passengers. Over 1,700 men were crowded into quarters intended for 600. Only 482 men walked off the ships in Osaka, Japan. Poor ventilation, no food, no water, and no place to lie down had taken a heavy toll.

When Jimmy reached the United States, he was decorated for bravery and given a six-day pass to see California. He and three friends drove up to Mt. Shasta to ski. There he beheld "a sight that restored [his] sanity." With seven years of hell behind him, Lake Shasta and the snow-capped mountain in front of him, Jimmy came face to face with a young deer. Only five feet away, the fawn stared straight into Jimmy's eyes. Tears flowed down his cheeks as he gazed at the most beautiful scene he had encountered in his twenty-four years of life.

After his experience at Mt. Shasta, Jimmy's life became less chaotic. He went back to the dark, damp coal mines with his father and brothers. Since mining coal is a "filthy, unsafe job and most people do not live to regret their old age in the mines," Jimmy soon headed north to Ohio and the steel mills. . . .

Jimmy's dream included having a home, a wife, and a daughter, but after marrying "Kat," two sons were born within three years. He loved his sons, yet his heart yearned for a daughter, one who would never engage in combat or shoot another human being. One evening two years later, a girl was born to him and his wife.

The birth certificate was not signed until Jimmy got home from work after midnight, eight hours after the birth. As he stared at his newborn daughter in amazement, he whispered, "She is the most beautiful sight I have ever seen." Recalling that earlier moment of overwhelming joy and peace, my father named me Shasta.

Questions for Discussion

1. Evaluate the effectiveness of Shasta's title. Give a reason for your opinion.

2. Contrast the death march and the drive up Mt. Shasta. Consider what awaited Jimmy at each place.

3. How are a new baby and a fawn similar? How are these two moments connected in the story?

4. Discuss the switch from third person to first person in the last line. Do you think third person throughout would have been more or less effective? Why?

5. Shasta could have ended with her father's death from black lung disease as his final walk through hell. Would this ending have been more or less effective? Why do you think so?

FOR YOUR REFERENCE: NARRATIVE ESSAYS IN THE READER

- "Rosetta Disk Is Foundation's Gift to Future Linguists," David Bank, page 555
- "Home for Christmas," Carson McCullers, page 559
- "The Art of Acknowledgment," Jean Houston, page 563
- "How to Get out of a Locked Trunk," Philip Weiss, page 567

Summary

The purpose of a narrative may be to reflect, entertain, inform, explain, or persuade. Narrative formats are used in college writing and on the job. A narrative about an experience or fictitious event does not always have a thesis statement; the thesis may be implicit. The action opening hooks readers' attention by showing a part of the action immediately. But opening with a quotation delays the action.

A narrative may be told in first person or in third person. Switches in person should be skillful and purposeful. Chronological order is common in narratives. The action begins and proceeds in a natural sequence. Sometimes the chronology is disrupted by a sudden shift to the past. If a flashback occurs, it should be for a crucial incident.

To write a narrative paper, select a topic you know well and can shape purposefully. Decide when the story should begin, perhaps starting with an action, a quotation, or a comparison. Dialogue, carefully edited, can advance the action and heighten interest.

Narrative endings vary. Usually, the complication, conflict, or problem is resolved. If not, there should be a clue so that the reader can surmise what will happen.

A narrative report arises from the need to record a real situation or event. When writing a report, consider the purpose and the audience. A report has three main sections: purpose and scope, body, and conclusion. All three sections have headings.

When revising, check the larger elements of the narrative first, particularly the order and development. Prune any surplus words or excessively long sentences that slow the pace of the narrative. Check the ending to be sure it is satisfying and complete.

Key Terms

action opening	flashback	reaction ending
chronological order	narrative	surprise ending
dialogue	narrative report	third-person narration
first-person narration	point of view	unity

Practice

Write a News Story

Assume you are a reporter for your campus or hometown newspaper. Write a news story. You may want to conduct interviews to gain specific details. The following suggestions may stimulate an idea you can use:

1. New construction, new business, or restaurant
2. Historical highlight: A story from the city's history

3. Profile of the president of the university or college
4. Student interviews about campus concerns
5. Plans for an activity such as May Day, a concert, or pig roast

Write a First-Person Narrative

Select an incident from your experience that may have caused you to laugh, to cry, to run, to show courage, or to learn. Then do some prewriting about the key events, including your reactions. After that, write a unified paragraph or short narrative. Perhaps one of the suggestions below will help you to find a suitable topic:

1. A learning experience—gulp!
2. Out of the mouth of a toddler . . .
3. Finding a . . .
4. A wonderful day
5. A surprise

Thirty Ideas for Narrative Papers

1. An incident on the job (a narrative report)
2. One evening as . . .
3. A new wife's (or husband's) first home-cooked dinner
4. Being stopped for a traffic violation
5. How I handled harassment on the job
6. A frightening experience at work
7. Learning how to drive
8. Fatherhood/motherhood is _____
9. How my mother met my father
10. My most embarrassing experience
11. My first taste of defeat
12. A prank that backfired
13. The first time I rode a . . .
14. How I met my husband/wife
15. My experience with . . .
16. My first encounter with a . . .
17. My worst date
18. I was my brother's keeper
19. The secret in . . .
20. There was a young woman who lived in a . . .

21. The day I won . . .
22. My favorite one-day trip
23. Revenge is not so sweet
24. Sadder, but wiser
25. The day the black sheep came home
26. The last time I . . .
27. _____ weren't meant for . . .
28. A strange experience or unusual occurrence
29. My first day on a new job
30. The lesson of the _____ experience

CHAPTER 11

$\mathcal{D}escription$

Conveying Impressions

The background must never swamp the action,
nor must the aura of a place interfere with
the progress of the story.

—Rosalind Laker
"Imagination and the Past," *The Writer*

The distant moan of a locomotive may take us back to a railroad siding where we picked and ate wild strawberries long ago. The fragrance of lilacs may remind us of the huge purple bush in grandmother's yard, where we frolicked with small cousins and rested on the lush grass. Descriptions such as these, based on seeing, hearing, touching, tasting, and smelling, allow the reader to visualize and share an experience vicariously.

WHAT EXACTLY IS DESCRIPTION?

Description has been defined by philosophers as "a mode of perception," a means of knowing. It is a way to impose order upon the confusing complexity of the real world and to understand it, at least partially. It allows the writer to record sensory details, to reflect on an experience and ponder its significance. Description is an excellent way to preserve oral family history and firsthand research.

See pages 115 and 116.

In primary research we *observe*, *describe*, *interpret*, and *write* our impressions of concrete details (obtained through the five senses) that we perceive firsthand. This four-stage process enables us to relate the physical parts of what we observe to the whole subject or unit. Then we can contemplate its meaning, whether it be a caterpillar or the earth's crust.

This chapter explains using description as a major writing strategy for various rhetorical situations. In much writing, however, description plays a minor role—supporting a major strategy such as narration, process analysis, or comparison.

PURPOSE OF DESCRIPTION

Whether you write a college paper, grant application, patient or client history, technical report, or other document, suitable descriptive details can strengthen your core idea. Successful description has a purpose: hand-picked details reinforce the thesis or the point of the description. In research, business, and technical writing, writers use description to help readers understand the material qualities and fundamental structure of physical objects, organisms, and phenomena. Descriptive details can provide concrete evidence to support a thesis.

In expressive writing such as personal essays and narratives, autobiographies, and poems, writers guide the emotional responses of readers by selecting sensory details to create a *dominant impression*.

CREATING A DOMINANT IMPRESSION

When description is the chief writing strategy, it conveys a dominant impression, a mood, that prevails throughout the piece for a purpose. Then sensory details unite to produce an overall mood, such as delight, fear, or curiosity—adding interest as well as evidence. This mood may be implied or expressed directly. In *Gift from the Sea*, Anne Morrow Lindbergh creates an implicit impression as she describes a shell, found on the beach, and compares the shell to her life:

> The shell in my hand is deserted. It once housed a whelk, a snail-like creature, and then temporarily, after the death of the first occupant, a little hermit crab, who has run away, leaving his tracks behind him like a delicate vine on the sand. . . . Did he hope to find a better home, a better mode of living? I too have run away, I realize, I have shed the shell of my life, for these few weeks of vacation.
>
> But his shell—it is simple; it is bare, it is beautiful. Small, only the size of my thumb, its architecture is perfect, down to the finest detail. Its shape, swelling like a pear in the center, winds in a gentle spiral to the pointed apex. Its color, dull gold, is whitened by a wash of salt from the sea. Each whorl, each faint knob, each crisscross vein in its egg-shell texture, is as clearly defined as on the day of creation. . . .
>
> My shell is not like this, I think. How untidy it has become! Blurred with moss, knobby with barnacles, its shape is hardly recognizable any more. Surely, it had a shape once. It has a shape still in my mind. What is the shape of my life?

As Lindbergh describes the shell, it becomes a symbol of her life. As she reflects, the images establish a thread of continuity, allowing the reader to sense her inner peace amid the problems of life. There is a tranquility, an acceptance of change, as she collects insights along with shells.

Subjective and Objective Description

Description may be subjective or objective. A *subjective* description, such as Lindbergh's, reveals how the writer feels and thinks about the subject. Subjectivity refers to a personal view, which includes attitude and opinion as well as fact.

The purpose of a subjective description is to share thoughts and feelings with the reader. But feeling must be kept within bounds so that it does not get out of control. Too much subjectivity can backfire. An essay with a dominant impression has a subjective slant.

In contrast, the tone of *objective* description is literal, factual, and fair. The tone is impartial and impersonal. In scientific and business writing, much description is based on unbiased, objective observation. Its aim is to reproduce for the reader exactly what the writer observed without reference to the writer's feelings about the subject.

See chapters
21 and 22.

In *Thinking in Pictures*, Temple Grandin objectively describes a demonstration of a machine built by Robert Richardson of Prescott, Arizona, for desensitizing unrideable horses:

> The wild horse was placed in a narrow stall similar to a horse trailer, with two gentle horses in adjacent stalls . . . wild horses will panic when they are alone. The horse's head protruded through a padded opening in the front of the stall, and a rear pusher gate prevented him from backing up and pulling his head inside. Sand slowly filled up the stall. . . . It wasn't until the sand came up to his belly that he jerked slightly, but then he appeared to relax. He seldom put his ears back, which is a sign of fear or aggression, and he never tried to bite anybody. He was alert and curious about his surroundings, and he acted like a normal horse in a stall. . . . He was free to move his head, and eventually he allowed people to touch his face and rub his ears and mouth. Touching that had been intolerable was now being tolerated.

WRITING A PAPER OF DESCRIPTION

Whether you have toured Ravenna, Italy, looking at mosaics, or never ventured beyond your city's limits, you have stored numerous sensory impressions. Perhaps you remember a lovely moment, painting, or place that might serve as a topic for a paper. Or perhaps you own an unsual object that has a story behind it. Think about the memory or object and its significance to you.

Prewriting

After you select a topic, mine your memory by prewriting. You might try asking yourself questions that involve the five senses, as in the example below. Flora Kyle recalls specific details of her grandfather crafting a hope chest.

Sight: What did I notice?

Grandfather was meticulous. Every joint had to be perfect.
the plane spewing wood curls from chestnut, maple, cedar boards
alternated woods in a chevron pattern on lid with an iron hinge
high luster of the finish
Aunt Lally put a wedding ring quilt she had made in the chest.

Sound: What did I hear?

whine of the saw

groan of the plane

scratch of sandpaper

pounding of hammer

Aunt Lally's words when she received chest on her sixteenth birthday

Smell: What did I smell?

aroma of cedar

smells of glue and shellac

fresh air when he opened the windows to let out fumes

Touch: How did the wood feel?

rough texture of boards

splinter in my finger

crispness of wood curls

satin smoothness of the hand-rubbed finish

Point of the Description

Chest is mine. Reminds me of Aunt Lally and my meticulous grandfather.

Determining the Dominant Impression

A hodgepodge of details without a central point will lack unity. Consider their overall meaning. Why is this topic significant to you? What is the dominant impression, the idea that links the details? The idea need not be dramatic or earth-shaking; it need only be important to you for a specific reason.

As you draft, you may uncover the wisp of a story. At first it may appear unimportant, or it may make you uncomfortable. But before tossing it away, take a second look. Paul Allen Dotson, Jr., drafted a description of a dining room light fixture. As he revised, he speculated about its meaning to him and realized it was more than just a beautiful object. There was a memory, an untold story, behind it—one he did not want to tell. But by referring to the story, he enriched the dominant impression.

The Crystal Chandelier

In the dining room of a house where I once lived hung a crystal chandelier. It was a gorgeous old-fashioned fixture with eight lights and numerous dangling crystals that sparkled with the colors of the rainbow. The chandelier had three settings: High, medium, and low. When it was set on high, my wife and I would entertain friends and relatives, balance our accounts, and write letters. When the chandelier was on medium, I would often lounge in a chair next to the stereo and listen to soft music while staring at the colors emanating from the crystals. Yet my favorite setting was low. There were nights I would arrive home before my wife and would prepare dinner for the two of us. When she would walk into the dining room, the colors from the crystals would shine on her hair; she would smile, and I would see the most beautiful woman in the world. Though we are no longer together, those moments under the crystal chandelier are among my fondest memories.

Although Paul merely hinted at the story in the last line, he enriched the description. Rarely is an entire story told. Someone once said that a story is like an iceberg: seven-eighths of it stays beneath the surface. The writer must decide how much to reveal. If you think there might be a story lurking in your prewriting notes, ask yourself these questions:

- Why do I have a special fondness for the object or impression?
- Did something happen that cast a shadow on or changed my life?
- How much do I want to say?
- Will that be enough? Will the ending seem complete?

Selecting a Vantage Point and Transition

You might think of a writer as holding a camera, aiming the lens in a certain direction to record an impression or a story. Wherever the writer is viewing the scene from is the *vantage point*. The writer may remain fixed in one spot or move around. A *fixed observer* describes only what can be seen from one position. A *moving observer* describes from more than one position. With each movement, the writer keeps the reader informed with transitional phrases such as "turning at the first country road," "reaching the summit," or "descending a narrow, crooked stairway."

Imagine in your mind's eye the position from which you will view your topic. Will you remain in one spot or will you move? Will you be close or distant? Will you be observing for a few moments or over a span of time? What would be the most interesting vantage point for the reader? What transitions will you need to keep readers informed of your movements?

See chapter 4.

Drafting an Introduction

Some openings take readers directly to a scene. There they observe a specific time and place through the writer's eyes. A short transitional phrase and past tense may set a historical scene. For example. "*In 1890 Central City had* dusty unpaved streets and 132 inhabitants, not counting 56 horses, 63 dogs, and 75 cats." Or a descriptive phrase and present tense may describe a current scene: "*Nestled in a valley in . . . is* a small village that still has a general store and a post office where patrons pick up their mail."

Sometimes a description opens with a specific thesis. More interesting is a vivid comparison. Jennifer Ramey begins her paper, "Maintaining a Marriage," with a simile, followed by a metaphor:

A good marriage is like a fine-tuned car. Care for it, work on it, and treasure it, and it will run well. Communication is the engine of a marriage. Effective communication goes beyond knowing a partner's favorite foods and activities. Heartfelt communication requires sensitivity—an awareness of the other person's feelings, embarrassments, concerns, and goals. Quality communication requires loyalty and listening with empathy, trying to understand what the other person is experiencing.

Organizing and Developing a Description

The organization of a description often arises quite naturally from the topic. If you describe an object, a place, an animal, or a person, then spatial order usually works well. In spatial order, details are arranged according to space or location. You can use spatial order to show direction: east to west, north to south, left to right, top to bottom, front to back, inside to outside, or vice versa. For instance, to describe an Irish setter, you might go from the head to the tip of the tail. As a moving observer, you might explore a haunted house, going in through the creaking front door, up the dusty staircase, and through a hall to a narrow stairway. At the top is an attic filled with who-knows-what.

Chronological order, a sequence of time, may be used to describe the changes in a neighborhood or a person. A street scene might be described from the wee hours of the morning to late at night.

Another possible order for description is from abstract to concrete or from general to specific (or vice versa). For example, to describe the disorder of a pack-rat's nest, you might begin with a general impression of the nest and the shock of finding this mess in your basement. Next might come a description of the items the rat had taken: an old spoon, a shiny silver button, a marble, and other trifles. Or if a topic requires emphasis, you might go from least to most important or from most to least important.

Comparing two views can give a fresh slant to an ordinary topic. For example, a tarnished silver belt buckle from a great-great-grandfather's Civil War uniform might be considered worthless by one cousin, but another might view it as priceless, a family heirloom. People, too, can be described from more than one vantage point, as Lori I. demonstrates.

My Fiery Grandma

My grandmother is like a brightly burning fire. She can be warm and welcoming, a "light" ever ready to give aid. However, she can also be cruel and destructive, freely turning emotions into ashes. When controlled, Grandma is a warm, gentle person. She doctors wounds with soft hands and a kindly smile. She can make a person feel safe and protected. She has offered food and shelter to those less fortunate than herself, allowing them to warm themselves at no cost, while still providing all the love her twelve grandchildren could want. She has encouraged hopes and dreams, as if they were dry wood she just needed to spark into life. To enter her presence is like coming into a fire-lit room after being in the cold. The fire is there, warming skin and bones while her welcome fills one with good cheer.

My grandmother is like a fire in less positive ways as well. When she is in one of her fiery moods, her tone and words can blister. The warmth, shelter, and love once freely offered sometimes flare into regret and bitterness, searing what was to an ash. Hopes and dreams she once nurtured can wither under a well-turned phrase. During these times she is like a house fire, destroying and burning everything and everyone in her path. No subject, person, or idea is safe from her at such times. Yet despite these vices, she is still "Gammy," and the entire family would be less joyful without her.

Writing a Conclusion

Successful endings give a sense of completion and satisfaction. In description, as in narration, the major point often appears at the end. The ending may be a brief summary that explains the point in an interesting way. Or the ending may sound optimistic as it looks to the future. A philosophical ending might relate physical details to an abstract thought. Anne Morrow Lindbergh is both optimistic and philosophical at the close of *Gift from the Sea:*

> The waves echo behind me. Patience—Faith—Openness, is what the sea has to teach. Simplify—Solitude—Intermittency . . . But there are other beaches to explore. There are more shells to find. This is only the beginning.

Sometimes a surprise or twist ending is effective. These endings require preparation. You cannot simply swoop down and attach an ending that is foreign to the description or story. You need to prepare the reader in small ways. Note that Paul mentions his wife early in "The Crystal Chandelier." He does not suddenly introduce her at the end. Effective endings are smooth; they grow out of whatever has preceded them.

Revising a Description

When revising a description, choose words that convey sharp, clear images— vibrant verbs, specific nouns, and modifiers that crackle with meaning. The audience should be able to visualize the spot, object, or person and savor the other sensory details. The aim is not only to increase interest but also to enhance the dominant impression.

In *The Elements of Style*, E. B. White warns against the use of meaningless modifiers. He calls *very, rather, little,* and *pretty* "the leeches that infest the pond of prose, sucking the blood of words." Beware, too, of stacking adjectives in a series; use one if needed, seldom two, rarely three.

Although the right adjective can convey an idea, an action verb can often convey it better. For example, the two sentences below carry the same idea, but the first slows the pace with a weak (*be*) verb, the adverb *very*, and two vague adjectives. The second version deletes the adverb and adjectives. A strong action verb and a specific noun replace them:

- The tomcat *was* very upset and vocal.
- The tomcat *hissed* his displeasure.

In the previous example, note the repetition of the *s* in the second sentence—the sound echoes the meaning. Such subtle surprises work well in prose if not overdone. As you revise, you may want to consult the following checklist:

CHECKLIST: REVISING A DESCRIPTION

1. Does the opening line arouse interest for this audience?
2. Is the vantage point suitable? Is any transition needed?
3. Is the written voice appropriate? Should it be more personal or friendly?
4. Is the imagery sharp and clear? Have I involved at least three senses?
5. Are all details effective? Could their order be improved?
6. Are most verbs in the active voice? Are nouns and adjectives specific?
7. Is the dominant impression clear and effective?
8. Does the ending seem complete?

TWO STUDENT PAPERS: DESCRIPTION

In the first paper, Jean Ice describes a favorite relative. She uses the concrete-to-abstract strategy, describing appearance before personality.

Aunt Marzia

Marzia was an elegant lady. Even as a young girl, she exhibited unusual characteristics for a country lass. Her coal-black hair glistened from regimental brushing and frequent shampooing. Her hair was a halo for a lovely face with arched eyebrows and curling lashes. Her eyes were light green or gray, depending upon the color of her apparel. Her high cheekbones gave her a slight resemblance to a Native American. Her mother was said to be of Indian ancestry.

Marzia was taller than most other women of this generation. She carried her height proudly. Her erect posture and uplifted chin gave her a regal air. Somewhat out of sync with her physical perfection was her quirky little walk. She turned each foot slightly to the side as she strolled the country lanes.

Marzia was different from other members of her family and from her classmates. The other school children wore plain homemade garments, but Marzia used her sewing skill to put tucks in her waists. She also put flounces in her skirts and attached lace or embroidery to her collars. Few people would have guessed her wardrobe was made from feed sacks.

Marzia adored her first name, but she abhorred the way it was pronounced "Marzie" by others. Even her older sisters Clara and Ara did not follow her wishes and mispronounced her name. This elegant lady was a perfectionist in many other ways. She seemed to believe it was her responsibility to reform others to her way of thinking. This was especially true of her nieces. There were only five of us, compared to many more nephews. She expected us girls to speak correctly, dress attractively, and excel in good manners. She tried to accomplish these objectives by correcting us whenever we made an error. Often I, the youngest niece, was overwhelmed by a miscue. Once I pronounced *chic* as "chick," confident that I was right. Consulting a dictionary, after she corrected me, proved how little I knew.

Marzia was well educated for her time and situation. She was graduated from high school when most students were satisfied to complete the eighth grade. She went to normal school and became a teacher in a one-room school. The school was on the outskirts of a very small town, composed mostly of people of color. Marzia prized her students, and they were very fond of her.

When Marzia decided to marry, she was forced to give up teaching; for years ago only single women were allowed to teach. Unlike her sisters, who married for security and a home of their own, Marzia married because of her love for a ne'er-do-well. Although he was short, unattractive, uneducated, and rough of manner and speech, he had a jolly personality, which attracted the young ladies. But even Marzia could not contend with the old demon—liquor. After three years of silent grief, she divorced this man. She was the only member of her family to be divorced.

Marzia lived a long and productive life in spite of the divorce. She was greatly loved by all her younger kin, who were so different from her. When Aunt Marzia died, we all missed her so much. Nobody ever took her place in my life; no one else reminded me that I could do better.

Questions for Discussion

1. Is Jean's dominant impression implicit or explicit?
2. How is the claim that Marzia is different and "elegant" supported?
3. Were you surprised about the way the nieces accepted her correction? Why or why not?
4. Jean mixes writing strategies. What order is used in her last three paragraphs?
5. What type of ending does she use?

In the second paper, student writer C. J. Banning presents an impressive number of vivid descriptive details. She uses comparison and contrast to explore the topic and to make her thesis all the more convincing.

Please, Do Not Forget Me

In England on a barren hillside, stands a long-forgotten castle that has given way to centuries of neglect. Fragments of its once stately gray stone walls litter the courtyard. A spire that once stood tall atop a tower now lies upon a heap of rubble. Windows that once gleamed in the sun are darkened with grime. Winged creatures of the night fly through broken windowpanes. The storeroom is dank and musty; gone are the fine foods and wines. Gone are the people who danced in the ballroom; gone is the grandeur of former years.

So, too, can be the life of a person suffering from severe depression. Often the person will go into seclusion, letting time and the world pass. Hiding in the dark recesses of the mind, the victim of depression cringes, hoping others will pass on by, paying no heed to the one that dwells within. Little by little, parts of the person are lost in the rubble of distress. Slowly, bit by bit, the self seems to be less and less. No longer does it feel that anyone might want anything it might be able to give. There is no room left for the food of good thoughts or warm feelings. The dark coldness of lost hope and worthlessness permeates the empty storage room. Unkempt thoughts weaken the body as well as the mind.

One summer day someone wonders how the old castle used to be. How had it looked with sturdy walls, clean windows, and polished floors? Had the steeple, standing tall and straight against the blue sky, seemed inviting to all who passed? Was the storeroom full, waiting for the banquets that were to come? Finally, someone decides to do something about the neglect. He picks up a stone and places it back into the wall, then another and another. He washes windows, and the sunlight once again streams through. He sweeps the dusty floor and dreams of the day the castle can be restored.

Despite protests, the victims of depression, too, need help and caring commitment to pick up the pieces of their lives, to wash their eyes and let in the light. They need help to discard the dark thoughts that flit about their minds, help to air the dark musty places that need a caring touch, help to let in a fresh dream of what they might be. Then, one piece at a time, their lives can be restored to become a little better, day after day.

Not all the castle walls and floors that are polished will shine as brightly as before. The storeroom will still have a faint mustiness, and a few stray creatures may venture in. But the castle can be a wonderful, grand place of peace.

Questions for Discussion

1. What is the impression in paragraph one? What words contribute heavily?
2. What specific details in the second paragraph link it to the first?
3. What do you notice in the third paragraph?
4. What advice does the writer give in paragraph four?
5. Does the writer seem to have firsthand or secondhand knowledge of the topic? Why do you think so?

FOR YOUR REFERENCE: DESCRIPTIVE ESSAYS IN THE READER

- "Caterpillar Afternoon," Sue Hubbell, page 572
- "One Writer's Beginnings," Eudora Welty, page 576
- "Dawn Watch," John Ciardi, page 579
- "Pedestrian Students," Liane Norman, page 583

Summary

Effective description has a purpose; it is not just a filler. You can use description as a major or minor writing strategy. Description often undergirds narration, comparison, persuasion, or another major strategy. The tone may be subjective or objective.

A paper of description has a dominant impression. You can select sensory details, referring to sight, sound, smell, touch, or taste, to enliven description. Strong verbs and specific nouns help description come alive. When planning a description, think about the vantage point or location from which you will observe the subject. Will you remain stationary or will you move around?

Sometimes there is a story connected with an object, place, or impression. Depending upon the situation, you might merely mention the story or you might develop it. Sometimes a story has a lesson or moral that will give depth to the paper.

You can organize descriptive details in spatial or chronological order, through comparison, or in another logical way. Devote care to beginnings and endings. Examine word choice to strengthen verbs and delete meaningless modifiers. Revision is an essential part of writing effective description.

Key Terms

dominant impression	objective tone	vantage point
fixed observer	sensory details	prose
moving observer	subjective tone	

Practice

Small Groups: *Devising Similes and Metaphors*

Directions: In groups of three or four, consider the items below. Select those that appeal to you and devise *unusual* comparisons that are similes and metaphors. Have fun! Appoint a recorder to save the best.

1. Fill in the blanks with a *fresh* comparison:
   a. He walked like a . . .   (Avoid clichés such as *duck.*)
   b. She ate like a . . .   (Avoid *horse.*)
   c. His tongue was as sharp as . . . (Not *knife*)
   d. He dressed like . . .   (Not a *hippie* or *hobo*)
   e. She was as proud as . . .   (Not *peacock*)
2. Comparisons with birds or insects: ladybug, hummingbird, dragonfly, house fly, termite, wasp, blue jay, woodpecker, meadow lark, canary, bobolink, ant, hoot owl, bumble bee, firefly, mosquito, or others. Here are two examples:

   Simile: His words bit like the sting of an angry wasp.
   Metaphor: His words stung.

Ideas for Writing a Paragraph

Directions: Be specific, using concrete words and vivid verbs. End with a thoughtful comment, perhaps about the function, meaning, or qualities of the object or person, *so that your paragraph has a point.*

1. Describe the vehicle you are driving or riding. What is the dominant impression of you in or on this vehicle?
2. Describe a prized object. Why is it special?
3. Describe the contents of your purse (if you have one). What is the dominant impression to a casual spectator?
4. Describe someone you know. What predominant qualities does he or she have?
5. Describe your favorite piece of old clothing. Why is it special?

Thirty Ideas for Descriptive Papers

1. My best boss
2. A family of bald eagles (or rabbits, ducks, etc.)
3. My first job ; *any job*
4. A shop in Chinatown
5. German Village in Columbus, Ohio
6. Riding a cable car in San Francisco
7. A favorite place to be alone
8. My father's toolbox
9. A moment to remember
10. A favorite hangout
11. Riding the rapids in Colorado
12. A ride on the canals of Amsterdam
13. A ride on the Staten Island ferry
14. The first time I . . .
15. The kindest person I know
16. An incident in . . .
17. Earliest childhood memory
18. My high school reunion
19. My _____ heritage
20. The best *worst* dog I ever had ; *pet*
21. The most courageous person I know
22. My neighborhood

23. A family heirloom and its significance to me
24. A favorite restaurant
25. My favorite vacation spot
26. A flower garden to attract butterflies
27. My mother's homemade bread
28. Butchering time on the farm
29. Picking apples (cherries or peaches)
30. My first apartment *, house, . . .*

CHAPTER 12

Process Analysis

Explaining How

It is far easier to discuss Hamlet's complexes than to write orders which ensure that five working parties from five different units arrive at the right time equipped with proper tools for the job.

— G. B. Harrison

Writing clear, concise directions is not always easy even for the professional. In the 1960s, before the public was familiar with photocopiers, Ohio State University placed a coin-operated copier in a campus library. The directions were so complicated that many users needed assistance from a librarian to complete the process of copying.

Perhaps you have worked with inadequate or nonexistent instructions and know how frustrating that can be. One young man, lacking any instruction, began a welding job only to find the equipment was different from that used on his previous job. He ruined $400 worth of equipment the first night. To write clear directions, you need to analyze the process.

WHAT IS PROCESS ANALYSIS?

A process is a series of steps, stages, phases, or natural changes that lead to a result. Daily you engage in processes, whether brewing coffee, shaving, or driving a car. On the job you may need to write instructions for operating software, explain a process or procedure to a new worker, or show someone how to operate a machine.

Process analysis is an explanation or description of sequential actions, operations, or changes that occur for a purpose. A paper of process analysis may explain how to do something, how a condition develops, how an organism grows, or how a phenomenon evolves. Regular occurrences in the natural world—such as digestion, icicles, and hurricanes—involve processes. For clarity, the process is explained in the order that changes/events normally occur. Some processes require one certain order; others can be done in more than one way.

Directions for Procedures

The simple experiments you conducted in high school science and chemistry labs were procedures. When you assemble shelving or pour a concrete patio, you also perform a procedure. To ensure good results, you follow the instructions carefully. If any steps are omitted or the order is reversed, the deviation may mar the final result. Some procedures, such as operating a chain saw, require warnings so that users take precautions. *Include a reason for each precaution so that users take heed.*

Other kinds of processes require multiple sets of directions, all of which have phases, steps, or stages. For instance, the production of steel and the publication of a book involve many processes and people. The *audience* for directions consists of the people who will be performing the procedure.

Use Second Person for Clarity   Directions for a procedure should be clear and concise. Therefore they are usually written in second person with *understood you*. Each step begins with an active verb: "*Insert* the tab . . . ," *Open* the chamber . . . ," "*Lift* the switch. . . ." Most instructions should be more than a brief list—they should explain according to readers' general level of knowledge. On the job, steps of a procedure are often simplified and numbered.

WORKPLACE CASE STUDY

ETHAN SOLVES THE OFFICE LOUNGE PROBLEM

The sink of the employee lounge is usually stacked full of dirty dishes. The room smells of stale coffee grounds. Green mold grows on uneaten lunches in the refrigerator. Although employees are assigned weeks to tidy the room, they often forget. Those who remember may wash only the dishes. Ethan has been asked to devise a new system.

After careful thought, Ethan gives each office employee a copy of a quarterly assignment sheet with his or her week marked in red. In a memo he asks the employees to add this date to their calendars. On the refrigerator, he posts a sign that reads: "On Fridays all lunch containers and open soda will be discarded." On a cupboard, he posts this notice:

Daily Cleaning Procedure

On your assigned day, please clean between 3 and 5 p.m. Then no one will be using the lounge. The following procedure will save time. (It should take 10–12 minutes.)

1. Close the drain and fill the sink with hot water.
2. Add detergent and let dishes soak.
3. Clear the table and counter of debris. Wash them off.

4. Wipe the microwave inside and out.

5. Wash dishes, rinse, and stack on drainboard.

6. To prevent fire unplug coffeemaker. Dispose of grounds.

7. Wash and rinse coffeemaker.

8. Dry dishes and put in cupboard.

9. FRIDAY: Throw out all lunch containers and open soda cans in the refrigerator. Wipe up crumbs and spills in the refrigerator.

The system has worked surprisingly well. Grumbling about clutter and odor has stopped. The lounge is a much more pleasant place to sit and relax.

Process Descriptions

The purpose of a process description is to describe a procedure, natural phenomenon, or other process for an audience who would like to know more about it but will not be performing the process. Therefore you supply just enough detail to provide an overview, state the function of each step or stage, and explain how each fits into the process. See page H-24.

Process descriptions are often written in narrative form, using either first- or third-person pronouns. Students in all academic disciplines analyze processes and write narratives. Sometimes the two overlap. For example, you might interview a patient, write a case history, and describe the onset of a health problem. Or you might narrate/explain how a hobby grew into a successful business.

Using First Person Student writer Janice D. uses first person and past tense to begin the story of how her rock garden evolved.

Gardening with Rocks

Rock gardening wasn't something I gave much thought to until a few years after we bought a house. I can remember the seller pointing out an overgrown bush in the front of the weedy yard, trying to use that as a selling point. Later my husband and I agreed "that will have to be the first thing to go." The first year we were so busy inside we didn't do much outside except to mow the lawn and kill the weeds. But over the next few years, we began to beautify the outside as well. We started small with a tree here, a few flowers and a rock there, which led to our lovely rock garden of today.

Using Third Person Process descriptions that are not drawn from a writer's personal experience are usually written in the third person. Present tense verbs in *active* voice are used for actions that recur: "The mollusk *opens* its shell . . . ," "Each year the tree *grows* new rings," "The furnace *melts* the glass. . . ." See "Caterpillar Afternoon," p. 572.

TRANSITION IN PROCESS ANALYSIS

A transition is a word, phrase, sentence, or paragraph that connects ideas, informing the reader of what is ahead. Transitions indicate shifts of meaning and relationships of time, location, sequence, similarity or difference, certainty or uncertainty. *Signpost transitions* appear at the beginning of sentences. This method is generally used in procedures. *Embedded transitions* appear at other places in a sentence, as explained in chapter 14.

For process analysis, use transitions that indicate *chronological* order. For procedures with major and minor steps, distinguish between them. For major steps, use numerical transitions (*first, second, third*, and so forth). For substeps, use other transitions of time, such as *then* or *next*. (Two or three *first's* and *second's* would be confusing.)

TRANSITIONS TO CLARIFY A PROCESS			
To Emphasize Major Steps or Stages		*To Indicate Substeps*	
first	(begin)	next	then
second		after that	later
third		while	when
fourth		meanwhile	as soon as
fifth	(finally)	during	after one hour

WRITING A PROCESS PAPER

The purpose of a process paper can be to provide directions for a procedure or to describe a process, according to the assignment. To fulfill either purpose, you first need to estimate how much readers know about the topic and whether they are likely to have performed or witnessed the procedure or process before. This estimate is particularly important for writing directions. It will help you in gauging not only the amount of explanation needed but also the need to include *precautions and a reason* at strategic points:

Warning: Perform the steps in the order given. Failure to do so may cause fire.

When writing directions, be specific. Otherwise, some users may decide to take unwise shortcuts. At tricky or risky points, include a reason for the step. For example, "Follow directions carefully *to obtain a smooth finish*. First, prepare surface. . . . Allow each coat of polyurethane to dry overnight. Between coats, sand with the grain of the wood, using 180 or 220 grit sandpaper. Remove dust each time, using a tack cloth or a vacuum cleaner."

Selecting a Topic and Prewriting

The topic for a process paper should be based on your personal experience or observation unless you plan to do research. The topic should be complex enough that readers won't find it obvious. You may find that narrowing the topic is essential: even a fairly simple process paper can become surprisingly lengthy. The subject should be one you know well. To develop your thinking skills, avoid a recipe or any other process you have learned from printed instructions.

The quickest way to start is to make a scratch outline, listing the steps or stages in sequence. Leave spaces to jot in brief explanations and insert necessary precautions or warnings at the beginning and at strategic points—not the end. *Many readers will not read the entire set of directions before they start.*

Drafting an Introduction

An introduction to a process paper may be as short as one sentence or as long as a paragraph, depending on the purpose for writing and the assignment. Particularly for directions, state the finished product or result of the process in the introduction. If you dive into the first step with no thesis statement, readers may become confused. The thesis should identify the process, make a claim, and specify the result, product, or benefit for the reader:

- White-water rafting can be an enjoyable experience for the beginner who is well prepared. (Claim/result: enjoyable experience)

- Setting up a backpacking tent correctly can net a good night's sleep. (Claim/result: good night's sleep)

The following student introductions illustrate just two of many options for an introduction.

Generalization Followed by Restriction An accurate generalization may be used for the beginning of a process analysis. Patricia Jones Black opens with a generalization followed by a restriction. Safety is her key idea. Since Patricia's introduction is only two sentences long, she chooses to combine it with the first point.

How to Process Green Beans

Home-grown green beans can be served year round when they are properly processed and stored. By following the twelve steps listed here, you can safely take green beans from the garden to the table several months later. First, pick beans that are plump and tender. Three to five pounds of beans will be needed for each quart to be processed.

Historical Opening Melinda Ham selected an unusual topic that carries a hint of nostalgia. She begins by describing the slow-paced life of pioneer days (a life without television, computers, or expensive toys).

Apple-Head Dolls: A Remnant of Yesteryear

Years ago when life was less complicated and most families lived miles away from their nearest neighbors, family entertainment was more often homespun than manufactured. Children had to invent their own games. Parents frequently made toys for their children out of natural materials because cash was scarce. One popular homemade toy was the apple-head doll. These dolls had wizened faces, like very wrinkled old people, with a variety of expressions. By following these simple instructions, you, too, can make an unusual doll for a child in your family.

Combining Second Person with Third Person   Note that Melinda begins the introduction by using third person. Then she skillfully switches to *second person in the middle of the final sentence* of the paragraph. This way she makes the pronoun shift smoothly.

Developing a Process Paper

As you draft, keep a specific audience in mind so that you will know how much explanation is needed. If you are writing directions, ask yourself, What points might be difficult, unclear, or risky? Present the steps in an orderly sequence so that the reader can understand and possibly duplicate the procedure. At the beginning, specify the equipment and material necessary to complete the process. In her paper on making apple-head dolls, Melinda Ham explains the process clearly, using numerical transitions and active verbs to indicate major steps. Her transitions are italicized here.

First, gather the necessary materials. An apple and cotton balls are needed for the face, hair, and beard of a male doll. Or you may wish to make a pair of dolls, male and female. The apple should be large because the head will shrink later. The body consists of a fine-gauge wire coat hanger, a large paper clip, clean cotton rags (an old sheet, pillowcase, or shirt), varnish or shellac, and scraps of fabric for clothing. Other items needed are a sharp paring knife, pliers, a small bowl, a bottle of pure lemon juice, plain table salt (not iodized), and about eighteen inches of heavy thread or fine cord.

Second, make the face of the doll. With the paring knife, thinly peel the apple. *Then* carve out the tiny eye sockets, nose, mouth, and ears. *After the head is carved*, place it in a small bowl. Pour one-fourth cup of lemon juice over the apple. Let set for thirty seconds, *then* rotate so that all sides are covered with juice. Wait one minute. To make the eyes, press two apple seeds horizontally into the carved sockets.

Aging is the *third* step. Unbend the paper clip, leaving the smallest "hook." Push the straight end of the clip into the top of the core down through the apple. *When the wire emerges*, bend it about an inch to make a right angle to support the apple. Loop a length of heavy thread over the top hook and tie a knot. *Next* suspend the thread from a window catch, away from direct sunlight, where the apple can hang for two to four weeks. *When the desired "wrinkling" occurs*, apply a thin coat of clear shellac or varnish to prevent further deterioration. Let dry overnight.

Fourth, add "hair" to the head. For a male, pull apart a cotton ball to form a beard. Glue around the jawline. A narrow strip of cotton around the back will form a fringe of hair around a bald spot. For a female doll, a large cotton ball (or two) will be needed for her hair, which can be arranged as desired.

Making the body is the *fifth* step. Use pliers to twist a thin wire coat hanger into a simple stick figure. Wrap strips of rags around arms and legs to give a rounded effect. Secure the rag strips with rubber bands or adhesive tape or both.

Creating clothing is the *sixth* step. Design simple clothes for the dolls. The male doll might wear a simple dark suit with a white shirt and perhaps a cap or hat. The female doll might wear a tiny apron, shawl or cape, sunbonnet, and long dress.

The final step is attaching the head. Attach the apple head firmly to the neck wire. Twist the clip wire tightly around the body wire so that the apple head will remain upright. If wire shows, cover with a necktie, shawl, or scarf.

Writing a Conclusion

An effective conclusion to a process analysis provides a sense of completion, often by referring specifically to the result of the process. If possible, end on a positive note. Even if the results of a procedure are negative, you might summarize what was learned, refer to a benefit or emotion, or add a bit of humor. Melinda ends by pointing out what makes apple-head dolls special.

Apple-head dolls are not only easy to make, but unusual. The face and expression of each doll will vary somewhat. The clothing can vary greatly. Apple-head dolls make attractive and distinctive gifts.

Revising a Process Paper

Clarity and completeness are the main qualities to check for as you revise your process paper. The following questions should be helpful.

CHECKLIST: REVISING A PROCESS PAPER

1. Who is the audience? (*Tip:* On your outline list age, experience, and any other relevant characteristics of the audience. Refer to the list as you revise your paper.)
2. Does the introduction establish the purpose and point out the product or result of the process?
3. Have necessary precautions been included at appropriate spots?
4. Are reasons included at strategic points?
5. Do transitions clearly distinguish major steps as well as substeps?
6. Is each step or stage of the process discussed in sufficient detail?
7. Does the conclusion complete the paper in a satisfying way?

TWO STUDENT PAPERS: PROCESS ANALYSIS

The purpose of Keith Witzel's paper was to explain how to replace a defective electrical outlet safely. He directed the paper to the average homeowner with relatively little experience in home repairs.

Replacing an Electrical Outlet Safely

Many people refuse to replace defective electrical connections in the home, either because of a lack of knowledge concerning the proper procedure or from fear of creating a fire hazard. By following a few simple guidelines, however, almost anyone can make minor repairs safely.

Most electrical circuits in the home are made up of general lighting circuits of either 15- or 20-amp circuits. These are the circuits used for small appliances, lamps, television, and others. These items are connected into the general lighting circuits by plugging into the wall outlet receptacles. If one of these receptacles becomes defective, it is a safe and simple process to replace it by following five main steps: First, assemble the necessary materials; second, shut off the house current; third, remove the receptacle; fourth, install the new receptacle; fifth, restore power and check the operation of the new receptacle.

First, assemble the necessary materials. These include a pair of needle-nosed pliers with a jaw approximately two inches long, tapering to a pointed end; a slotted screwdriver; a utility knife; and a new receptacle rated at 15 amps or 20 amps as required.

Second, shut off the power to the circuit that contains the defective receptacle. This is done by turning the main switch (marked on handle) to the "off" position on the circuit breaker or fuse box. Check to make certain that the electricity is off by trying to operate appliances in various locations of the house. They should not function.

Third, remove the cover plate from the defective receptacle by turning the screw in a counterclockwise direction. Remove the two screws that hold the receptacle outlet to the utility box (the small metal box mounted in the wall), and pull the receptacle from this box. There will be a white insulated wire, a black insulated wire, and possibly an uninsulated ground wire (depending on the age of the structure) attached to the receptacle. Remove these wires and discard the used receptacle.

Fourth, install the new receptacle and replace the cover. Before installation, inspect the black and white wires to ensure that each end is free of insulation for approximately five-eighths inch and the ends are formed into loops. These loops should be made in a clockwise direction. The purpose is to ensure that the wire is secured around the screw as the screw is tightened.

After that, install the wires to the new receptacle. The white wire is connected to the silver-colored side of the receptacle and the black wire to the brass-colored side. Tighten each screw firmly. Next, connect the uninsulated wire (if used) to the green screw on the bottom of the receptacle. Push the receptacle into the utility box and tighten, using the screws supplied with the new receptacle. Remount the receptacle cover, being careful not to overtighten this screw, which could cause the cover to crack.

Finally, restore power to the house and check the receptacle to see that it is functioning properly. If not, check to see that you have flipped all breaker switches.

If each of these steps is followed closely, you will have not only the satisfaction of doing the job yourself, but also the satisfaction of saving the cost of an electrician.

Questions for Discussion

1. Is Keith's paper a set of directions for a procedure or a process description? How do you know?

2. What transition does he use to indicate the substep of step four?

3. Does he provide any precautions or warnings? Where?

4. What type of ending does he use?

5. How clear do you find Keith's analysis? Is any step or substep unclear? If so, how might it be clarified?

In the next paper, Ann Kemmerley describes a procedure used at her job to make space for new books. Embedded and signpost transitions (both are italicized) provide tight links and clarify the steps for the reader.

How to Prepare Books for Sale at the Dorcas Carey Public Library

Many library books are read each year in the village of Carey. Some books, however, fail to be as popular as others and collect dust on the already crowded shelves. To dispose of the less popular works, the Dorcas Carey Public Library uses a *four-step process* to prepare books for sale.

"Weeding" is the term given to the *first step in this process*. Periodically, an assistant librarian looks through every book on a shelf for its last circulation date, found on the pocket inside the back cover. If this date goes back five years or more, the book is weeded from the shelf and placed in a stack beside the shelf. Often books will also be weeded if they are in poor condition because most people do not read books that are falling apart. This step of weeding is completed after the head librarian checks each book and decides whether to try the less popular work in another section or *to sell it*.

The books selected to be sold must then be prepared for sale. *This second step* includes ripping out the back pockets and marking out any identification. The back pocket, which holds the book's circulation card, is torn away from the page or cover where it is glued and thrown away. Any library identification, such as name and address or price, must be covered by a black marker. If this marking out is not done, a reader may confuse books bought at the book sale with those currently in circulation. An important part of this step is the saving of the circulation card, for it will be used in the *following steps*.

The removal or "pulling" of all the books' cards from the library's card catalog is the *third and lengthiest step*. In this step all cards pertaining to a book must be pulled from the drawers by tearing the lower hole. The circulation card saved in step two gives the information needed to complete this step. The circulation card's top line indicates the author, and its second line gives the title. The book's author card is pulled first. On the reverse side of this card may be a list of subjects related to the book. Each subject given is *then* found, and the cards pertaining to the book are pulled. The last card to be removed from the main card catalog is the title card. *Before step four*, it is necessary to pull another card for the book from the author file in the main office.

The fourth and final step in preparing books for sale is crossing them off in the accession books. The accession books list every book in a library according to an assigned number given at the time of purchase. This number is found on the circulation card's right side. The number is located in the accession book and "sold" is printed in the margin reserved for such remarks. At this time the circulation, author, subject, and title cards can be discarded, and books are ready for sale to the public.

The four steps for preparing books for sale are not complicated, but they do require some time. The effort put forth, however, is well worth the shelf space that can be used for new books (purchased with funds from the books sold) and the joy a reader receives from buying an inexpensive book to add to his or her own library.

Questions for Discussion

1. Is Ann's paper a set of directions for a procedure or a process description? How do you know?

2. How clear do you find Ann's analysis of the process? Is any step or substep unclear? If so, how might it be clarified?

3. Find some instances where Ann has taken time to explain the purpose for various steps and substeps. Do these explanations help you better understand the process? Do they ever make the process hard to follow? Explain your answer.

FOR YOUR REFERENCE:
PROCESS ANALYSIS ESSAYS IN THE READER

- "How to Cook a Carp," Euell Gibbons, page 586
- "Falling for Apples," Noel Perrin, page 590
- "Write Your Own Success Story," Carol Carter, page 594
- "How Do You Know It's Good?" Marya Mannes, page 600

Summary

A process analysis is a logical explanation of a process, giving either directions or a description. The analysis is arranged step by step in chronological order. Numerical transitions can mark major steps; other appropriate transitions can mark minor steps.

To write a process paper, keep a specific audience in mind so that you will know how much explanation is needed. Identify the topic and the result in the introduction. Develop the body with adequate details according to how much readers already know. Include precautions and warnings if needed. Possible endings include a summary, a reference to a benefit or emotion, and humor.

Key Terms

chronological order	major step	signpost transition
directions	numerical transition	substep
embedded transition	process analysis	transition
generalization	process description	

Test Yourself

True or False: Guidelines for Process Papers

Directions: Write T (true) or F (false) in the correct blank.

_____ 1. The finished product, result, or benefit of the process should be stated in the introduction.

_____ 2. Active verbs are best for explaining a process or procedure.

_____ 3. To be clear, steps should be parallel.

_____ 4. Numerical transition is recommended for processes with sub-steps.

_____ 5. Substeps should not be marked with numerical transitions.

_____ 6. When a writer uses "first," there should be a "second."

_____ 7. Instructions in manuals are prescriptive.

_____ 8. Precautions are necessary to forestall possible hazards.

Practice

Writing Ideas for Paragraphs

1. How to prune a shrub neatly and safely
2. How to bathe a dog with little fuss
3. How to make a paper airplane that will fly
4. How to tie a shoe (as explained to a five-year-old child)
5. How to reseed a lawn the easy way

Test Yourself Answers

All answers are true. This exercise can be used as a reference while writing a process paper.

Thirty Ideas for Process Papers

Describe or explain:

1. A natural process you have observed (butterfly hatching, erosion of a beach, aging of an oak tree, or other)
2. A procedure that you perform at work
3. How to have healthy house plants
4. How to install landscaping logs for a flower garden
5. How to water-ski, trim a poodle, or complete some other activity
6. How to bathe a bedfast patient (or an infant)

7. How to give a shot with minimum discomfort
8. How to construct a concrete patio
9. How to saddle a horse correctly
10. How to make a minor household repair (such as patching plaster)
11. Painting a house the professional way
12. Burglar-proofing your home
13. Grooming a horse for show
14. How to have a successful garage sale
15. How to cope with telemarketers
16. How to pack a suitcase efficiently
17. Weight lifting for beginners
18. How to raise big, beautiful roses
19. How to make ceramics
20. Touching up paint on a car
21. How to refinish antique furniture
22. Organizing a Neighborhood Watch program
23. How to preserve the natural beauty of a wood deck
24. Patching a bicycle tire
25. Fireproofing a home
26. How to select and eat crawfish Southern style
27. Quilting with little hand sewing
28. Fishing for bass
29. Racing a sailboat
30. How to make a Christmas wreath

CHAPTER 13

Illustration

Showing with Examples

Example moves the world more than doctrine.

—Henry Miller

For nearly fifty years Charles Schulz entertained Americans with the exploits of Charlie Brown, Snoopy, Lucy, Linus, and other characters in *Peanuts*. Schulz based many of his daily comic strips on examples taken from his own experience. He said, "If you were to read the strip, oh, for just a few months, you would know me because everything that I am goes into the strip." For instance, Charlie Brown's fear of rejection from the little red-haired girl originated from a refusal to a marriage proposal that Schulz once endured.*

PURPOSE OF EXAMPLES

Giving an example is an effective way to explain, convince, and lure a reader on. An appropriate example creates an impression by evoking an image in the reader's mind. The right selection of examples will help you demonstrate your knowledge, whether in an employment application letter, a technical report, or an essay exam, or a paper. Examples are valuable for explaining a concept, illustrating a problem, or supporting a reaction for papers in psychology, law enforcement, business management, literature, composition, philosophy, and other fields.

In the comic strip reprinted next, Charles Schulz took an incident from his boyhood, reacted, and explained what friendship meant to him. You might say that he derived a statement of his philosophy of life.

---

*Brendan I. Koerner, "Good grief! Charlie Brown says, 'So long,'" *U.S. News & World Report* 27 December 1999: 28.

Reprinted by permission of United Feature Syndicate, Inc.

ELEMENTS OF ILLUSTRATION

To illustrate or to exemplify simply means to clarify through example. You include impressions, facts, statistics, or expert opinion to lend substance to your writing, according to the rhetorical situation. The key is to choose examples that count, that enable your audience to understand what you mean and to see that you know what you are talking about. On the job you might use illustration to persuade, as in a proposal or grant application. In an academic paper or a personal essay, you might use illustration to explain (see "Envy" at the end of this chapter). Examples may relate an incident, compare, describe, or explain for a purpose. *Anecdotes* are brief stories, often humorous. An *analogy* is an extended comparison. *Historical examples* usually describe people or events. *Literary allusions* are examples taken from literature. *Hypothetical examples* are conjectures—supposedly true. However, real examples drawn from life are the most interesting and convincing.

WRITING A PAPER OF ILLUSTRATION

For a paper of illustration, you have a wide range of topic choices and organizational strategies. Select a topic you can develop with interesting examples. Then arrange the examples in an order that reflects your purpose.

Prewriting

The topic may be concrete or abstract, according to the assignment. When something is concrete, it is detectable through at least one of the five senses, often more. You can see, hear, feel, smell, or taste it. If you write about an abstract principle, you can clarify it with concrete examples familiar to the reader. You can cite a variety of examples as long as they all have a central thread.

Excellent illustrations can often be lifted from everyday life. For instance, if you have a family heirloom, memento, or special gift (possibly a music box), you might find a topic there. Perhaps your great uncle has a set of silver swords hanging over the fireplace. What do these objects represent to your family? Or perhaps your home has an unusual feature: a tower room, a secret room or passage, or something else. What is the story behind it?

Once you have chosen a topic, prewrite to form a pool of details. To start your creative juices flowing, write your topic at the top of a clean sheet of paper. Then jot down every idea that dives into your mind—anything that might be used as support. If you know the topic well, you will soon have a page of examples and details. To start prewriting, the following questions will be helpful:

- Why am I interested in the topic?
- What examples can I recall?
- Who is connected with the topic?
- Did he or she have a favorite saying, mannerism, or habit?
- How has he or she influenced me? Can I give an example?
- What changes have occurred; how do I feel about the changes?
- What is my main point?

Finally, draft a thesis that makes a point about your topic, ideally one that is unfamiliar to your readers.

Organizing and Developing a Paper of Illustration

To organize and develop your paper, choose an order, select examples, and weave explanation with examples, all the while focusing on your purpose and considering your audience.

See chapter 4.

Order   To organize a paper of illustration, select an order that suits your purpose and topic. You might organize examples chronologically or according to importance or in any other way that will advance your point. As you read the student papers in this chapter, notice the organizational strategies. Dixie O'Rourke uses chronological order, as shown in this outline:

Envy

   I. Introduction: Example of envy at age ten (very strong).

  II. Body

      A. Age thirteen. Envy had decreased somewhat.

      B. Example: Sudden change in Dixie's perspective.

      C. Today: Envy seldom occurs.

 III. Conclusion

Other topics can be organized according to some variation on order of importance. For a paper about exotic pets, you might move from relatively familiar examples to more surprising or outrageous ones. For a paper on natural cures for common ailments, you might move from examples of cures for minor ailments to examples of cures for more life-threatening ones. Such orders have the advantage of holding readers' attention by providing examples that increase in interest.

Relevant, Accurate, and Sufficient Examples   Every example you include should be *relevant* to your thesis, illustrating your main point in some way. Resist the temptation to include an example just because it is odd or funny. Illustrations should illuminate a point. Irrelevant examples distract from the thesis.

Check to see that examples are *accurate*. In attempting to be humorous or to dramatize a point, writers sometimes embellish examples, but extravagance can sabotage logic. An example may be dramatic, but it should not be too far-fetched or unusual—the one-in-a-million variety. To palm off an atypical example as typical is dishonest. If you generalize from an example, it should be *typical of its class*. When researching, consider the source of your statistics. Is it reliable? Is the information up-to-date?

How many examples will be sufficient? The answer depends on the nature of your thesis and the weight of the examples. The sheer number of examples is less important than their quality. Select impressive examples that will provide strong support for your thesis. A controversial or debatable thesis will require several high-quality examples to convince a skeptical audience. As a rule, when examples are brief, you need more than when they can be developed in detail.

In a paper entitled "The Talent Within," Nicole Vanderkooi cites several brief examples in each paragraph. Each example is clearly relevant. Her third paragraph appears here:

> Possessing a natural skill can be overpowering, a constant pressure. Children with such talent have expectations already set for them. At age six, Sarah Wells was told she had a promising future in gymnastics and was enrolled in nightly classes. Despite many strained muscles, injured ankles, and missed slumber parties, she persevered and gained confidence. Yet she endured many lows as well as highs; she became critical of herself. Constant pressure from her parents and coaches and a desire to win made her dream a reality. At thirteen, Sarah began her powerful run to the vault. To keep her lead in the meet, she had to score at least a 9.5. As her hands hit the leather, she felt the adrenaline pump, and she scored a perfect 10. A spectator cheered, "That's awesome!" Sarah Wells won the meet. By now her childhood was gone, but in its place was a confidence powered by success. To some people, that is robbery; to Sarah it is a rewarding way of life.

Weaving Examples with Explanation   As you draft, try to find an interesting approach to your topic. You might start with a series of short examples, eye-catching details drawn from everyday life. To connect the examples to your thesis, you will need to interlace them with explanation. Bryan Vaughn weaves example with explanation as he describes his perceptions of happiness:

> During my childhood, happiness meant anything from having waffles for breakfast to being able to stay outside after the streetlights came on, catching lightning bugs and playing tag. Early in my adolescence, happiness seemed to take on another meaning. Driving fast was my new source of happiness. I discovered that a motor could be affixed to just about anything. My first few inventions were just this side of lethal. When I consider these vehicles, it's a wonder I'm still alive today. I rode go-carts, three-wheelers, snowmobiles, motorcycles—anything I could put gas in, I drove.

During mid-adolescence, my perception of happiness changed again. Sports became my passion. For me, nothing could compare with the exhilaration of being part of a winning team. Our football team was the defending state champion. Our basketball team finished third in the state, and our baseball team was the conference champion. Happiness was being one of the main players on every team and having the potential to play college sports and possibly having a career in professional sports.

But those dreams ended during a football game when I received a severe spinal injury. After two months in the hospital, I was sent home—handicapped, but thankful. At this time happiness took on yet a new meaning: I was just glad to be alive and able to walk. . . .

As my life began to return to normal, I saw a new source of happiness. One day I saw, parked in front of a Sunoco station, a red 1969 Pontiac GTO Judge. That same day I bought "The Judge" and spent every spare minute working on it. . . . But later an old man drove out in front of me without warning and wrecked my happiness. . . . Although I bought another car, it was not the same as the Judge.

Now that I have matured to a ripe old twenty-two, the word *happiness* means much more than ever before. . . .

Writing a Conclusion

The conclusion for a paper of illustration, as with any essay, should provide a satisfying close. Ending on a positive note, especially after the recounting of a painful experience, is gratifying for the reader. Barb Bronson ends "Clipper Ship Mom" (see chapter 10) by continuing the comparison and expressing gratitude:

My clipper ship, my mom, has endured many rough storms. Every day I thank God that my mother stood fast. Words can never express how lucky I feel to have her. At the present Clipper Ship Mom and crew continue to sail steadfastly on course, but on different seas.

In a paper about a series of failures she faced, Phyllis Parks ends on an optimistic note, providing some specific examples of current successes:

Despite the failures I have experienced, all phases of my life have not been grim. My daughter from my first marriage has grown into a beautiful, healthy young lady. Fifteen months ago my new husband and I were married. I am also enrolled in college classes. Now I truly feel successful.

Sometimes writers tend to repeat their introductions in slightly different words or to summarize their body paragraphs. Try to find a more satisfying conclusion. Consider explaining a particular insight, noting an advantage, offering a suggestion, or expressing an opinion that is supported by your examples. Leave readers feeling they have learned something from the examples.

Revising a Paper of Illustration

After your first draft has cooled a bit, go back and read through the examples carefully. Try to distance yourself from each one so that you can evaluate it impartially. As you make revisions, consider the principles you have learned so far. The following checklist will help you revise.

CHECKLIST: REVISING A PAPER OF ILLUSTRATION

1. What is the main point of the paper? Is the point clear?
2. Is each example relevant, accurate, and valid?
3. Does each example add substance to my claim?
4. Do the examples create interest?
5. Are there enough examples?
6. Are examples arranged in a clear, logical order? Or could the order be improved?

TWO STUDENT PAPERS: ILLUSTRATION

In the first paper, Anita Ketcham describes her hobby in an unusual way, blending explanation with example. Her purpose was to entertain as well as inform.

Bathtub Solitude

An avid tennis player can be found lobbing away on the court; a woodworker may enjoy crafting furniture in a workshop; a gardener may relax by tending flowerbeds. I, too, have an enjoyable hobby—one that is not only relaxing and challenging but also educational. Like tennis, woodworking, and gardening, my hobby is done in the best possible place. That is why I do crossword puzzles in the bathtub.

As a mother of four young children, I rarely find time to sit down. Any time I do take for myself is soon interrupted. Mom sitting down is like a red flag waving, signaling a parade of little feet. This is why the bathtub is the perfect place to relax while working puzzles. There I cannot answer the telephone or pour a glass of milk or dress a Barbie doll. Those tasks have to wait. For a half hour, I escape to my own private retreat. Although it's not like Hawaii or the Bahamas, yet I am totally alone with my book and my bubbles, and it seems like heaven. The toughest problem I have to face is a six-letter word for supplication.

Working crossword puzzles is challenging. My favorites are the large "challenger" puzzles because the clues are difficult, requiring considerable thought. Still, I enjoy matching wits with the puzzlemaker. Some words can have several meanings and the clues can be ambiguous. A good puzzle solver learns to look at clues from different angles. For example, a five-letter word for the clue "drop a line" could be *write* or *angle*, but the answer the puzzlemaker wanted was *erase*. "Iron clothes" could be a clue for *press*; however, *armor* was the answer. A very difficult clue can be frustrating, especially for a puzzle printed in a newspaper because answers are not available until the next day. Although I rarely complete a difficult puzzle, I always try to improve my skills in order to do better with the next one.

Working crossword puzzles is educational. By using a dictionary often, I have expanded my vocabulary. Words such as *hirsute* and *litigious* have been added to my lexicon—as well as the word *lexicon*. And where else but in crossword puzzles could one find such a plethora of insignificant information? I know that Guido's note is an *ela*, but I do not know who Guido is. I know that the answer to "Roman bronze" is *aes* and that Caesar's road is an *iter*, should anyone ask. Not all of the knowledge I have gleaned from crossword puzzles is this trivial; some I have even found useful. Knowing that Siam is the former name of Thailand and that Istanbul was once Constantinople has helped me to defeat my husband during heated games of *Jeopardy*. He thinks he is married to a genius! I will never tell him my secret.

For my soon-to-be birthday, my husband will probably give me a bottle of bubble bath, the latest copy of *Dell Championship Crosswords*, and an hour to myself. Then I can enjoy some peace and quiet, sharpen my wits, and discover words new to me. All knocks on the door will be ignored. I will come out only when my toes are too wrinkled to stay longer.

Questions for Discussion

1. Look at Anita's opening. What expectation does she set up with the first three brief examples?
2. What comparisons do you see in paragraph two?
3. What is the purpose of the examples in paragraphs three and four?
4. Look at Anita's ending. How do the examples function there?

Next, Dixie O'Rourke offers a series of extended personal examples to show how she learned to control her emotions.

Envy

One evening without warning, envy crept into my young heart. The year was 1967. The place was a backyard ice rink at the home of my best friend, Sylvia. Although the time was only 5:00 p.m., dusk had already settled. Sylvia had just gone inside to eat dinner with her family in their comfortable brick home in a pleasant neighborhood.

Outside I continued to cut figure eights and spin on the ice while Sylvia ate dinner. As I paused to catch my breath, I found myself staring through the dining room window. Inside, the brightly lit room appeared warm and friendly as the family gathered around the table. Sylvia's father stood at the head, reading from the family Bible.

As I continued to window peek, I felt an overwhelming surge of envy and ill will. Suddenly, I was resentful not only of Sylvia's many possessions, but also of her intact family. I longed to live like Sylvia. This flood of painful feelings changed not only how I felt toward her, but also how I felt toward myself. The contentment of my childhood had shattered: I was ashamed of my house, my family, and myself.

Only ten years old, I was unable to deal with these new feelings of inferiority and kept them locked tightly within. I feared losing my best friend; I was afraid that if I told Sylvia how I felt, she might not like me anymore. I also feared telling my grandparents (with whom I resided); they might feel hurt and angry. So I told no one.

By junior high school, the feelings of shame and resentment had begun to diminish. Although I still felt pangs of envy when my friends flaunted their possessions, I had learned to control the envy so that it did not overwhelm me. The technique was simple—nothing new. I would count my blessings and thank God for each and every one of them. My grandparents had set a good example for me.

When I was thirteen, a sobering experience brought my perspective into a more realistic focus. During the school lunch hour, a group of students, whom I envied, gathered in front of the malt shop across from the school. This particular day the group welcomed and invited me to go with them to a carnival at a shopping center across town. The plan was to meet after school the next day and walk to the carnival. Knowing my grandfather's second job took him near the area, I offered the group a ride.

When school let out that afternoon, I ran home to plead for a ride and money for the carnival. Smiling, my grandmother lifted the lid of an old blue sugar bowl and gave me several silver coins. The next day grandpa drove his old Chevrolet, freckled with rust, to the school; and five of us piled in. When we reached a large parking lot, my friends hurried off toward the carnival without a word or backward glance to either of us.

Grandpa locked the car doors, bid me goodbye, and started toward the factory. As I watched him fade into the crowd, my eyes watered. Not one person had thanked him for the ride or waited for me. The envy I felt for that group fled. Suddenly, I felt proud of my grandfather even though he wore bib overalls and carried a lunch bucket. I felt fortunate to have both my grandparents.

Although I still feel a twinge of envy now and then, I no longer have the strong feelings of my youth. As my values have changed, I have focused my energies in a positive direction; presently, I'm working full time and attending classes for a nursing degree. Over the years, I have learned to subdue envy and to make the most of what I have.

Questions for Discussion

1. What do you notice about Dixie's opening?

2. How does she set the scene for the reader?

3. What do you notice about Dixie's vantage point? (See the second paragraph: "outside," "inside.")

4. What incident causes a sharp shift in Dixie's perspective?

5. Examine her conclusion. What do you notice?

FOR YOUR REFERENCE:
ILLUSTRATION ESSAYS IN THE READER

- "Mothers of Invention," Ethlie Vare & Greg Ptacek, page 606
- "Road Rage," Vest, Cohen, & Tharp, page 609
- "Black and Well-to-Do," Andrea Lee, page 615
- "Uptight Is Back in Style," Holman W. Jenkins, Jr., page 618

Summary

An illustration paper uses examples to explain, convince, or persuade, according to the rhetorical situation. The topic may be concrete or abstract; both kinds need concrete examples for support. Prewriting will help find raw material. The best examples are relevant, accurate, and adequate. The number needed depends not only on the type and quality of the examples but also on the topic, the purpose, and the audience.

Examples can be organized in various ways. Chronological order, concrete-to-abstract order, and comparison are often used. Examples integrated with explanation are effective. Ending on a positive note can provide a satisfying close.

As you revise your illustrations, weigh their effectiveness. Check the relevance, accuracy, quality, and number. Arrange in a logical order.

Key Terms

abstract	concrete	hypothetical example
analogy	example	illustration
anecdote	exemplification	literary allusion

Practice

Ideas for Writing

1. A pet food company is seeking winsome cats and dogs to be featured in television commercials. Write a letter explaining why your pet should be featured. Include examples of behavior and training.

2. Recently you purchased a home. Near the back fence, on a neighbor's property, stands an apple tree. Several limbs extend over the fence. Rotten apples, covered with insects, dot your lawn. Bees have stung your children twice. Legally, you can cut the tree back to the fence line, but for the sake of diplomacy, you prefer to talk to the neighbor. Map out your strategy by prewriting.

3. Describe a seemingly small incident such as a chance meeting or a sudden impulse that influenced your life.

4. Describe your first ride on a roller coaster.

5. Write an article for your campus newspaper using humorous examples to spoof a campus condition or a consumer product.

Thirty Ideas for Papers of Illustration

1. Optimism pays
2. How my view of work has changed

Not a "How to" essay

3. Soothing upset restaurant patrons is an art
4. Ways to save dollars at the supermarket
5. Beware of bargains in flea markets
6. How my parent's divorce affected me
7. Learning from hardship
8. Beware the pirates of the road
9. Aggressive drivers
10. What are good manners?
11. Easy ways to save money
12. An eccentric neighbor
13. Being a latchkey kid is not for the timid
14. Adversity can be an asset
15. How possessions complicate our lives
16. A wonderful friend
17. The most frugal person I know
18. Perils of baby-sitting
19. Common sense is in short supply

Go with what you KNOW

20. Avoiding common telemarketing scams
21. Common gardening mistakes
22. My Achilles heel
23. _____ is not my favorite television show
24. Ways to attract hummingbirds
25. Wardrobe basics that look smart and save cash
26. Visit Cincinnati's Gardens
27. View the wonders of West Virginia
28. The courage of a handicapped child
29. My grandmother's perseverance
30. My Father's Gift: Persistence

★ "Examples" ★

31. Part of Small / Large family
32. Only or one of many children
33. Books can change our lives
34. Learning to cope with _____ ....as a part of growing up
35. Experiences in childhood make lasting impressions?
36. Family gatherings can be .....?
37. Television shows can reflect real life.
38. People who have influenced my life
39. Experiences on vacation
40. Mexican food (3 types)

CHAPTER 14

Classification

Grouping and Dividing

Out of clutter, find simplicity.
—Albert Einstein

PURPOSE OF CLASSIFICATION

Classification allows us to establish order in our lives and to function effectively. For example, our linear measurement follows the U.S. Customary System. The division of distance into miles, furlongs, rods, yards, feet, and inches allows us to be specific. According to the Gregorian calendar, our year is divided into twelve months, each month into weeks, and each week into days. Each day is divided into hours, each hour into minutes, and each minute into seconds. That is just the beginning.

Everything on this planet can be classified in some way. The estimated five million species of life are divided into five formal classifications or kingdoms: animals, plants, fungi, bacteria, molds, etc. But we also classify in other ways. Vehicles are classified as sports cars, sedans, trucks, vans, SUVs, and the like. Then they are divided into subcategories. Credit card companies and manufacturers classify consumers in order to market their wares well. You classify when you sort and store, whether documents or laundry.

WHAT IS THE BASIS OF CLASSIFICATION?

Classification is a method of grouping and dividing items and ideas logically. To classify, you look for common features that certain elements or items have—a *principle of selection* that sets them off as a group. All members of the group must have this similarity. For example, lions, tigers, and house cats have enough similarity to be classified as felines (the principle of selection). Then felines can be

Unclassified Buckeye Fans

■■■○○■■○■○○■■○■■■■

Classified Buckeye Fans

Casual Fans   Concerned Fans   Ardent Fans

○○○○○○   ■■■■■■■■■■   ■■■■■■■

Fig. 14.1 Classification of Buckeye Fans.

subdivided into subcategories such as wild cats and domestic cats. Domestic cats can be subdivided further according to breed such as Manx, Persian, or Angora.

Student writer Jane Tinker informally classifies Ohio State football fans into three groups, according to their degree of "Buckeye Fever" (later in this chapter). Her principles of selection are "casual fans," "concerned fans," and "ardent fans" (see fig. 14.1).

WRITING A PAPER OF CLASSIFICATION

A paper of classification not only groups and divides but also analyzes, describes, and explains. The purpose and the topic determine the order.

Shaping a Topic to the Purpose and Audience

Many famous writers advise selecting a subject you know and care about. Then you can shape it to your purpose and the needs of the audience. Chances are that you already have a lode of details to be mined and classified. If you are a family history buff, you might describe your dominant impression of a quirky relative by grouping traits into well-defined categories. Or perhaps you live near a scenic area with little-known features that might attract tourists. If you were to write a brochure, what features would you describe and how would you classify them?

Observing at a restaurant buffet, Patricia Rush classified the members of "Annoying Eaters of America" as "inspectors, conversationalists, and gulpers." Her purpose was to amuse, and her audience was her classmates. Here is how she described the third group:

> Gulpers are the Indianapolis drivers of the table. To prepare for the race, they pile their platters high, thus cutting down on stops for refueling. They are determined to finish the meal first, even at the cost of indigestion. Stuffing their mouths and chomping, they shovel in the food and wash it down with great gulps of water. When every scrap is gone, they sometimes take a morsel of bread and swab their platters clean. Often their belches can be heard throughout the restaurant. Gulpers are usually males in ragged T-shirts and dingy jeans. For them, these garments may have more than one use; gulpers sometimes finish by wiping their hands across their chests or thighs.

GUIDELINES: CLASSIFICATION

1. ***Classify items according to the purpose and audience.*** Have a reason.

2. ***Avoid overlapping parts or categories.*** Be clear-cut.

3. ***Make each part or category large enough to contain a significant number.*** Have a minimum of three items or details in each category.

4. ***Make all parts parallel.*** All items in a category should be similar, having a common principle of selection. Then they will be parallel.

5. ***Organize all parts or categories to fit into one logical system.*** All the parts should fit together into one organized whole.

6. ***Arrange in a logical order.*** See "Seven Basic Orders," page 40.

Prewriting with the "Because" Technique

With a topic in mind, you can use any of the prewriting techniques you learned in chapter 3. Still another way of prewriting can be helpful: the "because" technique. This technique works well for topics that can be divided into advantages, benefits, or reasons. Just ask a question about the topic, then answer "because. . . ." Jot down your answer and ask "What else?" Repeat the sequence until you have enough material. After that, group the details logically into main points.

Let's assume you have a fourteen-year-old daughter, Kim, who has been invited to go riding with Brad, the sixteen-year-old next door. But you are convinced Brad is a reckless and irresponsible driver. Simply stating your belief and forbidding Kim to go may not carry much weight with her. You need evidence to support the claim and reinforce your decision. Prior to your talk, you use the "because" technique to help you classify relevant facts into main points:

Questions	*Answers*
1. Why does Brad seem irresponsible?	*Because* I have seen him speed by children on bikes, run stop signs and red lights. He brakes sharply, squealing his tires.
2. Are there any other reasons?	*Because* he has put several dents in his car although he's had it only three months. He backed into his mother's car last week.
3. What else?	*Because* he has been cited for speeding twice.

Your prewriting could continue until everything you know about Brad's driving has been listed. Then you could analyze the details and divide them into three categories such as: *speeding, carelessness,* and *ignoring traffic rules.*

Organizing a Classification Paper

Perhaps the most common order for a paper of classification is some order of degree: simple to complex, least to most important, easy to difficult, and so forth. To make a case against Brad as a driver you might organize points from the least to most dangerous aspects of his driving.

Brad is a reckless and irresponsible driver:

1. *Because he is careless.*
   Last week he backed into his mother's car.
   His car has several dents in it after only three months.
   He does not slow down for children on bicycles.

2. *Because he speeds.*
   He has had two speeding tickets.
   He drove 50 mph on a street posted at 35 mph.
   He turns corners too fast, squealing his tires.

3. *Because he often ignores other traffic rules.*
   He turns quickly without signaling to other drivers.
   He drove through a stop sign last week.
   He sometimes drives through red lights.

Drafting a Thesis Statement

The next step is to draft a tentative thesis. As you may recall, a thesis statement not only tells the reader the topic but also often suggests a logical order and hints at an attitude toward the topic. In a paper of classification, the thesis statement frequently sets up an order of degree, from least important to most important. Mark Newell uses this order to arrange his three main points in his thesis:

A good location, plenty of patience, and the right ammunition are three advantages I use to achieve successful squirrel hunting.

Not all thesis statement specify points or categories; some simply make a brief claim. For example, the parent might say, "You can't go out with Brad for three reasons."

Developing Main Points and Embedding Transition

As you draft, develop your main points with specific details, reasons, and explanations. Each paragraph should support the claim made in the thesis. And each paragraph should have a clear link to the thesis, either through signpost or embedded transition. Subtle transition is the mark of a proficient writer.

In the next example, Mark Brady begins by stating an opinion in the first sentence. In the second sentence he gives a fact. In the third sentence, the thesis, he supports opinion with three reasons (italicized):

> Upland bird hunting in Ohio is in a sad condition. Populations of three game birds—the ring-necked pheasant, the blue grouse, and the bobwhite quail—have dwindled. Three main factors for this decline are *the kind of hunters, increased pollution,* and *clearing of woods and underbrush for farming.*

Note how Mark returns to each of the main points of his thesis in the opening sentences of his body paragraphs:

> Along with the good *hunters* in the fields are a number of ignorant *hunters* who shoot every bird they can, despite the fact that they are exceeding the daily bag limit. . . .
>
> The second reason for the dwindling bird population is the *increased pollution* in our environment. . . .
>
> The *farmer* is probably the biggest reason for the declining bird populations. . . .

Again, in his conclusion, Mark reinforces each of his initial main points:

> Frankly, most of those concerned seem to contribute to poor hunting conditions. The *nonsportsman hunter* takes home more birds than allowed. The *manufacturers who make pesticides and weed sprays* sometimes fail to adequately check the long-term effects of products upon birds and their eggs. Many *farmers* clear their land and plow in the fall, not leaving cover or grain for the game birds. Surely we must work to solve this problem before it is too late.

Mark does an excellent job of connecting his thesis to the main points of his paper, using all four kinds of embedded transition: repetition of key terms, synonyms, pronoun and antecedent, and natural relationships.

FOUR KINDS OF EMBEDDED TRANSITIONS

1. **Repetition of key terms:** hunters, increased pollution
2. **Synonyms:** ignorant hunters, nonsportsman hunters
3. **Pronoun and antecedent:** hunters/they
4. **Natural relationships:** pollution/manufacturers/pesticides/sprays, nonsportsman/bag limit, farming/farmers

---

STUDENT ESSAY WITH THE MAIN POINTS IN THE THESIS

In the following essay, Michele Flahive states three main points in the thesis. She uses embedded transition to establish clear links from the thesis to body paragraphs. These links mark the path of the main idea and provide unity. Note how she repeats a key term (italicized) in the first sentence of each body paragraph:

Diamonds: A Girl's Summer Friend

As the batter walks up to the dusty plate on the diamond, she scans the outfield. Spying a vacancy between left and left center, she knows this is the best area to hit the ball. While the pitcher gets ready to make her move, the batter stands in position. In a slow pitch, the ball sails off into a perfect arc, dropping right where the batter wants it. With her heart pounding, she swings the aluminum bat and cracks the ball. Quickly, she runs three bases, listening to the cheers of teammates and hoping to reach home plate before the ball. For her the *challenge*, the *enjoyment*, and the *camaraderie* make softball a game worth playing.

The first game of the season seems always to pose a special *challenge*. The players often feel a bit rusty and nervous. Just walking onto the field and up to bat that first time takes strength of will. But once the umpire yells, "Play ball," the nervousness melts away and determination flows in. Enthusiasm for the game takes over.

Enjoyment of softball is the heart of the game. After a long day of work or school, it is a pleasure to leave the stress behind and walk out onto the diamond. Since both teammates and crowd are just out for an evening of recreation, there is no great pressure to win. The fun and action provide a refreshing reward at the end of a day.

The challenge and enjoyment would be incomplete without the *camaraderie* of teammates who share the same passion for a rousing game of softball. And when a member is feeling down for missing a ball or for striking out, words of encouragement flow from other members. Then too, there is a sense of unity as everyone plays together in the infield and outfield, backing each other up as needed.

As August slowly winds to an end, so must the summer softball season. It can be a sad time for many die-hard ball players who must leave the diamond and put away their gloves. Yet some players take heart, for not only does autumn bring bright foliage and cool evenings, but it also heralds the fall softball season!

Did you notice how Michele sets the scene and pulls the reader right into the action at the very beginning? With just a few concrete details, she creates an image of the dusty plate, batter with pounding heart, aluminum bat, sound of the bat hitting the ball, perfect arc, and cheers. This vivid description helps the reader to relive what she feels and sees as she walks up to the batter's box.

Making Main Points Parallel

See chapter 8.

When main points are parallel, the resulting balance strengthens transition, sentence structure, and unity. In the example below, note how Joanne M. Pohlman begins each main point with the same type of structure, a gerund phrase (italicized). Each main point in the body explains the matching point in her thesis:

Thesis: As a volunteer member of the National Ski Patrol, I earn the opportunity to meet many interesting people, learn challenging skills, and spend time with my family.

Parallel points:
1. *Joining the Central Division of the Patrol* has acquainted me with approximately eighty other patrollers. . . .
2. *Becoming a member of this national organization* takes more than being a proficient skier. My training. . . .
3. *Being able to ski with my family* is the main reason I chose to become a patroller.

Writing a Conclusion

A conclusion should flow logically and smoothly from the main idea. As a result, the reader should gain a sense of completeness or closure. To provide a satisfying ending, writers often allude to the thesis, as Joanne Pohlman does. At the end of the paper about skiing, she repeats the name of the organization and expresses appreciation:

> Finally, I feel fortunate to belong to the National Ski Patrol. Although I receive no wages, I do gain new friends, invaluable skills, and a closeness with my family that is priceless.

Revising the Paper

A paper of classification is more complex than those discussed in earlier chapters. The checklist below should help you to revise your paper successfully:

CHECKLIST: REVISING CLASSIFICATION PAPERS

1. Has the topic been narrowed to one item?
2. Is the introduction focused and interesting?
3. Do the main points follow the order set up in the thesis statement?
4. Are the main points linked with the thesis?
5. Are the main points parallel?
6. Are the main points well supported with specific details and examples?
7. Does the internal order of each paragraph flow well?
8. Can clarity be improved? Is more transition needed?

TWO STUDENT PAPERS: CLASSIFICATION

In the first paper, Nicole Vanderkooi's purpose is to inform, and her classmates are her audience. She describes three types of people a tourist might encounter on the streets of New Orleans.

The Melting Pot of New Orleans

The sweet voice of jazz and spicy smell of Cajun cuisine capture Nicole's senses as she walks through the French Quarter of New Orleans. People from every walk of life seem to wander these cobblestone streets. On the corner of Bourbon Street sits a vagrant, playing his harmonica. In a horse-drawn carriage, a tourist reclines, listening to the clip-clop of hooves and the driver's southern drawl. In an art gallery, a sightseer from New York purchases yet another work for his loft. Carrying a briefcase, a local businessman strides past the shops, bent on another destination.

Draped with tattered overcoats and wearing tennis shoes, the homeless of this elusive city often wear weathered grins amid week-old whiskers. Their daily hours are spent collecting tips for providing the pleasure of hearing their sultry saxophones. The night brings them home to humid, stagnant alleys and alcoves. These bumbling creatures usually walk alone, attended only by their instrument and ever-faithful bottle, enclosed in a brown paper bag.

Tourists and sightseers dot the avenues of New Orleans. At daybreak they begin to roam the high-priced novelty shops and spacious old plantations surrounding the area. Often dressed in walking shorts, they sport "I survived New Orleans nightlife" T-shirts and sun visors or sunglasses. Frequently, a woman is escorted by an overburdened man and a trusty guidebook. By night, infamous nocturnal pleasures entice many to partake in Cajun feasting and boisterous drinking.

Yet another colorful feature of this Louisiana melting pot is the local businessman. Attired in a single-breasted black suit, an ivory silk shirt, and a brilliant tie, this worldly person projects professionalism and sophistication. Finding him in an art gallery or trendy coffee shop, drinking a black brew from small cups is not unusual. At night he often dines at a specialty restaurant and listens to the rhythms of jazz. His companion may be a colleague or a breathtaking, well-dressed woman.

New Orleans graciously accepts the prize for the most captivating city. There musical vagrants, inquisitive visitors, and local residents catch the eye and capture the heart.

Questions for Discussion

1. What are Nicole's three categories? How does her way of introducing them differ from Joanne Pohlman's introduction (ski patrol)?

2. What kind of order does she use within each paragraph?

3. Where has Nicole used embedded transition to link body paragraphs to her thesis?

4. What kinds of specific details does Nicole use to describe each of her categories? Are the details comparable in each case? Why do you think so?

5. How does Nicole establish closure in her ending?

6. What else do you notice?

In the next paper, Jane Tinker classifies football fans into three categories. Her tongue-in-cheek tone and adroit use of concrete details enable readers to share her amusement.

Buckeye Fever

Every autumn for the past twelve years, I have witnessed an outbreak of "Buckeye Fever" in my neighborhood. The ailment seems to hit victims in varying intensities. They are the casual, the concerned, and the ardent fans of the Ohio State Buckeyes.

The mildest strain of Buckeye Fever is evident in the casual fans. When time permits, they enjoy watching the game on television or listening on radio. But if time is limited or the weather turns sunny and warm, they forsake the game without a second thought. If given tickets, they will go—they may even buy them occasionally. The casual fans usually know the names and numbers of a few star players. Some casual fans feel that if the Bucks lose the game, an afternoon's viewing time is wasted. Casual fans are not interested in watching the Saturday night replay, for they already know the result.

Buckeye Fever hits concerned fans with moderate severity. They watch or listen to every Buckeye game possible. With buddies they enjoy seeing the Bucks on television. Enthusiastic, the concerned fans enter into the game, yelling and screaming as excitement mounts. If they have to miss a game, they will tape it on the VCR to watch later. They will purchase tickets to a game if readily available, but they will not stand in line for hours. They know the names and numbers of all starting players and are also aware of the opponent's capabilities. If Ohio State loses, the concerned fans are very disappointed, but not upset if the game was well played.

The ardent fans have contracted a serious case of Buckeye Fever. This strain may be terminal to some relationships. On Friday nights, the ardent fans are planning and preparing their elaborate tailgate lunches for the next day's game. Early Saturday mornings they rise early to proudly display their scarlet and gray flags in a prominent place and to beat the traffic jam to home games or any other within driving distance. Their tickets have been purchased either by waiting long hours in line or by knuckling into scalpers.

Dressed in their red sweaters and gray pants, the ardent fans anticipate the glory of Buckeye victory. They know the names, numbers, and personal statistics of all fifty team players as well as the high school players being recruited for next season. Later the ardent fans watch the replay to relive moments of victory. Depending on the outcome of the game, the Buckeye coach is either a saint or a bum. When the Bucks lose, the ardent fans are furious; then they become depressed. The depression may last until the following Tuesday, when they begin to anticipate the upcoming game.

Despite the degree to which a fan catches the fever, they all agree that football can be a very exciting game to watch. And for them, no team is more exciting than the Ohio State Buckeyes.

Questions for Discussion

1. How does Jane's introduction to her three categories differ from Nicole's?
2. What principle of organization has Jane used for her paper?
3. Where has Jane used embedded transition to link body paragraphs back to her thesis?
4. Why do you think Jane devotes more attention to her final category than her first two?
5. How does Jane's ending differ from Nicole's?

FOR YOUR REFERENCE:
CLASSIFICATION ESSAYS IN THE READER

- "It's Only a Paper World," Kathleen Fury, page 621
- "Mind Over Munchies," Norman Brown, page 624
- "Where Do We Stand?" Lisa Davis, page 629
- "How Do We Find the Student?" James T. Baker, page 632

Summary

Classification helps us to organize our lives. Classification is the grouping and subdividing of various items or ideas into categories that form one system. Each category is regulated by a principle of selection.

To be effective, the topic should be shaped according to the purpose and audience. The "because technique" is a method of prewriting and scratch outlining. For a paper of classification, main points and categories are often organized according to importance.

To write well, a writer should know and care about the topic. For clarity, main points should be tightly linked to the thesis statement. An excellent means of connection is embedded transition. To support the thesis, body paragraphs should be fleshed out with facts, concrete details, and reasons. A reference to the thesis can establish closure at the end of a paper.

Key Terms

because technique	embedded transition	parallelism
classification	principle of selection	

Test Yourself

Embedded Transition

Directions: Examine Joanne Pohlman's thesis and main points about skiing (under "Making Main Points Parallel"). Identify each type of transition below: Repetition of key terms (R), synonym (S), pronoun/antecedent (P), or natural relationships (N). (To check your answers, turn to the end of the chapter.)

_____ 1. National Ski *Patrol*/Central Division of the *Patrol*

_____ 2. join/member

_____ 3. meet/become acquainted

_____ 4. interesting people/eighty other skiers

_____ 5. spend time with my *family*/ski with my *family*.

Classification

Directions: Analyze the statements below and classify them according to the listed categories. (Answers appear at the end of the chapter.)

cliché	common belief	myth
old saying	superstition	fad
stereotype	tradition	trend

_____ 1. "Punkers" dye their hair unusual colors such as green, orange, or purple.

_____ 2. Groups of people who ride motorcycles and wear black leather jackets are dangerous.

———— 3. Red sky at night; sailors' delight
Red sky in morning; sailors take warning.

———— 4. An unusual custom, hundreds of years old, survives in Olney, England. There, on the day before Lent, housewives bake pancakes and race to the church service, flipping the pancake three times or more during the contest.

———— 5. When a couple divorce, the mother should receive custody of very young children.

———— 6. To win at bridge, select a seat that is parallel with the bathtub in the house.

———— 7. Money is the root of all evil.

———— 8. According to Greek legend, Cerberus guarded the underworld, the realm of Hades, devouring anyone who tried to leave.

———— 9. Don't make mountains out of molehills.

———— 10. The middle class is gradually disappearing.

Practice

Collaborative Learning: Classification

Directions: Select the word in each group that is not in the same category as the other three words. Then compare your selections with other group members. Discuss disagreement. You may use dictionaries.

1. tanning lotion
   shaving cream
   toothpaste
   cleansing cream

2. hickory
   walnut
   elm
   oak

3. pearl
   ruby
   diamond
   emerald

4. lace
   snowflake
   frost
   water

5. crocus
   daffodil
   zinnia
   tulip

6. wolf
   coyote
   prairie dog
   dog

7. squirrel
   rat
   woodchuck
   fox

8. lion
   hyena
   leopard
   tiger

9. daisy
   rose
   chrysanthemum
   violet

Test Yourself Answers

Embedded Transition

1. *repetition of key term*
2. *natural relationship*

3. *synonym*

4. *natural relationship*

5. *repetition of key term*

Embedded Transition

1. *fad*

2. *stereotype*

3. *superstition/old saying*

4. *tradition*

5. *common belief/tradition*

6. *superstition*

7. *old saying, a misquotation of* "The love of *money is the root of all evil*" (*1 Timothy 6:10*)

8. *myth*

9. *cliché*

10. *trend*

Thirty Ideas for Classification Papers

When you develop your topic, you should have a definite audience in mind. In the suggestions that follow, some possible audiences are mentioned.

1. Classify the groups you belong to and explain why each is meaningful to you. *Audience:* Your parents who want you to study more.

2. Classify the voters in your town and discuss major characteristics of each group. *Audience:* Assume you are preparing a report for a politician who is planning to run for mayor.

3. Classify small cars (or some other vehicles) and evaluate them. *Audience:* Assume you are writing for readers of *Consumer Reports*.

4. For the home gardener, classify and describe hardy decorative plants that thrive in the sun, partial shade, and full shade.

5. Job considerations for an engineer (secretary or whom?)

6. Reasons I am thankful for living in the United States

7. Annoying drivers

8. Diets that don't work for me

9. Students in your classes

10. Interesting one-day trips within your state

11. Hazards in buying a used car (or anything else)

12. Computers

13. Fishing spots within your state

14. Caves in the United States
15. Checking accounts for students
16. Places to visit in Texas (or any other state)
17. Commercials that irritate
18. Types of homes available in the price range you can afford
19. Classification and evaluation of sports news shows
20. Friends
21. Childhood diseases (You might classify according to severity.)
22. Tourist attractions in your city or area
23. Classification and evaluation of local restaurants
24. Day care facilities in your area
25. Classification and evaluation of the major nonservice employers in your city
26. Kinds of patients/clients/customers
27. Relatives
28. Internet Service Providers (ISPs)
29. Kinds of computer/video games
30. Kinds of bosses you have had

CHAPTER 15

Comparison and Contrast

Explaining Likeness and Difference

Happiness is like a sunbeam,
which the least shadow intercepts.

—Chinese Proverb

A striking comparison can capture the essence of an idea in a single sentence. Comparing an abstract idea with a concrete image, as in the proverb above, explains the resemblance in a delightful way. We smile or sigh and think "How true." *Comparison* includes both likeness and difference with an emphasis on likeness. A *contrast* shows or emphasizes differences.

In our personal and business lives, we use comparison and contrast to make informed choices between alternatives, weighing advantages against disadvantages, pros against cons, possibilities against difficulties. Careful choices are essential to success in business. As Nancy Bazelon Goldstone notes in the beginning of *Trading Up*, much of our economy revolves around choices based on comparison and contrast:

> [The time is] 8:29 a.m.: the trading room of a large commercial bank on Wall Street. The room is filled with people. The United States government is about to release key information on the state of the economy. It is deadly quiet.
>
> The head foreign-exchange trader stands nervously behind his desk. He knows this information will move the dollar. If the data are good, the dollar will go up. The head trader will order his traders to telephone their counterparts at other banks and buy. If the numbers are very good, he will buy at least $100 million. If the numbers are bad, the dollar will fall; the head trader will sell. The decision to buy or sell must be made immediately because the price will begin to change the instant the information is released.

PURPOSE OF COMPARISON OR CONTRAST

Every paper of comparison or contrast needs a specific purpose according to the rhetorical situation. The fact that an instructor assigns the paper is not adequate. To determine the specific purpose, you might ask yourself, "Why might the audience like to read about this topic?"

Determining a Purpose

When a topic is unfamiliar to readers, your purpose in comparing or contrasting may be to inform them of significant distinctions between two subjects. When the topic is familiar, your purpose might still be informative; but to hold readers' attention, you should present new insights or a fresh perspective. To move beyond trite generalities, ask yourself, "How much do readers already know?"

Or the purpose of comparison or contrast might be to persuade. Then the strategy would be shaped to influence readers toward a certain viewpoint. For example, an employee might write a proposal comparing a present procedure to a proposed new procedure. The purpose would be to convince readers that the new procedure would save time and money. A third purpose of comparison or contrast might be to entertain by presenting the features of two subjects in an amusing way.

Comparison or contrast may have a dual purpose: to entertain and inform or to entertain and persuade or to inform and persuade. Drafting a purpose statement after you select a workable topic can help to clarify the purpose.

Selecting a Suitable Topic

Usually, differences are more interesting than similarities, but not always. Regardless, *the subjects to be contrasted or compared should be of the same species, class, or category*. Otherwise there would be no value in comparing them. For example, there would be no practical reason to compare hockey to stock car racing; the two are not in the same class of sports. Because the topics are so greatly different, you would be unable to find opposing points to match for a logical purpose. But if you wanted to compare different kinds of race car designs or perhaps compare hockey to soccer, you could find logical points of comparison or contrast.

- **Purpose:** To inform and to entertain the reader by comparing the behavior of the male and female praying mantis
- **Purpose:** To inform the reader of the advantages and disadvantages of Tax-Cut as opposed to Quicken
- **Purpose:** To inform and convince the reader that the way medical personnel are portrayed on television is often unrealistic

TRANSITION IN COMPARISON OR CONTRAST PAPERS

As you move from detail to detail while comparing or contrasting, you will need special transitions to indicate shifts in meaning. For your convenience, here are some transitions that point out likeness or difference:

Trans.

Similarity		*Dissimilarity*	
also	too	but	yet
and	both	in contrast	on the other hand
again	similarly	however	on the contrary
likewise	in addition	still	although
besides	then too	conversely	nevertheless

Now and then you may need a *transitional sentence* to bridge a gap in thought. For example, after discussing one horse, you might supply a sentence of transition to introduce another horse: "Whereas Rocket looked as if he had been groomed for the Kentucky Derby, Skip had the careless air of a beachcomber." Two other tips you may want to consider: (1) Place *also* or *however* within a sentence rather than at the beginning, where they may sound tacked on or out of place. (2) Substitute *too* or *then too* to avoid overuse of *also*.

PITFALLS TO AVOID IN COMPARISON OR CONTRAST PAPERS

In selecting a topic for a comparison or contrast paper, beware of three common pitfalls: overused topics, trite expressions, and hasty generalizations. Predictable topics such as "winter versus summer" or "a ranch house versus a two-story" can cause instructors to wince. The old axiom "Don't tell readers what they already know" still applies. When you select your topic, make it fresh by putting a new spin on an ordinary idea. For example, you might contrast a husband and a wife's views of buying an antique sofa for their home.

Trite expressions often infiltrate papers of comparison or contrast. Experienced writers avoid threadbare expressions and devise original comparisons, using concrete nouns, vivid adjectives, and active verbs to make the description come alive. Few readers enjoy frayed phrases like these:

different as day and night	a different story altogether
like two peas in a pod	are worlds apart
spitting image of his father	looked like twins

Hasty generalizations—exaggerated, unsupported claims—are another frequent pitfall in comparing or contrasting. Unintentionally, writers may repeat misstatements they have heard or think are probably true yet lack evidence to substantiate. Broad, general topics in particular can lead to unsupported generalizations. For example, a student who selected the topic "city life versus country life" generalized from stereotypes. The result was a series of overstatements, such as this one: City dwellers take little time to enjoy life and nature.

To sidestep hasty generalizations, first narrow your topic. Then check each claim carefully: Do you have adequate evidence to back up your statements? To be safe, avoid pronouncements about what a majority does or does not do. Writing about your own experience decreases the likelihood of blundering into unsupported generalizations.

ANALOGY: A SPECIAL KIND OF COMPARISON

Although the subjects of a comparison or contrast are usually of the same species, class, or category, a writer may choose to make an imaginative comparison, finding unusual likenesses in things that are of completely different categories. In "The Attic of the Brain," biologist and essayist Lewis Thomas compares the unconscious human mind with the attic of a house. In "Snapping the Leash," journalist Murray Kempton compares the darker forces of human nature to "a raging tiger" that each individual "spends [his or her] life building a cage to pen . . . in."

Such imaginative, nonliteral comparisons have much in common with the poetic devices of simile and metaphor. (See "Create a Simile or Metaphor" in chapter 5.) When extended over the course of a paragraph or an essay, comparisons like these become *analogies*. To be effective, an analogy should be consistent, apt, and fresh. It should also help readers see the subject in a new light. Note how the analogy of "cowboying" is used to illuminate the work of the writer:

> Both jobs—writing and cowboying—take up the whole mind and heart. . . .
> A good hand on a ranch requires vigilance, acute powers of observation, readiness to anticipate what might go wrong or what's coming next, a taste for recklessness, intuitive skills, patience, and what cowboys look for when they buy a horse: a lot of heart. Aspiring to those qualities as a rancher, I can only hope my writing will benefit as well.

> —**Gretel Ehrlich, "Life at Close Range"**

Analogies are often used to help explain something abstract in terms of something concrete. In this way they can play an important role in scientific and technical writing, as writers try to help readers understand ideas and concepts that are complex or difficult to grasp. Note how the next analogy illustrates the scale of geologic time:

> [G]eologists will sometimes use the calendar year as a unit to represent the time scale, and in such terms the Precambrian era runs from New Year's Day until well after Halloween. Dinosaurs appear in the middle of December and are gone the day after Christmas. The last ice sheet melts on December 31st at one minute before midnight, and the Roman Empire lasts five seconds.

> —**John McPhee, *Basin and Range***

In academic and professional writing, make sure that any analogies you devise have a clear explanatory purpose. Readers may not see the point of an analogy that is used primarily for decoration or entertainment.

WRITING A PAPER OF COMPARISON OR CONTRAST

Writing a paper of comparison or contrast is similar to writing a double paper of classification. You examine relationships between elements, distinguish the similarities and differences, then organize them in a logical order that reflects your purpose.

Gathering Information and Prewriting

If you were to compare two cars, the purpose might be to determine which one would better suit your needs and to inform an interested reader. To gather information, you might visit showrooms, talk to sales representatives, and drive the two cars. You could quote and identify the source in general terms such as "One salesperson said that. . . ." If, however, you were to read *Consumer Reports* or another publication, you would need to supply specific documentation, as explained in chapters 24 and 25.

To save time, prewrite details in parallel lists. Simply head two columns with the selected topics, then skip a space and start listing. Each time you write in a detail for one item, add a corresponding detail for the other. Placing the details side by side will make the lists parallel.

	Chevrolet Lumina	*Ford Taurus*
Features:	————	————
	————	————
	————	————
Price:	————	————
mpg:	————	————
Warranty:	————	————
Styling:	————	————
Handling:	————	————
Comfort:	————	————
Maintenance:	————	————

Next, classify details into categories. These categories can act as main points in your paper. For example, the price, expected cost of maintenance, and cost of operation (mpg) could be grouped under the category of economy.

After prewriting and grouping details, focus your paper with a thesis statement. Check to see that it (1) identifies a specific topic, (2) indicates similarity and/or difference, and (3) sets up an order of main points. Although not all thesis statements are this explicit, many instructors prefer such a clear focus, as in the following examples:

- **Thesis:** Although the Chevrolet Lumina and the Ford Taurus are similar in several respects, they vary in comfort, performance, and cost.
- **Thesis:** Whether I am in the mood for an exhilarating challenge or a leisurely ride through the woods, I have horses for each mood. (Kathy Burton)
- **Thesis:** Despite obvious differences, the two series *Earth's Children* and *The Hitchhiker's Guide to the Galaxy* have much in common. (Melissa Baker)

Organizing a Paper of Comparison or Contrast

The *block* and *alternating* methods are two basic ways to organize parallel points of comparison or contrast. For an easily understood topic, the block method is simple and suitable. This order lists all the pertinent points about the first subject in one block of parallel details, then lists the points about the second subject in corresponding order. This balanced arrangement ensures that the details are easy to follow.

Block Outline of Contrast

I. *Thesis statement:* Mr. Courtney and Mr. Graham, my former neighbors, contrasted greatly in appearance, demeanor, and friendliness.

II. Mr. Courtney (first subject)
   A. Appearance
      1. Meticulous. Clothes perfectly pressed.
      2. Clean-shaven. Hair neatly groomed.
      3. Short, trim, and muscular.
   B. Demeanor
      1. Solemn. Never seemed to smile. Eyes glared.
      2. Never out except to care for lawn. Swore and hurried.
      3. Children afraid of him. He scowled when greeted.
   C. Friendliness
      1. Unfriendly.
      2. Protected his privacy.

III. Mr. Graham (second subject)
   A. Appearance
      1. Clothes never hung quite right.
      2. Hint of a beard. Hair untidy.
      3. Tall and rather heavy.
   B. Demeanor
      1. Always smiling. Kind eyes.
      2. Often outside. Hummed, sang, worked in rose garden.
      3. Charmed children. Pitched ball, played hide-and-seek.
   C. Friendliness
      1. Regarded as grandparent by children.
      2. Concerned, a real neighbor.

IV. Conclusion

For a complex comparison, the alternating method is an effective way to organize. You explain comparable points paired in parallel order. In other words, you alternate the subjects. Because of frequent shifts from subject to subject, the alternating method requires more transition than the block method.

Outline of Contrast (Alternating Subjects)

I. Introduction

II. Appearance (first main point)
A.Mr. Courtney
B.Mr. Graham

III. Demeanor (second main point)
A.Mr. Courtney
B.Mr. Graham

IV. Friendliness (third main point)
A.Mr. Courtney
B.Mr. Graham

V. Conclusion

When only similarities are discussed, the pattern can be similar to one of the preceding examples for contrast. When you include both similarities and dissimilarities, the structure of the comparison becomes more complicated. Usually, similarities are discussed first, unless there is a reason for reversal.

Drafting an Introduction

Introductions of comparison or contrast papers can set the scene for the two subjects by revealing what, where, how, and when. Chuck Chesnut gives these details as he wryly contrasts two neighborhood animals. (His thesis is italicized.)

The Pet and the Pest

In my neighborhood there are several animals, but none quite like "the pet" or "the pest." When I walk out my back door and see or hear the pet, as I call him, I smile. He is a friendly old basset hound that lives in the next yard behind our house. But when I walk out my front door and see or hear the pest, my hackles rise. She is the high-strung miniature poodle that resides across the street. Some days I mutter, "The dog from Hell!" or something unprintable. *These dogs vary greatly not only to the eye and the ear but also to my sense of values.*

A narrative opening is an easy and effective way to set the stage for a comparison or contrast. Terri Bloomfield uses narration by presenting a few graphic details to describe a sudden change in her life:

My Life after Dealing with Death

As I pushed my Fiero up to sixty-five miles an hour, the possibility of being killed in an automobile accident was miles of thoughts away. Being young, I felt invincible—why should I worry about an unpleasant subject like death? In a few days, however, I had to confront that topic in an instant. On August 18, 1993, my best friend and my cousin were killed in an automobile accident. The realization of how quickly life can be snatched away changed my life, starting the moment I met death face-to-face.

Developing a Comparison or Contrast Paper

The order in which you develop your parallel points in a comparison or contrast depends upon the purpose and the audience. One technique, level of familiarity, starting with the familiar and going to the unfamiliar, is quite effective, allowing less explanation than the reverse requires. You use analogies, anecdotes, or examples to flesh out ideas. A topic that involves physical description will need numerous concrete details to support the main points. In the next example from "My Two Neighbors," Betty Fetter's precise descriptions enable the reader to visualize two individuals:

> Mr. Courtney was a meticulous person who seemed to reflect this quality in every aspect of his life. His clothes were always perfectly pressed, his face clean-shaven, and his hair neatly groomed. His short frame was trim and muscular despite his age. He seemed always to wear a solemn expression; I never once saw him smile. His glaring eyes echoed his disgust with people and his contempt for life.
>
> Seldom did I see Mr. Courtney outdoors except to care for his lawn. Despite the swearing and hurrying to get the job done, his yard was the best tended in the neighborhood. Local children never went near his house because they knew that the slightest transgression would be met with angry retribution. Mr. Courtney was a private person, and everyone treated him and his property with the respect he so vehemently demanded.
>
> Many times a greeting to Mr. Courtney would be answered with an angry scowl. Mr. Courtney was indeed an island unto himself. Every encounter with him would remind me of another, much more gentle, man—a very dear friend who had taught me the value of friendship and the real definition of the word *neighbor*.

Note that after the first block of details, Betty smoothly introduces the second block with "would remind me of another, much more gentle, man . . . ," leading into a description of Mr. Graham:

> If judged by first appearance, Mr. Graham would not have made a very good impression. His clothes, although neatly pressed, never hung quite right on his tall, rotund body. He seemed always to have a shadow of a beard, and his hair usually looked as if he had started to comb it but had been interrupted. He was, however, always smiling; and his love for people and life was reflected in his eyes.
>
> Many times I would hear Mr. Graham singing or humming while he worked in his garden or trimmed his rosebushes. He always worked with the same patience and deliberation, nurturing and caring for each plant. With this same calm concern, he charmed the children of the neighborhood. It was common to see him pitching a ball, playing hide-and-seek, or sitting on his porch with a group of children at his feet. The children regarded him as a grandparent and treated him with great respect, as did everyone in the neighborhood. He was a real neighbor to all, friend or stranger.

Writing a Conclusion

When the purpose of a comparison is to inform, a brief summary may be in order. In her conclusion, Betty not only summarizes but also shares insights gained from experience:

> Although Mr. Graham died a year ago, his memory will live in the hearts of the people who were lucky enough to have known him. For me, he made it easier to accept the Mr. Courtneys of the world. Mr. Graham knew the secret of happiness, and the values that he taught will remain a part of my life forever.

For a serious topic, a change of perspective can provide just the right note for ending. Terri Bloomfield concluded with this thought:

> After witnessing the death of my cousin and best friend, I cherish life much more. I know firsthand that life is precious and fragile. Now I never take today or tomorrow for granted. I feel as if I must appreciate life not only for myself, but for my cousin and my friend, too.

Revising a Paper of Comparison or Contrast

If you keep your outline handy as you revise, this will help you to maintain the balanced order that comparison and contrast require. The checklist that follows should also be helpful.

CHECKLIST: REVISING A PAPER OF COMPARISON OR CONTRAST

1. Is the thesis clear and specific?
2. Is the order of points in the thesis the same as their order in the body?
3. Are main points and paragraph details arranged in parallel form?
4. Does every paragraph have a topic sentence?
5. Does every topic sentence have adequate support?
6. Does the conclusion seem complete?
7. Have I fulfilled the purpose of the comparison or contrast?
8. Does anything else need to be said for this audience?

TWO STUDENT PAPERS: COMPARISON

In the first paper, Rosy Erdy looks at her parents' similarities and, more important, their differences. Her purpose is to inform; she envisions an audience of her descendants who will read the family history.

Parents through a Child's Eyes

The old axiom "opposites attract" certainly seems true in regard to my parents. Despite a physical resemblance, their differences far outnumber their likenesses. The most distinctive differences are in their childhood backgrounds, political views, and personalities.

Born only a year apart and in their middle seventies, my parents resemble one another. Both have thinning, silver-colored hair. Both are less than average height: Mom refers to herself as "petite"; Dad says he is "not tall." But these similarities are superficial.

The childhood backgrounds of my parents were certainly not alike. Growing up, Mom lived only in the city whereas Dad knew only the life on a farm. Mom was the first of her family to graduate from high school; Dad went to work immediately after completing the eighth grade at a rural school. A strong religious environment influenced Mom, whereas no visible religious commitments existed in Dad's family. Shortly after their marriage, however, Dad adopted Mom's religion. He still attends church regularly with her, but only half-heartedly.

My parents' political differences became quite apparent when I was very young because Mom is a loyal Democrat and Dad is a proud Republican. Every four years after a presidential election, they return from the polls loudly declaring that it is fruitless to vote. They know that the vote of one cancels out the vote of the other.

My parents' greatest difference is in personality. Mom has always been more friendly and outgoing whereas Dad tends to be shy. Mom seems to be always laughing, even with tears in her eyes, but Dad seems more serious. Mom demonstrates affection freely; Dad has difficulty in letting his emotions show. Years ago, Mom administered discipline, while Dad stayed in the background. Afterward he gave us emotional support on the sly.

Mom is forthright and open, but Dad is soft-spoken and reserved. Mom seems to have a strong opinion on everything; Dad tends to be quiet and easily swayed. No one in the family needs to worry about anything because Mom does it for us. If Dad ever worries, he keeps it well hidden. Privacy is not a word in Mom's vocabulary; it seems to be her God-given right as a mother to know everything about her family. On the other hand, Dad quietly respects everyone's privacy.

Despite their many contrasts, my parents have been married over forty years. They have been steadfast in their devotion to each other and to the family. As a result, my brother and I have been greatly influenced by the blending of their differences. From our wonderful parents, we have gained a balance and stability that has been transmitted to our own families' lives.

Questions for Discussion

1. What is the effect of including similarities? What would be the effect if Rosy had included only differences?

2. Which method of organization does she use?

3. Notice that she mixes a few first-person references with the third person. Are these necessary and effective? Why or why not?

4. Are her examples convincing support for her claims?

5. How would you describe the tone of the essay?

6. Comment on her conclusion.

The next paper, by Jeff Patten, contrasts two books by the same author. Jeff's purpose is to inform. His audience consists of readers who enjoy historical fiction.

I, Claudius and *Claudius the God*

In 1934 Robert Graves published a rather lengthy book of historical fiction entitled *I, Claudius*. The novel was written in such a manner as to have the reader believe it was an autobiography of the Roman Emperor Tiberius Claudius Drusus Nero Germanicus. *I, Claudius* takes the reader from the Emperor's earliest childhood remembrances up to the year 41 AD, when he became Emperor of the Roman Empire. It is there, minutes after Claudius's ascent to the throne, that the book ends.

This abrupt ending seemed to demand a sequel, and in 1935 Graves published *Claudius the God*. This second "autobiographical novel" chronicled the life of Claudius from his ascent to the throne to his murder. Although each of the novels was written about the same person, by the same author, there are few similarities. *I, Claudius* and *Claudius the God* seem similar only in the basic form in which they are written. They differ in readability, style, and entertainment value.

The two books resemble each other only in narrative autobiographical form. The reader experiences the life of ancient Rome, narrated through the thoughts and words of the Emperor Claudius. Graves has an almost mystical way of making the reader feel as if the Emperor Claudius had penned the words himself. The novels provide accounts of the seedy, scandalous lives of the ruling Caesars. Greek and Latin phrases reveal careful research. The historical accuracy makes the novels seem authentic.

There the resemblance ends. *I, Claudius* is an easily read, thoroughly engrossing book. Readers receive the impression of a smooth, flowing manuscript. They are led chronologically, with a few pauses for reflection, through the turmoil and pageantry of the Roman Empire and its rulers. *Claudius the God*, however, is a rather choppy, disjointed work. Readers are required to leap from one story line to another with little or no hint of a chronological advance. One can only speculate as to the reason. Yet one thing is certain. The readability and style of *I, Claudius* are far superior to its sequel.

Style is a significant difference between the two novels. Although both manuscripts were thoroughly researched, the historical data are presented in two very different ways. In *I, Claudius* the facts are colorful; the pompous and elegant lives of the ruling class make for fascinating reading. In contrast, the facts presented in *Claudius the God* seem dry and mundane; furthermore, the story line makes for dull reading.

The net result of these differences makes the books unequal in entertainment value. *I, Claudius*, whatever its historical worth, is a very good story. Even readers who ordinarily do not enjoy histories or autobiographies will likely enjoy this novel because it is so entertaining. The sequel, however, is a chore to read—much like reading a history textbook.

If it were not for the many weaknesses of *Claudius the God*, the set would make worthwhile reading. Robert Graves's prowess as a poet and distinguished writer shines brightly in his first novel, but fails miserably in the second.

Questions for Discussion

1. Why do you think Jeff spent two paragraphs on the introduction?
2. How are the two novels alike? How are they different?
3. What method of organization does Jeff use?
4. How would you characterize the tone of Jeff's essay?
5. Comment on the conclusion.

FOR YOUR REFERENCE:
COMPARISON AND CONTRAST ESSAYS IN THE READER

- "A Nonsmoker and a Smoker," Phillip Lopate, page 636
- "Americans: Conservationists or Champion Land Hogs?" Neil Pierce, page 640
- "Mother Tongue," Amy Tan, page 643
- "Women and Men Talking on the Job," Deborah Tannen, page 649

Summary

Your paper of comparison or contrast should have a specific purpose. Writing a purpose statement will help you to narrow the topic and focus your details. Transitions to indicate similarities and differences are especially important to help readers keep on track. Three common pitfalls to avoid are (1) stating the obvious, (2) trite expressions, and (3) hasty generalizations. Readers prefer fresh comparisons and vivid, accurate details. Using an analogy can help readers understand a difficult concept. Prewriting details in parallel lists will save you time. After that you can classify details into main points and write a thesis.

The block and alternating methods are two basic organizational strategies. The block method is suitable for easily retained material. The alternating method is better for complex material. Physical description requires concrete details for clarity. Transition between groups of details alerts the reader to shifts of meaning.

Take care in organizing and developing your introduction, body, and conclusion. Check your main points to be sure they are parallel. Your conclusion should contribute a sense of completeness.

Key Terms

alternating method	block method	contrast
analogy	comparison	hasty generalization

Test Yourself

Selecting a Topic for Comparison

Directions: Would the topics below be suitable for a 500-word paper of comparison? Mark them as suitable (S) or unsuitable (U). Check your answers with those that follow later.

_____   1. The courage of two men in history

_____   2. Two dogs I have owned

_____   3. Before and After: Stay-at-home Mom, then Career Woman

_____   4. Good and evil

_____   5. Tipping versus nontipping

Practice

Ideas for Writing

Directions: Select a topic from the list below (or one of your own) to contrast in a paragraph. Prewrite by making parallel lists of details.

1. Two service providers you have had

2. Two dogs (or cats) you have owned

3. Two methods of fishing

4. Two cars you have owned

5. Two brands of pizza

Test Yourself Answers

Items 1, 2, and 3 are suitable. Item 4 is too broad. Item 5 is probably unsuitable for most students. It is unlikely to elicit 500 words.

Thirty Ideas for Comparison or Contrast Papers

1. Two views of family reunions

2. Your life and your grandmother's or grandfather's life

3. Life before attending college and after

4. An owner's view of a property and a bank appraiser's view

5. A date that you enjoyed and one that you did not enjoy

6. Two news commentators

7. Two versions of an accident

8. Expectations of an event as opposed to what actually happened

9. Life before and after losing weight

10. A negative way and a positive way of coping with criticism
11. Two unusual restaurants
12. Two attitudes toward a family heirloom
13. Two favorite baseball pitchers
14. Two athletes in the same sport
15. Two football teams
16. Two celebrations of a holiday
17. Two unusual friends
18. Two neighborhoods you have lived in
19. Two roller coasters
20. Two presidents
21. A baseball team that went from the bottom to the top
22. Training methods at two places you have worked
23. Two people who have influenced your life
24. Living in the United States as compared to living in . . .
25. Two opposing views on buying term papers
26. Two very different bosses
27. Attitudes before and after an unsettling experience
28. Changes in attitude, thinking, or behavior
29. Two books on the same topic
30. Two special people or characters

CHAPTER 16

$\mathcal{D}$efinition

Identifying Basic Characteristics

The beginning of wisdom is the definition of terms.

—Socrates (470–399 BC)

PURPOSE OF DEFINITION

Clarity is crucial in communication. Undefined terms can lead to confusion, error, and problems. Definition at the right time can dissolve misunderstanding, improve communication, and promote safety. On the job you may write simple definitions or help write complex definitions in policies or reports—defining the background, objectives, success criteria, and scope of a project.

Learning to write clear definitions will sharpen your thinking and enable you to be more precise and accurate in your word choice. In college specific, complete definitions can improve your grades. On exams an instructor may ask such questions as "Can you define *irony*?" "What is 'tool steel'?" or "What is the essence of the accounting principle of materiality?" Yet the answers beginning writers commonly supply to such questions are vague descriptions, not clear definitions.

FORMAL SENTENCE DEFINITION

Providing a formal sentence definition on the spur of the moment is not easy. For example, a writing instructor had just explained formal sentence definition to his freshman composition class. He turned to a student who seemed half asleep and said, "Nick, will you please define *mammal* for me?"

Suddenly awake, the student stammered, "Er . . . a mammal is hairy; uh . . . it has a hard skeleton and provides milk."

With a twinkle in his eye, the instructor replied, "So far, you have not ruled out the coconut."

A formal sentence definition is a complete sentence that classifies something and then differentiates it from other members of its class. A formal sentence definition, which is more complete than a fragmentary dictionary definition, has four parts:

1. The term to be defined
2. A *be* verb—usually *is* or *are*
3. The classification (genus, class, or species)
4. The distinguishing features or characteristics

Below are two illustrations of the parts of a formal sentence definition:

Term	*Verb*	*Classification*	*Distinguishing Features*
A pelican	is	a large, web-footed water bird	with a distensible pouch hanging from its bill for catching and storing fish.
Lynxes	are	a species of wildcat in the Northern Hemisphere	which has a very short tail; tufted, tapering ears; and a ruff on each side of the face.

Note the distinguishing feature of each animal. There are many water birds with webbed feet, but only the pelican has a distensible pouch hanging beneath its bill. There are several species of wildcat in the Northern Hemisphere, but only the lynx has the slender tufted ears, unusual ruff, and very short tail.

To write a formal sentence definition about any concrete term, you might find these questions helpful:

1. What distinguishing features do all items in the class have?

2. How can similar items be ruled out?

3. What purpose or function does the item serve?

WRITING A SENTENCE DEFINITION

Start with a familiar object such as an apple. Consider: Which classification does an apple belong to? How do apples differ from other members of the class, such as plums, pears, and peaches? What are the distinguishing features of apples? Write a complete sentence that includes all four parts of the formal definition:

Term	*Verb*	*Classification*	*Distinguishing Features*
An apple	is	a/an _____	_____

An apple is a fruit, of course, but you might be more precise by stating the purpose: edible fruit. You might be more specific by giving its taxonomic category, the rose family. At first you may jot down features such as red and round. (Are all apples red? Round?) After you finish, see the example at the end of the chapter.

Two precautions will help you to sidestep common errors when writing formal sentence definitions:

1. *Do not define a term by repeating the term or using a derivation:*
   Avoid: A keystone is the key stone in an arch.
   Instead: A keystone is the central wedge-shaped piece at the top of an arch that holds the other stones in place.
2. *Avoid the phrase "is when" or "is where."* This usage is ungrammatical.
   Avoid: A greenbelt *is where* a band of parks, farmland, or unused land surrounds a community.
   Instead: A greenbelt is a band of parks, farmland, or unused land surrounding a community.

EXTENDED DEFINITION

The purpose of a paper of extended definition is to explain a term or concept clearly in an *original* way, drawing material primarily from your own experience. Research is generally limited to dictionaries, thesauruses, and books of quotations.

Consulting Sources

To gather ideas, consult two or three large dictionaries to discover what they say about your topic. Be sure to consult the unabridged *Oxford English Dictionary*, a set of several volumes, which traces the history of words introduced into the English language since AD 1150. There you may find an unusual detail to serve as an attention-getter for your introduction or an example for later use in your paper. Or you might trace the history of a word whose meaning has changed during your lifetime, your parents', or your grandparents'. Or you might trace a relatively new word.

Famous quotations can be found in the library or online. *Bartlett's Familiar Quotations, The Quotable Woman*, a Bible with a concordance, and similar references are quick and easy to use. Or you might interview people of various ages to gain insights about relatively recent connotations of a word.

Documenting Sources

See chapters 24 and 25.

If you decide to copy any material, be sure to set it off properly in your notes so that there is no confusion later. Legally, you are required to provide the following documentation:

1. Enclose short quotations with quotation marks.
2. Indent long quotations of five lines or more.
3. Specify the name of the author, the source, and the page. (Check with your instructor for the preferred format.)

Guidelines for Using Extended Definition

Readers tend to like a quotation that is appropriate but dislike a patchwork of quotations. They become impatient with old information unless it is a favorite story that merits retelling or a universal truth skillfully presented. Here are three guidelines for a paper of extended definition:

- **Use quotations for a purpose.** Use them to clarify and advance your discussion. Limit the number of quotations.
- **Use dictionary definitions for a logical reason.** Have a purpose, such as to clarify further or to disagree.
- **Include stereotypes or overstatement only for a purpose.** Perhaps you intend to disagree with a stereotype or to overstate to provoke amusement. If so, be sure the exaggeration is so great that readers will understand its purpose.

You can freshen an old topic by presenting it from your own point of view:

Stale: Growing old is a fear of many people. Many people believe they are old when they turn fifty.

Fresh: One chilly October morning, my fiftieth birthday tiptoed in. Glancing in the bathroom mirror, I suddenly felt old.

Careless use of stereotypes not only bores the audience, but it also injures a writer's credibility. Perceptive readers dismiss sweeping generalizations; they want the truth, not distortions. In the student examples below, can you spot the faulty stereotypes and other problems in logic?

- The elderly lead lonely, secluded lives, crisscrossed with financial worries.
- A mother's desired end is handling her three jobs well: housewife, mother, and career.

Both of these sentences exaggerate. Not all elderly people fit this pigeonhole. Not all mothers desire a career. Writers need to qualify generalizations—to identify opinions, perceptions, and inferences. Careless overstatement includes all-or-none claims that lack support, as in the following bloopers:

- "Friends are forever." (Question: Do all friends last a lifetime?)
- "Success is defined in as many different ways as there are people on earth." (Question: Does no one agree with anyone else?)

WRITING A PAPER OF EXTENDED DEFINITION

To learn as much as possible from writing a definition paper, select an abstract term for the topic. What do you feel strongly about? How does this topic relate to you? How does it affect your principles and values? How much support can you provide for your thesis? You will be wise to sidestep Herculean topics such as "time," "democracy," and others that are very broad. If you choose a term you have learned in another class, do not merely summarize other people's ideas—develop your own.

Narrowing a Topic and Prewriting

First, narrow the topic so that it can be covered adequately in the assignment. For instance, "discrimination" would be too broad. One student limited this topic to "prejudice against short men." He gave examples of how he copes with short-ness through elevator shoes, hairstyles, and dress. Then he explained how these changes have improved his life and gained him respect.

Next, consult your dictionary notes and think about them. Then prewrite to unearth examples, anecdotes, comparisons, cause-and-effect factors, or changes in meaning. Clustering is particularly helpful for prewriting about an abstract concept.

See chapter 3.

The two sample scratch outlines below are arranged according to order of importance:

Example I: **Professionalism at a Golf Club**

a. Ethics = respect

b. Customer service

c. Accuracy of records

d. Dress of personnel

Example II: **My Procrastination**

a. Examples: Cause

b. Effects

c. How I am overcoming

Drafting a Special Kind of Introduction

Opening with a quotation is one of the easiest ways for a beginning writer to achieve a polished introduction. A relevant quotation can set the tone and indicate the focus of the paper. The quotations that open the chapters of this book show how to format and document a quotation that precedes your main text. *Documentation:* Notice that because the quotations are indented and set apart from the text, quotation marks are not needed. The author's name appears beneath the quotation. Inclusion of the source is optional. Include dates of works written *before* the twentieth century.

Establishing Transition   To forge a link from an introductory quotation to the text of your paper, embed transition in your first sentence. Repeating a key term from the quotation or using a synonym or related word will establish a clear link. Try to be subtle. A direct reference, unless cleverly done, can mar the opening and stamp the work as that of an amateur. With thought, you can avoid weak transition, such as "In this quotation . . . ," "As stated in the quotation above, . . . ," or "I think the above quotation means. . . ."

In the following example, the student writer (who prefers to remain anonymous) uses an embedded transition in her first sentence. A related word (*alcoholism*) echoes a word in the quotation (*drunkenness*). Note, too, that the first sentence here is a formal sentence definition.

Living with an Alcoholic

Drunkenness . . . spoils health,
dismounts the mind, and unmans men.

—William Penn

Alcoholism is a disease caused by continual heavy drinking of alcoholic beverages. In the acute and chronic stages, alcoholism consists of symptoms ranging from the obvious to the obscure. Usually, it is not difficult to recognize a person who is inebriated; generally, staggering and slurring of speech are apparent. Accompanying neurological disorders such as tremors (shakes), hallucinations, and seizures are easily discerned. Hidden to the naked eye is the damage endured by the liver, stomach, and pancreas. Not only is excessive drinking devastating to the physical and mental health of the alcoholic, but it is also devastating to the alcoholic's family.

Living for eighteen years with my father, who was a severe alcoholic, was much like living with Dr. Jekyll and Mr. Hyde. The alcohol would turn my kindhearted, loving father into a brutal, hateful monster. Because of my father's unpredictable behavior, high anxiety and fear were normal, everyday emotions for me.

Did you notice that the first paragraph is written in *third* person? The writer gives general background information before narrowing the topic to the alcoholic's family. In the second paragraph, she shifts to *first* person because it reveals specific details about her life. See how she eases the shift from third person to first with a gerund phrase ("Living . . . with my father").

Did you note the simile in the second paragraph? The phrase "like living with Dr. Jekyll and Mr. Hyde" not only sets up a striking comparison but also establishes a natural relationship with "unmans men" in the opening quotation.

Developing an Extended Definition

The heart of any good piece of writing is vivid imagery. Concrete details and action verbs make writing come alive. Depending on the subject and purpose, a paper of extended definition may be developed by almost any strategy or combination of strategies—description, comparison, narration, examples, or explanation, for instance. There are five basic techniques for developing an extended definition.

Operational Definition   To define an operation, the writer tells (a) what the object being defined does, (b) how it works, and (c) the basic principle underlying its performance. For example, a one-sentence operational definition might state that a refrigerator is a mechanized box, powered by electricity or gas, that circulates coolant to a condenser to chill food, medicines, or other items. An expanded operational definition would explain in detail how a refrigerator works. Operational definitions are often used in technical writing.

Defining by Comparison   Comparison is useful for explaining abstractions, such as emotions. If you can find an object to compare an idea or emotion to, then this technique will help to clarify your definition. In the following example, Marjorie Holmes begins with concrete images before going to abstract feelings:

> What feeling is so nice as a child's hand in yours? [It is] so small, so soft and warm like a kitten huddling in the shelter of your clasp. A child's hand in yours— what tenderness it arouses, what power it conjures up. You are instantly the very touchstone of wisdom and strength.

Defining by Synonym   In defining by synonym, a writer provides another word or phrase that has the same meaning. The synonym can be included either in parentheses or as an appositive:

- Rocky Collins will fight F. G. Jones for the bantamweight (112 to 118 pounds) world title.
- At one time many people believed that human intelligence could be judged by phrenology, the study of the shape of the skull.

Defining by Negation   Another effective technique of definition is *negation* (denial). The writer begins by telling what the term is not. In a paper entitled "Fear of Failure," Phyllis Parks uses negation in her opening sentence:

> *Failure* is not a pretty word. The very mention of it creates images and feelings of someone who is inept and incompetent. The word itself strikes fear in my heart. Sometimes my life has seemed as though it has been one failure after another. But with time has come an appreciation for the value of failure.

In *Faith of My Fathers*, Senator John McCain begins his definition of *glory* by explaining what glory is not. Then he describes what glory means to him:

> Glory is not a conceit. It is not a decoration for valor. It is not a prize for being the most clever, the strongest, or the boldest. Glory belongs to the act of being constant to something greater than yourself, to a cause, to your principles, to the people on whom you rely, and who rely on you in return.

Weaving Example with Explanation   A lone example without interpretation may be of little use to readers. You cannot assume that every reader will see the connection you intend. You need to link the example to the main idea and comment appropriately. Chris Layman, a student writer, first uses negation. Then he weaves example with explanation in an extended definition of honesty:

> "Do as I say, not as I do," my parents would often say as I was growing up. However, admonitions such as this often fade from the mind whereas examples form

lasting impressions. As children grow they need models to follow. They need to determine how they will live their lives, what their values will be, and how they will treat other people. A father is a model that his children depend on to learn how to act within their society and to form their own set of values.

   Recently, my young son and I were in a store when he noticed a $100 bill lying on the floor. I had always told my son to be honest; now I could show him what honesty meant. Together we went to the store manager and put the money in his care, hoping the rightful owner would return to claim it. This incident allowed me to act as a role model for my son, and it set an example I hope he will follow throughout his life.

Including a Dictionary Definition

If a dictionary definition is *necessary* in your paper, you can easily identify the copied material by using quotations marks and by stating the source. The three examples that follow will not be suitable for every writing situation, but you can adapt them to fit your paper if appropriate.

- Although *Webster's College Dictionary* defines _____ as the "_____," this definition does not. . . .

- According to *Webster's New World Dictionary*, _____ is "_____," but that definition does not. . . .

- Meanings can change over time. The first edition of *The American Heritage Dictionary* defines _____ as "_____." The fourth edition, however, has added another meaning: "_____." We might go beyond these to say. . . .

To integrate other types of quotations into the text of your paper, see "Using Signal Phrases to Integrate Quotations into the Text," page 390.

Writing a Conclusion

A conclusion for a paper of definition should be brief and appropriate. One way to end is with a formal sentence definition. Another is to allude to an opening quotation. A third way is to summarize changes and end on a positive note.

Closing with a Formal Sentence Definition   Debby Ketcham concludes her paper with a formal sentence definition. The definition is followed by a sentence of summary and another of comment:

   Finally, poise is an inner mental balance, the ability to face new situations calmly, to hold one's temper, to cope with stress, and to deal with embarrassment. All these situations require a control over emotion and the ability to present a calm, tactful, polite manner. Poise is truly a valuable trait.

Alluding to an Opening Quotation   A reference to the beginning creates an "echo ending" and establishes closure. Using this technique, Penny Amrine repeats parts of a quotation by Joseph Conrad in her conclusion. In the last sentence she provides a formal sentence definition:

My loneliness did indeed wear a "mask." For months I had endured its "naked terror" without being able to identify its misleading appearance. Loneliness for me was life without intimate friends and relatives to lean on for love and companionship.

Ending with a Personal Lesson   Those of us who successfully survive a painful experience often extract a lesson, a bit of wisdom. The student who wrote "Living with an Alcoholic" summarized her insights:

> Over the years I have tried to educate myself on alcoholism. Counseling has helped me to understand how alcoholism victimizes the entire family. Now, at age 33, I realize that despite how it seemed at the time, my father was only a human being who was consumed by a dread disease.

The last line reveals the writer's compassion as well as her intellectual and emotional growth since those early years of torment. The implicit note of forgiveness and the gentle tone provide a positive ending to a wrenching topic.

Revising a Paper of Definition

To revise a paper of extended definitions successfully, you need to examine its many facets. The checklist below will enable you to scrutinize individual aspects.

CHECKLIST: REVISING EXTENDED DEFINITIONS

1. Is the topic narrow enough to be defined in a short paper?
2. Will the introduction interest the audience?
3. Have important terms been defined if they are apt to be unfamiliar to the average reader? Have terms with more than one possible meaning been explained fully?
4. Are all definitions necessary?
5. Do formal sentence definitions (if any) conform to the standard four-part format?
6. Does every detail, definition, and quotation support the thesis?
7. Are quotations worked smoothly into the text so that their point is clear in the paper? Has proper credit been given to each original source?
8. Have stereotypes and overstatement been avoided?
9. Is the organization of the paper clear?
10. Is the closing effective?

TWO STUDENT PAPERS: DEFINITION

Jeannine Caudill talked to her friends before she wrote the following paper, which is based on their experience as well as hers. Her purpose is to explain a term not found in the dictionary. Skillfully, she states several axioms (universal truths). Three questions begin her introduction.

Mother Love

Love cannot be forced, love cannot be
coaxed and teased. It comes out of
Heaven, unasked and unsought.

—Pearl Buck

What is mother love? Is it a feeling, an emotion, or the dedication of an entire lifetime? Is it bad or good, imaginary or genuine? One thing is certain; mother love is difficult to define, especially to those who have not experienced it. None of the dictionaries seem to think *mother* and *love* should be combined into the phrase *mother love*. Yet there is motherhood, mother lode, and motherland. Could any of these words be more fitting to combine with *mother* than the word *love*?

Psychiatrists define mother love, doctors prescribe it, lawyers divide it, children bask or drown in it, and fathers observe it. Perhaps even a mother cannot define it, but some still try. Love as only a mother can feel begins for some women with the first knowledge of pregnancy. For others, it comes with beholding the charm of their own soft, sweet-smelling baby. The baby does not have to be beautiful to inspire great love. Perhaps mother love at this stage of life is a myriad of feelings: infant dependency, mother's pride of accomplishment, and primitive emotions that have been basic to the human race since its beginning. Whatever the reasons, loving a baby seems very easy.

The real growth of mother love begins later. Much of the time during a child's life, no one seems to love him or her except the mother. True mother love develops over many years and through many trials. When a toddler throws a fit in a store, shouts a loud "No," or dampens a neighbor's carpet, mother love is put to a test. But even in this stage, the child is very appealing to her. Here a new facet of love begins, pride in the child's independence.

The early school years strain the most patient mother. After the thumb-sucking, leg-hugging, insecure years come the years of grade cards, teacher conferences, show and tell, and four hundred papers to be praised and hung up.

Many older mothers say to younger mothers, "If you think things are bad now, just wait till he's a teenager!" But the young mothers often counter with "Nothing could be worse." This lack of foresight must be a tool of Mother Nature. Otherwise, only the very brave would dare to have a child.

Mother love seems never to end. It usually begins with the birth of a child and continues to encircle and entwine the mother's heart down through the years. Strangely enough, the only person who can appreciate the real meaning of mother love is a mother.

Questions for Discussion

1. What do you notice about Jeannine's introduction?
2. Examine the first sentence of the second paragraph. What do you notice about the sentence structure?
3. Do Jeannine's examples ring true? Why or why not?
4. What does she do before she comments?
5. How would you describe the tone of the essay?

In the following paper, Ron Willetts cites a dictionary definition and parts of speech for *work* for a significant reason: He expands upon its meanings as a noun and as a verb. In the first main point, he uses narration and explanation to illustrate his early view of work. He defines later views by explanation, associations, and examples.

Changes in My View of Work

My friend there is a Hell . . . when a man has a family to support, has his health, and is ready to work, and there is no work to do. When he stands with empty hands and sees his children going hungry, his wife without the things to do with. I hope you never have to try it.

—Louis L'Amour

The *Oxford American Dictionary* defines work as a noun that means "Use of bodily or mental power in order to do or make something, especially as contrasted with play or recreation." Work is also defined as a verb: "to perform work, to be engaged in bodily or mental activity." Over the years I gradually learned to understand these concepts, but only when I became unemployed for an extended period did I understand L'Amour's definition.

When I was very young, work was not a verb, it was a noun, a place to go and a place to leave. My grandfather would come home from work in the evenings, and we would go through a ritual. As he drove his truck into the garage, I would be waiting. He would pick me up, and somewhere between the truck and the house, I would remove the hat from his head and transfer it to mine. Once inside, he would place his dinner bucket on a chair, and I would rummage through it for the leftover cookie, banana, or candy bar that was always there. At that time in my life, I did not have to worry; all my needs were taken care of.

When I became a young adult, the word *work* took on a new meaning. It was not only a noun, but suddenly a verb, a task to be performed for which one received some form of remuneration. This definition began to form when I was in the eleventh grade and began helping the janitors after school during basketball season. For sweeping the classrooms and dusting the teachers' desks, I received a modest sum and attended the home games at no cost. Thus work became associated with money. And money became closely associated with girls, cars, entertainment, and other necessities. At this time, work was a necessary evil, for it took time away from my social life.

When I became older, I found the word *work* had to be redefined once again. Along with being a place to go and an activity to perform, work became a goal. This new meaning became associated with other words such as wife, insurance, children, house, and friends. Between 1975 and 2000, work was no problem for me. If I changed jobs, the longest period of unemployment was two days. Once I quit one job on Friday and started a new one the following Monday.

In 2000, however, the story changed. Due to economic conditions, I became unemployed after working at a company for fifteen years. That company and my coworkers were as much a part of my life as my own family. I felt rejected and depressed. The severance pay ran out. The unemployment benefits were exhausted. The retirement fund vanished, and the bills began to pile up. I was no longer able to provide for my family. But then I thanked God we were living in modern times when it was acceptable for a married woman to work. Although my wife's income did not pay all the bills, it did allow us to feed the family and keep the electricity turned on.

Being unemployed for over two years creates a situation that at times is almost unbearable. Perhaps the worst part is being told that one cannot be hired because he is overqualified and undereducated. Being told that one could perform the task, but would not be satisfied with the job is enough to make a person ill. A man needs to be able to provide for his family.

Yes, my friend, there is a hell—I know, for I have been there. It is my sincere hope that I am the last person that has to define the lack of work as hell.

Questions for Discussion

1. Discuss the use of the dictionary definition in the introduction. Would the paper have been as effective without it? Why or why not?
2. Briefly summarize the changes in Ron's viewpoint.
3. What causes are specified?
4. Discuss the effectiveness of this ending. What device does he use?

FOR YOUR REFERENCE: DEFINITION ESSAYS IN THE READER

- "On Being 17," David Raymond, page 655
- "The Handicap of Definition," William Raspberry, page 659
- "Becoming Educated," Barbara Jordan, page 662
- "The Sweet Smell of Success Isn't All That Sweet," Laurence Shames, page 665

Summary

The general purpose of any definition is to explain and clarify. Clear definition is needed to forestall misunderstanding and mistakes. Formal sentence definitions are one-sentence definitions with four parts: the term, a *be* verb, the classification, and features that distinguish the subject from other members of the class. Extended definitions are explanations that may include description, comparison, anecdotes, reasons, examples, or formal definitions.

Keeping a specific audience in mind will help you avoid common problems: unnecessary definition, repeating common information unnecessarily, and using stereotypes or overstatement without a logical reason.

Key Terms

allusion   formal sentence definition

axiom   negation

extended definition   operational definition

Practice

Collaborative Exercise: Discerning Genuine Definitions

Directions: Identify the satisfactory definitions in the list below and mark with an S. Mark the unsatisfactory with a U. Discuss why they are unsatisfactory. (You may consult a dictionary.)

1. A sprinkling can is a utensil that is not a bucket, dishpan, or bowl.
2. A cut is when you slash open the skin.
3. A book is like a little golden door to opportunity.
4. The gemsbok of southern Africa is a large antelope with long, sharp, straight horns and a tufted tail.
5. Honey is a sweet gooey substance that is delicious on breakfast cereal.
6. "Monopoly" is a table game that resembles life because you trade, buy, and sell.
7. *Morale* refers to the condition of the spirits of individuals or employees.
8. The ruffed grouse, sometimes called "partridge" or "pheasant," is a North American game bird with spotted brown feathers.
9. Gelatin is a clear quivery substance, made in various colors.
10. A dandelion is a small edible weed with fuzzy yellow flowers and saw-toothed leaves.
11. Dissatisfied means not content.
12. A suitcase has a handle and is used to carry clothing.
13. A vacation is where you tire yourself out having fun so that you are glad to go home and go to work.
14. Empathy is as refreshing as pure cold water from a spring.
15. A fruitcake is a cake that contains fruit.

Collaborative Writing: Formal Sentence Definition

1. Appoint a recorder to jot down the comments of the group. Define one of the terms below in a formal sentence definition.

   dog   cow   cucumber   chair   couch

2. Ask each other questions to limit the term and identify the essential features. For example:
   a. How does a dog differ from a wolf or coyote?
   b. What kind of dog? Prairie dog? Wild dog? What?
   c. What is the purpose of the dog?

   (*Note:* You may want to limit the term to watch dog, police dog, Seeing Eye dog, hunting dog, or other kind of dog.)

3. Revise. Does the definition have all four parts? Does it read smoothly?

4. Repeat the procedure, using another term.

Ideas for Formal Sentence Definition

Directions: Write a formal sentence definition or a paragraph that includes a formal sentence definition. Select a concrete word from the list below or use one of your own.

oranges   ballpoint pen   drum   turnips   plums

Possible Answer for Writing a Sentence Definition (page 201)

An apple is an edible fruit of the rose family that can be red, yellow, green, or multicolored; when mature, the small seeds are encased in a core connected to a flexible stem at the top and the blossom end.

Thirty Ideas for Papers of Definition

1. What is the "positive attitude" that employers seek?
2. Ethics for the nurse (or other professional)
3. What is customer service?
4. Freedom (What kind or kinds?)
5. What is patriotism?
6. What does a college degree really mean?
7. What is professionalism?
8. Self-discipline
9. What is maturity?
10. Procrastination
11. Optimism
12. Attitude: Victim or winner?
13. A family value
14. Appreciation
15. Fear of . . .
16. Self-acceptance

17. What is integrity?
18. Jealousy/envy
19. Loyalty
20. What is an education?
21. Satisfaction
22. Ambition
23. What is marriage or commitment to another person?
24. Compassion
25. What is parenting?
26. Trust
27. Discrimination (What kind?)
28. What is happiness?
29. Anger
30. Responsibility

CHAPTER 17

Cause and Effect

Explaining Why

Our least deed, like the young of the land crab,
wends its way to the sea of cause and effect as soon
as born, and makes a drop there to eternity.

—Henry David Thoreau
Journal, March 14, 1838

Thoreau's observation reminds us that a single decision, action, or event can cause far-reaching effects. The relationship between cause and effect can be more intricate and extensive than we may imagine. Sometimes we lack complete information and see only part of an effect. Or we may assume a connection between two events where none exists. Or we glimpse only *short-term effects* while significant *long-term effects* remain hidden for years.

All the while there is the ever-present risk of blithely underestimating the repercussions of certain acts and of making unwise decisions based on unproved assumptions and ill-founded predictions.

PURPOSE OF CAUSAL ANALYSIS

The purpose of causal analysis is to determine whether or not a cause-and-effect relationship actually exists. If it does exist, precisely what is the connection between the cause and the effect? What happened to bring about the change?

Causal analysis allows you to reflect on an experience or event and to learn from the past. With study and practice, you can improve your ability to analyze cause-and-effect relationships. You can question doubtful information and withhold judgment until adequate proof of the final cause is available.

On the job you may analyze cause-and-effect relationships, then give input into decisions that will influence the profit or loss of your company. According to the rhetorical situation, you may write a recommendation, proposal, or report, based on your causal analysis. The greater your knowledge and insight, the more accurate the analysis will be.

WORKPLACE CASE STUDY

The Accident

Lisa was walking within the pedestrian lane of the large plant warehouse where she worked. The warehouse seemed even more noisy than usual. She was unaware that behind her a tow-truck driver violated company rules when he failed to sound his horn before coming around a corner. The next moment she heard the roar of a motor and glanced back. The vehicle hit her. A searing pain darted down her right leg. She crumpled and fell to the floor.

Lisa was rushed to the hospital, where a leg fracture and several deep cuts were treated. She was kept overnight. The emergency room physician said she would be unable to work for 8 weeks. A witness to the accident corroborated Lisa's report, saying she was in the safety lane. The driver did not sound his horn before coming around the corner very fast. Losing temporary control of the vehicle, he swerved into the safety lane and knocked her to one side.

ACTIVITY:

Assume the role of the supervisor. Write a summary of the accident in your own words and recommend action. The tow-truck driver was newly hired; he has worked only three days. The plant provides no training for tow-truck drivers.

WHAT IS CAUSAL ANALYSIS?

A *cause* influences or changes something or someone. The resulting change is called the *effect*. *Causal analysis* is an examination of effects that have one or more causes (conditions that may have contributed to the effect). To resolve a question of cause and effect, explore all the conditions that might have caused the effect. Since you already know the effect (by observation), start by noting its significant features. Then work backward through the chain of cause and effect. Describe the related condition(s). Then list possible explanations. Next, test each explanation and eliminate as many as possible. That should lead you to the cause(s). If not, keep searching.

For example, the supervisor of a department that spray-paints washing machines notices that the finish is uneven. He wonders what condition could have

---

STEPS IN CAUSAL ANALYSIS

1. Specify the effects. Separate from the presumed cause.
2. Examine the conditions that existed.
3. Ask whether or not these conditions could have caused the effect(s).
4. Think about possible explanations: What might have happened?
5. Test your theories. Did the presumed causes actually produce the effect?

---

caused this effect. Has an atmospheric change occurred? Is there a mechanical defect? Has human error interfered? Was the batch of paint too thin? Could multiple causes exist? Only after he has ruled out all other possibilities will he be able to pinpoint the cause(s).

A Reversed Chain of Cause and Effect

To trace a simple cause, start with the observed effect(s) and work *backward* through the chain until you find proof of the cause. In the example below, the gas hot water furnace requires electricity to operate the pump and thermostat.

EFFECT ➡	Condition ➡	Possibilities ➡	Test ➡	Cause
House is cold	<Furnace not working	<Electricity off?	(no)	
		<Gas line plugged?	(unlikely)	
		<Gas line shut off?	yes*	<Bill unpaid*

Note: Since the pilot light cannot be lit, you assume that the gas has been shut off. Checking through old bills reveals three are unpaid. But until you check with the gas company, you do not have actual proof of the cause.

Logical Principles of Cause-and-Effect Relationships

As you explore possible cause-and-effect connections, examine the logic of your conclusion or inference. Is it reasonable, sensible, and sound? Or has an error occurred? To be valid, a claim of causal relationship must be based on two essential standards.

Two Principles of Logic in Cause and Effect

- The cause is able to produce the effect.
- Other causes that might have produced the effect have been ruled out.

Two Fallacies to Avoid in Analyzing Cause and Effect

A systems analyst says that the most frequent mistake in logic that his team makes is to assume that because one event follows another, the first caused the second—even though there is no proof. This assumption is the *post hoc* fallacy; chronology is mistaken for causation. Events in a sequence do not always have a connection.

Another fallacy of cause and effect is the *non sequitur* (meaning *it is not necessarily true*). A non sequitur is also an assumption, but it does not involve chronology. Non sequiturs often occur in predictions. For example, it was once widely said that "a Catholic will never be elected president." Yet John F. Kennedy became the first Roman Catholic president of the United States. This common belief was disproved.

See chapter 20.

If we keep in mind that much of what we "know" is actually inference, theory, value judgment, or myth, we are more likely to pause and seek evidence before leaping to conclusions about why something happened.

WRITING A PAPER ANALYZING CAUSE AND EFFECT

A paper of causal analysis allows for a wide range of topics to be organized and developed in various ways. Every time you inquire about *how* or *why* something happened, you begin causal analysis. To prewrite, you might sketch a reverse chain of cause and effect as shown in the earlier diagram. Keep in mind the following principle: *Complex events, conditions, or situations seldom stem from a single cause.* Therefore don't halt your search too soon. You may find more than one cause.

Planning a Cause-and-Effect Paper

After you have sketched a cause-and-effect chain, consider how to organize details. The big question is this: *"What does the audience need to know?"* Your answer will help you decide what to include and where to start. Then set up a scratch outline in a way that seems logical. To begin, consider the following questions:

- Was there a single cause and single effect? Or were several factors involved?
- Will the major emphasis be on the specific phenomenon (cause)? Or will it be on the consequence (effect)?
- What kind of order will work best?

Chronological order is often simplest and most efficient. This way you discuss the cause before the effect. Sometimes *reverse chronological order* is used with effect before cause. If you have multiple causes and/or multiple effects, you may need to organize your main points by order of importance. Several possible strategies are presented here. If one seems to fit your topic, adapt it as needed.

Outline A: Single Cause with Multiple Effects
(chronological order)

Claim: High consumption of soft drinks containing sugar and caffeine contributes to overweight, other health problems, and mild addiction.

I. Introduction (specifies the cause): high consumption of soft drinks containing sugar and caffeine

II. Body (order of importance)
 A. Describes/explains effect no. 1: overweight
 B. Describes/explains effect no. 2: other health problems
 C. Describes/explains effect no. 3: mild addiction

III. Conclusion

Outline B: Single Effect Produced by Multiple Causes
(reverse chronological)

Claim: Many farmers in the South are diversifying crops to increase profits.

I. Introduction (specifies the effect): Many farmers in the South are decreasing the acreage allotted to tobacco in favor of vegetable crops. Fresh produce sold to urban markets yields more profit.

II. Body (order of importance)
 A. Cause no. 1: Nicotine has been identified as a cause of cancer.
 B. Cause no. 2: Many people have ceased smoking because of possible health hazards.
 C. Cause no. 3: Prospects for future tobacco markets are dim.
 D. Cause no. 4: High prices of fresh produce promise lucrative returns.

III. Conclusion

If you discuss both multiple causes and multiple effects, you will need a more complex outline. The block or alternating method might be used, depending on the rhetorical situation.

Outline C: Multiple Causes and Multiple Effects
(block method)

I. Introduction: who, what, and where?

II. Body: Explanation of causes and effects (why)
 A. Causes
 B. Effects

III. Conclusion (may be recommendation)

Once in a while you may need to explain a *series* of interrelated events. To emphasize the chronology of each cause and its immediate effect, you could use an alternating method. In other words, cause and effect would alternate in pairs in chronological order.

Outline D: Series of Events Linked to Each Other (alternating method)

I. Introduction: specifies nature of causal relationship
II. Body (chronological order)
   A. Cause no. 1
   B. Effect no. 1
   C. Cause no. 2
   D. Effect no. 2 (continue as needed)
III. Conclusion

Drafting an Introduction

See chapter 4.

The introduction may take various forms, depending on the emphasis and kind of causal relationships. For example, you might begin with a *narrative*, possibly an eyewitness account of an accident, then go on to describe the cause and effect(s). Your thesis could then link the cause with the effects you will focus on.

Or you might open by describing a specific effect, showing why it is important or interesting to consider what caused it. You might explain the effect by classifying *examples* and presenting *illustrations*. Or you might provide an overview of the causal relationship or suggest that the causes or effects will be surprising. Watch for a hook that will make your analysis meaningful for your readers.

Developing a Paper Analyzing Cause and Effect

Your purpose will help you to devise a suitable writing strategy to develop your paper adequately. Most topics will require a thorough explanation with specific details and examples that reflect the purpose. Usually, the primary purpose of causal analysis is to inform or to persuade. Even when the purpose is informative, the paper will still have an *argumentative edge*, or element of persuasion. It may range from a hint to much more. In short, whether *implicitly* or *explicitly*, you will argue for your claim that a cause has led or will lead to an effect. (The difference between an informative and a persuasive paper of causal analysis is a matter of degree and strategy, not necessarily content.)

To support your claim, you need convincing proof. For example, you might contend that action should be taken to keep sixteen-year-olds from driving after midnight because of an extremely high rate of accidents for that age group. To make your claim plausible, you would have to produce valid research and possibly expert opinion to indicate that the hours after midnight are a dangerous time for sixteen-year-old drivers to be out on the roads.

Writing a Conclusion

See chapter 4.

The conclusion of a cause-and-effect paper summarizes the consequence or result. It may mention a repercussion, influence, benefit, or implication for the future. Or there may be an allusion to the title or opening that establishes closure, as in "Silver Lining," below. Regardless, the ending should flow from the description of cause and effect and give a sense of completeness.

Revising a Cause-and-Effect Paper

As you start to revise your cause-and-effect paper, look at the larger items first. Pay particular attention to the strategy, logic, and writer's voice. After you are satisfied with these aspects, check the smaller aspects, as explained in chapter 5.

See "Editing," page 59.

The checklist below should be helpful.

CHECKLIST: REVISING A CAUSE-AND-EFFECT PAPER

1. Does the strategy emphasize the purpose?
2. Is the evidence adequate to support the claim?
3. If not, have I qualified my statements (with *seem* or *appear*, for example) to allow for chance?
4. Could another contributing cause exist?
5. Is the voice impartial and fair?
6. Is the connection clear? Have I explained enough?

TWO STUDENT PAPERS: CAUSE AND EFFECT

The purpose of both papers that follow is to inform classmates of the writer's perspective of a situation. Jo Rae Sloan begins with the cause and explains the effects.

Silver Lining

To a nineteen-year-old girl, owning her own vehicle oftentimes seems alluring. But once the dream becomes a reality, the resulting responsibilities may seem overwhelming at times. Several months ago I had an opportunity to buy a pickup truck with help from my mother. Having my own transportation is convenient, and I do take pride in my Chevy pickup; yet the upkeep and expense can be exasperating.

Before I bought a truck, I had to schedule my activities around the other family members. I had to borrow my mother's car and worry about the possibility of putting a dent in the fender before I returned. Now I can hop in my Chevy and go whenever I need or wish without a care. I am a cautious driver and have insurance. Although I still park in a far row of parking lots, away from other vehicles, I no longer worry about possible dents.

When I drove someone else's car, I did not really care how it looked. Once I owned my own vehicle, however, my feelings changed. I take pride in my Chevy truck. When I first purchased it, I took it to a body shop for a new paint job with stripes and for window tinting. Now I vacuum my truck every week as well as wash and wax it regularly. All this takes time and effort. The work and expense are much more than I bargained for.

In the "good old days," all of my extra cash went for clothes, cosmetics, and anything else I wanted. Not now—every cent seems to go to my truck. The expected expense is bad enough, but the unexpected expense can be heartbreaking to a full-time student with a part-time job. Insurance takes a big chunk of my earnings. Filling the gas tank is another regular expense, along with the cost of oil and periodic maintenance. The unexpected expense of a new tire, a muffler system, and other repairs has been formidable. Thank goodness, I live at home and don't have to make payments to a car dealer. My mother is willing to wait for a payment when necessary.

As a result of buying my truck, I have been forced to budget—I haven't bought any new clothes since graduation last June. Although I seldom have more than a few dollar bills and some silver lining my pockets, I have a wonderful sense of independence. My Chevy truck has transported me from adolescence to adulthood.

Questions for Discussion

1. What is the single cause of the effects Jo Rae describes?
2. How do her expectations compare with reality?
3. How does she feel about the effects at times? What is her overall feeling?
4. Does Jo Rae use the block or the alternating method of organization?
5. What is the effect of placing advantages before disadvantages?
6. What is the effect of the title? To what old saying does it allude?

In the next paper, Mary Ann Holvick also describes a single cause that produces multiple effects. First she explains her job; then she presents the benefits:

Why I Enjoyed Being a School Bus Driver

Often when two people are introduced, they initiate conversation by inquiring about each other's occupation. For six years my answer to that question produced raised eyebrows and caused my new acquaintances to exclaim, "You couldn't pay me enough to do that job!" Then I would explain that driving a school bus had rewards other than the usual monetary compensation: mastering a machine, enjoying nature, and participating in children's lives.

Achieving control of the school bus was an arduous task. I had to learn a maintenance routine which included checking all oil and fluid levels, inspecting all hoses and belts for signs of wear, and verifying that all lights and warning buzzers were functional. The most difficult aspect was backing the bus, thirty-eight feet long, from a narrow country road into a still narrower driveway. Yet I derived great satisfaction from knowing the children on the bus were safe because it was in top running condition, and I was confidently in control.

Nature rewarded me for my early morning hours with a spectacular array of sunrises, which fired the deep-textured woods and fence rows with iridescent colors. Although I had grown up in the country, I never tired of watching the trees, wildflowers, and farm crops grow, blossom, and display the triumphant colors of a purpose fulfilled. Under the cover of vegetation, animals and birds carried on their daily lives, unabashed by the passing of so many curious eyes. The children and I enjoyed sights such as a buck deer bounding across an open field, a skunk hunting for his insect breakfast, a flock of Canadian geese flying in formation, and a hawk carrying away his prey with victorious cries.

The children, however, were my constant source of delight. The younger ones were always eager to share their concerns with me. I became a doll fashion advisor and new clothes admirer. I sympathized with the losing Little League team and empathized with the disappointed owners of bologna sandwich lunches. I patched dozens of scraped knees and critiqued hundreds of homework papers. Grade cards were presented for approval; and, occasionally, love notes were dropped surreptitiously into my lap by red-faced little boys.

Older students generally remained aloof until desperation brought them to me, seeking advice about dating or dealing with unreasonable parents. For homecoming queens I saved newspaper pictures, and I congratulated teams for their athletic feats and scholastic achievement. And I worried over their safety each weekend when carloads of teenagers jammed the downtown square. Although I do not have any children of my own, I have loved several hundred boys and girls who made me a part of their lives.

If, like my new acquaintances, I had considered only the hard work involved in my job, then I would not have been a school bus driver. Of course, I received a monetary reward, but my real rewards were the physical discipline of driving, intimacy with nature, and the trusting love of the children.

Questions for Discussion

1. What is the cause in Mary Ann's paper?
2. What are the effects?
3. How does Mary Ann use description to convey her feelings about her job? Which examples do you find most vivid? Why?
4. What order is used to organize details relating to children? For organizing main points?
5. How would you describe the voice of the paper?

**FOR YOUR REFERENCE:
CAUSE-AND-EFFECT ESSAYS IN THE READER**

- "Spudding Out," Barbara Ehrenreich, page 668
- "Why Marriages Fail," Anne Roiphe, page 671
- "The Teacher Who Changed My Life," Nicholas Gage, page 675
- "The Emotional Quadrant," Elizabeth Kübler-Ross, page 680

Summary

Causal analysis is the study of relationships between two events or conditions, one of which is thought to have caused the other. Causal analysis enables us to learn from experience and to predict what may happen. Cause-and-effect relationships can be incredibly complex. We may assume a complex problem has a single cause, when, indeed, there are several causes. Often we see only the short-term effects. The long-term effects may not be apparent until years later.

Two basic principles of logic govern cause and effect: (1) the cause is able to produce the effect and (2) other causes that might have produced the effect have been ruled out.

As you analyze cause and effect, watch for two common fallacies: *non sequitur* and *post hoc*. As you try to determine why something happened, proceed carefully. Avoid making unfounded inferences or hasty generalizations. Proof is needed before you cite a cause. Sketching a reverse chain of cause and effect will help to distinguish the effects from the cause.

Depending on the purpose and audience, papers of cause-to-effect or effect-to-cause can be opened and developed in various ways. Description and comparison/contrast are often used. Various writing strategies can be combined. When revising your paper, keep the rhetorical situation in mind.

Key Terms

argumentative edge	effect	post hoc
causal analysis	long-term effect	short-term effect
cause	non sequitur	

Practice

Ideas for a Cause-and-Effect Paragraph

1. Haste makes waste
2. How learning to save (or not save) has affected my life
3. Honesty is the best policy
4. How an error in judgment caused . . .
5. How learning to _____ led to . . .

Group Exercise: Writing "If . . . Then" Statements

Directions: Discuss each claim and the implications that *logically* follow. Then write a series of inferences derived from each claim. (The hints will start your thinking.)

1. In 1998 a Canadian business group got a permit to export water from Lake Superior to Asia. After an outcry in Canada and the United States, Ontario canceled the permit in 1999. Now Global Water Corp. of Vancouver, British Columbia, has secured a permit to take water from a lake near Sitka, Alaska, to sell to China. Alaskans granted the permit because they regard water as a renewable resource.

   Claim: Alaska should not be allowed to export water to a foreign country. (How might it affect the local supply? Water table? Might depletion affect the rate of renewal? Why?)

- If Alaska exports water, then there will be _____ water available to _____.

  - If a _____ should occur in the lower United States, then _____.
  - If Alaska continues to export water over the years, then _____.

2. *Claim:* Exercise is good for you; therefore, you should exercise regularly. (What conditions are implicit in this statement? Think about the exceptions and fill in the blanks with logical answers.)

   - If you have no _____ [what?], then you should exercise regularly.
   - If you have _____, then you should _____ [consult whom?] before exercising.
   - If your _____ recommends _____, then you should _____ regularly.
   - If _____, then _____.

Thirty Ideas for Papers of Cause and Effect

1. How I have been influenced by social expectations of computer literacy
2. An act of kindness and its effect on me
3. The influence of my favorite teacher
4. Effects of having multiple credit cards
5. Effects of being a cheerleader/football player/band member
6. Peer pressure in high school
7. The effects of fatherhood on a sports enthusiast
8. The effect of a telephone stalker on my life
9. How reading influenced my life
10. Influences of an alcoholic parent on a family
11. How my thinking has changed since attending college
12. Grandmother's favorite proverb and its influence on me
13. Effect of being the oldest of _____ children
14. How cancer changed my home
15. Thirty seconds of success and its effect
16. Influence of my stay-at-home mother
17. A father's example
18. Changes in my neighborhood
19. Effects of winning
20. Effects of losing a job

21. How my parents' divorce changed my life
22. Three words that changed my life
23. How losing _____ pounds influenced my life
24. Effect of college classes on my self-esteem
25. Switching from fast food to healthy home cooking
26. Stress on a nursing assistant
27. How my parents' living through the 1960s influenced me
28. The effects of being raised in a _____ neighborhood
29. A dream can generate power
30. How the events of September 11, 2001, have influenced my life

Critical Thinking, Evaluation, and Argument

Part 4

CHAPTER 18

Problem Solving

A problem well stated is a problem half solved.
　　　　　　　—Charles F. Kettering

Businesses, industries, and other organizations frequently face major problems of costs, personnel, and service. Prices of materials and wages rise. Competitors cut prices. Inventories "shrink." Equipment malfunctions. Deliveries run late. Personnel make mistakes, and customers complain. Problems of some sort occur in every workplace. How these problems are solved can mean profit or loss. Therefore job applicants with effective problem-solving skills, as well as writing skills, have an edge in interviews.

DEWEY'S METHOD OF PROBLEM SOLVING

Since primeval times, people have been solving problems randomly, trying one plan, then another, seeking an effective solution. Over several centuries, many people have helped to formulate the basic rules of scientific research. By 1855 a basic procedure had come to be known as the "scientific method," which is still used in research.

In the early twentieth century, John Dewey, an American philosopher and educator devised an efficient problem-solving method, based on the scientific method. Dewey, however, omitted the step of formulating a hypothesis, a step that can hinder objectivity. The researcher who formulates a hypothesis risks finding support only for the theory and overlooking evidence against it.

Dewey's systematic six-step procedure has been widely adopted and adapted by educators, business personnel, and others, according to the rhetorical situation. This basic procedure is also practical for individual use, providing an effective way to organize research papers and reports that focus on a problem. The purpose is to inform the audience of possible alternatives for solving or alleviating it. A simplified version appears here:

See chapters 21 and 22.

1. *State the problem.* Identify it.
2. *Define the problem.* Limit its scope. Examine its history.
3. *Formulate criteria.* Devise standards to measure the problem.
4. *Propose alternatives.* Consider possible solutions.
5. *Evaluate alternatives.* Apply criteria to solution options.
6. *Recommend action.* Select best possible solution(s).

Dewey knew that a problem must be confronted and clearly identified before it can be solved. Once the problem is understood, a plan of attack can be devised. Finding practical solutions was Dewey's primary concern. His main criterion for evaluating an alternative was "Will it work?" He went to great lengths to be objective.

HOW CAN ONE BE OBJECTIVE?

To be objective, we must be willing to relinquish old biases, to question and to seek the truth. Basically, there are two general ways to obtain information: firsthand and secondhand. Both ways can present problems in terms of objectivity. Although we observe something firsthand, we may see only part of it and think we saw 100 percent. Or we may misinterpret the meaning of what we observed; we may make incorrect inferences and treat them as fact. Information gained secondhand is often subject to error and distortion. So how can one be as objective as possible and minimize the chances of error?

First, *we can reserve judgment.* We can hold back our opinions until they are solidly supported. We can listen to both sides of an issue and consider all facets of a problem. By reserving judgment, we can look for facts and comprehensive coverage before making decisions.

Second, *we can try to be impartial and fair.* We can remain open to new information. The fact that one deduction fits should not lead us to ignore other possibilities or conflicting viewpoints. Often someone with a different perspective can give valuable assistance in solving a problem and in averting mistakes.

Third, *we can qualify generalizations and refrain from embellishing facts.* We can distinguish inference from fact. We can also be alert for clever images that carry negativity and for cunning words that carry bias. To be objective, we must seek the truth.

See chapters 6 and 20.

Fourth, *we can keep in mind that no one is immune to mistakes.* To be human means to be susceptible to error. Although we think we understand something, our information may be only partial. When we attempt to explain, we may be able to tell what caused something, what affects it now, and what may affect it in the future. We may even be able to discuss its apparent effect on other things. Nonetheless, our understanding is inferential, incomplete, and inconclusive at some point. This awareness should keep us not only humble, but also alert.

WORKPLACE CASE STUDY

WRITING A COMPANY POLICY

A marketing firm has recently installed software that allows executives to access and monitor electronic communication. This installation was made because several employees were playing games, gambling, job hunting, shopping, and watching porn online instead of working. (Each visit to a Web site drags along the company name.)

An attorney has advised the firm to write a policy covering e-mail and Web use. To balance company interests and employee privacy, the attorney advised appointing a committee that includes rank-and-file employees.

ACTIVITY

Meet with your group to draft specific guidelines for e-mail and Web use. Consider these issues: Should employees be allowed to use e-mail for personal messages? To trade stock during work hours? To grocery shop or engage in other leisure activities? If so, what kind of activities and for how many hours? Include penalties for policy violations. Should the number and severity of the offenses be factors?

WRITING A PROBLEM-SOLVING PAPER

A problem-solving paper combines various writing strategies into a basic format that is suitable not only for some short papers but also for some research papers. The outline on pages 232 and 233 is based on Dewey's method of problem solving. This format generally follows Dewey's method of problem solving. Although you and your peers may use the same general pattern of organization, you will make individual decisions, according to the rhetorical situation.

Selecting a Topic and Prewriting

To find a topic for a problem-solving paper, you might begin by considering your experience, including work-related projects. Or perhaps you know of a family, a neighborhood, a community, or a city facing a problem. The problem should be significant, yet not too technical or complex. It should have at least three alternatives. That does not mean all alternatives must be feasible. Two or more can be ruled out, but one must provide a means to alleviate or to resolve the problem. Sometimes all alternatives may be needed. If the problem cannot be alleviated, look for another topic.

As you search for details to use in a problem-solving paper, watch for changes, increases or decreases, cause and effect, side effects, risks, advantages and disadvantages. Note that changes may be negative or positive and their effects may be simple or complicated. Advantages and disadvantages may be short-term or long-term. Asking questions will speed your search.

Questions to Discover Details for Problem Solving

- What exactly is the problem?
- When was it first noticed?
- What or whom does it affect?
- What are its effects? (Signs, symptoms, characteristics?)
- How far does it extend? (Scope?)
- What were the causes? (History?)
- What, if anything, has been done to alleviate the problem?
- What other alternatives exist?
- What are the advantages and disadvantages of each alternative?
- What is the best alternative? Or will a combination be needed?

See chapter 17.

Caution: Beware of oversimplification. Complex problems seldom have a single cause.

Making an Outline

Dewey's method of problem solving furnishes an easy and effective way to organize information clearly for an audience. You can adapt this method to most problems. Using the six steps, you can start your scratch outline. Steps 1 and 2 will form the introduction of the paper. Steps 3, 4, and 5 form the body. Step 6 forms the conclusion as shown here.

Introduction

| Step 1: | Identify the problem |
| Step 2: | Define the problem |

Body

Step 3:	Identify criteria
Step 4:	Propose alternatives
Step 5:	Evaluate alternatives

Conclusion

| Step 6: | Recommend action |

Following the order of the six steps will simplify organizing your paper. The working outline here illustrates how you might convert the six steps into an outline.

I. Introduction
   A. Attention-getting detail
   B. Description of the problem
   C. History of the problem
   D. Identification of the cause(s)

II. Body
   A. Specific criteria stated
   B. Alternative 1 and evaluation
   C. Alternative 2 and evaluation
   D. Alternative 3 and evaluation

III. Conclusion
   A. Recommendation or best alternative
   B. Relevant comment

TRANSITION IN A PROBLEM-SOLVING PAPER

A problem-solving paper requires transitions to signal cause-and-effect relationships. To direct the reader, place appropriate transitions near reasons why an event happened or a description of how it affected another event or situation:

therefore	one difficulty	an offshoot	one part
thus	an outcome	a consequence	one complication
affected	one effect	a by-product	one influence
two factors	an outgrowth	as a result	one proposal
three aspects	influenced	contributed	changed

Drafting an Introduction

Problem-solving papers can begin in several ways. You might open with an appropriate quotation or a brief dialogue that illustrates a vital aspect of the problem. Another way is to start with a narrative that describes the problem; then you might describe cause and effect. Keith Zuspan described an incident that happened where he worked:

Preventing an Expensive Problem

One of the most recent crises at ——— State Headquarters in ——— occurred in the executive building. A twenty-five-year-old air-conditioning unit failed to maintain the required cooling level in this large complex. When such an event occurs, it is imperative that the Building Operations Supervisor take action immediately. The supervisor must be able not only to recognize the potential risks, but also to correct the problem in the least amount of time and in the most efficient manner.

The introduction of a problem-solving paper sets the stage for the identification of criteria and a discussion of alternatives.

Identifying Criteria

To check decisions and to evaluate possible solutions to problems, we need to develop criteria. By identifying our own specific criteria, we can measure the existing alternatives and make more logical decisions than we might otherwise make.

What Are Criteria?   Instead of criteria, you may be used to talking about "guidelines," "specifications," "company policy," "diplomacy," or similar terms. All of these are criteria, used to weigh decisions and evaluate alternatives. Criteria are simply the factors that influence decision making and problem solving.

Daily life offers many opportunities to apply criteria. For instance, when planning a major purchase, you use criteria to weigh the advantages and disadvantages of comparable products. Before buying a new television set, you might consider some, or perhaps all, of the following criteria:

- screen size
- brand name
- price
- warranty
- quality of sound
- high definition

A criterion (the singular of criteria) is *one* standard, rule, principle, or test used to evaluate a decision or proposal. For example, *Merriam-Webster's Collegiate Dictionary*, Tenth Edition, defines *criterion* as "a standard on which a judgment or decision may be based."*

Dewey's first criterion—"Will it work?"—is a factor in solving any problem. Time is another important criterion to consider. Other common criteria are listed here:

- Is it cost-effective?
- Is it safe?
- Is it practical?
- Is it legal?
- Is it ethical?
- Is it fair?
- Is it appropriate?
- Is it beneficial in the short run? Long run?

Stating Criteria   To identify criteria, ask: "What factors will influence this decision?" Perhaps the simplest way to specify criteria is to pose each criterion as a question. In her paper Nancy Miller stated criteria as questions:

> Making our house more energy-efficient required careful consideration. When the alternatives to this problem were evaluated, three main questions were asked.

---

*By permission from *Merriam-Webster's Collegiate® Dictionary*, Tenth Edition. Copyright © 1999 by Merriam-Webster, Inc.

First, what is the cost? Second, how energy-efficient is the alternative? Third, will the alternative raise the equity in our home?

Another example was written by a mother who had recently lost her job through a layoff. Carol Walkins specified three concerns in her job search: day shift, pay scale, and location:

> A major problem that I faced was the possibility of having to work the evening or midnight shift if I found employment in another factory. With two elementary school children, I needed to be at home in the evenings in order to spend important time with them. Since my family depends on my income, I also had to find a job that would provide a pay scale similar to that of my former job. Location was another factor to be considered. My husband works locally, and we own our home. Therefore, moving was not an option.

For clarity in a problem-solving paper, some instructors prefer that students state criteria before alternatives. Regardless, do not confuse criteria with alternatives. Criteria are the factors or considerations that govern decisions. Alternatives are the options for action—possible solutions. In other words, criteria provide a means to weigh the benefits and risks of an alternative.

Proposing and Evaluating Alternatives

Usually, a problem-solving paper presents at least three alternatives. Perhaps two of the choices can be eliminated, leaving one that can best solve the problem. This does not mean that every problem can be solved with one alternative. Perhaps a combination will be needed. Or perhaps the best that can be done is to alleviate the problem.

After alternatives are determined, each possibility is evaluated according to criteria. In this fifth step, advantages and disadvantages become apparent. Upon a first glance, an alternative may seem to be a practical solution to a problem. After research and analysis, however, hidden disadvantages may emerge.

To evaluate alternatives for a paper, research the feasibility of each one. Do not assume there are no disadvantages. To be objective, a paper must specify disadvantages as well as advantages. (An omission of either would constitute card stacking. See chapter 20.) Then evaluate the alternatives according to the criteria. Note that a problem may have a short-term alternative and a long-term solution. When Carol analyzed her problem of unemployment, she found both:

> My first alternative was to collect the nine months of unemployment compensation that I qualified for. I could accomplish my household tasks during the day, leaving the evenings free for my children. Collecting unemployment and saving on babysitting fees would compensate for the weekly paycheck. Although the idea of staying home was appealing, collecting an unemployment check would be temporary and not a real solution to the problem.
>
> A second alternative was to go job hunting. Although it seemed like a logical solution, I knew that a good job would be difficult to find at this time. To secure

factory work with daytime hours would be almost impossible. Daytime office jobs were available, but I lacked the training needed to qualify. I realized that it was unrealistic to expect to find a suitable, well-paying job locally.

A third option was available, however. Because I had lost my job due to foreign trade, I was eligible for a new federal program under the Trade Readjustment Act. This program would pay for college tuition for two years as well as books and supplies. I could attend day classes while the children were in school. The plan would also pay a small allowance for living expenses for up to one year if grade and attendance requirements were maintained. Although this option would require a drastically revised family budget, I knew I could manage.

Carol combined steps 4 and 5 of the problem-solving method: she proposed an alternative, applied criteria, and evaluated. This order enabled her to avoid undue repetition. The parallelism of her points helped to make the paper clear and easy to read. The details prepared the audience for the conclusion.

Writing a Conclusion

The end of a problem-solving paper presents the recommendation the writer has prepared the reader to accept. In other words, the selected solution should flow logically from the discussion of alternatives. Some conclusions contain a call for action, perhaps pointing out the consequences of inaction. In his paper about the air-conditioning problem on the job, Keith Zuspan concluded by making a recommendation:

> Repairing the existing air-conditioning unit would, in fact, be the most efficient and economical method of regaining the desired environmental controls required for the complex. It is also the writer's opinion that by utilizing the in-house building mechanics to complete this project, additional money could be saved.

Other conclusions, like the ending of Nancy Miller's paper, summarize the action already taken and explain how a solution fits the criteria:

> After reviewing the three alternatives, we chose the third, which proved to be the most cost-effective as well as energy-efficient. By purchasing the siding and windows together, we received a discount. The new furnace also proved to be energy-efficient, and we saw a sizable reduction in heating expense in the first year after installation. This third option has also increased the home's equity dramatically, although part of the increase is due to inflation. In 1972 we paid just over seven thousand dollars for the house, and now, three decades later, the house is worth over sixty-five thousand dollars.

Revising a Problem-Solving Paper

See chapter 5. To produce your best work, allow plenty of time for revising, editing, and proofreading your problem-solving paper. The following checklist will help to ensure that you check strategic points:

> ### CHECKLIST: REVISING A PROBLEM-SOLVING PAPER
>
> 1. Is the problem clearly defined in the introduction? Are the causes and pertinent history of the problem explained?
> 2. Are specific criteria for evaluating alternative solutions identified? Are these criteria reasonable and adequate?
> 3. Are different alternatives for solving the problem identified and described?
> 4. Is one alternative recommended? Is it clear why this solution is best?
> 5. Is the conclusion effective? Does it flow logically from the body?
> 6. Have transitions been used effectively?

TWO STUDENT PAPERS: PROBLEM-SOLVING

In the first example, Rajini Maturu proposes a solution to a problem faced in her former workplace:

Unhappy Customers at the Bank of India

The Union Bank of India is a financial institution that has 1,000 branches all over India. In the city of Secunderabad, the Union Bank caters to the financial needs of local customers. There the branch manager has to tackle the problem of customer dissatisfaction toward the check-cashing procedure.

Presently, there are four staff members of the bank taking care of the four steps of the check-cashing routine. During the banking hours between 10 a.m. and 2:30 p.m., there are about seventy customers. The customer first presents the check to a clerk, who enters the check number and amount in a register. The clerk gives the customer a metallic coin, called a token, with a number.

Then the customer goes to another clerk, who debits the customer's account with the amount of the check. Next, an accountant verifies the customer's signature. Finally, the check is taken to the cashier, who identifies the customer by the token number and makes the payment. During this procedure each customer waits for at least thirty minutes to cash a check.

There are two important aspects to the problem of expediting the check-cashing procedure. One aspect is the cost involved in bringing about changes since the branch is allowed a budget of $2,000 dollars. The other aspect to be considered is the amount of time saved by introducing the changes.

A proposed solution is to increase the number of staff members. Three additional clerks could be appointed to handle the check cashing. The cost of this change would mean $500 per clerk. For three more clerks, the total cost would be $1,500, which is within the budget limit. The main drawback to this proposal is that the customers would still have to wait for at least fifteen minutes to cash their checks.

A second proposal is the opening of a teller counter. This would mean creation of a separate cubicle with ledgers containing customer information. The specimen signatures of the customers would be stored at the teller counter. Here the entire check-cashing procedure could be managed by one employee called the teller officer. When a check was presented for payment, the teller officer would scrutinize the customer's signature, enter the check amount in the cash register, and make payment to the customer. This proposal would cost $1,900; hence, the expenses would be within the budget. As all the operations would be managed by one employee, the check could be cashed in eight minutes. This would mean a considerable reduction in the customer's wait.

A third proposal is to computerize all the customer's records. With this method the check would be cashed in two minutes. This is the best proposal as far as the time element is concerned. The cost involved in purchasing the computers and training the clerks would be $4,000 dollars, however. The disadvantage to this proposal is that it does not meet the budget requirements.

The second proposal of creating a teller counter appears to be the most suitable action at this time. This proposal reduces the waiting period to cash a check from thirty minutes to eight minutes, and the expenses involved are within the budget specifications.

In the second example, Chris Hafley proposes a solution to a problem facing his community:

A Plan for Quality Emergency Care

In the small northwest Ohio city of ———, the city fire department provides emergency medical care for its residents and township residents. In the past decade, a need for more advanced prehospital intervention has developed. To provide better medical care, the city council elected to send ten of twenty Advanced Emergency Medical Technicians to paramedic school at Sandusky Providence Hospital.

Before these ten people graduate and begin to function as paramedics, a dilemma must be resolved as to how the Rescue Squad will respond to possible life-threatening medical and trauma emergencies. With only one paramedic on duty as part of a two-person team, it would be almost impossible for the squad to function properly and respond efficiently to all calls twenty-four hours a day. Therefore, a committee has been organized to investigate four possible solutions.

The criteria set up by the investigational committee for review of the recommendations were availability, training, and cost-effectiveness. The first solution suggested was to respond with an ambulance and two police officers. But the officers' level of medical training is limited to basic first aid and CPR training. They would not be much help with patients needing advanced life support. To upgrade all the officers' training to at least emergency medical technician would involve considerable expense to the city. This method would be the most expensive option of the four, costing initially $30,000 to certify all eighteen officers. There are many times, however, when officers are out on call and thus are unavailable.

The second option would be to arrange for one additional paramedic to be on call at home for twenty-four hours a day. This plan would cost approximately $27,000, but it would be the most effective as far as availability is concerned.

The third option would be to dispatch an additional ambulance as a backup system for the first ambulance. After researching this option, more people favored it than any of the others because of quality of assistance and cost-effectiveness. Personnel on the ambulance already have the necessary training. Availability, however, would be a problem at times since the ambulance personnel make numerous out-of-town transfers.

The fourth option would provide for the fire department pumper to respond along with the ambulance. Research shows that this alternative would be the most cost-effective. The idea is to have two firefighters cross-trained as Basic Emergency Medical Technicians. There would be two firefighter EMTs on each shift. This option would cut down the number of personnel to be trained and would be the least expensive way for the city to provide the additional staff to assist in medical emergencies. The initial cost would be about $12,000 for training. An advantage to using the firefighters would be that they are usually available to respond to medical emergencies with the ambulance.

After all the information was compiled and the alternatives were reviewed again and again, the review committee recommended both options three and four be implemented. Thus if the firefighters were unavailable, the second ambulance might possibly provide a backup.

Questions for Analysis

1. Does each paper provide a clear description of the problem?
2. Are the criteria clear?
3. Does the order of alternatives seem appropriate?
4. Are alternatives evaluated according to the criteria?
5. Does the conclusion seem logical and complete?
6. What are the chief differences in the way the two problems are solved?

FOR YOUR REFERENCE:
PROBLEM-SOLVING ESSAYS IN THE READER

- "How Do You Know It's Good?" Marya Mannes, page 600
- "Road Rage," Vest, Cohen, & Tharp, page 609
- "Why Marriages Fail," Anne Roiphe, page 671
- "The Emotional Quadrant," Elizabeth Kübler-Ross, page 680

Summary

John Dewey's method of problem solving is based on the scientific method. Objectivity is an essential aspect of problem solving. Although no one can be 100 percent objective, we can work to control our biases and mistakes.

Dewey's six steps of problem solving provide an easy and efficient way for you to organize a paper: (1) identify the problem, (2) describe the problem, (3) specify criteria, (4) propose alternatives, (5) evaluate alternatives according to the criteria, and (6) recommend the best alternative(s).

Criteria are standards of measurement—the factors or considerations that influence decision making. You apply criteria so that you can weigh the advantages and disadvantages of alternatives. This way you can evaluate the practicality of possible solutions to a problem.

For a problem-solving paper, you may need special transitions to show cause and effect. Your conclusion should flow logically from the body. The conclusion presents the solution you have prepared the audience to accept.

Key Terms

alternative	Dewey's method of problem solving	scientific method
criteria	firsthand information	secondhand information
criterion	objectivity	

Practice

Small Groups: Identifying Criteria

The following introduction to a problem-solving paper was written by Patricia Davis. After you read it, brainstorm possible criteria that would influence the final decision. One group member should record all of these. Finally, examine your list of criteria and decide which are most important in determining a solution.

A Pet for Aunt Emily

My aunt, although eighty-three years old and rather frail, is still able to care for herself. Aunt Emily lives alone in her own home on a limited income. Ordinarily, she is quite independent and self-sufficient, but last week she surprised me. When I dropped by, she asked for advice. Confiding that she was lonely, she explained she needed companionship and was thinking about getting a pet. But she was unsure about what sort of animal would be best for her. She asked me to help in deciding what kind of pet would be the most enjoyable and suitable.

Small Groups: Case Problems

Directions: Select *one* of the authentic cases below. Steps 1 and 2 of Dewey's problem-solving method are given. Supply steps 3, 4, 5, and 6.

1. You are a member of the committee selected to plan the office Christmas party. Your instructions are to eliminate past problems or cancel! In past years, employees have bought gifts for the president of the small marketing research firm. Some buy expensive gifts and appear to be currying favors, which causes grumbling. The owner gives everyone a small rolled ham and provides a lunch of finger food and fruit punch. But someone always spikes the punch with gin. Some employees have become boisterous. Last year a few became amorous, which led to a temporary separation of one couple. Devise a plan to prevent similar problems.

2. You are a computer and software sales rep. While running a booth at a trade show, you meet a woman who asks if you still have the same sales manager, J. D. Smith. When you reply "Yes," she says, "That's too bad." Then she tells about her boyfriend buying software out of the sales manager's home. You mull over the pros and cons of telling the owner, whom you admire and trust. You do not trust the sales manager because of his office pranks and complaints behind the owner's back. What other factors should you consider? Alternatives? What do you decide?

3. You are the assistant manager of a bookstore. One day you see the nine-year-old son of your best friend. He glances around and puts a book inside his jacket. Then he walks toward the door. Store policy requires that you alert another employee, stop shoplifters after they leave the store, and retrieve merchandise. You are to warn them that if they ever reenter, charges will be filed. Parents of children who shoplift are to be notified. To protect your friend and yourself from an awkward situation, you are tempted to ignore the incident. What factors should be examined? Is there a third alternative? What do you decide?

4. Your husband works nights. One evening you are alone except for your three-year-old child, asleep in her room. At eleven o'clock you hear a noise in the chimney of the fireplace. Terrified, you watch a small dark creature creep out and fly across the room. It perches in one corner near the ceiling. What will you do? What are your alternatives? What factors must be considered?

5. Your neighbors often stay out until 2:30 a.m. on weekends. They leave their Doberman tied out in the backyard, where he howls—keeping you awake until they take him in. You do not know if he is hungry or lonely. The dog does not recognize you, but from a distance he seems fairly friendly. What are your alternatives? What risks are involved?

Thirty Ideas for Problem-Solving Papers

1. A problem on the job
2. Stress management for nurses, police officers, or . . .
3. Relocating in a new community
4. Investigating alternatives for elder care
5. Coping with divorce
6. Security for twenty-four-hour businesses
7. Automobile security from theft
8. Spotting shoplifters
9. Mastering the fear of failure
10. Parking restrictions around campus

11. How can we attract new industries and businesses to the city?
12. How can we attract more tourists?
13. How can we raise funds to replace playground equipment in the city park?
14. Staffing athletic programs on a low budget
15. Inadequate child-care facilities for working parents
16. Registering for classes
17. Monitoring children's television viewing
18. Local litter control
19. Stray animal control
20. Drag racing on city streets
21. Relying on credit cards
22. Alcoholism in the family
23. Complaints and the apartment owner
24. Problems for families when women start careers
25. Coping with discrimination
26. Adjustment to college after _____ years
27. Good nutrition on a low budget
28. Breaking the nicotine habit
29. Safety when walking alone at night
30. Maintaining an exercise plan

CHAPTER 19

Shaping an Effective Argument

Truth is one forever absolute, but
opinion is truth filtered through the moods,
the blood, the disposition of the spectator.

—Wendell Phillips (1859)

Hardly a day passes without your persuading someone of something. It may be as trivial as convincing a friend to try a new restaurant or as significant as convincing an interviewer you are qualified for a position. On the job you may write a proposal, a request for new software, a grant application, or other document. In a college class you may be asked to write a persuasive essay, a reaction paper, or a paper of argument. Skill in argument and persuasion will enable you to become a more effective writer and speaker, both in college and in the workplace.

PURPOSE OF ARGUMENT

Although there are many types of argument, the general purpose of any serious argument is to convince readers to accept a belief, adopt a policy, or enact a decision, proposal, or law. In the strictest sense, the term *argument* refers to an assertion that is based on logic and proof, a rational appeal to the intellect.

According to the rhetorical situation, however, many arguments contain not only rational appeals but also ethical and emotional appeals. This chapter explains a classic argument model that includes appeals to logic, ethics, and emotions. This model is flexible, effective, and practical. It can be adapted in various ways for general use.

THREE CLASSIC APPEALS USED IN ARGUMENT

More than two thousand years ago, the Greek philosopher Aristotle defined three kinds of appeals that make up an argument: *logos* (logic), *ethos* (moral character or ethics), and *pathos* (emotion). Aristotle realized that logic alone is not always sufficient to persuade an audience. To be convincing, you must also gain credibility—the trust of your listeners or readers. To do so, you must be perceived as honest, fair, and responsive to moral obligations. Aristotle called this the appeal to *ethos*. In *Nicomachean Ethics*, he explains:

> Virtue then is twofold, partly intellectual and partly moral, and intellectual virtue is originated and fostered mainly by teaching; it demands therefore experience and time. Moral virtue on the other hand is the outcome of habit, and accordingly its name *éthike*, is derived by a slight variation from *éthos*, habit.

> —from *On Man and the Universe: Metaphysics, Parts of Animals, Ethics, Politics, Poetics.* Louise R. Loomis, Editor

Logical and ethical appeals are often enough to convince on some issues, but unless emotion moves an audience to act on other issues, the argument will be in vain.

WORKPLACE CASE STUDY

"You Got a Tiger by the Tail!"

Matthew Resome was a programmer at XYZ Company. Matt was a quiet guy with an excellent work record who got along well with other employees. For three years he had tried to work through the right channels to improve wages and working conditions. But neither had changed despite the fact that the company's sales had increased 55 percent during those years.

When Matt contacted the National Labor Relations Board (NLRB), they said that if he could secure seventy-five signatures on a petition, then they could come in and conduct a vote to unionize the plant. The company would have to provide a room with a booth where employees could come during work hours. Matt secured the required signatures, and two NLRB representatives conducted the vote at the plant. The vote failed.

The next morning J. B. Smith, the plant manager, told his assistant to fire Matt. The assistant, who had attended law school, refused. Using a *logical* appeal, he warned, "You can't do this. Federal laws prohibit discrimination against peaceful and acceptable union activities. You got a tiger by the tail! Let it go."

But four days later, the irate plant manager called Matt in and stated, "Your job has been phased out. We don't need you any more. You can clear out your desk and leave right now." Matt contacted the NLRB.

ACTIVITY

Assume the role of the NLRB investigator. Examine Matt's work record and investigate the events preceding the firing. Summarize the situation and write a letter to J. B. Smith. Inform him that to prevent legal action, the company must reinstate and reimburse Matt for all lost wages. The company has thirty days to consider the offer.

You can identify the three classic appeals by the questions they raise with readers:

- **Logical appeal:** Is the claim or petition factual and reasonable? True or false? Practical or impractical?
- **Ethical appeal:** Is it just or unjust? Honest or dishonest? Right or wrong?
- **Emotional appeal:** Do the words arouse such feelings as empathy and sympathy? Do they cause the reader to care about the subject?

The Logical Appeal

In most rhetorical situations, you will be expected to base your conclusions on sound reasoning and adequate proof. A logical argument appeals to the mind, using evidence, reasons, and examples to support a claim or proposition. Logical appeals are based on facts, sound inferences, and working theories. Reliable evidence may include established truths, primary sources, statistics, expert opinion, or personal experience.

Established Truths   Some evidence is so solidly grounded that no reasonable person will seriously debate it. In the examples below, the first three are *established facts*, which have been conclusively proven. The fourth example has been accepted as fact, based on the existing evidence.

- **Historical fact:** Meriwether Lewis and William Clark explored the northwestern United States from St. Louis to the Pacific Ocean.
- **Geographical fact:** The Mississippi River is joined by the Missouri, Illinois, and Ohio Rivers before it flows down to the Gulf of Mexico.
- **Scientific fact:** When a heavy object is dropped, it falls to the ground.
- **Scientific theory regarded as fact:** The sun's gravitation attracts the planets and keeps them in their paths. Stars are held on course by the pull of heavenly bodies.

Primary Sources   Research that is gathered firsthand carries more credibility than that filtered through secondary researchers. If you can obtain relevant documents, letters, autobiographies, or other primary source materials, these can lend strong support to your argument. Or you may choose to gather evidence firsthand yourself. For further explanation of and suggestions for primary research, see chapter 22, "Primary Research."

Statistics   Reliable statistical findings from recognized and reputable authorities can strengthen your argument. To be reliable, the findings should be based on samples that are representative and random. Yet some widely quoted findings are neither random nor representative, as explained in chapter 22.

Another problem in reliability occurs when the researcher who is under extreme pressure, such as meeting a deadline, falsifies results. When you find unusual conclusions, check to see if the results are consistent with those of others in the field. Unless an experiment can be duplicated under controlled laboratory conditions by qualified researchers, it cannot be accepted as evidence.

Expert Opinion   The opinion of a recognized authority in a field generally conveys credibility and enhances a argument. If you decide to use expert opinion, check out the person's qualifications first. Here the Internet is an invaluable and speedy resource for checking on well-known authorities. Interviewing can also be helpful for local issues. For instance, if you were arguing for a proposal to thwart break-ins and burglary, then the chief of police, sheriff, or mayor could be credible sources.

See "Watch for Credentials" chapter 23.

Personal Experience   The personal stories of people who have been involved in an accident, a tragedy, or natural phenomenon such as a tornado, can be powerful. A detailed description of such an event can have a strong emotional impact and buttress a logical argument. Personal experience stories should be used to supplement logical evidence, not supplant it. The experience should be significant and have a definite, relevant point.

Important Considerations   When you are presenting inconclusive evidence, avoid confusing theory with fact. Be accurate and precise so as not to overstate and weaken your case. For a reference list, see "Using Tentative Words to Discuss Findings and Theories," page 379.

Inferences are often confused with fact, and generalizations are often made from an invalid sample. For a further discussion of what constitutes reliable evidence, see chapters 6 and 20. To construct a flawless argument, you need to be able to recognize pitfalls in logic.

The Ethical Appeal

Ethical appeals are designed to strike a responsive chord in the minds of the readers, entreating them to do what is right, good, fair, and best. Ethics can be broadly defined as a set of moral values—principles of conduct for an individual, group, profession, or society. Sound ethics are essential for a well-constructed argument.

To be ethical, an argument must respect the rights and needs of the audience. In other words, deception to obtain a selfish aim is unethical—and often illegal. For example, a pastor of an Ohio church persuaded several elderly couples to donate their life savings to his church. However, he spent the money for expensive cars and other luxuries. Eventually, he was convicted of fraud and sent to prison.

An ethical appeal requires you to first demonstrate comprehensive knowledge of your subject. *You have an ethical obligation to give the reader the whole truth*, not just proof that will make your side of the argument *seem* convincing. In other words, if there are disadvantages to your proposal, you need to be honest about them. Second, you must approach the subject in an even-handed way, presenting differing viewpoints accurately and fairly. Your written voice must sound reasonable, controlled, and concerned.

The Emotional Appeal

Emotional appeals stir the feelings of readers with figurative language, connotation, and anecdote. Such appeals can be powerful, for they bypass the intellect. Emotional appeals work best, however, when used in moderation. They should also be ethical. Do not use an emotional appeal that gives you any misgivings or uneasiness.

Used wisely, emotion can motivate. For example, in the Workplace Case Study earlier, the assistant might have stressed his emotional appeal more. Instead of hinting with "You got a tiger by the tail!" he could have been more direct by saying, "You might lose your own job over this firing. Be careful." Perhaps the boss would have listened.

Using the Three Appeals

The bulk of your argument paper should be a logical appeal, based on sound logical proof. But keep in mind that credible persuasion rests on a blend of facts and ethical reasons, bonded with appropriate emotion. In other words, emotion usually plays a lesser role. To be effective, all three appeals must harmonize. An emotional appeal that conflicts with either a logical appeal or an ethical appeal is inappropriate.

GUIDELINES FOR USING PERSUASIVE APPEALS

1. *Alert the audience to a problem by using suitable emotion.*
2. *Use restraint.* Do not overstate. Exaggerated appeals can backfire.
3. *Do not circumvent an issue.* Focus your argument on the issue. Answer all of the opposition's points with solid evidence and reasons.
4. *Do not oversimplify.* Guard against either/or alternatives.
5. *Avoid conflicting appeals.* Contradiction undermines arguments.
6. *Show and tell.* Use examples and anecdotes to illustrate and heighten interest.
7. *Read aloud to check for objectivity.* Evidence should be presented honestly without slanting or manipulation. The writer's voice should sound fair and trustworthy.

UNDERSTANDING OPPOSING VIEWS AND OVERCOMING OBJECTIONS

Two landowners were involved in a boundary dispute that dated back to their grandfathers' time. Years before, a rail fence had been erected by one grandparent and moved by the other. At last one man consulted a lawyer. Relating the history of the argument, the client presented one view of the dispute. The lawyer assured him that the law was on his side and asked when he wanted to sue. The client replied, "Never, I just gave you the other guy's version."

Researching both views of an issue provides an opportunity not only to weigh the facts, but also to consider the priorities, values, and attitudes of readers who disagree. Sometimes readers may agree with a proposal, but not act. Then your first task is to discover the *area of resistance* and determine why they are reluctant. The second task is to prepare a persuasive strategy to overcome their objections and resistance. Once you understand the opposing view, you can decide how to shape the argument to emphasize advantages and benefits.

For example, voters may agree that more money is needed to fund local schools, but they may resist voting for a bond levy. How do you convince them that the proposed benefits justify the expense? An appeal combining logic, ethics, and emotion might be the most effective:

> Several of our school buildings are over seventy-five years old. They are drafty and expensive to heat; those big windows have single panes. The frames rattle. The electrical wiring is inadequate; there is no way to plug in computers. Plaster has fallen from some ceilings. Building now will avoid expensive renovations and save money in the long run, for construction costs continue to climb.
>
> The buildings are also overcrowded. For instance, in one building a class meets on the auditorium stage, another in the lunchroom, and two meet at the ends of halls. The children are distracted by passersby, and the acoustics are poor. The children have no place to put their coats.
>
> Our children deserve better. They deserve a place where they can concentrate and do their best. Our children are the future leaders of this country. Surely, we need to give them a chance for optimum learning. Won't you dig down in your pocket to come up with the extra dollars to make this dream come true? Vote yes for the school bond levy!

QUESTIONS TO ANALYZE AN AUDIENCE

1. How much does the audience know about the topic?
2. How strong is their disagreement or resistance?
3. If they agree on a proposal, why are they reluctant to act?
4. What is important to them?
5. What is important to me?
6. What change can I reasonably expect?

WRITING A CLASSIC ARGUMENT PAPER

Many times it is not enough to research the facts on an issue, for facts alone may not convince. People often act on perceptions and instincts that are not always logical. When a problem arises, you may have a practical solution and all the relevant facts; but unless you can tap into your audience's priorities and needs, chances are your proposal will be rejected. Therefore, careful audience analysis is essential to draft an effective strategy of argument. (For explanations of audience analysis, see chapters 1 and 31.)

The strategy you select will be determined by the purpose, the topic, and the amount of resistance to the proposition. Will the audience show reluctance, firm opposition, or downright hostility? As you shape your strategy, keep in mind the three classic appeals. Consider how they can help you focus your paper.

Selecting a Topic

The topic for an argument paper should be controversial and significant. A controversial topic has at least two points of view. To be significant, the disagreement would involve more than a definition of terms or a question of fact that could be easily checked. This means the topic would center on more than a simple question of truth or a matter of personal preference. For instance, to argue that computers can be fun would be unsuitable. Or to argue vaguely that U2 is better than the Beatles would be futile since this judgment hinges upon personal taste. But a paper that contains adequate support and criteria to evaluate the characteristics of both musical groups could yield a logical argument.

Claims of judgment involve an opinion or rating that is significant and logical, resting on facts and reasons. Aesthetic judgments evaluate the worth or value of music, art, and literature. Ethical judgments evaluate whether something is beneficial or harmful, humane or inhumane, moral or immoral, right or wrong. Functional judgments evaluate how well something or someone works. Arguments, including judgments, make five types of claims.

Five Basic Claims Made in Arguments

1. ***Claim of judgment:*** What is the writer's position on the issue? What are the criteria upon which the judgment is based?
2. ***Claim of fact:*** What is actually true? (Myth as opposed to fact or updates in scientific thinking might be typical examples.)
3. ***Claim of interpretation:*** What do the facts mean?
4. ***Claim of cause:*** Why did something happen? Why is it the way it is? (A valid hypothesis provides the simplest and best explanation.)
5. ***Claim of policy:*** What should be done? What is the best alternative to solve the problem? Or are there several acceptable alternatives?

Before an argument can be resolved, the participants must agree on a *basic premise* or *proposition* upon which the argument rests. For example, two students could agree on the basic premise that a college diploma should signify competency, although they disagree about how competency should be measured. Since they agree on the underlying belief, a logical argument could be constructed.

To write effectively about a value-laden topic, you must be open-minded, fair, and alert. Topics such as gun control, abortion, and religion carry emotional baggage that make them difficult to argue for three reasons: (1) rarely do the opposing views agree on a basic premise; (2) sources are often slanted toward one view; and (3) you must sift the evidence while keeping your own biases under control. Other topics for argument may have inherent hazards, too. For your consideration, some typical problems that students wade into are listed here:

Common Hazards in Selecting Topics for Argument

1. **The topic is too broad.** Subjects should be narrowed to a proposition that can be supported and discussed well in the allotted length.
2. **The topic is strictly informational.** A paper of argument does more than collect information. You strive to convince the reader of a proposition.
3. **The topic is hackneyed.** Sometimes students resurrect old papers or debate notes from high school. An important reason for assigning a paper of argument is to spur you to think and learn.
4. **Adequate support is unavailable.** If a topic is recent, you may find little data available. If a topic is heavily laden with emotion, you may find bias and fallacies in the sources.

Typically, instructors groan when they see old, overused topics such as capital punishment, legalizing illicit drugs, and the like. To be significant, a topic does not have to have worldwide or national implications—it may be a campus, community, or neighborhood issue. Such topics can yield fresh material.

CRITERIA FOR SELECTING AN ARGUMENT TOPIC

1. Is there disagreement about the subject or an area of resistance?
2. Is the issue significant and challenging?
3. Can I obtain enough factual information?
4. After research, will I be able to thoroughly understand the issue?
5. Can I write about the topic in a fair, objective tone?

Gathering Information and Prewriting

The more knowledgeable and sophisticated your readers, the more they will insist on adequate proof of a claim. Yet a writer seldom has all the facts needed to attain a comprehensive view of a controversial topic. To be knowledgeable and objective, you need information from a variety of sources and viewpoints. In the workplace, you may talk to personnel at other companies who have resolved a similar question or problem. You may also consult journals, trade magazines, or online services.

In a college class, you may be asked to take a position on a literary work and write a paper of argument. In that case, you examine the work closely, make notes, think, and write. Or you may be required to do a research paper with text citations and a list of works cited. To focus a search for information, you might begin by posing a controlling question.

Drafting a Controlling Question   A controlling question narrows the search for information and establishes the focus of a paper. This question limits the topic and aids in finding suitable source materials. After you write your controlling question, check to see whether or not it performs these two vital functions:

1. Identifies the *specific* topic and scope
2. Specifies the *direction* of the research

For controversial topics, the wording of the question should receive special attention. The words should be fair and objective. Notice how a few words can change the tone of a question:

Biased: Should students be *forced* to take achievement tests *every year*?

Neutral: Should achievement tests *be given yearly*?

A neutral controlling question will help you to analyze a controversy fairly. Rereading the question from time to time will aid you in withholding judgment until key facts and implications are clear. The researcher who maintains an open mind is more likely to appraise an issue impartially than is one who leaps to a quick decision.

Searching for Reliable Sources   You need to gain an accurate overview of an issue, not just gather evidence to bolster one point of view. Understanding varying views is necessary to shape a convincing argument. To compare accounts and judge credibility, read from several sources. Not all sources are authoritative or reliable. Some may contain incorrect or outdated information, logical fallacies, or bias.

As you select books, look at the back cover, in the foreword, or in the introduction for the writer's credentials. Is he or she an authority in the field? Then scan a few pages and listen to the tone of the writing. Does it sound objective or biased? Does the coverage seem slanted? Do the significant points of the controversy seem to be covered? If you find inconsistencies or differing interpretations, jot down page numbers and authors. These discrepancies should be mentioned in your paper.

To research a local issue, you might interview the people involved and read newspaper accounts. To research a topic in a specialized field, consult journals or trade publications for technical information and opinions of authorities. Popular magazines may give brief factual overviews of issues, but the treatment may be incomplete. (Also see "Selecting Suitable Sources" and "Evaluating Reliability of Internet Sources" in chapter 23.)

Note-Taking and Critical Reading   While interviewing and reading, gather facts, statistics, expert opinion, cause and effect, reasons, and examples that constitute support for *both* sides. You will need to know the points of the opposing side so that you can refute them effectively. If you cannot answer the opposition's points by citing stronger evidence and better reasons, then your argument will not be convincing.

Take care to represent differing views fairly. That does not mean you give them equal space; you condense their main points. Try to spot anything that seems illogical, biased, or irresponsible. Write your notes in the margins of a copy or on cards. For detailed suggestions for critical reading, see chapter 26.

Making Con/Pro Lists   You can simplify the task of organizing the chief points of a controversy by listing pros and cons while reading. To separate evidence against and for the proposition, just write *con* and *pro* at the top of a sheet of paper. Then as you read, list proof in two vertical columns, placing parallel points side by side. Leave plenty of white space between items to add notes. Follow each item with the name of the author and page number. This identification will save time later. The lists will resemble those below except that actual points and answers will be listed:

Con	Pro
Main point (Barnes 140)	Agrees with facts, then disagrees about implications (Aker 39)
Main point (Barnes 141)	Objection and answer (Berry 149)
Main point (Smith 33)	Objection and answer (Conroy 12)

Stating a Position

After you list the significant points of disagreement for an argument, your next task is to select the viewpoint you think is soundest. Then write a proposition, indicating your position on the issue.

Writing a Proposition   The thesis statement of an argument is called the *proposition*. The tone of this statement is usually serious and much stronger than that of an ordinary thesis. To draft a proposition, you might start by rewriting your controlling question, then exploring its implications:

Controlling question: Since privacy issues are involved, should telemarketing firms be subject to restrictions?

Possible thesis: Telemarketing is an invasion of privacy that should not be permitted.

Possible thesis: Telemarketing is a legal right that should not be abridged.

Taking a Position of Compromise   Sometimes you may not agree wholeheartedly with either view; you see some validity in both views. If you reach an impasse, try a middle-of-the-road approach. Can you think of a way to modify your stand with a compromise that is acceptable to you? The examples below may suggest some ideas:

Compromise: Telemarketing should not be permitted after 6 p.m.

Compromise: Telemarketing by computerized dialing should not be allowed.

Each time you revise your thesis, check it carefully. Does it say what you mean? Could the terminology be confusing to the reader? Does it need to be revised further? Creating a focused title may also be helpful at this point.

Writing a Focused Title   A focused title acts like a thesis statement, clearly stating the proposition. Focused titles can be quite beneficial. You can glance back at the title from time to time to ensure that the argument is staying on course. A focused title indicates a position.

Focused title: English Should Be Declared the Official Language of the USA

Focused title: The USA Does Not Need an Official Language

When an issue is heated, a writer may pose a question in the title to create a zone of neutrality. This zone allows the writer to present and evaluate the evidence before declaring a position in a *delayed thesis*. This *indirect approach* lowers the temperature of the argument and encourages consideration of differences. Although a neutral question title does not indicate a position, it does indicate a persuasive purpose:

Neutral question title: Should English Be Declared Our Official Language?

Although the neutral question title can be quite effective, your instructor may specify a focused title to simplify the writing of your paper. When misused, the neutral question title can lead to vague, rambling papers. Regardless of which kind of title you use, understanding the opposing view will assist in focusing your persuasive strategy.

Planning the Shape of an Argument

There is no "one size fits all" strategy of argument. Arguments come in all shapes and sizes, depending on the rhetorical situation. Thus a writer is left to devise a strategy that will accommodate the situation in the best possible way. The structure of a logical argument consists of four basic parts: (1) making a claim (stating the purpose), (2) anticipating objections from readers, (3) countering objections by supporting the claim with solid evidence, and (4) submitting a conclusion derived from the evidence.

Four Elements of a Logical Argument

Claim: The specific proposition of a writer is the claim. A claim may be made directly or indirectly.

Objections: Knowing the main points of the opponents helps a writer to answer objections effectively.

Evidence: A writer supports a claim with facts, interprets the facts, and explains—giving statistics, reasons, examples, or other evidence. (The most effective arguments contain an appeal designed to satisfy or benefit the reader.)

Conclusion: The end of an argument is often a restatement of the claim. It may be a summary of main points or a logical generalization. It may attempt to motivate the reader to act.

Direct or Indirect Order: Early or Delayed Thesis?

To organize an effective argument, you first consider whether to use direct or indirect order. In other words, will an early or a delayed thesis be most persuasive? How the four parts of the argument are arranged and developed depends on the implications of the topic and the probable impact on the audience. Think: How will the proposition be received by readers?

Direct Approach

If your readers are likely to be well informed and only mildly opposed to a proposition, you may decide to be direct and bring out the proposal early. Then the thesis can be stated in the introduction. Here is an example of a proposition that would probably meet with little resistance from employees who will readily accept change:

Early thesis: A new system of billing will speed up the collection process and save an estimated $50,000 annually in collection costs.

Indirect Approach

An indirect plan, on the other hand, allows you to delay your thesis until much later in the paper. A delayed thesis allows you to consider the main points of the other side before mentioning your points. This arrangement sets the stage for a congenial discussion. Often it is wise to treat an argument as a misunderstanding or as a difference in perception. This low-key approach is less likely to be perceived as threatening or combative. Any hint of antagonism, sarcasm, impatience, or superiority will undermine your stand. A reader who is patronized or derided may be offended. Negative undertones can sabotage the flawless logic of an argument.

Readers who are likely to be uninformed or hostile will require more facts and reasons than will readers who are well informed. You need to lay extra groundwork for your recommendation. The stronger the objection, the more time you will need to prepare them to accept the proposition. As long as the path of an argument is clear, the thesis statement may be postponed until the body or conclusion.

Delayed thesis: Genetic engineering of food crops can be beneficial.

Sometimes, however, a thesis is implicit (unstated). Still, the argument is focused on one unmistakable conclusion. Since arguments with implicit theses require considerable skill, they are best left to experienced writers. Most instructors require an explicit thesis to aid in establishing the direction of an argument. Regardless of the type of argument you write, stress the benefits, advantages, and strengths of your proposal.

FACTORS TO CONSIDER IN PLANNING AN ARGUMENT

1. What does the audience believe about the issue?
2. How does the audience feel about the issue?
3. Which order will be most effective: direct or indirect?
4. What kind of title will be most effective?
5. How much transition will be needed to make points of view clear?

Presenting Opposing Viewpoints   To set the tone for a calm, courteous discussion, place the opposing view *before* your own. This method acknowledges the main points of the opposition and shows that you have considered the evidence. This arrangement is akin to listening, indicating a willingness to suspend judgment. This makes your argument stronger, for it emphasizes your answers to the opposing point of view. (For help in keeping viewpoints clear see "Labeling Points of View," page 257.)

When you are *for* an issue, the argument seems simpler for most students to organize. *Then you take the pro side of the issue and place it second:*

(*Opposing view*) Opponents of gambling

(*Pro view*) Proponents of gambling

But when you are *against* an issue, setting up the terminology takes more thought. The order of the viewpoints is *reversed.* (Just remember that your view always comes second.) To prevent possible confusion in your notes, clearly label points of view and place them at the top of your lists of points:

(*Other view*) Proponents of gambling

(*Your view*) Opponents of gambling

After points of view are clearly identified, you consider whether to present the argument in block or alternating (point-by-point) form. An outline is essential to keep the argument on track.

Block and Alternating Organization   There are two basic ways to set up a controversial topic. The simplest is the block method. This way the main points of the opposing side appear in one chunk right after the introduction. One paragraph is usually adequate for this *summary of the opposing view.* Then in the next several paragraphs, you answer *all* the points raised and submit *evidence* to support your reasoning. The block method has an advantage in tone. Describing the opponent's view first not only conveys a sense of fairness but also postpones disagreement.

When an issue is complex, the alternating method is clearer than the block. The alternating pattern pairs one of the opposing points with one of yours, arguing

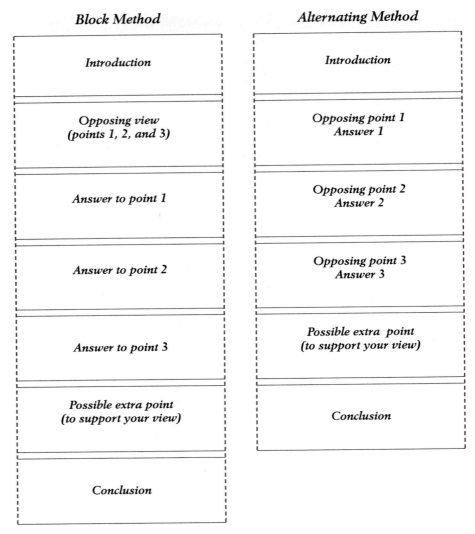

Fig. 19.1 Ways to organize an argument.

back and forth, emphasizing your answers. (In fig. 19.1, each box represents a paragraph, although others could be added.) A possible disadvantage of alternating is that disagreement emerges earlier than in the block method. Then too, the alternating method requires extra transition. (See "Labeling Points of View" on page 257.)

An unanswered point would pose a serious flaw in any argument. If you cannot answer a point adequately and should decide to reverse your original position in the argument, it is fine to do so. It shows you have an open, logical mind.

LABELING POINTS OF VIEW

If differing points of view go unlabeled, readers may become bewildered. To prevent confusion, identify the side holding each view *every time there is a shift from one to the other*. Four pairs of transitions appear below:

(con) adversaries   opponents   critics   opposition

(pro) advocates   proponents   supporters   sponsors

Select either *one pair* of terms or *two closely related pairs* and repeat them throughout your paper for clarity. To provide variety you might substitute *opponents* for the *opposition*. But abrupt shifts to dissimilar pairs would be distracting; the puzzled reader would have to stop and reread. Clarity is more important than variety.

When selecting labels for viewpoints, beware of slanting. For instance, a student writing about sex education called the opposition "right wingers" while labeling the other side "proponents." This mismatch of terms not only lacked parallelism but also revealed bias. Likewise, avoid the terms *liberals* and *conservatives*. These words have been bandied about so much their meanings have blurred. In some contexts, they have also taken on negative connotations.

To maintain an objective tone, try to avoid personal involvement in the argument. Two tips should be helpful: (1) Use third person, not first. (2) Try putting yourself in the role of a reporter writing a news item. This role should help you to distance yourself from the topic and avoid slanting.

Usually, main points are arranged in least- to most-important order so that the argument gradually builds. The best point is placed last, where it receives the most emphasis. To plan a paper on a controversy, the following questions will be helpful:

Questions for Shaping a Controversial Topic

1. What is at stake? Is there a hidden agenda?
2. Where is the best spot for the proposition? (Direct or indirect order?)
3. Is a definition needed?
4. How much background information will be needed?
5. Is there a common ground?
6. Can any concessions be made?
7. What are the advantages to accepting the proposition?
8. Are there disadvantages?
9. Will the block or alternating method be more suitable?
10. What is the best way to conclude the argument?

Drafting a Neutral Introduction

The purpose of an introduction is to present a factual overview of the argument. The introduction describes the issue and its origin, cause(s), and history. The introduction tells *when, who, what, how,* and perhaps *why,* defining the area of disagreement. The appeal is primarily logical: the tone is neutral. If readers are familiar with a topic, background information may be brief. If a topic is unfamiliar, the introduction should be more detailed. In the first example below, the writer describes a local problem that had been aired extensively by the media:

Curbing Overpopulation of Deer by "Harvesting"

The rapid growth of deer herds in Sharron Woods and Blacklick Park in Central Ohio poses problems. With no predators, the deer have multiplied to the point where they have stripped the woods and run out of food. Samuel B. Randall, attorney for Metro Parks, estimates that in the 700 acres of Sharron Woods, 375 deer live, which is "10 times the number the park can support." The controversy is over the means by which the deer herds will be decreased. One alternative is to let nature resolve the problem. Other alternatives are to use birth control or to move the deer. A fourth alternative, "harvesting," has led to requests for intervention. Recently, a Franklin Court judge declared he had no jurisdiction over the case (Candisky 1).

In the next student introduction, Pamela J. Van Camp begins with a definition. Then she gives logical reasons why so many people are turning to alternative medical treatments. At the end of the paragraph, she introduces the element of risk.

Alternative Medicine Has a Healthy Attraction

Alternative medicine is a term that describes nonconventional medical practices such as chiropractic, meditation, yoga, acupuncture, and herbal remedies. In the past two decades in the United States, more and more people are seeking alternative treatment. One reason for this growing trend is that people are looking for effective medical help without the side effects that often come with conventional medicine (Peeke 92). They are also attracted by the mind-body connection that alternative therapies claim to address for their total health (92). Many of the alternative medicine patients are well-educated people who pay for treatments out of pocket (Patel 49–50). Some are terminally ill and desperately seeking a cure even though it may carry a risk.

Finding Common Ground

Agreement sets the scene for mutual respect. A point of agreement or *common ground* increases the chances that a proposition will receive thoughtful consideration from readers who disagree. Common ground can be a shared interest, a belief, an understanding, or a goal.

A common ground prepares the reader for a reasonable argument. In a paper about aspartame, Rita Fleming provides facts and advantages before presenting disadvantages:

Nearly "180 times sweeter than sugar," aspartame is the most popular low-calorie sweetener available today. Each year over "100 million Americans consume carbonated beverages, iced tea, desserts, presweetened cold cereal and other products" sweetened with aspartame (Farber 52). NutraSweet has been referred to as a "dieter's dream" since it contains few calories, and many products containing aspartame have been labeled "low calorie" (*Sweeteners* 49).

To settle on a common ground, a writer not only presents facts but also listens to the connotations of words. Ill-chosen phrases can inflame feelings. But tactful words create an air of peaceful deliberation.

Acknowledging and Clarifying Points of Agreement

While analyzing the main points of the opposing view, watch for a way to grant a point or clarify what you mean. To show agreement with the opposition's point, acknowledge it with a word or phrase such as *certainly, granted, it is true, proponents agree,* or *advocates recognize.* Then present the related pro point. The following phrases or similar ones might be used according to the purpose:

- It is true that . . . but . . .
- Proponents realize that . . . , yet they believe . . .
- Supporters recognize . . . ; still they do not acknowledge . . .
- This is not say that . . . but to . . .
- _____ argues that . . .
- _____ claims that . . .but [include evidence] reveals . . .
- In short, the opponents believe . . . because . . .

Agreeing before disagreeing is not only fair but also tactically sound. Rita Fleming extends the common ground of her argument by conceding a point (italicized):

> Many consumers assume that when the FDA approves a product, it is safe for them to use. *True, aspartame has been generally accepted as harmless, and many people use it with "no apparent ill effects,"* but others do "complain of side effects." According to Richard Wurtman, a neuroscientist at the Massachusetts Institute of Technology, aspartame has been linked to "numerous side effects." Some of the most common are "seizures, migraine headaches and mood swings" (*Macleans'* 31, 32).

Refuting Opposing Points

To refute means to show that the information of claim is irrelevant or just partly true or completely false. In answering opposing points, avoid any hint of disrespect or antagonism; be respectful and friendly. When you show respect for the reader's points, your chances for acceptance of the proposition will increase. To be convincing, a writer needs adequate evidence. The opinion of just one authority is inadequate; multiple sources are required. Opinion must be substantiated by facts, reasons, and examples. As a rule, the more evidence, the more convincing the argument, but do not oversell.

Select the most noteworthy points of the argument. Use quality evidence. Weak evidence will not support a claim for very long. Careful readers will be apt to spot distortions, omissions, quotations taken out of context, or other problems. There must be solid proof that the proposition is logical, beneficial, and ethical. Only a sound, ethical argument will stand up under intense scrutiny. Examining the two student papers at the end of the chapter will help you see how to refute points well.

Dodging Fallacies

For an argument to be effective, the logic must be impeccable. A writer who misquotes, transposes statistics, misdiagnoses cause and effect, or trips over hasty generalizations may be perceived as careless, uninformed, biased, or manipulative. Although name-calling, exaggeration, or other blunders may be discounted in conversation, readers are unlikely to be so patient or forgiving. (See chapter 20 for more on fallacies.) Let's consider two fallacies from papers:

> The most annoying thing in the world is to pick up the telephone after a long day at work and find a telemarketer at the other end of the line.

> A voluntary national service would solve the United States' problems.

Both claims are hasty generalizations. Certainly there are greater annoyances than a telephone interruption, and no one action could possibly solve the numerous problems faced by the United States. Another common fallacy is assuming that a complex problem results from a single cause. *Rarely does a complex problem have only one cause.* For example, presidents are often blamed for problems existing long before they took office. The truth is that many factors influence complicated problems.

A final precaution to keep in mind is that *an analogy cannot constitute proof.* Although valid analogies are useful for explanation, they prove nothing.

Writing a Conclusion

A conclusion is the final nail in the building of an argument. The conclusion should be sound, appropriate, and complete. It should not stray into irrelevancies, fail to take a stand, or end abruptly. It should leave the reader persuaded that the reasoning is valid and worthy of consideration. If action is advocated, the tone should convey a sense of immediacy, a feeling that impels the reader to act. Rita Fleming closes with a reference to risk:

> Although the FDA has allowed aspartame to remain on the market, a look at the history of this chemical raises severe doubts about its long-term safety for everyone. The risks of using this product regularly far outweigh any advantages.

To be forceful and complete, most arguments need a restatement of the thesis. Restatement redirects the reader's attention to the proposition, as in the following example. Kathy Kerchner writes:

> Finally, the use of restraints is a prime concern in geriatric facilities. Research on physical or mechanical restraint use is vague, and more is needed. For many confused residents, restraints are harmful in the long run. If a restraint not only denies

freedom and dignity for the aged, but also leads to disorientation, then justification for use must outweigh possible consequences. Caregivers should exhaust all other alternatives before applying a restraint and continue to reevaluate its need from time to time.

Kathy's ending is one of compromise. She realizes that there is no one solution for all situations or all patients at all times. Still, she takes a firm stand, pointing out the dangers of long-term use of restraints.

Revising an Argument

Reviewing your outline will help you check the organization of your paper. Could the order be improved? Would any section or subsection fit better in another spot? Reread the paper and check it with the outline as you go. Do you see any discrepancies? This method forces you to look more closely at work that has become familiar. Using a checklist will help you guard against omissions.

CHECKLIST: REVISING AN ARGUMENT

1. Is the issue clearly defined?
2. Does the introduction have a neutral tone?
3. Has a common ground been established?
4. Are points of view clearly identified?
5. Are main points of the opposition presented fairly?
6. Is adequate evidence presented to refute each opposing point?
7. Is the logic sound and ethical?
8. Is the language calm and rational?
9. Does the conclusion restate the position?
10. Is the organization clear to the reader?

In summary, to build an effective argument about a controversial topic, you should (1) define the disagreement, (2) find the area of resistance or dissent, (3) respect the audience, and (4) ensure that evidence is logical and ethical.

TWO STUDENT PAPERS: CLASSIC ARGUMENT

Both papers are presented in MLA format for research papers without a cover page. They are reduced to show proportional margins for an 8½- by 11-inch page. Chapter 24 provides specific guidelines for research papers in MLA style. The first paper is by Bethany Shirk, who researched her questions on the legality of high-decibel noise and the effects of noise on human health.

Shirk 1

Bethany Shirk

Professor Nancy Gilson

Communications 112

3 May 2001

Automobile Stereo Speakers: Turn Them Down

The right of United States citizens to turn the volume of their automobile stereo speakers to any decibel level they choose is a controversial topic in courts today. Laws vary across the nation, but viewpoints generally fall into two directly opposed groups. Those who drive with high-powered stereos going full blast believe they have the right to play their music as loud as they like. Those outside the car, however, often say the level of sound is rude, unsafe, and threatening to their health.

Those who believe they have the right to listen to their car stereo at any volume are against legislation that would limit decibel levels. Marc Yarbrough, a twenty-year-old Aurora, Illinois, resident is quoted by the Chicago Tribune: "For police to be harassing people who spend time and money to make their cars sound better is senseless to me. There are much more important things that police should be worrying about."

For some drivers, pumping up the stereo is a form of entertainment. Dallas Wilson, who works in an electronics store and competes in car stereo sound competitions, said, "I will drop the windows, and I will crank my stereo to a point where I can enjoy my music at a loud volume" (Aurora). Although playing loud music is enjoyable for some people, many others believe the negative aspects outweigh the positive.

Those for legislation limiting car stereo sound believe that it is not only inconsiderate but also unethical to pollute the environment with unnecessary noise. One group, the Noise Pollution Clearinghouse (NPC) is seeking to advance the "ethic of the commons." They think that noise polluters mistakenly extend "their own private property rights to that [air space] which is publicly owned or cared for."

In other words, no one has the right to infringe on other people's rights by making loud noises that disrupt peace of mind and sleep (Protecting).

Proponents of legislation to control high-decibel noise from car stereos point out that the United States has been slow to take legal action against drivers who pollute the environment with loud music. Other countries have long had laws in place to control such noise. For example, in 1947 Bermuda passed The Road Traffic Act, which states that it is illegal to play a "car radio/tape player (or sound a vehicle-fitted alarm or bell) between midnight and 6 a.m." (sect. 19.2). The sound of car stereos is limited to a radius of 30 feet. Violators risk a fine of $50. Even bicycle riders are fined $25 if the bike causes "undue noise" (Answer).

In the United States, however, police in many cities have been slow to enforce noise ordinances. Although they have the power to determine what noise is disruptive and to decide what penalty to administer, they issue only a warning and tell the offender to turn down the music.

Still, some U.S. cities have drafted codes that specifically spell out violations and have begun to enforce them. For example, Cincinnati Municipal Code 910-7 states:

> No person, firm, or corporation shall operate or cause to be operated any . . . radio or other sound-producing or sound-amplifying instrument so as to emit loud and raucous noises or in any way create noise or sound in such a manner as to disturb the peace and quiet of a neighborhood or as to interfere with the transaction of business or other ordinary pursuits.

The cities of Pittsburgh, Buffalo, New York City, and Chicago have enacted much stricter laws against car stereo pollution. There police can impound offending vehicles and impose expensive fines ("Cut Volume").

Proponents also point out that sound from car stereos can be dangerous not only to the offender but also to other drivers on the

Shirk 3

road. Excessively high volume prevents the driver from hearing horns of other drivers or sirens of emergency vehicles such as fire trucks, police cars, and ambulances. Thus he (or she) may not move out of the way. Neither can the driver hear approaching trains over throbbing stereo speakers. Both situations can lead to tragic accidents.

The most common danger is to human health. Hearing is at risk when an individual is exposed to excessively loud noise over a length of time. Twenty-eight million people in the United States already have impaired hearing, and more than a third of the cases are believed to have been partly caused by loud noise (Colino 64). Hearing loss is not limited to the elderly. Nancy Nadler, director of the noise center at the League for the Hard of Hearing in New York City, says that "Hearing loss is also affecting younger people" (Colino 64).

Excessive noise contributes to many health problems other than hearing loss. The federal government estimates:

> More than one in three Americans is [sic] affected by noise pollution. Apart from hearing loss, excessive noise can cause lack of sleep, irritability, heartburn, indigestion, ulcers, and high blood pressure. Noise-induced stress can create severe tension in daily living and may contribute to mental illness. (Noise Pollution)

Many studies have linked noise pollution with hypertension, low birth weight, and impaired immune function (Colino 64). Arline Bronzaft, professor emerita of psychology at Lehman College, New York City, explains, "A person's pulse rate and blood pressure increase; adrenaline surges. Anything that puts added stress on the sympathetic nervous system . . . could lead to a breakdown of the body's systems" (Colino 64). In addition, William Clark, PhD, reports there is medical evidence that excessive noise has caused heart attacks in individuals with existing cardiac injury (Wilson 77).

Excessive volume from car stereos is not just a breach of etiquette and ethics. It is much more serious. High decibel sound can cause accidents involving other drivers on the road. Excessive noise can damage hearing and health. Cities and communities without

Shirk 4

noise-control ordinances should outlaw extremely loud sounds from car speakers. Then police should be advised to ticket those who violate the law and infringe upon the rights of other citizens.

Works Cited

"The Answer Man." <u>The Bermuda Sun</u> 2 Nov. 1998. 10 April 2001.
    <http://www.Bermudasun.org/issues/j28/ans.html>.

"Aurora Fighting Cars That Go Boom." <u>Chicago Tribune</u> 26 Mar.
    1996: 1.

Cincinnati, Ohio. "Cincinnati Municipal Code 910-7." <u>The City
    Bulletin</u> 14 July 1995: 1.

Colino, Stacey. "Sounding Off about Noise." <u>American Health for
    Women</u> Oct. 1997: 64.

"Cut Volume on Whining." <u>Chicago Sun-Times</u> 30 Sept. 1998: 41.

"Noise Pollution." <u>Electric Library.</u> 1998. Concise Columbia Electronic
    Encyclopedia, 4th. ed. 10 April 2001. <http://www.encyclopedia
    .com/articles/09313.html>.

"Protecting the Commons." [n.d.] Noise Pollution Clearinghouse
    10 April 2001. <http://www.nonoise.org/commons.htm>.

Wilson, Brenda L. "All Quiet on the Noise Control Front." <u>Governing</u>
    Sept. 1990: 77–78.

Questions for Discussion

1. Where is Bethany's thesis statement located?
2. Is there a common ground in this argument?
3. Is the argument clear?
4. Does she use block or alternating order?
5. Would another order be more effective? Why or why not?
6. Examine the conclusion. What does she do here?
7. What types of appeals do you see?
8. The third entry of Bethany's works cited list is for a government publication. How does this kind of entry differ from most?

Pickering 1

Cheryl Pickering

Professor Leslie Weichenthal

Communications 109

24 May 2001

Cockfighting Should Be Considered a Felony in Ohio

Cockfighting is a spectator sport that never appears on television. These contests generally take place in secluded spots at night, indoors or outdoors. In a pit or small arena, two roosters are turned loose to fight each other to the death (Allred 421). Often the spectators bet among themselves as to the outcome of the struggle. These roosters are fitted with gaffs, which are "thin, razor-sharp spurs" attached to the roosters' legs with "leather cuffs." The gaffs are "usually 1-1/8 to 2-3/4 inches long"; some are up to 4 inches long (Allred 424).

When the roosters attack each other with their feet, the gaffs cut the roosters repeatedly until one or both "bleed to death or suffer nerve damage" that leaves one unable to defend itself. Sometimes the gaffs become stuck in the other rooster, and the handlers must pull the gaff out without damaging the injured rooster any further. The fight is then resumed. When one rooster stops fighting or dies, the match is over (427).

In "Feathers and Blood," Rob Simbeck describes an illegal cockfight that he attended in Kentucky. Not only is the actual fight gruesome but often the preparation and aftermath are, too. Simbeck reports, "Some cockfighters routinely drug their roosters, using everything from speed and steroids to strychnine." After a fight when a rooster is not quite dead, his head is whacked on the edge of the concrete stoop, and he is thrown "onto a pile of carcasses near the door" (Simbeck 4).

Cockfighting is illegal in forty-seven states and a felony in nineteen states ("Put an End"). Randall Edwards and Jim Woods, staff reporters for the Columbus Dispatch, state that cockfighting is only a "fourth degree misdemeanor in Ohio, with a maximum penalty of thirty days in jail and a $250 fine" (4).

Yet Larry Cantrell, a cockfighting supporter, perceives the activity as "one of man's inherent rights." Cantrell was quoted in the Columbus Dispatch as saying, "I believe that man is a superior being. Everything put on earth is for man's use. . . ." Although Rev. David Couto, pastor of a Baptist church in Athens, Ohio, agrees with this basic premise, he disagrees with the interpretation of it. Rev. Couto points out that "Dominion doesn't mean being cruel. Dominion simply means reigning over. . . . Nowhere [in the Bible] can you find cruelty to animals sanctioned." Opponents generally agree that animal abuse should not be tolerated, regardless of who owns the roosters (Dispatch 1).

The owners of the gamecocks, however, say it is a "natural instinct" for the roosters to fight to the death (Allred 391). Glyde March, a veterinarian and retired professor of poultry science at The Ohio State University says it is "natural for one chicken to fight another. I don't see cruelty in it" (Blackford and Edwards 1). To cockfighting supporters, this activity is perfectly normal and should be allowed.

Opponents of this sport do not believe it is "natural" for roosters to fight with razor-sharp gaffs in a staged confrontation. Sandy Rowland, Director of the Great Lakes office of the Humane Society of the United States, feels that "forcing roosters to cut and slash one another to death is cruel and barbaric" (Associated Press 3). They believe the fights are cruel and inhumane. They feel that cockfighting should be declared a felony, not just a minor offense, and that fines should be more severe than they are at present for people who engage in this activity.

When there is betting of large sums on a cockfight, a fine of $250 and a sentence of thirty days in jail are inadequate deterrents. According to Fred Bailey, Director of the Ohio Department of Agriculture, "If you want to stop it [cockfighting], you're going to have to make it a felony" (Edwards 2). Rep. Dean Conley, D-Columbus agrees and calls for "stricter penalties" for those convicted of participating in cockfighting (Edwards and Woods 4).

Pickering 3

Animal abuse under the guise of recreation should not continue. Citizens should contact their state representatives and speak out. If cockfighting were declared a felony offense and if it carried higher fines and longer periods of incarceration, then more people would be deterred from watching and promoting this inhumane and illegal sport.

Works Cited

Allred, Kelli. "Cockfighting." Foxfire 8. Ed. Elliot Wigginton and Margie Bennett. Garden City: Anchor, 1983.

Associated Press. "Over 300 Arrested in Southern Ohio Cockfighting Raids." News Journal [Mansfield, OH] 13 May 1991: A3.

Blackford, Darris C., and Randall Edwards. "Supporters of Cockfighting Say It's One of Man's Inherent Rights." Columbus Dispatch 15 May 1991: A1.

Edwards, Randall. "Raids Are Not Expected to End Cockfighting in Ohio." Columbus Dispatch 19 May 1991: D2.

Edwards, Randall, and Jim Woods. "Lawmaker Seeks Stricter Penalties for Cockfights." Columbus Dispatch 14 May 1991: B4.

"Put an End to Cockfighting Abuses Once and for All!" 9 Feb. 2001. The Humane Society of the United States. 15 May 2001. <http://www.hsus.org/programs/government/state_nm_cockfight.html>.

Simbeck, Rob. "Feathers and Blood." Nashville Scene 12 June 2000: 1–9. 20 May 2001. <http://www.weeklywire.com/ww/06-12-00/nash_cover.html>.

Questions for Discussion

1. Is a detailed description of cockfighting helpful? Why or why not?
2. Where is Cheryl's thesis located? Does this location affect the tone?
3. How would you describe the tone of her argument?
4. Where does she begin to answer the proponents?
5. Does she use the block or the alternating method?
6. Does the argument rely primarily on a logical, ethical, or emotional appeal?
7. Is the argument convincing? Why or why not?

> **FOR YOUR REFERENCE:**
> **ARGUMENTATIVE ESSAYS IN THE READER**
>
> - "The New Case for Latin," Mike Eskenazi, page 683
> - "When the Lullaby Ends," Andrea Sachs, page 686
> - "Working at McDonalds," Amitai Etzioni, page 689
> - "The Other Difference between Boys and Girls," Richard M. Restak, page 693
> - "We Have No 'Right to Happiness,'" C. S. Lewis, page 698

Summary

A formal argument is based on a logical appeal. A *classic* argument combines three appeals: logical, ethical, and emotional. For an effective argument, assess the rhetorical situation and combine appeals appropriately.

An argument has a basic premise or underlying belief called the proposition. This belief is the starting point of the argument. Arguments can make any of five basic claims: claims of fact, interpretation, cause, judgment, or policy.

Before taking a definite stand, thoroughly research your topic. You might begin by writing a controlling question to direct your search. Making notes in a con/pro format will simplify your analysis of the issue.

An effective argument has four basic parts: claim (thesis), objection, evidence, and conclusion. For mild opposition, the thesis may be direct and early. For strong opposition, the thesis is generally indirect and delayed. An argument on an issue can be arranged in block or alternate block order. Main points are usually placed least to most important.

In the introduction of a classic argument, you describe the background of the issue and define disagreement. Then include areas of agreement, if any exist. In the next section, summarize opposing points if you use the block method. For the alternating method, place objections and refutation in pairs. Counter each objection with logical evidence. Use pairs of parallel transitions to clearly identify points of view.

Fallacies of hasty generalization, oversimplification, and overstatement are to be avoided. The conclusion of an argument should be suitable and complete.

To simplify revision, review your outline and check it against the order of your paper. Reread your argument to check the completeness of your answers to opposing points.

Key Terms

area of resistance	claim of fact	claim of policy
argument	claim of interpretation	classic argument
claim of cause	claim of judgment	common ground

compromise	ethical appeal (*ethos*)	persuasion
controlling question	indirect order	premise
delayed thesis	logical appeal (*logos*)	proposition
direct order	objection	refute
emotional appeal (*pathos*)		

Practice

Writing Exercise: Examining Opposing Points of View

Directions: Select a topic. Write two paragraphs from two *contrasting* points of view. Separate the paragraphs and indicate the person speaking. Be biased and emotional if the occasion calls for it.

1. *Animal Control.* Your town council is considering hiring an animal control officer because of complaints about stray cats, bats, and raccoons. You are a citizen with high property taxes who thinks the officer is unnecessary. You have varmint-proofed your home yourself and cats are not a problem. Next, write the view of a citizen who has had flowers dug up, sleep disturbed, and a car scratched by cats. Raccoons have invaded his attic, and he is afraid they may have rabies.

2. *Deadline.* At 4:30 p.m. your boss hands you ten pages of a draft with numerous red-penciled changes. The typed project report is due at 8 a.m. tomorrow. He plans to revise the last six pages while you correct the first ten pages. You have a dinner date and know the job will take at least an hour. You normally work until 5 p.m. Write your boss's view and your view.

3. *Dental charge.* A busy dentist has a policy that if a patient misses an appointment without canceling, a minimum charge of $25 is added to the bill. A woman who missed her appointment because she took her injured child (who suffered a broken arm) to the emergency room is protesting the extra charge. Write the dentist's view, then her view.

4. *Broken window.* A ten-year-old has just batted a softball through the thermopane window of a neighbor's house. It landed on the dining room table while she was entertaining dinner guests. One guest received a nick on the face from flying glass. Write the batter's version of the event and then the neighbor's.

5. *Ball game.* Imagine you are two reporters writing accounts of the same game. One reporter favors the hometown team; the other does not.

Workplace Issues for Discussion

1. You do not have enough money to buy your lunch. Is it all right to borrow $5 from your cash register and return the money after you get paid that evening? (You will be returning after dinner to work overtime.) Why or why not?

2. Is it all right to use your company's computer to print ten posters for a garage sale you are planning? Why or why not?

3. Is it ethical to use the company computer during work time to send several e-mail messages to friends? To chat online? Give reasons for your answer.

4. Two office mates (one is married) are having a romance that has affected their productivity. How should the employer intervene?

5. In a foreign country where bribes are a part of the economic system, is it all right for an American factory owner to offer a bribe to a purchasing agent? Why or why not?

Thirty Ideas for Papers of Argument

1. Should grizzlies be removed from the endangered species list?

2. Should violent "disturbed" students be permitted to attend public schools? What alternatives exist?

3. Refusal of insurance: Reasonable risk or genetic discrimination?

4. Nuclear Power: Revival or Relapse?

5. Should "nonalcoholic" beer (0.5 percent) be sold to minors?

6. Is computerized voting really tamperproof?

7. Should throwaway bottles be banned?

8. Does "zero tolerance" in public schools make sense?

9. Should children under sixteen be sentenced as adults?

10. Every home should have at least three smoke alarms.

11. Should athletic teams be suspended for repeated poor sportsmanship leading to violence?

12. Should procedures at fertility clinics be changed to decrease the likelihood of multiple births with more than three babies?

13. Should the legal driving age be lowered or raised?

14. Should sex education begin in kindergarten?

15. Do we need stronger cybercrime laws?

16. Should prison inmates be allowed to vote?

17. Should in-vitro fertilization be banned?

18. Should "great books" courses be revived in high schools?

19. Should power boats be permitted on environmentally threatened waters?

20. Should a "Shoot the Burglar" law be enacted?

21. Should perpetrators collect damages for injuries incurred during a crime?

22. Should classes for gifted students be continued/discontinued?

23. Should the growing of tobacco be subsidized?
24. Should children have recess in elementary schools?
25. Should surrogate births be legal?
26. Should profanity and sex on television be limited to late-night shows?
27. Should the number of dogs per household be limited?
28. Should copyright protection apply to Internet content?
29. Should cross-species cloning be banned?
30. Fashion: Should toddlers be turned into teenyboppers?

CHAPTER 20

Detecting Fallacies

Doubt is often the beginning of wisdom.

—M. Scott Peck
The Road Less Traveled and Beyond

You've probably seen dozens of stories circulating on the Internet, but how many have you questioned? Recently, a slanderous tale about a senator's being connected to the Black Panthers years ago has been making the rounds. One version is formatted as "The Rest of the Story" and attributed to Paul Harvey, which makes it seem more plausible. Yet a quick visit to a Web site that dispels urban myths and legends can establish the truth. The story is a distortion of an article that first appeared in 1998 in a major newspaper under the byline of a different writer. (See <http://www.urbanlegends.com>.)

To protect ourselves from propaganda, deceptive arguments, misinformation, and other fallacies, three precautions are essential:

1. Develop a healthy sense of skepticism. Don't believe everything you hear or read. The most convincing lies contain at least a few grains of truth.

2. Consider the documentation or lack of it (author, place, date). Lack of documentation should raise doubt about authenticity.

3. Check out a claim before you accept it as fact. Can you find the same information in a reputable source?

Studying the chief logical and emotional fallacies will help you to spot distortions in research, as well as daily life, and avoid them in your own writing. *Logical fallacies* often happen in three ways—through omission, oversimplification, and exaggeration. As we appraise an event or situation, we may overlook, ignore, or deemphasize a significant factor; or we may overemphasize another. Then we make incorrect assumptions. *Emotional fallacies* are more easily recognized by appeals to feelings. They contain a pitch designed to override logical judgment.

LOGICAL FALLACIES

Logical fallacies are false beliefs caused by errors in reasoning. Unless you stop to think and question, the errors may seem plausible and persuasive. Logical fallacies can be found in everyday conversation, talk shows, chat rooms, political speeches, advertising, published writing, and student papers. Histories, biographies, and other works may contain distortions, misinformation, or fabrications. There are eight common logical fallacies:

Eight Common Logical Fallacies

1. Card stacking
2. Either/or fallacy
3. False analogy
4. Red herring
5. Begging the question/circular argument
6. Hasty generalization
7. Non sequitur
8. The post hoc fallacy

Card Stacking

Card stacking (stacking the deck) is an act of slanting, distorting, or fabricating facts to suit the speaker's or writer's purpose. This fallacy involves misrepresentation, either intentional or unintentional. Although card stacking is unethical, scientific researchers have been known to fudge facts in order to support an illogical conclusion. To save time, they may take unethical shortcuts or falsify data. Or they may select only the facts that support a theory, omitting other evidence. Sooner or later such practices are generally discovered and discredited.

But what are we to make of polls and studies from reputable sources that report widely varying results? As you gather data, be aware that research methods can be flawed in various ways. The way that questions are worded can influence the answers that are given. Then, too, if respondents are asked to recall data or events, their memories may falter. The size and kind of population samples may also vary, resulting in different responses. Keep in mind that *the sample must represent the general population to produce reliable results.* (See "How Can One Be Objective?" in chapter 18 and "Observation" in chapter 22.)

Sometimes students unintentionally "stack the deck" while doing research for papers. They may have too few sources to provide objective coverage. Insignificant details may be exaggerated or significant details underemphasized. Important facts may be omitted through carelessness or insufficient research.

Either/Or Fallacy

The *either/or fallacy* occurs when we assume there are only two sides to an issue or two alternatives for a problem when there are actually more. Sometimes this fallacy is called the "fallacy of false alternatives." Basically, the either/or fallacy presents the writer's view as the only correct alternative. The either/or fallacy is a simplistic judgment that may occur from glancing at a problem and jumping to a conclusion. On bumper stickers you may have seen this fallacy in slogans such as "Make love, not war" and "America: Love it or leave it."

When speaking to voters, office seekers often oversimplify our country's policymaking process. For example, the either/or fallacy is apparent in this statement, voiced by a presidential candidate: "Either elect me and have a truly democratic government or elect one of my opponents and continue as we are." His either/or claim overlooks the possibility of change by other political candidates.

False Analogy

The fallacy of *false analogy* hinges upon an invalid comparison. Just as an invalid check will not clear a bank's requirements, neither will a false analogy clear a test of logic. In this fallacy two cases or items are compared and assumed to be similar although they are basically different. A conclusion that is true for one is assumed to be true for the other. You may have heard someone say, "We tried this before, and it didn't work." But conditions may have changed since the first attempt, or the way the alternative was applied may have counteracted its effectiveness. Two cases are seldom the same.

A false analogy exaggerates similarity, making the comparison illogical and unsound. The fundamental problem with a false analogy is that it ignores a basic difference in the two cases. For example, a few years ago a group of citizens who lived in an earthquake-prone state argued for underground rail systems, pointing out that such systems have worked well in other states. The analogy was false, however, since the successful systems were located in states with little earthquake activity. A false analogy can be revealed by pointing out a significant difference.

Red Herring

The fallacy called *red herring* drags in a side issue to distract the audience from the main issue. This fallacy is rather like the tactic that burglars in old movies often used, carrying steak along to throw to the watchdog before robbing the mansion. In the red herring fallacy, the writer suddenly tosses the reader a "bone," an irrelevant point, to avoid proving the original claim. In other words, the subject is abruptly changed in order to divert attention from the real issue.

Using the red herring fallacy, a speaker or writer attempts to prove a point by leapfrogging to an irrelevancy. For example, "the mayor is a man of integrity; he is a church member and a fine family man." But the discerning listener or reader knows the mayor's church membership and family status do not necessarily prove he has integrity. No real proof has been submitted.

Begging the Question/Circular Argument

In the fallacy of *begging the question*, or *circular argument*, the argument sidesteps the issue. Here the word *question* refers not to sentence structure, but to the subject under discussion. When a question is "begged," it is not discussed. To avoid giving a direct answer, people may hide their beliefs in a thicket of words. Begging the question in this case is simply empty talk that ducks the issue.

Statements that beg the question can be short or long. They may employ phrases such as "everyone knows," "the fact is," or "obviously" when the opposite is true. An example is "Everyone knows it is not safe to swim for an hour after eating." Students sometimes beg the question when writing essay answers on tests and exams. They pile up words in an attempt to disguise the fact they lack the answer—they neglect to provide support.

When an argument avoids confronting an issue by restating a premise, we call it *circular argument*. For example, "Football is entertaining because it is such an enjoyable sport" or "Irrelevant courses such as ancient history are a waste of time." In neither case has proof been offered. The reader is asked to agree with the first part of each statement. The argument moves in a circle by repeating the claim in different words. The issue is dodged, and the proposition is assumed to be true.

Hasty Generalization

A *hasty generalization* is a broad general statement that lacks adequate support. The writer misstates, exaggerates, or minimizes the facts. Hasty generalizations are assumptions that occur in various ways. Three of the most common are (1) presenting inferences as fact, (2) stereotyping, (3) taking a small or atypical sample of a group and generalizing about a larger group or population.

Hasty generalization can be averted by careful, accurate word choice to reflect the facts. You can identify opinions and qualify generalizations so that they are accurate. You can avoid absolute terms unless adequate evidence is available. When conducting research, you can secure a representative sample.

A hasty generalization may resemble the non sequitur somewhat (both contain inferences), but the hasty generalization does not set up a false cause and effect as the non sequitur does. Nor does the hasty generalization refer to specific instances as the non sequitur does.

See "Writing Responsibly," chapter 6.

Non Sequitur

Translated from Latin, the phrase *non sequitur* simply means "it does not follow." Such fallacies contain faulty assumptions about cause-and-effect relationships. In other words, a cause is asserted for an effect, but the effect "does not follow" logically from the cause. Non sequiturs may use words such as *because*, *therefore*, and *if . . . then*, and they may be attempts to persuade someone to do something. A student may claim, for example, "I should get an A on this paper because I spent thirty hours working on it and handed it in two days early." But the quality of the paper does not necessarily follow from either of the two reasons offered for a good grade.

Non sequiturs may appear in predictions: "Because Marilyn vos Savant is listed in the *Guinness Book of World Records* as having the highest IQ on record, she would make an excellent president." The fallacy here is in assuming that the chief requirement for the presidency is stellar intelligence. Jimmy Carter, for example, was highly intelligent, but many historians do not consider him to be among the better presidents.

Non Sequitur—A Grocer's "Mistakes"

Eddie Cantor credits much of his success as an entertainer to a grocer he once knew. Cantor, who was raised on the lower East Side of New York, would do errands for neighbors. In return, they would give him a hunk of cake, a slice of salami, or another treat. But they insisted he go to a grocery ten blocks away rather than to neighborhood stores.

One day Eddie went to a nearby store and bought exactly the same groceries, but the housewives knew and berated him. Baffled, he wondered how they knew. The next time at the distant store, he observed every move of the grocer. Eddie decided the man was near-sighted [a non sequitur]. An order might call for twelve buns, but the grocer put in thirteen. He put in five bananas instead of four. He did not stop at the quart line on the milk jug, but went over. Making another assumption, Eddie pointed out the "mistakes."

The grocer replied that he always put in a little more than was required. Long remembering the grocer's words, Cantor applied them not only to his personal life, but also to his career. After many years he went back, but the little grocery had disappeared. At last on the upper East Side, he found the grocer. The man had become the head of a large chain of supermarkets.

The Post Hoc Fallacy

One evening in New York City, so the story goes, a small boy kicked a lamppost. At that moment the lights went out all over the city; a power blackout had occurred. Yet the boy thought he had caused the power failure. This kind of thinking illustrates the post hoc fallacy: because one event follows another, the first is thought to have caused the second. But there is no evidence of a connection:

Facts:	Event A: Boy kicked lamppost.
	Event B: Power blackout.
Post hoc fallacy:	A caused B. (Because event B followed event A, A is assumed to have caused B.)

The full Latin name of this fallacy is *post hoc ergo propter hoc*, meaning "after this, therefore because of this." Although no proof is offered, this fallacy assumes that one event or condition was caused by another. The truth is that the two events or conditions only *correlate*, meaning they exist together but do not interact upon or influence one another.

We have all heard similar post hoc fallacies: Bad luck is often attributed to breaking a mirror, walking under a ladder, or stepping on a crack. And you probably know other fallacies based on superstitions. Hundreds, perhaps thousands, of years ago, these beliefs sprang up because two events happened one after the other. Perhaps someone broke a mirror and cut a foot severely. Someone else may have walked under a ladder and broken a leg soon after. In each case, the first event was blamed for causing the second.

The Pattern of Superstitious Thinking: A Post Hoc Fallacy

Part 1: Superstition: Handling toads causes warts. (A causes B.)

Part 2: Because Shawn handled a toad and the following week a wart appeared on his thumb, the toad caused the wart. (Therefore, A caused B.)

A systems analyst says that his subordinates seldom have trouble with any fallacy except the post hoc. Once in a while a team member will seize on an obvious but incorrect cause for a problem. The member errs in assuming two factors have a cause-and-effect relationship when they merely correlate.

To avoid confusing the fallacies of cause and effect, notice that post hoc involves two events that occur in a sequence whereas the non sequitur has only one. If a statement contains both fallacies, label it post hoc. For your convenience, the following list summarizes the main distinctions between post hoc and non sequitur.

Post hoc	*Non sequitur*
• Two sequential events or conditions. (A apparently caused B)	• Only one fact or event plus an inference.
• No proof that the first event caused (or will cause) the second.	• Only an opinion, often a prediction.

EMOTIONAL FALLACIES

Americans are bombarded with emotional fallacies every day. When we drive past a billboard, open a magazine, or turn on a television set, we are exposed to cleverly planned propaganda. Usually, the propaganda contains emotional fallacies designed to arouse strong feelings and impel us to buy products, donate money, or accept ideas. The propagandists know that if they can trigger strong feelings, then logic may be dethroned and emotion may rule. *Emotional fallacies not only conflict with logical thinking but also interfere with fairness and objectivity.*

Understanding these fallacies can help you to resist them and detect them in your research and writing. This is not to say that all emotional appeals are to be avoided. Some emotional appeals attempt to persuade honestly and fairly.

An emotional appeal may be warranted in an argument, but the emotion should be controlled and ethical. A modicum of emotion may also be appropriate in other kinds of writing. To decide, you need an alert eye and a sensitive ear. Deceit is never acceptable.

In most emotional fallacies, *transfer* plays an important role. Transfer is a device of association that uses the connotations of words and pictures to manipulate our responses. The idea is to carry positive connotations over to products, ideas, or people. Positive transfer presents products in the most attractive way possible with appealing names and surroundings. Commercials for some products, for instance, portray endearing family scenes—perhaps of children, puppies, or kittens. On the other hand, negative transfer is often used in political campaigns to disparage opponents, as in name-calling. Eight common emotional fallacies are discussed here:

Eight Common Emotional Fallacies

1. *Argumentum ad hominem*/straw man
2. Bandwagon
3. Plain folk appeal (*ad populum*)
4. Status appeal
5. Scare tactics
6. Testimonial
7. Improper appeal to authority
8. Glittering generality

Argumentum ad Hominem/Straw Man

In an *ad hominem* argument, a person's character or appearance is assaulted. Name-calling, mudslinging, and smear tactics are all forms of *argumentum ad hominem* ("against the man"). A sly variation of ad hominem uses derisive humor to discredit. A personal characteristic that is irrelevant to performance becomes the subject of joking. Former President Gerald Ford was ridiculed for his lack of physical coordination and former Vice President Dan Quayle for his misspelling of *potato*. Neither characteristic pertained to the ability to perform in office.

The *straw man* fallacy, a similar assault, is as flimsy as it sounds—lacking weight or evidence. The argument attacks an opponent or a group with a trumped-up charge or issue that is easily defeated or refuted. A classic example occurred back in the 1950s in a small city in the Midwest. A man who was running for mayor, a retired bank president, was the victim of a whispered attack. His opponents circulated a story that he was an active communist. It was said that he held "weekend 'Red' meetings in a party house beside his pond." When citizens demanded the sheriff investigate, he discovered that the so-called communist meeting was merely a bunch of buddies playing their weekly poker game.

Both *ad hominem* and straw man fallacies are unethical and impractical. The persons who indulge in name-calling, backbiting, and false charges endanger their own credibility and careers. Students who indulge lose points and credibility as writers.

Bandwagon

Another emotional fallacy urges everyone "to jump on the bandwagon," to go along with the crowd. *Bandwagon* is the fallacy of common practice—the "everyone's doing it, so you should, too," argument. Peer pressure is exerted to exploit the desire to belong to a group or to do what other people are doing. The fallacy also capitalizes on the belief that the majority knows best.

Ads and commercials using the bandwagon appeal often show large groups of happy people using the same product and enjoying the results. For example, ads for soft drink commercials feature explicit entreaties like "Join the Pepsi Generation." In McDonald's commercials about "happy meals" for children, bandwagon is implicit. The bandwagon fallacy focuses on common ties of family, nationality, race, age, religion, gender, job, or special interest. Thus the propagandist may call upon us as United States citizens, Polish Americans, Catholics, Protestants, men, women, baby boomers, truck drivers, or members of another group to do something.

Plain Folk Appeal/*ad Populum*

Awareness of the plain folk appeal, or *ad populum*, can be helpful in analyzing your reading audience. For example, this appeal is useful both in letter writing and argument. Establishing a common bond or "common ground" with the reader can have a positive and powerful influence.

The plain folk appeal stresses similarity to ordinary people or the so-called average citizen. A speaker wears ordinary clothing, adopts similar speech habits, and participates in everyday activities to show that someone of high status is just "a regular guy" at heart. For example, Fiorella La Guardia, who gained renown as mayor of New York City (1935–45), spoke three languages. When he visited various neighborhoods to campaign, he would vary his speech according to his audience. As a result, those who heard him felt he was one of them and truly their representative. The secret to effectiveness with the plain folk appeal is sincerity.

The plain folk appeal is seldom a problem in student essays, but you may encounter it being misused during your research. For now you should be prepared to recognize abuses and to apply the appeal appropriately.

Status Appeal

The old saying "keeping up with the Joneses" illustrates status appeal, or snob appeal as it is sometimes called. *Status appeal* is a pitch to better oneself by wearing stylish clothes, driving expensive cars, taking exotic vacations, or buying whatever a company sells that requires lavish spending. For example, a commercial for a well-known car uses status appeal: "It's the difference between just getting there and truly arriving." Such commercials feature attractive people, dressed in stylish attire, who purchase top-of-the-line luxuries. The implication is that the viewer can be like them by buying and using the manufacturer's product.

Status appeal is the opposite of plain folk. Whereas plain folk can arouse friendly feelings when appropriately used, status appeal may antagonize, even when used appropriately. The applications for status appeal are limited. Unless you are a marketing major who creates advertising copy or writes sales brochures or a business communications student who writes sales letters, you will probably not use the status appeal in your college writing. Nonetheless, you need to be aware of it so that you can recognize it and deal with it appropriately.

Scare Tactics

Daily we encounter appeals that use *scare tactics*. These appeals attempt to manipulate us into accepting a product, message, or person. Often the danger is exaggerated, and other alternatives do exist. For example, some insurance ads use scare tactics to sell policies. One ad showed a mother holding a young child in her arms with the caption "What will they do when you are gone?"

But scare tactics can also warn the public of possible hazards. For example, warnings about the dangers of small children drinking household cleaners or the danger of unhooked safety belts are a public service. In some cases, alarming statistics are given and frightening pictures shown (such as an accident caused by a drunk driver) to motivate people to protect themselves and their families.

In research papers, scare tactics are best avoided. A calm, objective tone and a logical approach that stresses benefits is the most effective way to persuade. In a process paper, a legitimate warning may be imperative.

Testimonial and Improper Appeal to Authority

Because Tiger Woods gives a testimonial for Titleist golf balls, a television viewer may be convinced to purchase some. Other athletes have plugged a variety of goods from shaving lotion to snuff. The *fallacy* inherent in a *testimonial* is the assumption that something is true or good just because a well-known person says so. Never forget that unless stated otherwise, the person giving the testimony has been paid by the sponsor.

Political testimonials for candidates are often given in election campaigns. Although a well-known public figure may endorse a relatively unknown candidate, we should keep in mind that endorsements are a form of patronage, an exchange of political favors. In student writing, testimonials seldom appear, but a related fallacy sometimes occurs—improper appeal to authority.

An *improper appeal to authority* is the giving of testimony by well-known persons about a particular field in which they are unqualified. The so-called authority, lacking relevant credentials, claims something is true. Some instances of this fallacy may be harmless; nonetheless, deception is inherent. For example, when physicians, researchers, or other professionals step outside their fields of expertise, their claims become meaningless. In writing papers, consider the qualifications of the researcher as well as the validity of the claim.

Glittering Generalities

Glittering generalities proffer fuzzy phrases that sound good but lack substance. In other words, these vague generalizations "glitter," but have little meaning. A glittering generality contains an undefined term. If people were called upon to define the term, they might respond with different definitions. For instance, what is a "red-blooded American"? The "American way"? "Good government"? "Old-fashioned goodness"? All of these phrases can be stretched to mean whatever a writer wants.

Glittering generalities use positive words to persuade us to accept a product or proposal without thinking. Loaded with positive connotations, these statements stir emotions and cloud thinking. Propagandists often use glittering generalities to appeal to our sense of fair play, brotherhood, or love. They sprinkle their talk with virtuous words like *liberty*, *loyalty*, *patriotism*, *progress*, *truth*, *honor*, or *justice*. These words suggest ideals that all "good" people believe in. Glittering generalities play on the emotions, urging us to do something without examining the facts.

CHECKLIST: USING APPEALS IN WRITING

To determine the difference between a legitimate appeal and propaganda, ask yourself these key questions:

1. Is the claim truthful and accurate? Does the writing represent the claim fairly?
2. Does it have the interest of the audience at heart? Will it really protect or benefit them? Or is there a sly attempt to manipulate?

DEALING WITH FALLACIES

Fallacies are dishonest arguments that cheat on the facts or use an overdose of emotion to beguile an audience. Although there may be temptations to resort to fallacious persuasion, this path is unwise from both an ethical and a practical standpoint. Ethically, we have the obligation to give readers and listeners the facts. In the long run, deception is invariably impractical. Chances are the truth will eventually emerge, and the reputation of an unethical writer or speaker will be tarnished.

You may become fascinated by finding and categorizing fallacies, but if you find it difficult to label a particular case, don't worry. Recognizing deceit, manipulation, and misstatement is what is important, not the label. By learning about fallacies, you can develop healthy skepticism as well as thinking skills.

This chapter is much more than an intellectual exercise. The most important lesson is to *apply* your learning. Thinking skills can be applied almost anywhere. Critical thinking is valuable in writing and revising papers, in your personal life, and in the workplace. Critical thinking can improve your self-image and professional image. Critical thinking used wisely can give you *power*.

Summary

Critical thinking requires distinguishing facts from fallacies. Logical fallacies contain errors in reasoning. Eight common logical fallacies are card stacking, either/or, false analogy, red herring, begging the question, hasty generalization, non sequitur, and post hoc. Some subcategories of these fallacies exist, too.

Critical thinking also requires recognizing emotional fallacies, appeals that are overstated and designed to manipulate. Emotional fallacies are propaganda techniques that attempt to overrule logic with a rush of feeling. Yet some emotional *appeals*, not fallacies, can be used with restraint in college speaking and writing. An emotional appeal should be appropriate, honest, and fair.

There are eight common emotional fallacies: *argumentum ad hominem*, bandwagon, plain folk, status appeal, scare tactics, testimonial, improper appeal to authority, and glittering generality. Positive or negative transfer usually appears in emotional fallacies.

It is both unethical and impractical to use fallacies in your writing. Understanding them can help you to avoid them as well as recognize deception and manipulation.

Key Terms

ad populum	either/or fallacy	plain folk
argumentum ad hominem	emotional fallacy	post hoc fallacy
bandwagon	false analogy	red herring
begging the question	glittering generality	scare tactics
card stacking	hasty generalization	status appeal
circular argument	improper appeal to authority	straw man
correlation	logical fallacy	testimonial
credibility	non sequitur	transfer

Test Yourself

Fallacy Review

_____ 1. A comparison that has more differences than likenesses.

_____ 2. Reasoning that states or assumes only two alternatives exist when there are actually more.

_____ 3. An attack upon a person's character.

_____ 4. Circular reasoning that assumes something is true and reads as if it were true. Circumvents the issue.

_____ 5. An appeal to follow the majority and do something because "everyone else is doing it."

_____ 6. Appeal based on the premise that the speaker/writer is one of the common people, an average citizen.

_____ 7. Overstatement, an inference, based on inadequate evidence.

_____ 8. (After this, because of this.) This fallacy assumes that because one event occurs after another, the first caused the second.

_____ 9. A side issue presented to distract from the main issue.

_____ 10. How can this chapter help you? State two ways.

Acceptable or Hasty Generalizations?

Directions: Mark A for acceptable generalization or H for hasty generalization. Then check your answers at the end of the chapter.

1. Pit bulls are killers.
2. Women tend to score higher on vocabulary tests than men.
3. Most teenage drivers today are more reckless than those of other decades.
4. Left-handed folks are better at arithmetic than right-handed.
5. Beef is a versatile and nutritious food.

Practice

Case Problems: Analyzing Logic

Directions: In small groups read the following cases aloud. Then discuss the main points and implications. Decide if the logic is valid or invalid. Give reasons for your decisions.

1. Is there a curse on presidents who are elected every 20 years, in years ending in zero? Since William Henry Harrison, elected 1840, all presidents elected in 20-year cycles have either died in office or been shot: Abraham Lincoln, elected in 1860; James Garfield, elected in 1880; William McKinley, elected in 1900; Warren G. Harding, elected in 1920; Franklin D. Roosevelt, reelected in 1940; John F. Kennedy, elected in 1960; Ronald

Reagan, elected in 1980 (seriously wounded but recovered). Just one other president died in office: Zachary Taylor, elected in 1850. Which fallacy is revealed in the idea of a curse?

2. After the November 2000 presidential election, Katherine Harris, Florida secretary of state, was disparaged by some journalists for her stand on ballot counting. Robin Givhan of the *Washington Post* described Harris at a press conference: "Her eyes, rimmed in liner and frosted with blue shadow, bore the telltale . . . spikes of false eyelashes. Caterpillars seemed to rise and fall with every bat of her eyelid, with every downward glance." What two fallacies are present in this comment?

3. In an essay entitled "Blue Jeans Are Here to Stay," a student made the following claims. Discuss their validity.

> The atmosphere at business meetings . . . is more casual when people dress in blue jeans. The fact that everyone feels comfortable eases the tension. Conversation is easily developed; ideas and thoughts flow more freely. The second factor that makes blue jeans popular is their quality. Everyone likes the thought of receiving the best value in clothing for the right price. Blue jeans have this feature. They are purchased for reasonable prices and provide excellent wear. . . .
>
> The most influential factor that causes people to buy blue jeans is their comfort in wearing. Most people like to feel good in the clothing they wear. Blue jeans are made to give this feeling to all who wear them. There is an exact size to provide everyone with a unique fit. Then they are pleased with themselves and present a cheerful attitude toward life.

Collaborative Learning: Identify the Fallacies

Directions: Identify the fallacy or propaganda device in each example.

1. As a burglar entered a home, a black cat dashed across the room. He opened a wall safe, emptied it, and continued to search. Suddenly, he was confronted by two policemen with drawn guns. At that moment he realized the cat was an omen. (The safe had an alarm.)

2. Mike wrote an argument paper using information from only two sources: a paid political advertisement and three pamphlets from the National Rifle Association. Discuss any problems you see in his sources and the quality of his evidence.

3. Excerpt from a student theme: "The mature person is *continuously* open, flexible, curious, and active." (*Hint:* See a dictionary.)

4. A ninety-year-old women makes her own wine using whole grapes. Recently she had a minor stroke, but is now completely recovered. She attributes her recovery to drinking three small glasses of her homemade wine daily. Do you agree with this reasoning? Why or why not?

5. Four-year-old Jill Smythe has won twenty beauty contests. Her mother has enrolled Jill at a school of dance, for she believes that Jill will become a movie star. Discuss this path of reasoning and where it leads.

Test Yourself Answers

Fallacy Review

1. *False analogy*
2. *Either/or fallacy*
3. Argumentum ad hominem
4. *Begging the question*
5. *Bandwagon*
6. *Plain folk*
7. *Hasty generalization*
8. Post hoc ergo propter hoc
9. *Red herring*
10. (a) *Increase your learning*
    (b) *Sharpen your thinking skills*
    (c) *Improve grades*
    (d) *Protect yourself against scams*

Acceptable or Hasty Generalizations?

1. H. *Three breeds of dogs are classified as pit bulls. Not all are dangerous.*
2. A. Fact. Tend to *qualifies the statement, indicating a majority.*
3. H. *Opinion, a value judgment.*
4. H. *No evidence to substantiate this statement.*
5. A. Fact. *Beef can be prepared in many ways; it contains many nutrients.*

Research Writing

Part 5

CHAPTER 21

Preliminary Considerations for Research

*Learning without thought is labour lost;
thought without learning is perilous.*

—Confucius (6th century BC)
Analects, 2.15, trans. James Legge

In the Information Age, learning often involves research. Professionals in business, law, engineering, medicine, and other fields gather, digest, and condense large quantities of information during the course of their work days. In your professional life, you may observe sites and situations, interview prospective employees, or survey a group to gather opinions. You may analyze annual reports, budgets, government documents, court cases, medical journals, or other records.

In your college classes, you gather information for research papers and reports. A research project can help you acquire a wide range of career skills. It can afford opportunities to develop the ability to

- Plan and schedule your time
- Observe, interview, and survey
- Locate information in the library
- Find information on the Internet
- Summarize, paraphrase, and quote
- Analyze and evaluate
- Provide proper documentation for sources
- Meet deadlines

PRIMARY AND SECONDARY RESEARCH

You can collect information in either of two general ways—primary research or secondary research—or combine the two. Collecting data firsthand is called *primary research*. You become the researcher and go to a *primary source*, one that has not been filtered through the eyes of another researcher. Whether you observe a class, interview someone, or survey a population sample, you conduct primary research. You may make careful notes, describing what happens and your perceptions. Or you may construct a questionnaire, administer it, and tabulate the responses. The data you collect becomes the basis of your report or paper.

Secondary research is the collecting of information that has passed through someone else's hands. You use *secondary sources;* someone else has conducted the research and recorded the original data. Usually, this information has been published and printed. You may find it in a library or on the Internet.

Basic Guidelines for Research

1. For research to be reliable, the researcher must be accurate and objective in presenting findings and interpreting results.
2. Sources must be clearly identified.
3. Primary sources are preferable to secondary sources.
4. Both primary and secondary research requires *documentation*, a listing of the source, the date, the author, and other related data. Omission of documentation can result in plagiarism.

See
chapter 24

A basic concept to remember throughout your project is that for research to be reliable, the researcher must be accurate and objective in presenting findings and in interpreting results.

The Path to Objectivity

There are three sides to every story—yours, mine, and all that lie between.

—Jody Kern

Recently a National Public Radio panel discussed whether or not a reporter has the right to include opinion in a news report of an overseas conflict. The question was this, Should he give only the facts or should he put himself into the story as well? Traditionally, reporting and other research have constituted a quest for truth, a search for facts, not an opportunity to express a personal view.

Researchers are still expected to step back from their own beliefs and emotions—to be as objective and unbiased as possible. To maintain professional integrity and reliability, they must be observant and open to new information. They must be competent and honest, able to identify and describe data accurately, and able to understand what is occurring. They must be willing to question their own perceptions, for optical illusions and misperception can occur.

To check for bias, researchers need to be keenly aware that observation, description, interpretation, and writing are *separate* stages of primary research (see fig. 21.1). Distortion can occur at any stage. To ensure accuracy, researchers check their perceptions, word choice, interpretation, and final draft carefully.

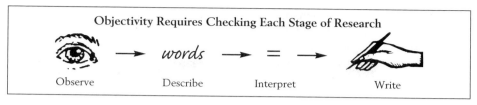

Figure 21.1 Path to objective research.

Fact or Idea?

Questioning the mental images, words, and inferences you derive through perception leads to objective writing. This doubting will help you differentiate fact from idea, which is not always easy. *Fact* is information generally accepted as real or true. But not all so-called facts are true. An *established fact* has been verified by substantial support/evidence. Some facts can be quickly verified through the five senses. Other facts are established through laboratory tests, control groups, and other measures.

In *The Modern Researcher*, fourth edition, Jacques Barzun defines an *idea* as "an image, inference, or suggestion that goes beyond the data [facts] nameable in conventional terms." This definition can guide you when the boundary between fact and idea blurs. Ask yourself if the information is entirely fact or if opinion has been injected. Is the information accepted by experts in the field as true or is it still in the realm of theory and unproven? Barzun explains, "An idea leads us on . . . . [It] suggests doubts and possibilities."

To test your alertness, consider the two sentences below. Which one is strictly fact? Which one mixes an idea with fact?

John F. Kennedy, a great president, was assassinated in 1963.

President John F. Kennedy was assassinated on November 22, 1963.

The first sentence contains the idea of greatness, which is a matter of opinion. Every word in the second sentence is factual. As you record data do not mix ideas in with your concrete facts. Ideas belong to a later stage, when you make inferences and derive a conclusion. Descriptions of observations should be precise and factual. Keep in mind, too, that the *image* you perceive may be incomplete or distorted, depending upon your vantage point and your knowledge of the subject. Try to ensure that you will see all that happens.

Second, *choose words carefully*. Use neutral, concrete words, not emotionally charged language. Some words carry extra baggage—hidden meanings, associations, or opinions. For example, there is a big difference between "dozens of black-and-orange ladybugs have crept under my back door" (fact) and "dozens of spotted beetles have invaded my home" (idea). As you record data, avoid using words that reveal your opinion.

Third, *check interpretations and inferences.* Do they seem logical and reasonable, considering the observable facts? Do the inferences account for all the loose ends? Or are there conflicting data? If so, the conflict should be noted and discussed.

Fourth, *be tentative* in presenting interpretations and inferences. Use qualifiers such as *indicate, suggest, may, appear,* and *tend.* Remembering these precautions will help you attain objectivity.

SCHEDULING RESEARCH TASKS

Regardless of whether you do primary or secondary research, your project will require considerable time. If you interview, you will need to set up appointments, construct a list of questions, tabulate responses, and write a report of your findings. For secondary research, you will need to locate materials in the library or on the Internet. Reading, analyzing, and writing will require much time.

Is a Schedule Really Necessary?

Procrastination may be tempting when the deadline for a research report or paper seems distant—perhaps a month or more away. Yet don't be lulled into complacency by believing you can draft a questionnaire or find all the books you need in an hour. Such misconceptions can lead to anxiety and even panic as your deadline looms.

A flexible schedule, tailored to your needs, can alleviate anxiety and increase efficiency. The first step is to list the tasks involved. The second step is to make a realistic estimate of the time required for each one. Keep in mind that if you are doing secondary research, you will need to locate specific information, compile source cards, read, and take notes. Writing a paper based on either primary or secondary research will require drafting, revising, editing and proofreading. If possible, allow a little leeway here and there in your schedule.

As a safeguard, plan research tasks so that your final draft can be completed a day or two early. That way you can revise, edit, and proofread thoroughly. And if a minor emergency should occur, you will not have to worry about finishing on time. Start soon so you will have the time to write a quality paper.

Will the Internet Cut Research Time?

If you are adept at searching the Web and if you can find reliable and substantial information on your topic quickly, then you may save time in locating materials. But if you are a novice in cyberspace, it may take longer to locate sources on the Net than in the library. Research opportunities on the Internet are limited for several reasons:

1. Some sources on the Web are not reliable. The individual who posts the information may not be an authority and may not cite the source fully.

2. Free information on the Internet may be scant and superficial.

3. Many databases require *paid subscriptions*. They are available only at libraries or to patrons who have contracted for them.
4. Instructors often limit the number of online sources for a paper.

TENTATIVE FIVE-WEEK SCHEDULE FOR SECONDARY RESEARCH

	Days Needed	Date to Complete
1. Select a topic. Locate materials. Do preliminary reading. Start note cards and source cards.	2–3	_____
2. Limit topic, read, and write a controlling question.	2	_____
3. Read. Start a scratch outline.	3	_____
4. As you read, continue making note and source cards.	3	_____
5. Revise outline. Write thesis and start draft.	3	_____
6. Reread notes. Refine outline. Finish first draft.	6	_____
7. Return unneeded materials. Get more if needed.	1	_____
8. Read. Revise draft. Print out.	4	_____
9. Revise draft. Check order and format. Print.	3	_____
10. Alphabetize source cards. Type list of works cited.	1	_____
11. Revise, edit, and proofread several times.	3	_____
12. **Tentative deadline:** Proof again. Print final copy.	1	_____
Final deadline: Submit research paper.		_____

A NOTE OF ENCOURAGEMENT

You can make your project satisfying and challenging by choosing a topic that interests you and pushes you to learn beyond what you already know. You can ease the pressure of the assignment by drafting a schedule early and by adjusting the schedule to your needs. A realistic plan for completing your project can enable you to become more efficient.

Hang in there! You should do just fine.

Summary

Primary research involves collecting data firsthand; you become the researcher. In secondary research, you gather information secondhand. Someone else has done the research.

For research findings to be reliable, the researcher must be accurate and objective. Facts should be entirely presented, not misrepresented. An established fact has been proven. But an idea mixes fact with unproven information or conjectures. As you record data, choose your words carefully, for they can carry hidden meanings and connotations. Double-check your inferences and interpretations.

A flexible schedule, tailored to your needs, can decrease anxiety and increase efficiency. If you are adept at using the Internet and fortunate, you can save time in locating research material. Otherwise, locating material in a library may be more efficient. A research project can challenge you to learn new skills.

Key Terms

documentation	objectivity	secondary research
established fact	primary research	secondary sources
idea	primary sources	

Practice

Drafting a Schedule

If your assignment calls for primary research, read chapter 22, "Primary Research: Observation, Interviews, and Surveys" before drafting your schedule. For secondary research, read chapter 23, "Secondary Research: Orientation: Locating Print and Electronic Sources."

1. Choose your research topic and determine the best method or combination of methods to accomplish your purpose.
2. Prewrite: List all the tasks you will need to complete.
3. Draft: Copy your tasks in the order they will be done. At the bottom of the sheet, write *deadline*, followed by the date due.
4. If your instructor has included checkpoints, include those dates.
5. Determine the number of days until your deadline. Now allot a few days to each task, making sure you do not run over the total number of days. Include a *tentative deadline* to allow for an emergency.
6. Check to see that your estimates are realistic. Revise as needed.

Primary Research

Observation, Interviews, and Surveys

A prudent question is one-half of wisdom.
> —Francis Bacon (1561–1626)

Recently a market research firm conducted focus groups of urban and suburban teens to determine what fads are in and what are out. The researchers asked questions, listened, and videotaped every word and gesture. From these observations, they will predict new teen trends in various products from fast food to jeans. Corporate clients will use the report to shape commercials and products to teen tastes.

OBSERVATION

Observation can be done in other ways. In "Caterpillar Afternoon," Sue Hubbell, a naturalist, tells how she chanced upon a queer object, which appeared to be a snakeskin, lying on a dirt road. But when she knelt down, she found it was a mass of small white, hairless caterpillars that exhibited unusual behavior, especially when disturbed. Quite curious, she examined them and later searched through her library until she found a book that mentioned experiments with pine processionaries by a nineteenth-century entomologist. Later in an interview with another naturalist, Hubbell learned that such a sight was quite rare. Thus she combined primary and secondary research. (Hubbell's story is located in the Reader.)

Observational research involves methodically watching a specimen, activity, interaction, or phenomenon and recording data. Observation can be done up close through the five senses or through cameras, tape recorders, X-ray machines, microscopes, radar, and other devices. The main advantage of observation is that the observer sees the subject firsthand. And if strict standards are maintained, findings can be quite reliable. The main disadvantage is that observation is limited to subjects verifiable through the senses. Observation is not a reliable method for testing attitudes or motives.

Selecting a Site

To accurately assess specimens, situations, or behavior, you need a certain amount of expertise. For instance, if enrolled in certain education courses, you might observe a class of schoolchildren. You could categorize their interactions with the teacher and each other, comment on patterns observed, and relate them to a course. Or as a student who has taken several college courses, you might observe the instructional styles of several professors who teach the same course and rate their effectiveness. This would require more than your opinion; you would need to survey other students, too. Then you could compare responses.

Or you might observe the instructional styles of one instructor who teaches in two areas, perhaps composition and speech. The findings for the two areas might vary considerably. The disparity might be due to greater competency in one area; attitude of the instructor and of the students toward the subject; potential to use audio-visuals, small groups, and humor; or other factors. Obtaining other students' opinion would make the research more valid.

Other projects for observation might be much simpler. You might watch various TV networks, perhaps ABC, CBS, and CNN, to see how each covers the same stories. Or you might watch several TV programs to classify and count actions that indicate courtesy as opposed to rudeness. Or you might play arcade games and categorize acts of violence and how they are treated. Is there fighting, blood, or killing? How much? Are gory scenes shown close up? How do characters respond to gore? How do the children/youth who play the games respond? Do the games seem to have redeeming value? If so, how would you rate them on a scale of one to ten?

Preparing to Observe

Some research requires obtaining permission and making appointments. If you would like to tape your observation, this privilege will require permission, which should be secured well in advance. Inquire as to when you should arrive and where you should sit so as to be unobtrusive.

Be prepared. Remember to take an extra pen and a note pad of convenient size. Devise a system to take notes, perhaps abbreviating, so that you can watch as much as possible. If you will be taping, check your supply of blank tapes and fresh batteries. Have the recorder working and ready to go with the flick of a switch. (Observing more than once will yield information to compare and to verify impressions.)

Keeping a Log

A detailed log of research data and results is essential. After you leave the site, rewrite and expand your notes as soon as possible. (The ability to recall falls off after one hour.) Flesh out the notes with precise details and examples of what happened. Your objective at this point is to record the facts, describing exactly what you saw and heard. Tell what occurred, under what conditions, the exact time of day, who was present, and other vital information. If an interaction occurred, describe it and the precise words said. Do not inject opinion.

Use quotation marks to enclose a comment or remark you include. Note non-verbal communication: gestures, frowns, smiles, touching, vocal intonations, and other nonverbal cues. Hold off on analysis and interpretation until you have the facts down on paper and have time to consider their meaning. To be as comprehensive and objective as possible, you need to look at the entire episode, not isolated fragments. The checklist below can help you expand your notes.

CHECKLIST: MAINTAINING OBJECTIVITY

1. Observation
   - What do I see?
   - What do I hear?
   - What do I smell?
   - What do I taste?
   - What do I perceive by touch?
   - Is anything else significant?

2. Description
   - What are the physical features?
   - What behavior is observable?
   - What interactions are occurring?
   - Would someone else agree?
   - Are the words neutral?

3. Interpretation
   - What might it mean?
   - What else might it mean?
   - Are the inferences logical?
   - Are the inferences unbiased?
   - Do inferences account for all events/behavior?

4. Writing
   - Is the description neutral?
   - Is the interpretation logical?
   - Does the conclusion flow logically from observable data?
   - Is the conclusion fair?

Later you can analyze and look for links—common threads and patterns of behavior. If you observed more than once, did similar or dissimilar interactions occur on different days? Describe your overall impression each time. Date each observation as to the hour. In some cases, morning or afternoon can make a difference in activities and behavior.

INTERVIEWS

An interview is sometimes defined as a conversation with a purpose. Employers conduct interviews to hire, appraise, debrief, and fire employees. Computer sales reps interview clients to ascertain system needs. Journalists interview, seeking news and feature stories. Policemen interview witnesses and interrogate suspects. Lawyers interview clients to establish a defense. As a part of your primary research, you might interview to learn more about a community problem, the history of your city, the underground railroad, or another topic.

Types of Interviews

Telephone interviews allow you to contact more people than face-to-face interviews do. But usually you gain less information since most people are less inclined to volunteer details to a faceless, unknown caller. Successful telephone interviews require lessening interviewees' suspicion and gaining their trust. Telephoning, however, may be a quick alternative when face-to-face interviews are canceled and you lack time to schedule more.

Talking face-to-face takes longer than telephoning but yields more information. Face-to-face interviews require planning and persistence. You have to call ahead, request appointments, and then travel. If an appointment is suddenly canceled, you may need to reschedule or find an alternative. Yet face-to-face interviews are worth the extra effort because you gain more details and make contacts that may prove beneficial.

Informational Interviewing   Informational interviews allow you to research family history, a product, or other topics. For a college research project, you might obtain pre-employment information about your career field. If you do, keep in mind that informational interviews are not a job search although they may lead to a position later. An employer is apt to be kindly disposed to someone who is motivated to conduct pre-employment research and to prepare a list of well-crafted questions. For example, you could ask about skills needed for a position, training offered, responsibilities, starting salary range, travel, chances for advancement, and related questions.

Before going to any interview, consider your choice of apparel carefully. If you are interviewing an elderly relative in her home, casual dress is appropriate. But if you are doing a pre-employment interview, dress just as if you were applying for a job. Before you leave, convey your appreciation to the interviewee.

Unstructured versus Structured Interviews   *Unstructured* interviews are casual with no set format. They may elicit information that would not surface in a structured interview, but they are time-consuming and difficult to compare if you are doing a series. In an unstructured interview, interviewer and interviewee often contribute equally to the conversation. Yet authorities on interviewing recommend a 30 to 70 percent ratio with the interviewer doing the least talking, according to Charles J. Stewart and William B. Cash, Jr., in *Interviewing: Principles and Practices*. The interviewer's prime task is to listen.

The *structured* interview is based upon a list of prepared questions that is used for every interview. This approach not only saves time but also assures coverage of all planned questions. A set of questions also provides a clear base for comparison.

Types of Questions

Well before your interviews start, read all you can on the subject to be discussed. You need to know enough to prepare a list of quality questions that will yield the information you seek. Using a format similar to that of a questionnaire will ease tabulation. Provide checklists for answers to allow comparison of responses. Leave an extra space after each question for comments. Include some open questions to elicit unanticipated information.

Open questions are broad and unlimited. Their flexibility allows the interviewee to answer in several ways—for example, "Can you tell me about the duties of a bank teller?" Open questions may begin with phrases such as *what happened, how do you see this*, or *what experience have you. . . .* Often they are used at the beginning of interviews to decrease tension.

Closed questions limit an interviewee's response; they are more specific. For example, "What does a bank teller do when the day's accounts do not balance?" or "After one year what are the promotional opportunities for a teller?" These questions are so limited they have only one answer. Degrees of openness vary, as shown in the following examples:

Open: What types of crime have occurred in this neighborhood?

Less open: What types of vandalism have occurred in this neighborhood this year?

Closed: Have you had any vandalism on your property this year?

Avoid a series of closed questions that might cause defensiveness and cut off the flow of information. If questions about sensitive topics are necessary, ask them near the end of the interview. Be discreet. For example, if you ask about income or age, have the respondent indicate a range rather than a specific figure.

Leading questions indicate an expected answer. They yield little information and lead to dead ends. In the examples below, the tip-off word is italicized:

- Do you *dislike* filling out all those government forms?
- Do you *enjoy* flying to consulting sites?
- This seems like a progressive company. *Would you agree?*

Make several copies of your set of questions so that you have a clean sheet for each interview. During the interview, briefly note replies. Expand your notes soon afterward. With permission, you may tape-record. Be wary of promising copies of the results unless you have the time and resources to duplicate, mail, or deliver.

GUIDELINES FOR INTERVIEWING

1. *Call for an appointment.* Give full name and college or university. State the purpose of the call. Use courtesy words. (Reduces suspicion of unknown callers.)
2. *Arrive a few minutes early* to catch your breath and relax a bit.
3. *Shake hands.* A woman should extend her hand first so that the other person knows she is comfortable shaking hands.
4. *Do not sit until invited.*
5. *Politely decline an offer of a beverage.* Don't chance a spill.
6. *Have a typed list of questions handy.* Leave spaces to jot brief notes. Bring a clipboard or tablet for support. (Never use a corner of the person's desk.)
7. *Do not stay over the appointed time.* Ask important questions first.
8. *Thank the interviewee before you leave.*
9. *Write up your notes soon after the interview.* Expand. Include the date, place, and name of interviewee. Use quotation marks to enclose exact words.
10. *Write a thank you note to the interviewee.* Although this last tip is optional, it may be wise to cultivate some contacts for future reference.

SURVEYS

Professional opinion polls and surveys are taken often. News organizations may survey a president's popularity every week; a magazine may survey readers' preferences; manufacturers may offer free coupons to entice you to reveal personal information. A survey requires a questionnaire, skillfully designed to yield the desired information. For your research project, you might conduct a student survey on campus. You would need good questions to elicit responses that reveal views and attitudes about a concern, a problem, an issue, or other topic. After you obtain the sample responses, you tabulate and interpret the results of the research.

Planning a Survey

An executive of ActivMedia, Inc., who designed the first marketing survey on the Internet, has valuable advice for students: "Have a *significant purpose* in mind as you draft questions. A major problem with many questionnaires is haphazard questions that yield trivial information. For example, a survey may find that graduates of Harvard are apt to come from affluent families—something anyone could easily guess. Make your search worthwhile."

Another major problem with some surveys is that the samples are neither random nor representative. For example, over the years Alfred Kinsey has been widely criticized for his statistical sampling. Vern L. Bullough, University of California, writes in the *Journal of Sex Research:* "It is quite clear that Kinsey's sample is not random and that it over represents some segments of the population. . . ."

Representative and Random Samples

A *representative* sample is a group that is typical of the general population in age, gender, education, socioeconomic status, and other significant characteristics. The size of a sample should be statistically significant. This means that a reasonable number of instances should be examined before any inference is made—the larger the sample, the better. Ten percent of the population is considered ideal, but few professional surveys have that many. *Still, the typicality of the sample is more important than size.* For example, to be typical, a campus survey would include students of both genders, various age ranges and ethnic groups, all programs, and day and evening classes. In other words, the sample should represent the mix of the larger campus population.

A sample is *random* if all members of the population have equal chances of being chosen. If not, the results do not reflect the opinion of the larger population, only the group sampled. Random sampling is not simple. Even if you were to select every thousandth name in a telephone directory, you would omit the poor, those too ill to answer, and others who do not have telephones. To obtain a random sample, consider the place, the day, the time, and any other factors that influence randomness. The checklist below will help you plan.

CHECKLIST FOR PLANNING A SURVEY

1. *Have a significant purpose.* Find an interesting project that will supply meaningful information.

2. *Determine how the survey can be representative and random.* How large will the survey be? (Check with your instructor.) Where and how will you conduct it?

3. *How much time will the survey take?* Consider that you will need to design a questionnaire, duplicate, administer, tabulate, and interpret in addition to writing. If you have to do research to pose questions, that takes time, too.

4. *How much will paper and copying cost?* If you research a topic for a business, supplies might be furnished. One student even received $100 for conducting a customer survey for a barber shop.

5. *Will there be an additional cost for distribution?* Some students have been dismayed to find they spend over $50 for copies, envelopes, stamps, and gas for distributing and picking up questionnaires.

Dear Student,

Help!!! Will you please take five minutes of your valuable time to assist a fellow student? I have to conduct a survey and write a report. Will you please complete this short questionnaire and drop it in the box labeled "Survey" in the student lounge by [date]?

Thanks loads,
[Your name]

Figure 22.1 Sample cover note for a questionnaire.

Constructing a Questionnaire

After you determine the topic, a group to sample, and a method of distribution, draft a set of questions. They should be appropriate for the topic, the situation, and the audience. Try to limit your questions to one page for easy answering. Next, write a brief set of *directions* for the questionnaire. Test the directions and questions to see whether or not they are clear and suitable. For some topics, you might seek feedback from half a dozen classmates; or you may need the expertise of an instructor or someone in the field.

Distributing Questionnaires

Mailing questionnaires is time-consuming and expensive. You need not only a cover letter but also a stamped, self-addressed envelope unless you plan to pick up the questionnaires. Another disadvantage is that mailed questionnaires usually have a low rate of return. Although dropping off and picking up takes time, the rate of return rises considerably. Handing out a questionnaire in a store, for return later, is apt to be unsuccessful. Instead, you might have customers write on a clipboard while you wait. One student set up a card table and chairs near the front of her parents' clothing store.

For a campus survey, you might select students at random in the student lounge, but you would need to spend equal time in the library and other places where students go. Otherwise, you would be unable to obtain a cross section. Or you might ask some instructors to distribute the questionnaire at the end of certain classes. If all students at your college are required to take freshman English, you might get a representative sample there. If you use that method, you will need a brief note to enlist cooperation and to direct respondents to an easily found box in the same building.

GUIDELINES FOR CONSTRUCTING QUESTIONNAIRES

1. Phrase questions clearly in *neutral* words. Be specific.
2. Ask for information that is easily recalled.
3. Keep questions *short*.
4. Ask only *one* question to a sentence.
5. Provide spaces, checklists, and multiple choices for *ease in answering.*
6. Plan *equal* ranges: 1–10; 11–20; 21–30. Error: 1–10; **10**–20; **20**–30
7. Use scale items (with a key) to circle for opinion:
   SA   A   N   D   SD
   SA = strongly agree, A = agree, N = neutral, D = disagree, SD = strongly disagree
8. Arrange questions in a *logical order.*
9. Place *sensitive* questions (age, salary, and so forth) near the end. Word them carefully.
10. Place any open-ended questions at the end for additional comments.
11. Limit questionnaire to one page if possible. (People dislike filling long forms.)
12. If space allows, add a one-line thank you.

WORKPLACE CASE STUDY

CINDY SURVEYS DRESS CODES FOR BANK EMPLOYEES

Cindy is majoring in business management. For her research project, she surveyed local bank managers to determine policies on attire.

SURVEY OF CLOTHING WORN BY LOCAL BANK EMPLOYEES

Directions: Please check *all* answers that apply to your bank.

1. Does the bank have a dress code?
   ☐ Dress code written in handbook or elsewhere.
   ☐ Unwritten dress code/guidelines given orally to employees.
   ☐ No dress code. Employees wear what they like.

continued

2. Indicate all suitable attire for employees Monday through Thursday:
   - ☐ suit
   - ☐ jacket & slacks
   - ☐ shirt/sweater, pants
   - ☐ women wear skirts
   - ☐ jeans
   - ☐ no expectations

3. If you have casual Fridays, please indicate all suitable attire for Friday:
   - ☐ jacket & slacks
   - ☐ shirt/sweater, jeans
   - ☐ shorts, miniskirts
   - ☐ T-shirt/sweatshirt

4. What is the bank's policy on jewelry and tattoos?
   - ☐ small earrings permitted
   - ☐ two per ear limit
   - ☐ no nose, tongue, or eyebrow piercing
   - ☐ no visible tattoos

5. Does the bank provide financial assistance to encourage professional attire?
   - ☐ gift certificate
   - ☐ clothing bonus
   - ☐ other _____
     (please explain)
   - ☐ no assistance

6. If an employee wears unsuitable attire, does the bank take action?
   - ☐ sends home without pay
   - ☐ sends home to change
   - ☐ gives warning
   - ☐ other _____
     (please explain)

7. If an employee persists in wearing unsuitable attire, does the bank take action?
   - ☐ may fire
   - ☐ places on probation
   - ☐ warns of possible firing
   - ☐ other _____
     (please explain)

8. Please indicate the approximate number of employees at this facility. (Do not count branch banks.)
   - ☐ 101 or more
   - ☐ 81–100
   - ☐ 61–80
   - ☐ 41–60
   - ☐ 21–40
   - ☐ 20 or fewer

9. Estimate the number of employees who have been notified of unsuitable attire in the past year:
   - ☐ 21 or more
   - ☐ 16–20
   - ☐ 11–15
   - ☐ 6–10
   - ☐ 1–5
   - ☐ none

10. Is your bank contemplating a change in the current policy on employee attire?
    - ☐ yes   *Comment:* _____
    - ☐ no   _____

Thank you for your courtesy and cooperation.

Drawing Conclusions from a Survey and Interviews

After you tabulate the results of your survey, you draw a logical conclusion, based on the findings. This step requires interpreting the results: What do they mean and what are the implications? Then you make a reasonable generalization and possibly a prediction or recommendation, depending upon the rhetorical situation.

Let's assume Cindy's survey revealed that each of the ten banks had 21 to 40 employees. Six banks had written policies governing attire. Each bank's manager estimated five or fewer instances of improper attire in the past year. Warnings had been effective; no one was discharged.

But four banks had no policy. In follow-up interviews with the managers of these banks, Cindy learned that some employees repeatedly wore beach sandals, sheer blouses, visible tattoos, ponytails, or unusual haircuts. They were warned, which would work for a while. Three managers estimated a dozen instances of improper dress had occurred; one manager estimated two dozen instances. Cindy concludes that written policies are more effective than unwritten policies.

MAKING AN OUTLINE

Next, Cindy makes a working outline for her report. She follows a basic report format and lists the tabulation of each question in the original order:

I. **Introduction:** Purpose and scope of the project (list of 10 banks)

II. **Method of research:** Survey of six banks and interviews with four other bank managers

III. **Body of report**
   A. Summary of results of survey (results converted to percentages)
   B. Additional findings obtained through six interviews

IV. **Conclusion:** Enforced policies with warnings and penalties do work.

V. **Recommendation:** Banks lacking a policy on proper work attire should appoint a committee composed of bank officials and employees to write one. The policy should consider not only clothing and shoes, but also jewelry, visible tattoos, body piercings, hairstyles and hair colors.

To see a primary research paper or report, turn to the end of this chapter. The section that follows will help you organize and interpret findings for your paper or report.

WRITING A PRIMARY RESEARCH PAPER OR REPORT

Whether you write a research paper or report, be sure you understand the assignment. Then examine your materials carefully. Do you have everything you need? If you made notes, have they been rewritten and amplified in your log so that you have all the data in front of you? If you used a set of questions, have they been tabulated? (For quick counting, use a blank copy of the questionnaire.)

If you did background reading, have you made a source card for each work (see chapter 23)? Is a list of works cited required (chapter 24), or can you state sources and dates in the text (see "Using Signal Phrases to Integrate Quotations into the Text," chapter 25).

Organizing and Interpreting Findings

Before starting to draft, consider what the findings of your research mean. Jot down your interpretation in a sentence or two. This prewriting exercise will help you focus on your thesis, the main idea of the research. Raw data is not sufficient to present in a paper or report. You not only summarize and explain the findings but also draw a conclusion. Then the reader who is unfamiliar with the subject will understand the purpose of the project and the meaning of the results.

Observation   If you observe a site or subjects, you might classify the examples from your log. Classification can help you organize by importance, such as *minor to major*, *mild to severe*, or in another way. For example, if you observe traffic at an intersection several times (for the purpose of proving that a stoplight is needed), you might begin by classifying your observations by the type of safety infraction. Then you could organize the categories according to severity of the consequences. Which infractions led to near misses? Which ones led to accidents? What was the extent of damages and injuries? Was a citation issued? Anything else?

If you observed animals or people, you might classify by physical characteristics, behavior, personality, or other traits that are relevant. For example, in a study of twins, physical characteristics and DNA results would be significant whereas for some other studies, these would be insignificant. What similarities and differences might you see? What categories of behavior would you note? Isolation? Positive interactions with others? Antisocial behavior? What else?

Next, look for patterns, trends, or tendencies. What links and connections can you spot? What do these seem to indicate? What logical inferences can you make? What is your overall impression?

Interviews and Surveys   After you add the responses to each question, convert the total into a percentage. Divide each total by the number of returned questionnaires. For example, if an item received 60 *yeses* out of 80 returns, divide 60 by 80, which equals 75 percent. (Divide the smaller number by the larger one.) Next consider whether a majority is large or small. Or is opinion almost evenly split? Look for attitudes, patterns, trends. Think about implications. What reasonable inferences can you derive from this data? What can you reasonably conclude? How will you state your findings in *tentative* terms, without overstating?

For example, two of the nation's top family scholars, Cynthia Harper at the University of California and Sara McLanahan at Princeton, conducted a longitudinal study, which was reported in the *Wall Street Journal* in December 1998. Using a large national database, Harper and McLanahan analyzed family breakdown and compared theories about "root causes" of crime. They found that "Boys raised outside of intact marriages are, *on average*, more than twice as *likely* as other boys to end up jailed, even after controlling for other demographic factors. Each year spent without a dad in the home increases the *odds* of future incarceration by *about* 5%." (The tentative words are italicized here. For a list of tentative terms, see chapter 25.)

To simplify drafting of your report, make a working outline, based on classification or whatever organizational strategy you select. If you used a questionnaire, you may want to follow the order set up there. (An example of an outline appears with the student report later in this chapter.)

How Research Papers and Research Reports Differ

Research papers and reports differ considerably in format. The chief difference is that a research paper does not have internal headings. A research report is usually divided into three sections or more, each preceded by a heading.

The introduction of a research paper states the purpose and often gives an overview of the research. The methodology may be placed there or in a preface or in a content note at the bottom of a page or at the end of the paper. The methodology tells what was observed or who was interviewed or who was surveyed. For a survey the date, demographics, and size of the sample should also be provided. (For several interviews, your instructor may require a list of sources at the end of the report. See chapter 24 for MLA or APA style.)

The first section of a report, often called the "Purpose and Scope," states the purpose and tells why the research was conducted. This section also sets forth the range (coverage of the topic) of the research and may include the methodology. Or it may be placed in a separate section. Regardless of where this essential information is placed, it should be specific. State how the observation was made and under what conditions. For an interview or survey, tell how it was conducted, number of questionnaires given out, and rate of return.

The body of the research paper contains the findings and the discussion. There data and examples are presented; data is interpreted; patterns and trends are described. For a report, this material is also placed in the body, but in one section or more. The section may be entitled "Results of the Survey" or another suitable heading.

The conclusion of an informative research paper is a short summary of the results, the chief idea. The conclusion of a problem-solving paper recommends an alternative. In an argument, the conclusion restates the proposition. The final section of a report is often entitled "Conclusion" or "Recommendations." *Conclusion* implies a summary. *Recommendations* are suggestions for action. In student research reports, recommendations are usually those of professionals, such as physicians, engineers, environmentalists, or others.

A research paper may not be quite as concise as a report. A paper may spend more time explaining data, including definitions and examples, and may include several direct quotations—significant responses to open-ended questions. The following paper and report show two of many ways to organize and format. The structure you use will vary, depending on the assignment, the topic, and the method(s) of research.

STUDENT PAPER BASED ON OBSERVATION

Janet Burks, a volunteer playground supervisor at her children's school, observed the situation described here. She used a problem-solving strategy to organize her paper.

Playground Supervision

There was an old woman who lived in a shoe;
She had so many children she didn't know what to do.

—Mother Goose

The old lady living in a shoe and a volunteer playground supervisor have a similar problem. Both have so many children they do not know what to do. Although Mother Goose does not tell readers how many children the old woman had, the number was certainly fewer than the 120 or so children for whom the playground supervisor is responsible.

What, specifically, can be done to solve this problem? Apparently, there are three possible solutions: soliciting additional volunteers, decreasing the number of children released for recess at any one time, or presenting a tax levy to pay the salaries for full-time supervisors. But any possible solution would be governed by two major constraints: cost and feasibility.

Presently, volunteers come to the playground to supervise during the hour-long midday recess (which includes lunch time). The supervisor's responsibility is to circulate among the children and either to help them or to maintain discipline. The job is physically, emotionally, and mentally draining because the supervisor's tasks vary all the way from tying a kindergartner's shoe to helping a child who has fallen off the slide to resolving disputes. During this vigil, children may approach the volunteer frequently with problems, complaints, or accident reports. The supervisor cannot be everywhere at once. Children can be hurt before he or she even knows about a fight.

A complication arises when the supervisor must handle an extreme disciplinary situation. He or she is not allowed to administer discipline, but instead escorts unruly (and often unwilling) children to the principal's office. While the supervisor is attending to one child, 119 or so are outside without supervision.

As the volunteer program has continued, more people have been quitting because of difficulties they confront. This factor has made the playground problem even worse. One proposal is to solicit the help of more volunteers. Having more would provide two supervisors each day. Then the child-to-supervisor ratio of 120 to 1 would decrease to 60 to 1. Although this proposal has the advantage of being inexpensive, it also has the disadvantage of being unlikely. Most parents are not volunteering to help (many work) and probably will not volunteer in the future.

A second proposal is to decrease the number of children released for recess at any one time. This proposal would involve shortening the midday recess to thirty minutes and staggering recess times. Only two classes (of the usual five) would be on the playground at once, cutting the number of children to supervise to approximately 40 per session. The others would return to their rooms for quiet play with teacher supervision. But the children would probably object, and teachers would not want to assume additional duties.

The third proposal would be to present a tax levy to pay the salaries of full-time supervisors. The rate per hour would be much less than the rate required to pay teachers to supervise the playground during their lunch break. At the same time, the rate would be high enough to attract people to the job. Full-time volunteers sometimes do not come. Then, too, full-time supervisors would have standard rules, which the volunteers do not have. The main disadvantage is voter reluctance to approve higher taxes.

The writer's recommendation is a combination of the first and third proposals. First, information concerning the problem could be distributed to parents. They would know that if enough volunteers were not found, then a tax levy would be necessary. The levy would provide the necessary funds for employing full-time supervisors.

Although the old lady in the shoe did not know what to do, let it not be said that the same is true of Sycamore's parents and teachers. Let us solve this problem together.

In the student report that follows, notice that there are two sections in the body, entitled "Background Reading and Reactions" and "Self-Evaluation: Progress toward Objectives." These headings reflect the nature of the assignment and of the research.

STUDENT REPORT BASED ON READING AND OBSERVATION

The following report by Lisa White, a nursing student, was written for an oral communications class. The project required reading one book or more, applying principles learned in class and through reading to either the student's personal or work life, and keeping a log. In their reports, students were to react to their reading, citing the most helpful ideas. Then they were to present and explain their findings as well as to evaluate progress toward their objectives. Before the project, they received an outline with suggested headings for formatting the report.

No list of references was required although sources were to be provided. Lisa supplied her source information in the text of the report.

NONVERBAL COMMUNICATION WITH GERIATRIC PATIENTS

Prepared for Betty M. Dietsch, Prof.
CM 116 Oral Communications
Individual Goals Project

Prepared by Lisa White
February 28, 2002

Outline of the Report

I. Purpose and Scope
II. Methods of Research
III. Background Reading and Reactions
  A. *How to Win Friends and Influence People*, by Dale Carnegie
  B. *Nonverbal Communication with Patients*, by Marion Nesbitt Blondis
  C. *How to Stop Worrying and Start Living*, by Dale Carnegie
  D. *How to Manage Conflict*, by William Hendricks
IV. Self-Evaluation: Progress toward Objectives
  A. Appraisal of Progress
  B. Examples of Progress
V. Conclusion

Nonverbal Communication with Geriatric Patients

I. PURPOSE AND SCOPE

Lake View Center (a pseudonym) is a geriatric care facility. The patients range from those needing postsurgical care to those needing care for Alzheimer's disease. As a nurse's aide, I daily encounter numerous situations that are taxing mentally, physically, and emotionally. Yet I lack the training to cope with them as I would like. I want to learn more about the importance of nonverbal communication and how to apply it to geriatric nursing. To become more skilled in interacting with patients and staff, I set the following objectives for this project:

1. To learn how to use nonverbal communication to enhance interactions with patients

2. To learn how to accept criticism

3. To develop ways to control anger

II. METHODS OF RESEARCH

Four library books supplied information on nonverbal communication. Most helpful were the specific suggestions that I could apply on the job. For three weeks (January 31 to February 19), I tried out the suggestions and kept a log. Every day after work, I recorded at least one incident, telling what happened, how I felt, how the other person reacted and seemed to feel. Then I stated what I had learned. As the days passed, I began to rate my progress. The log has twenty entries.

III. BACKGROUND READING AND REACTIONS

A. *How to Win Friends and Influence People,* Dale Carnegie, 1981 (1964).

In this early book, Carnegie offers some fundamental techniques for dealing with people. The first is to remember that the deepest urge in human nature is the desire to be important. Sometimes we forget that other people besides us need to feel important. The second technique is to remember that everyone wants to be appreciated in one way or another. We can remember to thank in small ways by words or by a quick note.

A third way to develop the best in another person is through encouragement. We all need to be encouraged, to know that we are heading in the right direction. Most helpful was Carnegie's reminder that other people need to feel important, too. I tend to get so wrapped up in trying to get everything done that I forget to try to help people feel valued, especially my patients.

B. *Nonverbal Communication with Patients,* Marion Nesbitt Blondis, 1977.

Blondis makes many excellent points about geriatric nursing. Her first suggestion is that when pausing to talk, one should speak patients' names, stand very close, look directly at them, and touch them lightly on the hand or arm. This sends a nonverbal message of "I am not too busy for you. You are important. I do care."

A second excellent point is that some elderly patients may not understand verbal communication due to hearing loss or mental impairment. But they are apt to note and understand nonverbal cues. Yet even when they understand, there is often a cultural gap of fifty or sixty years separating them from their young nurses. A word I say in one way may not be understood in the same context.

Third, patients will be more likely to judge us kindly when our nonverbal behavior is cheerful and effective. And it often seems that when one person is cheerful, the other person responds likewise. Fourth, Blondis warns that we should not confuse a patient's having a problem with the patient's being a problem. For example, some of the patients I take care of have been diagnosed as "hostile," "confused," or "senile." In reality, they may simply be unable to communicate verbally. Nevertheless, they still have thoughts and feelings.

C. *How to Stop Worrying and Start Living,* Dale Carnegie, 1984 (1970).

In his book, Carnegie explains several ways to accept and deal with criticism. The first is to remember that when we are "kicked" and criticized, it is often done because it gives the kicker a feeling of importance. Some people seem to derive satisfaction out of denouncing others who are better educated or more successful than they are. They are envious or jealous.

A second way to alleviate the sting of criticism is to remember that unjust criticism may be a compliment in disguise. We may just need to search for the motive behind it. If we keep that idea in mind, we will be less apt to worry so much about what some people say. A third suggestion is to just do the best we know how and can do when criticized unjustly—to retain dignity.

A fourth way is to keep a log of the foolish things we do and criticize ourselves for. After that, we can ask someone we respect and trust for unbiased, helpful, constructive criticism. I think this is a great idea because it helps us to improve.

D. *How to Manage Conflict,* William Hendricks, 1989.

Hendricks shares some practical tips on how to reduce and control anger through conflict management. His first suggestion is to have tolerance for diversity among people. We need to understand that other people's thoughts and ideas about issues may not reflect the same views we have. The second suggestion is to learn how to properly focus our anger on issues, not people. This concept is difficult to apply, at least for me. I find that venting my anger on people is much easier than focusing on the issue.

Third, Hendricks points out that repressing anger will eventually lead to an explosion. Basically what he is saying is that we need to find a healthy way to handle anger. A good way, I think, is through exercise, cleaning, crafts, or talking to a friend. This book has been very helpful because I have a quick temper.

IV. SELF-EVALUATION: PROGRESS TOWARD OBJECTIVES

A. Appraisal of Progress

Objective 1. I wanted to learn how to use nonverbal communication effectively on the job. Now when I talk to my patients, I look them in the face and smile. I speak in a cheerful tone. I also touch them on the hand to show I am not too busy for them and that I truly care. I have learned how powerful nonverbal cues can be.

Objective 2. I am learning to handle criticism in a calm, logical way. First, I assess the remark or comment to determine whether it is unjust or constructive criticism. If unjust, I take it as someone just being jealous or envious. If it is constructive criticism, I use it to improve myself and what I am doing. This procedure helps me to avoid taking offense.

Objective 3. I have been trying to focus my anger on the issue and not the person. I have also started activities to vent my emotion in a healthy manner. As soon as I get home after work, I exercise. Or if I am so angry, I cannot wait until I get home, I clean out the patients' closets. Talking to coworkers who have been in the same or a similar situation also helps.

B. Examples of Progress

Before I started this project, I used to become upset, worry, and sometimes cry. Now I do not let anybody's unjust criticism bother me. For example, a nurse at work was criticizing what I wear. I took it as her opinion and did not become upset. In fact, I used the "sponge" method, taught in class. I told her that she was probably right and that I probably could dress differently.

Another day a nurse criticized me because I was having trouble taking patients off the bedpan and in keeping their beds dry. As a result, they were angry and complaining. I asked her if she would show me how she did it. She explained and then showed me. As a result of her constructive criticism and instruction, I learned to do the chore better and patients stopped complaining.

My log contains many other examples of progress, but two are especially significant. One evening a patient began yelling at me for not putting her to bed when she wanted. I tried using nonverbal communication in order to make her feel more important. It worked! I looked her in the eye while smiling and touching her hand. I explained it would be some time before I could put her to bed, but I would come back as soon as I could. Suddenly, she smiled and said that would be fine. Ever since then she has not given me any more problems.

The most trying incident occurred when I was trying to put a patient to bed. She slapped my face, scratched my arms, and bit me. I felt like screaming and hitting her back, but did not. Instead, I walked up and down the halls until I cooled down a bit. Then I went back and cleaned out her closet. (I cleaned out a lot of closets before the project was finished.)

V. CONCLUSION

This project has given me the opportunity to learn more about an important part of communication and to improve my work habits. My supervisor noticed the improvement and commended me. I told her about the communication project, and she seemed quite interested. Although I am well pleased with my success, I plan to continue the project. I want to learn more about nonverbal communication and continue to gain skill in accepting criticism.

Summary

Primary research can be conducted firsthand through observation, interviews, surveys, or a combination of methods. Sometimes background reading is needed before primary research is begun. The purpose of the research should be significant and clear. The topic and scope of the research should be narrowed sufficiently. The student should be acquainted with basic research techniques and competent to observe, interview, or survey.

To be as objective and unbiased as possible, researchers should check their perceptions, word choice, and inferences carefully. Ideas should be distinguished from established facts. Objective research requires accurate record keeping, neutral reporting of results, and frequent checks to maintain accuracy.

Interviews can be unstructured with little preparation or structured with a set of prepared questions. Open questions provide flexibility in answering; closed questions limit responses. Leading questions indicate an expected answer and possible bias.

A survey sample should be large enough to be meaningful. It should also be random and representative of the general population. A well-crafted questionnaire asks pertinent questions with sensitive topics placed near the end. Items are clear and easy to answer. The method of distribution affects the rate of return.

The chief difference between a research paper and a research report is the format. Both state the purpose and scope of the research as well as findings and implications but in different ways.

Key Terms

closed question	leading question	random sample
established fact	open question	representative sample
idea	primary research	tentative

Thirty Ideas for Observation, Interviewing, and Surveys

Observation

1. Observe a neighborhood problem such as litter control. Discuss possible alternatives and recommend action to alleviate the problem.

2. Observe a crossing that needs a stoplight. Count the cars that pass through at peak times. Describe reckless driving. What else? You might send the report to the editor of a local newspaper.

3. Observe a family communication problem. What is happening? What alternatives might alleviate the problem?

4. Record anecdotes of family events you have witnessed. Find a central theme.

5. Local pollution problem: Combine observation with interviewing?

6. Observe a budget problem. Recommend cost-cutting actions. Pros and cons?

7. Preschool television: Time? Purpose? Themes? Hosts? Graphics? Value? Observe children viewing and record their responses, verbal and nonverbal.

8. Adult television: Observe *Oprah* or some other talk show for two weeks. Note the topics; guest(s); responses of host, guest(s), and audience. What values, patterns, and trends become apparent? What is your reaction to the show?

9. Adult television: Watch eight or more detective/murder shows. Note character traits and acts of violence. Categorize. What themes do you note? Devise criteria and rate the shows (see chapter 18).

10. Compare daily newscasts by different reporters. Divide topics: local, national, or international. Rate reporters and react (see Critical Reading in chapter 26).

Interviewing

11. Internet providers: Compare fees, support services, and freedom from junk e-mail. What else?

12. Jobs and salaries available locally in your career field. Will you need more training to qualify?

13. Qualities and training employers look for in _____ (your field).

14. Reasons why applicants are hired or not hired. What implications does this research have for you?

15. How important is writing skill in your field? What documents might you write on the job? What percentage of your time might be spent writing?

16. Tour assisted living facilities: Formulate a list of questions to find the best place for an elderly parent or grandparent. (Observe and interview.)

17. Tour day-care centers: Interview personnel and observe. Which would be the best emotionally and educationally for your child?

18. What do you see as your state's biggest concern? Interview state officials.

19. Interview an elderly relative. Ask about his or her youth, parents, and grandparents. Record and analyze the anecdotes for your family history.

20. Interview small businesses to discover the computers and software used.

Surveys

21. Conduct a campus survey on the need for more litter control, parking lot surveillance at night, or another concern.

22. Campus opinion poll: Survey reactions to a no-smoking or other policy.

23. Survey student satisfaction with the bookstore. Convenience of layout, hours, service, competitive pricing, friendliness? What else?

24. Survey of new computers: Cost? Features? Benefits? Suitability? What else?

25. Community poll: If your local library does not restrict Internet access for children, poll parents and determine what they would like to have done.

26. Community poll: How do parents feel about sex education in schools? When should it begin? Should the sexes be separated? What else?

27. Survey to determine major concerns of a community: More police/deputies? Repair of schools? New schools? Street repair? Vandalism? What?

28. Customer survey: Ask your store manager for permission and input.

29. Investment survey: Contact a dozen banks for data on CDs, money market accounts, savings accounts, and checking accounts. Compare benefits.

30. Survey businesses and companies about their desktop publishing. What documents are produced? How many persons do this? What else?

CHAPTER 23

Secondary Research

Locating Print and Electronic Sources

To be conscious that you are ignorant of the facts is a great step to knowledge.

—Benjamin Disraeli (1845)

An open mind is an asset for research. To be open does not mean you accept everything you read. It just means you give new information and opposing beliefs a fair hearing. You consider unfamiliar data and dissenting views rather than hastily rejecting them because they seem strange or different. You are willing to review a claim before you evaluate it. As you examine the evidence, you try to appraise the information impartially, yet question any point that seems doubtful. *The principal goal of research is to obtain an objective assessment of the facts—to discover the unvarnished truth.*

DETERMINING THE AIM OR PURPOSE

The first step to any research project is to determine the general aim or purpose. Your instructor may already have made this decision for you by assigning a particular kind of research paper. If not, consider whether you want to inform, investigate a problem, or persuade. All three kinds of papers require substantial reading, summary, paraphrase, quotation, and documentation of sources. As a result, the tone of research papers tends to be formal and less personal than undocumented papers.

Informative Research Papers

An informative research paper explores what is actually known about a topic and presents it in an objective manner. The paper ends with a logical conclusion, drawn from the research. The researcher boils down a wide range of information into a balanced summary, incorporating results of reputable studies and quoting opinion of authorities in the field, then points out the relevance to the reader.

For an informative research paper, you not only summarize and quote but also define, compare results, and paraphrase. You define terms not generally known and compare professional opinions. You report on areas of consensus or disagreement among experts. *You think about what the research means, how it can be applied, and what questions remain for future research.*

Research papers often require more than one kind of order. For example, you might use chronological order to summarize the onset of a disease and its symptoms, then use classification to list methods of treatment.

Problem-Solving Research Papers

Many topics for research papers center on problems. For example, you might investigate a business, medical, ethical, legal, social, or environmental problem. The problem might involve your campus, your community, your workplace, or a group to which you belong. You may do primary or secondary research or a combination of both.

See chapters 18, 22.

Like an informative paper, a problem-solving paper reports existing data and expert opinion. But it goes a step further: you evaluate the alternatives for solving or alleviating the problem. A *recommendation* may also be included. If your paper is based on secondary research, the recommendation is based on the majority opinion of experts in the field. If you conduct primary research yourself and if you are the expert, then you make the recommendation. A problem-solving paper often combines chronological order with description and classification.

Research Papers of Argument

An argument paper is quite different from either the informative or problem-solving paper. In a paper of argument, you briefly summarize a controversy and argue for a point of view, belief, or course of action. In other words, you take a stand and support it with facts, reasons, and examples. An argument may open with a chronological summary, then use illustration and classification to organize the supporting details.

The tone of the argument depends upon the purpose, the topic, and the audience. How will you approach the topic so that your argument is effective? A fair and reasonable tone, adequate and reliable evidence, and logical organization will help to insure that the argument is sound.

See chapter 19.

SELECTING AN APPROPRIATE TOPIC

Your research topic should be provocative, worthwhile, and challenging. This project should offer you the opportunity to learn and to draw a conclusion. Avoid a rehash of a topic you covered in high school or one well-covered in a single source. As you mull over choices, consider three important questions:

- Can you find a topic that stirs your curiosity?
- Is the topic significant?
- Can you locate conclusive support: data, studies, and expert opinion?

WHERE TO FIND POSSIBLE TOPICS

Check out the topic suggestions at the end of this chapter. You can also find ideas for topics in weekly newsmagazines such as *Time*, *Newsweek*, and *U.S. News and World Report*. Also try online subject directories.

For example, if several of your family members have the same health problem, you might investigate the cause, the effects, and current methods of treatment. You could consult reputable medical journals or books by physicians who specialize in that area. Some of these sources, such as the *New England Journal of Medicine*, are available online. For most health conditions, you should be able to find abundant and reliable information.

To determine whether or not a topic is feasible, do a *preliminary search* of possible sources. Can you secure enough information within a few days? If a topic is new or quite old, you may find few sources. For instance, if you wanted to investigate a medication awaiting government approval, you might find only the research of the company that had developed it. Findings from that research would not constitute valid support. Or if you wondered whether George Washington really wrote his farewell address, you might find only one book, written in 1859. Even though that book is comprehensive, it would not provide sufficient support for a research paper. (Ask your instructor how many sources are required.)

Finally, your topic should be appropriate for your current level of skill. Advanced writers who are familiar with research practices may want to select topics that involve extensive research, whereas beginning writers may prefer topics that are less complex or technical. Select material you can comprehend.

LIMITING THE TOPIC

Limiting the topic for a research paper can be intimidating—rather like picking up an octopus. The crux of the problem is this: Where and how do you grasp it? Where do you start?

Starting Points

For some topics, you may need to acquire more general knowledge of a subject before you can limit your topic. Reading an overview in an encyclopedia, an abstract, or digest is a quick and easy way to obtain leads. This broad view will list the main aspects of the topic. You can select one and search for more information on the narrowed topic. You may find that it, too, has several aspects that require narrowing the topic again. At the ends of articles, you may find lists of related sources and topics to investigate.

A good way to limit a subject is to consult the *Library of Congress Subject Headings*, a multivolume listing of headings used to catalog books. The *Library of*

> ## TIPS FOR USING KEYWORDS ONLINE TO NARROW A TOPIC
>
> The key words in the subheadings of the LCSH can help you limit a topic for an online search. Also see "Online Directories" later in this chapter.

Congress Subject Headings (LCSH) is a very large book, usually located adjacent to the reference section. In the LCSH, under the subject headings for books, you can find subheadings to use in your search. You can also consult an online directory such as Yahoo. There you can find general topics, which can be narrowed according to your purpose and audience.

Writing a Controlling Question

After finishing your preliminary reading and deciding on a topic, you may find that it is too broad. Writing a *controlling question* will help you narrow the topic. A controlling question establishes limits. For example, the subject of breast cancer is much too broad. But you could restrict it by asking, "What are the advantages and disadvantages of various methods of treating breast cancer?" Here are more examples of controlling questions:

- How effective is solar energy for heating new homes?
- What should parents look for when selecting day care?
- What ethical issues are at stake in fetal stem cell research?

A controlling question will help you focus your research by specifying the direction your paper will take. Formulating the question early can cut both search and writing time. Then as you examine materials, list possible main points and start a scratch outline.

CASE STUDY

FLORA NARROWS A VERY BROAD TOPIC

After preliminary reading on rain forests, Flora Kyle found that a number of rain forests exist around the world. She limited her topic to Amazon rain forests, but still she found too much information for the assignment of a 1,500–1,700-word paper. Feeling overwhelmed, she consulted her instructor, who suggested asking: How does deforestation of the Amazon rain forests affect residents of the United States? Then Flora was able to restate the question, limit her focus to three main reasons, and begin an outline:

continued

SCRATCH OUTLINE

Controlling Question: Why should U.S. citizens be concerned about deforestation of the Amazon rain forest?

1. Habitat of many plants and animals destroyed
2. Spread of disease from fleas and mites that leave the deforested area
3. Effect on the ozone layer by greenhouse gases produced by burning in the rain forest
4. Worldwide climate changes

SELECTING SUITABLE SOURCES

Not all sources are equally suitable for academic research. While most of us are inclined to smile or shrug when headlines of supermarket publications proclaim "Man frozen in block of ice for 500 years recovers," we are less skeptical of most other printed and Internet sources. To research effectively, however, we need to question and evaluate all sources carefully. This is not so simple. Three preliminary questions will help you select suitable sources:

1. *Is the source reliable?* Beware of any materials that do not include complete documentation. The date of the research, size of study, and names of researchers should be stated. If, however, authoritative groups such as the American Cancer Society, Mayo Clinic, and the U.S. Census Bureau publish documents without an author, you can depend on finding accurate information. Beware, too, of books without an author, especially those that promote the views of a cult or vendor.

2. *Does the source provide comprehensive and fair coverage?* Some sources, such as popular magazines, may give a brief overview of a topic or an issue. Coverage may be superficial with few details and omission of significant points. Even though an article may purport to give both sides of an issue, the treatment may slant toward one view. You need to ensure that your sources give full coverage of your topic.

3. *Is the source written on an appropriate level?* The source material you select should match the level of your intended audience. Reject any material that is overly simplified, directed toward adolescents, or too technical, intended for specialists in the field. For a research paper, you need solid, reliable evidence—statistics, findings, examples, and expert opinion that is clearly stated.

Once you begin gathering potential sources for your research paper, whether from a library or a Web site, you will need a working bibliography to organize them.

> ### CHECKLIST FOR PREVIEWING SOURCES
>
> 1. *Is the material current or outdated?* Some fields need frequent updating; others do not. Material should be current and appropriate for the field.
> 2. *Is the material relevant?* Scan the table of contents, preface, and index. Read chapter titles, scan paragraphs here and there, as well as subheadings. Consider your purpose and audience.
> 3. *Is the treatment of the topic evenhanded?* Differing viewpoints should be recognized and treated with respect. Consider the tone of the article.
> 4. *Is there solid support for the conclusions reached?* Watch for inconsistencies. Are any fallacies apparent?
> 5. *Is the source primary or secondary?* Try to obtain information from primary sources whenever possible.

See chapter 20.

See chapter 21.

Making a Working Bibliography

A working bibliography is a list of possible sources for you to consult. When you go to the library, take a pack of 3- by 5-inch index cards, rather than sheets of paper, so that you can start a bibliography. Cards work well because you can easily sort and alphabetize them. These source cards or your electronic file will help you find materials and develop an outline. Similarly, if you have a laptop computer or can work at a library computer, creating your list as a word processing file can save you time. The program will alphabetize your entries for you, and, when you are preparing your works cited or reference list, you will be able to cut and paste the sources you used from your working bibliography to your final list.

At this point, you may want to turn to chapter 24, which shows how to document sources required for research. You may follow the MLA or APA guidelines, depending on the course and the instructor. You might mark this chapter with a paper clip so that you can quickly refer to it while making your working bibliography.

How to Begin To keep track of your sources, copy all information for each source onto one card, using only one side. Copy the call numbers from the catalog card or index entry onto the upper right corner of the source card. Although you won't need this information for documentation, it will help you find your source. Underneath that, copy other pertinent information such as author, title, editor (if one), year of publication, publisher, city and state. Making a working bibliography will also give you a headstart on your works cited or reference list.

For any reference materials, make source cards, too. For computerized listings that can be printed, printouts will suffice temporarily, but make sure the information is complete. For any item you obtain through the Internet, *write down not only the usual information but also the address (URL) and access date*. Take pains to copy the URL exactly; extra spaces may hinder retrieval.

Making Source Notes

---

1. For *books*, you need:
   a. Full name(s) of author(s)
   b. Full title (including subtitle, if any)
   c. Editor(s) or translator(s)
   d. Total volumes and specific volume number(s) you will use.
   e. City of publication (if unfamiliar, also include state), name of publisher, date of publication

2. For *periodicals*, you need:
   a. Full name(s) of author(s)
   b. Full title of article (including subtitle, if any)
   c. Name of periodical
   d. Full date of periodical (for academic journals also include the volume and issue number, if listed)
   e. Inclusive page numbers (including section letters for newspapers)

3. For *special sources*, such as nonprint material and online sources, you need to jot down various items as explained in chapter 24. Note that nonprint sources such as tapes, compact discs, CD-ROM, television programs, and others have *no page numbers*.

NEVER POSTPONE NOTING A SOURCE

When you find a promising article, document, or book, make a source card or note and check out the publication right away. If the needed article is on the Internet, print it out immediately. If you delay, the materials may be gone—borrowed by someone else or deleted from the Web site. What you find on the Internet today may not be there tomorrow. *Be sure to obtain all essential documentation and keep it until your graded paper is returned.*

FINDING AND EVALUATING PRINT AND ELECTRONIC SOURCES AT THE LIBRARY

Not only do libraries have resources on the premises, but they also have access to resources at other libraries and to the Internet. Unless you are doing very advanced research, your college library should provide everything you need. As you search, do not assume a source is unavailable just because you cannot locate it. There may be a second copy elsewhere, or it may have been returned but not yet checked in. Then, too, older books and newspapers may be stored on microfilm or microfiche.

Be aware, too, that your library's central catalog may consist of one complete system or of segments, both printed and electronic. Ask at the information desk.

Finding Your Way around the Library

Many libraries provide a map of the facility and a brochure describing available services. Look for these materials near the main entrance or at the information desk. If you don't find what you need, inquire. There may be several computer areas, each with a different function. Usually, there are indexes, CD-ROMs, and an Internet connection.

Libraries have four excellent sources for beginning a search: general references, indexes, catalogs, and bibliographies. Sources may be available in print, on microfilm or microfiche, or online. If any of these resources is new to you, do not be dismayed. Library personnel tend to be quite helpful.

GUIDELINES: HOW TO MAKE A WORKING BIBLIOGRAPHY

1. *Start with the Library of Congress Subject Headings for listing of subjects.* If the listings are extensive, take to a nearby copier for duplication. If you don't find what you need, try a thesaurus for synonyms or an online directory.

2. *Seek an overview.* Read entries in dictionaries, encyclopedias, and other general references. Take brief notes.

3. *Use indexes, printed or online.* Indexes can help you find articles in newspapers, magazines, and journals. Make a source card for each promising title or print out relevant computer listings.

4. *Use the electronic central catalog or the Internet.* To find promising book titles, type in the subject listing. If you use a search engine, add the word *books*. (See "Finding and Evaluating Internet Sources," later in this chapter.)

5. *Make source cards or entries for your computer file.* Double-check to see that you have all needed information.

Preliminary Reading: General References

Brief preliminary reading in some general references will provide a quick overview of your topic and help you limit it. If the subject is not new, begin with short selections from dictionaries, encyclopedias, or abstracts. Many encyclopedias give not only an overview but also a bibliography for locating additional sources. For topics about North American subjects, *Encyclopedia Americana* is well respected. Even more comprehensive is the *Encyclopaedia Britannica*, which is more scholarly.

In addition, many encyclopedias and dictionaries are available on medical, legal, business, or other specialized topics. They range from the *Encyclopedia of Chemistry* to the *Encyclopedia of Advertising* to the *Encyclopedia of Rock, Pop, and Soul*. And, of course, some encyclopedias are available on CD-ROM and the Internet.

Electronic Central Catalog

After you have gained an overview of your topic, it is time to seek detailed material to flesh it out. Most libraries have transferred their old card catalogs to an *electronic central catalog*. This allows you to use a computer terminal to locate most of the holdings housed on the premises. You can search by subject, author, title, or keyword by pressing the appropriate keys. Most systems indicate the location of a book, availability, and date of return—if it has been borrowed.

Periodical Indexes and Abstracts

You can find recent information in newly published articles in periodicals (newspapers, magazines, journals, newsletters, and bulletins). To find these materials, consult indexes and abstracts. Indexes (printed, CD-ROM, and online) list articles alphabetically according to subject. Indexes give specific titles, authors, and publications—including magazines, newspapers, pamphlets, government publications, maps, pictures, records, tapes, films, and videos as well as books. Many specialized indexes list sources of information for science and technology, art, business, nursing, medicine, drama, education, and other areas.

Abstracts not only list subject headings but also summarize key information in a highly condensed form. For example, you might consult *Psychology Abstracts* (1927 to present) or *Historical Abstracts* (1955 to present).

General Indexes   General indexes list articles intended for a particular audience. For example, *The Readers' Guide to Periodical Literature* (1905 to present) lists hundreds of popular periodicals. Electronic directories list periodicals from the last decade or so, but if you want earlier articles, you will need to consult a print index.

The Magazine Index, often found in college libraries, is a microfilm index of hundreds of periodicals. Newspaper indexes, such as the *New York Times Index* and the *Wall Street Journal Index*, can also guide you to articles of general interest. All these indexes include scientific, technical, and literary articles, but they are not as extensive as those found in more specialized indexes. If you use popular sources, you will need to supplement them with more scholarly sources.

Specialized Indexes   To find technical or scholarly research and government publications, consult specialized indexes and abstracts. For example, *The Hu-*

manities Index (1974 to present) lists articles on archaeology, history, literature, the performing arts, philosophy, and religion. The *Social Sciences Index* (1974 to present) lists articles on economics, geography, government, law, political science, psychology, and sociology.

Prospective teachers might consult the *Education Index*. Medical technology students might search the *Cumulative Index to Nursing and Allied Health Literature*. The *Public Affairs Information Service* (PAIS) (1915 to present) carries subject listings of material by public and private agencies on economic and social concerns, international relations, and public administration.

Government Publications   These materials are cataloged according to a different system. Although there are indexes to these publications, such as the *Monthly Catalog of United States Publications* and *American Statistics Index*, the help of a librarian may be necessary.

Your library will not carry every periodical listed in every index. If you can't locate a periodical you need, ask if it can be borrowed from another library.

Bibliographies

These publications are similar to catalogs and indexes, but they may be more comprehensive. *Books in Print* lists every book in print in the United States, giving authors, titles, and subject area. *Paperbound Books in Print* is valuable in locating sources on recent topics. *The Bibliographic Index* is helpful for locating subjects you cannot find in other indexes.

Other sources may also use the LCSH as a guide, but often they have their own subject headings. Sometimes a thesaurus is handy for finding synonyms under which a subject may be listed.

TIP: DON'T OVERLOOK LIBRARY SOURCES ON CD-ROM

Your library may have considerable information available on CD-ROM. On CDs you can find such reference works as encyclopedias and *The Oxford English Dictionary*. You may also find back issues of *Time* magazine and other periodicals. In addition, there are interactive multimedia sources produced by the National Geographic Society and other educational publishers.

Finding Print Sources

To use materials that are stored on site, take your source cards or electronic catalog listings with you to the stacks. The stacks are the rows of shelves where less recent periodicals and books are stored. To find the correct row, look up at the outside ends of the stacks. There the subject listing or the range of call letters for each row is found.

The most recent periodicals are usually displayed on shelves in a reading area. They are arranged alphabetically according to title, left to right. The shelves, on which the latest copies rest, generally lift up. Underneath are recent copies. Older periodicals in the stacks are shelved by title and date or by subject, title, and date (alphabetically by title and numerically by year). They may be stored in open containers or in binders. Still older issues may be stored on microfilm or microfiche in drawers. (Ask a library assistant.)

Books are shelved in numerical order by call numbers as well as alphabetical order by the author's last name. If books or other materials cannot be found on a shelf or in a file, consult the electronic central catalog for availability. If materials have been loaned, you can reserve them or perhaps borrow another copy through an interlibrary loan network (ask a librarian). For new books on recent topics, check with a bookstore.

Skimming Sources and Evaluating Content

A brief preview in the library will save you from copying or lugging home irrelevant materials. Check the copyright date, and skim introductory pages to discover the author's credentials and what the book covers. Then read a page here and there to sample the depth and tone. To obtain a variety of viewpoints, look for materials by several authors. Although they may all cite classic research, their interpretations may differ somewhat. Each writer should also cite other research that contributes to the body of knowledge. (You may want to consult these sources, too.)

A Precaution

Prior to taking notes at the library, refer to chapter 25 so that you know what to look for and the expected procedure. Even though you may have written a research paper before, this one may differ considerably. Chances are that your English instructor will expect a different kind of paper.

Chapter 25 offers a way to save time by taking preliminary notes, summarizing, and paraphrasing. As you make notes, *always insert quotation marks around copied material immediately to avoid confusion*. Attempting to summarize and paraphrase when rushed can lead to borrowing the author's words without being aware of it. Careful documentation will help you to avoid unintentional plagiarism.

Borrowing Materials from Other Libraries

To locate materials at other campuses and libraries, you can use a computer connected to a local or regional network. Before searching, however, narrow your topic by writing a controlling question. For a search to be fruitful, the key words should be fairly specific.

Online Catalogs for Regional Networks   Colleges and universities with multiple campuses and libraries may have a regional network of computers that

GUIDELINES FOR EVALUATING SOURCES

- *When was the data collected?* Is it relevant? Scientific and technological data tend to change rapidly. Not all early sources are outdated; some are classics.

- *What is the author's professional status?* Look for a brief biography in the introduction of a book or article. What else has the author written? What are his or her professional credentials?

- *How credible is the publication?* To assess the credibility of a nontechnical book, consult *Book Review Digest*. For reviews of technical works, see *Technical Book Review Digest*. Match the copyright date of the book with the volume of the digest. You can also check the next volume after that date.

- *How much information is given about the research?* What were the characteristics of the sample or study group? Size? Was the sample representative of the general population? Have other researchers obtained similar results? If an experiment was controlled in a laboratory, have other qualified personnel been able to replicate the experiment?

- *If a topic is controversial, do sources examine various points of view?* A balance of viewpoints is necessary to give comprehensive coverage. Does the tone seem impartial or biased?

- *Are enough sources available to give comprehensive coverage?* A few articles, even well-detailed ones, are inadequate for a research paper. To understand the thinking in a field and find adequate coverage, you need numerous sources with a variety of viewpoints.

connects all the sites. This means you can order materials from the main campus when you are on a branch campus and vice versa. Or you may be able to access a statewide hookup of colleges and universities. You may find that you can access more than one network from the same computer terminal.

These networks allow patrons to borrow materials through an interlibrary loan system. A central catalog for each network appears on screen, giving the site (campus, college, or university) and whether or not the materials are available.

If you plan to order items from another site and face a deadline soon, be sure to ask about delivery dates and availability. You also need to inquire about notification. Does the library notify you of arrivals, or must you check a posted list? If you are to check a list, where will it be?

Requesting Materials via OCLC   Many public libraries belong to an international online network, called OCLC. If you are unable to locate materials, you may be able to order them there. This network makes difficult-to-obtain materials available through interlibrary loan. You can request that a librarian access the OCLC network, or you can reach the Web site **OCLC FirstSearch** <http://www .oclc.org/oclc/menu/eco.htm>.

FINDING AND EVALUATING INTERNET SOURCES

The Internet is a maze of private and commercial collections in cyberspace. The World Wide Web, a part of the Internet, is an electronic Wild West because of the lack of regulation. Since almost anything can be found there, reliability and quality are concerns for researchers. This chapter discusses Internet services that are directly related to research. You'll find tips for searching, evaluating Web sites, and judging reliability.

An Internet directory at the end of this chapter lists reliable Web sites for research. This is no guarantee you won't become sidetracked to an unreliable site. Just stay alert and apply the criteria for evaluation that are provided here.

Using Online Directories and Search Engines

Unlike most search engines, directories are organized according to *subject*. Search engines just pick out words from texts, regardless of what the words mean. Unless you are quite specific, the result is a flood of irrelevant references.

Online Directories   A quick way to focus a search is to write a controlling question and use an online directory, such as Yahoo. You can save time by taking the keywords from your question to activate the directory. Select at least two words to start. Connect the words with *and* (+) or enclose in quotation marks to avoid getting irrelevant pages. To narrow the search, use three to five words. *Place the most essential words first.*

Although using one keyword or a two-word phrase will take longer, it can help you narrow a topic. For example, an online directory found 110 subjects with 215 entries under the heading of "Amish." Only 8 appeared on the first screen, but one of those narrowed the topic to "Amish Social Life and Customs," which yielded 30 listings. From there, the search could be narrowed more.

Search Engines   Before using a search engine, narrow your topic. For some search engines, place quotation marks around the key phrase you type in the slot. All search engines are not equal. Different ones will yield different topics. Google, Looksmart, Excite, and Dogpile (a metasearch engine) are among the most popular. To locate a search engine, just preface the name with *http://www.* and then add *.com*. For example, the URL for Google is <http://www.google.com>.

SEVEN TIPS FOR SEARCHING THE INTERNET

1. **Before you start, check the spelling of your topic.** Typing errors and misspellings will interfere with the search.

2. **Before using a directory or search engine, read the help information.** All these vehicles vary somewhat.

3. **Try several search engines.** There are millions of sites on the Web; it is impossible for any one search engine to cover them all.

4. **If you cannot reach a URL, try at a different time or even several days later.** Heavy traffic flow and other factors can interfere with loading.

5. **When you find a relevant Web site, check for links to similar sites.** These leads may be significant.

6. **You may be able to guess a URL.** Add the name and domain name to the standard prefix of <http://www.> and guess at the suffix, as <http://www.microsoft.com>.

7. **Keep searching until you find quality material from reliable sources.**

Evaluating Web Sites

Although the need for controls on the Internet has been in the national spotlight, to date there are relatively few. Any individual who can construct a Web page can stake out a site and post almost anything—accurate or inaccurate; legitimate or fraudulent. Thus visitors must maintain vigilance, keeping an eye out for disclaimers, errors, and doubtful information.

Clues to Sponsors of Web Sites When visiting a Web site, look for the sponsor first. Sponsorship can give clues to the reliability of the posted information. Usually, the sponsor is listed on the home page. If you arrive on some other page, look for a link to go back. The suffix at the end of the URL is a clue to the type

Reprinted by permission of United Feature Syndicate, Inc.

of site. You can recognize private sites by scanning the URL. If you see a tilde (-), this indicates a personal page. If a tilde is part of an .edu URL, it usually indicates the page of a faculty member or a graduate student.

As you search, look for traditional sources. The last segment of the domain name of the URL can give you a clue. For example, in <http://www.mhhe.com>, the domain name <www.mhhe> tells you it is the address of a World Wide Web page, originated by a private company, McGraw-Hill. In the United States *.com* is used by companies; *.edu* is used by colleges and universities; *.gov* by government agencies; *.mil* by the military; *.net* by some Internet service providers; and *.org* by nonprofit groups.

Seven new domain name suffixes (TLDs), selected by the Internet Corporation for Assigned Names and Numbers (ICANN), recently went into effect: *.aero* (air-transport industry), *.biz* (businesses), *.coop* (cooperatives), *.info* (unrestricted use), *.museum* (museums), *.name* (individuals), and *.pro* (accountants, lawyers, physicians, and other professionals). For more information, see <http://www .dotcom.com/news/toplevel.html> and <http://www.icann.org/tlds>.

Additional hints for determining the source of a Web site include looking for a link that says "About This Page," "About Us," or "Home." Such links should take you to information about the sponsor. If there is no such link, try cutting the URL down to the domain name (using just the information before the first single slash).

AVOID PLAGIARIZING ONLINE MATERIALS

Warning If you stumble onto Web sites where you can view student papers or purchase professional research papers, beware. Some sites post a warning about *plagiarism;* others do not. Still, some errant students download and submit these papers to instructors, which is foolish and dangerous. Those who cheat not only rob themselves of an opportunity to learn, but they also run a high risk of detection and punishment for plagiarism. If you are tempted, consider these salient points:

- *Free student papers posted on the Internet tend to be mediocre*—replete with errors in content, sentence structure, spelling, and grammar.
- *Papers for sale tend to be poorly documented*, listing few sources. For example, one paper, "Evolution vs. Creationism," merely compares the content of two Web sites. Such methods constitute shoddy research.
- *Few students have the writing proficiency of professionals*. The differences in writing style are quite likely to be detected by experienced instructors.
- *Instructors can and do visit such Web sites.*
- *Instructors can purchase software that helps to detect plagiarism.*

Free or for a Fee?   Some newspapers, magazines, journals, and books offer sample articles or a chapter in order to encourage print or electronic subscription or sales. If the source is reputable (many periodicals are well-known) and the information is relevant, then use it. If you decide to purchase information by credit card, be sure that the site is secure. Why take unnecessary risks when you can obtain the same information from a library? At college and university libraries, you can access several subscription databases at no charge.

Evaluating the Reliability of Internet Sources

Unlike library books, periodicals, and other materials that have gone through a screening process to ensure reliability and accuracy, the Internet has no screen or controls. On the Net anyone with a computer and a modem can publish anything. Researchers need to scrutinize Web sites to see if they are accurate, expert, objective, timely, comprehensive, and responsible.

Check for a Monitor   Traditional sites of reputable companies, institutions, organizations, and government agencies are generally monitored for accuracy. For example, *Encyclopedia Britannica* is vetted (verified) by editors. Some medical Web sites are screened by physicians. Some sites are maintained by librarians. Some news articles such as those in the *New England Journal of Medicine*, the *New York Times*, and the *Wall Street Journal* cite sources. But these sites are in a minority. Thus the researcher must be alert to discrepancies and wary of unreliable sites.

Watch for Credentials   Look for the name and qualifications of the author of the information. Reputable medical advice is available from physicians who publish the full text of articles related to their speciality. Notice that these professionals provide their names, city, state, and credentials at the top of the articles they publish. You can check out the credentials of physicians by consulting the American Medical Association <http://www.ama-assn.org>. This site lists the education, residencies, and specialties of physicians.

Notice the Tone   Listen to the writer's voice. Are various theories, policies, methods, or other ideas discussed in an objective way? Or does the author seem bent on pushing an ideological or political agenda? Be suspicious if the document is filled with negativity or sensationalism. Watch out for special interests, such as informational advertisements and testimonials advocating a product. Before accepting any of these claims as fact, examine the source data. Have medicines been approved by the FDA? What side effects have occurred? If a study was done, who conducted it? Who paid for it? Companies that hire researchers may slant results to confirm their products.

Notice Dates   Look for dates on Web pages. Most reliable Web pages specify a date at the start or end. Lack of dates on a Web site and in the text of an article casts doubt on reliability.

> ### HOW TO FIND WEB PAGE DATES
>
> If the page lacks a date, you can sometimes find it by going to "Page Info" or "Document Info" on the "View" menu.

Evaluate the Coverage   To check comprehensiveness, look for a statement of purpose. What is the intent of the Web site? How specific is the material, and is it up-to-date? Does the material seem factual? If a treatment or topic is controversial, is the article well balanced, citing risks as well as advantages? Has the purpose been fulfilled? Finally, you can evaluate Internet information by comparing it to that gained from scholarly sources in a library. (See also "Guidelines: Evaluating Sources" earlier in this chapter.)

> ### GUIDELINES FOR EVALUATING THE RELIABILITY OF WEB SITES
>
> #### ACCURACY
>
> - Are sources of information properly cited?
> - Are there bibliographic links to check against library holdings?
> - Are spelling and grammar standard usage?
>
> #### EXPERTISE
>
> - Has the author been trained in this field?
> - Is the author a member of an academic or professional organization?
> - Has the document or site been reviewed by a peer or noted by a respected publication in print?
> - Has the author published in print or electronic format?
> - If the material is from a secondary source, are citations included for the original source?
>
> #### OBJECTIVITY
>
> - Does the language sound professional and fair?
> - Does the site contain informational advertisements, testimonials, or other commercial interests?
> - If research was conducted, who paid for it? (Be wary of studies paid for by the author or sponsor.)

TIMELINESS

- When was the site established?
- When was the material posted? Updated?
- Are there dead links on the page?

COVERAGE

- Is the material comprehensive, covering the main aspects of the topic?
- Does it give enough specific details to serve your purpose?
- Are references, bibliographies, or links included to access other current information on the topic? (Before deciding, check out the links to other pages.)

RESPONSIBILITY

- Is there a way to contact the author?
- Does the Web site list a Webmaster or a way to supply feedback?

Preserving Online Source Information

When you find a relevant and reliable article on the Internet, print it out immediately to ensure that you have all the information you need. If you wait, it may be gone when you return.

How Much Source Data Do You Need? Remember to obtain as much data about each source as possible. You will need it later to construct a works cited entry for each source. Find the author, title, date of publication, original source (if there is one), sponsor of the Web site, URL, and the date you visited. Most browsers show the URL, date, and page name as a header or footer when you print a page. (On Netscape, pull down the File menu, go to Page Setup and select Netscape Communicator to create the template for headers or footers.) You may have to hunt or follow links to find the other information.

SAVE YOUR INTERNET SOURCES AFTER TURNING IN A PAPER

Save your printed Internet source documents until after your paper is graded and returned. Your instructor may ask you to recheck a source or verify an item before a grade is placed on a paper. If you cannot provide evidence of sources, this lack may lead to embarrassing questions.

Balancing Library and Internet Sources

The library and the Internet each have strengths and limitations. As for which is the fastest, the time spent on research depends on the topic, your expertise, and luck. One important asset of the library is the staff. These professionals can help you find what you need quickly. On the Internet, you are usually on your own. There it is easy to lose your way; you may have to circumvent roadblocks that consume hours.

If searching for current information, you may want to start with the Internet, then search weekly newsmagazines or professional journals in the library. If you are researching an invention, historical data, or an event of even a few years ago, the library is the best place to start. *Use of back issues of periodicals is free at the library; on the Internet you often pay a fee.*

If you need to read and study an entire work, the library may be the best place to obtain a novel or play. But if you need to locate a particular item, say a line, in one of Shakespeare's plays, the Internet is generally faster. The Internet may also be quicker for finding a famous quotation, but the campus library may have a broader selection.

As a rule, the Internet offers a quick overview of a subject. It is not a substitute for the comprehensive sources available in the library. The Internet can supplement and enhance library research, not replace it.

DIRECTORY FOR INTERNET RESEARCH

Online Help for Searching

- **Search Engine Watch** <http://www.searchenginewatch.com>
- **Tool Kit for the Expert Web Searcher** by American Library Association <http://www.lita.org/committe/toptech/toolkit.htm>

Online Help for Evaluating Web Pages Critically

- **Checklist for Evaluating Web Resources** University of Southern Maine <http://library.usm.maine.edu/guides/webeval.html>
- **Widener Library** Hints for analyzing special pages with links to examples. <http://www2.widener.edu/Wolfgram-Memorial-Library/webevaluation/webeval.htm>

General Reference Web Sites

- **Argus Clearinghouse** Links to academic and general-interest sites. Run by librarians. <http://www.clearinghouse.net>
- **Encyclopedia Britannica** Links to expanded essays and related topics. Verified by editors. <http://www.britannica.com>

- **Librarian's Index to the Internet** This directory lists 7,000 sites relating to the arts, education, geography, literature, law, medicine, sports, other subjects. <http://www.lii.org/>
- **Merlot: Multimedia Educational Resource for Learning and Online Teaching** <http://www.merlot.org/home/SubjectCatIndex.po>
- **National Archives and Records Administration** <http://www.nara.gov/>
- **University of Michigan Documents Center** Government information. <http://www.lib.umich.edu/libhome/Documents.center/index.html#doctop>
- **WebGEMS: A Guide to Substantive Web Resources** <http://www.fpsol.com/gems/webgems.html>
- **The World Wide Web Virtual Library** <http://www.vlib.org/Overview.html>

Literature and Language Web Sites

- **The American Heritage Book of English Usage** Covers grammar, diction, style, words, gender, and pronunciation. <http://www.bartleby.com/64/>
- **Bibliomania** Browse the complete texts of literary classics, reference books, novels, short stories, drama, poetry, biographies, science texts, and other works. Keyword search available. <http://www.bibliomania.com/>
- **Famous quotations** (3 sites) <http://www.quotationspage.com>, <http://www.quoteland.com>, <http://www.bartleby.com/100/>
- **GreatBooks Online** Verse, fiction, nonfiction, reference, modern usage <http://www.bartleby.com>
- **Guide to Grammar and Writing** <http://webster.commnet.edu/grammar>
- **A Literary Index: Internet Resources in Literature** <http://www.vanderbilt.edu/AnS/english/flackcj/Litmain.html>
- **MagPortal.com** A categorized index of links to the latest magazine articles available on the Web. <http://www.magportal.com>
- **Merriam-Webster's Collegiate Dictionary** <http://www.m-w.com/dictionary>
- **Online Media Directory** of the Media Links database allows you to access newspapers from every continent. <http://www.mediainfo.com/emedia>

continued

- **Shakespeare's plays** This site allows you to locate a line in a play. <http://www.psrg.cs.usyd.edu.au/~matty/Shakespeare>
- **Voice of the Shuttle** Humanities research subject directory from the University of California at Santa Barbara. <http://vos.ucsb.edu/index.html>
- **Your Dictionary.com** Thesaurus, grammars, multilingual dictionaries, research, and more. <http://www.your dictionary.com/index.shtml>

Medical Web Sites

- **CancerNet** Run by the National Cancer Institute. Sections for patients, health professionals, and basic researchers. <http://cancer-net.nci.nih.gov>
- **HealthGate** Provides access to databases, such as CANCERLIT and MEDLINE. <http://www.healthgate.com/index.shtml>
- **Mayo Clinic** Doctors respond to short queries through "Ask Mayo." <http://www.mayohealth.org>
- **Medical World Search** of Katonah, N.Y., offers links to over 100,000 Web pages of information. <http://www.mwsearch.com>
- **Mental Health Net** lists 7,000 sites where you can obtain information on mental health. <http://www.cmhc.com>
- **New England Journal of Medicine** Offers a partial text or an entire text of some articles. <http://www.nejm.org>

Note: For career-related Web sites, see chapter 30.

Summary

The main goal of research is to discover the relevant facts. To plan a research project, first determine your aim or purpose. Is it to inform, investigate a problem, or to persuade? Next, choose a suitable topic and limit the scope. Then do a preliminary search to see if adequate sources are available.

The *Library of Congress Subject Headings* is an excellent place to begin. There you can find possible listings of sources, which can also help to narrow a topic. To gain an overview of a subject, read concise references such as dictionaries, encyclopedias, abstracts, or almanacs. Indexes and catalogs, including online directories, can provide convenient access to sources. Or you may find what you need on CD-ROM.

On-site periodicals and books are housed in the stacks. You need to make a source card or note for each potential source, including all pertinent bibliographic information. Or if you have a computer printout, make sure all necessary source data is listed.

Research on the Internet can supplement library research but rarely supplant it. When you select online documents, evaluate their reliability carefully. As a test, compare them with scholarly library sources.

If you decide to use material from a Web site, print it out and record the date you accessed it. Include the sponsor, author, and date of posting. You will need this information to document your research paper. Do not be tempted by unwise shortcuts that lead to plagiarism.

Key Terms

abstracts	electronic central catalog	preliminary research
access date	indexes	source cards
call letters	online directories	stacks
controlling question	periodicals	working bibliography

Practice

Preliminary Library Search

Directions: To become familiar with the resources available at a campus library, search the following sources. You can also start a working bibliography for your research paper. The completed search can count as a ten-point quiz.

1. *Determine which system of cataloging the library uses.* Write it here.

2. *Find your subject in the Library of Congress Subject Headings.* What headings could you use in your search? (If the library uses the Dewey Decimal system, you receive one free point.)

3. *Electronic Periodical Index.* Type in a subject. Select sources that might be useful. Print out a list. If the library is not computerized, use *The Readers' Guide to Periodical Literature.*

4. *Electronic Central Catalog or Network.* Select three books that might be useful. Print out (or copy) the bibliographic data. (If there is no electronic catalog, use the card catalog.)

5. *Encyclopedia.* Check an encyclopedia to find basic information on a topic. In three sentences, summarize the most important points. If a topic is not listed, try an almanac, atlas, or yearbook. Summarize the information in one sentence.

6. *Indexes.* Consult an index that is not computerized. It might be the *New York Times Index, Applied Science and Technology Index,* or another index. Find and copy an entry that might be relevant to your research.

7–10. List four sources of information not listed on this quiz that you might consult. Specify the general area of the library where the material is located.

Thirty Ideas for Research

1. What career opportunities will you be qualified for after graduation? Narrow the list to two or three, then discuss the advantages and disadvantages of each.

2. Investigate potential employers you might apply to after graduation. Discuss three or fewer. Cite advantages and disadvantages of each one. Or compare two.

3. How are robots used?

4. How practical are alternative fuel vehicles?

5. What possibilities exist for gene therapy? What risks does it pose?

6. Advances in laser eye surgery (or some other type)

7. What are the risks of various types of cosmetic surgery?

8. Methods of terrorism used in the United States and resulting precautions

9. What risks do alcohol and drug use pose to unborn children?

10. What are the chief factors that influence children's academic success?

11. What has happened in countries that have legalized drugs?

12. Guidelines for selecting a quality nursing home for an aged parent

13. What are the benefits and risks of common herbal supplements?

14. How practical is solar energy in home construction?

15. What has happened in countries that have socialized medicine?

16. Nutrition during pregnancy

17. Causes and prevention of burnout in nurses (or anyone else)

18. Pollution of the oceans (or another element of our environment)

19. Possible causes of and treatment for Alzheimer's (or another) disease

20. Are pet vaccinations really safe?

21. Effects of sleep deprivation

22. How important is exercise to health?

23. What should everyone know about heart disease?

24. How important is diet in preventing and treating cancer?

25. Effects of noise on hearing and emotional well-being

26. How do male and female brains differ?

27. How can obesity in children be prevented?

28. What alternatives exist for treating breast cancer?

29. Grounds for and consequences of divorce

30. Techniques for healing a marriage

Documenting Sources

*Every [person] has a right to [an] opinion, but
no [one] has a right to be wrong in . . . facts.*

—Bernard Baruch

In the workplace, accurate and complete information is essential not only in writing checks and invoices, but also in keeping records. Daily business and legal transactions must be preserved. Problems in safety, personnel, and other areas must be noted and investigated. Medical treatments, lab tests, and drug dosages must be logged. All this documentation constitutes proof. And proof must be provided for daily functioning as well as for complaints, disputes, or audits.

Inaccurate and inadequate documentation can result in cash imbalances, negative publicity, job loss, medical complications, and legal problems. Accurate and adequate documentation enhances credibility not only in the workplace, but also in college writing. Readers feel they can trust someone who supports a claim with substantial evidence.

WHAT IS DOCUMENTATION?

Careful documentation is a hallmark of professionalism. When a researcher provides source information, this process is known as *documentation*. It gives credit to the author and allows readers to check facts or to search further. Legally, you may use small parts of copyrighted works (less than 10 percent of the entire work) for research if the author does not prohibit such use, and if you document clearly what you summarize, paraphrase, or quote.

WHAT IS PLAGIARISM?

If you do not give credit to an author, the offense is *plagiarism*. Plagiarism is taking someone else's work and presenting it as your own. Whether intentional or unintentional, plagiarism is risky and impractical. Penalties for plagiarism in colleges and universities range from a failing grade to suspension. Usually, an experienced instructor who is familiar with a student's writing can detect plagiarism. Each writer has his or her own individual voice and style of expression. When plagiarized material from professional writers is added to most undergraduate writing, the additions are readily apparent.

FREQUENTLY ASKED QUESTIONS: SOURCE INFORMATION

1. Where are the publication date and the place of publication found?

   Answer: Near the beginning of the book, usually on the back of the title page.

2. What if there is more than one publication date?

   Answer: Use the most recent one.

3. What if more than one city of publication is given?

   Answer: Cite the first one.

4. What if the book has been published by two companies?

   Answer: List both publishers in the order given.

5. What if no date, page, publisher, or place of publication is given?

   Answer: Use n.d. to mean no date, n.pag. for no page, and n.p. for no publisher or no place.

6. What if a model for an entry is not given?

   Answer: Construct a model similar to the one most like it.

7. What title is used for the source page?

   Answer: If MLA style is used, the page is called "Works Cited." The APA style has a page called "References."

8. Are printed sources from the Internet documented just the same as other publications?

   Answer: No. Construct an example according to the Internet models.

9. What extra information do sources taken from the Internet require?

   Answer: Web publication date (if available), date of access, URL (Web address), and other data may be required.

10. Which style of documentation should be used on the job?

    Answer: Some large firms have their own style manuals. If not, and if no preference is expressed, use either the MLA or APA style.

Why take this unnecessary risk when you can easily avoid it? When making source cards or note cards and drafting your paper, you use the three forms of documentation listed below.

1. *Sources provided within the text.* Identify the author's name and other source information either in the text or in a parenthetical citation.
2. *Quotation marks.* Enclose copied words with quotation marks.
3. *List of sources.* Place a works cited list or a reference list (bibliographic data) at the end of a research paper to identify all sources mentioned, summarized, paraphrased, or quoted.

WHICH DOCUMENTATION STYLE IS APPROPRIATE?

Documentation styles vary according to disciplines. For disciplines and courses in the humanities, including freshman composition, the documentation style of the Modern Language Association (MLA) is widely recommended. For the social and behavioral sciences, the style of the American Psychological Association (APA) is generally used. Models for citations and entries for both styles appear in this chapter. For more detailed information, see the *MLA Handbook for Writers of Research Papers*, fifth edition, 1999, by Joseph Gibaldi, or the *Publication Manual of the American Psychological Association*, fifth edition, 2001. Both the MLA and the APA have web sites that offer information about their documentation styles. For the MLA, visit <www.mla.org>, and for the APA, visit <www.apastyle.org>. Some colleges and universities also post MLA and APA documentation models online.

For classes in other disciplines, your instructor may ask you to use some other citation style, such as the *Chicago Manual of Style* (CMS), often used in business, history, and other similar disciplines. The Council of Science Editors (CSE), formerly the Council of Biology Editors (CBE), style is used in the life sciences and explained in *Scientific Style and Format: The CBE Manual for Authors, Editors, and Publishers*, sixth edition, 1994. The Institute of Electrical and Electronic Engineers (IEEE) style is used in computer science and other fields.

MLA STYLE OF DOCUMENTATION

The MLA has endorsed a style of documentation that has been widely adopted for research in the humanities. The MLA style requires brief source references within the text of a research paper. The paper concludes with a list of sources entitled "Works Cited."

CHAPTER 24 MLA STYLE DIRECTORY

SECTION TITLE	PAGE
Parenthetical Citations: MLA Style	342
Using Notes with MLA Parenthetical Citations	346
Recommended Abbreviations for MLA Works Cited Entries	348
Preparing a List of Works Cited: MLA Style	347
1. Sample MLA Entries for Books and Other Nonperiodical Publications	349
2. Sample MLA Entries for Articles and Other Publications in Periodicals	352
3. Sample MLA Entries for Miscellaneous Print and Nonprint Sources	355
4. Sample MLA Entries for Electronic Sources	358

Parenthetical Citations: MLA Style

Source information placed within parentheses is called *parenthetical citation.* You will be using these citations throughout your research paper. For easy reading, keep citations brief. When feasible, insert the author's name into the text of your paper so that you can limit citations to just a page number. (Page numbers of cited material always appear in parentheses.) Key or match each of your citations to a source entry at the end of your paper. Several citations may refer to the same entry.

You may have used an earlier method of documentation that varied somewhat from the updated MLA style. As you construct MLA parenthetical citations to use in the text of your paper, keep these two guidelines in mind:

- Use a parenthetical citation *each time* a source is cited. Some paragraphs may need several citations. Rarely will you have a paragraph without a citation.

- If the source is from more than one page, cite the full range of pages (example: 19–23).

One Author   When you identify the author in your text, put only the page number in parentheses. When you do not mention the author's name, include the author's last name inside the parentheses, before the page number. Do *not* separate the two with a comma.

Theodore Bernstein, assistant managing editor of the <u>New York Times</u> for seven years, points out that the word <u>bandit</u> "has a flavor of heroism." Bernstein advises: "Avoid any suggestion of glorifying outlaws" (17).

One editor has advised against the use of the word <u>bandit</u>

because its "flavor of heroism" has the effect "of glorifying

outlaws" (Bernstein 17).

Work Cited

Bernstein, Theodore M. <u>Watch Your Language</u>. Great Neck, NY:

    Channel Press, 1958.

Two or More Works by the Same Author   To make citations for two or more works by the same author, place a comma after the author's name, followed by a condensed title and the page references: (Barrett, "Claw" 123) (Barrett, "Sickness" 103).

Works Cited

Barrett, Deirdre. "The Claw of the Panther: Dreams and the

    Body." <u>The Committee of Sleep</u>. New York: Crown, 2001.

———. "Mourning Sickness." <u>The Pregnant Man</u>. New York:

    Random House, 1998.

Two or More Authors   For works with two or more authors, include all last names; spell out *and:*

Four "aims of argument" are identified: inquiry, convincing,

persuasion, and negotiation" (Crusius and Channell 8).

Some researchers recommend "rapid-fire questioning" during

survey interviews (Kinsey, Pomeroy, and Martin 54).

For four or more authors, include only the first author's last name and the Latin abbreviation *et al.* ("and others"): (Klein et al. 53).

Works by Two Authors with the Same Last Name   When two authors have the same last name, give their full names in the text (preferred usage) with just the page number in each citation. If names are not given in the text, then include the first initial in the parenthetical citation: (G. Mueller 24), (A. Mueller 36).

Entire Work   When citing an *entire* work, not a specific page, state only the author's name in the text and, if helpful, the title. Be sure the source is on your works cited list.

H. W. Fowler's <u>Modern English Usage</u> reflects his spartan life.

Fowler believed in simplicity not only in living but also in writing

a sentence. Clarity had top priority.

One-Page Articles   It is not necessary to include the page number when referring to an article that is a page or less long.

> According to its secretary, Michael Heyman, "the story of the Smithsonian is also the story of its volunteers."

Work Cited

Heyman, Michael. "Smithsonian Perspectives." <u>Smithsonian</u>
> Apr. 1996: 16.

Source with No Author Given   For unsigned works, shorten long titles. Begin with the word by which the work is alphabetized in works cited: (DJIA).

Work Cited

"The DJIA through the Century." <u>Wall Street Journal</u> 28 May
> 1996: R29.

Corporate Author   Although a work by a group or an agency can be cited in parentheses, the preferred usage is to include the name in the text:

> Microsoft Corporation's 2001 annual report stated that Microsoft will continue "to work vigorously to resolve the remaining issues" of the antitrust lawsuit.

Work Cited

Microsoft Corporation. <u>2001 Annual Report</u>. Redmond, WA:
> Microsoft, 2001.

Indirect Source   When possible, use an original source rather than a secondhand one that quotes the original. If you are unable to obtain the original source and must use a secondary source, place *qtd. in* ("quoted in") before the citation for the secondary source.

> Ralph Waldo Emerson said, "Our best thoughts come from others" (qtd. in Cohen 9).

Work Cited

Cohen, Herb. <u>You Can Negotiate Anything</u>. New York: Bantam,
> 1980.

Quotations by Two or More Authors in One Sentence Follow each quotation with a separate parenthetical citation.

Zinsser says, "The most important sentence in any article is the first one" (59), and Bernstein suggests the writer "ask . . . what it is he is writing about" to find the focus for that sentence (75).

Two or More Sources in One Citation If you cite information from two or more sources, include identifying information for each source in your parenthetical citation, separated by semicolons.

All seem to agree that good writing is hard work (Bernstein 44; Trimble 54; Zinsser 33).

Work of More Than One Volume If your works cited list includes more than one volume of a multivolume work, include the volume number, separated from the page number by a colon: (Nicolson and Trautman 3: 25).

Literary Works Because classic prose works may appear in different editions, include chapter (*ch.*), book (*bk.*), and part (*pt.*) in addition to page numbers. Place extra information after the page with a semicolon between.

In the <u>Republic</u>, Plato has Socrates ask: "What do you consider to be the greatest blessing which you have reaped from your wealth?" (221; bk. 1)

Work Cited

Plato. "Republic." <u>Five Great Dialogues</u>. Trans. B. Jowett. Ed.
Louise Ropes Loomis. Roslyn, NY: Classics Club, 1942.

To cite classic verse plays, poems, and other works, leave out page numbers. Instead, give the division—canto, act, scene, book, part—and the line(s). Separate numbers by periods. For example, (*Waste Land* 1.35) refers to canto 1, line 35; (*Electra* 1.60) refers to scene 1, line 60. Note that the word *line* is spelled out in citations.

Dickinson ends her poem "Wild Nights—Wild Nights!" with a prayer: "Might I but moor--Tonight-- / In Thee!" (lines 11-12).

<u>Romeo and Juliet</u> provides one of Shakespeare's most quoted lines: "But soft! What light through yonder window breaks?" (2.2.2).

Nonprint Sources   Works taken from a Web site are cited just like printed works. If Internet sources are not marked with page numbers, paragraph or section numbers may be included. If so, include those numbers, preceded by the proper abbreviation (*par.* or *sect.*).

If a nonprint source (interview, television program, compact disc, CD-ROM, or other) lacks page numbers, you can omit a parenthetical citation if you state the author's name in the text. A works cited entry is still needed. If the author's or performer's name is not cited in the text, place it in a citation (Dave Matthews Band). For sound recordings, the medium (compact disc) is stated in the works cited entry:

Work Cited

Dave Matthews Band. "The Space Between." <u>Everyday</u>. Compact

disc. BMG/RCA, 2001.

Long Quotations   Quotations of five lines or more are set off, indented ten spaces. The parenthetical citation is placed one space after the final punctuation.

Charles C. Moskos summarizes the argument well:

> The principal argument raised against linking national
> service and federal educational aid is that it would have
> a regressive effect. . . . Students from wealthy families
> who do not need aid would be unaffected, while poor
> students would have to enter national service in order
> to get aid. (380)

Punctuation   For short quotations within the text, place a period or other punctuation *after* the parenthetical citation. For long block quotations, set off from the text, place the period one space *before* the parenthetical citation.

Using Notes with MLA Parenthetical Citations

Content notes and bibliographic notes can be used along with parenthetical citations to provide more information. To insert a note, place a superscript Arabic number at a suitable place in the text. Then at the bottom of the same page, place a matching number before the note. Keep the notes short and informative. Content notes and bibliographic notes can be mingled and numbered in sequence.

Content Notes   When a secondary source is cited, a content note can provide complete publication data on the original source. Or a necessary explanation may be included, as in the example below:

Several months ago when obesity specialist Dr. Frank Greenway from UCLA revealed that a thigh reduction cream really worked, several news accounts incorrectly reported reductions of as much as 1-1/2 inches. The fact was that the most a woman's thighs shrunk was 1-1/2 <u>centimeters</u> or approximately 1/2 inch. Furthermore, the safety of the cream has been questioned.[1]

Note

[1] Several news sources have pointed out this misstatement.

Bibliographic Notes   To provide evaluative comments on sources or for references having several citations, use notes.

The <u>Wall Street Journal</u> and many other newspapers carried articles about the resignation of David Howard, head of the District Office of Public Advocate, Washington, D.C., over his use of a standard word that sounded like a taboo term.[1]

Note

[1] For a sample of articles taken from editorial pages, see Dooling and Parker.

Works Cited

Dooling, Richard. "What a Niggling Offense! Oops, We Mean . . ." <u>Wall Street Journal</u> 29 Jan. 1999: A14.

Parker, Kathleen. "Must We Be So Niggling about Words?" <u>Marion Star</u> 7 Feb. 1999: A6.

PREPARING A LIST OF WORKS CITED: MLA STYLE

Use these general guidelines for the format of your works cited page.

1. Type *Works Cited*, centered, at the top of the page.
2. Alphabetize entries according to the last name of the author. When an author's name is not known, alphabetize by the first word in the title except for *a, an,* or *the.*

RECOMMENDED ABBREVIATIONS FOR MLA WORKS CITED ENTRIES

PUBLISHERS' NAMES

Shorten the names of publishers, omitting *Inc.*, *Company*, and so forth, and using only the first name when there is more than one name. *University Press* is shortened to *UP* (or *U of . . . P*). In some cases, initials are used. Some examples follow:

Appleton-Century-Crofts	Appleton
Beacon Press, Inc.	Beacon
Cambridge University Press	Cambridge UP
Henry Holt and Company	Henry Holt
Holt, Rinehart and Winston	Holt
New American Library	NAL
University of Chicago Press	U of Chicago P

STATES

Use state abbreviations without periods: NY, OH, CA.

GOVERNMENT PUBLICATIONS

Use the following abbreviations:

Congressional Record	Cong. Rec.
Government Printing Office	GPO
House of Representatives Report	H. Rept.
House of Representatives Document	H. Doc.
Library of Congress	LC
Senate Resolution	S. Res.
Senate Document	S. Doc.

3. Double-space the entire listing of works cited.

4. Do not indent the first line of an entry. Indent *five* spaces (or one-half inch on a word processor) for succeeding lines of the entry. This style of indention is called a "hanging indention."

5. Place a period after each subdivision of an entry and at the end of each entry.

6. Underline the title of an *entire* work, such as books, magazines, newspapers, plays, paintings, and others.

7. Place quotation marks around titles of short works that appear in longer works, such as articles, chapters, stories, poems, and songs.

8. Cite inclusive page numbers (121–28) for specific essays, articles, short stories, and so forth that appear in a book or periodical.

9. Number the works cited page using arabic numerals, just as the other pages of the paper.

10. Use shortened forms for the names of publishers and reference sources (see Recommended Abbreviations).

1. SAMPLE MLA ENTRIES FOR BOOKS

Include the author's name as it is printed on the title page. In the works cited entry, reverse the name and place a comma between the last and first part: Bickford, Scott, Jr. Except for Jr. and roman numerals (which are part of a name), leave out titles, affiliations, or degrees.

Underline the titles and subtitles of books. Separate the title and subtitle with a *colon* unless the main title ends with a question mark, an exclamation point, or a dash. An underline can be typed as a solid line under all the words in a title or name even when it contains a colon. Do *not* underline the period at the end of a title.

Specify the city of publication, publisher, and year of publication (or copyright date if the publication date isn't listed). You can omit the state, country, or province if there is no chance of confusion.

1.1. A Book by One Author

The last name of a single author comes first.

Clarke, Arthur C. <u>The Collected Stories of Arthur C. Clarke</u>.

New York: A Tom Doherty Associates Book, 2000.

1.2. Two or More Books by One Author

List the name once in the first entry (alphabetically by title). For the second entry, type three hyphens and a period instead of the name.

Goldberg, Natalie. <u>Wild Mind: Living the Writer's Life</u>. New York:

Bantam, 1990.

---. <u>Writing Down the Bones: Freeing the Writer Within</u>. Boston:

Shambhala, 1986.

1.3. A Book by Two or Three Authors

When there are two or three authors, reverse only the first name. Spell out *and*. Retain the title exactly as it appears on the book.

> Musciano, Chuck, and Bill Kennedy. HTML & XHTML: The
>
> Definitive Guide. 4th ed. Sebastopol, CA: O'Reilly, 2000.

1.4. A Book by Four or More Authors

For a book with four or more authors, you may include only the first author and add *et al.* ("and others"), or you may state all the authors in the order given on the title page.

> Burrows, Thomas D., et al. Video Production: Disciplines and
>
> Techniques. New York: McGraw-Hill, 2000.

1.5. Corporate Author: A Book by a Group

> Boston Women's Health Book Collective. Ourselves and Our
>
> Children. New York: Random, 1978.

1.6. Second or Later Edition of a Book

Specify any edition other than the first by number (2nd ed., 3rd ed.), by name (Rev. ed.), or by year (1990 ed.).

> Figler, Howard. The Complete Job-Search Handbook: Everything
>
> You Need to Know to Get the Job You Really Want. 2nd ed.
>
> Buffalo: Firefly Books, 1999.

1.7. A Work in a Compilation, Anthology, or Collection

Enclose in quotation marks the title of an essay, a short story, a poem, or other work collected in a book. The anthology title and editor(s) follow. State the inclusive page numbers for the specific piece at the end of the entry. If you are citing a previously published scholarly article, insert *Rpt. in* ("Reprinted in"), the title of the collection, and the new publication data.

> Maddox, Jack, and Rosa Maddox. "How We Got Over." Talk That
>
> Talk: An Anthology of African American Storytelling. Eds.
>
> Linda Goss and Marian E. Barnes. New York: Simon, 1989.
>
> 117-25.

1.8. A Book by an Anonymous Author

Go Ask Alice. New York: Prentice, 1971.

1.9. A Book with an Editor or Editors

Reed, Ishmael, Kathryn Trueblood, and Shawn Wong, eds. The
Before Columbus Foundation Fiction Anthology: Selections
from the American Book Awards, 1980-1990. New York:
Norton, 1992.

1.10. A Book with an Author and an Editor

Tolkien, J. R. R. Unfinished Tales. Ed. Christopher Tolkien. Boston:
Houghton, 1980.

1.11. A Book in Volumes

When using just one volume of a multivolume work, give that volume number before the place of publication.

Shakespeare, William. "Cymbeline." The Tragedies of
Shakespeare. Ed. Warren Chappell. Vol. 2. New York:
Random, 1944.

When using two or more volumes of a work, include the total number of volumes after the title.

Nicolson, Nigel, and Joanne Trautmann, eds. The Letters of
Virginia Woolf. 5 vols. New York: Harcourt, 1977.

1.12. An Article from a Reference Book

The place and publisher can be omitted for encyclopedias, dictionaries, and other well-known reference books. Page numbers can also be omitted if the entries are alphabetical. If the entry is signed, lead with the author's name.

"The Civil War." Encyclopedia Americana. 100th Anniversary
Library Edition. 1995.

1.13. An Introduction, Preface, Foreword, or Afterword

Start with the author of the piece and then identify what you are citing—for example, "Preface." If the book is by a different writer, include his or her name as shown in the following example.

Ehrlich, Gretel. Introduction. <u>My First Summer in the Sierra</u>. By
John Muir. New York: Penguin, 1987. vii-xvi.

1.14. A Translation or Edited Edition

Dostoevsky, Fyodor. <u>The Brothers Karamazov</u>. Trans. Constance
Garnett. Ed. Manuel Komroff. New York: NAL, 1957.

1.15. A Pamphlet

Treat a pamphlet as a book, even if very short.

Lazear, David G. <u>Teaching for Multiple Intelligences</u>. Bloomington:
Phi Delta Kappa, 1992.

1.16. Government Publications

When the writer is unknown, list the government agency as author. If two
or more works are issued by the same government agency, place three hyphens
in place of the author's name (---.). Repeat if the works are by the same agency
(---. ---.). Most congressional documents require the number and session of Congress, the house (S or HR), and the kind and number of publication (S. Res. 19,
H. Res. 49). The *Congressional Record*, however, requires just the date and page.

United States. Health Care Financing Administration. <u>Medicare &</u>
<u>You 2001</u>. Washington: GPO, 2001.

---. Dept. of Justice. <u>FBI National Academy Directory of Graduates</u>
<u>2001 Edition</u>. Quantico, VA.: FBI Academy, 2001.

1.17. Sacred Writings

The article, chapter, or "book" (as in books of the Bible) is placed before the
verses (if applicable). The title of the entire work follows. (Titles of sacred writings are not underlined or enclosed with quotation marks.) If the work has more
than one version, the abbreviation for the version is placed last.

Proverbs 22:1. Bible. KJV.

Genesis 1:3. Torah.

2. SAMPLE MLA ENTRIES FOR ARTICLES

Periodicals comprise journals, magazines, newspapers, newsletters, and similar publications. Scholarly journals, which are usually published quarterly, are
not aimed at a general audience. Since these articles often describe original

research and give professional opinion, they are valuable sources for research papers.

Works cited entries for articles in periodicals follow the general guidelines for books except that different publication information is provided, and inclusive page numbers (for the entire article) appear. For names of publications beginning with *the*, omit the first word: *Wall Street Journal.* For a daily periodical, put the day before the month and year with no intervening punctuation. As you consult various periodicals in your research, collect the following information on your note cards. Then you will be well prepared to construct works cited entries later.

1. Name of author (if given)
2. Title of article
3. Name of source (title of periodical)
4. Series (if one)
5. Volume number (scholarly journals only)
6. Issue number (if one)
7. Publication date
8. Edition (if given)
9. Inclusive page numbers of the article

2.1. Journal Article with Continuous Paging

Many scholarly journals use continuous paging, starting in January and continuing throughout the year. The volume number and year are sufficient (not issue or month).

Luna, Beatriz, and Mark N. Funglar. "Drug-Induced

Hyperglycemia." Journal of the American Medical

Association 286 (2001): 1945-48.

2.2. Journal Article with Each Issue Paged Separately

Include issue numbers for journals that do *not* number pages continuously. After the volume number, place a period and the issue number together with no space: 10.3 (indicating volume 10, issue 3).

Togger, Debra A., and Phyllis S. Breaner. "Metered Dose

Inhalers." American Journal of Nursing 101.10 (2001): 26-32.

2.3. Article from a Daily Newspaper

When a newspaper has different editions, specify the edition between the date and the page.

> Browning, E.S., and Ken Brown. "How Will You Know When It's
>
> Safe to Buy Stocks Again?" <u>Wall Street Journal</u> 9 Apr. 2001,
>
> Midwest ed.: A1.

2.4. Article from a Monthly Magazine

Include the cover date. Abbreviate all months except May, June, and July, using the first three letters. When the paging of an article is not consecutive, write only the first page number with a plus sign.

> Colón, Aly. "Avoid the Pitfalls of Plagiarism." <u>Writer</u> Jan. 2001:
>
> 8-9.

2.5. Article from a Weekly Newspaper or Weekly Magazine

> Begley, Sharon, and Michael Isikuff. "Anxious about Anthrax."
>
> <u>Newsweek</u> 22 Oct. 2001: 28-35.

2.6. An Anonymous Article

When the author of an article is unstated, begin with the title and alphabetize by the first significant word in the title.

> "Dill Soothes an Upset Tummy." <u>Organic Gardening</u> July/
>
> Aug. 2001:13.

2.7. Review

> Applebaum, Herbert A. Rev. of <u>Social Anthropology of Work</u>, ed.
>
> Sandra Wallman. <u>Current Anthropology</u> 21 (1980): 307-08.

2.8. Abstract and a Review

The abstract of the book appears before the abstract of the review. The periodical carrying the abstract and review is placed last. If the abstract has no review, omit *Rev. by*.

> Monti, Daniel J. <u>The American City: A Social and Cultural History</u>.
>
> Oxford, UK: Blackwell, 1999. Rev. by J. C. Schneider, <u>Journal</u>
>
> <u>of American History</u> 87 (2001): 1537-1538. <u>Book Review</u>
>
> <u>Digest</u> 97.6 (2001): 157.

2.9. An Editorial

When citing a signed editorial, start with the author's name, then the title. Next, write *Editorial* (no underlining or quotation marks). When the editorial is unsigned, start with the title.

> Maxwell, Bill. "The Messenger Takes a Pounding." Editorial. <u>The</u>
>
> <u>Marion Star</u> 26 Oct. 2001: 6A.

2.10. A Letter to the Editor

> Cooper, B. A. "Limit Trucks but Not Traffic." Letter. <u>Washington</u>
>
> <u>Post</u> 16 Oct. 2001: 22A.

2.11. Newsletter Article

> Guthrie, L. "Cemetery Report." <u>Ohio Genealogical Society</u>
>
> <u>Newsletter</u> 32.10 (October 2001): 168-169.

3. SAMPLE MLA ENTRIES FOR MISCELLANEOUS PRINT AND NONPRINT SOURCES

For broadcast, film, and recorded sources involving various personnel, you begin the entry with the name or title that is the primary subject of emphasis in your paper, as shown below:

> Stouffer, Marty. "Cutthroat Trout." 2 episodes. <u>Wild America</u>. PBS.
>
> WOSU-TV, Columbus, OH. 11 Sept. 1995-12 Sept. 1995.
>
> "Cutthroat Trout." 2 episodes. Marty Stouffer. <u>Wild America</u>. PPS.
>
> WOSU-TV, Columbus, OH. 11 Sept. 1995-12 Sept. 1995.

3.1. Television or Radio Programs

The items in a works cited entry for a television or radio program generally follow the order below. (Omit any items that are not relevant, but include relevant items such as performers, director, conductor, or number of episodes.)

1. Episode or segment title (Enclose in quotation marks. If there are two or more episodes, state the total.)
2. Author's name (in reverse order if it begins the entry)
3. Program title (underline)
4. Series title

5. Network (for example, CNN)

6. Local call letters and city (for example, WMAQ, Chicago)

7. Date of broadcast

Schama, Simon. "The Body of the Queen." 5 episodes. <u>A History of Britain</u>. Narr. Simon Schama. The History Channel. CNBC, Columbus, OH. 29 Oct. 2001.

"John Williams Gala Celebration." Comp. and Cond. John Williams. Host: Richard Dreyfuss. <u>Evening at the Pops</u>. PBS. WOSU-TV, Columbus, OH. 9 July 1993.

"Open Line." Host and prod. Fred Andrel. <u>News 820 Update</u>. WOSU-AM, Columbus, OH. 7 July 1993.

If a transcript is available online, provide the information.

Shaw, Bernard. "Clinton's Boom Era Not as Turbulent as LBJ's." Program segment. <u>Inside Politics</u>. CNN. 29 June 1999. Transcript. 1 July 1999. <http://www.cnn.com/ TRANSCRIPTS/9906/29/ip.06.html>.

For sound recordings of television or radio programs, see 3.2. For a videotape of a performance, see 3.3. For interviews conducted on television or radio, see 3.4.

3.2. Sound Recordings

If the recording is on compact disc, omit the medium. Specify audiocassette tape or LP. Also include manufacturer and date. The name you place first depends on whom you want to emphasize—composer, conductor, or performer.

McLachlan, Sarah. "Building a Mystery." <u>Mirrorball</u>. BMG/Arista, 1999.

Strauss, Edvard. "The Merry Widow Waltz." <u>Viennese Favorites</u>. LP. Cond. Arthur Fiedler. Boston Pops Orchestra. Audiocassette. RCA Victrola, 1983.

3.3. Film or Video Recording

Include all pertinent information in an order that reflects your emphasis. For video recordings, include the original date of release as well as the date the recording was released.

a. A Film Video Recording, or Performance

Enchanted April, Dir. Mike Newell. Perf. Miranda Richard

Josie Lawrence, Polly Walker, and Joan Plowright.

Screenwriter Peter Barnes. Warner Brothers, 1992.

If material is not a film, specify the medium. Some materials may include an original release date, perhaps in another form. For example, some laser discs contain films in IMAX. If material has an original release date, include that date before the medium.

b. Videocassettes, DVD, Laser Disc, or Filmstrip

MacArthur Foundation, J. D. and C. T., National Science

Foundation, and Jostens Foundation. Tropical Rainforest.

1992. Laser disc. Denver: Lumivision. 1994.

Those Wonderful Dogs. Narr. Richard Kiley. Writer and Prod.

Barbara Jampel. Music by Scott Harper. National

Geographic Society. 1989. Videocassette. Columbia Tristar,

1994.

3.4. Interviews

Published interviews are treated as excerpts from anthologies and periodicals. Broadcast interviews are treated as television or radio programs. Personal and telephone interviews are listed as such. In all cases, list the name of the person interviewed first.

MacLeish, Archibald. "Archibald MacLeish." Interview with

Benjamin De Mott. Writers at Work: The Paris Review

Interviews 5. Ed. George Plimpton. New York: Penguin,

1988. 23-48.

Senitko, Melanie. Personal interview. 27 Oct. 2001.

Witzel, Carol. Telephone interview. 29 Oct. 2001.

3.5. Cartoon

Schulz, Charles. "Peanuts." Cartoon. Marion Star 15 June 2002:

B13.

l legal citations, see the most recent edition of *The*
f Citation (Cambridge: Harvard Law Rev. Assn.).
line nor enclose in quotation marks any titles of
n the text or in the list works cited. Works of this
ɪs. The year is included when it is significant.

4.

FOR
S

ɔnly use six kinds of sources from the World
cles in periodicals, texts of books, reference databases, scholarly
projects, professional sites, and personal sites. Models for each are shown in the
following section.

Other types of electronic sources include CD-ROMs and diskettes. Increasingly, sources are available in multiple mediums. The content of documentation entries varies; include all the relevant items that are available. The guidelines on page 359 will alert you to needed information:

4.1. Online Database, Scholarly Project, Professional and Personal Sites

Start with the title of the article or document (if given). Next, give the project or database (underline). List the editor (if there is one). Supply any electronic publication information, such as version, number, date of latest update, and sponsor. Include the date of access and the URL.

a. Online Encyclopedia or Other Information Database

"D.C. Mail Being Sterilized." CNN.Comm. 25 Oct. 2001. Cable

　　　News Network. 25 Oct. 2001 <http://www.cnn.com/>.

"Wild Rice." The Columbia Electronic Encyclopedia, 6th ed.

　　　25 Oct. 2001 <http://www.encyclopedia.com>.

b. Scholarly Project

Ward, Mrs. Humphry. "The Story of Bessie Costrell." 1895.

　　　Victorian Women Writers Project. Ed. Perry Willett. 18 May

　　　1999. Indiana U. 11 June 1999 <http://www.indiana.edu/

　　　~letrs/vwwp/ward/bessie.html>.

MLA STYLE: DOCUMENTING ELECTRONIC SOURCES

1. *Name of the author, editor, compiler, and translator of the source, text, or project.* Reverse the name of the first (or only) person so that it can be alphabetized. (Use abbreviations such as ed., comp., tr.)

2. *Book title.* Underline both main title and subtitle.

3. *Title of an article, a poem, short story, or similar item* in a scholarly project, database, or periodical. Enclose with quotation marks.

4. *Title of the scholarly project, database, periodical, or professional or personal site.* Underline. If there is no title, write a description such as Home page.

5. *Edition, version, volume, or issue number.* If the version number is included in the title, do not repeat. For a journal, include the volume, issue, or any other number for identification.

6. *Dates of information.* Include the dates of posting, electronic publication, and most recent update, if there is one.

7. *Date of access.* Also include the date when you obtain the material.

8. *Article or work from a subscription service.* In addition to the work's title and author, provide the name of the database or service, the name of the subscriber (often a library), the date of access, and the subscriber's URL.

9. *Posted list or forum.* Supply the name of the list or forum.

10. *Range or number of pages, paragraphs, or sections.* Include if the material is numbered.

11. *Sponsor of the Web site.* Identify the individual, institution, organization, or agency sponsoring or associated with the Web site.

12. *Web address.* Place the URL of the source in angle brackets (< >), followed by a period when the URL is the final item. (For a subscription service, do likewise for the URL of the home page.)

13. When online material carries a printed source and date, cite that first, according to the MLA guidelines for books and periodicals (see 1.1 to 2.10 in preceding MLA discussion). Follow this information with the name of the sponsor, institution, agency, or organization; date of access; and URL.

14. Medium of publication (CD-ROM, diskette or other).

15. Other publication information such as publisher's name, place of publication, and copyright date.

c. Professional Site or Personal Site

First give the name of the person who created it (if given) and the title of the site (underline) with a description such as *Home page* (no underlining). Next give the sponsor of the site, the date of access, and the URL. (In the first example below, the sponsor is also the author, so no sponsor is listed.)

<u>Hopkins Information Technology Services Home Page</u>. Johns
    Hopkins University. 26 Oct. 2001 <http://webapps.jhu.edu/
    hitswebsite/>.

Barbour, Dennis. <u>Dennis Barbour Useful Links</u>. 7 Jan. 2001.
    Online Directory. 26 Oct. 2001 <http://www.hme.jhu.edu/
    ~dbarbour/links.h>.

4.2. Online Book

The book was originally published in 1878. The online source is based on Harper's 1892 edition.

James, Henry. <u>Daisy Miller</u>. 1878. New York: Harper, 1892. 1 Nov.
    2001 <http://www.newpaltz.edu/~hathaway/daisyO.html>.

4.3. Online Poem, Short Story, or Other Short Work within a Work

The first example is from an online anthology with the editor and sponsor listed. The second example is an electronic version of a printed book with the editors, place, and publisher listed.

Frost, Robert. "Mending Wall." <u>Modern American Poetry</u>. Ed.
    Cary Nelson. Oxford U. Press, 2000. 2 Nov. 2001 <http://
    www.english.uluc.edu/maps/poets/a_f/frost/wall.htm>.

Sawyer, Robert J. "Gators." <u>Urban Nightmares</u>. Eds. Josephas
    Sherman and Keith R.A. DiCandido. Bronx: Baen, 1997.
    2 Nov. 2001. <http://www.sfwriter.com/stgator.htm>.

4.4. Online Article in a Scholarly Journal

The online article below was printed in *American Psychologist*, Vol. 54, issue 10, October 1999. It had three pages. The site was accessed Oct. 26, 2001.

Parrott, Andy C. "Does Cigarette Smoking Cause Stress?"
    American Psychologist, 54.10 (Oct. 1999): 3 pp. 26 Oct. 2001
    <http://www.apa.org/journals/amp5410817.html>.

4.5. Online Article in a Newspaper

Tempest, Rone, and Richard Boudreaux. "Exiles Support Lead
    Role for Ex-King in Post-Taliban Era." Los Angeles Times
    25 Oct. 2001. 26 Oct. 2001 <http://www.latimes.com/news/
    nationworld/world/la-102601pakmeet.story>.

4.6. Online Article in a Magazine

Morse, Jodie. "Congress Tries to Tell the Bad Schools from
    the Mediocre." Time 27 July 2001. 26 Oct. 2001 <http://
    www.time.com/time/columnist/morse/article/
    0,9565,169152,00.htm>.

4.7. Online Abstract

Glenn, Melissa J., and Dave G. Mumby. "Place Memory Is Intact
    in Rats with Perirhinal Cortex Lesions." Behavioral
    Neuroscience 112.6 (1998): 1353-65. Abstract. 26 Feb. 1999.
    <http://www.apa.org/journals/bne/1298ab.html#6>.

4.8. Online Article from a Newsletter

Justice, Rod. "Hospital Workers Forget to Wash Hands between
    Patients." In Touch Newsletter 3.4 (2000). In Touch.
    26 October 2001 <http://www.intouchnews.com/
    sample.htm>.

4.9. Posting to a Discussion Group

Kasworm, Evelyn. "A Totally Implantable Artificial Heart." Online
    posting. 15 Oct. 2001. Evening Discussion Group, Div.
    of Medical Ethics of LDS Hospital. 26 Oct. 2001 <http://
    www.med.utah.edu/ethics/index.htm>.

4.10. E-Mail Communication

Dietsch, Betty M. "Note to Instructors." E-mail to Renée Deljon.

25 Oct. 2001.

4.11. Periodical Published on CD-ROM

Many newspapers, magazines, journals and other periodicals can be accessed from databases. Usually source information is provided at the beginning of the file.

Hansen, Robert W. "Stigma, Conflict, and the Approval of AIDS

Drugs." <u>Journal of Drugs</u> (Winter 1995): 129-39. CD-ROM.

UMI-ProQuest. 1995.

4.12. Nonperiodical Publication on CD-ROM

Some nonperiodical databases are published only once with no revisions or updates. Cite nonperiodical CD-ROMs the way you would cite a book but include the publication medium. (Usually, there is a publisher but no vendor.)

<u>1880 United States Census and National Index</u>. CD-ROM. Salt

Lake City: Intellectual Reserve, 2001.

"Making a Will." <u>Family Lawyer</u>. CD-ROM. Hiawatha, IA: Parsons

Technology, 1995.

4.13. Publication on CD-ROM or Diskette

Computer programs, languages, and other software on CD-ROM or diskette may be updated from time to time. For updates, specify the edition, version (if not in the title), or other update. Separate the publication information from the title of the product with a period.

<u>Dr. Solomon's Virex 6.1 for Macintosh</u>. CD-ROM. Sunnyvale, CA:

McAfee.com Corporation, 2001.

Bird, Alan. "TimeOut." <u>Quickspell</u> Diskette. San Diego: Beagle

Bros., 1987.

4.14. Article from an Online Service

To cite an article without a URL found through an online service a library subscribes to, include the author's name, the title of the work, publication information about the printed version (if given), the name of the database underlined (if known), the name of the service, the name of the library, and the date of access. Include the URL of the service's homepage (if known).

> Koehn, Nancy F. "Henry Heinz and Brand Creation in the Late
> Nineteenth Century: Making Markets for Processed Food."
> Business History Review 73.3 (1999): 349+, InfoTrac
> OneFile. InfoTrac. San Francisco Public Lib., 3 May 2002
> <http://infotrac.galegroup.com/>.

4.15. A Work in More Than One Publication Medium

Some stores offer bundles of software in one package. Follow the directions for a nonperiodical CD-ROM (4.12) and list the media in the package.

> Newman, John J. "Ohio." Uncle, We Are Ready! Registering
> America's Men 1917-1918. CD-ROM and book. North Salt,
> Utah: Heritage Quest, 2001.

4.16. Other Electronic Sources

To document other electronic sources, follow the general guidelines for citing print and electronic sources, but change the guidelines appropriately. For example, you may need to add a label such as *map* or *interview* (no quotation marks or underlining).

APA STYLE OF DOCUMENTATION

For research papers in the social and behavioral sciences, many instructors prefer the American Psychological Association (APA) style of documentation. The explanations and examples shown here follow the guidelines in the *Publication Manual of the American Psychological Association*, fifth edition, 2001.

CHAPTER 24 APA STYLE DIRECTORY

SECTION TITLE	PAGE
Parenthetical Citations: APA Style	364
Preparing a Reference List: APA Style	366
A. APA Entries: Periodicals	366
B. APA Entries: Books, Brochures and Government Publications	368
C. APA Entries: Audiovisual Media	371
D. APA Entries: Internet and Other Electronic Sources	372

Parenthetical Citations: APA Style

The APA style keys parenthetical citations in a text to a list of sources. Include the author's last name, the year of publication, the abbreviation for page (*p.* or *pp.* for pages), and the page number. Ampersands (&) are used instead of *and* in a parenthetical citation. *Chapter* is abbreviated *chap.* and *section* is abbreviated *sec.* in parenthical citations.

Single Author   The author's name is usually mentioned in the text, followed by parentheses containing the year of publication and page. If the entire work is cited, no page numbers are needed. If the author is not listed in the text, include the author's last name in the parenthetical citation.

Theodore Bernstein (1958, p. 17) points out that the word *bandit*

"has a flavor of heroism."

Research shows that experienced writers seem to have much

stronger revision habits than do student writers (Sommers, 1980).

Two or More Works by the Same Author   Different works by one author are distinguished by their dates. For multiple references in the same year by one author, add *a*, *b*, or *c* in lowercase letters: 2002a, 2002b, and so forth.

Two or More Authors   For a work with two authors, cite both names every time. For three to five authors, include all names the first time, arranged alphabetically. After that, cite only the first author's name followed by *et al.* For six or more authors, cite only the first author followed by *et al.* for all occurrences.

Rivers, Moss, and Wang (2000) claim. . . .

These findings have been labeled "ridiculous, perhaps

fraudulent" (King & Alberti, 2002, p. 322).

Works by Two Authors with the Same Last Name   Distinguish by using initials: "J. Neff (1999) and C. A. Neff (2000) also found. . . ."

Source with No Author Name Given   For unsigned sources, use an abbreviated version of the title. Place article titles in quotation marks, and underline or italicize book and pamphlet titles: "Timber Wolves," 2002), (*Recycling*, 1991).

Groups as Authors   In general, give the name of the group in full each time you cite it. If the name is long, abbreviate it in subsequent citations.

First reference: (American Association of Retired People [AARP],

2002)

Later references: (AARP, 2002)

Secondary Source   If you are citing an author quoted by another author, precede the secondary source with the phrase *as cited in*.

Jameson's findings (as cited in Baure & Dinks, 2001, p. 124).

Two or More Sources in One Citation   List alphabetically by authors' last names, separated by semicolons: (Adams, 2000; Coates & Tan, 2001; Martiniu, 1998). If citations include two works by the same author, list the dates, separated by commas: (Wiggins, 1989, 1991).

Personal Communications   E-mail, personal interviews, letters, and the like are cited only in the text, not on the reference list.

According to the hospital's chief administrator, the procedure is

no longer performed there (J. A. Wells, personal communication,

May 28, 2001).

Long Quotations   Quotations of forty words or more are double spaced and set off, indented five spaces. The parenthetical citation is placed one space after the final punctuation.

Moskos (2000) summarizes the argument well:

> The principal argument raised against linking national
>
> service and federal educational aid is that it would have a
>
> regressive effect. . . . Students from wealthy families who do
>
> not need aid would be unaffected, while poor students would
>
> have to enter national service in order to get aid. (p. 380)

PREPARING A REFERENCE LIST: APA STYLE

Preparing a reference list is tricky, so keep the models and general guidelines below handy. Double check the order of entries, punctuation, capitalization, parentheses, and brackets in each entry. All references cited in the text, except personal communication, belong in the reference list. Here are general guidelines for the format:

- Type *Reference List*, centered, at the top of the page.
- Double space entries.
- Alphabetize entries according to the authors' last names or, when no author is listed, the first major word of the title. Use initials and the surname. Omit suffixes such as *Jr.*
- After the author's name, enclose the date of publication (year, month, day) in parentheses, followed by a period.
- Do not indent the first line of each entry. Indent subsequent lines five spaces.
- Italicize the title of periodicals, volume numbers, and book titles. If your keyboard lacks an italicizing function, underline.
- Place nonroutine information that is necessary to identify and recover a source in brackets after the article title.
- Use arabic numerals for volume (e.g., 4, not IV). Retain roman numerals that are part of a title.

A. APA ENTRIES: PERIODICALS

Since entries for articles vary, check each item carefully after you type it, comparing it with the correct model in this section. Proofread again when you are fresh. The guidelines below will help you type your entries correctly.

- Capitalize only the first word of an article title or subtitle and proper nouns.
- Do not enclose article titles in quotation marks.
- Use an ampersand (&) instead of *and* when listing two or more authors.
- Italicize the name of the journal or magazine and the volume number. Omit *vol.*
- Spell out months.
- To list pages of newspapers, abbreviate as *p.* or *pp.*
- Place a range of pages at the end. Omit *p.* or *pp.* for references to journal and magazine articles.

1. Journal Article with Two Authors and Continuous Paging

Invert the names of both authors:

Luna, B., & Funglar, M. N. (2001, October 24/31). Drug-induced hyperglycemia. *Journal of the American Medical Association, 286*(16), 1945-1948.

Three to six authors: List all the names in a series.
More than six authors: List six names, then *et al.,* set off by a comma.

2. Journal Article with Each Issue Paged Separately

Include issue numbers in parentheses after the volume number with no space between: *7*(3).

Togger, D. A., & Breaner, P. S. (2001, October). Metered dose inhalers. *American Journal of Nursing, 101*(10), 26-32.

3. Magazine Article

Begley, S., & Isikuff, M. (2001, October 22). Anxious about anthrax. *Newsweek,* 28-35.

4. Anonymous Article

Dill soothes an upset tummy. (2001, July/August). *Organic Gardening,* 13.

5. Daily Newspaper Article Continued to Other Pages

Armour, S. (2001, October 30). Tough times for laid-off, low-income workers. *USA Today,* pp. 1A, 2A.

6. Newsletter Article

Guthrie, L. (2001, October). Cemetery report. *Ohio Genealogical Society Newsletter, 32*(10), 168-169.

7. Editorial

After the article title, place nonroutine information necessary for identification in brackets.

> Maxwell, B. (2001, October 26). The messenger takes a pounding [Editorial]. *The Marion Star,* p. A6.

8. Letter to the Editor

> Cooper, B. A. (2001, October 16). Limit trucks but not traffic [Letter to the editor]. *The Washington Post,* p. A22.

9. Abstract and Review from a Secondary Source (print periodical)

In scholarly research cite primary sources when possible (also see example 16). If an abstract has no review, omit *Review by*.

> Monti, Daniel, J. (1999). *The American city: A social and cultural history.* Review by J. C. Schneider (2001) in *Journal of American History, 87,* 1537-1538. Abstract and review obtained from *Book Review Digest, 2001, 97*(6), 157.

B. APA ENTRIES: BOOKS, BROCHURES, AND GOVERNMENT PUBLICATIONS

Entries for books include author, date, title, place of publication (city and state), and publisher. Use all the names in a publishing company (Simon & Schuster, not just Simon), but don't include *Publishing Company, Inc.* and other nonessential words. Retain *Books* and *Press.*

- Capitalize only the first word of the title and of the subtitle, as well as proper nouns.
- Use initials and the surname.
- Spell out the names of associations and university presses: National Audubon Society, Oxford University Press.
- Do not invert the names of editors. Identify the editor by (Ed.) after the surname.
- Italicize book titles (or underline if you lack that function). Do not enclose article or chapter titles in quotation marks.

10. A Book by One Author

> Clarke, C. A. (2000). *The collected stories of Arthur C. Clarke.* New York: Tom Doherty Associates.

11. Two or More Books by One Author

Books by the same author are listed according to date, from least to most recent. The author's name is repeated in each subsequent entry.

Goldberg, N. (1986). *Writing down the bones: Freeing the writer within.* Boston: Shambhala.

Goldberg, N. (1990). *Wild mind: Living the writer's life.* New York: Random.

12. A Book by Two or More Authors

Musciano, C., & Kennedy, B. (2000). *HTML & XHTML: The definitive guide* (4th ed.). Sebastopol, CA: O'Reilly.

13. A Book by an Unknown Author

Go Ask Alice. (1971). New York: Prentice-Hall.

14. Book, Revised or Later Edition

Figler, H. (1999). *The complete job-search handbook: Everything you need to know to get the job you really want* (2nd ed.). Buffalo: Firefly Books.

15. Article or Chapter in a Book

Cite the inclusive pages of the article or chapter in parentheses after the book title.

Ryan, T. (2001). Such a thing as destiny. In *The prize winner of Defiance, Ohio* (pp. 283-289). New York: Simon & Schuster.

16. A Work in an Anthology

If you consult one book of a multivolume set, capitalize the volume number (Vol. 5) and place it after the volume title without parentheses. The example below is for a single-volume anthology:

Maddox, J., & Maddox, R. (1989). How we got over. In L. Goss & M. E. Barnes (Eds.), *Talk that talk: An anthology of African American storytelling* (pp. 117-125). New York: Random House.

17. Published Interview

Begin with the name of the person interviewed and the date of the interview, then the title (if any), and the identifying information in brackets. Complete the entry by placing information identifying the source according to the guidelines for books (or periodicals, if the interview appeared in periodically published source).

> MacLeish, A. (1974, Summer). "Archibald MacLeish." [Interview with Benjamin De Mott]. In G. Plimpton (Ed.) (1988), *Writers at work: The Paris review interviews, 5* (pp. 23-48). New York: Penguin.

18. Review

> Applebaum, H. A. (1980) Looking at work from a social anthropological perspective [Review of the book *Social anthropology of work*]. *Current Anthropology, 21,* 307-308.

19. Dictionary or Encyclopedia

If a major reference work has a large editorial board, you may cite only the name of the executive editor and follow it with "et al." as in the first example.

Single Volume with Several Editors

> Pickett, J.P., et al. (Eds.). (2000). *The American heritage dictionary of the English language* (4th ed.). Boston: Houghton Mifflin.

No Author Given

> The Civil War. (1995). In *Encyclopedia Americana* (Vol. 6, pp. 782-819), Danbury, CT: Grolier.

20. Chapter in a Volume in a Series

> Moore, W. E. (1969). Social structure and behavior. In G. Lindzey & E. Aronson (Eds.), *The handbook of social psychology:* Vol. 4. *Group psychology and phenomena of interaction* (2nd ed., pp. 283-322). Reading, MA: Addison-Wesley.

21. Brochure, Corporate Author

Start with the publisher; then give the date and title. Identify the publication in brackets. List the place and author.

Personal Training Systems. (1992). *The official audio guide to Quicken for Macintosh* [Brochure]. San Jose, CA: Author.

22. Government Publications with a Group Author

Health Care Financing Administration. (2001). *Medicare & You 2001.* Washington, DC: U.S. Government Printing Office.

U.S. Department of Justice. (2001). *FBI National Academy Directory of Graduates 2001 Edition.* Quantico, VA: FBI Academy.

C. APA ENTRIES: AUDIOVISUAL MEDIA

For broadcast, film, and recorded sources, enclose in *parentheses* the contributing personnel and the date. Place the medium [Motion picture] or [Television broadcast] in *brackets*.

23. Motion Pictures

Indicate the specific medium in brackets. Include the city and producing organization, if available.

Newel, M. (Director), & Barnes, P. (Screenwriter). (1992). *Enchanted April* [Motion picture]. Burbank, CA: Warner Brothers.

24. Television Broadcasts

Identify a series of broadcasts in brackets [Television series] or give the number of episodes and transcript information, if available.

Schama, S. (Writer, narrator, & producer). (2001, October 29). The body of the queen [Television series, 5 episodes]. *A history of Britain.* Columbus, OH: The History Channel.

Shaw, B. (Reporter). (1999, July 1). Clinton's boom era not as turbulent as LBJ's [Television broadcast, transcript]. *Inside politics.* Atlanta: CNN.

25. Music and Audio Recordings

When referring to specific lyrics or compositions, begin with the lyricist/composer, followed by the original copyright date. Then provide recording information, including the date, if it is different from the copyright date. Or if appropriate, begin with the performer, conductor, or title. For nonmusical recordings, start with the original writer's name (if provided) or with the title. Include the medium and the number in brackets.

> Blitzstein, M. (1941). In the clear [Recorded by D. Upshaw]. On
>
> *I wish it so* [CD]. New York: Elektra Entertainment. (1994)
>
> *Official audio guide to Quicken.* (1992). [Cassette recording no.
>
> IQU4.00M-1-A]. San Jose, CA: Personal Training Systems.

D. APA ENTRIES: INTERNET AND OTHER ELECTRONIC SOURCES

When an Internet entry has a printed source, cite the print information (see examples 1–24) before online information. Provide the author, date of online publication, and sponsor of the site when possible. These three guidelines will be helpful:

- Place *Retrieved from* and the date before the URL. Do not use angle brackets or add a period.
- When no date is available, use (n.d.).
- Split URLs only at slash [/] marks.

Note that many types of electronic sources can be stored on an aggregated database. This term refers to a single searchable database with many parts. Basically, the database combines words with pictures and/or numbers. Whether you access information from a database stored on a CD-ROM, loaded onto a college or library server, or available on the Internet, you need to attach a retrieval statement to your entry.

First, identify the work, using the appropriate format. Then indicate where the source was *Retrieved from*, the date it was retrieved, and the name of the database. If there is an item or access number, place it at the end of the entry in parentheses. If you access the database online, also provide a URL that links to its main search page.

Internet Articles Based on a Print Source

If the print version has been unchanged on the Internet, no retrieval statement is necessary. Just add [Electronic version] after the article title. If page numbers are not given or if the format differs from the print version, add a retrieval statement with the date and URL.

Periodicals on the Internet

26. Article in a Journal

Parrott, A. C. (1999, October). Does cigarette smoking cause stress? [Electronic version] *American Psychologist, 54,* 817-820.

27. Article in a Magazine

Morse, J. (2001, July 27). Congress tries to tell the bad schools from the mediocre. *Time.* Retrieved November 3 from http://www.time.com/time/columnist/morse/article/ 0,9565,169152,00 htm

28. Article in a Newspaper

Tempest, R., & Boudreaux, R. (2001, October 25). Exiles support lead role for ex-king in post-Taliban era. *Los Angeles Times.* Retrieved October 26, 2001, from http://www.latimes.com/ news/nationworld/world/la-102601pakmeet.story

29. Article in an Internet-Only Newsletter

Justice, R. (n.d.) Hospital workers forget to wash hands between patients. *In Touch Newsletter.* Retrieved October 26, 2001, from http://www.intouchnews.com/sample.htm

30. Abstract

Glenn, M. J., & Mumby, D. G. (1998). Place memory is intact in rats with perirhinal cortex lesions. *Behavioral Neuroscience, 112,* 1353-1365. Abstract retrieved February 26, 1999, from http://www.apa.org/journals/bne/1298ab.html#6

Nonperiodical Documents on the Internet

31. Chapter or Section in an Internet Document

The book below was originally published in 1878. The online source is based on Harper's 1892 edition.

James, Henry. (1878) Part I. *Daisy Miller.* New York: Harper (1892).
Retrieved November 1, 2001, from http://
www.newpaltz.edu/~hathaway/daisyO.html

32. Online Anthology

Frost, R. (n.d.) "Mending Wall." *Modern American Poetry.*
C. Nelson (Ed.). Retrieved November 2, 2001, from Oxford
University Press Web site http://www.english.uluc.edu/
maps/poets/a_f/frost/wall.htm

33. Collection of Short Stories from a Book

Sawyer, R. J. Gators. (1997). In J. Sherman, & K. R. DiCandido
(Eds.) *Urban Nightmares.* Bronx: Baen. Retrieved
November 2, 2001, from http://www.sfwriter.com/
stgator.htm

34. Document Available on University Program or Department Web Site

Ward, H. (1999, May 18). The Story of Bessie Costrell. (1895). In
P. Willett (Ed.) *Victorian Women Writers Project.* Retrieved
June 11, 1999, from Indiana University Web site http://
www.indiana.edu/~letrs/vwwp/ward/bessie.html

35. Online Encyclopedia

Wild rice. (2001). *The Columbia electronic encyclopedia* (6th ed.).
Retrieved October 25, 2001, from http://
www.encyclopedia.com

36. Professional or Personal Site

Hopkins Information Technology Services. Home page. Retrieved
    October 26, 2001, from Johns Hopkins University Web site
    http://webapps.jhu.edu/hitswebsite/

Barbour, D. (2001, January 7) *Dennis Barbour useful links.* Online
    directory. Retrieved October 26, 2001, from http://
    www.hme.jhu.edu/~dbarbour/links.html

37. Message posted to an Online Forum or Discussion Group

Kasworm, E. (2000, October 15). A totally implantable artificial
    heart. Message posted to http://www.med.utah.edu/ethics/

38. E-Mail

Online correspondence between individuals is cited as *personal communication* in the text of your paper only, as shown below. List the initials of the sender and the exact date.

(C. M. Smith, personal communication, May 1, 2002)

Nonperiodical Publications on CD-ROM

Cite nonperiodical CD-ROMs the way you would cite a book title and author. Include the publisher and disc or item number (if there is one).

39. CD-ROMs

The example below refers to one disc of a set of CD-ROMs that is available at many public libraries. Since the sets are stored on the premises, there is no URL.

1880 United States Census and National Index. (2001). Retrieved
    November 1, 2001, from Family Search Family History
    Resource File [CD-ROM]. Salt Lake City, UT: Intellectual
    Reserve.

40. Daily Newspaper Article, Electronic Version Available by Search

Harlin, Kevin. (n.d.). Students develop 'smart parking' system. *New York Times*. Retrieved November 4, 2001, from http://www.nytimes.com

41. Material from an Electronic Database

Koehn, Nancy F. (1999). Henry Heinz and brand creation in the late nineteenth century: Making markets for processed food. *Business History Review 73*(3), 349+. Retrieved May 3, 2002, from *InfoTrac OneFile* database.

42. Computer Software and Computer Programs

Schulman, R., Schrader, J., & Jacobs, J. (1999). *Quicken Deluxe 99* [Computer software]. Menlo Park, CA: Intuit.

Summary

Accurate and complete documentation is essential both in the workplace and in college. The primary purpose of documentation is to supply source information for the reader and to give credit to the author. When material is borrowed without providing documentation, the offense is plagiarism.

Different styles of documentation are used for research papers. MLA documentation style requires a list of works cited that provides complete bibliographic information for each source used. Within the paper, parenthetical citations key each source to its works cited entry. Formats for entries vary according to the kind of work.

Both the MLA and APA styles use hanging indention. But APA parenthetical citations and source entries differ from those of the MLA in significant ways. Moreover, the APA list of sources is titled "References," and electronic entries require a retrieval statement.

To provide accurate and complete documentation, follow the required style guide carefully, using the correct model for each entry. Devote extra care to URLs.

Key Terms

aggregated database	document (v.)	parenthetical citation
APA style	documentation	plagiarism
bibliographic note	hanging indention	reference list
content note	MLA style	works cited

Practice

Recognizing Items That Need to Be Documented

Directions: Go to a library or use some of your own materials to create examples of entries for an MLA style list of works cited or an APA style reference list. Follow the textbook models carefully, checking format and punctuation.

1. Book by two or three authors
2. Book with an editor or editors
3. A work in an anthology by several authors
4. Book with several volumes
5. Article from a daily newspaper
6. Article from a monthly magazine
7. Article from a journal with continuous paging
8. Videotape
9. One author quoting another author
10. Internet source: published newspaper, magazine, or journal article
11. Internet source: article from a professional Web site

CHAPTER 25

Using Sources and Writing a Research Paper

I have lived in this world just long enough to look carefully the second time into things that I am the most certain of the first time.

—Josh Billings (1818–1885)
(Henry Wheeler Shaw)

See chapter 21.

See "The Logical Appeal," page 245.

Research can be scientific investigation, as in primary research, or scholarly inquiry, as in secondary research. Both kinds require a fair and thorough consideration of existing facts before reaching a conclusion. When doing any research, be open to new evidence even if it conflicts with what you believe. Withhold judgment until you have examined the facts, noted inferences, and labeled theories. Otherwise, expensive mistakes may be made.

WORKPLACE CASE STUDY

TRACKING THE TRUTH

As an employee was leaving a plant, security guards stopped him to search his briefcase. They found a $35 telephone. Assuming he had stolen the phone, the company fired him. Notices were placed on eleven bulletin boards and the electronic mail system, saying the phone was company property and the employee had violated work rule number 12 about theft. The employee filed suit against the company for libel.

At the trial a coworker testified to going with the defendant to a mall where he had purchased the phone. The defendant explained that his company phone had been damaged by a flood. But he had lost the sales slip for the new phone. His boss had said to just keep the phone. After the firing, the man had applied for a hundred jobs, but was rejected each time it was learned why he had been fired. The jury awarded the defendant $1.3 million in damages. The moral of this story is that an open mind is a prerequisite to tracking the truth.

RESEARCH READING

Reading for research, if you are absorbed in your topic, can be just as engrossing as the latest best-seller. By reading widely, you can gain not only a comprehensive view of your topic but also knowledge of the latest discoveries in a field. Research reading, however, requires an organized, analytical approach that reflects your purpose. At some points you need to be critical.

Examining Dates and Credentials

As new knowledge is discovered, previous knowledge may become dated. As you read, examine the dates of surveys, studies, and other research as well as the credentials of the writers and researchers. To find this background information, check the home page of a Web site and the preface, introduction, or any footnotes of printed materials.

CHECKLIST FOR EXAMINING SOURCES AND CREDENTIALS

1. Is the source primary or secondary? Is enough documentation provided?

2. Does the author/researcher have advanced degrees, licenses or certification, and a fine reputation in the field?

3. When was the study, poll, or other research conducted? Where? What was the size of the sample?

4. Does the interpretation of results seem logical? Does the language seem objective? Or does the writer seem to have a hidden agenda? For example, a nutritionist on a radio talk show recommended a vitamin preparation that he had invented.

5. Has other research reported similar or conflicting results? What do authorities in the field generally accept?

Using Tentative Words to Discuss Findings and Theories

The rhetorical situation of a research paper requires more precision in word choice than that of a less formal paper. As you read reputable accounts of polls, experiments, and studies, notice the tentative, or provisional, words that qualify discussions of results. These *uncertain* words indicate that evidence is *not* conclusive even though a growing body of research may indicate a conclusion or theory is probably true. Look at how the journal *Science* uses tentative words

TENTATIVE WORDS COMMONLY USED IN RESEARCH		
Verbs	*Nouns*	*Phrases*
indicates	indication	probable cause
found	findings	possible influence
may	possibility	apparently is
reported	report	is often a sign of
suggest	suggestion	could indicate
influence	influence	suggests that
theorize	theory	
imply	implication	
seems	symptoms	
appears	appearance	

(italicized here) to discuss results of several studies about the cause of perfect pitch:

> A research team from Düsseldorf, Germany, *may* have located the physical basis of one exceptional form of mental performance: perfect pitch—the ability to identify any musical note without comparison to a reference note. . . .
> A team led by neurologists Gottfried Schlaug and Helmuth Steinmetz of Düsseldorf's Heinrich Heine University *reports* that the planum temporale, a region of the brain cortex that processes sound signals, is far larger on the left side than on the right in professional musicians—and especially in those who have perfect pitch.

Overstatement undermines the credibility of research. Yet beginning writers sometimes assume that because a study or experiment *suggests* that something is true, it is, indeed, true. By the time they summarize their research notes, they have catapulted theory into the realm of fact. Often one word, *prove*, is what launches this assault upon truth. To discuss uncertain research findings competently, qualify your statements with tentative words. Use accurate terminology; examples are listed in the box.

Recognizing Information That Must Be Acknowledged

The rhetorical situation of a secondary research paper requires that the majority of what you write will be based on outside sources. Careless noting of sources can result in unintentional plagiarism. Perhaps knowing that the Latin *plagiarius* means "kidnapper" will remind you not to kidnap absentmindedly any original words. The penalties for this offense can be severe (see chapter 24). Take care in gathering all of the source information needed for parenthetical citations and works cited entries.

Restating Common Knowledge   Factual information that is familiar to the general public is considered common knowledge. For example, it is common knowledge that orange juice is high in vitamin C, that Thomas A. Edison perfected the incandescent lightbulb, and that Alfred Hitchcock directed suspense films. So if you come across such facts in your research, you will not be expected to acknowledge the source for them—*unless you decide to quote the source directly.* If you copy an author's words, you need to enclose them in quotation marks and cite the source. In your early efforts at research, it is best to cite the source of any piece of information that you were unaware of before your reading.

Acknowledging Everything Else   Practically all other information gathered in research requires documentation. Here is a list of items to watch for so that you can make a source card for each item:

- Historical information that is not commonly known
- Current information based on a writer's direct observation or reporting
- Statistics
- Surveys and opinion poll results. Give the researcher, date, place, size of sample, and any other pertinent information in the text of the paper if possible.
- Research results and interpretations. Give names of researchers, date.
- Expert opinion, estimates, predictions
- Theories. Identify the person who originated the theory, if possible.
- Artistic interpretations or criticisms
- Tables, charts, graphs, and other visual material
- Any statement that is subject to debate
- Footnote from printed material

Stating Your Own Ideas and Conclusions   If you combine primary research with secondary research, then you describe your findings in detail. You offer a logical interpretation of the evidence, taking into consideration the opinions of authorities. To start thinking, you might ask yourself, *"Why are the findings significant? What does it all mean? What are the implications?"* As a rule, informative secondary research papers by freshmen do not include personal opinion or reactions. If you are unclear on this point, be sure to ask your instructor.

A paper based on observation or a survey alone does not require a list of sources, but a series of interviews would need a list of sources. When primary and secondary research are both used, the source entries can be combined into one list.

See chapters 22 and 24.

TIPS FOR COMPILING A LIST OF SOURCES

- Start making source cards early. Note the author, publication, date, page numbers, or other source information.
- To make entries, find the correct model in chapter 24. Check the order and punctuation of each entry you construct.
- As you add more parenthetical citations to your paper, make a new source entry for each citation unless the source already has an entry.
- *Alphabetize* source cards before typing your list of sources.
- Double-space entries when typing your list of sources for your paper.

NOTE-TAKING, SUMMARIZING, PARAPHRASING, AND QUOTING

Take care to preserve the meaning of the original passage as you take notes, summarize, paraphrase, and quote. Distinguish fact from opinion. Transcribe numbers and other figures correctly. With thought and care, you can avoid four common problems in student research papers:

- pulling ideas out of context
- omitting significant information
- overuse of quotations
- inadequate documentation

An informative freshman research paper is usually expected to consist mainly of summary. Paraphrase appears at times, and short direct quotations are sprinkled at appropriate intervals. One or more long direct quotations may be used, depending on the assignment and the material. An example of an informative research paper appears at the end of this chapter. To see researched arguments, turn to chapter 19.

Note-Taking and Critical Reading

The most important requirement as you take notes, either in the margins of photocopies or on note cards, is to *insert quotation marks around any material that you intend to copy into your research paper or report.* This chapter explains how to integrate quotations into a paper as well as use ellipsis, brackets, and explanatory notes. For extensive help with note-taking, commenting, and reacting to ideas, see "Critical Reading" in chapter 26. The handbook provides grammar rules and examples, pages H-23 to H-39.

For sentence patterns, see chapter 8.

Summarizing

A summary condenses and restates. To summarize, you extract the main ideas of a passage and *convert them into your own words and sentence patterns*. You reduce the passage—perhaps several paragraphs or even several pages—by 50 to 75 percent. To focus on the main ideas of an original, reword the topic sentences. Use synonyms to replace major words (nouns, verbs, adjectives, and adverbs) and combine lesser ideas. Restructure sentences, retaining only the gist of the material.

Minor words such as articles (*a, an, the*), prepositions, and conjunctions may be repeated from the original if necessary to preserve the meaning. A thesaurus and dictionary can help you quickly find synonyms to replace the author's words. Examples of summary, paraphrase, and quotation follow. The original example is a story that has become a classic, involving a horse thought to have the ability to communicate with people.

Original

Herr von Osten purchased a horse in Berlin, Germany, in 1900. When von Osten began training his horse, Hans, to count by tapping his front hoof, he had no idea that Hans was soon to become one of the most celebrated horses in history. Hans was a rapid learner and soon progressed from counting to addition, multiplication, division, subtraction, and eventually the solution of problems involving factors and fractions. As if this were not enough, von Osten exhibited Hans to public audiences where he counted the number in the audience or simply the number of people wearing eyeglasses. Still responding only with taps, Hans could tell time, use a calendar, display an ability to recall musical pitch, and perform numerous other seemingly fantastic feats. After von Osten taught Hans an alphabet which could be coded into hoof beats, the horse could answer virtually any question—oral or written. It seemed that Hans, a common horse, had complete comprehension of the German language, the ability to produce the equivalent of words and numerals, and an intelligence beyond that of many human beings.

Mark L. Knapp
—Nonverbal Communication in Human Interaction

Summary

Mark L. Knapp tells an amazing story of a horse owned by Herr von Osten of Germany in the early 1900s. His owner taught Hans to do arithmetic, drummed out with a front hoof. Then von Osten began showing the horse in public, where Hans computed the total of persons with spectacles and did other tricks. He seemed to have learned the alphabet, for he could tap out a response to most queries. Many people were convinced Hans knew German well. In fact, he appeared brighter than many people (1).

The summary, less than half as long as the original, makes essentially the same points. Note that the source is clearly identified in the first sentence of the summary. At the end, the page number of Knapp's passage is placed in parentheses *before* the period. Synonyms replace major words that are not *generic* (the name of a category). Generic words such as *horse*, *musical pitch*, and *alphabet* have no close synonyms. Therefore they are included without quotation marks. (Don't assume that a word is generic; check in a dictionary. For example, Kleenex is not generic; *facial tissue* is generic.)

In the example of plagiarism below, major words have been copied when they should not have been. In addition, variations of major words have been used. For instance, Knapp writes "began training," and the unacceptable example uses "trained." The plagiarized portions are underlined.

Plagiarized Summary

According to Mark L. Knapp, in 1900 in Berlin, Germany, Herr von Osten *purchased* a horse. *When von Osten trained* the horse to *count* by rapping his hoof, he did not know that Hans would *become one of* the most famous horses *in history*. Hans was a *rapid learner and soon* could do arithmetic and other tricks. *After Herr von Osten taught Hans a coded alphabet, it seemed* Hans, a horse, understood German well and knew more than many people (1).

Paraphrasing

See chapter 8.

Paraphrase, which is longer than summary, is the restatement of an original passage. To paraphrase, *reword and use different sentence patterns*. Retain the meaning of the original; do not distort. Look up words that you do not know. As you paraphrase, take care to select accurate synonyms, not variations of the original words. For example, if an author uses *defend*, do not write *defending*. Find another word such as *protect*. Use paraphrase for the following reasons:

- **To emphasize important ideas.** Use paraphrase for significant points that will support your rhetorical purpose.
- **To clarify a difficult passage.** Reword and make ideas clearer.
- **To combine details.** You may want to condense lesser ideas.

If a passage seems impossible to paraphrase, you can include a few brief quotations, as in the following example, which might have been awkward to paraphrase. Note that even if you do not use a quotation, you still need to give the page number and make a works cited entry.

Paraphrase

To explain how animals "read" nonverbal signals, Mark L. Knapp tells a strange story of a horse bought by Herr von Osten in Berlin, Germany. While teaching the horse, Hans, to rap out numbers with a fore hoof, von Osten did not suspect that the animal would ever become famous. But Hans learned so fast that he could soon do arithmetic. When von Osten showed Hans in public, the horse "counted the number of people wearing eyeglasses." He could even "tell time," read a calendar, remember musical pitch, and do other tricks. When von Osten drilled the horse in the alphabet, tapped out with a hoof, Hans responded to almost any query. He appeared not only to understand German well, but also to know more than many people (1).

GUIDELINES: WRITING SUMMARIES AND PARAPHRASES

1. Read the entire original carefully several times so that you are sure you understand it completely. If you can mark the original, underline the topic sentences and key points for ease of reference.

2. Rewrite, retaining the order of the original. Changes in order may distort meaning.

3. Reread the original. Check to see that you have not changed the order or unwittingly copied material that should be paraphrased.

4. If you are unable to paraphrase difficult phrases, copy and enclose in quotation marks.

5. For a summary, reduce material by 50 percent or more. Paraphrase topic sentences, quoting key terms as needed. Restate major points. Combine and condense related ideas. Omit examples and minor details.

6. Cite source and pages.

7. Checkpoint. Is the summary or paraphrase clear? Has all important information been included? Are all spellings correct?

Using Quotations

Quotation is a respected practice that is used by educators, researchers, and other writers. Appropriate quotation in a research paper indicates responsible writing. Below are five reasons that you might include quotations. (The examples are from *The Writer*, January 2001.)

1. **To present technical words for which there is no accurate paraphrase.** Quoting the exact words prevents misunderstanding. In "Selling Your Work Online," Emily Vander Veer points out a new term:

   Stephen King single-handedly catapulted the term "e-publishing" into the mainstream last March when over half a million readers logged onto their computer and downloaded electronic copies of his novella *Riding the Bullet*.

2. **To allay any doubt about the accuracy of a surprising statement or evidence.** By giving the exact words, you avert the reader's suspicion. In "Take the Reader Along," Martha Sutro quotes a paradoxical truism to illustrate the risks that authors take in pitching their work to editors:

   Throughout the process, I remembered a helpful adage: "You have to increase your rate of failure in order to increase your rate of success." You have to be willing to put yourself out there.

3. **To capture the flavor of the original.** Paraphrase will often not do justice to a passage that is vivid and unusual. Aly Colón opens "Avoid the Pitfalls of Plagiarism" by quoting a distinctive phrase:

> Plagiarism is the "unoriginal sin," writes writing coach Roy Peter Clark, a senior scholar at the Poynter Institute, in an article first published in the March 1983 issue of *Washington Journalism Review*. And it seems to be a very common sin.

4. **To avoid an awkward or wordy paraphrase.** Do not abuse this privilege, however. Keep such quotations brief. Here Colón quotes a list of criteria rather than attempting to paraphrase it. Because the material is identified and indented, no quotation marks are required. It is treated as a long quotation:

> • Was there intent? Did the writer intend to pass the work off as his or her own?
>
> • If there was no intent, then did the writer's work habits and methods lead to unintended replication?

5. **To enhance your credibility as a writer.** By including quotations appropriately, you demonstrate professionalism.

Use quotations for a purpose. Keep most quotations brief, according to your assignment and the difficulty of the material. Technical material may require more quotation than usual.

Making Changes in Quotations

Your readers expect that what you enclose in quotation marks will be the exact words of the original source. Yet some quotations may be lengthy and wordy. To shorten a quotation, you may omit unnecessary words and replace them with an ellipsis as long as the meaning is not changed.

Ellipsis   An ellipsis (a set of three spaced dots) can replace wordy or irrelevant material you wish to omit at the beginning, middle, or end of a sentence. The result should still be a complete sentence. The example below, an excerpt from a *Wall Street Journal* article entitled "Chemicals Bad for Ozone Are Declining," by Amal Kumar Naj, shows an ellipsis:

> "Dr. Montzka said the measurements . . . make it possible to predict when the ozone layer will recover. He said the rate of recovery will depend on stratospheric temperature and chemical emissions from volcanoes" (B4).

To omit an entire sentence or more, use four dots. (The fourth dot is the period.) If you omit material and use an ellipsis, take care not to distort the meaning. (The example above shows the traditional MLA recommendations. If, however, your instructor wishes you to follow the latest MLA style, see the Handbook section of this text.)

Brackets   If you need to add something to a quotation for clarity or logic, you can insert the explanatory words within brackets [ ]. Originally, the paragraph below used *he*, which has been replaced with the name of the researcher:

> "Barring unusual changes in temperature and emissions, [Dr. Montzka] estimated that it will take 50 to 60 years before the Earth's ozone layer is restored to the levels before 1970."

When the verb tense of a quotation differs from the text of your paper, you can resolve this inconsistency by substituting another tense in brackets. In the example below, the original was written in the present tense. For the sake of logic, two changes to the past tense (in brackets) replace the original wording.

> Farley Mowat describes the clothes of the Ihalmiut, a tribe that became extinct in the 1950s, as "two suits of fur, worn one over the other. . . . The inner suit [was] worn with the hair of the hides facing inward and touching the skin while the outer suit [had] its hair turned out to the weather" (422).

Once in a while, you may find an error in grammar or spelling in one of your sources. To indicate that you are reproducing the original error rather than creating one of your own, you may insert the Latin word *sic* ("thus") in brackets after the error, as shown after this grammatical mishap:

> An example of the radical nature of the organization is this advice from a pamphlet it published: "Thieves should be punished by having there [*sic*] hands cut off."

Keep in mind, however, that some words have two or more correct spellings. It is always a good idea to check two dictionaries to be sure a word is actually misspelled or misused.

Quotation within a Quotation   When your source contains a quotation, change the double quotation marks in the original to single marks (' '). Then enclose the full quotation in double quotation marks, as shown below:

> In *Strictly Speaking* Edwin Newman writes: "Most conversation these days is as pleasing to the ear as a Flash-Frozen Dinner is to the palate, consisting largely of 'You've got to be kidding,' 'It's a bad scene,' 'How does that grab you?' 'Just for openers . . .'" (16).

MAKING A WORKING OUTLINE

Once you have completed the bulk of your research and note-taking, you can use your note cards to start a working outline. A simple way to start is to classify your note cards. Sort through the cards according to subject and place related items in piles. Then examine each pile and label it with a category under which all items will fit. After that, organize the categories into a possible order. If you become puzzled, ask yourself questions as you draft your outline.

QUESTIONS FOR DEVELOPING A THESIS AND AN OUTLINE

1. *What is the purpose of the paper?* How can I make the purpose clear?
2. *What are the main points of my research?*
3. *What thesis can serve as an umbrella for all the main points?* Do I have irrelevant material? Do I need to narrow the topic?
4. *Is chronological order visible anywhere?* Are there historical items to place in chronological order? Might they make an interesting introduction or should they come later? Will the overall order be chronological or just the introduction?
5. *How should the body of the paper be organized?* Should main points be arranged according to importance? Or should they go from concrete to abstract? Or would some other order, possibly problem solving, work best?
6. *Does the material seem comprehensive?* Are there significant gaps? Do I need more information to be complete?

When you are comfortable with a tentative order, number your note cards and copy the categories and subcategories into outline form. Leave spaces for adding items. By the end of the writing process, your working outline will have become a formal outline, ready for submission along with your paper, if required. (An example of an outline submitted with a student paper appears near the end of this chapter.)

DRAFTING A RESEARCH PAPER

As you begin to draft, keep in mind that your working outline is subject to change. In the course of getting your thoughts on paper, you may make slight changes or even find a different organization emerging. If so, take the time to rethink your working outline before continuing to draft.

Drafting a Thesis and Introduction

The sooner you can state a clear thesis, the sooner you can begin to organize and draft your research paper. If you are uncertain, reexamine your controlling question and rewrite it as a thesis statement. Or you might prefer to draft the introduction as a whole unit rather than in pieces. You may even find that your thesis has mushroomed out over several sentences as in Wilma Dunnington's introduction. Although her purpose is clearly informative, there is no one thesis sentence:

The Genome Project

Probably few readers can imagine a time when genetic profiles would be used as a basis for marriage or divorce, a time when genetic testing would be required by employers to screen applicants. It is easier to envision a world where children "diagnosed with cystic fibrosis would be spared their fate by a gene transplant," a world where cancers would be revealed and treated before a single cancer cell could grow (Bishop and Waldholz 22). These are the "threats and promises" of what could be the "most ambitious scientific research project ever undertaken" (22). The Human Genome Project is an effort to identify all of the genes in the human body.

In *Principles of Anatomy and Physiology*, Tortora and Anagnostakos report that the Human Genome Project will take an estimated fifteen years and cost three billion dollars. The overriding goal of the project is to "conquer genetic disease" (953). Marwick points out that in the human body are more than 100 thousand genes. Occasionally, a gene is injured, resulting in "abnormal features or disorders." Sometimes an embryo will not grow; other times children are born with defects. Some conditions caused by a damaged gene may not be apparent until a person becomes aged (3247).

Possible effects

Definition

Main goal

Explanation

Another way to begin an introduction is with a definition of a special term, followed by a brief history and explanation. Note, too, that Kathy Rummer includes a statement of purpose.

Dr. Nightingale: Nurse Practitioners in Primary Medical Care

The role of the nurse practitioner has evolved over several decades in response to a shortage of physicians and physician's assistants, escalating costs, and a shortage of affordable health care. A nurse practitioner (NP) is a registered nurse who has completed an "accredited two-year program of study and clinical practice," earned a master's degree in nursing, and passed a national exam ("Nurse Practitioners" 4). In California, for example, NPs are certified to provide basic medical care, prenatal care, and family planning assistance. They must pass a course in pharmacology and work for six months in an internship, receiving intense supervised training, before they can write prescriptions ("Need a" 4).

Definition

Example

The nurse practitioner program has evolved as a result of the short supply of physician's assistants (PAs). In 1965 the physician's assistant program was created to relieve the shortage of physicians. Using a physician's assistant for routine medical care freed physicians to concentrate on more complex medical problems (Sidel and Sidel 203, 204). But for some reason the program attracted relatively few medical students. In 1970 the American Medical Association asked the American Nurses Association (ANA) to supply nurses to be trained as physician's assistants. Instead of complying with the request, the ANA created its own alternative to the physician's assistant—the nurse practitioner (Sidel and Sidel 204).

History

The intent of the American Nurses Association was that this new health care professional's "training and philosophy [would reflect] nursing and not medicine" (Sidel and Sidel 204). Dock and Stewart point out that this philosophy is based on the "Nightingale concept" of nursing in which there is "neither independence nor subordination but interdependence and cooperation." According to the Nightingale philosophy, nursing is not a "subcaste of medicine." A nurse is not a "handmaid," but a "helpmate and partner" (367).

Purpose

For other kinds of openings, see chapter 4.

Using Signal Phrases to Integrate Quotations into the Text

Every quotation you use requires transition to weave it into your text. Usually, a *signal* phrase precedes the quotation. This introductory phrase signals the reader that a direct quotation will be presented. To keep your signal phrases strong and responsible, give the full name of the researcher, team, organization, study, or poll whenever possible. To identify a person, give degrees, position, or other credentials. The examples below illustrate signal phrases for introducing quotations:

- According to Dr. Sheila S. Smith, a psychologist at Blake University,
- A study by an Ohio State University medical team found ". . . ."
- In March 2002, the American Medical Association reported:
- James A. Bell, a scientist at Jones Laboratories of New York City, stated:
- Others, like Dr. H. R. Smythe, believe that ". . . ."

More examples of signal phrases can be viewed in student examples throughout the chapter as well as in the research paper at the end of the chapter.

Weak Phrases   Some popular magazines and newspapers omit vital source information. Instead, they substitute vague transitional phrases and the word *it.* All of the following examples are evasive and *inappropriate* for research papers and reports:

A study revealed . . .	(What study? Who conducted it?)
Experts/researchers/authorities say . . .	(Who? All?)
It is believed . . .	(Who believes?)
It is estimated . . .	(Who estimated?)
It is predicted . . .	(Who predicted?)
"In my opinion" or "I feel"	(So what?)

Short Quotations   Quotations of four lines or fewer (three for poetry) are considered short. You can use short quotations to identify special terms or include vivid words and difficult-to-paraphrase segments. Short quotations, too, require transition to link them to the text.

Sometimes you may lack the name of a researcher to use as a transition to a quotation. Often popular magazines summarize research, giving only a minimum of details about several studies. When April Rausch was confronted with this problem, she presented the vital information that was available, using two short quotations:

> In 1991, as reported by *USA Today*, thirty-seven babies in the United States died "while sleeping in bean-bag infant cushions." Although some of the babies were

VERBS IN SIGNAL PHRASES

The verb in a signal phrase should indicate the intent of the writer or speaker. Usually the verb is in the present tense unless the context requires the past tense (found, reported, stated). The reference list of verbs below are all in the present tense:

admits	concedes	discloses	holds	observes
agrees	concludes	disputes	highlights	refuses
argues	concurs	emphasizes	insists	refutes
believes	denies	finds	maintains	reveals
claims	disagrees	grants	notes	stresses

thought to have died of Sudden Infant Death Syndrome, others apparently smothered. After a research team headed by James S. Kemp and Bradley T. Thach tested bean-bag cushions from two makers, using rabbits, the Consumer Product Safety Commission cited the cushions as a potential "asphyxiation hazard." In late 1991 infant bean-bag cushions were removed from the market (*USA Today* 5).

Block Quotations   A block quotation is a long quotation of five lines or more (four for poetry). For a research paper (MLA style), double-space and indent block quotations *ten* spaces on the left margin, none on the right. Do *not* use quotation marks for a block quotation because the indentation and parenthetical citation alert the reader that the material has been borrowed. Careful writers use long quotations for a valid reason; overuse signals a hastily written paper. In the example below notice that (1) the source and author are identified in the text of the paper *before* the long quotation, (2) a *colon* is placed after the verb, (3) the period appears one space *before* the citation.

In <u>The Managerial Woman</u>, management consultants Margaret Hennig and Anne Jardim state:

>Studies of women who enroll in continuing college education programs show that many of the women who fail in these programs . . . have never discussed their goals with their husbands. The husbands never really understood why their wives had gone back to school, and the wives on their own had attempted to

> maintain the same level of housework they had been
> accustomed to. (212)

Inserting Explanatory Notes

Once in a great while you may have material that is useful in discussing your subject but that seems to interrupt the text. In such cases you have the option of including the information in an explanatory note. To do so, insert a superscript numeral at an appropriate point in your text. Then you can place the note either at the bottom of the same page or on a separate page, headed "Note" or "Notes." Begin the note with a matching superscript number (see "Content Notes" in chapter 24).

Writing a Conclusion

The conclusion of a research paper may be longer than those of the other papers you have been writing. A graceful ending of three to five (or more) sentences is usually expected. Although new information is not introduced in the conclusion, a writer may leave the reader with a new thought. A brief summary or reference to the future may be appropriate. Peggy Bean combines these three techniques in her closing:

> Although the fetal alcohol syndrome is a tragic disorder, it is also a preventable one. Therefore, it is important that the general public become aware of the risks ethanol poses to the developing fetus, especially to the fetus of a chronic alcoholic. Once families know the cause of this disorder, they can assist the alcoholic mother-to-be in securing professional help.

Bonnie L. Rice ends her research paper with a reference to the future and to what a reader might do to help in a similar situation:

> Efforts toward education, intervention, and prevention of adolescent suicide are being made. They must continue and expand. But can the individual do something to help? Yes, the greatest problem for the unhappy adolescent is isolation from close relationships; one person can be that caring friend who is missing from someone's lonely life.

Sometimes beginning writers tack on a quotation at the end without transition. Although the quotation may be appropriate, the gap between the body and the quotation halts the smooth flow of thought. To link a quotation to a conclusion, use a transitional segment, as italicized in the following example:

> *Child abuse is an ancient problem, but it is an occurrence that concerns us all, a problem that needs to be solved. For as James Agee wrote,* "In every child who is born, under no matter what circumstances, and of no matter what parents, the potentiality of the human race is born again; and in him, too once more, and of each of us, our terrific responsibility towards human life. . . ."

REVISING, EDITING, AND FORMATTING

When you finish the rough draft of your research paper, heave a sigh of relief, and take a break if possible. If not, perhaps you might alphabetize the entry cards for your works cited list and start typing that or do some other related chore. Before you start to revise your paper, however, you need to gain distance so that you can come back and examine it objectively.

Revising

Persistence, time, and care are the keys to successful revision and proofreading. Yet you may be so preoccupied with content that order, documentation, and mechanics receive low priority. Several revisions spaced over several days will catch more errors than one intensive session the night before a deadline. The checklist below will prove helpful in assisting a tired brain to focus during this all-important stage:

See chapter 5.

CHECKLIST: REVISING SOURCE-BASED PAPERS

1. Compare your outline and paper. Is the order the same? Is it sound?
2. Now read the paper aloud. Is the introduction interesting and complete?
3. Are the main ideas clear?
4. Is there sufficient transition? Is each quotation linked to the text?
5. Are there too many direct quotations? Should some be paraphrased or summarized instead?
6. Could the order of details within paragraphs be improved?
7. Is the conclusion logical and complete?

Checking Documentation

Every source you use in your research paper must be acknowledged according to a standard documentation style. Two of the most common—Modern Language Association (MLA) style and American Psychological Association (APA) style—are described in detail in chapter 24. Both use parenthetical citations within the text that are keyed to a complete bibliographical list.

In the course of drafting and revising, even the most conscientious writer may omit, misplace, or lose a text citation while rearranging sentences or paragraphs. If a problem occurs, don't panic! Remember you have your earlier drafts and note cards. Also check to see that every paragraph in your research paper has at least

> ### CHECKLIST: USING PARENTHETICAL CITATIONS
>
> 1. Is there a citation for every source used?
> 2. Does every parenthetical citation for a printed source include a page number (except for single-page sources and entire works)?
> 3. Is the name of the author/researcher/group included either in the parenthetical citation or in an introductory phrase?
> 4. If there is more than one source by the same author, does a short form of the title appear in parenthetical citations?

one text citation unless there is a reason for not including one. Remember, too, that if you split a paragraph you will probably have to make another citation.

Editing and Proofreading

See chapter 5. To catch errors in a research paper, proofread when you are alert. Go over your paper several times—one sitting is seldom enough. For example, watch to see that you have the correct spelling of prefixes, as in words beginning with per- and pre-. To attain the high grades that most students desire, revise and proofread several times. If you follow the editing guidelines outlined in chapter 5 and provide the necessary effort, your paper should be a success.

Using an Appropriate Format

Some instructors may give few or no instructions for formatting a research paper; others may give precise instructions. Most expect good quality white, 8½- by 11-inch paper. If you plan to use erasable paper or to submit a photocopy, check with your instructor first. A title (cover) page may or may not be required. Some instructors like the title page format commonly used in the workplace (see the research paper at the end of this chapter). The MLA style does not require a title page whereas the APA style does. Both styles require that you double-space the entire manuscript, including quotations and list of sources. Some instructors also prefer that you staple or use a paper clip rather than a binder to keep pages together.

Margins and Indentation   Standard specifications for research papers call for one-inch margins (top, bottom, and sides). Page numbers are placed one-half inch from the top right and flush with the right margin. Indent the first line of paragraphs one-half inch (five spaces on a typewriter). For long quotations, the MLA style indents one inch (*ten* spaces) from the left margin. The APA style, however, indents long quotations one-half inch (*five* spaces).

MLA Style Heading, Title, and Page Numbering If you decide not to have a title page, MLA style advises starting the first page of the manuscript with your name, your instructor's name, the course number, and the date on consecutive lines one inch from the top left margin. Next, center the title. Capitalize the first and last words and major words of the title. Do not italicize any words unless you mention a book title or use a foreign phrase or other wording that requires italicizing. (Never italicize your own title.) Page numbers, in the upper right corner, are preceded by the writer's last name. The top of the first page of a research paper, MLA style, looks like this:

Bellows 1

Susan N. Bellows

Professor Raintree

English Composition 112

May 15, 2002

New Sources of Antibiotics from Land and Sea

Many of the wonder drugs of former decades are losing their effectiveness as bacteria acquire immunity to certain antibiotics. Thus there is a never-ending search for new medicines to replace older ones that have become obsolete.

APA Style Headings, Title, and Page Numbering The APA style requires a title page with a "running head" (abbreviated title) of the first two or three words of the title, the full title, and the byline. The full title should summarize the main idea of the manuscript briefly and simply. The byline contains the writer's name and the institutional affiliation (college, university, or other site). In the byline use no extra words such as *by* or *from*. The preferred form of an author's name is first name, middle initial, and last name.

First, type the running head (the first two or three words of the title) and the page number one-half inch from the top right margin in upper and lowercase. Skip down about one third of the page and type the full title, centered in lowercase with capitals (if needed, on two lines, double-spaced). Double-space, then center the writer's name. Double-space again and center the name of the institution. The top of a title page, APA style, looks like this:

New Sources of Antibiotics   1

New Sources of Antibiotics from Land and Sea
Susan N. Bellows
Professor Raintree
English Composition 112
May 15, 2002

Page numbers in APA style are preceded by the running head from the title page on succeeding pages. This means that the first two or three words are taken from the title. Note that the page number appears five spaces after the head.

SAMPLE STUDENT RESEARCH PAPER: MLA STYLE

A complete student research paper using the Modern Language Association style follows. The outline appears before the paper by Lois J. Gordon. For specific guidelines regarding the parenthetical citations in this paper, see chapter 24.

Workers' Compensation: The Employee's Insurance Policy
by
Lois J. Gordon
CM 110 Research Writing
Professor Leslie Weichenthal
April 10, 2001

Gordon 1

Workers' Compensation: The Employee's Insurance Policy

<u>Thesis:</u> Over the years so many workers' compensation laws have been passed that volumes of information have accumulated, much of it written in legalese. Discerning what is directly relevant to an injured employee is an overwhelming task. And since laws differ so much from state to state, this paper is limited to an overview of workers' compensation in the United States, common problems in resolving claims, and basic suggestions for filing a claim.

I. Brief history of workers' compensation in the United States

II. Overview of workers' compensation

III. Common problems in resolving claims

   A. Prevalence of conditions causing musculoskeletal disorders and implementation of ergonomics rules. Explanation of ergonomics.

   B. Determining whether or not an injury is work-related

   C. Prevalence of fraud

   D. Employers, even when negligent, may contest claims.

   E. Genetic testing

IV. Suggestions for filing a claim

Workers' Compensation: The Employee's Insurance Policy

Before workers' compensation programs came into effect, injured employees had no recourse except to sue for coverage of their medical bills and lost wages. This chore was not only extremely difficult but also unpleasant because of possible retaliation from the employer. Then too, co-workers were often hesitant to testify on behalf of the employee. Awards hinged upon the expertise of the lawyers involved, not actual losses. Cases could take years to settle while legal costs accumulated for the injured employee (Williams 4).

In 1908 President Theodore Roosevelt proposed that workmen's compensation be applied to all workers (Williams 43). In 1912 an amendment to the Constitution of the United States established Workmen's Compensation, which was changed to Workers' Compensation on January 17, 1977. The 1912 amendment required employers to provide insurance for work-related diseases, injuries, or death caused by mental, physical, and emotional factors. No longer would employees be required to prove that their employers intentionally harmed them (Swisher 283). But this amendment does not cover all categories of workers. For example, migrant or seasonal farm workers may or may not be covered according to the state and the employer ("Texas" 1). Some states make other exceptions.

Now, nearly a century after Roosevelt's recommendation, the United States has fifty-three workers' compensation systems in various stages of development with assorted rules and provisions. Two federal programs cover federal employees and longshore workers. There are fifty state programs and another system that covers Washington, D.C., because workers' compensation is a form of insurance regulated by the state in which the company is located (Williams 43). Congress regulates only the transactions that are considered interstate ("Insurance" 1).

Over the years so many laws relating to workers' compensation have been passed that volumes of information have accumulated, much of it written in legalese. Discerning what is directly relevant to an injured employee is an overwhelming task. And since these laws

Gordon 3

differ so much from state to state, this paper is limited to an overview of workers' compensation, common problems in resolving
claims, and basic suggestions for filing a claim.

A short, convenient description of workers' compensation is that
it is an employee's insurance policy. An explicit definition of this term
is provided by William R. Tracey:

> Workers' compensation—Statutes passed by all states designed
> to protect workers from the hazards and consequences of acci-
> dents, injuries, illnesses, and death to themselves and their fami-
> lies as a result of their employment. Benefits are paid to workers
> suffering job-related physical, mental, or emotional accidents,
> injuries, disabilities, or disfigurement or who aggravate preexist-
> ing physical or mental conditions at work. In addition to death
> payments, they typically include weekly payments, based on
> earnings and size of family, medical and hospital bills, scheduled
> loss (amputation, loss of use, or loss of a bodily function), pay-
> ments for scarring, rehabilitation, retraining, settlements, travel
> expenses, and attorney fees paid to the employee or his or her
> surviving spouse or children. Businesses must either have ade-
> quate funds to pay claims or carry appropriate workers' compen-
> sation insurance coverage. The laws also provide some protec-
> tion to employers against excessive liability. (375)

Employees who are injured on the job or disabled from work-
related mental or emotional illnesses or diseases are eligible for
workers' compensation benefits, according to state regulations, the
employee's wages, and the severity of the disability. Financial benefits may be awarded in a lump sum or a weekly check. For example,
the DIA Circular Letter No. 303 (October 2, 2000) cited Massachusetts's weekly benefits as ranging from a minimum of $166.18 to a
maximum of $830.89. A statute mandates that the minimum benefit
be "at least 20% [of] the state average weekly wage" and the maximum benefit "be set at 100%" of the SAWW ("Maximum" 1). Other
common benefits include medical treatment, prosthetics, rehabilitation, living expenses, job retraining, and funeral expenses. Some

Gordon 4

states provide allotments for attorneys' fees except for frivolous claims. Such payments must be approved by the court before the case is heard.

United States federal regulations override state laws whenever there is a contradiction in rules. The Occupational and Safety Health Act (OSHA) was passed to protect workers' safety and health while in the workplace, regardless of the state. OSHA laws regulate private employers that conduct business in interstate traffic. The federal government has also established health and safety laws for its own agencies. To guarantee that regulations are being followed, the Secretary of Labor has the authority to inspect workplaces, investigate complaints, and make decisions about needed laws. A citation may be given to employers who violate regulations. Fines may be imposed; the amount varies according to duration and type of violations ("Workplace" 1).

Problems have long existed in workers' compensations systems in the United States. In 1970 a national commission was set up to evaluate all fifty-three systems (Williams 43). The commission discovered many deficiencies and recommended that every state be required to meet nineteen essential standards by July 1, 1975. Most states still have some standards to be met.

One of the major health problems of employees is a group of conditions classified as musculoskeletal disorders. According to the U.S. Bureau of Standards, musculoskeletal disorders traceable to the workplace are responsible for "a third of the occupational illnesses reported." These conditions range from carpal tunnel syndrome to back and neck injuries (Pramik 1). In response to this finding, President Clinton's administration enacted regulations on ergonomics that would require "companies to implement comprehensive programs to protect their workers from repetitive-motion injuries" by May 2001 ("Bush" A16). Almost two dozen states had begun making rules to meet the deadline when Congress repealed the legislation in March 2001. The reasoning was that implementing the programs would be so expensive that it would work an undue hardship on employers.

Gordon 5

Three states—North Carolina, California, and Washington—had already enacted the ergonomics regulations (Ergonomics B15).

Ergonomics includes everything from office furniture to the "walk through the parking lot to the relationships among co-workers." Adjustable chair seats and backs, improved keyboards, a track ball instead of a mouse, anti-glare screens, glasses to reduce eyestrain, and other features can alleviate strain and stress. Some companies furnish recreation rooms, weight rooms, and jogging tracks (Pramik H4).

Problems in resolving workers' compensation claims often arise when a determination is needed to prove an injury or disease is work-related. This decision is particularly difficult in cases where the employee uses a home computer or other appliance that may lead to musculoskeletal disorders. In such cases, a physician often considers the number of hours spent on each appliance and arrives at a split estimate. The decision becomes more complicated when employers urge the employee to see a company doctor. Although the law may state that an injured employee can see his or her own physician, employees may believe that this is their only choice. Even if they know better, they may feel pressured to see the company physician. Sometimes an injured employee sees several doctors who may disagree. Some states, like New York, require that an "impartial specialist" be appointed ("Rules" 1). Some states, such as California, identify specific criteria to classify the degree of incapacitation (Levels 1).

A big problem for employers and insurance companies is fraud. A 1998 industry estimate places the "price of fraudulent claims in the United States at about $120 billion a year." This problem is so widespread that even people in authority, including "police chiefs and priests," have been found guilty of "feigning injuries" and cheating on insurance claims. Employers can help to prevent phony claims by investigating incidents immediately—photographing the scene and interviewing eyewitnesses, as well as the victim. A variety of signs can signal fraud, particularly a history of filing accident claims (Anthony 1, 2).

Gordon 6

Even when negligence seems clear-cut, a employer may dispute the claim for fear the employee will seek a large settlement. For example, an employee stepped into a puddle on a sunken sidewalk on company property. Ice lay beneath the water, causing her feet to fly out from under her. She suffered a mild concussion. The company contested, claiming the accident was "an act of God." The agency settled in her favor, finding that the walk constituted a hazard and should have been repaired. She asked only for payment of medical costs, which was awarded ("Anonymous"). In other cases, of course, employees often do receive large awards.

Yet another complication in the resolution of workers' compensation claims is DNA testing. In February 2001, the U.S. Equal Employment Opportunity Commission called for a stop to genetic testing of employees by the Burlington Northern Santa Fe Railroad. The commission's lawsuit, filed in U.S. District Court in Sioux City, Iowa, said a "nationwide policy of requiring employees who have submitted claims of work-related carpal-tunnel syndrome . . . to provide blood samples for DNA tests" infringes on rights to privacy and freedom from discrimination (Chen B2). The next day the company halted the tests (Machalaba B10).

The general procedure for filing a claim for workers' compensation is similar throughout the U.S., although time limits and requirements vary. In Massachusetts, if an employee is unable to work for "five or more calendar days, or dies, as the result of a work-related injury or disease," the employer must submit a "First Report of Injury" to the Office of Claims Administration at the DIA, the insurer, and the employee within one week of the injury notification. Within 14 days of the report, the insurer must either settle the claim or contact the Department of Industrial Accidents [DIA], the employer, and the employee of the decision to deny the claim. A "pay without prejudice period" exists for 180 days, allowing the insurer to pay without accepting liability. This period encourages the early settlement of claims. After that other conditions and rules take effect ("Maximum" 1).

Gordon 7

    To obtain specific information about workers' compensation laws in a state of residence or employment, visit WorkersCompensation .com or another Web site written in plain English. (Government sites contain legalese.) Some employers furnish such information. Some basic suggestions for filing a claim, based on this research and my experience, are presented here:

1. When an accident or illness occurs, record the exact time, conditions, cause, and names of any eyewitnesses. Photograph the accident scene if possible.

2. Secure medical treatment. If an on-site specialist sees you, secure a second opinion from your own physician.

3. Report the accident or illness to the employer as soon as possible.

4. Do not sign a waiver or take a quick settlement until the extent of injury is known. Some injuries may not become apparent until weeks later.

5. Fill out all necessary forms neatly and completely. Be polite and cooperative in follow-up meetings.

6. If necessary, secure the services of a competent attorney. If the state pays the fees, this step will have to be preapproved by the court.

    Finally, an injured employee who is well-informed and proactive will have a better chance of resolving a claim fairly with a minimum of stress than the one who leaves everything to the employer and to chance.

Works Cited

Anonymous personal interview. 16 Mar. 2001. Marion, Ohio.

Anthony, Alanna. "Workers' Compensation Fraud." <u>Risk Management</u> Oct. 1998. 23 Mar. 2001. <http://proquest.umi.com/pqdlink>.

"Bush Could Move to Wipe Out Clinton's Final Actions." <u>Wall Street Journal</u> 19 Jan. 2001, Midwest ed.: A16.

Chen, Kathy. "U.S. Seeks to Halt Employee DNA Tests." <u>Wall Street Journal</u> 12 Feb. 2001, Midwest ed.: B2.

Gordon 8

"Ergonomics Rules Still Alive in Many States." <u>Wall Street Journal</u>
        14 Mar. 2001:B15.
"Insurance Law: An Overview." <u>LII: Law about . . . Insurance,</u> n.d.
        30 Mar. 2001 <http://www.secure.law.cornell.edu/topics/
        insurance.html>.
"Levels of Subjective Disability." <u>WorkersCompensation.com.</u> 2 Apr.
        2001 <http://www.workerscompensation.com/california/
        reference/qfacts/appe.htm>.
Machalaba, Daniel. "Burlington Northern Ceases Its Genetic
        Testing," <u>Wall Street Journal</u> 13 Feb. 2001, Midwest ed.: B10.
"Maximum and Minimum Benefits." [Massachusetts]
        <u>WorkersCompensation.com,</u> n.d. 3 Apr. 2001 <http://
        www.state.ma.us/wcac/ben-max.html>.
Pramik, Mike. "Health Risks Also Found in Modern Workplaces."
        <u>Columbus Dispatch</u> 3 Sept. 2000: H1, H4.
"The Rules of New York: Workers' Compensation Subchapter A,
        part 303." <u>WorkersCompensation.com,</u> n.d. 4 Apr. 2001 <http://
        www.workerscompensation.com/new_york/rules.htm>.
Swisher, Thomas R. <u>Ohio Constitution Handbook.</u> Cleveland:
        Baldwin, 1990.
"Texas Workers' Compensation Commission Rules."
        <u>WorkersCompensation.com.</u> 4 Apr. 2001 <http://
        www.workerscompensation.com/texas/rules/htm>.
Tracey, William R. <u>The Human Resources Glossary: A Complete Desk
        Reference for HR [Human Resource] Professionals.</u> New York:
        American Management, 1991.
Williams, C. Arthur, Jr. <u>An International Comparison of Workers'
        Compensation.</u> Boston: Kluwer, 1991.
"Workers' Compensation Overview" [Massachusetts].
        <u>WorkersCompensation.com,</u> n.d. 26 Mar. 2001 <http://
        www.state.ma.us/wcac/wc-over.html>.
"Workplace Safety: An Overview." <u>LII: Law about . . . Workplace
        Safety,</u> n.d. 28 Mar. 2001 <http://www.secure.law.cornell.edu/
        topics/workplace_safety.html>.

Summary

Effective research requires an open mind and a thorough consideration of available evidence. In reporting research findings and commenting on implications, you should use provisional words, such as *suggests* and *indicates*. While taking notes, be careful to use your own language, summarizing most of the time. If you copy, enclose the material in quotation marks to avoid confusion later.

Summary, paraphrase, and quotation all require documentation (author, source, date, etc). Use quotations for a good reason. Introduce them appropriately. If necessary, you can make minor changes to quotations using ellipsis to indicate omissions. Brackets can indicate substitutions or additions.

A working outline, based on your sorted note cards, is quite helpful when you begin drafting. The sooner you can state a thesis, the sooner you can begin to organize and draft. Use clear transitional phrases as you integrate summaries, paraphrases, and quotations into your draft.

Both short and long quotations require parenthetical citation. Although short quotations require quotation marks, block quotations do *not* require quotation marks. Instead, they are indented ten spaces on the left.

For every parenthetical citation, make a corresponding entry for your works cited or list of references, giving full bibliographic data as explained in chapter 24. Observing the guidelines for documentation and for good writing will help to make your research paper a success.

Key Terms

block quotation	generic term	secondary source
brackets	paraphrase	short quotation
citations	primary source	summary
ellipses	provisional	

Test Yourself

What Are the Facts about Documentation?

Directions: Fill in the blank with true (T) or false (F). To check your answers, turn to the end of this chapter.

_____ 1. Minor words such as *a, an, the, but, of, on* may be copied without documentation.

_____ 2. Plagiarism may be unethical, but it is legal.

_____ 3. Plagiarism refers only to copying from published works.

_____ 4. A general word that has no accurate synonym can be copied without documentation.

_____ 5. If an author's unique idea is used but not his or her words, the source must be identified.

_____ 6. All special terms should be set off with quotation marks the first time they are used.

_____ 7. A selection from an author's work may be copied if placed in quotation marks and if the source is identified.

_____ 8. If even a few of an author's major words are copied, they must have both quotation marks and a citation.

_____ 9. Quotation marks and documentation are both needed for copied material that is not indented.

_____ 10. If only statistics are copied, quotation marks are not used, but a source is supplied.

Practice

Transitional Phrases to Introduce Quotations

Directions: For the following items, write a transitional phrase to introduce the quotation. For help, see "Using Signal Words to Integrate Quotations into the Text," in chapter 25. (_Source for this exercise:_ Siebert, Al. _The Survivor Personality._ New York: Berkley, 1996. Both quotations appear on page 64 of Siebert's book.)

1. Quotation: "The most direct access to the subconscious mind is through dreams. When we fall asleep, our rational, logical thinking relaxes."

2. Quotation: "Our dreams contain information about what is happening in our lives, our bodies, and the world around us."

Writing a Summary

Directions: Write a summary following "Guidelines for Writing Summaries and Paraphrases" in this chapter. Your tasks are as listed:

1. Find a one- or two-page article (three pages if much space is taken by pictures) in a popular magazine. Or if you prefer, select a short article from a journal to be used for your research paper.

2. Duplicate the article on a copier. This copy will be turned in to the instructor along with the summary.

3. Reread the article. Underline each topic sentence and essential supporting data. Number each topic sentence for convenience in writing your summary.

4. To begin your summary, write an introductory sentence that gives the author's name and the source. (Turn back to "Using Signal Words to Integrate Quotations into the Text.")

5. Make one entry for a works cited list. Place at the bottom of your paper.

6. Staple the copy of the article to your completed summary.

Test Yourself Answers

1. true
2. false
3. false
4. true
5. true
6. true
7. true
8. true
9. true
10. true

Reading and Writing about Essays, Fiction, Plays, and Poetry

Part 6

CHAPTER 26

Reading and Responding to Essays

. . . the unexamined life is not worth living.

—Socrates
(in Plato, *Apology*)

You may read essays in magazines, on editorial pages of newspapers, or in literature and other classes. In college classes, essays may be referred to as readings. There you not only read but also respond in discussions, reaction papers, or essay exams. To assist you, this chapter presents an overview of essays and suggests strategies for critical reading. The chapter also explains how to write a paper of reaction and long essay exam answers.

WHAT TO EXPECT IN ESSAYS

An essay is a short literary composition that focuses on one major idea. Essays range all the way from lighthearted spoof to political commentary to serious argument. Essayists reflect, reminisce, discuss incidents, or argue about daily life, trends, justice, values, and other subjects. Their words may echo nostalgia or disgust, cheeriness or sadness, cheekiness or humility. Often the ideas in essays are universal and timeless. An essayist may marvel at nature's beauty or decry its despoilment, explore humane acts or condemn inhumane acts, search for a purpose in life or wonder if there is one.

Essays are usually nonfiction. They often appear in op-ed columns, meditations, memoirs, diaries, journals, and letters. But some essays are fiction. They may appear in such forms as fables, parodies, or satire. For example, in 1729 after three years of drought and poor crops, Jonathan Swift wrote a satire entitled "A Modest Proposal." The essay raised quite a stir because many people took it seriously. The offending segment follows:

> I have been assured by a very knowing American of my acquaintance in London, that a young healthy child well nursed is at a year old a most delicious, nourishing,

411

and wholesome food, whether stewed, roasted, baked, or boiled; and I make no doubt that it will equally serve in a fricassee or a ragout.

Although the general populace did not understand Swift's bitter irony, "A Modest Proposal" became famous. It is still widely read today as a classic example of satire.

Like fictional works, essays may contain figurative language and symbolism. Sometimes these devices are so cleverly used, the essay may seem like a short story. So how can you distinguish the two? First, check to see how the piece is categorized. In a magazine or book, turn to the table of contents or introduction. Consider that essays tend to be self-expressive and idea-centered. They often express an opinion about a significant topic. Stories, however, have a theme, which is invariably implicit. Rarely is there a direct attempt to share an opinion, as in an essay. (For short stories, see chapter 27.)

Purpose of Essays

The chief purpose of an essay is to explore an idea and reflect upon it. Sometimes an essayist may simply seek a means of fresh expression, not necessarily agreement. Other essayists seek to inform or entertain. Others attempt to persuade the reader to agree with a position on an issue.

Personal (informal) essays often expose a human frailty or condition and attempt to elicit empathy or sympathy from the reader. Some essayists go against popular opinion in an attempt to surprise, shock, or arouse public indignation. Some writers use humor not only to entertain but also to make a point.

Formal essays invariably have an earnest, intent purpose. The writer seeks to stimulate thought and persuade the reader to agree or at least consider a point of view. Holman and Harmon's *A Handbook to Literature* describes the formal (impersonal) essay as having "seriousness of purpose, dignity, logical organization, length. . . . The technique of the formal essay is now practically identical with that of all factual or theoretical prose writing in which literary effect is secondary to serious purpose."

Characteristics of Personal Essays

Personal essays often appear to be spontaneous as they meander in and through a subject or circle it, coming closer and closer to the heart of the discussion. Others move along a time line, narrating an incident. You can identify personal essays by their conversational tone, self-disclosure, humor, freshness, and casual structure. They tend to be subjective and honest, inspiring trust in the reader.

The personal essay is essentially self-revelation. The writer, like a friend, shares personal details, opinions, and biases. In *The Art of the Personal Essay*, editor Phillip Lopate explains:

> The hallmark of the personal essay is its intimacy. The writer seems to be speaking directly into your ear, confiding everything from gossip to wisdom. . . . At the core . . . is the supposition that there is a certain unity to human experience.

Characteristics of Formal Essays Despite the apparent spontaneity of many essays, the words are carefully chosen for a purpose. Typically, the language of a formal essay is restrained. Cynthia Ozick, in "Portrait of the Essay as a Warm Body" (*Atlantic Monthly*, Sept. 1998), describes a "genuine" essay as a "fireside [chat], not a conflagration or a safari." Ozick says these essays have power, derived from an alluring use of language. She explains, "I may not be persuaded by Emersonianism as an ideology, but Emerson—his voice, his language, his music—persuades me."

Point of View and Voice

The perspective of the writer usually permeates an essay, although other viewpoints may be present. The way the topic is viewed affects the voice you hear from the printed page. This written voice may sound informal or formal, humble or arrogant, friendly or cantankerous, cheerful or cranky—just as the human voice reflects a range of emotion. Once in a great while, an essayist will assume a *persona*, a fictitious narrator, to tell a story. To determine how the words should be taken, seriously or in jest, you need to listen carefully to the written voice.

Questions to Analyze Point of View and Voice

1. Whose perspective is presented?
2. How friendly does the speaker sound?
3. How is the subject treated? Seriously? Sympathetically? Ironically? With sly ridicule? How?
4. How does the speaker seem to feel about the subject?
5. Does the voice seem overly biased? Reasonably objective? How so?

In "A Ride through Spain," a descriptive essay by Truman Capote, the reader hears a light, conversational voice like that of a friend. Capote writes from the point of view of a passenger on the train. His written voice reveals enjoyment of the experience. The opening and ending of this informal essay appear here:

A Ride through Spain

Certainly the train was old. The seats sagged like the jowls of a bulldog, windows were out and strips of adhesive held together those that were left; in the corridor a prowling cat appeared to be hunting mice, and it was not unreasonable to assume his search would be rewarded.

Slowly, as though the engine were harnessed to elderly coolies, we crept out of Granada. The southern sky was as white and burning as a desert; there was one cloud, and it drifted like a traveling oasis. . . .

Ending It was like a party, and we all drifted back to the train as though each of us wished to be the last to leave. The old man, with my shirt like a grand turban on his head, was put into a first-class carriage. . . .

The train moved away so slowly butterflies blew in and out the windows.

Figurative Language

Comparison in the form of metaphor, simile, and analogy is often used in essays and other nonfiction writing. In the excerpt from "A Ride through Spain," Capote uses concrete images and figurative language, which enable the reader to share the train ride vicariously. Frequent similes ("sagged like the jowls of a bull dog") and other images enable the reader to visualize the trip and to sense the camaraderie of fellow travelers.

Assonance and other devices of sound contribute to the imagery and movement. An example of assonance appears in the last sentence. Here the sounds of the words reflect the movement of the train: the long *o* in *so* and *slowly* slows the rate of speech as do the three syllables of *butterflies* and the phrase *in and out the windows*. In fact, the language is rather like that of a lyric poem.

See chapter 28.

The Power of Plain Words

Many essays are more direct and plainspoken than Capote's "A Ride through Spain." In fact, the words of some may seem stark and unadorned. Nonetheless, the essays attain power as significant details accrue. The secret of that power resides in the telling—the skill of the essayist, not the method. Robert L. Rose, a staff writer for the *Wall Street Journal*, describes the predicament of a young mother in plain words:

Is Saving Legal?

A penny saved is a penny earned. Usually.

Take the case of Grace Capetillo, a 36-year-old single mother with a true talent for parsimony. To save on clothing, Ms. Capetillo dresses herself plainly in thrift-store finds. To cut her grocery bill, she stocks up on 67-cent boxes of saltines and 39-cent cans of chicken soup.

When Ms. Capetillo's five-year-old daughter, Michelle, asked for "Li'l Miss Makeup" for Christmas, her mother bypassed Toys 'R' Us, where the doll retails for $19.99. Instead, she found one at Goodwill—for $1.89. She cleaned it up and tied a pink ribbon in its hair before giving the doll to Michelle. Ms. Capetillo found the popular Mr. Potato Head at Goodwill, too, assembling the plastic toy one piece at a time from the used toy bin. It cost her 79 cents, and saved $3.18.

WHOSE MONEY?

Ms. Capetillo's stingy strategies helped her build a savings account of more than $3,000 in the last four years. Her goal was to put away enough to buy a new washing machine and maybe one day help send Michelle to college. To some, this might make her an example of virtue in her gritty North Side neighborhood, known more for boarded-up houses than high aspirations. But there was just one catch: Ms. Capetillo is on welfare—$440 a month, plus $60 in food stamps—and saving that much money on public aid is against the law. When welfare officials found out about it, they were quick to act. Ms. Capetillo, they charged, was saving at the expense of taxpayers.

Last month, the Milwaukee County Department of Social Services took her to court, charged her with fraud and demanded she return the savings—and thousands more for a total of $15,545. Ms. Capetillo says she didn't know it, but under the federal program Aid to Families with Dependent Children, she was ineligible for assistance after the day in 1985 when her savings eclipsed $1,000.

Uncle Sam wanted the money back.

"Tax dollars are going to support a person's basic needs on the AFDC program," says Robert Davis, associate director of the Milwaukee social services department. Federal rules, and the spirit of the program, don't intend for "people to take the money and put it in a savings account."

WELFARE'S ROLE

Ms. Capetillo's troubles began in 1988, when the social services department discovered the savings account she had opened in 1984. The tipoff: The department had matched its records with those supplied by her bank to the Internal Revenue Service.

Next, the sheriff department's welfare fraud squad went into action. Investigators contacted the M&I Bank two blocks from Ms. Capetillo's apartment and found she had "maintained $1,000 consistently" in her savings account from Aug. 1, 1985 through May 31, 1988.

In an interview that May with investigators, Ms. Capetillo admitted she hadn't reported the savings account to the department. After doing a little arithmetic, welfare officials figured she should repay $15,545—the amount of monthly aid she received after her bank balance passed $1,000. (The assistant district attorney later considered that harsh; he lowered the figure to $3,000.)

But the judge who got her case found it hard to believe Ms. Capetillo was motivated by fraud. Indeed, for Ms. Capetillo, thriftiness had been a way of life. Her father instilled the lessons of economizing, supporting his nine children on his modest income from a local tannery.

After Michelle was born, Ms. Capetillo began drawing aid—and saving in earnest. She says she rents the second floor of her father's duplex for $300 a month (though the welfare department says it suspects she was able to save so much by skipping at least some rent payments). In the summer, she looks for second-hand winter clothes and in the winter shops for warm-weather outfits to snare out-of-season bargains. When Michelle's T-shirts grew tight, her mother snipped them below the underarm so they'd last longer.

"She cared for her daughter well, but simply," says Donna Paul, the court-appointed attorney who defended Ms. Capetillo. "With inflation, all Grace could expect was for government aid to become more inadequate."

Now that Michelle is getting ready to enter the first grade, Ms. Capetillo says she will no longer have to stay home to care for the child. She says she plans to look for full-time work or go back to school to train to be a nurse's aide.

But her round face, framed by shoulder-length black hair, still brightens at the prospect of bargain-hunting. At her favorite supermarket, her eyes dart from item to item. She spots the display of generic saltine crackers. "See that? That's cheap," she pronounces, dropping a box in her grocery cart.

The total bill comes to $5.98, but Ms. Capetillo forgot the coupon that entitles her to free bacon for spending more than $5. She pockets the receipt, and vows to return for the bacon.

After the law caught up with her, Ms. Capetillo reduced her savings to avoid having her welfare checks cut off. She bought her new washing machine, a used stove to replace her hotplate, a $40 refrigerator and a new bedroom set for Michelle. But that didn't resolve the charge of fraud.

Finally, her day in court arrived. At first, Circuit Court Judge Charles B. Schudson had trouble figuring out Ms. Capetillo's crime. To him, welfare fraud meant double dipping: collecting full benefits and holding a job at the same time.

After the lawyers explained the rules about saving money, he made it clear he didn't think much of the rules. "I don't know how much more powerfully we could say it to the poor in our society: Don't try to save," he said. Judge Schudson said it was "ironic" that the case came as President Bush promotes his plan for Family Savings Accounts. "Apparently, that's an incentive that this country would only give to the rich."

THE LIMITS OF AID

Others differ. County welfare worker Sophia Partipilo says Ms. Capetillo's savings raise the question of whether she needed a welfare check at all. "We're not a savings and loan," says Ms. Partipilo, who handled the case. "We don't hand out toasters at the end of the month. We're here to get you over the rough times."

Ms. Capetillo could have fought the charge. Her lawyer and even the judge said later that there was a good chance a jury would have sided with the welfare mother. Even the prosecutor admits that had she simply spent the money, rather than saving it, she could have avoided a run-in with the law.

But for Ms. Capetillo, going to court once was enough. She was so frightened and her throat was so dry that the judge could barely hear her speak. She pleaded guilty to "failure to report change in circumstance." The judge sentenced her to one-year probation and ordered her to repay $1,000.

A few days later, Ms. Capetillo, who remains on welfare, returns from a shopping trip and is met by Michelle. Banana in hand, Michelle greets her mother with a smile and a gingerbread man she made at half-day kindergarten.

"Now you can see why I do what I do," says Ms. Capetillo.

Questions for Discussion

1. Think about the opening anecdote. How does it affect your opinion when you hear the charge against Ms. Capetillo?

2. What is the effect of giving the price of every item down to the penny?

3. To what did Mrs. Capetillo plead guilty? Why? Do you think she was guilty? Why or why not?

4. What is ironic about the case?

5. The author tells the story without interjecting opinion. Yet his opinion is apparent. Where and how?

CRITICAL READING

When you curl up with a novel or other leisure reading, you read primarily for pleasure. You may skim long descriptive passages and slow down to savor others. Rarely, if ever, do you take notes. *Critical reading* for college classes and the workplace, however, has other purposes that are much more demanding. Critical reading requires you to analyze and evaluate—to think about ideas and ponder their meaning.

Critical reading can be divided into three stages: prereading, rereading, and prewriting. Often the stages overlap. You can use prewriting notes to clarify and to question as you reread. They can provide the starting point for your draft. Prewriting is an integral part of critical reading.

Evaluating What You Read

Critical reading requires you not only to examine and weigh ideas but also to consider their implications. With a skeptical eye, you contemplate the writer's analysis, interpretation, or argument—while waiting to form an opinion. Give the author a fair hearing; hold off making a judgment until all evidence has been carefully reviewed.

With an open mind, scrutinize inferences, data, results of studies, claims, reasons, examples, or whatever the author offers. Try to determine the *reliability* of any quoted sources. Ask questions such as "Who did the study? When? Was the sample representative? Are the entire results presented or has something been pulled out of context?" Question and puzzle over any inconsistencies. Compare various accounts and interpretations of the same information.

See "The Logical Appeal," page 245.

Emotion can color the perceptions of a writer as well as a reader. When discussing an issue, the writer may not give an opposing belief a fair hearing. The critical reader's task, then, is to spot bias, illogic, and inaccuracy. This task requires knowledge, objectivity, and awareness of common fallacies and methods of propaganda.

See chapter 20.

A Strategy for Critical Reading

Some essays are relatively simple and easy to understand; others are complex and difficult. A methodical approach to critical reading can simplify the task and yield more insights than a haphazard approach. A good place to start is with a brief background of the author.

1. **Read a biographical sketch.** Reading a synopsis of an author's background can give you a sense of the culture and the era that influenced the essay. Sometimes background material appears just before or after the piece. Books of essays by the same author usually print biographical information in the introduction or preface. Encyclopedias also contain biographical sketches of well-known authors. Examine, too, the writer's credentials. Is he or she an authority in the field?

2. **Look for the date of the essay.** A biographical sketch may yield the year an essay was written. Some essays may refer to events, which can help to determine the year. Then ask yourself whether or not the message is timely or dated. Some essays, regardless of age, remain timeless and universal. They continue to have relevance down through the centuries.

3. **Consider the title and other clues.** Often essay titles not only identify the topic but also suggest an attitude or point of view. Sometimes a title is deliberately misleading, however. It may indicate a literal meaning when a significant symbolic meaning also exists, as in Philip Weiss's essay, "How to Get Out of a Locked Trunk," which is included in the Reader. Watch for clues that point to double meanings and layers of meaning.

   As you read the body of an essay, think how it fits with the title. If you find an odd description or an apparent meandering, ask yourself how this relates to the main idea. An analogy or other bit of symbolism may be hiding there.

4. **Preread to gain an overview.** Previewing can improve your comprehension and retention. Read quickly to gain an impression of the piece. Note headings or subheadings or italicized phrases. Notice ideas and names that are repeated.

5. **Consider tone and point of view.** Before you form an opinion, try to view the subject through the author's eyes. Read the entire piece before making a judgment. Consider how the written voice sounds. Is the author serious, joking, or ironic? Does the point of view seem sensible and logical? What values underlie the piece? For example, how does the author regard responsibility? Sanctity of human life? Other universal concerns?

6. **Reread to examine and understand.** Read the essay slowly the second time. Look for the thesis. If it is elusive, look in the first and the last paragraphs. Once in a while, a thesis is unstated and implied—with just a hint in the title or elsewhere.

7. **Start your prewriting notes.** Underline the thesis and mark any clues to it. Look for key points and underline them. Then ask yourself, "What is this essay about?" Keep in mind that the first idea may merely introduce the topic. The main idea may come later. Finally, summarize the main point of the essay in one sentence. That sentence will clarify the focus.

   Star any definitions or copy them onto note cards. Circle unfamiliar words and look them up. Question any information that omits significant details or raises doubt. Write your questions in the margins or on cards. You can also check to see if the author answers the questions you raise. These notes will help you to understand connections in the text and form a starting point for your draft.

   If you spot doubtful information, an apparent fallacy, or a contradiction, place a question mark beside it. Watch to see if the author provides sources for any information not generally known or accepted. If a claim differs from the general thinking of experts in the field, does the writer provide sufficient support to be convincing? Finally, ask yourself, "What is my overall impression of what the author is saying?" Jot down your perception in three sentences or less.

8. **Look for the premise of an argument.** Where is the starting point or basis of the discussion? On what vital point does the argument hinge? For

example, the *premise* of an animal rights proposal might be the belief that animals have a right to enjoy their lives. From this premise, the proponents might argue that animals should not be eaten.

But opponents might argue that this view conflicts with the traditional belief that humans should rule over animals and eat certain ones. If opposing factions cannot agree on a premise, they will be unable to convince the other side.

9. **Write a synopsis or make an outline.** In your own words, summarize the content of the essay in a paragraph or two. Scan each topic sentence so that all key ideas are included. Or if you prefer, make a brief outline. Either technique will help to clarify your understanding.

10. **Check out new or doubtful ideas further.** If a reading topic is unfamiliar, find out what other authors have written about it. Or set up telephone or face-to-face interviews with officials of local agencies or businesses who would know. To make an informed judgment, you need to gather sufficient evidence and weigh it impartially.

WRITING A PAPER OF REACTION OR ESSAY EXAM ANSWERS

In psychology, literature, philosophy, history, or other college courses, you may write short papers and essay exam answers that *react to ideas* in essays, short stories, histories, or other literature. In one or two pages, you are expected to respond to content, not structure. A paper of reaction and some examination questions require you to analyze the central idea of a reading and contribute an *informed opinion*. That opinion should be based on facts and reasons, not emotion. A written reaction is expected to be logical, focused, clear, and complete.

Two Types of Reactions

A reaction paper or an exam answer is a thoughtful response to a writer's ideas. The purpose is to present a point of view and persuade the audience that the response is sound and reasonable. This assignment allows considerable leeway in responding to a topic. Usually, a reaction is either a commentary or an argument, although the two are sometimes blended, depending on the rhetorical situation.

A Commentary   A reaction may be a *commentary* that considers *how* the reading presents the main idea. For example, you might discuss the originality of the piece, insights of the author, and the humor; then you give your response. On weightier matters, you would consider the facts and possible consequences or implications of the main idea. For example, you might discuss the implications for your field of study.

TASKS IN RESPONDING TO READINGS

- **Summarize:** To condense, giving only the chief points. The purpose of a summary is to show that you understand the main ideas and relationships between ideas of a work (see page 383).
- **Paraphrase:** To restate in your own words. The purpose of paraphrasing is generally to report or to clarify (see page 384).
- **Quote:** To copy someone's work and to give credit to the author. Requires quotation marks and source identification (see chapter 25).
- **Analyze:** To examine the parts of a whole. Analysis goes beyond a summary. You have to look closely at a work and think about what is happening. The purpose is to understand how the author achieves the effect (result). For example, you may be asked to analyze elements of structure or style.
- **Evaluate:** To rate, appraise, or judge. The purpose is to attach an opinion of value or worth to something. For example, problem solving and argument require evaluation.

When appropriate, you can allude to historical figures or literary characters or cite quotations. You might compare or contrast, discuss cause and effect, give real-life examples, or organize in any way that is effective. There is no special way to organize a reaction.

An Argument   A reaction is often an argument. It examines, interprets, evaluates, and states an opinion. To be effective, an argument requires specific facts and reasons to defend and support a stand on an issue. Although a reaction paper or an exam answer may not be a full-fledged argument, an element of persuasion is inherent in many assignments. When an assignment is not explained, you may have to interpret it, as in the following examples:

- React to the ethical questions that Andrea Sachs raises in "When the Lullaby Ends" (pp. 688–690). (*Here you are to consider questions of responsibility and of right and wrong. Then comment and supply reasons for your opinion.*)
- Many times welfare officials return children to their homes after the children are determined to have been sexually abused. State the rationale of the officials and your reaction. (*This question asks for a summary of the officials' reasons. Then you are to agree or disagree and give your reasons.*)

Other assignments clearly call for an argument. They require you to take a position, defend it, and provide logical reasons:

- Respond to Neal Peirce's "Americans: Conservationists or Champion Land Hogs?" (pp. 643–645). Did you like or dislike it? Why?

- React to James T. Baker's "How Do We Find the Student in a World of Academic Gymnasts and Worker Ants?" (pp. 632–635).

Do you agree or disagree with Baker's thesis? How do you feel about his tone?

Prewriting and Outlining

To expand your prewriting notes, look at your questions in the margins. Did the author answer them? If not, you might raise them in your draft. Did any of the author's statements seem doubtful or inconsistent? How might you check these? Were you impressed by any descriptions or insights? Can you think of further comments to make? Asking yourself more questions will help you to expand your prewriting notes and start drafting.

Questions for Prewriting

1. What is the main point of the essay?
2. Is the support convincing? Why or why not?
3. Has the writer omitted any significant facts? Are there implications or possible side effects that should be discussed?
4. What is especially interesting or challenging?
5. Is there any aspect I particularly like or dislike?
6. How does the author's voice sound?
7. How do I feel about the values underlying the essay? Why?
8. Might the ideas in the essay be applied to my field of study?

To make your draft go quickly, expand your working outline. If you haven't started an outline yet, just copy your thesis at the top of a clean sheet. Underneath, list your main points. Leave spaces between the points to add subpoints later. If a definition is required, write it on the outline. This framework will establish the direction of the paper. Although reactions are often responses to essays, they can also be responses to a piece of fiction.

Drafting

There is no one way to start a draft, but it helps to know where you are going. Look over your working outline. Will you be writing a commentary, argument, or combination? What order is indicated? Revise your outline so that it clearly reflects a suitable order.

Writing a Commentary   To begin a commentary, you might identify the author and title of the work, then add a statement about the piece. (*Tip:* In your prewriting notes, find the one-sentence summary of the author's main point.) When you agree with an author, you might comment on a significant point or statement, the research, or an example. Or you might discuss the implications for

---

WORKING OUTLINE FOR A PAPER OF REACTION

Question: Define *poetic justice* and explain how it functions in the "The Lady and the Tiger." What outcome would you predict?* Why? [In this short story by Frank Stockton, the main character has a chance to live and marry a lovely woman if he opens the right door. Behind one of the three doors lurks a tiger.]

WORKING OUTLINE:

Definition   1. Poetic justice—goodness is rewarded and evil is punished, often ironically.

Thesis   2. I think the tiger will come out the opened door.

Reasons   3. Why do I think so?
     a. Hints about "poetic justice." (Give examples)
     b. You can't believe the king—or his daughter? (Example)
     c. The princess is "semi-barbaric." (Explain)
     d. Nothing indicates she loves him so much she'll give him to another woman. She is jealous. (Give example)

Ending   4. Allude to "Nor hell a fury like a woman scorned." William Congreve, *The Mourning Bride* (1697) [Give the original source, regardless of where you find the line.]

*The word *predict* implies a reaction. The question calls for an opinion that will provide a logical outcome to the story.

---

you and your future career. The ending of a reaction paper can be brief, just a few well-stated sentences that give a sense of closure.

Planning an Argument   If you disagree with an author, then you need to construct a reasonable argument and provide adequate support. Before plunging into the fray, list pros and cons on your outline. In the first paragraph, identify the author and title and summarize the issue or controversy. The tone of this description should be neutral. Next, briefly summarize the author's position, taking care to be fair. After that, give your rebuttal, answering the main points of the other side. Cite facts and other logical support. Use a summary ending, restating your thesis.

A paper of reaction rarely requires research. Usually, you are expected to study only one reading and draw from your own experience. If you do consult outside sources, however, proper documentation is always required.

Revision and Editing

Before you revise and edit a paper of reaction, it is often helpful to reread the directions for the assignment. Then as you revise, check to see if you have fulfilled every one of them. Examine the organization, development, and logic of your paper. Would any sentence be more effective if moved elsewhere? Does more need to be said at any point? Is there needless repetition? Are the words clear?

Read your paper aloud to hear how your written voice sounds. Is the tone consistent with your purpose? Do you sound objective and knowledgeable? Can you find a better way to express an idea? Use a dictionary and a thesaurus to help you refine words so that you say what you intend in a suitable tone.

Edit each sentence with care. Even though you may have run a computer check for spelling, grammar, or punctuation, *proofread your paper carefully*. Software will not pick up all errors, and some packages may disagree with the rules your instructor advocates. Don't guess about spelling corrections—take a few seconds to open an up-to-date dictionary.

CHECKLIST FOR REVISING A REACTION PAPER

1. Is the thesis clear?
2. Is the order clear and logical?
3. Do I go beyond a summary and actually contribute to the discussion? Does my opinion sound informed?
4. If I am disagreeing, have I responded to all the writer's points?
5. Is my defense well supported?
6. Are facts correctly stated?
7. Are inferences logical and identifiable?
8. If there are allusions to other writers' works, have I given credit? If I consulted outside sources, are they properly documented?
9. Is my written voice appropriate?
10. Is there anything else that should be said?

STUDENT PAPER: REACTION

A college philosophy class was assigned a short paper of reaction with topics drawn from readings discussed in the classroom. One of the topics was to react to the philosophy of Martin Buber and to give practical applications. Scott Allen discusses the implication of Buber's beliefs for classroom teachers. He presents impressions, draws comparisons, and points out applications.

A Reaction to Martin Buber's Philosophy

SUMMARY/COMPARISON

Martin Buber's philosophy, as set forth in *Between Man and Man*, seems similar to Plato's in many respects. Although the philosophers disagree about the source of goodness, they both believe that goodness is an absolute, quite distinct from people.

They believe we strive to attain goodness by making wise choices. Buber's philosophy has important applications for teachers.

Buber feels that the formal teaching of values is worthless. Nonetheless, he believes that the teacher presents a selection from the real world and acts as a model to the pupil (indirect teaching). Buber develops the concept of "inclusiveness," which is the complete realization of the submissive person (i.e., the student).

To develop the mental powers to make good choices, Plato suggests the [direct] study of mathematics, philosophy, and other disciplines. Plato attempts to outline an ideal society where everyone can live peacefully and develop to the fullest capacity.

REACTION AND IMPLICATIONS

In the educational situation, this inclusiveness means that educators must beware of the dangers of such a relationship. They must refrain from arbitrariness and must exercise responsibility in interpreting the real world to the pupil. I agree: Teachers should consider the needs and rights of their pupils and try to respond in a way that will benefit them. This goal requires not only responsibility in the selection of classroom material but also fairness in grading, settling disputes, and other situations which arise. I concur with Buber's theory about the teaching of values: values are caught, not taught. A teacher should be of good character and should act as a role model for students.

How can educators accomplish this responsibility? Buber says they can do it by conscious and willed selection. In other words, educators should know what they want to achieve and select the proper means to achieve it. They should examine their basic principles and understand what is happening—not merely what they think they are doing. They must be objective as well as responsible.

Finally, Buber believes that "Life lived in freedom is personal responsibility or it is a pathetic farce" ("Education," Section III). Rousseau, in a similar vein, says that pupils are obliged to develop their intellectual powers to learn a vocation and provide for themselves. Like Buber, Rousseau is greatly concerned about the educator's responsibility of keeping evil away from pupils. This idea of personal responsibility involves intellectual self-discipline as well as physical self-discipline, but it helps us to gain self-respect and stature in the eyes of others. It helps us to find a purpose beyond ourselves—and perhaps that is what life is really all about.

CONCLUSION

In short, although Buber's traditional Judeo-Christian philosophy will not appeal to Ayn Rand fans or existentialists with leanings toward Nietzsche or Sartre, I believe it provides an excellent set of principles for undergirding education.

Summary

An essay is a short literary composition, usually nonfiction, on one topic. An essay reveals the writer's (and perhaps another) point of view on one subject. Essays range from formal to informal, from serious to humorous. The personal essay deals with everyday experience in a confidential manner, using a conversational tone.

Critical reading for college courses has three stages: prereading, rereading, and prewriting. These stages often overlap. The reader should be open to new and different ideas and alert for inconsistencies and fallacies. The reader should examine the logic and clarity of the writer's ideas. Using a strategy for critical reading simplifies the task.

In various college courses and in the workplace you may be required to react by speaking or writing. A paper of reaction presents a perspective based on logical reasoning. The paper is primarily an informed opinion—a commentary, not just a summary. A reaction paper is an analysis of the facts and their implications. Reaction papers require careful reading of the original source. If outside sources are consulted, they must be properly documented.

Key Terms

critical reading   informed opinion   premise
formal essay   personal essay   reaction

Practice

One-Minute Reactions

Directions: Select one of the following topics or another and write until your instructor tells you to stop.

1. Are you satisfied or dissatisfied with your state's highways? Why?
2. What is the most annoying problem in your neighborhood or city?
3. What is your favorite make of automobile? Why?
4. How would you describe the president? Why?
5. Did you ever get into mischief in school? How did you react?

Thirty Ideas for Reaction Papers

All of the essays mentioned below are located in the Reader. Or you may prefer to react to another of your choice.

1. React to Deborah Tannen's "Women and Men Talking on the Job." Do you agree or disagree? Why? Can you cite examples you have seen?
2. React to the analogy in Liane Norman's "Pedestrian Students and High-Flying Squirrels."
3. Respond to "Road Rage." Have you ever experienced a similar incident? What did you do?
4. React to "Mind Over Munchies" and Brown's treatment of the topic.

5. React to James T. Baker's "How Do We Find the Student?" Comment on the perspective of the author. Do you agree or disagree? Why?

6. React to Phillip Lopate's "A Nonsmoker with a Smoker." How do you feel about banning smoking? Why?

7. Respond to Barbara Jordan's "Becoming Educated." What does an education mean to you?

8. Respond to Euell Gibbons's "How to Cook a Carp." What do you think of his method of fishing? Would you have been willing to taste all the recipes?

9. React to Barbara Ehrenreich's "Spudding Out." Has this phenomenon changed in the past decades since her article was written? If so, how?

10. React to "It's Only a Paper World," by Kathleen Fury. Can you think of another type of office animal that she does not mention?

11. Respond to "Mother Tongue," by Amy Tan. Summarize her conclusions. Do you think her experience was unique or does it have widespread implications? Why?

12. In "The Handicap of Definition," William Raspberry discusses two stereotypes and the effects they have on black youngsters. Do you agree or disagree with his thesis that we define our success by our beliefs and goals? Why?

13. React to "The Sweet Smell of Success Isn't All that Sweet," by Laurence Shames. Do you agree or disagree with his thesis? What would you add?

14. React to "Why Marriages Fail," by Anne Roiphe. Can you cite any other reasons that marriages fail? Can you expand on Roiphe's points?

15. React to "Working at McDonald's." Do you agree or disagree with Etzioni? Why?

16. React to Andrea Lee's "Black and Well-to-Do." You might comment on the effect her sheltered lifestyle had upon her or any other element in the essay.

17. React to "We Have No 'Right to Happiness.'" What is C. S. Lewis's real point? Do you agree or disagree? Why?

18. React to Marya Mannes's "How Do You Know It's Good?" Comment on her criteria.

19. React to Jean Huston's "The Art of Acknowledgment." Have you ever had a similar experience? How did you cope?

20. Select any other essay you wish and react to it.

Other Suggestions

21. Listen to a television or radio talk show and react to a view about a significant issue.

22. Scan newspapers, magazines, or electronic bulletin boards for positions on political or educational issues, and react to one.

23. React to an unusual news item.

24. Turn to the opinion page of a newspaper. Read the columns and letters there. Then write a reaction to one.

25. Has a poem, story, or other piece of literature caused you to ponder an aspect of your life? Might you find a topic there?

26. React to a quotation that stimulated you to think about an idea.

27. React to an incident that seemed trivial but had unexpected results.

28. React to a favorite saying of someone who was significant in your life. How were you influenced?

29. Describe your reaction to a hardship as a child. Has your perception changed over the years? If so, how?

30. React to a local zoning decision, traffic routing, or other concern.

CHAPTER 27

Reading and Responding to
Short Stories, Novels, and Plays

Genuine literature informs while it entertains.
It manages to be both clear and profound.

—"Author's Note"
The Collected Stories
of Isaac Bashevis Singer

Why do we read literature? The written word can be far more alluring than a video or movie screen. Literature challenges us to create a world on the screen of the mind. There we can meet intriguing characters, participate in an exciting plot, explore new ideas and sensations. We can watch and wonder about the unfamiliar and untried without undergoing the risks of reality. More than this, we can share moments of human experience that help us reflect on the shape and direction of our own lives.

THE HUMAN CONDITION

Literature encourages us to consider large questions of our existence, arising from the human condition that all people experience: "Do we really have choices, or is life one great predestined plan?" "What is the purpose of living?" "What is worthwhile?" "What responsibilities do we have?" "What is happiness?" Literature allows us to explore universal dilemmas such as "What causes conflict between people who love each other?" "Is it wise to stand up for personal beliefs that differ from those of the mainstream?" "Should I risk danger to protect someone else's life?"

Literature enables us to laugh at the foolishness and smile at the cleverness of human behavior and thought. Literature often strips away layers that disguise intentions, motives, and values; it distinguishes the insignificant from the significant.

Reading literature helps us to encounter diverse cultures and viewpoints—to confront and interpret reality in a new light. But for literature to affect us deeply, we need to be engaged mentally as well as emotionally.

WHAT IS THE ROLE OF THE READER?

The reader plays an active role while reading literature. Meaning is not limited to the text of a work. As we read, we view ideas through our own window of experience—interpreting, inferring, evaluating—creating meaning. Our view is colored by our individual perception of the world, the topic, the treatment of the text, and the voice of the narrator. Many people assume a literary work has a single meaning or interpretation. The truth is that there is no one right answer about what a work means. Often a piece of literature is subtle, containing meanings of which the author is unaware.

Although readers create meaning to some extent, this is not an invitation to pull a passage out of context and distort it. Evidence found in the work must support the interpretation. This chapter explains an approach that is generally applicable to short stories, novels, and plays.

What Are the Major Characteristics of Novels?

A novel generally covers a much longer period than a short story or play. Novels of epic proportions may chronicle the life of the main character and the lives of descendants over several generations. Divided into chapters, novels usually have complex plots and subplots with many characters. The main characters tend to be well-developed; the reader learns of their quirks and peers into their personal lives. The action may take place in various locales, often far-flung. Yet the skillful author weaves all the elements together into a compelling tale that has unity and coherence.

The opening of a novel may contain lengthy description and proceed at a much slower pace than that of a short story or a play, where the action begins at once. The leisurely pace of some novels is due to the narrator's revelations about characters and a smaller percentage of dialogue. Once the conflict is introduced and the main character is beset with a problem, decision, or moral dilemma, the pace of the novel picks up. In the latter half, conflict builds to a climax, and the situation is usually resolved.

How Do Short Stories Differ from Novels?

Short stories have just a few pages for the action to unfold; every word must count. All descriptions and images must be essential. Time in a short story is constricted, often to a week or a day or less. There are few characters, and the reader is seldom told very much about them. Most of the meaning is derived from a juxtaposition of events, phrasing, and dialogue.

Yet the meaning may be puzzling. The reader must watch for clues, cleverly concealed throughout the plot. These short stories are like gemstones that must be carefully polished to reveal their brilliance. Although similar clues exist in novels, they are seldom so important to meaning as in the short story. Often plain, seemingly ordinary little stories are not ordinary at all. They may contain clues that reveal surprising intensity and depth.

How Does Reading a Play Differ from Reading a Novel?

Plays are meant to be seen and heard. When you read a play, you are more or less on your own, using a flashlight to view the action instead of watching it performed on a well-lit stage. You can't see the expressions on the faces of the characters or hear the intonations in their voices. In a novel there is a narrator who usually drops hints or explains from time to time. In a play there is no narrator.

Plays are usually divided into acts, which are divided into scenes. An introduction may precede the first act. Never skip this opportunity to preview the background, the plot, or other aspects. If the author is well known, you can consult an encyclopedia or look for a biography or review of the play. Otherwise, you are handed only a list of characters before the action of the play begins.

Scenes may shift abruptly with only a note such as "Venice. A street." Entrances, exits, and other sparse notes appear at intervals in parentheses. As you read, you are forced to rely chiefly on the words of the characters, which may be deceptive. A character may not tell the truth, or the words of the play may be from a different era. Shakespeare, for example, often uses common words, but they may have different meanings and connotations than do the same words today. Therefore the reader is often obliged to interrupt the passage and consult a footnote to understand. Drama is generally considered the most difficult of all literary writing because of its complexity and economy of form.

If you have a choice of plays and are relatively inexperienced, choose one that is straightforward with clear motivation. For example, *Julius Caesar* is easier than *Twelfth Night*. Yet *Twelfth Night* is easier than *Hamlet* or *Macbeth*. At times it is helpful to read puzzling bits of dialogue aloud and try to imagine the action in your mind's eye. What seems to be happening? Watch for subtleties and layers of meaning. Consider the craftmanship of the play. Three important features to keep in mind are the

- Sequencing of scenes (the pace of the action). For example, comedy may slow the pace in one scene, and a battle may rage in the next as in *Henry IV.*
- Character development. What motivates the characters? How do they change?
- Unveiling of the theme. At what points does the theme become visible? How? What is implied about the human condition?

READING AND TAKING NOTES

When you read an assigned short story, do you curl up in a comfortable chair and enjoy the tale? Or do you anxiously pore over every word and take elaborate notes that may never be used? For a short work, starting at the story level is not only more fun but also more practical. Once you gain a sense of the entire story, you can quickly reread and look more closely at the individual parts. The short story is an economical and enjoyable way to examine elements common to all literature. The short stories mentioned here are located in the Reader, where you can easily refer to them.

How to Start Prewriting

As you reread, make brief notes to mark clues and special passages that may lead to implicit ideas. Note-taking and questioning as you reread will simplify drafting later. (For convenience, make a copy to take notes on.) Here are some questions to help you start.

1. **Does anything seem *odd?*** If so write a question in the margin or on a file card. For example, in "Doves," by Ursula Hegi, there is a half-page description of stolen shoes. This seems odd in a story of just a few pages. On a card, you might ask, "What might stolen shoes and discarded shoes symbolize?"

2. **Do the title and ending contain clues?** Is there a hint in the title? How does the ending fit with the title? In many stories, the ending circles back to a previous part. If you become stumped, go back and reread the story, stopping to mark passages—anything that reminds you of something else. Circle words that seem linked to the central idea.

3. **What might the names mean?** Look up *names* of people, trains, ships, or other objects that appear in the story. Authors often select names with special meanings that tie into the theme. If you can't find a reference book on the meaning of names at the library, try your local bookstore for an inexpensive paperback such as *10,000 Baby Names,* by Bruce Lansky. These references give the origins of first names, their meanings, and famous namesakes.

4. **What motivates the character?** Think about the plot and ask questions. For example, "Why does Francine walk past the friendly, multi-colored parrot in the pet store to look at the gray doves? Why does she buy two? Why not one? What does this incident reveal about her?" Sometimes it is helpful to consult a dictionary. You may find connotations of a significant noun or symbolism that will lend insight.

5. **Is anything repeated or similar?** Watch for *repetition* of any sort and echoes of ideas. Place a question mark nearby. For example, in Baxter's "Scheherazade," the idea of *west* is repeated in *westward* and echoed in Pacific

Ocean (west ocean), zephyr (west wind), and Hawaii (west of the mainland). Why is *west* important? (*Hint:* The sun sets in the west. Sunset symbolizes _____ in the story?)

Unless you speed read, you may not have time to reread a novel or a play. Taking notes, questioning, and marking significant pages during a first reading may be a necessity. Mark long noteworthy passages with brackets so that you can go back and find them easily. Or if you do not own the book, list significant items and pages on file cards with an identifying phrase. Then insert the cards with one edge (your subject note) protruding from the top of the book. Since many instructors require page numbers of citations, start keeping track of them early.

Getting Ready to Draft

Once you have finished note-taking, consider individual elements that are interesting to you. Which one or ones would you like to write about? How do they influence the work? What will your thesis be? Writing a thesis early will provide a direction for your draft and save time.

To achieve a valid interpretation, look for a series of clues, a chain of evidence, upon which to base your thesis. Your discussion of the elements should be consistent with the total context. The best interpretations consider the entire work and offer an explanation of passages that may seem contradictory or inconsistent. That does not mean you have to refer to those you lack the resources or the ability to interpret. You can select another element you understand, perhaps in another work.

ELEMENTS OF LITERATURE

Short stories, novels, and plays have much in common despite obvious differences. All three genres have unity—a central idea and a pattern of development. All three may consider universal questions, current issues, or everyday incidents. All use figurative language and concrete images in varying degrees. All can be analyzed according to seven basic elements: point of view, setting, plot, character, symbolism, irony, and theme. These elements are intertwined and often impossible to discuss without reference to two or more.

Point of View

Point of view is revealed through the narrator's voice. An author selects either a first-person or third-person point of view for the narrator. This means that the narrator's voice is *not* the voice of the author. The narrator may be one of the characters or someone outside the work. When the story is presented through the eyes of *a* character, you gain an *inside* view. You have access to one person's thoughts and observations. F. Scott Fitzgerald's *The Great Gatsby* opens with the narrator reminiscing:

In my younger and more vulnerable years my father gave me some advice that I've been turning over in my mind ever since.

"Whenever you feel like criticizing any one," he told me, "just remember that all the people in this world haven't had the advantages that you've had."

He didn't say any more, but we've always been unusually communicative in a reserved way, and I understood that he meant a great deal more than that. In consequence, I'm inclined to reserve all judgments, a habit that has opened up many curious natures to me and also made me the victim of not a few veteran bores.

Whereas a first person narrator observes or participates in the action, a third-person narrator is *outside* the action. Usually, a third-person narrator enters the mind of just one character. But a third-person narrator with *limited omniscience* enters the minds of several characters. Sometimes a third-person narrator is *omniscient*, or all-knowing. You might think of an omniscient narrator as standing on a hill, looking down into the lives and minds of the characters, seeing everything that goes on.

Sometimes a story is told from *multiple viewpoints*. Two or more characters act as narrators, each giving a different version. In William Faulkner's novel *The Sound and the Fury*, four narrators give four points of view, each presenting bits and pieces of the same story. In addition, an appendix presents more details of the fictional family's history from an omniscient point of view. To discern the "truth" of this puzzling tale, the reader must filter the points of view and reconcile them with the history. Gauging the accuracy and truthfulness of a narrator, particularly one who is a character, is not always simple. Like human beings, characters may misjudge, understate, overstate, or deceive.

Setting

The time, place, weather, and culture of the characters make up the setting. Included in setting, too, are the objects and articles the characters have and use. Symbolism is often intermingled with setting to create a mood. For example, Thomas Hardy's novels take place on wild and stormy moors, which set the scene for passion and outbursts of temper. Savvy readers know that the storms are omens of stormy relationships or tragic events.

As you read, note the setting of each action and the implications. Consider the area, time of year, and weather, all of which create a mood. What objects are present? What familial, social, political, or religious obligations or conditions exist? How do they influence the plot and characters?

Plot

The series of actions or *conflict* that occurs in a narrative is called the plot. Broadly defined, plot includes not only physical action, but also words and thoughts. Conflict can arise not only from circumstance, but also from human motivation. The characters face an opponent or an impediment to a goal, which may be another individual, a natural force, an animal, societal rules and values, or an *internal conflict* over right and wrong. As the turmoil caused by the conflict increases, the suspense builds for the reader.

How the characters respond depends on the circumstances, their emotional makeup, and their values. Thus plot and character are intertwined. The physical action in *Romeo and Juliet*, for example, would have little meaning without the thoughts and feelings of the hero and heroine. Although a narrator may explain part of a plot, the readers should watch for clues to interpret the implicit ideas.

Plots generally take the form of straightforward narratives. Sometimes they may be structured as letters, diaries, or other "found" writings. For example, in Daniel Keyes's *Flowers for Algernon*, the diary form springs from the plot. The main character, a mentally handicapped man named Charlie, is asked by his doctor to prepare progress reports during the course of an experimental treatment. Early entries begin on a rudimentary level:

progris riport 2—martch 6

Dr. Strauss says I shud rite down what I think and evrey thing that happins to me from now on. I dont know why but he says its importint so they will see if they will use me. I hope they use me. Miss Kinnian says maybe they can make me smart. I want to be smart. My name is Charlie Gordon. I am 37 years old and 2 weeks ago was my birthday. I have nuthing more to rite now so I will close for today.

This early entry reveals not only Charlie's low level of understanding and education but also his desire to learn. Although Charlie is unable to explain what is happening, the phrase "use me" suggests to the alert reader that Dr. Strauss's purpose may not be in Charlie's best interest. After surgery and intensive training, Charlie's intelligence and learning escalate—revealed by later diary entries that are longer and more explicit. Toward the end, as Charlie deteriorates, the concluding entries parallel his condition.

Foreshadowing   When authors use *foreshadowing* in a plot, they scatter clues that hint of events to come. For example, in *Flowers for Algernon*, when Algernon the mouse begins to deteriorate, the alert reader suspects that Charlie will experience the same symptoms; for both have had the same operation. The drastic changes in Algernon foreshadow the plot's irrevocable conclusion. (See also "Writing about Symbols.")

Characters

The people in a narrative are the characters. To seem realistic, they are endowed with certain qualities and quirks. They may be portrayed as primarily good or evil, weak or strong, serious or fun-loving. Major characters are usually revealed indirectly through behavior whereas minor characters tend to be revealed directly through explanation. *Round characters* change and mature; they learn from events and circumstances. *Flat characters*, usually minor characters, do not change or grow. They may lack insight, remaining unaware and insensitive.

As you read, assess the characters. Do they seem true to life or stereotypic? Real people exhibit a blend of many traits. Do the characters act predictably or inconsistently? Are inconsistent acts explainable through motivation? Not every character needs to be well-developed, but all need to have a reason for their existence.

Symbolism

A symbol is something material that represents something else, usually an abstraction. A symbol may be a person, a place, an object, an action, or situation. *Universal symbols* are recognized worldwide, regardless of culture. One common example is ordinary water. Long used in the sacrament of baptism, water is universally regarded as a symbol both of purification and of life. More specifically, a bubbling fountain may represent youth and optimism. A stagnant pond may symbolize contamination or ebbing of life. Water may also signify sexuality. For example, lovers may meet by a placid lake, a river with rapids, or aboard ship on a storm-tossed sea. The condition of the water symbolizes the status of their relationship. When you think something might be a symbol, place a question mark beside it; or if you understand the symbol, make a note.

Irony

Irony refers to an inconsistency or incongruity between what is believed or expected and what is real. An event that is ironic is painfully contrary to what is expected. This means that simple unexpected events are not necessarily ironic. Sometimes irony takes the form of an unexpected twist of the plot or *situational irony*, as often found in the stories of Edgar Allan Poe or the films of Alfred Hitchcock. Using *dramatic irony*, a writer reveals to readers something that characters do not know, which creates suspense. *Verbal irony* involves saying something that is the opposite of what one means. Sarcasm is a form of verbal irony, fairly easy to detect, but much verbal irony is more subtle.

Writers often use irony to suggest human fallibility—the vanities, unwise judgments, and other limitations that keep us from recognizing the truth around us. Such susceptibility to error is at its most extreme in *cosmic irony*, or irony of fate. Cosmic irony is prevalent in Greek tragedies and other writings; the gods or destiny seem to control events so as to test and frustrate the protagonist.

Theme

The main idea embodied in a work of literature is called the theme. Some works have more than one theme. Theme reflects a universal belief about human life or "the human condition"—those experiences that are basic to the human race, regardless of color, class, or century. Theme may concern good or evil, love or hate, modesty or pride, or some other virtue or vice.

More often than not, theme is implicit. Theme can be implied through a series of events, actions, or dialogue. Theme may be revealed as an observation, insight, doctrine, or general principle by a character or the narrator. For example, a devout character might murmur, "Evil has its own reward," meaning "Evil will be punished, sooner or later." In much modern literature, themes are complex and cannot be reduced to a simple moral or proverb. Theme is the common thread that unifies the other elements; theme establishes order and coherence.

Figurative Language and Literary Devices

A figure of speech has a special meaning and construction that deviates from standard use of the language. *Similes* and *metaphors* are figures of speech that are unusual comparisons. Similes contain *like* or *as*; metaphors do not (for extensive examples, see the index). *Personification*, another common figure of speech, is the giving of human attributes to an object, abstraction, or animal. For example, the animals in George Orwell's *Animal Farm* represent people.

Special effects can be achieved with words by using *onomatopoeia, alliteration*, and *assonance*. These literary devices can emphasize and smooth phrases, as well as enhance the sound of words. All three devices are explained in chapter 28, since they are so often incorporated into poetry (see the analysis of a poem on page 451).

PREPARING AN ANALYSIS OF LITERATURE

When your instructor assigns a paper of analysis, sometimes called a "paper of explication," you will usually have leeway in choosing a topic. Whether the class has studied many selections or just one major work, there will be several options. Select a topic from a work that interests you, one that you clearly understand. You can discuss point of view, setting, plot, characterization, symbolism, irony, theme, or a combination. For example, you might compare and contrast two characters in one work, or you might compare the central characters of two works.

An analytical paper on a piece of literature responds to the form and content. You interpret the meaning and evaluate the significance of what happens. You can begin by examining certain elements and explaining their role. How do they influence the effect of the work? For example, how do the doves and the songs on the radio influence "Doves"? Before you start to draft, a few precautions are in order:

1. **Avoid giving the impression that there is only one valid interpretation of a work.** Shun phrases such as "obviously" and "it is evident that." Use tentative words that leave the interpretation open to other possibilities.

2. **Analyze the work objectively.** Veto any inclination to give harsh criticism or sweet adoration.

3. **Don't speculate about an author's intent.** Since a work may have a significance that the author was unaware of while writing, don't attempt to

TENTATIVE WORDS FOR INTERPRETING LITERATURE		
suggests	suggesting	implies
indicates	indicating	signals
possibly	apparently	foreshadows
probably	may	represents
not entirely	seems	appears
hints	connotes	gesture
symbolizes	clue	sign

mind-read. Instead, discuss the total effect. Describe the impression that is created. Supply reasons and examples.

Writing about Point of View

A narrator may describe the story from inside or outside the action. The following example from a student paper focuses on the perspective of a lonely narrator who is outside the family circle and other groups, looking in. Gradually, the perspective of *The Grass Harp* changes, and the development of the central character, Collin, changes, too.

The Grass Harp, by Truman Capote, is a beautifully written and sensitive account of a young boy, Collin, who becomes an orphan at age eleven. Collin goes to live with two aged cousins until he is eighteen. The novella chronicles the changes that occur in his life and the lives of people close to him. Written in first person with Collin as the narrator, the perspective of the book is cleverly done.

Collin is a shy boy who does not make friends easily and who remains on the outer fringes of most groups. He literally stays outside the action, a spectator most of the time. In the Talbo household, he lives with his cousins, Dolly and Verena, and the black maid, Catherine. Collin spends much of his time up in the attic, peering down through a knothole and cracks at the activities going on below. When the story opens, Collin is outside the action not only physically but also emotionally.

Collin is again a spectator when Riley Henderson, whom Collin greatly admires, confesses he is miserable. Riley would have killed himself if it were not for the responsibility of caring for his younger sisters. . . .

When Sister Ida invites the Judge and Dolly to go away with her, Collin feels left out, just as he has many times before; again he is on the outside of a circle, peering in. Again he is a spectator as he peers through a window at Riley, who is now his best friend and who is kissing a girl.

But later there are moments when Collin is accepted and moments when he is able to become an active participant. . . .

To start your prewriting notes on point of view, answer the questions in the checklist below after you complete your reading.

CHECKLIST: QUESTIONS FOR ANALYZING POINT OF VIEW

1. Who is telling the story?
2. Is the voice of the narrator consistent or does it change? If it changes, how?
3. How reliable is the narrator?
4. Should the narrator be taken literally? Or is the piece a satire, a tall tale, legend, myth, fable, or parable?
5. What is the effect of the narrator's voice?
6. Where is the narrator? Inside or outside the action? How does this perspective influence the plot, character, or theme?

Writing about Setting

To write about setting, take notes on the chief features of the place and time (era). Look for changes and contrasts in setting and wonder about their meaning. For example, if you were writing about *The Old Man and the Sea*, by Ernest Hemingway, you might examine how setting isolates the main character. You could explain how the old man copes with isolation and achieves a qualified success. Although you would also refer to plot, character, and symbolism, the focus would be on setting. Now let's take a look at how Hemingway sets the scene, introducing the main character and preparing for the dramatic action of the novel all in one paragraph.

> He was an old man who fished alone in a skiff in the Gulf Stream, and he had gone eighty-four days now without taking a fish. In the first forty days a boy had been with him. But after forty days without a fish the boy's parents had told him that the man was now definitely and finally *salao*, which is the worst form of unlucky, and the boy had gone at their orders in another boat which caught three good fish the first week. It made the boy sad to see the old man come in each day with his skiff empty and he always went down to help him carry either the coiled lines or the gaff and harpoon and the sail that was furled around the mast. The sail was patched with flour sacks and, furled, it looked like the flag of permanent defeat.

After you have taken notes on setting, you might reread them and write a quick draft, commenting on cause and effect and emphasizing your main idea. This exercise will spur thinking and should yield an overview of your forthcoming paper.

EXAMPLE OF A QUICK DRAFT

Hemingway's *The Old Man and the Sea* begins in a poor fishing village off the *Gulf Stream*. There superstition influences the thought and behavior of many residents, but not the old man. The belief in *salao*, or bad luck, has isolated him. Because he has had bad luck in fishing, going eighty-four days without a good fish, he

---

CHECKLIST: QUESTIONS FOR ANALYZING SETTING

1. What in the setting is particularly significant? Features of the landscape? Time of year? Weather? What?
2. Do any parts of the setting seem to be symbolic?
3. How does setting contribute to the tone or mood?
4. Does the setting change? How does this influence the plot and the characters?
5. Is there any foreshadowing (hints of what is to come)?

---

is shunned. The old man has even been separated from his former companion, the boy.

Alone on his skiff, the old man sits with his tattered flag and patched sail, which seem to be symbols—the sail "looked like a flag of permanent defeat." Two similarities between the boat and the old man stand out: both are old and both appear dysfunctional. Yet these appearances are deceiving. Despite the isolation and hardships imposed by weather, sea, and sharks, both endure. The old man continues his quest for a huge fish. Determined to succeed at any cost, he will not accept defeat.

Notes:

1. Need to discuss changes in setting at sea and effects on old man and the skiff.
2. Are sharks part of the setting? Not characters; must be setting.
3. Describe condition of the skiff, big fish, and old man when he returns to the harbor.
4. Is irony a significant element here?
5. What else should be mentioned?

Writing about Plot

An analysis of plot is usually combined with one or more of the other elements of literature. The examples that follow are from an analysis of a novel. The student writer discusses plot, character, and theme. The title alludes to a nursery rhyme character, as explained in the opening sentence. The ending also hints at the analogy.

Men, Chicks, and Eggshells

INTRODUCTION

Willie Stark, the main character of *All the King's Men*, by Robert Penn Warren, is the Humpty Dumpty who sits on top of the wall, the governorship of Louisiana. Here he reigns in his own anthropocentric world until he falls. The book has an epic quality in plot, character, and theme.

Willie is a farm boy with little education, but one who works hard and long to become a lawyer and achieve admittance to the bar. He believes in God, in honor, and in goodness. And at first he believes what people tell him. But Sadie Burke wises him up. He forsakes orange soda pop and a wholesome view of the world to embrace Scotch whiskey, a realistic view, and Sadie (as well as other mistresses). *[A major section of the paper, which appears later, emphasizes character, although plot is mentioned throughout the paper. In the conclusion the student writer reacts to the novel, giving her response to plot and character.]*

CONCLUSION

All the King's Men, like a mighty river, snatches up the reader and thunders to the inexorable finish. When released, the reader is purged and saddened by the tragic mess which some characters have made of their lives, yet gladdened by the few who retain integrity and develop responsibility.

Rereading your notes and prewriting will help you trace the development of the plot. Think about events that are examples of cause and effect. Consider character flaws, impulses, values, goals, issues, or coincidences that influence the outcome of the plot. The checklist below will assist you.

CHECKLIST: QUESTIONS FOR ANALYZING PLOT

1. What is the major conflict, dilemma, or problem?
2. What aspects of the plot create tension? How is it developed?
3. Who is involved and why?
4. Must the chief character make a difficult decision? What is it?
5. Does the chief character lose or triumph? Why or why not?

Writing about Character

Analyzing character takes time and thought. Consider whether or not the character seems true to life. Start with the external aspects and go to the internal qualities. To discover personality traits, notice how the character treats other people. How does he or she speak and act? Modestly or arrogantly? Kindly or rudely? Thoughtfully or impulsively? What motivates the character? Motivation is a strong determinant of behavior. What does he or she seek? For example, Willie Stark thirsts for political power, but attaining that power has a hidden price, an undesirable consequence:

Willie Stark is a complex character, a curious blend of good and evil, with Nietzsche-like overtones. As Stark gains power, he becomes a superman whose reign is based on *argumentum ad hominem*, blackmail, and the premise that all men have erred. Yet Stark has a curious code of honor: he never frames anybody. He believes framing is unnecessary; all he does is dig deeply until he finds something.

Although Stark manipulates people and abuses power, he does work for the ultimate good of the people as he conceives it. He provides social services and allocates funds for a lavish hospital, which will be free to the poor.

Stark has an unusual philosophy: "Goodness . . . You got to make it. . . . And you got to make it out of badness. . . . Because there isn't anything else to make it out of" (257). Although this idea is reminiscent of Romans 8:28 ("And we know that all things work together for good to them that love God, to them who are the called according to *His* purpose"), there is an essential difference that illustrates this character: Stark was a pragmatist who acted independently; he did not rely on his creator for direction.

To discuss character, make an assertion or claim about the character's role or personality. Then support this thesis with adequate examples and proof. You might examine how the character functions in the story. Is he the hero? Is she the heroine? Or does the character act as a *foil* or contrast for a major character? The questions in the checklist will help you to continue your analysis and start prewriting.

CHECKLIST: QUESTIONS FOR ANALYZING CHARACTER

1. How and where does the character live?
2. What is significant about his or her appearance? Attire?
3. What does the character say that makes an impression?
4. What motivates the main character? How are these motives revealed?
5. How does the character achieve desires and goals? What values are revealed here?
6. What do you notice about the characters and their relationships with each other? Do they change?
7. What similarities and differences do you see in the characters?
8. What do these things imply?
9. Do the characters seem convincing and realistic? Why or why not?
10. What else do you notice?

Writing about Symbols

Uncovering symbols can lead the reader to look beneath a surface meaning for a deeper abstract meaning. The names of characters and places are often symbolic: they represent some aspect of plot, characterization, or theme. In *Jane Eyre*, the mansion of Edward Rochester, Thornfield, is the site of much trouble and pain. Besides the obvious meaning (field of thorns), Rochester's mad first wife, who is imprisoned on the top floor, is a thorn in his life.

You may recall another symbol Charlotte Brontë used in this novel—the giant horse chestnut tree, which stood in the orchard at Thornfield for many years. Near this tree Edward proposed marriage to Jane without telling her he already had a wife. After Jane accepted his proposal, a storm arose and the huge tree "writhed and groaned." That night the tree, which symbolized Edward, was struck by lightning and split, *foreshadowing* the impending tragedy.

A paper on symbolism alone could be difficult and inappropriate for some works. Unless you are adept at interpreting symbols, you may want to widen the scope of your analysis to include other elements. To start thinking about possible symbols in a work, consider the questions below.

CHECKLIST: QUESTIONS FOR INTERPRETING SYMBOLS

1. What features, objects, or persons might be symbols?
2. Where and how do they appear?
3. Do any of the symbols change? How?
4. Are there any connections between the symbols? If so, how?
5. Are the symbols universal or individual? How are they related to the theme of the work?

Writing about Irony

Usually, an analysis of irony is combined with other elements, unless irony is dominant in a work. If irony is a significant part of a story, you may want to analyze and categorize the types of irony embedded in the work. In Jane Austen's *Pride and Prejudice*, for example, verbal irony and situational irony appear throughout the novel. Verbal irony is habitual for the narrator as well as for Elizabeth Bennet and her father. The novel opens with the narrator speaking:

> It is a truth universally acknowledged that a single man in possession of a good fortune must be in want of a wife.
> However little known the feelings or views of such a man may be on his first entering a neighbourhood, this truth is so well fixed in the minds of the surrounding families, that he is considered as the rightful property of some one or other of their daughters.

Later Mr. Bennet, who assumes the role of an ironic spectator, says, "For what do we live, but to make sport for our neighbors, and laugh at them in our turn?" Elizabeth, like her father, categorizes people into the simple and the complex, finding amusement in the follies of the simple. Situational irony appears in minor incidents such as Lydia repeating much of her mother's behavior. The major example of irony evolves around Elizabeth, who begins by detesting Mr. Darcy but who finally loves and marries him.

Hemingway uses cosmic irony in *The Old Man and the Sea*. Even though the old man succeeds in catching the great fish and in taking it home, fate extracts an exorbitant price for success: the sharks not only eat all the flesh off his prize, but the old man also dies soon after.

If you should decide to write about irony, the prewriting checklist will help you begin.

CHECKLIST: QUESTIONS FOR DETECTING IRONY

1. Are there any inconsistencies between expectations and outcomes in the plot that create situational irony?
2. Does the reader or a character know something that another does not?
3. Do any of the characters say the opposite of what they mean?
4. Does fate or cosmic irony play a role in the plot?
5. How does irony influence the work?

Writing about Theme

Theme is a continuing thread, the central meaning that winds through a work. A theme contains an observation about human life or the conditions that prevail. Usually, the theme is implicit and unstated, but you may find a theme directly stated, perhaps tucked into an obscure turn of the plot. In *All the King's Men*, an explicit statement of the theme reposes in a journal entry of a man long deceased:

> . . . the world is like an enormous spider web and if you touch it, however lightly, . . . the vibration ripples to the remotest perimeter and the drowsy spider feels the tingle . . . springs out to fling the gossamer coils about you . . . then injects the black, numbing poison under your hide. It does not matter whether you meant to brush the web of things. . . . what happens always happens. (188)

Briefly summarized, the theme is that even small unintentional acts and events can have consequences that reverberate, setting up a chain of cause and effect in our lives and the lives of others. (Willie Stark and others touch the web of circumstance.)

To write about theme, consider that it results from other elements. Look for a series of events and ideas that seem to be connected. Are there sets of circumstances that seem significant? What do they say about human life or values? Also keep in mind that there is not just one way to set forth a theme; readers' statements of theme from the same work will vary. Although theme is sometimes difficult to state, you can start your prewriting notes by answering the questions in the checklist.

CHECKLIST: QUESTIONS FOR FINDING CLUES TO THEME

1. Does a set of related events, decisions, behavior, or symbols seem noteworthy? What might they mean?
2. What do characters feel strongly about? What is important to them?
3. What values are revealed by their responses?
4. What happens that strengthens or weakens human character? Could a universal statement be made about this?
5. What other aspects of plot and character challenge, entertain, or disgust readers? What do all these aspects seem to say about human life?

Revising

Accuracy, reasonableness, and fairness are key qualities to aim for in revising the draft of an analytical paper. Scrutinize your draft and add tentative words, qualifying phrases, and textual evidence to support claims and inferences. The following checklist will help you to avoid going out on the proverbial limb.

CHECKLIST FOR REVISING AN ANALYSIS OF LITERATURE

1. Is the thesis of my analysis clear? What elements will be discussed in the paper?
2. Is there enough evidence to support my thesis?
3. Are my main points clearly related to the thesis?
4. Is the discussion organized in a clear, logical order?
5. How familiar will the audience be with the work? How much do I need to explain?
6. How does the tone of the analysis sound? Is it serious? Is it overly critical or overly favorable?
7. Do I include at least one significant example (preferably more) to support each inference?
8. Are examples labeled correctly? (To check, see "Elements of Literature," near the beginning of this chapter.)
9. Has each inference been identified by a qualifier such as *indicates*, *suggests*, or another tentative term?
10. Do I explain how elements contribute to meaning?
11. Might I have overlooked any symbols or irony?
12. Have I identified the theme of the work?

Student Paper: Literary Analysis

The writer of the next paper had difficulty in limiting her topic because Updike's story has such splendid unity. Each element is tightly linked to another. She wanted to focus on symbolism but found that impossible to discuss without mentioning plot and character. And since much of the symbolism of the games was ambiguous, she selected only the clearest symbols.

Breaking Up Is Hard to Do

John Updike's short story "Still of Some Use" focuses on one day in the lives of a divorced couple and their children. The plot is simple, but the characterization and symbols are complex. Foster, his former wife, and their two grown sons are cleaning out the attic of the vacant house they once shared. The older son's girlfriend is also helping. Near the end, the former wife's friend Ted arrives. The story is revealed through Foster's eyes, although the omniscient narrator occasionally interjects a helpful comment.

To glimpse the conflicting emotions of the characters, the reader must peel back layers of symbolism, double meanings, and other clues. Implicit is an analogy between the contents of the attic and the former marriage: both are obsolete—the last tangible remnants of their lives together are being hauled to the dump. The characters' responses to this event vary. The older son seems unmoved, but the younger son, Tommy, is visibly upset. Although the older son and his girlfriend notice, neither seems empathetic. He remarks that Tommy has been "mooning over old stuff." She says Tommy is "very sensi-tive."

But the boys' mother is concerned and asks Foster to "talk to Tommy." She adds, "This is harder on him than he shows." Although Foster has kept a tight rein on his emotions, his inner conflict becomes evident when, "in a kind of agony," he shouts, "What shall we do with all these games?"

When his sons respond, "Trash 'em" and "Toss 'em," Foster is stunned. He stares at the "sad wealth of abandoned playthings" and remembers how "their lives had touched these tokens and counters once." He wishes they had played with them more often. Foster's former wife, too, seems reluctant to discard the games, asking, "Would Goodwill want them?"

Nor does she seem altogether happy about severing the marriage ties. Small clues hint at her emotional conflict. When Foster asks how she can bear to leave the house, she seems to reply a bit too quickly and flippantly to be convincing, saying, "Oh, it's fun once you get into it. Off with the old, on with the new." This response sounds defiant. She seems to still care for Foster. For instance, when he sits staring out the attic window, she asks, "What's the matter?" After listening a moment, she says, "You better stop now; it's making you too sad." Later she shares her drink with Foster—a gesture of intimacy.

There is little doubt about how Foster feels about the divorce. When he and his former wife are alone in the attic, regret overwhelms him. He looks at her, and the "attic tremble[s] slightly." Later he seems almost desperate as he begs, "Give me one sip." Only minutes before he had refused a drink. Does he want only to press his lips where hers have been?

Clearly, Foster is reluctant to part with the past. He wonders: What if they had "avoided divorce"? Then all the games would have stayed in the attic, their "sorrow [imperfections] unexposed." This passage suggests Foster would have preferred to remain in a marriage with his imperfections unexposed (to him).

So what does the reader actually learn about the breakup of the marriage? Not much, although the use of symbols is lavish. The most vivid is the image of games plummeting from the upstairs window to the truck bed: they "exploded," scattering "laughing children," "curious little faces," "hieroglyphs . . . whose code was lost." Like the games, the marriage undoubtedly started out with high expectations, but somehow the code to an enduring relationship was lost (or never found). Finally, the marriage "exploded" in divorce, scattering children and parents. Now the house is empty and the stove disconnected—just as the marriage has been abandoned and the family relationships disconnected.

The games, "aping the strategies of the stock market, of crime detection, of real estate speculation, of international diplomacy and war," seem to represent elements that marred the marriage. But the connection remains hazy and unclear. Had Foster speculated and lost family funds? What else happened? "War" seems to symbolize discord in the marriage.

The word *token* appears several times, suggesting Foster's minimal participation in the family. There are other hints he may have spent little time interacting with other family members: he says "he had not played enough with these games," and "now no one wanted to play." Yet he had spent many hours building a bookcase "so not a nailhead marred its smoothness." Did he devote more attention to objects than to family relationships? Was he an introvert who liked to go off alone? A stronger hint is that Foster never mentions his former wife's or his older son's names. This omission suggests that his relationships with them were not close.

In contrast, Ted is a "radiant brute," an extrovert, full of vitality and confidence, friendly even to Foster. Ted seems to prize time with his own children, visiting them instead of helping with the attic. He is charming and complimentary to Foster. Unlike Foster, Ted takes the initiative. Already he seems to have made himself a member of the family group: he gives fatherly advice, "Don't dawdle till the dump closes" and wipes away "a smudge of dirt along her [Mrs. Foster's] jaw." He even thanks Foster for helping clean the Foster attic, which seems unusual.

Foster realizes his former wife and Ted are now a "couple." Like the "cardboard spacemen" in the discarded games, Foster seems to feel he is a cardboard man, taking up space in a house no longer his. He feels he's "on the wrong square." He feels discarded—of no use as a husband or father. But as he is leaving, Tommy asks him to ride along to the dump. Foster declines, then asks, "This depresses you?"

Tommy admits, "Kind of," and adds, "It's changed since you left. They have all these new rules." Although Tommy is apparently talking about the dump, his face is clouded as if he's about to cry. His words seem to mirror a double meaning: Ted and his mother have new rules, and Tommy misses his father.

Foster senses these undercurrents, for suddenly he changes his mind and his mood. He jokes, "You win. I'll come along. I'll protect you." Foster seems pleased at the request—as if he is "still of some use."

The human desire to be needed and to be useful is a major theme in Updike's complex and disturbing story. Closely allied is the theme that divorce is not the perfect solution in such a situation. And even under amicable circumstances, divorce is never easy.

—Mae Mattix

Summary

By reading literature, we can gain a different perspective on the world and our own lives. Although readers create meaning to some extent, they should rely on evidence found in the work to support their interpretations. Good short stories are concise; every word is essential to the meaning. Novels have the same basic elements as a short story but are much more complex. Plays are meant to be performed; directions are infrequent. The reader must rely mainly on dialogue. Careful note-taking and prewriting are necessary to prepare a draft.

A paper of analysis is often assigned after reading literature. A literary analysis discusses elements of a work and explains how they influence meaning. The paper cites portions of the original text and interprets their function. An analysis is an informed opinion, based on parts of the work in regard to the total content.

The form of a work affects the meaning. Literature takes many forms—novels, short stories, plays, diaries, and letters, for example. The narrator of a fictional work is not the author. The narrator may be a character or an omniscient observer who knows all and who stands outside the action. Or the narrator may have limited omniscience. There may be more than one narrator. The alert reader watches for clues to the "truth" of a story. Literature often reveals meaning indirectly through symbols, irony, and other devices. To write a paper of analysis, discuss significant elements of a work such as setting, plot, characters, or theme.

A paper of analysis requires several readings of the original source and adequate evidence from the source to support inferences and interpretation. The tone should be serious and professional.

FOR YOUR REFERENCE:
SHORT STORIES AND NARRATIVES IN THE READER

- "Story of an Hour," Kate Chopin, page 711
- "Doves," Ursula Hegi, page 703
- "Scheherazade," Charles Baxter, page 707
- "Still of Some Use," John Updike, page 714
- "The Well-Baked Man," page 721
- Genesis 1–2, page 723
- The Koran, page 730

Key Terms

character	irony	round character
conflict	narrator's voice	setting
flat character	omniscient observer	symbolism
foil	plot	theme
foreshadowing	point of view	the human condition

Twenty-Five Ideas for Papers of Literary Analysis

The short stories, narratives, and questions in the Reader can stimulate ideas for papers. Other suggestions for topics are listed below.

1. Analyze the main character of "Doves." How is Francine like the doves? How do they influence her?
2. Analyze the setting, symbolism, and theme of "Doves."
3. Discuss the characterization and plot of "Story of an Hour."
4. Discuss the plot and irony in "Story of an Hour."
5. Compare and contrast the leading characters of "Doves" and "Story of an Hour." Discuss the fantasy that each has and how it influences the outcome of the story.
6. Discuss the influence of *setting* on plot and character in "Scheherazade."
7. Discuss the title, plot, and symbolism of "Scheherazade."
8. Compare the reality of the plot of "Scheherazade" with the fantasy the old woman creates.
9. Analyze the main character in "Scheherazade." Consider the line "It was like combat of a subtle kind."
10. Compare and contrast Foster and his former wife in "Still of Some Use."
11. Compare Foster with Francine ("Doves"). How are they similar in personality and behavior? How do they differ? (*Hint:* Consider initiative.)
12. Discuss the influence of setting, plot, and characterization in "Still of Some Use."
13. Analyze the plot and characterization of "Still of Some Use." Do you think there is hope for reconciliation in this story? Provide reasons and examples for your position.
14. Analyze the main character in "Still of Some Use."
15. Discuss the irony of a work and how it influences plot and character.
16. Compare and contrast the creation account in Genesis 1 and 2 with the account in the selections from the Koran.
17. Discuss the irony in the "The Well-Baked Man." What are the implications for us?
18. Analyze the King James and the Torah versions of Genesis 1–2: 3. What differences do you see? How and why are they significant?
19. Secure a copy of the Bible and read Genesis 3. What relevance does the chapter hold for us today? Consider the behavior of Eve and Adam and their attitude toward responsibility as well as any other topics in the account.
20. Secure a copy of the Koran. Read chapter 15, where there are more details of the creation, the disobedience of Iblis (Satan), and his fate. Then compare and contrast this section with the account in Genesis 3.

21. Compare two short stories with similar themes.

22. Analyze the symbolism in a work and explain how it is related to the theme.

23. Discuss the characterization of a novel. What motivates the main character? How are the other characters depicted? Do they seem realistic and convincing? Why or why not?

24. Select a short story that contains suspense. Analyze how the author creates the suspense. Do you notice any foreshadowing or symbolism? Give specific examples.

25. Compare two characters from different works.

CHAPTER 28

Reading and Responding to Poetry

The poet is the stained glass window
that transmits sunlight just as
ordinary windows do, but colors it
as it passes through.

—Robert Hillyer, *In Pursuit of Poetry*

Poetry has taken a backseat in an age of electronic gadgets and cyberspace. We whiz from our homes to our jobs to other places in a whirlwind of activity. At night we tap away at a computer keyboard or collapse in front of the tube. If we read, it's often the headline news or the comics or self-help books, which poet Tess Gallagher calls "hamburger stands of the soul." Gone are the leisurely evenings and Sunday afternoons spent reading and staring into a wood-burning fire. Now there just doesn't seem to be time to read poetry and ponder tendrils of meaning.

Yet poetry can help us discover a hidden dimension of ourselves. Poetry can connect us more closely to nature and to the human race. In reading a poem, we can peer through a new window on our existence, savoring beauty taken for granted, sharing the warmth of unselfish love or the frigid chill left by death. Poetry acts as a link to the past by recapturing the pleasures and the pains of an earlier age. A poem can reach into the future, kindling desires, fueling dreams—providing the spark that transforms a wish into reality. A poem can fill the present with delight, appreciation, and anticipation. Poetry can yield contentment and acceptance of things we cannot change.

Here the purpose of reading poetry is *not* to classify dozens of literary devices or to analyze meter or to hunt for a message. *The purpose is to enter a poem, to experience it, to look at its parts, and to marvel at its artistry.* Despite careful analysis, any such knowledge is always incomplete. We can never comprehend all there is to know about a work of art—not that all poems are art. But if we approach each one as if it were, then we are more apt to give it a fair hearing.

HOW CAN A READER GET HOLD OF A POEM?

Great poetry has an essence that is elusive. Unlike expository writing, which is primarily concerned with fact and explanation, poetry is primarily feeling. With a few words poets may sketch scenes or wisps of ideas, leaving the reader to fill in the rest. For the most part, poets show rather than tell. And the more passionate their feelings, the simpler their statements. Consider the closing couplet of Countée Cullen's "Yet do I marvel":

> Yet do I marvel at this curious thing:
> To make a poet black and bid him sing.

Readers familiar with the history of the Black experience in the United States will immediately recognize the *paradox*, strange but true, posed in this poem, which was written about 1920. But someone unfamiliar with this period would be unable to fill in the gaps or fully appreciate Cullen's lines. Every word counts; every word is in perfect alignment and tension. The poet has said just enough in a unique and thoughtful way, balancing expectation with surprise.

When readers are required to analyze a poem, they often begin with the question "What does the poem mean?" In the title of his famous textbook, John Ciardi suggests a more effective starting point: "*How* does a poem mean?" For the meaning of a poem is derived not only from its words, but also from its structure. Ciardi also suggests that to study a poem, the reader adopt a playful attitude—for much poetry, like dance, is "a performance" to be appreciated for the pleasure it brings. Ciardi believes the "best any analysis can do is to prepare the reader to enter the poem more perceptively."

To experience joy in comprehending a poem, we need a sense of curiosity, of wonder, and of play. For poets often frolic with words, pairing them in unexpected ways. A sense of play permeates the next poem. To appreciate the structure and sound, read it aloud.

On the Vanity of Earthly Greatness
by Arthur Guiterman

The tusks that clashed in mighty brawls
Of mastodons, are billiard balls.

The sword of Charlemagne the Just
Is ferric oxide, known as rust.

The grizzly bear whose potent hug
Was feared by all, is now a rug.

Great Caesar's bust is on the shelf,
And I don't feel so well myself.

Notice that the poem is composed of four rhyming *couplets*. (A couplet is a set of two successive lines.) Listen to the pace of the words, their slowness or quickness. The first line of each couplet tends to be slow and ponderous whereas the second is quick, especially the last phrase. Hear the sound and movement of certain words: "tusks that clashed," "billiard balls," and "grizzly bear whose potent hug." Note that other words suggest a lack of motion: "rust," "now a rug," and "bust is on the shelf." Each couplet contains surprises not only in sound but also in meaning.

Questions for Discussion

1. Where does the biggest surprise occur?
2. What is the effect of the last line?
3. Does the poem seem to have a purpose other than to provoke amusement?
4. What do you notice about the title that is very different from the poem?
5. How would you state the main idea of Guiterman's poem?

The next poem by Carl Sandburg is more explicit and quite different in tone. Yet despite the macabre images, there is a spirit of sly playfulness, revealed in the grim irony and choice of narrator.

Grass

Pile the bodies high at Austerlitz and Waterloo.
Shovel them under and let me work—
          I am the grass; I cover all.

And pile them high at Gettysburg
And pile them high at Ypres and Verdun.
Shovel them under and let me work.
Two years, ten years, and passengers ask the conductor:
          What place is this?
          Where are we now?

          I am the grass.
          Let me work.

Questions for Discussion

1. What has happened at all the places Sandburg names?
2. Who is the narrator? What is the "work"?
3. What is the significance of the passengers' questions to the conductor? What is the irony here?
4. How is "Grass" similar to "On the Vanity of Earthly Greatness"?
5. How do the treatments of the topic differ?

You may feel frustrated as you try to interpret the layers of meaning and glimpse the core of an apparently simple poem. But if you approach a poem as a work of art with form, sound, movement, and meaning and if you examine its parts with care, then you will begin to see its fusion and unity. Then you will be better prepared to appreciate its artistry.

READING NARRATIVE POEMS

Narrative poems are like miniature stories. They begin with a place and a situation. Often the scene is set very simply with a sparseness of detail. Characters are briefly introduced, and the action begins. The movement is usually from specific to general. Concrete details or symbols often hint of a greater meaning, a *universal truth*, at the end. The length of a narrative poem may vary from an anecdote such as Countée Cullen's "Incident" to a very long ballad such as "The Rime of the Ancient Mariner."

Cullen was born in Louisville, Kentucky, in 1903. By 1925 he had become the most renowned Black writer in North America. Cullen completed theological study at Morgan State College in Baltimore. There he was a Methodist pastor for two years. Then he moved to New York City, where he formed a storefront mission and became politically active. His poem "Incident" deserves several readings.

As you examine this poem, keep in mind that understatement provides a wellspring of power for English poetry. *Understatement*, however, requires the reader to look beneath the surface of a poem to glimpse its essence. To assist in detecting understatement, keep a dictionary handy. Look up any unfamiliar words or any that might have more than one meaning. Consider all meanings of a word; poets often select ambiguous words that create layers of meanings. Also consider the historical period and the cultural norms that existed then:

Incident

by Countée Cullen

Once riding in old Baltimore,
   Heart-filled, head-filled with glee,
I saw a Baltimorean
   Keep looking straight at me.

Now I was eight and very small,
   And he was no whit bigger,
And so I smiled, but he poked out
   His tongue, and called me, "Nigger."

I saw the whole of Baltimore
   From May until December;
Of all the things that happened there
   That's all that I remember.

Questions to Analyze "Incident"

1. Vocabulary: *glee, incident.* (Also see *incidental.*)
2. How would you describe the tone of verse one?
3. What line in verse one conveys strong feeling?
4. Where does Cullen pair expectation with surprise? What is the effect?
5. Comment on the movement of the poem. (*Hint:* Examine the changes in tone from verse to verse.)
6. Ordinarily, a rollicking rhyme structure is not used in a serious poem. Why does it work well here? (*Clue:* Children's poems often use rhyme.)
7. Is this a child's poem? Why or why not?

READING LYRIC POEMS

Originally, lyric poems were sung by the Greeks to the accompaniment of a lyre, a stringed instrument. Lyric poetry, which includes most short poems, covers a broad array of subjects and forms. Rather than telling a story as narrative poetry does, lyric poetry expresses a state of mind, revealing thought and feeling. Since there is no plot, word choice and imagery must be unique in a lyric poem.

Special Effects with Words

Poets select words not only for meaning but also for sound, movement, and color. All four aspects are inseparable. *Alliteration* (repeated consonant sounds), *assonance* (repeated vowel sounds), and rhyme are the most common devices of sound. Another device is *onomatopoeia*, whereby the sound of the word mimics its denotation. Listen to *hum, buzz,* and *crack* as you say them. These words sound like the actions they represent. Onomatopoeia supplies vitality to any poem.

Action verbs also give vitality to poetry, enhancing the image and varying the pace. Words may skip or skitter, slink or slither, sprint or stroll across a page. Let's pause for a moment and consider the verb pairs in the previous sentence. First, visualize the difference in movement between *skip* and *skitter.* A child might skip down a sidewalk, but an autumn leaf skitters across a lawn, blown by the wind in quick irregular spurts.

Next listen to the sounds of the verb pairs. Notice the repetition of *sli* in *slink* and *slither,* which adds smoothness to their sound. Similarly, *ski* is repeated in *skip* and *skitter.* But the third pair sets up a little surprise. Instead of exact repetition at the beginning of the words, the *t* sound comes at a different place in each word: *sprint, stroll.* Finally, listen to the pace. The first word in each verb pair quickens the pace whereas the second slows it. For example, *sprint* with its short *i* is much quicker to say than *stroll* with the long *o* and *ll* sounds.

When you consider adjectives such as *red* and *ruby* or *green* and *emerald*, you can note contrasts in color as well as sound and pace. The eye easily detects that red and green offer an array of shades whereas *ruby* and *emerald* are each a specific shade. As you listen to the sounds, you can hear the quickness of *red* and *green*. *Ruby* and *emerald* sound slower and richer.

Imagery in Lyric Poems

Our cave-dwelling ancestors drew primitive sketches to represent activities and events in their lives. Similarly, poets sketch images with words to represent significant occurrences, ideas, and emotions. In a poem with a single image, all words contribute. *Haiku*, an ancient Japanese form of lyric verse, always focuses on a single image. The form generally consists of three lines of seventeen syllables, based on a metaphor. Implicit in the image is a comparison. Typical haiku describe nature or the seasons, much like the following examples:

The Barley Field
by Joso

Bent down by the rain,
   the ripe barley makes this
     such a narrow lane!

The Barley Field
by Sora

Up the barley rows,
   stitching, stitching them together
     a butterfly goes.

If you have seen wheat or oats growing in a field, then you can easily visualize the field of barley, which also grows in willowy stalks. To compare the two poems, jot down differences in the spaces below, beginning with concrete details. Then ask: How do the details influence the effect of each poem?

	(Joso)	(Sora)
Angle of stalks	_____	_____
Width of rows	_____	_____
Image (metaphor)	_____	_____
Punctuation	_____	_____
Connotations	_____	_____
	_____	_____
Repetition	_____	_____
Literary devices	_____	_____
	_____	_____
Tone	_____	_____

Poems with more than one image lack the splendid unity of poems with a single image. Yet multiple images can be skillfully unified by a central theme. All connotative meanings must, as Ciardi points out, "combine the overtone themes of the words and the images into a single unity." Otherwise, utter confusion could result. To better understand this fusion of multiple images, you might think of a

sunburst: all points are separate, but they fuse at the core. So too, multiple images are separate, yet they meet in a central idea.

Emily Dickinson, famous for her lyric poems, was born in 1830 in Amherst,
Massachusetts. She was educated at Amherst Academy and Mount Holyoke
Seminary. Her innovative style, characterized by whimsical daring and nimble
skill, became a strong influence on twentieth-century poets. Yet Emily Dickinson
was practically unknown at the time of her death; only a few of her poems had
been published in a local newspaper:

[I taste a liquor never brewed]

by Emily Dickinson

I taste a liquor never brewed,
From tankards scooped in pearl;
Not all the vats upon the Rhine
Yield such an alcohol!

Inebriate of air am I,
And debauchee of dew,
Reeling, through endless summer days,
From inns of molten blue.

When landlords turn the drunken bee
Out of the foxglove's door,
When butterflies renounce their drams,
I shall but drink the more!

Till seraphs swing their snowy hats,
And saints to windows run,
To see the little tippler
Leaning against the sun!

Questions to Analyze "I taste a liquor never brewed"

1. Vocabulary: *tankard, debauchee, foxglove, seraphs, tippler.*

2. What does verse one reveal about the "liquor"?

3. What literary devices do you see?

4. Verse two sets the scene and indicates the central theme of the poem.
   How would you state it? (You may want to skip on, then answer later.)

5. How does the poet use signs of intoxication to indicate her mood? How
   does this influence the tone of verses one and two? How do the images in
   verses three and four differ? (*Clue:* places)

6. What attitude is shown in verse four?

7. What is the central idea that unifies the series of images?

8. Why might this poem have seemed daring in the late 1800s?

Although a spirit of play is less apparent in the poetry of Archibald MacLeish, still it is there. MacLeish won the Pulitzer Prize for poetry in both 1933 and 1953. He was not only a distinguished poet but also an author and statesman, working for UNESCO and other organizations. Born in Glencoe, Illinois, MacLeish graduated from Yale University and obtained a law degree from Harvard, where he became a professor. His most famous poem, "Ars Poetica" (Latin for *poetics*, the theory of writing poetry), written in 1926, contains a series of images. These involve sight, sound (or the lack of it), movement, and touch as well as meaning. Think about the texture of the images. What qualities do they have in common?

Ars Poetica
by Archibald MacLeish

A poem should be palpable and mute
As a globed fruit,

Dumb
As old medallions to the thumb,

Silent as the sleeve-worn stone
Of casement ledges where the moss has grown—

A poem should be wordless
As the flight of birds.
*

A poem should be motionless in time
As the moon climbs,

Leaving, as the moon releases
Twig by twig the night-entangled trees,

Leaving, as the moon behind the winter leaves,
Memory by memory the mind—

A poem should be motionless in time
As the moon climbs
*

A poem should be equal to:
Not true.

For all the history of grief
An empty doorway and a maple leaf.

For love
The leaning grasses and the two lights above the sea—

A poem should not mean
But be

Questions to Analyze "Ars Poetica"

1. Vocabulary: *palpable, mute, medallion, casement, be* ("to have life or reality")

2. Why is *palpable* an excellent word for this poem? (Consider the medical meaning of the word as well as the old Latin.)

3. Consider the sound and imagery of "globed fruit," "sleeve-worn stone," "moon climbs," and "poem." What do you notice?

4. What do you notice about the pace of the pair of lines below?
     A poem should be wordless
     As the flight of birds.

5. What words convey the idea of silence?

6. The final line has no period. What is the effect? (*Clues:* What does a period do? What idea is conveyed through "motionless in time" and "history" that is similar to ending without a period?)

7. What else do you notice?

8. Each couplet specifies a quality that a poem should have. What are the qualities?

9. The final verse summarizes the meaning of the poem. How would you paraphrase it?

The Mysterious Fact of Poetic Energy

Josephine Jacobsen has not only won numerous awards but also published ten books of poetry and served two terms as Poetry Consultant to the Library of Congress. She writes: "Poetry is energy, and it is poetic energy that is the source of that instant of knowing that the poet tries to name" (*The Writer*, January 1999). Jacobsen speaks of "the mysterious fact" that selected words, arrayed in an unusual rhythm, begin a "chain reaction explained by nothing in the words themselves or in their content." The cadence of the lines and the idea, perfectly expressed, can haunt us with their beauty and mystery.

For Jacobsen, an instant of knowing was followed by a strange chain reaction. She tells of stumbling upon an old cemetery in New Hampshire fifty years ago. Among the overgrown and broken tombstones, she saw a stone with a pair of clasped hands carved above a woman's name, a date, and two lines of poetry:

> It is a fearful thing to love
> What Death can touch.

These eleven words haunted Jacobsen; she tried to trace them but could not. Much later she wrote a lyric poem about a wartime cemetery and quoted the epitaph. Five years had passed when she read a review of *Agamemnon*, a New York verse-play by William Alfred. The play, at its climax, included the two lines from the tombstone. Jacobsen recognized the lines and wrote Alfred, asking their source, but he did not know. He had taken them from her poem. The energy in those eleven words had struck the poet-dramatist with such force that he placed them at the end of his play.

Jacobsen concludes: "A knowledge of what we already knew [before the poet said it] becomes for an instant so devastatingly fresh that it could be contained no more than a flash of lightning." Good poetry prompts that flash of knowing.

PREPARING AN ANALYSIS OF A POEM

As you browse through poems, choose one you like that offers possibilities for serious discussion. A fairly short poem is usually preferable to a long one, for even a short poem can be complex. You may find different versions of the same poem or possibly different titles. For example, one of William Wordsworth's poems has been widely printed under two different titles: "Daffodils" or "I wandered lonely as a cloud." (Sometimes brackets are placed around the title of a poem when it is reprinted to indicate it was originally untitled.)

See chapter 23

Developing Your Analysis

Do a little research on the poet. After that, reread the poem silently. Then reread it aloud and listen to the sound and movement. Who is speaking? Watch for clues to how the speaker feels about the subject. If the poem has rhyme, is there a pattern to the rhyme? Next, count the number of syllables in each line and write them at the side to determine how the lines compare. Do any have the same number of syllables? Is there a pattern to the arrangement of the lines?

After that, study the definitions and connotations of key words to see how they contribute to the meaning. Write the definitions and connotations near each word. Next, look for similes, metaphors, analogies, personification, symbols—or any other device that links one part of the poem with another. (For more about figurative language, see chapter 27.) Jot brief notes as you go. Write any questions you have at the bottom of the page or on the reverse side. You may find the answers later, or you might discuss the questions with someone else. By the time you have finished, you should have accumulated a page of notes to serve as raw material for a rough draft. (see "Critical Reading" in chapter 26.)

Finally, reread the poem aloud to reassemble the parts in your mind and focus on the effect of the entire work. As you do, chances are that you will begin to see how the parts fuse into a central image or theme.

Organizing the Paper

Although there are many aspects to poetry, first-year college students are usually not expected to cover all of them. Often an analytical paper on a poem is only one or two pages long. If your instructor allows a choice, select major elements

TIPS FOR ANALYZING A POEM

1. *Make a copy of the poem, enlarging it, but leaving 1½-inch margins.* The copy will provide a handy way to make notes and gain an overview.

2. *Read biographical sketches.* Gaining insight into an author's back ground and the spirit of the times is often helpful in understanding a work. Encyclopedias offer easy access to brief biographies. Some poetry books include abstracts of poets' lives. Or you may find a book-length biography.

3. *Hold off on interpretation.* Going into a poem with preset ideas can close the mind. Withhold judgment, be open to newness.

4. *Look up unfamiliar words.* Read all definitions listed for a word. Poets often select words with double or triple meanings to enrich a poem. Jot definitions near the example if possible.

5. *Examine the words.* What is the level of language? Is dialect, jargon, or other special terminology used? What does this usage imply?

6. *Listen to the feeling behind the words.* How does the voice of the narrator sound? From what point of view or perspective is the voice speaking? Listen to the nuances of the words. What emotion do you sense?

7. *Listen for devices of sound and movement.* Do you notice rhyme? Alliteration? Assonance? Onomatopoeia? Any other device? How does the rhythm (pattern of sound) of the poem reinforce the meaning?

8. *Look for figurative language.* Are there similes, metaphors, personification, symbolism, or other devices that contribute to an image?

9. *Notice punctuation.* Poetry, like prose, is punctuated for a reason. Consider the effect of punctuation—or the lack of it—upon meaning.

10. *Keep the context of the poem in mind while looking at its parts.* Try to discover how each part is linked to the whole.

11. *Consider possible meanings.* Read the poem aloud. What does the imagery suggest? What do the words say? Might there be more than one interpretation? If so, which one fits best and why? Review your notes.

12. *What is the total effect of the poem?* What is your response to it?

that interest you. Then explain your impression of the way various elements contribute to the unity and meaning of the poem.

GUIDELINES: ORGANIZING AND DEVELOPING A POETIC ANALYSIS

1. Identify the poem as narrative or lyric. If a special type, specify.
2. Follow the order of the poem as nearly as possible.
3. Explain how the word choice, symbolism, or other elements contribute to the overall effect of the poem.
4. Cite examples of elements.
5. State your perception of the central idea.
6. Describe your response to the poem.

If the poem is short, include the entire text in your paper. If the poem is over half a page, attach a copy to your paper unless the poem is in your textbook. To quote fewer than four lines, use quotation marks and indicate line breaks by a slash mark: "Inebriate of air am I / And debauchee of dew." (*Note:* One space is placed before and after each slash.) If you quote four lines or more of poetry, indent and treat as a long direct quotation (with no quotation marks).

Revising an Analysis of a Poem

Even though your paper of analysis is only a page or two, check the organization and revise carefully. The following questions will help you revise your draft. Select the items that pertain to your subject.

CHECKLIST: REVISING AN ANALYSIS OF A POEM

1. Do I have a clear thesis?
2. Do I follow a logical order?
3. Have I discussed the central image (or series of images)?
4. Are any symbols present? Have I explained how they contribute?
5. Have I discussed the devices of sound in the poem?
6. Are there any similes, metaphors, or personification not yet discussed?
7. Have I pointed out connections between related ideas?
8. Have I considered how the poem appears on the page? How many stanzas there are? Their length and any other significant aspects?
9. Have I interpreted the central idea of the poem?

STUDENT PAPER: ANALYSIS OF A POEM

The following example shows one way to organize an analytical paper. A poem of this length usually appears on a separate page, before the analysis. (Wordsworth's poem was written about 1800 in the British Lake District.)

[I wandered lonely as a cloud]
by William Wordsworth

I wandered lonely as a cloud
That floats on high o'er vales and hills,
When all at once I saw a crowd,
A host of golden daffodils;
Beside the lake, beneath the trees
Fluttering and dancing in the breeze.

Continuous as the stars that shine
And twinkle on the milky way,
They stretched in never-ending line
Along the margin of a bay:
Ten thousand saw I at a glance,
Tossing their heads in sprightly dance.

The waves beside them danced; but they
Outdid the sparkling waves in glee;
A poet could not but be gay
In such a jocund company;
I gazed—and gazed—but little thought
What wealth the show to me had brought:

For oft, when on my couch I lie
In vacant or in pensive mood,
They flash upon that inward eye
Which is the bliss of solitude;
And then my heart with pleasure fills,
And dances with the daffodils.

Form and Meaning in "I wandered lonely as a cloud"

Every time I read William Wordsworth's poem "I wandered lonely as a cloud," it is a source of pleasure. The dazzling beauty of the daffodils is one that any reader can readily conceive and enjoy. But this lyric poem is much more than a vivid description, with contrasts of sight and sound. The poem is alive with motion.

In the first line the narrator compares himself to the cloud that "floats high." The tone of this line and the next differs greatly from that of other lines. The narrator's loneliness is juxtaposed to the happy sight of a "host of golden daffodils . . . Tossing their heads in sprightly dance."

Light radiates throughout the poem in the words *golden, stars, shine, twinkle, milky way, sparkling waves,* and *flash.* Alliteration in *stars, shine, stretched, saw, sprightly* and in *Ten thousand . . . Tossing* focuses on this glorious sight.

Assonance contributes not only to the unity of the poem but also to the sound, varying the pace. The repetition of the long *o* in *lonely*, *floats*, *o'er*, and other examples slows the lines and suggests aloneness. The long *a* in *gazed* and its repetition reflect the narrator's reluctance to leave. In contrast is the short, quick *e*, in "Beside the lake, beneath the trees."

Personification and movement are major features of the poem. The daffodils toss their heads, dance, and laugh with *glee*. Movements of dance are conveyed by the words. *Fluttering* suggests short spurts of movement; *dancing*, a smooth glide. The rhyme scheme and the length of lines mimic the dance of the daffodils. Although the end rhyme is exact, the pattern of rhyming varies in the third stanza. No stanza has the same pattern, although some have the same number of syllables per line. These lines suggest the movement of dancers to music.

If there is a theme to the poem, it might be stated as "Beauty can nourish the spirit" or "Drink in every drop of beauty and store it to cheer the soul."

—Bettina Dietrich

Summary

Perhaps the best way to approach a poem is to regard it as a work of art until evidence to the contrary is found. Poems may be narrative or lyric. Poetry tends to be indirect, showing more than telling. Form and meaning are intertwined. Concrete language, imagery, figures of speech, and devices of sound and movement contribute to the meaning of a poem.

To write an analysis of poetry, select a fairly short poem that you like. As you read it aloud, listen to the sound and movement. Watch for clues to the speaker's attitude toward the subject. Count the syllables in each line. Is there rhyme? A rhyme scheme? Figures of speech? What else do you notice? To organize your paper, follow the order of the poem as much as possible. Take examples from the poem and explain how they contribute to the meaning. You might end by describing your response to the poem.

Key Terms

alliteration	lyric poetry	paradox
assonance	narrative poetry	understatement
couplet	onomatopoeia	universal truth
haiku	pace	

Practice

Ideas for Writing

1. React to the two haiku entitled "The Barley Field." Which do you prefer? Why? Write a short essay giving your response.

2. Analyze Emily Dickinson's poem "I taste a liquor never brewed."

3. Analyze another poem in this chapter and explain how some elements contribute to meaning.

4. Read and analyze another poem of your choice.

5. Research the life of your favorite poet and select one poem that reveals his or her philosophy. Write a short paper that summarizes his life and philosophy. Relate the poem to the philosophy.

Essay Exam Writing, Employment Writing, and Oral Presentations

Part 7

CHAPTER 29

Writing Effective Essay Exams

Procrastination is the thief of time.

—Edward Young
  Night Thoughts (1742–46) 1.393.

Many students procrastinate when preparing for examinations. They wait until the night before and drink cola or coffee by the quart to stay awake while they study. During the exam they are so exhausted they can barely keep their eyes open, much less focus scattered thoughts to write complete essay answers. Pulling an all-nighter is not an effective way to study for any exam, particularly essay exams, which often require analytical thinking and synthesis of ideas. To write effective essay answers, you need to prepare well throughout the term.

PREPARING FOR EXAMS

Excellent preparation is probably the best way to decrease anxiety before an exam. Good study habits not only decrease stress but also yield better grades than cramming. The rule of thumb for college study is "two hours out of class for every hour in class." This means that if you're taking sixteen hours of classes per week, you study thirty-two hours per week. About ten days before final exams, start allowing extra time for review every day. Allotting this much time for study requires skillful planning.

Time Management

If finding thirty-two hours a week to study seems impossible, don't despair. There are 168 hours in a week and many practical ways to become efficient. The first is simple—just resolve early in the term to manage your time wisely and improve your study habits. The second step is to take control of your time by setting priorities and making a schedule.

Setting Priorities and Scheduling   Two keys to efficient scheduling are *rating your priorities early* in the term and *disciplining yourself* to follow through. Decide which of your activities are most important. Mark them high priority (HP). Place these items on a monthly calendar. (One big sheet for each month allows you to quickly check each day to see what is coming up.) Include exam dates as well as deadlines for papers and projects. Include work and high-priority personal activities, too. If two high-priority items conflict on the same date, plan ahead so that one can be rearranged or completed early.

Shuffle medium priorities (MP), those that are less urgent or less important, around high priorities. Postpone low-priority (LP) items until after your final exam. Be ruthless in assessing priorities if you are serious about earning good grades. Even though you might prefer to hang out with friends, go to a concert, or build a new deck, put study time first. Activities will wait; exams will not.

Second, make a detailed *weekly calendar* so that you can develop a routine. Otherwise, there may be a tendency to forget. Mark your class hours, study times, work hours (if you have a job), and other high-priority items. A routine can help you become more efficient. But keep in mind that a schedule is simply a tool to organize your day and serve as a reminder. It should be flexible enough to accommodate a change when necessary. You should leave a little flextime in case of an emergency.

Third, make a *to-do list* for high-pressure days when you have a dozen things pending. Carry the day's list with you as a reminder. As you complete an item, cross it off. If something does not get done, place it on your agenda for the following day. Making a to-do list the night before decreases stress and increases your sense of being in control.

Setting priorities and following a schedule can help you develop a "can-do" attitude. Then you can enjoy the confidence and satisfaction that flow from being in control of your time.

Timesavers   There are four relatively painless ways to save time. Studying during your *prime time* is the most effective way. Your prime time is the portion of the day when you are most alert and able to retain what you read. Long ago I learned that, for me, one hour of study in the early morning was more effective than two hours late at night. Night owls may find the reverse is true. Whenever possible, use your prime time to study.

Another way to become more efficient is to study at odd moments. Then you can make *double use* of time. While a carpool buddy drives (or on weekend trips), hit the books! Or you might tape your class notes and listen while you drive. Study on breaks, during lunch, and for the five minutes or so before a class begins. Study while waiting for appointments, at airports, or during flights. Can you think of other ways to double up and use "lost time"?

A third way to devote more time to study is to obtain help, especially during exam week. A study buddy can ask questions and help you think through major concepts. If you are responsible for a family, is there someone who might assist at home? Might you trade child care with a friend? (Retired parents or grandparents can also provide help.)

Finally, when your schedule is squeezed, be ready to forgo leisure *temporarily*. Discipline yourself to say no to television, to hanging out with friends, and to must-see films when you need to study. (Films will come back later on video.) Giving high priority to learning will help you achieve your college and career goals.

Reviewing for Essay Exams

If you have studied regularly throughout the term, attended classes, taken good notes (and perhaps typed them each evening), then a week or so of review should be enough. Cramming should be unnecessary. The suggestions that follow can help you to organize your review time.

1. *Plan the review*. To start your review, first scan the table of contents of your textbook. There you can gain an *overview* of material assigned during the term. Note how the chapters are divided into major and minor categories. Second, *mark HP by the categories (or chapters) that will need extensive review*. Mark others either MP or LP. Then review the high-priority sections first, the medium-priority next, and the low-priority (material you know well) last. That way if you run out of time, you will have reviewed the most difficult chapters.

2. *Think and question*. As you review, think about the major ideas and how they are related. Since you will not have time to reread all the assigned material, pay close attention to textbook headings. *Turn the headings into questions* and try to answer orally. If you can't answer a question, scan the section for the answer. Better yet, make up several essay questions and write out the answers. This practice will force you to examine and synthesize ideas in your own words as you strive for complete answers.

   As you review your notes, highlight major points the instructor has emphasized. In a history, sociology, psychology, art, philosophy, literature, or other course, consider *causes, influences*, and *trends. How have they affected the culture?* Consider how people and events are linked. What changes have occurred? Making a diagram or outline can help you visualize and retain this information.

3. Use *memory aids*. In science, geography, composition, and other courses, you may review processes and memorize information. Then it is important to know the steps of the process and understand how the steps influence the result. A course may require you to memorize statistics, definitions, rules, principles, or other information.

   Any way that you can think of to divide material into smaller recognizable units will make it easier to retain. Some students make *flashcards* (from index cards) to review definitions, dates, and rules, putting a few on each card. Some use *color coding* to group items in a list. For example, one student divided a list of twelve items into two columns. Then she tinted the first three items red, the second group green, the third yellow, and the fourth group orange. The colors helped her to visualize the list.

Making acronyms can also help you to remember. For example, if you have four items, such as communication skills, to learn, memorize the first letter of each one as a reminder: **RSRR**

- Restatement/paraphrasing
- Summarizing
- Responding to nonverbal cues
- Responding to feelings

A traditional method of review that works well for many students is recitation. You say answers aloud to yourself or to someone else. Recitation can be combined with flashcards and color coding. Just say the answer before you look at the cards or colored lists.

Some students prefer to type an outline of their notes, particularly of difficult material. For them, an outline condenses and makes remembering easier. It also saves time in reviewing. You may find that certain methods work better for certain types of material. Try to discover a combination that works well for you.

4. *Encourage yourself.* If you have followed your study schedule rather well and completed your high- and medium-priority tasks this term, commend yourself! These achievements take self-discipline, which is not easy. If you haven't done so well, resolve to turn over a new leaf and begin now!

As you review each lesson, *give yourself positive feedback and encouragement.* Visualize yourself completing the exam successfully. Refuse to succumb to negative thoughts and the "what if" syndrome. ("What if I can't remember the answer? What if I fail?") Negative thinking is a dead end. It sabotages your time and ability to concentrate. From time to time, reward yourself with brief breaks. A glass of ice water and a bit of exercise will help you think more clearly.

Predicting Essay Exam Questions

Attending class regularly, particularly the sessions before exams, is advisable. Many instructors share study hints and sample questions during classes before an exam. Have a pen poised, ready to record even the casual remarks an instructor makes about an exam. Listen carefully for hints that may be disguised by a joking manner—for example, "Memorize the headings!" Translated, this usually means you need to study the major ideas of the textbook. If in doubt ask, "Do you mean word for word?"

Or an instructor may smile and say, "Just remember *everything* I've covered in the lectures!" This means you can depend heavily on your notes—if they are complete. If not, try to secure a good copy from someone else. Beware, however, of letting your own notes out of your sight unless you have them on a computer disk in a safe place. There is the danger of notes not being returned or of their being lost or stolen.

Some instructors may prepare a short study guide. Others may volunteer only the time of the exam and vague suggestions for study. In either case, feel free to ask reasonable questions: Will dictionaries, spelling checkers, or thesauruses be allowed? Will the exam be on paper or computer? Will the exam contain only essay questions or a combination?

Open Book Exams   Be forewarned that a question about open book exams may evoke laughter. To the uninitiated, an open book exam sounds as if it would not require much study. But the truth is that you have to prepare just as much or even more! Although textbooks are permitted during an open book exam, the odds are stacked against your having time to use them.

Open book exams are so long that if you spend time searching for answers, finishing the exam is doubtful. Once I saw three fellow students come in with textbooks loaded with colored slips of paper and topical references. During the exam they rapidly flipped pages, hunting for answers. None of the three completed the exam. There is no substitute for well-planned study and review.

Two Types of Essay Questions

Exam questions may be broad or narrowly focused. Broad questions allow leeway in answering. They may ask you to *trace or state* influences, developments, or history. Such questions require listing a series of significant events or changes in *chronological* order and explaining their evolution, as in the question below:

- Trace the development of computers from the first practical model up to the present.

Or you may be asked to *analyze, discuss, explain, comment on,* or *account for* influences, changes, or trends, as in this question:

- Analyze the influence of World War II on women's lives from 1941 to 1950.

Narrowly focused questions are more specific. Sometimes they use some of the same words but narrow the scope of the answer. They may ask you to *identify, cite, compare, contrast, list, argue, defend, justify, support, evaluate,* and so on. These questions may be stated in one sentence or in more than one, as in the following examples:

- Discuss the roller-coaster performance of the Dow Jones Index in 2002 and cite the chief causes of its many fluctuations.
- Contrast Walter Mitty's real life with his secret life. Give two major reasons why he feels the need to escape from reality.

Taking Essay Exams

To perform at your best level, get a full night's rest before an exam. Eat lightly on exam day, but avoid meal skipping. Going without food can lower the blood sugar, which can result in fatigue and inability to concentrate. Daily exercise, even walking a few blocks before the exam, contributes to a sense of well-being and helps to control *test anxiety*. Deep breathing and drinking cold water can also help you feel more alert and less anxious. Rested and energized, you will be able to think more clearly.

Arrive about five minutes early with all your supplies on exam day. If you arrive too early, you may find yourself listening to someone wail about the upcoming exam. Take two pens (one may run dry), plenty of theme paper (the instructor may not supply it), a dictionary, and anything else you will need. If the exam is on a computer with a spelling checker, some supplies may seem unnecessary but still may be useful.

Check the chalkboard for messages. Sometimes an instructor has been detained, or the exam has been moved to another room. Yet some students may sit and chat, not thinking to glance at the board.

TIPS FOR WRITING ESSAY ANSWERS

1. **Preview the test.** Scan the entire test. If you have a choice of questions, say five of seven, mark out the two you will not answer. *Do not spend time on extra questions for which you will receive no credit.*

2. **Plan your time according to the worth of the questions.** If all questions are weighted equally, allot equal time. If a question is worth more than the others, allot more time there.

3. **Start with the easiest question.** Answering one completely will boost your confidence.

4. **When stalled for an answer, move on to another question or take a quick break.** Walk down the hall, breathe deeply. You may think of the answer. If not, move on and do your best.

5. **Keep your exam until the last possible moment.** Do not leave early. Instead, go back and check your answers. If you see any omissions or think of significant details, add them.

6. **If you see you are running out of time, start outlining your answers.** It is better to earn partial points than to leave a question blank and earn none.

Avoid bringing coffee, soft drinks, or food to class. If you are nervous or some-one bumps you, drinks may spill. Crumbs and smears may stick to exams. Then too, food wrappings can be noisy and distracting to other students who are trying to concentrate.

WRITING COMPLETE ESSAY EXAM ANSWERS

Before writing an exam answer, read the entire question. Two major causes of low grades on essay exams are that students omit parts or misread the question. Hurrying through instructions is a path to disaster. Be sure that you understand what is required. A minute spent reading and considering a question can make the difference between an incomplete answer and a complete one.

To answer essay questions completely, you need to follow directions, orga-nize, and provide adequate support. You may need to supply a definition or ex-ample, compare or contrast, classify, formulate a persuasive argument, or apply some other writing strategy. Instructors expect you to cite significant points and explain connections clearly without becoming entangled in trivial details. Clear, concise answers are better than long rambling padded ones. Strive for quality, not quantity.

Understanding the Question

To answer essay questions completely, you need to know the precise mean-ings of certain verbs commonly used on exams. These words contain clues to the writing strategy that will best organize an essay answer. Listed below are defini-tions of verbs frequently found on essay exams:

Definitions of Common Verbs in Essay Questions

Account for: to explain, as a cause and its effect; to justify

Analyze: to examine the parts of and determine their connections

Clarify: to explain; to present details, reasons, or examples

Defend, justify, support: to give reasons for; to offer evidence

Define: to give the meaning; to describe basic characteristics

Discuss: to examine and consider; to present details and reasons

Evaluate: to examine advantages and disadvantages; rate or judge

Explain: to make clear; to define or offer reasons

Identify: to define; to give the characteristics of

Trace: to track or explain in chronological order

Every word of an essay question should be read carefully. Then think about the meaning. Even if you draw a blank, do not panic. Reread the question. Mark key words and phrases so that you can quickly refer to them when needed. These

WRITING STRATEGIES SUGGESTED BY KEY PHRASES

Key Phrases	Writing Strategies
Trace, give the history of	Narration
Provide details, describe	Description
Explain, list, provide examples of	Illustration
Discuss or analyze the parts of	Division-classification
Analyze, explain how, show how	Process analysis
Discuss advantages/disadvantages	Comparison-contrast
Show similarities/differences	Comparison-contrast
Account for, analyze the results of	Cause-effect
Discuss or explain reasons for	Cause-effect
Identify, clarify, explain the term	Definition
Defend, evaluate, justify, support	Argument-persuasion

words will direct your answer and indicate the strategy of writing you need to organize your answer.

Drafting Complete Essay Answers

As soon as you are clear about what a question requires, begin prewriting in the margins or on the back of the exam. Then identify your main points and number them. This start can serve as a working outline. Write your first draft on the exam paper or in the exam booklet; rarely is there enough time to recopy. Instead, use any extra time to check and edit your answers. Instructors are more concerned with accuracy, completeness, and correctness than with neatness.

Paragraph Essays   Usually, the instructor gives out a sheet with half a dozen essay questions or else writes them on the chalkboard. From the list, you select one or more, as directed. To begin an essay paragraph, write a clear topic sentence. To organize support sentences, refer to your working outline.

As you draft, keep in mind the *basic pattern of claim and evidence*. In other words, every detail and example in the paragraph should support the claim of the topic sentence. Use complete sentences. Fragments can lead to confusion and a loss of points. At the end of your answer, leave a few lines in case you think of more information later.

When you are faced with writing several essay exam answers, focus on one question at a time. If you should think of information for another question before you finish the first, jot down the idea and put it aside. Continue this way, using your prewriting and outlining to organize each answer. The precautions that follow will also help you write complete essay answers.

PRECAUTIONS FOR WRITING COMPLETE ESSAY ANSWERS
1. *Heed directions:* Listen to oral instructions. Check the blackboard for any corrections. Read exam questions twice.
2. *Highlight* or *underline* key terms.
3. *Number the parts* of multifaceted questions.
4. *Check off numbers* of parts after you answer each one.
5. *When finished with the exam,* check the answers you are least sure of. If you think of more information, add. Proofread.

SAMPLE PARAGRAPH ESSAY

The three-part essay question below calls for definition, contrast, and division. The one-paragraph answer opens with a definition before the topic sentence. The support sentences follow.

Question: Define *information interview.* How does it differ from an employment interview? State three specific advantages of this interview.

      Answer: An information interview is a meeting with an employer for the

Definition   direct purpose of gaining information about a career field, not to get a job.

Contrast   The information interview has three distinct advantages. It provides first-

Topic Sentence hand information about a position you hope to be working in some day. It

Support   allows you an inside look at a company to see whether or not you would enjoy working there. It allows access to employers whom you might not be able to contact otherwise. You may even be asked to bring your résumé or

Example   to come in for an employment interview. In fact, that is what happened to me last week. Tomorrow I start my new job as a medical transcriptionist.

Summary   The information interview is truly an excellent technique for uncovering the "hidden jobs" that are never advertised.

Long Exam Essays   Instead of several paragraph essays, you may be asked to write an in-class paper. Always state your thesis early. Questions about literature usually ask you to analyze elements of fiction such as theme and character. They may ask about symbolism, irony, or other devices (see chapters 27 and 28).

Some essay questions may call for a *reaction.* A written reaction goes a step further than an analysis. A paper of reaction includes an opinion based on facts. If you are asked to react to a reading, you respond to the main *idea* and add your well-reasoned opinion (see chapter 26).

Summary

Procrastination leads to ineffective study. Instead, start early in the term to manage your time well. Set priorities and make schedules to increase your efficiency. Make a monthly calendar, weekly calendar, and a daily to-do list. Use your prime time for study, make double use of time, get help, and limit leisure activities when necessary.

Regular study throughout the term is probably the best way to decrease test anxiety as well as earn good grades. Developing a "can-do" attitude can alleviate anxiety and improve study habits. Following the tips for taking essay exams can assist you in controlling anxiety and in using exam time wisely.

Understanding and predicting types of essay questions can help you write complete answers. Read the entire question carefully. Mark the key words because they imply a writing strategy for your answer. Prewrite before drafting. Emphasize quality, not quantity.

Paragraph essays should start with a topic sentence. Long essays need a thesis sentence. Some questions may require a paper of reaction, which includes a well-reasoned opinion.

Key Terms

analyze	explain	rationale
defend	identify	reaction
define	justify	trace
evaluate	priorities	

Practice

Make Your Own Study Questions

To master the suggested study techniques for essay exams, make up your own study questions. Base them on the headings in this chapter. Leave spaces for your answers. After you have finished, check your answers with the text to see that you have included all significant points.

Draft an Essay Exam Answer

Sample Exam Question: Identify the chief obstacles you face when preparing for an essay exam. Which suggestions in this chapter might you adopt to alleviate these concerns and improve your study habits? Write a well-developed paragraph, citing specific details, reasons for your answer, and a plan for effective study.

Employment Writing for the Twenty-First Century

I hope I shall possess firmness and virtue enough to maintain what I consider the most enviable of all titles, the character of an "Honest Man."

—George Washington (1732–99)

With the Information Age, our culture has catapulted into cyberspace. From the World Wide Web, you can research companies, read job listings, and secure résumé help. You can even post your own résumé on the Web, if you wish. Posting requires an Internet version, a plain text document that can be sent through e-mail or cut and pasted into online forms. But don't be misled into thinking an Internet posting is a one-hour shortcut to a job. Richard N. Bolles, whose *Net Guide* includes "The Fairy Godmother Report on Résumé Sites," says the chances are that an Internet résumé will go unread.

I. WRITING AN EFFECTIVE RÉSUMÉ

Bolles's report emphasizes the fact that most job seekers need a printed résumé for mailing and faxing. If they apply to large companies that screen résumés with software, they will also need a scannable résumé. And since many companies request a résumé be sent by electronic mail, a third version may be required.

Compiling different versions of a résumé is not as complicated as you might think, for all versions have the same basic content. Only the format is varied. This chapter presents up-to-date suggestions for printed, scannable, and electronic résumés. It also explains writing letters for employment and compiling a list of references. Included, too, are Web sites where you can secure career information without charge (see the directory on page 501).

REASONS RÉSUMÉS ARE CULLED

As you assemble your personal data on your education, experience, and skills, double-check all dates carefully. As employers scan your résumé and check your references, they watch for discrepancies, which may indicate carelessness or dishonesty. For example, one woman learned her résumé had been weeded out for an accounting position because she had accidentally misstated the date of her college graduation by one year. Other common reasons for discarding résumés are

- *Not following employers' directions.* For example, employers often request a cover letter to be e-mailed before a résumé.
- *Problems in format.* A résumé should be clear and legible. E-mail and scanners require special precautions.
- *Skimpy listing of skills and experience.* Develop your presentation in a positive way.
- *Spelling and grammatical errors.* Employers consider such errors inexcusable. Most positions for college graduates require accuracy and writing competency.

TWO POPULAR STYLES OF PRINTED RÉSUMÉS

Résumé styles evolve over the years, sometimes rather quickly. Often the ones found in books become outdated. For example, renditions of the simplified and functional résumés from the 1980s and early 1990s are not the same as today's styles.

The suggestions in this chapter focus on providing necessary dates as well as accomplishments and skills directly related to the job objective. Many employers have said these résumés rank among the best they have seen. Two popular styles for printed résumés are explained: the chronological and the functional. The basic principles for writing résumés apply to both styles, regardless of whether they are faxed, scanned, or e-mailed.

The Chronological Résumé

The *chronological* résumé style emphasizes solid qualifications and achievement over several years in one career field. This style highlights education and work experience, setting forth what the applicant has accomplished. If you have had steady work in your chosen career field, progressed upward, and acquired the skills for your targeted position, then the chronological style is probably the best choice for you.

The content of the chronological résumé is similar to that of the functional résumé. The chief difference is that the chronological places more emphasis on work experience and less on skills.

The Functional Résumé

The *functional* résumé style emphasizes skills and abilities—not when, where, or how you obtained them. Dates are de-emphasized because there is no long work history. Often new college graduates have minimal work experience; this way they can fill out their résumé with groups of skills. As for older students who have worked many years, they need go back only ten years or fifteen years if the job was in their targeted field. Usually, it is to their advantage to emphasize transferable skills rather than experience in another field.

The beauty of the functional résumé style is that it allows you to list competencies acquired from hobbies, volunteer work, and college courses. A functional résumé has other advantages, too. If you lack paid work experience in your chosen career field, if you plan to change careers, or if you have hopped from job to job, then these facts are minimized.

Gaps in employment are less noticeable on a functional résumé. If you have dropped out of the workforce for family obligations, health problems, or other reasons, then these irregularities need not raise red flags on a functional résumé. This style emphasizes capabilities and skills—what you can do. The flexibility of the functional style makes it the best choice for most students.

RESEARCH AND PREWRITING FOR A RÉSUMÉ

The purpose of any résumé is to obtain an interview. To succeed, you need to package your qualifications in the most appealing way possible as long as the résumé does not deviate from the truth. Writing an effective résumé requires knowledge, skill, effort, and sincerity. You need to have a general knowledge of your career field, know what employers want, have certain skills, and present yourself well. From your résumé and during interviews, prospective employers will be trying to predict how you will fit in with the company and how you will perform.

The first step to a successful résumé is preliminary research. You need background knowledge of your career field, of working conditions, and of existing positions. New jobs are being created constantly.

Gaining an Overview of a Career Field

Although the Internet has a wealth of resources, you can fritter away hours online. But in an hour or less, you can gain an overview of a field and the range of positions within it at your campus library or career center. CD-ROMs can provide profiles of career fields on state and national levels. A computerized index or the *Readers' Guide to Periodical Literature* will assist you in locating articles in journals and magazines. The *Occupational Outlook Handbook* and the *Dictionary of Occupational Titles* define conventional jobs as well as many not commonly known. To locate these or other materials, ask the reference librarian.

After a preliminary search, you should have a general idea of the field and the employment opportunities there. The second phase of your research is to gather specifics. Read the help-wanted ads in newspapers, in the back pages of journals and some magazines, and on the Internet. Print out copies of the ads that interest you so that you will know how to focus your résumé and use the correct terminology. This research will acquaint you with the expectations of employers.

Identifying Employers' Needs

The more you know about the qualifications that employers seek, the better you can tailor your résumé to fit a company's specific needs. It also helps to have an understanding of problems that employers commonly face but seldom discuss with applicants: absenteeism, dishonesty, lack of confidentiality, and low productivity. Such items compose an invisible agenda that directs the appraisal of résumés and applicants.

If you can adroitly show on your résumé how a company can benefit from hiring you, the targeted job may well be yours. As you research, watch for answers to the following questions:

1. What are the main duties of the positions?
2. What skills, qualities, and habits do potential employers seek?
3. What keywords recur in help wanted ads?
4. Which kind of position is likely to be most appropriate for me?

Identifying Qualifications

A giant first step toward compiling an effective résumé is the identification of *transferable skills*, skills that can be applied on another job. A skill is an "art, trade, or technique, particularly one requiring the use of the hands or body," developed through practice. Thinking tasks are also skills—analytical tasks such as problem solving, decision making, designing, and the like. After identifying skills, you can devise ways to attest to positive personal qualities and desirable work habits.

Transferable skills will become the heart of your printed résumé. To identify your skills, examine your experience in the workplace, in college, and during leisure hours. You can start by brainstorming. Take three sheets of paper and write three headings: "Work Skills," "Academic Skills," and "Leisure Skills." On the "Work Skills" page, jot down duties and tasks performed from both paid and unpaid jobs. (Include military service and volunteer work.) Leave an inch or so of space between items to add more details later. On the second sheet, list tasks performed during academic training. On the third sheet, list hobbies and any skills you may have developed during leisure hours. To prod a sluggish memory, you might ask yourself questions.

Workplace Skills   As the questions below indicate, workplace skills include many abilities and responsibilities. Some may have been listed in your job description, but others may have been additional tasks you took on.

- *What problems have I helped to solve or alleviate?* Include cost control, procedural changes, security, troubleshooting, or others.
- *What tasks can I perform effectively?* Include record keeping, accounting, and other procedures such as specific software applications.
- *What equipment can I operate, maintain, or repair?* Include everything from oscilloscopes to cash registers to tractors.
- *What systems, layouts, or operations have I designed or executed?*
- *Have I ever taken an inventory, audited, or researched?* Include online research, lab or legal research, surveys, or other.
- *What oral communication skills have I developed?* Have I conducted meetings? Given public presentations? Taught or trained? Screened applicants? Greeted clients? Do I speak a second language well?
- *What tasks have required interpersonal skill?* Handling difficult clients or patients? Resolving problems? Negotiating? Making collections?
- *What have I done that demonstrated responsibility?* Supervised or managed? Reorganized a department? Expanded? Resolved disputes? Budgeted? (State amount if large.) Hired? Fired? Scheduled? Coordinated projects?
- *What writing did I do on the job?* Minutes or memos? Letters or newsletters? Procedures or manuals? Reports or proposals? Patient charts?
- *How else have I contributed to the success of projects and operations?* Decreased costs? Increased profits? Improved client or community relations?
- *Did I receive training in the military or in special courses on the job?*
- *Do I have any special licenses or certifications?*

Academic Skills   Think of your college courses as training, but do *not* list courses. Look for *skills* you have gained—that's what employers want to know. Consider, too, any skills developed from internships, clinics, or other educational outside work. You might start by asking yourself questions such as these:

- *What equipment have I learned to operate?* Repair? Maintain? Improve?
- *What procedures have I performed?* Medical, legal, accounting, or others?

- *How have I used management skills?* What projects have I completed? Include work with campus organizations, fundraising, events planning, tutoring, counseling, case work, and other projects.

- *What oral communication skills and interpersonal skills have I honed?* Giving presentations? Empathetic listening, questioning, or nonverbal communication? Recognition of communication barriers? Business etiquette? Telephoning? Group dynamics? Instructing clients, handling complaints, crisis intervention, or others?

- *What research and writing skills have I demonstrated?* Include online research, paralegal and other specialized research, research papers, business report writing, independent study projects, published work in campus newspapers or magazines, and the like.

- *What other specialized training do I have?* Include skills such as "calculate depreciation," "compile federal tax returns," "build prototypes," "diagnose electrical failures." Include knowledge from courses in business ethics, law, CPR, and other areas relevant to your field.

Personal Skills   You may have acquired planning, leadership, financial, teaching, human relations, or other skills during leisure hours. Consider activities and memberships in high school, college, or community organizations as well as hobbies. To start a train of thought, review the previous questions about work and academic skills. You may have developed some of those skills during your leisure hours. Then ask yourself other questions such as these:

- *What projects have I completed for my family and home?* You might list compiling a family genealogy, remodeling a kitchen, or building a patio. Or perhaps you transferred all your household accounts to a computer file.

- *What community projects have I participated in?* Planning? Serving on committees? Managing a scout troop or other youth group? Coaching a team? Assisting in a day care center? Counseling on a hotline? Judging contests? Writing a newsletter? Conducting meetings? Organizing?

- *Have I developed special skills?* Photography, music, drawing, designing, writing, cooking, sewing, woodworking, working with software or others?

- *What special training have I received?* Have I worked as a volunteer firefighter, librarian, pianist or other position? Do I have CPR or EMT training? Certification or special licenses such as a pilot, chauffeur, or other?

- *Do I have other knowledge derived from adult education courses, seminars, workshops, conferences, or special projects?*

Compiling a comprehensive skills list will require more than one session. Time is needed to mull over your experience. When you finish, you may have twenty or more specific, transferable skills (some students identify more than fifty). After that, pinpoint items that indicate positive qualities and work habits.

Personal Qualities and Work Habits   Employers look for positive personal qualities such as reliability, confidentiality, honesty, and flexibility. However, you won't claim these directly on your résumé. Avoid trite, unsubstantiated claims such as "work well with people," "honest," and "hard-working." Instead, give specific examples that imply or indicate these intangible qualities and sound work habits. For example, you might list items similar to the following:

- Never missed a day's work in five years
- Met all deadlines for reports and projects
- Collected cash receipts and made bank deposits
- Entrusted with keys to open and close business
- Maintained and monitored confidential client files
- Received two promotions within one year
- Acted as supervisor during boss's two-month leave

Or perhaps you had a special security clearance or special bonding. You may have had independent access to computer codes, valuable merchandise, confidential formulas, procedures, or other private information. One applicant identified flexibility as a quality needed in all her positions. After pondering how to present this item effectively, she wrote the following summary (company names omitted) and placed it directly before "References upon request":

FLEXIBILITY:

> During 12 years' experience, have performed backup work, acting in various capacities. At _____, handled major "touchy" accounts. At _____ Corp., substituted for Accounts Payable and Payroll Clerks. At _____, filled in for Manager's Secretary. All these jobs, as well as the present job of Production Coordinator at _____, require flexibility, tact, and maturity.

DRAFTING A RÉSUMÉ

The major parts of a résumé are *job objective, work experience, education, skills,* and, in some cases, *accomplishments.* The job objective always comes first, but other major parts follow in most- to least-important order, according to the applicant's qualifications. In other words, you organize these sections to your best advantage, using either the chronological or functional résumé styles.

Within sections containing dates—for example, education and experience—dates are arranged in *reverse chronological order*. Thus the most recent date is listed first. Other information such as military service, memberships, and personal data follows the major sections. You can draft each section separately. In fact, it is not uncommon for the job objective to be drafted last. For clarity and ease of reference, let's start with the job objective.

The Basic Job Objective

Years ago a job objective was very brief, perhaps just a word or two, stating the general position, such as "typist." By the 1980s, job objectives had expanded into a short paragraph. Later some experts suggested omitting the objective if the position was mentioned in the cover letter. *But this suggestion proved impractical because some companies discard cover letters after an initial reading.*

Today job objectives are essential to focus the résumé. They state the job title; type of business, industry, or institution the applicant is seeking (optional); and job reference number, if there is one. Good job objectives steer away from personal needs; they do *not* refer to *I* or *me*. They contain carefully worded fragments. The examples that follow are *basic job objectives:*

- Pediatric nursing position #2023
- Environmental coordinator for waste management company
- Account representative for an insurance agency

Advice and examples vary as to the length of a basic job objective, but a range of three to six words seems to be average. The objectives focus on one position or one branch of an occupational field. If you are qualified for two distinct positions or occupational areas, then compile two résumés, each with a different objective and focus. The basic job objective is widely used for both simplified and functional résumés.

Effective job objectives avoid trite, vague, and misdirected phrases such as "desire to work for a company that is a leader in the field" or "to gain experience and eventually assume an administrative position." If the job objective is expanded, the focus should not be on the applicant's personal needs but on serving the company.

The Service-Oriented Job Objective

If you are compiling a functional résumé, consider a *service-oriented job objective*, which can be custom-tailored for a particular company. This job objective acts as an abbreviated thesis statement with three parts:

- Specific position with reference number, if there is one
- Type of business, industry, or institution (optional, especially when applying to a position with a reference number)
- Major skill areas of the applicant

Prewriting can speed the narrowing and drafting of your objective. Shy away from using the phrase *entry-level;* career consultants warn against it. Just start by asking yourself questions and jotting down answers:

1. What position do I want? How specific should I be?
2. What kind of facility, business, or industry do I want to work for? Or does it matter?
3. What major skill areas do employers seek for this position?
4. Do my qualifications fit the objective? (If not, look for another position.)
5. Is the terminology correct for the field?

SERVICE-ORIENTED OBJECTIVES

A service-oriented objective identifies the position and states how you can benefit the employer:

- Pediatric nursing position #2023. Skilled in postsurgical and terminal care.
- Junior accounting position #1021. Well-versed in medical terminology and corporate accounting applications.
- Assistant manager. Use major software applications for small businesses. Skilled in oral and written communication.
- Medical laboratory technician. Prefer clinic or hospital that is seeking superior accuracy, reliability, and interpersonal skills.

Grouping and Sharpening Skills

If you are fortunate enough to have some work experience in your career field, group those work skills underneath the name of the employer. This arrangement is common to the chronological résumé. If you are compiling a functional résumé, your next task is to revise and regroup your prewritten skills:

1. *Sort skills into categories according to the needs and requirements of potential employers.* (This means that work, academic, and leisure skills will be mixed.)
2. *Strategically arrange the skills into neat columns with general category headings.* Place the most important details at the beginning of each category.
3. *Begin each skill entry with an appropriate action verb.*
4. *If you have five or more impressive skills or honors, you may be able to title them "Accomplishments" or "Achievements."*

You can impress potential employers by labeling groups of skills with an eye to their needs. For example, create headings that highlight skills: computer, research, leadership, communication, public relations, marketing, accounting, supervision, management, or another.

Combining Skill Groups   If a group of skills looks skimpy, combine it with a related group. Then add a dual heading, as in the following example:

Accounting/Computer Skills

- Post accounts receivable and payable
- Compile daily sales record
- Bill customers and answer questions
- File social security and annuity payments
- Make out payroll
- Compile weekly, quarterly, and annual reports
- Know basic business laws and regulations
- Write documentation and footnote balance sheets
- Use TaxCut, TurboTax, Quicken, and Word

Adding Action Verbs   Action verbs can make skills attractive, parallel, and convincing. "Type 70 wpm" is a skill, but "fast typist" is a vague claim. "Managed 15 employees" indicates a skill; "excellent manager" is a claim. (Skills are written in the present tense if you still have them.) Select accurate, positive verbs. Careless word choice can paint an applicant as naïve, unqualified, or arrogant.

ACTION VERBS FOR RÉSUMÉS

calculate	establish	maintain	record
compute	expand	operate	refine
conduct	implement	organize	reorganize
coordinate	increase	originate	repair
create	initiate	plan	research
decrease (costs)	innovate	prepare	schedule
develop	install	produce	support

Citing Accomplishments   Employers seek to hire people who can cut costs, solve problems, and perform quality work. If you have five or more such distinctive achievements, you may list these separately immediately after the job objective. The manager of mail services for a large corporation labeled her accomplishments a "Record of Productivity," which she placed before work experience.

Record of Productivity

- Streamlined entire mail services operation for corporate headquarters of _____, Inc. This changeover included reorganizing job duties of all mail room personnel, developing new procedures, and reorganizing the physical layout for greater efficiency.
- Despite a 25% increase in mail flow, maintained quality service with no additional personnel. Increased number of in-house mail services for employees.
- Wrote and justified proposal for $80,000 for new equipment through equivalent savings in one year's time.
- As benefits approver at _____, maintained 97% accuracy and production criteria.
- At _____ Corporation, changed all accounts receivable functions from manual to computerized system.

To identify potential achievements on your skills lists, search for superior work, particularly any regarding finances or saving of resources, personnel, or time. Then *add a second part that provides specific data.* This addition can sometimes expand a skill to an accomplishment:

- *Skill:* Decreased costs
  Add: 20% through selective bulk buying
- *Skill:* Generated sales
  Add: of $950,000 during the past year
- *Skill:* Computerized outdated inventory system,
  Add: cutting storage time by one third

To fill out a list of accomplishments, you may also include honors, awards, and other distinctions you've received. Yana Parker suggests writing PAR (Problem-Action-Results) statements in *24 Hot Tips on Résumé Writing.* (To see examples, visit her Web site, listed later.) PAR statements can be included under accomplishments.

Discovery Questions for Finding Accomplishments

1. Have I received recognition at work for distinguished service, perfect attendance, highest sales, or exceeding production quotas?
2. Did I earn distinction in high school, in college, or in the community? (Consult your old newspaper clippings, certificates, trophies, scholarship awards, and the like.)

3. What difficult or long-term projects have I completed?

4. What significant problems have I solved?

5. Have I done anything else noteworthy?

EDUCATION

For higher education, provide names and addresses (optional) of institutions, dates, degrees, and major(s). Also state your minor concentration if relevant. Specify grade point average (GPA) if B+ or higher. GPA is usually stated in decimals such as "3.35/4.0," the second figure indicating the scale. If the GPA of your major is higher, you can cite it: "Major GPA 3.6/4.0."

List teaching certificates, nursing licensure, and other professional certification with education. For younger applicants, a high school degree can be included if space allows. You might include items such as "Took college preparatory courses," "Wrote for school newspaper," "Trained in debate." You can also list high school honors here. (Do not note a GED.)

WORK EXPERIENCE

Experience in your targeted field should be emphasized by allotting more space than for other jobs. If you have had steady employment, include the employers' names and dates with months (Dec. 1997–July 1999). State promotions; for example: "Hired as crew member. In six months, promoted to assistant manager." After that, you can list work skills.

FREQUENTLY ASKED QUESTIONS ABOUT WORK EXPERIENCE

1. *How far back should I go on work experience?* To avoid age discrimination (if you're over 40), you may want to list only your last three jobs or the last ten years. That is usually enough unless you have earlier work in your targeted field. Label that section as "Recent Work History" or "Relevant Work Experience."

2. *Should any work experience ever be omitted?* Employment of one month or less can be omitted.

3. *How can I make a job title sound better?* Retitle jobs such as dishwasher, cleaning lady, yard man, and bartender. For example, kitchen assistant, housekeeper, greenskeeper, and server.

4. *What if I have no work experience?* Your best bet may be to head for the campus placement service or an employment agency to ask about temporary or part-time work in your targeted field.

Include minor job experience because it indicates a desire to work and familiarity with the work world. If you have served in the military, place that under work experience. State term of service, branch, and rank upon leaving. List travel or training relevant to your job objective. If you have held a succession of minor, unrelated jobs, or have large gaps in employment, provide a short summary with a range of dates. At the end of the summary, insert a sentence *telling what you have learned:*

Summary of Work Experience

Jan. 1998–May 2002

> During college years, held part-time and temporary employment at a fast food restaurant, service station, car wash, and campus library. Developed initiative and accuracy. Learned to budget, schedule, catalog books, find answers to research questions, and provide courteous customer service.

OTHER INFORMATION ON A RÉSUMÉ

Use extra space on your résumé for minor, but significant, information. Employers look for well-rounded applicants who can interact well. Possible items to list include the following, in this order:

- *Honors or awards.* If not listed elsewhere, group honors such as "Employee of the Month," "Top Salesperson of the Year," civic awards, dean's list, and other distinctions under "Honors."
- *Memberships.* Memberships in service clubs and professional organizations imply commitment to a community and a career. Do not list lodges, religious affiliations, or any membership that might arouse prejudice.
- *Activities and interests.* Include only those that are relevant.
- *References.* Place "References upon request" last.

Your résumé should use positive words. Label layoffs as "downsizing." Do not mention firings, demotions, ethnicity, handicaps, age, or medical disabilities. (Note: a disability or medical condition that *might interfere with performance* must be disclosed before a position is accepted.) Although employers often request salary information, the routine advice of career consultants is to withhold it until the interview. Otherwise, you might price yourself out of a job or be hired at a low rate. (Research the salaries in your field and locale.)

ORGANIZING RÉSUMÉS

The job objective is the first item on any résumé after your name, home address, and home telephone number. (Do not give a work telephone number, address, or e-mail.) Next is the section on accomplishments, if there is one.

ROBERT A. MICHAELS   (303) 222-3333   rmichaels@service.net
3945 East Front Street
Denver, CO 80200

Objective: Assistant systems manager. Experience in management information
systems, network communication, problem solving

Accomplishments
- Microsoft Certified Systems Engineer
- Created motivational plan that led to increased sales of 20%
- Customized software for company and client needs
- Graduated *summa cum laude*
- Won the *Wall Street Journal* award for student achievement

Computer Skills
- Use Microsoft Office XP and Great Plains accounting software with
  e-commerce
- Design systems and create documentation
- Program in Oracle, SQL, C++, and Visual Basic
- Use PowerPoint in training sessions
- Perform user setup and maintenance on NT Server
- Detect and solve problems in software
- Improve systems of computer security

Experience

PROTECH ELECTRONICS, INC.

April 2002   Administrative assistant to the president
to   - Perform financial analysis
present   - Assist in interviewing and hiring
- Assist in pricing and purchasing stock
- Track and report inventory
- Provide support for sales representatives
- Train employees
- Write brochures and design training literature
- Write proposals for potential users
- Write business letters and reports with graphics
- Make informative and persuasive presentations
- Provided support for end users
- Handle complaints and work out compromises
- Designed customer survey, compiled results, and wrote report

Fig. 30.1 Chronological résumé with strong work experience in desired field
(continued on next page).

Arrange the major sections of work experience, education, and skills in *most- to
least-important* order. To decide the best arrangement for your résumé, ask yourself, "Which sections will be most important to potential employers?"

Organizing a Chronological Résumé

After the job objective and accomplishments, the next major part of a
chronological résumé is usually a *reverse chronological* listing of work experience

Robert A. Michaels   3945 East Front Street

XYZ ELECTRONICS COMPANY

July 1999
to
March 2002

Hired as a sales representative. Promoted to sales manager after one year.

- Supervised five employees.
- Hired, dismissed, and trained personnel
- Sold, installed, and provided support for systems/software
- Made minor repairs on PC desktop computers
- Revised performance evaluation procedure
- Assisted potential users in defining systems needs
- Answered application and support questions for customers
- Designed local area networks

WENDY'S

May 1997
to
June 1999

Hired as customer-service representative. Promoted to assistant manager after six months.

- Supervised six employees
- Kept sales records
- Ordered supplies
- Worked late shifts
- Balanced cash register
- Made bank deposits
- Opened and closed store

Education   **OLYMPIA UNIVERSITY**

June 2003   Bachelor of Science, Computer Science, GPA 3.8/4.0

Majors: Database Management Network Administration

Member   Small Business Association

References upon request

Fig. 30.1 continued from previous page.

(most recent first). Achievements, including promotions, are listed under each employer. But for a teaching position that requires a certain degree and certification, *education* could come next, particularly for a recent graduate with only a few years' teaching experience.

The general rule for both chronological and functional résumés is to place the most important major section first and the least important last. When (relevant) work experience is placed before education, then a general list of skills is sometimes listed near the end of a simplified résumé. (For an example of a chronological résumé, see fig. 30.1.)

MELODY A. SMITH
612 Greenlawn Drive
Marion, Ohio 43302
(614) 555-0755

OBJECTIVE: Paralegal position. Trained in research,
communications, and computer applications.

- -

EDUCATION: **Marion Technical College,** Marion, Ohio 43302
Associate of Applied Business Degree
Dec. 2002   Major: Paralegal Studies, GPA 3.6/4.0

PARALEGAL TRAINING
- Investigated legal problems
- Drafted contracts
- Prepared memoranda
- Applied problems in tort law
- Practiced basic accounting principles
- Attended legal education seminars
- Increased knowledge of criminal law
- Drafted complaints and responses
- Drafted and executed wills according to Ohio law
- Researched and wrote argument paper
- Prepared partnership agreements
- Implemented debt-collection practices

COMMUNICATION SKILLS
- Gave presentations successfully
- Wrote collection letters
- Coordinated workers' compensation presentation
- Conducted survey of opportunities for paralegals
- Trained in questioning and active listening
- Received practice in accepting criticism

COMPUTER SKILLS
- Conduct legal research using LEXIS
- Operate PC and Macintosh computers
- Use Access, Excel, and Word
- Solved tax problems on PC/TaxCut

Fig. 30.2 Functional résumé with no paid work experience in desired field (continued on next page).

Organizing a Functional Résumé

The functional résumé style is quite flexible, suitable for anyone who lacks the qualifications needed for the chronological style. If you are close to graduation and have little work experience, you can emphasize your academic achievement by using the following order: *education, skills, work experience.* Degreed ap-

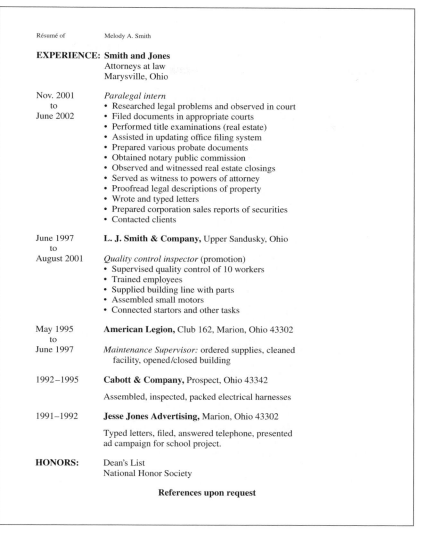

Résumé of   Melody A. Smith

EXPERIENCE: Smith and Jones
Attorneys at law
Marysville, Ohio

Nov. 2001   *Paralegal intern*
to   • Researched legal problems and observed in court
June 2002   • Filed documents in appropriate courts
                 • Performed title examinations (real estate)
                 • Assisted in updating office filing system
                 • Prepared various probate documents
                 • Obtained notary public commission
                 • Observed and witnessed real estate closings
                 • Served as witness to powers of attorney
                 • Proofread legal descriptions of property
                 • Wrote and typed letters
                 • Prepared corporation sales reports of securities
                 • Contacted clients

June 1997   **L. J. Smith & Company,** Upper Sandusky, Ohio
to
August 2001   *Quality control inspector* (promotion)
                 • Supervised quality control of 10 workers
                 • Trained employees
                 • Supplied building line with parts
                 • Assembled small motors
                 • Connected startors and other tasks

May 1995   **American Legion,** Club 162, Marion, Ohio 43302
to
June 1997   *Maintenance Supervisor:* ordered supplies, cleaned
                   facility, opened/closed building

1992–1995   **Cabott & Company,** Prospect, Ohio 43342

                 Assembled, inspected, packed electrical harnesses

1991–1992   **Jesse Jones Advertising,** Marion, Ohio 43302

                 Typed letters, filed, answered telephone, presented
                 ad campaign for school project.

HONORS: Dean's List
                 National Honor Society

                 References upon request

Fig. 30.2 continued from previous page.

plicants who are switching career fields might also use this order, particularly if their educational record matches well with the new career field.

If you will be competing with applicants who have higher degrees than you and if you have some work in your targeted field, you can use a different arrangement: *skills, work experience, and education.* College students who are *not* close to graduation but who have some work experience in their chosen field can use this same order. (For examples of functional résumés, see figs. 30.2 and 30.3.)

Résumé of:	**JANE E. DOE**	(213) 121-2121
	124 Plum Tree Lane	jdoe@service.net
	Arizona City, AZ 85223	

| **Objective:** | Assistant manager of retail store that requires good management, communication, and computer skills. |

Graduation: June 2001	Washington Community College
	Associate of Applied Sciences in Business
	Majors: Business management/Accounting GPA 3.75

MANAGEMENT SKILLS

- Trained in small business management
- Assist in managing store; supervise three employees
- Balance cash register, make bank deposits
- Open and close store, order stock, take inventory
- Resolve complaints, make collections, handle shoplifters
- Organized softball league for girls 8 to 17
- Supervised Vacation Bible School for 150 children
- Headed United Way campaign

COMMUNICATION SKILLS

- Apply active listening and questioning skills daily
- Use nonverbal communication and empathy daily
- Deal with difficult people pleasantly
- Practice telephone etiquette daily. Fluent in Spanish
- Write effective memos, business letters, and reports
- Make effective presentations
- Served as president of Parent-Teacher Association two years
- Taught adult education oil painting classes five years

COMPUTER/ACCOUNTING SKILLS

- Use TaxCut, Word, Excel, and Quicken software
- Compile federal, state, and city tax returns
- Trained in cost and tax accounting
- Post accounts receivable and payable, sales records
- Operate PC desktop and Macintosh computers

| **Employment:** 2000 to present | Derrick's Designer Shop |
| | Sales representative. Act as manager in his absence |

| **Interests:** | Toastmasters International member, reading, gardening, painting |

References upon request

Fig. 30.3 Functional résumé with strong part-time experience.

> ### CASE STUDY
>
> ### MARK FOCUSES HIS FUNCTIONAL RÉSUMÉ
>
> Mark, a young graduate with a bachelor's degree but little work experience, saw an ad for a position that sounded interesting. The employer was seeking someone with three strengths: initiative, computer skills, and writing skills. Since Mark was strong in all three areas, he used these categories in his service-oriented job objective and skill headings. He kept the same order as the ad. Under the first heading, *initiative*, Mark mixed his work experience and honors in reverse chronological order:
>
> - Arose at 3:00 a.m. as disk jockey for one year during college
> - Worked till midnight on weekends at Burger King for two years
> - Maintained a college GPA of 3.5/4.0
> - Awarded full-tuition scholarship for high school GPA of 4.0/4.0
> - Worked Saturdays as an assistant bookkeeper for two years
> - Managed paper route for two years
>
> Under *computer skills* Mark listed specific skills gained from management information systems courses. Under *writing skills* he grouped research, documentation, and writing skills, listing a 50-page marketing research paper. After that he listed *education* and date of graduation. His effort won an interview and a job offer. He had tailored his qualifications to the employer's needs.

Scannable Résumés

Sometimes human eyes never see a résumé. If your résumé will be scanned, prepare a scannable version that will keep it from being tossed out. Streamline your printed style résumé. Keep margins rather narrow and do not center anything. (Length is seldom a concern.) Use a clear size 12 font such as Arial, Courier, or Verdana. *The general rule is "the plainer, the better."* That means no fancy fonts, bullets, italics, underlining, parentheses, brackets, graphics—anything that might end up as gibberish. Then place a keyword summary of your qualifications at the top of page 1.

Keyword Summary   Read ads and job boards to find the skills and abilities employers seek for a type of job. Then match these words with your qualifications and copy them into your summary. The more matches you can provide, the more the scanner will select and the better your chances of having your résumé read. (You can use hyphens in place of bullets to set off items.)

A KEYWORD SUMMARY

- 3 years' purchasing experience—vendors and wholesalers
- 2 years' client/customer service—corporate accounts
- Gave on-site training seminars—installations, setups
- Wrote brochures, bulletins, reports, technical manuals
- Computer applications: MS Word, Excel, Powerpoint, Visual Basic

---

Editing and Printing   After you finish your scannable version, run a spelling check and proofread it again. Then save as a text file (or ASCII or DOS). Name it *resume.txt* Use any text editor (such as Appletext, MS Word, or Notepad) to edit the resume.txt. file to resemble your original résumé. Print your scannable résumé, using a high-resolution laser printer. Do not bend or fold the résumé. Place it in a large manila envelope to protect it.

For online help, see the Internet Career Directory on page 501.

E-Mail Résumés

If you have a choice between submitting an e-mail résumé or a scannable résumé by mail, take e-mail. Scanning managers of GTE and other companies prefer e-mail résumés because there is less chance for error when storing in a database. In fact, many ads specify, "a plain text document sent in the body of your [e-mail] message." This means the résumé is *not* sent as an attachment. Attached files can be cumbersome to download and print out.

Preparation   An e-mail résumé does not need a keyword summary. Just add your e-mail address to your printed résumé. Then streamline it as you would for a scannable version—taking out italics, underlining, parentheses, brackets, graphics, bullets, centering, or anything that might become illegible. Run a spelling check and proofread thoroughly. Save the résumé into a text file (see "Scannable Résumés"). In this plain form, the résumé can be copied, pasted into e-mail, and read by unknown software.

Before e-mailing your résumé, however, insert your cover letter into the message first. (Employers prefer to see the cover letter beforehand.) If the length of the two documents together overwhelms your e-mail capacity, then send the two documents separately. For online help see page 501.

Internet Posting   You can post your e-mail résumé at one or more sites on the Internet if you wish. Before you do, you may want to delete your name, address, and telephone number. It is best to get a separate e-mail address and use your initials for this résumé. To obtain free e-mail, visit <http://www.emailaddresses .com/>.

FORMATTING A PRINTED RÉSUMÉ

Since your printed résumé is your ambassador, an immaculate appearance is imperative. Purchase high-quality twenty-pound bond paper. Buy enough so that you have matching paper for cover and follow-up letters. White is best for résumés that will be duplicated or scanned. Otherwise, ivory is suitable. Employers tend to dislike unusual colors and extravagant layouts. You can vary the format by using capital letters, oversize letters, boldface, or underlining for headings. You can lead into each skill entry with a bullet (oversize dot), followed by one space.

To give a picture-frame look, use the same size margins all around. Triple-space between sections, if possible, and double-space between subsections. You can center major headings or locate them at the side or mix the two arrangements. Work with your résumé until you have an effective layout that enhances your qualifications.

Never send pale or smudged copies to an interviewer. Avoid script and difficult-to-read fonts. Select a popular font that is neat and clear; use a laser printer if possible. For students, a résumé of one or two pages is adequate. Yet expectations for acceptable résumés vary among employers, particularly government agencies. If your résumé is to work efficiently for you, determine what each employer expects and do your best to meet those expectations.

REVISING, EDITING, AND PROOFREADING A RÉSUMÉ

To appraise your work critically, imagine you are an employer, reading the résumé of an unknown applicant. How would the document appear? Neat and attractive? Well-organized? Well-developed? Chances are that a superficial résumé, hastily compiled, will not yield interviews. Employers assume a résumé reflects the intellect, competency, and attitude of the applicant. Take time to revise as much as necessary so that your résumé will outclass the competition and earn you the opportunities you deserve.

Checking Layout and Order

Layout does make a difference. The *white space* throughout the résumé, not just the margins, influences appearance, readability, and credibility. Neat, aligned columns provide a balanced look. A crowded résumé is more difficult to read than a well-spaced one. For ease in reading, place dates on the left except when you want to de-emphasize them.

If your résumé runs more than one page, your name and a page number should appear at the top of the second page and any succeeding pages. (You can reduce the type one or two sizes for the name there.) This precaution will prevent loss or confusion when the interviewer compares applicants' qualifications.

The order and size of sections, words at the beginning of columns, type size, and capitals influence the emphasis of your résumé. Revise until you attain an appropriate balance. The following checklist can help in examining your résumé.

CHECKLIST: REVISING LAYOUT, ORDER, AND EMPHASIS

1. Is the layout attractive, well balanced, and easy to read? Is every column aligned? Is there enough white space?
2. Are sections arranged in most- to least-important order?
3. Are dates arranged in reverse chronological order?
4. Could the order within skill lists be improved?
5. Does each skill start with an action verb?
6. Are all major sections well developed, positive, and accurate?
7. Are minor sections relevant?

Adjusting Length of Printed Résumés

"How long should a résumé be?" is a common question with no definite answer. Although many employers prefer one-page résumés for *entry-level* employees, this preference does not rule out longer résumés for applicants with extensive qualifications. Two-page résumés are increasingly common for newly graduated applicants. If you plan a second page, it should have sufficient information. A fraction of a page may appear to be the result of poor planning.

When expanding your résumé to fill a second page, be careful not to indulge in puffery. Wordiness and irrelevant details will detract from your purpose. A concise one-page résumé is far better than a puffed two-page one. The following options should help you to find more material and adapt the format, if you need a second page:

Ways to Expand a Résumé

1. *Review the suggestions for identifying skills to find more.* Also consider adding more minor categories if relevant.
2. *Add white space.* Have you triple-spaced between sections? Have you centered your heading? A centered heading takes more space than one aligned on the left with items beside it. (See figs. 30.1, 30.2, and 30.3 for use of headings and white space.)
3. *Expand the margins,* keeping the same size all around.
4. *Expand a summary of minor work experience.* If you have such a summary, you might expand it by adding names of employers.

5. *If you are not working, you can supply the addresses and telephone numbers of previous employers.* If working, reserve this information for a sheet of references.

6. *If you are not working and have an extra half page or so,* you might add your list of references (explained later in this chapter) to the second page of the résumé.

On the other hand, if you must cut the length of your résumé, start with the first suggestion below. Then go down the list only as far as needed; don't toss out good material unnecessarily. To adjust the length, you have several options:

Ways to Cut the Length of a Résumé

1. *Group similar skills on one line.* This technique is simple and quick.

2. *Narrow the margins and place major headings to the far left.* If you have centered the first heading with "Résumé of" above your name, you can conserve space by placing it on the same line as your name.

3. *Omit some minor items.* High school data and activities are optional.

4. *Summarize unrelated work experiences.* Beware of cutting too much; work experience of any kind can be an asset.

5. *Reduce size of type.* To save space, you might list skills in ten-point type with skill headings in twelve-point.

6. *Last resort:* Double-space between sections. The résumé will not be quite as attractive or clear as when triple-spaced.

Scrutinizing Word Choice

Extra words dilute meaning. To interviewers, vague wordy phrases may imply that the applicant lacks confidence and competence. When reviewing the skill lists on your résumé, weigh every word. Delete unnecessary words and qualifiers, such as *very*, and unneeded prepositional phrases.

Weak and Wordy Phrases

have a knowledge of	know about	familiar with
provided assistance	exposed to	very good with
acquainted with	had exposure to	worked on

Instead of the first phrase above, say *know.* Instead of "provided assistance," say *assisted.* Instead of "had exposure to," say *used* or *operated. Tip:* Watch for *of, to, on, with,* and other prepositions that often indicate unnecessary words.

Eagle-Eyed Proofreading

You know and I know that errors can creep into a draft for a multitude of reasons, but that does not excuse them in an employer's eyes. Serious applicants take the time and expend the effort to proofread the finished résumé several times when they are fresh and alert. Otherwise, they are unlikely to nab every error. Although a spelling checker can catch misspellings, it cannot monitor usage. An eagle eye is needed to detect inappropriate words. If you have the slightest doubt about spelling or usage, consult a dictionary at once. And run a spelling check before every printout.

Consistent Punctuation   To ensure clarity and readability, set off fragments that are in paragraphs with periods. Fragments listed in columns do *not* require periods. Be consistent in punctuation and concentrate on clarity.

Other Problems   Notice that some software packages have strange names with capital letters in the middle. If you don't have access to the box, look in catalogs or stop by an electronics store. The spelling of compound words is also a slippery slope; some are hyphenated—others are not. (Consult an up-to-date dictionary.) Finally, check to see that colloquial words and slang have not crept into your résumé.

CHECKLIST: EDITING AND PROOFREADING A RÉSUMÉ

1. Are all dates accurate?
2. Are months as well as years specified for education and related work experience?
3. Is there any duplication of skills? (If so, cut.)
4. Is every word positive or neutral?
5. Is every word spelled and hyphenated correctly?
6. Are punctuation and capitalization consistent and correct?

A Note of Encouragement

As you pore over help wanted ads and job boards, don't become discouraged if your qualifications are not a perfect fit for a position. Keep in mind that the best-qualified applicant is not always hired. An applicant may be ruled out after a reference check or offered another position, leaving the job open. If you are eager to learn and sincere—even though you may lack a desired skill—you may still have a chance.

Employers often provide in-house training or pay for off-site seminars and courses to upgrade employees' skills. Instead of looking for a perfect match, they look at an applicant's present skills and *potential* to develop more. That is why it is important to state your qualifications in the best way possible so that they reflect your initiative, dependability, and integrity. Then in your cover letter and interview, you can indicate your willingness to learn and expend the necessary effort. *Note:* Exploring the company Web site is an excellent way to prepare.

INTERNET CAREER DIRECTORY

Multiple Resources: The sites below provide free, up-to-date help for your career search. View sample job objectives, résumés, letters, and interviewing tips. You can also post your résumé or search for a job.

- **BrassRing** Includes tips on salary issue <http://brassring.com>
- **HRS Federal Job Search** Government jobs <http:www.hrsjobs.com>
- **JobStar Central** Excellent resource <http://jobstar.org>
- **411 Jobs: the Career Directory** Site links <http:www.411jobs.net>
- **Links to Nifty Places on the Web** Yana Parker provides direct links to many career sites. <damngood.com/jobseekers/links.html>
- **The Monster Board** Many job listings <http://www.monster.com>
- **Proven Résumés.com** Excellent resource <http:www.provenresumes.com>
- **Rebecca Smith's eRésumés** Electronic résumés <http://www.eresumes.com>

Special Career Guides are available free at the following sites:

- **CareerCity** Cover letter tutorial <http://www.careercity.com>
- **24 Hot Tips on Résumé Writing** by Yana Parker. <http:wwwdamngood.com>
- **The Net Guide: Your Résumé** Includes Richard N. Bolles's "The Fairy Godmother Report on Résumé Sites" <http://www.JobHuntersBible.com>
- **Writing Effective Letters** by Florida State University. Includes "Twenty-eight Common Mistakes," the "Friendship Letter," and others. <http://www.careerlab.com/letters/link002.htm>

II. WRITING LETTERS AND OTHER CORRESPONDENCE FOR EMPLOYMENT

Effective business letters can help you win the job you want. A neat format; well-organized content; and correct grammar, punctuation, and spelling convey an air of professionalism. The subtle aspects of your written voice that reveal attitude also influence whether or not you will be considered for a position.

Neat handwriting is essential for some tasks, such as writing numbers, invoices, notes, and prescriptions. Regardless of the position you apply for, take extra pains to sign application forms and letters neatly. Employers often draw inferences from incidentals, even messy, illegible signatures. Always take the time to produce your best work when corresponding with potential employers whether through regular mail or e-mail.

WRITING E-MAIL MESSAGES

E-mail provides such convenience, economy, and speed that we tend to use it automatically—without the care we would give to a business letter. To save time, some writers clip their e-mail so much that it is difficult to decipher. Such carelessness and spur-of-the-moment reactions can lead to embarrassment and other problems that are beyond the scope of this book. Still, five basic reminders are in order:

- All e-mail in your computer at work is the legal property of your employer. And your home computer may be confiscated.
- E-mail can be intercepted by your employer or by third parties on the Internet. In fact, the *New York Times* once fired 22 people for e-mailing offensive jokes. Such firings are not unusual at companies with harassment policies.
- E-mail can be misdirected to the wrong person through various errors.
- E-mail is often copied and sent on to dozens of people.
- E-mail messages linger. You may think you erase them through deletion, but this is not always true. And a copy, which may end up in court, is always stored on your provider's server.

Therefore it is essential to keep this lack of privacy in mind. Although writing e-mail may seem intimate and personal, it is like carrying on a conversation in a public place. You might think of e-mail as a memo that can be sent around, passed out at meetings, or tacked to a bulletin board. Unless you revise carefully, it may come back to haunt you.

Without the standard openings, closings, and courtesy words used in business letters, e-mail may sound curt and abrupt. Some folks try to soften the tone with smiley faces and the like. But recipients may not care for the cutesiness, which is unsuitable for business messages. It is far better to take a few minutes to be cautious and complete.

WRITING AN EFFECTIVE
COVER LETTER FOR A RÉSUMÉ

When hundreds of people vie for a single position, a résumé cover letter may be the only document in a job packet that an interviewer reads. If a cover letter contains even a whiff of incompetence or dishonesty the résumé may well be

GUIDELINES FOR E-MAIL MESSAGES

1. *Keep e-mail short and focused.* Include a subject line. If you have two detailed topics to discuss, consider sending two messages.

2. *Start with a pleasant greeting:* "Hello," "Hi," "[name]," "Good morning!" "Dear Director," or whatever fits the occasion.

3. *Be friendly and courteous.* When appropriate, start with "Thank you for. . . ." If you make a request, ask a question with a question mark and include "May I" or "Will you please."

4. *Place the important part first unless it is negative.* In that case, build up to the bad news.

5. *After you have made your point, close.* Don't ramble on.

6. *End on a positive note,* even if you say no more than "Bye" or "Take care." For a more professional tone, use "Best regards," "Best wishes," or a similar suitable close.

7. *Don't send e-mail when very tired.* Avoid writing messages when exhausted, particularly those that are work-related.

8. *Reread each e-mail carefully before sending.* A hasty message may not say what you intend or carry the desired tone. *Tip:* Set your e-mail spelling checker (if possible) to scan outgoing messages. This step will provide a second chance to revise.

9. *Wait 24 hours before replying to an irritating message.* Choose your words carefully. Reread several times. Consider how the reader may take them and whether the message merits a reply. Silence may be the best, and safest, response.

10. *Send e-mail by blind carbon copy (Bcc) when appropriate.* Some Internet messages accumulate long strings of names and addresses. Before forwarding, remove the string and direct the message by using "Bcc," not "To." This small courtesy will be appreciated by friends. It will also increase readability.

tossed aside, unread. Regardless of whether a résumé is mailed, faxed, e-mailed, or delivered in person, a cover letter is usually expected.

As you write your cover letter, keep in mind that the primary purpose is to motivate the interviewer to read your résumé. Express interest in the position, present an overview of your credentials, and make a courteous request for an interview. The tone of a well-written cover letter is professional and confident, never desperate, half-hearted, or arrogant. A confident letter may spark confidence in its reader—exactly the effect you wish to achieve. Like other business letters, cover letters have three basic parts: introduction, body, and closing.

Effective Introductions

A pet peeve of interviewers is triteness in cover letters. Imagine having to read dozens of letters that begin: "I saw your ad in . . ." or some other predictable phrase. To make a cover letter stand out, hook the reader's interest with your very first words. Select them judiciously: the wrong words may steer you into a low-paying position. If you have experience in your desired field, shy away from "entry-level" or "trainee." These words peg you as having minimal skills and lacking experience. For inexperienced applicants, however, an entry-level position in your chosen field affords an opportunity to gain practical knowledge and skill.

A simple way to get up-to-date information about employers' needs is to clip job descriptions and ads. Underline the skills and abilities required for positions you would like. After that, draft an introduction that suggests how your training and experience meet those needs. Be sure that your description truly reflects your qualifications.

When you are applying for a particular position, specify the exact job title and number (if there is one) in the introduction of your cover letter. Otherwise, you can be less specific. To create a distinctive opening that will work for you, adapt one of the four basic openings for cover letters.

The Name Opening   You are fortunate, indeed, if you can begin with the name of a person the employer knows, one who has referred you or who will recommend you. Often a referral will open doors that might otherwise remain closed. If you learn of an available position from an executive or from someone else the employer respects, seize the opportunity! First, state the name of the person making the referral. Then mention the position and give the main areas of your qualifications.

- Jason Blank, systems manager of Incatech, advised me of an opening in your company for a junior accountant. He recommended I apply, for he is familiar with my accounting background and computer experience.
- Cynthia Jones, vice president of Blink's Advertising, has suggested I apply for the position of copywriter at your company. The requirements she mentioned match my training and experience in advertising.

The Creative Opening   To find just the right detail for an unusual opening, search your résumé and memory. Watch local papers for news items about potential employers, possibly the arrival of a new business or the expansion of a local company. Then match your experience, activities, and talent so as to spark the interest of an interviewer:

- Perseverance does pay off. After five years of attending night classes, working as a restaurant manager, and providing for a family, I am graduating *magna cum laude* with a B.S. degree in restaurant management. Would these qualifications plus confirmed workaholic tendencies equip me for the position of manager of your hotel's dining room?

- After Hastings, Holby, and Haberman move to the new downtown location, they may need more personnel. If so, please consider my legal training and work experience, which should qualify me for a paralegal position.

The Summary Opening   Although traditional, the summary opening can be quite workable when your strongest qualifications are linked to the desired position. You might give two or three main points taken from the headings of your résumé. But be sure the points are clearly connected to the current needs of potential employers. In the following summary openings, notice that the focus is upon *how the applicant can serve the employer:*

- Training in social work, an internship in student admissions, and a bachelor's degree in psychology should help me fulfill the responsibilities of Human Services Coordinator for Blinhard University.

- My management skills in nursing have been honed by supervision of nursing personnel, development of nursing policies and procedures, and preparation of six-figure budgets. This background, along with a recently acquired M.S.N. degree should qualify me for Director of Nursing at Memorial Hospital.

The Question Opening   Opening with a question is a popular method, but a word of caution is advisable. Some personnel directors say that question openings are "overused" and frequently "filled with clichés." One interviewer even went so far as to say he tossed letters that opened with stereotypic questions into the wastebasket unread. Still, an original question opening can serve as an attention-getter if it is fresh, appealing, and relevant.

Whatever opening you use, avoid any hint of overconfidence or presumption. Note, for example, that the sample introductions here use phrases such as "*should* qualify me for the position" rather than "*will* qualify me." At the same time, an opening that seems doubtful or anxious is not likely to open many doors. Striking the proper balance can be tricky, so thoughtful applicants evaluate and revise their openings carefully, using their own words and avoiding trite phrases.

The Body of the Letter

The body of a cover letter explains the qualifications mentioned in the introduction. When you develop these points, retain the order set forth in your opening. After summarizing the highlights from the résumé, conclude the body with an *indirect* reference to the résumé. A direct reference, such as "Please see the enclosed résumé," is awkward. An indirect reference is worked smoothly into a sentence in a dependent clause or phrase. The indirect references below are italicized:

- Since age fifteen, I have been working. During these years I have dealt with the public and gained significant insights into providing customer service. For me, the customer is really number one. Supervision of eight employees has also offered opportunities to polish my interpersonal skills, *as indicated on the enclosed résumé.*

- On June 12, 2002, I will graduate *summa cum laude* from Buckeye University with a bachelor of arts degree in education. There I concentrated in English, specifically the teaching of high school literature and composition. In my senior year, I won first prize in the National Arts and Letters contest involving five area colleges. Seven poems have been published in little magazines *as explained in the enclosed résumé.*

How to Handle the Salary Question

Although an ad may request "desired salary" or "salary history," you are not obligated to divulge your answer. In a cover letter, you might give an expected salary range, such as "$26,000 to $29,000" or "upper 20s." But before you do, consider that your answer may jeopardize your chances of being hired. The risk is twofold: If your figure is too high, employers may conclude you are overqualified or overpriced; if too low, they may think you underqualified. Even if you are aware of current salary ranges, a small business may not be able to comply.

In a telephone conversation, you might say that salary is "open" or sidestep questions about salary history (another can of worms) until the interview. In the conclusion of a cover letter, you can postpone your answer tactfully:

- At your convenience, may I set up an interview to discuss my qualifications, including expected salary [or salary history, if requested]? My telephone number is (000) 910-6721, and I'm available after 6:30 p.m.

Sooner or later, you will confront the question of salary. Rather than be unprepared, begin to research salaries in your field; then you'll know what you can expect locally, statewide, or nationally. Information about salary ranges can be gained from libraries, friends, employment agencies, information interviews, and temporary employment.

Effective Conclusions

The end of a cover letter is rather like a goodbye. As such, it should be brief, cordial, and courteous. Courtesy is integral to good business relations, yet many applicants fail to include courtesy words in cover letters. Instead, they border on arrogance without realizing it, sounding presumptuous or overly forceful. One applicant concluded with "I will be in town Tuesday and will stop by . . . ," presuming that he would be welcomed. Others thank in advance, assuming they will gain an interview, unaware that busy interviewers may take offense.

> **CHECKLIST: EFFECTIVE CONCLUSIONS**
>
> 1. Is there a courteous request for an interview?
> 2. Is a home telephone number included? Protect your privacy and your job. Giving a work number poses hazards.
> 3. Did you specify the hours you can be reached at home?

You can transform a demand into a polite request with just a few courtesy words and a question mark:

- Demand: "Call me at . . ."
- Polite request: "Will you please call me at . . . ?"

A question with a question mark is more polite than a statement. A question is a request whereas a statement often sounds like a demand. You can set an appropriate tone in your letters by using questions with courtesy words such as *may, please, appreciate, appreciation,* and *your convenience.* Let consideration shine through your words as in the following examples:

- May I have an appointment at a convenient time to further explain how I might serve your company as a junior accountant? Please dial (611) 121–2121 anytime Saturday or Monday through Thursday from 4:30 to 9:30 p.m.
- If you think there might be a place for me in your firm, will you please call (402) 555-2626? I can be reached in person after 4 p.m. weekdays and 8–11:30 a.m. Saturdays, or you may leave a message, and I will promptly return your call.

Other Considerations

A job search may require dozens of mailings and many interviews before the right position is found. The wisest course may be to write two basic cover letters and see which elicits more responses. Each time you contact a potential employer, customize the basic letter with the current date and correct inside address and salutation as well as any other suitable changes. A cover letter should be limited to one uncrowded page with "picture frame" margins and plenty of white space. Before mailing, proofread your letter carefully, and check to see that it is signed. When contacting several employers, be sure each letter is inside the correct envelope and signed.

E-mail Cover Letters   If an employer requests an e-mail résumé, then prepare a cover letter for e-mail, too. You can take your printed cover letter and save another version as a plain text document (explained in "Scannable Résumés" and "E-Mail Résumés"). Then e-mail the cover letter before the résumé, preferably in the same message.

CHECKLIST: REVISING A COVER LETTER

1. Does the introduction focus on the employer's needs?
2. Does the introduction set up the main points of the body?
3. Does each paragraph center on one main idea?
4. Is the material well organized?
5. Are qualifications linked to job requirements?
6. Is the résumé referred to indirectly at the end of the body?
7. Is the tone confident without sounding overly confident?
8. Is an interview *requested* in the closing?
9. Has a telephone number been included? A time to call?
10. Are the words polite and appreciative? Do they conform to standard usage?

Tips for Writing an Effective Cover Letter

1. *Secure the name of the interviewer.* If unknown, call the company. If impossible to secure a name, send to "Human Resources Director." "Dear Director" can serve as your salutation.
2. *Write in a confident, courteous tone.*
3. *Individualize the letter.* Avoid trite phrases and examples from books on the Internet. Be original.
4. *Type an individualized letter for each company.* Form letters without an inside name and address are inappropriate and ineffective.
5. *Sign each letter neatly in black ink to match the type.* Never leave a letter unsigned. Employers tend to view the omission as carelessness and a disregard for detail.

Revising a Cover Letter

Rarely is an excellent cover letter dashed off in a few minutes. Examine, revise, and proofread your draft several times. Whether or not you are granted an interview may hinge upon how effective your cover letter is.

FORMAT FOR A BUSINESS LETTER

All business letters contain similar elements, but the positioning of the elements differs slightly. Letters typed with letterheads often follow the *block format* (fig. 30.4) with the date and all other typed elements aligned at the left margin.

124 Plumtree Lane
Arizona City, AZ 85223
February 1, 2002

Sally Chen, President
Sally's Tall and Short Shop
332 Main Street
Anywhere, U.S.A. 00000

Dear Ms. Chen:

As an artist, I have developed a keen eye for detail, line, and color. This ability, along with my academic training and work experience, should qualify me for the position of manager of Sally's Tall and Short Shop.

At Washington Community College, I earned an Associate of Applied Business degree with a major in business management. There I received training in small business management, business law, cost and corporate accounting, computing and filing of tax returns. I operate IBM and Macintosh computers and use PC TaxCut, WordPerfect, and Lotus 1-2-3 software. Training in interpersonal communication, including active listening and questioning, has helped prepare me to serve customers well.

For four years at Derrick's Designer Shop, I arranged window displays weekly, assisted customers, assisted in shop security, balanced the cash drawer, opened and closed the store, and made bank deposits. Whenever the owner was away, I managed the shop, supervising eight employees. Other experience is explained on the enclosed résumé.

May I have an appointment to discuss my qualifications and salary history? My telephone number is (000) 121-1212. I am available Mondays, Tuesdays, and Thursdays 4:30 to 9:30 p.m. or anytime Friday or Saturday morning.

Sincerely,

Jane A. Doe

Fig. 30.4 Cover letter with creative opening and reference to salary history. (Block format)

The *modified block format* (shown in fig. 30.5) is most common for letters that are *not* typed on letterhead stationery. Then the typed signature may be followed by a line of type indicating the writer's business title. A business title accords respect.

Modified Block Form

Heading: At the top right-hand corner of the margin, place your own address and the date.

331 Cherry Lane
Wintoska, Oregon 47000
March 27, 2002

Ms. Cheryl Withers
Office Manager
Baywood and Goldberg
1221 North Main Street
Wintoska, Oregon 47000

Dear Ms. Withers:

When an old and respected law firm like Baywood and Goldberg advertises for a junior accountant, I am interested. My three years' work experience and my training in accounting and information systems should enable me to perform successfully for you.

As the only accountant for a hardware store, I assume many responsibilities. During my first year, I streamlined bookkeeping operations by converting a manual arrangement to a computerized system. At that time I also wrote a proposal for a federally funded small business loan that won the owner a low-interest loan. Daily I handle accounts receivable and accounts payable. I write collection letters and call customers who are behind in their payments. Weekly I make out the payroll and handle insurance payments. Weekly and monthly balance sheets are also compiled. Quarterly, I write reports and file tax returns.

On June 10, 2003, I will graduate from Franklin University with a bachelor's degree in accounting. There I have received training not only in cost and corporate accounting, but also in finance and business law. Since my minor is in data processing, I am familiar with a wide range of microcomputers and accounting software, as explained on the enclosed résumé.

At your convenience, would it be possible to set up an appointment to discuss how I can serve your firm? Salary is open. Will you please call (000) 389-4689 between 5:30 and 9:00 p.m. Monday through Wednesday or weekends?

Sincerely,

Rosalind Caton-Green

Fig. 30.5 Cover letter with summary opening. (Modified block with indented paragraphs)

Inside Address: Type the recipient's name and address—just as they appear on the envelope—several spaces below the heading at the left-hand margin.

Salutation: Use business title. The salutation falls two spaces below the heading, also at the left margin. The salutation is always followed by a colon.

Body: Body paragraphs are single-spaced, with double-spacing between paragraphs. Indentation is optional.

Complimentary close: A close such as "Sincerely" or "Best regards" is separate and double-spaced after the final body paragraph. The closing is aligned with the heading and followed by a comma.

Signature: Leave four lines after the complimentary close for the handwritten signature. Below this space, place the typed signature.

PACKAGING JOB SEARCH DOCUMENTS

A positive first impression is important not only for applicants but also for their job-search packet. Chances are the applicant will never meet the interviewer unless the documents in the packet are immaculate. Erasures, strikeovers, and smudges are verboten. The résumé, cover letter, and other items should be perfectly printed by a laser printer (if possible), high-quality inkjet printer, or an up-to-date electric typewriter, preferably on *white* 20-pound bond paper. White paper transfers more clearly than colored when duplicated or scanned or faxed. Use a clear, conventional type style. Italics or unusual fonts are difficult for a scanner to read.

When finally satisfied with the quality of your résumé and cover letter, place them inside an 8½- by 11-inch manila envelope, unfolded. This precaution will protect against weather, wrinkling, fingerprints, or dropping. If you are employed, do *not* enclose a sheet of references, lest your employer be contacted prematurely. One applicant made this unfortunate mistake, only to find he had no job with either firm. The interviewer had telephoned the employer immediately, and the man was fired upon his return an hour later.

If unemployed, you can enclose references along with the résumé and cover letter; yet this is unnecessary, since most employers wait until after an interview to run a reference check. If you enclose letters of recommendation, do *not* send the originals, which could disappear into an employer's file. When an employer wants a grade transcript, order one and arrange to have it mailed directly to the company. Because oversized envelopes require extra postage, you can conserve by using standard envelopes for mailings to companies that seem less desirable.

PROVIDING A LIST OF REFERENCES

When you walk into an interview with an up-to-date, well-organized sheet of references, you have a definite advantage. This preparation not only boosts your confidence, but also indicates to the interviewer your ability to plan ahead and organize. Yet relatively few job seekers are aware of the full significance of this important job search tool, nor do they think to add financial references to the usual list of former employers, teachers, and the like. However, financial references are significant. From the employer's point of view, someone who is financially stable seems more likely to be trustworthy and reliable.

GUIDELINES: COMPILING A LIST OF REFERENCES

1. *Request permission before using names.* With teachers and others you have not seen for many years, try to meet in person to make sure you are remembered. Otherwise, telephone. If you must write, enclose a stamped, self-addressed envelope and politely request an early reply. (Employers expect to be contacted; it is unnecessary to ask for their permission, although you may.)

2. *Be sure the person is willing to give you a reference.* If you sense reluctance or a lack of enthusiasm, ask someone else. A lukewarm response can do harm.

3. *Employment references.* From your last two positions, list supervisors. If you know employees at the company to which you are applying who would give favorable references, include their names, too.

4. *Other references.* Include coworkers, teachers, coaches, scout leaders, or anyone else who can attest to your good qualities—except relatives and the clergy. For financial references, list banks, charge accounts, or paid-up loans.

5. *Indicate in parentheses your relationship to the reference.*

6. *Organize the list of references in most- to least-important order.* Put employers first, character references second, and financial references third.

7. *Include complete addresses and telephone numbers.*

8. *Include your name, address, and telephone number.* Place this information at the top of the sheet in a centered heading like the one on a résumé.

9. *If working, take precautions.* Across the top, before the heading with your name, type in capital letters: "PLEASE DO NOT CONTACT MY CURRENT EMPLOYER UNTIL THE FINAL STAGES OF INTERVIEWING." If using a computerized résumé service, ask that neither your résumé nor reference list be sent to your present employer.

WRITING A LETTER OF APPRECIATION

Several applicants had interviewed for the position of Financial Aid Director at Marion Technical College, but the search committee could not agree. Then a letter of appreciation for the interview arrived from Andrew Harper, who was the only applicant to send a thank you. The committee reevaluated his credentials and

1122 Valley Road
Clearview, Washington 98222
February 6, 2002

Dr. Margaret Berman
Mad River Medical Association
1555 Main Street
Wenatchee, Washington 98555

Dear Dr. Berman:

Thank you for the opportunity to discuss the possibility of working at Mad River Medical Association. I enjoyed meeting with you and your staff; the friendly atmosphere and organization impressed me. After interviewing with you, I am even more eager to become a part of your medical team.

Once my program at Marion Technical College is complete on March 19, 2002, I will be available for employment. If accepted for the position of medical secretary, I am prepared to put all my efforts into achieving the goals set by your practice and to serving your patients accordingly.

If you should need any further information concerning my credentials, please contact me at (000) 365-1111 any time convenient for you.

Sincerely,

Trena M. Craig

Fig. 30.6 Letter of appreciation.

called him for a second interview. Andy got the job. That one brief letter tipped the scales in his favor. Why? What is significant about a letter of appreciation?

First, a letter of appreciation reveals a sincere interest in a position. Since most applicants interview for several positions and seldom send follow-up notes, an employer does not know whether or not they are genuinely interested. Second, a thank you conveys a message, implying the sender is considerate and appreciative. It also suggests motivation, perseverance, and a positive attitude. Third, the letter indicates good human relations skills. (See fig. 30.6 for an example.)

There is no standard format for a letter of appreciation, but *timing* and *tone* are important. Mail your letter either the day of the interview or the next day. But keep your priorities straight: accuracy is more important than same-day mailing. Read the letter aloud to gauge the tone. Edit and proofread several times. Be sure the tone mirrors *enthusiasm*, not the image of a forlorn applicant sitting by a silent telephone. Avoid phrases such as "I'll be waiting to hear from you," "If you are interested, please call me," or "I eagerly look forward to hearing from you," which may suggest doubt or anxiety.

To write a successful letter of appreciation quickly, follow the outline below, including any of the six parts that are relevant to your situation.

Outline: Letter of Appreciation

1. Thank you

2. I'm interested

3. I enjoyed . . . (or was impressed by . . .)

4. I'm available (give date)

5. Another item you might like to know (optional)

6. If you need more information (give telephone number and time to call)

WORKPLACE CASE STUDY

CONNECT THE DOTS

During an interview, Valerie L. was asked if she had any grant-writing experience. She replied, "No, but I have had considerable experience writing letters, reports, and other documents. I would be glad to learn."

After the interview, Valerie went to the library, where she looked at sample grants. She realized that they were similar to the proposals she had written at her previous job. In her letter of appreciation, she mentioned going to the library, the similarity between grants and proposals, as well as her proposal-writing experience.

She was hired.

Moral: Connect the dots of your experience to the job you apply for. Do not assume the interviewer will make the connections.

WRITING A LETTER OF ACCEPTANCE

Often employers notify successful applicants by telephone. If you should be called, be sure the terms of the job offer are clear before accepting. Acceptance over the telephone is an oral contract. If you have other offers pending, you might ask for a day or two to decide.

Dear Ms. Hendricks:

Thank you for the job offer. The staff nurse position, evening shift, on the surgical floor will not only be challenging, it will also offer numerous opportunities to learn. The salary of $_____ per hour with $_____ on weekends is more than acceptable.

On June 12, I will arrive early to fill out the insurance forms, receive instructions, and begin.

I am looking forward to working with you and the other members of the staff at Belvedere General Hospital.

Cordially,

Jonathan Jones

Fig. 30.7 Abbreviated letter of acceptance.

After making a decision, call in your acceptance and send a letter accepting the job offer and the terms (see fig. 30.7). Specify the primary provisions of the offer and keep a copy. This letter not only protects the employer but it also protects you by forestalling misunderstanding or friction later.

Outline: Letter of Acceptance

1. Thank you or an expression of appreciation
2. Acceptance of the offer (Sound pleased)
3. Main points of the job offer
4. Date and time to begin work
5. Courtesy closing

WRITING A LETTER OF REFUSAL

Never let the door slam on a job offer. Courtesy is important even in a refusal, for some day you may wish to reapply at the company. A refusal should be made promptly so that the company can continue the search. The refusal can be made over the telephone, but unless you are adept at speaking off the cuff, it is wiser to mail a decision.

Begin by tactfully expressing appreciation for the offer. But avoid an overly enthusiastic tone that might mislead the reader into thinking the letter is an acceptance. Provide a general reason for the refusal, without mentioning anything that might seem negative about the company or the offer. Close with a positive comment. (See fig. 30.8.)

Dear Ms. Plymale:

Thank you for the informative tour of Tucker & Taylor's downtown facility and for the attractive offer of the junior accounting position.

I have, however, accepted another offer that is more consistent with my career goals.

Your time, consideration, and courtesy are appreciated.

Sincerely,

Rafael Perez

Rafael Perez

Fig. 30.8 Abbreviated letter of refusal.

Outline: Refusal of a Job Offer

1. Expression of appreciation for the job offer
2. Brief refusal
3. General reason for the refusal (optional)
4. Courtesy closing

WRITING A LETTER OF RESIGNATION

Business etiquette requires that when an employee accepts another position, the present employer be notified in writing. Appreciation should be expressed, and the date of leaving specified. A letter of resignation should be sent to the head of the department. If you are asked to go within the hour, don't be surprised or take offense. Many companies require that personnel working with computer records or other data requiring security depart immediately. Sometimes, however, when there is no immediate replacement, the employee is asked to stay longer.

Try to leave on a friendly footing. Even if your employer does not take your resignation well, retain your dignity. If you are treated unprofessionally, be very careful that bitterness does not seep into your letter of resignation. Later you will be glad you retained your professional demeanor.

Sometimes an employee is fired and given the opportunity to write a letter of resignation. Although this event is disheartening, the employee should take advantage of the offer unless prepared to contest the termination in court. A letter of resignation is a protection not only for the employer, but also for the discharged

Mr. James Jones
Sales Manager
Mazdex, Incorporated
111 East Main Street
Anywhere, USA

Dear Jim:

My five years with Mazdex have been challenging and rewarding. This association has provided an opportunity for applying and developing my skills as well as gaining practical knowledge of the business world. It is with reluctance that I tender my resignation, effective immediately.

I have decided it is time to turn my career in a slightly different direction as an accounting software trainer/sales consultant. My experience with Mazdex has provided me with valuable skills and contacts.

Finally, Jim, I appreciate your assistance and training. You have helped to make our association pleasant and productive. I look forward to dealing with Mazdex in a different capacity.

Sincerely,

John R. Smith

Fig. 30.9 Abbreviated letter of resignation.

employee. It gives the appearance of leaving of one's own accord, which will work to an advantage in future employment interviews.

Outline: Letter of Resignation

1. Express appreciation (possibly regret).
2. State the exact date of leaving.
3. If another job has been accepted, give a reason for leaving. State in general terms such as "opportunity" or "generous offer."
4. If you want to take accrued vacation time or holidays off, specify.
5. Keep the letter positive and end on an upbeat note.

The letter shown in fig. 30.9 was written by a company's star sales representative who had been asked to tender his resignation. A powerful client had complained over a refusal to be given a large discount and had arranged a deal with the sales manager. Then the client demanded the sales representative be fired, and the manager complied. Although filled with indignation, the discharged employee knew his future career depended upon subordinating feelings and conducting himself in a professional manner. To gain control, he waited a day to write the letter.

Summary

In today's changing job market, you may need two or three versions of your résumé: printed, scannable, and e-mail. Two popular résumé styles are the chronological and functional. Both list the basic categories of education, work experience, and skills but in different formats.

You have accumulated many transferable skills, but unless you clearly link them to job requirements in your chosen field, your résumé may be ineffective. Research your career field to discover which skills are in demand and the correct terminology to use. Identify your work, academic, and leisure skills. Begin each skill with an action verb.

To be effective, a résumé needs a job objective. Revision, editing, and proofreading are essential. The layout should be attractive, with plenty of white space for easy reading. Do not use first person. Proofread carefully. Every word must be spelled correctly.

The purpose of a cover letter is to motivate an employer to read the résumé. To be effective, use one of four basic openings: name, summary, creative, or question. Your introduction should indicate interest in the position and set up the main points you will develop.

Develop each main point into a paragraph in the body of the letter. The last body paragraph should contain an indirect reference to your résumé. In the conclusion *ask* for an interview courteously. Specify a home telephone number and times of availability.

If a letter and résumé are to be mailed in a standard envelope, fold them correctly. Mail or hand-deliver your cover letter and résumé unless the employer asks for something else. E-mail cover letters require special preparation.

Before using references, secure permission to ensure all referrals are positive. Type a list of references to present in an interview. After an interview, send a letter of appreciation to the potential employer. When a job is offered, send a letter of acceptance or refusal. Notify your present employer of your decision to leave with a letter of resignation.

Key Terms

academic skills	functional résumé	name opening
accomplishments	leisure skills	puffery
basic job objective	letter of acceptance	question opening
chronological résumé	letter of appreciation	service-oriented objective
courtesy closing	letter of refusal	summary opening
cover letter	letter of resignation	transferable skills
creative opening	list of references	work skills

Practice

Collaborative Exercise: Revising Skills Lists

Directions: Working with a partner, check each other's drafts of skills. Questioning your partner will help each of you to find more transferable skills and an action verb for each skill.

1. Is the item a claim or a skill?
   Note: A skill tells what one can *do:* "type 60 wpm" and "monitored cash drawer" are skills. But "work well with others" and "honest" are vague claims. Instead, cite specific duties that point to a skill or an ability: *Example* of an interpersonal skill: "Resolved customer complaints."
2. Does each item begin with an action verb?
3. What else did you do that required accuracy, responsibility, communication skill, tact, problem solving, or trustworthiness?
4. How can that task be reworded for your skills list?
5. Is there anything else that you did at work, in class, or during leisure hours that might be transferable?

Collaborative Exercise: Revising a Job Objective

Directions: Using the criteria below, critique the job objectives of your group members. Place a question mark after any word or phrase that does not sound appropriate. Make suggestions.

1. Is the objective limited to *one* position or area?
2. Does the objective focus on service to an employer?
3. Is the objective written in third person?
4. Is the objective written as a fragment, not a sentence?
5. Are the skills in the objective the same as those in the skill headings?
6. Is the wording correct and appropriate?

CHAPTER 31

Oral Presentations

You gain strength, courage, and confidence by every experience in which you really stop to look fear in the face. . . . You must do the thing you think you cannot do.

—Eleanor Roosevelt

In a survey of 480 companies, the National Association of Colleges and Employers asked what qualities were considered most important when hiring. The most frequent response was "communication skills." Employers want applicants who can write well and speak effectively. To help meet this need, more and more colleges and universities are incorporating speaking skills, including oral presentations, into courses across the curriculum. But many students quake at the thought of standing before a group and making a presentation.

WHETHER SPEAKING TO SIX OR TO SIXTY . . .

If your heart does a rapid tango and your face pales at the thought of giving an oral presentation, you will be glad to know that these responses are common and surmountable. And the fundamentals of speaking are easy to learn. In fact, many students discover they are better speakers than writers.

Whether facing six classmates or coworkers, or sixty participants at a training seminar, you can learn to speak with confidence. The first key is to get your fear under control. By giving yourself a pep talk and applying the many tried-and-true tips in this chapter, you can ease the task of giving an oral presentation. The second key is to practice enough but not too much. We'll talk more about this point later.

The third key is to think of the audience as friends with whom you will share some interesting information. If you are enthusiastic, they will sit up and listen. Finally, the chances are good that your college classmates will be an empathic audience, because they will be presenting, too. They are apt to encourage you by listening attentively, providing the kind of support they will want when they are doing the speaking. Now are you ready to start?

HOW DO WRITING AND SPEAKING DIFFER?

See chapter 1.

If you are asked to present a paper orally to the class, rest assured that you have already accomplished a big chunk of the work. With a little tweaking, you can adapt the paper for presentation to a live audience. To start, you need to consider how your role as writer changes to that of speaker. For both rhetorical situations, the purpose and the topic remain the same, but three other factors—occasion, audience, and voice—change dramatically, as shown in the box on page 522.

Writing and Speaking: Comparing Two Types of Rhetorical Situations

Three basic elements differ in the rhetorical situations of writing and speaking: the occasion, audience, and voice. These differences influence how an effective presenter prepares and how an audience receives the message.

Occasion	Purpose	Topic	Audience	Voice
• Writing	Same	Same	• Readers *see* words	*Writer's* voice
• Speaking	Same	Same	• Listeners *see* actions *hear* words	*Speaker's* voice

In a paper the content, punctuation, and spelling are important. *In an oral presentation, however, the content and delivery are important.* Thus this chapter contains an overview of revising a paper for presentation as well as guidance for delivering the presentation. You will see examples of purpose statements, thesis statements, introductions, conclusions, and a sample student speech. Specific tips for preparing notes and audiovisuals; practicing; and improving eye contact, articulation, and vocal variety are also provided.

Presenting versus Reading

Any effective presentation requires that the speaker exude the energy, enthusiasm, and vocal variety found in animated conversation. Eye contact, facial expression, gestures, and tone of voice can make words come alive. A compelling speaker can make a message vibrant and persuasive in a way that differs radically from the mechanical reading of the same message.

Yet students who lack training in oral communication are often unsure of what is expected. Some assume they can just stand up and read their paper aloud.

PREPARING A PAPER FOR ORAL PRESENTATION

If you are asked to present a paper orally, don't panic! No radical changes are required. Here is an overview of the necessary steps. Tips and examples appear later in the chapter.

1. **Mark up your paper as you simplify and condense.** Most papers, especially research-based papers, will need to be simplified and condensed. Working on a printed copy of your paper, highlight the thesis, and sharpen it further (see "Define the Purpose" on page 525). Highlight statistics and brief anecdotes that lend support for your main point. Delete minor details and less relevant examples. Put brackets around extended discussions or complicated points, and jot summaries in the margins. Watch for an unusual fact or arresting quotation. Divide long sentences into shorter ones.

2. **Prepare an outline.** Outline main points and significant subpoints (see "Outlining" in chapter 5).

3. **Plan an attention-getting introduction.** To help make your opening attention-getting, in addition to starting with a catchy quotation or example, emphasize a vital link to tie the topic to the listeners. Build your introduction around (frame your presentation with) the ways your audience will be able to use the information you're providing.

4. **Plan an effective and memorable conclusion.** Summarize the main idea, and then give your audience something extra that's memorable. You might add a bit of wisdom, a provocative thought, or a look toward the future.

5. **Prepare your notes.** Using note cards, sheets of paper, or the notes pages tool of presentation software, work from your marked-up paper and written plans to prepare notes. Outline your main points and significant subpoints.

6. **Prepare audiovisuals.** People like to see as well as hear. If you are talking about coaching Little League baseball, wear your official shirt and bring a ball and bat. If you have access to PowerPoint or another presentation software program you may want to use it to visually (and auditorily) support your thesis (see "Creating Effective Audiovisuals").

7. **Time the presentation.** Pause slightly between sentences. If allowed four to six minutes, aim for five. The extra minute will give you time to pause for emphasis (or laughs). If needed, cut or condense points.

8. **Practice but do not overpractice.** Practice enough times so that you're comfortable but not so many that you memorize every word. Your presentation will seem fresh and spontaneous.

9. **Revise troublesome phrases.** Mark any words that cause stumbling. Use a thesaurus to find synonyms, so you can recast and shorten awkward or confusing sentences. Find words you can use comfortably and pronounce easily.

10. **Check arrangements and arrive early.** Have your notes and audiovisuals in order. Test projection and computer equipment to make sure it's hooked up and working properly. Good preparation will ease your mind.

At a Society of Technical Communication conference in Chicago, a scientist made this mistake. After five minutes of his droning, people began to leave. As he continued in a monotone, bowed head with no eye contact, more and more left. By the end of the hour, two thirds of the audience had gone.

By applying the guidelines in this chapter, you will be spared the embarrassment this man must have endured. As you gain experience in presenting, you will appear more confident and knowledgeable during job interviews. If asked to introduce yourself, report on a team project, give a sales presentation, or summarize a research paper or project, you will be able to smile, control the butterflies, and do a creditable job.

FOUR TYPES OF ORAL PRESENTATIONS

A speaker can choose from four types of oral presentations: *manuscript, memorized, extemporaneous*, and *impromptu*. Successful reading of a manuscript takes skill, training, and charisma. Memorized presentations are hazardous because they often lack spontaneity. Then too, nervousness can cause forgetfulness.

The most effective type of prepared presentation is extemporaneous. The secret of success for this type of presentation is sufficient preparation and speaking in a *conversational* manner. Although the presenter may glance at notes, the tone is informal and friendly. An impromptu speech is a spur-of-the-moment talk, given without more than a few moments of preparation. For example, you speak impromptu when introducing yourself to the class, when escorting visitors around your workplace, or when filling in for a master of ceremonies who is late or unexpectedly unable to attend an event. As you develop skill in speaking extemporaneously, your ease in impromptu speaking will increase.

PLANNING AN EXTEMPORANEOUS PRESENTATION

The first step toward an effective extemporaneous presentation is to analyze the rhetorical situation. The setting may impose limitations that can be circumvented, but if the presentation is inappropriate for the occasion and the audience, it has little chance for success.

Preview the Setting

To begin planning any presentation, find out where it will be held and the nature of the space. How large is the room? How will the seating be arranged? Is there a lectern for notes? Will you be using a microphone? Can projectors or any other necessary equipment be reserved? Is an Internet connection available? Are electrical outlets near the lectern, or are extension cords available? Is the lighting satisfactory?

The closer you can be to the audience, the more intimate and informal the setting. A semicircle is ideal because it allows you to establish eye contact with everyone. For very large audiences, a center aisle is desirable so that you can actually walk into the audience and involve individuals, particularly if there is a question-and-answer session.

If you will be using a microphone, try to practice at least a few minutes beforehand. Familiarizing yourself with the room and the equipment will not only diminish the fear of the unknown but also allow you to plan around any deficiencies and tailor the presentation to the setting.

Assess the Audience

Before definitely settling on a topic, consider the attitudes, beliefs, and values of the people to whom you will speak. Find out as much as you can about their demographics—age range, gender, ethnicity, occupation, education, or other relevant cultural factors. Then estimate how the audience will be likely to react to your topic. To analyze the audience, you might start with the familiar pattern of *who, what, why, where, when,* and *how:*

- Who will be attending? How many? (All men? All women? Mixed group?)
- What special interests or concerns do they have? (Consider age, education, culture.)
- Why will I be making the presentation? (What do they expect and want?)
- How much does the audience *already know* about the topic?
- How do they *feel* about the topic? (Is the topic charged with emotion?)
- When will the presentation occur? How will the time of day, current events, or even upcoming holidays affect it?

The answers to these questions will guide you in planning your approach—thinking about how you can stimulate their interest. If you lack a topic or decide to switch to another, see "Thirty Ideas for Oral Presentations" at the end of the chapter.

CASE STUDY

Murphy's Law in Action

Skipping audience analysis can invoke Murphy's law: "If anything can go wrong, it will." One student, who skipped this step, asked in a strong confident voice, "How many of you have tried to quit smoking?" Only two of twenty-five classmates raised their hands. When the presenter realized that almost all of her audience were nonsmokers, her face paled and her voice wavered. Her enthusiasm fled. The response of the audience was polite but lukewarm. With an audience of smokers, the presentation had the potential to earn an A; as it was, it earned a C.

Consider the Occasion

When and why a presentation is given influences the length, approach to the topic, and organization. In the classroom, oral presentations will be much shorter than those generally given at work, for clients or prospective customers, or in the community. For a class you might give a one- to three-minute practice speech or a lab report. A graded presentation might run from 4 to 8 minutes, depending on the time available and the size of the class. The purpose and audience will influence how you shape and organize the material for the presentation.

Define the Purpose

The *general* purpose of an oral presentation may be to inform, to persuade, to inspire, to dedicate, to celebrate, to entertain, to express appreciation, or a combination of these purposes. The general purpose indicates the type of presentation. The *specific purpose statement* has three parts: purpose, topic, and desired result. Once you define your specific purpose, you can write a clear thesis statement reflecting that purpose. The thesis statement is the central idea you want to convey.

Specific Purpose Statements

- [purpose] [topic]
  The purpose is to *inform* the audience about *common spiders* and
  [desired result]
  show how to determine friend from foe.

- [purpose] [topic]
  The purpose is to *persuade* the audience that since *most spiders are*
  [desired result]
  harmless and beneficial, they should not be killed.

Thesis Statements

- Common spiders are harmless and easily distinguished from several poisonous varieties. (Informative)
- We should not kill beneficial and harmless spiders. (Persuasive)

Notice that the examples above illustrate how the same subject can be approached in different ways, according to your general purpose. Before starting your outline or notes, write a specific purpose statement. It will clarify your intent and help you stay on track. Your thesis can be written later.

Select an Appropriate Topic

For a successful classroom presentation, the topic should be suitable for both you and the audience. Never speak on a subject that causes you to feel uneasy; discomfort blunts enthusiasm and dulls a presentation. Select a topic you can discuss rationally without excessive emotion—one that offers an opportunity for listeners to learn as well as to enjoy. Opinions about issues such as gun control, abortion, religion, and politics tend to be deeply ingrained and highly charged. There is little chance of changing anyone's mind; in fact, a shouting match may erupt and distract from your presentation.

Chances are that if you have already prepared a paper for another class, and it has been graded, then the topic is suitable for an oral presentation. If in doubt, ask your instructor. The following tips will help you to adapt the paper or select an entirely new topic.

Get Off the Beaten Path   Topics that have been highly publicized tend to make boring presentations. For example, most people already know quite a bit about cancer, AIDS, illegal drugs, and various kinds of abuse. Unless you can provide additional information that is fresh and interesting, the audience will be unlikely to listen closely. You may need to research your topic further (see chapter 23).

Sometimes you can freshen an old topic by researching the latest discoveries, such as advances in medicine. Or if you decide to look for another topic, you might share an area of personal expertise that would interest the audience, such as desktop publishing, genealogical research, or building a musical instrument.

Link the Topic to the Audience   During the introduction, effective presenters establish a link between the audience and the topic. To include listeners, use personal pronouns *(you, your, we, us)*. State an advantage, benefit, or reason for them to listen. To search for a connection, you might ask yourself.

- Why should the audience listen to me?
- What benefit can they derive? (Learn, improve, enjoy, or what?)
- How can I make them eager to listen? (Look for the unusual or amusing.)

Role-Play   You might ask the class to assume a role. A bank manager wanted to practice a presentation she would be giving at work. Before the presentation, she asked the class to pretend they were managers of local branch banks who were attending a training seminar. This role-playing heightened their interest, and their attentive feedback enabled her to give an excellent presentation.

CASE STUDY

FINDING A LINK TO THE AUDIENCE

A student who collected antique glass wanted to share his hobby but doubted that the men in the audience would be interested. When he sought help in finding a link, his instructor asked, "What are men generally interested in?"

The student thought a moment, smiled, and replied, "Money?"

"Right! You could present antique glass not only as fun but also as an investment. Have you ever made a profit this way?"

"Yes, just last week," he replied. "I was driving through a village and spotted a general store. On a dusty bargain table I found a lovely old glass bowl that was hand signed. It cost just $5, but a catalog lists it for $100!" That anecdote became the opening for his presentation.

Audience Analysis: Make a Brief Written Plan

Writing down a plan or an overview of the rhetorical situation for your presentation will help to clarify the steps of preparation. In fact, your instructor may require that a plan be handed in. Below is a sample format for such a plan or overview.

Presentation Plan/Rhetorical Situation Overview

1. General purpose: to _____
   Specific purpose: to _____

2. Demographics of audience:
   Estimated age range: _____ to _____ Gender: _____
   Relevant cultural factors: _____

3. What does the audience know about the topic? _____

4. What else can you tell them? _____

5. How does the audience *feel* about the topic? _____
   Any touchy aspects? If so, what? _____

6. What are the implications of your audience analysis for this presentation?
   _____

7. *If* you use an argument format, how will you establish common ground? (See chapter 19.)

_____

8. What audiovisual will you use? _____ When and how will you use it? _____

9. What factors influence your credibility? _____

10. What will be your biggest challenge? Why? _____

_____

CREDIBILITY, ORGANIZATION, AND DEVELOPMENT

The aim of an extemporaneous presentation is to talk *with* an audience in a forthright manner, not *at* them. This requires showing respect for their integrity, intelligence, and values. To gain the trust of the audience and establish credibility, you need to show regard for accuracy, for ethics, and for the listeners. A knowledgeable presenter who is poised, prepared, and considerate will earn respect. Preparation includes not only collecting reliable information, planning, organizing, and practicing but also giving attention to other factors that influence credibility.

Considering Credibility

Your *credibility* (estimate of trustworthiness by the audience) is based upon the quality of the information you present and the way you present it. To gain

See chapter 25.

trust and respect, you need to sound as if you know and believe what you say. That means you collect reliable information, identify sources, and radiate sincerity.

Your credibility emanates not only from thorough preparation and reliable information but also from professional demeanor and energy level. A clear confident voice, proper pronunciation, and correct grammar promote respect. Appropriate attire and a neat appearance also contribute to credibility. Look professional, not flashy. To feel tip-top and maintain your energy level, get a full night's rest and eat breakfast. To decrease anxiety, do some form of exercise.

Organizing an Informative Presentation

Clarity, logical reasoning, and flexibility are the chief factors to keep in mind as you organize an oral presentation. Depending upon the rhetorical situation, an informative presentation can be organized in various ways. For example, to ex-

See chapter 12.

plain a training procedure, use chronological order just as you would in a process paper.

See "The Seven Basic Orders," chapter 4.

If you are explaining something by giving three reasons, characteristics, or other categories, you could arrange them according to importance. To describe the layout and features of a historical park, you could use spatial order or a combination of orders. As you practice a presentation, revise the order as needed.

Organizing a Persuasive Presentation

A low-key argument is generally more effective than direct confrontation. The wise presenter downplays disagreement by starting with a neutral overview of an issue. A wise strategy is to follow with a point that both sides agree on. This *common ground* sets the stage for discussion. Next, state the points of the opposition *fairly* before presenting your points.

See chapter 19.

Treating an issue as a problem to be resolved will establish an air of objectivity and fairness. Try to find a common goal. Use the pronoun *we* whenever possible: "*We* all want Children's Services to keep on serving needy children in Hardin County. The question is, How do *we* continue services after the present operating levy expires?" This attitude will foster respect for the other side and keep tempers banked. To elicit cooperation, *ask* questions such as "What are the alternatives?" "What are the advantages and disadvantages of each alternative?" "What is the best overall solution?"

To shape an effective argument, determine the *area of resistance* and find a way around it. Why does the other side reject a proposal? Often the area of resistance is cost. You might point out "The operating levy on the ballot is a renewal. It will not increase your taxes." List the benefits and conclude with a summation such as "Anything worthwhile is going to cost money. Let's not be penny-wise and pound foolish. Let's plan for the future."

Considering Ethics, Logic, and Emotion

An important factor in any presentation is the blending of logic, ethics, and emotion. Yet there is no quick formula. First of all, appeals should be ethical. Second, most classroom presentations will require that logic predominate and emotion remain subordinate. Emotion should be subtle and suitable, used to reinforce the central point. The emphasis should be on facts, data, details, reasons, and examples.

Choosing the Right Words

When considering words, select a level of formality that is appropriate for the topic and the audience. This guideline rules out nonstandard English for classroom presentations. Informal Standard English is generally suitable for these presentations. Contractions will lend a conversational tone. If you need a technical term that the audience may not know, define it and perhaps give a brief example.

See chapter 2.

Sometimes you can make a presentation come alive with a vivid comparison—a simile, metaphor, or analogy. John F. Kennedy, in his inaugural address on January 20, 1961, used striking imagery. The excerpt that follows contains two metaphors:

> To our *sister republics* south of the border, we offer a special pledge: to convert our good words into good deeds—in a new alliance for progress—to assist free men and free governments in casting off the *chains of poverty*.

See
chapter 9.
Shy away from buzz words, slang, and clichés that may not be understood by some generations or ethnic groups. Avoid stereotypes and any language that might offend.

Improving Transition

To track the main idea, listeners need guide words even more than readers do. When there is a shift in meaning, place a transitional word or phrase at the head of the sentence. For example, *"But* the proponents believe that . . ." If you use chronological order or an order of importance, begin with numerical transition (*first, second, third*). For other situations involving time, you can insert transitions of time: *fifty years ago, today,* or *in the future.* If you speak of different places, begin with phrases such as *in Europe* or *at Madiera Beach.* (For lists of transitions, see the index.)

OPTIONS FOR INTRODUCTIONS AND CONCLUSIONS

Unless you plan carefully, the closing of your presentation may be the only part that an audience remembers. Unless you hook their attention early, some may daydream for the entire presentation. The attention of others may fade in and out like a weak radio signal. A successful introduction has three key ingredients:

1. **Attention-getter.** It must relate to the topic.
2. **Topic.** State the topic and the thesis unless there is a logical reason for delaying the thesis.
3. **Link the topic to the audience.** Whet their curiosity and interest.

Introductions

An attention-getter hooks listeners and stimulates interest, perhaps through a reference to the occasion, an anecdote or example, unfamiliar facts or fragments of history, a startling statistic or opinion, an intriguing question, an apt quotation, or original humor—something that happened to you.

Refer to the Occasion   Does the day of the presentation have historical significance? Is the occasion special for the audience or just for you? A reference to the occasion can provide an effective entry into the main idea. On September 7, 1953, George Meany, president of the American Federation of Labor broadcast a message to our nation. He began by defining the day:

> Labor Day is the one national holiday which does not commemorate famous heroes or historic events. It is dedicated to the millions of men and women who work for wages, the people who have built America's towns and cities, the skilled and unskilled laborers who are responsible, in large measure, for the miracle of American

industrial progress. As the representative of nine million of these working men and women, it is my purpose to report to you on the issues which are of supreme importance on this Labor Day.

Offer an Anecdote or Example   A personal story that illustrates the main point allows you to ease into the topic. For example, if your purpose was to inspire and pay tribute, you might begin, "My uncle would have scoffed if someone had said he had great courage. He would have replied, 'I just did what needed to be done.'" Then the story or example would follow.

Provide an Unfamiliar Fact or Bit of History   Little-known information about a famous person, event, or place can provide an interesting opening. For example, an article from the *Wall Street Journal* (16 October 1998) could serve as an opening for a persuasive presentation:

> Our Congressional Cemetery, 191 years old and located near Capitol Hill, has sunk into obscurity and decay. In fact, this cemetery—where John Philip Sousa, Mathew Brady, and other noted persons lie—was cited in 1997 as "one of the nation's 11 most endangered historic places." That fall volunteers worked for two days cutting shrubbery and sprucing up the grounds. Retired FBI agents placed a bench and fence on J. Edgar Hoover's plot, but major improvements are needed.

Give a Surprising Statistic or Opinion   To capture attention, begin with an unexpected fact or statement. This opening is handy if the topic is familiar to the audience. To interest them, you need something different, a fresh angle or an unusual comment to make them sit up and listen. Consider the following example:

> When my great-grandmother traveled from Pennsylvania to Ohio in a covered wagon in the 1800s, the family had to buy safe drinking water along the way. A typhoid epidemic was raging and people were dying. Today many of us are faced with polluted drinking water on a lesser scale, and we may not even know it. Arsenic is a naturally occurring element in our soil that flows into well water and reservoirs.

Ask a Question   Asking a *rhetorical question*, one you will answer in the presentation, can stimulate curiosity about the topic. For instance, if you were going to talk on beekeeping, you might ask, "Did you know that worker bees have to put the queen on a diet before she can fly and start a new hive? Normally, she is too heavy. They have to keep her from eating until she is light enough to fly."

Or you might ask a question and take an answer from the audience. If you take individual responses, limit to three. Call on people who are unlikely to toss in a joke or hog the stage. The safest way is to ask a direct question of the entire audience, one that requires a brief yes or no, such as "How many of you have bought a lovely house plant only to have it die within a short time?" Then raise your own hand to indicate a show of hands.

Find an Apt Quotation   The right quotation at the beginning can lend a professional touch. In the first line of the introduction, repeat a key word or phrase from the quotation. This repetition will provide a direct lead to the main idea. If you cannot create a link, find a quotation that is relevant.

Use Humor   Using humor is like lighting a fire—you need to know what you are doing, or you may be burned. Original humor is best, especially brisk one-liners that bring you quickly to the main idea. Do not tell irrelevant jokes just because they are funny. Keep anecdotes and jokes short. A long-winded tale can create a top-heavy presentation. If you direct good-natured humor toward someone, choose a close friend or the head of the company—a self-confident person who will not take offense. Or better yet, tell jokes on yourself. The audience will love it, and it will keep you humble. Avoid ethnic, sexist, and off-color jokes. Be professional.

GUIDELINES FOR USING HUMOR

Inappropriate humor can blast a speaker's credibility. If you intend to use humor in a presentation, appraise it carefully, and follow these guidelines:

1. **Be original and relevant.** Relate humor closely to the main idea.
2. **Use humor like salt—sparingly.** Keep jokes and stories brief.
3. **Be kind.** Avoid remarks that might offend individuals or groups.
4. **Practice your timing.** If people do not laugh, go right on.
5. **Practice your punch line.** Pause before the punch line. Then say it clearly. Do not rush. Emphasize the important words.

Conclusions

In a serious presentation, the conclusion has two prime functions: to summarize and to provide closure. For most informative and persuasive presentations, the ending should *restate the main idea.* As you restate the thesis, allude to the importance of the topic to the audience. Be concise. Three guidelines can help you avoid common problems:

- Do not end abruptly.
- Do not introduce new points.
- Do not ramble.

To devise an effective closing, think about the impression you want to leave. What do you want listeners to remember? Six common endings are listed here. They can be combined in various ways, depending upon the presentation.

Summarize   For emphasis in a serious presentation, remind listeners of the thesis, either directly or by allusion. When you repeat the main idea, listeners are more apt to remember it. Or summarize your main points if appropriate. To spice up a summary ending, combine it with another type of closing.

End with a Quotation   A relevant quotation can provide a thoughtful conclusion. Do not quote an entire poem—use only a few lines that apply to the central idea of the presentation. If you began with a quotation, do not end with another. Chances are the two will conflict and detract from the presentation.

Loop to the Introduction   Allude to the opening in some way for closure. If you began with a rhetorical question, you might answer it briefly in the conclusion. If you began with a quotation, you might repeat a key phrase. Or if you began with a story, you might quickly finish it as Paul Harvey does in "the rest of the story."

Pose a Challenge or Question   A challenge or provocative question can motivate an audience. This ending is often used to persuade. For example, a presentation that reports the progress on a volunteer playground project might end with appreciation, a summary, and a question (note the emotional appeal):

> We appreciate your generosity. You have opened your pocketbooks and lent your hands. The job is almost complete. Will you come once more to help rake the site and spread mulch this Saturday or Sunday? Seeing the delight on the children's faces when they can use this playground will make you glad you did.

Call for Action   A persuasive presentation requires a restatement of the proposition. Often a call for action is also included to motivate the audience. For example, "Tonight set your alarm ten minutes early. Then stop by the voting booth on your way to class or to work. You owe it to yourself and your country."

Refer to the Future   Mentioning the future can lend an optimistic note. In "I Have a Dream," Martin Luther King combined three techniques in his ending: he summarized the main idea, alluded to the future, and quoted from an old song. Note, too, the use of *we* to unite listeners:

> When we let freedom ring, when we let it ring from every village and every hamlet, from every state and every city, we will be able to speed up that day when all of God's children, black men and white men, Jews and Gentiles, Protestants and Catholics, will be able to join hands and sing in the words of the old Negro spiritual, "Free at last! free at last! Thank God almighty, we are free at last!"

PREPARING NOTES AND AUDIOVISUALS

Preparing careful notes and effective audiovisuals can enhance your presentation. Although some experienced speakers manage without notes, most carry them as insurance. Even professional presenters are not immune to sudden memory loss. Confidently, one presenter strode up to the lectern without his notes because he had practiced well. But when he looked out over a sea of 500 faces, his mind went blank. While the audience waited, he walked back to his chair for the notes. That was a humbling experience.

Notes on Paper or Cards?

By now you should be convinced that notes are essential, even if your instructor does not require them. The one remaining question is whether to put the notes on paper or file cards. If you ever present a seminar, you might decide to type your outline on paper, double spaced in large type. If you're using presentation software, the program will include options for preparing notes.

A few sheets of paper are simpler to handle than a dozen note cards unless there will be air blowing near you. (Overhead projectors, for instance, can scatter pages.) Number the sheets in the upper right corner. Place them in a neat pile on one side of the lectern before you begin. As you finish covering the points on each page, *slide the page to the other side of the lectern while looking at your audience.* Continue in this way, and the audience will be unlikely to notice your notes. This method takes more skill and practice than using a few note cards.

For classroom presentations, carefully prepared note cards are easy to use. You just lay out the cards and leave them alone during the presentation. Six large cards will usually fit neatly on a lectern. Although six may seem like quite a few, beware of crowding words. *You need to be able to scan the cards quickly without picking them up or bending over.* Note cards should be legible from three feet away (unless you are very short).

TIPS FOR MAKING NOTE CARDS

1. **Use large 5- by 8-inch cards.** For easy reading, avoid crowding.
2. **Number the cards in the upper right corner.** Avoid mixups.
3. **Use an outline format.** Leave blank space to add key phrases later.
4. **Print neatly with black ink in large letters.** Use broad strokes.
5. **Use numbers or bullets to list points.** Enhance visibility.
6. **Use only one side of each card.** Turning cards over diverts attention.

Creating Effective Audiovisuals

Chances are that you will have a software program such as PowerPoint at your disposal for use in a presentation. Or you might use an overhead projector, a flip chart, a VCR, a tape player, or other audiovisual. (A chalkboard is not recommended because it lacks novelty and requires turning your back while the audience waits.)

The purpose of an audiovisual is to enhance a presentation, not overpower it. Avoid clutter. As you plan graphics, check to see that each frame or sheet conveys a single idea. If you have several statistics or other complex items, prepare a handout to distribute before you begin. *Do not interrupt your presentation to pass out materials.* Less relevant information can be left near the door to be picked up later.

GUIDELINES FOR PLANNING AUDIOVISUALS

1. **Make sure an AV will not harm the audience or make them squirm.** No snakes, guns, explosives, volatile liquids, or other dangerous items.

2. **Predict the effect of the AV and test it.** Be sure there are no trouble spots. *Run unusual ideas past your instructor.*

3. **Limit the number of AVs and keep them fairly simple.** Otherwise, you may feel like a juggler with too many balls in the air.

4. **Limit tapes and videos to one minute in a five- to seven-minute presentation.**

5. **Make graphics neat and attractive.** Plan layouts so they are clear, uncluttered, and pleasing to the eye. Limit to one idea each.

6. **Use color for a purpose.** Human eyes, like those of bees, are attracted to red and black. Use red for emphasis and dark colors for lettering.

7. **Check to see that visuals are clear to persons seated in the back row.** If you are discussing a small object, show an enlargement.

8. **Retain the element of surprise!** Keep visuals hidden until you use them. For example, reverse posters until you are ready to show them.

PRACTICING A PRESENTATION

Planning and practice are essential for an effective presentation. Last-minute attention to equipment and materials, hurrying, and dropping or misplacing items can give the impression of carelessness and incompetence. Careful preparation will boost your confidence and help fend off mishaps.

Practice your presentation several times, using your note cards and audiovisuals, but do not overpractice, or it may sound memorized. To lend a natural conversational tone, you might imagine you are talking to friends. *Act as if you feel calm, even if you don't.* If you have the opportunity to videotape a practice session, do so. Then you can critique your eye contact, posture, gestures, vocal variety, and use of notes and audiovisuals.

Using Audiovisuals

Plan how and when to use audiovisuals so that the audience does not have to wait. Can you set up and adjust PowerPoint, the VCR, or any projectors before class? How will you prop up the antique doll? Can you get an easel so that the poster will not flop over? Other questions to consider are when to bring out objects and how long to leave them out.

As you speak, *look at the audience, not the visuals*. When using an overhead projector, use a pencil to point on the transparency. When slides or other visuals are projected on a screen behind you, use a longer object to point to areas of the screen. That way you can glance at it and look at the audience, not the screen. If you are describing an unfamiliar object or craft, such as punched tin, bring it out early. If the object will not distract, leave it out the entire time. Or some objects are more effective shown only at the end.

One student, who had won several trophies showing her horse, did not want to appear to be bragging, so she decided to display just one trophy. First she described the fun of displaying the horse in the ring; then she explained the unglamorous work behind the scenes. At the end she held up a large trophy and said, "But all the hard work was worthwhile, for I won first prize!" By then she had charmed the audience, and they were glad her efforts had been rewarded.

Revising Note Cards

As you practice your presentation, highlight key points on your notes with a colored marker. If you quote someone, highlight it. If certain terms are difficult to recall, print them in red. Reword any phrases or sentences that cause stumbling. Write the revision on your note card. Star the spots where audiovisuals will come. On the final card or page, write out the last sentence you want to say as a safety blanket. If your notes become messy from revision, recopy them as necessary for easy reading.

Improving Eye Contact, Posture, and Gestures

Before you ever open your lips, you send silent messages that enhance or diminish your credibility. Your eye contact, posture, and gestures greatly affect your presentation. Do you look at the audience—or do you stare at a point on the back wall? Do you stand erect or slumped? Do you have notes in hand ready to lay out, or do you fumble through a briefcase, backpack, or handbag?

Eye Contact   Smile and establish eye contact immediately before you say a word. During the presentation, look at one person for several seconds before moving on. Look at various people in different parts of the room, not just the front row. Avoid eye dart. You may *glance* at your note cards from time to time, but do not linger. Their purpose is merely to remind you of the next idea.

Gestures   Like your words, your gestures should appear spontaneous and natural. You might rest one hand on the lectern, but do not clutch it with both hands. The purpose of a lectern is to hold notes, not to lean on or hide behind.

Once in a while you may want to walk out from behind the lectern, but beware of purposeless movement and repetitive gestures. Consider, too, that some gestures may have negative or humorous connotations. Three common stances have been identified as detrimental for speakers:

- **The Fig Leaf** Avoid standing with hands clasped in front.
- **Parade Rest** Avoid standing with hands clasped behind the back like a general reviewing the troops.
- **Closed Mind** Avoid crossed arms on the chest. This posture may suggest coldness and a reluctance to admit new information.

While you speak, let you arms hang loosely at your sides so that you can use them naturally. Avoid nervous habits that dispel the illusion of spontaneity and distract. Common habits include scratching the nose, twisting long hair or beard, fidgeting with earrings, jingling coins, taking glasses on and off, or waving a note card around.

Improving Vocal Variety

The human voice is an instrument that conveys distinctive speech sounds that vary in volume, rate, and pitch. When we are relaxed and happy, the sounds are more pleasing than when we are tired or upset. Fear, anxiety, and anger tighten the vocal cords, producing a higher, thinner pitch than normal. With practice you can gain greater control of your voice. Volume and rate are easier to control than pitch, but all can be improved to some extent. Taping an entire presentation allows you not only to time it but also to hear how you sound.

Volume A presenter's voice should be loud enough to be heard by everyone in the room, unless a microphone is available. Volume is seldom a problem for male voices, but some female voices are barely audible. Women often need to speak louder than normal. To project your voice to the back row, you need plenty of air in the lungs. Shallow breathing interferes with vocal variety and quality. Try varying your volume according to the effect you wish to create. Emphasize important words. Be careful that your voice does not trail off at the ends of sentences, making them inaudible.

Rate "Mallspeak" or immature speech patterns may be a concern for some readers. In "Taking Aim at Student Incoherence" (*Chronicle of Higher Education* 26 March 1999), Alison Schneider cites this sample, delivered breathlessly: "Okay. Today I'm going to be talking to you guys about malaria." During the presentation the student fidgeted and giggled, ending with "So, in conclusion, I'd just like to say, malaria, you know, is the most prevalent of all tropical diseases."

Speaking too fast, fidgeting, and giggling may be due to nervousness or feelings of inadequacy, intensified by habit. If you have any of these concerns, give yourself a little pep talk. Reassure yourself that these minutes are yours and you have an interesting topic to share. The audience is alert and waiting. You don't have to race to the finish line. Don't be afraid to pause at the right places, including a slight pause after periods. Pausing after an important point gives emphasis and allows the audience time to absorb the idea. Knowing that it is all right to pause naturally may help you delete unintentional fillers such as *uh, um, okay,* or *you know.*

Articulation Practice and pausing can alleviate slurring (running words together) or other problems in articulation. The lips, the tongue, and the teeth form speech sounds—they articulate the words. At the same time, the mouth has to open wide enough to let the words out or mumbling occurs. And *it must be empty*—chewing gum, candy, or cough drops interfere with clear delivery.

Common concerns are slurring and addition of or omission of syllables. Tape yourself and then check a dictionary for problem words. Listed here are common mispronunciations and the correct pronunciations:

Incorrect	*Correct*
acrost	a-cross'
ath-*a*-lete	ath'lete
fishin'	fish'ing
gonna	go'ing to
pitchur	pic'ture
wanna	want to

Pitch Pitch refers to the lowness or highness of the voice. We all have a natural pitch that varies according to our emotions and health. Other factors also influence pitch. For example, if we ask a question, our voice goes up at the end of the sentence. At the end of a declarative sentence, the voice goes down. Most speakers, when relaxed, vary their pitch naturally. Those that speak in a monotone can add expression to their words through vocal exercise and practice (see the exercises at the end of the chapter).

GIVING A PRESENTATION

Enthusiasm and *sincerity* are two keys to an effective presentation. Enthusiastic speakers know and care about their topics. They vary their volume, rate, and pitch just as they would in casual conversation. Chances are that if you like your topic and prepare well, your enthusiasm will radiate from your face and your voice. And if you truly believe what you are saying, your sincerity will be apparent.

Arrive Early

Go early to the room where you will speak. Erase the chalkboard if necessary. Check to see that the equipment you need is in working order. (One mortified student forgot to plug in the VCR.) If you are supposed to sign equipment out somewhere else, go get it.

Take a Deep Breath . . .

When introduced, take a deep breath and approach the lectern. Put down your notes or, if you're using note cards, lay them out in sequence. Then look out over the audience and smile. Chances are that some people will smile back. If you come across as a friendly person, listeners will be more apt to give you their undivided attention. For some topics, smiling may be inappropriate.

On the job or in a community setting, extend an appropriate greeting, such as "Good Morning" or "Welcome." You may want to thank someone who has assisted or the group for inviting you. In the classroom these little courtesies are not expected.

Don't Apologize Unnecessarily

Even if you feel unprepared, rushed, or nervous, don't apologize or toss in unnecessary comments. Just ignore your feelings and begin with your planned opening. Once you get past that and the audience responds, speaking will become easier. If you should mispronounce a word, just correct yourself and go on. Avoid weak, *ineffective* remarks such as these:

- Uh, I guess I'm a little nervous.
- I didn't have as much time to prepare as I would have liked.
- I regret I am not an expert on this topic (false modesty).

Adapt to the Audience

Watching the audience will take your mind off yourself. Are they listening attentively? Or do they slump in their seats, gaze at the ceiling, or fidget? To regain lost attention, you can move out from behind the lectern, use more gestures, increase volume, or lower your voice to a whisper.

Handle unexpected incidents with poise. If a transparency falls, let it lie unless you need it. If the bulb in an overhead projector burns out, flip the switch for the spare bulb. If there is none, continue anyway. If computer equipment malfunctions, take a moment to resolve the problem, and if the problem can't be fixed within those couple of moments, go on without your computerized audiovisuals. Seldom is there cause to interrupt a presentation. In the unlikely event of a power outage, sonic boom, fire alarm, or a storm alert, stop and wait. Then when you resume the presentation, you might toss in a quick joke. The audience will admire your calm, professional demeanor and ability to function under duress.

End Purposefully and Gracefully

The last few words of a presentation tend to linger in the minds of the audience. Once in a while, an inexperienced presenter will skid to an abrupt stop with "That's it" or "that's all." Some go to the other extreme—tacking on afterthoughts, irrelevant jokes, or stories. Such tactics throw a presentation off balance and weaken its impact. Know when to stop.

Be Prepared for Questions

After a presentation, you may have the opportunity to say, "Are there any questions?" If so, listen carefully to the entire question before responding. Maintain eye contact. If the question is unclear, restate it as a question. If you don't know the answer, ask for a phone number or an e-mail address so that you can get back to the person.

Student Sample: A Persuasive Presentation

Carol Witzel gave the following presentation extemporaneously. She had outlined it on note cards but wrote out the draft later, when requested.

Give It More Respect!

Do you know what the hottest part of your body is? Do you know what part is the most dangerous if it becomes infected? The answer to both questions is your mouth, specifically your gums and teeth. Are you surprised? Like Rodney Dangerfield, your mouth and its contents get little respect. After you hear of my unfortunate experience, you should accord this part of your body much, much more respect.

During a regular checkup two years ago, my physician said that he did not like the looks of my gums and that I should have a dentist take a look at them. Immediately, I made an appointment with my regular dentist. I told him my mouth had a metallic taste, and my teeth seemed to hurt often. During the exam the dentist told me not to worry, everything was fine. He did not bother to take x-rays.

One year passed and the symptoms worsened. By then my gums were bleeding when I brushed my teeth. When I opened my mouth in cold air, my face and teeth hurt. I decided it was time to consult a different dentist. The second dentist did a quick exam—the results were dismal. Several teeth had advanced decay. Worst of all, my gums were in an advanced stage of periodontal disease or gingivitis. Gingivitis is inflammation and infection of the gingiva or gums. There are five stages of the disease, and I was in stage four.

What I needed was minor surgery on the gums to clear away the infection. Then he put in seven crowns to correct the problems with decayed teeth. After that came bridge work, which involved three additional crowns and two pontics (false teeth). The bridge was made to cover the loss of two teeth due to poor care. Correcting all these problems cost nearly $7,000.

Today you cannot tell my natural teeth from the crowns or bridgework. My teeth no longer hurt when I drink hot or cold liquids. I can actually breathe through my mouth without severe pain emitting from teeth to all points on my face.

Now you are probably wondering how you can prevent some of the problems I've experienced. The first step is to have regular dental checkups with a responsible dentist. Second, take good daily care of your teeth and mouth. Third, watch for any of these five symptoms:

1. **Bleeding in the mouth.** Have it checked just as you would if some other part of your body was bleeding regularly.

2. **A metallic taste.** If you already have fillings, this could mean you have decay under the filling, and the old filling is leaking.

3. **Extreme sensitivity** to hot and cold temperatures.

4. **Chronic bad breath.**

5. **Chronic tiredness, headaches, or white spots on the gums** could indicate infection. Those who use tobacco should watch these signs closely because of the risk of cancer in the mouth.

If your dentist does not stress good gum care, maybe you should consider finding another dentist. Just remember that your mouth is the gateway to your body. To have good health, respect and maintain your mouth, gums, and teeth. You will be glad you did!

Questions for Discussion

1. How does Carol involve the audience in her opening?
2. What common order does she use to present information?
3. What signpost transitions indicate this order?
4. Can you find the transitional sentence that she uses to go from talking about herself to explaining about good dental care?
5. What do you notice about her ending?

Summary

Three elements of the rhetorical situations for writing and speaking differ greatly: occasion, audience, and voice. These elements influence the preparation and delivery of an effective presentation. There are four types of presentations: manuscript, memorized, extemporaneous, and impromptu.

As you plan your extemporaneous presentation, check out the setting as well as the audience so that you can tailor your approach to the topic. Define the purpose, and be sure that your topic is suitable. If you do further research, secure reliable information and sources. To adapt a paper for presentation, condense and simplify according to the rhetorical situation.

In the opening, link the presentation to the audience. Organize main points clearly. Plan a suitable closing. Prepare notes in outline form. Keep audiovisuals simple and purposeful, and practice using them. Practice the entire presentation several times, but do not memorize it word for word.

Good eye contact, erect posture, appropriate gestures, and a neat appearance add to a presenter's credibility. Vocal variety and clear articulation add interest and clarity. A presenter should act calm and professional with no apologies or unnecessary remarks. At the conclusion of serious presentations, the main idea should be restated for emphasis. If questioned afterward, listen carefully and show respect.

Key Terms

articulation	common ground	impromptu
audience analysis	credibility	pitch
audiovisual	demographics	purpose statement
closure	extemporaneous	rhetorical situation

Practice

Exercise: Articulation

To improve your articulation, say the alphabet aloud. Exaggerate each letter and say it distinctly. Listen and think about the position of your tongue and lips. They must be in the right position for a letter to be clear. To form an *l*, the tip of the tongue touches the roof of the mouth, and the mouth opens slightly. The *r* sound rumbles deep in the throat as the tongue is held up slightly and the mouth curls down, slightly open.

If dropping of *g*'s is a problem for you, practice words ending with *-ing* and think about the position of your tongue and mouth as you say them correctly, emphasizing *-ing*. As you attain greater self-awareness, your vocal variety will improve.

Exercise: Volume, Rate, Pitch

To improve vocal variety, you might read aloud to a child. To relax the vocal cords, exaggerate the sounds and have fun. *Goldilocks and the Three Bears* provides excellent practice, allowing the reader to assume different voices. Baby Bear's words tumble out in a high squeaky pitch. Mother Bear articulates clearly at a moderate rate in a medium-pitched voice. Papa Bear speaks in a slow, deep-pitched voice that rumbles with authority. (If the child can read, she can take Goldilocks's part. A boy might prefer a role in *The Three Little Pigs*.)

Ungraded Presentations

The chief purpose of an ungraded presentation is to alleviate speech fright. A one- or two-minute practice speech can use the basic claim-and-evidence order (opinion and support). For example, you might disagree with a news item, magazine article, political decision, or movie review. Give reasons. Close with a complete sentence, such as "See *Clint Rides Again* only if you want to be bored stiff." Or you might use one of the ideas below or one of your own.

1. Funny, exciting, or embarrassing moment
2. An unusual ancestor, neighbor, or boss
3. An incident: How your spouse proposed, prank at summer camp, et cetera
4. Description: Your best teacher, first job, first car
5. Anecdote: a lost pet, special birthday, or disastrous first date

Thirty Ideas for Oral Presentations

Informative Topics

1. Present a research-based paper or project to the class (condense and simplify).
2. Present a lab report. Describe the process that you observed.
3. Do home computers really need anti-virus protection? (Cite experts.)
4. Practice a presentation you will be giving at work or elsewhere.

5. Inform employees of a new company policy (privacy, Internet use, or sexist jokes).
6. Present tips for improving something.
7. Describe your job and three things you have learned.
8. Suggest ways to cut utility bills.
9. Explain what to look for in a diamond.
10. Describe an inexpensive weekend at _____.
11. Suggest three interesting one-day trips to lesser-known spots.
12. Explain how to find time to exercise.
13. Provide information about what everyone should know before going white-water rafting.
14. Describe factors to consider when buying a new computer, car, camping equipment, or other item.
15. Explain how to refinish old furniture.
16. Describe your hobby.
17. Suggest three excellent restaurants in _____.
18. Warn about faked auto accidents.
19. Tell about collecting antique boxes (or anything else).
20. Explain three ways to make house plants thrive.

Persuasive Topics

21. Research a timely issue and take a position.
22. Get a physical exam regularly.
23. Voting is a responsibility.
24. Neuter your pet.
25. Cut your sugar intake.
26. Preserve a historical landmark.
27. Take steps to prevent fires in your home.
28. Instant replay should (should not) be used by football referees.
29. Prevent skin cancer.
30. Be an organ donor.

The Reader

Alternate Contents: The Readings by Theme   549
Introduction to the Reader   553
   How Do Essays and Short Stories Differ?   553
   Critical Reading   553
   Second Guessing   554

NARRATION: RECOUNTING EVENTS   555
   DAVID BANK, Rosetta Disk Is Foundation's Gift to Future Linguists   555
   CARSON MCCULLERS, Home for Christmas   559
   JEAN HOUSTON, The Art of Acknowledgment   563
   PHILIP WEISS, How to Get Out of a Locked Trunk   567

DESCRIPTION: CONVEYING IMPRESSIONS   572
   SUE HUBBELL, Caterpillar Afternoon   572
   EUDORA WELTY, One Writer's Beginnings   576
   JOHN CIARDI, Dawn Watch   579
   LIANE ELLISON NORMAN, Pedestrian Students   583

PROCESS ANALYSIS: EXPLAINING HOW   586
   EUELL GIBBONS, How to Cook a Carp   586
   NOEL PERRIN, Falling for Apples   590
   CAROL CARTER, Write Your Own Success Story   594
   MARYA MANNES, How Do You Know It's Good?   600

ILLUSTRATION: SHOWING WITH EXAMPLES   606
   ETHLIE VARE AND GREG PTACEK, Mothers of Invention   606
   JASON VEST, WARREN COHEN, AND MIKE THARP, Road Rage   609
   ANDREA LEE, Black and Well-to-Do   615
   HOLMAN W. JENKINS, JR., Uptight Is Back in Style   618

CLASSIFICATION: GROUPING AND DIVIDING   621
   KATHLEEN FURY, It's Only a Paper World   621
   NORMAN BROWN, Mind Over Munchies   624
   LISA DAVIS, Where Do We Stand?   629
   JAMES T. BAKER, How Do We Find the Student?   632

COMPARISON AND CONTRAST:
EXPLAINING LIKENESS AND DIFFERENCE   636
   PHILLIP LOPATE, A Nonsmoker and a Smoker   636
   NEAL PEIRCE, Americans: Conservationists or Champion
   Land Hogs?   640
   AMY TAN, Mother Tongue   643
   DEBORAH TANNEN, Women and Men Talking on the Job   649

DEFINITION: IDENTIFYING BASIC CHARACTERISTICS   655
   DAVID RAYMOND, On Being 17, Bright, and Unable to Read   655
   WILLIAM RASPBERRY, The Handicap of Definition   659
   BARBARA JORDAN, Becoming Educated   662
   LAURENCE SHAMES, The Sweet Smell of Success Isn't All
   That Sweet   665

CAUSE AND EFFECT: EXPLAINING WHY   668
   BARBARA EHRENREICH, Spudding Out   668
   ANNE ROIPHE, Why Marriages Fail   671
   NICHOLAS GAGE, The Teacher Who Changed My Life   675
   ELISABETH KÜBLER-ROSS, The Emotional Quadrant   680

SHAPING AN EFFECTIVE ARGUMENT   683
   MIKE ESKENAZI, The New Case for Latin   683
   ANDREA SACHS, When the Lullaby Ends   686
   AMITAI ETZIONI, Working at McDonald's   689
   RICHARD M. RESTAK, The Other Difference Between Boys
   and Girls   693
   C. S. LEWIS, We Have No 'Right to Happiness'   698

SHORT STORIES AND CREATION NARRATIVES   703
   Short Stories
   URSULA HEGI, Doves   703
   CHARLES BAXTER, Scheherazade   707
   KATE CHOPIN, Story of an Hour   711
   JOHN UPDIKE, Still of Some Use   714

   Creation Narratives
   Introduction: The Search for Our Beginnings   719
   PIMA INDIAN LEGEND, The Well-Baked Man   721
   GENESIS 1–2:3   723
      From the *Torah*   723
      From the *Bible* (KJV)   726
   Selected Verses. From the Koran   730

ALTERNATE CONTENTS: THE READINGS BY THEME

CREATION AND TEMPTATION

Genesis 1–2, from the *Torah*   723

Genesis 1–2, from the *Bible* (KJV)   726

Selected Verses, from the *Koran*   730

The Well-Baked Man, related by the Pima   721

C. S. LEWIS, We Have No "Right to Happiness"   698

ANNE ROIPHE, Why Marriages Fail   671

MYSTERIES OF THE HUMAN BODY

NORMAN BROWN, Mind Over Munchies   624

LISA DAVIS, Where Do We Stand?   629

ELISABETH KÜBLER-ROSS, The Emotional Quadrant   680

DAVID RAYMOND, On Being 17, Bright, and Unable to Read   655

RICHARD M. RESTAK, The Other Difference between Boys and Girls   693

CULTURAL RULES OF FORM AND BEHAVIOR

KATE CHOPIN, The Story of an Hour   711

LISA DAVIS, Where Do We Stand?   629

BARBARA EHRENREICH, Spudding Out   668

HOLMAN W. JENKINS, JR., Uptight Is Back in Style   618

ANDREA LEE, Black and Well-to-Do   615

PHILLIP LOPATE, A Nonsmoker with a Smoker   636

WILLIAM RASPBERRY, The Handicap of Definition   659

AMY TAN, Mother Tongue   643

DEBORAH TANNEN, Women and Men Talking on the Job   649

JASON VEST, WARREN COHEN, and MIKE THARP, Road Rage   609

LANGUAGE USE AND ABUSE

DAVID BANK, Rosetta Disk Is Foundation's Gift to Future Linguists   555

ELISABETH KÜBLER-ROSS, The Emotional Quadrant   680

JEAN HOUSTON, The Art of Acknowledgement   563

ANDREA LEE, Black and Well-to-Do   615

C. S. LEWIS, We Have No "Right to Happiness"   698

WILLIAM RASPBERRY, The Handicap of Definition   659

AMY TAN, Mother Tongue   643

DEBORAH TANNEN, Women and Men Talking on the Job   649

CHANGES AND CHALLENGES

JAMES T. BAKER, How Do We Find the Student?   632

CAROL CARTER, Write Your Own Success Story   594

MIKE ESKENAZI, The New Case for Latin   683

NICHOLAS GAGE, The Teacher Who Changed My Life   675

BARBARA JORDAN, Becoming Educated   662

LIANE ELLISON NORMAN, Pedestrian Students and High-Flying Squirrels   583

DAVID RAYMOND, On Being 17, Bright, and Unable to Read   655

ELISABETH KÜBLER-ROSS, The Emotional Quadrant   680

ETHLIE VARE and GREG PTACEK, Introduction of Mothers of Invention   606

EUDORA WELTY, One Writer's Beginnings   576

PROBLEMS, SOLUTIONS, AND CONSEQUENCES

CHARLES BAXTER, Scheherazade   707

KATE CHOPIN, The Story of an Hour   711

MIKE ESKENAZI, The New Case for Latin   683

EUELL GIBBONS, How to Cook a Carp   586

SUE HUBBELL, Caterpillar Afternoon   572

HOLMAN W. JENKINS, JR., Uptight Is Back in Style   618

ELISABETH KÜBLER-ROSS, The Emotional Quadrant   680

MARYA MANNES, How Do You Know It's Good?   600

DAVID RAYMOND, On Being 17, Bright, and Unable to Read   655

ANNE ROIPHE, Why Marriages Fail   671

JOHN UPDIKE, Still of Some Use   714

JASON VEST, WARREN COHEN, and MIKE THARP, Road Rage   609

PHILIP WEISS, How to Get Out of a Locked Trunk   567

THINKING ABOUT CONTEMPORARY ISSUES

CAROL CARTER, Write Your Own Success Story   594

MIKE ESKENAZI, The New Case for Latin   683

AMITAI ETZIONI, Working at McDonalds   689

KATHLEEN FURY, It's Only a Paper World   621

URSULA HEGI, Doves   703

PHILLIP LOPATE, A Nonsmoker with a Smoker   636

NEAL PEIRCE, Americans: Conservationists or Champion
  Land Hogs?   640

ANDREA SACHS, When the Lullaby Ends   686

LAURENCE SHAMES, The Sweet Smell of Success Isn't All
  That Sweet   665

ETHLIE VARE and GREG PTACEK, Introduction of Mothers
  of Invention   606

JOHN UPDIKE, Still of Some Use   714

EVALUATING CLAIMS AND EVIDENCE

AMITAI ETZIONI, Working at McDonald's   689

C. S. LEWIS, We Have No "Right to Happiness"   698

MARYA MANNES, How Do You Know It's Good?   600

RICHARD M. RESTAK, The Other Difference between Boys
  and Girls   693

LAURENCE SHAMES, The Sweet Smell of Success Isn't All
  That Sweet   665

HARMONY WITH NATURE AND WITH SELF

JOHN CIARDI, Dawn Watch   579

URSULA HEGI, Doves   703

JEAN HOUSTON, The Art of Acknowledgement   563

CARSON MCCULLERS, Home for Christmas   559

NOEL PERRIN, Falling for Apples   590

LAURENCE SHAMES, The Sweet Smell of Success Isn't All
  That Sweet   665

EUDORA WELTY, One Writer's Beginnings   576

ETHICS: SEARCHING FOR ANSWERS

JEAN HOUSTON, The Art of Acknowledgement   563

WILLIAM RASPBERRY, The Handicap of Definition   659

C. S. LEWIS, We Have No "Right to Happiness"   698

ANDREA SACHS, When the Lullaby Ends   686

Introduction to the Reader

The forty-five essays, short stories, and creation narratives in this reader have been carefully selected not only for quality but also for interest. They cover unusual topics, ranging from the best way to cook a carp to philosophical issues such as "Do we have a right to happiness?" and "How did the human race originate?" All of the readings should stimulate thinking and questioning; for they open windows on different eras, cultures, personalities, problems, and points of view.

HOW DO ESSAYS AND SHORT STORIES DIFFER?

An essay is a short literary composition that focuses on a single idea. Usually, the author's opinion is present. For example, the author may speculate about the meaning of an event or a course of action and possible consequences. An essay of argument may question one viewpoint and offer another. Essays tend to be direct, with the thesis clearly stated. They are organized in various ways, depending on the purpose and the subject.

[See page 411.]

A short story is a fictitious narrative that has a beginning and an end and is constricted by time. For example, Kate Chopin's story occurs in just one hour. Other short stories may span a day or a few days, seldom more than a week. A good short story is compressed, giving only necessary details. The reader must interpret clues and ferret out the theme, the meaning that underlies the plot. After reading a short story, go back and consider how certain objects, dialogue, and actions contribute to the meaning. Every detail should have a reason for being.

CRITICAL READING

As you examine and discuss these readings, you will learn much about the craft of writing. You'll notice how writers use openings to set the stage for an idea and endings to conclude gracefully. You'll gain skill in scrutinizing logic and in spotting the clever use of literary devices. In short, you will learn to read critically—analyzing and evaluating not only content but also structure. A strategy for critical reading is explained in chapter 26. This strategy outlines three stages of critical reading—prereading, rereading, and prewriting—and gives helpful steps to apply as you read.

As you read, think, and discuss, take note of a significant distinction: The *writer's purpose* and the *writer's intent* are not the same. The writer's purpose is usually *stated* in an essay. You can find the purpose in the thesis statement, if there is one. A good thesis statement makes it clear whether the purpose of a piece is to entertain, inform, define, persuade, or combine some of these functions. When the purpose is stated, then it is possible to evaluate whether the writer has achieved what he or she set out to do.

On the other hand, we seldom know what a writer has intended, for *intent is rarely stated*. Unless an author spells out his or her intentions, we cannot be sure of what they are. They may, in fact, be quite different from the stated purpose.

SECOND GUESSING

Sound critical reading does not second guess an author's intent. A writing may be richer and deeper than a writer consciously intends. It is not unusual for authors to admit they were unaware of certain symbols or themes in their works until someone pointed them out. All we can logically evaluate is what the writer has *achieved*.

The more experience readers gain, the more they will notice. Perhaps the best piece of advice is to read quickly for enjoyment the first time. Then go back, reread, and ponder the piece. The better you understand the effect of a work, the more you will enjoy and appreciate its artistry.

ESSAYS

Narration

Recounting Events

Rosetta Disk Is Foundation's Gift to Future Linguists

David Bank

The Rosetta Stone is the key to ancient languages used in Egypt. This black granite slab was found in 1799, half-buried in the mud at the mouth of the Nile delta, by a French officer in Napoleon's army. In 1801 it was taken by the British and later placed in the British Museum. Upon the Rosetta Stone are three identical texts, carved in Egyptian hieroglyphics, Greek, and Demotic—the popular language of Egypt during the reign of Ptolemy Epiphanes IV from 203 to 181 B.C. His son, Ptolemy V, began to rule at age thirteen; during his reign, a council of priests inscribed a decree on the stone about 196 B.C. A French scholar, Jean François Champollion, first translated the Greek portion. Then gradually he decoded the rest, publishing the results in 1822.

Linguists now estimate that one language is lost every ten days worldwide. To offset this loss, the Rosetta Project, a global collaboration, is creating an archive of 1000 languages on a three-inch nickel disk, encased in a glass ball. In the future when our digital computers become obsolete, the disk will provide a key to the languages of the twenty-first century. David Bank, the author of this article, is a staff reporter for the Wall Street Journal. *He has also published* Breaking Windows: How Bill Gates Fumbled the Future of Microsoft *(2001).*

Around 196 B.C., a council of ancient Egyptian priests inscribed a decree on   1
a granite slab affirming the rule of 13-year-old Ptolemy V and providing three
translations, including one in a form of ancient Greek. After Napoleon's troops in
Egypt recovered the slab, the Rosetta Stone, in 1799, linguists used the Greek to
unlock the Egyptian hieroglyphics, whose meaning had been lost for centuries.

Now, a small San Francisco foundation is leading an effort to create a modern Rosetta Stone, a collection of 1,000 translations of the first three chapters of the book of Genesis into languages from Abkhaz to Zulu. The foundation's far-thinking backers hope the project will help decoders in the distant future recover languages of our own day, many of which will certainly be lost.

"If it's good with three, why not with 1,000?" asks Stewart Brand, best known as the founder of the Whole Earth Catalog and now a board member of the Long Now Foundation, which is coordinating the Rosetta Project. "In the fullness of time, civilizations come and go. It would be good to have better re-start capabilities."

When the collection is completed next year, roughly 30,000 pages of linguistic submissions will be inscribed by ion beams in tiny text onto three-inch nickel disks and encased in glass balls. The technology provider, Norsam Technologies, of Hillsboro, Ore., says tests show the disks will last at least 1,000 years, withstanding salt water, sunlight and nuclear radiation using the technology, developed at the Los Alamos nuclear labs. The foundation will distribute 1,000 disks to libraries and museums, and sell them to individuals around the world, all under the archival principle, *Lots of Copies Keep Stuff Safe.*

The hope is that at least some of the disks will survive and prove useful to future archaeologists. The glass balls encasing the disks are rudimentary magnifying glasses. Larger text in eight languages spirals around the edge of the disk as a kind of hint to discoverers to magnify the disks further. The Rosetta Project backers assume future generations will at least have a 1,000-power microscope to enlarge the tiny type. They won't need what will surely be long-lost technology: the personal computer, a Windows operating system or even electricity. The information will be presented in plain text, not digital bits.

Linguistic experts say by 2100, up to 90 percent of the world's 6,000 to 7,000 languages are in danger of becoming moribund, or even extinct, as industrialization and globalization reach every corner of the globe. Most of the world's recent losses come in once language-rich regions of the world, such as Papua New Guinea, Indonesia and Nigeria. One language becomes moribund every 10 days, on average, experts say, meaning that children no longer learn it and speak it.

With modest funding—$165,000 over two years from the Lazy Eight Foundation, of Denver, Colo.—the project is attracting submissions by linguists from around the world. No single expert could possibly check every submission, so the Rosetta Project relies on a network of linguists to correct each others' work.

Mr. Mason began by collecting nearly 1,000 translations of the world's most widely translated text, Genesis, mainly from Bible societies. The decision to use a biblical text generated a heated debate within the foundation over its religious associations, but Mr. Mason says the availability of translations made it the only practical choice. The next most-translated text, the Universal Declaration of Human Rights, has been translated into about 300 languages.

The project's Web site, www.rosettaproject.org, is becoming one of the broadest collections of language information on the Internet. Jim Mason, the anthropologist directing the project, calls it "the Linux of linguistics," referring to the open-source operating system developed collaboratively over the Internet. "A large collection of languages is way too complex for one person, or even one group of people to tackle," Mr. Mason says. "The only way to do it is create a global collaboration."

In technology terms, Mr. Mason describes the Rosetta Project as a "platform" able to support a wide variety of activities. It includes a range of material in each language, including indigenous creation stories, terms for colors, the so-called Swadesh list of the 100 words that occur in almost every language and "orthographies" describing writing and speaking styles.

The project began as a demonstration of possibilities for long-term data preservation. The record of the digital age—dependent on ever-changing computer platforms and formats—promises to be startlingly impermanent. Older media aren't much better. Newspapers and videotapes have a life expectancy of less than 30 years. Acid-free paper and some types of microform can last up to 500 years but are susceptible to heat, humidity, scratching and sunlight. History has shown that libraries burn down, museums are neglected and time capsules are forgotten.

"We're building amnesia into our civilization, which is probably a non-robust thing to do," remarks Mr. Brand.

The Long Now Foundation's focus on the far distant future is meant to stretch the time-horizon of planners, executives and leaders by 100 or 500 years, if not by 10,000. (It's already working on the deca-millenium bug, referring to the current year as 02001.) Its most well-known project is a "10,000-year clock" currently in several prototype forms, including one at the National Museum of Science and Industry in London. It ticks once a year, has a century hand that advances every 100 years and tolls every 1,000 years.

The Rosetta Project is a kind of complement. "It's very hard to send information into the future," says Kevin Kelly, a foundation board member and former executive editor of Wired magazine. "It's even harder to send values, or any kind of information that's embedded in a culture."

Other board members include musician Brian Eno, futurist Paul Saffo, Stanford University Librarian Roger Kennedy, and old-timers Danny Hillis, a pioneer in supercomputing, Mitch Kapor, a founder of Lotus Development Corp., pundit Esther Dyson and Doug Carlston, the co-founder of Broderbund Software.

The first and so far only completed submission is for Degema, spoken by about 22,000 people in two communities in Nigeria. A Nigerian linguist studying in Japan, Ethelbert Kari, prepared a detailed description of the language, pronunciation and common words. There were originally three dialects of Degema, but one became extinct when its speakers adopted Kalabari, the language of the Abonnema people.

"If one is a native speaker of a language, one will soon realize how sad and hopeless it is not to be able to speak or think in that language again," Mr. Kari said in an e-mail exchange. "Indeed, this pain is hanging upon the faces of many speakers who have lost their languages."

There is no complete survey of the world's languages, says Doug Whalen, vice president of research at Yale University's Haskins Laboratories and the founder of the Endangered Language Fund. The fund has distributed about $60,000 to help in such projects as recording elderly speakers of Dakota and a video drama in Choctaw, both Native American languages, but it has resources to capture no more than a handful of languages. The Rosetta Project is useful in focusing attention on the long-term preservation of keys to unlocking language fragments that might survive into the future.

"I'm happy preserving samples for 100 years, but thinking about what we'd like to leave for 10,000 years, that's a different picture," Dr. Haskins says. "If this was all that remained of these languages, it's really not enough to preserve them. It doesn't stop the extinction, but it's better than nothing."

Reflecting and Interpreting

1. Consider that the first paragraph could have been omitted. What valuable functions does it perform?
2. Which text will be inscribed in 1000 languages on the Rosetta Disk? Despite the controversy, why was it finally selected?
3. What other material will be included?
4. In creating the disk, what two assumptions have linguists made?
5. How many languages do linguists estimate exist? In what areas of the world are languages rapidly becoming "moribund"?
6. Which group of languages in the United States is disappearing? Which two of these are mentioned in the article?
7. What five problems commonly interfere with long-term data preservation? Which medium will last up to 500 years under optimum conditions?
8. What five languages do you think will be the most predominant 50 years from now? Why? What methods of data preservation can you envision for the future?
9. Jim Mason, the anthropologist directing the project, calls it "the Linux of linguistics." What literary device is this?
10. Examine the rhetorical structure of Bank's article. Which method of organization does he use to open? What other rhetorical strategies does he combine?

A Writer's Response

Make a list of the documents in your family that you would like to see preserved for at least one hundred years. Since most paper will disintegrate much sooner than that, how can you easily and inexpensively make copies on acid-free paper (available at most office supply stores)? If you don't have the equipment, do you know someone who does?

Home for Christmas

Carson McCullers

Nestled among Carson McCullers's memories was one drawn from her childhood in Georgia. Through twelve-year-old eyes, she described her family's preparations for the Christmas season, a season so special that she and her siblings sang carols in August to break the monotony of summer. This anecdote, first printed in her autobiography, reveals how she began to ponder the mystery of time. McCullers (1917–67) was also the author of several acclaimed works of fiction, including The Heart Is a Lonely Hunter *(1940),* Reflections in a Golden Eye *(1941),* A Member of the Wedding *(1946), and* The Ballad of the Sad Cafe *(1951).*

Sometimes in August, weary of the vacant, broiling afternoon, my younger brother and sister and I would gather in the dense shade under the oak tree in the back yard and talk of Christmas and sing carols. Once after such a conclave, when the tunes of the carols still lingered in the heat-shimmered air, I remember climbing up into the tree-house and sitting there alone for a long time.

Brother called up: "What are you doing?"

"Thinking," I answered.

"What are you thinking about?"

"I don't know."

"Well, how can you be thinking when you don't know what you are thinking about?"

I did not want to talk with my brother. I was experiencing the first wonder about the mystery of Time. Here I was, on this August afternoon, in the tree-house, in the burnt, jaded yard, sick and tired of all our summer ways. (I had read *Little Women* for the second time, *Hans Brinker and the Silver Skates*, *Little Men*, and *Twenty Thousand Leagues under the Sea*. I had read movie magazines and even tried to read love stories in the *Woman's Home Companion*—I was so sick of everything.) How could it be that I was I and now was now when in four months it would be Christmas, wintertime, cold weather, twilight and the glory of the Christmas tree? I puzzled about the *now* and *later* and rubbed the inside of my elbow until there was a little roll of dirt between my forefinger and thumb. Would the *now I* of the tree-house and the August afternoon be the same *I* of winter, firelight and the Christmas tree? I wondered.

My brother repeated: "You say you are thinking but you don't know what you are thinking about. What are you really doing up there? Have you got some secret candy?"

September came, and my mother opened the cedar chest and we tried on winter coats and last year's sweaters to see if they would do again. She took the three of us downtown and bought us new shoes and school clothes.

Christmas was nearer on the September Sunday that Daddy rounded us up   10
in the car and drove us out on dusty country roads to pick elderberry blooms.
Daddy made wine from elderberry blossoms—it was a yellow-white wine, the
color of weak winter sun. The wine was dry to the wry side—indeed, some years
it turned to vinegar. The wine was served at Christmastime with slices of fruitcake when company came. On November Sundays we went to the woods with
a big basket of fried chicken dinner, thermos jug and coffee-pot. We hunted partridge berries in the pine woods near our town. These scarlet berries grew hidden
underneath the glossy brown pine needles that lay in a slick carpet beneath the
tall wind-singing trees. The bright berries were a Christmas decoration, lasting in
water through the whole season.

In December the windows downtown were filled with toys, and my brother
and sister and I were given two dollars apiece to buy our Christmas presents.
We patronized the ten-cent stores, choosing between jackstones, pencil boxes,
water colors and satin handkerchief holders. We would each buy a nickel's
worth of lump milk chocolate at the candy counter to mouth as we trudged from
counter to counter, choice to choice. It was exacting and final—taking several
afternoons—for the dime stores would not take back or exchange.

Mother made fruitcakes, and for weeks ahead the family picked out the nut
meats of pecans and walnuts, careful of the bitter layer of the pecans that lined
your mouth with nasty fur. At the last I was allowed to blanch the almonds,
pinching the scalded nuts so that they sometimes hit the ceiling or bounced across
the room. Mother cut slices of citron and crystallized pineapple, figs and dates,
and candied cherries were added whole. We cut rounds of brown paper to line
the pans. Usually the cakes were mixed and put into the oven when we were in
school. Late in the afternoon the cakes would be finished, wrapped in white
napkins on the breakfast-room table. Later they would be soaked in brandy. These
fruitcakes were famous in our town, and Mother gave them often as Christmas
gifts. When company came thin slices of fruitcake, wine and coffee were always
served. When you held a slice of fruitcake to the window or the firelight the slice
was translucent, pale citron green and yellow and red, with the glow and richness
of our church windows.

Daddy was a jeweler, and his store was kept open until midnight all Christmas week. I, as the eldest child, was allowed to stay up late with Mother until
Daddy came home. Mother was always nervous without a "man in the house."
(On those rare occasions when Daddy had to stay overnight on business in Atlanta, the children were armed with a hammer, saw and a monkey wrench. When
pressed about her anxieties Mother claimed she was afraid of "escaped convicts
or crazy people." I never saw an escaped convict, but once a "crazy" person did
come to see us. She was an old, old lady dressed in elegant black taffeta, my
mother's second cousin once removed, and came on a tranquil Sunday morning
and announced that she had always liked our house and she intended to stay with
us until she died. Her sons and daughters and grandchildren gathered around to
plead with her as she sat rocking in our front porch rocking chair and she left
not unwillingly when they promised a car ride and ice cream.) Nothing ever hap-

pened on those evenings in Christmas week, but I felt grown, aged suddenly by trust and dignity. Mother confided in secrecy what the younger children were getting from Santa Claus. I knew where the Santa Claus things were hidden, and was appointed to see that my brother and sister did not go into the back-room closet or the wardrobe in our parents' room.

Christmas Eve was the longest day, but it was lined with the glory of tomorrow. The sitting-room smelled of floor wax and the clean, cold odor of the spruce tree. The Christmas tree stood in a corner of the front room, tall as the ceiling, majestic, undecorated. It was our family custom that the tree was not decorated until after we children were in bed on Christmas Eve night. We went to bed very early, as soon as it was winter dark. I lay in bed beside my sister and tried to keep her awake.

"You want to guess again about your Santa Claus?"   15

"We've already done that so much," she said.

My sister slept. And there again was another puzzle. How could it be that when she opened her eyes it would be Christmas while I lay awake in the dark for hours and hours? The time was the same for both of us, and yet not at all the same. What was it? How? I thought of Bethlehem and cherry candy, Jesus and skyrockets. It was dark when I awoke. We were allowed to get up on Christmas at five o'clock. Later I found out that Daddy juggled the clock Christmas Eve so that five o'clock was actually six. Anyway it was always still dark when we rushed in to dress by the kitchen stove. The rule was that we dress and eat breakfast before we could go in to the Christmas tree. On Christmas morning we always had fish roe, bacon and grits for breakfast. I grudged every mouthful—for who wanted to fill up on breakfast when there in the sitting-room was candy, at least three whole boxes? After breakfast we lined up, and carols were started. Our voices rose naked and mysterious as we filed through the door to the sitting-room. The carol, unfinished, ended in raw yells of joy.

The Christmas tree glittered in the glorious, candlelit room. There were bicycles and bundles wrapped in tissue paper. Our stockings hanging from the mantle-piece bulged with oranges, nuts and smaller presents. The next hours were paradise. The blue dawn at the window brightened, and the candles were blown out. By nine o'clock we had ridden the wheel presents and dressed in the clothes gifts. We visited the neighborhood children and were visited in turn. Our cousins came and grown relatives from distant neighborhoods. All through the morning we ate chocolates. At two or three o'clock the Christmas dinner was served. The dining-room table had been let out with extra leaves and the very best linen was laid—satin damask with a rose design. Daddy asked the blessing, then stood up to carve the turkey. Dressing, rice and giblet gravy were served. There were cut-glass dishes of sparkling jellies and stateliness of festal wine. For dessert there was always sillabub or charlotte and fruitcake. The afternoon was almost over when dinner was done.

At twilight I sat on the front steps, jaded by too much pleasure, sick at the stomach and worn out. The boy next door skated down the street in his new Indian suit. A girl spun around on a crackling son-of-a-gun. My brother waved sparklers. Christmas was over. I thought of the monotony of Time ahead, unsolaced by the distant glow of paler festivals, the year that stretched before another Christmas—eternity.

Reflecting and Interpreting

1. What do you notice about McCullers's first sentence? How do the length and punctuation affect the pace? Is the pace of the second sentence similar or different? How do the two sentences set the scene?

2. What do you notice about the next six lines? Describe their effect.

3. What do you learn about the narrator in paragraph 7? Does she seem to be an average twelve-year-old? How would you describe her?

4. What seems to be the essence of Christmas for the author?

5. The episodes that McCullers recounts occurred in 1929. Consider paragraphs 10 to 14. What strikes you as unusual or interesting? What do you learn?

6. Beginning in September, the entire family helped to prepare for the Christmas season. List the steps that the author describes.

7. What privileges did Carson enjoy as the eldest child? How did these privileges affect her?

8. The mystery of time is referred to again in paragraph 17. What is this mystery? How does her perception of time on Christmas Eve differ from her sister's?

9. The author uses sensory language to create vivid scenes. Which scene particularly stands out in your mind? What words help to create the image?

10. Examine the last paragraph. What does McCullers mean by "paler festivals"? How does she feel about these days as compared to Christmas? Why?

A Writer's Response

1. Does one particular Christmas stand out in your collection of memories? Write a description of a particular scene, using active verbs and specific adjectives as McCullers does.

2. With your group, discuss the factors that influence our perception of time. Have you ever gone through periods in your life when time seemed to slow drastically? How does a vacation affect the passing of time for you? What inferences can you draw from this discussion in regard to happiness, well-being, and the use of time?

The Art of Acknowledgement

Jean Houston

Life is like a roller-coaster that can take us from the depths of despair to the apex of joy—if we can just hang on. Clinging precariously, some hardy souls survive alone; others derive strength from the support of a family member, friend, or teacher. In this excerpt from The Possible Human *(1982), Jean Houston, a social scientist, describes the visiting professor who enabled her to surmount a devastating experience during her college years. This tale reminds us that we all have the ability to give a priceless gift. Houston is also the author of* A Mythic Life *(1996),* The Search for the Beloved *(1997),* The Passion of ISIS and OSIRIS *(1998),* A Passion for the Possible *(1998), and* Jump Time *(2000), as well as coauthor of seven books and numerous other publications.*

I was eighteen years old and I was the golden girl. A junior in college, I was   1
president of the college drama society, a member of the student senate, winner
of two off-Broadway critics' awards for acting and directing, director of the class
play, and had just turned down an offer to train for the next Olympics (fencing).
In class my mind raced and dazzled, spinning off facile but "wowing" analogies to
the kudos of teachers and classmates. Socially, I was on top of the heap. My advice was sought, my phone rang constantly, and it seemed that nothing could
stop me.

I was the envy of all my friends and I was in a state of galloping chutzpah.

The old Greek tragedies warn us that when hubris rises, nemesis falls. I was
no exception to this ancient rule. My universe crashed with great suddenness. It
began when three members of my immediate family died. Then a friend whom I
loved very much died suddenly of a burst appendix while camping alone in the
woods. The scenery of the off-Broadway production fell on my head and I was left
almost blind for the next four months. My friends and I parted from each other,
they out of embarrassment and I because I didn't think I was worthy. My marks
went from being rather good to a D-plus average.

I had so lost confidence in my abilities that I couldn't concentrate on anything
or see the connections between things. My memory was a shambles, and within
a few months I was placed on probation. All my offices were taken away; public
elections were called to fill them. I was asked into the advisor's office and told that
I would have to leave the college at the end of the spring term since, clearly, I
didn't have the "necessary intelligence to do academic work." When I protested
that I had had the "necessary intelligence" during my freshman and sophomore
years, I was assured with a sympathetic smile that intellectual decline such as this
often happened to young women when "they became interested in other things;
it's a matter of hormones, my dear."

Where once I had been vocal and high-spirited in the classroom, I now   5
huddled in my oversized camel's-hair coat in the back of classes, trying to be as

nonexistent as possible. At lunch I would lock myself in the green room of the college theater, scene of my former triumphs, eating a sandwich in despondent isolation. Every day brought its defeat and disacknowledgments, and after my previous career I was too proud to ask for help. I felt like Job and called out to God, "Where are the boils?" since that was about all I was missing.

These Jobian fulminations led me to take one last course. It was taught by a young Swiss professor of religion, Dr. Jacob Taubes, and was supposed to be a study of selected books of the Old Testament. It turned out to be largely a discussion of the dialectic between St. Paul and Nietzsche.

Taubes was the most brilliant and exciting teacher I had ever experienced, displaying European academic wizardry such as I had never known. Hegel, gnosticism, structuralism, phenomenology, and the intellectual passions of the Sorbonne cracked the ice of my self-noughting and I began to raise a tentative hand from my huddle in the back of the room and ask an occasional hesitant question.

Dr. Taubes would answer with great intensity, and soon I found myself asking more questions. One day I was making my way across campus to the bus, when I heard Dr. Taubes addressing me:

"Miss Houston, let me walk with you. You know, you have a most interesting mind."

"Me? I have a *mind?*"   10

"Yes, your questions are luminous. Now what do you think is the nature of the transvaluation of values in Paul and Nietzsche?"

I felt my mind fall into its usual painful dullness and stammered, "I d-don't know."

"Of course you do!" he insisted. "You couldn't ask the kinds of questions you do without having an unusual grasp of these issues. Now please, once again, what do you think of the transvaluation of values in Paul and Nietzsche? It is important for my reflections that I have your reactions."

"Well," I said, waking up, "if you put it that way, I think . . ."

I was off and running and haven't shut up since.   15

Dr. Taubes continued to walk me to the bus throughout that term, always challenging me with intellectually vigorous questions. He attended to me. I existed for him in the "realest" of senses, and because I existed for him I began to exist for myself. Within several weeks my eyesight came back, my spirit bloomed, and I became a fairly serious student, whereas before I had been, at best, a bright show-off.

What I acquired from this whole experience was a tragic sense of life, which balanced my previous enthusiasms. I remain deeply grateful for the attention shown me by Dr. Taubes. He acknowledged me when I most needed it. I was empowered in the midst of personal erosion, and my life has been very different for it. I swore to myself then that whenever I came across someone "going under" or in the throes of disacknowledgment, I would try to reach and acknowledge that person as I had been acknowledged.

I would go so far as to say that the greatest of human potentials is the potential of each one of us to empower and acknowledge the other. We all do this throughout our lives, but rarely do we appreciate the power of the empowering that we give to others. To be acknowledged by another, especially during times of confusion, loss, disorientation, disheartenment, is to be given time and place in the sunshine and is, in the metaphor of psychological reality, the solar stimulus for transformation.

The process of healing and growth is immensely quickened when the sun of another's belief is freely given. This gift can be as simple as "Hot Dog Thou Art!" Or it can be as total as "I know you. You are God in hiding." Or it can be a look that goes straight to the soul and charges it with meaning.

I have been fortunate to have known several of those the world deems   20
"saints": Teilhard de Chardin, Mother Teresa of Calcutta, Clemie, an old black woman in Mississippi. To be looked at by these people is to be gifted with the look that engenders. You feel yourself primed at the depths by such seeing. Something so tremendous and yet so subtle wakes up inside that you are able to release the defeats and denigrations of years. If I were to describe it further, I would have to speak of unconditional love joined to a whimsical regarding of you as the cluttered house that hides the holy one.

Saints, you say, but the miracle is that anybody can do it for anybody! Our greatest genius may be the ability to prime the healing and evolutionary circuits of one another.

It is an art form that has yet to be learned, for it is based on something never before fully recognized—deep psychological reciprocity, the art and science of mutual transformation. And all the gurus and masters, all the prophets, profs, and professionals, can do little for us compared to what we could do for each other if we would but be present to the fullness of each other. For there is no answer to anyone's anguished cry of "Why am I here, why am I at all?" except the reply, "Because I am here, because I am."

Reflecting and Interpreting

1. Notice the title. *Acknowledgement* is not commonly used in this way. What word would you use instead?

2. In the second paragraph, Houston says she was in a state of "galloping chutzpah." What does she mean?

3. Houston says, "I felt like Job and called out to God, 'Where are the boils?'" (See Job 2:1–10.) What do Houston's comparison and question reveal?

4. In the third paragraph, there is a sudden change in tone. What does Houston mean when she refers to hubris? Does this passage remind you of an old saying? (See Proverbs 16:18.) How does this proverb apply to Houston?

5. What do you think she means when she says, "I existed for him in the 'realest' of senses, and because I existed for him I began to exist for myself"? How does Dr. Taubes's attention affect Houston?

6. Houston says, "I acquired . . . a tragic sense of life, which balanced my previous enthusiasms" (paragraph 17). Can you explain this idea in your own words?

7. How would you describe Houston's attitude as she looks back on this troubling experience? Does she retain a sense of humor? Find examples to support your claim.

8. Comment on Houston's last statement, which seems puzzling and somewhat contradictory to the ideas expressed in the essay.

9. Notice Houston's alternating of colloquialisms with literary allusions. For example, what is the effect of "wowing" and "on top of the heap" in one paragraph and "hubris" and "nemesis" in another?

10. Note how she contrasts the "before and after" at several points. What is the effect of these contrasts as opposed to a simple chronological narrative?

A Writer's Response

Have you ever undergone a distressing experience and been helped by someone? Or perhaps you have been able to "prime the healing and evolutionary circuits" of someone. Describe what happened in an essay.

How to Get Out of a Locked Trunk

Philip Weiss

Metaphor plays a prominent role in this essay. By the end, the astute reader knows there is a deeper meaning to the experience than what is apparent. Weiss blends humor, suspense, and romance while explaining a process (in fact, several versions of it). In this clever piece, originally published in Harper's *magazine and later in* The Best American Essays *(1993), Weiss begins with an investigation of one process of escape and uses it to reflect on another. He has written for* The New York Times Magazine, The New York Observer, Jewish World Review, *and other publications. Weiss is the author of* Religion & Art *(1964),* Modes of Being *(1968),* Art Deco Environment *(1976), and* Cock-A-Doodle-Doo *(1995).*

On a hot Sunday last summer my friend Tony and I drove my rental car, a '91   1
Buick, from St. Paul to the small town of Waconia, Minnesota, forty miles south-west. We each had a project. Waconia is Tony's boyhood home, and his sister had recently given him a panoramic postcard of Lake Waconia as seen from a high point in the town early in the century. He wanted to duplicate the photograph's vantage point, then hang the two pictures together in his house in Frogtown. I was hoping to see Tony's father, Emmett, a retired mechanic, in order to settle a question that had been nagging me: Is it possible to get out of a locked car trunk?

We tried to call ahead to Emmett twice, but he wasn't home. Tony thought he was probably golfing but that there was a good chance he'd be back by the time we got there. So we set out.

I parked the Buick, which was a silver sedan with a red interior, by the grave-yard near where Tony thought the picture had been taken. He took his picture and I wandered among the headstones, reading the epitaphs. One of them was chillingly anti-individualist. It said, "Not to do my will, but thine."

Trunk lockings had been on my mind for a few weeks. It seemed to me that the fear of being locked in a car trunk had a particular hold on the American imag-ination. Trunk lockings occur in many movies and books—from *Goodfellas* to *Thelma and Louise* to *Humboldt's Gift*. And while the highbrow national news-papers generally shy away from trunk lockings, the attention they receive in local papers suggests a widespread anxiety surrounding the subject. In an afternoon at the New York Public Library I found numerous stories about trunk lockings. A Los Angeles man is discovered, bloodshot, banging the trunk of his white Eldo-rado following a night and a day trapped inside; he says his captors went on joy-rides and picked up women. A forty-eight-year-old Houston doctor is forced into her trunk at a bank ATM and then the car is abandoned, parked near the

Astrodome. A New Orleans woman tells police she gave birth in a trunk while being abducted to Texas. Tests undermine her story, the police drop the investigation. But so what if it's a fantasy? That only shows the idea's hold on us.

Every culture comes up with tests of a person's ability to get out of a sticky   5
situation. The English plant mazes. Tropical resorts market those straw finger-grabbers that tighten their grip the harder you pull on them, and Viennese intellectuals gave us the concept of childhood sexuality—figure it out, or remain neurotic for life.

At least you could puzzle your way out of those predicaments. When they slam the trunk, though, you're helpless unless someone finds you. You would think that such a common worry should have a ready fix, and that the secret of getting out of a locked trunk is something we should all know about.

I phoned experts but they were very discouraging.

"You cannot get out. If you got a pair of pliers and bat's eyes, yes. But you have to have a lot of knowledge of the lock," said James Foote at Automotive Locksmiths in New York City.

Jim Frens, whom I reached at the technical section of *Car and Driver* in Detroit, told me the magazine had not dealt with this question. But he echoed the opinion of experts elsewhere when he said that the best hope for escape would be to try and kick out the panel between the trunk and the backseat. That angle didn't seem worth pursuing. What if your enemies were in the car, crumpling beer cans and laughing at your fate? It didn't make sense to join them.

The people who deal with rules on auto design were uncomfortable with my   10
scenarios. Debra Barclay of the Center for Auto Safety, an organization founded by Ralph Nader, had certainly heard of cases, but she was not aware of any regulations on the matter. "Now, if there was a defect involved—" she said, her voice trailing off, implying that trunk locking was all phobia. This must be one of the few issues on which she and the auto industry agree. Ann Carlson of the Motor Vehicle Manufacturing Association became alarmed at the thought that I was going to play up a nonproblem: "In reality this very rarely happens. As you say, in the movies it's a wonderful plot device," she said. "But in reality apparently this is not that frequent an occurrence. So they have not designed that feature into vehicles in a specific way."

When we got to Emmett's one-story house it was full of people. Tony's sister, Carol, was on the floor with her two small children. Her husband, Charlie, had one eye on the golf tournament on TV, and Emmett was at the kitchen counter, trimming fat from meat for lunch. I have known Emmett for fifteen years. He looked better than ever. In his retirement he had sharply changed his diet and lost a lot of weight. He had on shorts. His legs were tanned and muscular. As always, his manner was humorous, if opaque.

Tony told his family my news: I was getting married in three weeks. Charlie wanted to know where my fiancée was. Back East, getting everything ready. A big-time hatter was fitting her for a new hat.

Emmett sat on the couch, watching me. "Do you want my advice?"

"Sure."

He just grinned. A gold tooth glinted. Carol and Charlie pressed him to yield his wisdom. 15

Finally he said, "Once you get to be thirty, you make your own mistakes."

He got out several cans of beer, and then I brought up what was on my mind.

Emmett nodded and took off his glasses, then cleaned them and put them back on.

We went out to his car, a Mercury Grand Marquis, and Emmett opened the trunk. His golf clubs were sitting on top of the spare tire in a green golf bag. Next to them was a toolbox and what he called his "burglar tools," a set of elbowed rods with red plastic handles he used to open door locks when people locked their keys inside.

Tony and Charlie stood watching. Charlie is a banker in Minneapolis. He en- 20 joys gizmos and is extremely practical. I would describe him as unflappable. That's a word I always wanted to apply to myself, but my fiancée had recently informed me that I am high-strung. Though that surprised me, I didn't quarrel with her.

For a while we studied the latch assembly. The lock closed in much the same way that a lobster might clamp on to a pencil. The claw portion, the jaws of the lock, was mounted inside the trunk lid. When you shut the lid, the jaws locked on to the bend of a U-shaped piece of metal mounted on the body of the car. Emmett said my best bet would be to unscrew the bolts. That way the U-shaped piece would come loose and the lock's jaws would swing up with it still in their grasp.

"But you'd need a wrench," he said.

It was already getting too technical. Emmett had an air of endless patience, but I felt defeated. I could only imagine bloodied fingers, cracked teeth. I had hoped for a simple trick.

Charlie stepped forward. He reached out and squeezed the lock's jaw. They clicked shut in the air, bound together by heavy springs. Charlie now prodded the upper part of the left-hand jaw, the thicker part. With a rough flick of his thumb, he was able to force the jaws to snap open. Great.

Unfortunately, the jaws were mounted behind a steel plate the size of your 25 palm in such a way that while they were accessible to us, standing outside the car, had we been inside the trunk the plate would be in our way, blocking the jaws.

This time Emmett saw the way out. He fingered a hole in the plate. It was no bigger than the tip of your little finger. But the hole was close enough to the latch itself that it might be possible to angle something through the hole from inside the trunk and nudge the jaws apart. We tried with one of my keys. The lock jumped open.

It was time for a full-dress test. Emmett swung the clubs out of the trunk, and I set my can of Schmidt's on the rear bumper and climbed in. Everyone gathered around, and Emmett lowered the trunk on me, then pressed it shut with his meaty hands. Total darkness. I couldn't hear the people outside. I thought I was going to panic. But the big trunk felt comfortable. I was pressed against a sort of black carpet that softened the angles against my back.

I could almost stretch out in the trunk, and it seemed to me I could make them sweat if I took my time. Even Emmett, that sphinx, would give way to curiosity. Once I was out he'd ask how it had been and I'd just grin. There were some things you could only learn by doing.

It took a while to find the hole. I slipped the key in and angled it to one side. The trunk gasped open.

Emmett motioned the others away, then levered me out with his big right forearm. Though I'd only been inside for a minute, I was disoriented—as much as anything because someone had moved my beer while I was gone, setting it down on the cement floor of the garage. It was just a little thing, but I could not be entirely sure I had gotten my own beer back. 30

Charlie was now raring to try other cars. We examined the latch on his Toyota, which was entirely shielded to the trunk occupant (i.e., no hole in the plate), and on the neighbor's Honda (ditto). But a 1991 Dodge Dynasty was doable. The trunk was tight, but its lock had a feature one of the mechanics I'd phoned described as a "tailpiece": a finger-like extension of the lock mechanism itself that stuck out a half inch into the trunk cavity: simply by twisting the tailpiece I could free the lock. I was even faster on a 1984 Subaru that had a little lever device on the latch.

We went out to my rental on Oak Street. The Skylark was in direct sun and the trunk was hot to the touch, but when we got it open we could see that its latch plate had a perfect hole, a square in which the edge of the lock's jaw appeared like a face in a window.

The trunk was shallow and hot. Emmett had to push my knees down before he could close the lid. This one was a little suffocating. I imagined being trapped for hours, and even before he had got it closed I regretted the decision with a slightly nauseous feeling. I thought of Edgar Allan Poe's live burials, and then about something my fiancée had said more than a year and a half before. I had been on her case to get married. She was divorced, and at every opportunity I would reissue my proposal—even during a commercial. She'd interrupted one of these chirps to tell me, in a cold, throaty voice, that she had no intention of ever going through another divorce: "This time, it's death out." I'd carried those words around like a lump of wet clay.

As it happened, the Skylark trunk was the easiest of all. The hole was right where it was supposed to be. The trunk popped open, and I felt great satisfaction that we'd been able to figure out a rule that seemed to apply about 60 percent of the time. If we publicized our success, it might get the attention it deserved. All trunks would be fitted with such a hole. Kids would learn about it in school. The grip of the fear would relax. Before long a successful trunk-locking scene would date a movie like a fedora dates one today.

When I got back East I was caught up in wedding preparations. I live in New York, and the wedding was to take place in Philadelphia. We set up camp there 35 with five days to go. A friend had lent my fiancée her BMW, and we drove it south with all our things. I unloaded the car in my parents' driveway. The last thing I pulled out of the trunk was my fiancée's hat in its heavy cardboard shipping box. She'd warned me I was not allowed to look. The lid was free but I didn't open it. I was willing to be surprised.

When the trunk was empty it occurred to me I might hop in and give it a try. First I looked over the mechanism. The jaws of the BMW's lock were shielded, but there seemed to be some kind of cable coming off it that you might be able to manipulate so as to cause the lock to open. The same cable that allowed the driver to open the trunk remotely . . .

I fingered it for a moment or two but decided I didn't need to test out the theory.

Reflecting and Interpreting

1. Where is the thesis statement located?
2. Do you see any foreshadowing? (Hint: Notice where he parks the Buick.)
3. In paragraph 5 there is a hint that the essay may be about more than finding a way out of a locked trunk. Where is the hint?
4. Can you see a link between the epitaph on the tombstone and Emmett's bit of wisdom? If so, what is it?
5. What qualities does the narrator see in Charlie and Emmett that he would like to develop?
6. Climbing out of the trunk, he was "disoriented . . . someone had moved my beer. . . ." What does this incident suggest about his personality?
7. Examine paragraph 34. What is the implication?
8. By the end of the story, do you see any change in Weiss? If so, what?
9. In Philadelphia, he decided he "didn't need to test out the theory" on the BMW his fiancée had borrowed. What are the implications of this decision?
10. What does Weiss mean by "You would think such a common worry would have a ready fix . . . something we should all know about." What might it symbolize?

A Writer's Response

1. Freewrite about physical states that mimic social or emotional entrapment.
2. *Small Groups:* The steps of the process are intermingled with a narrative. What are the six steps?

Description

Conveying Impressions

 ## *Caterpillar Afternoon*

Sue Hubbell

Sue Hubbell is a naturalist, a commercial beekeeper, who lives in the Ozark Moun-tains. She is the author of seven books, including A Book of Bees *(1988),* On This Hill-top *(1991),* Waiting for Aphrodite *(2000), and* Shrinking the Cat *(2001). One day as Hubbell was walking down a dusty country road, she spied what appeared to be a snake skin lying in the road. Curious, she bent down and saw, instead, a strange procession of maggoty-like caterpillars. "Caterpillar Afternoon," from* A Country Year *(1999), illus-trates one way primary and secondary research can be combined.*

A year ago, on an afternoon late in springtime, I was walking on the dirt road   1
that cuts across the field to the beehives. I noticed a light-colored, brownish dap-pled something-or-other stretched across the roadway ahead of me, and decided that it was a snakeskin. I often find them, crumpled husks shed by snakes as they grow. They are fragile and delicate, perfect but empty replicas of the snakes that once inhabited them. I started to turn it over with the toe of my boot, but stopped suddenly, toe in air, for the flecked, crumpled-looking empty snakeskin was moving.

It gave me quite a start and I was amused at my own reaction, remembering that Ronald Firbank wrote somewhere that the essence of evil was the ordinary become unnatural, the stone in the garden path that suddenly begins to move.

I squatted down to see what queer thing I had here, and found that my sup-posed snake skin was a mass of maggoty-like caterpillars, each one no more than half an inch long. They were hairless, with creamy white smooth skin, black heads and brown stripes along their backs. They were piled thickly in the center, with fewer caterpillars at the head and rear end of the line, which was perhaps eighteen inches long. They moved slowly, each caterpillar in smooth synchrony with its fellows, so that a wave of motion undulated down the entire length of the line.

They seemed so intensely social that I wondered what they would do on their own. I gently picked up half a dozen or so, and isolated them a few inches from the column. Their smooth, easy movements changed to frantic, rapid ones, and they wriggled along the ground quickly until they rejoined the group. They certainly were good followers. How did they ever decide where to go? The single caterpillar in the lead twisted the forepart of his body from side to side as though taking his bearings; he appeared to be the only one in the lot capable of going in a new direction, of making a decision to avoid a tuft of grass here, of turning there. Was he some special, super-caterpillar? I removed him from the lead position and put him off to the side, where he became as frantic as had the others, wriggling to rejoin the group somewhere in the middle, where he was soon lost to view, having turned into just another follower. At the head, the next caterpillar in line had simply assumed leadership duties and was bending his body from side to side, making the decision about the direction the column was to take. I removed three leaders in a row with the same result: each time, the next caterpillar in line made an instant switch from loyal and will-less follower to leader.

What were they doing? Were they looking for food? If so, what kind? What manner of creature were they? The beework that I had set out to do could wait no longer, so I went back to the hives. When I returned along the road, the caterpillars, if that is what they were, had disappeared. 5

Back in my cabin, none of the books on my shelves were much help explaining what I had seen, except one by Henri Fabre, the nineteenth-century French entomologist who had conducted one of his famous experiments with pine processionaries, one of the Thaumatopoeidae. Fabre's caterpillars were *Thaumatopoea processionea*, "the wonder maker that parades"; eventually they become rather undistinguished-looking moths.

The pine processionaries are a European species, but their behavior was similar to that of my caterpillars, although not identical. Pine processionaries travel to feed in single file, not massed and bunched, but they do touch head to rear and have only one leader at a time. Fabre found them so sheeplike that he wondered what they would do if he could somehow manage to make them leaderless. In a brilliant experiment, he arranged them on the upper rim of a large vase a yard and a half in circumference, and waited until the head end of the procession joined the tail end, so that the entire group was without a leader. All were followers. For seven days, the caterpillars paraded around the rim of the vase in a circle. Their pace slowed after a while, for they were weary and had not been able to feed, but they continued to circle, each caterpillar unquestioningly taking his direction from the rear of the one in front, until they dropped from exhaustion. However, even Fabre never discovered what it was that could turn one caterpillar into a leader as soon as he was at the head of the line.

It was not until several months later, when I was talking to Asher, that I was able to find out anything about the caterpillars I had found in the roadway. He said that I probably had seen one species or another of sawfly larvae. They are gregarious, he told me, and some are whitish with brown stripes. Sure identification could only be made by counting the pairs of their prolegs, and of course I had not known enough to look at them that closely. Asher said that they were a rare sight and that I would probably never see them again, but if I did I should gather up a few and put them in a solution of 70 percent alcohol; then he would help me identify them. He had read about Fabre's experiment too, but knew nothing more about their behavior.

He added, "If you ever find out what makes processionary caterpillars pro-sesh, please enlighten me. Maybe it's the same thing that makes people drive in Sunday traffic or watch TV or vote Republican."

It is springtime again. I would like to count the caterpillars' prolegs and am   10
prepared to pickle a few to satisfy my curiosity, but mostly I should just like to watch them again. This time I should let the beework go. I should like to know where these caterpillars go, and what it is they are looking for. I wonder if I could divide them up into several small columns that would move along independently, side by side. I have more questions about them than when I first saw them.

This spring I often walk along, eyes to the ground, looking for them. There may have been nobler quests—white whales and Holy Grails—and although the Ahabs and Percivals of my acquaintance are some of my most entertaining friends, I am cut of other stuff and amuse myself in other ways. The search for what may or may not be sawfly larvae seems quite a good one this springtime.

Reflecting and Interpreting

1. What two strategies of exposition does Hubbell use to explain her research?
2. Note the distinctive way that Hubbell describes the caterpillars. What device does she use in the third sentence?
3. What was unusual about the physical appearance of the caterpillars?
4. What spur-of-the moment experiments did Hubbell conduct? How did the individual caterpillars react?
5. What paragraph presents the questions that Hubbell wants to research?
6. What transition shifts the reader to the next scene, where Hubbell continues her research?
7. How and when did Hubbell gain more specific information about the kind of caterpillars she had seen? By what name are they tagged?
8. What had Henri Fabre discovered in the nineteenth century about a similar caterpillar?
9. What experiment does Hubbell plan to do if she ever finds more of these strange caterpillars?
10. Do you see any similarities between the behavior of the caterpillars and some people? What kinds of events can cause people to suddenly become leaders?

A Writer's Response

1. Have you ever been thrust into a circumstance where you suddenly had to assume a leadership role? If so, write an essay describing your experience.

2. *Small Groups:* Have you ever seen something that appeared to be something else at first? What does this reveal about the process of perception? Can you list a few precautions to promote objectivity? (After the group is finished, turn to "Checklist: Maintaining Objectivity" in chapter 22.)

✍ *One Writer's Beginnings*

Eudora Welty

Eudora Welty (1909–2001) published her first short story in 1936. After writing short fiction for ten years, she published a novel, Delta Wedding, *in 1946. She has written twenty-six books, receiving a Pulitzer Prize in 1971. In 1980 she received the National Medal for Literature and the Presidential Medal of Freedom. In this excerpt from* One Writer's Beginnings *(1984), she explores the connection between reality and the imagination in an attempt to trace her origin as a writer.*

I had the window seat. Beside me, my father checked the progress of our train   1
by moving his finger down the timetable and springing open his pocket watch. He explained to me what the position of the arms of the semaphore meant; before we were to pass through a switch we would watch the signal lights change. Along our track, the mileposts could be read; he read them. Right on time by Daddy's watch, the next town sprang into view, and just as quickly was gone.

Side by side and separately, we each lost ourselves in the experience of not missing anything, of seeing everything, of knowing each time what the blows of the whistle meant. But of course it was not the same experience: what was new to me, not older than ten, was a landmark to him. My father knew our way mile by mile; by day or by night, he knew where we were. Everything that changed under our eyes, in the flying countryside, was the known world to him, the imagination to me. Each in our own way, we hungered for all of this: my father and I were in no other respect or situation so congenial.

In Daddy's leather grip was his traveler's drinking cup, collapsible; a lid to fit over it had a ring to carry it by; it traveled in a round leather box. This treasure would be brought out at my request, for me to bear to the water cooler at the end of the Pullman car, fill to the brim, and bear back to my seat, to drink water over its smooth lip. The taste of silver could almost be relied on to shock your teeth.

After dinner in the sparkling dining car, my father and I walked back to the open-air observation platform at the end of the train and sat on the folding chairs placed at the railing. We watched the sparks we made fly behind us into the night. Fast as our speed was, it gave us time enough to see the rose-red cinders turn to ash, each one, and disappear from sight. Sometimes a house far back in the empty hills showed a light no bigger than a star. The sleeping countryside seemed itself to open a way through for our passage, then close again behind us.

The swaying porter would be making ready our berths for the night, pulling   5
the shade down just so, drawing the green fishnet hammock across the window so the clothes you took off could ride along beside you, turning down the tight-made bed, standing up the two snowy pillows as high as they were wide, switch-

ing on the eye of the reading lamp, starting the tiny electric fan—you suddenly saw its blades turn into gauze and heard its insect murmur; and drawing across it all the pair of thick green theaterlike curtains—billowing, smelling of cigar smoke—between which you would crawl or dive headfirst to button them together with yourself inside, to be seen no more that night.

When you lay enclosed and enwrapped, your head on a pillow parallel to the track, the rhythm of the rail clicks pressed closer to your body as if it might be your heart beating, but the sound of the engine seemed to come from farther away than when it carried you in daylight. The whistle was almost too far away to be heard, its sound wavering back from the engine over the roofs of the cars. What you listened for was the different sound that ran under you when your own car crossed on a trestle, then another sound on an iron bridge; a low or a high bridge—each had its pitch, or drumbeat, for your car.

Riding in the sleeper rhythmically lulled me and waked me. From time to time, waked suddenly, I raised my window shade and looked out at my own strip of the night. Sometimes there was unexpected moonlight out there. Sometimes the perfect shadow of our train, with our car, with me invisibly included, ran deep below, crossing a river with us by the light of the moon. Sometimes the encroaching walls of mountains woke me by clapping at my ears. The tunnels made the train's passage resound like the "loud" pedal of a piano, a roar that seemed to last as long as a giant's temper tantrum.

But my father put it all into the frame of regularity, predictability, that was his fatherly gift in the course of our journey. I saw it going by, the outside world, in a flash. I dreamed over what I could see as it passed, as well as over what I couldn't. Part of the dream was what lay beyond, where the path wandered off through the pasture, the red clay road climbed and went over the hill or made a turn and was hidden in trees, or toward a river whose bridge I could see but whose name I'd never know. A house back at its distance at night showing a light from an open doorway, the morning faces of the children who stopped still in what they were doing, perhaps picking blackberries or wild plums, and watched us go by—I never saw with the thought of their continuing to be there just the same after we were out of sight. For now, and for a long while to come, I was proceeding in fantasy.

Reflecting and Interpreting

1. What do we learn about Welty and her father in the first and second paragraphs? Do they seem similar or different? How?

2. As Welty attempts to trace her origins as a writer, why does this train trip seem significant?

3. How do Welty's childhood dreams differ from the reality of the train?

4. The description of the porter making up the berths is filled with similes and metaphors. Which ones do you especially like?

5. Welty spends a paragraph describing the sounds of the engine, rails, whistle, and structures that vary the "pitch, or drumbeat, for your car." What device is used here? What do these details reveal about her, even as a child?

6. Note the alternating of images when she describes riding in the sleeper. How do these images and sounds reflect the rhythm of the train?

7. Is the essay written, for the most part, from the point of view of a ten-year-old or from an adult in retrospect? Where does a shift occur? What was "his fatherly gift"? Why does Welty seem to need that?

8. Images that connote safety and seclusion while experiencing the world from a distance appear throughout this essay. Which ones do you notice?

9. Welty was interested in photography. How is this excerpt of her writing like a series of photos?

10. What might the author mean at the end when she says, "For now, and for a long while to come, I was proceeding in fantasy"?

A Writer's Response

1. Describe a trip you took as a child that was memorable. Use vivid images and sensory language to recapture the experience and your feelings at the time.

2. Welty opens with "I had the window seat." Later she says, "I saw it going by, the outside world, in a flash." You might say we all have a window seat from which we view life as it flashes by. Select one vivid "flash" from your window on life to describe in an essay.

Dawn Watch

John Ciardi

A renowned poet, essayist, and translator, John Ciardi (1916–86) wrote over fifty books. He received the Prix de Rome of the American Academy of Arts and Letters, the Harriet Monroe Memorial Award, and the NCTE Award for Children's Poetry. He first published a book of poems entitled Homeward to America *(1940). Two years later he enlisted in the Army Air Force and served with distinction as an aerial tail gunner during World War II. He taught at Harvard and Rutgers; spent twenty years as poetry editor for the* Saturday Review *magazine; wrote children's books, poetry textbooks, and others; and translated* The Divine Comedy *and other classic works. Some of his well-known works are* Mid-Century American Poets *(1950),* How Does a Poem Mean *(1959),* Selected Poems *(1984),* Saipan: The War Diary of John Ciardi *(1988),* The Birds of Pompeii *(1988), and* The Selected Letters of John Ciardi *(1991), some of which were published posthumously. In this essay from* Manner of Speaking *(1972), Ciardi praises a magical time of day.*

Unless a man is up for the dawn and for the half hour or so of first light, he   1
has missed the best of the day.

The traffic has just started, not yet a roar and a stink. One car at a time goes by, the tires humming almost like the sound of a brook a half mile down in the crease of a mountain I know—a sound that carries not because it is loud but because everything else is still.

It isn't exactly a mist that hangs in the thickets but more nearly the ghost of a mist—a phenomenon like side vision. Look hard and it isn't there, but glance without focusing and something registers, an exhalation that will be gone three minutes after the sun comes over the treetops.

The lawns shine with a dew not exactly dew. There is a rabbit bobbing about on the lawn and then freezing. If it were truly a dew, his tracks would shine black on the grass, and he leaves no visible track. Yet, there is something on the grass that makes it glow a depth of green it will not show again all day. Or is that something in the dawn air?

Our cardinals know what time it is. They drop pure tones from the hemlock   5
tops. The gang of grackles that makes a slum of the pin oak also knows the time but can only grate at it. They sound like a convention of broken universal joints grating uphill. The grackles creak and squeak, and the cardinals form tones that only occasionally sound through the noise. I scatter sunflower seeds by the birdbaths for the cardinals and hope the grackles won't find them.

My neighbor's tomcat comes across the lawn, probably on his way home from passion, or only acting as if he had had a big night. I suspect him of being one of those poolroom braggarts who can't get next to a girl but who likes to let on that he is a hot stud. This one is too can-fed and too lazy to hunt for anything. Here he comes now, ignoring the rabbit. And there he goes.

As soon as he has hopped the fence, I let my dog out. The dog charges the rabbit, watches it jump the fence, shakes himself in a self-satisfied way, then trots dutifully into the thicket for his morning service, stopping to sniff everything on the way back.

There is an old mountain laurel on the island of the driveway turnaround. From somewhere on the wind a white morning-glory rooted next to it and has climbed it. Now the laurel is woven full of white bells tinged pink by the first rays through the not quite mist. Only in earliest morning can they be seen. Come out two hours from now and there will be no morning-glories.

Dawn, too, is the hour of a weed I know only as day flower—a bright blue button that closes in full sunlight. I have weeded bales of it out of my flower beds, its one daytime virtue being the shallowness of its root system that allows it to be pulled out effortlessly in great handfuls. Yet, now it shines. Had it a few more hours of such shining in its cycle, I would cultivate it as a ground cover, but dawn is its one hour, and a garden is for whole days.

There is another blue morning weed whose name I do not know. This one   10
grows from a bulb to pulpy stems and a bedraggled daytime sprawl. Only a shovel will dig it out. Try weeding it by hand and the stems will break off to be replaced by new ones and to sprawl over the chosen plants in the flower bed. Yet, now and for another hour it outshines its betters, its flowers about the size of a quarter and paler than those of the day flower but somehow more brilliant, perhaps because of the contrast of its paler foliage.

And now the sun is slanting in full. It is bright enough to make the leaves of the Japanese red maple seem a transparent red bronze when the tree is between me and the light. There must be others, but this is the only tree I know whose leaves let the sun through in this way—except, that is, when the fall colors start. Aspen leaves, when they first yellow and before they dry, are transparent in this way. I tell myself it must have something to do with the red-yellow range of the spectrum. Green takes sunlight and holds it, but red and yellow let it through.

The damned crabgrass is wrestling with the zinnias, and I stop to weed it out. The stuff weaves too close to the zinnias to make the iron claw usable. And it won't do to pull at the stalks. Crabgrass (at least in a mulched bed) can be weeded only with dirty fingers. Thumb and forefinger have to pincer into the dirt and grab the root-center. Weeding, of course, is an illusion of hope. Pulling out the root only stirs the soil and brings new crabgrass seeds into germinating position. Take a walk around the block and a new clump will have sprouted by the time you get back. But I am not ready to walk around the block. I fill a small basket with the plucked clumps, and for the instant I look at them, the zinnias are weedless.

Don't look back. I dump the weeds in the thicket where they will be smothered by the grass clippings I will pile on at the next cutting. On the way back I see the cardinals come down for the sunflower seeds, and the jays join them, and then the grackles start ganging in, gatecrashing the buffet and clattering all over it. The dog stops chewing his rawhide and makes a dash into the puddle of birds, which splashes away from him.

I hear a brake-squeak I have been waiting for and know the paper has arrived. As usual, the news turns out to be another disaster count. The function of the wire services is to bring us tragedies faster than we can pity. In the end we shall all be inured, numb, and ready for emotionless programming. I sit on the patio and read until the sun grows too bright on the page. The cardinals have stopped singing, and the grackles have flown off. It's the end of birdsong again.

Then suddenly—better than song for its instant—a hummingbird the color   15
of green crushed velvet hovers in the throat of my favorite lily, a lovely high-bloomer I got the bulbs for but not the name. The lily is a crest of white horns with red dots and red velvet tongues along the insides of the petals and with an odor that drowns the patio. The hummingbird darts in and out of each horn in turn, then hovers an instant, and disappears.

Even without the sun, I have had enough of the paper. I'll take that hummingbird as my news for this dawn. It is over now. I smoke one more cigarette too many and decide that, if I go to bed now, no one in the family need know I have stayed up for it again. Why do they insist on shaking their heads when they find me still up for breakfast, after having scribbled through the dark hours? They always do. They seem compelled to express pity for an old loony who can't find his own way to bed. Why won't they understand that this is the one hour of any day that must not be missed, as it is the one hour I couldn't imagine getting up for, though I can still get to it by staying up? It makes sense to me. There comes a time when the windows lighten and the twittering starts. I look up and know it's time to leave the papers in their mess. I could slip quietly into bed and avoid the family's headshakes, but this stroll-around first hour is too good to miss. Even my dog, still sniffing and circling, knows what hour this is.

Come on, boy. It's time to go in. The rabbit won't come back till tomorrow, and the birds have work to do. The dawn's over. It's time to call it a day.

Reflecting and Interpreting

1. Ciardi's essay has an argumentative edge that is apparent in his thesis statement. Where is it?

2. What is the dominant impression of "Dawn Watch"?

3. Can you find similes?

4. Can you find an example of personification?

5. Throughout the essay, Ciardi's carefully chosen words create sensory descriptions that convey an essence of the scene. How many types of appeals to the senses can you find?

6. What is the primary order used to organize details?

7. Ciardi alternates subjectivity with objectivity at times in his description. Can you find examples of each?

8. Instead of presenting only beautiful images of the morning, Ciardi pairs negative images with positive ones and presents other unusual contrasts. What are the effects?

9. Does Ciardi make his reversed schedule seem logical? Has he supplied enough support for his claim to be convincing? Give reasons for your answer.

10. Describe the voice of the writer. Where does he seem to be poking fun at himself?

A Writer's Response

1. Whether you agree or disagree with Ciardi's belief that early morning is the best time of all may depend upon whether you are a "lark" or "night owl." What time of day do you like best? Why?

2. List favorite spots where you can be alone. Focus on one and freewrite about the atmosphere there, incorporating as many sights, sounds, and other sensory images as possible. Next add a chronological structure, similar to Ciardi's, describing the "events" of a typical visit from beginning to end. How does the passing of time affect what happens there? What time of day is best? Rewrite your draft into a revised essay.

Pedestrian Students and High-Flying Squirrels

Liane Ellison Norman

So what do high-flying squirrels and many college students have in common? What is a significant difference? Liane Ellison Norman creates this unique analogy to illustrate a common view of first-year college students, intent on obtaining the necessary skills to land a good job. Thought-provoking, the essay examines certain traditional beliefs and questions their practicality. Norman is also the author of Hammer of Justice: Molly Rush and the Plowshares Eight *(1989),* Mathland: The Expert Version *(1994),* Mathland: The Novice Version *(1994) and* Stitches in Air: A Novel about Mozart's Mother *(2001).*

The squirrel is curious. He darts and edges, profile first, one bright black eye   1
on me, the other alert for his enemies on the other side. Like a fencer, he faces both ways, for every impulse toward me an impulse away. His tail is airy. He flicks and flourishes it, taking readings of some subtle kind.

I am enjoying a reprieve of warm sun in a season of rain and impending frost. Around me today is the wine of the garden's final ripening. On the zucchini, planted late, the flagrant blossoms flare and decline in a day's time.

I am sitting on the front porch thinking about my students. Many of them earnestly and ardently want me to teach them to be hacks. Give us ten tricks, they plead, ten nifty fail-safe ways to write a news story. Don't make us think our way through these problems, they storm (and when I am insistent that thinking *is* the trick, "You never listen to us," they complain). Who cares about the First Amendment? they sneer. What are John Peter Zenger and Hugo Black to us? Teach us how to earn a living. They will be content, they explain, with know-how and jobs, satisfied to do no more than cover the tedium of school board and weather.

Under the rebellion, there is a plaintive panic. What if, on the job—assuming there is a job to be on—they fearlessly defend the free press against government, grand jury, and media monopoly, but don't know how to write an obituary? Shouldn't obituaries come first?

I hope not, but even obituaries need good information and firm prose, and   5
both, I say, require clear thought.

The squirrel does not share my meditation. He grows tired of inquiring into me. His dismissive tail floats out behind as he takes a running leap into the tree. Up the bark he goes and onto a branch, where he crashes through the leaves. He soars from slender perch to slender perch, shaking up the trees as if he were the west wind. What a madcap he is, to go racing from one twig that dips under him to another at those heights!

His acrobatic clamor loosens buckeyes in their prickly armor. They drop, break open, and he is down the tree in a twinkling, picking, choosing. He finds what he wants and carries it, an outsize nut which is burnished like a fine cello, across the lawn, up a pole, and across the tightrope telephone line to the other side, where he disappears in maple foliage.

Some inner clock or calendar tells him to stock his larder against the deep snows and hard times that are coming. I have heard that squirrels are fuzzy-minded, that they collect their winter groceries and store them, and then forget where they are cached. But this squirrel is purposeful; he appears to know he'd better look ahead. Faced with necessity, he is prudent, but not fearful. He prances and flies as he goes about his task of preparation, and he never fails to look into whatever startles his attention.

Though he is not an ordinary pedestrian, crossing the street far above, I some-times see the mangled fur of a squirrel on the street, with no flirtation left. Even a high-flying squirrel may zap himself on an aerial live wire. His days are danger-ous and his winters are lean, but still he lays in provisions the way a trapeze artist goes about his work, with daring and dash.

For the squirrel, there is no work but living. He gathers food, reproduces,   10
tends the children for a while, and stays out of danger. Doing these things with style is what distinguishes him. But for my students, unemployment looms as large as the horizon itself. Their anxiety has cause. And yet, what good is it? Ten tricks or no ten tricks, there are not enough jobs. The well-trained, well-educated stand in line for unemployment checks with the unfortunates and the drifters. Neither skill nor virtue holds certain promise. This being so, I wonder, why should these students not demand, for the well-being of their souls, the liberation of their minds?

It grieves me that they want to be pedestrians, earthbound and always care-ful. You ask too much, they say. What you want is painful and unfair. There are a multitude of pressures that instruct them to train, not free, themselves.

Many of them are the first generation to go to college; family aspirations are in their trust. Advisers and models tell them to be doctors, lawyers, engineers, cops, and public-relations people; no one ever tells them they can be poets, phi-losophers, farmers, inventors, or wizards. Their elders are anxious too; they reject the eccentric and the novel. And, realism notwithstanding, they cling to talis-manic determination; play it safe and do things right and I, each one thinks, will get a job even though others won't.

I tell them fondly of my college days, which were a dizzy time (as I think the squirrel's time must be), as I let loose and pitched from fairly firm stands into the space of intellect and imagination, never quite sure what solid branch I would light on. That was the most useful thing I learned, the practical advantage (not to mention the exhilaration) of launching out to find where my propellant mind could take me.

A luxury? one student ponders, a little wistfully.

Yes, luxury, and yet necessity, and it aroused that flight, a fierce unappeasable   15
appetite to know and to essay. The luxury I speak of is not like other privileges of wealth and power that must be hoarded to be had. If jobs are scarce, the heady regions of treetop adventure are not. Flight and gaiety cost nothing, though of course they may cost everything.

The squirrel, my frisky analogue, is not perfectly free. He must go on all fours, however nimbly he does it. Dogs are always after him, and when he barely escapes, they rant up the tree as he dodges among the branches that give under his small weight. He feeds on summer's plenty and pays the price of strontium in his bones. He is no freer of industrial ordure than I am. He lives, mates, and dies (no obituary, first or last, for him), but still he plunges and balances, risking his neck because it is his nature.

I like the little squirrel for his simplicity and bravery. He will never get ahead in life, never find a good job, never settle down, never be safe. There are no sure-fire tricks to make it as a squirrel.

Reflecting and Interpreting

1. Examine the first sentence of the essay. Is this sentence significant, or is it merely specifying a characteristic of a squirrel? Give a reason for your answer.

2. Why is the second paragraph relevant? Would some other season have done just as well to set the scene? Why or why not?

3. What is the fear that Norman senses in many of her students? What do they assume they should be learning about writing? (What does *obituary* symbolize?)

4. How are the squirrel's activities that Norman observes similar to those of college students?

5. Is Norman advising students not to listen to advisers' and parents' advice about an occupation? What is she recommending?

6. Why is Norman sad? What does she mean when she says students "want to be pedestrians"? (Check the adjective meaning of this word.) What does she say was the most practical advantage she gained in college?

7. Norman says she had "a fierce unappeasable appetite to know and to essay." What does she mean? (Check the verb meaning of *essay*.) How are these qualities related to finding and keeping a job? Or are they?

8. What qualities does Norman admire in the squirrel? She ends with "There are no sure-fire tricks to make it as a squirrel." Is she just being flippant, or is there a deeper meaning here? Why or why not?

9. How does the tone change in the paragraphs where Norman considers the squirrel and then her students? See paragraphs 1, 4, and 8 for examples.

10. What rhetorical strategies are used in this essay along with description?

Small Group Discussion

1. With your group, discuss whether or not most jobs are entirely "safe." Once you get the necessary skills in your field, will you be immune to job turnover? Before answering, list major factors that affect the job market. What are they?

2. What personal qualities are necessary to survive fluctuations in the job market? How will the qualities that Norman mentions help us to regain our equilibrium after a downsizing?

Process Analysis

Explaining How

How to Cook a Carp

Euell Gibbons

This essay has the air of an old-time western movie with cowhands sitting around a campfire in the evening, spinning yarns. Only this time, they vie with each other to describe the best way to cook a carp—a fish that has been commonly regarded in the United States as a "trash fish," unfit for eating. Born in Clarksville, Texas, Euell Gibbons (1911–75) worked as a cowboy, carpenter, harvest hand, and trapper. He served a two-year hitch in the U.S. Army from 1934 to 1936. During World War II, he helped build ships for the U.S. Navy. When he was thirty-six years old, he enrolled at the University of Hawaii as a freshman. He later taught, wrote, and lectured about wild foods and living off the land. His amusing narratives include Stalking the Wild Asparagus *(1962), from which "How to Cook a Carp" has been taken;* Stalking the Blue-Eyed Scallop *(1964);* Stalking the Healthful Herbs *(1966); and* Euell Gibbons' Beachcomber's Handbook *(1967). More than thirty years later, these books were reprinted.*

When I was a lad of about eighteen, my brother and I were working on a   1
cattle ranch in New Mexico that bordered on the Rio Grande. Most Americans
think of the Rio Grande as a warm southern stream, but it rises among the high
mountains of Colorado, and in the spring it is fed by melting snows. At this time
of the year, the water that rushed by the ranch was turbulent, icy-cold and so silt-
laden as to be semisolid. "A little too thick to drink, and a little too thin to plow"
was a common description of the waters of the Rio Grande.

A few species of fish inhabited this muddy water. Unfortunately, the most
common was great eight- to ten-pound carp, a fish that is considered very poor

eating in this country, although the Germans and Asiatics have domesticated this fish, and have developed some varieties that are highly esteemed for the table.

On the ranch where we worked, there was a drainage ditch that ran through the lower pasture and emptied its clear waters into the muddy Rio Grande. The carp swimming up the river would strike this clear warmer water and decide they preferred it to the cold mud they had been inhabiting. One spring day, a cowhand who had been riding that way reported that Clear Ditch was becoming crowded with huge carp.

On Sunday we decided to go fishing. Four of us armed ourselves with pitchforks, saddled our horses and set out. Near the mouth of the ditch, the water was running about two feet deep and twelve to sixteen feet wide. There is a saying in that part of the country that you can't get a cowboy to do anything unless it can be done from the back of a horse, so we forced our mounts into the ditch and started wading them upstream, four abreast, herding the carp before us.

By the time we had ridden a mile upstream, the water was less than a foot 5 deep and so crystal clear that we could see our herd of several hundred carp still fleeing from the splashing, wading horses. As the water continued to shallow, our fish began to get panicky. A few of the boldest ones attempted to dart back past us and were impaled on pitchforks. We could see that the whole herd was getting restless and was about to stampede back downstream, so we piled off our horses into the shallow water to meet the charge. The water boiled about us as the huge fish swirled past us and we speared madly in every direction with our pitchforks, throwing each fish we managed to hit over the ditch bank. This was real fishing— cowhand style. The last of the fish herd was by us in a few minutes and it was all over, but we had caught a tremendous quantity of fish.

Back at the ranch house, after we had displayed our trophies, we began wondering what we were going to do with so many fish. This started a series of typical cowboy tall tales on "how to cook a carp." The best of these yarns was told by a grizzled old *vaquero*, who claimed he had made his great discovery when he ran out of food while camping on a tributary of the Rio Grande. He said that he had found the finest way to cook a carp was to plaster the whole fish with a thick coating of fresh cow manure and bury it in the hot ashes of a campfire. In an hour or two, he said, the casing of cow manure had become black and very hard. He then related how he had removed the fish from the fire, broken the hard shell with the butt of his Winchester and peeled it off. He said that as the manure came off the scales and skin adhered to it, leaving the baked fish, white and clean. He then ended by saying, "Of course, the carp still wasn't fit to eat, but manure in which it was cooked tasted pretty good."

There were also some serious suggestions and experiments. The chief objection to the carp is that its flesh is full of many forked bones. One man said that he had enjoyed carp sliced very thin and fried so crisp that one could eat it, bones and all. He demonstrated, and you really could eat it without the bones bothering you, but it was still far from being an epicurean dish. One cowboy described the flavor as "a perfect blend of Rio Grande mud and rancid hog lard."

Another man said that he had eaten carp that had been cooked in a pressure cooker until the bones softened and became indistinguishable from the flesh. A pressure cooker is almost a necessity at that altitude, so we had one at the ranch house. We tried this method, and the result was barely edible. It tasted like the poorest possible grade of canned salmon flavored with a bit of mud. It was, however, highly appreciated by the dogs and cats on the ranch, and solved the problem of what to do with the bulk of the fish we had caught.

It was my brother who finally devised a method of cooking carp that not only made it fit for human consumption, but actually delicious. First, instead of merely scaling the fish, he skinned them. Then, taking a large pinch, where the meat was thickest, he worked his fingers and thumb into the flesh until he struck the median bones, then he worked his thumb and fingers together and tore off a handful of meat. Using this tearing method, he could get two or three goodsized chunks of flesh from each side of the fish. He then heated a pot of bland vegetable shortening, rubbed the pieces of fish with salt and dropped them into the hot fat. He used no flour, meal, crumbs or seasoning other than salt. They cooked to a golden brown in a few minutes, and everyone pronounced them "mighty fine eating." The muddy flavor seemed to have been eliminated by removing the skin and the large bones. The forked bones were still there, but they had not been multiplied by cutting across them, and one only had to remove several bones still intact with the fork from each piece of fish.

For the remainder of that spring, every few days one or another of the cow-   10
boys would take a pitchfork and ride over to Clear Ditch and spear a mess of carp. On these evenings, my brother replaced the regular *cocinero* and we enjoyed some delicious fried carp.

The flavor of carp varies with the water from which it is caught. Many years after the above incidents I attended a fish fry at my brother's house. The main course was all of his own catching, and consisted of bass, catfish and carp, all from Elephant Butte Lake farther down the Rio Grande. All the fish were prepared exactly alike, except that the carp was pulled apart as described above, while the bass and catfish, being all twelve inches or less in length, were merely cleaned and fried whole. None of his guests knew one fish from another, yet all of them preferred the carp to the other kinds. These experiences have convinced me that the carp is really a fine food fish when properly prepared.

Carp can, of course, be caught in many ways besides spearing them with pitchforks from the back of a horse. In my adopted home state, Pennsylvania, they are classed as "trash fish" and one is allowed to take them almost any way. They will sometimes bite on worms, but they are vegetarians by preference and are more easily taken on dough balls. Some states allow the use of gill nets, and other states, because they would like to reduce the population of this unpopular fish, will issue special permits for the use of nets to catch carp.

A good forager will take advantage of the lax regulations on carp fishing while they last. When all fishermen realize that the carp is really a good food fish when prepared in the right way, maybe this outsized denizen of our rivers and lakes will no longer be considered a pest and will take his rightful place among our valued food and game fishes.

Reflecting and Interpreting

1. In what general locale does the story take place? Where on the ranch do the cowboys start their fishing trip?

2. What is the effect of including the common description of the waters of the Rio Grande in the spring? How does it influence the tone?

3. How does Gibbons's use of first person influence the narrative? How would it have differed if it he had used third person?

4. In paragraph 4, a common saying is included. What is the effect?

5. What is the chief objection to eating a carp? What two methods are tried to overcome these objections but are unsuccessful?

6. An old *vaquero* claims that he has discovered the best way to cook a carp. How does he claim to have done it? Is there anything that makes you doubt the story?

7. What method does Gibbons's brother devise that makes the carp delicious and easy to eat? The removal of what two parts improves the flavor? Later Gibbons finds another significant factor that influences the flavor. What is it?

8. What proof does Gibbons offer to support his claim that carp is a "fine food fish"?

9. The actual procedure of cooking a carp successfully is not explained until paragraph 9. How do paragraphs 1 through 8 function?

10. Gibbons's books were first published in the 1960s and reprinted over thirty years later. How do you explain the popularity of his writing?

A Writer's Response

1. Alone or with your group members, write a step-by-step analysis of something you do. For example, you might consider a morning or evening ritual such as caring for a pet or a Sunday afternoon activity. Create a list of the steps in chronological order. Then discuss ways in which you can use point of view and humor to make the essay more engaging.

2. Try rewriting some of Gibbons's paragraphs using third person only. For instance, rewrite paragraph 1, deleting all first-person pronouns (*we*, *I*, etc.). How difficult is this rewriting? How does the third-person point of view change those paragraphs?

Falling for Apples

Noel Perrin

Noel Perrin has served as an associate editor for the journal Medical Economics. *Since 1959 he has taught English at Dartmouth College in New Hampshire. Twice a Guggenheim Fellow, Perrin also received a Fulbright Fellowship to teach one year at the University of Warsaw. His writings include articles, essays, novels, and a history of Japan—over fifteen books. Some of the best known are* First Person Rural: Essays of a Sometime Farmer *(1980),* Second Person Rural *(1981),* A Reader's Delight *(1988),* Life with an Electric Car *(1994),* Last Person Rural *(1996), and* A Child's Delight *(1997). In this excerpt from* Second Person Rural, *Perrin describes an early way of making apple cider.*

The number of children who eagerly help around a farm is rather small. Willing helpers do exist, but many more of them are five years old than fifteen. In fact, there seems to be a general law that says as long as a kid is too little to help effectively, he or she is dying to. Then, just as they reach the age when they really could drive a fence post or empty a sap bucket without spilling half of it, they lose interest. Now it's cars they want to drive, or else they want to stay in the house and listen for four straight hours to The Who. That sort of thing.

There is one exception to this rule. Almost no kid that I have ever met outgrows an interest in cidering. In consequence, cider making remains a family time on our farm, even though it's been years since any daughter trudged along a fencerow with me, dragging a new post too heavy for her to carry, or begged for lessons in chainsawing.

It's not too hard to figure out why. In the first place, cidering gives the child instant gratification. There's no immediate reward for weeding a garden (unless the parents break down and offer cash), still less for loading a couple of hundred hay bales in the barn. But the minute you've ground and pressed the first bushel of apples, you can break out the glasses and start drinking. Good stuff, too. Cider has a wonderful fresh sweetness as it runs from the press.

In the second place, making cider on a small scale is simple enough so that even fairly young children—say, a pair of nine-year-olds—can do the whole operation by themselves. Yet it's also picturesque enough to tempt people of any age. When my old college roommate was up last fall—and we've been out of college a long time—he and his wife did four pressings in the course of the weekend. They only quit then because I ran out of apples.

Finally, cider making appeals to a deep human instinct. It's the same one that makes a housewife feel so good when she takes a bunch of leftovers and produces a memorable casserole. At no cost, and using what would otherwise be wasted, she has created something. In fact, she has just about reversed entropy.

Cidering is like that. You take apples that have been lying on the ground for a week, apples with blotches and cankers and bad spots, apples that would make a supermarket manager turn pale if you merely brought them in the store, and out of this unpromising material you produce not one but two delicious drinks. Sweet cider now. Hard cider later.

The first step is to have a press. At the turn of the century, almost every farm family did. They ordered them from the Sears or Montgomery Ward catalogue as routinely as one might now order a toaster. Then about 1930 little presses ceased to be made. Pasteurized apple juice had joined the list of American food-processing triumphs. It had no particular flavor (still hasn't), but it would keep almost indefinitely. Even more appealing, it was totally sterile. That was the era when the proudest boast that, let's say, a bakery could make was that its bread was untouched by human hands. Was touched only by stainless-steel beaters and stainless-steel wrapping machines.

Eras end, though, and the human hand came back into favor. One result: in the 1970s home cider presses returned to the market. They have not yet returned to the Sears catalogue, but they are readily available. I know of two companies in Vermont that make them, another in East Aurora, New York, and one out in Washington state. If there isn't someone making them in Michigan or Wisconsin, there soon will be. Prices range from about 175 to 250 dollars.

Then you get a couple of bushels of apples. There *may* be people in the country who buy cider apples, but I don't know any of them. Old apple trees are too common. I get mine by the simple process of picking up windfalls in a derelict orchard that came with our place. I am not choosy. Anything that doesn't actually squish goes in the basket.

With two kids to help, collecting takes maybe twenty minutes. Kids tend to be less interested in gathering the apples than in running the press, but a quiet threat of no-pickee, no-pressee works wonders. Kids also worry about worms sometimes, as they scoop apples from the ground—apples that may be wet with dew, spiked with stubble, surrounded by hungry wasps. Occasionally I have countered with a short lecture on how much safer our unsprayed apples are than the shiny, worthless, but heavily sprayed apples one finds in stores. But usually I just say that I have yet to see a worm in our cider press. That's true, too. Whether it's because there has never been one, or whether it's because in the excitement and bustle of grinding you just wouldn't notice one little worm, I don't dare to say.

As soon as you get back with the apples, it's time to make cider. Presses come in two sizes: one-bushel and a-third-of-a-bushel. We have tried both. If I lived in a suburb and had to buy apples, I would use the very efficient third-of-a-bushel press and make just under a gallon at a time. Living where I do, I use the bigger press and make two gallons per pressing, occasionally a little more.

The process has two parts. First you set your pressing tub under the grinder, line it with a pressing cloth, and start grinding. Or, better, your children do. One feeds apples into the hopper, the other turns the crank. If there are three children present, the third can hold the wooden hopper plate, and thus keep the apples from bouncing around. If there are four, the fourth can spell off on cranking. Five

10

or more is too many, and any surplus over four is best made into a separate crew for the second pressing. I once had two three-child crews present, plus a seventh child whom my wife appointed the official timer. We did two pressings and had 4¼ gallons of cider in 43 minutes and 12 seconds. (Who won? The second crew, by more than a minute. Each crew had one of our practiced daughters on it, but the second also had the advantage of watching the first.)

As soon as the apples are ground, you put the big pressing plate on and start to turn the press down. If it's a child crew, and adult meddling is nevertheless tolerated, it's desirable to have the kids turn the press in order of their age, starting with the youngest: at the end it takes a fair amount of strength (though it's not beyond two nine-year-olds working together), and a little kid coming after a big one may fail to produce a single drop.

The pressing is where all the thrills come. As the plate begins to move down and compact the ground apples, you hear a kind of sighing, bubbling noise. Then a trickle of cider begins to run out. Within five or ten seconds the trickle turns into a stream, and the stream into a ciderfall. Even kids who've done it a dozen times look down in awe at what their labor has wrought.

A couple of minutes later the press is down as far as it will go, and the container you remembered to put below the spout is full of rich, brown cider. Someone has broken out the glasses, and everybody's having a drink.   15

This pleasure goes on and on. In an average year we start making cider the second week of September, and we continue until early November. We make all we can drink ourselves, and quite a lot to give away. We have supplied whole church suppers. One year the girls sold about ten gallons to the village store, which made them some pocket money they were prouder of than any they ever earned by baby-sitting. Best of all, there are two months each year when all of us are running the farm together, just like a pioneer family.

Reflecting and Interpreting

1. How would you describe the tone of the first paragraph?
2. Where is the thesis statement located?
3. What are the advantages of cider making, according to Perrin?
4. What piece of equipment is needed to make apple cider? Comment on Perrin's style as opposed to that of an instruction manual. How do the tone and explanations differ?
5. What part of the process seems to intrigue the participants? Why? How does it change the usual behavior of children?
6. Perrin's imagery appeals to four of our senses. What are they? What significant characteristic of cider (and apples) has been omitted?
7. Perrin gives five basic steps of cider making. Can you find the five steps?
8. At the end, Perrin cites his favorite reason for cider making? What is it?
9. Notice the title. Normally, we speak of fallen apples. What happens here?

10. To be successful, a writer must be competent and knowledgeable about his topic. How would you rate Perrin's expertise on cider making? As a writer? Give reasons for your answers.

A Writer's Response

Have you ever watched or helped in making apple butter, butchering a hog, smoking hams, drying string beans, quilt making, or another activity that was done in a traditional way? Write a paper explaining the process. Include interesting related details as Perrin does. Try to toss in a bit of humor.

Write Your Own Success Story

Carol Carter

Coasting through high school, seldom studying, seventeen-year-old Carol Carter was yanked from a career disaster by a conversation with her brother. This vivid essay from Majoring in the Rest of Your Life: Career Secrets for College Students *(1999) relates how she suddenly changed direction, "determined to learn all she could." Since graduating from the University of Arizona, Carter has also written* Student Planner *(1998) and* Keys to Success *(2000). She has coauthored and collaborated on more than a dozen other books designed to help students increase their effectiveness.*

Who am I to talk to high school graduates and college freshmen about plan- 1
ning? As a high school student in Tucson, Arizona, I never planned. I just coasted along letting things happen to me. Sure, I was spontaneous. I spent weeknights talking on the phone and studied only when I felt like it—i.e., seldom. On weekends my friends and I roamed shopping malls and partied in the mountains. The typical irresponsible high school student.

And then BOOM. The ax fell. The ax was not some accident, scandal, or divine intervention. It was simply a conversation with my older brother Craig during the first week of my senior year in high school. Our talk changed the course of my life.

At seventeen, I was intimidated by my four older brothers. I saw them as bright, motivated, and respected achievers—the opposite of me. Whenever one of them asked me about what I was doing or thinking, I'd answer with a one-liner and hope he'd soon leave me alone.

This conversation with Craig was different. He didn't give up after five minutes despite my curt, vague responses.

"Carol, what are you interested in?"   5

"I dunno."

"What do you think about all day?"

"I dunno."

"What do you want to do with your life?"

"I'll just let things happen."   10

Craig persisted. His voice grew indignant. He criticized me for talking on the phone, for spending too much time at pep rallies and rock concerts, for not studying, for not challenging myself. He pointed out that I hadn't read an unassigned book in three years. He asked if I intended to approach college the way I'd approached high school—as one continuous party. If so, he warned, I'd better start thinking of a career flipping burgers at the local hamburger stand because no respectable employer would ever take me seriously. He asked me if that was what I wanted to do with my life. He cautioned that out of laziness and lack of planning I would limit my options so narrowly that I would never be able to get a real job. I had wasted three years of high school, he said. College was a new start, since employers and graduate schools seldom check as far back as high school for records. So he advised me to quit making excuses, decide what I wanted and plan how to achieve it. My only limitations would be self-imposed.

Craig then left my room—sermon completed. I didn't speak to him before he flew back to New York that afternoon to finish his senior year at Columbia. I hated him for interfering in my life. He made me dissatisfied with myself. I was scared he was right. For the first time, I realized that "typical" was not necessarily what I wanted to be.

The next day, still outraged but determined to do something, I went to the library and checked out six classics: *Pride and Prejudice* by Jane Austen; *The Great Gatsby* by F. Scott Fitzgerald; *A Farewell to Arms* and *For Whom the Bell Tolls* by Ernest Hemingway; *A Portrait of the Artist as a Young Man* by James Joyce; and *Sister Carrie* by Theodore Dreiser. Then I wrote down in a notebook a few goals that I wanted to accomplish. They all seemed boldly unattainable: earn straight A's (previously I had made B's and C's), study every week including one weekend night, keep reading classics on my own. If I couldn't make it in my senior year of high school, why should I waste time and money in college? I'd beat fate to the door and begin my career at the hamburger stand directly.

Three weeks later I got a letter from Craig. He knew how angry I was with him. He told me our conversation wasn't easy for him either but if he hadn't cared, he wouldn't have bothered to say anything. He was right. I needed that sermon. If I didn't come to terms with my problems, I could never have moved from making excuses to making things happen.

I worked hard and got results. The second semester of my senior year I made   15
all A's (except for a B in physics). I finished the six classics and others as well. I started reading newspapers and magazines. I had to move the *Vogue* on my nightstand to make room for *Time, Harper's,* and *Fortune.* I found that I could set goals and attain them, and I started to realize that I wasn't so different from my brothers after all.

To my utter astonishment, I discovered that for the first time I enjoyed learning. My world seemed to open up just because I knew more about different kinds of people, ways of thinking and ways of interpreting what I had previously assumed to be black-and-white. (If you are a shy person, joining a club and getting to know—and actually like—a few people whom you originally perceived as unfriendly or uninteresting may astonish you as much as my newfound appreciation for learning astonished me.)

The summer before college, I thought about what I wanted to do with my life, but couldn't decide on a direction. I had no notion of what I wanted to major in. What to do . . . what to do?

I turned to Craig, a phone call away in New York City. He told me not to worry in my first year of college about what I wanted to do. The main priority: learn as much as I could. College, he told me, was my golden opportunity to investigate all kinds of things—biology, psychology, accounting, philosophy. He told me I'd become good at writing and critical thinking techniques—skills that would help me learn any job after graduation. And though I could continue to expand my educational horizons throughout life, college was the best opportunity to expose myself to the greatest minds and movements of our civilization.

Craig also warned me that being a scholar, though important, wouldn't be enough. (He had just graduated from Columbia as a Phi Beta Kappa, but since he hadn't gained any real-world experience in college, it took him several months to find his first job.) To maximize options upon graduation, I would have to do three things:

1. Learn as much as possible from classes, books, professors, and other people
2. Participate in extracurricular activities
3. Get REAL-WORLD experience by working part-time and landing summer internships

If I did these three things reasonably well, Craig assured me, I could choose   20
from a number of career opportunities at the end of my senior year. And even if I only did two of the three full-force and one half-speed, I'd be in good shape. The effort in each area, and a modest outcome, was an attainable goal. That way I could balance my college experience and open options for the future.

Craig advised me that I should look ahead and develop a plan of action for each of my four years of college. He told me that foresight—the ability to consider the bigger picture beyond short-term challenges and intermittent goals—is invaluable in most jobs; it distinguishes outstanding people from the rest of the pack. . . . Most important, you'll learn that everyone—including YOU—has his or her own set of skills, abilities, passions and talents to tap. Finding the career and lifestyle that allows you to cultivate and nurture them is one of the most important success secrets.

So Take Action!

A good way to start is to assess your shortcomings and strengths. As I've already told you, one of my shortcomings in high school was not learning all I could from my classes and teachers. Your shortcoming may have been that you focused entirely on your studies without developing many outside interests. Someone else may feel that he concentrated so much on an outside activity—such as training for a particular sport—that he had no time for studies or friends. What was your major shortcoming in high school?

Now think about three things:

1. What pleased you in high school?
2. What could you have done better?
3. What do you want to improve upon in the future?

Identifying these areas will help you strike a good balance during college.   25
Once you get in the habit of analyzing past experiences, you will have a clearer notion of what you do and don't want in the future. That's important.

As a high school senior, a college freshman, or a college senior, the next thing you must do is decide to take action. Don't worry if you don't know what you want to do. Just commit yourself to the process. If you do, you'll eventually find out which careers might be best for you and how you could best prepare for them.

RECAP: The priorities

1. Gain knowledge

2. Participate in activities

3. Get REAL-WORLD experience

Making It Happen

"Luck is the residue of design," said Branch Rickey, known as the baseball mahatma for his strategic methods for playing and organizing baseball. He developed the farm system on which the minor leagues were formed. His PLANS OF ACTION took a handful of disjointed teams in faraway cities and banded them into an organization which has left its mark on American culture.

Nothing happens magically. If you want to be a success, you are going to have to take personal responsibility for your life. Why do some graduates get twenty job offers and others receive none?

While successful people may appear lucky, they, in fact, illustrate the maxim   30
that "luck favors the prepared mind."

Joe Cirulli agrees. He is the owner of the successful Gainesville Health and Fitness Center in Florida. Early on in his life, exercise was a priority, an essential part of his day. So he followed his interests and put his talents to work to start his own health club. While many other clubs have folded around him, he has experienced enormous success—his membership continues to grow, and he is able to keep his club filled with the best equipment and the most knowledgeable professionals.

When Joe was twenty, he worked as an assistant manager and a sales representative for a health club. One of his responsibilities was to train new sales representatives for the club. He worked hard to prepare them for their jobs only to have to compete with them once they were trained.

He remembers talking with the vice president of the company about his frustration. The vice president, a person Joe respected, advised him to keep on putting his best efforts into his work. "Right now you may not see the benefit of your hard work, but one day you will."

Joe followed his advice. Less than five years later his skill at training people in the health club industry paid off—he was able to put his expertise to work for his own health club. "Knowing how to motivate employees to do their best, to care about the quality of their work, and to care about our customers has had an enormous impact on the success of my own company."

Joe believes the secret to his success is giving 100 percent of himself in every-   35
thing he does. "Success is the culmination of all your efforts. There are thousands of opportunities for people who give their all."

How do you arrange to have the most options when you leave college? Plan, develop foresight, and take charge of your life, and you will become one of the lucky ones. Most important, decide that you want to succed—and believe it.

Charles Garfield a clinical psychologist who has spent his career studying what motivates people to superior effort, says that the drive to excel comes primarily from within. Can "peak performances" be learned? Yes, says Garfield. High achievers are not extraordinarily gifted superhumans. What they have in common is the ability to cultivate what the German writer Johann Wolfgang von Goethe termed "the genius, power, and magic" that exists in all of us. These doers increase the odds in their favor through simple techniques which anyone can cultivate:

1. Envision a mission
2. Be result-oriented
3. Tap your internal resources
4. Enlist team spirit
5. Treat setbacks as stepping stones

First Things First

The first thing to keep in mind when planning: accept the world the way it is. Your plans should be based on a realistic assessment of how things are, not some starry-eyed vision of how they should be. You can dream, but there's a happy medium between cold reality and pie in the sky. That's why you must be open to opportunity. Indeed, you must create it. Although you can't change the hand you were dealt, you can play it as wisely as possible.

So start today. Start now.

The more questions you ask now, the better prepared you'll be in four years. 40 You don't want to be stuck in a boring job or wondering why you can't find work.

Are you going to make mistakes? I hope so, unless you're not of the human species. Making mistakes is the process by which we learn. And whenever we're disappointed by the outcome, we have to maintain a positive attitude, log the information, and keep going. The key is to learn from mistakes without letting them slow us down.

Reflecting and Interpreting

1. What rhetorical strategy does Carter use in the first sentence? What is the effect?
2. How did Carol's careless attitude in high school affect her self-image?
3. What three main points did Craig make in his criticism?
4. How did Carol react to her brother's advice? Why? What did she do the next day?
5. What three things did Carol discover about herself?
6. When Craig pointed out that high grades alone were not enough to land a job, what three actions did he recommend?

7. What four actions does Carol recommend readers take to "have the most options when you leave college"?
8. Does the author seem convincing? Why or why not?
9. What type of support does she provide other than personal experience?
10. What is appealing about her writing style?

A Writer's Response

What is the most significant point that you derived from this essay? Did you learn anything that can help you be more successful in college? On the job? What do you plan to do differently to improve your grades and chances for success? Write an essay that responds to these questions and any other points Carter raised.

How Do You Know It's Good?

Marya Mannes

What makes writing, art, music, or theater good? One popular approach denies the existence of any valid criteria to measure the quality of a work. This approach claims that decisions about value are merely a matter of personal taste. But Marya Mannes disagrees, saying there are standards to determine value. She says that the prime function of art is "to create order out of chaos — again, not the order of neatness or rigidity or convention or artifice, but the order of clarity. . . ." There is room for "incredible diversity of forms" within a universal pattern and rhythm. Mannes (1904–90) was born into a family of prominent musicians and chemists. She was a columnist, editor, and television commentator for PBS. She wrote two novels, Message from a Stranger *(1948) and* They *(1968), as well as an autobiography,* Out of My Time *(1971). Best known was her collection of essays,* But Will It Sell? *(1964), in which "How Do You Know It's Good?" was first published.*

Suppose there were no critics to tell us how to react to a picture, a play, or a   1 new composition of music. Suppose we wandered innocent as the dawn into an art exhibition of unsigned paintings. By what standards, by what values would we decide whether they were good or bad, talented or untalented, successes or failures? How can we ever know that what we think is right?

For the last fifteen or twenty years the fashion in criticism or appreciation of the arts has been to deny the existence of any valid criteria and to make the words "good" or "bad" irrelevant, immaterial, and inapplicable. There is no such thing, we are told, as a set of standards, first acquired through experience and knowledge and later imposed on the subject under discussion. This has been a popular approach, for it relieves the critic of the responsibility of judgment and the public of the necessity of knowledge. It pleases those resentful of disciplines, it flatters the empty-minded by calling them open-minded, it comforts the confused. Under the banner of democracy and the kind of equality which our forefathers did *not* mean, it says, in effect, "Who are you to tell us what is good or bad?" This is the same cry used so long and so effectively by the producers of mass media who insist that it is the public, not they, who decides what it wants to hear and see, and that for a critic to say that *this* program is bad and this program is good is purely a reflection of personal taste. Nobody recently has expressed this philosophy more succinctly than Dr. Frank Stanton, the highly intelligent president of CBS television. At a hearing before the Federal Communications Commission, this phrase escaped him under questioning: "One man's mediocrity is another man's good program."

There is no better way of saying "No values are absolute." There is another important aspect to this philosophy of *laissez faire:* It is the fear, in all observers of all forms of art, of guessing wrong. This fear is well come by, for who has not heard of the contemporary outcries against artists who later were called great? Every age has its arbiters who do not grow with their times, who cannot tell evolution from revolution or the difference between frivolous faddism, amateurish experimentation, and profound and necessary change. Who wants to be caught *flagrante delicto* with an error of judgment as serious as this? It is far safer, and certainly easier, to look at a picture or a play or a poem and to say "This is hard to understand, but it may be good," or simply to welcome it as a new form. The word "new"—in our country especially—has magical connotations. What is new must be good; what is old is probably bad, and if a critic can describe the new in language that nobody can understand, he's safer still. If he has mastered the art of saying nothing with exquisite complexity, nobody can quote him later as saying anything.

But all these, I maintain, are forms of abdication from the responsibility of judgment. In creating, the artist commits himself; in appreciating, you have a commitment of your own. For after all, it is the audience which makes the arts. A climate of appreciation is essential to its flowering, and the higher the expectations of the public, the better the performance of the artist. Conversely, only a public ill-served by its critics could have accepted as art and literature so much in these last years that has been neither. If anything goes, everything goes; and at the bottom of the junkpile lie the discarded standards too.

But what are these standards? How do you get them? How do you know they're the right ones? How can you make a clear pattern out of so many intangibles, including that greatest one, the very private I? 5

Well for one thing, it's fairly obvious that the more you read and see and hear, the more equipped you'll be to practice that art of association which is at the basis of all understanding and judgment. The more you live and the more you look, the more aware you are of a consistent pattern—as universal as the stars, as the tides, as breathing, as night and day—underlying everything. I would call this pattern and this rhythm an order. Not order—an order. Within it exists an incredible diversity of forms. Without it lies chaos. I would further call this order—this incredible diversity held within one pattern—health. And I would call chaos—the wild cells of destruction—sickness. It is in the end up to you to distinguish between the diversity that is health and the chaos that is sickness, and you can't do this without a process of association that can link a bar of Mozart with the corner of a Vermeer painting, or a Stravinsky score with a Picasso abstraction; or that can relate an aggressive act with a Franz Kline painting and a fit of coughing with a John Cage composition.

There is no accident in the fact that certain expressions of art live for all time and that others die with the moment, and although you may not always define the reasons, you can ask the questions. What does an artist say that is timeless; how does he say it? How much is fashion, how much is merely reflection? Why is Sir Walter Scott so hard to read now, and Jane Austen not? Why is baroque right for one age and too effulgent for another?

Can a standard of craftsmanship apply to art of all ages, or does each have its own, and different, definitions? You may have been aware, inadvertently, that craftsmanship has become a dirty word these years because, again, it implies standard—something done well or done badly. The result of this convenient avoidance is a plenitude of actors who can't project their voices, singers who can't phrase their songs, poets who can't communicate emotion, and writers who have no vocabulary—not to speak of painters who can't draw. The dogma now is that craftsmanship gets in the way of expression. You can do better if you don't know *how* you do it, let alone *what* you're doing.

I think it is time you helped reverse this trend by trying to rediscover craft: the command of the chosen instrument, whether it is a brush, a word, or a voice. When you begin to detect the difference between freedom and sloppiness, between serious experimentation and ego-therapy, between skill and slickness, between strength and violence, you are on your way to separating the sheep from the goats, a form of segregation denied us for quite a while. All you need to restore it is a small bundle of standards and a Geiger counter that detects fraud, and we might begin our tour of the arts in an area where both are urgently needed: contemporary painting.

I don't know what's worse: to have to look at acres of bad art to find the little good, or to read what the critics say about it all. In no other field of expression has so much double-talk flourished, so much confusion prevailed, and so much non-sense been circulated: further evidence of the close interdependence between the arts and the critical climate they inhabit. It will be my pleasure to share with you some of this double-talk so typical of our times.   10

Item one: preface for a catalogue of an abstract painter:

"Time-bound meditation experiencing a life; sincere with plastic piety at the threshold of hallowed arcana; a striving for pure ideation giving shape to inner drive; formalized patterns where neural balances reach a fiction." End of quote. Know what this artist paints like now?

Item two: a review in the *Art News:*

". . . a weird and disparate assortment of material, but the monstrosity which bloomed into his most recent cancer of aggregations is present in some form everywhere. . . ." Then, later, "A gluttony of things and processes terminated by a glorious constipation."

Item three, same magazine, review of an artist who welds automobile fragments into abstract shapes: 15

"Each fragment . . . is made an extreme of human exasperation, torn at and fought all the way, and has its rightness of form as if by accident. *Any technique that requires order or discipline would just be the human ego*. No, these must be egoless, uncontrolled, undesigned and different enough to give you a bang—fifty miles an hour around a telephone pole. . . ."

"Any technique that requires order or discipline would just be the human ego." What does he mean—"just be"? What are they really talking about? Is this journalism? Is it criticism? Or is it that other convenient abdication from standards of performance and judgment practiced by so many artists and critics that they, like certain writers who deal only in sickness and depravity, "reflect the chaos about them . . ."? Again, whose chaos? Whose depravity?

I had always thought that the prime function of art was to create order *out* of chaos—again, not the order of neatness or rigidity or convention or artifice, but the order of clarity by which one will and one vision could draw the essential truth out of apparent confusion. I still do. It is not enough to use parts of a car to convey the brutality of the machine. This is as slavishly representative, and just as easy, as arranging dried flowers under glass to convey nature.

Speaking of which, i.e., the use of real materials (burlap, old gloves, bottle-tops) in lieu of pigment, this is what one critic had to say about an exhibition of Assemblage at the Museum of Modern Art last year:

> Spotted throughout the show are indisputable works of art, accounting for a 20
> quarter or even half of the total display. But the remainder are works of non-art, anti-
> art, and art substitutes that are the aesthetic counterparts of the social deficiencies
> that land people in the clink on charges of vagrancy. These aesthetic bankrupts . . .
> have no legitimate ideological roof over their heads and not the price of a square in-
> tellectual meal, much less a spiritual sandwich, in their pockets.

I quote these words of John Canaday of *The New York Times* as an example of the kind of criticism which puts responsibility to an intelligent public above popularity with an intellectual coterie. Canaday has the courage to say what he thinks and the capacity to say it clearly: two qualities notably absent from his profession.

Next to art, I would say that appreciation and evaluation in the field of music is the most difficult. For it is rarely possible to judge a new composition at one hearing only. What seems confusing or fragmented at first might well become clear and organic a third time. Or it might not. The only salvation here for the listener is, again, an instinct born of experience and association which allows him to separate intent from accident, design from experimentation, and pretense from conviction. Much of contemporary music is, like its sister art, merely a reflection of the composer's own fragmentation: an absorption in self and symbols at the expense of communication with others. The artist, in short, says to the public: If you don't understand this, it's because you're dumb. I maintain that you are not. You may have to go part way or even halfway to meet the artist, but if you must go the whole way, it's his fault, not yours. Hold fast to that. And remember it too when you read new poetry, that estranged sister of music.

> A multitude of causes, unknown to former times, are now acting with a com-
> bined force to blunt the discriminating powers of the mind, and, unfitting it for all vol-
> untary exertion, to reduce it to a state of almost savage torpor. The most effective of
> these causes are the great national events which are daily taking place and the in-
> creasing accumulation of men in cities, where the uniformity of their occupations pro-
> duces a craving for extraordinary incident, which the rapid communication of intelli-
> gence hourly gratifies. To this tendency of life and manners, the literature and
> theatrical exhibitions of the country have conformed themselves.

This startingly applicable comment was written in the year 1800 by William Wordsworth in the preface to his "Lyrical Ballads"; and it has been cited by Edwin Muir in his recently published book, *The Estate of Poetry*. Muir states that poetry's effective range and influence have diminished alarmingly in the modern world. He believes in the inherent and indestructible qualities of the human mind and the great and permanent objects that act upon it, and suggests that the audience will increase when "poetry loses what obscurity is left in it by attempting greater themes, for great themes have to be stated clearly." If you keep that firmly in mind and resist, in Muir's words, "the vast dissemination of secondary objects that isolate us from the natural world," you have gone a long way toward equipping yourself for the examination of any work of art.

When you come to theatre, in this extremely hasty tour of the arts, you can   25
approach it on two different levels. You can bring to it anticipation and innocence, giving yourself up, as it were, to the life on the stage and reacting to it emotionally, if the play is good, or listlessly, if the play is boring; a part of the audience organism that expresses its favor by silence or laughter and its disfavor by coughing and rustling. Or you can bring to it certain critical faculties that may heighten, rather than diminish, your enjoyment.

You can ask yourselves whether the actors are truly in their parts or merely projecting themselves; whether the scenery helps or hurts the mood; whether the playwright is honest with himself, the characters, and you. Somewhere along the line you can learn to distinguish between the true creative act and the false arbitrary gesture; between fresh observation and stale cliché; between the avant-garde play that is pretentious drivel and the avant-garde play that finds new ways to say old truths.

Purpose and craftsmanship—end and means—these are the keys to your judgment in all the arts. What is this painter trying to say when he slashed a broad band of black across a white canvas and lets the edges dribble down? Is it a statement of violence? Is it a self-portrait? If it is *one* of these, has he made you believe it? Or is this a gesture of the ego or a form of therapy? If it shocks you, what does it shock you into?

And what of this tight little painting of bright flowers in a vase? Is the painter saying anything new about flowers? Is it different from a million other canvases of flowers? Has it any life, any meaning, beyond its statement? Is there any pleasure in its forms or texture? The question is not whether a thing is abstract or representational, whether it is "modern" or conventional. The question, inexorably, is whether it is good. And this is a decision which only you, on the basis of instinct, experience, and association, can make for yourself. It takes independence and courage. It involves, moreover, the risk of wrong decision and the humility, after the passage of time, of recognizing it as such. As we grow and change and learn, our attitudes can change too, and what we once thought obscure or "difficult" can later emerge as coherent and illuminating. Entrenched prejudices, obdurate opinions are as sterile as no opinions at all.

Yet standards there are, timeless as the universe itself. And when you have committed yourself to them, you have acquired a passport to that elusive but immutable realm of truth. Keep it with you in the forest of bewilderment. And never be afraid to speak up.

Reflecting and Interpreting

1. Where is the thesis statement located?
2. Mannes says a denial of the existence of criteria to evaluate the arts has been popular for several reasons. What are they?
3. What is the general fear of observers of all forms of art? Yet what danger lies in accepting a critic's verdict of "exquisite complexity" without evaluation?
4. Mannes says that appreciation is necessary for the arts to flower. How do the expectations of the public influence art? Are there any other factors that Mannes does not mention?
5. What two basic criteria can be used to judge any piece of art? (Hint: See paragraphs 6 and 7.)
6. What does Mannes mean when she says, "The dogma now is that craftsmanship gets in the way of expression."
7. How does Mannes define *craft*? She says that an audience needs to be able to distinguish what from what?
8. Mannes gives a final piece of advice. What is it?
9. Mannes suggests we ask, "What does an artist say that is timeless; how does he say it?" Using these guidelines, how would you explain Jane Austen's popularity?
10. What four steps does Mannes suggest the reader take to acquire the standards needed to distinguish good art from bad?

Small Group Discussion

With your group explore the criteria you use to rate a film as good or bad—one that you would or would not recommend to friends. Have a recorder jot down the proceedings and tabulate the votes for each criterion. After the discussion, the recorder should read the results.

Illustration

Showing with Examples

Introduction of Mothers of Invention

Ethlie Ann Vare and Greg Ptacek

Sometimes an author's best fuel is a powerful load of examples and dry wit, especially when those examples loudly decry the opposition's assertions. In this excerpt from Mothers of Invention *(1988), Vare and Ptacek effectively shoot down an unjust stereotype, presenting impressive facts. They have also coauthored* Women Inventors and Their Discoveries *(1993),* Patently Female: More Women Inventors and Discoveries *(1998), and* Patently Female *(2001). Vare has also written* Adventurous Spirit *(1992) and* Diva: Barbra Streisand and the Making of a Superstar *(1996) as well as television scripts. Ptacek has collaborated on four other books, consulted on a feature film, and written scripts for fitness videos.*

The first inventor introduced in every grammar-school primer is Eli Whitney, the genius who invented the cotton gin in 1793. Fact is, Mr. Whitney *didn't* invent the cotton "engine" in 1793—or any other year. Eli Whitney built a device conceived, perfected, and marketed by Mrs. Catherine Littlefield Greene, a Georgia belle who, unlike her Massachusetts-born houseguest, was quite familiar with the cotton boll.

Some accounts have it that Mrs. Greene handed Whitney a virtual set of plans for the cotton gin; others believe she "merely" suggested the idea and financed the work. Either way, Catherine Littlefield Greene somehow got lost on her way to those sixth-grade history texts.

Women have been inventing in America [since] before there was a United States, and in other parts of the world [since] before there was an America.

Catherine Littlefield Greene is not the only innovative lady whose accomplishments have slipped through the cracks. Western society has decreed that women do not invent despite facts to the contrary, and makes it a self-fulfilling prophecy by overlooking a few of those facts.

Even in our Smithsonian Museum, the painting honoring America's great inventors—"Men of Progress" by John Lawrence Mott, c. 1856—depicts exactly that: men, all white, and all over the age of forty. By 1856 a young widow named Martha Coston had already patented the Navy's signal flare; Ada Lovelace had designed the prototype computer; Mary Montagu had introduced smallpox inoculation; Nicole Clicquot had invented pink champagne and Elizabeth Flanagan the cocktail; and a Madame Lefebre synthesized the first nitrate fertilizer.

Nor can we look back and laugh at nineteenth-century male chauvinism. In his 1957 book *Inventors and Inventions*, C. D. Tuska, then director of RCA patent operations, said: "I shall write little about female inventors . . . most of our inventors are of the male sex. Why is the percentage [of women] so low? I am sure I don't know, unless the good Lord intended them to be mothers. I, being old-fashioned, hold that they are creative enough without also being 'inventive.' They produce the inventors and help rear them, and that should be sufficient."   5

By 1957 Eleanor Raymond and Maria Telkes had perfected solar heating; Grace Murray Hopper created the basis of computer software; Melitta Bentz invented the modern coffeepot; Mary Engle Pennington developed refrigeration; Margaret Knight invented the square-bottomed bag; Katherine Burr Blodgett patented invisible glass; Gladys Hobby produced the first usable penicillin; Kate Gleason designed the first tract housing; and Hattie Alexander had cured meningitis.

The National Inventors' Hall of Fame in Washington, D.C., boasted a total of fifty-two inductees in 1984; none was a woman. William Coolidge, the inventor of the vacuum tube, is mentioned . . . but not Marie Curie, who invented what we now call the "Geiger" counter and discovered radioactivity. Enrico Fermi makes the grade for building the first atomic reactor . . . but not Lise Meitner, who first created—and named—nuclear fission. Leo Bakeland is honored for inventing Bakelite . . . but not Madame Dutillet, who created cultured marble a century before. . . .

Since 1880, the U.S. Patent Office has officially recognized not only mechanical devices as inventions per se, but also substances, techniques, and processes. . . .

In this volume, we expand the definition of Inventor to include the Discoverers, those who advanced humankind by recognizing the value of things that were in front of everyone else all along.

The list of female inventors includes dancers, farmers, nuns, secretaries, actresses, shopkeepers, housewives, military officers, corporate executives, schoolteachers, writers, seamstresses, refugees, royalty, and little kids. All kinds of people can and do invent. The idea that one's gender somehow precludes the possibility of pursuing any technological endeavor is not only outdated but also dangerous. In the words of 1977 Nobel Prize winner Rosalyn Yalow: "The world   10 cannot afford the loss of the talents of half of its people if we are to solve the many problems which beset us."

Reflecting and Interpreting

1. What do you note about the pairing of facts in the first paragraph? Read the last two lines and the second paragraph aloud. How would you describe the tone?

2. Can you find a thesis statement in this essay? How does the delay affect the effectiveness of the opening?

3. What is a "self-fulfilling prophecy" (paragraph 3)?

4. What other groups of inventors were ignored by artist John Lawrence Mott, whose painting hangs in the Smithsonian Museum?

5. We tend to think of the latter half of the twentieth century as being enlightened. What evidence do the authors cite that indicates stereotypes about women inventors were widespread at that time?

6. Were the omissions that the authors speak of generally true for your school's history books? Were any women inventors mentioned? If so, which ones do you recall?

7. Look at each place where the authors list women inventors. Note how assertions about male inventors contrast with lists of women whose lives disprove the assertions. Do the contrasts always follow the same structure? Map the examples to show two ways they are presented.

8. Although twentieth-century history books recognize the work of Marie Curie, she has never received what honor that the authors think she deserves?

9. What is the stereotype that long governed the recognition of inventors and discoverers? By 1977 this assumption had run aground. How do you know?

10. Typically, fewer girls than boys take electives in mathematics and science. More men than women obtain degrees in medicine, biochemistry, and engineering. Might these facts influence the number of people who become inventors? Why or why not?

A Writer's Response

1. Discrimination appears in many shapes and forms. Have you ever been a victim? How did you cope? Write an essay, giving at least three examples.

2. Since the equal rights movement began, many changes have occurred. Has your life been affected by this movement? If so, how? Write an essay based on examples. (You might contrast your opportunities with those of a parent.)

Road Rage

Jason Vest, Warren Cohen, and Mike Tharp

Have you ever been crowded onto the shoulder of a road, insulted, or assaulted by an angry driver? If so, you were a victim of "road rage," an ever-increasing phenomenon that sometimes results in fatalities. Vest, Cohen, and Tharp researched this problem for U.S. News & World Report *and reported their findings in an article first published June 2, 1997. Jason Vest is a Washington D.C.-based reporter who has also written for several on-line publications. Warren Cohen is a journalist who has taught at Northwestern University in Evanston, IL and Columbia College in Chicago. He contributed to* Merchants of Misery *(1996). Mike Tharp is West Coast Correspondent for* U.S. News and World Report. *He has worked in Japan and served as President of the Foreign Correspondents' Club of Japan.*

Some of the incidents are so ludicrous you can't help but laugh—albeit nervously. There was the case in Salt Lake City, where 75-year-old J. C. King—peeved that 41-year-old Larry Remm Jr. honked at him for blocking traffic—followed Remm when he pulled off the road, hurled his prescription bottle at him, and then, in a display of geriatric resolve, smashed Remm's knees with his '92 Mercury. In tony Potomac, Md., Robin Ficker—an attorney and ex-state legislator—knocked the glasses off a pregnant woman after she had the temerity to ask him why he bumped her Jeep with his.

Other incidents lack even the element of black humor. In Colorado Springs, 55-year-old Vern Smalley persuaded a 17-year-old boy who had been tailgating him to pull over; Smalley decided that, rather than merely scold the lad, he would shoot him. (And he did. Fatally—after the youth had threatened him.) And last year, on Virginia's George Washington Parkway, a dispute over a lane change was settled with a high-speed duel that ended when both drivers lost control and crossed the center line, killing two innocent motorists.

Anyone who spent the Memorial Day weekend on the road probably won't be too surprised to learn the results of a major study to be released this week by the American Automobile Association. The rate of "aggressive driving" incidents—defined as events in which an angry or impatient driver tries to kill or injure another driver after a traffic dispute—has risen by 51 percent since 1990. In those cases studied, 37 percent of offenders used "firearms" against other drivers, an additional 28 percent used other weapons, and 35 percent used their cars.

Fear of (and participation in) aggressive driving has grown so much that in a poll last year residents of Maryland, Washington, D.C. and Virginia listed it as a bigger concern than drunk driving. The Maryland highway department is running a campaign called "The End of the Road for Aggressive Drivers," which, among other things, flashes anti-road-rage messages on electronic billboards on the interstates. Delaware, Pennsylvania, and New Jersey have initiated special highway patrols targeting aggressive drivers. A small but busy community of therapists and scholars has arisen to study the phenomenon and counsel drivers on how to cope. And several members of Congress are now trying to figure out ways to legislate away road rage.

Lest one get unduly alarmed, it helps to put the AAA study's numbers in context: Approximately 250,000 people have been killed in traffic since 1990. While the U.S. Department of Transportation estimates that two-thirds of fatalities are at least partially caused by aggressive driving, the AAA study found only 218 that could be directly attributable to enraged drivers. Of the more than 20 million motorists injured, the survey identified 12,610 injuries attributable to aggressive driving. While the study is the first American attempt to quantify aggressive driving, it is not rigorously scientific. The authors drew on reports from 30 newspapers—supplemented by insurance claims and police reports from 16 cities—involving 10,037 occurrences. Moreover, the overall trendlines for car accidents have continued downward for several decades, thanks in part to increases in the drinking age and improvements in car technology like high-mounted brake lights.   5

But researchers believe there is a growing trend of simple aggressive behavior—road rage—in which a driver reacts angrily to other drivers. Cutting them off, tailgating, giving the finger, waving a fist—experts believe these forms of nonviolent fury are increasing. "Aggressive driving is now the most common way of driving," says Sandra Ball-Rokeach, who codirects the Media and Injury Prevention Program at the University of Southern California. "It's not just a few crazies—it's a subculture of driving."

In focus groups set up by her organization, two-thirds of drivers said they reacted to frustrating situations aggressively. Almost half admitted to deliberately braking suddenly, pulling close to the other car, or taking some other potentially dangerous step. Another third said they retaliated with a hostile gesture. Drivers show great creativity in devising hostile responses. Doug Erber of Los Angeles keeps his windshield-wiper-fluid tank full. If someone tailgates, he turns on the wipers, sending fluid over his roof onto the car behind him. "It works better than hitting the brakes," he says, "and you can act totally innocent."

Mad Max

While the AAA authors note there is a profile of the lethally inclined aggressive driver—"relatively young, poorly educated males who have criminal records, histories of violence, and drug or alcohol problems"—road-rage scholars (and regular drivers) believe other groups are equally represented in the less violent forms of aggressive driving. To some, it's tempting to look at this as a psychologically mysterious Jekyll-and-Hyde phenomenon; for others, it's simply attributable to "jerk drivers." In reality, there's a confluence of emotional and demographic factors that changes the average citizen from mere motorist to Mad Max.

First, it isn't just your imagination that traffic is getting worse. Since 1987, the number of miles of roads has increased just 1 percent while the miles *driven* have shot up by 35 percent. According to a recent Federal Highway Administration study of 50 metropolitan areas, almost 70 percent of urban freeways today—as opposed to 55 percent in 1983—are clogged during rush hour. The study notes that congestion is likely to spread to currently unspoiled locations. Forty percent of the currently gridlock-free Milwaukee County highway system, for example, is predicted to be jammed up more than five hours a day by the year 2000. A study by the Texas Transportation Institute last year found that commuters in one-third of the largest cities spent well over 40 hours a year in traffic jams.

Part of the problem is that jobs have shifted from cities to suburbs. Commu-   10
nities designed as residential suburbs with narrow roads have grown into "edge cities," with bustling commercial traffic. Suburb-to-suburb commutes now account for 44 percent of all metropolitan traffic versus 20 percent for suburb-to-downtown travel. Demographer and *Edge City* author Joel Garreau says workers breaking for lunch are essentially causing a third rush hour. He notes that in Tysons Corner, Va., it takes an average of four traffic signal cycles to get through a typical intersection at lunchtime. And because most mass transit systems are of a spoke-and-hub design, centering on cities and branching out to suburbs, they're not really useful in getting from point A to point B in an edge city or from one edge city to another. Not surprisingly, fewer people are relying on mass transit and more on cars. In 1969, 82.7 percent drove to work; in 1990, 91.4 percent did. Despite the fact that the Washington, D.C., area has an exemplary commuter subway system, it accounts for only 2 percent of all trips made.

Demographic changes have helped put more drivers on the road. Until the 1970s, the percentage of women driving was relatively low, and many families had only one car. But women entered the work force and bought cars, something developers and highway planners hadn't foreseen. From 1969 to 1990 the number of women licensed to drive increased 84 percent. Between 1970 and 1987, the number of cars on the road more than doubled. In the past decade, the number of cars grew faster (17 percent) than the number of people (10 percent). Even carpooling is down despite HOV lanes and other preferential devices. The cumulative effect, says University of Hawaii traffic psychology professor Leon James, is a sort of sensory overload. "There are simply more cars—and more behaviors—to deal with," says James.

As if the United States couldn't produce enough home-grown lousy drivers, it seems to be importing them as well. Experts believe that many immigrants come from countries that have bad roads and aggressive styles. It's not just drivers from Third World countries, though. British drivers are considered among the safest in Europe, yet recent surveys show that nearly 90 percent of British motorists have experienced threats or abuse from other drivers. Of Brits who drive for a living, about 21 percent report having been run off the road. In Australia, one study estimates that about half of all traffic accidents there may be due to road rage. "There are different cultures of driving all over the world—quite clearly, if we mix new cultures in the melting pot, what we get is a culture clash on the roadway," says John Palmer, a professor in the Health Education and Safety Department at Minnesota's St. Cloud University.

The peak moment for aggressive driving comes not during impenetrable grid-locks but just before, when traffic density is high but cars are still moving briskly. That's when cutting someone off or forcing someone out of a lane can make the difference (or so it seems) between being on time and being late, according to Palmer.

Unfortunately, roads are getting more congested just as Americans feel even more pressed for time. "People get on a time line for their car trips," says Palmer. "When they perceive that someone is impeding their progress or invading their agenda, they respond with what they consider to be 'instructive' behavior, which might be as simple as flashing their lights to something more combative."

Suburban Assault Vehicles

This, uh, "instruction" has become more common, Palmer and others specu- 15
late, in part because of modern automotive design. With hyperadjustable seats, soundproof interiors, CD players, and cellular phones, cars are virtually comfort-able enough to live in. Students of traffic can't help but wonder if the popularity of pickup trucks and sport utility vehicles has contributed to the problem. Sales have approximately doubled since 1990. These big metal shells loom over every-thing else, fueling feelings of power and drawing out a driver's more primal in-stincts. "A lot of the anecdotal evidence about aggressive driving incidents tends to involve people driving sport utility vehicles," says Julie Rochman of the Insur-ance Institute for Highway Safety. "When people get these larger, heavier ve-hicles, they feel more invulnerable." While Chrysler spokesman Chris Preuss dis-counts the notion of suburban assault vehicles being behind the aggressive-driving phenomenon, he does say women feel more secure in the jumbo-size vehicles.

In much of life, people feel they don't have full control of their destiny. But a car—unlike, say, a career or a spouse—responds reliably to one's wish. In auto-mobiles, we have an increased (but false) sense of invincibility. Other drivers be-come dehumanized, mere appendages to a competing machine. "You have the il-lusion you're alone and master, dislocated from other drivers," says Hawaii's James.

Los Angeles psychologist Arnold Nerenberg describes how one of his recent patients got into an angry road confrontation with another motorist. "They pulled off the road and started running toward each other to fight, but then they recog-nized each other as neighbors," he says. "When it's just somebody else in a car, it's more two-dimensional; the other person's identity boils down to, 'You're some-one who did something bad to me.'"

How can aggressive driving be minimized? Some believe that better driver's education might help. Driver's ed was a high school staple by the 1950s, thanks to federal highway dollars given to states. But a 1978 government study in De Kalb County, Ga., found no reduction in crashes or traffic violations by students who took a driver's ed course compared with those who didn't. Rather than use these results to design better driver's ed programs, the feds essentially gave up on them and diverted money to seat belt and anti-drunk-driving programs. Today, only 40 percent of new drivers complete a formal training course, which may be one reason 20 percent to 35 percent of applicants fail their initial driving test.

The Inner Driver

But governments are looking anew at the value of driver's education. In April, Michigan passed sweeping rules that grant levels of privilege depending on one's age and driving record. States with similar systems, like California, Maryland, and Oregon, have seen teen accident rates drop.

Those who lose their licenses often have to return to traffic school. But some   20
states have generous standards for these schools. To wit: California's theme schools. There, errant drivers can attend the "Humor's My Name, Traffic's My Game," school, in which a mock jury led by a stand-up comic decides who the worst drivers are; the "Traffic School for Chocoholics," which plies errant drivers with chocolate and ice cream; and the gay and lesbian "Pink Triangle Traffic School."

But the real key to reducing road rage probably lies deep within each of us. Professor James of the University of Hawaii suggests that instead of emphasizing defensive driving—which implies that the other driver is the enemy—we should focus on "supportive driving" or "driving with the aloha spirit." Of course that's hard to do if (a) someone has just cut you off at 60 mph or (b) you live in Los Angeles instead of Hawaii. Nerenberg, the Los Angeles psychologist, has published an 18-page booklet called "Overcoming Road Rage: The 10-Step Compassion Program." He recommends examining what sets off road rage and to "visualize overcoming it." Other tips: Imagine you might be seeing that person at a party soon. And remembering that other drivers "are people with feelings. Let us not humiliate them with our aggression." In the chapter titled, "Peace," he suggests, "Take a deep breath and just let it go." And if that doesn't work, the windshield-wiper trick is pretty clever.

Reflecting and Interpreting

1. Comment on the incidents described in the opening. Do you think such conflicts are common or isolated? Do they seem to occur more often in certain areas? If so, where?

2. How does the American Automobile Association define an "aggressive driving" incident?

3. When does the peak moment for aggressive driving occur?

4. What do the authors cite as major causes of the increase in aggressive driving?

5. Do the authors of the AAA research believe that aggressive drivers tend to have criminal records, histories of violence, or drug or alcohol problems?

6. What did the drivers in focus groups set up by the University of Southern California admit?

7. How does the type of vehicle seem to influence a driver's feelings and behavior?

8. Since 1987, the miles of roadway in the USA have increased by 1%, but the miles driven have increased 35%. What conclusions can you draw from these statistics?

9. What is the predominant rhetorical strategy used in this article?

10. How do the authors support their claims?

Small Group Discussion

1. What tends to set off road rage? What can a driver do to forestall arousing his or her own impatience and irritating other drivers?

2. Discuss possible ways of self-preservation when risky on-the-road situations occur. How can you diffuse the wrath of a driver? What should you do if that person signals you to stop?

3. Have you ever witnessed an incident of road rage? If so, write an essay describing what happened. Is there a moral to the tale?

Black and Well-to-Do

Andrea Lee

Too often in the past, blacks have been dogged by stereotypes. In this essay Andrea Lee strikes a different note as she describes her life in the upper-middle-class integrated suburb of Yeadon, on the edge of Philadelphia. Sheltered from prejudice, she attended Quaker schools and spent summers on Martha's Vineyard. At Harvard, she earned both bachelor's and master's degrees. She and her husband spent nearly a year in Russia in 1978–79, where she started writing Russian Journal *(1981). In 1984 she received the Jean Stein Award and American Academy and Institute of Arts and Letters award. She is a staff writer for* The New Yorker.*

I grew up in the kind of town few people believe exists: a black upper-middle-class suburb full of colonial-style houses and Volkswagen Rabbits. Yes, Virginia, there is a black bourgeoisie, it has existed for years, and it summers on Martha's Vineyard.

The Philadelphia suburb of Yeadon, my home through childhood and adolescence, is one of many black enclaves that someday will make a very interesting study for a sociologist.

After World War II, housing speculators found it profitable to scare off white residents and sell whole streets of Yeadon to black professionals who were as eager as anyone else at that time to pursue the romantic suburban dream of field-stone patios and eye-level ovens. In the 1950's, half the black doctors and lawyers in Philadelphia crowded into this rather small town, which was one of the few integrated suburbs, and we Yeadon kids grew up with tree houses and two-car garages and fathers who commuted into the city.

Our parents had a vision of pastoral normalcy for their children that was little different from the white ideal laid out in the Dick and Jane readers. Their attempts to provide this and to protect us from the slightest contact with race prejudice left us extraordinarily, perhaps unhealthily, sheltered: We were sent to Quaker schools and camps where race and class were discounted with eager innocence. When the Yeadon Civic Association (my father was president) discovered that a local swimming club was discriminating against blacks, the parents in my neighborhood simply built another club, which they christened "The Nile Swim Club." When we asked about the name, my father explained gravely: "This is a club only for Egyptians."

Childhood in Yeadon was a suburban idyll of shady streets and bicycles and ice cream from a drugstore called Doc's. This was the early 1960's, and as my friends and I grew older, we became dimly aware that the rest of the world was not necessarily Yeadon. Most of our parents were active in the civil rights movement, and at gatherings we listened avidly to their campaign references: Birmingham, Selma, Greensboro.

Occasionally, we kids would travel into the city and stare in horrified fascination at slums. When my generation of Yeadon preppies was graduated from high school in the late 1960's and early 1970's, however, we quickly realized that our vague concern was not enough, and many of us became radicalized. (Most of us were attending Ivy League colleges, and this increased our sense of guilt.)

During college holidays, Yeadon's driveways were colorful with dashikis and other, more complicated African garments, and a great deal of talk went on about the brothers and sisters of the urban community. Yeadon parents were edgy and alienated from their children at this time, and a common conversation between mothers began: "Yes, she used to look so sweet, and now she's gone and gotten one of those . . . Afros."

In the 1970's, our guilt evaporated, and Yeadon became a place where parents vied with one another to produce tidbits about surgeon daughters and M.B.A. sons. Now, early in the 1980's, I find that in some circles, Yeadon is a synonym for conservatism and complacency, a place famed as being the hunting-ground of the AAP (Afro-American Prince or Princess), but I don't care.

Yeadon was a great town to grow up in, was as solid a repository of American virtues and American flaws as any other close-knit suburban community; moreover, it had, and still has, its own peculiar flavor—a lively mixture of materialism, idealism, and ironic humor that prevents the minds of its children from stagnating. I feel a surge of well-being when I return there in the summer to hear the symphony of lawn mowers and to find that the Nile Swim Club remains "for Egyptians only."

Reflecting and Interpreting

1. Examine the first paragraph. What tone does "Yes, Virginia, there is . . ." set?
2. What is the "romantic suburban dream" that Lee speaks of?
3. What types of people lived in Yeadon? Describe their lifestyle.
4. How were Lee and other children in Yeadon sheltered from racial prejudice?
5. How did the youth of Yeadon become aware of racial prejudice?
6. What message was implicit in Lee's father's explanation of the name of the swim club?
7. What did the new swim club symbolize? Why was it unusual and significant?
8. Why did Lee and her friends feel guilty when they were attending Ivy League colleges?
9. How does Lee feel about Yeadon and her childhood there?
10. Andrea Lee has two degrees from Harvard and is a staff writer for *The New Yorker*. After reading this essay, what do you think were the prime factors that influenced her success?

A Writer's Response

1. Write an essay describing the place where you grew up. How did you feel about it? Have your feelings stayed the same or changed over the years?

2. *Small Groups:* What kinds of discrimination exist? What changes of societal attitudes have occurred there during your lifetime? What other changes would you like to see?

Uptight Is Back in Style

Holman W. Jenkins, Jr.

It may be time to iron those white shirts and air out the mothballs from your business suits. During economic slowdowns, dressing up may be a way to "look less expendable." Recent surveys report a decline in the wearing of "business casual" for several significant reasons. Although relatively few employers have dress codes, many have expectations about how their staff should look. Holman W. Jenkins, Jr., a member of the editorial board of The Wall Street Journal, *writes a column entitled "Business World." In 1994 and 1995 he worked in Hong Kong as an editor of the Asian* Wall Street Journal. *In 1997 he received the Gerald Loeb Award for distinguished business and financial coverage. The following column was published November 21, 2001.*

In this week of Thanksgiving, more than a few restuffed shirts of the business world will give praise to their God or gods for a merciful termination of the business casual trend. Sure, corporate leaders might have done more to stand up for the right of business people to dress like business people, but they were terrorized by the young mullahs of dotcomdom.

It turns out that the old and moldy traditionalists had a point. People who look sloppy work sloppy, or at least that's been the conclusion of a growing number of business types, reminding us why we zipped ourselves into monkey suits in the first place.

Jack Mitchell, whose family runs the business-friendly Mitchells and Richards stores in suburban Connecticut, and who therefore has done more than his share of zipping up the corporate class for battle, cites a conversation with an unnamed CEO of a Wall Street bank at the height of the fad: "I hate it, Jack," he complained, "but I can't mandate a suit and tie. It's too political."

Some have tried: In a memo to his troops last summer, Michael MacDonald, head of North American sales for Xerox, noted that although everyone might enjoy dressing casually for reasons of comfort and convenience, "I am personally asking each of you in jobs requiring direct customer contact to dress in business attire at all times." This, he added, would "show the world 'we mean business.'"

Dressing up is a pain, which was reason enough for employees, when they had the upper hand, to oppose dressing up. Managers who surrendered to their demands tried to rationalize by saying employees would be more productive and happy, but their main hope was that they wouldn't lose out in recruiting in what until last year was an ultra-tight job market.

A much-cited survey by Jackson Lewis, a law firm specializing in employment suits, last year marked an incoming tide of disillusionment. In the minds of many respondents, business casual had become associated with an unhealthy increase in absenteeism and "flirtatious behavior," among other workplace ills.

The Society for Human Resource Management; meanwhile, found for the first time in a decade a decline in the number of companies indulging casual dress. After rising from 24% to 94% between 1992 and 1999, last year the number dropped to 87%.

Data from the battlefront confirms the trend is in reverse. Over the summer Joe Blair, who runs Individualized Shirts, the country's biggest maker of custom shirts, noticed a 12% increase in orders for the color white. Of his CEO-heavy client list, he says, "They're tired of the way they look. How many khakis and golf shirts can you do? The CEO sets the example and it trickles down."

Business casual, like disco, will not disappear but is being reined in after having its moment of untrammeled fadhood. In the weeks before Sept. 11, rumors were rife that a blue-chip Wall Street investment bank would announce a new, suits-only policy. It didn't happen and perhaps was never likely—business casual is too much seen as an employee perk and therefore difficult to withdraw without risking a labor uprising. Besides, people nowadays consider their dignity infringed when employers tell them how to dress. Better to let the message seep around by example and innuendo.

President Bush wears suits and expects his staff to dress up, unlike the Clin-   10
tonites, who showed up at the office on Saturdays in their bathrobes. After Sept. 11, a bracing sense of life's seriousness has reinforced the trend. With layoffs looming, dressing up to look less expendable has struck many employees as the better part of valor, while others have been donning suit and tie to sneak out at lunch for safety-net interviews.

It could also be that employees, noticing what eyesores their co-workers had become decided on their own to take business casual out behind the dumpster and shoot it as a project in workplace beautification.

One big problem with business casual was that few men knew how to do it well. The one-plus-one challenge of matching a tie to a suit was hard enough for male employees. When it became the three-dimensional chess of trying to get shirt, slacks, sweater, shoes, belt and socks all pulling in the same direction, despite the deceptive use of the word "casual," the style was a source of anxiety and despair for many worker drones. Interestingly, one of the earliest opponents of the trend was a female investment banker of our acquaintance who saw the decline in formality as a setback to her efforts to tamp down the juvenility of her colleagues.

A second problem is what Mr. Mitchell, the Connecticut clothier, calls the Clark Kent syndrome. Even CEOs who never leave the office had to keep several changes of wardrobe on hand to conform to the sartorial styles of important clients. And where once a single suit and a few ties would get business travelers through a week of sales calls, now they had to haul multiple changes of disguise or risk being seen as a toff or a slob, depending on the dress code of his customers.

Many got it wrong no matter what they did. One partner at a New York private equity firm points out that it became so difficult to guess what appropriate dress might be that every meeting necessarily had to start with a Japanese-style ritual of apology: "Sorry, we screwed up and wore suits and you didn't (or vice versa)."

Showing up in the wrong attire could be worse than a faux pas. The same in-   15
vestment banker tells of visiting a Midwest company with his retinue of spread-
sheet nerds in Wall Street pinstripes. The local CEO took him aside and said,
"Don't come back here looking like that!" The mere appearance of men in suits
was enough to spark office gossip that bankers had arrived to put the company up
for sale.

A living society is one that allows the pendulum to swing. Even as grownups
were dressing down in the 1990s, schools, especially in minority neighborhoods,
were bringing back uniforms as a way to reinforce a sense of serious purpose. It's
not supposed to be fun (though a few weirdos seem to enjoy it anyway). Of
course some of us will always consider dressing up (also, bathing and shaving) a
dubious expenditure of time. But that doesn't mean we don't appreciate it when
other people take the trouble to look their best.

Reflecting and Interpreting

1. What do you notice about the word choice in the title and first two
   paragraphs?
2. How would you describe the tone of paragraphs 1 and 2?
3. What is the conclusion of a "growing number of business types"? Have you
   noticed any sign of this trend in your workplace or city? If so, what has
   changed?
4. When Jenkins cites the results of the Jackson Lewis survey (paragraph 6), notice his choice of words. If he had said "led to," instead of "had become associated with" how would the meaning have changed? What does his wording
   reveal about his research technique?
5. Although some companies have tried to change dress habits by direct request, this avenue has not been too successful. Why? What seems to be the
   best way for a CEO to institute such a change?
6. What three main problems arise when men don "business casual" wear?
7. Sometimes wearing a traditional business suit can meet with a negative response. Can you cite some examples? What insight can you derive from these
   examples?
8. Can you find an example of irony?
9. What is the purpose of wearing a traditional business suit?
10. How does Jenkins's writing style reflect the content of the column?

A Writer's Response

Write an essay describing proper attire for an employment interview in your
career field. If you are unsure, telephone employers or talk to instructors in that
field. (Dress may vary according to area or company.)

Classification

Grouping and Dividing

 ## *It's Only a Paper World*

Kathleen Fury

Even if you have never worked in an office, you will appreciate Kathleen Fury's spoof of the innovations people use to channel the never-ending flow of paper. She is a native New Yorker (born 1941) who graduated from Purdue University. She has worked as a writer and editor for Redbook, Savvy, *and* Ladies Home Journal. *She has published* Dear 60 Minutes *(1985);* Forever Young, A Guide to Life After 50 *(1996); and contributed to* Death, then what? *(online anthology). She has also written for* TV Guide, Cat Quotes, New Woman, *and other magazines. For years she contributed regular columns to* Working Woman, *one of which appears here.*

Many experts claimed that the computer age heralded the advent of the paperless office. Clearly, this is not to be. If anything, offices are overwhelmed by even more paper, much of it now with sprocket holes.

Humankind is adapting, fortunately. According to the dictates of our varied individual natures, we have developed ways of copying with our changing ecosystem.

The beaver uses paper to build. It may not be exactly clear to observers just what she's building, but deep in her genetic code she knows.

On one side of the typical beaver's desk leans a foot-high stack of papers. Close by is a vertical file stuffed with bulging folders, some waving in the air, unable to touch bottom. In between, the beaver constructs a clever "dam" to prevent the entire structure from falling over: Her two-tier In/Out box supports the pile and allows movement of papers from one place to another.

Incredibly, to nonbeaver observers, the beaver has an uncanny ability to lo-   5
cate a two-month-old report buried within the pile. With deft precision, she can
move her hand four millimeters down the pile and extract what she's looking for,
confident that the dam will hold.

In this way, the beaver has evolved a protective mechanism that makes her
invaluable within the organization, for nobody else, including her secretary, can
find anything on her desk. When the beaver goes away on vacation, her department simply ceases work until she returns. She is thus assured that the cliché "nobody's indispensable" doesn't apply to her.

The squirrel's desk, by contrast, is barren. Throughout the year, in all kinds of
weather, the squirrel energetically stores away what her brain tells her she may
need someday. In her many file cabinets, drawers and book-cases she neatly stores
memos, letters, printouts and receipts she believes will nourish her in the months
and years to come.

Unlike her co-worker the beaver, the squirrel does not always know exactly
where she has hidden a particular item. She knows she *has* it but is not skilled at
remembering the exact location.

Like the maple tree, which produces enough seeds to reforest a continent, the
squirrel illustrates nature's method of "overkill." By saving and storing everything,
she increases her chance of retrieving something.

Of necessity, squirrels have developed the ability to move through a wide ter-   10
ritorial range. When a squirrel moves on to another job, as she tends to do rather
often due to lack of space, management must hire a special team of search-and-
destroy experts to go through her files.

Nature's scavengers, her "clean-up crew," crows are regarded with wary ad-
miration by squirrels and beavers, who recognize their contribution to keeping
the corporate ecosystem tidy.

Crows are responsible for such paper-management advice as "Act on it—
or throw it away." They are deeply drawn to paper shredders, trash compactors
and outsized waste receptacles and will buy them if they happen to work in
purchasing.

Crows belie the common epithet "birdbrained," for it has taken centuries of
evolution to create a mind disciplined enough to know with certainty that it is
OK to throw the CEO's Statement of Corporate Policy in the wastebasket after
a glance.

Other species, who must adapt to the corporate food chain, quickly learn not
to address any crow with a sentence that begins, "Do you have a copy of . . . ?"

The clever bees are among the wonders of the corporate world. A bee neither   15
hoards nor destroys paper; she redistributes it, moving from office to office as if
between flowers.

Her methods are various and unpredictable, but there is no madness in them.
Sometimes she arrives in an office with paper in hand and, distracting a colleague
with conversation, simply leaves the paper inconspicuously on his desk. Sometimes she moves paper through seemingly legitimate channels, sending it through

interoffice mail with ingenious notes like "Please look into this when you get a chance." More often, she employs the clever notation invented by bees, "FYI."

Whatever her method, she ensures that paper floats outward and does not return to her. Students of human behavior have come to call this crosspollination "delegation," though to the bee it is simply a genetic imperative.

While others of the species hoard, distribute and destroy paper, the possum follows the evolutionary dictates of all marsupials and carries it with her.

Instead of a pouch, the office possum has a briefcase—in some cases, several. It is large and soft sided to accommodate her needs. Some possums, as an auxiliary system, carry handbags large enough to hold legal-size files. When a possum needs to retrieve paper, she goes not to a file cabinet or an In box but to her bags. She protects her paper by carrying it with her at all times—to her home, to the health club, to lunch.

Though she has no natural predators, the possum's habits create special risks. 20 She must spend considerable time at the lost-and-found department of theaters and restaurants and knows by heart the telephone number of the taxi commissioner. One of her arms is longer than the other.

But in nature, all things serve a purpose. And if the office burned down, the lowly possum would be the sole possessor of the paper that is the raison d'être of all the other animals.

Reflecting and Interpreting

1. Can you find an example of foreshadowing?
2. How does paragraph 2 function? What is the analogy that is introduced here?
3. How can you identify a "beaver"? What special ability does she have? Why is she indispensable?
4. Why is the squirrel's desk bare? How efficient is the squirrel?
5. Why do other office worker's never ask a "crow" for anything?
6. What are some clues that can help you spot a "possum"?
7. Notice the references to genetics and evolution throughout the essay. How do these function?
8. What literary device is the basis for Fury's classifications?
9. Can you find instances of irony in the essay?
10. Why is the last paragraph effective?

A Writer's Response

Can you think of another type of office worker, unnamed by the author? If so, write a paragraph describing this creature. Give the advantages and disadvantages of his or her method of managing the flow of paper.

Mind Over Munchies

Norman Brown

"Food cravings are like fingerprints," or so Norman Brown has decided. We all have individual food cravings that surface, perhaps at a particular time of day or under certain conditions. He presents research about "comfort foods," "mood foods," and "happy foods" but with no definitive results. Although researchers do not agree about what causes food cravings, they do agree that excessive cravings of certain foods and nonfoods are a good reason to consult a physician. "Mind over Munchies" was first published in Northwest Airlines *(June 1992) and later in* The Thoughtful Reader *(1994).*

Got any favorite foods? They can reveal a lot about your personality, say experts who have been digging into our "edible complex" ever since Cleopatra's milk baths and fig outs. Not surprisingly, those gastronomical urges are also the subject of considerable debate. 1

Some researchers believe there are strong physiological links to food cravings. But others feel that our urges are not that deep-rooted or overwhelming. How much is scientific fact—and should we be that concerned about "mood foods" which are supposed to make us happier, smarter or sexier?

Current research lends support to both sides. Scientists now believe that food cravings are a smorgasbord of biological and psychological events that help the body regulate its intake of nutrients. The notion, though controversial, has obvious appeal. Whether you crave a pizza or nachos, it's comforting to think the body is getting a desired carbohydrate fix—or quick salt injection.

Food cravings are like fingerprints. In those sluggish hours when there's nothing better to do than imagine the perfect entrée, our choices are as varied as they are precise: McDonald's fries, subgum chow mein, or chocolate chip cookies.

Necessary Comforts

"Comfort foods are really an individual thing," says Dr. Kelly Brownell, professor of nutrition at Yale University in New Haven. He compares cravings to a wave in the ocean—starting small, building to a peak, then rapidly subsiding. If you track where you are in the cycle, or if the urge strikes at the same time each day, you can ward it off by taking a brisk walk. 5

Brownell admits he's not sure whether cravings are in the head or stomach. "It's possible that there's nothing physiological about them," he says. "Even if you buy that argument, our protein intake is amazingly steady. What varies wildly is fat and sugar consumption—and which foods you choose depends on habit."

In a survey for the *Wall Street Journal*, half of all respondents said they did seek solace in food when depressed. First choice: ice cream or chocolate bars (with 34 percent of the vote). Pizza, beer, soft drinks, hot soup, peanut butter and burgers completed the list of comforting edibles.

Other scientists agree that what we eat (or don't eat) is often rooted in the nurturing, warmth and security we felt in childhood. "Some cravers want a little taste of what Mom gave them to feel better," explains Dr. Tom Castonguay, associate professor of nutrition at the University of Maryland. "Others use food to be bad."

The very word "craving" conjures up an addiction, but that's not the kind of thing a person with a sweet tooth is experiencing. "Cravings are not that deep-rooted or overwhelming," says Castonguay. "But people are making money talking about them in that way."

Eat for Success?

Every fad diet for "cravers" that hits the bookstores claims to rely on scientific   10
proof and it all has to do with those elusive brain chemicals that can send you to the sack—or to the refrigerator. Among the strongest proponents of "mood foods" is Dr. Judith Wurtman, nutritional biochemist at the Massachusetts Institute of Technology.

Her research over the past several years seems to indicate that irrational desires for certain foods may indeed be biologically based. Carbohydrate cravers, she says, feel calmer—and less tired and depressed—after satisfying their need.

Wurtman notes that dietary needs vary from person to person, but suggests that carbohydrate craving may be linked to the activity of serotonin, a chemical produced in the brain when sugar or starch is ingested. When cravers were given a substance that increases serotonin, she says, "the cravings went down to nothing."

Her books and advice have become immensely popular, but she's quick to point out that food is not a panacea for all our ills. "There are myths to confront," says Wurtman. One is that sugar causes anxiety. Her research has shown that sugar or starch actually has a calming effect and may be an unconscious attempt at self-medication.

She advises stress-plagued executives to cut down on "dumb" foods and eat smart: low-fat carbohydrates like bananas and crackers to chase away tension, or high-protein snacks (peanut butter or cottage cheese) for the alertness chemicals dopamine and norepinephrine.

Happy Foods

Campbell Soup Co. is also investigating how food may affect people's moods,   15
and is doing research projects with Tufts University School of Medicine. "We feel mood is going to be really big in the 90s and that positioning foods as making one smarter or happier could be a gold mine," says Tony Adams, marketing research chief.

The company is studying carbohydrates, caffeine and other components of food. "But the research puts some folks at Campbell in a nervous mood. "People here worry about making claims," says Adams. "We'll have to be careful to separate fact from witch doctoring."

Other researchers think carbohydrate cravers may be deluding themselves. What they really yearn for are those fat-sugar mixtures, says Dr. Adam Drewnowski, nutrition professor at the University of Michigan School of Public Health.

"Hardly anyone craves pure carbohydrates such as macaroni or cabbage," he says. "But almost everybody can identify with an uncontrollable desire for a Snickers bar or piece of cheesecake." He has demonstrated that such food cravings can be blocked by the drug naloxone, which is also given to addicts to ease opiate cravings.

Other scientists are studying a hormone (cholecystokinin) that may hold the key to why we pig out. They believe that the hormone, secreted during digestion, sends signals to the brain that cause the can't-eat-another-bite sensation. The trick in stopping binges is to make this reaction happen sooner—not later.

And behaviorists argue that we *learn* our food fixations. "Taste may be more   20 addictive than calories or nutrients," says Dr. Stephen Chang, food science professor at Rutgers University. The brain is more interested in what's happening on the tongue than in the stomach. "If the tongue is happy, then the brain will be happy," he says.

Brain Chemicals

Drewnowski and others speculate that in some people, food cravings increase the output of endorphins, mood-altering brain chemicals with potent effects similar to narcotics. Not only do endorphins soothe headaches and calm frazzled nerves, they can sweep us into euphoria—or kindle destructive behavior such as excruciating workouts or compulsive gambling.

Childbirth would be unbearable without the easing effects of these natural opiates, which increase four or five times during labor. After the baby is born, endorphins return to their former levels. Not surprisingly, people with chronic pain have only half the endorphins of a healthy person.

It's not that cravings are significantly more common during pregnancy. Rather, women are more likely to satisfy them at that time, explains Dr. Judith Rodin, professor of psychology at Yale. Pregnant women do require the extra salt and calories that pickles and ice cream provide as fetal development begins.

Aversions, the flip side of cravings, are particularly strong during the first trimester. Since that's when the fetus is most vulnerable, aversions to coffee or alcohol are very protective, says Rodin.

When food cravings (or aversions) have an obsessional quality, or are persis-   25 tent, it may indicate a more serious eating disorder such as bulimia or anorexia, she says. For most of us, cravings are either short-lived or the result of temporary stress.

Food intolerances also can cause anxiety, food cravings and obesity. Additives, irritants and toxins are common culprits. But there may be an acquired biochemical defect, such as the inability to digest milk sugar (lactase deficiency). Finding *healthy* ways to boost our moods through endorphins and other brain chemicals could even keep us from falling into dangerous addictions.

Mood Medicine

Food cravings can be the undoing of even the most conscientious eaters. So, how do we deal with them? "You can't control the fact that cravings occur," says Dr. Harvey Ross, psychiatrist and author of *The Mood Control Diet* (Prentice Hall, 1990). "But you can control how you react to them."

His research shows that certain foods, or substances concentrated from them, can be used in the same way as drugs to improve your sleep or the way you handle stress. Avoiding "trigger" foods can be effective in treating disorders as varied as depression and yeast infections.

The most controversial aspect of food cravings or intolerances is the claim that they are often the underlying causes of such disorders as hypoglycemia (low blood sugar), allergies, anemia, and chronic fatigue. Most allergists dispute such claims, but additional studies may eventually bear out many of them.

If you find yourself craving inordinate amounts of the following, consult your   30
physician to rule out any serious medical condition:

Salt. Excessive cravings can be a sign of adrenal insufficiency in which tissues and blood are depleted of saltwater, and blood pressure plummets.

Water. Constant thirst may signal juvenile or adult-onset diabetes. Weight loss may also occur despite constant hunger or voracious eating.

Sugar. Severe cravings may be a symptom of reactive hyperglycemia and the body's inability to maintain adequate levels of blood sugar (glucose).

Ice. Persistent need can be a sign of anemia (sore mouth or tongue) or chronic kidney disease due to disturbances in blood chemistry.

Nonfoods. Abnormal cravings for items such as laundry starch by pregnant   35
women and paint chips by children is known as pica. Fetal risk and lead poisoning are possible effects.

Reflecting and Interpreting

1. What rhetorical device does Brown use in the first and second paragraphs?

2. Dr. Judith Wurtman advises eating certain foods to alleviates stress and increase alertness. What are they? What four examples does she give?

3. Dr. Wurtman claims that sugar has a calming effect. Do you agree or disagree? Is it possible that different people react differently to sugar?

4. What hormone is thought to "hold the key to why we pig out"? Yet what do behaviorists argue as being more "addictive than calories and nutrients"?

5. Researchers speculate that in some people, food cravings increase the output of endorphins, mood-altering brain chemicals. How can endorphins affect us?

6. What is the most controversial aspect of food cravings or intolerances?

7. The author cites five kinds of cravings that deserve the attention of a physician. What are they?

8. You may have to hunt to find Brown's thesis. What is the main idea of this essay? How would you state it in your own words?

9. Although the author cites research, this is not a technical article. How does he achieve the light tone?

10. How would you rate Brown's objectivity in presenting this research?

A Writer's Response

1. Before your group begins, appoint someone to chart categories of individual food cravings and the times they occur. Then share experiences. What factors seem to affect your cravings? Do you attempt to control them? What seems to work best? After the discussion, tally the responses and read them to the group.

2. What are your favorite foods? Do you experience cravings at particular times? Do you think they reveal anything about your personality? Write a short essay analyzing and classifying your eating habits.

Where Do We Stand?

Lisa Davis

Have you noticed any slight differences in behavior or conversational style among students of varying cultures on your campus? In this essay, first published in In Health *magazine, Lisa Davis discusses how different spatial needs and eye contact can cause hasty judgments and misunderstanding. Davis graduated with a B.A. in psychology from the University of California and an M.S. in Education and Psychology from California State University. She has served as advisor to the San Joaquin Family Preservation and Family Support Program and received awards from the Sierra Health Foundation (1995), City of Manteca (1995), University of California (1992), and an Excellence award (1998). Davis has published* Journeys Within: Source Book of Guided Meditations *(1997) and several health articles for various publications.*

Call it the dance of the jet set, the diplomat's tango: A man from the Middle East, say, falls into conversation with an American, becomes animated, takes a step forward. The American makes a slight postural adjustment, shifts his feet, edges backward. A little more talk and the Arab advances; a little more talk and the American retreats.

"By the end of the cocktail party," says Middle East expert Peter Bechtold of the State Department's Foreign Service Institute, "you have an American in each corner of the room, because that's as far as they can back up."

What do you do when an amiable chat leaves one person feeling vaguely bullied, the other unaccountably chilled? Things would be simpler if these jetsetters were speaking different languages—they'd just get themselves a translator. But the problem's a little tougher, because they're using different languages of space.

Everyone who's ever felt cramped in a crowd knows that the skin is not the body's only boundary. We each wear a zone of privacy like a hoop skirt, inviting others in or keeping them out with body language—by how closely we approach, the angle at which we face them, the speed with which we break a gaze. It's a subtle code, but one we use and interpret easily, indeed automatically, having absorbed the vocabulary from infancy.

At least, we *assume* we're reading it right. But from culture to culture, from group to group within a single country, even between the sexes, the language of space has distinctive accents, confusing umlauts. That leaves a lot of room for misinterpretations, and the stakes have gotten higher as business has become increasingly international and populations multicultural. So a new breed of consultants has appeared in the last few years, interpreting for globe-trotters of all nationalities the meaning and use of personal space.

For instance, says international business consultant Sondra Snowdon, Saudi Arabians like to conduct business discussions from within spitting distance—literally. They bathe in each other's breath as part of building the relationship.

"Americans back up," says Snowdon, "but they're harming their chances of winning the contracts." In seminars, Snowdon discusses the close quarters common in Middle Eastern conversations and has her students practice talking with each other at very chummy distances.

Still, her clients had better be careful where they take their shrunken "space bubble," because cultures are idiosyncratic in their spatial needs. Japanese subways bring people about as close together as humanly possible, for instance, yet even a handshake can be offensively physical in a Japanese office. And, says researcher and writer Mildred Reed Hall, Americans can even make their business counterparts in Japan uncomfortable with the kind of direct eye contact that's normal here.

"Not only do most Japanese businessmen not look at you, they keep their eyes down," Hall says. "We look at people for hours, and they feel like they're under a searchlight."

The study of personal space got under way in the early 1950s, when anthropologist Edward Hall described a sort of cultural continuum of personal space. (Hall has frequently collaborated with his wife, Mildred.) According to Hall, on the "high-contact" side of the continuum—in Mediterranean and South American societies, for example—social conversations include much eye contact, touching and smiling, typically while standing at a distance of about a foot. On the other end of the scale, say in Northern European cultures, a lingering gaze may feel invasive, manipulative or disrespectful; a social chat takes place at a remove of about 2½ feet.

In the middle-of-the-road United States, people usually stand about 18 inches 10
apart for this sort of conversation—unless we want to win foreign friends and influence people, in which case, research shows, we'd better adjust our posture. In one study, when British graduate students were trained to adopt Arab patterns of behavior (facing their partners straight on, with lots of eye contact and smiling), Middle Eastern exchange students found them more likable and trustworthy than typical British students.

In contrast, the misuse of space can call whole personalities into suspicion: When researchers seated pairs of women for conversation, those forced to talk at an uncomfortably large distance were more likely to describe their partners as cold and rejecting.

Don't snuggle up too fast, though. Men in that study were more irritated by their partners when they were forced to talk at close range. Spatially speaking, it seems men and women are subtly foreign to each other. No matter whether a society operates at arm's length or cheek-to-jowl, the women look at each other more and stand a bit closer than do the men.

Anthropologist Hall suggests that a culture's use of space is evidence of a reliance on one sense over another: Middle Easterners get much of their information through their senses of smell and touch, he says, which require a close approach; Americans rely primarily on visual information, backing up in order to see an intelligible picture.

Conversational distances also tend to reflect the standard greeting distance in each culture, says State Department expert Bechtold. Americans shake hands, and then talk at arm's length. Arabs do a Hollywood-style, cheek-to-cheek social kiss, and their conversation is similarly up close and personal. And, at a distance great enough to keep heads from knocking together—about two feet—the Japanese bow and talk to each other. On the other hand, the need for more or less space may reflect something of a cultural temperament. "There's no word for privacy in Arab cultures," says Bechtold. "They think it means loneliness."

Whatever their origin, spatial styles are very real. In fact, even those who set   15
out to transgress find it uncomfortable to intrude on the space of strangers, says psychologist John Aiello at Rutgers University. "I've had students say, 'Boy, that was the hardest thing I ever had to do—to stand six inches away when I was asking those questions.'"

Luckily, given coaching and time, it seems to get easier to acculturate to foreign habits of contact. Says Bechtold, "You often see men holding hands in the Middle East and walking down the street together. It's just that they're concerned and don't want you to cross the street unescorted, but I've had American pilots come in here and say, 'I don't want some SOB holding my hand.' Then I see them there, holding the hand of a Saudi."

"Personal space isn't so hard for people to learn," Bechtold adds. "What is really much harder is the business of dinner being served at midnight."

Reflecting and Interpreting

1. How does Davis classify people in this essay?
2. What divisions of conversational distances are discussed?
3. What is unusual about the way the first example is given? Describe the tone.
4. How does Davis establish credibility in the second paragraph and again later?
5. What function does paragraph 3 serve?
6. Davis makes unusual comparisons. Identify the literary devices in "a zone of privacy like a hoop skirt" and "bathe in each other's breath."
7. How do the personal space needs of Americans and those of Middle Eastern people generally differ? What American habits make Japanese uncomfortable?
8. Who studied the use of personal space? At what average distance do Americans converse? How does this distance vary with gender?
9. What danger exists in nonverbal communication?
10. How do greetings and other habits influence personal space? How does this vary from culture to culture? Is it difficult to learn about this topic? To adapt?

A Writer's Response

In your future career, will it be beneficial for you to be keenly aware of cultural diversity? Why or why not? Write an essay explaining your point of view.

How Do We Find the Student in a World of Academic Gymnasts and Worker Ants?

James T. Baker

Categorizing individuals is risky business, especially if you are not a member of the group you are classifying. Study carefully how James Baker delineates types of college students he has known and think about the implications. This essay, in which Professor Baker reveals as much about himself as about his students, was first published in The Chronicle of Higher Education. *Baker has also written* Brooks Hays *(1989),* Studs Terkel *(1992), and* Eleanor Roosevelt: First Lady *(1998). He coauthored* A Headstart: Study Tips for the Student of Western Civilization: A Brief History since 1300 *(1998).*

Anatole France once wrote that "the whole art of teaching is only the art of awakening the natural curiosity of young minds." I fully agree, except I have to wonder if, by using the word "only," he thought that the art of awakening such natural curiosity was an easy job. For me, it never has been—sometimes exciting, always challenging, but definitely not easy.

Robert M. Hutchins used to say that a good education prepares students to go on educating themselves throughout their lives. A fine definition, to be sure, but it has at times made me doubt that my own students, who seem only too eager to graduate so they can lay down their books forever, are receiving a good education.

But then maybe these are merely the pessimistic musings of someone suffering from battle fatigue. I have almost qualified for my second sabbatical leave, and I am scratching a severe case of the seven-year itch. About the only power my malaise has not impaired is my eye for spotting certain "types" of students. In fact, as the rest of me declines, my eye seems to grow more acute.

Has anyone else noticed that the very same students people college classrooms year after year? Has anyone else found the same bodies, faces, personalities returning semester after semester? Forgive me for violating my students' individual "personhoods," but reality makes it so tempting to see them as types. Doubtless you will recognize at least some of them. They have twins, or perhaps clones, on your campus, too.

There is the eternal Good Time Charlie (or Charlene), who makes every party on and off the campus, who by November of his freshman year has worked his face into a case of terminal acne, who misses every set of examinations because of "mono," who finally burns himself out physically and mentally by the age of 19 and drops out to go home and recuperate, and who returns at 20 after a long talk with Dad to major in accounting.

There is the Young General Patton, the one who comes to college on an R.O.T.C. scholarship and for a year twirls his rifle at basketball games while loudly sniffing out pinko professors, who at midpoint takes a sudden but predictable, radical swing from far right to far left, who grows a beard and moves in with a girl who refuses to shave her legs, who then makes the just as predictable, radical swing back to the right and ends up preaching fundamentalist sermons on the steps of the student union while the Good Time Charlies and Charlenes jeer.

There is the Egghead, the campus intellectual who shakes up his fellow students—and even a professor or two—with references to esoteric formulas and obscure Bulgarian poets, who is recognized by friend and foe alike as a promising young academic, someday to be a professional scholar, who disappears every summer for six weeks ostensibly to search for primeval human remains in Colorado caves, and who at 37 is shot dead by Arab terrorists while on a mission for the C.I.A.

There is the Performer—the music or theater major, the rock or folk singer—who spends all of his or her time working up an act, who gives barely a nod to mundane subjects like history, sociology, or physics, who dreams only of the day he or she will be on stage full time, praised by critics, cheered by audiences, who ends up either pregnant or responsible for a pregnancy and at 30 is either an insurance salesman or a housewife with a very lush garden.

There is the Jock, of course—the every-afternoon intramural champ, smelling of liniment and Brut, with bulging calves and a blue-eyed twinkle, the subject of untold numbers of female fantasies, the walking personification of he-man-ism—who upon graduation is granted managerial rank by a California bank because of his golden tan and low golf score, who is seen five years later buying the drinks at a San Francisco gay bar.

There is the Academic Gymnast—the guy or gal who sees college as an obstacle course, as so many stumbling blocks in the way of a great career or a perfect marriage—who strains every moment to finish and be done with "this place" forever, who toward the end of the junior year begins to slow down, to grow quieter and less eager to leave, who attends summer school, but never quite finishes those last six hours, who never leaves "this place," and who at 40 is still working at the campus laundry, still here, still a student. 10

There is the Medal Hound, the student who comes to college not to learn or expand any intellectual horizons but simply to win honors—medals, cups, plates, ribbons, scrolls—who is here because this is the best place to win the most the fastest, who plasticizes and mounts on his wall every certificate of excellence he wins, who at 39 will be a colonel in the U.S. Army and at 55 Secretary of something or other in a conservative Administration in Washington.

There is the Worker Ant, the student (loosely rendered) who takes 21 hours a semester and works 49 hours a week at the local car wash, who sleeps only on Sundays and during classes, who will somehow graduate on time and be the owner of his own vending-machine company at 30 and be dead of a heart attack at 40, and who will be remembered for the words chiseled on his tombstone:

All This Was Accomplished Without Ever Having So Much as Darkened The Door Of A Library

There is the Lost Soul, the sad kid who is in college only because teachers, parents, and society at large said so, who hasn't a career in mind or a dream to follow, who hasn't a clue, who heads home every Friday afternoon to spend the weekend cruising the local Dairee-Freeze, who at 50 will have done all his teachers, parents, and society said to do, still without a career in mind or a dream to follow or a clue.

There is also the Saved Soul—the young woman who has received, through   15 the ministry of one Gospel freak or another, a Holy Calling to save the world, or at least some special part of it—who majors in Russian studies so that she can be caught smuggling Bibles into the Soviet Union and be sent to Siberia where she can preach to souls imprisoned by the Agents of Satan in the Gulag Archipelago.

Then, finally, there is the Happy Child, who comes to college to find a husband or wife—and finds one—and there is the Determined Child, who comes to get a degree—and gets one.

Enough said.

All of which, I suppose, should make me throw up my hands in despair and say that education, like youth and love, is wasted on the young. Not quite.

For there does come along, on occasion, that one of a hundred or so who is maybe at first a bit lost, certainly puzzled; who may well start out a Good Timer, an Egghead, a Performer, a Jock, a Medal Hound, a Gymnast, a Worker Ant; who may indeed have trouble settling on a major, who will be distressed by what sometimes passes for education, who might even be a temporary dropout; but who has a vital capacity for growth and is able to fall in love with learning, who acquires a taste for intellectual pleasure, who becomes in the finest sense of the word a Student.

This is the one who keeps the most jaded of us going back to class after class,   20 and he or she must be oh-so-carefully cultivated. He or she must be artfully awakened, given the tools needed to continue learning for a lifetime, and let grow at whatever pace and in whatever direction nature dictates.

For I try always to remember that this student is me, my continuing self, my immortality. This person is my only hope that my own search for Truth will continue after me, on and on, forever.

Reflecting and Interpreting

1. Do you agree with Anatole France's definition of the art of teaching? Why or why not?
2. What is the question behind the opening paragraph? In paragraph 2?
3. The third paragraph is self-deprecating. How does he feel? Yet he makes a claim. What is it?
4. Paragraphs 5 to 16 set forth categories of students. Are all categories equally well done? Are any underdeveloped? Do any overlap or lack clarity?

5. What is the tone of the description about the "Lost Soul"?

6. What literary device is present in the description of the Jock?

7. Evaluate the objectivity of each category. Is Baker harder on some types of students than others? Which remarks border on insult?

8. In using humor there is always the risk of offending someone. How did you feel when you read his classifications? Would the humor be suitable for Baker's intended audience of college faculty?

9. Can you recognize yourself or your peers in any of these categories? What are the categories? What does this say about Baker's essay?

10. Did your response change when you came to the last four paragraphs? Why or why not? What does the author reveal about himself and his values?

A Writer's Response

1. Turn the tables on Baker! Sort professors into categories similar to his categories for students. Add a final, positive example, called "The Teacher." For help in writing the essay, see chapter 14.

2. Would you have liked a different ending for Baker's essay? Perhaps you could allude to the title in some way or write an ending that has universal appeal.

3. *Small Groups:* Discuss how you decide when someone is crossing the line on humor in writing or in conversation. Can you devise some guidelines?

Comparison–Contrast

Exploring Likeness and Difference

 ## A Nonsmoker with a Smoker

Phillip Lopate

Phillip Lopate, a well-known essayist, is the author of Against Joie de Vivre: Personal Essays *(1989), from which this essay is taken. Lopate, a nonsmoker, ponders his thoughts on smoking, contrasting the feelings and views of smokers and nonsmokers. He creates a kaleidoscope of images which cause us to feel—not merely see—first one side of smoking and then the other. The result? A remarkably balanced viewpoint. Lopate is also a poet, fiction writer, literary and film critic, as well as editor of several anthologies of essays. He has published several books, including* The Ordering Mirror: Readers and Contexts *(1993),* Totally, Tenderly, Tragically: Essays and Criticism from a Lifelong Love Affair with the Movies *(1998), and* John Koch: Painting a New York Life *(2001).*

Last Saturday night my girlfriend, Helen, and I went to a dinner party in the Houston suburbs. We did not know our hosts, but were invited on account of Helen's chum Barry, whose birthday party it was. We had barely stepped into the house and met the other guests, seated on a U-shaped couch under an A-framed ceiling, when Helen lit a cigarette. The hostess froze. "Uh, could you please not smoke in here? If you have to, we'd appreciate your using the terrace. We're both sort of allergic."

Helen smiled understandingly and moved toward the glass doors leading to the backyard in a typically ladylike way, as though merely wanting to get a better look at the garden. But I knew from that gracious "Southern" smile of hers that she was miffed.

As soon as Helen had stepped outside, the hostess explained that they had just moved into this house, and that it had taken weeks to air out because of the previous owner's tenacious cigar smoke. A paradigmatically awkward conversation about tobacco ensued: like testifying sinners, two people came forward with confessions about kicking the nasty weed; our scientist-host cited a recent study of indoor air pollution levels; a woman lawyer brought up the latest California legislation protecting nonsmokers; a roly-poly real estate agent admitted that, though he had given up smokes, he still sat in the smoking section of airplanes because "you meet a more interesting type of person there"—a remark his wife did not find amusing. Helen's friend Barry gallantly joined her outside. I did not, as I should have; I felt paralyzed.

For one thing, I wasn't sure which side I was on. I have never been a smoker. My parents both chain-smoked, so I grew up accustomed to cloudy interiors and ever since have been tolerant of other people's nicotine urges. To be perfectly honest, I'm not crazy about inhaling smoke, particularly when I've got a cold, but that irritating inconvenience pales beside the damage that would be done to my pluralistic worldview if I did not defend smokers' rights.

On the other hand, a part of me wished Helen *would* stop smoking. That part 5 seemed to get a satisfaction out of the group's "banishing" her: they were doing the dirty work of expressing my disapproval.

As soon as I realized this, I joined her in the garden. Presently a second guest strolled out to share a forbidden toke, then a third. Our hostess ultimately had to collect the mutineers with an announcement that dinner was served.

At the table, Helen appeared to be having such a good time, joking with our hosts and everyone else, that I was unprepared for the change that came over her as soon as we were alone in the car afterward. "I will never go back to that house!" she declared. "Those people have no concept of manners or hospitality, humiliating me the moment I stepped in the door. And that phony line about 'sort of allergic'!"

Normally, Helen is forbearance personified. Say anything that touches her about smoking, however, and you touch the rawest of nerves. I remembered the last time I foolishly suggested that she "think seriously" about stopping. I had just read one of those newspaper articles about the increased possibility of heart attacks, lung cancer, and birth deformities among women smokers, and I was worried for her. My concern must have been maladroitly expressed, because she burst into tears.

"Can't we even talk about this without your getting so sensitive?" I had asked.

"You don't understand. Nonsmokers never understand that it's a real addic- 10 tion. I've tried quitting, and it was hell. Do you want me to go around for months mean and cranky outside and angry inside? You're right, I'm sensitive, because I'm threatened with having taken away from me the thing that gives me the most pleasure in life, day in, day out," she said. I shot her a look: careful, now. "Well, practically the most pleasure. You know what I mean." I didn't. But I knew enough to drop it.

I love Helen, and if she wants to smoke, knowing the risks involved, that remains her choice. Besides, she wouldn't quit just because I wanted her to; she's not that docile, and that's part of what I love about her. Sometimes I wonder why

I even keep thinking about her quitting. What's it to me personally? Certainly I feel protective of her health, but I also have selfish motives. I don't like the way her lips taste when she's smoked a lot. I associate her smoking with nervousness, and when she lights up several cigarettes in a row, I get jittery watching her. Crazy as this may sound, I also find myself becoming jealous of her cigarettes. Occasionally, when I go to her house and we're sitting on the couch together, if I see Helen eyeing the pack I make her kiss me first, so that my lips can engage hers (still fresh) before the competition's. It's almost as though there were another lover in the room—a lover who was around long before I entered the picture, and who pleases her in mysterious ways I cannot.

A lit cigarette puts a distance between us: it's like a weapon in her hand, awakening in me a primitive fear of being burnt. The memory is not so primitive, actually. My father used to smoke absentmindedly, letting the ash grow like a caterpillar eating every leaf in its path, until gravity finally toppled it. Once, when I was about nine, my father and I were standing in line at a bakery, and he accidentally dropped a lit ash down my back. Ever since, I've inwardly winced and been on guard around these little waving torches, which epitomize to me the dangers of intimacy.

I've worked hard to understand from the outside the satisfaction of smoking. I've even smoked "sympathetic" cigarettes, just to see what the other person was experiencing. But it's not the same as being hooked. How can I really empathize with the frightened but stubborn look Helen gets in her eyes when, despite the fact we're a little late going somewhere, she turns to me in the car and says, "I need to buy a pack of cigarettes first"? I feel a wave of pity for her. We are both embarrassed by this forced recognition of her frailty—the "indignity," as she herself puts it, of being controlled by something outside her will.

I try to imagine myself in that position, but a certain smugness keeps getting in the way (I don't have that problem and *am I glad*). We pay a price for our smugness. So often it flip-flops into envy: the outsiders wish to be included in the sufferings and highs of others, as if to say that only by relinquishing control and surrendering to some dangerous habit, some vice or dependency, would one be able to experience "real life."

Over the years I have become a sucker for cigarette romanticism. Few Hollywood gestures move me as much as the one in *Now Voyager*, when Paul Henreid lights two cigarettes, one for himself, the other for Bette Davis: these form a beautiful fatalistic bridge between them, a complicitous understanding like the realization that their love is based on the inevitability of separation. I am all the more admiring of this worldly cigarette gallantry because its experiential basis escapes me.

The same sort of fascination occurs when I come across a literary description of nicotine addiction, like this passage in Mailer's *Tough Guys Don't Dance:* "Over and over again I gave them up, a hundred times over the years, but I always went back. For in my dreams, sooner or later, I struck a match, brought flame to the tip, then took in all my hunger for existence with the first puff. I felt impaled on desire itself—those fiends trapped in my chest and screaming for one drag."

"Impaled on desire itself"! Such writing evokes a longing in me for the centering of self that tobacco seems to bestow on its faithful. Clearly, there is something attractive about having this umbilical relation to the universe—this curling pillar, this spiral staircase, this prayer of smoke that mediates between the smoker's inner substance and the alien ether. Inwardness of the nicotine trance, sad wisdom ("every pleasure has its price"), beauty of ritual, squandered health—all those romantic meanings we read into the famous photographic icons of fifties saints, Albert Camus or James Agee or James Dean or Carson McCullers puffing away, in a sense they're true. Like all people who return from a brush with death, smokers have gained a certain power. They know their "coffin nails." With Helen, each cigarette is a measuring of the perishable, an enactment of her mortality, from filter to end-tip in fewer than five minutes. I could not stand to be reminded of my own death so often.

Reflecting and Interpreting

1. What is the effect of the anecdote as an opening to the essay?

2. How does Lopate feel about an issue on which most people have clear-cut opinions? Describe the tone.

3. What happens after Helen leaves the room?

4. Comment on the contrast between Helen's behavior and her feelings.

5. Lopate admits that he has selfish reasons for wanting Helen to quit smoking. What are they? Comment on the image near the end of paragraph 11.

6. Can you find two vivid similes that dramatize Lopate's deep feelings about *tobacco?*

7. What is the "cigarette romanticism" that he mentions? Do you think it is still prevalent? Why or why not?

8. Despite Lopate's attraction to a smoker and smoking, he does not smoke. Why?

9. After reading the essay, how do you feel about the author? How does he sound?

10. For Lopate, cigarettes have also acquired a deadly symbolism: "an enactment of . . . mortality." Where does he explain this?

A Writer's Response

1. Using some of Lopate's techniques, compare and contrast two views in an essay. For example, you might discuss a habit you disapprove of but, nonetheless, tolerate in someone you love.

2. *Small Groups:* Summarize the viewpoint of the host and hostess, listing their reasons. Then summarize the view of smokers. Now analyze. Which reasons are based on fact? On emotion? What about etiquette? Who was being rude?

Americans: Conservationists or Champion Land Hogs?

Neal R. Peirce

Are you dismayed at the deterioration and urban sprawl as you drive through many American cities? Journalist Neal R. Peirce is greatly concerned because conservationists are losing the tug of war over land use. In this essay, originally printed in the Washington Post, *he advocates political action to preserve cities and slow the disappearance of the countryside. Peirce has written or collaborated on nineteen books, including* The Electoral College Primer *(2000),* Boundary Crossers: Community Leadership for a Global Age *(1997),* Citistates: How Urban America Can Prosper in a Competitive World *(1994), and* Breakthroughs: Re-Creating the American City *(1993).*

Check in almost any region you like and you discover that Americans *say* they want diverse, colorful, people-friendly, well-used downtowns and neighborhoods. [1]

A rush of "Vision 2000" or "2020" plans have been produced by broad-based citizen committees—some acting independently, some with government support—from Seattle to Orlando, Indianapolis to Louisville, Chattanooga to Tempe, Ariz. Almost all place high value on historic preservation, lively streets, and public transit accessibility.

Nor, do we seem to like the idea of endless suburban sprawl. Our vision statements endorse preservation of open space in and around our regions.

Yet there's a deep chasm between what Americans say we want and what, as consumers choosing places to live and work, we actually do.

We may indeed be the champion land hogs of history. Our urban areas devour land four to eight times faster than their population grows. The New York area's population increase over the past 25 years has been only 5 percent, but the developed land has increased by 61 percent, devouring nearly 25 percent of the region's forests and farmland. [5]

And while we say we like—even romanticize—old-style town life, we accept suburban development patterns of rigidly compartmentalized, single-purpose land uses that destroy community by obliging us to drive everywhere.

We say we value public transit, but we stick to our private cars. During the 1980s, while mass transit systems languished, the number of Americans driving their cars all alone to work soared by 22 million, or 35 percent, several million more than the 18 million workers added to the national work force.

We call for preserving the open countryside, but we rush to the new subdivisions and "edge cities." Virtually all European "citistates" have set up and enforce urban growth boundaries. But not us. Only Oregon enforces truly strict growth boundaries around its cities.

Real estate expert Christopher Leinberger traces multiple stages of U.S. commercial development. From the old downtowns, we began to branch out in the '60s to close-in commercial centers like Bala Cynwyd near Philadelphia and the northern reaches of Phoenix's seemingly interminable Central Avenue. Then, from the mid '70s through the '80s, development exploded into such mega-developments as Tysons Corner, Va., in the Washington suburbs, King of Prussia, Pa., Denver's Tech Center and Bellevue across Lake Washington from Seattle.

Yet another wave began in the late '80s—to such distant development centers as Houston's 290 corridor, Loudoun County, Va., (an hour's congested drive from Washington), and Mesa outside of Phoenix. 10

In the meantime, our inner cities have suffered immense disinvestment and have lost hundreds of thousands of jobs.

And what next? When the recession truly ends, will investment in our downtowns and older suburbs pick up again? Are we ready to reject exploitative sprawl?

Probably not, say most of the experts. "Now that so many jobs have moved to the fringe," predicts Leinberger, "new housing can go another 20 miles out. There will be a leapfrog effect."

Metropolitan Cleveland provides a typical example. As long as most jobs were in or near downtown Cleveland, a 30-minute commute limited people to fairly close-by suburbs in Cuyahoga County.

But now, with the interstates complete and so-called "edge city" commercial 15 centers sprung up around the regional periphery, the 30-minute commuting range has moved far beyond Cuyahoga County. And potential new suburbs show up as an eerie blob on the planners' maps, spreading far out into still-rural areas of Lorain, Medina, Summit, Portage, Geauga and Lake Counties.

"Edge cities," reports EcoCity Cleveland Journal, "not only make it possible for suburbia to chew up more woods and farmlands. They also promote more commuting across suburbs, more congestion on suburban and rural roads, more energy consumption and pollution, and a more dispersed population that cannot be served by mass transit."

To that, one must add the gruesome social cost as new job locations proceed farther and farther out into the countryside. Some inner-city folks might have found a way to get to jobs in a Country Club Plaza beside Kansas City, or Towson near Baltimore, or L.A.'s Century City. But it's virtually impossible for them to get to such distant places as Ontario (34 miles from L.A.), or Hoffman Estates—the spot 37 miles from Chicago's Loop to which Sears escaped, jettisoning practically all its Chicago work force.

Our land use practices threaten social conflagration in our cities. But corporate America doesn't seem to care. Not a single major corporate relocation in America in the last four years, notes Leinberger, "has gone anywhere except the absolute metropolitan fringe."

In the boardrooms, the distant "campus-like" settings may seem to make sense—the land, after all, is cheap and easily assembled, and it turns out that the executives, with uncanny regularity, live nearby.

But the public costs—despair in the inner cities, environmental degradation, undermining of older neighborhoods and suburbs—are frightening. Romantic visions about our communities need to be transformed into tough political action that sets meaningful growth boundaries around our burgeoning citistates—and insists that *all* developers and corporations honor them. 20

Reflecting and Interpreting

1. Where is the thesis statement? How does it function in that spot?
2. How does the rate of land consumption by the encroachment of "edge cities" compare with the increase in population? What accounts for this?
3. How many cars does the average family own where you live? How do multiple cars contribute to the loss of the countryside?
4. What does Peirce mean by the "gruesome social cost" of this phenomenon?
5. How has this pattern of growth affected the environment?
6. What can businesses and manufacturers do to promote ride sharing? What rule was enacted to limit traffic in Manhattan after September 11, 2001?
7. The author criticizes suburban development patterns of "rigidly compartmentalized, single-purpose land" (zoning for single homes). What countertrend does he neglect to mention?
8. What action does the author advocate to conserve land and preserve cities? Do you know of any other measures that some cities have taken?
9. Do you see any risks in placing restrictions other than zoning on businesses and industries? What might happen?
10. Does Peirce use the block or alternate block organization in this essay? How would the essay have been changed if he had used the other method?

A Writer's Response

Compare and contrast the city you live in as it was thirty years ago with how it is today. Is it suffering from urban blight? Have any steps been taken?

Mother Tongue

Amy Tan

Born and raised in California, Amy Tan (1952–) graduated from high school in Montreux, Switzerland. She earned a master's degree in linguistics from San Jose State University. Her first novel The Joy Luck Club *(1988), brought her international acclaim. Her other works include* The Kitchen God's Wife *(1991),* The Hundred Secret Senses *(1995),* The Bonesetter's Daughter *(2001), and two children's books—*The Moon Lady *and* The Chinese Siamese Cat. *Tan's books have been translated into twenty languages. This essay first appeared in* Threepenny Review *(1989).*

I am not a scholar of English or literature. I cannot give you much more than 1 personal opinions on the English language and its variations in this country or others.

I am a writer. And by that definition, I am someone who has always loved language. I am fascinated by language in daily life. I spend a great deal of my time thinking about the power of language—the way it can evoke an emotion, a visual image, a complex idea, or a simple truth. Language is the tool of my trade. And I use them all—all the Englishes I grew up with.

Recently, I was made keenly aware of the different Englishes I do use. I was giving a talk to a large group of people, the same talk I had already given to half a dozen other groups. The nature of the talk was about my writing, my life, and my book, *The Joy Luck Club*. The talk was going along well enough, until I remembered one major difference that made the whole talk sound wrong. My mother was in the room. And it was perhaps the first time she had heard me give a lengthy speech, using the kind of English I have never used with her. I was saying things like, "The intersection of memory upon imagination" and "There is an aspect of my fiction that relates to thus-and-thus"—a speech filled with carefully wrought grammatical phrases, burdened, it suddenly seemed to me, with nominalized forms, past perfect tenses, conditional phrases, all the forms of standard English that I had learned in school and through books, the forms of English I did not use at home with my mother.

Just last week, I was walking down the street with my mother, and I again found myself conscious of the English I was using, the English I do use with her. We were talking about the price of new and used furniture and I heard myself saying this: "Not waste money that way." My husband was with us as well, and he didn't notice any switch in my English. And then I realized why. It's because over the twenty years we've been together I've often used that same kind of English with him, and sometimes he even uses it with me. It has become our language of intimacy, a different sort of English that relates to family talk, the language I grew up with.

So you'll have some idea of what this family talk I heard sounds like, I'll quote 5 what my mother said during a recent conversation which I videotaped and then transcribed. During this conversation, my mother was talking about a political gangster in Shanghai who had the same last name as her family's, Du, and how the gangster in his early years wanted to be adopted by her family, which was rich by comparison. Later, the gangster became more powerful, far richer than my mother's family, and one day showed up at my mother's wedding to pay his respects. Here's what she said in part:

"Du Yusong having business like fruit stand. Like off the street kind. He is Du like Du Zong—but not Tsung-ming Island people. The local people call putong, the river east side, he belong to that side local people. That man want to ask Du Zong father take him in like become own family. Du Zong father wasn't look down on him, but didn't take seriously, until that man big like become a mafia. Now important person, very hard to inviting him. Chinese way, came only to show respect, don't stay for dinner. Respect for making big celebration, he shows up. Mean gives lots of respect. Chinese custom. Chinese social life that way. If too important won't have to stay too long. He come to my wedding. I didn't see, I heard it. I gone to boy's side, they have YMCA dinner. Chinese age I was nineteen."

You should know that my mother's expressive command of English belies how much she actually understands. She reads the *Forbes* report, listens to *Wall Street Week*, converses daily with her stockbroker, reads all of Shirley MacLaine's books with ease—all kinds of things I can't begin to understand. Yet some of my friends tell me they understand 50 percent of what my mother says. Some say they understand 80 to 90 percent. Some say they understand none of it, as if she were speaking pure Chinese. But to me, my mother's English is perfectly clear, perfectly natural. It's my mother tongue. Her language, as I hear it, is vivid, direct, full of observation and imagery. That was the language that helped shape the way I saw things, expressed things, made sense of the world.

Lately, I've been giving more thought to the kind of English my mother speaks. Like others, I have described it to people as "broken" or "fractured" English. But I wince when I say that. It has always bothered me that I can think of no way to describe it other than "broken," as if it were damaged and needed to be fixed, as if it lacked a certain wholeness and soundness. I've heard other terms used, "limited English," for example. But they seem just as bad, as if everything is limited, including people's perceptions of the limited English speaker.

I know this for a fact, because when I was growing up, my mother's "limited" English limited *my* perception of her. I was ashamed of her English. I believed that her English reflected the quality of what she had to say. That is, because she expressed them imperfectly her thoughts were imperfect. And I had plenty of empirical evidence to support me: the fact that people in department stores, at banks, and at restaurants did not take her seriously, did not give her good service, pretended not to understand her, or even acted as if they did not hear her.

My mother has long realized the limitations of her English as well. When I   10
was fifteen, she used to have me call people on the phone to pretend I was she.
In this guise, I was forced to ask for information or even to complain and yell at
people who had been rude to her. One time it was a call to her stockbroker in
New York. She had cashed out her small portfolio and it just so happened we
were going to go to New York the next week, our very first trip outside California. I had to get on the phone and say in an adolescent voice that was not very
convincing, "This is Mrs. Tan."

And my mother was standing in the back whispering loudly, "Why he don't
send me check, already two weeks late. So mad he lie to me, losing me money."

And then I said in perfect English, "Yes, I'm getting rather concerned. You
had agreed to send the check two weeks ago, but it hasn't arrived."

Then she began to talk more loudly. "What he want, I come to New York tell
him front of his boss, you cheating me?" And I was trying to calm her down, make
her be quiet, while telling the stockbroker, "I can't tolerate any more excuses. If I
don't receive the check immediately, I am going to have to speak to your manager
when I'm in New York next week." And sure enough, the following week there
we were in front of this astonished stockbroker, and I was sitting there redfaced
and quiet, and my mother, the real Mrs. Tan, was shouting at his boss in her impeccable broken English.

We used a similar routine just five days ago, for a situation that was far less
humorous. My mother had gone to the hospital for an appointment, to find out
about a benign brain tumor a CAT scan had revealed a month ago. She said she
had spoken very good English, her best English, no mistakes. Still, she said, the
hospital did not apologize when they said they had lost the CAT scan and she had
come for nothing. She said they did not seem to have any sympathy when she told
them she was anxious to know the exact diagnosis, since her husband and son had
both died of brain tumors. She said they would not give her any more information until the next time and she would have to make another appointment for
that. So she said she would not leave until the doctor called her daughter. She
wouldn't budge. And when the doctor finally called her daughter, me, who spoke
in perfect English—lo and behold—we had assurances the CAT scan would be
found, promise that a conference call on Monday would be held, and apologies
for any suffering my mother had gone through for a most regrettable mistake.

I think my mother's English almost had an effect on limiting my possibilities   15
in life as well. Sociologists and linguists probably will tell you that a person's developing language skills are more influenced by peers. But I do think that the language spoken in the family, especially in immigrant families which are more in-
sular, plays a large role in shaping the language of the child. And I believe that it
affected my results on achievement tests, IQ tests, and the SAT. While my English skills were never judged as poor, compared to math, English could not be
considered my strong suit. In grade school I did moderately well, getting perhaps
B's, sometimes B-pluses, in English and scoring perhaps in the sixtieth or seventi-
eth percentile on achievement tests. But those scores were not good enough to

override the opinion that my true abilities lay in math and science, because in those areas I achieved A's and scored in the ninetieth percentile or higher.

This was understandable. Math is precise; there is only one correct answer. Whereas, for me at least, the answers on English tests were always a judgment call, a matter of opinion and personal experience. Those tests were constructed around items like fill-in-the-blank sentence completion, such as, "Even though Tom was _____, Mary thought he was _____." And the correct answer always seemed to be the most bland combinations of thoughts, for example, "Even though Tom was shy, Mary thought he was charming," with the grammatical structure "even though" limiting the correct answer to some sort of semantic opposites, so you wouldn't get answers like, "Even though Tom was foolish, Mary thought he was ridiculous." Well, according to my mother, there were very few limitations as to what Tom could have been and what Mary might have thought of him. So I never did well on tests like that.

The same was true with word analogies, pairs of words in which you were supposed to find some sort of logical, semantic relationship—for example, "*Sunset* is to *nightfall* as _____ is to _____." And here you would be presented with a list of four possible pairs, one of which showed the same kind of relationship: *red* is to *stoplight, bus* is to *arrival, chills* is to *fever, yawn* is to *boring.* Well, I could never think that way. I knew what the tests were asking, but I could not block out of my mind the images already created by the first pair, "*sunset* is to *nightfall*"— and I would see a burst of color against a darkening sky, the moon rising, the lowering of a curtain of stars. And all the other pairs of words—red, bus, stoplight, boring—just threw up a mass of confusing images, making it impossible for me to sort out something as logical as saying: "A sunset precedes nightfall" is the same as "a chill precedes a fever." The only way I would have gotten that answer right would have been to imagine an associative situation, for example, by being disobedient and staying out past sunset, catching a chill at night which turns into feverish pneumonia as punishment, which indeed did happen to me.

I have been thinking about all this lately, about my mother's English, about achievement tests. Because lately I've been asked, as a writer, why there are not more Asian Americans represented in American literature. Why are there few Asian Americans enrolled in creative writing programs? Why do so many Chinese students go into engineering? Well, these are broad sociological questions I can't begin to answer. But I have noticed in surveys—in fact, just last week—that Asian students, as a whole, always do significantly better on math achievement tests than in English. And this makes me think that there are other Asian-American students whose English spoken in the home might also be described as "broken" or "limited." And perhaps they also have teachers who are steering them away from writing and into math and science, which is what happened to me.

Fortunately, I happen to be rebellious in nature and enjoy the challenge of disproving assumptions made about me. I became an English major my first year in college, after being enrolled as pre-med. I started writing nonfiction as a free-lancer the week after I was told by my former boss that writing was my worst skill and I should hone my talents toward account management.

But it wasn't until 1985 that I finally began to write fiction. And at first I   20 wrote using what I thought to be wittily crafted sentences, sentences that would finally prove I had mastery over the English language. Here's an example from the first draft of a story that later made its way into *The Joy Luck Club*, but without this line: "That was my mental quandary in its nascent state." A terrible line, which I can hardly pronounce.

Fortunately, for reasons I won't get into today, I later decided I should envision a reader for the stories I would write. And the reader I decided upon was my mother, because these were stories about mothers. So with this reader in mind—and in fact she did read my early drafts—I began to write stories using all the Englishes I grew up with: the English I spoke to my mother, which for lack of a better term might be described as "simple"; the English she used with me, which for lack of a better term might be described as "broken"; my translation of her Chinese, which could certainly be described as "watered down"; and what I imagine to be her translation of her Chinese if she could speak in perfect English, her internal language, and for that I sought to preserve the essence, but neither an English nor a Chinese structure. I wanted to capture what language ability tests can never reveal: her intent, her passion, her imagery, the rhythms of her speech and the nature of her thoughts.

Apart from what any critic had to say about my writing, I knew I had succeeded where it counted when my mother finished reading my book and gave me her verdict: "So easy to read."

Reflecting and Interpreting

1. Note how the author opens the first two paragraphs. What parallel pattern does she use to precede the definition? ("I am not . . . I am.") What technique is this?

2. How does Amy Tan define *writer*?

3. How did her mother's English influence Amy?

4. Amy Tan and her husband sometimes use her "mother's tongue" to communicate when they are alone. Why?

5. Does Amy's mother's English reflect the depth of her understanding of the language? How do you know?

6. How do the public and hospital employees react to Mrs. Tan's broken English?

7. What does Amy Tan notice about math and English test scores of Asian students? How does this affect course scheduling in high schools?

8. How does Amy Tan react to disillusionment?

9. What advantages does Standard English have over broken English?

10. If this essay had been written in third person by a biographer, how would that change have affected the essay?

A Writer's Response

1. Have you ever turned disillusionment or failure into something positive? Write an essay describing how you achieved this feat.

2. *Small Groups:* How many tips for good writing can you glean from this essay?

Women and Men Talking on the Job

Deborah Tannen

Do you ever wonder how you can be more persuasive in presenting your ideas? If so, Deborah Tannen, a linguistics professor at Georgetown University in Washington, DC has a book for you. Her seventeen works not only cover a range of communication styles but also offer fascinating insights and helpful suggestions. You Just Don't Understand *(1990) held the top spot on the bestseller list for eight months and remained on the list for nearly four years. Some of her better known books include* That's Not What I Meant! *(1987),* The Argument Culture *(1999),* I Only Say This Because I Love You *(2001), and* Talking from 9 to 5: Women and Men in the Workplace: Language, Sex, and Power *(2001). This essay is taken from an earlier edition of* Talking from 9 to 5 *(1994).*

Negotiating Styles

The managers of a medium-sized company got the go-ahead to hire a human-resources coordinator, and two managers who worked well together were assigned to make the choice. As it turned out Maureen and Harold favored different applicants, and both felt strongly about their preferences. Maureen argued with assurance and vigor that the person she wanted to hire was the most creative and innovative, and that he had the most appropriate experience. Harold argued with equal conviction that the applicant he favored had a vision of management that fit with the company's, whereas her candidate might be a thorn in their side. They traded arguments for some time, neither convincing the other. Then Harold said that hiring the applicant Maureen wanted would make him so uncomfortable that he would have to consider resigning. Maureen respected Harold. What's more, she liked and considered him a friend. So she felt that his admission of such strong feelings had to be taken into account. She said what seemed to her the only thing she could say under the circumstances: "Well, I certainly don't want you to feel uncomfortable here; you're one of the pillars of the place. If you feel that strongly about it, I can't argue with that." Harold's choice was hired.

In this case, the decision-making power went not to the manager who had the highest rank in the firm (their positions were parallel) and not necessarily to the one whose judgment was best, but to the one whose arguing strategies were most effective in the negotiation. Maureen was an ardent and persuasive advocate for her view, but she assumed that she and Harold would have to come to an agreement in order to make a decision, and that she had to take his feelings into account. Since Harold would not back down, she did. Most important, when he argued that he would have to quit if she got her way, she felt she had no option but to yield.

What was crucial was not Maureen's and Harold's individual styles in isolation but how their styles interacted—how they played in concert with the other's style. Harold's threat to quit ensures his triumph—when used with someone who would not call his bluff. If he had been arguing with someone who regarded this threat as simply another move in the negotiation rather than as a nonnegotiable expression of deep feelings that had to be respected, the result might have been different. For example, had she said, "That's ridiculous; of course you're not going to quit!" or "If that's how shallow your commitment to this firm is, then we'd be better off without you," the decision might well have gone the other way.

When you talk to someone whose style is similar to yours, you can fairly well predict the response you are going to get. But when you talk to someone whose style is different, you can't predict, and often can't make sense of, the response. Hearing the reaction you get, if it's not the one you expected, often makes you regret what you said. Harold later told Maureen that he was sorry he had used the argument he did. In retrospect he was embarrassed, even a bit ashamed of himself. His retrospective chagrin was like what you feel if you slam down something in anger and are surprised and regretful to see that it breaks. You wanted to make a gesture, but you didn't expect it to come out with such force. Harold regretted what he said precisely because it caused Maureen to back down so completely. He'd known he was upping the ante—he felt he had to do something to get them out of the loop of recycling arguments they were in—but he had not expected it to end the negotiation summarily; he expected Maureen to meet his move with a balancing move of her own. He did not predict the impact that personalizing his argument would have on her. For her part, Maureen did not think of Harold's threat as just another move in a negotiable argument; she heard it as a personal plea that she could not reject. Their different approaches to negotiation put her at a disadvantage in negotiating with him.

"How Certain Are You Of That?"

Negotiating is only one kind of activity that is accomplished through talk at work. Other kinds of decision making are also based as much on ways of talking as on the content of the arguments. The CEO of a corporation explained to me that he regularly has to make decisions based on insufficient information—and making decisions is a large part of his work life. Much of his day is spent hearing brief presentations following which he must either approve or reject a course of action. He has to make a judgment in five minutes about issues the presenters have worked on for months. "I decide," he explained, "based on how confident they seem. If they seem very confident, I call it a go. If they seem unsure, I figure it's too risky and nix it."

Here is where the rule of competence and the role of communication go hand in hand. Confidence, after all, is an internal feeling. How can you judge others' confidence? The only evidence you have to go on is circumstantial—how they talk about what they know. You judge by a range of signs, including facial expression and body posture, but most of all, speech. Do they hesitate? Do they speak or swallow half their words? Is their tone of voice declamatory or halting? Do they make bald statements ("This is a winner! We've got to go for it!") or hedge ("Um . . . from what I can tell, I think it'll work, but we'll never know for sure until we try")? This seems simple enough. Surely, you can tell how confident people are by paying attention to how they speak, just as you can tell when someone is lying.

Well, maybe not. Psychologist Paul Ekman has spent years studying lying, and he has found that most people are very sure they can tell when others are lying. The only trouble is, most can't. With a few thus-far inexplicable exceptions, people who tell him they are absolutely sure they can tell if someone is lying are as likely to be wrong as to be right—and he has found this to be as true for judges as for the rest of us.

In the same way, our ability to determine how confident others are is probably quite limited. The CEO who does not take into account the individual styles of the people who make presentations to him will find it difficult, if not impossible, to make the best judgment. Different people will talk very differently, not because of the absolute level of their confidence or lack of it, but because of their habitual ways of speaking. There are those who sound sure of themselves even when inside they're not sure at all, and others who sound tentative even when they're very sure indeed. So being aware of differences in ways of speaking is a prerequisite for making good decisions as well as good presentations.

Feasting On Humble Pie

Although these factors affecting decision making are the same for men and women, and every individual has his or her own style, it seems that women are more likely to downplay their certainty, men more likely to downplay their doubts. From childhood, girls learn to temper what they say so as not to sound too aggressive—which means too certain. From the time they are little, most girls learn that sounding too sure of themselves will make them unpopular with their peers. Groups of girls, as researchers who have studied girls at play have found, will penalize and even ostracize a girl who seems too sure she's right. Anthropologist Marjorie Harness Goodwin found that girls criticize other girls who stand out by saying, "She thinks she's cute," or "She thinks she's something." Talking in ways that display self-confidence are not approved for girls. . . .

The expectation that women should not display their own accomplishments   10
brings us back to the matter of negotiating that is so important in the workplace. A man who owned a medium-sized company remarked that women who came to ask him for raises often supported their requests by pointing to a fellow worker on the same level who earned more. He considered this a weak bargaining strategy because he could always identity a different co-worker at that level who earned less. They would do better, he felt, to argue for a raise on the basis of how valuable their own work is to the company. Yet it is likely that many women would be less comfortable "blowing their own horn" than making a claim based on fairness.

Follow the Leader

Similar expectations constrain how girls express leadership. Being a leader often involves giving directions to others, but girls who tell other girls what to do are called "bossy." It is not that girls do not exert influence on their group—of course they do—but, as anthropologists like Marjorie Harness Goodwin have found, many girls discover they get better results if they phrase their ideas as suggestions rather than orders, and if they give reasons for their suggestions in terms of the good of the group. But while these ways of talking make girls—and, later, women—more likable, they make women seem less competent and self-assured in the world of work. And women who do seem competent and self-assured are as much in danger of being negatively labeled as are girls. After her retirement, Margaret Thatcher was described in the press as "bossy." Whereas girls are ready to stick this label on each other because they don't think any girls should boss the others around, it seems odd to apply it to Thatcher, who, after all, was the boss. And this is the rub: Standards of behavior applied to women are based on roles that do not include being boss.

Boys are expected to play by different rules, since the social organization of boys is different. Boys' groups tend to be more obviously hierarchical: Someone is one-up, and someone is one-down. Boys don't typically accuse each other of being "bossy" because the high-status boys are expected to give orders and push the low-status boys around. Daniel Maltz and Ruth Borker summarize research by many scholars showing that boys tend to jockey for center stage, challenge those who get it, and deflect challenges. Giving orders and telling the others what to do are ways of getting and keeping the high-status role. Another way of getting high status is taking center stage by telling stories, jokes, and information. Along with this, many boys learn to state their opinions in the strongest possible terms and find out if they're wrong by seeing if others challenge them. These ways of talking translate into an impression of confidence.

The styles typical of women and men both make sense given the context in which they were learned, but they have very different consequences in the workplace. In order to avoid being put in the one-down position, many men have developed strategies for making sure they get the one-up position instead, and this results in ways of talking that serve them well when it comes to hiring and promotion. In relation to the examples I have given, women are more likely to speak in the styles that are less effective in getting recognized and promoted. But if they speak in the styles that are effective when used by men—being assertive, sounding sure of themselves, talking up what they have done to make sure they get credit for it—they run the risk that everyone runs if they do not fit their culture's expectations for appropriate behavior: They will not be liked and may even be seen as having psychological problems.

Both women and men pay a price if they do not behave in ways expected of their gender: Men who are not very aggressive are called "wimps," whereas women who are not very aggressive are called "feminine." Men who are aggressive are called "go-getters," though if they go too far, from the point of view of the viewer, they may be called "arrogant." This can hurt them, but not nearly as much as the innumerable labels for women who are thought to be too aggressive— starting with the most hurtful one: bitch.

Even the compliments that we receive are revealing. One woman who had   15
designed and implemented a number of innovative programs was praised by
someone who said, "You have such a gentle way of bringing about radical
change that people don't realize what's happening—or don't get threatened by
it." This was a compliment, but it also hinted at the downside of the woman's
gentle touch: Although it made it possible for her to be effective in instituting the
changes she envisioned, her unobtrusive style ensured a lack of recognition. If
people don't realize what's happening, they won't give her credit for what she has
accomplished.

Not only advancement and recognition, but hiring is affected by ways of
speaking. A woman who supervised three computer programmers mentioned
that her best employee was another woman whom she had hired over the objections of her own boss. Her boss had preferred a male candidate, because he felt
the man would be better able to step into her supervisory role if needed. But she
had taken a dislike to the male candidate. For one thing, she had felt he was in-
appropriately flirtatious with her. But most important, she had found him arrogant, because he spoke as if he already had the job, using the pronoun "we" to refer to the group that had not yet hired him.

I have no way of knowing whether the woman hired was indeed the better of
these two candidates, or whether either she or the man was well suited to assume
the supervisory role, but I am intrigued that the male boss was impressed with the
male candidate's take-charge self-presentation, while the women supervisor was
put off by it. And it seems quite likely that whatever it was about his way of talking that struck her as arrogant was exactly what led her boss to conclude that this
man would be better able to take over her job if needed.

Reflecting and Interpreting

1. Why did Maureen favor one candidate? Why did Harold favor the other?
   What do you think Harold meant by "a thorn in the side"?

2. How did Harold view his threat? How did Maureen view it? How did her
   perception and assumption weaken her position in negotiating?

3. What other insights did you gain from the anecdote about Maureen and
   Harold?

4. Paragraph 1 relates an anecdote. What does paragraph 2 do?

5. What is the factor that influences the accuracy of our predictions of another's
   responses?

6. What visible signs can you use to evaluate a person's confidence?

7. What is a prerequisite for making good decisions as well as good presentations?

8. What suggestion is given for people who are asking for raises?

9. How do boys and men gain status in a social group?

10. Reread paragraph 16, where only the supervisor's view is given. Why might the applicant have flirted with her and used "we," although he had not been hired yet?

A Writer's Response

Have you ever noticed an instance when gender expectations influenced communication? When and where did it occur? Have you noticed differences in communication styles between young women and older women? Young men and older men? If so, how did they differ? Write an essay, providing examples and an analysis.

Definition

Identifying Basic Characteristics

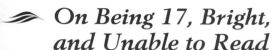

On Being 17, Bright,
and Unable to Read

David Raymond

Someone who has experienced a disability can give an insider's view, providing insights that increase an outsider's understanding in a way that a technical definition cannot. David Raymond was a junior in high school when his essay on dyslexia was published in the New York Times. *Dyslexics think in pictures and experience problems in perceiving letters or numbers. Words may appear jumbled, upside down, backwards, or in other ways that hinder reading. Symptoms vary in range and intensity. Special programs are now available to help dyslexics.*

One day a substitute teacher picked me to read aloud from the textbook. 1
When I told her "No, thank you," she came unhinged. She thought I was acting smart, and told me so. I kept calm, and that got her madder and madder. We must have spent 10 minutes trying to solve the problem, and finally she got so red in the face I thought she'd blow up. She told me she'd see me after class.

Maybe someone like me was a new thing for that teacher. But she wasn't new to me. I've been through scenes like that all my life. You see, even though I'm 17 and a junior in high school, I can't read because I have dyslexia. I'm told I read "at a fourth-grade level," but from where I sit, that's not reading. You can't know what that means unless you've been there. It's not easy to tell how it feels when you can't read your homework assignments or the newspaper or a menu in a restaurant or even notes from your own friends.

My family began to suspect I was having problems almost from the first day I started school. My father says my early years in school were the worst years of his life. They weren't so good for me, either. As I look back on it now, I can't find the words to express how bad it really was. I wanted to die. I'd come home from school screaming, "I'm dumb. I'm dumb—I wish I were dead!"

I guess I couldn't read anything at all then—not even my own name—and they tell me I didn't talk as good as other kids. But what I remember about those days is that I couldn't throw a ball where it was supposed to go, I couldn't learn to swim, and I wouldn't learn to ride a bike, because no matter what anyone told me, I knew I'd fail.

Sometimes my teachers would try to be encouraging. When I couldn't read 5 the words on the board they'd say, "Come on, David, you know that word." Only I didn't. And it was embarrassing. I just felt dumb. And dumb was how the kids treated me. They'd make fun of me every chance they got, asking me to spell "cat" or something like that. Even if I knew how to spell it, I wouldn't; they'd only give me another word. Anyway, it was awful, because more than anything I wanted friends. On my birthday when I blew out the candles I didn't wish I could learn to read; what I wished for was that the kids would like me.

With the bad reports coming from school, and with me moaning about wanting to die and how everybody hated me, my parents began looking for help. That's when the testing started. The school tested me, the child-guidance center tested me, private psychiatrists tested me. Everybody knew something was wrong—especially me.

It didn't help much when they stuck a fancy name onto it. I couldn't pronounce it then—I was only in second grade—and I was ashamed to talk about it. Now it rolls off my tongue, because I've been living with it for a lot of years— dyslexia.

All through elementary school it wasn't easy. I was always having to do things that were "different," things the other kids didn't have to do. I had to go to a child psychiatrist, for instance.

One summer my family forced me to go to a camp for children with reading problems. I hated the idea, but the camp turned out pretty good, and I had a good time. I met a lot of kids who couldn't read and somehow that helped. The director of the camp said I had a higher I.Q. than 90 percent of the population. I didn't believe him.

About the worst thing I had to do in fifth and sixth grade was go to a special 10 education class in another school in our town. A bus picked me up, and I didn't like that at all. The bus also picked up emotionally disturbed kids and retarded kids. It was like going to a school for the retarded. I always worried that someone I knew would see me on that bus. It was a relief to go to the regular junior high school.

Life began to change a little for me then, because I began to feel better about myself. I found the teachers cared; they had meetings about me and I worked harder for them for a while. I began to work on the potter's wheel, making vases and pots that the teachers said were pretty good. Also, I got a letter for being on the track team. I could always run pretty fast.

At high school the teachers are good and everyone is trying to help me. I've gotten honors some marking periods and I've won a letter on the cross-country team. Next quarter I think the school might hold a show of my pottery. I've got some friends. But there are still some embarrassing times. For instance, every time there is writing in the class, I get up and go to the special education room. Kids ask me where I go all the time. Sometimes I say, "to Mars."

Homework is a real problem. During free periods in school I go into the special ed room and staff members read assignments to me. When I get home my mother reads to me. Sometimes she reads an assignment into a tape recorder, and then I go into my room and listen to it. If we have a novel or something like that to read, she reads it out loud to me. Then I sit down with her and we do the assignment. She'll write, while I talk my answers to her. Lately I've taken to dictating into a tape recorder, and then someone—my father, a private tutor or my mother—types up what I've dictated. Whatever homework I do takes someone else's time, too. That makes me feel bad.

We had a big meeting in school the other day—eight of us, four from the guidance department, my private tutor, my parents and me. The subject was me. I said I wanted to go to college, and they told me about colleges that have facilities and staff to handle people like me. That's nice to hear.

As for what happens after college, I don't know and I'm worried about that.   15
How can I make a living if I can't read? Who will hire me? How will I fill out the application form? The only thing that gives me any courage is the fact that I've learned about well-known people who couldn't read or had other problems and still made it. Like Albert Einstein, who didn't talk until he was 4 and flunked math. Like Leonardo da Vinci, who everyone seems to think had dyslexia.

I've told this story because maybe some teacher will read it and go easy on a kid in the classroom who has what I've got. Or, maybe some parent will stop nagging his kid, and stop calling him lazy. Maybe he's not lazy or dumb. Maybe he just can't read and doesn't know what's wrong. Maybe he's scared, like I was.

Reflecting and Interpreting

1. Rather than calling on one person to read, what might the teacher have done?
2. At no point does the author give the technical definition of dyslexia. Should he? What is the effect of this omission?
3. What is dyslexia? Does it vary in how it affects people?
4. What experience was a turning point for David? How did it help?
5. What changes occurred in David's life during junior high school?
6. Why is he confident that he can graduate from college? What does he fear?
7. Why does he mention Albert Einstein and Leonardo da Vinci?

8. David includes many colloquialisms in the essay. How do "blow up" and "didn't talk as good as other kids" affect the tone?

9. What is the author's purpose in writing the essay?

10. What factor do you think is most influential in David's or anyone's success?

A Writer's Response

Have you had a long, difficult experience that makes you somewhat of an expert? Write an essay that gives an insider's view. If you haven't, perhaps a close family member has. How did the problem affect you and other family members?

The Handicap of Definition

William Raspberry

Born in a small town in Mississippi in 1935, William Raspberry knows firsthand about the various connotations that have been attached to his race. In this essay, taken from Instilling Positive Images *(1982), he explores various meanings of* black. *At the end he issues a challenge to blacks and mainstream Americans to expect more from black youth, encourage them, and expand the definition of* black. *Raspberry worked his way through Indiana Central College as a reporter, photographer, and editor for the* Indianapolis Recorder. *After a two-year stint in the Army, he joined* The Washington Post, *where he writes a column, now syndicated in 225 newspapers. He has won "Journalist of the Year" (1965), a Citation of Merit in Journalism (1967), and the Pulitzer Prize for Distinguished Commentary (1994). He has also published* Looking Backward at Us *(1991).*

I know all about bad schools, mean politicians, economic deprivation and racism. Still, it occurs to me that one of the heaviest burdens black Americans—and black children in particular—have to bear is the handicap of definition: the question of what it means to be black.

Let me explain quickly what I mean. If a basketball fan says that the Boston Celtics' Larry Bird plays "black," the fan intends it—and Bird probably accepts it—as a compliment. Tell pop singer Tom Jones he moves "black" and he might grin in appreciation. Say to Teena Marie or The Average White Band that they sound "black" and they'll thank you.

But name one pursuit, aside from athletics, entertainment or sexual performance in which a white practitioner will feel complimented to be told he does it "black." Tell a white broadcaster he talks "black," and he'll sign up for diction lessons. Tell a white reporter he writes "black," and he'll take a writing course. Tell a white lawyer he reasons "black" and he might sue you for slander.

What we have here is a tragically limited definition of blackness, and it isn't only white people who buy it.

Think of all the ways black children can put one another down with charges of "whiteness." For many of these children, hard study and hard work are "white." Trying to please a teacher might be criticized as acting "white." Speaking correct English is "white." Scrimping today in the interest of tomorrow's goals is "white." Educational toys and games are "white."

An incredible array of habits and attitudes that are conducive to success in business, in academic, in the non-entertainment professions are likely to be thought of as somehow "white." Even economic success, unless it involves such "black" undertakings as numbers banking, is defined as "white."

And the results are devastating. I wouldn't deny that blacks often are better entertainers and athletes. My point is the harm that comes from too narrow a definition of what is black.

One reason black youngsters tend to do better at basketball, for instance, is that they assume they can learn to do it well, and so they practice constantly to prove themselves right.

Wouldn't it be wonderful if we would infect black children with the notion that excellence in math is "black" rather than white, or possibly Chinese? Wouldn't it be of enormous value if we could create the myth that morality, strong families, determination, courage and love of learning are traits brought by slaves from Mother Africa and therefore quintessentially black?

There is no doubt in my mind that most black youngsters could develop their   10
mathematical reasoning, their elocution and their attitudes the way they develop their jump shots and their dance steps: by the combination of sustained, enthusiastic practice and the unquestioned belief that they can do it.

In one sense, what I am talking about is the importance of developing positive ethnic traditions. Maybe Jews have an innate talent for communication; maybe the Chinese are born with a gift for mathematical reasoning; maybe blacks are naturally blessed with athletic grace. I doubt it. What is at work, I suspect, is assumption, inculcated early in their lives, that this is a thing our people do well.

Unfortunately, many of the things about which blacks make this assumption are things that do not contribute to their career success—except for that handful of the truly gifted who can make it as entertainers and athletes. And many of the things we concede to whites are the things that are essential to economic security.

So it is with a number of assumptions black youngsters make about what it is to be a "man": physical aggressiveness, sexual prowess, the refusal to submit to authority. The prisons are full of people who, by this perverted definition, are unmistakably men.

But the real problem is not so much that the things defined as "black" are negative. The problem is that the definition is much too narrow.

Somehow, we have to make our children understand that they are intelligent,   15
competent people, capable of doing whatever they put their minds to and making it in the American mainstream, not just in a black subculture.

What we seem to be doing, instead, is raising up yet another generation of young blacks who will be failures—by definition.

Reflecting and Interpreting

1. Where is the transitional sentence that spans the chasm between the positive examples and the negative ones?

2. How does the construing of saving money, pleasing the teacher, educational toys, and speaking correct English as "white" prove detrimental to blacks?

3. What reasons does Raspberry cite for blacks' success in basketball? Do you agree or disagree? Why?

4. What rhetorical strategy does Raspberry use in paragraph 9?

5. What image, in particular, is harmful for young black males?

6. Notice the three-word sentence "I doubt it" in paragraph 11. What is the effect?

7. See paragraph 15. In 1987 Raspberry pinpointed a crucial aspect of the problem: For most black children, the subculture is their world, meaning they do not see themselves as an integral part of a larger society. Do you think this perspective has changed since 1987? Since September 11, 2001? How?

8. How would you classify Raspberry's ending? (Hint: See "Writing an Effective Conclusion," chapter 4.)

9. How would you describe the writer's voice? How does the tone differ from that of many other black writers?

10. Raspberry says that "an incredible array of habits and attitudes are conductive to success in business, in academia, and in the nonentertainment professions." Can you specify some of these?

A Writer's Response

How does a person's attitude and behavior define his or her chances for success? Write an essay explaining these vital influences. Cite positive and negative examples as Raspberry does.

✍ *Becoming Educated*

Barbara Jordan

Barbara Charline Jordan (1936–96) was born in an all-black neighborhood in Houston, Texas. In an era when relatively few women attended college, she earned a bachelor's degree from Texas Southern University and a law degree from Boston University Law School (1959). Seven years later she became the first black woman to be elected to the Texas Senate. In 1972 she won a seat in the U.S. House of Representatives, where she served on the Judiciary Committee. Her powerful speech in favor of impeaching President Nixon during the Watergate affair gained national attention. Some constituents were so impressed with her dedication and ethics that they urged her to run for president, but she declined. In 1978 she left Congress to teach at the University of Texas at Austin. In 1992 at the Democratic National Convention, she spoke eloquently about making the American Dream come true for both whites and blacks. Her Selected Speeches *(1999) was published posthumously. In this extract from her autobiography,* Barbara Jordan: A Self Portrait *(1979), she defines what an education means to her.*

So I was at Boston University in this new and strange and different world, and   1
it occurred to me that if I was going to succeed at this strange new adventure, I would have to read longer and more thoroughly than my colleagues at law school had to read. I felt that in order to compensate for what I had missed in earlier years, I would have to work harder, and study longer, than anybody else. I still had this feeling that I did not want my colleagues to know what a tough time I was having understanding the concepts, the words, the ideas, the process. I didn't want them to know that. So I did my reading not in the law library, but in a library at the graduate dorm, upstairs where it was very quiet, because apparently nobody else there studied. So I would go there at night after dinner. I would load my books under my arm and go to the library, and I would read until the wee hours of the morning and then go to bed. I didn't get much sleep during those years. I was lucky if I got three or four hours a night, because I had to stay up. I had to. The professors would assign cases for the next day, and these cases had to be read and understood or I would be behind, further behind than I was.

I was always delighted when I would get called upon to recite in class. But the professors did not call on the "ladies" very much. There were certain favored people who always got called on, and then on some rare occasions a professor would come in and would announce: "We're going to have Ladies Day today." And he would call on the ladies. We were just tolerated. We weren't considered really top drawer when it came to the study of the law.

At some time in the spring, Bill Gibson, who was dating my new roommate, Norma Walker, organized a black study group, as we blacks had to form our own. This was because we were not invited into any of the other study groups. There were six or seven in our group—Bill, and Issie, and I think Maynard Jackson—and we would just gather and talk it out and hear ourselves do that. One thing I learned was that you had to talk out the issues, the facts, the cases, the decisions, the process. You couldn't just read the cases and study alone in your library as I had been doing; and you couldn't get it all in the classroom. But once you had talked it out in the study group, it flowed more easily and made a lot more sense.

And from time to time I would go up to the fourth floor at 2 Rawley Street to check on how Louise was doing. She was always reading *Redbook*. Every time I was in there and wanted to discuss one of the cases with her, she was reading a short story in *Redbook*. I don't know how she could do that. She was not prepared in class when the professors would call on her to discuss cases, but that did not bother her. Whereas it was a matter of life and death with me. I had to make law school. I just didn't have any alternatives. I could not afford to flunk out. That would have been an unmitigated disaster. So I read all the time I was not in class.

Finally I felt I was really learning things, really going to school. I felt that I was getting educated, whatever that was. I became familiar with the process of thinking. I learned to think things out and reach conclusions and defend what I had said.

In the past I had got along by spouting off. Whether you talked about debates or oratory, you dealt with speechifying. Even in debate it was pretty much canned because you had, in your little three-by-five box, a response for whatever issue might be raised by the opposition. The format was structured so that there was no opportunity for independent thinking. (I really had not had my ideas challenged ever.) But I could no longer orate and let that pass for reasoning. Because there was not any demand for an orator in Boston University Law School. You had to think and read and understand and reason. I had learned at twenty-one that you couldn't just say a thing is so because it might not be so, and somebody brighter, smarter, and more thoughtful would come out and tell you it wasn't so. Then, if you still thought it was, you had to prove it. Well, that was a new thing for me. I cannot, I really cannot describe what that did to my insides and to my head. I thought: I'm being educated finally.

Reflecting and Interpreting

1. In the first paragraph, what do we learn about Barbara Jordan's early education? What decision does she make? What does this reveal about her attitude?

2. Why doesn't she study in the law library? What does this reveal about her?

3. How does the professor at Boston University treat women in his classes? What is "Ladies Day"?

4. Why do Jordan and her friends form a study group? Describe the results.

5. How does Louise differ from Barbara Jordan? What is the effect of including this paragraph in the essay?

6. How has Jordan gotten along in former debate classes? How does her performance change at Boston University Law School?

7. How does Jordan feel as a result of this experience?
8. In one brief paragraph, Jordan defines what becoming educated means to her. Can you find it?
9. How would you describe Jordan's attitude toward learning?
10. How would you describe the writer's voice in this essay?

A Writer's Response

1. In a paragraph, define and explain what an education means to you.
2. *Small Groups:* What were your early expectations for your college courses? What was the reality? Are there any similarities between Jordan's experience at Boston University and your college experience? If so, what?

The Sweet Smell of Success Isn't All That Sweet

Laurence Shames

Dozens of definitions of "success" reverberate across our culture, influencing our values and choice of careers. In this essay, Laurence Shames mentions several current definitions of that illusive concept, but he believes that a "noble failure" is better. Shames, a graduate of New York University, is best known for his eight mystery novels, of which Mangrove Squeeze *(1998),* Welcome to Paradise *(1999), and* The Naked Detective *(2001) are the latest. He has also written nonfiction for* McCall's, Saturday Review, Vanity Fair, The New York Times, *and others. His two nonfiction works,* The Big Time: The Harvard Business School's Most Successful Class and How It Shaped America *(1986) and* The Hunger for More: Searching for Values in an Age of Greed *(1991) reveal his concern with values.*

John Milton was a failure. In writing "Paradise Lost," his stated aim was to 1 "justify the ways of God to men." Inevitably, he fell short of accomplishing that and only wrote a monumental poem. Beethoven, whose music was conceived to transcend Fate, was a failure, as was Socrates, whose ambition was to make people happy by making them reasonable and just. The inescapable conclusion seems to be that the surest, noblest way to fail is to set one's own standards titanically high.

The flip-side of that proposition also seems true, and it provides the safe but dreary logic by which most of us live: The surest way to succeed is to keep one's strivings low—or at least to direct them along already charted paths. Don't set yourself the probably thankless task of making the legal system better; just shoot at becoming a partner in the firm. Don't agonize over questions about where your talents and proclivities might most fulfillingly lead you; just do a heads-up job of determining where the educational or business opportunities seem most secure.

After all, if "success" itself—rather than the substance of the achievements that make for success—is the criterion by which we measure ourselves and from which we derive our self-esteem, why make things more difficult by reaching for the stars?

What is this contemporary version of success really all about?

According to certain beer commercials, it consists in moving up to a premium 5 brand that costs a dime or so more per bottle. Credit-card companies would have you believe success inheres in owning their particular piece of plastic.

If these examples sound petty, they are. But take those petty privileges, weave them into a fabric that passes for a value system and what you've got is a national mood that has vast motivating power that can shape at least the near future of the entire country.

Under the flag of success, modern-style, liberal arts colleges are withering while business schools are burgeoning—and yet even business schools are having an increasingly hard time finding faculty members, because teaching isn't considered "successful" enough. Amid a broad consensus that there is a glut of lawyers and an epidemic of strangling litigation, record numbers of young people continue to flock to law school because, for the individual practitioner, a law degree is still considered a safe ticket.

The most sobering thought of all is that today's M.B.A.'s and lawyers are tomorrow's M.B.A.'s and lawyers: Having invested so much time and money in their training, only a tiny percentage of them will ever opt out of their early chosen fields. Decisions made in accordance with today's hothouse notions of ambition are locking people into careers that will define and also limit their activities and yearnings for virtually the rest of their lives.

Many, by external standards, will be "successes." They will own homes, eat in better restaurants, dress well and, in some instances, perform socially useful work. Yet there is a deadening and dangerous flaw in their philosophy: It has little room, little sympathy and less respect for the noble failure, for the person who ventures past the limits, who aims gloriously high and falls unashamedly short.

That sort of ambition doesn't have much place in a world where success is   10
proved by worldly reward rather than by accomplishment itself. That sort of ambition is increasingly thought of as the domain of irredeemable eccentrics, of people who haven't quite caught on—and there is great social pressure not to be one of them.

The result is that fewer people are drawn to the cutting edge of noncommercial scientific research. Fewer are taking on the sublime, unwinnable challenges of the arts. Fewer are asking questions that matter—the ones that can't be answered. Fewer are putting themselves on the line, making as much of their minds and talents as they might.

The irony is that today's success-chasers seem obsessed with the idea of *not settling.* They take advanced degrees in business because they won't settle for just a so-so job. They compete for slots at law firms and investment houses because they won't settle for any but the fastest track. They seem to regard it as axiomatic that "success" and "settling" are opposites.

Yet in doggedly pursuing the rather brittle species of success now in fashion, they are restricting themselves to a chokingly narrow swath of turf along the entire range of human possibilities. Does it ever occur to them that, frequently, success is what people settle for when they can't think of something noble enough to be worth failing at?

Reflecting and Interpreting

1. Consider the way the three examples in the first paragraph are presented. How would you describe the writer's voice?

2. What kind of success is described in the second paragraph?

3. How is success related to self-esteem? Is one's perception of oneself and one's success always realistic? Why?

4. What does Shames mean by "noble failure"? What assumptions does he make?

5. He points out a "great social pressure" to be a success in the eyes of the world. Do you see a greater pressure that influences you and your friends?

6. How do you reconcile his example of "reaching for the stars" by "making the legal system better" (paragraph 2) with his apparent disdain in paragraph 9, where he includes "perform socially useful tasks"?

7. Examine paragraph 11. What factors influence people to take on the challenge that he speaks of?

8. What strategies of exposition are used in this essay?

9. How would you summarize Shames' definition of success?

10. His definition of success seems limited to an either/or proposition. Do you agree or disagree? Why?

A Writer's Response

Write an essay defining your vision of success. How do you measure success? What internal and external rewards are included in your definition?

Cause and Effect

Explaining Why

Spudding Out

Barbara Ehrenreich

Growing up in Montana and earning a doctorate at Rockefeller University helped to shape Barbara Ehrenreich's perspective on American life. She has studied a wide range of social and political issues from gender to public health as well as written thirteen books and collaborated on many more. Her latest works include The Snarling Citizen *(1995),* Blood Rites: Origins and History of the Passions of War *(1998),* Nickel and Dimed: On (Not) Getting By in America *(2001), and* Untitled on Poverty *(2002). This essay is from* The Worst Years of Our Lives *(1991).*

Someone has to speak for them, because they have, to a person, lost the power to speak for themselves. I am referring to that great mass of Americans who were once known as the "salt of the earth," then as "the silent majority," more recently as "the viewing public," and now, alas, as "couch potatoes." What drives them—or rather, leaves them sapped and spineless on their reclining chairs? What are they seeking—beyond such obvious goals as a tastefully colorized version of *The Maltese Falcon?*

My husband was the first in the family to "spud out," as the expression now goes. Soon everyone wanted one of those zip-up "Couch Potato Bags," to keep warm in during David Letterman. The youngest, and most thoroughly immobilized, member of the family relies on a remote that controls his TV, stereo, and VCR, and can also shut down the neighbor's pacemaker at fifteen yards.

But we never see the neighbors anymore, nor they us. This saddens me because Americans used to be a great and restless people, fond of the outdoors in all of its manifestations, from Disney World to miniature golf. Some experts say

1

there are virtues in mass agoraphobia, that it strengthens the family and reduces highway deaths. But I would point out that there are still a few things that cannot be done in the den, especially by someone zipped into a body bag. These include racquetball, voting, and meeting strange people in bars.

Most psychologists interpret the couch potato trend as a negative reaction to the outside world. Indeed, the list of reasons to stay safely tucked indoors lengthens yearly. First there was crime, then AIDS, then side-stream smoke. To this list should be added "fear of the infrastructure," for we all know someone who rashly stepped outside only to be buried in a pothole, hurled from a collapsing bridge, or struck by a falling airplane.

But it is not just the outside world that has let us down. Let's face it, despite   5
a decade-long campaign by the "profamily" movement, the family has been a disappointment. The reason lies in an odd circular dynamic: we watch television to escape from our families because television shows us how dull our families really are.

Compare your own family to, for example, the Huxtables, the Keatons, or the peppy young people on *Thirtysomething*. In those families, even the three-year-olds are stand-up comics, and the most insipid remark is hailed with heartening outbursts of canned laughter. When television families aren't gathered around the kitchen table exchanging wisecracks, they are experiencing brief but moving dilemmas, which are handily solved by the youngest child or by some cute extraterrestrial house-guest. Emerging from *Family Ties* or *My Two Dads*, we are forced to acknowledge that our own families are made up of slow-witted, emotionally crippled people who would be lucky to qualify for seats in the studio audience of *Jeopardy!*

But gradually I have come to see that there is something besides fear of the outside and disgust with out families that drives us to spudhood—some positive attraction, some deep cathexis to television itself. For a long time it eluded me. When I watched television, mainly as a way of getting to know my husband and children, I found that my mind wandered to more interesting things, like whether to get up and make ice cubes.

Only after many months of viewing did I begin to understand the force that has transformed the American people into root vegetables. If you watch TV for a very long time, day in, day out, you will begin to notice something eerie and unnatural about the world portrayed therein. I don't mean that it is two-dimensional or lacks a well-developed critique of the capitalist consumer culture or something superficial like that. I mean something so deeply obvious that it's almost scary: when you watch television, you will see people doing many things—chasing fast cars, drinking lite beer, shooting each other at close range, etc. But you will never see people *watching television*. Well, maybe for a second, before the phone rings or a brand-new, multiracial adopted child walks into the house. But never *really watching*, hour after hour, the way *real* people do.

Way back in the beginning of the television era, this was not so strange, because real people actually did many of the things people do on TV, even if it was only bickering with their mother-in-law about which toilet paper to buy. But modern people, i.e., couch potatoes, do nothing that is ever shown on television (because it is either dangerous or would involve getting up from the couch). And what they do do—watch television—is far too boring to be televised for more than a fraction of a second, not even by Andy Warhol, bless his boredom-proof little heart.[1]

So why do we keep on watching? The answer, by now, should be perfectly obvious: we love television because television brings us a world in which television does not exist. In fact, deep in their hearts, this is what the spuds crave most: a rich, new, participatory life, in which family members look each other in the eye, in which people walk outside and banter with the neighbors, where there is adventure, possibility, danger, feeling, all in natural color, stereophonic sound, and three dimensions, without commercial interruptions, and starring . . . us.

"You mean some new kind of computerized interactive medium?" the children asked hopefully, pert as the progeny on a Tuesday night sitcom. But before I could expand on this concept—known to our ancestors as "real life"—they were back at the box, which may be, after all, the only place left to find it.

Reflecting and Interpreting

1. Why is the title of the essay particularly fitting?
2. Examine the first paragraph. Can you summarize Ehrenreich's thesis in one sentence?
3. Who are the "silent majority" that Ehrenreich refers to?
4. What effects of long hours of television viewing does she mention?
5. What are three causes of the couch potato trend according to Ehrenreich?
6. Consider the time restrictions on a TV drama series. How does that factor affect the content as compared to real life?
7. Can you find any irony in the essay?
8. How would you describe the tone?
9. What seems to be the purpose of the essay?
10. Considering that Ehrenreich wrote this commentary over a decade ago, do you think the viewing habits of Americans have changed? If so, how?

A Writer's Response

How has technology affected your life? Consider your television viewing, computer use, cell phone use, and any other appliance that you use for recreation. Write an essay analyzing the cause and effects you see in your life.

---

[1] Pop artist Andy Warhol (1930?–1987) made a series of lengthy films that was deliberately designed to be extremely boring, a task obviously requiring great resistance to boredom.

Why Marriages Fail

Anne Roiphe

Born in New York City, Anne Roiphe graduated from Sarah Lawrence College with a BA degree. In the past four decades, she has published a dozen fiction and nonfiction books, as well as collaborated on several others. Her latest works include If You Knew Me *(1995),* Lovingkindness *(1997),* Fruitful: Living the Contradictions: A Memoir of Modern Motherhood *(1997),* For Rabbit, with Love and Squalor: An American Read *(2000), and* 1185 Park Avenue: a Memoir *(2000). In this essay, which first appeared in* Family Weekly *(27 Feb. 1983), she analyzes the factors that lead to divorce.*

These days so many marriages end in divorce that our most sacred vows no longer ring with truth. "Happily ever after" and "Till death do us part" are expressions that seem on the way to becoming obsolete. Why has it becomes so hard for couples to stay together? What goes wrong? What has happened to us that close to one-half of all marriages are destined for the divorce courts? How could we have created a society in which 42 percent of our children will grow up in single parent homes? If statistics could only measure loneliness, regret, pain, loss of self-confidence and fear of the future, the numbers would be beyond quantifying.

Even though each broken marriage is unique, we can still find the common perils, the common causes for marital despair. Each marriage has crisis points and each marriage tests endurance, the capacity for both intimacy and change. Outside pressures such as job loss, illness, infertility, trouble with a child, care of aging parents and all the other plagues of life hit marriage the way hurricanes blast our shores. Some marriages survive these storms and others don't. Marriages fail, however, not simply because of the outside weather but because the inner climate becomes too hot or too cold, too turbulent or too stupefying.

When we look at how we choose our partners and what expectations exist at the tender beginnings of romance, some of the reasons for disaster become quite clear. We all select with unconscious accuracy a mate who will recreate with us the emotional patterns of our first homes. Dr. Carl A. Whitaker, a marital therapist and emeritus professor of psychiatry at the University of Wisconsin explains, "From early childhood on, each of us carried models for marriage, femininity, masculinity, motherhood, fatherhood and all the other family roles." Each of us falls in love with a mate who has qualities of our parents, who will help us rediscover both the psychological happiness and miseries of our past lives. We may think we have found a man unlike Dad, but then he turns to drink or drugs, or loses his job over and over again or sits silently in front of the T.V. just the way Dad did. A man may choose a woman who doesn't like kids just like his mother or who gambles away the family savings just like his mother. Or he may choose a slender wife who seems unlike his obese mother but then turns out to have other addictions that destroy their mutual happiness.

A man and a woman bring to their marriage bed a blended concoction of conscious and unconscious memories of their parents' lives together. The human way is to compulsively repeat and recreate the patterns of the past. Sigmund Freud so well described the unhappy design that many of us get trapped in: the unmet needs of childhood, the angry feelings left over from frustrations of long ago, the limits of trust and the recurrence of old fears. Once an individual senses this entrapment, there may follow a yearning to escape, and the result could be a broken, splintered marriage.

Of course people can overcome the habits and attitudes that developed in childhood. We all have hidden strengths and amazing capacities for growth and creative change. Change, however, requires work—observing your part in a rotten pattern, bringing difficulties out into the open—and work runs counter to the basic myth of marriage: "When I wed this person all my problems will be over. I will have achieved success and I will become the center of life for this other person and this person will be my center, and we will mean everything to each other forever." This myth, which every marriage relies on, is soon exposed. The coming of children, the pulls and tugs of their demands on affection and time, place a considerable strain on that basic myth of meaning everything to each other, of merging together and solving all of life's problems.

Concern and tension about money take each partner away from the other. Obligations to demanding parents or still-depended-upon parents create further strain. Couples today must also deal with all the cultural changes brought on in recent years by the women's movement and the sexual revolution. The altering of roles and the shifting of responsibilities have been extremely trying for many marriages.

These and other realities of life erode the visions of marital bliss the way sandstorms eat at rock and the ocean nibbles away at the dunes. Those euphoric, grand feelings that accompany romantic love are really self-delusions, self-hypnotic dreams that enable us to forge a relationship. Real life, failure at work, disappointments, exhaustion, bad smells, bad colds and hard times all puncture the dream and leave us stranded with our mate, with our childhood patterns pushing us this way and that, with our unfulfilled expectations.

The struggle to survive in marriage requires adaptability, flexibility, genuine love and kindness and an imagination strong enough to feel what the other is feeling. Many marriages fall apart because either partner cannot imagine what the other wants or cannot communicate what he or she needs or feels. Anger builds until it erupts into a volcanic burst that buries the marriage in ash.

It is not hard to see, therefore, how essential communication is for a good marriage. A man and a woman must be able to tell each other how they feel and why they feel the way they do; otherwise they will impose on each other roles and actions that lead to further unhappiness. In some cases, the communication patterns of childhood—of not talking, of talking too much, of not listening, of distrust and anger, of withdrawal—spill into the marriage and prevent a healthy exchange of thoughts and feelings. The answer is to set up new patterns of communication and intimacy.

At the same time, however, we must see each other as individuals. "To 10 achieve a balance between separateness and closeness is one of the major psychological tasks of all human beings at every stage of life," says Dr. Stuart Bartle, a psychiatrist at the New York University Medical Center.

If we sense from our mate a need for too much intimacy, we tend to push him or her away, fearing that we may lose our identities in the merging of marriage. One partner may suffocate the other partner in a childlike dependency.

A good marriage means growing as a couple but also growing as individuals. This isn't easy. Richard gives up his interest in carpentry because his wife, Helen, is jealous of the time he spends away from her. Karen quits her choir group because her husband dislikes the friends she makes there. Each pair clings to each other and are angry with each other as life closes in on them. This kind of marital balance is easily thrown as one or the other pulls away and divorce follows.

Sometimes people pretend that a new partner will solve the old problems. Most often extramarital sex destroys a marriage because it allows an artificial split between the good and the bad—the good is projected on the new partner and the bad is dumped on the head of the old. Dishonesty, hiding and cheating create walls between men and women. Infidelity is just a symptom of trouble. It is a symbolic complaint, a weapon of revenge, as well as an unraveler of closeness. Infidelity is often that proverbial last straw that sinks that camel to the ground.

All right—marriage has always been difficult. Why then are we seeing so many divorces at this time? Yes, our modern social fabric is thin, and yes the permissiveness of society has created unrealistic expectations and thrown the family into chaos. But divorce is so common because people today are unwilling to exercise the self-discipline that marriage requires. They expect easy joy, like the entertainment on TV, the thrill of a good party.

Marriage takes some kind of sacrifice, not dreadful self-sacrifice of the soul, 15 but some level of compromise. Some of one's fantasies, some of one's legitimate desires have to be given up for the value of the marriage itself. "While all marital partners feel shackled at times, it is they who really choose to make the marital ties into confining chains or supporting bonds," says Dr. Whitaker. Marriage requires sexual, financial and emotional discipline. A man and a woman cannot follow every impulse, cannot allow themselves to stop growing or changing.

Divorce is not an evil act. Sometimes it provides salvation for people who have grown hopelessly apart or were frozen in patterns of pain or mutual unhappiness. Divorce can be, despite its initial devastation, like the first cut of the surgeon's knife, a step toward new health and a good life. One the other hand, if the partners can stay past the breaking up of the romantic myths into the development of real love and intimacy, they have achieved a work as amazing as the greatest cathedrals of the world. Marriages that do not fail but improve, that persist despite imperfections, are not only rare these days but offer a wondrous shelter in which the face of our mutual humanity can safely show itself.

Reflecting and Interpreting

1. Reread the first paragraph. What rhetorical strategy is used here? How does it function?

2. In paragraph 3, Roiphe cites expert opinion. Why?

3. Do you agree or disagree with Dr. Whitaker's theory? Why?

4. What is the basic marriage myth that Roiphe wrote about two decades ago? Do you think the myth still exists? Why or why not?

5. What five qualities does Roiphe identify that are essential for a marriage to endure? Can you think of any others?

6. What pretense does a partner often use to "solve old problems"? How effective is it? What are the risks? (Think about the opening sentence.)

7. What are some of the factors that have created more tension in marriages than those of a century ago?

8. Roiphe says that divorce is so common for one chief reason. What is it? What can couples do to evade divorce? Can you think of some ways that she does not name?

9. What is the basic question that couples must resolve in order for a marriage to succeed?

10. What advantages does a successful marriage offer a family? Consider effects on children, education, health, and others.

A Writer's Response

1. If you are married, analyze the growth that you have attained since your wedding vows. Write an essay analyzing the cause and effects. If you are single, describe the kind of marriage you would like to have some day. Then analyze the responsibilities you will need to assume and the changes you will need to make.

2. *Small Groups:* Roiphe points out that growth must take place for a marriage to succeed. What kind of growth does she mean? How do changes in perception and perspective figure in? Can you give some examples?

The Teacher Who Changed My Life

Nicholas Gage

Running barefoot through minefields with his three sisters, Nicholas Gage left his Greek village to escape Communist guerrillas. The children stayed in a refugee camp until their father, who lived in the United States, located them. When nine-year-old Nicholas Gage arrived in the U.S., he did not expect to be placed in a class for the mentally retarded. Non-English speaking, he and his sisters learned English. Four years later, Gage met a teacher who changed his life. He won a scholarship to Boston University and later attended Columbia's Graduate School of Journalism. He worked for the Associated Press, Boston Herald Traveler, Wall Street Journal, *and the* New York Times, *which sent him to Greece as a foreign correspondent. His first book* Eleni *(1987), was a bestseller and was later produced as a film. He has written ten other books, including* Hellas: A Portrait of Greece *(1987),* Greece: Land of Light *(1998), and* Greek Fire *(2001). The following excerpt is from his second book,* A Place for Us *(1990).*

The person who set the course of my life in the new land I entered as a young   1 war refugee—who, in fact, nearly dragged me onto the path that would bring all the blessings I've received in America—was a salty-tongued, no-nonsense schoolteacher named Marjorie Hurd. When I entered her classroom in 1953, I had been to six schools in five years, starting in the Greek village where I was born in 1939.

When I stepped off a ship in New York Harbor on a gray March day in 1949, I was an undersized 9-year-old in short pants who had lost his mother and was coming to live with the father he didn't know. My mother, Eleni Gatzoyiannis, had been imprisoned, tortured and shot by Communist guerrillas for sending me and three of my four sisters to freedom. She died so that her children could go to their father in the United States.

The portly, bald, well-dressed man who met me and my sisters seemed a foreign, authoritarian figure. I secretly resented him for not getting the whole family out of Greece early enough to save my mother. Ultimately, I would grow to love him and appreciate how he dealt with becoming a single parent at the age of 56, but at first our relationship was prickly, full of hostility.

As Father drove us to our new home—a tenement in Worcester, Mass.—and pointed out the huge brick building that would be our first school in America, I clutched my Greek notebooks from the refugee camp, hoping that my few years of schooling would impress my teachers in this cold, crowded country. They didn't. When my father led me and my 11-year-old sister to Greendale Elementary School, the grim-faced Yankee principal put the two of us in a class for the mentally retarded. There was no facility in those days for non-English-speaking children.

By the time I met Marjorie Hurd four years later, I had learned English, been 5 placed in a normal, graded class and had even been chosen for the college preparatory track in the Worcester public school system. I was 13 years old when our father moved us yet again, and I entered Chandler Junior High shortly after the beginning of seventh grade. I found myself surrounded by richer, smarter and better-dressed classmates who looked askance at my strange clothes and heavy accent. Shortly after I arrived, we were told to select a hobby to pursue during "club hour" on Fridays. The idea of hobbies and clubs made no sense to my immigrant ears, but I decided to follow the prettiest girl in my class—the blue-eyed daughter of the local Lutheran minister. She led me through the door marked "Newspaper Club" and into the presence of Miss Hurd, the newspaper adviser and English teacher who would become my mentor and my muse.

A formidable, solidly built woman with salt-and-pepper hair, a steely eye and a flat Boston accent, Miss Hurd had no patience with layabouts. "What are all you goof-offs doing here?" she bellowed at the would-be journalists. "This is the Newspaper Club! We're going to put out a *newspaper*. So if there's anybody in this room who doesn't like work, I suggest you go across to the Glee Club now, because you're going to work your tails off here!"

I was soon under Miss Hurd's spell. She did indeed teach us to put out a newspaper, skills I honed during my next 25 years as a journalist. Soon I asked the principal to transfer me to her English class as well. There, she drilled us on grammar until I finally began to understand the logic and structure of the English language. She assigned stories for us to read and discuss; not tales of heroes, like the Greek myths I knew, but stories of underdogs—poor people, even immigrants, who seemed ordinary until a crisis drove them to do something extraordinary. She also introduced us to the literary wealth of Greece—giving me a new perspective on my war-ravaged, impoverished homeland. I began to be proud of my origins.

One day, after discussing how writers should write about what they know, she assigned us to compose an essay from our own experience. Fixing me with a stern look, she added, "Nick, I want you to write about what happened to your family in Greece." I had been trying to put those painful memories behind me and left the assignment until the last moment. Then, on a warm spring afternoon, I sat in my room with a yellow pad and pencil and stared out the window at the buds on the trees. I wrote that the coming of spring always reminded me of the last time I said goodbye to my mother on a green and gold day in 1948.

I kept writing, one line after another, telling how the Communist guerrillas occupied our village, took our home and food, how my mother started planning our escape when she learned that the children were to be sent to re-education camps behind the Iron Curtain and how, at the last moment, she couldn't escape with us because the guerrillas sent her with a group of women to thresh wheat in a distant village. She promised she would try to get away on her own, she told me to be brave and hung a silver cross around my neck, and then she kissed me. I watched the line of women being led down into the ravine and up the other side, until they disappeared around the bend—my mother a tiny brown figure at the end who stopped for an instant to raise her hand in one last farewell.

I wrote about our nighttime escape down the mountain, across the minefields   10
and into the lines of the Nationalist soldiers, who sent us to a refugee camp. It was
there that we learned of our mother's execution. I felt very lucky to have come to
America, I concluded, but every year, the coming of spring made me feel sad because it reminded me of the last time I saw my mother.

I handed in the essay, hoping never to see it again, but Miss Hurd had it published in the school paper. This mortified me at first, until I saw that my classmates reacted with sympathy and tact to my family's story. Without telling
me, Miss Hurd also submitted the essay to a contest sponsored by the Freedoms
Foundation at Valley Forge, Pa., and it won a medal. The Worcester paper wrote
about the award and quoted my essay at length. My father, by then a "five-and-
dime-store chef," as the paper described him, was ecstatic with pride, and the
Worcester Greek community celebrated the honor to one of its own.

For the first time I began to understand the power of the written word. A
secret ambition took root in me. One day, I vowed, I would go back to Greece,
find out the details of my mother's death and write about her life, so her grandchildren would know of her courage. Perhaps I would even track down the men
who killed her and write of their crimes. Fulfilling that ambition would take me
30 years.

Meanwhile, I followed the literary path that Miss Hurd had so forcefully set
me on. After junior high, I became the editor of my school paper at Classical High
School and got a part-time job at the Worcester *Telegram and Gazette*. Although
my father could only give me $50 and encouragement toward a college education,
I managed to finance four years at Boston University with scholarships and part-
time jobs in journalism. During my last year of college, an article I wrote about
a friend who had died in the Philippines—the first person to lose his life working
for the Peace Corps—led to my winning the Hearst Award for College Journalism. And the plaque was given to me in the White House by President John F.
Kennedy.

For a refugee who had never seen a motorized vehicle or indoor plumbing until he was 9, this was an unimaginable honor. When the Worcester paper ran a
picture of me standing next to President Kennedy, my father rushed out to buy
a new suit in order to be properly dressed to receive the congratulations of the
Worcester Greeks. He clipped out the photograph, had it laminated in plastic and
carried it in his breast pocket for the rest of his life to show everyone he met. I
found the much-worn photo in his pocket on the day he died 20 years later.

In our isolated Greek village, my mother had bribed a cousin to teach her to   15
read, for girls were not supposed to attend school beyond a certain age. She had
always dreamed of her children receiving an education. She couldn't be there
when I graduated from Boston University, but the person who came with my father and shared our joy was my former teacher, Marjorie Hurd. We celebrated not
only my bachelor's degree but also the scholarships that paid my way to Columbia's Graduate School of Journalism. There, I met the woman who would eventually become my wife. At our wedding and at the baptisms of our three children,
Marjorie Hurd was always there, dancing alongside the Greeks.

By then, she was Mrs. Rabidou, for she had married a widower when she was in her early 40s. That didn't distract her from her vocation of introducing young minds to English literature, however. She taught for a total of 41 years and continually would make a "project" of some balky student in whom she spied a spark of potential. Often these were students from the most troubled homes, yet she would alternately bully and charm each one with her own special brand of tough love until the spark caught fire. She retired in 1981 at the age of 62 but still avidly follows the lives and careers of former students while overseeing her adult stepchildren and driving her husband on camping trips to New Hampshire.

Miss Hurd was one of the first to call me on Dec. 10, 1987, when President Reagan, in his television address after the summit meeting with Gorbachev, told the nation that Eleni Gatzoyiannis' dying cry, "My children!" had helped inspire him to seek an arms agreement "for all the children of the world."

"I can't imagine a better monument for your mother," Miss Hurd said with an uncharacteristic catch in her voice.

Although a bad hip makes it impossible for her to join in the Greek dancing, Marjorie Hurd Rabidou is still an honored and enthusiastic guest at all family celebrations, including my 50th birthday picnic last summer, where the shish kebab was cooked on spits, clarinets and *bouzoukis* wailed, and costumed dancers led the guests in a serpentine line around our Colonial farmhouse, only 20 minutes from my first home in Worcester.

My sisters and I felt an aching void because my father was not there to lead   20 the line, balancing a glass of wine on his head while he danced, the way he did at every celebration during his 92 years. But Miss Hurd was there, surveying the scene with quiet satisfaction. Although my parents are gone, her presence was a consolation, because I owe her so much.

This is truly the land of opportunity, and I would have enjoyed its bounty even if I hadn't walked into Miss Hurd's classroom in 1953. But she was the one who directed my grief and pain into writing, and if it weren't for her I wouldn't have become an investigative reporter and foreign correspondent, recorded the story of my mother's life and death in *Eleni* and now my father's story in *A Place for Us*, which is also a testament to the country that took us in. She was the catalyst that sent me into journalism and indirectly caused all the good things that came after. But Miss Hurd would probably deny this emphatically.

A few years ago, I answered the telephone and heard my former teacher's voice telling me, in that won't-take-no-for-an-answer tone of hers, that she had decided I was to write and deliver the eulogy at her funeral. I agreed (she didn't leave me any choice), but that's one assignment I never want to do. I hope, Miss Hurd, that you'll accept this remembrance instead.

Reflecting and Interpreting

1. Where is Gage's thesis statement?
2. Although this essay is primarily about a teacher that Gage had the year he was thirteen, he talks about virtually his entire life. Why?

3. What order does Gage use to present the events of so many years? At times he uses what device to weave in past events? How does he accomplish these shifts so that readers can easily follow?

4. How did Miss Hurd (later Mrs. Rabidou) occasionally make a "project" of one of her students?

5. What are stories of "underdogs"? Can you think of one of our presidents who was an underdog?

6. What skills did Gage develop as a result of Miss Hurd's instruction? How did one of her assignments change his life?

7. Trace Miss Hurd's influence on Gage after he left her junior high class.

8. When Gage uses "salty-tongued, no-nonsense" to describe Miss Hurd, what do you think he means? What other glimpses of her personality do you gain not only from her interaction with Gage but also with other students?

9. An excerpt from Gage's book *Eleni* was quoted on national television. Who referred to it? What was the occasion? How did one of her assignments change his life?

10. How would you describe Gage's attitude and the tone of the essay?

A Writer's Response

1. Have you ever changed schools and felt uncomfortable among students who seemed quite different? Describe the experience and how you adjusted. Was any particular person helpful in making you feel comfortable? Write an essay describing the experience and how it affected you.

2. Consider the people who have influenced your life. Write an essay identifying the incidents that were particularly significant to you. Explain why.

The Emotional Quadrant

Elisabeth Kübler-Ross

"Big boys don't cry!" We've all heard it, and perhaps some of us have said it without an inkling of the possible effects on a child who has a vital need to cry. The following essay by Elisabeth Kübler-Ross, one of the world's foremost authorities on death and dying, traces the effect of a parent's death on a young child. Kübler-Ross, born in Zurich, Switzerland in 1926, received her M.D. from Zurich University in 1957. Four years later she became a naturalized American citizen. A physician, educator, and writer, she published her watershed work, On Death and Dying, *in 1969. Since then she has published twelve other books, including* On Life After Death *(1991),* On Children and Death *(1997),* Working It Through *(1997),* Remember the Secret *(1998),* The Tunnel and the Light *(1999), and* Life Lessons *(2000).*

Very young children have no fear of death, although they have the two innate   1
fears of sudden loud noises and of falling from high places. Later on children are
naturally afraid of separation, since the fear of abandonment and the absence of
a loving caretaker is very basic and meaningful. Children are aware of their dependency, and those who have been exposed to early traumas in life are scarred.
They will need to relive the trauma and learn to let go of the panic, pain, anxiety
and rage of the abandonment.

These violent feelings arise often, not solely when a member of the family
dies. Abandonments of all sorts happen thousands of times over in our society,
and if the loss is not associated with the death of a loved one, few people will recognize this. The emergency support systems or shoulders to lean on will not be
called into action, and there will be no sympathy visits by neighbors. So the child
who feels abandoned in some manner is left vulnerable; his future mind-set could
include a general mistrust, a fear of ever allowing a close relationship, an alienation from the person who is blamed for the separation, and a deep grief over the
absence of love.

Rene was such a child, and he needed thirty years to heal. He was only five
years old when his father told him to get into the car, because they were going
somewhere together. Rene was very excited. His father had been drinking for
many years; his mom had been in and out of mental hospitals, and there had
been very little laughter and happiness in his life. And now his dad was going to
take him somewhere. He did not dare to ask him where they were going. To the
zoo? To the park? To a football game? He could not understand why Dad had
come home in the middle of the week, but he knew that his mom was very sick
again, because she had slept all day and never came down even to fix him a
sandwich.

In the car, Rene and his father approached a huge building and parked. His
father silently opened the car door and let Rene out. The father was very quiet;

he did not even smile once. Rene wondered if his father was mad at him. He remembered he had fixed his own breakfast. He had even put the dishes in the sink. He was never noisy when his mom and dad had their fights, and he stayed in the den and out of the way. He had not heard them fighting today, and therefore Rene had hoped it would be a good day.

His dad took him by the hand and led him into a strange room with a funny   5
smell. A Catholic sister came and talked to his father, but no one talked to him. Then his father left the room, and a short time later the sister left also. Rene sat very quietly and waited, but no one came. Maybe his dad had to go to the bathroom. Finally he got up, and out the window he saw his dad walking out of the house toward the car. He ran as fast as he could: "Dad, Dad, don't leave me!" But the car door shut, and he saw the old familiar car turn the corner—out of sight.

Rene never saw his mother again. She returned to the mental hospital, where two years later she killed herself. He didn't see his father again for many years. It was much later that a strange woman came to visit him one day; she told him that his dad had married her and that they had planned to take him out of the home of the sisters to see if it could "work out."

Rene tried to please his dad in every way he could. He painted the new house and worked every free moment he had to get a nod of approval from him. But his dad remained as silent as he had always been. This silence always brought back to Rene the memory of that nightmarish day when he had been taken away from home without so much as an explanation, much less a good-bye or last hug from his mom.

His father never said "thank you" or "I am pleased with you," just as he never brought up the reasons for Rene's placement in the home and the lack of warning. So Rene grew up trying to please, not knowing that the fear of rejection and abandonment was still with him in adulthood. But Rene was afraid of alcoholism, afraid of mental illness, afraid of getting close to anyone. His whole life consisted of work and more work to please his father. He never allowed himself to get angry, to speak up, to express displeasure. The only time his face lit up was at the sight of a parent playing with a child in the park or swinging on a swing in a schoolyard. He spent his free time in those places, vicariously enjoying the laughter of these children, unaware of why he could not experience love and laughter in his own life.

As a mature adult he took an opportunity to look at his pain, anguish, despair, and incomprehension of this totally unexpected abandonment in early childhood, and he emerged a free man. It took him only one week, touched by others who shared their agonies in a safe place where it was regarded as a blessing to get rid of old tears and anger. During that week, Rene felt loved unconditionally. This man has just resolved his conflicts and has begun to understand his inability to trust and relate.

If someone—preferably his parents—had talked with this little boy and   10
made an effort to understand his play, his drawings, his sullen withdrawal and isolation, much pain and unresolved conflict, carried within for decades, could have easily been avoided. You think those things happened in the last century? No, they still happen every day in our society.

Many, many adults suffer from never having resolved the hurts of their child-hood. So children need to be allowed to grieve without being labeled crybaby or sissy, or hearing the ridiculous statement "Big boys don't cry." If children of both sexes are not allowed to express their natural emotions in childhood, they will have problems later on in the form of self-pity and many psychosomatic symp-toms. Grief and fear, when allowed to be expressed and shared in childhood, can prevent much future heartache.

Reflecting and Interpreting

1. In the anecdote about five-year-old Rene, from whose point of view is the story told? What is the effect?
2. Where is the thesis statement?
3. How does Rene try to win his father's approval?
4. Describe Rene's early home life and his relationship with his father. Did the relationship improve when his father remarried? How effective is this ex-tended example in supporting the thesis?
5. As an adult, what three things did Rene fear?
6. Although the essay devotes only one paragraph to the startling change in Rene, what can we surmise?
7. What danger does Dr. Kübler-Ross point to in the conclusion of her essay?
8. The author says that after a week of treatment, "Rene felt loved uncondition-ally." What does this phrase mean to you?
9. When tragedy strikes in a family, why should it be discussed with even very young children?
10. The author does not define "emotional quadrant" in this essay. Consider the meaning of *quadrant*. To what does emotional quadrant seem to refer?

A Writer's Response

1. Has something ever happened to you that you felt you could not tell anyone? What was the effect on your peace of mind and behavior? What finally hap-pened? Write an essay describing the event and your reaction to it.
2. Perhaps you have survived a traumatic event with the support of kind friends and family. Write an essay describing the experience and its effect on you.

Shaping an Effective Argument

The New Case for Latin

Mike Eskenazi

During the past few decades, Latin was considered a dead language and rarely taught except in a few private schools and colleges in the USA. Now it is being resurrected in grades 3 through 7 in many private, public, and home schools. In this essay from Time *(11 December 2000), reporter Mike Eskenazi describes the third-grade classroom he visited in Fairfax City, Virginia, where Latin is taught orally. The purpose is to increase students' reading skills and test scores. Eskenazi has reported for* CNN News. *He writes regularly for* Time *magazine and* Time.com.

Amy High is decked out in the traditional pink dress and golden stole of   1
ancient Rome. She bursts into a third-grade classroom and greets her students:
"*Salvete, omnes!*" (Hello, everyone!) The kids respond in kind, and soon they are
studying derivatives. "How many people are in a duet?" High asks. All the kids
know the answer, and when she asks how they know, a boy responds, "Because
duo is 'two' in Latin." High replies, "*Plaudite!*" and the 14 kids erupt in applause.
They learn the Latin root *later*, or side, and construct such English words as bi-
lateral and quadrilateral. "Latin's going to open up so many doors for you," High
says. "You're going to be able to figure out the meaning of words you've never seen
before."

High teaches at Providence Elementary School in Fairfax City, Va., which has
a lot riding on the success of her efforts. As part of Virginia's high-stakes testing
program, schools that don't boost their scores by the year 2007 could lose state
funding. So Fairfax City, just 18 miles southwest of the White House, has up-
graded its two crumbling elementary schools with new high-tech television stu-
dios, computer labs and one very old feature—mandatory Latin.

Here lies one of the more counter-intuitive developments of the standardized-testing movement: Though some critics complain that teachers are forced to dumb down their lessons and "teach to the test," some schools are offering more challenging course work as a way of engaging students. In the past three years, scores of elementary schools in high-stakes testing states such as Texas, Virginia and Massachusetts have added Latin programs. Says Allen Griffith, a member of the Fairfax City school board: "If we're trying to improve English skills, teaching Latin is an awfully effective, proved method."

This is not your father's Latin, which was taught to élite college-bound high schoolers and drilled into them through memorization. Its tedium and perceived irrelevance almost drove Latin from public schools. Today's growth in elementary school Latin has been spurred by new, interactive oral curriculums, enlivened by lessons in Roman mythology and culture. "One thing that makes it engaging for kids is the goofy fun of investigating these guys in togas," says Marion Polsky, author of *First Latin: A Language Discovery Program*, the textbook used in Fairfax City.

Latin enthusiasts believe that if young students learn word roots, they will be able to decipher unfamiliar words. (By some estimates, 65% of all English words have Latin roots.) Latin is an almost purely phonetic language. There are no silent letters, and each letter represents a single sound. That makes it useful in teaching reading. And once kids master the grammatical structure of Latin—which is simple, logical and consistent—they will more easily grasp the many grammatical exceptions in English. 5

In the 1970s and '80s, the U.S. government funded Latin classes in underperforming urban school districts. The results were dramatic. Children who were given a full year of Latin performed five months to a year ahead of control groups in reading comprehension and vocabulary. The Latin students also showed outsize gains in math, history and geography. But Congress cut the funding, and nearly all the districts discontinued Latin.

Some curriculum experts have examined the evidence and still favor modern languages instead of Latin. John Chubb, chief executive of the Edison charter schools, said the company decided to make Spanish, not Latin, mandatory in its elementary schools because "we want our kids to be socialized to the outside world."

Still, Griffith, the Fairfax City school-board member, believes that "so far, the Latin looks like a good investment." He took encouragement from the confident smiles of Amy High's students each time they correctly responded to a question. "They're so receptive," says High. "They don't even know they're learning."

Reflecting and Interpreting

1. What type of opening does Eskenazi use? What is the effect?

2. How does Latin open doors for students?

3. How do the new Latin programs differ from the old method of rote memorization?

4. What is significant about the grammatical structure of Latin, as opposed to the structure of English?

5. How would you state the old case against Latin? Why was it neglected in the twentieth century?

6. In earlier government-funded Latin programs in urban schools, what were the results? Why were the programs discontinued?

7. Why do the Edison charter schools prefer to teach Spanish?

8. What is accomplished by Eskenazi's including actual quotations from those involved in the Latin programs?

9. Look at the final sentence. What does this sentence indicate?

10. Many Latin words have been incorporated into the English language and used regularly. How many of these terms are familiar to you: *antebellum, bona fide, carpe diem, caveat emptor, e pluribus unum, modus operandi, persona non grata, quid pro quo, and vox populi?*

A Writer's Response

Have you or has anyone in your family learned a foreign language? Are you learning one now? Has learning another language helped in deciphering unfamiliar English words? Would learning another language be valuable for your future career?

When the Lullaby Ends

Andrea Sachs

Should someone be allowed to return a child to an adoption agency if the child turns out to be defective? That is the question Andrea Sachs raises in this essay. A member of the New York Bar, the Illinois Bar, and the United States Supreme Court Bar, Sachs has a degree not only in law but also in journalism. Sachs has written for the Los Angeles Times, *the* Washington Post, New York Newsday, *the* Columbia Journalism Review, *and the* American Bar Association Journal. *Currently, she covers the Supreme Court and legal issues for* Time *magazine. In 2000 she received special recognition for her reporting for an article in* Time.

Most eleven-year-olds don't have a lawyer, but Tony is a special case. His   1
adoptive parents decided five years after his adoption that Tony had not properly "bonded" with them, and returned him to the state in March. They kept Sam, Tony's natural younger brother. Patrick Murphy, the Chicago public guardian who was appointed to serve as Tony's attorney, says the youngster is an "absolute joy to be around." But there have been scars. Says Murphy: "One of the tragic things is that Tony blames himself."

Tony is one of at least 1,000 children adopted in the U.S. each year who will be returned to agencies by their new parents. Some are sent back because of unmet expectations, others because they have severe emotional problems the parents cannot handle. In a risk-averse age when consumer standards have become more exacting and family commitments seem less binding, there is a danger that adopted children could be viewed as commodities that come with an implied warranty. The problem presents a major challenge for the legal system. "This is not a question of damaged goods; it's a matter of what's in the best interest of the child," says Neil Cogan of Southern Methodist law school.

Social workers used to believe that all an adopted child needed was a loving home. But now many admit that even the most committed parents may be overwhelmed by unexpected problems. In 1986 Dan and Rhonda Stanton adopted a blond baby girl they named Stacey René. "We thought we had a perfect baby because she didn't cry," says Dan, an insurance agent in suburban Dallas. Their contentment faded as the months passed and Stacey did not develop properly. She didn't babble and laugh like their friends' babies and couldn't pinch with her individual fingers. The tentative diagnosis: Rett's syndrome, a rare genetic disorder in which the brain stops growing. Devastated, the Stantons took Stacey back to the agency and have not seen her since. "We made a commitment to her, but we were not able to live up to that commitment," says Rhonda. "She turned out to be totally different from what we thought we had adopted."

If adoptive parents are saddled with an unforeseen defect, who should shoulder the load? Most experts put the onus on the adoptive parents. "Families, having decided to do an adoption, assume a certain risk," says Professor William Winslade of the University of Texas Medical School in Galveston. "If it is an incredibly difficult burden, it seems unfair not to give parents, who have provided the benefit to society by making the adoption, some special help. But I don't think the burden should be totally given back to the state either. Parents adopt because they want the joys—and the sorrows—of having children."

About 2% of all adoptions in the U.S. fail. But for older children and children   5
with special needs, the numbers are far higher. For children older than two, 10% of the adoptions are dissolved. For ages 12 to 17, the rate shoots up to around 24%. This poses a special problem, since healthy adoptable babies are increasingly scarce due to the fact that more single women now opt to have abortions or to keep their infants. More families are therefore adopting older or handicapped children. This seems to be a main cause of the growing return-to-sender phenomenon.

As the problem of disrupted adoptions spreads, specialists are looking more closely at agency methods. One cause for failure is a practice that Berkeley Professor Richard Barth describes as "stretching." In essence, it is a bait-and-switch game: would-be parents are encouraged to adopt a child different from the one they wanted by the withholding of some negative information. For example, a couple who want a baby are persuaded to take an older child and never told that several earlier placements have not worked out because of emotional problems. Though the motive is benevolent—finding a home for a hard-to-place child— Barth regards the tactic as unethical.

Some disappointed parents have begun to fight back in the courts. The notion of "wrongful adoption"—which claims that agencies are liable for damages if they place children without fully disclosing their health backgrounds—is gaining legal recognition. Frank and Jayne Gibbs of Philadelphia are suing two agencies for $6 million, following their adoption of a seven-year-old boy who turned out to be violently disturbed. After the adoption, say the couple, they discovered that he had been horribly abused, including an attempt by his natural mother to cut off his genitals.

Many states have passed medical disclosure laws, which make it easier to obtain accurate information about a child. Agencies themselves are attempting to gather more data. The Golden Cradle adoption agency, in Cherry Hill, N.J., requires natural mothers to fill out 10-page medical histories that ask about everything from hay fever and heavy drinking to Down's syndrome and blood transfusions. Genetic counselors are often called in as consultants. "We believe an ounce of prevention is worth a pound of cure," says agency supervisor Mary Anne Giello.

Still, there are no warranties on adoptions. Those who set out looking for perfect "designer" children are likely to be disappointed. Nor is it possible—or even necessary—to know everything about a child. "People shouldn't get the idea that they can't be parents unless they have a DNA portrait of a kid," says Professor Joan Hollinger of the University of Detroit law school. Instead, adoptive parents, armed with as much information as possible, should face the inevitable mysteries—just as all parents do.

Reflecting and Interpreting

1. Examine the first paragraph. Does it raise any questions in your mind? Is there anything more you would like to know about that particular case?

2. Approximately how many adopted children are returned each year? What are three reasons children are returned?

3. Which age range of children has the greatest rate of return? Which factors might lead to their return? Are these factors similar to the ones that natural parents face?

4. What, according to Neil Cogan of Southern Methodist law school, is the key question that should be asked when an adopted child is about to be returned?

5. Should an alternative or support be offered to adoptive parents in these circumstances? If so, what?

6. Who should assume the responsibility for unforeseen problems in children? What do most experts say in answer to this question?

7. What factors contribute to the growing problem of returns?

8. Define "stretching" as practiced by some adoption agencies. Is this an ethical tactic?

9. What is "wrongful adoption"?

10. If agencies allow the return of adopted children, should a time limit be set? If so, what is a reasonable limit? (Answers may vary.)

A Writer's Response

1. Should adoptive parents be allowed to return children? Write an essay taking a stand on this question and defend your position. To gain more information, you may want to do research.

2. *Small Groups:* What can a couple do to forestall unnecessary risks in adopting a child? Should they depend only on the agency to provide information? Should they be allowed access to the medical histories of the parents?

Working at McDonald's

Amitai Etzioni

Dr. Etzioni, who has taught at Columbia University, Harvard Business School, and George Washington University, served as Senior Advisor to the White House (1979–1980). The recipient of many awards, he is the author of nineteen books. They include The Moral Dimension: Toward a New Economics *(1988),* The Spirit of Community *(1993),* The New Golden Rule *(1996), and* The Limits of Privacy *(1999). He has also published articles in* The New York Times, The Washington Post, *and* The Wall Street Journal. *This essay first appeared in* The Miami Herald. *In the headnote, Etzioni gave credit for contributions from his teenage son, Dari.*

McDonald's is bad for your kids. I do not mean the flat patties and the white-flour buns; I refer to the jobs teen-agers undertake, mass-producing these choice items.   1

As many as two-thirds of America's high school juniors and seniors now hold down part-time paying jobs, according to studies. Many of these are in fast-food chains, of which McDonald's is the pioneer, trend-setter and symbol.

At first, such jobs may seem right out of the Founding Fathers' educational manual for how to bring up self-reliant, work-ethic-driven, productive young-sters. But in fact, these jobs undermine school attendance and involvement, im-part few skills that will be useful in later life, and simultaneously skew the values of teen-agers—especially their ideas about the worth of a dollar.

It has been a longstanding American tradition that youngsters ought to get paying jobs. In folklore, few pursuits are more deeply revered than the newspaper route and the sidewalk lemonade stand. Here the youngsters are to learn how sweet are the fruits of labor and self-discipline (papers are delivered early in the morning, rain or shine) and the ways of trade (if you price your lemonade too high or too low . . .).

Roy Rogers, Baskin Robbins, Kentucky Fried Chicken, et al., may at first seem   5
nothing but a vast extension of the lemonade stand. They provide very large num-bers of teen jobs, provide regular employment, pay quite well compared to many other teen jobs and, in the modern equivalent of toiling over a hot stove, test one's stamina.

Closer examination, however, finds the McDonald's kind of job highly uned-ucational in several ways. Far from providing opportunities for entrepreneurship (the lemonade stand) or self-discipline, self-supervision and self-scheduling (the paper route), most teen jobs these days are highly structured—what social scien-tists call "highly routinized."

True, you still have to have the gumption to get yourself over to the ham-burger stand, but once you don the prescribed uniform, your task is spelled out in minute detail. The franchise prescribes the shape of the coffee cups; the weight, size, shape and color of the patties; and the texture of the napkins (if any). Fresh coffee is to be made every eight minutes. And so on. There is no room for initiative, creativity, or even elementary rearrangements. These are breeding grounds for robots working for yesterday's assembly lines, not tomorrow's high-tech posts.

There are very few studies of the matter. One of the few is a 1984 study by Ivan Charper and Bryan Shore Fraser. The study relies mainly on what teen-agers write in response to questionnaires rather than actual observations of fast-food jobs. The authors argue that the employees develop many skills such as how to operate a food-preparation machine and a cash register. However, little attention is paid to how long it takes to acquire such a skill, or what its significance is.

What does it matter if you spend 20 minutes to learn to use a cash register, and then—"operate" it? What "skill" have you acquired? It is a long way from learning to work with a lathe or carpenter tools in the olden days or to program computers in the modern age.

A 1980 study by A. V. Harrell and P. W. Wirtz found that, among those stu-   10 dents who worked at least 25 hours per week while in school, their unemployment rate four years later was half of that of seniors who did not work. This is an impressive statistic. It must be seen, though, together with the finding that many who begin as part-time employees in fast-food chains drop out of high school and are gobbled up in the world of low-skill jobs.

Some say that while these jobs are rather unsuited for college-bound, white, middle-class youngsters, they are "ideal" for lower-class, "non-academic," minority youngsters. Indeed, minorities are "over-represented" in these jobs (21 percent of fast-food employees). While it is true that these places provide income, work and even some training to such youngsters, they also tend to perpetuate their disadvantaged status. They provide no career ladders, few marketable skills, and undermine school attendance and involvement.

The hours are often long. Among those 14 to 17, a third of fast-food employees (including some school dropouts) labor more than 30 hours per week, according to the Charper-Fraser study. Only 20 percent work 15 hours or less. The rest: between 15 and 30 hours.

Often the stores close late, and after closing one must clean up and tally up. In affluent Montgomery County, Md., where child labor would not seem to be a widespread economic necessity, 24 percent of the seniors at one high school in 1985 worked as much as five to seven days a week; 27 percent, three to five. There is just no way such amounts of work will not interfere with school work, especially homework. In an informal survey published in the most recent yearbook of the high school, 58 percent of the seniors acknowledged that their jobs interfere with their school work.

The Charper-Fraser study sees merit in learning teamwork and working under supervision. The authors have a point here. However, it must be noted that such learning is not automatically educational or wholesome. For example, much of the supervision in fast-food places leans toward teaching one the wrong kinds of compliance: blind obedience, or shared alienation with the "boss."

Supervision is often both tight and woefully inappropriate. Today, fast-food chains and other such places of work (record shops, bowling alleys) keep costs down by having teens supervise teens with often no adult on the premises.

There is no father or mother figure with which to identify, to emulate, to provide a role model and guidance. The work-culture varies from one place to another: Sometimes it is a tightly run shop (must keep the cash registers ringing); sometimes a rather loose pot party interrupted by customers. However, only rarely is there a master to learn from, or much worth learning. Indeed, far from being places where solid adult work values are being transmitted, these are places where all too often delinquent teen values dominate. Typically, when my son Oren was dishing out ice cream for Baskin Robbins in upper Manhattan, his fellow teen-workers considered him a sucker for not helping himself to the till. Most youngsters felt they were entitled to $50 severance "pay" on their last day on the job.

The pay, oddly, is the part of the teen work-world that is most difficult to evaluate. The lemonade stand or paper route money was for your allowance. In the old days, apprentices learning a trade from a master contributed most, if not all, of their income to their parents' household. Today, the teen pay may be low by adult standards, but it is often, especially in the middle class, spent largely or wholly by the teens. That is, the youngsters live free at home ("after all, they are high school kids") and are left with very substantial sums of money.

Where this money goes is not quite clear. Some use it to support themselves, especially among the poor. More middle-class kids set some money aside to help pay for college, or save it for a major purchase—often a car. But large amounts seem to flow to pay for an early introduction into the most trite aspects of American consumerism: flimsy punk clothes, trinkets and whatever else is the last fast-moving teen craze.

One may say that this is only fair and square; they are being good American consumers and spend their money on what turns them on. At least, a cynic might add, these funds do not go into illicit drugs and booze. On the other hand, an educator might bemoan that these young, yet unformed individuals, so early in life driven to buy objects of no intrinsic educational, cultural or social merit, learn so quickly the dubious merit of keeping up with the Joneses in ever-changing fads, promoted by mass merchandising.

Many teens find the instant reward of money, and the youth status symbols it buys, much more alluring than credits in calculus courses, European history or foreign languages. No wonder quite a few would rather skip school—and certainly homework—and instead work longer at a Burger King. Thus, most teen work these days is not providing early lessons in the work ethic; it fosters escape from school and responsibilities, quick gratification and a short cut to the consumeristic aspects of adult life.

Thus, parents should look at teen employment not as automatically educational. It is an activity—like sports—that can be turned into an educational opportunity. But it can also easily be abused. Youngsters must learn to balance the quest for income with the needs to keep growing and pursue other endeavors that do not pay off instantly—above all education.

Go back to school.

Reflecting and Interpreting

1. To what audience is the essay addressed? How does that change in the final sentence?

2. How would you define the work ethic? What values are implied? Consider that in earlier times it was often referred to as the "Puritan work ethic."

3. What three claims does the author make about jobs in fast-food chains? Are the claims limited to Manhattan or are they broad generalizations?

4. The author cites two studies with which he disagrees. What evidence does he submit for his opinion? How convincing are his replies?

5. Consider that not all students participate in after-school activities. They hang out at malls, in homes with no parents present, or in the streets. What fallacy is implicit in the thesis statement?

6. Do teens learn different values from spending money they have earned than they learn from spending an allowance provided by their parents? If so, do the values always differ in the way Etzioni says? What evidence is submitted?

7. See paragraph 16. Is one example adequate to support the either-or claim of sometimes a "tightly-run shop" or "sometimes a rather loose pot party interrupted by customers"? What further evidence would you like to see?

8. Etzioni says that 20% of working students work 15 hours or less. Will that prevent them from doing homework? How would you categorize his claim that it will?

9. Is alternating or block order used to present the argument?

10. Examine paragraph 21. How does the tone differ from that of earlier claims?

A Writer's Response

1. Did you hold a job while going to high school? If so, how many hours per week did you work? How did you spend (or save) your money? How would you say that working influenced you? Write an essay describing the cause and effects.

2. If you did not have a job during high school, how did you spend your time after school and weekends? Do you view this time as well spent? How did it affect your values? Write an essay describing the effects of this leisure.

3. *Small Groups:* What primary research could Etzioni have done to provide stronger support for his thesis?

The Other Difference
between Boys and Girls

Richard M. Restak

A practicing neurologist in Washington, DC, Richard Martin Restak is interested in the philosophical aspects of scientific research. He is a consultant to the Council for Science and Society (London) and a visiting lecturer for numerous colleges, universities, the Central Intelligence Agency, NASA, and other organizations. He is the author of ten books, including Premeditated Man *(1975),* The Infant Mind *(1980),* The Self Seekers *(1982),* The Brain Has a Mind of Its Own *(1991),* The Modular Brain *(1994),* Brainscapes *(1995), and* Older and Wiser *(1997), as well as coauthor of* Brainmakers *(1994), and* The Longevity Strategy: How to Live to 100 Using the Brain-Body Connection *(1998). In the following article, first printed in the* Washington Post, *Restak recommends social and educational changes because men and women do not think alike.*

Boys think differently from girls. Recent research on brain behavior makes   1
that conclusion inescapable, and it is unrealistic to keep denying it.

I know how offensive that will sound to feminists and others committed to overcoming sexual stereotypes. As the father of three daughters, I am well aware of the discrimination girls suffer. But social equality for men and women really depends on recognizing these differences in brain behavior.

At present, schooling and testing discriminate against both boys and girls in different ways, ignoring differences that have been observed by parents and educators for years. Boys suffer in elementary school classrooms, which are ideally suited to the way girls think. Girls suffer later on, in crucial ways, taking scholarship tests that are geared for male performance.

Anyone who has spent time with children in a playground or school setting is aware of differences in the way boys and girls respond to similar situations. Think of the last time you supervised a birthday party attended by five-year-olds. It's not usually the girls who pull hair, throw punches or smear each other with food.

Usually such differences are explained on a cultural basis. Boys are expected   5
to be more aggressive and play rough games, while girls are presumably encouraged to be gentle, nonassertive and passive. After several years of exposure to such expectations, the theory goes, men and women wind up with widely varying behavioral and intellectual repertoires. As a corollary to this, many people believe that if child-rearing practices could be equalized and sexual stereotypes eliminated, most of these differences would eventually disappear. As often happens, however, the true state of affairs is not that simple.

Undoubtedly, many of the differences traditionally believed to exist between the sexes are based on stereotypes. But despite this, evidence from recent brain research indicates that many behavioral differences between men and women are based on differences in brain functioning that are biologically inherent and unlikely to be modified by cultural factors alone.

The first clue to brain differences between the sexes came from observations of male and female infants. From birth, female infants are more sensitive to sounds, particularly to their mother's voice. In a laboratory, if the sound of the mother's voice is displaced to another part of the room, female babies will react while male babies usually seem oblivious to the displacement. Female babies are also more easily startled by loud noises. In fact, their enhanced hearing performance persists throughout life, with females experiencing a fall-off in hearing much later than males.

Tests involving girls old enough to cooperate show increased skin sensitivity, particularly in the fingertips, which have a lower threshold for touch identification. Females are also more proficient at fine motor performance. Rapid tapping movements are carried out quickly and more efficiently by girls than by boys.

In addition, there are differences in what attracts a girl's attention. Generally, females are more attentive to social contexts—faces, speech patterns and subtle vocal cues. By four months of age, a female infant is socially aware enough to distinguish photographs of familiar people, a task rarely performed well by boys of that age. Also at four months, girls will babble to a mother's face, seemingly recognizing her as a person, while boys fail to distinguish between a face and a dangling toy, babbling equally to both.

Female infants also speak sooner, have larger vocabularies and rarely demonstrate speech defects. Stuttering, for instance, occurs almost exclusively among boys.

Girls can also sing in tune at an earlier age. In fact, if we think of the muscles of the throat as muscles of fine control—those in which girls excel—then it should come as no surprise that girls exceed boys in language abilities. This early linguistic bias often prevails throughout life. Girls read sooner, learn foreign languages more easily and, as a result, are more likely to enter occupations involving language mastery.

Boys, in contrast, show an early visual superiority. They are also clumsier, performing poorly at something like arranging a row of beads, but excel at other activities calling on total body coordination. Their attentional mechanisms are also different. A boy will react to an inanimate object as quickly as he will to a person. A male baby will often ignore the mother and babble to a blinking light, fixate on a geometric figure and, at a later point, manipulate it and attempt to take it apart.

A study of nursery preschool children carried out by psychologist Diane McGuinness of Stanford University found boys more curious, especially in regard to exploring their environment. McGuinness' studies also confirmed that males are better at manipulating three-dimensional space. When boys and girls are asked to mentally rotate or fold an object, boys overwhelmingly outperform girls. "I folded it in my mind" is a typical male response. Girls, when explaining how

10

they perform the same task, are likely to produce elaborate verbal descriptions which, because they are less appropriate to the task, result in frequent errors.

In an attempt to understand the sex differences in spatial ability, electroencephalogram (EEG) measurements have recently been made of the accompanying electrical events going on within the brain.

Ordinarily, the two brain hemispheres produce a similar electrical background that can be measured by an EEG. When a person is involved in a mental task—say, subtracting 73 from 102—the hemisphere that is activated will demonstrate a change in its electrical background. When boys are involved in tasks employing spatial concepts, such as figuring out mentally which of three folded shapes can be made from a flat, irregular piece of paper, the right hemisphere is activated consistently. Girls, in contrast, are more likely to activate both hemispheres, indicating that spatial ability is more widely dispersed in the female brain.

When it comes to psychological measurements of brain functioning between the sexes, unmistakable differences emerge. In 11 subtests of the most widely used test of general intelligence, only two subtests reveal similar mean scores for males and females. These sex differences have been substantiated across cultures and are so consistent that the standard battery of this intelligence test now contains a masculinity-femininity index.

Further support for sex differences in brain functioning comes from experience with subtests that eventually had to be omitted from the original test battery. A cube-analysis test, for example, was excluded because, after testing thousands of subjects, a large sex bias appeared to favor males. In all, over 30 tests eventually had to be eliminated because they discriminated in favor of one or the other sex. One test, involving mentally working oneself through a maze, favored boys so overwhelmingly that, for a while, some psychologists speculated that girls were totally lacking in a "spatial factor."

Most thought-provoking of all is a series of findings by Eleanor Maccoby and Carol Nagly Jacklin of Stanford on personality traits and intellectual achievement. They found that girls whose intellectual achievement is greatest tend to be unusually active, independent, competitive and free of fear or anxiety, while intellectually outstanding boys are often timid, anxious, not overtly aggressive and less active.

In essence, Maccoby and Jacklin's findings suggest that intellectual performance is incompatible with our stereotype of femininity in girls or masculinity in boys.

Research evidence within the last six months indicates that many of these brain sex differences persist over a person's lifetime. In a study at the University Hospital in Ontario that compared verbal and spatial abilities of men and women after a stroke, the women did better than men in key categories tested. After the stroke, women tended to be less disabled and recovered more quickly.

Research at the National Institute of Mental Health is even uncovering biochemical differences in the brains of men and women. Women's brains, it seems, are more sensitive to experimentally administered lights and sounds. The

15

20

investigator in charge of this research, Dr. Monte Buchsbaum, speculates that the enhanced response of the female brain depends on the effect of sex hormones on the formation of a key brain chemical. This increased sensibility to stimuli by the female brain may explain why women more often than men respond to loss and stress by developing depression.

It's important to remember that we're not talking about one sex being generally superior or inferior to another. Rather, psychobiological research is turning up important functional differences between male and female brains. The discoveries might possibly contribute to further resentments and divisions in our society. But must they? Why are sex differences in brain functioning disturbing to so many people? And why do women react so vehemently to findings that, if anything, indicate enhanced capabilities in the female brain?

It seems to me that we can make two responses to these findings on brain-sex differences. First, we can use them to help bring about true social equity. One way of doing this might be to change such practices as nationwide competitive examinations. If boys, for instance, truly do excel in right-hemisphere tasks, then tests such as the National Merit Scholarship Examination should be radically redesigned to assure that both sexes have an equal chance. As things now stand, the tests are heavily weighted with items that virtually guarantee superior male performance.

Attitude changes are also needed in our approach to "hyperactive" or "learning disabled" children. The evidence for sex differences here is staggering: More than 95 percent of hyperactives are males. And why should this be surprising in light of the sex differences in brain function that we've just discussed?

The male brain learns by manipulating its environment, yet the typical student is forced to sit still for long hours in the classroom. The male brain is primarily visual, while classroom instruction demands attentive listening. Boys are clumsy in fine hand coordination, yet are forced at an early age to express themselves in writing. Finally, there is little opportunity in most schools, other than during recess, for gross motor movements or rapid muscular responses. In essence, the classrooms in most of our nation's primary grades are geared to skills that come naturally to girls but develop very slowly in boys. The results shouldn't be surprising: a "learning disabled" child who is also frequently "hyperactive."

"He can't sit still, can't write legibly, is always trying to take things apart, won't follow instructions, is loud, and, oh yes, terribly clumsy," is a typical teacher description of male hyperactivity. We now have the opportunity, based on emerging evidence of sex differences in brain functioning, to restructure elementary grades so that boys find their initial educational contacts less stressful.

At more advanced levels of instruction, efforts must be made to develop teaching methods that incorporate verbal and linguistic approaches to physics, engineering and architecture (to mention only three fields where women are conspicuously underrepresented and, on competitive aptitude tests, score well below males).

The second alternative is, of course, to do nothing about brain differences and perhaps even deny them altogether. Certainly there is something to be said for this approach too. In the recent past, enhanced social benefit has usually resulted from stressing the similarities between people rather than their differences. We ignore brain-sex differences, however, at the risk of confusing biology with sociology, and wishful thinking with scientific facts.

The question is not, "Are there brain-sex differences?" but rather, "What is going to be our response to these differences?" Psychobiological research is slowly but surely inching toward scientific proof of a premise first articulated by the psychologist David Wechsler more than 20 years ago:

"The findings suggest that women seemingly call upon different resources or   30
different degrees of like abilities in exercising whatever it is we call intelligence. For the moment, one need not be concerned as to which approach is better or 'superior.' But our findings do confirm what poets and novelists have often asserted, and the average layman long believed, namely, that men not only behave, but 'think' differently from women."

Reflecting and Interpreting

1. What is Restak's thesis? What does he say is the reason for basic differences between boys and girls?

2. How does the second paragraph contribute to Restak's credibility?

3. How does paragraph 4 function? Why is it included?

4. What sexual differences have been observed in tests with newborns and infants?

5. Restak says that schooling and testing discriminate against both boys and girls in different ways. What does he mean?

6. What differences in spatial reasoning between the sexes have been found?

7. Although girls have superior fine motor skills, boys tend to be much more interested in computer games than girls. What does Restak say that would explain this difference?

8. What biochemical differences have been found between men's and women's brains?

9. What caution does Restak give?

10. What are two alternative ways of responding to these findings? Which does he advocate?

A Writer's Response

1. Have you ever been unable to do something that most other children (or adults) can do? Write a paragraph describing this situation and how you coped with it. Did it affect your later life? If so, how? Or perhaps you have had a family member or friend who underwent such an experience. Can you describe it?

2. *Small Groups:* Consider the pros and cons of Restak's recommendations for changes in education (paragraphs 23 through 27). Do they seem advisable to you? Why or why not?

We Have No "Right to Happiness"

C. S. Lewis

What exactly is the "pursuit of happiness," which we claim as a right? Does it have limits? In this essay C[livel] S[taples] Lewis (1898–1963) raises questions of morality that are even more pertinent today than four decades ago. A writer of world renown, Lewis also taught literature courses at Oxford and Cambridge Universities. His work includes adult fiction, children's books, poetry, and numerous books and essays on Christianity. Some of his best known works are The Allegory of Love: A study in Medieval Tradition *(1936),* The Screwtape Letters *(1942),* Mere Christianity *(1943),* Miracles: A Preliminary Study *(1947), and the seven* Chronicles of Narnia *(1950–1956).*

"After all," said Clare, "they had a right to happiness."   1

We were discussing something that once happened in our own neighborhood. Mr. A. had deserted Mrs. A. and got his divorce in order to marry Mrs. B., who had likewise got her divorce in order to marry Mr. A. And there was certainly no doubt that Mr. A. and Mrs. B. were very much in love with one another. If they continued to be in love, and if nothing went wrong with their health or their income, they might reasonably expect to be very happy.

It was equally clear that they were not happy with their old partners. Mrs. B. had adored her husband at the outset. But then he got smashed up in the war. It was thought he had lost his virility, and it was known that he had lost his job. Life with him was no longer what Mrs. B. had bargained for. Poor Mrs. A., too. She had lost her looks—and all her liveliness. It might be true, as some said, that she consumed herself by bearing his children and nursing him through the long illness that overshadowed their earlier married life.

You mustn't, by the way, imagine that A. was the sort of man who nonchalantly threw a wife away like the peel of an orange he'd sucked dry. Her suicide was a terrible shock to him. We all knew this, for he told us so himself. "But what could I do?" he said. "A man has a right to happiness. I had to take my one chance when it came."

I went away thinking about the concept of a "right to happiness."   5

At first this sounds to me as odd as a right to good luck. For I believe—whatever one school of moralists may say—that we depend for a very great deal of our happiness or misery on circumstances outside all human control. A right to happiness doesn't, for me, make much more sense than a right to be six feet tall, or to have a millionaire for your father, or to get good weather whenever you want to have a picnic.

I can understand a right as a freedom guaranteed me by the laws of the society I live in. Thus, I have a right to travel along the public roads because society gives me that freedom; that's what we mean by calling the roads "public." I can also understand a right as a claim guaranteed me by the laws, and correlative to an obligation on someone else's part. If I have a right to receive £100 from you, this is another way of saying that you have a duty to pay me £100. If the laws allow Mr. A. to desert his wife and seduce his neighbor's wife, then, by definition, Mr. A. has a legal right to do so, and we need bring in no talk about "happiness."

But of course that was not what Clare meant. She meant that he had not only a legal but a moral right to act as he did. In other words, Clare is—or would be if she thought it out—a classical moralist after the style of Thomas Aquinas, Grotius, Hooker and Locke. She believes that behind the laws of the state there is a Natural Law.

I agree with her. I hold this conception to be basic to all civilization. Without it, the actual laws of the state become an absolute, as in Hegel. They cannot be criticized because there is no norm against which they should be judged.

The ancestry of Clare's maxim, "They have a right to happiness," is august. In words that are cherished by all civilized men, but especially by Americans, it has been laid down that one of the rights of man is a right to "the pursuit of happiness." And now we get to the real point. 10

What did the writers of that august declaration mean?

It is quite certain what they did not mean. They did not mean that man was entitled to pursue happiness by any and every means—including, say, murder, rape, robbery, treason and fraud. No society could be built on such a basis.

They meant "to pursue happiness by all lawful means"; that is, by all means which the Law of Nature eternally sanctions and which the laws of the nation shall sanction.

Admittedly this seems at first to reduce their maxim to the tautology that men (in pursuit of happiness) have a right to do whatever they have a right to do. But tautologies, seen against their proper historical context, are not always barren tautologies. The declaration is primarily a denial of the political principles which long governed Europe: a challenge flung down to the Austrian and Russian empires, to England before the Reform Bills, to Bourbon France. It demands that whatever means of pursuing happiness are lawful for any should be lawful for all; that "man," not men of some particular caste, class, status or religion, should be free to use them. In a century when this is being unsaid by nation after nation and party after party, let us not call it a barren tautology.

But the question as to what means are "lawful"—what methods of pursuing happiness are either morally permissible by the Law of Nature or should be declared legally permissible by the legislature of a particular nation—remains exactly where it did. And on that question I disagree with Clare. I don't think it is obvious that people have the unlimited "right to happiness" which she suggests. 15

For one thing, I believe that Clare, when she says "happiness," means simply and solely "sexual happiness." Partly because women like Clare never use the word "happiness" in any other sense. But also because I never heard Clare talk about the "right" to any other kind. She was rather leftist in her politics, and would have been scandalized if anyone had defended the actions of a ruthless man-eating tycoon on the ground that his happiness consisted in making money and he was pursuing his happiness. She was also a rabid teetotaler; I never heard her excuse an alcoholic because he was happy when he was drunk.

A good many of Clare's friends, and especially her female friends, often felt—I've heard them say so—that their own happiness would be perceptibly increased by boxing her ears. I very much doubt if this would have brought her theory of a right to happiness into play.

Clare, in fact, is doing what the whole western world seems to me to have been doing for the last forty-odd years. When I was a youngster, all the progressive people were saying, "Why all this prudery? Let us treat sex just as we treat all our other impulses." I was simple-minded enough to believe they meant what they said. I have since discovered that they meant exactly the opposite. They meant that sex was to be treated as no other impulse in our nature has ever been treated by civilized people. All the others, we admit, have to be bridled. Absolute obedience to your instinct for self-preservation is what we call cowardice; to your acquisitive impulse, avarice. Even sleep must be resisted if you're a sentry. But every unkindness and breach of faith seems to be condoned provided that the object aimed at is "four bare legs in a bed."

It is like having a morality in which stealing fruit is considered wrong—unless you steal nectarines.

And if you protest against this view you are usually met with chatter about the legitimacy and beauty and sanctity of "sex" and accused of harboring some Puritan prejudice against it as something disreputable or shameful. I deny the charge. Foam-born Venus . . . golden Aphrodite . . . Our Lady of Cyprus . . . I never breathed a word against you. If I object to boys who steal my nectarines, must I be supposed to disapprove of nectarines in general? Or even of boys in general? It might, you know, be stealing that I disapproved of. 20

The real situation is skillfully concealed by saying that the question of Mr. A.'s "right" to desert his wife is one of "sexual morality." Robbing an orchard is not an offense against some special morality called "fruit morality." It is an offense against honesty. Mr. A.'s action is an offense against good faith (to solemn promises), against gratitude (toward one to whom he was deeply indebted) and against common humanity.

Our sexual impulses are thus being put in a position of preposterous privilege. The sexual motive is taken to condone all sorts of behavior which, if it had any other end in view, would be condemned as merciless, treacherous and unjust.

Now though I see no good reason for giving sex this privilege, I think I see a strong cause. It is this.

It is part of the nature of a strong erotic passion—as distinct from a transient fit of appetite—that it makes more towering promises than any other emotion. No doubt all our desires make promises, but not so impressively. To be in love involves the almost irresistible conviction that one will go on being in love until one dies, and that possession of the beloved will confer, not merely frequent ecstasies, but settled, fruitful, deep-rooted, lifelong happiness. Hence *all* seems to be at stake. If we miss this chance we shall have lived in vain. At the very thought of such a doom we sink into fathomless depths of self-pity.

Unfortunately these promises are found often to be quite untrue. Every experienced adult knows this to be so as regards all erotic passions (except the one he himself is feeling at the moment). We discount the world-without-end pretensions of our friends' amours easily enough. We know that such things sometimes last—and sometimes don't. And when they do last, this is not because they promised at the outset to do so. When two people achieve lasting happiness, this is not solely because they are great lovers but because they are also—I must put it crudely—good people; controlled, loyal, fairminded, mutually adaptable people.

If we establish a "right to (sexual) happiness" which supersedes all the ordinary rules of behavior, we do so not because of what our passion shows itself to be in experience but because of what it professes to be while we are in the grip of it. Hence, while the bad behavior is real and works miseries and degradations, the happiness which was the object of the behavior turns out again and again to be illusory. Everyone (except Mr. A. and Mrs. B.) knows that Mr. A. in a year or so may have the same reason for deserting his new wife as for deserting his old. He will feel again that all is at stake. He will see himself again as the great lover, and his pity for himself will exclude all pity for the woman.

Two further points remain.

One is this. A society in which conjugal infidelity is tolerated must always be in the long run a society adverse to women. Women, whatever a few male songs and satires may say to the contrary, are more naturally monogamous than men; it is a biological necessity. Where promiscuity prevails, they will therefore always be more often the victims than the culprits. Also, domestic happiness is more necessary to them than to us. And the quality by which they most easily hold a man, their beauty, decreases every year after they have come to maturity, but this does not happen to those qualities of personality—women don't really care twopence about our *looks*—by which we hold women. Thus in the ruthless war of promiscuity women are at a double disadvantage. They play for higher stakes and are also more likely to lose. I have no sympathy with moralists who frown at the increasing crudity of female provocativeness. These signs of desperate competition fill me with pity.

Secondly, though the "right to happiness" is chiefly claimed for the sexual impulse, it seems to me impossible that the matter should stay there. The fatal principle, once allowed in that department, must sooner or later seep through our whole lives. We thus advance toward a state of society in which not only each man but every impulse in each man claims *carte blanche*. And then, though our technological skill may help us survive a little longer, our civilization will have died at heart, and will—one dare not even add "unfortunately"—be swept away.

Reflecting and Interpreting

1. Examine paragraph 3. What irony do you see?

2. What implicit question is the central idea of this essay? (Look at the first sentence and the title.)

3. Can you find an example of negation, a technique of definition?

4. Is there a difference between a right to happiness and the right to pursue happiness? If so, what is it?

5. Clare believes that "behind the laws of the state there is a Natural Law." Does Lewis agree or disagree? Why?

6. In paragraph 10 Lewis begins to trace the history of Clare's belief and where it leads. What is the pivotal question on which he disagrees?

7. How does Lewis view the marrige vow?

8. What kind of happiness does Lewis believe Clare means? Why does this kind raise moral questions?

9. What does Lewis say is necessary for two people to achieve lasting happiness?

10. What six rhetorical patterns does Lewis combine to organize his complex argument?

A Writer's Response

Lewis says that "women are more naturally monogamous than men; it is a biological necessity." Write an essay agreeing or disagreeing with his position. Cite facts and examples to support your claim.

Doves

Ursula Hegi

When Tearing the Silence: Being German in America *(1997) was selected for Oprah Winfrey's book club, Ursula Hegi gained widespread fame. Hegi has also written two collections of short stories:* Unearned Pleasures *(1997) and* Hotel of the Saints: Stories *(2001). She has also written five novels:* Stones from the River *(1994),* Salt Dancers *(1995),* Intrusions *(1997),* Floating in My Mother's Palm *(1998), and* The Vision of Emma Blau *(2001). Hegi was born in Germany after World War II; at age eighteen she immigrated to the United States. Now a professor at Eastern Washington University, she teaches creative writing. "*Doves,*" the story which appears here, was first published in* Prairie Schooner 65, *no. 4 (Winter 1992).*

Francine is having a shy day, the kind of day that makes you feel sad when the elevator man says good afternoon, the kind of day that makes you want to buy two doves.

Her raincoat pulled close around herself, Francine walks the twelve blocks to Portland Pet And Plant. She heads past the African violets, past the jade plants and fig trees, past the schnauzers and poodles, past the hamsters and turtles, past the gaudy parrot in the center cage who shrieks: "Oh amigo, oh amigo . . ."

What Francine wants are doves of such a smooth gray that they don't hurt your eyes. With doves like that you don't have to worry about being too quiet. They make soft clucking sounds deep inside their throats and wait for you to notice them instead of clamoring for your attention.

Six of them perch on the bars in the tall cage near the wall, two white with brownish speckles, the others a deep gray tinged with purple. Above the cage hangs a sign: Ring Neck Doves $7.99. Doves like that won't need much; they'll turn their heads toward the door when you push the key into the lock late in the afternoon and wait for you to notice them instead of clamoring for your attention.

"Oh amigo, oh amigo . . . ," screeches the parrot. Francine chooses the two smallest gray doves and carries them from the store in white cardboard boxes that look like Chinese takeout containers with air holes. The afternoon has the texture of damp newspaper, but Francine feels light as she walks back to her apartment.

In her kitchen she sets the boxes on top of her counter, opens the tops, and waits for the doves to fly out and roost on the plastic bar where she hangs her kitchen towels. But they crouch inside the white cardboard as if waiting for her to lift them out.

She switches on the radio to the station where she always keeps it, public radio, but instead of Tuesday night opera, a man is asking for donations. Francine has already sent in her contribution, and she doesn't like it when the man says, "None of you would think of going into a store and taking something off the shelves, but you listen to public radio without paying. . . ." The doves move their wing feathers forward and pull their heads into their necks as if trying to shield themselves from the fund-raising voice.

Francine turns the dial past rock stations and commercials. At the gaudy twang of a country-western song, the doves raise their heads and peer from the boxes. Their beaks turn to one side, then to the other, completing a nearly full circle. Low velvet sounds rise from their throats. Francine has never listened to country-westerns; she's considered them tacky, but when the husky voice of a woman sings of wanting back the lover who hurt her so, she tilts her head to the side and croons along with the doves.

Before she leaves for her job at K-Mart the next morning, Francine pulls the radio next to the kitchen sink and turns it on for the doves. They sit in the left side of her double sink which she has lined with yellow towels, their claws curved around folds of fabric, their eyes on the flickering light of the tuner that still glows on the country-western station. When she returns after working all day in the footwear department, they swivel their heads toward her and then back to the radio as if they'd been practicing that movement all day.

At K-Mart she finds that more people leave their shoes. It used to be just once   10 or twice a week that she'd discover a worn pair of shoes half pushed under the racks by someone who's walked from the store with stolen footwear. But now she sees them almost every day—sneakers with torn insoles, pumps with imitation leather peeling from the high heels, work shoes with busted seams—as if a legion of shoe thieves had descended on Portland.

Francine keeps the discarded shoes in the store's lost and found crate out back, though no one has ever tried to claim them. But some are still good enough to donate to Goodwill. She murmurs to the doves about the shoes while she refills their water and sprinkles birdseed into the porcelain soap dish. Coming home to them has become familiar. So have the songs of lost love that welcome her every evening. A few times she tried to return to her old station, but as soon as the doves grew listless, she moved the tuner back. And lately she hasn't felt like changing it at all. She knows some of the lines now, knows how the songs end.

Francine has a subscription to the opera, and after feeding the doves, she takes a bubble bath and puts on her black dress. In the back of the cab, she holds her purse with both hands in her lap. Sitting in the darkened balcony, she feels invisible as she listens to *La Traviata*, one of her favorite operas. For the first time it comes to her that it, too, is about lost love and broken hearts.

In the swell of bodies that shifts from the opera house, Francine walks into the mild November night, leaving behind the string of waiting taxicabs, the expensive restaurants across from the opera house, the stores and the bus station, the fast-food places and bars.

A young couple saunters from the Blue Moon Tavern hand in hand, steeped in amber light and the sad lyrics of a slow-moving song for that instant before the door closes again. Francine curves her fingers around the doorhandle, pulls it open, and steps into the smoky light as if she were a woman with red boots who had someone waiting for her. Below the Michelob clock, on the platform, two men play guitars and sing of betrayed love.

On the bar stool, her black dress rides up to her knees. She draws her shoulders around herself and orders a fuzzy navel, a drink she remembers from a late night movie. The summer taste of apricots and oranges soothes her limbs and makes her ease into the space her body fills.   15

A lean-hipped man with a cowboy hat asks Francine to dance, and as she sways in his arms on the floor that's spun of sawdust and boot prints, she becomes the woman in all the songs that the men on the platform sing about, the woman who leaves them, the woman who keeps breaking their hearts.

Reflecting and Interpreting

1. What do you learn in the first two sentences about the setting and the main character?

2. Why is Francine attracted to the doves rather than the parrot? What does the narrator say?

3. What does the parrot screech at her? Notice that he repeats the same words in paragraph 5. What do they mean (translated)? What is their significance?

4. What is the significance of paragraph 6? What do you learn about Francine and the doves?

5. What do you learn about Francine's values in paragraph 7?

6. A paragraph and a half is spent describing shoes, which seems odd in a story so short. Do you see any similarities between the shoes and something else? Hint: consider their condition.

7. How does the footwear in Francine's fantasy differ from the shoes left at K-Mart? What connotations do the red boots carry?

8. How does Francine feel as she dances? How has she changed since she bought the doves?

9. What kind of night is described? Compare this night with the day the story opens.

10. What is the theme of this story?

A Writer's Response

Have you ever made a small purchase or made a slight variation in your daily routine that has had far-reaching effects? Or perhaps you made a small decision that led to a big change. What motivated or inclined you to take the action that initiated the change? Share your experience with your group.

Scheherazade

Charles Baxter

A prolific writer, Charles Baxter is the director of the M.F.A. program in creative writ-ing at the University of Michigan. Baxter is the author of three novels, Shadow Play *(1994),* First Light *(1995), and* The Feast of Love *(2001). He has also written four col-lections of short stories:* A Relative Stranger *(1991),* Harmony of the World *(1997), Be-lievers (1998), and* Through the Safety Net *(1998). Five of his stories have been selected for* Best American Short Stories. *"Scheherazade," which appears here, was first published in* A Relative Stranger.

She leaned down to adjust his respirator tube and the elastic tie around his   1
neck that kept it in place. "Don't," he said, an all-purpose warning referring to
nothing in particular, and she heard Muzak from down the hall, a version of "Star-
dust" that made her think of cold soup. A puddle outside his window reflected
blue sky and gave the ceiling of his room a faint blue tint.

He was looking sallow and breathing poorly; she would have to lie again to
perk him up.

"Do you remember," she said, sitting in the chair next to his chair, "my goodness, this would have been fifty years ago, that trip we made to Hawaii?"

"Don't remember it," he said. "Don't think I've been there."

"Yes, you have," she said, patting his hand where the wedding ring was. "We   5
took the train, it had 'Zephyr' in its name somewhere, one of those silver trains
that served veal for dinner. We had a romantic night in the Pullman car; I expect
you don't remember that."

"Not just now," he said.

"Well, we did. We took it to Oakland or San Francisco, I forget which, and
from there we took the boat to Honolulu."

"What boat? I don't remember a boat. Did it have a name?"

She leaned back and stared at the ceiling. Why did he always insist on the
names? She couldn't invent names; that always caused her trouble. And her bifo-
cals were hurting her. She would have to see that nice Dr. Hauser about them.
"The name of the ship, dear, was *Halcyon Days*, not very original, I must say; we
were on the C deck, second-class. The first night out you were seasick. Then you
were all right. The ship had an orchestra and we danced the fox-trot. You flirted
with that woman whose room was down the hall. You were quite awful about it."

The outline of a smile appeared on his face. "Who?"   10

She saw the smile and was pleased. "I don't remember," she said. "Why should
I remember her name? She was just a silly woman with vulgar dark-red hair. She
let it fly all over her shoulders."

"What was her name?"

"I told you I don't remember."

"Please," he said. His mouth was open. His filmy eyes looked in her direction.

"All right," she said. "Her name was Peggy."   15

"Peggy" he said, briefly sighing.

"Yes, Peggy," she said, "and you made yourself quite ridiculous around her, but I think she liked you, and I remember I once caught you two at the railing, looking at the waters of the Pacific go by as the ship churned westward."

"Was I bad?"

"You were all right, dear. You were just like any man. I didn't mind. Men are like that. You bought her drinks."

"What did she drink?"   20

"Old-fashioned," she said, but she felt herself going too far and hauled herself back in. "What *I* minded was that she would not always close the door to her stateroom. You would look in, and there she was."

"Yes," he said. "There she was."

"There she was," she continued, "in her bathrobe, or worse, with that terrible red hair of hers billowing down to her shoulders. In her white bathrobe, and you, standing in the hallway like any man, staring at her."

"You caught me."

"Yes, I did, but I didn't blame you. You were attractive to women."   25

"I was?"

"Yes, you were. You were so handsome in those days, and so witty, and when you sat down at the piano and sang those Cole Porter tunes, it was hard for women to resist."

"Could I play the piano?" He was smiling, perhaps thinking of the Pacific, or Peggy.

"Very well, dear. You could play and sing. Though I've heard better, I have certainly heard worse. You sang to me. You'd sing to anybody."

"To Peggy?"   30

"To anyone," she said. When she saw his smile fade, she said, "And to her, too. In an effort to charm. You sang 'You're the Top.' I daresay she liked it. Who knows what trouble you two got into? I was not a spy. All I know now is, it's been over fifty years."

He closed his eyes and stretched his thin legs. She saw a smile cross his face again and was pleased with herself.

"In Hawaii," she said, "we stayed at the Royal Palm Hotel." Although she had once been on a ship, she had never been in Hawaii and was speaking more slowly now as she tried to see the scene. "It was on the beach, the famous one with the name, and the sands were white, as white as alabaster. We played shuffleboard."

"I remember that," he said.

"Good. We drove around the island and climbed the extinct volcano, Mount   35
Johnson. There's a lake inside Mount Johnson, and you went swimming in it, and there were large birds, enormous blue birds, flying over our heads, and you called them the archangel birds and said that God had sent them to us as a sign."

"A sign of what?"

"A sign of our happiness."

"Were we happy?"

"Yes," she said. "We were."

"Always?"   40

"It seems so to me now. Anyway, Mount Johnson was one day, and on another day we went diving for pearls. You found an oyster with a pearl in it. I still wear it on a pin."

He looked over at her and searched her face and chest and arms.

"Just not today," she said. "I'm not wearing it today."

The sound of the oxygen hissing out of the respirator tube fatigued her. She would not be able to continue this much longer. It was like combat of a subtle kind. She hurried on. "On the island we picked enormous flowers, and every evening we sat down for dinner by the water, and you put a gardenia in my hair one night. We ate pineapples and broke open coconuts, and at moonrise the sea breezes came in through the window of our room where we were lying on the bed. We were so in love. We had room service bring us champagne and you read poetry to me."

"Yes," he said. "What did you look like?"   45

She clasped her hands in her lap. "I was beautiful." She paused. "You said so."

"The sound," he said.

"What sound?"

"There was a sound."

"I don't remember a sound," she said.   50

"There was one," he insisted.

"Where?"

"In the room."

"Yes?"

"It came in through the window," he whispered.   55

"From where?"

"From the sea. Do you hear it?"

"No."

"Listen."

She sat listening. The Muzak from the hallway had fallen silent. From outside   60
there was a faint, low humming.

"Hear it?"

"Yes," she said faintly.

"I heard it first there. In Hawaii."

"So did I."

"I feel a little better," he said. "I feel sleepy."   65

"Go to sleep, dear," she said. "Take a little nap."

"You'll be back?"

"Yes, tomorrow."

"Where else did we go?"

"We went," she said, "to Egypt, where we crawled through the pyramids. We   70
went through the fjords in Norway. We saw wonders. We saw many wonders."

"Tell me tomorrow."

"I will." She kissed him on the forehead, stood up, and walked to the doorway. She looked back at him; he seemed to be about to fall asleep, but he also seemed to be listening to the sound. She gazed at him for a moment, and then went down the hallway, past the nurses, bowing her head for a moment before she went out the front door to the bus stop, thinking of tomorrow's story.

Reflecting and Interpreting

To understand the allusion in the title of "Scheherazade," the reader needs to know that it alludes to the *Arabian Nights*, a collection of 200 folktales. The *Arabian Nights* begins with a story about King Shahriyar, who has vowed to marry a new wife every night and have her beheaded in the morning. When Scheherazade becomes his bride, however, she tells him a tale that is so entertaining he lets her live another day so that she can finish it. Her storytelling continues for one thousand and one nights. By that time the king is so in love with her that he lets her live.

1. Describe the setting of "Scheherazade." (Consider the weather outside as well as the atmosphere inside.)
2. What in the story indicates that the old man is terminally ill? (Hint: Think about the title.)
3. Why does the old woman tell her husband the tale about their going to Hawaii? Is this the first time that she has lied to him?
4. With a dictionary, look up the meaning of the names of the train and the ship. How do these names form a connection to the setting and the old man?
5. What direction did the ship head? What other connections do you see to this direction?
6. What are the archangel birds a sign of? Was the marriage always a happy one?
7. Examine the description of Hawaii. Do you notice any symbolism?
8. What does "It was like combat of a subtle kind" refer to? Who (or what) was the old woman's adversary?
9. What does the old woman's tale reveal about her?
10. What element of this story lends a note of universality?

A Writer's Response

The author is very careful to name objects but not the main characters. What is the effect of calling them *she* and *he* rather than giving their names? Does this detract or enhance the image of the hospital room for you? Why?

The Story of an Hour

Kate Chopin

A prolific writer, Kate Chopin (1850–1904) did not start until age 38, when she wrote her first poem "If It Might Be" and began the story "Euphrasie." She married at age 20 and had six children before her husband died in 1882. In 1889 the poem and two stories, "Wiser than a God" and "A Point at Issue" were published and well received. In 1890 her novel, At Fault, *appeared in print. She was unable to find a publisher for another novel,* Young Dr. Gosse *and destroyed the manuscript. Other successful writing— "Désirée's Baby" (1893),* Bayou Folk *(1894), "Athénaise" (1895), and* A Night in Acadie *(1897)—made her acclaimed in St. Louis, where she lived. In 1899, however, the reviews of* The Awakening *were scathing. Critics hailed it as "immoral," and her popularity faded. In the past few decades, her writing has again gained favor in the United States.*

Knowing that Mrs. Mallard was afflicted with a heart trouble, great care was taken to break to her as gently as possible the news of her husband's death. 1

It was her sister Josephine who told her, in broken sentences: veiled hints that revealed in half concealing. Her husband's friend Richards was there, too, near her. It was he who had been in the newspaper office when intelligence of the railroad disaster was received, with Brently Mallard's name leading the list of "killed." He had only taken the time to assure himself of its truth by a second telegram, and had hastened to forestall any less careful, less tender friend in bearing the sad message.

She did not hear the story as many women have heard the same, with a paralyzed inability to accept its significance. She wept at once, with sudden, wild abandonment, in her sister's arms. When the storm of grief had spent itself she went away to her room alone. She would have no one follow her.

There stood, facing the open window, a comfortable, roomy armchair. Into this she sank, pressed down by a physical exhaustion that haunted her body and seemed to reach into her soul.

She could see in the open square before her house the tops of trees that were all aquiver with the new spring life. The delicious breath of rain was in the air. In the street below a peddler was crying his wares. The notes of a distant song which some one was singing reached her faintly, and countless sparrows were twittering in the eaves. 5

There were patches of blue sky showing here and there through the clouds that had met and piled one above the other in the west facing her window.

She sat with her head thrown back upon the cushion of the chair, quite motionless, except when a sob came up into her throat and shook her, as a child who has cried itself to sleep continues to sob in its dreams.

She was young, with a fair, calm face, whose lines bespoke repression and even a certain strength. But now there was a dull stare in her eyes, whose gaze was fixed away off yonder on one of those patches of blue sky. It was not a glance of reflection, but rather indicated a suspension of intelligent thought.

There was something coming to her and she was waiting for it, fearfully. What was it? She did not know; it was too subtle and elusive to name. But she felt it, creeping out of the sky, reaching toward her through the sounds, the scents, the color that filled the air.

Now her bosom rose and fell tumultuously. She was beginning to recognize   10
this thing that was approaching to possess her, and she was striving to beat it back with her will—as powerless as her two white slender hands would have been.

When she abandoned herself a little whispered word escaped her slightly parted lips. She said it over and over under her breath: "free, free, free!" The vacant stare and the look of terror that had followed it went from her eyes. They stayed keen and bright. Her pulses beat fast, and the coursing blood warmed and relaxed every inch of her body.

She did not stop to ask if it were or were not a monstrous joy that held her. A clear and exalted perception enabled her to dismiss the suggestion as trivial.

She knew that she would weep again when she saw the kind, tender hands folded in death; the face that had never looked save with love upon her, fixed and gray and dead. But she saw beyond that bitter moment a long procession of years to come that would belong to her absolutely. And she opened and spread her arms out to them in welcome.

There would be no one to live for during those coming years; she would live for herself. There would be no powerful will bending hers in that blind persistence with which men and women believe they have a right to impose a private will upon a fellow-creature. A kind intention or a cruel intention made the act seem no less a crime as she looked upon it in that brief moment of illumination.

And yet she had loved him—sometimes. Often she had not. What did it mat-   15
ter! What could love, the unsolved mystery, count for in face of this possession of self-assertion which she suddenly recognized as the strongest impulse of her being!

"Free! Body and soul free!" she kept whispering.

Josephine was kneeling before the closed door with her lips to the keyhole, imploring for admission. "Louise, open the door! I beg; open the door—you will make yourself ill. What are you doing, Louise? For heaven's sake open the door."

"Go away. I am not making myself ill." No; she was drinking in a very elixir of life through that open window.

Her fancy was running riot along those days ahead of her. Spring days, and summer days, and all sorts of days that would be her own. She breathed a quick prayer that life might be long. It was only yesterday she had thought with a shudder that life might be long.

She arose at length and opened the door to her sister's importunities. There   20
was a feverish triumph in her eyes, and she carried herself unwittingly like a god-

dess of Victory. She clasped her sister's waist, and together they descended the stairs. Richards stood waiting for them at the bottom.

Some one was opening the front door with a latchkey. It was Brently Mallard who entered, a little travel-stained, composedly carrying his grip-sack and umbrella. He had been far from the scene of accident, and did not even know there had been one. He stood amazed at Josephine's piercing cry: at Richards' quick motion to screen him from the view of his wife.

But Richards was too late.

When the doctors came they said she had died of heart disease—of joy that kills.

Reflecting and Interpreting

1. Might there be more than one kind of "heart trouble" involved?
2. Often denial is the first stage of grief. How does Mrs. Mallard react to the news?
3. Describe the scene outside her open bedroom window. How does that scene symbolize what she is experiencing?
4. As she sits, facing the window, Mrs. Mallard feels ambivalent. Why? (Consider the lines in her face and "fearfully.")
5. How does her outlook on life change? How does this change affect her behavior?
6. Reread the story. Do you see any foreshadowing?
7. Do you notice any changes in the way the narrator refers to the main character? What is the significance of these various forms?
8. How does the staircase function in the story?
9. How is the story ironic?
10. What is curious about the use of "abandonment" and "abandoned"? How do these words relate to the ending—or do they?

A Writer's Response

Essay or Small Group: Consider that this story was written in 1894. How do you think it might have been received by the general public if it had been published then? What is your reaction to the story?

Still of Some Use

John Updike

In an interview for Salon magazine, Dwight Garner wrote: "There is indeed something snow-capped and oddly angelic about [John] Updike; he seems to hover over the contemporary literary scene like an apparition from another era, the last great American man of letters." In 1981 John Updike (1932–) won the Pulitzer prize for Rabbit Is Rich, *the third of a series of Rabbit novels. Over four decades, Updike has written nearly fifty books, which include eighteen novels, several collections of short stories, poems, and criticism. Some of his best known works include* Rabbit Run *(1960),* Pigeon Feathers *(1962),* Couples *(1968),* Bech: A Book *(1970),* Bech Is Back *(1982),* In the Beauty of the Lilies *(1997), and* Bech at Bay: A Quasi-Novel *(1998). His latest book of poems is a* Child's Calendar *(2000). The following short story was first published in* Trust Me *(1987).*

When Foster helped his ex-wife clean out the attic of the house where they   1
had once lived and which she was now selling, they came across dozens of forgotten, broken games. Parcheesi, Monopoly, Lotto; games aping the strategies of the stock market, of crime detection, of real-estate speculation, of international diplomacy and war; games with spinners, dice, lettered tiles, cardboard spacemen, and plastic battleships; games bought in five-and-tens and department stores feverish and musical with Christmas expectations; games enjoyed on the afternoon of a birthday and for a few afternoons thereafter and then allowed, shy of one or two pieces, to drift into closets and toward the attic. Yet, discovered in their bright flat boxes between trunks of outgrown clothes and defunct appliances, the games presented a forceful semblance of value: the springs of their miniature launchers still reacted, the logic of their instructions would still generate suspense, given a chance. "What shall we do with all these games?" Foster shouted, in a kind of agony, to his scattered family as they moved up and down the attic stairs.

"Trash 'em," his younger son, a strapping nineteen, urged.

"Would the Goodwill want them?" asked his ex-wife, still wife enough to think that all of his questions deserved answers. "You used to be able to give things like that to orphanages. But they don't call them orphanages anymore, do they?"

"They call them normal American homes," Foster said.

His older son, now twenty-two, with a cinnamon-colored beard, offered,   5
"They wouldn't work anyhow; they all have something missing. That's how they got to the attic."

"Well, why didn't we throw them away at the time?" Foster asked, and had to answer himself. Cowardice, the answer was. Inertia. Clinging to the past.

His sons, with a shadow of old obedience, came and looked over his shoulder at the sad wealth of abandoned playthings, silently groping with him for the particular happy day connected to this and that pattern of colored squares and arrows. Their lives had touched these tokens and counters once; excitement had flowed along the paths of these stylized landscapes. But the day was gone, and scarcely a memory remained.

"Toss 'em," the younger decreed, in his manly voice. For these days of cleaning out, the boy had borrowed a pickup truck from a friend and parked it on the lawn beneath the attic window, so the smaller items of discard could be tossed directly into it. The bigger items were lugged down the stairs and through the front hall; already the truck was loaded with old mattresses, broken clock-radios, obsolete skis and boots. It was a game of sorts to hit the truck bed with objects dropped from the height of the house. Foster flipped game after game at the target two stories below. When the boxes hit, they exploded, throwing a spray of dice, tokens, counters, and cards into the air and across the lawn. A box called Mousetrap, its lid showing laughing children gathered around a Rube Goldberg device, drifted sideways, struck one side wall of the truck, and spilled its plastic components into a flower bed. A set of something called Drag Race! floated gently as a snowflake before coming to rest, much diminished, on a stained mattress. Foster saw in the depth of downward space the cause of his melancholy: he had not played enough with these games. Now no one wanted to play.

Had he and his wife avoided divorce, of course, these boxes would have continued to gather dust in an undisturbed attic, their sorrow unexposed. The toys of his own childhood still rested in his mother's attic. At his last visit, he had crept up there and wound the spring of a tin Donald Duck; it had responded with an angry clack of its bill and a few stiff strokes on its drum. A tilted board with concentric grooves for marbles still waited in a bushel basket with his alphabet blocks and lead airplanes—waited for his childhood to return.

His ex-wife paused where he squatted at the attic window and asked him,   10
"What's the matter?"

"Nothing. These games weren't used much."

"I know. It happens fast. You better stop now; it's making you too sad."

Behind him, his family had cleaned out the attic; the slant-ceilinged rooms stood empty, with drooping insulation.

"How can you bear it?" he asked, of the emptiness.

"Oh, it's fun," she said, "once you get into it. Off with the old, on with the   15
new. The new people seem nice. They have *little* children."

He looked at her and wondered whether she was being brave or truly hardhearted. The attic trembled slightly. "That's Ted," she said.

She had acquired a boyfriend, a big athletic accountant fleeing from domestic embarrassments in a neighboring town. When Ted slammed the kitchen door two stories below, the glass shade of a kerosene lamp that, though long unused, Foster hadn't had the heart to throw out of the window vibrated in its copper clips, emitting a thin note like a trapped wasp's song. Time for Foster to go. His dusty knees creaked when he stood. His ex-wife's eager steps raced ahead of him down through the emptied house. He followed, carrying the lamp, and set it finally on the bare top of a bookcase he had once built, on the first-floor landing.

He remembered screwing the top board, a prize piece of knot-free pine, into place from underneath, so not a nailhead marred its smoothness.

After all the vacant rooms and halls, the kitchen seemed indecently full of heat and life. "Dad, want a beer?" the bearded son asked. "Ted brought some." The back of the boy's hand, holding forth the dewy can, blazed with fine ginger hairs. His girl friend, wearing gypsy earrings and a NO NUKES sweatshirt, leaned against the disconnected stove, her hair in a bandanna and a black smirch becomingly placed on one temple. From the kind way she smiled at Foster, he felt this party was making room for him.

"No, I better go."

Ted shook Foster's hand, as he always did. He had a thin pink skin and silver hair whose fluffy waves seemed mechanically induced. Foster could look him in the eye no longer than he could gaze at the sun. He wondered how such a radiant brute had got into such a tame line of work. Ted had not helped with the attic today because he had been off in his old town, visiting his teen-aged twins. "I hear you did a splendid job today," he announced.

"They did," Foster said. "I wasn't much use. I just sat there stunned. All these things I had forgotten buying."

"Some were presents," his son reminded him. He passed the can his father had snubbed to his mother, who took it and tore up the tab with that defiant-sounding *pssff*. She had never liked beer, yet tipped the can to her mouth.

"Give me one sip," Foster begged, and took the can from her and drank a long swallow. When he opened his eyes, Ted's big hand was cupped under Mrs. Foster's chin while his thumb rubbed away a smudge of dirt along her jaw which Foster had not noticed. This protective gesture made her face look small, pouty, and frail. Ted, Foster noticed now, was dressed with a certain comical perfection in a banker's Saturday outfit—softened blue jeans, crisp tennis sneakers, lumberjack shirt with cuffs folded back. The youthful outfit accented his age, his hypertensive flush. Foster saw them suddenly as a touching, aging couple, and this perception seemed permission to go.

He handed back the can.

"Thanks for your help," his former wife said.

"Yes, we do thank you," Ted said.

"Talk to Tommy," she unexpectedly added, in a lowered voice. She was still sending out trip wires to slow Foster's departures. "This is harder on him than he shows."

Ted looked at his watch, a fat, black-faced thing he could swim under water with. "I said to him coming in, 'Don't dawdle till the dump closes.'"

"He loafed all day," his brother complained, "mooning over old stuff, and now he's going to screw up getting to the dump."

"He's very sensi-tive," the visiting gypsy said, with a strange chiming brightness, as if repeating something she had heard.

Outside, the boy was picking up litter that had fallen wide of the truck. Foster helped him. In the grass there were dozens of tokens and dice. Some were engraved with curious little faces— Olive Oyl, Snuffy Smith, Dagwood—and others with hieroglyphs—numbers, diamonds, spades, hexagons—whose code was lost. He held out a handful for Tommy to see. "Can you remember what these were for?"

"Comic-Strip Lotto," the boy said without hesitation. "And a game called Gambling Fools there was a kind of slot machine for." The light of old payoffs flickered in his eyes as he gazed down at the rubble in his father's hand. Though Foster was taller,, the boy was broader in the shoulders, and growing. "Want to ride with me to the dump?" Tommy asked.

"I would, but I better go." He, too, had a new life to lead. By being on this forsaken property at all, Foster was in a sense on the wrong square, if not *en prise*. He remembered how once he had begun to teach this boy chess, but in the sadness of watching him lose—the little furry bowed head frowning above his trapped king—the lessons had stopped.

Foster tossed the tokens into the truck; they rattled to rest on the metal. "This depresses you?" he asked his son.

"Naa." The boy amended, "Kind of."   35

"You'll feel great," Foster promised him, "coming back with a clean truck. I used to love it at the dump, all that old happiness heaped up, and the seagulls."

"It's changed since you left. They have all these new rules. The lady there yelled at me last time, for putting stuff in the wrong place."

"She did?"

"Yeah, it was scary." Seeing his father waver, he added, "It'll only take twenty minutes." Though broad of build, Tommy had beardless cheeks and, between thickening eyebrows, a trace of that rounded, faintly baffled blankness babies have, that wrinkles before they cry.

"O.K.," Foster said. "You win. I'll come along. I'll protect you."   40

Reflecting and Interpreting

"Still of Some Use" is a rather puzzling story because so much that is important is left unsaid. The reader must watch for clues and listen to the nuances of dialogue to detect the turbulent emotions beneath the calm exterior of the main characters. As you make inferences, be sure to base each one on evidence from the story. Qualify your statements to make them tentative as you discuss the questions that follow.

1. Only one of Foster's family members is named. What does the lack of names imply?

2. What does Foster discover as he flips the games down to the truck?

3. Why are Foster's old toys and bookcase significant in the story? (Consider their condition.)

4. What does Foster's sarcastic response to his ex-wife indicate?

5. How does Foster feel about his ex-wife? What signs do you see?

6. Why might Foster's wife drink beer when she does not like it? What does her sharing her drink with him indicate?

7. What change does Foster show in his conversation with Tommy?

8. How are the title, the first paragraph, and the last sentence linked?

9. What is the analogy that underlies this story?

10. What themes do you see?

Small Group Discussion

With your group, discuss the change in societal attitudes toward divorce. In the 1930s, divorce was relatively rare and viewed askance. Now at the turn of the twenty-first century, divorce is commonplace, with nearly half of all marriages disintegrating. What causes have contributed to the change? What subtle changes often occur in the way children are regarded and treated after divorce? Should any changes be made in laws regarding marriage and divorce?

CREATION NARRATIVES

Introduction

The Search for our Beginnings

*Earth with its mountains, rivers and seas, Sky with its sun, moon,
and stars: in the beginning all these were one, and the one was Chaos.
Nothing had taken shape, all was a dark swirling confusion, over and
under, round and round. For countless ages this was the way of the
universe, unformed and illumined, until from the midst of Chaos came
P'an Ku. . . . [H]e raised his great arm and struck out blindly in the
face of the murk, and with one great crashing blow he scattered the
elements of Chaos.*

> —Cyril Birch
> from "Heaven and Earth and Man,"
> Chinese Myths and Fantasies (1996)

Practically every culture has a creation story that has been passed down
orally through the mists of time. Often the narrative has been recorded on stone,
clay tablets, papyrus, leather, or some other material. The latest innovation—
designed to preserve languages, as well as creation narratives—is a nickel disk that
is encased in a glass ball, the Rosetta Disk. (See the first essay in the Reader.)

Tribal stories of human origins vary considerably, but most have a watery element with the earth being created by hand, often from clay or mud. Sometimes
an animal—for example, a duck, frog, or toad—dives deep into the water to
bring up mud, perhaps with a root, from which springs all the plants and trees of
the earth. Many such narratives describe a single creator who makes and popu-
lates the earth with animals and humans in that order.

Some creation stories describe how animals and humans spoke one language
and lived peaceably in the beginning. American Indian legends often refer to animals that speak and to the mysterious power that resides in nature. Mountains,
rocks, and rivers are thought to be inhabited by spirits. Some Indian legends also
mention trickery, often to deceive evil spirits and accomplish some good act.
Some like "The Well-Baked Man," which appears in this section, contain wry
humor.

Other creation narratives, written in a much different vein, have been recognized for their moral and spiritual significance and incorporated into various religious writings. The creation account by the ancient Hebrews and Greeks, which has been translated into hundreds of languages, is the basis of many scriptures.

The most widely discussed and disputed is the Bible. Two versions of Genesis 1–2 are included here: the Torah and the King James. Comparable verses have been selected from the Koran (also translated as the Qur'an).

The Well-Baked Man

Pima Indian Legend

The legend of the "The Well-Baked Man," related by the Pima Indians, is based on fragments recorded in 1880. Apparently, it was borrowed from the early Pueblo, a nearby tribe, who lived in Arizona and New Mexico. The Pueblo have long been not only farmers but also craftsmen, noted for their fine jewelry, baskets, and pottery. The Pima have a history of farming, diverting river water to irrigate their crops. The Pima tribe, according to oral tradition, originated in the Salt River valley and spread to the Gila River. Formerly this area, which lies south of Phoenix, Arizona, belonged to Mexico. The Piman language is spoken by the Pima Indians, the Papago of Arizona, and the Yaqui of Mexico.

The Magician had made the world but felt that something was missing. 1
"What could it be?" he thought. "What could be missing?" Then it came to him that what he wanted on this earth was some beings like himself, not just animals. "How will I make them?" he thought. First he built himself a *horno*, an oven. Then he took some clay and formed it into a shape like himself.

Now, Coyote was hanging around the way he usually does, and when Magician, who was Man Maker, was off gathering firewood, Coyote quickly changed the shape of that clay image. Man Maker built a fire inside the *horno*, then put the image in without looking at it closely.

After a while the Magician said: "He must be ready now." He took the image and breathed on it, whereupon it came to life. "Why don't you stand up?" said Man Maker. "What's wrong with you?" The creature barked and wagged its tail. "Ah, oh my, Coyote has tricked me," he said. "Coyote changed my being into an animal like himself."

Coyote said, "Well, what's wrong with it? Why can't I have a pretty creature that pleases me?"

"Oh my, well, all right, but don't interfere again." That's why we have the dog; 5
it was Coyote's doing.

So Man Maker tried again. "They should be companions to each other," he thought. "I shouldn't make just one." He shaped some humans who were rather like himself and identical with each other in every part.

"What's wrong here?" Man Maker was thinking. Then he saw. "Oh my, that won't do. How can they increase?" So he pulled a little between the legs of one image, saying: "Ah, that's much better." With his fingernail he made a crack in the other image. He put some pleasant feeling in them somewhere. "Ah, now it's good. Now they'll be able to do all the necessary things." He put them in the *horno* to bake.

"They're done now," Coyote told him. So Man Maker took them out and made them come to life.

"Oh my, what's wrong?" he said. "They're underdone; they're not brown enough. They don't belong here—they belong across the water someplace." He scowled at Coyote. "Why did you tell me they were done? I can't use them here."

So the Magician tried again, making a pair like the last one and placing them   10
in the oven. After a while he said: "I think they're ready now."

"No, they aren't done yet," said Coyote. "You don't want them to come out too light again; leave them in a little longer."

"Well, all right," replied Man Maker. They waited, and then he took them out. "Oh my. What's wrong? These are overdone. They're burned too dark." He put them aside. "Maybe I can use them some other place across the water. They don't belong here."

For the fourth time Man Maker placed his images inside the oven. "Now, don't interfere," he said to Coyote, "you give me bad advice. Leave me alone."

This time the Magician did not listen to Coyote but took them out when he himself thought they were done. He made them come to life, and the two beings walked around, talked, laughed, and behaved in a seemly fashion. They were neither underdone nor overdone.

"These are exactly right," said Man Maker. "These really belong here; these I   16
will use. They are beautiful." So that's why we have the Pueblo Indians.

—Based on fragments recorded in the 1880s.

Reflecting and Interpreting

1. When the story opens, what has the Magician already created? What else does he desire?

2. A conflict occurs. What is it and what results?

3. Even after Coyote's trickery, the magician seems to depend on him. What is the second result?

4. How reliable is Coyote's judgment in the third baking?

5. The ending has an amusing twist. What is the theme behind it?

6. Do you see any instances of irony?

7. What aspect of the legend reveals that the Magician has mercy and consideration?

8. What actions indicate that the Magician has a plan for his human beings?

9. Words from certain cultures have long been integrated into other languages. Do you see any evidence of such borrowing in this story?

10. Often myths and legends are woven around existing elements of a culture. Can you find elements of the Pueblo culture?

A Writer's Response

Read Genesis 1–2. Write an essay comparing and contrasting these two creation narratives.

Genesis 1–2

Genesis *is the first book of the* Pentateuch, *the five early books of the* Torah *and the* Bible. *Although Moses has long been ascribed authorship, many scholars now believe that these five books were written over an extended period by various authors. Parts may have been written as late as the fifth century B.C. Early stone tablets from Sumeria, Babylon, and other civilizations carry narratives similar to biblical accounts of the Garden of Eden, the Great Flood, and others in the Old Testament.*

The Dead Sea Scrolls, the earliest existing biblical scripts, were handwritten on leather and sealed in large jars over 2,000 years ago. Written in Hebrew, Greek, and Aramaic, the manuscripts contain portions from all of the five early books, as well as writings by the Essenes, a religious sect. These fragments of scripture were evidently hand copied from earlier manuscripts. Through history there have been numerous translations. In 1611, James I of England authorized a version of the Bible that is still in use today.

The Hebrew Bible includes thirty-six books, but not the New Testament. The Holy Bible includes both the Old and New Testaments. The Roman Catholic Church, the Greek Orthodox Church, and some Protestant denominations also include the Apocrypha. Included here are two versions of Genesis 1–2. The first is a modern translation from the Torah; *the second is from the King James Version.*

Genesis 1–2 From the Torah

1 When God began to create*a* the heaven and the earth—²the earth being unformed and void, with darkness over the surface of the deep and a wind from*b* God sweeping over the water—³God said, "Let there be light"; and there was light. ⁴God saw that the light was good, and God separated the light from the darkness. ⁵God called the light Day, and the darkness He called Night. And there was evening and there was morning, a first day.*c*

⁶God said, "Let there be an expanse in the midst of the water, that it may separate water from water." ⁷God made the expanse, and it separated the water which was below the expanse from the water which was above the expanse. And it was so. ⁸God called the expanse Sky. And there was evening and there was morning, a second day.

1

---

a Others "In the beginning God created"
b Others "the spirit of"
c Others "one day"

⁹God said, "Let the water below the sky be gathered into one area, that the dry land may appear." And it was so. ¹⁰God called the dry land Earth, and the gathering of waters He called Seas. And God saw that this was good. ¹¹And God said, "Let the earth sprout vegetation: seed-bearing plants, fruit trees of every kind on earth that bear fruit with the seed in it." And it was so. ¹²The earth brought forth vegetation: seed-bearing plants of every kind, and trees of every kind bearing fruit with the seed in it. And God saw that this was good. ¹³And there was evening and there was morning, a third day.

¹⁴God said, "Let there be lights in the expanse of the sky to separate day from night; they shall serve as signs for the set times—the days and the years; ¹⁵and they shall serve as lights in the expanse of the sky to shine upon the earth." And it was so. ¹⁶God made the two great lights, the greater light to dominate the day and the lesser light to dominate the night, and the stars. ¹⁷And God set them in the expanse of the sky to shine upon the earth, ¹⁸to dominate the day and the night, and to separate light from darkness. And God saw that this was good. ¹⁹And there was evening and there was morning, a fourth day.

²⁰God said, "Let the waters bring forth swarms of living creatures, and birds that fly above the earth across the expanse of the sky." ²¹God created the great sea monsters, and all the living creatures of every kind that creep, which the waters brought forth in swarms; and all the winged birds of every kind. And God saw that this was good. ²²God blessed them, saying, "Be fertile and increase, fill the waters in the seas, and let the birds increase on the earth." ²³And there was evening and there was morning, a fifth day.

²⁴God said, "Let the earth bring forth every kind of living creature: cattle, creeping things, and wild beasts of every kind." And it was so. ²⁵God made wild beasts of every kind and cattle of every kind, and all kinds of creeping things of the earth. And God saw that this was good. ²⁶And God said, "Let us make man in our image, after our likeness. They shall rule the fish of the sea, the birds of the sky, the cattle, the whole earth, and all the creeping things that creep on earth." ²⁷And God created man in His image, in the image of God He created him; male and female He created them. ²⁸God blessed them and God said to them, "Be fertile and increase, fill the earth and master it; and rule the fish of the sea, the birds of the sky, and all the living things that creep on earth."

²⁹God said, "See, I give you every seed-bearing plant that is upon all the earth, and every tree that has seed-bearing fruit; they shall be yours for food. ³⁰And to all the animals on land, to all the birds of the sky, and to everything that creeps on earth, in which there is the breath of life, [I give] all the green plants for food." And it was so. ³¹And God saw all that He had made, and found it very good. And there was evening and there was morning, the sixth day.

2 The heaven and the earth were finished, and all their array. ²On the seventh day God finished the work which He had been doing, and He ceased*a* on the seventh day from all the work which He had done. ³And God blessed the seventh

5

---

a Or "rested"

day and declared it holy, because on it God ceased from all the work of creation which He had done. [4] Such is the story of heaven and earth when they were created.

When the LORD God made earth and heaven—[5] when no shrub of the field was yet on earth and no grasses of the field had yet sprouted, because the LORD God had not sent rain upon the earth and there was no man to till the soil, [6] but a flow would well up from the ground and water the whole surface of the earth— [7] the LORD God formed man[b] from the dust of the earth.[c] He blew into his nostrils the breath of life, and man became a living being.

[8] The LORD God planted a garden in Eden, in the east, and placed there the man whom He had formed. [9] And from the ground the LORD God caused to grow every tree that was pleasing to the sight and good for food, with the tree of life in the middle of the garden, and the tree of knowledge of good and bad.

10

. . . .

[15] The LORD God took the man and placed him in the garden of Eden, to till it and tend it. [16] And the LORD God commanded the man, saying, "Of every tree of the garden you are free to eat; [17] but as for the tree of knowledge of good and bad, you must not eat of it; for as soon as you eat of it, you shall die."

[18] The LORD God said, "It is not good for man to be alone; I will make a fitting helper for him." [19] And the LORD God formed out of the earth all the wild beasts and all the birds of the sky, and brought them to the man to see what he would call them; and whatever the man called each living creature, that would be its name. [20] And the man gave names to all the cattle and to the birds of the sky and to all the wild beasts; but for Adam no fitting helper was found. [21] So the LORD God cast a deep sleep upon the man; and, while he slept, He took one of his ribs and closed up the flesh at that spot. [22] And the LORD God fashioned the rib that He had taken from the man into a woman; and He brought her to the man. [23] Then the man said,

> "This one at last
> Is bone of my bones
> And flesh of my flesh.
> This one shall be called Woman,[e]
> For from man[f] was she taken."

[24] Hence a man leaves his father and mother and clings to his wife, so that they become one flesh.

[25] And they were both naked, the man and his wife, and were not ashamed.

---

[b] Heb 'adam
[c] Heb 'adamah

Genesis 1–2 From the Bible (King James Version)

Genesis 1: KJV

1 In the beginning God created the heaven and the earth. 1

2 And the earth *was* without form, and void; and darkness was upon the face of the deep. And the Spirit of God moved upon the face of the waters.

3 And God said, Let there be light: and there *was* light.

4 And God saw the light, that it *was* good: and God divided the light from the darkness.

5 And God called the light Day, and the darkness he called Night. And the 5 evening and the morning were the first day.

6 And God said, Let there be a firmament in the midst of the waters, and let it divide the waters from the waters.

7 And God made the firmament, and divided the waters which *were* under the firmament from the waters which *were* above the firmament: and it was so.

8 And God called the firmament Heaven. And the evening and the morning were the second day.

9 And God said, Let the waters under the heaven be gathered together unto one place, and let the dry *land* appear: and it was so.

10 And God called the dry *land* Earth; and the gathering together of the wa- 10 ters called he Seas: and God saw that *it was* good.

11 And God said, Let the earth bring forth grass, the herb yielding seed, *and* the fruit tree yielding fruit after his kind, whose seed *is* in itself, upon the earth: and it was so.

12 And the earth brought forth grass, *and* herb yielding seed after his kind, and the tree yielding fruit, whose seed *was* in itself, after his kind: and God saw that *it was* good.

13 And the evening and the morning were the third day.

14 And God said, Let there be lights in the firmament of the heaven to divide the day from the night; and let them be for signs, and for seasons, and for days, and years:

15 And let them be for lights in the firmament of the heaven to give light 15 upon the earth: and it was so.

16 And God made two great lights; the greater light to rule the day, and the lesser light to rule the night: *he made* the stars also.

17 And God set them in the firmament of the heaven to give light upon the earth,

18 And to rule over the day and over the night, and to divide the light from the darkness: and God saw that *it was* good.

19 And the evening and the morning were the fourth day.

20 And God said, Let the waters bring forth abundantly the moving creature   20
that hath life, and fowl that may fly above the earth in the open firmament of
heaven.

21 And God created great whales, and every living creature that moveth,
which the waters brought forth abundantly, after their kind, and every winged
fowl after his kind: and God saw that it *was* good.

22 And God blessed them, saying, Be fruitful, and multiply, and fill the waters in the seas, and let fowl multiply in the earth.

23 And the evening and the morning were the fifth day.

24 And God said, Let the earth bring forth the living creature after his kind,
cattle, and creeping thing, and beast of the earth after his kind: and it was so.

25 And God made the beast of the earth after his kind, and cattle after their   25
kind, and every thing that creepeth upon the earth after his kind: and God saw
that it *was* good.

26 And God said, Let us make man in our image, after our likeness: and let
them have dominion over the fish of the sea, and over the fowl of the air, and over
the cattle, and over all the earth, and over every creeping thing that creepeth
upon the earth.

27 So God created man in his *own* image, in the image of God created he him;
male and female created he them.

28 And God blessed them, and God said unto them, Be fruitful, and multiply,
and replenish the earth, and subdue it: and have dominion over the fish of the sea,
and over the fowl of the air, and over every living thing that moveth upon the earth.

29 And God said, Behold, I have given you every herb bearing seed, which *is*
upon the face of all the earth, and every tree, in the which *is* the fruit of a tree
yielding seed; to you it shall be for meat.

30 And to every beast of the earth, and to every fowl of the air, and to every   30
thing that creepeth upon the earth, wherein *there is* life, I *have given* every green
herb for meat: and it was so.

31 And God saw every thing that he had made, and, behold, it was very good.
And the evening and the morning were the sixth day.

Genesis 2: KJV

1 Thus the heavens and the earth were finished, and all the host of them.

2 And on the seventh day God ended his work which he had made; and he
rested on the seventh day from all his work which he had made.

3 And God blessed the seventh day, and sanctified it: because that in it he had
rested from all his work which God created and made.

4 These *are* the generations of the heavens and of the earth when they were   35
created, in the day that the LORD God made the earth and the heavens,

5 And every plant of the field before it was in the earth, and every herb of the
field before it grew: for the LORD God had not caused it to rain upon the earth,
and *there was* not a man to till the ground.

6 But there went up a mist from the earth, and watered the whole face of the
ground.

7 And the LORD God formed man *of* the dust of the ground, and breathed into his nostrils the breath of life; and man became a living soul.

8 And the LORD God planted a garden eastward in Eden; and there he put the man whom he had formed.

9 And out of the ground made the LORD God to grow every tree that is   40 pleasant to the sight, and good for food; the tree of life also in the midst of the garden, and the tree of knowledge of good and evil. . . .

15 And the LORD God took the man, and put him into the garden of Eden to dress it and to keep it.

16 And the LORD God commanded the man, saying, Of every tree of the garden thou mayest freely eat:

17 But of the tree of the knowledge of good and evil, thou shalt not eat of it: for in the day that thou eatest thereof thou shalt surely die.

18 And the LORD God said, *It is* not good that the man should be alone; I will make him a help mate for him.

19 And out of the ground the LORD God formed every beast of the field,   45 and every fowl of the air; and brought *them* unto Adam to see what he would call them: and whatsoever Adam called every living creature, that *was* the name thereof.

20 And Adam gave names to all cattle, and to the fowl of the air, and to every beast of the field; but for Adam there was not found an help meet for him.

21 And the LORD God caused a deep sleep to fall upon Adam and he slept: and he took one of his ribs, and closed up the flesh instead thereof;

22 And the rib, which the LORD God had taken from man, made her a woman, and brought her unto the man.

23 And Adam said, This *is* now bone of my bones, and flesh of my flesh: she shall be called Woman, because she was taken out of Man.

24 Therefore shall a man leave his father and his mother, and shall cleave   50 unto his wife: and they shall be one flesh.

25 And they were both naked, the man and his wife, and were not ashamed.

Reflecting and Interpreting

1. What does the word *genesis* mean? Consider the meanings of *generate* and *generation*. What common link do all three words have?

2. List the eight actions accomplished in six days. As you list them, do you notice anything that is puzzling? Do you have an explanation?

3. After each creation, God looked at it and assessed it. What opinion did he give?

4. What command did God give to animals, fish, fowl, and humans? What did he do before giving the command?

5. State two ways in which humans were made special.

6. Do you see anything puzzling in Genesis 1:26?

7. What did God create last? How is that creation to be regarded?

8. What happened on the seventh day? What does *sanctify* mean?
9. What do you learn about the form and nature of God from this account?
10. How does the sequence of the Genesis account of creation fit with what you have learned in biology?

A Writer's Response

Read the creation narrative from the modern version of the Torah and from the King James Version of the Bible. What small differences do you note in language and style? Which version do you prefer? Why? Write an essay discussing the differences and citing reasons for your preference.

❧ *The Koran*

The Koran or Qur'an (meaning "recital"), the sacred scripture of Islam, consists of 114 chapters and over 400 pages. It is regarded by Muslims as the latest supplement to the Old and New Testaments. The traditional view of its origin is that Mohammed (A.D. 570–632) recited the exact words of Allah (Arabic for God). Sources disagree about who was the first to record Mohammed's sermons and how they evolved to become The Koran. Over a span of twenty years or so (possibly 610 to 632), the verses were recorded, a few at a time, perhaps on palm leaves and sheep blade bones. Later the verses were collated and recopied on scrolls of papyrus.

Mohammed was a merchant who claimed to be a descendant of Abraham. When Mohammed was about forty years old, he reported seeing the angel Gabriel, while praying in a cave near Mount Hira. The angel relayed a message from Allah, which was implanted in Mohammed's mind. Later when the angel came again, Mohammed was told to wash his clothes, praise Allah, and preach to the people (who worshipped many gods). He was to tell them that Allah was the supreme ruler of the universe, all knowing and all powerful, and that they were to do His will. Although Mohammed won a few converts, crowds mocked and scorned him. After being stoned, he fled to Medina, where the people welcomed him. There his preaching was so moving and powerful that he was crowned king. Then he ordered all idols demolished, alms given to the poor, and killing of baby girls to cease.

The earliest traces of the Koran are inscriptions on coins and the Dome of the Rock. These inscriptions vary little from today's canonical text. Early Greek writings confirm that Mohammed lived but note his death in 634. By the eighth century, The Koran was a subject of argument between Christians and Muslims. By the early ninth century, there were over a dozen versions of The Koran, due to contention about the meaning and what should belong. Interpretations varied, mainly because early manuscripts lacked vowels and diacritical marks. Ninth century records also indicate that The Koran was being used in some legal decisions. By the tenth century, although many forgeries existed, a standard version had been established. Because the Koran contains repetitive references to the creation, only selected verses are printed here.

The Koran: Selected Verses

Translator, Abdullah Yusuf Ali

The Heifer

2:22 Who has made the earth your couch, and the heavens your canopy; and sent down rain from the heavens; and brought forth therewith fruits for your sustenance; then do not set up rivals unto Allah when you know (the truth). . . .   1

2:29 It is He Who hath created for you all things that are on earth; moreover His design comprehends the heavens, for He gave order and perfection to the seven firmaments; and of all things He has perfect knowledge. . . .

2:31 And He taught Adam the nature of all things; then He placed them before the angels, and said: "Tell me the nature of these if you are right."

2:32 They said: "Glory to Thee, of knowledge We have none, save what Thou Hast taught us: In truth it is Thou Who art perfect in knowledge and wisdom.". . .

2:35 We said: "O Adam! you and your wife dwell in the Garden: and eat of　5 the bountiful things therein (as where and when) you will, but do not approach this tree, or you will run into harm and transgression."

Al-'Imran, or The Family of 'Imran

3:59 The similitude of Jesus before Allah is as that of Adam; He created him from dust, then said to him: "Be." And he was.

The Heights

7:54 Your Guardian-Lord is Allah, Who created the heavens and the earth in six days, and is firmly established on the throne (of authority): He draweth the night as a veil o'er the day, each seeking the other in rapid succession: He created the sun, the moon, and the stars, (all) governed by laws under His command. Is it not His to create and to govern? Blessed be Allah, the Cherisher and Sustainer of the worlds!

The Rocky Tract

15:26 We created man from sounding clay, from mud moulded into shape;

15:27 And the Jinn race [angels], We had created before, from the fire of a scorching wind.

Luqman, the Wise

31:10 He created the heavens without any pillars that you can see; He set on　10 the earth mountains standing firm, lest it should shake with you; and He scattered through it beasts of all kinds. We send down rain from the sky, and produce on the earth every kind of noble creature, in pairs.

Adoration

32:4 It is Allah Who has created the heavens and the earth, and all between them, in six Days, and is firmly established on the Throne (of Authority): you have none, besides Him, to protect or intercede (for you): will you not then receive admonition? . . .

32:7 He Who has made everything which He has created most good: He began the creation of man with (nothing more than) clay,

32:8 And made his progeny from a quintessence of the nature of a fluid despised:

32:9 But He fashioned him in due proportion, and breathed into him something of His spirit. And He gave you (the faculties of) hearing and sight and feeling (and understanding): little thanks do you give!

Ya-Sin

33:33 A Sign for them is the earth that is dead: We do give it life, and pro-   15
duce grain therefrom, of which you do eat.

33:34 And We produce therein orchards with date-palms and vines and We
cause springs to gush forth therein:

33:35 That they may enjoy the fruits of this (artistry): it was not their hands
that made this: will they not give thanks?

36:36 Glory to Allah, Who created in pairs all things that the earth produces,
as well as their own (human) kind and (other) things of which they have no
knowledge.

The Crowds

39:5 He created the heavens and the earth in true (proportions): He makes
the Night overlap the Day, and the Day overlap the Night: He has subjected the
sun and the moon (to His law): Each one follows a course for a time appointed.
Is not He the Exalted in Power—He Who forgives again and again?

39:6 He created you (all) from a single person: then created, of like nature,   20
his mate; and he sent down for you eight head of cattle in pairs: He makes you,
in the wombs of your mothers, in stages, one after another, in three veils of darkness. Such is Allah, your Lord and Cherisher: to Him belongs (all) dominion. There
is no god but He: then how are you turned away (from your true Center)? . . .

39:21 Don't you see that Allah sends down rain from the sky, and leads it
through springs in the earth? Then He causes to grow, therewith, produce of
various colors: then it withers; you will see it grow yellow; then He makes it dry
up and crumble away. Truly, in this, is a Message of remembrance to men of
understanding.

Reflecting and Interpreting

1. Why is the title of the Koran especially significant?
2. Examine verse 2:22. What does "then set not up rivals unto Allah when you
   know (the truth)" mean?
3. What three steps in the process of creating Adam are stated?
4. What poetic device do you see in chapter 7, verse 54?
5. What verses indicate that Allah is merciful?
6. What verse indicates that limits were placed on Adam's knowledge?
7. Do you see anything puzzling about verse 7:54?
8. Do you see any puzzling omission in this creation account?
9. What do you learn about the form and nature of Allah from this account?
10. Examine verse 39:21. What is the implication here?

A Writer's Response

Compare and contrast the Genesis account of creation with the account in
the Koran.

The Handbook

A Brief Guide to
Grammar, Punctuation,
Mechanics, and Usage

HANDBOOK DIRECTORY

INTRODUCTION

1. **Punctuation** H-2
   1a. Comma H-2
   1b. Semicolon H-4
   1c. Colon H-5
   1d. Apostrophe H-6
   1e. Dash H-7
   1f. Parentheses H-8
   1g. Brackets H-9
   1h. Hyphen H-9
   1i. Slash H-10
   1j. Quotation Marks H-11
   1k. Italics (Underlining) H-13
   1l. Ellipses H-14
   1m. Period H-15
   1n. Question Mark H-16
   1o. Exclamation Point H-16

2. **Capitalization** H-16

3. **Abbreviations** H-19
   3a. Guidelines for Using Abbreviations H-19
   3b. Common Abbreviations and Reference Terms H-20

4. **Numbers** H-21

5. **Grammar and Usage** H-23
   5a. Sentence Fragments H-23
   5b. Comma Splices and Fused (Run-on) Sentences H-25
   5c. Pronouns H-26
   5d. Verbs H-31
   5e. Use *Like* Correctly H-37
   5f. Modifiers H-37

6. **Spelling** H-39
   6a. Spelling Tips H-39
   6b. Association Aids to Improve Spelling H-40
   6c. Other Spelling Aids H-41
   6d. Six Ways to Improve Spelling H-42

7. **Glossary of Usage** H-44

INTRODUCTION

This brief, concise handbook is a handy guide to frequently asked questions about standard written English. Here you can quickly find established rules, conventions, and examples that will help you to write correct and effective sentences. Whether you write essays, papers, letters, reports, or other documents, you can find answers to most of your writing questions either in this reference section or in related parts of the textbook.

WHAT IS THE BEST WAY TO USE THIS HANDBOOK?

To find quick answers to usage questions, first turn to the Handbook Directory, which appears on the opposite page. Next, scan the headings to locate the section you need and the page number, such as H-2. Then turn to that page and skim the rules until you find the appropriate information. Or you may wish to brush up on all of the rules in a particular section. If you desire more help, look for cross-references in the handbook that direct you to other sections of the text where you'll find related information.

Another way to locate related discussions in various chapters is to consult this book's subject index. For example, cross-references and the index indicate that chapter 25 provides extra help with ellipsis, brackets, and quotation marks. Chapter 8 explains voice of verbs, *be* verbs, sentence structure, adverb and adjective clauses, commas, and editing. For more help with word choice, you could turn to chapters 6 and 9, and for an overview of revising, editing, and proofreading, chapter 5.

SHOULD A WRITER EVER BREAK A RULE?

If you deliberately break a stylistic rule, it should be done for a purpose that promotes effective writing. To estimate how effective the writing will be, consider the rhetorical situation (chapter 1). You might ask yourself two key questions: What do readers expect? Is the writing appropriate for the occasion? If readers expect standard written English and you punctuate creatively, they may think you are uneducated. As a result, your ideas may not receive the attention they deserve.

When in doubt about questions of grammar, mechanics, punctuation, and usage, consult this book, your instructor, the campus writing center, or an online writing lab (OWL). For example, you might visit the one hosted by Purdue University at <http://owl.english.purdue.edu>.

1. PUNCTUATION

1a. COMMA (,)

The primary task of the comma is to clarify by indicating sentence structure. Commas should be used for a reason. (The old general rule to insert a comma for a pause does not always work.) In fact, many comma errors are due to unnecessary commas. To guide you, here are three don'ts:

▶ Do not place a comma before a parenthesis.

▶ Do not place a comma between a verb and a direct object.

▶ Do not insert a comma if you lack a reason.

1. **Use a comma to separate coordinate words, phrases, or clauses in a series.**

▶ The Delany children were named *Lemuel, Sarah, Elizabeth, Julia, Henry, Lucius, Manross, Hubert, Laura,* and *Samuel.* [a series of nouns]

▶ A 1994 book by Sadie and Bessie Delany *made the best-selling nonfiction list, ran as a successful play,* and *won several awards.* [a series of verb phrases]

▶ Sarah "Sadie" Delany, *by completing high school, graduating from Columbia University's Teachers College,* and *circumventing prejudice,* gained a teaching position in an all-white New York City school during the Depression. [a series of participial phrases]

▶ *If Sadie had accepted the stereotypes of the time, if she had succumbed to the racial barriers, if she had rejected the long hours of work and study,* she would have remained in the South, uneducated and unknown. [a series of adverb clauses]

(For more information on coordination, see "Parallelism with Items in a Series," chapter 8.)

2. **Use a comma to separate addresses, dates, and titles.**

▶ In the late 1890s Henry and Nanny Delany lived with their ten children in a small house on the campus of *Saint Augustine's School, Raleigh, North Carolina.*

▶ Elizabeth "Bessie" Delany was born on *September 3, 1891.*

▶ In 1918 Henry Beard Delany, *Jr.,* encouraged his sister to become a dentist, too.

▶ Bessie Delany, *D.D.S.,* became the second black woman licensed in New York City to practice dentistry.

3. **Place a comma before a coordinating conjunction that joins independent clauses (clauses that could be complete sentences).**

The coordinating conjunctions are *for, and, nor, but, or, yet, so*. (See chapter 8 for more on joining independent clauses.)

▶ In 1869 the territory of Wyoming granted women the right to vote, *but* Amendment 19 to the Constitution did not become law until August 1920.

4. Use a comma to separate an introductory subordinate clause from the main part of the sentence.

When the introductory clause is short and will not be misread, the comma may be omitted. (See chapter 8 for more on subordinate clauses.)

▶ *After Victoria Claflin Woodhull became one of the first two female stockbrokers in the United States*, she became, in 1872, the first woman to run for the presidency.

5. Use a comma after an introductory participial phrase or infinitive phrase.

▶ *Living in Tasmania and southern Australia*, wombats are marsupials that feed on roots, leaves, and vegetables.

▶ *To see a wombat*, you must look at night.

6. Use a comma after two or more introductory prepositional phrases or a long introductory prepositional phrase (a good rule of thumb is four words or more).

▶ *In the icy waters of the North Atlantic*, the savage wolf fish grows up to three feet long. *Along the sea bottom*, the sea robin walks on its breast fin rays, looking for food.

7. Use commas to set off transitional expressions and conjunctive adverbs.

Transitional expressions include phrases such as *in fact* and *for example*. Conjunctive adverbs include words such as *however, consequently*, and *therefore*.

▶ *Finally*, the flood waters receded after ten days of rain.

▶ It was, *in fact*, the worst flooding on record in the region.

▶ Flooding is common in the area; *consequently*, people are being discouraged from rebuilding homes there.

8. Use commas to set off nonessential (nonrestrictive) elements.

Use a comma to set off tag words such as *well, yes*, and *isn't it* at the beginning or end of a sentence.

▶ *Yes*, you really did win a new Lexus.

▶ You are a very lucky fellow, *aren't you?*

Use a pair of commas to set off nonessential phrases that interrupt the flow of a sentence.

- ▶ One department head, *working late*, inadvertently erased the weekly sales report.
- ▶ Ricardo Alvarez, *a business owner*, joined our Toastmasters' Club last week.
- ▶ Our students, *who come from surrounding counties*, usually commute daily.

9. **Use a comma to set off a contrasting expression.**

- ▶ My billfold is lying on the dresser, *not the chair*.

10. **Use a comma to prevent misreading.**

Sometimes a comma is needed for clarity.

- ▶ Inside, the stereo was going full blast.
- ▶ Outside, the children were roaring around the house on their motorbikes.

11. **Use commas to set off a speaker tag or source tag from a direct quotation.**

A speaker tag or source tag identifies the speaker or writer and includes a verb of saying, such as *said*, *called*, *asked*, or *wrote*.

- ▶ *Derek yelled*, "Get out! The rear tire is on fire!"
- ▶ "The law must be stable," *wrote Roscoe Pound*, "but it must not stand still."

Note that when the speaker tag follows a quotation or part of a quotation, the comma preceding it is placed inside the quotation marks.

1b. SEMICOLON (;)

Basically, the semicolon has only two uses. If you understand the rules governing it, you should be able to use the semicolon with confidence. Remember that the semicolon is a stronger mark of punctuation than the comma and that it is used for the *larger* divisions within a sentence.

1. **Use a semicolon to connect two closely related independent clauses not joined by a comma and a coordinating conjunction (*and, but, or, nor, for, so,* and *yet*).**

- ▶ Representatives from every state attended the Democratic Convention; the majority voted against "open rule."

2. **Use a semicolon between two independent clauses joined by a conjunctive adverb or other transitional expression.**

   ▶ Sue is an accounting major; *however*, she plans to switch to data processing.

   ▶ Kevin was not feeling well; *nonetheless*, he went to the dance.

   Note that using a comma instead of a semicolon before a conjunctive adverb such as *nevertheless, however,* or *therefore* at the junction of two independent clauses results in an error called a comma splice. For more on comma splices, see section 5b. in this handbook. (See chapter 8 for more on joining independent clauses.)

3. **Replace commas with semicolons for clarity when items in a series contain commas.**

   ▶ Here is our new slate of officers: *Jean Henson, president; Mike Henry, vice president; Scott Trainor, treasurer; and Mary Wiley, secretary.*

4. **If there are commas within the independent clauses of a sentence, use a semicolon rather than a comma before the coordinating conjunction.**

   ▶ The Harvest House, a new restaurant on Center Street, features ethnic foods; and the crowds, surprisingly large for a small town, flock in.

1c. COLON (:)

A colon is used after an independent clause to signal that something will follow.

1. **Use a colon to precede a list or series that does not fit smoothly into a sentence.**

   ▶ Sue ordered the following items: *one pair of scissors, two yards of denim, one thimble, and one tape measure.*

   ▶ Nanette will need these tools: *needle-nose pliers, a monkey wrench, a claw hammer, and a hacksaw.*

   However, do not use a colon after a verb or preposition.

   Incorrect

   ▼ My grocery list included: zucchini, papaya, mangoes, and sunflower seeds. [The colon is not needed.]

2. **Use a colon to formally introduce a quotation.**

   ▶ My point can be summarized in the words of Edward Haines: "With every civil right there has to be a corresponding civil obligation."

3. **Use a colon between independent clauses when the second explains the first.**

  ▶ Jim has a real problem: his hair started falling out last month.

  ▶ "Let the world slip: we shall ne'er be younger." (William Shakespeare, *The Taming of the Shrew*)

4. **Use a colon in biblical references, expressions of time, and after salutations in business letters.**

  Use a colon between chapter and verse numbers of the Bible.

  ▶ Psalm 27:3

  Use a colon between the hour and the minute in referring to time.

  ▶ 6:05 p.m.

  Use a colon after the salutation of a business letter.

  ▶ Dear Manager Brown:

1d. APOSTROPHE (')

The apostrophe has three basic uses: to form possessives, to form a few plurals, and to indicate omissions.

1. **Use an apostrophe with *s* to form the possessive of singular nouns and irregular plural nouns not ending in *s*.**

  ▶ today's fashions   ▶ my mother's life   ▶ the city's attractions

  ▶ men's clothing   ▶ children's toys   ▶ mice's lifespans

  Note that when adding *s* to form the possessive sounds awkward in speech, some writers add only an apostrophe in writing: *Mr. Rogers' neighborhood, Charles' sons*. But it is never incorrect to add both an apostrophe and *s* for such words. Whichever practice you adopt, be consistent.

2. **Add only an apostrophe to form the possessive of a plural noun ending in *s*.**

  ▶ boys' jeans   ▶ horses' manes   ▶ butterflies' wings

3. **Indefinite pronouns (*anyone, everyone, everybody, nobody, one*) in the possessive case are treated like singular nouns and require an apostrophe before *s*.**

  ▶ Everyone's invitation was mailed.   ▶ Each one's jacket was labeled.

  ▶ Anybody's guess is as good as mine.   ▶ No one's car was ticketed.

4. **To show joint possession and to show possession with hyphenated terms and names of organizations, make only the last word possessive.**

   ▶ Bill and Thad's boat
   ▶ father-in-law's car
   ▶ Cutter and Holt's Welding Company

5. **To show individual possession, use an apostrophe with each name.**

   ▶ Sue's and Joan's themes are late.

6. **Use an apostrophe to form the possessive of words referring to time or to amounts of money.**

   ▶ a minute's rest   ▶ a week's wages   ▶ one cent's worth
   ▶ two hours' work   ▶ one month's rent   ▶ two cents' worth
   ▶ three days' pay   ▶ two years' time   ▶ a dime's worth

7. **Use an apostrophe to form the plurals of numbers, letters, symbols, and words referred to as words. (Sometimes the apostrophe is omitted if there is no problem of clarity.)**

   ▶ My house number is simply three 7's, or 777.
   ▶ *Occasionally* is spelled with two *c*'s and one *s*.
   ▶ How many ='s should there be in this equation?
   ▶ Ashley had three *and*'s in one sentence.

8. **Use an apostrophe to replace omitted letters or numbers in a contraction.**

   ▶ They don't know when they'll be called back to work. [*do not; they will*]
   ▶ Terry can't go until tomorrow. [*cannot*]
   ▶ It's his turn. [*It is*]
   ▶ The class of '89 is planning a reunion. [*1989*]

   NOTE: Do not confuse *it's* with the possessive pronoun *its*, which does not require an apostrophe: "The cat lost its catnip mouse." (*Its*, like *his* and *hers*, is in the possessive case.)

1e. DASH (—)

Dashes, parentheses, and brackets share a basic function: to set off information from the rest of the sentence. But these marks of punctuation differ in effect. Dashes emphasize material whereas parentheses de-emphasize. Brackets are generally used to enclose clarifying information in direct quotations.

The dash is informal punctuation that indicates an interruption of a sentence. A dash can signal a break in thought or provide special emphasis. Often used in pairs, dashes are bold and dramatic—as long as they are used sparingly. (In typing, use two hyphens without spacing to make a dash.)

1. **Use a dash or a pair of dashes to emphasize an appositive or other explanatory material.**

   ▶ "Soon members of the PMAC—referred to as the Derg—were dispatching their 'enemies' without trials."

   ▶ "There was not—and never had been—a Communist Party in Ethiopia: the country was linked to the West and dependent on free-world aid."

   ▶ "Soon he realized that his one hope was to make contact with two notorious smugglers who might guide him out—an idea fraught with risk."

   ▶ "He had to do this—regardless of the consequences."

Note: The preceding examples of dashes are taken from "Escape from Ethiopia," by Trevor Armbrister.

2. **For clarity, use a dash or a pair of dashes to set off nonrestrictive (nonessential) elements containing commas.**

   ▶ The Kincaid triplets—Jane, Janice, and Jeanette—enrolled in Miss Hickman's first-grade class.

3. **Use a dash or a pair of dashes to set off interrupters or to indicate a pause.**

   ▶ Sarah has twenty—yes, twenty—Angora cats!

   ▶ He's a nuisance—just a big, fat freeloader.

1f. PARENTHESES ( )

For a discussion of the basic functions and different effects of parentheses and dashes, see the first paragraph of section 1.e. in this handbook.

1. **Use parentheses to enclose (and de-emphasize) nonessential material.**

   ▶ The United States two-cent piece (issued in 1864) was the first coin with the motto "In God We Trust."

2. **Use parentheses to enclose explanations or definitions.**

   ▶ The *New York Times* and five other metropolitan daily newspapers have joined in a WWW (World Wide Web) site called CareerPath, featuring employment advertisements.

▶ Since the World Wide Web has no central organization, you need a "search engine" (a special site that locates other sites) to surf the Web.

▶ Semicolons have two basic uses (see section 1b.).

3. **In some documentation styles, use parentheses to enclose reference information such as page numbers or dates.**

(For more information on documentation styles, see chapters 24 and 25.)

▶ In *The Laughter Prescription*, Dr. Lawrence J. Peter advises making "yourself the target of your own quips" (146).

4. **Occasionally an entire sentence or more is enclosed in parentheses as a kind of aside.**

▶ In a Pullman berth, a man can truly be alone with himself. (The nearest approach to this condition is to be found in a hotel bedroom, but a hotel room can be mighty depressing sometimes, it stands so still.)

Note: The preceding sentence is from E. B. White, "Progress and Change."

1g. BRACKETS [ ]

1. **Use brackets to insert explanatory material in quotations.**

(For more information on using brackets in quoted material, see chapter 25.)

▶ "In a Pullman berth [a curtained bunk on a sleeping car of a train], a man can truly be alone with himself. . . ."

2. **For clarity, use brackets instead of parentheses to enclose material already within parentheses.**

▶ We should be sure to give Emanuel Foose (and his brother Emilio [1812–1882] as well) credit for his role in founding the institute.

(For more examples with brackets, see "Making Changes in Quotations," chapter 25.)

1h. HYPHEN (-)

1. **Use a hyphen to divide a word at the end of a line.**

At least one syllable of three or more letters should be before the division: *con-sequently*.

2. **Use a hyphen in spelled-out compound numbers from twenty-one through ninety-nine.**

3. **Use a hyphen in spelled-out fractions.**

- ▶ one-fourth
- ▶ two-thirds
- ▶ five-eighths
- ▶ four and one-third

4. **Use a hyphen between two or more words used together as a modifier before a noun (unless the first word ends in *ly*).**

- ▶ thought-provoking speech
- ▶ problem-solving quiz
- ▶ rosy-cheeked baby
- ▶ lightly salted peanuts
- ▶ all-out effort
- ▶ on-the-job training
- ▶ up-to-date data
- ▶ highly rated programs

However, do not hyphenate such modifiers when they do not precede the noun they modify.

- ▶ The quiz was on problem solving.
- ▶ The baby was rosy cheeked.
- ▶ Training was conducted on the job.
- ▶ The data were up to date.

5. **Use a hyphen with certain prefixes.**

These include *ex-* and *self-* with the exceptions of *selfless, selfsame*. There is no hard-and-fast rule about other prefixes such as *anti-, co-, pre-, pro-, re-*, and *well-*. Check an up-to-date dictionary, and, if given a choice, be consistent.

- ▶ anti-intellectual
- ▶ co-owner
- ▶ ex-president
- ▶ pre-election
- ▶ self-denial
- ▶ well-being

NOTE: Always use a hyphen when the word to be prefixed begins with a capital as in *pro-American, non-British,* or *mid-July*.

6. **Use a hyphen to avoid doubling a letter and to avoid confusion.**

- ▶ semi-invalid [avoids *semiinvalid*]
- ▶ re-enlist [avoids *reenlist*]
- ▶ re-form [avoids confusion with *reform*]

1i. SLASH (/)

1. **In certain situations, such as highly informal writing or technical papers, use a slash to replace *or*, which is ordinarily required to show alternatives.**

- ▶ all ready/already
- ▶ radio/television
- ▶ to/too/two

NOTE: Many readers object to the use of *and/or*. Often *and* or *or* is sufficient.

2. **Use a slash to separate elements in certain expressions.**

   ▶ Dates: 1998/99
   ▶ Fractions: 1/4
   ▶ Places: Dallas/Fort Worth

3. **Use slashes (with a space on each side of the slash) in prose to indicate divisions between lines of poetry.**

   (See "Preparing an Analysis of a Poem," chapter 28.)

   ▶ Shakespeare writes: "Like as the waves make towards the pebbled shore, / So do our minutes hasten to their end. . . ."

1j. QUOTATION MARKS (" ")

Although quotation marks have more than one use, they usually indicate the beginning and end of someone's exact words. Dialogue requires quotation marks. Citations require quotation marks (see chapter 25). Quotation marks may also be used to indicate words used in special ways. Titles of short written works or parts of works are enclosed with quotation marks.

1. **Use quotation marks in dialogue to enclose the exact words of a speaker.**

   ▶ Phoebe called, "Sparky, bring that shoe back here!"
   ▶ "Come on, Sparky," she cajoled, "bring the shoe back, and I'll give you some Teeny Bits."

2. **Use quotation marks to enclose short direct quotations.**

   Short is defined differently in different documentation styles. The most commonly used style in English, that of the Modern Language Association (MLA), defines *short* as four lines or less. (Long quotations are indented. For more on quoting sources, see chapter 25.)

   ▶ In *The Conduct of Life*, Emerson wrote as follows: "The art of conversation, or the qualification for a good companion, is a certain self-control, which now holds the subject, now lets it go, with a respect for the emergencies of the moment."

3. **Use quotation marks to enclose the titles of parts of books and periodicals.**

   Because this rule is often confused, here is an informal guideline that will help you remember the principle: Underline (italicize) the title or name of a whole item; use quotation marks around the title of a part. The lists below indicate how the guideline applies:

Underline "Whole" Items	*Use Quotation Marks for "Parts"*
book title	chapter or story title
songbook title	song title
poetry book title	poem title
title of a very long poem [e.g., *Paradise Lost*]	
name of a newspaper	comic, article, or feature title
name of a magazine	article, feature, or story title
pamphlet title	speech, short report
name of a plane, ship, or train	
title of a film, painting, record album, television or radio program	title of an episode of a radio or television series

Finally, a writer does not underline or use quotation marks with his or her own title at the beginning of a work. (See also section 1k. on italics [underlining].)

4. **Use single quotation marks to enclose a quotation within a quotation.**

   If a quotation occurs within a quotation already marked with double quotation marks, enclosed the inside quotation in single quotation marks. This will sometimes result in three quotation marks at the end of the quotation.

   ▶ "You must have read Eiseley's 'The Real Secret of Piltdown,'" Bill's friend observed.

   NOTE: In ordinary American usage, the only exceptions to the use of double quotation marks for main, or outside, quotations are long quotations (block quotations), which are not placed within quotation marks because they are indented. (For more information on quoting sources, see chapter 25.)

5. **Traditionally, quotation marks were used to enclose words discussed as words. However, many writers now prefer italics for this purpose (see also section 1k., Italics).**

   ▶ "Computer" is derived from the Latin verb *computare*.

6. **Use quotation marks to enclose words used in a special or ironic sense.**

   ▶ What chain of events caused the sinking of an "unsinkable" ship such as the *Titanic?*

   NOTE: Do not use quotation marks for emphasis. The effect can be unintentionally ironic and humorous: Jordan Bailey, "President"; "I'm sure your 'wife' will enjoy the ring you bought at our store."

7. **Use other punctuation with quotation marks correctly.**

Commas and periods always go *inside* closing quotation marks (except in one documentation situation). Colons and semicolons always go *outside* closing quotation marks. The rule for all other punctuation is that if the punctuation is part of the quotation, it goes inside, and if it is not part of the quotation, it goes outside.

▶ "Reading *Space Technology* gives me the insider's view," he says, adding, "It's like having all the top officials sitting in my office for a discussion."

▶ He said, "I will pay the full amount"; this certainly surprised us.

▶ She has two favorite "sports": eating and sleeping.

1k. *ITALICS* (<u>UNDERLINING</u>)

Italics is a typeface that slants to the right (*Moby Dick*). If your keyboard does not have italics, underline instead. Italics and underlining can indicate foreign words; special names of vehicles, vessels, or artworks; words used as words; and titles of long works. Since many foreign words have been adopted into English, check a dictionary to see whether or not they should be italicized. Direct quotations in another language are not italicized.

1. **Use italics (underlining) for titles of long works.**

For a discussion of when to use italics and when to use quotation marks in titles, see section 1j.3 of this handbook. The treatment of titles differs from one documentation style to another. (For more information on titles of sources in research papers, see chapter 25.) Listed here are the most common kinds of works with italicized titles:

books: *A Tale of Two Cities*

Exception: Do not use italics (or underlining) for the names of sacred books: the Bible (or the Holy Bible), the New Testament, the Koran, and so forth.

long poems: *Paradise Lost, The Iliad, The Wasteland*

newspapers and magazines: the *New York Times; National Geographic*

pamphlets: *Letters from an American Farmer*

vessels (planes, trains, ships, spacecraft): the *Titanic;* the *Burlington Zephyr; Challenger*

plays: *Hamlet; The Music Man*

comic strips: *Doonesbury*

films and television and radio programs: *Aladdin; The X-Files; A Prairie Home Companion*

albums and long musical works: *Thriller;* Mahler's *Symphony No. 9*

paintings and sculpture: da Vinci's *Mona Lisa;* Michelangelo's *David*

software: *Windows 98; PageMaker 6.5*

2. **For clarity, use italics for words discussed as words, particularly when quotation marks are used in the same sentence for another purpose.**

   ▶ The word *boudoir* comes from an Old French verb, meaning "to pout or sulk."

3. **Use italics for emphasis, but do so sparingly.**

   ▶ Trust me—take Route 315, *not* Route 23.

   ▶ What is the *evidence* for that position?

11. ELLIPSIS (. . .)

An ellipsis is a set of three spaced dots that indicate an omission. When an omission occurs at the beginning of a quotation, an ellipsis is *not* necessary; but an omission in the middle or at the end requires an ellipsis. To shorten a quotation, you can use an ellipsis as long as you do not distort the meaning. When omitting a word, phrase, sentence, or more, be guided by integrity: Is the result fair to the author? Is it grammatically correct?

You should be aware that the fifth edition of the *MLA Handbook* now includes the use of brackets to distinguish between your ellipses and the spaced periods that sometimes appear in works. Your instructor may follow that style. But the examples that follow reflect *traditional* Modern Language Association recommendations. The first two are based on an excerpt from Linda Ryberg's "The Midwest Salutes its Swedish Roots" in *Midwest Living.*

Original:

   ▶ A harsh first winter on the windswept Illinois prairie in 1846 couldn't stop a tiny group of Swedish immigrants from prospering in the town they founded and named Bishop Hill. After all, they'd crossed the Atlantic, sailed the Great Lakes, and walked 160 miles southwest from Chicago to get there.

1. **Use an ellipsis to show an omission in the middle of a quotation.**

   ▶ Tracing the history of an Illinois town, Linda Ryberg writes: "A harsh first winter . . . in 1846 couldn't stop a tiny group of Swedish immigrants from prospering in the town they founded and named Bishop Hill."

2. **Use an ellipsis to show an omission at the end of a quotation.**

   ▶ Linda Ryberg, tracing the history of Bishop Hill, Illinois, explains that in 1846 a small band of Swedish settlers "crossed the Atlantic, sailed the Great Lakes, and walked 160 miles southwest from Chicago. . . ."

► Linda Ryberg, tracing the history of Bishop Hill, Illinois, explains that in 1846 a small band of Swedish settlers "crossed the Atlantic, sailed the Great Lakes, and walked 160 miles southwest from Chicago . . ." (40).

NOTE: Since there is no parenthetical reference in the first example, the sentence period is placed flush against the last word within the quotation marks. In the second example, however, the sentence period is placed after the parenthetical reference of this short quotation. (For information on using ellipses in long quotations, see chapter 25.)

3. **Use a whole line of ellipsis points to indicate omission of a line or more in quoted poetry.**

► William Wordsworth was a poet of the city as well as the countryside. While crossing Westminster Bridge, in London, he wrote:

Earth has not anything to show more fair:
Dull would he be of soul who could pass by
A sight so touching in its majesty:
. . . .
Ne'er saw I, never felt, a calm so deep!

4. **Use an ellipsis to indicate a pause or hesitation, but use this device sparingly.**

► Don't swim in this water . . . unless you're fond of sharks.

1m. PERIOD (.)

1. **Use a period at the end of statements, mild commands, and indirect questions.**

► The temperature in the cave is a constant 58 degrees.
► As you tour the cave, please stay on the marked trail.
► Many people have asked how the cave was first discovered.

2. **Use a period (or periods) with some abbreviations.**

If an abbreviation comes at the end of a sentence, use only one period. (For more on abbreviations, see section 3 of this handbook.)

3. **Use a period as a decimal in numbers.**

► 1.06   ► 0.910   ► $149.95

1n. QUESTION MARK (?)

1. Use a question mark at the end of a direct question or request.

► Will you please pick up a roll of stamps on your way?

► A group of citizens discussed the question, "Does our town need a city manager instead of a mayor?"

2. Use a question mark after each elliptical question in a series.

► Should obscenity be controlled on the Internet? If so, by whom? How?

3. Use a question mark in parentheses after an item that is of doubtful accuracy.

► The tunnel from his cell, disguised by a huge poster, was started in 2001(?) but was discovered only after he had fled.

1o. EXCLAMATION POINT (!)

An exclamation point indicates strong emotion: pain, fear, surprise, indignation, or excitement. An exclamation point cannot bolster a weak statement nor make an argument more convincing. Use exclamation points sparingly; otherwise, they lose their power.

1. Use an exclamation point to add force to a command or expression of emotion.

► "Ouch!"

► "Help!" Jimmy screamed. "The horse is standing on my foot."

► WATCH OUT! Deer Crossing

2. CAPITALIZATION

If you become lost in the thicket of capitalization, first consult an up-to-date dictionary. If you should find more than one way to capitalize, then let your audience be your guide. In other words, when you are writing for an employer, follow conventional business and technical usage. When writing a college research paper, follow the style manual your instructor recommends.

You may be surprised at certain variations in capitalization. One of the most striking differences concerns the names of software. Business and technical personnel generally follow the spelling of the manufacturer, even if it means placing a capital in the middle of a brand or trade name: for example, *InfoTrac*. Fortunately, the capitalization of most words is standard and can usually be found in a good desk dictionary.

Once you master the following standard rules of capitalization, you will be able to capitalize most words without consulting other sources.

1. **Capitalize the first word of a sentence.**

   ▶ The sentence above is an example; so is this one.

   NOTE: In most writing, capitalization of a sentence following a colon is optional, but be consistent. Some documentation styles specify whether such sentences should be capitalized, so if you are writing a research paper following a particular documentation style, see the appropriate guidelines. The Modern Language Association specifies that the second sentence is capitalized if it enunciates a rule or principle, but not if it simply elaborates on the first sentence.

2. **Capitalize proper nouns and trade names.**

   Capitalize the names of people; places; political, racial, and religious groups; institutions and organizations; sacred writings; brand and trade names; ships, planes, and trains; monuments; awards; and specific academic degrees and courses.

▶ Karen O'Neill	▶ University of Michigan
▶ the Dead Sea Scrolls	▶ Catholic, Protestant, Jewish
▶ the Bible (or the Holy Bible)	▶ the Koran
▶ Twenty-first Street	▶ United States Post Office
▶ Colorado River	▶ the Spirit of St. Louis
▶ the South	▶ Purina Cat Chow
▶ Congress	▶ League of Women Voters
▶ Calculus 101	▶ Master's of English Education

   EXCEPTIONS: Do not capitalize directions, ideologies, or philosophies (unless derived from the name of an individual—Marxism, for example).

   ▶ After Ken left Philadelphia, he drove *south*.

   ▶ Shelly is an *idealist*.

   ▶ Many Russians feel they were better off under *communism*.

3. **Capitalize proper adjectives and abbreviations.**

   Capitalize adjectives and abbreviations derived from proper nouns.

▶ the French language	▶ Palestinian soldiers
▶ Cooper's hawk	▶ Appalachian quilt
▶ Japanese maple	▶ Boston terrier
▶ IRS	▶ UCLA

NOTE: There are exceptions: for example, *Venice* but *venetian blind*, *French door* but *french fry*. If in doubt, check a dictionary. See also section 3, Abbreviations.

4. **Capitalize official and personal titles.**

Capitalize a title (or rank) immediately before the name of a person.

- ▶ Dr. Stephanie Winters
- ▶ Justice Sandra Day O'Connor
- ▶ General Colin Powell
- ▶ Mr. Jacob Turner

- ▶ Professor Celia Kincaid
- ▶ President Dwight Eisenhower
- ▶ Reverend Jamison
- ▶ Ms. Shannon Maguire

EXCEPTION: When no name is given, do *not* capitalize a title.

- ▶ The professor encouraged the class to share their opinions.
- ▶ The president of the United States visited flood victims.

5. **Capitalize titles of literary and other artistic works.**

Ordinarily, capitalize the first and last words as well as all major words in the title of a literary or artistic work.

- ▶ Last week Jack read the autobiography of William O. Douglas, *Go East, Young Man: The Early Years.*
- ▶ Erma J. Fisk's *The Peacocks of Baboquivari* is an unusual story of an elderly woman who lived alone for five months in the foothills of Arizona, recording and banding birds.
- ▶ At the Louvre, we saw Leonardo Da Vinci's *The Mona Lisa.*

NOTE: Rules for capitalizing titles of works differ from one documentation style to another. If you are writing a research paper and following a particular style, check the appropriate guidelines.

6. **Capitalize calendar items and historical periods.**

Capitalize months, special weeks, days, holidays, and historical periods.

- ▶ April
- ▶ Tuesday
- ▶ Easter
- ▶ the Renaissance

- ▶ New Year's Day
- ▶ Right-to-Read Week
- ▶ Middle Ages
- ▶ the Great Depression

EXCEPTIONS: Do not capitalize seasons or centuries.

- ▶ our spring break   ▶ the twentieth century   ▶ in the winter

7. **Capitalize events and documents.**

Capitalize wars, treaties, constitutions, and other important events and documents.

- ▶ World War II
- ▶ World Series
- ▶ Rose Bowl game
- ▶ the Louisiana Purchase

- ▶ Treaty of Versailles
- ▶ United States Constitution
- ▶ Magna Carta
- ▶ Battle of Gettysburg

EXCEPTIONS: Do not capitalize laws, theories, or hypotheses:

- ▶ nature's laws
- ▶ code of Hammurabi

- ▶ theory of relativity
- ▶ Mendelian principles

3. ABBREVIATIONS

When writing, avoid unnecessary abbreviations and use them appropriately. Use only conventional abbreviations that can be easily understood. Except for addresses and documentation, spell out the names of countries, states, and possessions in the United States. In desk dictionaries and many other reference sources, you will find a key to the abbreviations used, either in the front or back of the publication. (For abbreviations used in MLA works cited entries and in APA entries, see chapter 24.)

3a. GUIDELINES FOR USING ABBREVIATIONS

Abbreviation styles may differ significantly from one dictionary to another or from one documentation style to another. If you are writing a research paper and following a particular style, check the appropriate guidelines. *Generally, use abbreviations in a table and a list of works cited, but not in the text of a research paper.* If you do use an abbreviation in the text, be sure to define it. The examples that follow are based upon the *MLA Handbook for Writers of Research Papers*, 5th ed., by Joseph Gibaldi.

1. **Use no periods or spaces between abbreviations of most letters that are capitalized.**

FBI	IBM	MD	BA
PSAT	PhD	RN	AD
IRS	EST	DNA	BC

Some exceptions:

U.S.S.	Scott Felder, Jr.	Mr. Daley
N.P.	S.S.	
J. R. Smith	Ms. Jones	

2. **Use a period after each lowercase letter of most abbreviations that represent a word.**

p.m.	ed.	s.t.
a.m.	r.s.v.p.	e.g.
n.p.	p.p.a.	

There are many exceptions:

2nd	mph	rpm

3. **Use a period after most abbreviations that end with lowercase letters:**

govt.	Eng.	wk.	Wed.	assn.
dept.	mkt.	mo.	Mar.	biog.
Mar.	obs.	yr.	fig.	introd.
adj.	arch.	ed.	def.	cont.

3b. COMMON ABBREVIATIONS AND REFERENCE TERMS

AD	*anno Domini* (in the year of the Lord). Precedes numerals (AD 16). Follows centuries (eighth century AD).
arch.	archaic
BC	before Christ. Follows numerals (23 BC)
c., ca.	*circa:* "about"; used with approximate dates
comp., comps.	compiled by, compiler(s)
Cong.	Congress
Cong. Rec.	Congressional Record
e.g.	*exempli gratia:* "for example"
et al.	*et alii:* "and others"
ex., exs.	example(s)
DA, DSI	Dissertation Abstracts, Dissertation Abstracts International
diss.	dissertation
doc.	document
H. Doc.	House of Representatives document
ibid.	*ibidem:* "in the same place"
i.e.	*id est:* "that is" (set off by commas)
ips	inches per second (refers to tape recordings)

LC	Library of Congress
ms., mss.	manuscript(s)
par.	paragraph
pref.	preface, preface by
pt.	part
rept., repts.	reported by, report(s)
rpt.	reprint, reprinted by
S. Doc.	Senate document
sec., sect.	section
sic	thus in the source (place in square brackets as an editorial note, otherwise in parentheses)
S. Rept.	Senate report
var.	variant

4. NUMBERS

Two basic systems for numbers above ten exist. Choose the system that is appropriate for your audience, and follow it consistently. Many writing handbooks tell you to spell out numbers that can be expressed in two words or less: *one hundred* but *101*. Other guides, especially in business and technical writing, tell you to spell out numbers up through ten and use numerals for numbers above ten: *ten* but *11*. Both systems call for consistency and specify numerals in certain situations and spelled-out numbers in others. Here are some general guidelines:

1. **Begin sentences with spelled-out numbers.**

Never begin a sentence with a numeral. Either spell out the number, or invert the sentence if the number is too large to spell out.

▶ Seventy-five students were enrolled in Keyboarding 101 last quarter.
▶ Last semester 250 students were enrolled in Economics 101.

2. **Spell out round numbers.**

Round numbers (tens, hundreds, thousands, and so forth) and approximations should be spelled out.

▶ Experts estimate that we have enough coal to last two hundred years.

3. **Combine numerals and words to avoid large figures with many zeros.**

▶ 25 million   ▶ 300 billion   ▶ 100 trillion

4. **Be consistent in writing numbers in parallel constructions.**

   ► Sue bought three books, four pens, and two notebooks.
   ► The English department ordered 36 manila folders, 210 red pencils, and 15 large packages of typing paper.
   ► The chef ordered 18 heads of lettuce, 7 pounds of carrots, 6 bunches of celery, and 7 cabbages.

   NOTE: If a small number is used in the same sentence with a large number but in a different context, the smaller number can be spelled out.

   ► Those *two* technicians are operating $12,000 computers.

5. **If two numbers occur together, either spell out the smaller number or recast the sentence to separate them.**

   ► In 2001, 9,785 students registered for fall quarter. [may be confusing]
   ► In fall quarter 2001, there were 9,785 students registered. [preferable]
   ► *four* 15-cent stamps
   ► 20 *five*-inch nail files

6. **Use numbers correctly in addresses.**

   Except for the house number *one*, express house numbers as numerals. If a street name is a number less than eleven, spell out the number. If the street name is eleven or higher, use a hyphen preceded and followed by a space to separate the house number from the street number.

   ► One Blaine Avenue
   ► 9 Blaine Avenue
   ► The furniture is to be delivered to 454 East Fifth Street.
   ► Grace lives at 1310 - 121st Street.

7. **Use numerals in dates, measurements, and decimals.**

   ► March 15, 2002 or 15 March 2002 [not March 15th, 1999]
   ► 6 feet 2 inches tall, 7 square feet, 3 inches, 4 minutes
   ► The temperature was 110 degrees [or 110°] Fahrenheit.
   ► The average age of our students is 27.5 years.

8. **For percentages, use the percent symbol or spell out *percent* as appropriate.**

   In ordinary usage, use a figure, followed by the word *percent* spelled out. In business usage, figures are sometimes used with the symbol for percent. The symbol for percent is always used in charts and tables.

▶ Ordinary usage: 50 percent

▶ Business usage: 50 percent or 50%

▶ Technical usage: 50%

▶ Charts and tables: 50%

9. **Ordinarily, use numerals for sums of money.**

▶ $1.38 $454.06 $1,564

▶ $5, $10 [zeros are usually omitted for even amounts]

▶ eighty-nine cents [amount less than a dollar in ordinary prose]

▶ $0.89, 89¢, or 89 cents [business usage]

NOTE: In legal documents, spell out sums of money and then write the numerals in parentheses: "I agree to pay a monthly rental fee of one hundred ten dollars ($110)."

10. **Use numerals appropriately in expressions of time.**

Use numerals except when the word *o'clock* is used: 6 p.m.; six o'clock.

11. **Use numbers in fractions appropriately.**

Except in technical usage and in charts and tables, simple fractions are usually written out: one-third, one-eighth. Fractions mixed with whole numbers are written as numerals: $28\frac{1}{2}$ cubic inches. (If the keyboard does not have a fraction key, a hyphen is added to make such mixed numbers clear: 28-1/2 cubic inches.)

NOTE: Instead of ordinary fractions, use decimals to express precise amounts. If a decimal fraction has a value less than one, place a zero before the decimal point: 0.628.

5. GRAMMAR AND USAGE

The guidelines presented here are generally used for college composition in the United States, although some instructors may vary them slightly to fit various rhetorical situations. If you are in doubt, check with your instructor.

5a. SENTENCE FRAGMENTS

Traditionally, sentence fragments have been frowned on and complete sentences advocated except in dialogue, conversation, and other informal situations. In formal writing, fragments are avoided in all but a few special circumstances.

✗ *Definition:* A fragment is a portion of a sentence that is punctuated as if it were an entire sentence. Lacking a subject, a verb, or both, a fragment is an incomplete thought. A fragment may be a word, a phrase, a dependent clause, or any combination of words that deviate from the basic subject-verb (or verb-subject) sentence pattern.

Usage: A general guideline for using fragments is to consider the rhetorical situation and use a fragment only for a purpose. The most important special uses of the fragment are answers to questions, exclamations, and requests, or commands.

▶ When is the next meeting? Next Thursday at 2:30 p.m. [fragment answer to question]

▶ What a shame!   ▶ No! Not really! [exclamations]

▶ No smoking.   ▶ Ready, get set, go! [requests or command.]

If you decide to use a fragment, be sure (1) your reader will approve, (2) you know how to avoid unintentional fragments, (3) the fragment is appropriate in the context. To be effective, a fragment should have a purpose.

1. **Avoid using *-ing* words or infinitives as main verbs, thus creating a fragment.**

   Incorrect

   ▼ *Driving* 100 miles a day to and from classes, *doing* complex assignments, and *raising* a family. I found that my undergraduate days were exhausting. [The first group of words is a fragment.]

   ▼ Jim and Shane stayed home last night. The reason *being* that they were broke. [The second group of words is a fragment.]

   ▼ First, the proper equipment *to get* out on the lake or pond. A canoe with a paddle or chest waders will do the job. [The first group of words is a fragment.]

   Correct

   ▶ *Driving* 100 miles a day to and from classes, *doing* complex assignments, and *raising* a family, I found that my undergraduate days were exhausting. [Join the fragment to the sentence with a comma.]

   ▶ Jim and Shane stayed home last night *because* they had no money. [The fragment and the sentence could be joined with a comma, but the result would be wordy.]

   ▶ First, *gather* the proper equipment to get out on the lake or pond. Either a canoe with a paddle or chest waders will do the job. [Add a verb to the first word group; the subject is understood to be *you*, meaning "you gather."]

2. **Avoid treating phrases that merely add additional details as complete sentences.**

Incorrect

▼ Then there is the high-speed driver. *A real maniac.*

▼ Kevin called his father collect last night. *To ask for a loan.*

▼ The company refused to honor the warranty. *Even though I purchased the lawn mower only six months ago.*

Correct

► Then there is the high-speed driver, a real maniac.

► Kevin called his father collect last night to ask for a loan.

► The company refused to honor the warranty even though I purchased the lawn mower only six months ago.

3. **Avoid treating dependent clauses as complete sentences.**

Incorrect

▼ *After I learned the market price for comparable antique tables.* I decided to rescue mine from the attic and refinish it.

Correct

► After I learned the market price for comparable antique tables, I decided to rescue mine from the attic and refinish it. [The introductory adverb clause is made a part of the sentence with a comma.]

5b. COMMA SPLICES AND FUSED (RUN-ON) SENTENCES

how 2 ind. Clauses joined together incorrectly

Beginning writers sometimes omit punctuation between clauses in a compound sentence. (See chapter 8 for more on compound sentences.) This error results in a *fused sentence*, sometimes called a *run-on sentence*. A related error is the *comma splice*, which occurs when two clauses are joined (spliced) with a comma. Never use the comma alone to punctuate a long compound sentence. If you use a comma, you must also have a coordinating conjunction. Note also that a semicolon is required before a conjunctive adverb such as *however* or *therefore*. The examples below will help to clarify punctuation of compound sentences:

1. **Punctuate sentences correctly to avoid comma splices.**

Incorrect

▼ Terrariums are costly at a flower shop, they are inexpensive to make at home.

▼ Terrariums are costly at a flower shop, however, they are inexpensive to make at home.

Correct

▶ Terrariums are costly at a flower shop, *but* they are inexpensive to make at home. [Coordinating conjunction and a comma]

▶ Terrariums are costly at a flower shop; however, they are inexpensive to make at home. [A semicolon replaces the coordinating conjunction and comma.]

2. **Punctuate sentences correctly to avoid fused (run-on) sentences.**

Incorrect

▼ The ordinance won wide support it was passed by a two-thirds vote.

Correct

▶ The ordinance won wide support; it was passed by a two-thirds vote. [semicolon added]

5c. PRONOUNS

Pronouns have different uses and therefore have different forms. A pronoun that is a subject is in the *subjective* case; a pronoun that shows ownership is in the *possessive* case; and a pronoun that acts as an object is in the *objective* case.

Pronouns also show person. *First person* refers to the individual who is speaking: *I (We)* will leave soon. *Second person* refers to the individual spoken to: *You* are very thoughtful. *Third person* refers to the people or things spoken about: *She (He, It, They)* will arrive soon. The following table will help you review the uses of pronouns.

1. **Use the correct case of pronouns.**

Subjective case. Use the subjective case for the following:

Subjects of main or subordinate clauses

▶ *I* will act as chairman during Brad's absence.

▶ Jane's party was the best *I* have ever attended.

Appositives identifying words in the subjective case

▶ Only two people—*Ray and I*—decided to go.

Subject complements following linking verbs

▶ The winners were *he* and Joan.

Case of Pronouns

	Subjective	*Possessive*	*Objective*
Singular			
First person	I	my, mine	me
Second person	you	your, yours	you
Third person	he, she, it	his, her, hers, its	him, her, it
Plural			
First person	we	our, ours	us
Second person	you	your, yours	you
Third person	they	their, theirs	them

[handwritten marginalia: preach, teach, give comands]

[handwritten marginalia: inappropriate]

Possessive case. Use the possessive case for the following:

To designate ownership

▶ That hat is *hers*.

▶ The committee was late in finishing *its* report.

Before a gerund (a verb form used as a noun)

▶ *Your* not writing upset Mother.

▶ *Her* drum playing angers the neighbors.

Objective case. Use the objective case for the following:

Direct objects, indirect objects, and objects of prepositions

▶ Bradley hit *it* over third base. [direct object]

▶ Jack sent *her* flowers. [indirect object]

▶ The letter was addressed to *me*. [object of preposition]

Appositives identifying objects

▶ The club elected two new members, Erin and *her*.

NOTE: After *than* or *as*, use the pronoun case that correctly completes your meaning.

▶ My mother understands my sister better than *I*. ("than I do")

▶ My mother understands my sister better than *me*. ("than she understands me")

Notice that *we* or *us* before a noun takes the same case it would if you dropped the noun.

▶ *We* students have complained to the administration about this problem before.

▶ It is difficult for *us* registered Independents to affect the primary process.

2. **Make sure that what each pronoun refers to is clear.**

Since a pronoun is a substitute for a noun or a noun phrase, a pronoun's meaning is apparent only when the reader or listener knows to what the pronoun refers. In other words, a pronoun should have a clear antecedent.

Unclear

▼ The law firm of Creager and Colvin failed after *he* withdrew the operating capital and fled to Switzerland.

▼ Teresa proofread my paper, but she didn't find a single *one*.

▼ He believes in reincarnation, but he does not believe that *they* appear to the living.

▼ *It* said in the newspaper that the election would be close.

Clear

▶ The law firm of Creager and Colvin failed after *Colvin* withdrew the operating capital and fled to Switzerland.

▶ Teresa proofread my paper, but she didn't find a single *error*.

▶ He believes in reincarnation, but he does not believe that *the dead* appear to the living.

▶ The newspaper reported that the election would be close.

3. **Make pronouns and their antecedents agree in gender, person, and number.**

Pronouns must have the same gender, person, and number as the word or phrase they refer to. Because gender and person seldom pose problems with pronouns (but see section 5c.4 on sexist usage), the discussion here is limited to agreement in number. The rule is simple: Use plural pronouns to refer to plural antecedents. Use singular pronouns to refer to singular antecedents.

Indefinite pronouns

Most indefinite pronouns indicate number. The plural forms seldom pose problems, but the singular forms are confusing, sometimes violating logic. For example, the word *everyone* means all, but *everyone* is singular and *all* is plural. An easy way to recall these eccentricities of usage is to remember that any pronoun containing *one* or *body* is singular. Listed below are the most common singular pronouns:

anyone	everybody	somebody
anybody	everyone	one
either	someone	each
neither	no one	

If you have trouble with *either, neither,* or *each,* then mentally add *one* and think: *either one, neither one, each one.* Likewise, in a word that has the suffix *body,* substitute *one:* for *anybody,* think *anyone;* for *somebody,* think *someone.*

Compound antecedents

In general, use a plural pronoun to refer to compound antecedents linked by *and:*

▶ George and Martha are taking *their* time.

However, when a compound antecedent is preceded by *each* or *every,* use a singular pronoun:

▶ Every cafe and restaurant in town has seen *its* business suffer.

Use a singular pronoun to refer to singular antecedents linked by *or* and *nor.* Use a plural pronoun to refer to plural antecedents linked by *neither* and *nor:*

▶ A dog or a cat has *its* special needs during warm summer months.

▶ Neither friends nor family members gave *their* approval to the marriage.

4. Avoid sexist use of pronouns.

Since the early 1970s we have become more aware that the English language discriminates against women in many ways. Some people object to word forms that contain the generic form *man* (meaning all people—the human race) and the use of the pronoun *he* when the referent could be female, as in "Everyone brought *his* toothbrush." Some people attempt to solve this dilemma by using *he/she* or other combinations, but none of these coinages is generally accepted. How then can writers best handle the problem of sexist language?

Use *he or she* and *his or her* sparingly. One *he or she* or one *his or her* will not disrupt the flow of a sentence, but the repeated use of these terms can distract the reader. Instead, rewrite sentences to avoid male and female pronouns. You can omit the third-person pronoun, repeat the noun, or make the entire sentence plural. Consider the following correct examples:

▶ If a person is insincere, chances are that *his or her* insincerity will be detected.

▶ If a person is insincere, chances are that *the* insincerity will be detected. [preferable]

▶ If *people* are insincere, chances are that *their* insincerity will be detected. [preferable]

As a way of avoiding sexist usage, people sometimes use the plural *their* when a singular personal pronoun such as *his* or *her* is called for. This colloquial usage is heard in sentences such as "*Everyone* should remember to take *their* ground cloth and hunting knife." But for most writing, this sentence would be considered incorrect. Standard usage would be as follows:

▶ *Everyone* should remember to take a ground cloth and hunting knife.

▶ *All* should remember to pack *their* rain gear.

▶ Not *one* of the runners felt *she* had run *her* best. [All the runners are women.]

▶ Not *one* of the alumni remembered to wear *his* old football jersey.

5. Use relative pronouns correctly.

There are only six relative pronouns, easily memorized because five begin with *w: who, whom, whose, which,* and *what.* The other one is *that. Which, what,* and *that* have the same form for all three cases. *Who* is in the subjective case, *whose* is in the possessive case, and *whom* is in the objective case.

▶ *Who* is calling? [subject]

▶ *Whose* gerbil is that? [possessive]

▶ To *whom* it may concern: [object of preposition]

Relative pronouns are used to introduce adjective clauses. Sometimes these pronouns cause problems in punctuation and usage. In the first example that follows, the adjective clause (italicized) is nonessential—unimportant to the main idea of the sentence; *which* is used and the phrase is set off by commas. In the second sentence, the adjective clause is necessary for the sentence to be clear and complete; *that* is used and no commas are needed.

▶ A dog, *which had no collar,* followed me home. [nonessential clause]

▶ The dog *that is wearing the collar* is mine. [essential clause]

NOTE: Who and *whom* generally refer only to people. *Which* and *that* refer to animals, places, or things. Sometimes *who* is used to refer to animals with names, but such usage is unusual.

6. Avoid inappropriate shifts of person.

A careless shift in person can confuse your reader. Maintain a consistent point of view by writing in the same person: first person (*I, we*), second person (*you*), or third person (*he, she, it, they*).

Inappropriate

▼ *I* always spend the morning hours on work that requires mental effort, for *your* mind is freshest in the morning.

Revised

▶ *I* always spend the morning hours on work that requires mental effort, for *my* mind is freshest in the morning.

5d. VERBS

All verbs have four basic forms. These principal parts are *the infinitive, present participle, past,* and *past participle.* These basic forms can be varied by the addition of helping verbs (*is, are, was, were, be, been, has, have, had,* etc.) or the preposition *to. To* indicates the infinitive, which is in the present tense.

Four Principal Parts

Infinitive	Present Participle	Past	Past Participle
(to) live	(is) liv*ing*	liv*ed*	(has, have, or had) liv*ed*

Six Troublesome Verbs

Present tense	Past tense	Past participle
lie (to recline)	lay	(has, had) lain
lay (to place an object)	laid	laid
sit (to take a seat)	sat	sat
set (to place an object)	set	set
rise (to get up)	rose	risen
raise (to lift)	raised	raised

1. **Use verb forms correctly.**

Try to be consistent in using verb forms. If you have a question, consult a dictionary. Once in awhile, you may find that two or more forms are considered acceptable. Since verbs are the most complex part of speech in the English language, a full treatment of the topic is impossible here. Only commonly misused forms are discussed.

The "troublesome six" verbs

Six verbs, sometimes called "the troublesome six," are outlined in the preceding table. Use the correct form of these verbs. Remember that *lay, set,* and *raise*—when used in the active voice—all require direct objects and that *lie, sit,* and *rise* do not take objects. This guideline should help prevent confusion. In the examples below, the direct objects are italicized.

Direct Objects	*No Direct Objects*
Please lay the *book* there.	Lie down, Rover.
Sharon laid her *coat* on the bed.	Sue has lain in the sun two hours.
Barry set his *briefcase* on my desk.	Harry sat there.
Jim raised the *blind*.	The sun rises at 6:30 a.m.

Four more verbs requiring caution

Try to be consistent in your choice of tense. Four verbs—*can, may, will,* and *shall*—are frequently misused because people mix tenses improperly. But if you understand the principal parts of verbs and remember the groupings listed below, you should be able to use these verbs correctly.

Present tense	Past tense
can	could
may	might
will	would
shall	should

If you have a question about the tense of a verb, consult your dictionary. Be aware that two or more forms are sometimes considered acceptable.

Principal parts of irregular verbs

The following list of irregular verbs and their principal parts is based on the *American Heritage Dictionary,* 3rd edition. The verbs are used with helping verbs (such as *is, are, was, were, have, has, have been*) to form tenses.

Present	Present Participle	Past	Past Participle
bear	(is, are) bearing	bore	(has, have, had) borne
beat	beating	beat	beaten
become	becoming	became	become
begin	beginning	began	begun
bite	biting	bit	bitten
blow	blowing	blew	blown
break	breaking	broke	broken
bring	bringing	brought	brought
burst	bursting	burst	burst
buy	buying	bought	bought
catch	catching	caught	caught
choose	choosing	chose	chosen
come	coming	came	come
cut	cutting	cut	cut
creep	creeping	crept	crept
dive	diving	dived	dived, dove
do	doing	did	done
draw	drawing	drew	drawn
drink	drinking	drank	drunk

Present	Present Participle	Past	Past Participle
drive	driving	drove	driven
eat	eating	ate	eaten
fall	falling	fell	fallen
find	finding	found	found
fling	flinging	flung	flung
fly	flying	flew	flown
forget	forgetting	forgot	forgot, forgotten
freeze	freezing	froze	frozen
get	getting	got	gotten, got
give	giving	gave	given
go	going	went	gone
grow	growing	grew	grown
hang (suspend)	hanging	hung	hung
hang (execute)	(is being) hanged	hanged	hanged
hit	hitting	hit	hit
hurt	hurting	hurt	hurt
keep	keeping	kept	kept
know	(is) known	knew	known
lead	leading	led	led
leave	leaving	left	left
lend	lending	lent	lent
let	letting	let	let
pay	paying	paid	paid
lose	losing	lost	lost
ride	riding	rode	ridden
ring	ringing	rang	rung
rise	rising	rose	risen
run	running	ran	run
say	saying	said	said
see	seeing	saw	seen
shake	shaking	shook	shaken
shine (the sun)	shining	shone	shone
shine (to polish)	shining	shined	shined
sing	singing	sang or sung	sung
sink	sinking	sank or sunk	sunk
speak	speaking	spoke	spoken

Present	Present Participle	Past	Past Participle
spring	springing	sprang, sprung	sprung
stand	standing	stood	stood
steal	stealing	stole	stolen
sting	stinging	stung	stung
strike	striking	struck	struck
swear	swearing	swore	sworn
swim	swimming	swam	swum
swing	swinging	swung	swung
take	taking	took	taken
teach	teaching	taught	taught
tear	tearing	tore	torn
tell	telling	told	told
throw	throwing	threw	thrown
wear	wearing	wore	worn
write	writing	wrote	written

2. Use *be* correctly.

The verb *be* should not be used as if it were a complete verb. Except in a few special instances (see the discussion of the subjunctive mood in section 5d.6), some other form of *be* or a helping verb such as *will* is required.

Nonstandard

I *be* a college student.

I *be* going there.

Mrs. Beck, you *be* leaving soon?

Standard

I *am* a college student.

I *am* going there.

Mrs. Beck, *will* you *be* leaving soon?

3. Make subjects and verbs agree in number.

Use singular verbs with singular subjects; use plural verbs with plural subjects. Verb agreement is sometimes a problem, particularly for international students. But if you remember—when using the third person—that adding an *s* to a verb makes it singular, this principle should help. (Adding an *s* to a noun makes it plural.) Here are some third-person examples:

Singular	Plural
is	are
was	were
has	have
skates	skate

Words between the subject and verb

Words and phrases that appear between the subject and the verb sometimes mislead. In the following sentences, the verbs are plural to agree with the plural subjects:

▶ The letters, along with the package, *were* mailed today.

The word *package* is not the subject. But because *package* comes immediately before the verb, it may seem natural to use *was*. This is not correct. In the following sentence *were* is correct:

▶ The letters and the package *were* mailed this morning.

▶ The package and the letters *were* mailed this morning. [preferable]

Compound subject linked with or or nor

Another troublemaker is the sentence that has a singular and a plural subject without *and*. Then the subject nearest the verb determines the agreement of the verb:

▶ Neither the cookies nor the fruitcake *was* fresh.

▶ Neither the fruitcake nor the cookies *were* fresh.

Inverted word order

In questions and in statements beginning with *there*, the subject usually follows the verb. Be careful that the verb agrees with the subject.

▶ *Are* the photocopies ready to be picked up? (photocopies *are*)

▶ There *is* only one clerk at work today. (clerk *is*)

Relative pronoun subjects

In a clause beginning with a relative pronoun—*who, which,* or *that*—look for the pronoun's antecedent to decide whether the verb is singular or plural.

▶ People who *litter* should be fined heavily. (people *litter*)

▶ This house, which *needs* some work, could be a bargain. (house *needs*)

4. **Use the active voice of verbs unless there is a good reason for using the passive voice. (See chapter 8.)**

Use the active voice in most sentences. The active voice occurs when the subject is the doer of the action expressed by the verb. The passive voice occurs when the subject is not the doer of the action expressed by the verb.

▶ Sergei Grinkov *won* an Olympic gold medal twice. [active voice]

▶ Twice an Olympic gold medal *was won* by Sergei Grinkov. [passive voice]

5. **Avoid inappropriate shifts of tense, voice, or mood.**

Inappropriate shifts in the tense, voice, or mood of verbs can be distracting and even confusing for the reader.

Inappropriate

▼ Before he *went* to class, he *drinks* three cups of coffee. [needless shift from past to present tense]

▼ A cocoon was sighted on a liatris plant, and in the spring a beautiful moth crept out. [needless shift from active to passive voice]

▼ *Go* to school, and *you should* take an umbrella. [needless shift from imperative to indicative mood]

Appropriate

▶ Before he goes to class, he *drinks* three cups of coffee. [both verbs in present tense]

▶ On a liatris plant, I *found* a cocoon; and in the spring a beautiful moth *crept* out. [both verbs in past tense and active voice]

▶ Go to school and *take* an umbrella. [both verbs in imperative mood]

6. **Use the subjunctive mood correctly.**

The subjunctive mood is the form of a verb used to express doubt, desire, probability, a condition contrary to fact, or a hypothetical situation. The subjunctive appears in three ways: (1) in *if* clauses indicating unreal conditions; (2) in *that* clauses after verbs expressing requests, suggestions, wishes, or commands; and (3) in a few idioms.

Unreal conditions

▶ My husband acted as though he *were* an expert at ironing until he scorched a shirt.

▶ In Chicago's traffic jams, I felt as if I *were* having a bad dream.

▶ Terry could fix that leak if he *were* here.

That clauses after verbs expressing requests, suggestions, wishes, or orders

► Her boss asked that she *remain* in the building during her coffee break.

► The company requires that I *be* on duty at 8:00 a.m.

► The committee agreed that Jane *be* given released time to complete the project.

► Henry moved that the meeting *be* adjourned.

A few idioms

► If this *be* true ► Far *be* it from me

► *Come* what may ► Long *wave* the stars and stripes!

5e. USE *LIKE* CORRECTLY

1. **Use *like* as a preposition.**

► Jenny looks *like* her aunt.

► *Like* me, Bill enjoys jazz.

► It is not *like* him to be late.

► I feel *like* resting.

► It looks *like* rain.

► He walks *like* a duck.

2. **Use *like* as an adjective to mean "similar, equal, or alike."**

► I used one-half cup of butter and a *like* amount of flour.

► My grandmother used to say, "*Like* father, *like* son."

3. **Use *as if*, not *like*, as a conjunction to connect two clauses.**

Incorrect

▼ None of the teenagers lit their cigarettes *like* they were used to smoking.

▼ Hazel acted *like* she was angry with me.

Correct

► None of the teenagers lit their cigarettes *as if* they were used to smoking.

► Hazel acted *as if* she were angry with me.

5f. MODIFIERS

One frequent error, found not only in student writing but also in advertisements, newspaper articles, and other media, is tangled syntax or scrambled word order. Words or phrases are misplaced in sentences; sometimes important words are omitted. These offenses interfere with clarity and violate logic. Two common offenders are discussed here: misplaced modifiers and dangling modifiers.

1. **Avoid misplaced modifiers.**

Misplaced modifiers are simply modifying words or phrases (adjective or adverb) that are out of place. They sneak into places where they do not belong. For example, *only* is an impudent pest that cuts into line ahead of other words. Although *only* may seem small and harmless in the wrong place, don't overlook its misbehavior. Yank it back where it belongs, close to the word it limits. Consider some examples:

Misplaced

▼ "Who says kids *only* like junk food?" [an ad for spaghetti]

▼ "If *only* your feet could talk." [an ad for a podiatrist]

▼ "If you *only* inspect your draft sentence by sentence, you can easily overlook how its parts work together." [a textbook]

Revised

▶ Who says kids like *only* junk food?

▶ If your feet could *only* talk.

▶ If you inspect your draft *only* sentence by sentence, you can easily overlook how its parts work together.

The adverbs *almost* and *even* are other frequent offenders. Like *only*, they should be placed exactly before the word they modify.

Misplaced

▼ She *almost* used the entire bottle of bath oil for one bath.

▼ I *even* felt worse after I took the medicine.

Revised

▶ She used *almost* the entire bottle of bath oil for one bath.

▶ I felt *even* worse after I took the medicine.

Clauses and phrases may also be misplaced in sentences, often leading to unintentionally humorous misreadings:

Misplaced

▼ Jane wore a flower in her hair *that was pink*. [What was pink?]

▼ Dick kept an odd-shaped piece of jade in his jacket pocket, *which he considered lucky*. [What was lucky?]

▼ A spider dropped off the piano bench as I opened the door *into a large web*. [Did the spider web have a door?]

▼ I easily spotted the rare bird *using high-powered binoculars*. [Was the bird using binoculars?]

Revised

▶ In her hair Jane wore a flower that was pink. [Or: In her hair Jane wore a pink flower.]

▶ Dick kept an odd-shaped piece of jade, which he considered lucky, in his jacket pocket.

▶ As I opened the door, a spider dropped off the piano bench into a large web.

▶ Using high-powered binoculars, I easily spotted the rare bird.

2. **Avoid dangling modifiers.**

Dangling modifiers are phrases that lack a referent: the noun or pronoun needed to make the phrase clear and logical has been omitted. Usually, dangling modifiers cling precariously at the beginning of a sentence. Here are two examples from student papers:

Dangling

▼ When only a youngster in grade school, *my father* instructed me in the art of boxing. [Who was in grade school?]

▼ After standing up well under the two-year exposure test, the *manufacturers* were convinced that the paint was sufficiently durable. [The manufacturers stood up well?]

Revised (referent added)

▶ When *I was* only a youngster in grade school, my father instructed me in the art of boxing.

▶ After *the paint* stood up well under the two-year exposure test, the manufacturers were convinced that it was sufficiently durable.

NOTE: Whenever you include an *-ing* phrase (participial phrase) at the beginning of a sentence, check to see that the word it modifies immediately follows it. If not, rewrite the sentence to make that word the subject of the first clause. Probably the best way to find tangled syntax is to read your writing aloud and listen carefully. Does each sentence make sense? Beware of answering in the affirmative too quickly. Writers know what they mean. *The question is whether each sentence will be clear and logical to readers.*

6. SPELLING

6a. SPELLING TIPS

Many people feel inferior because they are poor spellers. They feel less intelligent than people who spell accurately. But not all very bright people are good spellers. For example one ninth-grader, a physician's daughter, was a brilliant student except for her spelling. Her themes were filled with misspelled words. Once, after she had corrected a theme, a word was misspelled in a different way. When asked why she hadn't used a dictionary, she replied, "Oh, I asked Dad." This example illustrates the need for spelling tip number one: *Use a dictionary; don't ask someone how to spell a word.*

The mystery of poor spelling has not been completely solved. But we do know that incorrect pronunciation sometimes leads to incorrect spelling. Students who mispronounce words frequently misspell those same words. The left list below contains some words that are commonly misspelled due to mispronunciation:

Incorrect	*Correct*
Artic	Arctic
congradulations	congratulations
discribe	describe
goverment	government
enviroment	environment
convience	convenience
secratary	secretary
wreck havoc	wreak havoc
procede	proceed
reciept	receipt
then (used in comparison)	than

If you are unsure of the spelling or pronunciation of a word, look it up in a dictionary. Then practice writing and saying the word correctly.

The best spellers are those who can visualize words. During spelling bees, students can write words on scraps of paper, in the air, or on a corner of the blackboard to see how the words look. Remembering the appearance of a word can help in recalling the correct letters.

If you can strengthen your mental images of any problem words, you can improve your spelling. One way is to keep a list of words that you misspell frequently and practice writing them. (Chances are there will be fewer than a dozen.) After you look up the correct spelling of each word on your list, write each one at least a dozen times.

6b. ASSOCIATION AIDS TO IMPROVE SPELLING

One way to improve spelling is to devise an association that will help you recall the correct spelling. For example, one student who had difficulty with the word *occasion* could not remember whether it had two *c*'s and one *s* or vice versa. She looked the word up several times until she devised this sentence: "Twenty-one is a special occasion." Twenty-one (21) reminded her that occasion had 2 *c*'s and 1 *s*. Listed below are some other associations to help you recall certain spellings.

▶ A *secretary* is a keeper of *secrets*. [An *e* follows the *r* in both words.]

▶ *separate* has *a rat* in it. [An *a* follows the *p*.]

▶ *there, their, they're*

    there: Without the *t*, *there* becomes *here*. [Both words refer to location.]

    their: Without the *t*, *their* becomes *heir*. [Both words refer to ownership.]

    they're: This is a contraction of *they are*. [The apostrophe indicates that *a* has been omitted.]

▶ *principal and principle:* The following sentence should help you remember that *principal* refers to someone or something of importance: "The *principal* points of his speech were. . . ." On the other hand, *principle* refers to a code, law, or doctrine.

    The *principal* of our school was a *pal* to the students.

    The Tenth Commandment is a difficult *principle* to follow.

▶ *prejudice:* Just remember that *prejudice* means to *pre-judge* something.

▶ *stationery* and *stationary:* Remember that you write on an envelope. [Both *envelope* and *stationery* have *e*'s.] Something *stationary* stays in one place. [two *a*'s]

▶ *maneuver:* When you are riding a horse, the mane is in front of you. Just remember that the *mane* is before the *u*.

You may want to devise your own association aids for words that give you trouble.

6c. OTHER SPELLING AIDS

▶ Only one English word ends in *sede: supersede*. Only three words end in *ceed: exceed, proceed, succeed*. All other words of similar sound end in *cede: precede, recede*, and so forth.

▶ Drop the final *e* in most words when the suffix you are adding begins with a vowel: *chang(e)ing, hop(e)ing, purchas(e)able*. (In a few instances, however, the final *e* is kept: *changeable, knowledgeable, peaceable*. And some words can be spelled either way: *salable, saleable; livable, liveable*.) Usually the final *e* is kept when the suffix begins with a consonant: *hopeful, vengeful, homeless*.

▶ *Pre* means "before." *Per* means "through, to, for, by each," or "by means of." *Pro* means "in favor of" or "acting as."

    preschool: before school

    perceive: to become aware of directly through the senses

    procapitalism: in favor of capitalism

▶ Plurals of words ending in *y* are formed as follows: When a consonant precedes the final *y*, change the *y* to *i* and add *es: company, companies; lady, ladies; cherry, cherries.* Exception: plurals of proper names, for instance *the Kelleys.* When a vowel precedes the *y*, keep the *y* and add *s: monkeys, attorneys, byways.*

▶ To form the plural of nouns ending in *ch, s, sh, x,* and *z,* add *es: matches, gases, bushes, taxes, buzzes.* This rule also applies to the singular forms of verbs ending in these letters.

▶ When adding a suffix that begins with a vowel, double a final consonant if the word meets all of these criteria: (1) It is one syllable or is stressed on the final syllable; (2) there is only one vowel in the word or in the final syllable; (3) the word or syllable ends in a single consonant. The following words meet all these criteria: *rap, rapped, rapping; occur, occurred, occurrence; fit, fitter, fittest; repel, repelling, repellent.* Note that for words ending in *e,* the *e* is dropped but the remaining consonant is never doubled: *write, writing* (not *writting*).

▶ A modification of this rule applies when the pronunciation of the word changes after the suffix is added. For example, *infer* becomes *inferring* (doubled final consonant) because the stress remains on the final syllable; but it becomes *inference* (no double consonant) because here the stress shifts to the first syllable. A related modification is seen in words such as *offer, offered, offering* and *order, ordered, ordering.* The stress is always on the first syllable, and thus the consonant is not doubled.

6d. SIX WAYS TO IMPROVE SPELLING

Probably the biggest factor in any improvement is motivation. If you resolve to refine your spelling skill and follow a plan, you will become a better speller. Here are six techniques to aid you:

1. **Use a dictionary to check words if you are unsure of their spelling.** Carry a spelling checker or pocket dictionary and keep a desk dictionary in a convenient place at home. But remember that computer spelling checkers are limited in their helpfulness. (see "Glossary of Usage" pages H-44–H-49 — for similar words that are commonly confused.)

2. **Pronounce words correctly.** If you leave out letters or syllables in pronunciation, you may leave them out when writing the word.

3. **Compile your own spelling list.** Review this daily for a few weeks. Look at each word. Then shut your eyes and see if you can spell it correctly.

4. **Write misspelled words correctly several times so that you can visualize their correct spelling in your mind.**

5. **Familiarize yourself with the memory association aids.** Then devise some aids of your own.

6. As a last resort, if you cannot recognize misspelled words, ask someone to mark them. Then get out the dictionary and correct the spellings yourself. With practice, your spelling ability will improve, and you will be able to catch more of your errors.

7. GLOSSARY OF USAGE

Some words in the English language are commonly confused because they look or sound alike. Other words used in conversation are sometimes mistaken for standard usage. This glossary will help you select the appropriate word for your college and business writing. The recommendations here are based on usage listed in current dictionaries. For clarity, misspellings and other unaccepted variations are listed after the standard word.

a, an   Use *a* before words starting with a consonant sound. Use *an* before words starting with a vowel sound.

- a bristlecone pine, a history, a quail, a sinkhole
- an aardvark, an egg, an infant, an honorable man

accept, except   *Accept* means "to believe," "to approve," or "to take" (as take an offered gift). *Except* means "without" or "excluding."

- Can he *accept* constructive criticism?
- All the children *except* Jane are here.

access, excess   The noun *access* is the "ability or right to enter, to use, or to approach." The verb *access* is used in a technological sense, as "to locate data." *Excess* means "too much" or "exceeding that which is normal and sufficient."

- It is impossible to gain direct *access* to the freeway from here.
- Lucinda can *access* those files easily.
- She stored the *excess* bread dough in the refrigerator.

adapt, adept, adopt   *Adapt* means "to make suitable for a specific situation." *Adept* means "very skilled; proficient." *Adopt* means "to take up and use as one's own," as an idea, word, or the like. *Adopt* also refers to the process of child adoption.

- Do you think you can *adapt* the part to make it fit?
- Jeff is *adept* at programming.
- When customers complain, Sarah *adopts* the tactic of "A soft answer turneth away wrath."

adverse, averse   *Adverse* means "harmful or unfavorable." *Averse* means "unwilling" or "disinclined."

- William has surmounted *adverse* circumstances before.
- Mike is *averse* to risk taking.

advice, advise   *Advice* is a noun that means "a view, opinion, or judgment." *Advise* is a verb that means "to counsel," "to inform" or "to recommend."

- His *advice* was to look for another job.
- I really don't know what to *advise*.

affect, effect   *Affect* is a verb meaning "to change or to influence." *Effect* is usually used as a noun to mean "result." As a verb *effect* means "to make" or "to implement."

- How will that *affect* your decision?
- What will be the *effect* of that decision?
- Can you *effect* an improvement in that procedure?

all ready, already   *Already* refers to time, meaning "previously." *All ready* means "prepared" or "available for action."

- Did you *already* clock out?
- Are you *all ready* to leave?

all right   *All right* means "satisfactory" or "proper." *Alright* is a common misspelling.

- It is *all right* to go in the kitchen; the floor is dry.

all together, altogether   *All together* means "in a group." *Altogether* means "completely."

- The birds huddled *all together* to keep warm.
- Joe's answer was not *altogether* right.

allusion, delusion, illusion An *allusion* is "a reference" (often to a literary work). A *delusion* is a "mistaken idea." An *illusion* is "an erroneous perception of reality."

- He made an *allusion* to Hamlet.
- He suffers from the *delusion* that he is immortal.
- The ghost was an *illusion*, created with special lighting.

allot, a lot *Allot* means "to parcel out" or "to give a certain portion." *A lot*, used to mean "a large extent, amount, or number," is informal. *Alot* is a common misspelling.

- The government *allots* only one per family.
- He has *a lot* of confidence.
- Jill's grandmother is *a lot* better.

among, between Use *among* when referring to three or more units or people. Use *between* when referring to only two.

- Let's keep this secret *among* our family members.
- *Between* you and me, I like his beard.

amount, number *Amount* refers to a quantity or weight. *Number* refers to a numeral, unit, or indefinite quantity of items or individuals.

- The recipe called for a small *amount* of black pepper.
- The crowd *numbers* in the thousands.

an, a See *a, an*.

any, any other *Any* means "one, some, every, or all." *Any other* is used in a comparison. Do not substitute *any* (by itself), which in the following example would mean that Brian was faster than himself.

- Brian was faster than *any other* runner in his age group.
- You may select *any* of the top prizes.

anyone, any one *Anyone* is a pronoun that means "any person" or in some instances, "everyone." *Any one* means "whichever one (just one) of a group." *Any one* can refer to a person or a thing.

- *Anyone* may come, not just members.
- *Any one* of the band members can carry the flag.

appraise, apprise *Appraise* means "to evaluate or estimate the value." *Apprise* means "to give notice to or inform."

- Will you *appraise* this emerald ring for me?
- Did you *apprise* the prisoner of his rights?

assure, ensure, insure *Assure* means "to inform positively." *Ensure* means "to make sure or certain." *Insure* means "to cover with insurance." *Insure* also means "to make certain, especially by taking precautions."

- I *assure* you that every precaution will be taken.
- Checking the map beforehand will *ensure* that you find the right road.
- Did you *insure* the contents of your house?

averse See *adverse, averse*.

awhile, a while *Awhile* is an adverb that means "a short time." *A while*, which consists of an article and a noun, means "a period of time." (The preposition *for* may be used with *a while*.)

- He stopped *awhile* to rest. (not *for awhile*)
- Don't rush off—stay for *a while*.

beside, besides *Beside* means "next to." *Besides* means "also."

- The scissors are lying *beside* my sewing basket.
- *Besides* my fishing equipment, I'm taking a picnic lunch.

between See *among, between*.

breath, breathe *Breath* is a noun; *breathe* is a verb. Both refer to inhalation and exhalation.

- The speech instructor advised taking a deep *breath* before starting to speak.
- *Breathe* deeply as you work out.

capital, capitol *Capital* refers to the "official place or city of government" or an "amount of money." *Capitol* refers to the "building that houses the official government offices."

- Denver is the *capital* of Colorado.
- We need more *capital* to fund the project.
- Sue visited the *capitol* building during her trip to the state *capital*.

censor, censure *Censor* is "to examine books, films, or other materials to remove or suppress what is considered objectionable." *Censure* is "to criticize severely or blame."

- The school board plans to *censor* books purchased for the school.
- The editorial *censured* a city council member for his failure to attend meetings regularly.

cite, sight, site *Cite* means "to quote." *Sight* refers to the ability to see or view. *Site* refers to location, as a building site.

- Can you *cite* his exact words?
- Can you *sight* Venus above the evening horizon?
- They selected a lovely wooded *site* for their new home.

complement, compliment *Complement* means "to complete or bring to perfection." *Compliment* means "to express praise."

- That floral arrangement *complements* your table setting.
- Brad *complimented* Cindy on her new shoes.

conscience, conscious *Conscience* is "the awareness of a moral or ethical aspect of one's conduct" and the desire "to prefer right over wrong." *Conscious* refers to "awareness of one's environment and existence."

- Jeannette returned the wallet to its owner to relieve her *conscience*.
- Is the patient *conscious* yet?

continual, continuous *Continual* means "recurring regularly or often." *Continuous* means "uninterrupted."

- Uncle Jake's *continual* complaining made our visit unpleasant.
- The flow of fresh air throughout the building is *continuous*.

council, counsel *Council* refers to a group of people who are delegated "to serve in an administrative, legislative, or advisory capacity." *Counsel*, as noun or verb, refers to advice.

- Anthony is a member of the town *council*.
- The admissions office *counsels* students.
- Lawyers charge for their *counsel*.

criteria, criterion A *criterion* is a "standard, rule, or test upon which a judgment or decision can be based." *Criteria* is the plural of *criterion*.

- She gave only one *criterion* for the job: a strong back.
- He stated six *criteria* for the upcoming performance evaluation.

delusion See *allusion, delusion, illusion*.

effect, affect See *affect, effect*.

emigrate, immigrate When people *emigrate*, they leave their homeland to reside elsewhere. When they *immigrate*, they enter a different country to reside.

- My paternal ancestors, five brothers, *emigrated* from Wales in the late 1700's.
- They *immigrated* to the United States and traveled to the territory that later became Ohio.

eminent, imminent *Eminent* means "of high rank, station, or quality." *Imminent* means "about to occur, impending."

- Today is the birthday of that *eminent* inventor Thomas A. Edison.
- Skating on thin ice poses an *imminent* danger.

enthusiastic *Enthusiastic*, meaning to have great excitement or interest, is standard usage. Enthused is used only colloquially.

- Cody was *enthusiastic* about traveling to the Rocky Mountains.

except See *accept, except.*

excess See *access, excess.*

explicit, implicit *Explicit* means fully and clearly expressed; leaving nothing implied." *Implicit* means "implied or understood though not directly expressed."

- The doctor's directions were *explicit:* "Take one tablet with a full glass of water after meals."
- The company president has *implicit* trust in Sheila's judgment.

farther, further *Farther* refers to "physical distance" and *further* to a nonphysical dimension such as distance in time.

- We drove *farther* than usual the second day of our trip.
- If we go *further* back a few generations, we find other family members who also suffered from breast cancer.

fewer, less *Fewer* is used in comparisons to refer to "individual units, things that can be counted." *Less* is used in comparisons to mean a smaller amount or "a mass of measurable extent."

- *Fewer* people attended the state fair this year than last year.
- Opals cost much *less* than diamonds of the same size.

flaunt, flout *Flaunt* means "to parade or display ostentatiously." *Flout* means "to show contempt for" or "to scorn."

- Lorrie *flaunted* her new engagement ring.
- Timothy *flouted* the dress code.

further See *farther, further.*

get *Get* means "to receive" or "to bring." Avoid the many colloquial uses of *get* in college and business writing. (See a dictionary for other examples of colloquial usage.)

- Standard: Will you *get* a gallon of milk when you go out?

- Colloquial: I hope the frost doesn't *get* our garden.
- Colloquial: That really *gets* to me!

good, well *Good* is an adjective meaning "positive or desirable." *Well* is often used as an adverb to mean "satisfactorily or sufficiently" or "skillfully or proficiently." *Well* is also used as an adjective to mean "a satisfactory condition; right or proper."

- Jerry received *good* news this morning.
- Jeremy did *well* on his calculus exam.
- Henry is *well;* he has completely recovered from pneumonia.
- The project is going *well.*

hanged, hung People are *hanged.* Objects are *hung.*

- The convicted murderer was *hanged.*
- Derek *hung* the painting over the fireplace.

idea, ideal An *idea* is "a thought." An *ideal* is "a principle" or "a conception or model of something in its absolute perfection."

- Suddenly he had a delightful *idea.*
- Her *ideal* husband would be a wonderful father.
- Always be true to your *ideals.*

illusion See *allusion, delusion, illusion.*

implicit See *explicit, implicit.*

its, it's *Its* is the possessive form of *it.* *It's* is a contraction of *it is.*

- The dog has lost *its* collar.
- *It's* over seventy miles to the next town.

leave, let *Leave* means "to go out or away from." *Let* means "to permit or allow."

- Will you *leave* Jiffy at the kennel when you go to the lake?
- Please *let* me help you with those packages.

less See *fewer, less.*

let See *leave, let.*

loose, lose *Lose* is a verb meaning "to mislay." *Loose* is an adjective meaning "not tight" or "unconfined."

- Did you *lose* an earring?
- My watchband is too *loose*.
- An orangutan was *loose* in the park.

medium, media *Medium* is (1) an "intermediate course," the midpoint between two extremes; (2) a way that something is "transmitted or carried"; (3) "an agency by which something is accomplished or conveyed or transferred." *Media* is the plural of *medium* and takes a plural verb.

- The Internet is a *medium* that relays daily stock market reports.
- The *media* frequently refer to the escapades of the royal family.

moral, morale *Moral* is an adjective that refers to "judgment of the goodness or badness of human action and character." *Morale* is a noun that means "the state of the spirits of a person or group."

- The *moral* code of society seems to be changing.
- Employee *morale* is high at XYZ Company.

number See *amount, number*.

passed, past *Passed* is a verb that means "having moved on; proceeded." *Past* as an adverb means "beyond" and as a noun or adjective refers to time that is over. Do not write "*past* history" because all history is past.

- Jerry *passed* the bakery without stopping.
- Jerry drove *past* the bakery without stopping.
- Let's forget the *past* and look to the future.

patience, patients *Patience* is the ability to "bear pain, provocation, or annoyance with calmness." *Patients* refers to people who "receive medical attention, care, or treatment."

- *Patience* is a quality that is learned.
- The physician saw thirty-seven *patients* yesterday.

personal, personnel *Personal* refers to the private matters of an individual. *Personnel* refers to a group of people who work for an organization. (Note that *personnel* has two *n*'s.)

- Please don't ask *personal* questions.
- Their *personnel* are very courteous.

precede, proceed *Precede* means "to go before." *Proceed* means "to go" or "to continue."

- The Rose Bowl game *precedes* the Orange Bowl game.
- Let's *proceed* with the meeting.

principal, principle (see "Association Aids to Improve Spelling," page H-44.)

quiet, quite *Quiet* means "free of noise." *Quite* means "very; entirely."

- Our dorm is rarely *quiet*.
- Your homemade apple pie is *quite* tasty.
- It is *quite* all right to park there.

quotation, quote *Quote* is a verb that means "to repeat or copy the words of (another)," usually citing the source. *Quotation* is a noun meaning "the act of quoting" or "a passage quoted."

- Do you plan to *quote* John F. Kennedy in your speech?
- A *quotation* from Winston Churchill might make an effective introduction.

real, really *Real* is an adjective meaning "genuine or authentic," "free of pretense or falsehood." (Avoid using *real* to mean "very.") *Really* is an adverb meaning "truly; genuinely."

- Her diamond is *real*.
- *Really*, I can't go with you.

regardless *Regardless* means "in spite of everything; anyway." Irregardless is redundant and nonstandard.

- Many people neglect to buckle their seat belts, *regardless* of the danger.

sight See *cite, sight, site.*

sometime, some time, sometimes *Sometime* means "an indefinite or unstated time." *Some time* refers to an amount of time. *Sometimes* means "occasionally."

- Stop in *sometime.*
- I haven't seen him for *some time.*
- *Sometimes* I feed the elephants at the city zoo.

stationary, stationery *Stationary* means "not moving" or "not capable of being moved." *Stationery* refers to writing materials.

- The tables in that restaurant are *stationary.*
- Would you like some monogrammed *stationery* for Christmas?

than, then *Than* is a conjunction indicating a comparison. *Then* is an adverb indicating time.

- Harrison likes pistachio ice cream better *than* chocolate.
- I will meet you *then.*

their, there, they're *Their* is the possessive form of *they. There* is an adverb that refers to place. (*There* can also be used in several other ways.) *They're* is a contraction of *they are.*

- *Their* cars are parked on the street.
- Do you see that ten-dollar bill lying *there* in the grass?
- *They're* the third couple from the left.

to, too, two *To* is a preposition meaning "toward," "in contact with," "in front of," or "constituting"; or it can be the sign of an infinitive. *Too* means "also" or "more than enough." *Two* is the whole number following *one;* a couple.

- I walked *to* the town square.
- *To* ensure you arrive safely, check the cable that is towing your glider.
- May I go, *too*?
- *Two* robins built a nest.

try to *Try to* means "to attempt." Try and is not generally accepted usage.

- *Try to* pull up the cap of the bottle after the arrows meet.

two See *to, too, two.*

which, who Use *which* when referring to an object or an animal. Use *who* when referring to a person. (For more information about usage, see section 5c. on pronouns.)

- The black horse, *which* is near the barn, belongs to Stanley.
- *Who* did you say is calling?

who, whom *Who* is in the subjective case, *whom* in the objective case.

- These are the men *who* you thought were responsible. [*who* were responsible]
- These are the men *whom* you chose for the job. [you chose *whom*]

who's, whose *Who's* is a contraction of *who is* or *who has. Whose* is the possessive form of *who.*

- *Who's* the best candidate for the position?
- *Whose* dalmatian is that?

your, you're *Your* is the possessive form of *you. You're* is the contraction of *you are.*

- Will you take *your* car?
- *You're* the winner of a trip to Tahiti.

Credits

Photo Credits

Author-Title Index

*Student writers and works are indicated by an asterisk.

Agamemnon (Alfred), 458–59
Alfred, William, 458–59
All the King's Men (Warren), 439, 443
*Allen, Robin, 62
*Allen, Scott, 423–24
*"Alternative Medicine Has a Healthy Attraction" (Van Camp), 258
"Americans: Conservationists or Champion Land Hogs?" (Peirce), 197, 420, 640–42
*Amrine, Penny, 207–08
Analects (Confucius), 289
*"Annoying Eaters of America" (Rush), 174
*Anonymous, 205, 208
Apology (Plato), 411
*"Apple-Head Dolls: A Remnant of Yesteryear" (Ham), 156–57
Aristotle, 243–44
"Ars Poetica" (MacLeish), 457
"The Art of Acknowledgement" (Houston), 134, 563–65
The Art of the Personal Essay (Lopate), 412
Atchity, Kenneth, 22
"The Attic of the Brain" (Thomas), 189
*"Aunt Marzia" (Ice), 145–46
Austen, Jane, 442
*"Automobile Stereo Speakers: Turn Them Down" (Shirk), 262–65

*"Babysitting for Grandfather" (Yeoman), 53, 55, 62
Bacon, Francis, 295
Baker, James T., 181, 421, 632–34
*Baker, Melissa, 191
Bank, David, 134, 555–58
*Banning, C. J., 146–47
The Barley Field (Joso), 455
The Barley Field (Sora), 455
Bartlett's Familiar Quotations, 202
Baruch, Bernard, 339
Barzun, Jacques, 291
Basin and Range (McPhee), 189
*"Bathtub Solitude" (Ketcham), 168–69
Bauer, Fred, 22
Baxter, Charles, 431, 447, 707–10
*Bean, Peggy, 392
"Becoming Educated" (Jordan), 211, 662–63
Beecher, Henry Ward, 66

Berger, Stuart M., 17
Bernstein, Theodore, 5
Best Spiritual Writing 2000 (Moore), 123
Billings, Josh (See Henry Wheeler Shaw)
Black and Blue (Quindlen), 25
Black and Well-to-Do (Lee), 170, 615–16
*Black, Patricia Jones, 155
*Bloomfield, Terri, 192–93, 194
Bolles, Richard N., 477
Bradley, Bill, 22
Brady, James, 22
*Brady, Mark, 177
Bramson, Robert M., 99, 100
*"Breaking the Habit" (Taylor), 43
*"Breaking Up Is Hard to Do" (Mattix) 445–46
*Bronson, Barbara, 125–26, 128, 167
Brontë, Charlotte, 442
Brown, Norman, 181, 624–27
Buber, Martin, 423
Buck, Pearl, 209
*"Buckeye Fever" (Tinker), 174, 180–81
Bullough, Vern L., 301
*Burks, Janet, 308–09
*Burton, Kathy, 191

Calero, Henry H., 84
Capote, Truman, 413, 437
Carter, Carol, 160, 594–98
Carton, Barbara, 16, 17
Cash, William B., 299
"Caterpillar Afternoon" (Hubbell), 147, 295, 572–74
*Caudill, Jeannine, 42, 209
The CBE Manual for Authors, Editors, and Publishers, 341
Ceremony (Wilbur), 78
*"Changes in My View of Work" (Willetts), 210–11
"Chemicals Bad for Ozone Are Declining" (Naj), 386
*Chesnut, Chuck, 192
Chesterfield, Lord, 92
Chicago Manual of Style, 341
Chinese Proverb, 186
Chopin, Kate, 447, 553, 711–13
Christie, Agatha, 26
Churchill, Winston, 99

Ciardi, John, 117, 147, 451, 455, 579–81
"Clearness" (Wilbur), 78
*Cleveland, Sharon K., 88
*"Climb Aboard!" (Goings), 79–80
*"Clipper Ship Mom" (Bronson), 125–26, 128, 167
*"Cockfighting Should Be Considered a Felony in Ohio" (Pickering), 266–68
*Coffey, Kim, 61
Cohen, Warren, 170, 239, 609–13
The Collected Stories (Singer), 428
Confucius, 289
Conrad, Joseph, 207–08
Coping with Difficult People (Bramson), 99, 100
*Cordle, Kathy, 39
*"The Crystal Chandelier" (Dotson), 141–42, 144
Cullen, Countee, 451, 453
*"Curbing Overpopulation of Deer by 'Harvesting'," 258

*D., Janice, 153
Davis, Lisa, 181, 629–31
*Davis, Patricia, 240
"Dawn Watch" (Ciardi), 117, 147, 579–81
"Dealing with Rejection" (Atchity), 22
Declaration of Independence, 100
Dewey, John, 229–32, 234, 239, 240
*"Diamonds: A Girl's Summer Friend" (Flahive), 178
Dickinson, Emily, 456
*Dietrich, Bettina, 463
Dillard, Annie, 118–19
Disraeli, Benjamin, 316
"Don't Blame the Editors" (Wilson), 6
*Dotson, Paul Allen, Jr., 141
"Doves" (Hegi), 431, 436, 447, 703–05
*"Dr. Nightingale: Nurse Practitioners in Primary Medical Care" (Rummer), 389
Dubus, Andre, 85
*Dunnington, Wilma, 388
*Dyer, Sonny, 81

Ecclesiastes, 22
*Edington, Janet, 38
Ehrenreich, Barbara, 223, 668–70
Ehrlich, Gretel, 189

Einstein, Albert, 173
The Elements of Style (White), 144
"The Emotional Quadrant" (Kübler-
    Ross), 223, 239, 680–82
*"Envy" (O'Rourke), 169–70
*Erdy, Rosy, 194–95
Eskenazi, Mike, 269, 683–84
Essay on Criticism (Pope), 12
Etzioni, Amitai, 269, 689–92
*"The Eye of the Beholder" (Walker),
    89

Faith of My Fathers (McCain), 206
"Falling for Apples" (Perrin), 160, 590–
    92
A Farewell to Arms (Hemingway), 102
Faulkner, William, 24, 433
*"The Fearsome Rabbit" (Cleveland),
    88
Fenton, Gary, 61
*Fetter, Betty, 193–94
Fitzgerald, F. Scott, 432–33
*Flahive, Michele, 177
*Fleming, Rita, 258–59, 260
Flesch, Rudolf, 104
Flowers for Algernon (Keyes), 434
*"Form and Meaning in 'I wandered
    lonely as a cloud'" (Dietrich),
    462–63
Fury, Kathleen, 181, 621–23

Gage, Nicholas, 223, 675–78
Gallagher, Tess, 450
*"Gardening with Rocks" (D.), 153
Genesis 1–2 KJV, 447, 726–28
Genesis 1–2 from the Torah, 447, 723–
    25
*"The Genome Project" (Dunnington),
    389
"Gettysburg Address" (Lincoln), 99
*Giacalone, Paul, 39, 43
Gibaldi, Joseph, 341
Gibbons, Euell, 160, 586–89
Gift from the Sea (Lindbergh), 139, 144
*"Give It More Respect" (Witzel, C.),
    540
*Goings, Bonita M., 80
Goldstone, Nancy Bazelon, 186
Gone with the Wind, 130
Gordon, Lois J., 396–405
Grandin, Temple, 140
"Grass" (Sandburg), 452
The Grass Harp (Capote), 437
The Great Gatsby (Fitzgerald), 432
*Gruber, Kristi, 88
Guiterman, Arthur, 451

*Hafley, Chris, 238–39
Hakluyt, 104
*Ham, Melinda, 155, 156–57
Hamlet (Shakespeare), 430
A Handbook to Literature (Holman and
    Harmon), 412
"The Handicap of Definition"
    (Raspberry), 117, 211, 659–60
Harrison, G. B., 151
Hegi, Ursula, 431, 447, 703–705
Hemingway, Ernest, 102, 443, 438,
    443
Herriot, James, 104
Hillyer, Robert, 450
Holman and Harmon, 412
Holmes, Marjorie, 206
*Holvick, Mary Ann, 222–23

*"Home Alone" (Omaits) 87
"Home for Christmas" (McCullers),
    134, 559–62
*"Hooked on a Tradition" (Patrick), 38
Houston, Jean, 134, 563–65
"How Do You Know It's Good?"
    (Mannes), 160, 239, 600–04
"How Do We Find the Student in a
    World of Academic Gymnasts
    and Worker Ants?" (Baker), 181,
    421, 632–34
How to Cook a Carp (Gibbons), 160,
    586–89
*"How to Get the Best Shine from
    a Coin-Operated Car Wash"
    (Gruber), 88
"How to Get Out of a Locked Trunk"
    (Weiss), 134, 418, 567–71
*"How to Prepare Books for Sale at the
    Dorcas Carey Public Library"
    (Kemmerley), 159–60
*"How to Process Green Beans" (Black),
    155
How to Read a Person Like a Book
    (Nierenberg and Calero), 84
Hubbell, Sue, 147, 295, 572–74
"The Human Cost of an Illiterate Soci-
    ety" (Kozol), 84–85
Huxley, Aldous, 108

*"*I, Claudius* and *Claudius the God*"
    (Patten), 196
*I., Lori, 143
*Ice, Jean, 145–46
"Imagination and the Past" (Laker), 138
"In a 24-Hour Workplace, Day Care
    Is Moving to the Night Shift"
    (Carton), 16
"Incident" (Cullen), 453
In Pursuit of Poetry (Hillyer), 450
"In Step with: Linda Ronstadt" (Brady),
    22
Interviewing: Principles and Practices
    (Stewart and Cash), 299
"Is Saving Legal?" (Rose), 414–16
"I taste a liquor never brewed"
    (Dickinson), 456
"It's Only a Paper World" (Fury), 181,
    621–23
"I wandered lonely as a cloud"
    (Wordsworth), 462

Jacobson, Josephine, 458–59
Jane Eyre (Bronte), 441–42
Jenkins, Jr., Holman W., 170, 618–20
*Jones, Mark, 89
Jordan, Barbara, 211, 662–63
Joso, 455
Julius Caesar (Shakespeare), 430
*"Just a Walk" (Scharf), 128, 130

Kelly, James, 104
*Kemmerley, Ann, 159
Kempton, Murray, 189
Kennedy, John F., 99, 115, 218
*Kerchner, Kathy, 260–61
Kern, Jody, 290
*Ketcham, Anita, 168–69
*Ketcham, Debbie, 207
Kettering, Charles F., 229
Keyes, Daniel, 434
*"Kicking the Habit" (Cordle), 39
King, Martin Luther, 533
Knapp, Mark L., 383

Koran, the (the Qur'an), Selections
    from, 447, 730–32
Kozol, Jonathan, 84–85
Kübler-Ross, Elisabeth, 223, 239, 680–
    82
*Kyle, Flora, 140–41

Laker, Rosalind, 138
L'Amour, Louis, 210
*Layman, Chris, 206–07
Lee, Andrea, 170, 615–16
Legge, James, 289
Letter to His Son (Chesterfield), 92
"Life at Close Range" (Ehrlich), 189
The Lives of a Cell (Thomas), 117
Levy, Matthys, 126
Lewis, C. S., 269, 698–701
Lewis, Sinclair, 69
Lincoln, Abraham, 85, 99, 115
Lindbergh, Anne Morrow, 139, 144
"Living Like Weasels" (Dillard), 118–19
*"Living with an Alcoholic"
    (Anonymous), 205, 208
Loomis, Louise R., 244
Lopate, Phillip, 197, 412, 636–39

Macbeth (Shakespeare), 430
MacLeish, Archibald, 457
Main Street (Lewis), 69
*"Maintaining a Marriage" (Ramey),
    142–43
"The Maker's Eye: Revising Your Own
    Manuscript" (Murray) 49
Mannes, Marya, 160, 239, 600–04
*Mattix, Mae, 445–46
Maturu, Rajini, 237–38
McCain, John, 206
McCullers, Carson, 134, 559–62
McPhee, John, 189
Meany, George, 530–31
*"The Melting Pot of New Orleans"
    (Vanderkooi), 179–80
Miller, Henry, 163
*Miller, Nancy, 234–35, 236
"Mind Over Munchies" (Brown), 181,
    624–27
*MLA Handbook for Writers of Research
    Papers*, 341
The Modern Researcher (Barzun), 291
"A Modest Proposal" (Swift), 411–12
*Moore, Roger, 56–59
Moore, Thomas, 123
*"Mother Love" (Caudill), 42, 209
"Mothers of Invention" (Vare and
    Ptacek), 170, 606–08
"Mother Tongue" (Tan), 117, 197,
    643–47
*"The Mulberry Tree" (Russell), 129,
    130, 132–33
Murray, Donald, 49
My American Journey (Powell), 82
*"My Fiery Grandma" (I.), 143–44
*"My Life after Dealing with Death"
    (Bloomfield), 192–93
*"My Two Neighbors" (Fetter), 193–94

Naj, Amal Kumar, 386
"The New Case for Latin" (Eskenazi),
    269, 683–84
*Newell, Mark, 176
Newman, Edwin, 413
Nierenberg, Gerald I., 84
Night Thoughts (Young), 467
"A Nonsmoker with a Smoker"
    (Lopate), 197, 636–39

Nonverbal Communication in Human Interaction (Knapp), 383
*"Nonverbal Communication with Geriatric Patients" (White), 309–13
Norman, Liane Ellison, 147, 583–85

Object Lessons (Quindlen), 25
The Old Man and the Sea (Hemingway), 438–39, 443
*"The Old Rocking Chair" (Schnitzler), 87
*Omaits, Suzanne, 87
"On Being 17, Bright, and Unable to Read" (Raymond), 211, 655–57
*"On-the-Job Cursing" (Silverman), 112
"On the Vanity of Earthly Greatness" (Guiterman), 451
One True Thing (Quindlen), 25
*"One Writer's Beginnings" (Welty), 147, 576–77
*O'Rourke, Dixie, 169–70
"The Other Difference between Boys and Girls" (Restack), 269, 693–97
Ozick, Cynthia, 413

*"Parents through a Child's Eyes" (Erdy), 195
*Parks, Phyllis, 167, 206
*Patrick, Kenny, 38
*Patten, Jeff, 196
Peck, Scott M., 273
"Pedestrian Students and High-Flying Squirrels" (Norman), 147. 583–85
Peirce, Neal, 197, 420, 640–42
Penn, William, 205
*"People Who Flock to Swap Meets" (Moore), 56–59
Perrin, Noel, 160, 590–92
*"A Pet for Aunt Emily" (Davis), 240
*"The Pet and the Pest" (Chestnut), 192
Phillips, Wendell, 243
*Pickering, Cheryl, 266–68
Pima, 447, 721–22
Plato, 411
*"Playground Supervision" (Burks), 308–09
*"Playing Possum" (Dyer), 81
*"Please, Do Not Forget Me" (Banning), 146–47
*Pohlman, Joanne M., 178, 179
Pope, Alexander, 12
"Portrait of the Essay as a Warm Body" (Ozick), 413
Powell, Colin, 3, 82
*"Preventing an Expensive Problem" (Zuspan), 233
"The Price of Love" (Bauer), 22
Pride and Prejudice (Austen), 442
Ptacek, Greg, 170, 606–08
Publication Manual of the American Psychological Association, 341

The Quotable Woman, 202
Quindlen, Anna, 25
Qur'an, the (the Koran), Selections from, 447, 730–32

*Ramey, Jennifer, 142
Raspberry, William, 117, 211, 659–60
*Rausch, April, 390
Raymond, David, 211, 655–57
*"A Reaction to Martin Buber's Philosophy" (Allen), 423–24

*"Replacing an Electrical Outlet Safely" (Witzel, K.), 158
Restak, Richard M., 269, 693–97
*Rice, Bonnie L., 392
Rico, Gabriele, 26
"A Ride through Spain" (Capote), 413, 414
The Road Less Traveled and Beyond (Peck), 273
"Road Rage" (Vest, Cohen, and Tharp), 170, 239, 609–13
"Rocky Mountain High" (Kelly), 104
Roiphe, Anne, 223, 239, 671–73
Romeo and Juliet (Shakespeare), 434
Rose, Robert L., 414–16
"Rosetta Disk Is Foundation's Gift to Future Linguists" (Bank), 134, 555–58
*Rummer, Kathy, 389
"Run-of-the-Mill Miracle" (Fenton), 61
*Rush, Patricia, 174
*Russell, Betty, 132–33

Sachs, Andrea, 269, 420, 686–88
*"Safety First!" (Edington), 38
Salvadori, Mario, 126
Sandburg, Carl, 452
*Scharf, Shasta, 130, 133–34
"Scheherazade" (Baxter), 431, 447, 707–10
Schneider, Alison, 537
The School Segregation Decision of 1954 (Warren), 18
*Schnitzler, Michael, 87
Schulz, Charles, 164
*Seigneur, Patty, 90
Shakespeare, William, 430
Shames, Lawrence, 211, 665–66
Shaw, Henry Wheeler, 378
*Shirk, Bethany, 262–65
*"Silver Lining" (Sloan), 221–22
Silverman, Rachel Emma, 112
Singer, Isaac Bashevis, 428
*Sloan, Jo Rae, 221–22
*Smathers, Nancy, 82
"Snapping the Leash" (Kempton), 189
Socrates, 200, 411
Sora, 455
The Sound and the Fury (Faulkner), 433
*Spillman, John, 61
"Spudding Out" (Ehrenreich), 223, 668–70
Steinbeck, John, 25
Stevenson, Adlai, 116
Stewart, Charles J., 299
"Still of Some Use" (Updike), 445–46, 447, 714–17
"Story of an Hour" (Chopin), 447, 711–13
"The Strychnine Episode at Darrowby" (Herriot), 104
"The Sweet Smell of Success Isn't All that Sweet" (Shames), 211, 665–66
Swift, Jonathan, 411–12

*"The Talent Within" (Vanderkooi), 166
Tan, Amy, 117, 197, 643–47
Tannen, Deborah, 197, 649–53
*Taylor, Sue, 43
"The Teacher Who Changed My Life" (Gage), 223, 675–78
Tharp, Mike, 170, 239, 609–13
Thinking in Pictures (Grandin), 140

Thomas, Lewis, 117, 189
Thoreau, Henry David, 215
*"Through a Child's Eyes" (Smathers), 82
Time Present, Time Past (Bradley), 22
*Tinker, Jane, 174, 180–81
*"The Trials of Tia" (Giacalone), 39
Trading Up (Goldstone), 186
Twain, Mark, 5
Twelfth Night (Shakespeare), 430

Updike, John, 32, 445–46, 714–17
"Uptight Is Back In Style" (Jenkins), 170, 618–20
"Under the Lights" (Dubus), 85
*"Unhappy Customers at the Bank of India" (Maturu), 237–38

Van Camp, Pamela J., 258
*Vanderkooi, Nicole, 166, 179–80
Vare, Ethlie Ann, 170, 606–08
*Vaughan, Bryan, 166–67
Vest, Jason, 170, 239, 609–13

*Walker, Peggy, 89
*Walkins, Carol, 235–36
Wallace, Lew, 69
Warren, Earl, 18
Warren, Robert Penn, 439–40
Washington, George, 477
"Watch Your Language" (Bernstein), 5
"We Have No Right to Happiness" (Lewis), 269, 698–701
Weiss, Philip, 134, 418, 567–71
"The Well-Baked Man" (Pima), 447, 721–72
Welty, Eudora, 147, 576–77
What Your Doctor Didn't Learn in Medical School (Berger), 17
"When the Lullaby Ends" (Sachs), 269, 420, 686–88
"Where Do We Stand" (Davis), 181, 629–31
*White, Dana, 25
White, E.B., 144
*White, Lisa, 309–13
*"Why I Enjoyed Being a School Bus Driver" (Holvick), 222–23
Why Buildings Fall Down (Levy and Salvadori), 126
"Why Marriages Fail" (Roiphe), 223, 239, 671–73
Wilbur, Richard, 78
*Willetts, Ronald, 210–11
Wilson, Sloan, 6
*Witzel, Carol, 540
*Witzel, Keith, 157
"Women and Men Talking on the Job" (Tannen), 197, 649–53
Wordsworth, William, 462
"Working at McDonald's" (Etzioni), 269, 689–92
"Write Your Own Success Story" (Carter), 160, 594–98
The Writer (Laker), 138
Writers at Work: First Series (Faulkner), 24

*Yeoman, John, 53, 55, 62
"Yet do I marvel" (Cullen), 451
Young, Edward, 467

*Zachman, Diane, 42
*Zuspan, Keith, 233, 236

Subject Index

A, an, H-44
Abbreviations, 348, H-19–H-21
Absolute terms, 72–74
Abstract words, 115–116
Abstracts, library, 324–325
Academic background; *see* Résumés
Accept, except, H-44
Access, excess, H-44
Accuracy, 66–74
    determining fact, 67–68
    of examples, 166
    revising for, 72–75
    sources of misinformation, 70–72
Acknowledgment; *see* Documentation
Action verbs, 123, 129, 144
Active voice (verbs), 93–94
Ad populum fallacy, 280; *see also* Emotional fallacies
Adapt, adept, adopt, H-44
Adjective clauses, 97–98, 103
Adjectives, 99, H-37–H-39
Adverb clauses, 98
Adverbs, H-3, H-5, H-37–H-39
Adverse, averse, H-44
Advice, advise, H-44
Affect, effect, H-44
"Against the man," 279–280; *see also* Emotional fallacies
Agreement
    in argument, 258–259
    of pronouns, H-28–H-29
    of verbs, H-34–H-35
All ready, already, H-44
All right, alright, H-44
All together, altogether, H-44
Alliteration, 61, 436, 453
Allot, a lot, alot, H-45
Allusion, delusion, illusion, H-45
Allusions, literary, 164
Alternating vs. block organization, *use in*
    argument papers, 255–257
    causal analysis papers, 219–220
    comparison/contrast papers, 191–192
Alternatives, false, 274–275; *see also* Logical fallacies
American Psychological Association (APA), 341; *see also* APA style
Among, between, H-45
Amount, number, H-45
Analogies, 164, 189, 260
Analogy, false, 275; *see also* Logical fallacies

Analysis; *see* Literary analysis; Poetic analysis
Anecdotes, 37, 164
Antecedents, H-28–H-29, H-35
Anthologies, citing, 350, 369
Anxiety; *see* Writer's block
Any, any other, H-45
Anyone, any one, H-45
APA style, 363–376; *see also* Style guides
    audiovisual media, 371–372
    books, brochures, 368–371
    electronic sources, 372–376
    government publications, 368–371
    parenthetical citations, 364–365
    periodicals, 366–368
    reference lists, 366–376
    in research papers, 394–396
    style directory, 364
Apostrophes, H-6–H-7
Appeal vs. propaganda, 282
Appositives, 103, H-8, H-26–H-27
Appraise, apprise, H-45
Argument, 243–268
    appeals, 243–247
    audience, 245–249, 254
    circular, 275–276
    claims, 249, 253
    common ground, 258–259
    compromise in, 252–253, 260–261
    critical reading of, 418–419
    drafting, 422
    evidence, 245–246, 259–260
    logical, 253–254
    opposing views, 247–248, 259–260
    organization of, 253–257
    premise, 249, 419
    readings, 683–702
    sample papers, 261–268
    tone, 220, 255
    writing process, 248–261
    use in
        reaction papers, 420–421
        research papers, 317
Argumentum ad hominem, 279–280; *see also* Emotional fallacies
Articles (periodical), 344, 352–355, 366–368
Articulation, 538
Assonance, 436, 453
Assumption and writer's voice, 13
Assure, ensure, insure, H-45

Audience
    assessing, 7
    clarity, 80
    defined, 6
    exploratory drafts, 33–34
    resistance in, 529
    considered in
        argument papers, 245–249, 254
        causal analysis papers, 218
        classification papers, 174
        comparison/contrast papers, 186, 193
        narration papers, 127, 131
        oral presentations, 521, 524–525, 529, 539
        process analysis papers, 152, 157
Audiovisual media; *see also* Electronic sources
    documentation style, 355–357, 371–372
    in oral presentations, 522, 534–536
Author citations, 380–381; *see also* Citations; Reference lists; Style guides
Authority, improper appeal to, 281–282
Author's background, evaluating, 417
Averse, adverse, H-44
Awhile, a while, H-45

Bandwagon fallacy, 280; *see also* Emotional fallacies
Be verbs, 94, H-34
"Because" technique, 175–176
Begging the question, 275–276; *see also* Logical fallacies
Beside, besides, H-45
Between, among, H-45
Bias; *see* Point of view
Bibliographies, 321–322, 323, 325; *see also* Research papers; Style guides
Block vs. alternating organization, *use in*
    argument papers, 255–257
    causal analysis papers, 219–220
    comparison/contrast papers, 191–192
Books, 349–352, 368–371
Brackets, 387, H-9
Brainstorming, 27–28; *see also* Prewriting
Breath, breathe, H-45
Broadcast sources, 355–356, 371

Brochures, citing, 352, 368–371
Business letters
  accepting position, 514–515
  appreciation, 512–514
  formatting, 508–511
  refusing position, 515–516
  resigning position, 516–517

Cadence, 458, 523
Capital, capitol, H-46
Capitalization, H-16–H-19
Card stacking, 274; *see also* Logical
  fallacies
Careers, researching, 479–480, 501; *see
  also* Résumés
Cartoons, citing, 357
Case (pronouns), H-26–H-27
Catalogs, library, 324
Causal analysis, 215–223; *see also*
  Cause and effect
  logical fallacies, 218
  order in, 218–220
  principles of logic, 217
  purpose for writing, 215–216, 220
  sample papers, 221–223
  writing process, 218–221
Cause and effect; *see also* Causal analysis
  vs. correlation, 278
  defined, 216
  non sequitur fallacy and, 276–277
  post hoc fallacy and, 277–278
  in problem solving papers, 233
  readings, 668–682
CBE (Council of Biology Editors), 341;
  see also Style guides
Censor, censure, H-46
Characters in literary analysis, 434–
  435, 440–441
Chicago Manual of Style (CMS), 341;
  see also Style guides
Chronological order
  defined, 40
  example of, 57
  use in
    causal analysis papers, 218–220
    process analysis papers, 154
    résumés, 478–479, 484, 490–491
Circular argument, 275–276
Citations, 202–203, 204; *see also* Parenthetical citations
Cite, sight, site, H-46
Civil Rights Act of 1964, 111
Clarity, 80, 105, 235
Classification, 173–181
  "because" technique, 175–176
  order in, 174–175, 176
  parallelism in, 178–179
  in primary research papers, 306
  readings, 621–635
  sample papers, 179–181
  transitions, embedded, 176–178
  writing process, 174–179
Clauses
  adjective, 97–98, 103
  adverb, 98
  dependent, 97–98
  essential/nonessential, 97, H-8
  independent, 94–98, H-2, H-4–
    H-6
  restrictive/nonrestrictive, H-8
  subordinate, 100, H-3
Clichés, 114
Closure; *see* Conclusions

Clustering, 26–27, 204; *see also*
  Prewriting
CMS (*Chicago Manual of Style*), 341;
  see also Style guides
Coherence, 81–82
Colloquial usage, 14; *see also* Writer's
  voice
Colons, 96, H-5–H-6
Comma splices, 96, H-25–H-26
Commas, 96, H-2–H-4; *see also* Clauses
Commentary, 419–420, 421–422
Common ground, 258–259, 529
Common knowledge, citing, 381
Comparison, 101–102, 186
Comparison/contrast, 186–197
  by analogy, 189
  commonality required in subjects, 187
  in definition papers, 206
  order in, 191–192
  parallelism in, 193
  pitfalls in, 188–189
  readings, 636–654
  sample papers, 194–197
  transitions, 187–188
  writing process, 190–194
Comparison/contrast paragraphs,
  defined, 89
Complement, compliment, H-46
Complexity, order of, 40–41
Compound antecedents, H-29
Compromise, 252–253, 260–261
Computers, 42–43, 51–52
Conciseness, 117
Conclusions
  effectiveness, 42–43
  objectivity, 297
  perspective, 194
  revising, 56
  of surveys, 305
  thesis statement in, 42, 179
  use in
    argument papers, 254, 260–261
    causal analysis papers, 220–221
    classification papers, 179
    comparison/contrast papers, 194
    cover letters, 506–507
    definition papers, 207–208
    description papers, 144
    illustration papers, 167
    oral presentations, 522, 532–533,
      539
    problem solving papers, 236
    process analysis papers, 157
    research papers, 392
Concrete words, 115
Conflict, 433–434
Conjunctions
  coordinating, 95–97, H-2–H-5
  parallel correlative, 101–102
  subordinating, 98
Conjunctive adverbs, H-3, H-5
Connotations, 109
Conscience, conscious, H-46
Context and interpretation, 429
Continual, continuous, H-46
Contractions and apostrophes, H-7
Contrast; *see* Comparison/contrast
Controlling questions, 251, 319–320
Conversational tone, 523
Coordinating conjunctions, 95–97,
  H-2–H-5
Corporate authorship, 344, 350, 365,
  370

Correlation vs. cause and effect, 278
Correlative parallel conjunctions, 101–
  102
Correspondence; *see* Business letters;
  Cover letters; E-mail; Résumés
Cosmic irony, 435
Council, counsel, H-46
Council of Biology Editors (CBE), 341;
  see also Style guides
Council of Science Editors (CSE; for-
  merly CBE), 341
Couplets in poetry, 451
Courtesy words, 109–110
Cover letters, 502–510
Creation narratives, *readings,* 719–732
Credibility; *see also* Documentation;
  Evidence
  accuracy, 66–67
  of author, 417
  of narrator, 433
  overstatement, 380
  point of view, 125
  stereotypes, 203
  considered in
    argument papers, 244, 246
    oral presentations, 527, 536
    résumés, 497
Criteria, 234–235
Criteria, criterion, H-46
Critical reading, 382, 416–419, 553–
  554
Criticism; *see* Writer's block
CSE (Council of Science Editors; formerly CBE), 341; *see also* Style
  guides

Dashes, H-7–H-8
Dates, H-22
Deadwood, editing out, 102–103
Decimals, H-15, H-22
Definition, 200–211
  extended, 202–203
  formal sentence definitions, 200–202
  readings, 655–667
  sample papers, 209–211
  types, 206
  writing process, 203–208
Definition paragraphs, 89
Delusion, illusion, allusion, H-45
Demographics, 300–307
Denotations, 108–109
Dependent clauses, 97–98
Description, 138–147
  dominant impression, 139–140, 141–
    142
  in introductions, 38
  objectivity in, 297
  readings, 572–585
  sample papers, 145–147
  subjectivity/objectivity, 139–140
  vantage point, 142
  writing process, 140–145
Descriptive paragraphs, 87
Dewey's method, 229–230, 231–233
Dialect, 15; *see also* Writer's voice
Dialogue, 129
Dictionaries, use of, 14–15, 16, 18
Dictionary of Occupational Titles (U.S.
  Department of Labor), 111
Direct objects, H-2, H-31
Documentation; *see also* Style guides
  defined, 339
  FAQs, 340

Documentation (*continued*)
  of research, 290
  of sources, 320
  styles compared, 341
  considered in
    definition papers, 202–203, 204
    research papers, 393–394
Domain names, 330
Dominant impression, 139–140, 141–142, 174
Drafting
  argument papers, 422
  essay exams, 474–475
  narration papers, 127–128
  paragraphs, 83–86
  reaction papers, 421–422
  research papers, 388–393
  résumés, 483–489
Drafts, 8–9, 32–45
  clarifying, 55–59
  exploratory, 33–36
  narrowing the topic, 33–34
  organization of, 39–42
Dramatic irony, 435

Edited American English; *see* Professional English
Editing, 9, 59–62; *see also* Proofreading; Revision
  reaction papers, 422–423
  research papers, 393–396
  résumés, 497–500
Editorial philosophy, 5, 67
Education; *see* Résumés
Effect, affect, H-44
Effects, 215
Either/or fallacy, 274–275; *see also* Logical fallacies
Electronic sources, citing, 358–363, 372–376; *see also* Audiovisual media
Ellipses, 386, H-14–H-15
E-mail, 497, 502–503, 507
Embedded transitions, *use in*
  classification papers, 176–178
  coherent paragraphs, 82
  definition papers, 204
  process analysis papers, 154
Emigrate, immigrate, H-46
Eminent, imminent, H-46
Emotional fallacies, 273, 278–282; *see also* Logical fallacies
  argumentum ad hominem ("against the man"), 279–280
  bandwagon, 280
  glittering generality, 282
  plain folk appeal (*ad populum*), 280
  scare tactic, 281
  status appeal, 280–281
  straw man, 279–280
  testimonial, 281–282
Emotions; *see* Speaker's voice; Tone; Writer's voice
Emphasis, H-7, H-14
Employers, 480
Employment writing; *see* Business letters; Cover letters; E-mail; Résumés
Ensure, insure, assure, H-45
Enthusiastic, enthused, H-46
Essay exams, 467–475
Essays, 411–424
  critical reading, 416–419

point of view, 413
sample paper, 423–424
vs. short stories, 553
types, 412–413
writing process, 419–421
Essential/nonessential clauses, 97, H-8
Established facts, citing, 291
Ethics, 529
Ethos (moral character, ethics), 243–244, 246
Euphemisms, 110–111
Evaluation, 234–235
Evidence; *see also* Credibility; Documentation
  in argument papers, 245–246, 254, 259–260
  in support sentences, 79
  types of, 68
Exaggeration, 273
Examples, 163–170
  hypothetical, 164
  use in
    causal analysis papers, 220
    definition papers, 206–207
    illustration papers, 166–167
Exams, 467–475
Except, accept, H-44
Excess, access, H-44
Exclamation points, H-16
Experience, 246, 488–489
Explanatory notes, 392
Explication; *see* Literary analysis; Poetic analysis
Explicit, implicit, H-47
Exploratory drafts, 33–36
Expository writing, 66–67, 95, 451
Eye contact, 536

Facts
  characteristics, 70
  determining, 67–68
  vs. ideas, 291–292
  sources of errors, 70–72
  vs. theory, 245
  use in
    argument papers, 245, 249
    narration papers, 123
Fallacies
  defined, 282
  detecting, 273
  emotional fallacies, 273, 278–282
    argumentum ad hominem ("against the man"), 279–280
    bandwagon, 280
    glittering generality, 282
    plain folk appeal (*ad populum*), 280
    scare tactic, 281
    status appeal, 280–281
    straw man, 279–280
    testimonial, 281–282
  logical fallacies, 218, 260, 273–278
    begging the question, 275–276
    card stacking (stacking the deck), 274
    either/or, 274–275
    false analogy, 275
    hasty generalization, 276
    non sequitur, 218, 276–277
    post hoc, 277–278
    red herring, 275
  False alternatives, 274–275; *see also* Logical fallacies
  False analogy, 275

Familiarity, organization by, 193
Fanboys (coordinating conjunctions), 95
Farther, further, H-47
Fewer, less, H-47
Fiction; *see* Literary analysis; Poetic analysis
Figurative language, 414, 436
Film sources, 356–357, 371
First person, 153, H-26–H-27; *see also* Person
Flaunt, flout, H-47
Foreshadowing, 434, 439, 442
Formal English, 18–19
Formal essays, 412–413
Formal sentence definition, 200–201
Formality, levels of, 16–19, 80
Formation, order of, 40–41
Formatting
  business letters, 508–511
  research papers, 393–396
  résumés, 497
Fractions, H-10, H-23
Freewriting, 26; *see also* Prewriting
Further, farther, H-47

Gathering information, 250–252; *see also* Prewriting; Primary research; Secondary research
Gender-neutral language, 111–113, H-29–H-30
Generalities, glittering, 282; *see also* Emotional fallacies
Generality, order of, 40–41
Generalizations, 203, 230; *see also* Hasty generalizations
Gestures, 536–537
Get, proper use, H-44
Good, well, H-47
Government publications, citing, 352, 368–371
Grammar and usage rules, H-23–H-39

Haiku, 455
Hanged, hung, H-47
Hasty generalizations, 276; *see also* Logical fallacies
  source of misinformation, 71–73
  use in
    argument papers, 260
    comparison/contrast papers, 188–189
Headings, formatting, 395–396
Helping verbs, H-31
Human condition, 428–429
Humor, 532
Hung, hanged, H-47
Hyphens, H-9–H-10
Hypothetical examples, 164

I, overuse of, 102–103
I rule, 37
Idea, ideal, H-47
Idea vs. fact, 291–292
IEEE (Institute of Electrical and Electronic Engineers), 341; *see also* Style guides
Illusion, allusion, delusion, H-45
Illustration, 163–170
  examples in, 166–167
  order in, 165
  readings, 606–620
  sample papers, 168–170
  writing process, 164–168

Illustration (*continued*)
  use in
    causal analysis papers, 220
    problem solving papers, 233
Illustration paragraphs, 88–89
Imagery in lyric poetry, 455–458
Immigrate, emigrate, H-46
Imminent, eminent, H-46
Impersonal essays, 412–413
Implicit, explicit, H-47
Importance, order of, 40
Impression, dominant, 141–142
Inclusive language, 111–113, H-29–
    H-30
Indefinite pronouns, H-6, H-28–H-29
Independent clauses, 94–98, H-2, H-4–
    H-6
Inferences; *see also* Interpretation
    in argument papers, 246
    characteristics, 70
    defined, 68
    fact and, 292
    objectivity in, 297
    source of misinformation, 74
Infinitives, H-3, H-31
Informal essays, 412
Informal Standard English, 16–17
Inner censor, 32; *see also* Brainstorming;
    Drafts
Institute of Electrical and Electronic
    Engineers (IEEE), 341; *see also*
    Style guides
Insure, assure, ensure, H-45
Intent of author, 554
Interlibrary loan, 326–327
Internet; *see also* Online sources
    compared with library research, 334
    directory of sources, 334–336
    evaluating web sites, 329–333
    online directories, 328
    research time, 292–293
    for résumé posting, 497
    URL explained, 329–330
Internet Corporation for Assigned
    Names and Numbers (ICANN),
    330
Interpretation; *see also* Inference
    claim in argument, 249
    context, 429
    fact and, 292
    objectivity in, 297
Interviews
    documentation style, 357, 370
    as primary research, 298–300
    writing the results, 306–307
In-text citations; *see* Parenthetical
    citations
Introductions
    drafting, 36–39
    revising, 55
    use in
      argument papers, 258
      causal analysis papers, 220
      comparison/contrast papers, 192–
        193
      cover letters, 504–505
      definition papers, 204–205
      description papers, 142–143
      narration papers, 127–128
      oral presentations, 522, 530–532
      problem solving papers, 233–234
      process analysis papers, 155–156
      research papers, 388–389

Irony, 435, 442–443
Irregular verbs, H-32–H-34
Italics, H-11–H-12, H-13–H-14
Its, it's, H-47

Job objectives; *see* Résumés
Journalism, 67; *see also* Expository
    writing
Journals; *see* Periodicals
Judgment, 230, 249

Keyword summary; *see* Résumés

Language
    figurative, 414, 436
    inclusive, 111–113, H-29–H-30
    trite, 114, 188
Leave, let, H-47
Legal references, citing, 358
Less, fewer, H-47
Letters; *see* Business letters; Cover
    letters; E-mail; Résumés
Library of Congress Subject Headings
    (LCSH), 318–319, 325
Library research, 322–328, 334
Like, use of, H-37
List-making, 28–29; *see also* Prewriting
Literary allusions, 164
Literary analysis, 428–446; *see also*
    Poetic analysis
    characters, 434–435, 440–441
    documentation, 345
    elements of literature, 432–436
    genres, 429–430
    literary devices, 435–436, 441–443;
      see also specific devices
    narrator, 432
    plot, 433–434, 439–440
    point of view, 432–433, 437–438
    reader's role, 429–430
    sample paper, 445–446
    setting, 433, 438–439
    writing process, 431–432, 436–444
Literature; *see* Literary analysis
Logic, 243–246, 529
Logical fallacies, 218, 260, 273–278;
    see also Emotional fallacies
    begging the question, 275–276
    card stacking (stacking the deck),
      274
    either/or, 274–275
    false analogy, 275
    hasty generalization, 276
    non sequitur, 218, 276–277
    post hoc, 277–278
    red herring, 275
Logos (logic), 243–246
Logs, research, 296–297
Loose, lose, H-48
Lyric poetry; *see* Poetic analysis

Magazines; *see* Periodicals
Manuscript presentation, 523
Materiality, order of, 40–42
Measurements, H-22
Medium, media, H-48
Memorized presentation, 523
Memory aids, 469
Metaphors, 61, 436
Misinformation, sources of, 70–74
Misreading, and comma usage, H-4
*MLA Handbook for Writers of Research
    Papers,* 341

MLA style, 341–363; *see also* Style
    guides
    abbreviations, 348
    articles, 352–355
    audiovisual media, 355–357
    bibliographic notes, 347
    books, 349–352
    content notes, 346–347
    electronic sources, 358–363
    government publications, 352
    pamphlets and brochures, 352
    parenthetical citations, 342–347
    periodicals, 344
    quotation example, 386
    reference lists, 347–363
    in research papers, 394–396
    sample research paper, 397–405
    style directory, 342
Modern Language Association (MLA),
    341; *see also* MLA style
Modifiers; *see also* Adjectives; Adverbs;
    Clauses
    hyphens with, H-10
    meaningless, 144
    rules for, H-37–H-39
Money, notation rules, H-23
Mood (verbs), H-36
Moral, morale, H-48
Motivation of characters, 441
Movement in narration, 127
Music sources, citing, 356, 372

Narration, 123–134
    dialogue in, 129
    point of view, 125–126, 133
    readings, 555–571, 703–718, 719–
      732
    sample papers, 132–134
    stories vs. reports, 131
    writing process, 127–131
    use in
      causal analysis papers, 220
      comparison/contrast papers, 192–
        193
      problem solving papers, 233
      process description papers, 153
Narrative paragraphs, 86–87
Narrative poetry; *see* Poetic analysis
Narrator, 430, 432–433, 438; *see also*
    Point of view
Negation, 206
New York Times, editorial philosophy, 5
Newspapers; *see* Periodicals
Non sequitur fallacy, 218, 276–277; *see
    also* Logical fallacies
Nonessential elements, H-3
Nonessential/essential clauses, 97, H-8
Nonrestrictive elements, H-3
Nonrestrictive/restrictive clauses, H-8
Note taking, 382, 431
Notes; *see also* Style guides
    bibliographic, 347
    content, 346–347
    explanatory, 392
    for oral presentations, 533–534, 536
    source, 322
Nouns, 100
Novels, 429–430
Number, amount, H-45
Numbers, H-9, H-21–H-23

Objections, 253
Objective case, H-26–H-27

Objectivity; *see also* Accuracy; Credibility; Point of view; Subjectivity
  checklist for, 297
  hindered by hypothesis, 229–230
  optimizing, 230
  considered in
    problem solving papers, 235–236
    research papers, 290–291
Observation, 295–298, 306
Observers, fixed/moving, 142; *see also* Narrator
Occasion, 521, 525; *see also* Rhetorical situation
Offensive language, 112–113
Omission, 273, H-14
Omniscience of narrator, 433
Online Computer Library Center (OCLC), 327–328
Online sources, 328, 358–363, 372–375; *see also* Internet
Online writing labs (OWLs), H-1
Onomatopoeia, 436, 453
Open book exams, 471
Openings; *see* Introductions
Operational definition, 205–206
Opinion polls, 300–307
Opinions, expert, 246
Opposing views, 247–248, 255, 259–260
Oral presentations, 520–541
  audience, 521, 524–525, 529, 539
  audiovisual media, 534–536, 534–536
  credibility, 528, 536
  extemporaneous, 523–524
  notes, 533–534, 536
  planning, 524–529
  sample paper, 540–541
  speaker's voice, 537–538
  speaking vs. writing, 521–523
  types, 523
Order; *see also* Organization
  parallelism, 192
  thesis and, 254
  types, 40–42, 257
  use in
    argument papers, 253–257
    causal analysis papers, 218–220
    classification papers, 174–175, 176
    comparison/contrast papers, 191–192
    description papers, 143–144
    illustration papers, 165
    narration papers, 128–129
    oral presentations, 528–529
    problem solving papers, 229–231, 231–233
    process analysis papers, 151, 154
    research papers, 317
Organization; *see also* Order
  alternating vs. block, *use in*
    argument papers, 255–257
    causal analysis papers, 219–220
    comparison/contrast papers, 191–192
  résumés, 489–495
  writing, 39–42
Outlining
  aid in revision, 51, 53–55
  essay exams, 474
  problem solving papers, 232–233
  reaction papers, 419, 421

research, 305
  research papers, 387–388
Oversimplification, 273
Overstatement
  in argument papers, 246–247
  credibility, 380
  in extended definitions, 203
  source of misinformation, 71

Pagination, 395–396
Pamphlets, citing, 352, 368–371
Paradox in poetry, 451
Paragraphs, 78–90
  elements, 78–80
  qualities for effectiveness, 80–83
  topic sentences, 83–85
  types, 86–90
Parallelism, 99–102
  use in
    classification papers, 175, 178–179
    coherent paragraphs, 82
    comparison/contrast papers, 193
    problem solving papers, 236
Paraphrasing, 384–385
Parentheses, H-8–H-9
Parenthetical citations, 380–381, 394; *see also* Citations; Reference lists; Style guides
Participles, H-3, H-31
Passed, past, H-48
Passive voice (verbs), 93–94
Pathos (emotion), 243–244, 247
Patience, patients, H-48
Peer review, 63–64
Percentages, H-22–H-23
Periodic sentences, 104
Periodicals
  documentation style, 344, 352–355, 366–368
  journals, 30
  library research, 324–325
Periods, H-15
Permission, 296
Person; *see also* Point of view; Pronouns
  pronouns, H-26–H-27, H-30
  use in
    definition papers, 205
    literary analysis papers, 432
    process analysis papers, 152
    process description papers, 153
Persona, 413
Personal communication, 365
Personal essays, 412
Personal, personnel, H-48
Personification, 436
Perspective, 53–55, 194, 230; *see also* Point of view
Phrases
  parallel, 100
  prepositional, 99, 103, H-3
  signal, 390, 391
Plagiarism; *see also* Credibility
  avoiding, 326, 380–381
  defined, 339–340
  of online sources, 330
  in summarizing, 384
Plain folk appeal, 280; *see also* Emotional fallacies
Plays, 429–430
Plot, 433–434, 439–440
Plurals, H-7

Poetic analysis, 450–463; *see also* Literary analysis
  imagery, 455–458
  lyric poetry, 454–459
  narrative poetry, 453–454
  poetic energy, 458–459
  reading poetry, 451–459
  sample paper, 462–463
  writing process, 459–462
Point of view; *see also* Person
  defined, 69
  vantage point, 142
  considered in
    argument papers, 257
    essays, 413, 418
    literary analysis papers, 432–433, 437–438
    narration papers, 125–126, 133
Position of emphasis, 105
Possessive case, H-26–H-27
Possessives, H-6–H-7
Post hoc fallacy, 218, 277–278; *see also* Logical fallacies
Posture, 536–537
Precede, proceed, H-48
Prefixes, H-10
Premises, 249, 419; *see also* Thesis statements
Prescriptive tone, 20–21
Prewriting, 8–9, 24–30
  classification papers, 175–176
  comparison/contrast papers, 190–191
  critical reading, 417–419
  definition papers, 204
  description papers, 140–141
  essay exams, 474
  illustration papers, 164–165
  literary analysis papers, 431–432
  narration papers, 127
  problem solving papers, 231–233
  process analysis papers, 155
  reaction papers, 418, 421
  research papers, 306
  résumés, 479–483
Primary research, 295–313; *see also* Documentation; Research papers; Secondary research; Sources
  four stages, 138
  interviews, 298–300, 306–307
  objectivity, 290–292
  observations, 295–298, 306
  paper vs. report, 307
  sample papers, 308–313
  scheduling, 292–293
  surveys, 300–305, 306–307
  writing the results, 305–307
Primary sources, 289–290
Principal, principle, H-41
Problem solving, 229–239
  alternatives, 235–236
  Dewey's method, 229–230
  evaluation criteria, 234–235
  objectivity, 230, 235–236
  in research papers, 308, 317
  sample papers, 237–239
  writing process, 231–237
Problem statements, 38
Process analysis, 151–160
  audience, 152, 157
  order in, 151, 156
  procedures, 152–153
  readings, 586–605

Process analysis (*continued*)
  sample papers, 157–160
  transitions, 154, 156
  writing process, 154–157
Process analysis paragraphs, 88
Process description, 153
Professional English, 17–18
Pronouns; *see also* Person; Writer's voice
  formality of writing, 17
  indefinite, H-6, H-28–H-29
  in introductions, 37
  relative, 97–98, H-30, H-35
  rules for, H-26–H-30
Pronunciation and spelling, H-40
Proof; *see* Evidence
Proofreading, 59, 62–63, 497–500; *see also* Editing; Revision
Propaganda vs. appeal, 282
Propositions, 249; *see also* Thesis statements
Publication Manual of the American Psychological Association, 341; *see also* APA style
Punctuation; *see also specific marks*
  clauses, 98, H-2–H-6, H-8
  compound sentences, 96
  dialogue, 129
  parallel construction, 101
  quotation marks, H-13
  rules for, H-2–H-16
Purpose, for writing, 4–5
  argument, 243
  causal analysis, 215–216, 220
  clarity, 80
  classification, 174
  comparison/contrast, 186–187, 193
  definition, 200
  description, 139
  determining, 316
  exploratory drafts, 33–34
  illustration, 163
  narration, 127, 131
  oral presentations, 525–526
  point of view, 125
  process description, 153
  related to topic, 187
  thesis statement, 128, 554
Purpose statements, 187

Qualifications; *see* Résumés
Qualifying terms and accuracy, 72–74
Question marks, H-16
Questioning, 29, 299; *see also* Prewriting
Questionnaires, 302–304
Questions
  controlling, 251, 319–320
  elliptical, in series, H-16
  essay, 473–474
  open, closed, leading, 299
  in oral presentations, 540
Quiet, quite, H-48
Quotation marks, H-11–H-13
Quotation, quote, H-48
Quotations
  altering, 386–387
  in definition papers, 203
  documentation of, 346, 365
  integrated into text, 390–392
  punctuation, H-5, H-11–H-13
  reasons for using, 385–386

Random sample, 301
Reaction papers, 411–424

argument in, 420–421
commentary in, 419–420
critical reading for, 416–419
essays, 411–416
sample paper, 423–424
writing process, 419–423
Reader's role, 429–430
Real, really, H-48
Red herring, 275; *see also* Logical fallacies
Reference lists; *see also* Parenthetical citations; Style guides
  books, 368–371
  electronic sources, 372–376
  in research papers, 381–382
References on résumés, 489, 511–512
Regardless, irregardless, H-48
Regional usage, 15; *see also* Writer's voice
Relative pronouns, 97–98, H-30, H-35
Representative samples, 301
Research logs, 296–297
Research papers; *see also* Bibliographies; Documentation; Primary research; Secondary research
  argument in, 317
  documentation style, 394–396
  drafting, 388–393
  evaluating research, 379
  order in, 317
  problem solving in, 317
  revision checklist, 393
  writing process, 378–396
Resistance, 248–249, 529
Restrictive/nonrestrictive clauses, H-8
Résumés, 477–500
  cover letters, 502–508
  education, 488
  electronic, 495–497
  experience, 481, 483, 488–489
  functional, 479, 492–495
  organization of, 489–495
  packets, 511
  references, 489, 511–512
  skills, 480–483, 485–488
  writing process, 479–483, 483–489
Reverse chronological order, 40
  use in
    causal analysis papers, 218–220
    résumés, 484, 490–491
Reviewing, 469–470
Revision, 8–9, 49–59
  defined, 50
  five steps, 50–52
  at the paragraph level, 56
  refocusing, 53–55
  sentences, 92–106
  applied to
    argument papers, 261
    causal analysis papers, 221
    classification papers, 179–181
    comparison/contrast papers, 194–196
    cover letters, 508–509
    definition papers, 208
    description papers, 144–145
    illustration papers, 167–168
    literary analysis, 444
    narration papers, 131–134
    poetic analysis, 461–463
    problem solving papers, 236–237
    process analysis papers, 157
    reaction papers, 422–423

research papers, 393–396
résumés, 497–500
Rhetorical situation, 4–8
  breaking rules, H-1
  effect on survey conclusions, 305
  organization of writing, 528
  point of view, 125
  revision, 49
  speaking vs. writing, 521
  considered in
    argument papers, 253
    causal analysis papers, 215–216
    comparison/contrast papers, 186
    illustration papers, 164
    narration papers, 127–128
    oral presentations, 524, 531
    problem solving papers, 229
    reaction papers, 419
    research papers, 379–380, 380–382
Role-play, 527
Rules, breaking, H-1

Sacred writings, 352
Salary queries, 506
Sampling, 301
San Jose Mercury News, editorial philosophy, 67
Sarcasm and irony, 435
Scare tactics, 281; *see also* Emotional fallacies
Scheduling, 292–293, 301
Scientific method; *see* Dewey's method
Scientific Style and Format: The CBE Manual for Authors, Editors, and Publishers; see also Council of Science Editors (CSE); Style guides
Scratch outlining; *see also* Prewriting
  causal analysis papers, 218
  definition papers, 204
  examples of, 28–29, 57
  process analysis papers, 155
  research papers, 319–320
Search engines, 328–329
Second person, 152, H-26–H-27; *see also* Person
Secondary research, 316–336; *see also* Documentation; Primary research; Research papers; Sources
  Internet research, 328–334
  library research, 322–328, 334
  objectivity, 290–292
  plagiarism, 320, 330
  sample paper, 396–405
  topic, 317–320
Secondary sources, 344, 365, 368
Semicolons, 96, H-4–H-5
Sentences, 92–106; *see also* Topic sentences
  concluding, 79–80
  emphasis within, 105
  formal sentence definition, 200–201
  fragments, 97, H-23–H-25
  fused (run-on), 96, H-25–H-26
  parallel construction, 99–102
  punctuation, 96–98, 101
  style, 104–105
  types of, 94–98
  wordiness, 102–103
Series, punctuation with, H-2, H-5
Setting, 433, 438–439, 524
Sexist language, 111–113, H-29–H-30

t stories, 429–430, 453, 553
adings, 703–718
("thus"), 387
it, site, cite, H-46
gnpost transitions, 81, 154
imiles, 61, 436
Simplification/oversimplification, 273
Sincerity, 280; see also Tone
Single quotation marks, H-12
Site, cite, sight, H-46
Site selection, for observational re-
  search, 296
Situational irony, 435
Slashes, H-10–H-11
Sometime, some time, sometimes, H-49
Source notes, 322, 333
Source-based papers; see Research
  papers
Sources; see also Documentation; Style
  guides; specific sources
  in argument papers, 245
  evaluating, 251, 320–322, 326–327,
    417
  evaluation checklist, 379
  indirect, 344, 365
  miscellaneous, 346, 355–358
Spatial order, 40
Speaker's voice, 521, 537–538; see also
  Writer's voice
Specificity in language, 116
Speed, in oral presentations, 537–538
Spelling, H-39–H-43
Stacking the deck, 274; see also Logical
  fallacies
Stacks, library, 325–326
Stationary, stationery, H-41, H-49
Statistics, 245–246
Status appeal, 280–281; see also Emo-
  tional fallacies
Stereotypes, 71, 188, 203
Straw man, 279–280; see also Emo-
  tional fallacies
Structured interviews, 298–299
Studying, 467–473
Style; see Bibliographies; Parenthetical
  citations; Reference lists; Sources
Style guides; see also Documentation
  APA, Publication Manual of the Amer-
    ican Psychological Association,
    341; see also APA style
  CBE (CSE), Scientific Style and For-
    mat: The CBE Manual for Au-
    thors, Editors, and Publishers, 341
  CMS, Chicago Manual of Style, 341
  IEEE, Institute of Electrical and Elec-
    tronic Engineers, 341
  MLA, Modern Language Association
    Handbook for Writers of Research
    Papers, 341; see also MLA style
Subjective case, H-26–H-27
Subjectivity, 139–140, 412–413; see
  also Objectivity
Subjunctive mood (verbs), H-36–H-37
Subordinate clauses, 100, H-3
Subordinating conjunctions, 98
Summarizing, 383–384, 385
Superstition, 278
Support sentences, 79
Surveys, 300–307
Suspense, building, 130
Symbolism, 433, 435, 441–442
Synonyms, 206
Syntax, 104–105

Technical jargon, 113–114
Telephone interviews, 298
Tense (verbs), 100, 153, H-31
Tentative terms, 306–307, 379–380,
  437
Test anxiety, 472
Testimonial, 281–282; see also Emotional fallacies
Than, then, H-49
That, which, 98, H-30
That, who, H-30
Their, there, they're, H-41, H-49
Themes in literary analysis, 435–436,
  443–444
Then, than, H-49
Thesis statements; see also Topics
  defined, 35–36
  delayed, 253
  implicit, 254
  narrowing the topic, 33
  organization of argument, 254
  purpose of writing, 128, 554
  qualified generalizations in, 72
  revising, 55
  use in
    argument papers, 252–253
    classification papers, 176
    comparison/contrast papers, 190–
      192
    conclusions, 42, 179
    description papers, 139
    essay exams, 475
    essays, 418
    literary analysis papers, 432
    narration papers, 127–128
    oral presentations, 525–526
    process analysis papers, 155
    research papers, 388–389
They're, their, there, H-41, H-49
Third person, 153, H-26–H-27; see also
  Person
Time management, 467–469
Time, notation rules, H-23
Timing oral presentations, 522
Titles; see also Style guides
  in argument papers, 253
  focusing, 53
  formatting, 395–396
  quotation marks with, H-11–H-12
To, too, two, H-49
Tone; see also Speaker's voice; Writer's
  voice
  point of view, 125
  prescriptive, 20–21
  subjectivity/objectivity, 70
  considered in
    argument papers, 254, 255
    essays, 412–413, 418
    oral presentations, 523, 529
Topic sentences
  functions, 78–79
  implied, 85
  positioning, 83–85
  qualified generalizations in, 72
  revising, 56
  unifying paragraphs, 80
  use in
    classification papers, 174
    essay exams, 474
    illustration papers, 164
    process analysis papers, 155
Topics; see also Thesis statements
  concrete/abstract, 164

limiting, 318–320, 323
narrowing, 33, 83
  in argument papers, 251
  in definition papers, 205
  related to purpose, 187
  selecting, 5–6, 188, 317–318
  considered in
    oral presentations, 525–526
    problem solving papers, 231–232
Transfer, in emotional fallacies, 279
Transferable skills; see Résumés
Transitional paragraphs, 90
Transitions
  defined, 154
  embedded, 82
  punctuation, H-3, H-5
  signpost, 82
  use in
    classification papers, 176–178
    coherent paragraphs, 81–82
    comparison/contrast papers, 187–
      188
    definition papers, 204–205
    oral presentations, 530
    problem solving papers, 233
    process analysis papers, 154, 156
Translated works, 352
Trite language, 114, 188
Trust and accuracy, 66
Truth and accuracy, 66–67
Try to, try and, H-49
Two, to, too, H-49

Underlining, H-11–H-12, H-13–H-14
Understatement, 453
Unity within paragraphs, 80
Universal resource locators (URL),
  329–330
Universal truth, 453
Unstructured interviews, 298–299

Value judgments, 69, 70
Vantage point; see Point of View
Variety in sentence structure, 94–98
Verbal irony, 435
Verbs
  action, 123, 129, 144
  revising sentences, 93–94
  rules for, H-31–H-37
  tense, 100, 153, H-31
  use in
    essay questions, 473
    lyric poetry, 453
    parallel construction, 100
    process description papers, 153
    résumés, 486
    signal phrases, 391
Viewpoint; see Point of view
Vocabulary, 15–16, 116–117
Voice; see Speaker's voice; Writer's
  voice
Voice (verbs), 93–94, 100, 153, H-36

Wall Street Journal, editorial philosophy,
  67
Web sites, 329–333
Well, good, H-47
When, who, what, how, why, 258
Which, that, 98, H-30
Who, that, H-30
Who, what, when, where, why, how, 29,
  124–125, 524–525
Who, which, H-49

Who, whom, 98, H-30, H-49
Who's, whose, H-49
Word as word, H-12, H-14
Word choice, 7–8, 108–118; *see also*
    Verbs; Writer's voice
  abstractions, 115–116
  clarity, 80
  clichés, 114
  conciseness, 117
  denotations vs. connotations, 108–
    109
  editing, 60–62
  inclusive language, 111–113
  negativity/positivity, 109–110
  objectivity, 291
  specificity, 116
  standard and nonstandard usage,
    14–16
  technical jargon, 113–114
  considered in
    description papers, 144
    essays, 414
    narration papers, 129
    oral presentations, 529–530
    research papers, 379–380
    résumés, 499

Wordiness, sources of, 102–103
Work experience; *see* Résumés
Working bibliographies, 321–323
Working outlines, 57
Works cited; *see* Reference lists
Writer's block, 24–25, 126
Writer's voice, 6–8, 12–23; *see also*
    Speaker's voice
  clarifying, 55
  colloquialisms, 19–20
  determining, 21
  pronouns, 20
  vs. speaker's voice, 521
  tone, 20–21, 70
  writing compared with conversation,
    14
  considered in
    argument papers, 246
    causal analysis papers, 221
    essays, 413, 418
Writing
  occasion for, 4
  online writing labs, H-1
  vs. speaking, 521–523
Writing process
  breaks, 33, 51–52

  stages, 8–9; *see also specific stages*
  writer's block, 24–25, 126
  considered in
    argument papers, 248–261
    causal analysis papers, 218–223
    comparison/contrast papers, 190–
      197
    definition papers, 203–208
    description papers, 140–147
    essay exams, 472–475
    essays, 419–421
    literary analysis papers, 436–444
    narration papers, 127–132
    poetic analysis papers, 459–463
    problem solving papers, 231–239
    process analysis papers, 152–160
    reaction papers, 419–421
    research papers, 378–405
    résumés, 479–489

You understood, 152
Your, you're, H-49

INVITATION FOR SUBMISSIONS

Instructors are invited to submit student writing for possible publication in future editions of *Reasoning and Writing Well*. All submissions will be read and carefully considered. Entire papers, as well as sample paragraphs, introductions, and conclusions are welcome.

All submissions should be typed, double-spaced, and accompanied by the following information:

- The student writer's name, permanent street address, e-mail address, and telephone number
- The submitting instructor's name, school affiliation, telephone number, and email address

Please send submissions to either the street or e-mail address below, or fax them to 415.989.7702.

Renee Deljon, Senior Development Editor, Composition
McGraw-Hill Higher Education
55 Francisco Street, 2nd floor
San Francisco, CA 94133

renee_deljon@mcgraw-hill.com